UNIVERSITY CASEBOOK SERIES

READINGS AND MATERIALS

TAX POLICY

by

PHILIP D. OLIVER
Professor of Law
University of Arkansas at Little Rock

FRED W. PEEL, JR.
Ben J. Altheimer Professor of Law Emeritus
University of Arkansas at Little Rock

WESTBURY, NEW YORK

THE FOUNDATION PRESS, INC.

1996

 TEXT IS PRINTED ON 10% POST
CONSUMER RECYCLED PAPER

With love and respect,

we dedicate this book to our wives and daughters,

Ranko and Dorothy Oliver, and Evelyn and Ellen Peel,

and to our parents,

Bobby and Bruce Oliver, and Bessie and Fred W. Peel, Sr.

PREFACE

Tax policy is the preeminent policy course in the curriculum of most schools. There are several reasons for this. First is the unrivaled impact of tax law. With the possible exception of criminal law, it is the most important branch of law. The Department of Commerce estimates that taxes at all levels take approximately 31 percent of gross domestic product.[a]

With taxes claiming nearly one dollar in three, it is hardly surprising that tax law affects almost all aspects of life. Taxes affect our employment decisions, the form of our compensation, when we retire, our decisions about savings and investments, and all manner of business decisions. Less obviously, taxes also affect such things as where we live (both the political jurisdiction and the type of housing). Taxes profoundly influence marital and family relationships as well. No other branch of law even begins to have the broad economic *and* social impact of tax law.

All these dollars mean that tax policy is a central political issue for every presidential administration, and in every Congress—and in every legislature, town hall, and county supervising board. A student of politics or government will find no better laboratories than tax policy debates, which are played out for high stakes both politically and financially. On the practical side, anyone attempting to influence politicians (as well as judges and administrators) who make tax decisions goes better armed with an understanding of policy issues. Arguments founded in self interest or client interest are more persuasive when framed with reference to broader values.

At the same time, development of tax policy is more than just a fight about dollars, or about political power. Through the decades, the debate over tax policy issues has generated the country's richest policy literature, and it continues to do so. The debate is sophisticated and nuanced, combining elements of pure theory with considerations of political practicality and public acceptance. Study of the reasoning in tax policy literature will serve a student who would attempt to reason, and to persuade, in any area.

For these reasons, the study of tax policy is not just for tax specialists, but is valuable to students who do not plan to specialize in tax. Tax policy issues are not simple, but we believe this book will be fully accessible to a reader who has taken any tax course at the undergraduate, graduate, or law school level.

---

a. The Department of Commerce estimates that 1995 gross domestic product amounted to $7.246 trillion, and that receipts by federal, state, and local governments totalled $2.268 trillion, or 31.3 percent. U.S. DEP'T. OF COM., SURV. OF CURRENT BUS., vol. 76, no. 4, April, 1996, tbl. 1.1, at 12, tbl. 3.1, at 17.

v

PREFACE

* * *

In writing this book, we faced the initial task of limiting the number of topics to keep the book of manageable size. We expect that many professors will supplement these materials to cover one or more topics that we have omitted.

We begin in Part I with five chapters addressing fundamental issues concerning the country's basic tax, the federal income tax. Here we cover such issues as whether tax rates should be progressive or flat, and whether we should treat taxpayers as individuals or as parts of family groups. We also explore the social and economic ramifications of the nontaxation of imputed income.

In Part II, we consider an idea that has been gathering force both in the literature and in the political sphere—replacement of the income tax with some form of consumption tax, either the value added tax used in much of the world or a largely untested form of consumption-type income tax. Part III provides an opportunity to examine in detail three aspects of the tax treatment of wealth transferred by reason of death.

In Part IV, we begin with a chapter on tax expenditures—which take the form of credits, exclusions, or deductions—then follow with two chapters covering an exclusion (for personal injury awards) and a deduction (for state and local taxes). There are other important exclusions—employer-provided health insurance, for example, which is a multi-billion-dollar tax expenditure. We find the exclusion for personal injury awards more interesting, because while it *may* be a tax expenditure, it may instead merely recognize that an accident victim should not be taxed because being compensated for an injury entails no element of profit. Similarly, a chapter on any of the other major personal deductions (medical expenses, interest, or charitable contributions) could have been included, but we preferred the deduction for state and local taxes because it raises unique federalism issues.

Part V is directed to three important topics in the taxation of business and investment income—capital gains and losses, the double tax imposed on doing business in the corporate form, and what to do about inflation. Finally, in Part VI, we close with a chapter devoted to the framework in which the tax legislative process operates.

Once we had chosen the topics for our chapters, we attempted to read every policy article relating to a chapter's subject matter, and were never confronted with a shortage of potential excerpts. The challenge was to choose from a wealth of high-quality materials, and then to trim their well-crafted presentations without losing the essence of the argument. We present a blend of academic and non-academic pieces. Where possible, we have selected recent materials. Our principal criterion for selection, however, has been compiling materials that explain an issue and present a range of views to the reader, as clearly and simply as the complexity of the issue permits.

At the beginning of each subchapter, we provide a textual introduction to place the excerpts in context. The subchapters close with notes and questions, which serve to review and examine the ideas presented in the excerpts, as well as to present the views of other commentators whose work was not excerpted.

We suggest that the reader examine the note on Editorial Conventions, at page xxxix, before beginning.

We shall appreciate any comments, suggestions for improvement, or suggestions for items that might profitably be included in a future edition (including reprints). Please send these to Oliver.

*   *   *

During this book's six-year gestation period, many people have made valuable contributions, which we wish to acknowledge. We are aware of the risk that we shall fail to mention some who should be mentioned, and we apologize in advance.

First, we are thankful to the many students at seven law schools whom we have had the opportunity to teach in courses and seminars on tax law and policy. Their insights and questions have helped shape these materials.

Professors Jonathan Forman, David Hudson, Douglas A. Kahn, Edward J. McCaffery, Richard Ruggles, Alan S. Schenk, L. Scott Stafford, William J. Turnier, Bernard Wolfman, and Lawrence A. Zelenak each made valuable comments on drafts of one or more chapters.

We appreciate the support of the administration at the University of Arkansas at Little Rock School of Law, including Dean William H. Bowen, former Dean Howard B. Eisenberg, Associate Dean Charles W. Goldner, Jr., and Robert Fleming, Director for Nonacademic Affairs. The UALR Law Library staff proved unfailingly helpful. In particular, Professor Melissa Serfass was "unstumpable" for finding answers and obtaining requested sources. Nicana Sherman handled our numerous interlibrary loan requests. Clarice Anderson, faculty secretary, and her predecessor, Juaniece Ammons, each performed a thousand valuable tasks.

This book could not have been completed without the dedicated work of a large number of present and former UALR law students. Research assistance was provided by Dawn Bohanan, Karla Burnett, Jonnie Dolan, Kristen Craig Gould, Gordon LeMaire, David Martin, Danny Rasmussen, Gregory Taylor, Andrea Wood Van Deventer, and Elisa White. The great amount of technical work required in converting excerpted materials from photocopies to a computerized format, and subsequently of putting the entire book into camera-ready form, was principally carried out by Dawn Bohanan, Gordon LeMaire, and Julian Summers, with assistance from Kevin Beckham,

vii

Sherry Burnett, Charles Harmon, Elizabeth Johnston, and Ellen Kreth. Elisa White proofed and reviewed for form the entire book. Gordon LeMaire, Lindsey Sloan, and Elisa White obtained approvals for the reproduction of copyrighted materials.

We hope that those who worked on this book will find the final product worthy of their efforts. The defects that remain are entirely our responsibility. To some degree, we can be even more specific. While this book has very much been a joint project, and every sentence has been evaluated by both of us (and not infrequently debated between us), Peel played the primary role in selecting excerpts for, and writing a first draft of, Chapters 1, 2, 4, 5, 11, 14, 15, 16, and 17. Oliver played the primary role in selecting excerpts for, and writing a first draft of, Chapters 3, 6, 7, 8, 9, 10, 12, and 13. In addition, Oliver handled administrative matters and supervised the technical production of the book.

Finally, we are appreciative of the support and sacrifices of our wives and families.

PHILIP D. OLIVER FRED W. PEEL, JR.
Little Rock, Arkansas Burlingame, California

June, 1996

SELECTIONS AND COPYRIGHT ACKNOWLEDGEMENTS

Chapter 1: THE INCOME TAX AND FISCAL POLICY

Robert Eisner, *We Don't Need Balanced Budgets*, WALL STREET JOURNAL, January 11, 1995. Copyright © Dow Jones and Company, Inc. Reprinted with permission.

Donald W. Kiefer, *Whatever Happened to Counter-Cyclical Economic Stimulus*, NATIONAL TAX ASSOCIATION FORUM, Winter 1993. Copyright © 1993 by the National Tax Association-Tax Institute of America. Reprinted with permission.

James Tobin, *Policy for Recovery and Growth*, Statement to President-elect Clinton's Economic Conference (1992).

Allen D. Manvel, *Federal Revenue Changes, 1972-1992*, 57 TAX NOTES 959 (1992). Reprinted with permission. Copyright © 1992. Tax analysts.

Edward M. Gramlich, *Savings, Investment, and The Tax Reform Act of 1986*, National Tax Association-Tax Institute of America 79th Annual Conference (1986). Copyright © 1986 by the National Tax Association-Tax Institute of America. Reprinted with permission.

Richard Ruggles, *Accounting for Saving and Capital Formation in The United States, 1947-1991*, 7 JOURNAL OF ECONOMIC PERSPECTIVES 3 (1993). Copyright © 1993, American Economics Association. Reprinted with permission.

Chapter 2: WHEN SHOULD INCOME BE TAXED?

Henry C. Simons, PERSONAL INCOME TAXATION (1938). Copyright © 1938 by The University of Chicago. All rights reserved. Published February 1938. Third Impression 1955. Composed and printed by The University of Chicago Press, Chicago, Illinois, U.S.A. Reprinted with permission.

Henry C. Simons, FEDERAL TAX REFORM (1950). Copyright 1950 © by The University of Chicago. All rights reserved. Published 1950. Composed and printed by The University of Chicago Press, Chicago, Illinois, U.S.A. Reprinted with permission.

Mark L. Louie, *Note, Realizing Appreciation Without Sale: Accrual Taxation of Capital Gains on Marketable Securities*, 34 STANFORD LAW REVIEW 857 (1982). Reprinted with the permission of the Stanford Law Review and the Fred B. Rothman Co. Copyright © 1982 by the Board of Trustees of the Leland Stanford Junior University.

Marvin A. Chirelstein, FEDERAL INCOME TAXATION (7th ed. 1994). Copyright © 1994, Foundation Press. Reprinted with permission.

Fred W. Peel, Jr., *Capital Losses: Falling Short on Fairness and Simplicity*, 17 BALTIMORE LAW REVIEW 418 (1988). Copyright © 1988 University of Baltimore Law Review. Reprinted with permission.

Victor Thuronyi, *The Concept of Income*, 46 TAX LAW REVIEW 45 (1990). Copyright © 1990 by the New York University School of Law. Reprinted with permission.

J. Gregory Ballentine, *Three Failures in Economic Analysis of Tax Reform*, NATIONAL TAX ASSOCIATION-TAX INSTITUTE OF AMERICA 79TH ANNUAL CONFERENCE (1986). Copyright © 1986 by the National Tax Association-Tax Institute of America. Reprinted with permission.

Chapter 3: IMPUTED INCOME

Richard Goode, *Imputed Rent of Owner-Occupied Dwellings Under the Income Tax*, 15 JOURNAL OF FINANCE 504 (1960). Copyright © 1960 by the Journal of Finance, Stern School of Business. Reprinted with permission.

Thomas Chancellor, *Imputed Income and the Ideal Income Tax*, 67 OREGON LAW REVIEW 561 (1988). Reprinted with permission. Copyright © 1988 by the University of Oregon.

Michael J. McIntyre and Oliver Oldman, *Taxation of the Family in a Comprehensive and Simplified Income Tax*, 90 HARVARD LAW REVIEW 1573 (1977). Copyright © 1977 by the Harvard Law Review Association. Reprinted with permission.

William A. Klein, *Tax Deductions for Family Care Expenses*, 14 BOSTON COLLEGE INDUSTRIAL & COMMERCIAL LAW REVIEW 917 (1973). Copyright © 1973 by Boston College Law School. Reprinted with permission.

Daniel C. Schaffer and Donald H. Berman, *Two Cheers for the Child Care Deduction*, 28 TAX LAW REVIEW 535 (1973). Copyright © 1973 by the New York University School of Law. Reprinted with permission.

Edward J. McCaffery, *Taxation and the Family: A Fresh Look at Behavioral Gender Biases in the Code*, 40 UCLA LAW REVIEW 983 (1993). Originally published in 40 UCLA Law Review 983 (1993), Copyright © 1993, The Regents of the University of California. Reprinted with permission.

Chapter 4: PROGRESSIVE TAX RATES

J B McCombs, *An Historical Review and Analysis of Early United States Tax Policy Scholarship: Definition of Income and Progressive Rates,* 64 ST. JOHN'S LAW REVIEW 471 (1990). Originally published in 64 St. John's Law Review 471 (1990), Copyright © The St. John's Law Review Association. Reprinted with permission.

Dan Throop Smith, *High Progressive Tax Rates: Inequity and Immorality?*, 20 UNIVERSITY OF FLORIDA LAW REVIEW 451 (1968). Copyright © 1968 University of Florida Law Review. Reprinted with permission.

Charles O. Galvin and Boris I. Bittker, *The Income Tax: How Progressive Should it Be?*, Second Lecture, by Boris I. Bittker (1969). Copyright © 1987 the American Enterprise Institute for Public Policy Research. Reprinted with the permission of the American Enterprise Institute for Public Policy Research, Washington, D.C.

Charles E. McLure, Jr., *Comments on Fundamental Tax Reform*, NATIONAL TAX ASSOCIATION-TAX INSTITUTE OF AMERICA 78TH ANNUAL CONFERENCE (1985). Copyright © 1985 by the National Tax Association-Tax Institute of America. Reprinted with permission.

Shoup Mission, REPORT ON JAPANESE TAXATION (1949).

Eugene Steuerle & Michael Hartzmark, *Individual Income Taxation, 1947-79*, 34 NATIONAL TAX JOURNAL 145 (1981). Copyright © 1981 by the National Tax Association-Tax Institute of America. Reprinted with permission.

U.S. Treasury, TAX REFORM FOR FAIRNESS, SIMPLICITY, AND ECONOMIC GROWTH (1984).

Chapter 5: TAXING FAMILIES

Poe v. Seaborn, 282 U.S. 101 (1930).

Staff of the Joint Committee on Taxation, INCOME TAX TREATMENT OF MARRIED COUPLES AND SINGLE PERSONS (1980).

Daniel R. Feenberg & Harvey S. Rosen, *Recent Developments in the Marriage Tax*, 48 NATIONAL TAX JOURNAL 91 (1995). Copyright © 1995 by the National Tax Association-Tax Institute of America. Reprinted with permission.

Boris I. Bittker, *Federal Income Taxation and the Family*, 27 STANFORD LAW REVIEW 1389 (1975). Reprinted with the permission of the Stanford Law Review and the Fred B. Rothman Co. Copyright © 1975 by the Board of Trustees of the Leland Stanford Junior University.

Lawrence Zelenak, *Marriage and the Income Tax*, 67 SOUTHERN CALIFORNIA LAW REVIEW 339 (1994). Reprinted with permission of the Southern California Law Review. Copyright © 1994 Southern California Law Review. Reprinted with permission.

Marjorie E. Kornhauser, *Love, Money, and the IRS: Family, Income-Sharing, and the Joint Income Tax Return*, 45 HASTINGS LAW JOURNAL 63 (1993). Copyright © 1993 by University of California, Hastings College of the Law. Reprinted from Hastings Law Journal Vol. 45, No. 1, pp. 63, 63-77, 92-105, by permission.

Fred W. Peel, Jr., *An Approach to Income Tax Simplification*, 1 UNIVERSITY OF ARKANSAS AT LITTLE ROCK LAW JOURNAL 1 (1978). Copyright © 1978 by the Board of Trustees University of Arkansas. Reprinted with permission.

H.R. 1215, THE CONTRACT WITH AMERICA TAX RELIEF ACT OF 1995, House Report No. 84, 104th Cong., 1st Sess. (1995).

Lawrence Zelenak, *Children and the Income Tax*, 49 TAX LAW REVIEW 349 (1994). Copyright © 1994 by the New York University School of Law. Reprinted with permission.

Joseph Pechman, FEDERAL TAX POLICY (5th ed. 1987). Copyright © 1987 by The Brookings Institution. Reprinted with permission.

Alicia H. Munnell, *The Coming of Age of the Earned Income Tax Credit*, NATIONAL TAX ASSOCIATION FORUM (Winter, 1994). Copyright © 1994 by the National Tax Association-Tax Institute of America. Reprinted with permission.

H.R. 1215, THE CONTRACT WITH AMERICA TAX RELIEF ACT OF 1995, House Report No. 84, 104th Cong., 1st Sess. (1995).

Chapter 6: VALUE ADDED TAXES

Richard W. Lindholm, *The Origin of the Value-Added Tax*, 6 JOURNAL OF CORPORATION LAW 11 (1980). Copyright © 1980 by the University of Iowa. Reprinted with permission.

COMMITTEE ON WAYS & MEANS, HEARING ANNOUNCEMENT ON THE TAX RESTRUCTURING ACT OF 1979, Statement By Representative Al Ullman (D., Oregon), (H.R. 5665), 96th Cong., 1st Sess. (1979).

U.S. Treasury, TAX REFORM FOR FAIRNESS, SIMPLICITY, AND ECONOMIC GROWTH (1984).

American Bar Association, VALUE ADDED TAX: A MODEL STATUTE AND COMMENTARY (1989). Copyright © 1989 American Bar Assoication. Reprinted with permission.

Charles E. McLure, Jr., THE VALUE-ADDED TAX: KEY TO DEFICIT REDUCTION? (1987). Copyright © 1987 the American Enterprise Institute for Public Policy Research. Reprinted with the permission of the American Enterprise Institute for Public Policy Research, Washington, D.C.

John F. Due, *Economics of the Value Added Tax*, 6 JOURNAL OF CORPORATION LAW 61 (1980). Copyright © 1980 by the University of Iowa. Reprinted with permission.

Alan Schenk, *Value Added Tax: Does this Consumption Tax Have a Place in the Federal Tax System?*, 7 VIRGINIA TAX REVIEW 207 (1987). Copyright © 1987 the Virginia Tax Review. Reprinted with permission.

Joseph Isenbergh, *The End of Income Taxation*, 45 TAX LAW REVIEW 283 (1990). Copyright © 1990 by the New York University School of Law. Reprinted with permission.

Michael J. Graetz, *Revisiting the Income Tax vs. Consumption Tax Debate*, 57 TAX NOTES 1437 (1992). Reprinted with permission. Copyright © 1992. Tax Analysts.

Chapter 7:   A CONSUMPTION-TYPE INCOME TAX

William D. Andrews, *A Consumption-Type or Cash Flow Personal Income Tax*, 87 HARVARD LAW REVIEW 1113 (1974).   Copyright © 1974 by the Harvard Law Review Association. Reprinted with permission.

Alvin Warren, *Would a Consumption Tax Be Fairer than an Income Tax?*, 89 YALE LAW JOURNAL 1081 (1980). Copyright © 1980 The Yale Law Journal Company.   Reprinted by permission of The Yale Law Journal Company and the Fred B. Rothman Company from the Yale Law Journal, Vol. 93, pages 259-286.

Alan Gunn, *The Case for an Income Tax*, 46 UNIVERSITY OF CHICAGO LAW REVIEW 370 (1979).   Copyright © University of Chicago. Reprinted with permission.

U.S. Treasury, TAX REFORM FOR FAIRNESS, SIMPLICITY, AND ECONOMIC GROWTH (1984).

Edward J. McCaffery, *Tax Policy under a Hybrid Income-Consumption Tax*, 70 TEXAS LAW REVIEW 1145 (1992). Published originally in 70 Texas Law Review 1145 (1992).   Copyright © 1992 by the Texas Law Review Association. Reprinted with permission.

Robert E. Hall & Alvin Rabushka, THE FLAT TAX (2d ed. 1995). Reprinted from *The Flat Tax*, second edition, by Robert E. Hall and Alvin Rabushka, with the permission of the publisher, Hoover Institution Press. Copyright © 1995 by the Board of Trustees of the Leland Stanford Junior University.

Alliance USA, *Unlimited Savings Allowance (USA) Tax System*, 6 TAX NOTES 1482 (1995). Reprinted by permission. Copyright © 1995. Tax Analysts.

Rudolph G. Penner, *Is Radical Tax Reform in Our Future?*, 21 NATIONAL TAX ASSOCIATION FORUM, SPRING 1995. Copyright © 1995 by the National Tax Association-Tax Institute of America. Reprinted with permission.

John S. Nolan, *The Merit of an Income Tax Versus a Consumption Tax*, 12 AMERICAN JOURNAL OF TAX POLICY 207 (1995). Copyright © 1995 by the American College of Tax Counsel, Inc. Reprinted with permission.

Chapter 8: LIFE INSURANCE

Charles E. McLure, Jr., *The Income Tax Treatment of Interest Earned on Savings in Life Insurance, in* THE ECONOMICS OF FEDERAL SUBSIDY PROGRAMS: A COMPENDIUM OF PAPERS SUBMITTED TO THE JOINT ECONOMIC COMMITTEE OF THE CONGRESS OF THE UNITED STATES, Part 3 (1972).

Andrew D. Pike, *Reflections on the Meaning of Life: An Analysis of Section 7702 and the Taxation of Cash Value Life Insurance*, 42 TAX LAW REVIEW 491 (1988). Copyright © 1988 by the New York University School of Law. Reprinted with permission.

U.S. Treasury, TAX REFORM FOR FAIRNESS, SIMPLICITY, AND ECONOMIC GROWTH (1984).

Chapter 9: INCOME TAX TREATMENT OF PROPERTY TRANSFERRED AT DEATH OR BY GIFT

Joint Committee on Taxation, GENERAL EXPLANATION OF THE TAX REFORM ACT OF 1976, 1976-3 C.B. 564-71.

Lawrence Zelenak, *Taxing Gains at Death*, 46 VANDERBILT LAW REVIEW 361 (1993). Copyright © 1993 by the Vanderbilt Law Review, Vanderbilt University School of Law. Reprinted with permission.

Louis M. Castruccio, *Becoming More Inevitable? Death and Taxes . . . and Taxes*, 17 UCLA LAW REVIEW 459 (1970). Originally published in 17 UCLA Law Review 459 (1970). Copyright © 1970, by The Regents of the University of California. Reprinted with permission.

Dan Subotnik, *On Constructively Realizing Constructive Realization: Building the Case for Death and Taxes*, 38 KANSAS LAW REVIEW 1 (1989). Copyright © 1989 Kansas Law Review. Reprinted with permission.

Joseph M. Dodge, *Beyond Estate and Gift Tax Reform: Including Gifts and Bequests in Income*, 91 HARVARD LAW REVIEW 1177 (1978). Copyright © 1978 by the Harvard Law Review Association. Reprinted with permission.

David M. Hudson, *Tax Policy and the Federal Income Taxation of the Transfer of Wealth*, 19 WILLAMETTE LAW REVIEW 1 (1983). Copyright © 1982

Chapter 10: TRANSFER TAXES AND WEALTH TAXES

Louis Eisenstein, *The Rise and Decline of the Estate Tax*, 11 TAX LAW REVIEW 223 (1956). Copyright © 1990 by the New York University School of Law. Reprinted with permission.

Mark L. Ascher, *Curtailing Inherited Wealth*, 89 MICHIGAN LAW REVIEW 69 (1990). Copyright © 1990 by the Michigan Law Review Association. Reprinted with permission.

Michael J. Graetz, *To Praise the Estate Tax, Not to Bury It*, 93 YALE LAW JOURNAL 259 (1983). Copyright © 1983 The Yale Law Journal Company. Reprinted by permission of The Yale Law Journal Company and the Fred B. Rothman Company from the Yale Law Journal, Vol. 93, pages 259-286.

Joel C. Dobris, *A Brief for the Abolition of All Transfer Taxes*, 35 SYRACUSE LAW REVIEW 1215 (1984). Copyright © 1984 by the Syracuse Law Review. Reprinted with permission.

Harry J. Rudick, *A Proposal for an Accessions Tax*, 1 TAX LAW REVIEW 25 (1945). Copyright © 1945 by the New York University School of Law. Reprinted with permission.

John E. Donaldson, *The Future of Transfer Taxation: Repeal, Restructuring and Refinement, or Replacement*, 50 WASHINGTON & LEE LAW REVIEW 539 (1993). Copyright © (1993) by John E. Donaldson. Reprinted with permission. All Rights Reserved. This article originally appeared in 50 Washington & Lee Law Review 539 (1993).

George Cooper, *A Voluntary Tax? New Perspectives on Sophisticated Estate Tax Avoidance*, 77 COLUMBIA LAW REVIEW 161 (1977). This article originally appeared in 77 Columbia Law Review 161 (1977). Copyright © 1977 by the Columbia Law Review. Reprinted with permission.

Daniel Q. Posin, *Toward a Theory of Federal Taxation: A Comment*, 50 JOURNAL OF AIR LAW AND COMMERCE 907 (1985). Copyright © 1985 by the School of Law, Southern Methodist University. Reprinted with permission.

Chapter 11: TAX EXPENDITURES

Stanley S. Surrey, PATHWAYS TO TAX REFORM (1973). Reprinted by permission of the publishers from Pathways to Tax Reform by Stanley S. Surrey, Cambridge, Mass. Harvard University Press, Copyright © 1973 by the President and Fellows of Harvard College.

Office of Management and Budget, ANALYTICAL PERSPECTIVES, BUDGET OF THE UNITED STATES GOVERNMENT, FISCAL YEAR 1995, (1994).

Douglas A. Kahn & Jeffrey S. Lehman, *Tax Expenditure Budgets: A Critical View*, 54 TAX NOTES 1661 (1992). Reprinted with permission. Copyright © 1992. Tax Analysts.

Boris I. Bittker, *Accounting for Federal "Tax Subsidies" in the National Budget*, 22 NATIONAL TAX JOURNAL 246 (1969). Copyright © 1969 by the National Tax Association-Tax Institute of America. Reprinted with permission.

Chapter 12: PERSONAL INJURY AWARDS

J. Martin Burke & Michael K. Friel, *Tax Treatment of Employment-Related Personal Injury Awards: The Need for Limits*, 50 MONTANA LAW REVIEW 13 (1989). Copyright © 1989 by the Montana Law Review. Reprinted with permission.

Paul B. Stephan III, *Federal Income Taxation and Human Capital*, 70 VIRGINIA LAW REVIEW 1357 (1984). Reprinted with permission of the Virginia Law Review and the Fred B. Rothman Company. Copyright © 1984 the Virginia Law Review.

Jennifer J.S. Brooks, *Developing a Theory of Damage Recovery Taxation*, 14 WILLIAM MITCHELL LAW REVIEW 759 (1988). Copyright © 1988 by William Mitchell College of Law (William Mitchell Law Review). Reprinted with permission.

Joseph M. Dodge, *Taxes and Torts*, 77 CORNELL LAW REVIEW 143 (1992). Reprinted with the permission of the Cornell Law Review and the Fred B. Rothman Company. Copyright © 1992 by Cornell University.

Thomas D. Griffith, *Should "Tax Norms" Be Abandoned? Rethinking Tax Policy Analysis and the Taxation of Personal Injury Recoveries*, 1993 WISCONSIN LAW REVIEW 1115. Copyright © 1993 by the Board of Regents of the University of Wisconsin System; Reprinted by permission of the Wisconsin Law Review.

Lawrence A. Frolik, *The Convergence of I.R.C. § 104(a)(2),* Norfolk & Western Railway Co. V. Liepelt *and Structured Tort Settlements: Tax Policy "Derailed,"* 51 FORDHAM LAW REVIEW 565 (1983). Copyright © 1983 by the Fordham Law Review. Reprinted with permission.

Chapter 13: FEDERAL TAX TREATMENT OF STATE AND LOCAL TAXES

U.S. Treasury, TAX REFORM FOR FAIRNESS, SIMPLICITY, AND ECONOMIC GROWTH (1984).

Senate Committee on Finance, Senate Report No. 99-313, 99th Cong., 2d Sess. (1986)

Nonna A. Noto & Dennis Zimmerman, *Limiting State-Local Tax Deductibility: Effects among the States*, 37 NATIONAL TAX JOURNAL 539 (1984). Copyright © 1984 by the National Tax Association-Tax Institute of America. Reprinted with permission.

William J. Turnier, *Evaluating Personal Deductions in an Income Tax—The Ideal*, 66 CORNELL LAW REVIEW 262 (1981). Reprinted with the permission of the Cornell Law Review and the Fred B. Rothman Company. Copyright © 1981 by Cornell University.

J B McCombs, *A New Federal Tax Treatment of State and Local Taxes*, 19 PACIFIC LAW JOURNAL 747 (1988). Copyright © 1988 by the University of the Pacific, McGeorge School of Law. Reprinted with permission.

Walter W. Heller, *Deductions and Credits for State Income Taxes*, House Comm. on Ways & Means, 1 Tax Revision Compendium 419 (1959).

Chapter 14: CORPORATIONS AND DIVIDENDS

Joseph A. Pechman, FEDERAL TAX POLICY, (5th ed. 1987). Copyright © 1987 by The Brookings Institution. Reprinted with permission.

U.S. Treasury, TAX REFORM FOR FAIRNESS, SIMPLICITY, AND ECONOMIC GROWTH (1984).

Alvin C. Warren, Reporter, AMERICAN LAW INSTITUTE REPORTER'S STUDY OF CORPORATE TAX INTEGRATION: SUMMARY AND PROPOSALS (1993). Copyright © 1993 by the American Law Institute. Reprinted with permission.

American Institute of Certified Public Accountants, STATEMENT OF TAX POLICY: INTEGRATION OF THE CORPORATE AND SHAREHOLDER TAX SYSTEMS (1993). Reprinted with permission from STATEMENT OF TAX POLICY: INTEGRATION OF THE CORPORATE AND SHAREHOLDER TAX SYSTEMS, Copyright © 1993 by the American Institute of Certificate Public Accountants, Inc.

U.S. Treasury, REPORT ON INTEGRATION OF THE INDIVIDUAL AND CORPORATE TAX SYSTEMS, (1992).

Fred W. Peel, Jr., *A Proposal for Eliminating Double Taxation of Corporate Dividends*, 39 TAX LAWYER 1 (1985). Copyright © 1985 American Bar Association. Reprinted with permission.

Bernard Wolfman, *Self-Help Integration (LLCs) or Otherwise*, 62 TAX NOTES 769 (1994). Copyright © 1994 by Bernard Wolfman. Reprinted with permission.

William D. Andrews, Reporter, AMERICAN LAW INSTITUTE REPORTER'S STUDY OF THE TAXATION OF CORPORATE DISTRIBUTIONS, APPENDIX TO SUBCHAPTER C PROPOSALS (1982). Copyright © 1982 by the American Law Institute. Reprinted with permission.

Michael J. Graetz, *The Tax Aspects of Leveraged Buyouts and Other Corporate Financial Restructuring Transactions*, 42 TAX NOTES 721 (1989). Reprinted with permission. Copyright © 1989. Tax Analysts.

Chapter 15: CAPITAL GAINS AND LOSSES

Jane G. Gravelle & Lawrence B. Lindsey, *Capital Gains*, 38 TAX NOTES 397 (1988). Reprinted with permission. Copyright © 1988. Tax Analysts.

Calvin H. Johnson, *Seventeen Culls from Capital Gains*, 48 TAX NOTES 1285 (1990). Reprinted with permission. Copyright © 1990. Tax Analysts.

Fred W. Peel, Jr., *Capital Gains: Falling Short on Fairness and Simplicity*, 17 UNIVERSITY OF BALTIMORE LAW REVIEW 418 (1988). Copyright © 1988 by the University of Baltimore Law Review. Reprinted with permission.

DISCUSSION BY CCH TAX ADVISORY BOARD ROUNDTABLE, Vol. 79, No. 26, Pt. 2, May 27, 1992. Reproduced with permission from CCH Tax Advisory Board Roundtable published and copyrighted by CCH INCORPORATED, 2700 Lake Cook Road, Riverwoods, Illinois 60015.

Congressional Budget Office, INDEXING CAPITAL GAINS (1990).

Testimony of Michael J. Boskin, *Tax Incentives for Increasing Savings and Investments*, Hearings Before the Senate Committee on Finance, 101st Cong., 2d Sess. (1990).

H.R. 1215, THE CONTRACT WITH AMERICA TAX RELIEF ACT OF 1995, House Report No. 84, 104th Cong., 1st Sess. (1995).

James M. Poterba, *Capital Gains Tax Policy Toward Entrepreneurship*, 42 NATIONAL TAX JOURNAL 375 (1989). Copyright © 1989 by the National Tax Association-Tax Institute of America. Reprinted with permission.

Gerard M. Brannon, *Bringing Taxes Home: Capital Gains on Residences, in* THE CAPITAL GAINS CONTROVERSY: A TAX ANALYSTS READER (1974). Reprinted with permission. Copyright © 1974. Tax Analysts.

H.R. 1215, THE CONTRACT WITH AMERICA TAX RELIEF ACT of 1995, House Report No. 84, 104th Cong., 1st Sess. (1995).

Chapter 16: RESPONDING TO PRICE LEVEL CHANGES

Henry J. Aaron, ed., INFLATION AND THE INCOME TAX, (1976). Copyright © 1976 by The Brookings Institution. Reprinted with permission.

Calvin Engler & Mitchell L. Engler, *Taxation of Capital Gains—Let's Be Fair*, 50 TAX NOTES 1303 (1991). Reprinted with permission. Copyright © 1991. Tax Analysts.

New York State Bar Association Section on Taxation Ad Hoc Committee, *Report on Inflation Adjustments to the Basis of Capital Assets*, 48 TAX NOTES 759 (1990). Reprinted with permission. Copyright © 1990. Tax Analysts.

U.S. Treasury, REPORT ON TAX REFORM FOR FAIRNESS, SIMPLICITY, AND ECONOMIC GROWTH (1984).

Michael C. Durst, *Inflation and the Tax Code: Guidelines for Policymaking*, 73 MINNESOTA LAW REVIEW 1217 (1989). Copyright © 1989 by the Minnesota Law Review Foundation. Reprinted with permission.

Chapter 17: TAXES AND THE LEGISLATIVE PROCESS

Kenneth W. Gideon, *Tax Policy at the Treasury Department: A 20-Year Perspective*, 57 TAX NOTES 889 (1992). Reprinted with permission. Copyright © 1992. Tax Analysts.

Ronald A. Pearlman, *The Tax Legislative Process: 1972-1992*, 57 TAX NOTES 939 (1992). Reprinted with permission. Copyright © 1992. Tax Analysts.

Michael D. Bopp, *The Roles of Revenue Estimation and Scoring in the Federal Budget Process*, 56 TAX NOTES 1629. Reprinted with permission. Copyright © 1992. Tax Analysts.

Randall Strahan, *Discussion: Gramm-Rudman-Hollings and Tax Policy*, NATIONAL TAX ASSOCIATION-TAX INSTITUTE OF AMERICA, 82ND ANNUAL CONFERENCE (1989). Copyright © 1989 by the National Tax Association-Tax Institute of America. Reprinted with permission.

John F. Witte, *A Long View of Tax Reform*, 39 NATIONAL TAX JOURNAL 255 (1986). Copyright © 1986 by the National Tax Association-Tax Institute of America. Reprinted with permission.

Jeffrey H. Birnbaum, *Showdown at Gucci Gulch*, 40 NATIONAL TAX JOURNAL 357 (1987). Copyright © 1987 by the National Tax Association-Tax Institute of America. Reprinted with permission.

Gerard M. Brannon, *Some Economics of Tax Reform, 1986*, 39 NATIONAL TAX JOURNAL 277 (1986). Copyright © 1986 by the National Tax Association-Tax Institute of America. Reprinted with permission.

Stanley S. Surrey, *The Congress and the Tax Lobbyist—How Special Tax Provisions Get Enacted*, 70 HARVARD LAW REVIEW 1145 (1957). Copyright © 1957 by the Harvard Law Review Association. Reprinted with permission.

SUMMARY OF CONTENTS

TABLE OF CONTENTS

PART II: CONSUMPTION TAXES

PART V: TAXATION OF BUSINESS AND INVESTMENT INCOME

PART VI: ENACTING TAX LAW

EDITORIAL CONVENTIONS

Each chapter is divided into subchapters. Except for the introductory subchapter, which may be entirely textual, subchapters begin with textual introduction, follow with excerpts of works originally published elsewhere, and conclude with notes and questions. Each chapter ends with a selected bibliography of materials that might serve as a starting point for research on tax policy issues in the area of the chapter's subject.

Necessarily, all excerpts have been tightly edited. Most footnotes and other citations to authority, including many cross references, are deleted without indication. Other deletions in text are indicated by three asterisks (* * *). Where the excerpted work quotes yet another source, and the author of the excerpted work excised a portion of the quoted source, we differentiated such deletions by use of ellipses (. . .).

We have corrected clear errors in excerpted works, occasionally without indication, more frequently by insertion of bracketed language. Bracketed language is used more frequently to clarify or simplify. Use of brackets implies no criticism of the authors or editors of the original sources; usually it was the editing for inclusion in this book that necessitated clarification.

We employ three types of footnotes. Numbered footnotes are those used in original sources, and retain the original numbering. Authors of most materials excerpted are identified, usually by position at time of original publication, by asterisk footnotes. All other footnotes added by the editors are lettered footnotes. Lettered footnotes that fall within excerpts are further identified as editors' footnotes by adding "(Eds.)."

Unless the context indicates otherwise, our references to "sections" are to the Internal Revenue Code at date of submission for publication (June, 1996). Authors of materials excerpted frequently refer to the Internal Revenue Code in existence at the time their work was originally published; on occasion, we have added footnotes or bracketed material to indicate current law, but usually we have concluded that such an addition would be more distracting than valuable.

TAX POLICY

*

PROLOGUE

THE CANONS OF TAXATION

Taxes are what we pay for civilized society.[a]

A necessary consequence of the coming of civilization is the organization of some sort of government, and with it associated expenses. Bearing those expenses requires some form of taxation. Different governmental and societal structures produce different tax systems. The tax system, even of an advanced society, need not depend on objective law:

> In the old Chinese system, quotas of tax liability were parceled out to the Provinces on the basis of the Emperor's opinion of what each Province should pay. The Province did the same to the districts, which did the same to the chos (groups of 100 hos), which did the same to the hos (groups of 100 families). The ho leader assessed on each of his 100 families the tax liability he thought each should pay, based on his intimate knowledge of each.[b]

The United States, which prides itself on having a "government of laws" and not a "government of men," obviously prefers a taxing system based on laws of general application. Nevertheless, if one assumed good faith on the part of each official involved, the ancient Chinese system could be viewed as extremely just, because it allows consideration of individual factors that could not be recognized in a tax statute.

We shall not devote much attention to how taxing decisions are made or how much should be collected in taxes, although these important matters are addressed in Chapters Seventeen and One, respectively. Rather, given the assumed need for substantial revenues, we shall ask what substantive decisions about the structure of taxation should be made—what decisions would serve well our large, complex, and diverse society and economy.

The primary criteria to be applied in wisely structuring taxes are open to debate and are a central focus of this book. Perhaps the most important is equity—but, like beauty, tax equity lies in the eye of the beholder. Another factor is the effect of taxing decisions on the economic well being of individual taxpayers and of the entire society. This is likely to be tied to notions of economic efficiency versus economic distortions, and of structuring

---

a. Justice Oliver Wendell Holmes, *in* Compania General de Tabacos de Filipinas v. Collector of Internal Revenue, 275 U.S. 87, 100 (1927) (dissenting).

b. Herbert Stein, *What's Wrong with the Federal Tax System?*, *in* HOUSE COMM. ON WAYS AND MEANS, 86th Cong., 1st Sess., 1 TAX REVISION COMPENDIUM 107, 110 (1959).

taxes so as not to encourage unproductive decisions and actions. Another important criterion must be administrability. For example, a tax that in theory seems just and wise, but whose collection depends *entirely* on self assessment by taxpayers, is in practice likely to be inequitable and to raise little revenue.

The most famous set of criteria for tax policy are the canons stated in 1776 by Adam Smith in his keynote for the age of capitalism, *The Wealth of Nations*:

> Before I enter upon the examination of particular taxes, it is necessary to premise the four following maxims with regard to taxes in general.
>
> I. The subjects of every state ought to contribute towards the support of the government, as nearly as possible, in proportion to their respective abilities; that is, in proportion to the revenue which they respectively enjoy under the protection of the state. * * *
>
> II. The tax which each individual is bound to pay ought to be certain, and not arbitrary. The time of payment, the manner of payment, the quantity to be paid, ought all to be clear and plain to the contributor, and to every other person. * * *
>
> III. Every tax ought to be levied at the time, or in the manner, in which it is most likely to be convenient for the contributor to pay it. * * *
>
> IV. Every tax ought to be so contrived as both to take out and to keep out of the pockets of the people as little as possible, over and above what it brings into the public treasury of the state.[c]

Testifying before the Ways and Means Committee in 1959, Professor Neil Jacoby placed Adam Smith's call for proportional taxation in historical context, and suggested additional and competing criteria for good tax policy:

> When Smith wrote, * * * the British revenue system consisted almost entirely of customs duties, excises, and real property taxes and was highly regressive. * * * Smith's demand that taxes should be "proportional" to the revenues was quite radical for its time. * * * Of course, we have long since abandoned the view that flat proportionality in personal income is equitable. * * *
>
> John Stuart Mill [writing in 1897] was among the first of the British economists to argue explicitly for use of the tax system to mitigate great inequalities in personal income and wealth, although he was careful to note that progression should not "impair the motives upon which society depends for keeping up (not to say increasing) the produce of its labor and capital."[d]

---

c. ADAM SMITH, THE WEALTH OF NATIONS 777-78 (1776).

d. Neil H. Jacoby, *Guidelines of Income Tax Reform for the 1960's, in* HOUSE COMM. ON WAYS AND MEANS, 86th Cong., 1st Sess., 1 TAX REVISION COMPENDIUM 157, 158-60 (1959).

When Professor Jacoby appeared before the Ways and Means Committee, progressive tax was at its zenith in American history: top federal income tax rates exceeded 90 percent. "Flat proportionality" has made a comeback in American politics, however. A recurring proposal in recent years, including in the 1996 presidential campaign, has been the implementation of some form of proportional, or "flat," tax.

Wilbur Mills, long-time chairman of the Ways and Means Committee, provided his own list of criteria at the same 1959 hearings:

> [T]ax reform must seek, among other things, (1) a tax climate more favorable to economic growth; (2) greater equity through closer adherence to the principle that equal incomes should bear equal tax liabilities; (3) assurance that the degree of progression in the distribution of tax burdens accords as closely as possible with widely held standards of fairness; (4) an overall tax system which contributes significantly to maintaining stability in the general price level and a stable and high rate of use of human and material resources; (5) a tax system which interferes as little as possible with the operation of the free market mechanism in directing resources into their most productive uses; and (6) greater ease of compliance and administration.[e]

As Chairman Mills' formulation suggests, tax policy concerns in recent decades have brought the matter of incentives to the fore. We are acutely aware that taxing an activity discourages it, and wish to structure our tax system in a way that does not discourage such beneficial activities as work, saving, and investment. At the same time, as economist David Ricardo made clear nearly two centuries ago, the effort can be only to create a tax that is *relatively* neutral, because we can never fully succeed in removing the undesired disincentives of taxation:

> There are no taxes which have not a tendency to lessen the power to accumulate. All taxes must either fall on capital or revenue. If they encroach on capital, they must proportionably diminish that fund by whose extent the extent of the productive industry of the country must always be regulated; and if they fall on revenue, they must either lessen accumulation, or force the contributors to save the amount of the tax, by making a corresponding diminution of their former unproductive consumption of the necessaries and luxuries of life. Some taxes will produce these effects in a much greater degree than others; but the great evil of taxation is to be found, not so much in any selection of its objects, as in the general amount of its effects taken collectively.[f]

---

e. Wilbur Mills, *Foreword, in* HOUSE COMM. ON WAYS AND MEANS, 86th Cong., 1st Sess., 1 TAX REVISION COMPENDIUM ix (1959).

f. DAVID RICARDO, THE PRINCIPLES OF POLITICAL ECONOMY AND TAXATION 95 (Everyman's Library ed. 1992) (1817).

Finally, the student of tax policy must remember that consideration of change to an existing tax provision entails somewhat different considerations from those presented at the time of enactment. At a time in which every election seems to be a referendum on sweeping tax change, Professor Walter Blum's admonition is pertinent: "In respect to taxation there is, generally speaking, considerable gain in merely preserving ancient rules intact and avoiding change."[g] Dr. Herbert Stein explained why this is so:

> In general, there is a tendency for the market to adjust to different tax treatments of incomes from different sources in such a way as to reduce the net effects on income after tax. * * *
>
> This is one aspect of the more general and very important proposition: Old taxes are good taxes. The economic system has adjusted to them so as to reduce discriminatory effects they might have had when first introduced. Moreover old taxes often, although not always, have a degree of acceptance they did not have when first imposed. Therefore the considerations relevant to the removal of some tax provision that has been in effect for some time are very different from the considerations that would be relevant to its initial adoption.[h]

At the same time, the maxim that "old taxes are good taxes" cannot be taken to an extreme, or it would forever lock in any existing tax provision, however unjust or unwise.

With these very general guidelines and admonitions in mind, we approach the study of tax policy.

---

g. Walter J. Blum, *Tax Policy and Preferential Provisions in the Income Tax Base, in* HOUSE COMM. ON WAYS AND MEANS, 86th Cong., 1st Sess., 1 TAX REVISION COMPENDIUM 77, 78 (1959).

h. Stein, *supra* note b, at 112.

PART I

INTRODUCTION TO THE INCOME TAX

The federal tax system is overwhelmingly based on income. The individual income tax accounts for nearly half of all federal revenues.[a] When combined with the corporate income tax and with the Social Security tax and related social insurance taxes, which are also income-based, the total rises to over ninety percent.[b] Moreover, it is fair to say that the popular perception of "federal taxes" is that of income taxes, as opposed to tariffs, estate and gift taxes, or any of a number of other levies that account for relatively small amounts.

Most of Parts III, IV, and V of this book deal with particular income tax issues. The first five chapters, however, deal with fundamental issues relevant to the income tax as a whole.

Chapter One deals with the role of the income tax in implementing fiscal policy. This involves understanding the role of balanced budgets, the impact of budget surpluses and deficits on the economy, and the extent to which fiscal policy should (and can) be used to control the direction of the economy. The conventional government budget is contrasted with a capital budget, under which capital expenditures would be accounted for over a number of years.

Chapter Two discusses when income should be measured and subjected to tax. The discussion revolves around the Haig-Simons definition of income, which has become the standard used by most academics in judging the income tax system. Both the practical shortcomings of the Haig-Simons definition and its merits and flaws at a theoretical level are described. The Haig-Simons approach is contrasted with the present generally applicable requirement of realization in determining income subject to tax.

Chapter Three deals with the outer limit of income subject to tax, addressing the benefits received from ownership of property and from the performance of services for one's self or family. Although it is not practical to tax such "imputed income," not doing so has important consequences affecting the equity of the income tax. Indirectly, the failure to tax imputed income affects society quite broadly, influencing the type of housing we live

---

a. In 1994, the individual income tax generated $543 billion, or approximately 43.2 percent of total federal revenues of $1.258 trillion. U.S. BUREAU OF THE CENSUS, STATISTICAL ABSTRACT OF THE UNITED STATES, tbl. 518, at 334 (115th ed. 1995).

b. In 1994, payroll taxes amounted to $461 billion, and corporate income taxes to $140 billion. These taxes, when combined with the individual income tax, generated approximately 91 percent of federal revenues. *Id.*

in, the choice between work and leisure, and the decision of wives (principally) to enter the paid labor force.

Chapter Four discusses how the national income tax burden should be divided among taxpayers with different incomes. This involves arguments for and against progressivity in the tax rate structure. The issues include equity between taxpayers with different levels of income, whether generalized conclusions as to the marginal utility of additional income are valid, the practical problems caused by differing tax rates, and the problem of arriving at a cap for top rates.

Chapter Five deals with the choice of the taxable unit: the individual; married couples; families extended to include children; or other, less conventional, arrangements. This chapter brings together issues discussed in Chapter Three, dealing with imputed income (important in the family context); and in Chapter Four, covering progressivity (the primary reason that the choice of taxable unit is important). The issues raised in Chapter Five involve equity between differently situated taxpayers, whether sociological considerations should be taken into account, the extent to which common law or community property law in the various states should impact the federal choice of taxpaying unit, and the relevance of family arrangements outside the standard husband-wife-children relationships. Special problems involving children—their tax rates, personal and dependency exemptions for them, and the earned income tax credit—are also presented.

CHAPTER ONE

THE INCOME TAX AND FISCAL POLICY

To raise taxes to reduce demand encounters at the outset a problem of understanding. That, in the event of insufficient demand and depression, taxes should be cut and public outlays increased in order to increase aggregate demand and employment is now widely accepted. There is an inherent logic to the procedure. This is also true of cutting public expenditures to counter inflation—were this only possible. However, the logic of increasing taxes is by no means so evident.[a]

A. OBJECTIVES OF AN INCOME TAX

The obvious objective of an income tax is to raise revenue. The first question is: How much revenue? Intuitively, the answer is "enough to cover the government's expenditures," but the answer perhaps is simplistic on two counts. First, it is not necessarily true that the level of taxation should be controlled by the level of expenditures any more than that the level of expenditures should be determined by the amount of revenue the government receives. Even more basically, the intuitive answer assumes that revenues and expenditures should balance, but that assumption may be unwarranted. Most of the discussion of deficit versus balanced budget is premised on an implicit assumption that total receipts should equal total expenditures each year, but that is, itself, not beyond question. Indeed, should a balanced budget even over the long term be viewed as necessary or desirable?

Assuming a balanced budget to be desirable, a possible alternative to a crude test of gross receipts versus gross expenditures would be a budget modeled on business practice. Businesses do not attempt to cover capital improvements by current receipts. Instead, they capitalize purchases of assets that have useful lives of more than one year. These capital expenditures are factored into business budgets over the estimated lives of the assets, using some more or less arbitrary method of depreciation or amortization. Even households treat outlays for big assets that will last for years—such as homes—differently from expenditures for current consumption. Discussing these and other issues, Professor Eisner argues against a proposed balanced budget amendment in the first excerpt below.

A government budget based on the business mode is called a *capital budget*. If it were to be adopted for the federal government, it would be a

---

a. John Kenneth Galbraith, The Affluent Society 242 (1958).

difficult concept to quantify. For example, how rapidly should government office buildings be depreciated? Should benefits from expenditures on intangibles such as education of children be capitalized? Without replacing the present budget, perhaps a parallel capital budget could be set up that would put deficit financing in better perspective.

The present conventional budget has practical uses; for one, the conventional deficit or surplus provides a measure of the federal government's impact on the economy. It does not, however, give an accurate picture of the timing of the impact on the economy of particular budgetary items, such as savings and loan bailout costs. There the impact on the economy was felt when improvident loans were made by the savings and loan associations, not at the later date when the government's obligations to the insured depositors were formally taken into account.

Planned manipulation of revenues, expenditures, and the gaps between them (surplus or deficit) are the major tools in *fiscal policy*. The government is committed to some form of fiscal policy management, a commitment enshrined in the Full Employment Act of 1946. At a popular level, presidents and their political parties win or lose elections depending upon whether the country is prosperous or in recession.

Fiscal policy means the use of taxes and the overall level of government expenditures to manage the economy. Fiscal policy is not consistent with consistently balanced annual budgets. In recent years economists have become less certain of their ability to manage the economy through use of the tools of fiscal policy. The article by Donald W. Kiefer summarizes changes in attitudes toward fiscal policy management over a twenty-year period, and discusses various reasons that have led many economists to discard the Keynesian economic models of the 1960s and before, and now to think that it is very difficult to use fiscal policy in a constructive manner.

James Tobin was a member of the Council of Economic Advisers that made the 1962 Report quoted in the Kiefer excerpt. In his statement presented to President-elect Clinton's 1992 Economic Conference, which follows the Kiefer article, Professor Tobin continues to advocate the counter-cyclical fiscal policy that Dr. Kiefer criticizes.

WE DON'T NEED BALANCED BUDGETS
Robert Eisner[*]
Wall Street Journal, January 11, 1995, at A14

It has been suggested that we combine two of the currently proposed amendments to the U.S. Constitution: Put into the supreme law of the land a requirement that the public schools have prayers for a balanced budget.

---

[*]. At time of original publication, Professor Emeritus at Northwestern University and a past president of the American Economic Association.

Since ordering a balanced budget is like commanding the tides to retreat, we may, after all, require some kind of divine intervention.

The "balance" apparently contemplated is an equality between federal government outlays (expenditures) and revenues (tax receipts). But both of these are variable and quite beyond the short-run control of the government. Tax receipts, of course, go up and down with the state of the economy. And some outlays—for unemployment insurance, for example—go down and up with the economy, too.

Each additional percentage point of unemployment is associated with at least $50 billion of additional deficit, as revenues shrink and outlays grow. If unemployment were to rise from the current 5.4% to, say, the 7.6% of June 1992, the deficit could be expected to rise by more than $110 billion. What would the law then tell us to do? Tell taxpayers to try harder? Stop some "entitlement" checks (for unemployment insurance, Social Security, Medicare and Medicaid)? Or pray?

Balancing Checkbooks

It is widely asserted: "I balance my checkbook. Why can't the government balance its?" But we would not dream of keeping our checkbooks balanced the way a balanced budget would require the government to. We borrow to buy houses and automobiles and to send our kids to college. If we lose our job or suffer a financial reversal, we may well borrow to tide ourselves over to a better time. In 1993, net borrowing of the U.S. government was $256 billion; that of private households was $294 billion. How about an amendment to ban individual borrowing for any purpose unless three-fifths of both houses of the Congress make an exception?

And how many businesses could get along without borrowing? Borrowing to invest and expand is the hallmark of business success. U.S. Treasury debt is now some $3.5 trillion. U.S. nonfinancial business owes more than $3.8 trillion. And private households owe about $4.5 trillion.

But government debt is somehow viewed as different. We are told that state governments balance their budgets and are widely required to do so in their constitutions. The great majority of state governments, though, have separate capital budgets. They balance only their operating or current budgets and borrow—that is, run deficits—for capital expenditures.

To require the federal government, which keeps no separate capital budget, to keep revenues equal to outlays would mean that all public investment would have to be financed out of current taxes. But capital investment is intended to offer benefits in the future. To ask current taxpayers to meet all of that burden is unfair, and most are likely to refuse —with the result that public investment in infrastructure, research, education and crime-fighting is likely to be starved.

Government debt is indeed different from private debt. In fact, it is its opposite! For every borrower there must be a lender. The federal debt of savings bonds and Treasury bills, notes and bonds is overwhelmingly owned by the private sector and our state and local governments. Eliminate or reduce the federal debt and we eliminate or reduce our own assets. It is widely asserted that we are currently leaving a debt of $3.5 trillion for our children and grandchildren to pay. But we are leaving the bulk of that amount (minus the minor portion owned by foreigners) to our children and grandchildren as their assets of Treasury securities.

The real question about government deficits should be: What would be the effect on the economy of the drastic deficit reduction necessary to get to "balance"? Government bonds are wealth to their holders and if the government spends more than it is taking in, it adds to their wealth. With government deficits, the rest of us are getting more from the government than we are giving. As this increases our purchasing power, the deficits and debt are fueling private spending and thus keeping American business prosperous. Eliminating the deficits and debt may well cut that prosperity short.

It is argued that deficit-induced private spending and private lending to government hold down private investment. The facts, though, appear otherwise. Bigger structural federal deficits have indeed encouraged consumption, but my own work with data of the past 40 years has shown that the deficits and increased consumption have in fact also increased gross private domestic investment. It should not be hard to understand why. If the government, by running a deficit, leaves our after-tax income higher and we go out and buy Buicks, Fords and Chryslers, the auto companies invest more, not less. And if government belt-tightening and/or tax increases to balance the budget leave us with less, so that we don't buy those new cars, the companies will surely invest less.

This is not an argument for unlimited deficits. They can be too large, and induce too much spending. A good rule of thumb would be similar to that for any household or business. Run deficits—borrow—to the extent that your debt stays in line with your income, and except when pressed by temporary hard times, use your borrowing not for current expenses but for investment.

For our federal government, with the national income growing at 6% per year on average (and more at the moment), that means that the debt can grow at 6% per year and keep the roughly 50% debt-to-GDP ratio from growing. (That ratio, while twice what it was before the 1980s, is less than half of what it was just after World War II.) But this implies a permanent deficit equal to 3% of GDP, or currently just about the $203 billion we had in fiscal 1994, and more than the $167 billion projected for 1995. By this rule of thumb, we are already in balance and heading into "surplus," a situation where the debt-to-GDP ratio will be declining.

Repeated assertions to the contrary notwithstanding, it is hardly clear, then, that a balanced budget—as opposed, for example, to merely keeping the debt from outrunning our income—is desirable. But suppose the balanced budget amendment became the law of the land. How would it be enforced? What would we do if a downturn in the economy created a deficit? Would we put the tax-collectors or Congress in jail for violating the Constitution?

Or should we, in a time of recession, cut government payments to people or raise taxes? Almost everyone recognizes that this would be exactly the wrong thing to do. Would three-fifths of Congress vote then to waive the balanced budget requirement, or would a politically minded minority refuse to do so?

Given the economic hardship and political difficulty in reaching and maintaining a balanced budget, we can look for all kinds of evasive tricks. A major one, already anticipated by most of our governors, would be to foist federal outlays off on the states. The federal government currently gives grants-in-aid of $200 billion a year to state and local governments. We could eliminate the deficit by canceling them.

The federal government could also substitute regulations and mandates for its own outlays, requiring private business and individuals or state and local governments to make expenditures and thus save the federal budget. * * *

Creative Accounting

Or we could go in for all kinds of creative accounting. My own preference, as suggested above, would be to set up a separate capital budget and include only depreciation, not new capital outlays, in the current budget, which would be what we would balance. Will the new constitutional amendment not only require a balanced budget but prescribe the accounting rules by which it should be measured?
* * *

Economists and politicians have varying views on these matters. But surely it is improper to sanctify any economic philosophy or ideology and put it into our long-lasting and very difficult-to-change Constitution. * * *

WHATEVER HAPPENED TO COUNTER-CYCLICAL ECONOMIC STIMULUS
Donald W. Kiefer[*]

National Tax Association Forum, Winter 1993, at 1-5

Mr. Clinton has said he is committed to substantial deficit reduction during his first term. While a fully developed economic program has yet to be articulated, the plan for fiscal policy apparently involves essentially no change—or perhaps a small increase—in the deficit in the first year (compared to baseline), followed by substantial reductions in the deficit during the next three years.

---

[*]. At time of original publication, Senior Specialist in Economic Policy, Congressional Research Service, Library of Congress.

Thus, the fiscal program is focused primarily on long-term growth. Despite the program's conception in a presidential campaign that began during a recession, and despite Mr. Clinton's emphasis on job creation, the fiscal program is not an old-time Keynesian counter-cyclical economic stimulus. And while some economists called for an economic stimulus early in 1992, the recommended policy was long-term investment programs that would be deficit financed in the short-run. There have been no proposals for an across-the-board tax cut to stimulate the economy.

Why not? In the 1960s and 1970s several tax cuts were implemented to boost the economy out of periods of slow growth or recession, and a tax increase was adopted to restrain inflation. In the 1980s and 1990s fiscal policy has not been used for counter-cyclical purposes. What has changed?

In short, Murphy's Law struck with a vengeance; everything that could go wrong did. Four important factors are highlighted in this article (not necessarily in order of importance): 1) collapse of the theoretical underpinnings of counter-cyclical fiscal policy, 2) structural changes in the economy, 3) policy disappointments, and 4) the current policy setting.

Collapse of the Theoretical Underpinnings of Counter-Cyclical Fiscal Policy

The high confidence in counter-cyclical fiscal policy in the 1960s and early 1970s was based on Keynesian macroeconomics, the theoretical structure built on the writings of John Maynard Keynes. Two elements were crucial. The first was the notion that fiscal policy—primarily increases or decreases in the government deficit—could stimulate or restrain short-term economic growth. The second element was not actually derived from the writings of Keynes, but was appended later and became a key underpinning of both "Keynesian" fiscal policy and counter-cyclical monetary policy theory. This was the Phillips Curve, the notion that there was a stable tradeoff between inflation and unemployment.

The Phillips Curve implied that lower unemployment would result in higher inflation and vice versa. According to this relationship, for example, if unemployment were maintained at a low level, inflation would be higher than at higher unemployment rates but would remain at a relatively constant rate. The implication of this relationship was that policy makers could choose a point along the inflation/unemployment tradeoff that they believed to be optimal and adjust policy to achieve it. In the early 1960s, policy makers chose to strive for "full employment," which was typically defined as an unemployment rate of 4 percent. This was thought to be the level at which most unemployment would be frictional or structural.

In 1967, in his presidential address to the American Economic Association, Milton Friedman argued that the Phillips Curve relationship is incorrect. He posited a "natural unemployment rate" that would exist if the economy were in equilibrium. This natural rate is determined by real factors in the economy—the composition of the labor force, the nature of the unemployment compensation system, and the pace of technological change, for example—but not by the rate of inflation.

Friedman argued that any tradeoff between unemployment and inflation is strictly a short-term phenomenon. If policy attempted to keep unemployment below the natural rate, the inflation rate would rise. But soon the expected rate of inflation would rise to match the actual inflation rate, and as that happened equilibrium would be restored in the economy and unemployment would return to the natural rate. At the new equilibrium, unemployment would again be at the natural rate, but it would be paired with a higher rate of inflation. Attempting to keep unemployment permanently below the natural rate would require continuously increasing inflation. The implications were that macroeconomic policy actually could do rather little to affect the unemployment rate, at least in the long term, and that the inflationary effects of reducing unemployment were much greater than previously believed.

Friedman's interpretation and conclusions were not immediately accepted by the mainstream of the economics profession. During the 1970s, however, the advent of "stagflation" (simultaneous increases in unemployment and inflation) forced a broad re-examination of the unemployment/inflation relationship. Stagflation is inconsistent with the Phillips Curve, but it is not inconsistent with the natural rate of unemployment hypothesis. Today the natural rate hypothesis is the most widely held view, although there are significant competing theories. In general, the theory serves relatively well in providing an explanation of the observed relationship between unemployment and inflation over the post-war period. * * *

Friedman's theoretical contribution was notable not only because it introduced the concept of the natural rate of unemployment, but also because of its attention to expectations, how they are formed, and how they affect behavior. Prior to this time, most economic theory ignored expectations or relied on a simplistic view of how expectations are formed. Typically, expectations were assumed to be based on simple extrapolations of past trends; any new information—such as a policy change—that should affect the course of the economy was assumed to be ignored until its effects appeared in the trends of economic data. But during the last two decades a new branch of economic theory has been developed, based on the assumption that economic agents form their expectations rationally, that is, incorporate all relevant information. Some of the early contributions to this rational expectations school of thought did serious damage to the first element of Keynesian economics that provided the basis for counter-cyclical fiscal policy: the notion that such policy could stimulate or restrain short-term economic growth.

In one of the most provocative papers, Sargent and Wallace in 1975 developed the argument that in a world of rational expectations, systematic counter-cyclical policy has no real effects on the economy. In such a world, events that are known beforehand have no economic effect because they are already factored into expectations. Only events that come as complete surprises (or the aspects of events that are surprises) can have economic effects. This implies that systematic counter-cyclical policy can have no effect because it will be fully anticipated; people will adjust their behavior to offset the policy and still achieve their objectives.

Shortly thereafter, the empirical foundations of counter-cyclical policy were attacked, using a rational expectations framework. In what became known as the "Lucas Critique," Robert Lucas argued that the econometric evidence supporting the effectiveness of counter-cyclical policy was flawed because the models used to estimate the policy effects were misspecified. Specifically, the parameters in the models depend on the structure of the economy; they depend on behavioral patterns that are based, in part, on expectations. Prior procedure had been to estimate an econometric model based on historical data, and then use the estimates to stimulate the effects of policy changes. Lucas pointed out that a policy change alters the structure of the economy and the expectations that the model parameters. Hence, simulations based on the historical relationships are invalid.

These papers and others—together with applied research finding disappointing effects of the counter-cyclical fiscal policies enacted in the 1960s and 1970s * * * destroyed essential elements of Keynesian economics as understood in the 1960s. The Keynesians had no immediate response to the criticisms. An effort ensued to reexamine and rebuild macroeconomic theory from the ground up, paying closer attention to the optimizing behavior of economic agents that produces the hypothesized macroeconomic relationships. This effort has become known as building the "micro foundations of macro-economics." The process is still underway, but it is unlikely to yield a single general model of the economy that enjoys the support of a substantial majority of the economics profession, as the Keynesian model once did. Instead, several different paradigms are being developed.

While space does not permit reviewing these paradigms, their implications for the points developed here can be summarized. The natural rate of unemployment hypothesis, or some variant thereof, is consistent with most of the new models. While only one of the new paradigms fully incorporates rational expectations, virtually all serious economic modeling in the last two decades has incorporated expectations—how they are formed and how they affect behavior—in one form or another. (The rational expectationists got their comeuppance in the early 1980s when the recessions were far more severe than they predicted would result from a pre-announced tightening of monetary policy to squeeze the inflation out of the economy.) And while early in the process new models were developed within which counter-cyclical policy could affect short-term economic growth even with rational expectations, in none of the current models is counter-cyclical policy as strong or as efficacious as it was believed to be in the Keynesian models of the 1960s.

Structural Changes in the Economy

Important structural changes in the economy have occurred since the 1960s, some of which have weakened the effectiveness of counter-cyclical fiscal policy. More specifically, in 1971 flexible exchange rates replaced the earlier system of fixed rates of exchange between currencies. The international capital market also has developed very rapidly in the last few decades as a result of advances in telecommunications and computerization. These changes have resulted in more efficient capital markets, but they also have weakened the ability of fiscal policy to affect domestic economic activity.

A tax cut to stimulate the economy, for example, will increase the budget deficit and result in higher interest rates. The higher interest rates will attract capital in the international capital markets as investors in other countries shift assets to earn the higher rate of return. With flexible exchange rates, the greater inflow of foreign capital will drive up the value of the dollar in relation to other currencies. This will make foreign goods and services cheaper to Americans and U.S. goods and services more expensive to foreigners. Hence, U.S. net exports will decline, offsetting the initial effects of the fiscal stimulus. This effect is sometimes characterized as "exporting the stimulus" because the decrease in net exports (increase in imports) will create jobs in other countries. (Under fixed exchange rates, the greater demand for dollars in the foreign exchange markets would force an expansion of the money supply; this monetary expansion would reinforce the fiscal stimulus.)

These effects can be seen in the U.S. experience during the 1980s. We incurred sustained, historically large Federal budget deficits, even during periods of fairly robust economic growth. These large deficits were accompanied by unusually high real interest rates. We changed from a capital exporting country into a capital importing country so quickly and drastically that we now are a net debtor to other nations of the world. As the dollar rose dramatically on the foreign exchange markets early in the decade, U.S. companies had difficulty selling exports and competing against imports, and "international competitiveness" became a policy issue. And despite the sustained unprecedented budget deficits, the economy did not overheat and become inflationary.

Another important structural change affecting fiscal policy is the indexation of the Federal individual income tax. Until the mid-1980s, the individual income tax burden increased automatically each year as a result of inflation—the so-called "bracket creep" phenomenon. Periodic counter-cyclical tax cuts enacted during recessions or stagnant periods offset the bracket creep that occurred during the growth years. Unless inflation got really out of hand, tax increases to restrain the economy were not needed; in a politically convenient fashion they occurred automatically due to bracket creep.

Now, however, the income tax is indexed for inflation; bracket creep is largely a phenomenon of the past (though real income growth still results in bracket creep). In this setting, a counter-cyclical tax cut has to be followed by a counter-cyclical tax increase to avoid a long-term reduction in government revenues. Given the difficulty with which our political structure confronts a tax increase (or spending cut), counter-cyclical fiscal policy implies pro-cyclical legislative gridlock.

Policy Disappointments

The third factor affecting the use (or nonuse) of counter-cyclical fiscal policy is that we tried it and it didn't work, or at least it didn't work as well as expected. The three major counter-cyclical fiscal policies implemented during the 1960s and 1970s—the 1964 tax cut, the 1968 surtax, and the 1975 tax cut—were the subject of much economic research. While this research cannot be reviewed here in detail, three general conclusions from the research can be summarized.

First, the magnitude of the peak effect of a tax increase or decrease, in terms of the change in real GDP, is only about equal to or somewhat smaller than the size of the tax change itself. This contrasts to earlier beliefs that the tax change multiplier could be as high as 2 or 3.

Second, the effectiveness lags for tax changes are longer than had been expected. Tax cuts or increases had been expected to have rather immediate effects. Instead, the effects grow slowly, peaking in the second or third year after implementation when economic stimulus or restraint may no longer be needed (or appropriate).

Third, in the short-run period when the effect of a tax increase or decrease is desired, a permanent tax change has more effect than a temporary tax change (both the 1968 surtax and the 1975 tax cut were temporary). In the first year, a temporary tax change probably has no more than half the effect of a permanent tax change. This finding is consistent with the theoretical developments in the 1970s and 1980s concerning the role of expectations in determining the effects of policy changes. Earlier theory, however, did not distinguish between permanent and temporary tax changes in terms of their effectiveness.

Another lesson was learned from the enactment of the 1975 tax cut: it is frequently impossible to know the stage of the business cycle early enough, and to design and implement legislation quickly enough, to offset an economic fluctuation.

The state of the economy was debated throughout 1974 during the first episode of stagflation in the aftermath of the 1973 OPEC oil price increase. Some people maintained the economy was overheating and that policy should aim to slow it down. Others believed it was slipping into recession. In October 1974 President Ford, siding with the first group (which was probably the majority of observers at that point), proposed a surtax to curb inflationary pressures. * * * It soon became clear, however, that the economy was, in fact, sliding into deep recession. In January 1975, the President recommended a tax cut to stimulate the economy out of the recession. It was enacted with uncharacteristic speed; the President signed the tax cut legislation on March 29, 1975, only 10 weeks after recommending it.

Despite the speed with which the 1975 tax cut was enacted, its implementation came after the recession had ended. With the advantage of hindsight and data that were unavailable concurrently, the recession was eventually dated as lasting from November 1973 to March 1975. The initial implementation of the tax cuts under the legislation did not occur until May 1975. Hence, the recession ended before the tax cut was put into effect. (It is possible, however, that the tax cut contributed to the end of the recession by giving a boost to expectations.)

The Current Policy Setting

Because of the factors summarized above—revisions in economic theory, structural changes in the economy, and disappointing policy experiences—views about the efficacy of counter-cyclical fiscal policy have changed substantially since the 1960s. One way to discern this change is to contrast statements of the Council of Economic [Advisers] (CEA) in the 1960s and 1980s.

In the 1962 *Economic Report of the President*, the CEA—comprised of Walter Heller, Kermit Gordon, and James Tobin—made the following statements:

> To capitalize on the potential gains of stabilization requires skillful use of all economic policy, particularly budget and monetary policy. (p. 70)

> To be effective, discretionary budget policy should be flexible. In order to promote economic stability, the government should be able to change quickly tax rates or expenditure programs, and equally able to reverse its actions as circumstances change. (p. 72)

In the report, the President proposed that he be given stand-by authority to temporarily reduce individual income tax rates by as much as five percentage points and to initiate temporary capital improvement projects as counter-cyclical measures.

The views of the 1982 CEA—comprised of Murray Weidenbaum, Jerry Jordan, and William Niskanen—also expressed in the *Economic Report of the President*, are in sharp contrast:

> Although the Federal Government is the appropriate agent for stabilizing the economy, the limits of such action must be understood. This Administration believes that "fine tuning" of the economy—attempting to offset every fluctuation—is not possible. The information needed to do so is often simply not available, and when it becomes available it is quite likely that underlying

conditions will already have changed. As a result, a policy of fine tuning the economy is as likely to be counterproductive as it is to be helpful. Though it is necessary for the government to have macro-economic policies, including both monetary and fiscal policies designed to achieve some desired growth of income, such policies are not suitable for correcting small fluctuations in economic activity. (p. 36)

While these statements were written by different economists working for different Administrations representing different political parties, the most important reason for their differences is probably the broadly changed views regarding counter-cyclical policy. Despite their differences, the statements in the two reports probably reflected the mainstream view of economists at the time they were written.

During the 1980s there was almost no discussion of counter-cyclical fiscal policy in the U.S. In terms of major tax legislation, the 1980s were the most active decade in the post-war period, but none of the tax changes was aimed at short-term stimulus or restraint of the economy. The legislation was aimed primarily at encouraging economic growth, tax reform, or raising revenue to reduce the budget deficit.

The deficit has itself become an independent reason for the disuse of counter-cyclical fiscal policy, at least on the stimulative side. The deficit has grown to such enormous proportions that significantly increasing it to stimulate the economy is no longer a serious policy option. Given the size of the deficit, the relevant fiscal policy question is not how to design and implement a stimulative deficit increase, but rather when and by how much the deficit can be reduced without causing intolerable contractionary effects.

It should be noted, however, that even though *discretionary* counter-cyclical fiscal policy is no longer in vogue, the Federal budget still contains a number of *automatic* stabilizers. The progressive income tax, for example, automatically claims a larger portion of income as incomes rise and a smaller portion as incomes fall. Welfare programs and unemployment compensation automatically increase payments to individuals as the economy slows down and reduce the payments as the economy speeds up. These programs result in significant automatic increases or decreases in the size of the deficit at different points in the business cycle. Hence, fiscal policy does not remain neutral with regard to the business cycle even though new fiscal policy legislation may not be enacted specifically to counter a given economic turn.

POLICY FOR RECOVERY AND GROWTH
James Tobin[*]

Statement to President-elect Clinton's Economic Conference (1992)

The United States suffers simultaneously from two macro-economic maladies. One is short-run and cyclical; the other is long-run and secular. The first is demand-side; the second is supply-side. The first is that spending on goods and services currently falls well short of the economy's capacity to produce them. The second is that productive capacity itself had been falling behind the needs and aspirations of the nation. The first has resulted in a shortage of jobs. The second is eroding the quality and real wages of jobs.

The great challenge of the Clinton Administration will be to provide remedies for both maladies. It won't be easy. The key to job creation in 1993 and 1994 is more spending, private or public, domestic or foreign, consumption or investment. The key to better real wages over the next two decades is faster growth of productivity, requiring greater national saving and investment.

Growth of the capacity of the economy determines the trend of real Gross Domestic Product (GDP) over the decades, across business cycles. Potential GDP at full employment—now about 5½ percent unemployment—grows nowadays at about 2 ½ percent per year. Half of that is due to the normal increase of the labor force, the other half to productivity. Productivity is growing much more slowly than before 1973, and more slowly than in other economies today. This is the long-run, supply-side malady. We need to raise productivity and the speed of its growth for the benefit of future Americans.

The short-run demand-side problem is that we haven't even kept up with the growth of capacity. 2 ½ percent is the sustainable growth rate. If GDP rises at that pace, it will just absorb the influx of new workers and the unemployment rate will remain constant. If GDP grows more slowly or actually declines, the unemployment rate will increase. The 2 ½ percent sustainable rate, not zero, is par for the U.S. economy. Relative to that par, we've been in recession—call it "growth recession"—for nearly four years; although GDP change was positive in most quarters, growth was usually slower than 2 percent annual rate. That is why unemployment increased by two percentage points, about 2 ½ million workers. As a result, GDP has by now fallen 5 or 6 percent below capacity.

To catch up in four years, we have to grow faster than the sustainable rate, indeed on average 1 ½ percentage points faster. GDP growth averaging 4 percent will be needed to bring the unemployment rate back down to 5 ½ percent in 1996, by creating 8 ½ or 9 million jobs—for roughly 5 or 5 ½

---

[*]. At time of original publication, Yale University economist and Nobel laureate who was a member of the Council of Economic Advisers under President Kennedy.

million new workers, 1 million persons re-entering the labor force, and the 2 ½ million now unemployed.

Will this catch-up recovery occur on its own? Or do we need fiscal stimulus to pep up demand for goods and services and for labor? There is, I believe, a strong case for stimulus. The labor market is weaker than the unemployment rate suggests. The number of employed workers involuntarily confined to part-time jobs is abnormally large. Job vacancies, as indicated by the Help-Wanted Index, are extraordinarily scarce. Defense cutbacks and corporate downsizings are destroying jobs irreversibly; to an unusual extent hirings in this recovery will have to be truly new jobs.

     * * *

Why can't the Federal Reserve do the job by itself, without fiscal help? One impediment is the banks' "credit crunch." Short-term interest rates are already very low. It may be that the Fed acted so little and so late from 1989 on that, as in 1930-31, they destroyed business and consumer expectations of recovery and let the economy slip out of their grasp. And after all, in virtually every previous cyclical recovery since World War II, monetary policy has had active fiscal help.

Nevertheless, the Fed * * * should lower rates further. The new President and Treasury Secretary will want to do their best to induce the Fed to be accommodative and to help reassure the bond markets. After all, no inflation cloud darkens the sky, and congestion of the capital markets is at least as distant as full recovery. * * *

Fiscal policy for recovery is bound to raise the budget deficit temporarily. (Among the virtues of an Investment Tax Credit is that it delivers a big bang of demand stimulus per dollar of lost tax revenue.) I recommend stimulus of $60 billion a year for the two years 1993 and 1994, about 1 percent of GDP, capable thanks to secondary "multiplier" effects of adding 1.5 percent to GDP demand, a modest amount relative to the 6% shortfall of GDP from its potential. The ratio of federal debt to GDP, which rose from 25 percent to 50 percent over the past twelve years, would be about one percentage point higher than otherwise. That price is worth paying for assuring a vigorous recovery.

Fiscal stimulus for recovery should be combined with credible deficit-reduction policies to be phased in later, so far as possible enacted in 1993. For deficit control as well as for its own sake, nothing is as important as health care reform. Otherwise federal outlays for Medicare and Medicaid will bust the budget throughout this decade, in particular rising by nearly 2 percent of GDP from 1996 to 2002.

In today's weak economy, immediate fiscal austerity would be counter-productive. It would raise unemployment. It would actually reduce investment for the future, thus doing harm rather than good to coming generations. The story will be different in robust prosperity three or four years from now. Once the economy is again producing at capacity, there will be no room for additional productive investment unless other demands on GDP are reduced,—that is, unless the country saves more. Federal deficit reductions are the prime way to raise national saving —provided they occur at the expense of private and public consumption and provided that the Fed lowers interest rates enough to channel saving into investment rather than going to waste in unemployment.

In the meantime the Clinton administration has the opportunity to provide in constructive ways the fiscal stimulus needed for recovery. * * *

Notes and Questions

1. Professor Eisner says that, if the government spends more than it is taking in, it is adding to the wealth of its bondholders. In fact, of course, the bondholders' wealth would not have disappeared had the government not needed to borrow it, they simply would have invested it differently. Professor Eisner probably is making the point that Americans, in the aggregate, owe most of the federal debt to themselves.

2. Professor Eisner suggests that the government deficit appears larger than it actually is, because the conventional budget requires current accounting of capital expenditures. Should the government have a separate capital budget?

3. Most discussions of government budgets focus on deficits, with a balanced budget usually the assumed ideal. What would be the consequences of a budget surplus?

4. Professor Eisner was particularly disdainful of attempting to mandate a balanced budget by constitutional amendment. (He referred to one proposal that would require a three-fifths-majority votes in Congress to allow a deficit.) Do you agree with Eisner?

5. Automatic counter-cyclical adjustments, such as higher income taxes during economic upturns and increased unemployment compensation payments during downturns, clearly have failed to prevent booms and recessions in the economy. Does this mean that John Maynard Keynes and Keynesian successors were mistaken as to the ability of government to successfully use fiscal policy?

6. Professor Eisner discounted concern about borrowing by the federal government by noting that households and private businesses each borrow comparable amounts. Does this data show that federal borrowing is not a matter of serious concern, or that borrowing on all levels, and not just by the federal government, is excessive?

7.   Dr. Kiefer argued that economists are much less sanguine than earlier about fiscal policy playing an effective role. First, he pointed to "the collapse of the theoretical underpinnings of counter-cyclical fiscal policy." What did he mean by this?

8.   Why do floating foreign exchange rates (in effect since 1971), and more efficient capital markets, make fiscal policy less likely to be effective?

9.   Dr. Kiefer quoted the 1962 *Economic Report of the President*, which was highly supportive of fiscal policy, and contrasted the 1982 report, whose authors thought that "fine tuning" the economy was impossible. Do you think that Professor Tobin, a member of the Council of Economic Advisers in 1962, would agree with Dr. Kiefer that fiscal policy likely cannot play a helpful role in fine tuning the economy?

10.   Note that the Clinton administration did not take Professor Tobin's advice to provide a government spending stimulus to the economy, but it did follow his suggestion of phasing in deficit-reduction policies.

B.   THE MIX OF REVENUE SOURCES

Federal government revenues come from a variety of sources. These shift over time in response to changes in government policy and in the composition of the economy. Without making a systematic attempt to separate changes as a result of higher levels of economic activity from changes in statutory rules, Dr. Allen Manvel describes and places in perspective the mixture of revenue sources in 1972 and in 1992:

FEDERAL REVENUE CHANGES, 1972-1992
Allen D. Manvel[*]
57 Tax Notes 959, 959-61 (1992)

Budget receipts in fiscal 1992 totaled nearly $1.1 trillion—up fivefold from the 1972 aggregate of $207 billion. During the same interval, the economy (gross domestic product, or GDP), as measured in current dollars, also expanded fivefold. That change mainly reflected price inflation—more than threefold in the 20-year period—but was bolstered also by a 58-percent growth in "real" or constant-dollar GDP (which in turn was traceable, in part, to a significant expansion of the nation's work force, reflecting a 21-percent

---

[*]. At time of original publication, retired Division Chief of the U.S. Census Bureau and regular Tax Notes columnist.

growth of population). Average annual percentages of change for the 20-year period, accordingly, were:

Federal receipts	8.6
Current-dollar GDP	8.5
Price inflation	6.1
Constant-dollar GDP	2.3
Population	1.0

Year-to-year changes in these measures, however, occurred variably, rather than uniformly, and, thanks mainly to the curtailment of inflation in the 1980s, the 1972-1982 and 1982-1992 periods involved markedly different developments, as shown by the following figures:[2]

	1972-82	1982-92
Percent change:		
Federal receipts	198	74
Current-dollar GDP	173	87
Price inflation	124	45
Constant-dollar GDP	23	29
Rate of change:		
Federal receipts	11.5	5.7
Current-dollar GDP	10.6	6.5
Price inflation	8.4	5.6
Constant-dollar GDP	2.1	2.6

During the past two decades, total federal receipts moved quite closely with the economy, and amounted annually to between 18 and 20 percent of GDP, except for two years—1976 (17.7 percent) and 1981 (20.2 percent). At first glance, this record of overall revenue stability may seem inconsistent with the story of hyperactive tax legislating laid out in C. Eugene Steuerle's recent incisive volume, which deals with the 1980s as "the tax decade."[3] But the story is more complex. First, when one goes below the aggregate to consider particular revenue sources, one finds—as reflected in table 1—that their relative importance has been altered sharply by developments of the past two decades. Second, it will be found that these changes occurred mainly because of the differing responsiveness of particular types of taxes to inflation and other economic changes, rather than as the planned result of tax legislation.

* * *

During the past two decades, the yield of social insurance taxes and contributions out paced the rate of increase in GDP by 53 percent, so that in 1992, they accounted for more than one-third of all budget receipts, compared with one-quarter in 1972. (See columns 3 and 4 of table 1.) The social

---

2. The figures pertain to fiscal years, as reported in tables 1.1, 1.2, and 1.3 of the *Budget of the United States Government, Fiscal Year 1993, Supplement, February 1992*.

3. C. EUGENE STEUERLE, THE TAX DECADE (HOW TAXES CAME TO DOMINATE THE PUBLIC AGENDA), Washington, D.C. The Urban Institute Press, 1992.

insurance sources amounted to some $1,600 per capita in fiscal 1992, or $556 more per capita than would have been realized at the 1972 rate of collection. All other sources together supplied about $2,600 per capita in fiscal 1992, which was less by about one-sixth, or $480 per capita, than if their yield had kept pace with the growth of the economy.

The following comments refer to the several major kinds of budget receipts. * * *

Estate and gift taxes probably constitute the most clearly and strongly "progressive" element of the federal revenue system, but their yield is small —one percent of all receipts in fiscal 1992—and has diminished sharply (in relative terms) during the past two decades. Coverage of these taxes is severely limited by a "unified tax credit" that, in effect, exempts $600,000 of any estate or gift from taxation. This exemption was provided by the Tax Act of 1981, and is more than three-and-one-half times as generous as the credit that previously applied. The 1981 change far more than compensated for the potential effect of price inflation upon the tax base. The 1981 Tax Act also reduced top rates of the estate and gift taxes.

Excise taxes supplied $46 billion of federal revenue in fiscal 1992, or 4.3 percent of the total. Every major excise tax component has lagged in yield far behind economic change, so that excise collections in fiscal 1992 were down, in relative terms, by 42 percent from the 1972 level. The drop would have been even greater if it had not been for statutory rate increases enacted at various times during the past decade.

Since 1991, the federal excise tax on cigarettes has been 42 cents per pack, as against 16 cents per pack between 1984 and 1991, and eight cents per pack for many years before 1984. The federal gasoline tax also went up in 1991, to 14 cents per gallon as compared with nine cents between 1984 and 1990, and four cents for a long period before 1984. And liquor tax rates, which had been nearly unchanged for a long time, were increased slightly in the mid-1980s and more sharply beginning with 1991. Nonetheless, in the context of drastic price inflation, and with less prevalent cigarette smoking, some decline in per capita liquor consumption, and improved highway mileage by passenger cars, the collections from each of these major kinds of federal excises have dropped off sharply, relative to GDP. (See column 8 of table 1.)

The *corporate income tax* has also diminished sharply in relative yield. In fiscal 1992, this source accounted for only one-eleventh of all federal receipts, as against nearly one-sixth 20 years before. Although some portion of the past two decades' relative shrinkage *may* have resulted from tax law changes, most of it has apparently resulted from a major change in the composition of corporate finance—involving far more use of borrowing and less reliance on equity financing. Accordingly, in relation to gross domestic product, corporate profits have diminished, while corporate outlays for interest have moved up strongly.

Table 1 -- Composition of Federal Budget Receipts, Fiscal Years 1972 and 1992

	Amount (bil. $)		Percentage		Percent of gross domestic product			Percent change 1972-92	Change in amount, 1972-92	
	1972	1992	1972	1992	1972	1992	Change, 1972-92		Bil. $	Per Capita[3]
All budget receipts	207.3	1,079.7	100.0	100.0	18.10	18.41	+0.31	+2	+18.18	+71
Individual income tax	94.7	468.5	45.7	43.4	8.27	7.99	-0.28	- 3	-16.42	-64
Corporation income tax	32.2	99.2	15.5	9.2	2.81	1.69	-1.12	- 40	-65.69	-257
Social insurance taxes and contributions	52.6	411.3	25.4	38.1	4.59	7.01	+2.42	+53	+141.93	+556
OASDI (& RR retirement)	40.9	304.7	19.7	28.2	3.57	5.20	+1.63	+46	+95.60	+374
Hospital insurance	5.2	79.0	2.5	7.3	0.45	1.35	+0.90	+200	+52.79	+207
Unemployment insurance	4.4	23.3	2.1	2.2	0.38	0.40	+0.02	+5	+1.17	+5
Other (Federal employees' retirement contributions)	2.1	4.6	1.0	0.4	0.18	0.08	-0.10	- 56	-5.87	-23
Excise taxes	15.5	46.0	7.5	4.3	1.35	0.78	-0.57	- 42	-33.43	-131
Alcoholic beverages	5.0	8.2	2.4	0.8	0.44	0.14	-0.30	- 68	-17.60	-69
Tobacco products	2.2	4.9	1.1	0.5	0.19	0.08	-0.11	- 58	-6.45	-25
Highways	5.3	17.4	2.6	1.6	0.46	0.30	-0.16	- 35	-9.38	-37
Airports, airways	0.7	5.2	0.3	0.5	0.06	0.09	+0.03	+50	+1.76	+7
Other excises	2.3	10.3	1.1	1.0	0.20	0.17	-0.03	- 15	-1.76	- 7
Estate and gift taxes	5.4	11.1	2.6	1.0	0.47	0.19	-0.28	- 60	-16.42	- 64
Miscellaneous sources (including customs)	6.9	43.7	3.3	4.1	0.61	0.74	+0.14	+21	+8.21	+32

Sources: 1972 data (and 1992 GDP amount) from *Budget of the United States Government, Fiscal Year 1993, Supplement, February 1992,* tables 1.2, 2.1, 2.4, and 2.5; 1992 receipts data from *Monthly Treasury Statement . . ., August 1992,* with extrapolations for September 1992.

2. Difference between actual 1992 amount that would have been received at the 1972 rate of collection, relative to GDP.

3. Based on estimated mid-1992 population of 255.5 million.

Although the *individual income tax* was by far the leading source of federal revenue in 1992, as also in 1972 (and in previous years back to before World War II), its yield failed to keep pace with the 1972-1992 expansion of GDP, by about $16 billion, or $64 per capita. During the 1970s, the yield of the individual income tax was strongly bolstered by inflation-spurred "bracket creep," and, despite some legislated rate cuts, its yield moved up to reach an all-time high of 9.6 percent of GDP in fiscal 1981. The relative shrinkage of the next 11 years, down to the 1992 rate of 8.27 percent of GDP, resulted mainly from the 1981 Tax Act, which cut applicable rates and provided for indexing of exemptions and tax brackets—a change which, from 1984 on, sharply reduced the tendency toward "bracket creep." Treasury Department estimates suggest that individual income tax revenue in fiscal 1989 was about 36 percent less than it would have been in the absence of tax law changes enacted in the preceding eight years.

As previously noted, *social insurance sources* experienced a strong yield increase during the 1972-1992 interval and expanded from 4.6 to 7.0 percent of GDP. This rise was in part a result of the Social Security Amendments of 1983, but most of it occurred as the "automatic" response to economic expansion (and inflation) of the provisions that govern the bulk of social insurance financing. Those provisions are explicitly structured to carry out the original mandate of the Social Security law that the trust funds concerned be kept out of the red. Under those provisions, there have been successive increases in payroll tax rates, and successive increases also in the annual pay ceiling for their application (reflecting the year-to-year rise in prices as measured by the cost-of-living index). It may be noted that these indexing arrangements have the opposite effect from that of the indexing that applies to the individual income tax—tending to enhance rather than curtail the rate of collections in response to price inflation.

Notes and Questions

11. Over the 1972-92 period, federal tax receipts roughly matched the growth of the economy as measured by gross domestic product (GDP), but rose more rapidly than the rate of inflation. Which comparison is more important in measuring whether the government's tax bite is growing?

12. Many excise taxes are *specific*: the tax is expressed as a stated amount per unit (a specified number of cents per package of cigarettes or gallon of gasoline). Other excise taxes are *ad valorem*—for example, a tax expressed in terms of a percentage of the charge for long distance telephone calls. Why do revenues from specific excise taxes tend to lag both the rate of growth of the economy and the rate of inflation?

13. Why does the increased reliance of corporations on debt adversely affect corporate income tax receipts?

14. Dr. Manvel largely attributes the relatively slow growth of individual income tax receipts in the 1982-92 period to the elimination of "bracket creep" (a topic discussed in greater detail in Chapter Sixteen). What is meant by bracket creep, and what effect did the 1981 tax act have on it?

15. As a percentage of total budget receipts, income taxes declined significantly between 1972 and 1992. Social insurance taxes and related outlays, on the other hand, increased greatly in importance. What implications do these changes have on the use of taxes to implement fiscal policy goals?

C. USE OF FISCAL POLICY TO CHANGE SOCIAL OR ECONOMIC BEHAVIOR

The broadest and least controversial fiscal policy goals (at least in terms of desirability) are to achieve something approaching full employment coupled with relative price stability. In addition, other, more specific goals have been proposed. Some have been implemented, at least in part. Some of these objectives are quite broad, such as increasing savings and/or investment; encouraging home ownership; and redistributing wealth or, at least, reducing differences in income levels. Other objectives are much narrower. These include targeting depressed geographic areas, supporting a domestic maritime industry, and encouraging the development of oil and gas reserves. Carrying out policies to achieve these objectives raises issues of fairness between taxpayers in the favored categories and those left out.

The articles excerpted in this subchapter deal with a broad goal of fiscal policy that has gotten increasing attention in recent years, the encouragement of savings. This is in response to a widespread understanding that the savings rate has sharply declined in the United States. This objective is used to justify more liberal tax treatment for Individual Retirement Accounts (IRAs) and, in a broader context, to justify proposals to shift an increased share of the tax burden from income to consumption. (Consumption taxes are discussed in Chapters Six and Seven.)

SAVINGS, INVESTMENT, AND THE TAX REFORM ACT OF 1986
Edward M. Gramlich[*]

National Tax Association-Tax Institute of America

79th Annual Conference 13-19 (1986)

One of the oldest questions in public economics is whether to tax income or consumption. The difference is saving, which at least until recently equaled investment. This implies that the question of whether consumption or income is the appropriate tax base gets very close to the question of

---

[*]. At time of original publication, Congressional Budget Office and The University of Michigan.

whether inducements for saving or investment should be provided in an income tax.

While this is a very old question, it is still a timely one. The present U.S. tax system can be thought of as an income tax, though it has certain features conferring consumption-tax-like treatment. The Economic Recovery and Tax Act of 1981 (ERTA) strengthened these consumptive-tax-like features, or inducements to save and invest, to such a degree that some effective tax rates on corporate investment actually became negative. That Act was also arguably the cause of the high deficits that have plagued the U.S. economy ever since. On the one hand, the deficits have appeared to cause a sharp fall in the share of U.S. output devoted to domestically-owned capital accumulation. On the other hand, they have led to a succession of tax changes that tightened up on savings and investment incentives. This process culminated in the massive Tax Reform Act of 1986 (TRA), which removed virtually all of the incentives that had not in the meantime become sacred cows.

This story suggests that the U.S. cannot get its tax Act together on saving-investment incentives. The U.S. first gave significant tax advantages with its right hand but simultaneously hurt investment worse by large deficits with its left. It then progressively took away these incentives with its right hand as it was trying to reduce deficits to increase domestically-owned capital formation with its left. What is going on?

One thing I do not do in the paper is to explain what is going on. In this messy world of tradeoffs, conflicting choices, imperfect understanding of the issues and politics, it is safe to say that nobody can really explain why all the changes have been made. But I do try to ask and answer three basic questions in the recent tax treatment of saving/investment:

1. Whether it is now appropriate for the U.S., a country with a personal and corporate income tax, to promote saving/investment.

2. Whether it is appropriate to promote saving/investment through the tax system or in some other way.

3. What are the likely effects of all the changes in saving/investment inducements in TRA on national saving and capital formation rates?

All three questions are posed from both a closed and a small open economy perspective.

Should Saving/Investment Be Promoted?

The saving/investment issue is one of the most basic in economics. Yet one of the most difficult to discuss objectively. Beginning with definitions, the standard national income accounts identity shows that private plus government savings equals the sum of capital investment plus the export surplus. When a country has an export surplus, it is by definition increasing its claim on foreigners, or lending abroad. These new international assets should be added to its domestic capital formation in deriving the impact of its saving on national net worth. Conversely, when a country has an import surplus, as does the U.S. right now, it is borrowing from abroad to put its domestic capital in place, and this borrowed capital should be deducted from total capital formation to determine the change in national net worth.

Either way, the newfound importance of trade and capital flows with other countries requires that physical capital formation be distinguished from wealth accumulation, or domestically-owned capital formation. In either case, wealth accumulation, not capital formation, is the best measure of how much of the nation's output is being diverted from present-day consumption to the provision of the future.[2] In either case incentives that promote saving must also be distinguished from incentives that promote investment. Since the two are no longer the same, incentive effects will not be either.

The more difficult question is the normative one of how much a country *should* save, or devote to wealth accumulation. At least four types of answers have been provided in the economics literature, none with absolutely compelling logic.

The market answer

The first impulse of American economists and politicians these days is to ask what "the market" would do. By this standard, the tax system should be neutral with respect to saving and investment and fiscal policy should be too. National saving rates would equal private saving rates, and each generation would pay for its public goods.

While the standard has superficial plausibility, there are many problems with it. First off, how can a country with both an income and a corporate tax ever attain neutrality, given the well-known double taxation of both dividend and interest income? Second, one can think of many other actions taken by government, such as in its public provision for retirement or its own investment portfolio, that have non-neutral effects on saving and investment. * * *

[S]omething that might be called "pragmatic neutrality" can be achieved by setting the long run governmental budget deficit equal to zero. But even this standard remains surprisingly amorphous as a pragmatic guide to policy. Does this government deficit that is set to zero include state and local deficits or not, their trust fund surpluses or not, it is a capital or a current operating deficit, correcting for the cycle or not, corrected for inflation-induced capital gains on debt or not, corrected for capital gains in assets or not? These questions are not answered by the underlying logic, but each one turns out

---

2. The statement is not meant to downgrade the usefulness of other measures. If one were interested in labor income or labor productivity, one should focus on capital put in place in the United States. And, the fact that borrowed capital has less impact on long term living standards than does domestically-owned capital does not obviously mean that it has no impact. Given that lack of saving, the fact that the U.S. *is able to* borrow from foreigners does keep U.S. living standards now and in the future above what they should be otherwise.

to matter enormously in practice. We are left with as many questions as we started with.

The time series answer

According to this standard, society might be thought of as an intergenerational compact where the generations cannot determine their proper saving rate, but they can agree to do whatever their parents did. If their parents devoted ten percent of national output to wealth accumulation, they should too. Under this standard, whatever exists is right, and changes in saving, particularly declines, are inappropriate.

As with the market standard, the problems with a time series standard are obvious. Should a generation forced to defend its homeland be held to the same standards as its parents, who may have lived in more peaceful times? More relevant to today's problems, what about a generation that finds itself with a costly strategic deterrence burden? What if there are new resource discoveries that promise to shift living standards up in the future? Or depletion that promises to shift down living standards? There may be some horizontal equity argument for the time series standard, but it is only if many important factors are held constant, factors that cannot possibly be held constant in real life.

The cross section answer

According to this standard, the U.S. is in a competitive rat-race for international markets, and should save as much as its neighbors. Which neighbors? And in a world of fluctuating market exchange rates, why keep up? If for some reason the U.S. gradually loses competitiveness, or has creeping inflation, its currency will slowly decline so as to maintain purchasing power parity. This implies a slow increase in relative prices for foreign goods, but so what? Relative prices change all the time. The cross section answer also leaves much unanswered.

The theoretical answer

Growth theorists have long recognized the existence of a "golden rule" of capital accumulation.[5] That yields a savings rate that, if maintained, maximizes the path of consumption per capita over time. * * *

In addition to the bizarre spectacle of having basic political questions being decided by assumptions from abstract growth models, one can raise the same problems as with the time series standard—why should society save at the same rate over time?

So none of these answers is fully, or perhaps even partially, convincing. A true skeptic will come out of this discussion believing that there is no proper savings rate policy, and by implication no limit from these considerations on government budget deficits.[6] But for those with any

---

5. Edmund S. Phelps, "The Golden Rule of Capital Accumulation: A Fable for Growthmen," *American Economic Review*, September, 1961, vol. 51, pp. 638-642.

6. There could be other limits. If, for example, the interest burden grew steadily as a share of GNP, the government could be put in a position of having either to repudiate its debt, or to

inclination at all to make subjective normative judgements about fiscal policy, it is interesting to note that at least for the early 1980s, all four standards clearly point to the fact that the U. S. should raise its national saving (wealth accumulation) rate. For the market standard, since 1980 deficits by any measure have risen sharply, and overall fiscal policy is definitely nonneutral—[the data] strongly suggest that these deficits have reduced the national wealth accumulation rate well below the private rate. The same numbers show a sharp drop in the national wealth accumulation rate, which argues for a higher saving by the time series standard. And even before the drop occurred, the U.S. was under-saving by both cross section and theoretical standard. Something as subjective as the proper saving rate can never be conclusively determined, but there does seem to be very strong evidence that the U.S. should try to save more than it now is, at least as much as the country did back in the 1960s.

          * * *

Implications

The clearest message here is that national saving is important, there are many reasons to believe that the U.S. is not doing enough of it lately, and that this is a good reason why the country should continue its difficult fight against government budget deficits.

But it becomes much more difficult to discern the impact of TRA in this fight. * * * TRA has eliminated some investment incentives and made many offsetting changes in saving incentives. * * * [T]here seems to be no substitute for honest-to-goodness deficit reduction, however painful that may be, as a way to increase national saving rates.

ACCOUNTING FOR SAVING AND CAPITAL FORMATION
IN THE UNITED STATES, 1947-1991
Richard Ruggles[*]

7 Journal of Economic Perspectives 3, 3, 12-16 (1993)

This paper is concerned with accounting for the saving and capital formation taking place in different sectors of the U.S. economy. In brief, where does saving arise and where is it used? Do some sectors save more than they spend for capital formation and thus are net lenders? Do other sectors save less than is required for their capital formation and thus are net borrowers? The U.S. national income accounts contain the basic data relating to these questions. However, at several points, these data must be recast in order to yield analytically useful results. When such a reformulation is made, the conclusions that can be drawn differ strikingly from much of the currently received conventional wisdom.

---

monetize it (and repudiate it through inflation). At present this interest burden growth in the United States has been contained, and we are now in the position of deciding whether there are other, more subjective, reasons for reducing deficits.

     *. At time of original publication, Professor Emeritus of Economics, Yale University.

* * *

Summary and Conclusions

The reformulation of the household sector account to take into account their ownership of houses and their actual receipts of pension benefits, indicates that, on balance, households have not been net providers of saving to other sectors in the economy. Although the gross saving of both the enterprise and household sectors approximate their capital formation, it does not mean that there is no inter-sectoral financing. Many households may be the source of finance for small business or venture capital. Conversely, many enterprises may extend consumer credit to households or finance owner-occupied housing mortgages.

Given the observed patterns of sector saving and capital formation three sets of questions need to be examined. First, how robust are the empirical findings about sector saving and capital formation? Are the observations relating to sector net borrowing and net lending valid even if more restrictive or broader concepts of saving and capital formation are used? Second, how relevant are the data on sectoral saving and capital formation to questions of the determinants of saving and capital formation in the economy? Are increased saving and capital formation both necessary and sufficient for productivity and economic growth? Finally, what are the implications of the cyclical changes in sectoral saving and capital formation for economic policy? What policies should be followed to ensure a high level of economic activity without inflation?

Robustness of the Empirical Findings

The absolute differences observed between saving and capital formation—that is, net lending and net borrowing—for the different sectors * * * are unaffected by differing definitions of saving and capital formation. * * *

Even if the concept of enterprise capital formation were to be expanded to include intangible capital such as research and development, worker training, environmental improvements and repair and maintenance, enterprise sector net lending and net borrowing would not be affected. * * * Indeed, even employing net saving and net capital formation concepts would not alter the empirical findings relating to sector net lending and sector net borrowing.

Relevance of Sector Saving and Capital Formation

These findings are directly relevant to understanding the process of saving and capital formation in the economy. The conventional view that saving by individuals provides the basis for enterprise capital formation is contradicted by the evidence. On balance, households are not net lenders to enterprises or government. For many enterprises, capital consumption allowances and retained earnings are the major source of funds for capital formation. The role of reserves held by employer pension and insurance funds against future liabilities also should be recognized as having a central role in the behavior of financial markets as a source of funds. Finally, from the volatile behavior of capital formation, it appears that the willingness of enterprises to undertake capital formation is, in most periods, a more important determinant than the availability of funds provided by saving in the economy. The balance sheets of many enterprises indicate that they have financial resources available to undertake capital formation in periods when nevertheless they are contracting their capital outlays.

Economic theory generally views capital as tangible goods yielding a flow of future services and representing a factor of production. However, many tangible goods, such as shopping malls, housing, consumer durables, public facilities and some highways, may primarily yield a flow of consumption services. Such consumption services are useful and important, but they may not have significant impact on increasing productivity and sustained growth in the economy. On the other hand, many other kinds of current expenditures for such things as research and development, employee training, education, [and] improvement of the environment may make major contribution to future increases in productivity.

Thus, the emphasis on the importance of saving and capital formation for economic growth and productivity may be misplaced. The production of some tangible producer and consumer goods, while important for economic growth, are not the sole determinants of productivity and development of the economy. More emphasis needs to be directed to encouraging and developing those economic and social activities that are recognized as having a significant impact on the productivity of the economic system.

The Cyclical Implications of Sectoral Saving and Capital Formation

The cyclical patterns of saving and capital formation of households, enterprises and government have important implications for economic policy directed at maintaining full employment and price stability. In periods of recession, households reduce their expenditures on consumer durables and their purchases of new owner-occupied housing. One consequence is that their borrowing for such expenditures decline, while at the same time their previous level of repayment on consumer debt and mortgages continues. Enterprises selling to consumers face a slackening in their sales and rising excess capacity, and as a consequence their profits and retained earnings decline and at the same time they also reduce their capital expenditures and their employment. The government in this situation is faced with declining tax revenues and rising needs of recession-related expenditures, with the consequence that government deficits increase.

It is apparent in this situation that although there has been a decline in saving in each sector, it has not been the cause of the decline in capital formation, income and employment. Efforts to stimulate saving in the expectation that it will induce more capital formation are misguided. Policies that raise income and profits and encourage spending and capital formation are needed. Thus, in recession, tax reductions and expansion of government expenditures on infrastructure are appropriate.

Because state and local governments are not permitted to indulge in fiscal policy, they are required to have balanced budgets. This means that in periods of economic decline, they must raise taxes and reduce their expenditures. This has the perverse effect of accentuating the decline in the economy. During this last recession, many economists and business leaders have urged that such balanced budget policies also be adopted by the federal government—thus prohibiting it also from engaging in fiscal policy. The extent to which fiscal policy should be used to stimulate the economy can be questioned, but unenlightened contractionary policies should not be taken by governments in periods of recession.

Finally, the analysis also has implications for saving and capital formation policies in periods of economic boom. During periods of economic expansion, both households and enterprises expand their capital formation. The increases in tax revenues and imports act as automatic stabilizers to some extent, but speculative expansions of capital expenditures (especially in the area of building construction) may result in rising prices and unsustainable levels of capital formation. The consequence may be overexpansion and economic collapse, such as occurred during the saving and loan crisis. Again, the major policy effort should not be directed to encouraging sectoral saving by offering incentives such as reductions in capital gains taxation, but rather at curbing investment in speculative capital that result in unwarranted and/or undesirable capital formation.

The major lesson from the analysis of sectoral saving and capital formation is that in peacetime and in periods of recession, the major focus should be on stimulating useful capital formation rather than encouraging saving. The encouragement of saving is appropriate in periods when large expenditures for such things as national defense are unavoidable and they generate income that exceeds the availability of consumable goods in the economy. During World War II, the restriction of spending and encouragement of saving was appropriate, but in today's economic climate, new policies are required.

Concluding Thoughts

Both economic theory and national accounting have failed to provide an adequate understanding of the process of saving and capital formation. To a major extent, this failure has been due to the simplistic formulations of saving and capital formation by both neoclassical and Keynesian economic theory. Reformulations of economic theory are needed so that the institutional aspects of modern economic systems can be taken into account.

The viability of capitalist market economies depends on their achieving levels of saving and capital formation that are compatible with economic growth and full employment equilibrium without inflation. The primary tools for achieving and maintaining such an equilibrium have been monetary and fiscal policy. However, past experience suggests that simple guidelines relating to regulation of the money supply or control of the federal budget are not sufficient for this task. * * *

Notes and Questions

16. Dean Gramlich discussed four theories for deciding how much the United States "should" save, but found flaws with each theory. How then, was he able to arrive at the conclusion that the level of saving should be increased?

17. Dean Gramlich noted that the seemingly simple principle of balancing the budget "remains surprisingly amorphous as a pragmatic guide to policy." Why?

18. Both Gramlich and Ruggles make the frequently ignored point that the budgets of state and local governments are relevant to carrying out fiscal policy, as well as to the measurement of savings. For example, if fiscal policy calls for a governmental deficit while states and localities are operating at a surplus, an expansionary federal fiscal policy must more than offset the state and local surplus before it can become an effective stimulus.

19. In measuring the fiscal impact of states and localities, current cash flow is all important. For purposes of determining proper fiscal policy, state and local expenditures for capital projects count toward a deficit, while taxes imposed to amortize the debt over a period of years count toward a surplus. This is true even if the state or locality regards its budget as balanced. Because many states use a capital budget, both expenditure on a capital project and repayment over a period of years may be consistent with a state constitutional requirement that the state's budget be "in balance."

20. Recalling the debate from Subchapter A, observe that Professor Ruggles appears to favor an active fiscal policy, rejecting the view that the federal government, like the states, should follow a balanced budget policy that would prevent an expansionary fiscal policy in time of recession.

21. Professor Ruggles contends that we should be interested in capital formation rather than saving. Moreover, government policy should be directed to encourage specific types of capital formation. Which types of capital formation are less important, and which more important, according to Ruggles?

22. Monetary policy, such as relaxing or restricting credit and lowering or raising interest rates, appears to be more effective in restricting the economy than in stimulating it, at least over the short run. Monetary policy

has been compared to a string, which can be used to hold back the economy, but cannot be used successfully to push the economy.

While fiscal policy may in theory be effective in both expansion and contraction, politically it is much easier to cut taxes or raise expenditures than the contrary.

23. If the rate of savings is of concern, would it be better to tackle it by cutting the federal deficit rather than attempting to increase private savings by offering tax benefits (such as more liberal treatment of IRAs)—which themselves will increase the deficit?

24. Professor Ruggles concluded that households have not been net providers of savings to other sectors of the economy. What are the more important financial sources of capital formation, according to Ruggles? Would Ruggles focus tax benefits on sectors of the economy other than households to achieve more capital formation?

Selected Bibliography

Aaron, Henry J., *Lessons for Tax Reform, in* DO TAXES MATTER? THE IMPACT OF THE TAX REFORM ACT OF 1986 50 (Joel Slemrod ed., 1990).

ALESINA, ALBERTO & ROBERTO PEROTTI, THE POLITICAL ECONOMY OF BUDGET DEFICITS, (National Bureau of Economic Research, Working Paper No. 4637, 1994).

AUERBACH, ALAN J., THE U. S. FISCAL PROBLEM: WHERE WE ARE, HOW WE GOT HERE AND WHERE WE'RE GOING, (NATIONAL BUREAU OF ECONOMIC RESEARCH, WORKING PAPER NO. 4709) (1994).

BOSWORTH, BARRY P., TAX INCENTIVES AND ECONOMIC GROWTH, Chapters 1, 3, and 6 (1984).

Buchanan, James M., *Clarifying Confusion about the Balanced Budget Amendment*, 48 NAT'L TAX J. 347 (1995).

Eisner, Robert, *We Don't Need Balanced Budgets*, WALL ST. J., Jan. 11, 1995, at A14.

GALBRAITH, JOHN KENNETH, THE AFFLUENT SOCIETY, Chapter XVII (1958).

Gramlich, Edward M., *Savings, Investment, and the Tax Reform Act of 1986*, NATIONAL TAX ASSOCIATION-TAX INSTITUTE OF AMERICA, 79TH ANNUAL CONFERENCE 13-19 (1986).

Kiefer, Donald W., *Whatever Happened to Counter-Cyclical Fiscal Policy*, NAT'L TAX ASS'N F., Winter 1993, at 1-5.

Lav, Iris J. & James R. St. George, *Will Curbs on Unfunded Mandates Protect States from the Impact of a Federal Balanced Budget Amendment?*, 48 NAT'L TAX J. 337 (1995).

Manvel, Allen D., *Federal Revenue Changes, 1972-1992*, 57 TAX NOTES 959 (1992).

Poterba, James M., *Balanced Budget Rules and Fiscal Policy: Evidence from the States*, 48 NAT'L TAX J. 329 (1995).

Ruggles, Richard, *Accounting for Saving and Capital Formation in the United States, 1947-1991*, 7 J. ECON. PERSP. 3 (1993).

SAMUELSON, PAUL A., ECONOMICS: AN INTRODUCTORY ANALYSIS, Chapter 12 (1948).

Schultz, Charles L., *The Balanced Budget Amendment: Needed? Effective? Efficient?*, 48 NAT'L TAX J. 317 (1995).

Steuerle, Gene, *What Should Be Done If a Surplus Arises?*, 70 TAX NOTES 463 (1996).

Tobin, James, *Policy for Recovery and Growth*, Statement to President-elect Clinton's Economic Conference, December 5, 1992.

——, TWO REVOLUTIONS IN ECONOMIC POLICY: THE KENNEDY AND REAGAN ECONOMIC REPORTS (1988).

CHAPTER TWO

WHEN SHOULD INCOME BE TAXED?

Under the definition of "income" most widely accepted by economists, an increase in the taxpayer's net worth during the relevant accounting period constitutes income, and a decline in net worth is an offset against income. * * *

Other than by negative inference, the Code does not expressly require realization as a prerequisite for taxing income, but realization is nevertheless so basic to the taxing structure of existing law that the general principle is simply not challenged.[a]

A. INTRODUCTION

The rules for measuring income for tax purposes are derived from the rules that evolved as generally accepted accounting principles. The objectives of the accounting principles, however, differ from the objective of measuring income to be subjected to tax. For accounting purposes, profit or loss is computed so owners of a business and prospective lenders or investors can know how well, or how poorly, the business is doing. Similarly, accounting defines the assets and liabilities of a business to serve the needs of its owners, its creditors, and its prospective investors.

For tax purposes, the objective is to measure profit to determine the portion to be paid as income tax. Timing is extremely important for this purpose. If a taxpayer can postpone income tax liability arising from a profit that produces cash receipts or that changes the nature of an investment which will result in higher investment yields, the taxpayer then can earn subsequent profits on what is, in essence, the Government's share. How important this is depends on the length of deferral, and on the current levels of tax rates and interest rates.

Taxpayers can postpone tax liability if they can speed up business expense deductions so that the deductions precede actual cash outlays—for example, by setting up a reserve for anticipated expenses. On the receipts side, tax liability can be postponed if the benefits from appreciation in the value of assets can be converted into additional earning potential before the appreciation in value has been taken into account.

---

a. Boris I. Bittker & Martin J. McMahon, Jr., Federal Income Taxation of Individuals ¶3.2 (2d ed. 1995).

Notes and Questions

1.   An appreciation of the importance of the time value of money is extremely important in the study of tax law and policy. As indicated above, three variables are involved. First is the amount deferred, which, in the case of a deferred tax obligation, is usually dependent on the marginal rate of tax. The value of deferring an obligation to pay a given amount depends upon the length of the deferral, and the assumed rate at which money can be invested over the deferral period. Consider the value to a taxpayer of postponing payment of a $1,000 tax versus paying the $1,000 currently. If one assumes a five percent rate of interest and a five-year deferral, the present value of the obligation shrinks to $784; if the assumed rate of interest is 10 percent, the present value is $614; and a 30-year deferral reduces the present value to only $231. If the rate of interest is assumed to be 10 percent, the five-year deferral reduces the present value of the obligation to $621, the 10-year deferral to $386, and the 30-year deferral to a mere $57. Observe that a very lengthy deferral—for example, the purchase of a deductible IRA by a young person, who pays tax many years later during retirement—removes the bulk of the tax burden if a modest rate of interest is assumed, and virtually eliminates the tax if a higher rate is assumed. But even a one-year deferral has noticeable value; if 10 percent interest is assumed, the present value of the deferred $1,000 obligation is reduced to $909.[b]

2.   For business accounting purposes it is useful to match receipts and expenses in order to measure profit or loss on a particular segment of business operations, either for an operating division or for a time segment. Should such matching be the standard for measuring taxable income?

B.   THE HAIG-SIMONS DEFINITION OF INCOME

Subject to very limited exceptions,[c] the present tax system does not take appreciation in value into account until the appreciation has been realized—typically by sale of the appreciated asset.

Professor Henry Simons, an economist, challenged the conventional accounting definition of income.   Departing from the constraints of realization, he wrote: "Personal income may be defined as the algebraic sum of (1) the market value of rights exercised in consumption and (2) the change in the value of the store of property rights between the beginning and end of the period in question."[d] In recognition of earlier work, this is sometimes referred to as the Schanz-Haig-Simons definition or, more frequently, the Haig-Simons definition.   In the first excerpt, written in 1938, Professor

---

b. All figures in this note are taken from MICHAEL J. GRAETZ & DEBORAH H. SCHENK, FEDERAL INCOME TAXATION: PRINCIPLES AND POLICIES 853 (Appendix A, Table 1) (1995).

c. The mark-to-market method, which taxes unrealized appreciation, can be applicable to securities dealers and with respect to commodity contracts. See sections 475 and 1256.

d. HENRY C. SIMONS, PERSONAL INCOME TAXATION 50 (1938).

Simons strongly criticized the accountants' definition of income. In the second excerpt, published posthumously in 1950, he presented a set of examples that he thought demonstrated the unfairness of postponing until realization the treatment of appreciation in value as income.

Even if one assumes the theoretical validity of the Haig-Simons definition, significant practical problems limit its utility. Mr. Louie's note focuses on marketable securities, an area in which the Haig-Simons definition could realistically be implemented because market prices are known and valuation problems would be minimized. The excerpt, however, summarizes practical advantages and disadvantages of taxing unrealized appreciation in general.

Application of a pure form of the Haig-Simons definition is impractical because it would require annual appraisal of assets. There is also the possibility that it would be unconstitutional, a topic addressed by Marvin Chirelstein in the final excerpt of this subchapter. In *Eisner v. Macomber*,[e] the Supreme Court endorsed realization as a constitutional requirement for taxing income. Is this 1920 decision still binding? Professor Chirelstein thinks the answer is clearly "no," but he does not assume that Congress should tax unrealized appreciation even if the Constitution permits it to do so.

PERSONAL INCOME TAXATION
Henry C. Simons[*]
Pages 80-83 (1938)

We turn now to brief consideration of the familiar criterion of realization. A standard manual on our federal income tax quotes Professor Haig's definition of income and then remarks: "It should include the word realized"[53]—as though the omission were only a careless oversight! This view is widely held by accountants, by the courts, and even by some economists. It derives clearly enough from the conventional practices of financial accounting. The accountant, faced with problems of valuation for which data are often meager, has developed and followed religiously a rule-of-thumb procedure which sacrifices relevance to "accuracy." Instead of attempting the best estimates which can be made, he is usually content to employ figures already available in his accounts and thus to minimize demands upon mere judgment.[54]

---

e. 252 U.S. 189 (1920).

*. At time of original publication, Professor of Economics, University of Chicago.

53. Montgomery, *Income Tax Procedure* (New York, 1926), p. 590. One wonders how Haig may react to his colleague's proposal to destroy his definition by introducing an innocent little participle. Likewise, one might wish to know with what feeling Schanz may have read Max Lion's essay in the volume dedicated to Schanz (*Beitrage zur Finanzwissenschaft*) [Tubingen 1928], II, 273-300). Lion * * * finds that Schanz is not clearly free from the careless error which Montgomery has noted in Haig!

54. One might say that he often eschews valuation entirely. At least, one finds difficulty in

His methods appear to be founded upon profound mistrust of both his professional colleagues and his employers. The reputable accountant never loses sight of the fact that his income statements are influential in matters of dividend policy. Income, for him, is perhaps only what may be reported safely to unsophisticated directors as income. He aims, it would seem, never to ascertain what income is, in any really definable sense, but rather to devise rules of calculation which will make the result a minimum or at least give large answers only in the future. Conventional accounting, moreover, not only employs a procedure with a markedly conservative bias but promptly repudiates this procedure whenever it shows signs of working the other way. When prices drawn from actual transactions on his books afford excessive estimates, the accountant promptly appeals to the market for his valuations.

That such worship of conservatism—and professional conspiracy against truth—is an unmixed evil, in a world of corruptible accountants and optimistic directors, one may hesitate to assert. Where such rule-of-thumb procedure is so universal, however, there is undue resistance to departure from it where different methods are clearly desirable. Furthermore, there is in many quarters a disposition to maintain that methods of calculation deemed expedient in business indicate exhaustively the real meaning of income. It is easy for most people to elevate rules-of-thumb into logical necessities; and persons do seriously maintain, with more than verbal paradox, that income not realized is not income. Our comments need imply no criticism of the accountant's practical wisdom; yet one may lament the effects of his practice and preaching upon unwary minds, especially in a world where courts insist upon investing somewhat technical terms with their connotations in everyday usage.

Advocates of the recurrence criterion have undertaken to construct a concept of personal income from that of productivity or yield from things. Those who emphasize realization are attempting to define personal income in terms of transaction profit. In either case, it simply cannot be done. If all business ventures were initiated and completed within the fiscal period, the realization criterion would lead to no serious confusion. But, in a world where ventures often have neither beginning nor end within the lives of interested parties, it is hard to argue that one may grow richer indefinitely without increasing one's income. Furthermore, since transaction income implies no imputation to preassigned periods of time, how may one develop from it a conception wherein such imputation is fundamental?

The emphasis of accounting upon the transaction of sale would be fairly appropriate for merely merchandising enterprises, if only prices were extremely stable. It is always more appropriate to merchandising than to manufacture and, in general, is least expedient for enterprises where the

---

the idea that an inventory is being "valued" when different parts of an inventory of identical goods are priced differently—as is approved practice.

selling function is least important. But surely no adequate conception of annual, personal income can be built around the notion of transaction profit. To be sure, one never knows the final result of a business venture until it is completed. But the whole notion of accrual must be abandoned if one adheres rigorously to the test of realization. The argument that recognition of appreciation involves "anticipation of profit" which may never be obtained, fails to recognize the fundamental continuity of economic relations and ignores the essential value implications of income.

    * * *

accrual is a form of realization

FEDERAL TAX REFORM
Henry C. Simons[*]
Pages 61-67 (1950)

At risk of laboring the obvious, let us now indicate, in terms of some extreme possible cases, how existing procedure actually works. For this purpose, it seems best to proceed in terms of the law as it stood before 1920, since the "realization procedure" with which we are mainly concerned was simpler under earlier legislation and, while becoming more complicated, has persisted throughout the years substantially unaltered in its essential features. In some of the cases, incidentally, it may be useful to think of "the corporation" as an investment-trust, widely diversified, with many large shareholders subject to high surtaxes and with a numerous minority interest as well.

Case I.—A very wealthy diversifying "operator" might, through a most profitable life, show little or no taxable income at all, while living like a king and steadily increasing his net worth. The trick, of course, is simply to "realize" all of one's losses on investments and none of one's gains; or—in an irresistible phrasing—to have and to hold all faithful (appreciated) investments till death (do us part) and to divorce opportunely all unfaithful (depreciated) shares. The appreciation, as potentially taxable gain accrued, vanishes completely at the moment of parting of body and soul. Save for death duties (which of course depend on current value, not at all on the decedent's unrealized gains or losses) the next generation can start all over, and with greatly elevated "bases" for future loss realizations.

Hold gains + sell losses

Case II.—Saving through unrealized appreciation (undistributed corporate earnings) *vs.* other savings: the income tax as spending tax on some, as income tax on others.

Jones and Smith are born on the same day, inherit estates of $2.5 millions simultaneously, hold common stocks in companies which each year earn exactly 4 per cent, and die simultaneously. Each maintains the same consumption outlay or living scale throughout life—"spending," say, $50,000 per year—and reinvests any residual income each year.

---

[*]. At time of original publication, Late Professor of Economics, University of Chicago.

Payout of
Divs triggers
realization
currently

By corp not
Distributing
all income
Corp saves
money for
investor & he
avoids cur-
rent pymt
of taxes on
total income

Those whose
earnings are
wages are
tax disadvan-
taged compared
to those who
say their
whole thb
postpone
realzn

Jones invests entirely in companies which (irregularities aside) pay out all their earnings in dividends. Thus, at 4 per cent, his income is exactly $100,000 every year. He pays his income tax each year on that amount (say, a tax of $35,000, or an average rate of 35 per cent) and reinvests what's left ($100,000 - $50,000 - $35,000 = $15,000) in additional stock of the same companies.

Smith, on the other hand, puts his $2.5 millions all in a big investment-trust corporation—which, as it happens, owns the same stocks as Jones and in the same proportions. The corporation earns exactly 4 per cent, of course, but invariably pays out only two-thirds of its earnings in dividends, reinvesting the other one-third. Smith thus has a "real income" each year of $100,000 but a taxable income of only $66,667. Letting the corporation do his saving for him, he is able to exclude his savings from income tax, confining his taxable income (i.e., dividends) to the amount he needs to meet his taxes and his consumption outlays. Thus the taxes (at an average rate of 25 per cent) might amount to $16,667.

Thus, Smith with the same initial wealth and real income as Jones, and the same "spendings," has much more left ($33,333 *vs.* $15,000!) for reinvestment the first year, consequently more income each year thereafter and, so, still more to reinvest than Jones. When they die, Smith will be enormously wealthier than Jones; and the little Smiths and little Joneses will thereafter be regarded as belonging to families at different social and economic levels.

Now Jones may, in the circumstances, be called either stupidly scrupulous about eschewing avoidance opportunities or just plain stupid. Consider, however, what he could have done to keep up with Smith (Smith's wealth-headstart apart) if his income had been a salary income; if it had come from a partnership (say, a law firm); or how he could have exploited the avoidance opportunity if his wealth and income had initially been smaller, and his income not such as to permit much saving. "The richer you are, the faster you should be allowed to get richer," says our realization procedure, while the bracket-rates raucously dissent.

Case III.—Capital-gain income versus other income: taxable income excluding saving and much of "spendings," i.e., excluding even much income realized and consumed.

Brown and Gray each inherit $2.5 million simultaneously at age 21. Both consume their whole real incomes throughout life, saving nothing but preserving their estates intact, and then die simultaneously. They are equally successful in their investments, getting yields, including imputed earnings undistributed, of 4 per cent annually. (We may conveniently assume that changing market values of their shares reflect, at least at death, merely changes of book-values, i.e., undistributed corporate earnings.)

Brown invests exclusively in businesses which pay out regularly their full (and stable) earnings. Thus, his taxable income is $100,000. After paying his income tax (say $35,000), he spends all the rest ($65,000).

Gray puts his estate entirely in shares of an investment company, whose portfolio has, it happens, the same composition as Brown's. By tacit understanding among executives and the numerous shareholders, this company pays no dividends at all but maintains the market price of its shares at the current break-up value. * * * Gray's share in earnings is, of course, $100,000 per year; the market price of his shares rises by 4 per cent (compounded) annually. To meet his living expenses, i.e., to "realize" his full annual income, *he sells each year 4 per cent of his (then remaining) shares.*

The arithmetic here gets a bit complicated as the years pass. The crucial point, however, should be apparent, Gray's taxable income will never even approximate his stable real income of $100,000. Maintaining his capital at the same level as Brown's, he can spend far more than Brown and leave him far behind in the social game of invidious consumption. Thus, in the first year, Gray sells (almost) 4 per cent of his shares for $100,000. His gain *on these shares* is 4 per cent or only $4,000, which *is* his total *taxable* income for the first year. Compound interest makes for arithmetic complexity from here on. However, his taxable income for the second year will be only a bit over $8,000; for the third year, $12,000 plus; and so on, until, in the seventeenth year, it reaches about $50,000, or half of Brown's! Taking account of family exemptions and progressive rates, one sees that while Brown pays tax of, say, $35,000 every year, Gray pays a few *hundred* dollars at first, pays more each year until, in the seventeenth year, he is paying perhaps $12,000, and would get up to, say, $20,000 (taxable income of $75,000) only after his shares had quadrupled in price (35 years, at 4 per cent compounded). Remember that the two taxpayers started with the same wealth, got the same return on their investments, and kept at the same wealth level. Brown has $65,000 left to live on each year after taxes. Gray has over $99,000 left to "spend" the first year, $88,000 in the seventeenth year, and still $80,000 in the thirty-fourth year!

Adding insult to injury, present law says that only half of Gray's realized capital gains shall be treated as income![f] Thus, he pays *on* only $2,000 the first year; *on* $25,000 in the seventeenth year; *on* $37,500 in the thirty-fourth year * * *—while Brown pays on $100,000 every year! * * *

Case IV.—Income without any taxable income: borrowing against security appreciation (undistributed earnings).

It should be evident on reflection that even Gray is only a novice at tax avoidance. What small taxes he pays, relative to Brown, are actually quite needlessly paid in his circumstances. Our *Case IV* may start exactly as did

---

f. Under present law, all capital gain is subject to tax, but section 1(h) provides a maximum rate of 28%, which benefits taxpayers subject to marginal rates above 28%. (Eds.)

Case III—down to, but not including, the last sentence of the third paragraph.

In the present case, "Gray," being possessed of abundant collateral and good reputation, evades all the arithmetic of compound interest, simply retaining all his shares until death and borrowing from his bank each year to the amount of their appreciation. For convenience, suppose that he pays interest to the bank at the same rate (4 per cent) as the yield (appreciation) of his investment-trust shares. Thus, each year he borrows $100,000 *plus* what he needs to pay interest on his outstanding bank loan and "spends" the $100,000. He lives well, maintains his capital quite intact (his securities rise in value just as much as his bank debt increases), *and has no taxable income whatever*.

Indeed, "Gray" has now over-worked his avoidance scheme. His taxable income, by virtue of interest payments, is actually *negative* at the start and will become an enormous negative quantity if he doesn't wake up and read the law! In other words, he will simply be squandering large available interest deductions.[g] Since the income tax rudely refuses to pay people for having negative incomes (and the case of "Gray" before the relief authorities clearly is not strong), some use must be found for the deductions. Two possibilities are evident, both calling for some reversal of the prestidigitation by which his income was rendered legally not-income.

"Gray" may "realize" enough income by selling shares to cover not only his deductions but also his personal exemptions, which would also be squandered otherwise. The alternative, however, is much better—if one looks beyond technicalities. What "Gray" really should do is to talk his fellow stockholders and directors into a less Spartan dividend policy for the investing company. Moderation of the no-dividend policy will diminish risks of *ad hoc* revision of the law * * * and markedly reduce the "lightning hazard" (Section 102).[h] If all the large shareholders acquire sufficient bank debts, they can shift gradually to a dividend policy which will seem quite moderate and inoffensive, even to zealous Bureaucrats or Congressmen, and yet never expose them (*or their heirs!*) to "those awful surtaxes."

Case V.—Income without any taxable income and without borrowing.

Here is not one case but a whole congeries of cases, involving combinations of practices highlighted in the foregoing examples, and overlapping notably with *Case I*, all involving highly prosperous persons but not income taxes.

---

g. At the time Professor Simons wrote, all interest was deductible. Under present law, "personal interest" is nondeductible (section 163(h)) and "investment interest" is currently deductible only to the extent of investment income (section 163(d)). (Eds.)

h. Section 102 of the 1939 Code was the predecessor of present section 531, which imposes an additional tax on unreasonable accumulations of corporate earnings. The reference to "lighting hazard" is Professor Simons' assessment that the slight risk of the accumulated earnings tax actually being applied is comparable to the risk of being struck by lightning. (Eds.)

Clearly, the borrowing devices in *Case IV* are "accidental" or unessential. More realistic alternatives, preferable to the taxpayer, are clearly available (with small change in Gray's total arrangements). If, besides large investment-company holdings, Gray had a diversified portfolio of other investment assets, he could easily "realize" his full income from the reinvesting company by selling *other* assets, in annual no-net-gain packets of appropriate size. Any dividend or interest receipts (or salary, for that matter) could be offset fully by choosing packets showing suitable net losses. (Section 117 now rather queers this trick;[i] but there remains the possibility of borrowing enough to offset such income items by interest deductions, i.e., of using the *Case IV* tricks as far as need be.) But enough of such slumming expeditions into income-tax operations.

offsetting gains w/ losses

* * *

The cases considered above are symptomatic, not merely descriptive. They should suffice to persuade people that something is rather fundamentally wrong with our income tax, present and past, to support our diagnosis, and to establish a *prima facie* case for the surgical or remedial measures here prescribed. Surely there is something radically wrong with a law under which such flagrant avoidance is legal and feasible—under which the cases described *could* occur, whether or not they do occur frequently or at all.

* * *

NOTE, REALIZING APPRECIATION WITHOUT SALE: ACCRUAL TAXATION OF CAPITAL GAINS ON MARKETABLE SECURITIES
Mark L. Louie[*]
34 Stanford Law Review 857, 861-71 (1982)

The realization requirement is a significant administrative rule in any income tax system; it determines what increments of wealth will be presently taxed and what increments will be taxed in the future. The realization requirement enables taxpayers to strategically target gains and losses for particular tax years. This Part discusses the advantages and disadvantages of requiring the taxpayer to recognize all income in the year it accrues.

The Advantages of Annually Taxing Appreciation

The federal tax system relies primarily on the personal income tax to generate governmental revenues, and generally favors taxing the appreciation of capital assets in the year the appreciation occurs.[19] Taxing without regard to realization has three principal advantages: It broadens the

---

i. Section 117(d) of the 1939 Code limited the deductibility of capital losses. Present section 1211(b) limits an individual's capital loss deduction to the amount of capital gain plus $3,000. See Chapter Fifteen for further discussion of this limitation. (Eds.)

*. Student author.

19. R. MUSGRAVE & P. MUSGRAVE, PUBLIC FINANCE IN THEORY AND PRACTICE (2d ed. 1980), at 231.

tax base, it improves the equity of the tax system, and it encourages efficient asset sales.

Broadening the income tax base

Under an income tax, income is taxed unless substantial policy reasons justify excluding it from the tax base. The annual appreciation in the value of capital assets is part of the tax base and should be taxed unless doing so can be shown to be substantially disadvantageous. Eliminating the realization requirement for capital assets would result in unrealized capital gains being included in the tax base; exclusion reduces the size of the tax base and forces the remaining items to bear a higher tax rate.

Improving the equity of the income tax

A second advantage of eliminating the realization requirement is that it would improve the equity of the tax system. Wealth in the United States is generally more concentrated than income.[22] Because of the realization requirement, the wealthiest members of society can defer the payment of taxes on substantial amounts of unrealized capital gains income. This ability to defer taxes amounts to an interest-free loan from the government to the taxpayer; consequently, the realization requirement allows the wealthy to keep more funds invested, increases the return on their initial investment, and allows them to defer even more taxes. Furthermore, when they eventually sell their capital assets, the deferral means that fewer real dollars are paid in taxes. The result is that the effective rate of tax on the appreciation of capital assets is much lower than the nominal rate.

The principle of vertical equity requires that individuals be taxed according to their ability to pay. Well-to-do taxpayers have a greater ability to pay than low-income taxpayers, and therefore should bear relatively larger tax burdens. The realization requirement allows well-to-do taxpayers to defer payment of taxes on unrealized capital gains income and, in some cases, to escape payment of taxes entirely through section 1014's stepped-up basis at death. * * * Eliminating the realization requirement would improve the general equity of the income tax by increasing its progressivity.

The "lock-in" phenomenon

The realization requirement and the stepped-up basis at death combine to lock investors into their investment portfolios. Because taxpayers do not have to pay taxes on the increase in value of an asset until they sell or exchange it, taxpayers will resist selling appreciated property even though they may have better available investments, or are in need of cash. The investors are said to be "locked in" because of the tax penalty that they would incur if they were to sell their property and realize the gains. If the investor is well-to-do and elderly, the lock-in problem becomes even more acute: The

---

22. The wealthiest 20% of American households hold roughly 76% of all net wealth, and the wealthiest 1% hold 20% of all net wealth. By contrast, the 20% of the population with the highest money incomes received only 41% of all money income. R. MUSGRAVE & P. MUSGRAVE, *supra* note 19, at 348.

incentives to hold an asset until death so that the basis can be increased to market value—allowing the unrealized gain to escape taxation entirely—become even greater.

The lock-in problem not only inconveniences investors who would prefer to sell their appreciated assets, but also impedes the flow of capital from one investment to another. Older investments that are no longer as profitable as newer ones tend to be kept longer, and new investments have more difficulty attracting capital than would be optimal. Eliminating the realization requirement would mean that capital gains income would be taxed regardless of whether the asset had been sold. Taxpayers would therefore have no incentive to retain less profitable investments to avoid paying taxes, and the lock-in phenomenon would be eliminated.

Problems With Taxing Appreciation

Although eliminating the realization requirement will increase the theoretical accuracy of the tax system, in application it could encounter significant problems. These problems relate to the valuation of capital assets, the "paper" nature of unrealized capital gains, the effect on the capital markets, and the economic responses of private parties to the change in the tax rules.

Valuation and liquidity

One argument against taxing unrealized capital appreciation is that capital assets cannot be accurately valued until they are sold. Some assets are easier to value than others. Closing stock prices appear in the financial sections of major newspapers and are accurate indicators of value. Valuing real estate or partnership interests, on the other hand, requires an appraisal and involves significant administrative costs. Silver and art collections are still harder to value, the results even more uncertain, and the attempt to value even more expensive.

The difficulty of valuation is linked to the liquidity of the asset: The less liquid an asset, the harder it is to value and the less reliable is the result. * * * [S]tocks, bonds, and other marketable securities are very easy to value and can readily be converted into cash; therefore, valuation and liquidity problems do not pose a barrier to including their appreciation in the tax base.

Paper gains and cash flow problems

Even if valuation could be performed accurately, the gain is only a "paper gain"—one that accrues even though the taxpayer receives no cash. This paper gain can be lost at any time until the taxpayer sells the underlying asset. Shareholders with substantial paper gains in one year are at risk until they liquidate their investment; they can easily lose the profit if the market falls in subsequent years. If the asset is illiquid and the investor is unable easily to convert the asset to cash, or if he can do so only at a substantial cost, taxing the unrealized capital gains income may create inequity.

Because a paper gain does not generate cash, taxing such a gain can create cash squeezes. Taxpayers may have tax liabilities, but not the cash necessary to pay them. To pay their taxes, they will be forced to sell some of their assets. If the taxpayers cannot borrow against their unrealized gains, they will have to sell assets they otherwise would have retained.

Effect on equity markets

Annually taxing stock appreciation would drive down stock prices, or at least cause them to increase less rapidly, because it would reduce a stockholder's after-tax return. Corporations that raise capital in the equity markets would therefore find equity capital to be relatively more expensive; they would have to sell more shares at a lower price to raise the same amount of capital.

For most large corporations, increasing the cost of equity capital would not be troublesome because capital requirements can be met by borrowing funds and using retained earnings. But some sectors of the economy must frequently go to the equity markets and would be particularly hurt by an appreciations tax. Public utilities, for example, have an enormous need for capital and frequently go to the equity and debt markets. Similarly, high-growth companies must frequently raise additional equity capital and could be adversely affected by an appreciations tax. Because of their rapid expansion, high-growth companies may not be able to generate enough capital through retained earnings and debt to finance optimal or efficient rates of growth. These firms are forced to go to the equity markets. And in the case of smaller high-technology firms and start-up companies, debt capacity is limited and equity capital may be the only viable alternative.

The higher cost of equity capital can be expected to cause some corporations to decide not to issue equity and to delay or curtail expansion plans and purchases of capital equipment. Investors who were willing to take a certain amount of risk for a given return may be unwilling to take as much risk when an appreciations tax reduces the after-tax rate of return. As a result, less growth will occur in some of the most dynamic and productive sectors of the economy.

Corporations currently in need of capital have a number of incentives to borrow rather than to sell equity: Interest is deductible, investment bankers charge substantially smaller underwriting fees, and debt does not dilute equity ownership interests. Taxing the appreciation of corporate stock would give corporations yet another reason to prefer debt. Although dividends are now taxed twice—once at the corporate level and once at the individual level—retained earnings are exempt from the individual tax. Stock appreciation reflects, in part, the increased value of a company due to retention and investment of earnings. Taxing the annual appreciation of corporate stock would eliminate a portion of the present favorable tax treatment of retained earnings, but interest payments would still be deductible. A corporation would prefer a higher debt/equity ratio.

A primary reason that corporations are interested in obtaining debt financing is that the leverage provided by borrowed funds increases return on equity so long as the firm's before-tax rate of return is greater than the interest rate it must pay on the funds that it borrows. But lenders require borrowers to make interest payments regardless of the borrower's financial condition. Interest payments are fixed costs, whereas dividend payments are not. * * * [T]he presence of fixed interest costs and the smaller equity base cause a leveraged firm's return on equity to fluctuate much more than its earnings before interest and taxes. Increasing a firm's debt levels thus leads to a more volatile after-tax earnings record, which means the investment is riskier.

* * * This suggests that corporations will not be willing to raise large amounts of capital by borrowing. But an appreciations tax will make raising equity capital seem relatively expensive, and the corporations may be reluctant to pay the returns that the equity markets demand. With less new capital raised through debt and less new capital raised through equity, there could be less investment and slower economic growth, particularly in the sectors most dependent on equity.

An appreciations tax also seems likely to increase the pressures for higher dividend payments, further reducing a corporation's available cash. Under current tax law, dividends are taxed twice, while retained earnings are taxed only at the corporate level. With an appreciations tax, both retained earnings and dividends would be taxed twice, and the bias against paying dividends would be reduced. In addition, shareholders, especially those with substantial holdings, could be expected to demand higher dividends to provide cash to pay the appreciations tax. * * *

Private responses to changed rule

Since some assets are more liquid and more easily valued than others, most proposals to eliminate the realization requirement target specific groups of assets. To avoid thorny valuation and liquidity problems, these proposals would tax only the appreciation of those capital assets that are easily valued and relatively liquid. Other capital assets would continue to be taxed as they are under the current tax law. Unfortunately, the decision to tax only some assets' capital appreciation probably would cause private investors to shift their funds from assets subject to the appreciations tax into assets not subject to the tax, thereby distorting optimal investment behavior.

In tax law, the problem of drawing lines between taxed and untaxed behavior is troublesome because there are powerful financial incentives to be on the untaxed side of the line, and large amounts of capital tend to flow from more heavily taxed investments into those less heavily taxed. If only stocks traded on major exchanges were taxed, there would be a tremendous incentive not to be listed on the exchanges. If shares of all publicly held corporations were taxed, there would be a drive to "go private" or stay private. If commercial real estate is taxed and residential real estate is not, capital will flee the commercial real estate market into the residential market. Arbitrary line-drawing in the tax area creates substantial economic distortion; any division between those assets made subject to the appreciations tax and those assets not made so should seek to minimize this distortion.

* * *

FEDERAL INCOME TAXATION
Marvin A. Chirelstein[*]
Pages 71-73 (7th ed. 1994)

It is important to remind oneself at the outset that realization is strictly an administrative rule and not a constitutional, much less an economic, requirement of "income." Early cases, like *Macomber*, do give support to the idea that the Constitution limits "income" to realized gains, but at present most tax commentators would be likely to feel that the Congressional taxing power is not seriously restricted by such an implied requirement, and that Congress is free to treat gains and losses as "realized" pretty much whenever it chooses. Congress could surely tax property appreciation at gift or at death if it desired to do so, and while a gift or bequest can be regarded as a realization event through semantic manipulation, it is difficult to suppose at this late date that the constitutionality of taxing such appreciation would depend on whether gifts and bequests could be forced into the mold of "realization."

Assuming, moreover, that "income" refers to the annual increase in one's disposable wealth, then, from an economic standpoint, a stock owner whose unsold shares have appreciated in value by $1,000 over the course of a year has just as much "income" as a stock owner who receives $1,000 in dividends or a speculator who sells his shares and realizes $1,000 of trading profits. The latter two, of course, are taxed currently, while the former, owing to the realization requirement, is permitted to treat his gain as exempt from tax until he disposes of his appreciated shares. Yet the increase in disposable wealth is identical for each, though reflected in cash in the latter cases and in kind in the former. To be sure, stock that has gone up one year may go down the next and finally be sold for no more than the original purchase price. But the same is true for the trader who sells his stock at year-end and reinvests the gain in other shares which subsequently decline, or of the dividend-recipient whose company sustains an operating loss in the period following. We may indeed wish to do something about fluctuating income through the adoption of an averaging device of some sort but the possibility that income will fluctuate from year to year, or that gains *may* be succeeded by losses, can hardly be taken to show that the taxpayer has not been enriched when the value of his property appreciates. * * *

---

[*]. At time of original publication, Professor of Law, Columbia University

Yet all this argumentation should not be taken to mean that an overall change in the realization requirement is contemplated or even desirable. Our tax system does not reach mere changes in property value, and apart from recurring proposals to treat gifts and bequests as realization events, few commentators would suggest that the realization requirement should be materially altered. The difficulty of making annual property appraisals may be the chief reason for this attitude of acceptance; the absence of ready cash to pay the tax on property appreciation and the consequent "forced liquidation" of assets to meet tax obligations is another. To be sure, neither reason is especially compelling where readily marketable property (*e.g.*, listed securities) is concerned; nor, as has been seen, does the law shrink from taxing compensation even when received in kind. Still, the justifications for a realization requirement seem reasonably strong to most observers, and as stated, no overall change is imminent. My main purpose here, in any case, is not to question realization as a policy matter; rather, my object is to stress that because the realization requirement exists, the income tax is a tax on *transactions* instead of being a tax on income in the economic sense. Dividends, interest and rents, gains on sales of property, salaries, wages and fees—all these are taxable because they occur through the medium of an "exchange." Property appreciation, though undoubtedly an enrichment to the property owner, is exempt from tax precisely because the transactional aspect is thought to be lacking.

[The application of the realization requirement] in close cases is fairly arbitrary. In that respect, as in others, realization bears a resemblance to the problem of cost-recovery. Once again, what is chiefly at stake from the taxpayer's standpoint is the anticipation or deferral of tax payments—that is, the timing of taxable income. An investor who sells appreciated property for cash pays a tax on the appreciation currently and can reinvest only the after-tax proceeds. An investor who retains his appreciated property—or who can somehow dispose of it without triggering off a "realization"—pays no tax and therefore has more available for reinvestment. Although unrealized appreciation may be taxed in the future if the property is sold, the postponement can be of considerable value to the property-owner, as has been seen, and it is often worth his while to litigate when the application of the realization rule is in doubt.

Stock Dividends

In *Eisner v. Macomber*, the Supreme Court was required to decide whether a common stock dividend could constitutionally be taxed as "income" to the shareholder-recipients. The taxpayer owned 2,200 shares of Standard Oil common stock. Standard Oil declared a 50% stock dividend and the taxpayer received 1,100 additional shares of which about $20,000 in par value represented earnings accumulated by the company since the effective date of the original income tax law. The statute then applicable expressly included stock dividends in income, in effect taxing such dividends in much the same way as dividends in cash.   In a lengthy opinion by Justice Pitney—matched by an interminable dissent from Justice Brandeis—the Supreme Court held that stock dividends could not be treated as income within the meaning of the 16th Amendment:

> We are clear that not only does a stock dividend really take nothing from the property of the corporation and add nothing to that of the shareholder, but that the antecedent accumulation of profits evidenced thereby, while indicating that the shareholder is the richer because of an increase of his capital, at the same time shows he has not realized or received any income in the transaction.

The Brandeis dissent—based more on concepts of corporate finance than taxation—argued in effect that a stock dividend is really a two-step affair consisting of (I) a cash distribution, followed by (ii) a purchase of additional shares through the exercise of stock subscription rights.   Looked at in that way, stock dividends are actually the equivalent of cash dividends and are therefore properly taxable.

     * * *

Notes and Questions

3.   In the excerpt from his 1938 book, Professor Simons harshly criticizes the approach of accountants in failing to use market value of assets when it is higher than cost.   If viewed as criticism of the accounting profession, is this criticism deserved?

4.   Professor Simons argues that adherence to the realization rule leads to "defin[ing] personal income in terms of transaction profit."   Similarly, Professor Chirelstein states that "because the realization requirement exists, the income tax is a tax on *transactions* instead of being a tax on income in the economic sense."   Are these observations accurate?

5.   Professor Simons is amused at the results of traditional procedures of inventory valuation during periods of extreme inflation.   Can business accounting, using the Last In, First Out (LIFO) method, measure merchandising profit in periods of inflation?

6.   In assessing Professor Simons' 1950 condemnation of the realization principle, it should be remembered that he is condemning the more-or-less "pure" form of the realization principle that existed in the years immediately following 1913, and not always actual law as it existed even in 1950 (and even less today).   Thus, it might be argued that it has been possible to close off many of the worst abuses of the "pure" realization system without abandoning its relative simplicity.

7.   Is Professor Simons' Case I still an accurate criticism of the law?

8. Observe that several of Professor Simons' schemes would depend upon full deduction of interest expense, regardless of the purpose to which the borrowed funds are put (for example, consumption). Current law limits deductions for "investment interest" and denies deductions for "personal interest." Section 163(d) and (h).

Even assuming that all interest were deductible, should we be alarmed by the tax avoidance scheme of Case IV?

9. Although Professor Simons uses examples of income earned by corporations, the examples do not acknowledge the potential for double taxation at the corporate and shareholder level. This issue is discussed in Chapter Fourteen.

10. Treatment of long term capital gain is not as lenient now as it was when Professor Simons wrote his Case III, though present section 1(h) is more favorable for long term capital gains than the top marginal tax rate on ordinary income. If "Gray" desires to sell part of his stock each year he may find it advantageous to invest in corporations that reinvest all their earnings instead of paying out dividends. One might think such corporations would be vulnerable to the section 531 tax on unreasonable accumulations, particularly since section 532(c) now makes the tax applicable to widely owned corporations. In fact, however, the Revenue Service does not attempt to apply the tax to widely held corporations.

11. What does Professor Simons mean by the observation, at the end of Case II: "'The richer you are, the faster you should be allowed to get richer,' says our realization procedure, while the bracket-rates raucously dissent."?

12. Mr. Louie states at the outset that there is a prima facie case for taxing unrealized appreciation because unrealized appreciation "is part of the tax base." Is this a valid point?

13. Clearly, deferral of income tax on realized income amounts to an interest-free loan from the government in the amount of the deferred tax. Is Mr. Louie correct in asserting that the government's failure to tax unrealized appreciation currently amounts to an interest-free loan?

14. The lock-in phenomenon discussed by Mr. Louie is discussed generally in Chapter Fifteen and, with particular reference to stepped-up basis at death, in Chapter Nine. Treating death as a realization event would solve a major part of the lock-in problem more easily than would abandoning the realization requirement.

15.   Both the Louie and Chirelstein excerpts describe the "paper gain" argument in favor of realization: that prior to realization the taxpayer has only a paper profit that remains at risk in the market.   Is Professor Chirelstein correct in arguing that this is not basically different from the situation where a taxpayer sells an asset at a profit, reinvests the proceeds, and then risks losing the reinvested profit?

16.   Most legal scholars agree with Professor Chirelstein that *Eisner v. Macomber* was wrongly decided.   Even if the realization requirement is accepted, taxing stock dividends might be considered valid now on the grounds that there is no constitutional objection to looking through the corporate shell and taxing shareholders on corporate earnings, whether or not distributed.   This approach, however, would leave unanswered the question of the constitutionality of taxing unrealized appreciation in general.

17.   Readers who are persuaded that taxation of unrealized appreciation is theoretically appealing but would be a nightmare in operation should be interested in David Shakow's detailed proposal for taxing many types of unrealized appreciation.[j]   Professor Shakow asserted that taxing unrealized appreciation would combat economic inefficiencies associated with the realization rule, such as the lock-in problem, and that it would be fairer in levying equal taxes on those who enjoyed equal amounts of appreciation, whether or not realized.[k]   Moreover, he asserted that significant simplification would result, in part because taxing of unrealized appreciation would logically lead to other changes, such as elimination of favorable treatment for capital gain, removal of most statutory rules related to corporation-shareholder relationships, and elimination of many statutory details related to capitalization, depreciation, and depletion.[l]

Professor Shakow recognized that taxation of unrealized appreciation "has never attracted a large group of adherents because its twin problems of valuation (How can all assets be valued every year?) and liquidity (How can taxpayers pay taxes if they do not sell their assets?) have never been solved."[m]   The bulk of his article addressed these practical problems (and others, including transition to the proposed system).   He argued that current taxation of unrealized appreciation was not just theoretically correct, but administratively feasible.   Professor Shakow summarized his valuation proposals as follows:

Some assets—notably owner-occupied residences and inexpensive consumer items—would be excluded from the system completely.

---

j. David J. Shakow, *Taxation Without Realization: A Proposal for Accrual Taxation*, 134 U. Pa. L. Rev. 1111 (1986).

k. *Id.* at 1114-15.

l. *Id.* at 1116.

m. *Id.* at 1113.

Items that are particularly difficult to value—notably closely held stock and collectibles—would be taxed only on realization, but with an adjustment to the final gain or loss that is intended to compensate for the fact that interim gains and losses were not taxed annually. The realization rules for such assets, however, would not include all the special nonrecognition rules of current law. Certain business assets—notably inventories, accounts receivable, and depreciable personal property—could be included in the system through modified versions of current law already applied to them that approximate accrual taxation. Other intangible assets—good will and going concern value—would not be treated on an accrual basis. Business and investment liabilities would generally be incorporated in the system.[a]

C. CRITIQUES OF THE HAIG-SIMONS APPROACH

Aside from questions of practicality, the principle of taxing appreciation in value before realization can be challenged. In the first excerpt below, Peel argues that an unrealized "paper profit" does not warrant the imposition of tax currently. Currently taxing the asset's yield—which does not violate the realization rule—is sufficient.

The Haig-Simons definition is, in part, a visceral reaction of unfairness to a situation in which two persons with equal amounts of realized income are taxed the same though the assets of one of the two have vastly appreciated in value. This is, however, only one aspect of the failure of an income tax to take into account differences in wealth that affect the burden of the tax. For example, the burden of a 40 percent income tax on income of $100,000 is much greater on a taxpayer worth only $200,000 than on a taxpayer worth $1 million. This difference exists whether the $1 million represents unrealized appreciation, savings from previously taxed earnings, or an inheritance.

Most scholars have embraced the Haig-Simons definition of income as the ideal, or goal, for tax policy. This is acknowledged by Professor Victor Thuronyi, even as he contends that the Haig-Simons formulation in fact leaves considerable ambiguity in its definition of income.

Even though the Haig-Simons definition is generally considered administratively impractical, it nonetheless remains the ideal for most academicians. Consequently, tax systems and tax revision proposals are tested against it, and a change is accepted or rejected (at least among academics, if not in Congress) depending upon whether or not it brings the tax system closer to the Haig-Simons ideal. In the final excerpt, J. Gregory Ballantine argues that the theory of second best does not support this approach.

---

a. *Id.* at 1183.

CAPITAL LOSSES: FALLING SHORT ON FAIRNESS AND SIMPLICITY
Fred W. Peel, Jr.[*]

17 Baltimore Law Review 418, 423-24 (1988)

Some opposition toward allowing the taxpayer to time his realization of capital losses to offset other income probably stems from a belief that unrealized gains and losses should be taken into account annually. Such belief is part of the Haig-Simons definition of the ideal income tax base. This definition has been accepted as the ideal with a surprising lack of critical analysis. One critic who does recognize the impracticality of its general application has noted that, logically, the second best tax system is not necessarily the system that comes closest to the Haig-Simons definition.[34] Nevertheless, Haig-Simons as the ideal has received more acceptance than it deserves.

Market value of property is determined by either current yield or anticipated demand or a combination of these two factors. The current yield itself is taxed presently. To the extent that the value of property is determined by current yield, taxation of both current yield and accretion in value of the underlying asset that is a reflection of the yield would be unfair. Except in the case of collectors' items, to the extent that an asset's appreciation in value has not been accompanied by a commensurate current yield, the owner of the asset has received no benefit beyond a feeling of satisfaction at having made a shrewd investment.

An unrealized gain unaccompanied by current benefit is, in common terminology, a "paper profit." Entirely aside from the administrative problems of annual valuation involved in applying the Haig-Simons definition, the principal problem with such definition is the absence of any benefit to the owner that justifies the imposition of an income tax on an unrealized accretion in value. Thus, the theoretical basis for this component of the Haig-Simons definition of income is at least questionable.

      * * *

THE CONCEPT OF INCOME
Victor Thuronyi[**]

46 Tax Law Review 45, 45-47, 61-62 (1990)

The concept of income serves as a touchstone against which the rules of the current income tax can be evaluated and is, therefore, of critical importance in the debate over what those rules should be. The meaning of

---

[*]. At time of original publication, Ben J. Altheimer Professor of Law Emeritus, University of Arkansas at Little Rock.

34. Bittker, *A "Comprehensive Tax Base" as a Goal of Income Tax Reform*, 80 HARV. L. REV. 925, 983 (1967).

[**]. At time of original publication, Associate Professor of Law, State University of New York at Buffalo (on leave; temporarily serving as Counsel (Taxation), International Monetary Fund).

income is also of interest to those charting the distribution of income, so as to have a quantitative measure of the degree of economic inequality in a society. * * *

Given the importance of these uses of the income concept, the manner in which income is defined can make a difference. For example, if it is considered desirable for the income tax to approximate the ideal concept of income as closely as possible, it becomes important whether that ideal treats gifts and bequests as income. Moreover, the pattern of income distribution and the effects of a change in tax or other policy on that distribution can vary significantly depending on how income is defined.

The income concept that is now widely accepted by analysts was formulated by Henry Simons in the 1930's, and is commonly referred to as Haig-Simons income, to acknowledge the prior contribution of Robert Haig.[5] It holds that an individual's income is the sum of his consumption plus accumulation during the taxable period. Despite its wide acceptance, Haig-Simons income remains elusive and ambiguous, since the terms "consumption" and "accumulation" are open-ended. In light of the slipperiness of these terms, some writers have questioned whether the Haig-Simons formulation is, at base, a coherent one and is really helpful in deciding what is income.[6] Indeed, one noted economist has concluded that "the problem of *defining* individual income, quite apart from any problem of practical measurement, appears in principle insoluble."[7] Despite these theoretical objections, the term "economic income," or Haig-Simons income, is commonly employed as if it were a relatively well-defined or well-understood concept. The fact that some use economic income as a workable concept while others question its validity suggests that the nature of the concept is not well understood and has not been fully explored, despite the inordinate volume of literature on the subject. This article begins with an inquiry into the nature of the income concept appropriate for tax policy. A selective survey of the extensive literature on the definition of income suggests that there is confusion about the philosophical groundwork supporting the Haig-Simons concept, largely because the concept was borrowed from economics to be used in law. While the language used to define income has meaning in economic theory, that meaning collapses when it is applied in the real world.

An adequate groundwork for the income concept, however, can be provided by basing it on tax fairness. This approach can be traced to the

---

5. See, e.g., Pechman, Comprehensive Income Taxation: A Comment, 81 HARV. L. REV. 63, 64-65 (1967). Some writers have referred to the "Schanz-Haig-Simons" definition of income to acknowledge the contribution of George von Schanz. E.g., S. Surrey & P. McDaniel, Tax Expenditures 4 (1985).

6. See, e.g., Bittker, A "Comprehensive Tax Base" As a Goal of Income Tax Reform, 80 HARV. L. REV. 925 (1967).

7. N. Kaldor, An Expenditure Tax 70 (1955).

seminal work by Simons, although Simons' reliance on the fairness criterion was ambiguous. While fairness may seem hopelessly vague, this article argues that the vagueness can be reduced by articulating criteria to be used in making judgments about fairness. Many of the arguments in the literature over how Haig-Simons income should be interpreted are, in fact, grounded in fairness concerns. The Haig-Simons formulation has survived over the years because people generally have considered it to be fair. Thus, the proposed fairness inquiry is not a complete departure from the types of arguments that have been made in deciding what is income. Rather, the focus on fairness is intended to sharpen and clarify the debate, and to make explicit what previously has been implicit.

     * * *

Income is not an "elegant" concept. It is by its nature highly practical, flexible and ad hoc. If it is determined, for example, that medical expenses should not be deducted in determining income, it is not because the concept of a deduction for medical expenses is completely antithetical to a comprehensive income tax, but rather because, on balance, it is considered more equitable to determine income without such a deduction. The definition of income must take into account the fact that many criteria that might be used in determining taxable capacity are not measurable and, accordingly, cannot be incorporated into the income concept, or are measurable, but deficient for one reason or another. The Simons definition of income is misleading in this respect, since it looks fairly elegant. Indeed, Simons defended his definition on the basis that it was elegant.[64] Any hope of elegance should, however, be dispelled quickly when consideration is given to exactly what the terms "consumption" and "wealth" in his definition mean.

Not only are these terms inherently vague, but also the very notion of capital maintenance on which the Simons definition of income rests is arbitrary. If income is defined as the amount that an individual could have consumed while leaving his capital intact, this at first seems a straightforward idea. But now consider what is meant by maintaining capital intact. What it ultimately might mean is that income is the amount that an individual could spend during a period while still being as well off (in a financial sense) at the end of the period as at the beginning. But if the fair market value of an individual's capital is maintained, is he necessarily as well off at the end as at the beginning? If interest rates have declined, the individual's initial capital may have gone up in value. But if this increase in value is consumed, the remaining capital will produce an income stream lower than the income stream that would have been produced if the rate of interest had not declined. The individual is less well off in the sense that his capital can now provide a smaller amount of annual consumption in the future. He is as well off only in the sense that if he liquidated his capital,

---

64. H. SIMONS, PERSONAL INCOME TAXATION 125 (1938).

he could buy the same amount of present consumption as he could have at the beginning of the period. While income can be defined in terms of the amount that could be consumed while maintaining the fair market value of the individual's capital intact, this means that two individuals with the same income may, in a certain sense, not be equally well off (even in purely financial terms).

* * *

THREE FAILURES IN ECONOMIC ANALYSIS OF TAX REFORM
J. Gregory Ballentine[*]

National Tax Association-Tax Institute of America
79th Annual Conference 3, 4-5 (1986)

Income Tax Reform and the Theory of Second Best

The third failure that I will discuss is different. It applies to the principles used to design good income tax policy, and it arises from ignoring an existing, well understood economic principle: the theory of second best. Early on in the practical discussion of tax reform it was agreed—wisely, in my view—that income taxation, rather than consumption taxation, would form the basis for designing tax reform. The first best income tax rule is essentially given by the Haig-Simons definition of income. That is, first best income tax policy implies measuring Haig-Simons income for all individuals and taxing that income.

In my experience at Treasury, the "right" practical tax policy—as opposed to the political compromise that might be required—was always defined as an application of the Haig-Simons first best rule, with little or no thought given to second best issues. Treasury I demonstrated that same approach: it essentially proposed applying the first best, Haig-Simons rule everywhere it was deemed feasible, with no regard for the fact that major deviations from the first best rule are inevitable.

While optimal tax formulas derived from sophisticated second best modeling are often quite arcane and not practical, there is a clear general lesson from the theory of second best that has not permeated most practical discussions of income tax reform and that is inconsistent with the Treasury approach. That lesson is that, if constraints prevent application of the first best rule in major areas, then, in general, the second best policy will require deviations from the first best rule in many other areas where the constraints do not apply.[2]

Owner occupied housing and other non-business capital is a salient example of the need for a second best approach to income tax reform. A

---

*. At time of original publication, principal, KPMG Peat Marwick, Washington, D.C.

2. While this general point has not been influential in most tax policy discussions, it has not been entirely ignored. In my view, the clearest and most compelling explanation of it is given by Boris Bittker in "A Comprehensive Tax Base as a Goal of Income Tax Reform," 80 HARV L. REV. 925 (1967).

practical constraint of income tax reform is that the imputed income on owner occupied housing will remain tax exempt. This is no minor constraint: approximately 30-35 percent of the depreciable capital stock of the U.S. is owner occupied housing. Given this major tax exemption for non-business capital, at the minimum there should be no presumption that the practical goal for income tax reform involves applying the Haig-Simons rule to the taxation of business capital income. Nonetheless, that is precisely the presumption inherent in Treasury I. Further, suggestions that the taxation of business capital should be reduced to offset the inevitable business/non-business tax distortion are usually treated as proposals to shift the basic system to *consumption* taxation, rather than as proposals to improve the practical design of an *income* tax in a second best world. Yet it is in the latter context that proposals for tax incentives for business investment have their most compelling practical justification.

Second best analysis is not only needed for major issues such as the treatment of business capital income; many smaller issues can benefit from such analysis. An excellent example comes from Bittker's article and Treasury I. Following Haig-Simons definition of income, Treasury I proposed taxing scholarship and fellowship income in excess of the amount used for tuition.[3]

The rationale given for this proposal was essentially that scholarship and fellowship payments are part of Haig-Simons income and, therefore, should be taxable.

In dealing with this same case, Bittker pointed out that most state universities, in effect, provide scholarships and fellowships to in-state students through reduced charges for tuition, room, and board. For example, room, board, and tuition of the University of Virginia for a Virginia resident is approximately $4000 per school year. At many comparable private institutions, room, board, and tuition may be $16,000 or more. Surely, one of the practical constraints of our tax system is that we will not impute scholarship income to in-state students attending the University of Virginia and tax that income. Once that fact is recognized, it is not so clear that taxing explicit scholarships and fellowships is good income tax policy. Of course, one may still conclude that taxing a portion of explicit scholarship or fellowship income is good tax policy, but that conclusion cannot be based on the simple assertion that scholarships fit the Haig-Simons definition of income just like wages. A more sophisticated rationale weighing different, but inevitable, distortions from the Haig-Simons rule is needed.

* * *

---

3. Indeed, Treasury I argued that "[i]n theory" *all* scholarship and fellowship income should be taxed. The continued exclusion for scholarships used to pay tuition was, apparently, a concession to concerns about public acceptance. See *Tax Reform For Fairness, Simplicity, and Economic Growth*, U.S. Treasury, Vol. 2, p. 58.

Notes and Questions

18. Peel argues that unrealized appreciation is attributable to some combination of two factors—increased yield or anticipated demand. Why does he contend that this means that unrealized appreciation should not be taxed?

19. Is Professor Thuronyi's approach of interpreting the Haig-Simons definition of income by basing it on tax fairness a helpful one?

20. Professor Thuronyi posits the case of a bondholder whose bonds rise in value due to a decline in interest rates. In what sense is the bondholder not better off as a result of the increased value?

21. Mr. Ballantine appears to assume, *arguendo*, that the Haig-Simons definition is the theoretical ideal, but in the real world unattainable. Does this mean that the real-world tax system should attempt to come as close as possible to the ideal? If the Haig-Simons definition of income is ideal, and that definition would include scholarships, does this mean that scholarships should be taxed?

Selected Bibliography

Auerbach, Alan J., *Retrospective Capital Gains Taxation*, 81 AM. ECON. REV. 167 (1991).

Ballentine, J. Gregory, *Three Failures in Economic Analysis of Tax Reform*, *in* 79th ANN. CONF., NAT'L TAX ASS'N 3 (1986).

Bittker, Boris I., *Comprehensive Income Taxation: A Response*, 81 HARV. L. REV. 1032 (1968).

——, *A "Comprehensive Tax Base" As a Goal of Income Tax Reform*, 80 HARV. L. REV. 925 (1967).

CHIRELSTEIN, MARVIN A., FEDERAL INCOME TAXATION (7th ed., 1994), Part A, Sec. 5.

Cunningham, Noel B. & Deborah H. Schenk, *How to Tax the House that Jack Built*, 43 TAX L. REV. 447 (1988).

Fellows, Mary Louise, *A Comprehensive Attack on Tax Deferral*, 88 MICH. L. REV. 722 (1990).

Ginsburg, Martin et al., *Reexamining Subchapter C: An Overview and Some Modest Proposals to Stimulate Debate*, *in* INVITATIONAL CONFERENCE ON SUBCHAPTER C 1, 6-7 (1987).

Goode, Richard, *The Economic Definition of Income*, *in* COMPREHENSIVE INCOME TAXATION (Joseph A. Pechman ed., 1977).

Halperin, Daniel I., *Interest in Disguise: Taxing the "Time Value of Money*,*"* 95 YALE L.J. 506 (1986).

Johnson, Calvin H., *The Undertaxation of Holding Gains*, 55 TAX NOTES 807 (1992).

Klein, William A., *Timing in Personal Taxation*, 6 J. LEGAL STUD. 461 (1977).

Louie, Mark L., Note, *Realizing Appreciation Without Sale: Accrual Taxation of Capital Gains on Marketable Securities*, 34 STAN. L. REV. 857 (1982).

Musgrave, R.A., *In Defense of an Income Concept*, 81 HARV. L. REV. 44 (1967).

Pechman, Joseph A., *Comprehensive Income Taxation: A Comment*, 81 HARV. L. REV. 63 (1967).

Peel, Fred W., Jr., *Capital Losses: Falling Short on Fairness and Simplicity*, 17 U. BALT. L. REV. 418 (1988).

. Shakow, David J., *Taxation Without Realization: A Proposal for Accrual Taxation*, 134 U. PA. L. REV. 1111 (1986).

Simon, Karla W., *Revenue or Religion? Issues and Answers on Tax Deferral*, 68 TAXES 1015 (1990).

SIMONS, HENRY C., FEDERAL TAX REFORM 6-67 (1950).

——, PERSONAL INCOME TAXATION 41-58, 80-83 (1938).

Slawson, David, *Taxing as Ordinary Income the Appreciation of Publicly Held Stock*, 76 YALE L.J. 623 (1967).

Strnad, Jeff, *Periodicity and Accretion Taxation: Norms and Implementation*, 99 YALE L.J. 1817 (1990).

Thuronyi, Victor, *The Concept of Income*, 46 TAX L. REV. 45 (1990).

Warren, Alvin C., Jr., *Financial Contract Innovation and Income Tax Policy*, 107 HARV. L. REV. 460 (1993).

——, *The Timing of Taxes*, 39 NAT'L. TAX J. 499 (1986).

CHAPTER THREE

IMPUTED INCOME

Imputed income may be defined * * * as a flow of satisfactions from durable goods owned and used by the taxpayer, or from goods and services arising out of the personal exertions of the taxpayer on his own behalf.

Imputed income is non-cash income or income in kind. But all non-cash income, or income in kind, is not included in the category of imputed income. * * *

Imputed income is * * * a species of the genus income in kind, and its distinguishing characteristic is that it arises outside the ordinary processes of the market.[a]

A. INTRODUCTION

Neither of the two broad categories of imputed income—that arising from property and that arising from services—is included in the base of the federal income tax. The classic example of *imputed income from property* is the economic benefit arising from the taxpayer's ownership of his residence. The taxpayer who purchases a home for $100,000 receives as a return on her investment the right to live rent-free, and tax-free, in a $100,000-home. By contrast, if the taxpayer had invested the money in securities, using the income generated to rent a residence, she would have been taxed on the income but have received no offsetting deduction for the expenditure. While housing is the most important example, imputed income from property arises from the ownership of any tangible asset of long life, such as an automobile or refrigerator, or even a tennis racket or ash tray.

Imputed income from services is the economic value of services rendered by the taxpayer for the benefit of himself or his family, or of others whom the taxpayer wishes to benefit. For example, the taxpayer who mows his own lawn or waxes his own car confers an economic benefit upon himself, without the burden of taxation. By contrast, if the taxpayer works in the market, then uses his earnings to pay someone to mow the lawn or wax the car, he will be taxed on his income and receive no deduction for his payment. The classic and most important example of imputed income from services are the household and child care services rendered by a housewife to her family.

It is important to keep in mind the distinction between imputed income and other types of *income in kind*. While imputed income arises from the

---

a. Donald B. Marsh, *The Taxation of Imputed Income*, 58 POL. SCI. Q. 514 (1943).

taxpayer's use of his own property or services to benefit himself (and members of his family or household), income in kind can be a method of payment for a transaction with another. For example, if an employee is allowed to live rent-free in a house owned by his employer, this in-kind benefit is not imputed income and, unless it fits within an exception to the general rule,[b] is included in the employee's gross income.

B. IMPUTED INCOME FROM PROPERTY

Serious proposals have been made to include in the tax base major categories of imputed income from property, particularly housing. As discussed in the following excerpts, this has been done in some jurisdictions and proposed for the United States. (Note that since Dr. Goode wrote, the United Kingdom has ceased including such imputed income in its tax base.)

Assuming it is decided that the failure to tax imputed income is a problem (and there is no unanimity on this question), it remains uncertain what, if anything, should be done about the problem. Although taxing the imputed income may be the most obvious remedy, others have been proposed, notably allowing renters some form of benefit to offset the perceived advantage of owner-occupiers. Doing nothing may emerge as not only the most likely course of action, but the best.

IMPUTED RENT OF OWNER-OCCUPIED DWELLINGS
UNDER THE INCOME TAX
Richard Goode[*]

15 Journal of Finance 504, 504-07, 512-14, 518-25 (1960)

Most economists agree that the rental value of a dwelling is part of the income of an owner-occupant. The services of the dwelling give the owner power to satisfy his wants, and that power is susceptible of valuation in terms of money.[1] In support of the view that the imputed rent of owner-occupied houses is income, the British Royal Commission on the Taxation of Profits and Income advanced two arguments: (1) the owner could rent his house if he wished, and his failure to do so indicates that the value of the occupancy to him must be at least equal to the rent foregone; and (2) an owner-occupant is better off than a tenant with the same money income.[2] The commission might have added that the homeowner has the alternative of investing his capital in other assets, and the choice of a house shows that

---

b. Section 119 excludes from income the value of lodging under certain circumstances. Note that this exclusion does not mean that the value of the lodging is imputed income.

*. At time of original publication, Brookings Institution.

1. In his classic definition, Haig said: ". . . Income becomes the increase or accretion in one's power to satisfy his wants in a given period in so far as that power consists of (*a*) money itself, or, (*b*) anything susceptible of valuation in terms of money" (see Robert Murray Haig, "The concept of Income—Economic and Legal Aspects," in *The Federal Income Tax*, ed. Haig [New York: Columbia University Press, 1921], p.7).

2. *Final Report* (Cmd. 9474 [June, 1955]), pp. 249-50.

he considers the return from it superior to the yield of other income-producing investments.

The imputed rent of owner-occupied houses is taxable income in the United Kingdom and many other countries. In the United States, however, imputed rent has never been included in the base of the federal income tax. The state of Wisconsin taxed the estimated rental value of owner-occupied residential property under its original income tax law of 1911 but discontinued this practice in 1917. Many economists have favored the inclusion of imputed rent in taxable income for purposes of the federal tax. In 1921 Haig concluded that this income should be taxed "if it is practicable to evaluate it."[3] Taxation of imputed rent has been recommended by Simons, Vickrey, Pechman, and others.[4]

The usual proposal is for the taxation of net rent, defined as imputed gross rent minus necessary expenses of ownership. The expenses consist of interest on mortgage debt, property taxes, depreciation, repairs and maintenance, and casualty insurance. * * *

Discriminatory Effects of the Exclusion of Imputed Rent and of Deductions for Interest and Taxes

The omission of imputed net rent from taxable income and the deductions for mortgage interest and property taxes on owner-occupied dwellings impair the uniformity of the income tax by producing differences in the taxation of persons with equal real incomes and by altering the usual relation between the tax liabilities of persons at different income levels. First and most obviously, the exclusion and deductions favor homeowners and discriminate against renters. The part of the owner's income which takes the form of imputed net rent and his expenditures for mortgage interest and property taxes are free of tax. The renter must use taxable income to pay his full housing costs. Second, the investor in an owner-occupied house is favored in comparison with other investors. * * *

Among owner-occupants, the exclusion and personal deductions favor those with high incomes compared with those in lower brackets. This is true because the value of an exclusion or deduction from taxable income varies directly with the marginal tax rate. * * *

The present arrangement also favors persons with a high preference for housing as against those who care less for this form of consumption. It favors those who like accommodations of a kind that are easily owner-occupied compared with those who have other tastes. For example, families

---

3. *Op. cit.*, p. 24.

4. Henry C. Simons, *Personal Income Taxation* (Chicago: University of Chicago Press, 1938), p. 211, and *Federal Tax Reform* (Chicago: University of Chicago Press, 1950), p. 36; William Vickrey, *Agenda for Progressive Taxation* (New York: Ronald Press, 1947), pp. 18-24; Joseph A. Pechman, "Erosion of the Individual Income Tax," *National Tax Journal*, X (March, 1957), 14-15, and "What Would a Comprehensive Individual Income Tax Yield?" in House Ways and Means Committee, *Tax Revision Compendium* (1959), 1, 261-62.

who prefer to live in the suburbs are favored compared with others who prefer a residential hotel in the central city. The benefits of the exclusion and deductions are more easily available to persons who lead settled lives than to those whose occupation requires them to move frequently.

Ownership of consumer durable goods resembles homeownership, in that the investment in the durables yields a real return which is not subject to income tax. The same general argument can be made for taxing the imputed service value of consumer durables as for including imputed net rent of owner-occupied houses in taxable income. [C]onsumers' investment in durables is large, although smaller than their investment in dwellings. Nevertheless, an attempt to tax the service value of consumer durables is seldom recommended because of administrative difficulties. The renting of consumer durables is less prevalent than the renting of dwellings, and the problem of discrimination between renters and owners is less acute for durables than for houses. In addition to renters of equipment, however, there are many consumers who obtain through the market services similar to those provided by durables. The patrons of commercial laundries and public transportation, for example, suffer a discrimination compared with owners of home laundry equipment and automobiles which is similar to that experienced by tenants compared with homeowners. It seems likely that ownership of durables is positively correlated with homeownership and that the effects of omitting imputed returns on the two kinds of investment are generally cumulative rather than offsetting.

* * *

The Effect on Housing Consumption and Homeownership of the Exclusion and Deductions

* * *

The tax saving due to the exclusion and deductions may be viewed as a reduction in the price of housing services for owner-occupiers who are subject to income tax or who would be subject to tax if imputed rent were included in the tax base. Inasmuch as the prices of rental housing and other goods and services are not directly affected by the exclusion, the price of housing services from owner-occupied dwellings is reduced relative to the prices of rental housing and all other goods and services. * * *

The presumption is that the changes in relative prices cause a shift from renting to owning one's dwelling and an increase in the total amount of housing services consumed relative to other goods and services. For these shifts to occur it is not necessary that consumers calculate the effect on relative prices of the income tax advantages of homeownership and adjust their budgets accordingly. Many may be conscious of the tax value of the deductions for interest and taxes, but probably only a sophisticated few recognize the significance of the exclusion. * * *

As an influence on decisions to buy houses, the deductions for interest and taxes seem to be more important than the exclusion of imputed net rent.

One reason is that, in the aggregate, the deductible items are substantially larger than net rent. A second reason is that net rent is likely to be especially small, relative to interest and property taxes, for new buyers. Most new buyers have smaller equities in their houses than the average for all owner-occupiers. * * *

Policy Implications

In appraising the economic significance of the omission of imputed rent from taxable income it is necessary to ask whether the stimulation of housing consumption and the promotion of homeownership are recognized objectives of public policy. If these are policy objectives, a further question is whether the present tax treatment is an appropriate and effective means of achieving them. If they are not specifically intended, the changes in consumption and ownership patterns impair the efficiency of resource allocation, and the question is whether the loss is great or small.

Much support can be found for the view that the improvement of housing standards is highly desirable, and there are some indications that public opinion and government policy accord a special status to housing. The emphasis, however, has usually been on slum clearance and the provision of minimum facilities for low-income groups and the elderly rather than on a general increase in housing consumption. At times, the promotion of housing construction has been favored as a means of stimulating general economic activity. The encouragement of homeownership appears to attract wide social approval. Homeownership is often thought to be associated with active interest and participation in community affairs and thus to have important intangible values. * * *

On the assumption that promotion of homeownership is a policy objective, the present income tax provisions work in the right direction but may be inefficient. The strongest stimulus to homeownership is given where least needed—to those with high incomes and high marginal rates of tax. * * * It seems entirely possible that the federal government could give broader and more effective encouragement to homeownership and housing by increasing expenditures for housing programs in an amount equal to the revenue loss attributable to the failure to tax imputed rent.

Implications of Revising the Income Tax Treatment of Owners and Renters

The present discrimination between homeowners and renters could be eliminated by broadening the income tax base to include imputed rent or could be reduced by allowing tenants to deduct rental payments from taxable income. Another approach would be to eliminate the personal deductions that owners are now allowed for payments of interest and property taxes, without requiring net imputed rent to be included in taxable income. These revisions would differ considerably in revenue implications, administrative complexity, and effectiveness in equalizing taxation of different groups.

Taxation of Imputed Rent

The only exact method of eliminating the discriminations between homeowners and renters would be to include in taxable income the net rental value of owner-occupied dwellings. * * *

Administrative problems would be involved. * * * The unique problem would be the estimation of gross rental value. Estimates have always been important in the allocation, between activities and over time, of contractual outlays or receipts. Depreciation allowances are an outstanding example. The items, however, can nearly always be traced back, if necessary, to transactions involving the payment or receipt of money or the exchange of property. The estimation of the gross rent which an owner-occupied dwelling would command could not be referred so directly to a market transaction. It would not be especially difficult to make fairly accurate estimates. They are prepared, as a matter of course, by FHA appraisers and others. But a higher standard of accuracy is demanded for income tax assessments than for mortgage appraisals and many other valuations. The estimation of imputed rent would involve the federal income tax authorities in a new kind of problem, and it would be necessary to deal with a large number of cases. * * *

It has been suggested that, in order to minimize the administrative difficulties involved in determination of imputed net rent, the figure be approximated by taking a standard rate of return on the owner's equity in the property, while allowing no deduction for interest, depreciation, and other costs. * * * The simplicity of this approach, however, is deceptive. In most cases the determination of capital value and owner's equity would not be much easier than the direct estimation of gross rental value. The difficulty of keeping assessments up to date would be the same under the modified computations as if an exact computation of imputed rent were required. In view of the rapid changes in property values that often occur and the experience of depreciation and obsolescence, it would be seriously objectionable to take as the owner's equity original cost minus current mortgage debt. * * *

The experience of the United Kingdom in taxing imputed rent does not shed much light on the practicability of doing so in the United States. In the United Kingdom, rent of owner-occupied dwellings has been included in Schedule A income from the beginning of the income tax, and its taxation is in accord with tradition rather than an innovation. The British custom of referring to the value of a house as its annual rent rather than its capital value may also contribute to popular acceptance of the inclusion of imputed rent in taxable income. Property taxes (local rates) are assessed against rental value rather than capital value. * * *

The administrative problems that would be presented by the measurement of imputed net rent with reasonable accuracy do not appear to be insuperable or even intrinsically very difficult. These problems, however, would be novel for the federal tax authorities. The staff that would be required for satisfactory administration of this provision would probably be large relative to the total administrative force for the income tax. The public would no doubt find the new provisions complicated and distasteful. With due regard for institutional and political considerations, the taxation of imputed rent must be considered difficult but not impossible.

Deduction of Rent

Under the Civil War income tax, tenants were allowed to deduct annual rental payments on their residences, beginning with the act of 1863. All taxpayers were allowed to deduct all federal, state, and local taxes and interest payments. Imputed rent was not taxable. The deduction for rent was intended to place tenants and homeowners in the same position, but it actually favored tenants, since the deduction of gross rent exceeded the sum of the deductions and exclusion allowed owner-occupants. Gross rent covers depreciation and repairs and maintenance, which were not deductible by owner-occupants, as well as taxes and interest, which were deductible. The Civil War tax, nevertheless, appears to have resulted in much more nearly equal treatment of renters and owner-occupants than has been achieved in the modern income tax law. Although allowance of a deduction for rent would reduce present inequalities and would involve no special administrative difficulties, it cannot be recommended in view of its revenue cost and the favoritism it would show to housing compared with other forms of consumption. * * * It might be feasible to modify the approach by allowing tenants to deduct only adjusted net rent, defined as gross rent minus an allowance for depreciation and other costs not deductible by owner-occupants. This would approximately equalize the taxation of renters and owners but would not avoid discrimination in favor of housing. * * *

Policy would cause a shift in consumption of more rental "goods"

Disallowance of Personal Deductions for Interest Payments and Taxes

Another approach would be to discontinue the personal deductions for payments of interest and property taxes with respect to owner-occupied dwellings without requiring imputed rent to be reported for tax purposes. Although it would be quite appropriate to allow deductions for interest and taxes if imputed rent were included in taxable income, it is illogical to allow the deduction (from other income) of costs associated with the realization of non-taxable income. Congress has explicitly denied deductions for interest on "indebtedness incurred or continued to purchase or carry" tax-exempt securities (*Internal Revenue Code*, Sec. 265). * * *

illogical to allow deduction of costs assoc w/ realization of nontaxable income

Quantitatively, the elimination of personal deductions for mortgage interest and property taxes on owner-occupied houses would achieve much of the results that could be obtained by taxation of imputed net rent. * * * There would, nevertheless, be significant difference between the two approaches.

The disallowance of the interest deduction would lessen the discrimination between renters and those who own their dwellings subject to heavy mortgages. * * * On the other hand, the elimination of the interest deduction would not affect the tax liability of persons owning their houses free of mortgage debt and hence would do nothing to reduce the present discrimination between this group and renters. Among homeowners, the interest deduction has the merit of recognizing that owners with mortgages are less favorably situated than those without mortgages. Denial of the deduction would remove a difference in taxable income of the two classes of owners which corresponds to a difference in their real income. * * *

IMPUTED INCOME AND THE IDEAL INCOME TAX
Thomas Chancellor[*]
67 Oregon Law Review 561, 605-09 (1988)

Can the failure to tax net imputed rent be properly viewed as a violation of horizontal equity, discrimination against renters, or a distortion in the efficient allocation of resources?

The difference in tax treatment between home ownership and renting a home is illustrated by the following example which assumes that imputed rent is not taxed. At the beginning of the year George and Mary each have $100,000 (after taxes) to invest. Mary spends $40,000 to purchase a home for her own use and she invests the rest in a bond paying eight percent, the going pretax rate on safe investments. George invests his entire $100,000 in bonds, paying eight percent. To simplify the example, assume that there is no inflation and that net income is taxed at a flat rate of fifty percent. George's interest of $8000 per annum is subject to tax and he therefore has $4000 available to pay rent (a net after-tax return of four percent on his investment). As for Mary, she has no taxable income from her home ownership but she would be responsible for paying property taxes and insurance, maintaining the house, and establishing a reserve for depreciation to rebuild the house at the end of its forty-year useful life. Assume these expenses total $2400 per year: property taxes, $700; insurance and maintenance, $700; and depreciation (2.5% per year), $1000. George desires to rent a house, identical to Mary's, owned by Charles (the landlord) who recently purchased it for $40,000. Assume that the landlord's expenses will be the same as those incurred by Mary on her home. Since the established after-tax rate of return is four percent, Charles will expect the same return. Therefore, he will demand a gross rent of $5600 to achieve a net after-tax return of $1600 (four percent on his investment).[156] George will not be able

---

[*]. At time of original publication, Professor of Law, University of Utah.

156.	Gross rent	$5600
	Property taxes	(700)
	Insurance and maintenances	(700)
	Depreciation (2.5% per year)	(1,000)
	Taxable income	$3200
	After-tax income	$1600 (4% on 40,000)

to rent the house if his only source of payments is his after-tax return from the $100,000 investment because he will have only $4000. By contrast, Mary will be able to pay for the $2400 of owner expenses from the $2400 after-tax return she receives from her remaining $60,000 investment.[157]

The foregoing example demonstrates that for an annual rent of $4000, Charles, as an investor, would be unwilling to pay $40,000 for the house as rental property because it would not yield the established after-tax return of four percent. How much would Charles pay for the house if the maximum obtainable rent was $4000 per annum? With the assumption that expenditures for property taxes, maintenance, and insurance remain constant regardless of price, an investor requiring a four percent after-tax return would pay no more than $24,762 for the house as a rental property.[158] If owner-occupied housing could be completely isolated from the owner-landlord market there would be no tax disadvantage to renters. The purchase price of owner-occupied housing would exceed the price of identical rental housing. George could use the after-tax income ($4000) from his $100,000 to rent a house from Charles which the latter had purchased for $24,762. Mary would use her $100,000 to buy an identical house for $40,000 and pay the taxes, maintenance, and insurance with the after-tax income on her remaining $60,000. Under these circumstances, therefore, there would be no tax advantage to home ownership.[159]

The difficulty is that the two markets cannot be isolated. Because imputed rent from home ownership is not taxed, an owner-occupier will pay more for a given house than a taxpayer who will be an owner-landlord. Owner-occupiers will bid up the price of new and existing single-family housing well beyond the level that could be justified as an investment. Over time, single-family residences would be owned by owner-occupiers rather than owner-landlords.

The failure to tax imputed rent changes the equilibrium that would otherwise exist between consumer assets and investment assets in a nontax world. Does this justify taxing imputed rent? A desire to remove allocative

[handwritten margin note: Sellers of Houses would maximize profits by selling to owner/occupier]

In this and the following examples assume the entire cost basis is allowable to the depreciable improvements. This avoids the necessity of allocating the purchase price between land and improvements.

157. Mary's gross income is $4800 (.08 x 60,000); after-tax net income is $2400. It is here assumed that, contrary to current law, property taxes are not deductible by an owner-occupier such as Mary. Thus the nondeductible expenses for taxes, maintenance, insurance and the reserve for depreciation total $2400.

158. This value was calculated as follows: X is the price Charles would pay for the house as rental property; .08X (required pretax return) equals $4000 (gross rent) minus .025X (annual depreciation) and less $1400 (real property taxes, insurance, and maintenance). Solving for X: $24,762.

159. Home ownership offers a variety of important psychic benefits (*e.g.*, long-term security; freedom to make improvements) that may enhance the value of a house to an owner-occupier. * * * This suggests that in a world with no taxes the rent paid by a long-term tenant should be somewhat less than the owner-occupier's amortized cost for the same house because a rental arrangement may be less attractive than owner occupancy.

inefficiencies may be a reason to reject income as the tax base, but once we have accepted income as the tax base, allocative efficiency should not be a criterion in the definition of income. An acknowledged feature of an income tax is that it encourages consumption over investment. The favorable treatment of home ownership and other consumer asset ownership (as compared to ownership for investment) is merely a manifestation of this difference.

It is frequently asserted that the difference in treatment between homeowners and renters constitutes horizontal inequity. As described above, a system that does not tax imputed rent results in an incentive to own rather than rent housing. Is that fact alone enough to justify including imputed rent in an ideal tax base? I think not. The principle of horizontal equity demands that people with equal income be taxed the same. Proponents of taxing imputed income argue that imputed rent must be treated as income so that renters and owner-occupiers have the same income. The existence of horizontal equity depends on the fundamental threshold issue: is the benefit of using an owned asset to be treated as income? Only if the answer to that question is "yes" must the imputed benefit be taxed to achieve horizontal equity. It is circular to argue that the answer to that question must be "yes" in order to justify equalizing the incomes of renters and owner-occupiers. In the end, horizontal equity is a question of subjective judgment which should not be allowed to trump the definition of income.

Only if one views owner-occupied housing as an investment is taxing imputed rent mandated. In that case, the tax law would be making one form of investment more favorable than another. Since an investment, if successful, produces new purchasing power, the purchase of a consumer asset is the antithesis of investment; housing and other consumer assets are a form of consumption, not a form of investment. The owner-occupier and the owner-landlord are not similarly situated.

                    * * *

Notes and Questions

1. Through most of its history, the British income tax system included the rental basis of owner-occupied housing in the tax base. The imputed rental values were not updated after 1939, and, on account of inflation, "became increasingly ludicrous."[e] By 1963, adjustment to current rental values would have resulted in significantly increased taxes; the government instead opted to drop imputed rent from the tax base altogether.[f]

---

e. J.A. KAY & M.A. KING, THE BRITISH TAX SYSTEM 55 (1986).
f. Id.

2. Do you agree with Dr. Goode that "[t]he omission of imputed rent from taxable income * * * favor[s] homeowners and discriminates against renters"? Contrast the reasoning of British commentators Kay and King:

> What the tax system favours is owner-occupation, not owner-occupiers, and this distinction is not always made clear. * * *
>
> [New purchasers of housing are] faced with buying houses at prices which have been forced up by the tax-stimulated demand for them: prices which reflect the capitalized value of the tax concessions. * * * Thus current house-buyers obtain relatively little benefit from the concessions. Indeed they may be worse off, since young married couples are forced to save for deposits towards house purchases at a time in their lives when incomes are low, outgoings high, and large compulsory savings of this kind inappropriate. * * *
>
> [T]his account demonstrates why tax capitalization is such a dangerous trap: although we believe it would be better if the system had never incorporated these concessions, it does not seem that it would now be either equitable or desirable to withdraw them. The losses from doing so would be principally borne by those who are currently struggling to meet the initial mortgage repayments on a house—people who have derived little benefit from the concessions and who may have actually suffered from them.[g]

3. Would the objection to taxation of imputed income from housing raised by Kay and King be met if the change were phased in over a period of many years?

4. Professor Chancellor demonstrates rather convincingly that a rational taxpayer should be willing to pay more for a house to live in than for the same house to rent out in a market transaction. Given the impossibility of isolating the two markets, this suggests a constant pressure in favor of housing becoming owner-occupied. What tax treatment seems to lead to this result?

5. Keep in mind that economic models can never be sufficiently nuanced to tell the whole story. For example, Professor Chancellor's figures assumed that his hypothetical house would encounter real economic depreciation of 2.5 percent per year regardless of ownership, and that this accurately-computed cost would be deductible by the landlord. But what if the tax system allows landlords depreciation deductions greatly in excess of economic depreciation? For example, many buyers appear to think that no depreciation at all is to be expected—that housing is more likely to increase in value than to

---

g. *Id.* at 56-57.

decrease—yet the tax system allows depreciation, currently over 27.5 years,[h] and recently over as little as 15 years.[i] Tax deductions for depreciation are not allowed to owner-occupiers. Generous tax treatment for depreciation, taken alone, should result in landlords being willing to pay more for housing than would owner-occupiers. This factor would appear to partially counter the favorable treatment afforded the imputed income of owner-occupiers.

The most constant influence of the tax system may be not so much discrimination favoring owner-occupiers vis-a-vis landlords and renters, but a bias in favor of housing as compared to other assets.

6. In principle, there seems to be little or no difference between imputed income from housing and from consumer durables. Administrative difficulties in comparison to revenue generated appear to be much greater with regard to consumer durables, however. If it were conceded that imputed income from consumer durables is not to be taxed, would considerations of fairness and consistency require that imputed income from housing also be exempt?

7. Does the failure to tax imputed income from housing result in a misallocation of resources to housing? To a particular type of housing?

8. Professor Chancellor concludes that the failure to tax imputed income from owner-occupied housing is problematic if we view such housing as an investment, but not if it is viewed as consumption. What is his argument?

9. Is political and social stability improved if a significant portion of the population lives in owner-occupied housing? If so, does this justify the current favorable treatment of housing, including the exclusion of imputed income from the tax base?

10. Elderly taxpayers are more likely than others to have lived in a house long enough to have accumulated significant equity, and thus may benefit disproportionately from the exclusion of imputed rent from income. Does this justify the exclusion?

11. The national saving rate of the United States is among the lowest of industrialized nations. Home mortgage payments, each of which includes a payment of principal, can be viewed as a form of forced savings. Is

---

h. Section 168(c)(1).

i. A 15-year depreciation period for real property was adopted in the Economic Recovery Tax Act of 1981, and remained in force until enactment of the Tax Reform Act of 1984. The 1984 Act extended the recovery period to 18 years, and subsequent statutes have extended the recovery period to its present 27.5 years for residential real estate, and 39 years for nonresidential real estate. Section 168(c)(1).

favorable treatment of housing justified in order to encourage saving? Is Dr. Goode correct in asserting that the exclusion of imputed income from the tax base is not important to the decision to purchase a house?

12. If the United States decided to include imputed income from owner-occupied housing in the tax base, how should the program be structured? Are the administrative problems overwhelming?

13. Suppose we conclude that imputed rent should be taxed in theory, but that such a tax is impracticable. Should we then consider a more workable "proxy"? Dr. Goode mentions two possibilities—allowance of some deduction for rent paid, and removal of deductions for mortgage interest and real estate taxes on personal residences. Does either of these appear attractive?

14. In Canada, imputed income is not taxed, but no deduction is allowed for mortgage interest and property taxes on the taxpayer's home. At least with respect to owner-occupied housing, the Royal Commission on Taxation recognized the theoretical correctness of taxing imputed income and the severe discrimination that resulted from not doing so, but concluded that "the determination of this net income for owner-occupied dwellings, even if arbitrary rules were adopted, would be fraught with uncertainly and would entail detailed administrative examination."[j] The Royal Commission asserted that the inequity of not taxing this imputed income was less severe in Canada than in the United States, because Canada allows no deduction for interest and property taxes on the taxpayer's residence.[k] Is this assertion always correct?

15. Many bank depositors receive low or no interest on their demand deposits, but are rewarded by receiving free or discounted check printing, checking account services, safety deposit boxes, and the like. Should these services be viewed as imputed interest income?[l]

16. Apart from issues of policy, the Constitution may restrict possible choices. A strained argument might be made that failure to include imputed income in the tax base might be viewed as impermissible discrimination. That argument was rejected by the Supreme Court shortly after ratification of the Sixteenth Amendment, in *Brushaber v. Union Pacific R.R.*[m] The

---

j. 3 REPORT OF THE ROYAL COMMISSION ON TAXATION 48 (1966).

k. *Id.* at 49.

l. For further discussion, *see* Melvin I. White, *Consistent Treatment of Items Excluded and Omitted from the Individual Income Tax Base, in* HOUSE COMM. ON WAYS AND MEANS, 86TH CONG., 1ST SESS., 1 TAX REVISION COMPENDIUM 317, 323-25 (1959).

m. 240 U.S. 1 (1916).

United States Supreme Court upheld the 1913 income tax, rejecting the plaintiff's argument that "[i]f the renter cannot deduct as an expense what he pays as rent, the owner, who has no such expense, should be charged with the rental value of his home . . ."[n] "[S]ince the *Brushaber* case there can be no serious constitutional objection to the exclusion of imputed income, but the question remains as to the constitutionality of its *in*clusion."[o]

While Congress is thus free not to tax imputed income—and there are now eight decades of practice to build on the *Brushaber* decision—there is a more serious possibility that Congress is barred from including at least some forms of imputed income from property because it does not constitute "income" under the Sixteenth Amendment. Almost certainly, Congress could not tax imputed income from services. The constitutionality of taxing imputed income from owner-occupied housing is placed in question by the Supreme Court's sixty-year-old dicta in *Helvering v. Independent Life Ins. Co.*: "If the statute lays taxes on the part of the building occupied by the owner or upon the rental value of that space, it cannot be sustained, for that would be a direct tax requiring apportionment."[p] The Court concluded that Congress had intended no such tax, and thus its holding did not reach the constitutional issue.

C. IMPUTED INCOME FROM SERVICES

Unlike the situation regarding imputed income from property, there is no realistic thought of imposing a tax on any form of imputed income from services. If nothing else—and there is much else—while the constitutionality of taxing imputed income from property may be questionable, it almost certainly would be unconstitutional to tax imputed income from services.

Nonetheless, the inquiry into the theoretical correctness of regarding these benefits as income informs our understanding of the nature of income and, more concretely, may lead us to conclude that certain "second best" approaches, which *are* workable and constitutional, are appropriate. With respect to imputed income from home ownership, for example, a possible "proxy" would be to allow a deduction for rent. Similarly, while there is no realistic consideration of taxing a family for the benefit conferred by a housewife and mother, should that failure to tax be offset by allowing a deduction for the expense of a maid and nanny employed by a working mother?[q] Such a provision might be thought of as a "proxy" for taxing the

---

n. Transcript of Record at 21, Brushaber v. Union Pacific R.R., 240 U.S. 1 (1916) (No. 140).

o. Bruce L. Balch, *Individual Income Taxes and Housing*, 11 NAT'L TAX J. 168, 170 (1958).

p. 292 U.S. 371, 378 (1934).

q. This text and the articles excerpted generally discuss the issue in terms of a working mother rather than a working father. In most couples, if one spouse is considering not working in the market, that spouse will be the wife. Similarly, where small children requiring custodial care are in a home headed by a single parent, it is usually the mother. Fathers are much more likely to occupy either of these roles than in decades past, but still less frequently than mothers.

imputed income generated by "nonworking" wives and mothers. That is, assume that we would prefer to tax the imputed income generated by a housewife, but we cannot for administrative, political and constitutional reasons. On this assumption, we think families with housewives are being given unfairly favorable treatment. Can we end the perceived unfairness indirectly, by proxy, by giving the family that does not have a housewife a deduction for purchasing the services that many housewives perform?

Present law (section 21) allows a credit for a portion of a taxpayer's expenses for child care or care of an adult unable to care for himself. If the taxpayer pays for care of such a "qualifying individual," the credit also covers payments for household services. The credit is limited to expenses that enable the taxpayer to work, and, in furtherance of that limitation, the amount of expenditure qualifying for the credit cannot exceed the earned income of the taxpayer or, if married, the earned income of the lower-earning spouse. In no event can qualifying expenditures exceed $4,800 ($2,400 where only one qualifying individual is present). Of the qualifying expenditures, the taxpayer's credit ranges from a maximum of 30 percent for taxpayers with adjusted gross income of $10,000 or less, decreasing to 20 percent when AGI exceeds $28,000.

The first three excerpts speak in terms of deductions rather than credits for child care and household services, in part because they were written when predecessors to section 21 were in effect.[r] The policy discussion remains almost unchanged, and therefore these articles continue to be relevant.

TAXATION OF THE FAMILY IN A COMPREHENSIVE AND SIMPLIFIED INCOME TAX
Michael J. McIntyre[*] & Oliver Oldman[**]
90 Harvard Law Review 1573, 1607-15, 1617-20 (1977)

A direct corollary of our conclusion [earlier in the article] that one-half of the consolidated marital income of a couple should be attributed to each of the spouses is that equal-income couples should pay equal taxes. * * *

The analysis is identical if "father" and "husband" are substituted for "mother" and "wife."

r. Congress initially allowed a tax concession for such expenses by enactment of section 214 in 1954, which allowed a sharply limited deduction. The provision was liberalized in 1963, 1964 and, most importantly, in 1971. By 1971, the limitations on deductibility were similar to the present limitations on expenditures qualifying for the credit. The use of a deduction made a qualifying dollar of expenditure of greater value to a high-bracket taxpayer; the present provision reverses this preference. On the other hand, high-income taxpayers could claim no deduction at all; present law allows even the millionaire a credit of 20 percent of qualifying expenses. For further discussion of the development and details of section 214, see William A. Klein, *Tax Deductions for Family Care Expenses*, 14 B.C. INDUS. & COM. L. REV. 917, 917-32 (1973) and Alan L. Feld, *Deductibility of Expenses for Child Care and Household Expenses: New Section 214*, 27 TAX L. REV. 415 (1972).

*. At time of original publication, Professor of Law, Wayne State University.

**. At time of original publication, Learned Hand Professor of Law and Director of the International Tax Program, Harvard Law School.

In this Part, we reexamine the proposition that couples with equal monetary income should pay equal taxes in light of the arguments made for adjusting the burdens on one- and two-job couples on account of perceived differences in the imputed income typically available to each. If imputed income should be taxed under the CTB [comprehensive tax base] ideal, and if two-job couples have less imputed income than one-job couples, then our decision to tax equally couples with equal monetary income discriminates against two-job couples.[117]   Hence, consideration of the issue of imputed income, although principally a problem of defining the appropriate tax base, has implications for the attribution of income within the family.

The case for including at least some self-performed services in income is illustrated by the following example: A_1 and B_1 are married and each has a forty-hour-a-week job with an annual salary of $10,000. At the end of a work day, A_1 and B_1 are seldom in the mood to cook; instead they either eat out at a restaurant or heat up in the oven a frozen convenience dinner purchased at the supermarket. They also hire a maid to clean the house and handle other domestic chores and they send their dirty clothes to the laundry. A_2 and B_2 are married. A_2 has a full-time job paying $20,000 a year and B_2 has no employment outside the home. B_2 spends a good bit of time, however, baking bread, cooking fancy meals, canning fruits and vegetables, cleaning the house, sewing, and doing laundry.

If the services performed by B_2 in the above example produce taxable income as a matter of definition under the CTB ideal, then the value of the services should in principle be included in the pool of income attributed to A_2 and B_2 under the scheme of taxation proposed * * * . We conclude that the pattern of distribution of imputed income from self-performed services is so complex that the failure to take imputed income into account in determining relative tax burdens leads to no particular disadvantage for two-job couples.
    * * *

According to Simons, the definition of income (1) should be objective rather than subjective; (2) should be quantitative and measurable; and (3) should have a minimum number of implicit arbitrary distinctions. These three minimum tests for an acceptable definition of income provide a convenient framework for an analysis of the case for taxing the imputed income from self-performed services.

The variety of self-performed services which in some sense constitute income range from the sublime to the ridiculous, from the priceless private poetry of an Emily Dickinson to the thumb-sucking of a small child. Putting a handle on the self-performed service concept is something like defining a capital gain: we think we know what we mean, but if we articulate a definition, we end up with either nothing fitting the description or everything

---

117. Although the discussion is framed in terms of the possible disparity in treatment of one-job and two-job couples in the failure to tax imputed income, similar considerations have been raised as to the comparative treatment of single individuals and one-job couples.

fitting it.   For example, which if any of the following services should be taxable: Getting up in the morning? Doing exercises? Singing in the shower? Grooming oneself? Fixing breakfast? Chewing food? Processing it within the stomach? Walking to work? Baking bread? Growing roses? Fixing the car? Driving in the country? Watching T.V.? Reading a novel? Reading bedtime stories to one's children? Playing backgammon?

As these examples illustrate, almost every activity we undertake is in some sense a self-performed service, since the possibility of imposing a market model on nonmarket activity has no logical limits.   A general inclusion of all imputed income from personal services in the definition of taxable income would cause the definition to fail all three of Simons' tests, since it would present hopeless problems of subjectivity and measurement and would require entirely ad hoc decisionmaking. At a minimum, therefore, some categories of imputed income ought to be excluded from the tax base.

* * *

Take an apparently minor item such as shaving. At the minimum market price of $2 per shave, imputed income from shaving would exceed $700 per year for a person who shaves daily. Similarly the imputed income from dressing oneself each day, measured by the market price for a valet, would be in the thousands of dollars. In fact, potential income from even a narrow definition of self-performed services would be likely to exceed salary income for a majority of taxpayers. * * *

The practical policy choice is between ignoring imputed income from self-performed services entirely or employing some indirect method of taxation. All indirect methods require a discernible pattern, since they cannot operate unless there is some factor other than the imputed income item itself for identifying who is being disadvantaged. That factor would be used as a proxy for the presence or absence of the benefits of a particular type of self-performed service.

* * *

A challenge to our tentative conclusion that couples with equal monetary income should pay equal tax is dependent, therefore, on a showing that the exclusion of certain items of imputed income from the tax base results in a definite pattern of discrimination against two-job couples.[127]

---

127. Whether or not a pattern of discrimination exists must be judged according to fairness criteria, not efficiency criteria. Much of the support for tax measures in favor of two-job couples nevertheless rests on considerations of efficiency. In analyzing the economic component of the choice between working in and working outside the market, economists find it useful to include income from self-performed services within the concept of income, since the optimum choice for efficiency purposes is the one which maximizes the total of market and nonmarket income. The failure to tax certain types of self-performed services probably creates a distortion in the labor market in favor, for example, of a woman working in the home rather than working at a job which pays a taxable salary. The utility of including self-performed services in the income concept for purposes of eliminating this distortion, however, has no bearing on the merits of including it in income for purposes of determining fairness. Arguments addressed to the social and economic consequences of a particular mode of taxing self-performed services have usually

Estimating the Patterns of Imputed Income from Self-Performed Services of One-Job and Two-Job Married Couples

Our analysis of imputed income was prompted by the concern that equal tax treatment of couples with equal monetary income might discriminate against two-job couples. As discussed above, a claim of discrimination depends on the existence of identifiable patterns in the distribution of imputed income which disadvantage two-job couples. A stereotyped view of the activities of working and nonworking wives might suggest that a clear pattern exists. In this Section, we attempt to go behind the stereotype.
* * *

To avoid some of the definitional ambiguities discussed above, we will be concerned exclusively with a limited group of self-performed services which many taxpayers commonly purchase in the market—"household services," such as cooking, cleaning, sewing, and caring for children; and "handy-person services," such as shoveling snow, fixing the television, and repairing the roof. In examining the widely held perception that one-job couples have more imputed income from these services than two-job couples have, we are unable to refer to existing empirical studies. * * *

First, we can find no predictable difference between one- and two-job couples in the consumption of self-performed child-care services. Obviously, and most importantly, such services are rarely performed by couples without children, in which case disparity between one- and two-job couples is nonexistent. In addition, when there are children a substantial amount of child-care services are performed by both two-job couples and one-job couples.[128] It is true that some one-job couples and even more two-job couples

---

sidestepped the issue of fairness and instead have focused on considerations of efficiency or social engineering. Proposals for accomplishing these nontax goals should be subjected to a tax expenditure analysis and must be justified, if at all, under budget criteria, not tax criteria. A discussion of the merits of proposals for adjusting the burden of one-job and two-job couples on efficiency grounds is beyond the scope of this Article.

If we did reach the merits, we would begin by examining the implicit assumption of all efficiency arguments—that the maximization of economic goods is a desirable social goal. We would want to see what the arguments are for encouraging market activity at the expense of leisure and self-performed services. Our suspicion is that giving money rewards for some kinds of activities but not for others already distorts the choice among activities in favor of paying jobs. There are a number of possible gains in a tax system which counteract this distortion. We think, for example, that citizen participation in the political processes of the country is desirable and is inhibited by the economic incentives which pull people away from volunteer political work. On the other hand, we can appreciate arguments for encouraging market behavior in other situations. None of the efficiency literature we have seen addresses itself, however, to this fundamental point. For a discussion of efficiency arguments, see H. Rosen, Application of Optimal Tax Theory to Problems in Taxing Families and Individuals (U.S. Dep't of Treasury, OTA Paper 21, November 1976) (also referring to much of the literature on the subject).

128. Some studies have been made on the patterns of child-care arrangements of working mothers with small children. The most common arrangement is for the child-care to be provided by either the father or another relative. According to a 1973 survey, 49% of working mothers paid nothing for child-care, and in a large number of other cases, the out-of-pocket expenses were "very small," because the services were provided by relatives. In 26% of white two-job families

purchase child-care services in the market. Those who purchase probably have less self-performed child-care services than those couples with children who do not purchase. But the ratio of purchased as opposed to self-performed child-care services may be more closely related to inclination than to whether both spouses work, especially if child-care services are defined more meaningfully than as one parent's mere physical presence for long stretches of time.

* * *

The one advantage which a one-job couple consistently has over a two-job couple is the extra time available for nonemployment activity. Although it cannot be assumed that this time is in fact used to perform services the couple would otherwise have to purchase in the market, some advocates of a tax allowance for two-job couples assert that leisure itself constitutes "consumption," and thus should be taxable. Treating leisure as consumption for tax purposes raises most of the problems of treating self-performed services as income. First of all, what is the policy reason for wanting small children, retired persons, students, and the unemployed—those most likely to have substantial amounts of leisure "income—to pay an increased share of the tax burden? * * *

Indirect Methods for Taxing Imputed Income from Self-Performed Services

Despite the preceding analysis, some may still feel that an ideal income tax somehow must take self-performed services into account. In this Section, we assume the validity of that perception and consider practical proposals for taking it into account. Since direct taxation of imputed income is universally acknowledged to be unfeasible, the objective is to find some indirect method of approximating the distribution of tax burdens which would result from direct taxation. We will discuss the merits of three possible indirect methods of taxing imputed income: a deduction for cash outlays for the purchase of personal services, an earned income allowance, and adjustments in the rate schedule. Given the conceptual problems with any definition of imputed income and the complex patterns of distribution of self-performed services among the groups of taxpayers, any indirect method of adjusting burdens will be crude indeed. The most that can be hoped for is a system which reduces the perceived disproportionate burden arguably imposed currently on two-job couples without creating greater unfairness for other taxpayers. We conclude that none of these proposals achieves even that limited goal.

Deductions for Purchases of Personal Services

Amounts spent on personal services—to hire a maid or gardener, for example—normally constitute consumption, and the income which finances

---

and 14% of black two-job families surveyed, the mother and father arranged working hours [so] that they could handle their child-care requirements themselves. Child-care in the home is also apparently preferred by the majority of two-job and one-parent families. *See* Woolsey, *Pied Piper Politics and the Child-Care Debate*, DAEDALUS, Spring 1977, at 127, 130-32.

the consumption is taxable. If many taxpayers receive these same benefits tax-free by performing the services themselves, a deduction for cash outlays for services may be in some circumstances a satisfactory indirect method of taxing self-performed services. The function of the deduction would be to equalize the tax treatment of purchased services and self-performed services by in effect making both kinds of services exempt from tax.

A deduction for cash outlays for personal services is defensible in an ideal income tax only if the amount spent to purchase services is a good proxy for differences in the distribution of self-performed services. For example, if all taxpayers either mow their own lawn or hire someone to do it, and if the amount of mowing which must be done is about the same for all taxpayers, then a deduction for the costs of hiring someone else to mow has about the same effect on relative tax burdens as including imputed income from mowing in taxable income. On the other hand, if a significant number of taxpayers do not have a lawn to mow, or mow it very infrequently, then a deduction for the purchase of mowing services is not an acceptable indirect method for taxing self-performed mowing services. The higher tax rates necessitated by the deduction unfairly increase the tax burden on persons who do not mow.[136]

This example illustrates that while a deduction for purchases of any type of services is fair as between persons who typically perform the services themselves and those who purchase, a deduction is unfair as between those who purchase and those who neither purchase nor perform the services themselves. A deduction for mowing is unfair to most renters; a deduction for shoveling snow is unfair to taxpayers in the South.

Of greater practical significance, a deduction for child-care expenditures is unfair to those without children, assuming that the purpose of the deduction is to make allowance for the failure of the tax system to tax imputed income from child-care services. If self-performed child-care services are to be treated as income, the proper adjustment is a large deduction for taxpayers without children, with a more modest deduction for those with children who purchase child-care services.

This analysis suggests that a minimum requirement for permitting a deduction for cash outlays for services must be that the service in question

---

136. Assume a universe with only three taxpayers, M, H, and N, each with pecuniary income of 100. The required revenue yield of the tax system is 30. Assume M mows his lawn, H hires someone to mow, and N has no lawn and never purchases lawn mowing services or performs them himself. If mowing for oneself should be taxable in an ideal income tax system, then M should pay more tax than H or N, and H and N should pay the same tax. If only H is allowed a deduction for mowing, then the tax on M and N will be increased to make up for the revenue loss. This is fair to M, who has more "income" than H, but unfair to N, who has the same income as H. The only fair solution is to give the deduction to both H and N. Assume further that H purchases some mowing services and also performs some for himself. The only way to approximate the "ideal" solution of taxing mowing services would be to give a big deduction to N (perhaps 30), a smaller deduction to H (say 10) and no deduction to M.

is one which virtually all taxpayers either perform themselves or purchase in the market. This requirement, although a necessary one, is not, however, a sufficient one to identify the purchases for which a deduction is an acceptable "second best" adjustment for the failure to tax self-performed services directly. Cooking may be the most pervasive example of a service which is either performed or purchased. A deduction for amounts spent at restaurants is, however, a poor index of the value of the self-performed services of those who eat at home. Amounts spent at restaurants vary considerably even among persons who frequently eat out; those who eat at expensive restaurants should not be allowed a tax benefit which is only vaguely related to the value of the self-performed cooking services of persons who eat at home. Cleaning house is another chore which is widely purchased or performed for oneself. The allowable deduction would have to be small, however, to avoid unfairness to people with small houses, people without children, and people with a high tolerance for untidiness.[137]

* * *

TAX DEDUCTIONS FOR FAMILY CARE EXPENSES
William A. Klein[*]

14 Boston College Industrial & Commercial Law Review 917,
917-19, 932-35, 937-40 (1973)

Prior to 1954 the only Code section under which a deduction for dependent-care expenses might plausibly have been allowed was the general provision, the predecessor of section 162, allowing a deduction for the "ordinary and necessary expenses [of] carrying on any trade or business."[2] The leading case denying the deduction under that language was *Henry C. Smith*.[3] While the opinion is not enlightening, it is sufficiently provocative to warrant careful examination. The facts are simply stated. Mr. and Mrs. Smith were both employed and filed a joint return[4] in which they claimed a

---

137. A maid service deduction, if regarded as an indirect method of taxing self-performed housecleaning services, should of course be available to all taxpayers, not simply those with a qualifying dependent for whom the expense is somehow job-related. *See* I.R.C. § 44A [and present section 21]. We suspect, however, that a deduction for maid services, if divorced from the business expense rationale which in part explained the political acceptability of the present household services credit, would be perceived by the public as a subsidy to the rich, who are more likely to pay for the performance of housework than are poorer people regardless of whether both spouses work. The problem of an apparent lack of equivalence between self-performed and purchased services may be particularly blatant here even though theoretically the two groups are being treated alike. It is unclear how a system of deductions could deal with this problem.

    *. At time of original publication, Professor of Law, University of California, Los Angeles.

    2. Int. Rev. Code of 1939, § 23(a)(1). In one case, in a rather unique set of circumstances, a deduction for child care expenses was claimed as a medical expense under the predecessor of § 213, on the theory that the taxpayer's health was imperiled by the necessity of caring for the children. The deduction was denied. Ochs v. Commissioner, 195 F.2d 692 (2d Cir. 1952).

    3. 40 B.T.A. 1038 (1939), aff'd per curiam, 113 F.2d 114 (2d Cir. 1940).

    4. The case arose before the era of split income, but even then married couples were permitted to file a joint return and in certain circumstances could gain a modest advantage by

deduction for the expense of hiring someone to care for their young child. According to the opinion of the Board of Tax Appeals, the Smiths' argument was simply that "but for" the fact that Mrs. Smith was working the child care expense need not have been incurred.[5] Since there was no suggestion that the Smiths would have hired a caretaker for the child even if one of them had been unemployed, the "but for" argument seemed to have considerable force, and the Board's rebuttal to this argument missed the point. Adopting a *reductio ad absurdum* approach, the Board stated that if the Smiths' argument were accepted, then a deduction for food and shelter should also be allowed as a business expense since without food and shelter a person would be physically unable to work. The obvious irrelevance of that observation lies in the fact that the cost of food and shelter is unavoidable for nonworkers as well as workers, whereas child care expenses are unavoidable only for workers.[6]

The Board's attack on the "but for" argument would have been more persuasive if it had been launched from another angle. The Board neglected the fact that child care expenses are not incurred by all workers, but only by those who have children. The expense, therefore, is attributable not only to the decision to work—taking children as given—but also to the decision to have children—taking work as given. In other words, the expense at issue can be looked upon in part as a cost of working and in part as a cost of having children—that is, as a trade or business expense and a personal expense—but not as either one alone. Such an observation scarcely resolves the question of deductibility, but at least it avoids spurious causative analysis and brings into sharper focus the central issue of the case.

Passing from its discussion of the "but for" or causative argument, the Board referred to the notion of the wife (not, it may be noted, the husband) as a provider of "services as custodian of the home and protector of its children," and pointed out that ordinarily these services are provided without financial reward. To use the jargon of the present-day economist, the nonworking spouse, husband or wife, provides imputed income in the form of services to the household or family. What is curious about the Board's observation is that it may be used to support rather than undercut the allowance of a deduction for child care expense. Because the cash income of the working wife is taxed while the imputed income of the nonworking wife is not, a deduction for child care can be defended as a means of mitigating the inequality in tax results. This argument seems to have escaped the Board.

　　　　* * *

---

doing so.

5. It was no doubt a sign of the times that the possibility was not even considered that Mr. Smith, rather than Mrs. Smith, could have been the child's caretaker.

6. The Board might have found in the denial of deductions for commuting expenses a more useful example for rebuttal.

As suggested earlier, child care expenses are not strictly comparable to business expenses such as wages, costs of goods sold, and so forth, because the former are incurred only by a certain class of earners—those with children—and that class is defined by a nonbusiness phenomenon. Such a characterization, however, does not require disallowance of the deduction for dependent care expenses in the interests of economic neutrality. In other words, the admitted distinction between dependent-care and other business-related expenses does not necessarily require that any deduction for the latter be characterized as a "subsidy" to child-bearing any more than a deduction of wages by a manufacturer is a "subsidy" to manufacturing.[85] To reach general conclusions regarding the proper characterization or treatment of the dependent care deduction, in relation to the goal of economic neutrality, would require an economic analysis far more detailed and sophisticated than seems justified for the purposes of this article.[86] I offer the suggestion, however, that anyone who attempts such an analysis will quickly discover that the issues cannot be resolved easily or in simple terms, but that if one makes certain assumptions[87] it is plainly the case that the dependent care deduction is not a "subsidy." Even if it were feasible to engage here in a complete inquiry into what would be an economically neutral tax rule for the dependent care expenses there is reason to doubt the value of such an effort, since other provisions of the tax law[89] as well as other social and economic pressures are blatantly non-neutral as they relate to the work and childbearing decisions.

One can, nonetheless, make certain limited but valuable observations about the effect of the deduction on decisions to work and decisions to have children. We can begin by asking what effects a deduction for dependent care expenses will have on a person's decision to work, given the fact that the

---

85. No one would bother to observe that a deduction for wages means more to a high-bracket manufacturer than to a low-bracket manufacturer, but the same kind of observation about the dependent care deduction has been made (indeed, belabored) by some sophisticated tax experts.

86. The kind of analysis I refer to would require examination of the kinds of decisions that would be made—in all types of individual circumstances, with and without a tax system and with and without a deduction—as to whether or not to work, and for how many hours, and whether or not to have children. The variety of types of individual circumstances (including, for example, different states of mind about work and child bearing, and different family circumstances) is large, and the analysis is complicated by the fact that our interest is in a deduction, but the deduction can be examined only in the context of a tax system and that tax system itself has significant effects on the work decision and, possibly, on the childbearing decision.

87. One such assumption would be that the decision whether or not to work arises after a decision to have children has already been made and carried out (as where a widow with young children seriously contemplates working only after the death of her husband); another, that the child care services provide no personal gratification.

89. For example, the provisions that make it advantageous for married couples to file joint returns (Int. Rev. Code of 1954, § 1) have the effect of imposing on the secondary worker (in our society, usually the childbearing wife) a marginal tax rate determined with reference not to his or her own income but rather with reference to that income plus the income of the primary worker.

family has a dependent requiring care during working hours. Once we take such a dependent as given, and once we assume that the dependent care services provide the taxpayer with no significant personal benefit,[91] the financial reward from working, the amount that provides the incentive to work, is the net figure arrived at by subtracting the dependent care expenses from earnings (net of other expenses). If the deduction were disallowed, a person would be taxed on more than his or her net income, and for such persons the financial reward of working would be reduced to a net figure below that of other persons with similar net incomes but with no dependents needing care. This observation by itself implies an economic distortion. Moreover, if the deduction is allowed the financial reward for working will be increased for those people who hire others to perform dependent care services, but, disregarding the possibility of a personal return from the purchase of such services,[92] the effect of allowing the deduction will certainly not be to increase the financial reward of working above what it would be in the absence of any tax system. On certain assumptions, then, the tax rule permitting the deduction is economically neutral.

> * * *

Fairness

One's views on whether fairness requires that the income tax system include a provision for deduction of the expenses of caring for dependents can be significantly affected by the kind of comparison one makes in examining the issue. In most economic analyses it seems to be assumed that all adults are married and have children and that the only relevant variable is whether or not the wife works. The children are taken as given, but the wife's job is not.[107] The comparison is then drawn between two families with dependent children and with equal total earnings; in one of the families the wife does not work while in the other she does. Unfairness results from the fact that the nonworking wife performs child care services for the family unit. That family is therefore said to have imputed income from those services—income that should be taxed in the interests of fairness but cannot be taxed because of other considerations. On the other hand, the family with the working wife must pay for child care services with after-tax dollars. To reduce the

---

91. For purposes of the present analysis I will assume away the possibility of personal benefit. To the extent that the dependent care services provide personal gratification, the offset for the cost of those services should be reduced by the value of that personal benefit. * * * [T]he assumption of no personal benefit worth worrying about does not seem highly unrealistic, particularly since many people enjoy caring for children. Still, that assumption is weakened if we also assume that a significant amount of housework will be provided by the provider of dependent care: such provision must be classified as personally gratifying.

92. See note 91 supra.

107. See, e.g., W. Vickrey, Agenda for Progressive Taxation 32-33 (1947); M. White, Proper Income Tax Treatment of Deductions for Personal Expense, 1 Tax Revision Compendium, House Comm. on Ways and Means, 86th Cong., 1st Sess. 365, 371-72 (1959).

unfairness resulting from the nontaxation of imputed income to the first family, the deduction for child care expenses is offered to the second family.

A similar conclusion can be reached more directly simply by observing that the family with a working wife must of necessity incur an expense that the other family does not incur and that the purchase of the service, by hypothesis,[110] does not provide the family purchasing the service with any personal benefit. However, stating the comparison in this manner should give us pause. In one sense it is true that the expense is one that "must of necessity" be incurred, but in another sense it is not. The correctness of the conclusion may be thought to depend on one's time perspective. The expense is necessary at a given point in time only because the couple had previously made a decision to have children.

To pursue this last point from a different perspective, consider a comparison between two families, one consisting of husband and wife, without children, and the other of husband, wife and child. Assume also that in both families the wife is working. Obviously the childless couple avoids an expense that the couple with a child must incur. But what is the significance of that observation? One approach is to conclude that the couple with the child has an added expense stemming in part from their decision to have children. Another approach is to take the perspective of the childless couple and conclude that one consequence of their decision to remain childless is that they save money on child care. It seems perfectly reasonable and just that their saving should be available to them for other pleasures. From this perspective, fairness does not seem to require a deduction for child care expenses.

With this perspective in mind we can profitably return to the original comparison of the two couples, both with children, only one of which has a working wife. Assume that the couple with the working wife made a deliberate, conscious decision to have a child, knowing that one of the costs of that decision would be the expense of hiring baby sitters while both the husband and wife were working. In this situation it would appear that the child care expense is more properly regarded as a cost of having children—a cost of personal consumption—and not a cost of working. On this assumption, then, it would be difficult to argue that fairness requires a deduction of the child care expense for such a couple, except for the troublesome fact that their counterpart family with the wife not working has the benefit of the wife's untaxed services in kind.[116] However, this result is

---

110. See note 91 supra. There appears to be no disagreement over the proposition that the expense should not be deductible to the extent that the service relieves that family of an expense that it would have incurred regardless of the job, or to the extent that it provides the family with a personal benefit. Obviously it will be difficult to draw the distinctions suggested by this statement and arbitrary rules will be required. The phase-out of the deduction as income rises above $18,000 is such a rule and seems to me to be a sensible one, though perhaps a bit generous.

116. Suppose that all women worked and that the only variable was whether they bore children

part of a much broader problem, which is that many taxpayers or taxpaying couples with identical earnings have different amounts of free time available either for leisure or for the performance of services for themselves; this is a general problem of tax policy, not limited to the area of child care. It creates a dilemma for which there is no entirely satisfactory solution.

The preceding analysis should suggest that the question of fairness is subject to the same complexities and uncertainties as is the question of economic effects. Consequently I will venture only this tentative generality: if we assume that childbearing will increasingly be seen as a conscious, volitional phenomenon, and if we assume that people as time goes by will increase their leisure time in proportion to their working time, the "fairness" argument for allowing the deduction for child care expenses will weaken.[118]

The deduction for household expenses again requires only brief comment. In the first place, whatever may be the justification for a deduction for such expenses on grounds of fairness, there is no defense whatever for conditioning the deduction on having a qualifying dependent in the household. Second, it may be true that the allowance of the deduction improves the fairness of the system by offsetting the advantage a couple can achieve where one spouse stays home and performs untaxed services for the family. At the same time, however, household chores, unlike dependent care duties, can be accomplished after working hours and on the weekends. Thus the major effect of allowing the deduction may be simply to allow people to purchase more leisure time. The potential invidious effects of this phenomenon are aptly described by the economist Richard Goode:

> Even if certain expenses could be identified as costs, a deduction for them would be unfair to families—usually those with low and low-middle incomes—in which the household work is done by the working wife or other family members in the evenings or on weekends compared with families which hire household help and enjoy more leisure. The practical effect of an allowance for expenses for household help would be discrimination in favor of upper-middle income groups.[120]

* * *

---

and retained responsibility for them. In such circumstances, I can think of no sound basis for allowing a deduction for child care expenses unless there were some good reason for wanting to increase the population.

118. My analysis implicitly dismissed two theories of childbearing that might have required more attention in an earlier time or in other countries. Both theories would deny that children are produced for the personal gratification of the parents. One would assert that children are produced as economic assets with future returns to the parents and the other would claim that children are produced out of a sense of obligation to God or society.

120. R. Goode, The Individual Income Tax 81 (1964).

TWO CHEERS FOR THE CHILD CARE DEDUCTION
Daniel C. Schaffer & Donald H. Berman[*]

28 Tax Law Review 535, 536-40, 542-45 (1973)

There is certainly no principle in our tax law that every expense combining business and pleasure is nondeductible. The cost of a meal taken while traveling away from home in the pursuit of a trade or business, the expense of a drink over which business discussions take place, the premium paid for first class air travel—all have a personal element and all are deductible. * * *

The truth is that we have no one guiding principle with which to determine whether expenses which are for personal and business purposes at the same time are deductible. To the extent that the problem is resolvable at all, each such deduction must be viewed ad hoc, and the advantages and disadvantages of allowing it considered.

We suggest that the deduction for child care can be defended as promoting the efficient allocation of labor. We take it as a postulate that taxpayers should be allowed to choose among available jobs according to the interplay of their personal preferences and the wage offered for each job, and that the tax system should distort this choice as little as is practically possible. * * *

[M]others are given the choice between work in the labor force, the income from which is taxable, and child care, the imputed income from which is not taxed. This is hardly a neutral system of taxation. It may induce a mother whose productivity in the labor force is higher than her productivity as a mother (measured by the fair market value of her services as a mother) to stay out of the labor force, even if she prefers paying work to caring for her children. This would be an irrational allocation of labor. Normally, the price system would attract such a woman into the labor force but may be frustrated when the income from one kind of work is taxed, and that from another is not. This observation is by no means original. Vickrey made it in 1947,[17] and he may not have been the first.

A misallocation may exist even if the value of the mother's services in the home and in the labor force are the same, or the former is higher than the latter. There are two reasons: (1) The mother may prefer a job in the labor force to homemaking. Quite apart from productivity there is something wrong with a tax system that for no particular purpose diverts people into work they would otherwise choose not to do; (2) Even if a mother likes housework as much as labor force work and renders services in the home which the market would value as highly as her work in the labor force, she might prefer a cash wage to a return in the form of housework accomplished. A housewife both renders and (with her family) consumes her services. As

---

*. At time of original publication, both authors were professors at Northeastern University School of Law.

17. VICKREY, AGENDA FOR PROGRESSIVE TAXATION 44-45 (1947).

a consumer, she may prefer the goods and services she can buy with a cash wage to her achievements in her home, even though the market would place the same value on each. This is no more than to say that given the same incomes, we might each spend them differently. An educated woman may be worth $15,000 per annum in the market both as a nanny and as, say, a computer programmer; she may like both jobs equally; but she may prefer to earn $15,000 in cash, spend $5,000 to hire child care inferior (in the market's view, and perhaps her own) to what she could provide to her children herself, and spend the remaining $10,000 on other pleasures. The income tax ought not to impede this choice.

A way to make the tax system more neutral as to a mother's choice of work would be to tax the imputed income which she generates. The difficulty of valuation of her services, the fact that we would be increasing a family's tax at just the moment when current policy calls for the tax to decrease—upon the birth of a child—and, if the tax is large enough, the family's problem of finding cash to pay tax on income which is neither in cash or in kind, all make this impractical. The only other solution is a child care deduction or credit of some kind. Those who see the deduction as one for a personal expense would say that it reduces the rate of income tax imposed on a mother's earned income below that imposed on other taxpayers. The justification is that the usual rates of income tax would have an unusually deterring effect on the entrance into the labor force of one who could work (as a mother) without being taxed at all.

We do not know if the theoretical disincentive which arises from taxing the labor force income, but not the imputed child care services income of a mother, really results in a large misallocation of labor. We can calculate the income tax penalty for entering the labor force in the case of any given mother, if we value her child care services and know her income tax bracket, but we do not know whether the income tax penalty influences a mother's choice of work often, sometimes, rarely or never. * * * What is important is to understand what questions we should be asking in evaluating [the child care deduction]. This is not to revert to the question of whether the deduction is really "personal." If every mother in the United States were in the labor force full-time, it would be clear that the unneutrality of the income tax was not misallocating labor, but the problem of whether child care was a personal or business expense to these mothers would remain.

* * *

We have been assuming that a mother's decision to stay at home or go out to work will be an efficient decision if she simply takes into account her own preferences, the value of her services in the home and the wage she can earn in the labor market. But suppose that her decision hurts or helps the rest of us (including her children), because children raised by surrogate parents tend to be juvenile delinquents (or, in the alternative, model citizens). Then the wages and costs which the wife faces will not reflect the costs and benefits of her decision to society. Because the costs and benefits of her decision are "externalized," that is, borne by others, including perhaps her children, rather than herself, her decision cannot be expected to maximize welfare. It is common in such cases to resolve the conflict with a tax subsidy or penalty. Parents may choose not to pay for their children's education. The rest of us feel so strongly affected by this decision that we [both pay for] the child's education and compel it. There is nothing wrong with asking whether a mother's entering the labor force has so great an effect, for good or for ill, on the rest of us that we would prefer to pay her to stay in her home or to get out of it. But this is hardly an issue for tax lawyers to resolve. [The child care deduction] should indeed be discussed in terms of its effects on children and on the rest of us, but as tax lawyers we bring very little expertise to the discussion. The question is important, but it is for someone else to answer. We *would*, however, ask those who favor a subsidy to keep mothers in the home why they think that the tax rates found in section 1(a) of the Internal Revenue Code are a proper measure of that subsidy.

* * *

Conclusion

Perhaps the most vulnerable point in our defense of [the child care deduction] is that our argument may imply something that no tax lawyer (including ourselves) would agree to for a moment: All personal expenses for services should be deductible. If the failure to tax the imputed income of a mother who stays home and cares for her children while taxing her income if she enters the labor force may result in a misallocation of labor, why is that not equally true of every other service which a taxpayer renders to himself and his family, the imputed income from which is not taxed? If a deduction for a mother's cost of employing others to care for her children is a defensible device to correct the possible misallocation of her labor, why should not, on the same grounds, every taxpayer who is in the labor force be able to deduct the cost of employing another to perform personal services for him?

To be more specific, a taxpayer may have to choose between spending a Saturday cleaning his house, mowing his lawn, washing his car, shopping and washing his laundry, on the one hand, and working overtime at his job, on the other. That his imputed income from performing chores goes untaxed while his overtime pay is taxed, may lead him to perform chores himself even though he is both more efficient and happier on his job, in which case his labor is misallocated. * * *

When a taxpayer employs another to wash his car or mow his lawn, he cannot argue that the expenditure is even partly a business one in the sense of the tax law. It is purely personal, not partly personal and partly business. This is because the taxpayer cannot argue that "but for" hiring someone to do his personal chores, he could not work overtime. The taxpayer cannot make the but for argument because he is free to work overtime and leave his personal chores undone. He may not enjoy driving a dirty car or having an unmowed lawn, but that is his personal choice. He is not forced to choose between doing his chores and working at his job. A mother's position is quite different; where her husband holds a job, she could not possibly be expected to leave her child unattended in order to enter the labor force, if only because to do so would in most cases violate state law. In the child care case (but not in the case of mowing the lawn or washing the car), the taxpayer could not work but for her expenditure. Of course, a but for relationship between expense and income is not *sufficient* to make the expenditure deductible (if it were we could all deduct the cost of our food and clothing), but it is *necessary*.   Thus the child care deduction fits into a different legal category—that of mixed business and personal expenses —than do deductions for other services.

* * *

TAXATION AND THE FAMILY: A FRESH LOOK AT BEHAVIORAL GENDER BIASES IN THE CODE
Edward J. McCaffery[*]

40 UCLA Law Review 983, 1001-05, 1055-58 (1993)

The failure to tax imputed income contributes to a bias against labor force participation by secondary earners. This failure has long been noted as a theoretical shortcoming of the tax system, although it is widely believed that its existence is of practical necessity. "Imputed income" is the value that flows from owner-supplied resources or labor.

Consider the basic accounting identity that sets income equal to the sum of consumption plus savings: all income must be either spent or saved. The present income tax may be viewed as an attempt to capture all items of savings and consumption measured over a set period of time, typically the taxable year. Imputed income, however, constitutes an entire class of items that never materialize into a visible cash stream, because the individual supplies her own consumption. Imagine a taxpayer who is handy around the home—perhaps she paints the house. Were she not so talented, she would have to earn the money to pay the painters—assume a fee of $1000. That $1000, however, would be taxable, as consumption, so that the taxpayer would have to earn $1000 *after* taxes in order to pay the painters. By painting her house on her own, she has performed services worth $1000, and she has the equivalent amount of consumption value, but she has been able to do so with *before* tax value.

The relevance of imputed income to married couples is clear, although the precise effects are highly contextual and complex. Virtually all of the

---

*. At time of original publication, Associate Professor of Law, University of Southern California Law Center.

services that the spouse who stays at home performs constitute untaxed imputed income. The demand for such services increases, first with marriage, and later, dramatically, with children. Consider a scenario where a secondary earner in a family with young children leaves the home to go to work. The family would then have to pay for a variety of services—child care and housekeeping among them—with after-tax dollars. By performing these services herself, the wife obtains a tax benefit for the family: it is precisely as though she were receiving a discount of her marginal tax rate. Thus, at a 33% tax rate, a wife would have to earn $15,000 merely to replace $10,000 worth of services that she had been supplying to the home. It is therefore not surprising that economists have now been studying the elasticity of nonmarket, as well as market, work to tax rates, and have found distinct gender-based patterns. Indeed, this distinction between market and nonmarket work reveals the normative biases of the more traditional variants of the "labor-leisure" distinction, which quite often divided time into market work and all else.

Calibrating the effects of a bias in favor of imputed income is a difficult undertaking. These effects are, as demonstrated above, a function of the tax rates facing the worker. But they also depend on the actual amount of imputed income generated by a potential worker; the costs of alternatives to the imputed income—such as child care provided by other family members, for example; and the utilities of money income and leisure. What is important is to set the imputed income phenomenon in a *behavioral* context, as opposed to the distributive setting where traditional tax policy discussions have located it for years. Measuring levels of imputed income for purposes of making static distributive comparisons is difficult. One could attempt to make crude *a priori* guesses about the levels, or try to devise some technique to measure exact amounts, or develop some proxy for getting at imputed income. Alternatively, one could realize that imputed income is one of the factors that makes the classical ability-to-pay income taxation model impossible of attainment.

What are less difficult to measure, and perhaps more important to see, are the behavioral effects flowing from the fact that the marginal-earner spouse must compare after-tax labor market income with before-tax imputed earnings. This is especially important for the current problem, because it will be comparatively easy to ascertain the steps necessary to put single- and dual-earning families on nominally equal footing: reforming social security, the treatment of mixed business-personal costs, and the like. But even once those steps are taken that will move the law toward its stated ideal of equal taxation for equal-earning couples, the largely invisible imputed income effect, tilting towards single-earner households, will remain.

Some may argue that the imputed income effects benefit families by encouraging personal care of children and other dependents. But when the effects are examined from the perspective of the behavioral impact on familial structure, what is disturbing is the push towards a gender division of labor. In the traditional single-earner household, the wife's imputed income effect will be measured relative to her *husband's* income. Given that the wife is apt to have less market power, and perhaps be socialized into the role of care-provider, it becomes more likely that it will be she who takes advantage of the imputed income bonus. Note the irony: The more the husband is taxed, the more we "pay" the wife to stay home and, perhaps, the more the man works to compensate for the loss due to taxes.

One solution to the behavioral aspects of the imputed income problem clarifies these points. A *subsidy* to secondary earners, financed by a higher rate on primary earners, would move the law in a new direction. This change would not entirely remove the imputed income effect—no traditional income tax will—but it shifts its incidence and degrees. If the wife stays home full time, she will effectively be taxed by forgoing the subsidy available to her if she works. On the other hand, if the husband cuts back on his labor market hours to help with the children and the housework, he will receive a full imputed income bonus—possibly higher than exists under current law, given the need to raise rates on primary earners. Details and magnitudes aside, this type of solution could begin unravelling centuries of gendered patterns. * * *

Choice of Family Structure

The problem of taxation and the family may be approached as one of an individual's freedom of choice regarding family structure. Current institutions push for traditional single-earner families, and away from more modern conceptions. * * *

In a first-best world or from the vantage point of the hypothetical original position, the concern with freedom to choose family structure might indeed lead to taxing equal-earning couples equally, or ignoring marriage altogether in the allocation of tax burdens. But in the present tense, the ideal would require greater sensitivity to impediments to married women's participation in the labor market, and to the deeply entrenched sexual division of familial labor. At a minimum, it would purge the law of those biases where two-earner families are treated worse than single-earner ones —changing social security, the child care credit, fringe benefit rules, and so forth. But full implementation of the notion would undoubtedly go beyond these preliminary steps, to move to correct and reverse deep-seated patterns of gender discrimination, and to look closely at the questions of ex ante incentives. * * *

One problem that the ideal of freedom to choose family structure encounters is that there are many types of family, defined functionally. It is not enough to talk just of literal marriage *vel non*, or to ask whether a household has one or two earners. At the most fundamental level, we are concerned with the human bonds that familial structures foster and nurture. As a practical proxy for these types, simple one- and two-earner marriages have been used throughout most of this Article. Indeed, much could be gained by acknowledging the factual prevalence and normative appeal of the two-earner model, and, in the face of laws and reality slanted against it, taking steps to place it on a genuinely equal footing with the traditional single-earner model. These steps may not be enough, however. * * *

Gender Bias and Inequality

A second general nonwelfarist approach, suggested by the above discussions, is to finesse the particular questions of family structure altogether, and instead look directly to the issue of women's rights. A good deal of the problems with present familial arrangements can be seen as a direct or indirect function of the pervasive gender bias in society. Women are the marginal workers; women are put to the hardest choices between parenting and working; women bear the greatest burden of juggling the two realms; and women suffer most when marriages break up, or fail to come about in the first place. All three of the dominant incentive effects discussed affect women especially painfully. Women are hurt by the failure of marriage, especially among the lower classes. Women are the stay-at-home spouse in traditional single-earner families. And women pay the greatest price for being on the cuff of an all-or-nothing labor decision that discourages part-time labor. Both symptomatic and causative of these problems and patterns is the fact that the dominant images of family, and the basic structure of our laws, have arisen out of a highly gendered, patriarchic world. If we take steps to alleviate these problems by empowering women, we will create the conditions under which a nongendered family model or models can arise, *whatever* they happen to be. In this manner, we can remain "neutral" regarding choice of family structure, without ignoring the gendered nature of society that makes the static neutrality of tax policy such a misguided idea.

Equality between the genders, although it is of course sadly far from the norm in either theory or practice, is an idea with obvious normative appeal. But even if we aim for equality between the genders, and not a neutrality between family types directly, we still want to look closely at the particular tax rules regarding family. As shown throughout this Article, the problems of married women are not the same as the problems of women generally; the family is not an institution we can simply ignore. Unmarried women suffer much less labor market discrimination. The situation of married mothers may lie at the center of the self-perpetuating cycle of socialized gender roles. Marriage neutrality alone is not enough. If our goal were to eliminate gender biases in the workplace and the gendered structure of the sexual division of labor, a perfectly good idea to study, for example, is an earned income credit targeted to secondary earners.

* * *

Notes and Questions

17. In a portion of their article not excerpted above, Professors McIntyre and Oldman favor imposing an equal tax burden on all married couples of a given income level. How might untaxed imputed income be viewed as making such an approach unfairly favor one-earner couples vis-a-vis two-earner couples? One-earner couples vis-a-vis singles? Do you agree with McIntyre and Oldman that no "pattern" of unfairness would result?

18. Should a credit or deduction be available for the expenses of child care? Should the deduction or credit be available even if a healthy parent is neither working nor studying (*e.g.*, is a housewife)? Is your answer to either question influenced by whether you think the value of a nonworking parent's services to the family should, in theory, be taxed?

19. If untaxed imputed income of nonworking parents justifies (as a proxy for taxing the imputed income) a child care deduction for working parents, what about childless taxpayers who generate absolutely no untaxed imputed income from child care? Do you agree with the argument of Professors McIntyre and Oldman that "[i]f self-performed child-care services are to be treated as income, the proper adjustment is a large deduction for taxpayers without children, with a more modest deduction for those with children who purchase child-care services"? (This argument is not put forward seriously, of course, but only in an attempt to refute the idea that imputed income from child care justifies a deduction for those who purchase child care services.)

20. Professor Klein's article emphasizes that our societal expectations of the norm may strongly influence choices made in the tax laws and, in turn, the tax laws along with other societal factors may influence decisions about having children and about working. Clearly, our society is not now typified by the so-called "traditional" family, consisting of a working husband and a nonworking wife who cares for their children. Is today's norm one in which virtually all adults work, some having children and others remaining childless? Or would a more correct description be that virtually all adults become parents, some continuing to work and others staying home to care for their children? What tax policies are suggested by each paradigm?

21. Even if a norm existed, it would not necessarily provide an answer. Professors Schaffer and Berman argue that "[i]f every mother in the United States were in the labor force * * * the problem of whether child care was a personal or business expense to these mothers would remain." Do you agree?

22. Are present tax policies, including the failure to tax imputed income generated by housewives, consistent with the view that "a woman's place is

in the home"? Or, by contrast, does the child care credit subsidize mothers who prefer to work outside the home? Or both? Should the tax laws be neutral, as Professors Schaffer and Berman "postulate," or should they subsidize the decision to stay home or to work?

23. Professor McCaffery argues that the tax law tends to influence married women, in particular, toward work in the home, and that the influence increases as their husband's taxable income rises. Why is this so?

24. Professor McCaffery acknowledges that any system of income taxation cannot entirely remove incentives in favor of imputed income. (All agree that direct taxation of imputed income is not under serious consideration.) Nevertheless, he directly challenges the neutrality postulate of Professors Schaffer and Berman (see Note #22 above), and favors an active role for the law to reduce such incentives in the case of married women. What effect would his proposed tax subsidy for secondary workers (usually wives) have? Would the proposed tax subsidy mean higher tax rates for taxpayers who cannot, or do not, qualify for the subsidy (one-earner couples, for example)? Is his proposed subsidy system fair? Is Professor McCaffery correct that "disturbing is the push toward a gender division of labor," or, by contrast, is his proposal objectionable precisely because it would inefficiently lead to reduced specialization of husbands and wives? Would it lead to better child care or worse? Again, this proposal raises the issue of whether the tax system should be neutral toward the wife's decision to enter the labor force, or encourage or discourage that decision, and makes clear the impact of tax law on the structure of society.

25. What of allowing a deduction for household care? Given that all families, with or without children, must either perform or pay for some amount of household care, should we account for the difference between performing (and generating untaxed imputed income) and paying for (with after-tax dollars) by allowing a deduction for payments? If we are concerned that this would unfairly benefit high-income taxpayers, can this objection be met by allowing the deduction but increasing the progressivity of the tax rates? Does this provide a perfect example of imputed income, which might be accounted for by allowing a deduction to those who hire others to perform the work?

26. At present, section 21 allows, under certain circumstances, a credit for household expenses as well as dependent care, but only if the taxpayer maintains a household with a child or other "qualifying individual." Focusing only on household expenses, is there any justification for tying the credit to whether the taxpayer supports a qualifying individual? If the expense of maids should give rise to a tax benefit (perhaps as a proxy to the untaxed

imputed income of those who care for their own houses), should it be available to all taxpayers, regardless of family status?

27. At present, many persons who provide services in the home are paid in cash, with payors and payees colluding to evade income taxes and Social Security taxes. To the degree that such payments are deductible or creditable by the payor, the payor has a strong incentive not to allow the fraud to take place. (For example, taxpayers claiming the credit under section 21 must report the Social Security number of the recipient of their payments; this, in turn, greatly increases the chance that the recipient will report and pay tax on the payment.) Does this justify some form of deduction or credit?

28. In a 113-page article, Professor Norman Lane argues that his "exchange model" of income is useful "both as a precis of our existing tax law and as a normative ideal."[s] Under this model, "[o]nly transactions which derive from the production and exchange process ought to increase the aggregate tax base."[t] This result is justified by the enormous increase in productivity and wealth occasioned by use of markets and specialization. With regard to imputed income from services,[u] Professor Lane argues that not only does it lie outside the proper scope of taxable income, but that no serious misallocation of resources results from this demarcation:

> [T]he exchange model sharply distinguishes between satisfying present wants through direct effort to that end, and satisfying them by participating in markets. The individual who grows his own vegetables in his home garden and cooks them on his own range is not taxed on the value of his output, while the individual who works for wages and purchases vegetables at the store must confront a tax wedge between the two activities. The exchange model assumes, quite reasonably, that technological conditions are such that the latter route provides far more vegetables per unit of time expended than the former even after the tax is paid.[v]

Is this persuasive in the case of vegetables grown in the back yard? In the case of a housewife's services to her family?

---

s. Norman H. Lane, *A Theory of the Tax Base: The Exchange Model*, 3 AMER. J. TAX POL'Y 1, 18 (1984).

t. *Id.*

u. Professor Lane's treatment of imputed income from housing and other consumer durables is somewhat more complex. *See id.* at 34-41.

v. *Id.* at 23.

Selected Bibliography

See also bibliography for Chapter Five.

Aaron, Henry, *Income Taxes and Housing*, 40 AM. ECON. REV. 789 (1970).

ANDO, ALBERTO ET AL., THE STRUCTURE AND REFORM OF THE U.S. TAX SYSTEM 91-95, 183-88 (1985).

Balch, Bruce Lee, *Individual Income Taxes and Housing*, 11 NAT'L TAX J. 168 (1958).

Bittker, Boris I., *A "Comprehensive Tax Base" as a Goal of Tax Reform*, 80 HARV. L. REV. 925, 947-48 (1967).

——, *Federal Income Taxation and the Family*, 27 STAN. L. REV. 1389 (1975).

Chancellor, Thomas, *Imputed Income and the Ideal Income Tax*, 67 OR. L. REV. 561 (1988).

Comment, *The Constitutionality of the Taxation of Imputed Income*, 9 VALPARAISO U. L. REV. 221 (1974).

Comment, *Taxation of Imputed Income*, 1959 DUKE L.J. 476.

Feld, Alan, *Another Word on Child Care*, 28 TAX L. REV. 546 (1973).

——, *Deductibility of Expenses for Child Care and Household Services: New Section 214*, 27 TAX L. REV. 415 (1972).

GOODE, RICHARD, THE INDIVIDUAL INCOME TAX 117-25 (Rev. ed. 1976).

——, *Imputed Rent of Owner-Occupied Dwellings Under the Income Tax*, 15 J. FIN. 504 (1960).

Haskell, Mark A. & Joel Kauffman, *Taxation of Imputed Income: The Bargain-Purchase Problem*, 17 NAT'L TAX J. 232 (1964).

Klein, William A., *Deductions for Family Care Expenses*, 17 B. C. INDUS. & COM. L. REV. 917 (1973).

Kindahl, James K., *Housing and the Federal Income Tax*, 8 NAT'L TAX J. 376 (1955).

Lane, Norman H., *A Theory of the Tax Base: The Exchange Model*, 3 AM. J. TAX POL'Y 1 (1984).

Marsh, Donald B., *The Taxation of Imputed Income*, 58 POL. SCI. Q. 514 (1943).

McCaffery, Edward J., *Taxation and the Family: A Fresh Look at Behavioral Gender Biases in the Code*, 40 UCLA L. REV. 983 (1993).

McIntyre, Michael J. & Oliver Oldman, *Taxation of the Family in a Comprehensive and Simplified Income Tax*, 90 HARV. L. REV. 1573 (1977).

Newman, Joel S., *Transferability, Utility, and Taxation*, 30 KAN. L. REV. 27, 46-48 (1981).

Oliver, Philip D., *Section 265(2): A Counterproductive Solution to a Nonexistent Problem*, 40 TAX L. REV. 351, 394-96 (1985).

Pechman, Joseph A., *What Would a Comprehensive Individual Income Tax Yield?*, in HOUSE COMM. ON WAYS AND MEANS, 86TH CONG., 1ST SESS., 1 TAX REVISION COMPENDIUM 251, 261-62 (1959).

Popkin, William D., *Household Services and Child Care in the Income Tax and Social Security Laws*, 50 IND. L.J. 238 (1975).

Ruhtenberg, Joan, Note, *Federal Income Tax Discrimination Between Homeowners and Renters: A Proposed Solution*, 12 IND. L. REV. 583 (1979).

Robert W. Tinney, *Imputed Rent on Owner-occupied Homes*, *in* STUDIES IN SUBSTANTIVE TAX REFORM 125-37 (Arthur B. Willis, ed., 1969).

ROYAL COMMISSION ON THE TAXATION OF PROFITS AND INCOME [Great Britain], FINAL REPORT 249-50 (1950).

ROYAL COMMISSION ON TAXATION [Canada], REPORT, vol. 3, ch. 8 (1966).

Schaffer, Daniel C. & Donald H. Berman, *The Child Care Deduction and the Progressivity of the Income Tax: A Reply to Professor Feld*, 28 TAX L. REV. 549 (1973).

———, *Two Cheers for the Child Care Deduction*, 28 TAX L. REV. 535 (1973).

SIMONS, HENRY, PERSONAL INCOME TAXATION 110-24 (1938).

VICKREY, WILLIAM, AGENDA FOR PROGRESSIVE TAXATION 17-52 (1947).

White, Melvin I., *Consistent Treatment of Items Excluded and Omitted from the Individual Income Tax Base*, *in* HOUSE COMM. ON WAYS AND MEANS, 86TH CONG., 1ST SESS., 1 TAX REVISION COMPENDIUM 317, 322-27 (1959).

Wolfman, Brian, Comment, *Child Care, Work, and the Federal Income Tax*, 3 AM. J. TAX POL'Y 153 (1984).

CHAPTER FOUR

PROGRESSIVE TAX RATES

*Unlike proportionality, progression provides no principle which tells us what the relative burden of different persons ought to be. * * * [T]he argument based on the presumed justice of progression provides no limitation, as has often been admitted by its supporters, before all incomes above a certain figure are confiscated, and those below left untaxed.*[a]

A. INTRODUCTION

The choice of appropriate tax levels involves a variety of often contradictory considerations. Public acceptance is of prime importance.

The primary concept underlying progressive taxation is ability to pay. In its simplest form, that means leaving a taxpayer with enough income after tax to support at least a rudimentary subsistence level. This has been institutionalized by the computation of a nationwide poverty level. Beyond this, ability to pay has provided the rationale for progressive tax rates.

Simple revenue needs underlie the choice of tax levels. Revenue needs were of overwhelming importance in setting high tax rates during World War I and World War II. When the factors of ability to pay and public acceptability were factored in, it was predictable that the wartime rates also would be sharply progressive.

In wartime and peacetime a variety of other consideration are taken into account. Federal tax decisions must take into account the revenue needs of state and local governments. Consideration must be given to the pressure of high tax rates to encourage tax evasion, or, at the least, to lead to elaborate and often uneconomic tax avoidance. Efforts must be made to minimize distortion of market choices. In a market-driven economy, taxes that distort market choices result in investment decisions that fail to maximize the economy's potential. Taxes also affect incentives to work, though here it is more difficult to determine their impact. There is the obvious effect of discouraging more work when the alternative is tax-free leisure (the "substitution effect"), but in a society with highly developed consumer demand there is an alternative pressure to work harder to earn enough after-tax income to achieve a desired standard of living (the "income effect"). The best example of the latter is the increase in the number of two-earner families.

The Tax Reform Act of 1986 revised the size and pattern of the tax rate schedules, and in so doing it changed drastically the frame of reference for

---

a. Friedrich A. Hayek, quoted in 69 TAX NOTES 1674 (1995).

103

debate on progressivity. Under the impetus of a drive for a broad-based flat
rate tax, but also under the constraint to produce a revenue-neutral bill, in
1986 Congress enacted a three-bracket system (zero tax, 15 percent, and 28
percent), dropping the top rate from 50 percent. The top rate has since been
increased, but it is difficult to imagine a top rate as high as the 91 percent
in effect in the 1950s and early 1960s. In the present climate of opinion, it
is hard to foresee an income tax (at least in peacetime) that will tax personal
income at an explicit rate higher than 50 percent.

B. PROGRESSIVITY: PROS AND CONS

This subchapter surveys the arguments for and against the desirability
of a progressive income tax. For the most part, the arguments are wide-
ranging, not limited by the frame of reference the 1986 Tax Reform Act has
set for us.

The principle of tax rates keyed, at least to some degree, to ability to pay
is not seriously challenged. Even a flat rate tax with a liberal exemption is
a progressive tax.[b] Consequently, the discussion revolves around the
appropriate formula establishing the degree of progression and, perhaps more
importantly, the search for a rationale for a cap on the top rate.

Professor J.B. McCombs' article reviews the theoretical arguments on
progressivity, with particular attention to the influential book written by
Professors Walter J. Blum and Harry Kalven, Jr. in 1953, *The Uneasy Case
for Progressive Taxation*. (The Blum and Kalven book questioned the
theoretical basis for progressivity.) The selection by Professor Dan Throop
Smith, an economist and at one time the principal expert on tax policy in the
Treasury, challenges progression in principle. His discussion, however, is
directed primarily to setting rational limits on the degree of progressivity.

The selection by Professor Boris Bittker, law professor and co-author of
the seminal treatise on the corporate income tax, argues that proportionality
is no more logical than progressivity, so there is no reason to put the burden
of proof on proponents of progressivity. He also argues that a progressive
income tax is counterbalanced by other, regressive federal, state, and local
taxes.

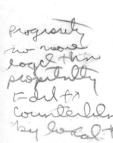

---

b. See the discussion of flat tax proposals in Chapter Seven.

AN HISTORICAL REVIEW AND ANALYSIS OF
EARLY UNITED STATES TAX POLICY SCHOLARSHIP:
DEFINITION OF INCOME AND
PROGRESSIVE RATES
J.B. McCombs[*]

64 St. John's Law Review 471, 512-25 (1990)

Blum and Kalven: The Critical View

In 1953, Professors Walter J. Blum and Harry Kalven, Jr., wrote a short book critiquing progressive taxation. They did not quickly convert the nation to proportionate taxation, but perhaps they demonstrated that Henry Simons was right in his contention that progressivity is an issue more concerned with ethics than rationality.

Blum and Kalven seemed to prefer Simons' approach. In 1963, when the book was reprinted, they recorded some additional thoughts on the view of progressivity as an ethical issue.

> Ten years ago we were puzzled as to why Henry Simons' bluntness had not had more impact on the tone of discussions in the United States. Writing in the late thirties, he exasperatedly asserted that the whole superstructure of sacrifice and ability-to-pay theorizing was simply nonsense and that the case for progression was no more and no less than the case for mitigating "unlovely" economic inequality.[157]

The authors claimed to have approached their topic with a bias favoring progressivity. Appropriately, Blum and Kalven's *The Uneasy Case for Progressive Taxation* begins with a careful definition of the central issue, particularly with reference to the difference between progression arising from a constant rate tax with a personal exemption, and the type of progression (relative to both total and taxable incomes) obtained from actually graduating the statutory marginal rates. The former is defined as degression. Based upon their conclusion that "[i]t is almost unanimously agreed that some exemption keyed to at least a minimum subsistence standard of living is desirable,"[160] the authors put aside the issue of degression and focused their attention on the latter form of progression.

The authors discussed three general objections often lodged against progressivity. First, they pointed to the additional complication progressivity adds to an income tax and its administration. Income splitting and other problems related to identifying the proper taxpayer fit into this category. Progressivity also creates the problem of identifying or defining the appropriate taxable unit in family matters. With a flat tax, husbands, wives,

---

[*]. At time of original publication, Assistant Professor of Law, University of Nebraska College of Law.

157. W. BLUM & H. KALVEN, JR., THE UNEASY CASE FOR PROGRESSIVE TAXATION (1953), at xiv.

160. *Id.*, at 4.

and children can be taxed together or separately with no difference in impact or tax liability. The difference between married, single, and head-of-household taxpayers would disappear (except with respect to the appropriate size of the exemption). Splitting income among different years is the temporal equivalent of splitting income among different individuals, and it is aggravated (though not created) by a progressive rate structure. Under a flat tax, the seemingly inescapable year-end ritual of deciding whether to accelerate deductions into the expiring year and delay income into the coming year, or vice versa, becomes purely a matter of the time value of money. The question of the year in which the individual will be in a higher tax bracket drops out of the equation.

And one of the few plausible arguments, if not the only one, for special treatment of capital gains stems from this characteristic of progression. Because a capital gain may have been in the making for many years, it seems unfair to tax all of it as the income of a single year.[163]

The authors also implied that the reduced importance of timing, which would result from elimination of progressive rates, would allow repeal of the rules for the net operating loss carry back and carry forward, installment sale method, last-in first-out ("LIFO") inventory method, and carryover of capital losses. Such an implication is not sound, however, for several reasons: the installment sale method is motivated in large part by a sympathy for the taxpayer who has a realized gain that is much greater than his cash from the transaction; the LIFO method is driven by desire to reduce the effective tax rate on inflationary gain by delaying the tax as long as possible; and net operating loss and capital loss carryover provisions are primarily based on the government's reluctance to give immediate refunds for such losses.

The second general objection to progressivity is that it is "politically irresponsible." This is the "tyranny of the majority" argument, which questions the right of the majority to impose such a burden on the higher-income minority. The response to this, which the authors acknowledged, is that such an objection applied to every decision made by a democratic government. The authors made reference to constitutional limitations on the power of the majority in certain areas, such as free speech, which merely highlights the fact that those who framed and adopted our Constitution never deemed the upper end of a highly paid person's income to rank with the fundamental individual freedoms protected by the Bill of Rights.

The third general objection to progressivity is that it reduces total national output. Blum and Kalven noted that a progressive tax is not the only type that can reduce the productivity of our economy:

---

163. *Id.*, at 16-17.

It is worth a reminder that the disadvantages of progression, as well as its advantages, in this connection and in all others, are to be assessed only by contrasting a progressive system which raises a given amount of revenue to a proportionate one which raises an identical amount of revenue.[170] Nevertheless, the comparable progressive tax will subject the most highly paid (and therefore, arguably, most productive) citizens to a higher marginal tax rate than would the revenue-equivalent proportionate system.

One fundamental assumption that the authors made regarding productivity deserved more thought than it received. They asserted that "[i]t is not difficult to concede that money is the dominant stimulus to work in our society."[171] Others would disagree with this assumption, however, especially with respect to high income individuals. It ignored the large number of "workaholics" in higher income strata. It also gave inadequate attention to the nonmonetary rewards that often flow from highly paid positions. Simons, whom the authors quote only briefly on this point, saw money as only one stimulus at work in our society.

It also can reasonably be argued that much of the interest of the rich in money is in having *relatively* more than their peers. This is a corollary to Simons' assertion that "[p]overty, want, and privation are in large measure merely relative."[173] Because a rational, progressive income tax will not upset the relative pre-tax order (of rich, richer, richest), this kind of egotistical stimulus to working will not be impaired by progressive taxation.

Another element in the productivity debate is the possible discouragement of saving and investing. There is widespread agreement that progressive taxation has a negative effect on capital accumulation and that such accumulation is an important element in economic growth. Simons wrote that "[w]ith respect to capital accumulation, however, the consequences are certain to be significantly adverse;"[174] but that, in his opinion, the incremental loss of productivity is probably justified by the reduction of inequality. Blum and Kalven agreed with him on the first conclusion but parted company with him on the second. They identified two phases in the formation of "real capital": the decision of an individual with discretionary income to save, rather than consume, a part of it; and the decision by that same, or another, person to invest those savings in a business or other venture. The authors recognized that the effect of progressive taxation on the decision to save is unclear. Some people save in response to the rate of interest their savings can earn. For high income people who save for this reason, the incentive to save is reduced by the higher tax rates that

---

170. *Id.* at 21.
171. *Id.* at 22.
173. H. SIMONS, PERSONAL INCOME TAXATION: THE DEFINITION OF INCOME AS A PROBLEM OF FISCAL POLICY 25 (1938).
174. *Id.* at 21.

accompany a progressive system (as opposed to a proportionate system that generates equal revenue). On the other hand, other people save to accumulate a specific amount of money for retirement. For them, reduction in rate of return due to the tax burden will actually force them to save more to achieve the same retirement goal. The authors recognized that, since the magnitudes of these two savings incentives are unknown, the net effect on saving of a particular tax rate is also unknown.

Blum and Kalven's analysis of the effects of progressivity on investment (*i.e.*, risk-taking) is not applicable under the current United States tax system with its extremely wide rate brackets. If one thinks back (or forward) to a rate structure containing a large number of relatively narrow brackets, however, the discussion is valuable. Under such a system, if an investment is successful, the profit will push the investor into a higher tax bracket and such profit will be taxed at a rate higher than the investor normally experiences. If the investment is unsuccessful, the loss will pull the investor down to a bracket lower than normal. As a result, the government takes a higher than normal percentage of investment profits, while it absorbs through loss deductions a lower than normal percentage of investment losses (assuming full deductibility of losses). Again, Blum and Kalven distinguished between high tax rates in general and high tax rates generated by progressivity. While a high tax rate itself may discourage investment, its impact is enlarged by a progressive system. Ultimately, the "relatively wealthy," a significant source of investment funds, are taxed under progression at rates higher than the single rate prevalent under a proportionate tax rate.

Blum and Kalven identified the effect of progressivity on levels of saving and investment as central to the debate over progressivity, and referenced Simons' idea of government capitalism. Thus, it may be in order to consider the capital formation issue more broadly, and in a modern context. Simons did not go into much detail in his discussion of government capital formation, but he did suggest that the government might appropriately purchase all regulated utilities. This, he believed, could be accomplished without a major overthrow of our economic system. If inadequate capital formation is a valid concern, however, perhaps we should be searching for possible ways to implement Professor Simons' concept of government capitalism, structured in ways and within limits that impose acceptably small costs in terms of greater government control over the private economy.

It is not at all clear that changing from progressive to proportionate taxation will increase private capital formation sufficiently to satisfy those who are concerned about it. Indeed, progressivity of federal taxes was reduced by the several tax reform acts of the 1980s, yet Congress is still grappling for ways to increase the United States saving rate. One point remains clear—taxes are not the only significant variable in capital formation. Cultural attitudes toward consumption and saving are also important ingredients.

Desire to retain progressive taxation, therefore, might not be the only force leading to endorsement of government capitalism. For example, in the United States, gradual changes in cultural attitudes could, over a span of multiple generations, produce a situation in which people save a lower percentage of their incomes than did their grandparents under otherwise identical circumstances. Furthermore, despair over the chances of economic development in the third world outstripping population growth could convince industrialized nations to assume the role of capitalists for less developed countries.

On the subject of a reduction in production caused by a progressive tax, the parallel between the Blum and Kalven team and Henry Simons continues, despite their inapposite conclusions on progression. The continuation of these diametric conclusions gives some validity to Simons' claim that progressivity ultimately rests upon an ethical judgment rather than logical reasoning.

In contrast, a number of theories have been advanced in support of a progressive income tax. One is the suggestion that a progressive tax is highly sensitive to contraction and expansion of the overall economy, and that it reacts to each in an appropriate manner. During a recession, for example, revenues produced by a progressive tax will fall faster than those from a proportionate tax, leaving more money in the private economy at a time when it is especially needed. During an expansion, revenues produced by a progressive tax grow faster than the economy, and faster than revenues from a proportionate tax, reducing the likelihood that the economy will become "overheated" and inflationary. During recession and expansion, these effects occur more quickly than federal spending changes could be made, and also reduce the amount of spending and monetary adjustments necessary to stabilize the economy.

The sacrifice theory is another supportive theory. According to Blum and Kalven, "[i]t ignores the benefits received from government and treats taxes as though they were a confiscation of property. The problem then becomes one of confiscating in an equitable manner."[182]

Although the term "equality of sacrifice" is often used in this context, it is used generally to describe a condition under which each person suffers a proportionate, rather than truly equal, sacrifice. If "sacrifice" is taken to mean the number of dollars surrendered, then proportionate sacrifice theory simply leads to proportionate taxation. If, however, sacrifice is to be measured in terms of potential satisfaction surrendered to the government, and if that meaning is combined with the theory of declining marginal utility

---

182. W. BLUM & H. KALVEN, JR., *supra* note 157, at 39.

of money, then proportionate sacrifice in terms of potential satisfaction will require progressive surrender in terms of dollars.

Blum and Kalven separated the truly equal sacrifice idea from that of proportionate sacrifice, although the distinction is difficult to discern. They demonstrated that the truly equal sacrifice approach does not necessarily lead to progressive rates. Simons has already stated that if the utility curve for money slopes downward only gradually, a goal of equal sacrifice will produce regressive tax rates. Blum and Kalven added that:

> This is an important step since it is one thing to assume that the utility of money declines but quite another to assume the rate at which it declines. Clearly, the fewer the demands the argument makes on knowledge of the slope of the curve, the stronger the argument will be.[185]

Both of these sacrifice theories involve a two-step process. First, each must establish a normative proposition of how the sacrifice of paying taxes should be shared. Second, a tax rate structure that achieves the proposed sharing must be shown. The equal sacrifice theory is strong on the first step and weak on the second. The proposal that a sacrifice for the good of the group should be borne equally by all its members is, superficially, very appealing. As discussed above, however, under this theory, support for progression depends upon the idea that the marginal utility of money decreases faster than income increases, and this supposition is subject to serious challenge.

Conversely, the proportional sacrifice theory as an argument for progression is strong on the second step, but at first glance seems weak on the first. Assuming for a moment the normative proposition that each person should suffer a proportionate sacrifice to pay for government expenditures, progressive taxation with respect to income is necessary and appropriate to achieve that goal. Any normal, declining marginal utility curve for money will support the claim for progression. Under any normal, downward sloping utility curve, even a gentle slope, a tax that takes twenty percent of income from both high income and low income taxpayers will be proportionate with respect to dollars but regressive with respect to satisfaction sacrificed. Because the high income individual will pay the tax with less valuable (*i.e.*, less satisfying) dollars, that person will sacrifice a lower percentage of his satisfaction. It is very clear that progressive tax rates are necessary to achieve proportionate sacrifice.

---

185. W. BLUM & H. KALVEN, JR., *supra* note 157, at 41. In my opinion, the equal sacrifice approach must be abandoned, because, as stated by British economist A.C. Pigou, "[i]n order to prove that the principle of equal sacrifice necessarily involves progression we should need to know that the last £10 of a £1000 income carry less satisfaction than the last £1 of a £100 income; and this the law of diminishing utility does not assert." A.C. PIGOU, A STUDY OF PUBLIC FINANCE 86 (3d rev. ed. 1962). Personal reflection leads to the intuitive conclusion that the utility curve for money does not decline that steeply. At least, many reasonable people could so conclude, which takes the strength out of this theory's support for progression.

The more difficult part of the analysis is to make a compelling argument for the first step, *i.e.*, the proposition that taxpayers should suffer a proportionate, rather than equal, sacrifice of the potential satisfactions represented by their incomes. Surprisingly, Blum and Kalven presented a convincing argument that proportionate sacrifice is the superior choice.

> Any theory of equalizing the sacrifice of taxpayers implicitly assumes that the taxes are a necessary evil falling upon a distribution of money, and therefore upon a distribution of satisfactions, which [distributional pattern] is otherwise acceptable. With this assumption the problem is not to use the tax system to adjust existing inequalities in that distribution but simply to leave all taxpayers equally "worse off" after taxes. The vice of the equal sacrifice formula is that it is regressive when measured by satisfactions and this becomes compellingly clear if large enough sacrifices are exacted equally from each taxpayer. The corresponding virtue of the proportionate sacrifice formula is that it remains neutral as to the relative distribution of satisfactions among taxpayers. Under it they are all equally "worse off" [in terms of satisfaction, not dollars] after taxes.[188]

In *The Uneasy Case for Progressive Taxation*, one can discern strength in each of the two steps that are required to support progressive taxation with the proportionate sacrifice theory. Although Blum and Kalven were not fully convinced by their own arguments, upon close analysis their arguments on behalf of the proportionate sacrifice theory are compelling. They summarize them as follows:

> [The proportionate sacrifice theory] makes relatively few demands on knowledge about the utility curve for money, other than that it declines; and it narrows considerably the issue between progressive and proportionate taxation. As between one who favors proportional taxation on grounds of its neutrality and one who favors the proportionate sacrifice standard on grounds of its neutrality there is only the issue of whether there is a meaningful and sufficiently ascertainable money utility curve for all taxpayers.[189]

The only remaining difficulty is how to devise a specific rate schedule that implements the proportionate sacrifice theory. To remain true to the reasoning behind the theory, some estimated utility curve for money must be constructed. It seems likely that there have been many years in which the United States statutory rates have been much more progressive than could be justified under this theory, with any reasonably estimated money utility curve.

---

188. W. Blum & H. Kalven, Jr., *supra* note 157, at 43-44.
189. *Id.* at 44-45.

Furthermore, even if it could be proven that the actual shape of the utility curve for money justifies rates above fifty percent, it is still possible to reject such high rates under this theory by following Carver's lead.[c] He began with the minimum sacrifice theory, which endorses the most extreme form of progressivity, and then superimposed a rate-limiting theory that considered the burden on others from the overall productivity loss caused by the extremely high rates.   His second step could be added to the proportionate sacrifice theory in the same manner. In this way, with some estimates of productivity losses caused by various rates, one could construct a declining marginal utility curve for money that maps the "boundary," below which one is not willing to follow the proportionate sacrifice theory. If the utility curve for money declines so steeply that the proportionate sacrifice theory prescribes unacceptably high rates at some income levels, Carver's theory of productivity losses can be used to constrain the rates ultimately selected to more reasonable levels.

One objection to progressivity raised by Blum and Kalven was that even if these various theories have some validity as general arguments in favor of progression, none gives any hint of what the theoretically justifiable rate structure should be. Properly conceived, their objection should not be used as a general argument against progressive taxes, but is valid only against highly progressive taxes. If it is agreed that the proportionate sacrifice theory demonstrates only that the ideal rate structure is progressive and nothing about the proper degree of progressivity, then it is highly likely that a moderately progressive set of rates will be closer than a strictly proportionate tax to the unknown theoretical ideal. As the proposed rate structure becomes more progressive, this likelihood is reduced. Seligman made an argument of this nature, without identifying the fact that the likelihood of being near the ideal varies when the proposed progressivity is changed.[194]   As long as the argument is restricted to the defense of

---

c. The reference to Carver is to a Nineteenth Century writer cited by Blum and Kalven: Carver, *The Ethical Basis of Distribution and Its Application to Taxation*, 6 ANNALS 95 et seq. (July, 1895). (Eds.)

194. *See* E.R.A. SELIGMAN, PROGRESSIVE TAXATION IN THEORY AND PRACTICE 293-94 (2d ed. 1908). Seligman wrote:

> It may, indeed, frankly be conceded that the theory of faculty cannot determine any definite rate of progression as the ideally just rate. To this extent there seems to be some degree of truth in Mill's contention that progressive taxation cannot give that "degree of certainty" on which a legislator should act; as well as in McCulloch's assertion that when we abandon proportion we "are at sea without rudder or compass." It is true that proportion is in one sense certain, and that progression is uncertain. The argument, however, proves too much. An uncertain rate, if it be in the general direction of justice, may nevertheless be preferable to a rate which, like that of proportion, may be more certain without being so equitable. . . . In truth, a strict proportional tax, if we accept the point of view mentioned above, is really more arbitrary as over against the individual taxpayers, than a *moderately* progressive tax. The ostensible "certainty" hence involves a really greater arbitrariness.

moderately progressive rates, it provides the better response to this issue. With this in mind, Blum and Kalven seem almost disingenuous in their complaint that the perfect proportionate sacrifice rate package cannot be determined.

* * *

HIGH PROGRESSIVE TAX RATES: INEQUITY AND
IMMORALITY?
Dan Throop Smith[*]

20 University of Florida Law Review 451, 452-63 (1968)

As on all issues of tax policy, progressivity must be appraised from the standpoint of equity, economic effects, revenue, and administrative complications. The equity and economic issues were stated in a condensed form by three children in a one-room school in Montana where the author had the challenge of discussing tax policy at the invitation of his daughter, the teacher. In response to the question: What would be a fair tax on a family with an income of 5,000 dollars if a family with 2,000 dollars income paid 200 dollars? The first child said, "500 dollars," thereby showing a predisposition for proportional burdens and perhaps a desire to make use of a newly-acquired familiarity with percentages. A second child immediately disagreed, with the comment that the payment should be more than 500 dollars because "each dollar isn't so important" to the family with the larger income. A third child agreed but with the reservation that the additional tax over 500 dollars shouldn't be "too much more or they won't work so hard." Elaborate theoretical structures concerning diminishing utility and incentives and disincentives are all really refinements of the quasi-intuitive opinions of those children and may not lead to any greater certainty.

The diminishing marginal utility of successive units of any single product is a familiar fact and has been an integral part of economic theory for about a century. But extension of this concept from a single commodity to income in general, which represents a claim on all commodities present and future and gives a choice between consumption and savings, is questionable in principle and quite unsatisfactory in practice if one hopes to measure the *rate* of decrease in marginal utility. The concept becomes even less suitable as a basis for public policy when one attempts to extend it to interpersonal comparisons. Though there is probably agreement that there is some decline in marginal utility for an individual's income, as well as for specific items of consumption, and that a decline also exists when one considers a total amount of income distributed among many people, there is no agreement on or even basis for determination of the extent of decrease. Though some progression would generally be regarded as more equitable

---

Id. (emphasis added [by Professor McCombs]).

[*]. At time of original publication, Professor of Finance, Harvard Graduate School of Business Administration.

than a proportionate tax, it is quite possible that under political pressure and confusion about the extent of changes in tax rates as well as the absolute level of rates, progressivity may be carried to such excesses that it is more inequitable than proportionality.

Quite apart from uncertainty about the degree of decline in the marginal utility of income, there is no agreement concerning whether it would be more equitable to strive for minimum aggregate sacrifice or equal proportionate sacrifice among taxpayers. The former sounds plausible and has in fact been advocated by some writers, but a strict application of it would mean that taxes would equalize incomes down to the point where the required revenue was secured. There would be a 100 per cent tax on all incomes (or other tax base) above that point, with no tax on lesser amounts. This follows logically from the proposition that any dollar of a larger income represents less want-satisfying power than any dollar of a small income. Until the largest income is brought down to the level of the next largest income, any taxation of the next largest involves greater sacrifice than additional taxation of the remaining balance of the largest.[5]

The idea of equalization of net incomes through taxation to the point where adequate revenue is secured is for many a valid *reductio ad absurdum* of the whole idea of progression. If one contemplates a so-called negative income tax at the bottom end of the scale, taxation under this concept would become a device for complete equalization of after-tax net incomes. Even the most ardent equalizers, or the most rigorous logicians, usually stop short of 100 per cent marginal tax rates, if only on pragmatic grounds.

The alternative standard of equal proportional sacrifice throws one back to the confusion about the rate of decrease in marginal utility. No basis of psychological measure has yet been found to remove the uncertainty that impelled McCulloch to make his much quoted statement about progression almost a century and a quarter ago that "the moment you abandon . . . the cardinal principle of exacting from all individuals the same proportion of

---

5. In a simplified example, if an income distribution consisted of one income of $150,000, two of $100,000 each, ten of $50,000 each, and eighty-seven of $20,000 each, and only $50,000 revenue was required, it should all come from the income of $150,000 under the theory of minimum aggregate sacrifice, since even the 50,000th dollar from it presumably represents less satisfaction than any one of the dollars of the person with an income of $100,000. If total revenue requirements do not exceed $200,000, all revenue should come from the three incomes above $50,000 and reduce them to that level. Only if total revenue required exceeded $590,000 would there be any tax on incomes of $20,000; equalization down to that level would produce $590,000. If $690,000 were required, incomes would be equalized down to $19,000. Alternatively, one might try to attain equal marginal sacrifice, recognizing that a small payment by someone with the smaller income may represent no more *relative* sacrifice than some part of the large payment by the person with the larger income. In the example above, a $10,000 tax on the incomes of $100,000 might involve the same relative sacrifice as a $30,000 tax on an income of $150,000, to produce $50,000 of revenue. But marginal utilities and sacrifices are elusive, if not nebulous.

their income or their property, you are at sea without rudder or compass, and there is no amount of injustice or folly you may not commit."[6]

A precise analysis in terms of equity is made even more difficult by the need to relate tax burdens to benefits from government services. Though taxation is the means to pay for government services, which, hopefully, are confined to the activities providing general benefit which can only, or most effectively, be provided collectively, government services in fact give direct benefits in varying degrees to individuals. In many respects the services are intended to help those who can least afford to help themselves and hence any attempt to match taxes against benefits would contravene the very purpose of the government program. But enough of the services are quasi-commercial, or yield benefits that do not have to involve a redistribution of income to be effective, to make a comparison of taxes to benefits not wholly irrelevant. Though theoretically valid, an attempt to carve out and value a segment of individual benefits from the body of general benefits is as frustrating as an attempt to establish the shape of a curve representing the declining utility of income. The existence of this two-fold problem further weakens any confidence one might have in any scientific establishment of equity in a tax system.

Quite apart from equity, one may argue that progressive taxation is justified by the need to reduce inequality and thereby establish a more attractive society (some refer to a more aesthetically satisfying society), the need to reduce social and political tensions, and the need to create greater equality of opportunity. All these are valid and appealing objectives, but some are purely subjective, and the role of taxation in others is quite indeterminate. They cannot, however, be brushed aside as irrelevant. Blum and Kalven conclude that an extensive analysis simply:[7]

> [S]uggests the tantalizing combination of plausible, ingenious and improbable ideas which make up the case for progression in terms of sacrifice and ability to pay. It likewise suggests why these notions have such a stubborn appeal. But it tends to demonstrate that the hold of these notions on the general public must derive from the fallacies that have frequented the theories and not from their truths which are difficult to drive to and once found would not support any firm conviction about the validity of the progressive principle.

When one turns to the economic significance of progression, the analysis must be made from several standpoints, only two of which are simple and straightforward. The revenue from a progressive income tax invariably fluctuates more with changes in national income than does a proportional tax. It thus exerts a counter-cyclical effect and is referred to as an automatic

---

6. J. McCulloch, Taxation and the Funding System 142 (1845).
7. W. Blum & H. Kalven, The Uneasy Case for Progressive Taxation 68 (1953).

stabilizer.[8] On this point, the facts and conclusions seem incontrovertible, though opinions differ on their importance. Many other counter-cyclical forces are available, including timely changes in tax rates and structures by legislation.

A second fairly certain economic result of progression in taxation is that it favors consumption over saving because of a somewhat higher marginal propensity to save from larger and from increasing incomes. In the 1930's with the prevalence of the fallacy of the mature economy and the presumption that savings would always outrun investment opportunities, progressive taxation was regarded as especially suitable to reduce those incomes that were most likely to be saved. With the more recent emphasis on the need for investment to increase productivity and minimize inflationary effects of large annual increases in wage rates, a tax factor that discriminates against potential savings is more likely to be regarded as undesirable. From this standpoint, the very high degree of progression seems particularly unfortunate when it exists in some of the underdeveloped countries that so desperately need both capital and enterprise even to maintain their present low per capita incomes.

The effects of progression on incentives for work and investment are more important and less clear than the effects on fluctuations in revenue and on the availability of net incomes most likely to be saved. Extreme critics are disposed to say that high progression will so destroy incentives that an economic system will grind to a halt. This is manifestly absurd, but the fact of continued growth in countries with high marginal tax rates is no reason to ignore their possible adverse influence on the amount and direction of human effort and investment. With a better tax structure, the growth might be greater.

Personal activity is stimulated by many incentives, among which pecuniary reward is only one. The old presumption of the "economic man," concerned only with maximizing the material gains from his efforts, has long been superseded. An entire field of study has been developed around human behavior in large and small organizations, with much of the analysis devoted to the nonpecuniary satisfactions and dissatisfactions in job situations. Perhaps surprisingly, more attention has been given to people employed in routine work than to those in higher levels of management and entrepreneurship. It is the latter who have the greater opportunities for such nonpecuniary rewards as power, prestige, and the satisfaction of one's

---

8. In economic terms, a "counter-cyclical factor" is one that operates in the opposite direction from the familiar cyclical forces. An increase in welfare payments during a recession is counter-cyclical to the decrease in private income from employment and investment. An automatic stabilizer is one that arises without the need for new legislation or administrative action. Progressivity in income taxation has an automatic stabilizing effect in that revenues fall off more sharply than total personal income in a recession because it is the highest segments of income that are subject to the highest tax rates; government expenditures are thus likely to be covered by deficit financing, which in turn is likely to have an expansionary effect.

various desires and talents for creative and socially constructive activity and whose motivations therefore are presumably the more complex. But it is now so clear that material rewards are by no means so dominant that any analysis of the effects of taxation which is based on the assumption that it operates on a simple "economic man" is woefully inadequate. Since taxation operates primarily to modify the pecuniary rewards of work, the effects of taxation should be appraised with full appreciation of the fact that pecuniary rewards are not necessarily dominant. Subject to this broad and important reservation, the direction of the effects of progressive taxation are quite clear.

By progressively reducing the net return from any given increment of gross income or gain, progressive taxation discourages additional efforts or activities, or a change in the direction of efforts or activities, which might be prompted by greater material rewards. It is always important to note the marginal rate of tax. Too often, defenders of the existing pattern of progression brush aside criticism by noting that the average rate of tax is lower than the marginal rate of tax. This is, of course, true by definition. The average rate gives a quick indication of the fractions of a total income taken by taxation and left for consumption or saving. But it gives virtually no indication about the effects of taxation on incentives.

A moment's reflection will indicate the difference, for example, of the effects on incentives if one compares two people each with taxable income of 20,000 dollars and each subject to an average tax rate of 50 per cent. In one case the tax is a flat 50 per cent; in the other the tax is 20 per cent on the first 10,000 dollars and 80 per cent on the second 10,000 dollars. They each pay a total tax of 10,000 dollars and have a net income of 10,000 dollars, but the first man can keep 50 cents of each extra dollar earned while the second man can keep only 20 cents on each dollar. In virtually all respects regarding incentives, it is the marginal rate of tax on increments of income that is significant.

On a transitory basis, an increase in taxation, through greater progression or a general increase in rates, may stimulate greater effort to maintain an existing standard of living. Two people may react quite differently to a tax structure depending, among other things, on their status under an earlier tax structure. The standards of living of executives and professional people with similar incomes differ on the basis of the scale of expenditure to which they became accustomed under lower taxes. * * *

The possibility of extra income for extra effort varies greatly with the line of activity. An executive does not have the chance for increments of income from overtime or secondary employment. Even independent professional men may have commitments to established clients or patients that require full-time availability and hence activity. But the author recalls having heard, at the end of World War I, the phrase "income-tax golfer" used to describe those who opted for more recreation in preference to full activity in business or professional work. And it is not uncommon for even academic people to remark in casual conversations that they have declined an invitation to speak or prepare a paper because the honorarium was so reduced by income taxation. It would be interesting and useful to know whether it is the reduced absolute level of the net honorarium or the fact that a major fraction of a given amount had to be paid in taxes that was the principal disincentive. For most people, both aspects probably have some importance.

* * *

Investments, in contrast to personal activity, do not typically yield non-pecuniary rewards that offset or compensate for lack of material gain. To be sure, ownership of land may provide prestige and emotional satisfaction, as well as an inflation hedge. * * * [T]here is no general nonpecuniary pressure of capital to become active. Idle capital does not get bored or develop a sense of frustration because of its wasted talents. In brief, investment is much more susceptible to purely pecuniary calculations and hence to tax influences than personal activity.

The higher the marginal tax rate the greater the inducement to move away from investments that yield regular taxable income toward either tax-exempt bonds or equity investments that have prospects for capital appreciation. The supply of tax-exempt bonds is so large that it exceeds the demand by high-bracket investors and for many years the yield has had to be high enough to attract medium-bracket investors, with a resulting large tax advantage to the intra-marginal holders. (With top-grade municipals selling to yield about 70 per cent of that on AAA corporate bond yields, the two types give an equivalent yield of an investor subject to a 30 per cent marginal tax, assuming that the securities are equally attractive except for the different tax status. But an investor taxed at a 70 per cent marginal rate would secure a net income 2.33 times higher than that on taxable bonds.) The reduction in the top bracket rate from 91 to 70 per cent between 1964 and 1966 had little effect on the yield differential.

* * *

The fact of the lower tax on capital gains profoundly influences both the direction and the total amount of investment. The reason for the effect on the direction of investment is self-evident. The higher the spread between the marginal rate on income and the capital gains rate, the greater the influence in favor of the capital gains. The effect on total investment is less obvious, but it arises from the fact that taxation at full rates would require liquidation of more capital to pay the tax when investment is shifted from one asset to another. Also, if the rates are very high, it might force some capital funds into idleness because net yields would be inadequate to compensate for the risk and effort of investment.

The greater attraction of capital gains would appear to increase the supply of funds for equity-type and higher-risk investments which, in turn, permits the financing of innovation and new ventures. From this standpoint, the shift in direction of investment because of high marginal rates on regular income may actually foster economic development, so long as the capital gains rate is not unduly repressive. But against the favorable influence on the direction of investment must be set the unfavorable impact on the supply of savings. Thus, though the direction of investment may be improved, the total amount of investment may be reduced, with the net effect indeterminate. With a somewhat higher marginal propensity to save from higher and growing incomes, progressive taxation hits disproportionately the segments of income most likely to be saved.

Each country has its own set of tax-sheltered investments, depending on the details of its tax laws. Real estate investments receive especially favorable treatment in this country, as do many aspects of agriculture. Tax-exempt mergers are favored over taxable sales of companies to new owners who would continue them as independent entities. Particular forms of capital structures are encouraged and others discouraged, especially in closely controlled corporations. Even a company with no growth can be made attractive if an older generation in a family takes senior securities that are retired with retained earnings, thereby increasing the value of a highly-leveraged common stock held by a younger generation.

Religious institutions, by an unjustified exemption from the tax on unrelated business income applicable to other tax-exempt organizations, are put in a position to pay higher prices than other potential purchasers of business concerns and to do so in a manner that is least likely to build up the enterprise after purchase. Cooperatives are favored over fully-taxable businesses. Extractive industries receive differential tax treatment with consequent lower prices to consumers or higher returns to investors. The list could be extended almost indefinitely. Some of the differential effects are intended and others arise from general provisions of the law. But they are all made more significant by high and progressive tax rates.

Among the economic effects of high and progressive rates, one must include the diversion of intelligence and effort into attempts to minimize taxes. Whenever a tax rate exceeds 50 per cent, it becomes more important to save a dollar of taxes than to earn a dollar of income, and this fact cannot fail to divert attention from truly productive activities. Though the incomes of those concerned with tax minimization enter the gross national product as fully as do those of all other producers of goods and services, their contribution to the general welfare seems at best ambiguous.

Progression typically contributes a very minor fraction of total revenue. When government expenditures amounted to 10 per cent of the gross national product or less, it would have been possible to construct a tax system that would have received most of the revenue from the higher brackets in a generally low-rate tax structure. But when expenditures absorb 25 or 30 per cent of the gross national product, the bulk of the revenue must come from the great mass of taxpayers. The higher income rates contribute only a very minor fraction of the total yield. * * * One can say categorically that progression, with all its distorting effects, is not required to provided adequate revenue. It must be justified on other grounds.

Nor can progressive rates be said to facilitate tax administration, either for tax collectors or taxpayers. The result is quite clearly the contrary. Not only do differences in rates complicate calculations, they make impossible a really effective system of withholding and, by encouraging shifts to tax-sheltered activities and investments, require loophole-closing amendments to the laws, which further complicate it. Or conversely, Congress is moved to adopt special relief provisions because the full burden of high-bracket rates is recognized as intolerable for certain types of incomes, and the special relief provisions are likely to be as complicated as those that close loopholes; in fact, adoption of a relief provision is likely to be followed by or itself be complicated by the need to prevent abuse of it. Progressive rates clearly and markedly complicate the tax law and its administration.

The existence of personal exemptions in the individual income tax provides a very real form of progression in average effective rates toward the bottom of the income scale since those whose incomes are just above the exemption pay only a very small tax. Progression from this source is quite pronounced until the taxable income is several times the personal exemption. And this sort of progression does simplify tax administration by making unnecessary the filing of many returns. One thus must distinguish between progression that arises automatically from the existence of a basic exemption and progression arising from a progressive rate structure. The former, a sort of built-in progression, is usually simplifying; the latter is almost inevitably complicating.

Probably the most serious burden that high progressive rates place on the tax administration comes from the strain on taxpayer morale. Our whole system relies heavily on self-assessment and tax evasion is generally still regarded as socially reprehensible in our country. But when marginal tax rates are made quasi-confiscatory for long periods, as distinct from short periods of war or other national emergency, tax evasion may come to be condoned by both the private and public conscience. And once a part of a tax is flouted with impunity, the rest of the tax system is in peril. * * *

As one appraises the present status of progressivity in tax rates, the principal problems seem to arise from what may be referred to as the "each and every" fallacy. Progression has been so vociferously advocated and so indiscriminately accepted that it has become a virtual fetish in political life, with two unfortunate results. There is, first, a presumption that each and every tax should be in and of itself progressive. Sales and property taxes are criticized and at times rejected because they are not progressive. Surely it is the distribution of the local tax burden that must be judged in the light of equity and consistency with social policy. It seems as ridiculous to insist that every tax be progressive as it would be to insist that everything in a meal be salted because salt is a necessary item in a diet. The result of the obsession about progression is a very real political difficulty in developing a balanced tax structure.

Total revenue requirements are so large that no one tax, not even a "least bad" income tax, should be relied on as a sole or even dominant source of funds. With a combination of taxes, rates on each one can be kept from becoming excessive, and the inevitable defects of each may hopefully balance out the defects of the others. The rates of those taxes most suitable for progression can be set to give whatever degree of progression is deemed appropriate in the composite burden.

The author favors a maximum marginal income tax rate of 50 per cent on grounds of equity and social policy. This rate also seems to have merit on economic grounds for reasons already enumerated. A limitation to this figure in no sense suggests approval of all aspects of conspicuous consumption by the very rich, which after all may seem no more foolish or offensive than the forms of conspicuous consumption of those with modest or even small incomes. But taste in consumption is an individual matter, and the income tax is both an inefficient and an inappropriate device for regulation.

When there is a happy coincidence of large potential revenue and a consensus on the need for regulation, selective excises may be used advantageously, as has been done in the liquor and tobacco taxes. But it is doubtful whether the tax system should be regarded as a principal instrument for solving social problems. Fines and penalties directly imposed are preferable to special taxes and tax credits in the control of pollution of the environment. * * * An attempt to find ways to modify tax systems to make them help at least in a small way in dealing with the population explosion—the greatest social problem of all—without adding to the individual problems of the disadvantaged, should be regarded by tax theorists and technicians as a major challenge. * * *

The second manifestation of the "each and every" fallacy appears when tax rates are changed. Very high marginal rates have developed because of confusion over the form of a tax increase. In 1932, when the range of rates was from 1.5 to 25 per cent, the bottom rate was raised to 4 per cent to secure more revenue. The percentage increase in the rate was applied to the top rate, pushing it to 63 per cent, an increase that from one point of view might be considered merely proportionate. But in terms of the impact on net income it was almost fantastically progressive. At the bottom, net income was reduced from 98.5 cents to 96 cents, or by a little over 2.5 per cent, while at the top it was reduced from 75 cents to 37 cents or by more than half. A continued application of this "proportionate" form of tax increase would have pushed the top rate to 315 per cent when the bottom rate rose to 20 per cent.

In fact, even an increase of an equal number of percentage points is highly progressive when added to an existing progressive rate structure. One percentage point added to a 14 per cent rate reduces net income from 86 to

85 or by 1.16+ per cent, while the same one percentage point addition to a 70 per cent rate reduces the net income from 30 to 29 or by 3.33 per cent.

The proposal to increase tax liabilities by a uniform percentage has the effect of greatly increasing the progressivity of the tax system. A 10 per cent increase in liabilities would push the bottom rate from 14 to 15.4 per cent the top rate from 70 to 77 per cent. A 40 per cent increase in liabilities would leave the bottom rate at 19.6 per cent, below the 20 per cent level at which it recently stood, while pushing the top rate to 98 per cent![d]

* * *

On reductions of rates the reverse analysis can be applied. A reduction from 90 to 70 per cent increases marginal net income three-fold while a complete abolition of a bottom rate of 20 per cent could no more than increase income by 25 per cent. To a considerable extent, the very high marginal tax rates have arisen from confusion about the arithmetic and definitions regarding equal, proportionate, and progressive changes in rates when the changes are made in a rate structure that is already highly progressive. Protagonists of each position make the calculations to fit their program, but the fetish of progressivity too often obliterates reasoned analysis and comparisons.

Progressivity in income and inheritance taxation, though universally adopted and almost universally supported in theoretical literature, lacks a solid base for a rational determination of the appropriate degree of progression. A succession of standards has been advanced in attempts to give precision to the concept of ability to pay, which is generally presumed to support progressive taxation. But none of these standards has received general acceptance even by those who intuitively favor progression on grounds of equity and support it as a matter of social policy. The economic effects of progression are more likely to be harmful than beneficial. Its revenue importance is negligible. It complicates tax administration and, when pushed to excess, strains taxpayer morale.

Some element of progression appeals to an almost intuitive sense of fairness, which is widely held. It is also consistent with a social policy of preventing indefinitely large accumulations of wealth. But progression as it exists is the result of the play of political forces in an area that has lacked clear definitions and analysis. In its excesses it may indeed approach inequity and immorality.

---

d. A 10% increase in tax liabilities applied to 1996 tax rates would raise the bottom rate from 15% to 16.5%, and the top rate from 39.6% rate to 43.56%. A 40% increase in tax liabilities applied to 1996 tax rates would raise the bottom rate from 15% to 21%, and the 39.6% rate to 55.44%.

THE INCOME TAX: HOW PROGRESSIVE SHOULD IT BE?*
Charles O. Galvin & Boris I. Bittker
Second Lecture, by Boris I. Bittker
Pages 25-43 (1969)

As a lawyer and teacher of law, my professional focus on federal income taxation has given me an understanding of the impact of progression on the tax structure; but when this brings me up against the moral and economic foundations of progression, I am a layman—at most, an educated layman—with no expertise or professional discipline to guide me in choosing among the conflicting claims with which this area abounds.

* * * I believe that in the choice of an income tax rate schedule, one cannot avoid, in the end, a decision that rests more on faith, personal preference, or fiat than on logic. I will pursue the road of rationality as far as I can trace its tracks; but for me, the final destination is not attained without wandering in the wilderness with only one's soul for guidance.

* * * [T]he concept of progression has evoked an immense body of literature, characterized by a wealth of ingenious theories and a paucity of consensus among the theoreticians. In the time allotted to me, I cannot review, let alone analyze, these efforts to support or undermine progression. Fortunately, however, this task was undertaken only 17 years ago [in 1952] by Professors Walter J. Blum and Harry Kalven, of the University of Chicago Law School, in their painstaking examination of the intellectual history of progression, *The Uneasy Case For Progressive Taxation.*[2] Like them, I find the economic arguments, whether based on theoretical models or empirical evidence and whether concerned with stability, growth, productivity, or incentives, to be rather inconclusive; and I have no special competence for resolving the conflicting assertions of economic experts. I would like, therefore, to devote myself primarily to the question of fairness, which all commentators, even those who hold strong views about the economic impact of progression, agree is of major importance.

In this emphasis on the moral issues, I follow Blum and Kalven, who set the stage for their analysis with these introductory remarks:

> Like most people today we found the notion of progression immediately congenial. Upon early analysis the notion retained its attractiveness, but our curiosity as to the source of its appeal increased. The somewhat paradoxical character we detected in the topic is suggested by certain aspects of its literature. A surprising number of serious writers note that progression seems to be

---

*. This book provides the text of a debate, sponsored by the American Enterprise Institute, between Dean Galvin (who favored a flat-rate income tax) and Professor Bittker (who spoke in favor of progressivity). The excerpted material is from Professor Bittker's presentation. At the time of the debate, Professor Bittker was Southmayd Professor of Law at Yale University.

2. Walter J. Blum and Harry Kalven, Jr., *The Uneasy Case for Progressive Taxation* (Chicago: University of Chicago Press, 1953), reprinted from 19 U. CHI. L. REV. 417 (1952).

instinctively correct, although they then go on to explore it on rational grounds.   More striking is the fact that the most devastating critics of the defenses for progression are almost invariably its friends. It is close to the truth to say that only those who ultimately favor progression on some ground have been its effective critics on other grounds. It is as though those who have most clearly detected the weaknesses of various lines of analysis previously offered to support progression were under a compulsion to find some new way to justify it rather than give it up. The hunch that there must be some basis on which an idea as initially attractive as progression can be justified is stubborn indeed.[3]

By way of conclusion, they sum up their quest in these words:

> The case for progression, after a long critical look, thus turns out to be stubborn but uneasy. The most distinctive and technical arguments advanced in its behalf are the weakest. It is hard to gain much comfort from the special arguments, however intricate their formulations, constructed on notions of benefit, sacrifice, ability to pay, or economic stability. The case has stronger appeal when progressive taxation is viewed as a means of reducing economic inequalities. But the case for more economic equality, when examined directly, is itself perplexing. And the perplexity is greatly magnified for those who in the quest for greater equality are unwilling to argue for radical changes in the fundamental institutions of society.[4]

The strength of conviction in this area is amply demonstrated by the reviews of the Blum-Kalven study. John Chamberlain, in whose eyes the Sixteenth Amendment "legalizes a theft," welcomed the book for conferring "academic recognition" on "the intellectual sapping operation against the progressive principle."[5] Randolph Paul, on the other hand, asserted that the book "has confirmed rather than shaken my belief that there should be more, rather than less, progression in the American tax system."[6]

In addition to commentators like Chamberlain and Paul, both of whom found support for their contradictory conclusions in the Blum-Kalven book, there was a third group, who felt that instinct, not reason, is bound to be controlling in choosing one rate structure rather than another. * * *

I would like to make three principal points in support of my own predilection for a progressive federal income tax rate structure.

My first point is that there is no magic in the idea of proportionality, as distinguished from progression: put another way, if the case for progression is "uneasy," so is the case for a proportional rate schedule. In Dan Smith's

3. *Ibid.*, pp. 2-3.
4. *Ibid.*, pp. 103-04.
5. Book review, 21 U. CHI L. REV., 1954, p. 502.
6. Book review, 67 HARV. L. REV., 1954, pp. 725, 730.

anecdote [concerning the Montana school children; see Smith excerpt], the first child favored a proportional tax, *viz.*, a $500 tax on the $5,000 family, given that the $2,000 family was to pay $200. As Mr. Smith suggests, this conclusion may have reflected no more than the child's fascination with percentages or fractions, leading to a result that was arithmetically "correct," without regard to any other considerations. Perhaps, however, the use of a precise rule rather than a discretionary judgment stemmed from the same desire for certainty that led J. R. McCulloch, a century ago, to insist, in a much-quoted remark, that a departure from proportionality would be disastrous:

> The moment you abandon . . . the cardinal principle of exacting from all individuals the same proportion of their income or their property, you are at sea without rudder or compass, and there is no amount of injustice or folly you may not commit.[7]

Whether or not this conviction that proportionality is an indispensable navigational instrument was endorsed by Dan Smith's Montana schoolchild, it has found much favor among theoreticians.

I think it is fair to say that all, or nearly all, commentators on the principle of progression have assumed that it must meet the burden of proof. Conversely, they have accepted the fairness of proportionality as self-evident, needing no affirmative justification; so that proportionality is to be qualified or rejected as the governing principle only if a convincing case can be made for adopting a progressive rate structure. (Regression, however, is ordinarily rejected out-of-hand.) This acceptance of proportionality may be explicit, as in McCulloch's case, or implicit, as where persuasive objections to progression are thought to end the matter, on the unarticulated premise that proportionality needs no defense. Sometimes this bias in favor of proportionality is buttressed by the argument that progression, lacking an internal limiting principle, invites the majority to oppress the minority, and hence must be resisted at all cost as an irretrievable step on the road to tyranny. This argument, applicable to all exercises of governmental power, seems quite inconclusive to me, especially since the abuse that is feared could be accomplished, even with proportional taxation, by an unfettered use of the expenditure power to redistribute wealth.

It is also argued that progression is responsible for many complications in the income tax law and difficulties in its administration, creating a prima facie case for proportionality. * * * [P]roportionality would not contribute very much to simplicity. Timing questions, if they involve postponement or acceleration of tax for more than a year or two, would continue to perplex us; and income-splitting issues are inevitable once we decide to allow personal exemptions and a standard deduction. They are also inevitable if progression in the income tax rate schedule is accepted as a counterweight to regressive

---

7. *Supra*, note 1, p. 45.

tendencies in other taxes, an aspect of progression that is tolerated, even favored, by some of the most vigorous opponents of progression per se.[8]

In my view, therefore, the premise that a proportional tax rate is presumptively fair, with its corollary that a progressive rate is ipso facto suspect, has been an important obstacle to the process of judgment in this area, at least among theoreticians. I do not quarrel with the Blum-Kalven conclusion that the case for progression is "uneasy," in the sense that the arguments for progression are not wholly conclusive and sometimes carry implications that the advocates of progression are not willing to press to their logical extremes. An equally painstaking examination of the case for a proportional rate structure, however, would in my opinion have ended with the same inconclusive verdict, *viz.*, that the case for proportionality is "uneasy." * * *

Let me expand on my heresy, *viz.*, that proportionality is no more entitled to a presumption of fairness than progression; and, conversely, that the case for proportionality must be tested by the same canons of criticism as the case for progression. What could be more clearly "proportional" than a per capita tax: one man, one dollar? Let us suppose that the amount to be raised by taxation in the United States is $200 billion, averaging out to $1,000 per person. If we pursued the principle of proportionality with sufficient enthusiasm we could raise the amount required by imposing a tax of $1,000 on every man, woman, and child, collecting this amount by levying on his or her property or wages and compelling those who could not pay to perform services to the value of $1,000. A more refined system, still adhering to the principle of proportionality, would be to exempt all persons who could not pay either in cash or in services, and divide the aggregate burden per capita among the others.

Is it not clear that such a head tax, whether crude or refined, would be instinctively rejected by almost everyone—despite its faithful adherence to the principle of proportionality? And is it not almost as clear that today's rationale for rejecting this proportional allocation of the tax burden would be that it disregarded ability to pay? And that an earlier generation of theorists would have argued that the hypothetical tax was unfair because it was not geared to the unequal benefits received from government by the taxpayers? And that a third group of commentators would argue that equality of sacrifice is the only fair principle of tax allocation, and that the head tax, though ostensibly the same for every taxpayer, actually calls for unequal sacrifices because $1,000 means more to a poor man than to a rich man? And that a fourth group would criticize the proposed head tax because it does nothing to reduce economic inequality?

---

8. Friedrich A. Hayek, "Progressive Taxation Reconsidered," in Sennholz, ed., *On Freedom and Free Enterprise* (Princeton: Van Nostrand, 1956), pp. 265, 269-70.

Those who are familiar with the intellectual history of progression will recall that "ability to pay," "payments in accord with benefits received," "equality of sacrifice," and "reduction of inequality" are the principles that, with various refinements and in various combinations, are regularly used to support progressive tax rates. As Blum and Kalven have pointed out, if these ideas are relentlessly subjected to rigorous analysis, they have shortcomings. For example, if a progressive income tax with rates ranging from 10 to 70 percent requires a taxpayer with $10,000 of income to pay $1,000 of tax and a millionaire taxpayer to pay $700,000, we cannot know—other than by intuition—whether their "sacrifices" are equal.[9] And "ability to pay," taken as a normative standard rather than as a credit manager's assessment of collectibility, is merely another label for "sacrifice." Finally, "benefit" theory (which I will refer to again later) is similar to "sacrifice" theory in calling for interpersonal comparisons that are in the end intuitive rather than logical: who *really* knows whether the millionaire taxpayer is getting benefits from the government that are worth 700 times as much as the benefits received by the $10,000 taxpayer? As for distributive justice, if a progressive rate structure is favored as a means of reducing inequalities of income or wealth, Blum and Kalven properly point out that this indicates a dissatisfaction with the market's allocation of rewards; and they ask the advocates of progression * * * why they do not follow the logic of this approach to the point of demanding more "radical changes in the fundamental institutions of the society."[10]

While this summary does complete justice neither to the traditional arguments in favor of progression nor to the Blum-Kalven replies, my point is that the same arguments and same criticisms are applicable to the decision to employ an income tax rather than a head tax—or, for that matter, a tax on sales, luxuries, real property, capital gains, or inheritances—to distribute the burden of government expenditures. In short, the case for *every* tax base and *every* rate schedule is "uneasy," since interpersonal comparisons cannot be avoided.

* * * [A] presumption of fairness is no more appropriate in deciding whether to tax income at progressive rather than proportionate rates than in deciding whether to levy an income tax rather than a head tax. One cannot avoid interpersonal comparisons in deciding whether to levy a head tax, an income tax, a sales tax, or a property tax; and, once *that* nettle has been grasped, there is no justification for employing a presumption rather

---

9. See the conclusion of Henry Simons, in *Personal Income Taxation* (Chicago: University Press, 1938), p. 7:

> One derives practical implications from the criterion of equality, or proportionality, of sacrifice precisely in proportion to one's own knowledge of something which no one ever has known, or ever will know, anything about. Perhaps this goes far toward explaining the popularity of these doctrines among academic writers.

10. *Supra*, note 1, p. 104.

than discretion in fixing the rate schedule for whatever tax base is adopted. If, having candidly acknowledged the difficulties in making interpersonal comparisons, we prefer an income tax to a head tax on "ability to pay" or "equal sacrifice" grounds, the use of a proportional rate in no way purges our decision of any of its uncertainties.

* * * [T]he maxim, "When in doubt, stick with proportionality," is no better guide than "When in doubt, divide the tax burden on a per capita basis." The policy maker *must* exercise judgment in deciding which tax base and which tax rate is best. * * *

In the hope that I have dismantled an obstacle to a fair assessment of graduated income tax rates, I would like now to offer several independent grounds for favoring a substantial degree of progression.

First, progression in the federal income tax serves to counterbalance regressive tendencies in other federal, state, and local taxes. Even those who favor an allocation of the nationwide tax burden that is proportionate to the taxpayer's income are ordinarily prepared to accept progression in one tax structure if it serves only to counterbalance regression elsewhere.

In applying this limited principle, of course, one encounters both conceptual and computational difficulties. If local property taxes are treated as though paid solely by homeowners, tenants, and consumers, this type of tax will seem more regressive than if one assumes that its burden falls partly on the owners of real estate. Conversely, if the corporate income tax is allocated wholly to shareholders, its impact will be more progressive than if it is thought to fall partly on employees and consumers.

Conclusions about the degree of actual progression in the tax system are also heavily affected by the way one defines the base against which the aggregate tax burden is calculated. It is of course familiar learning that the progressive rates of existing law apply to a less-than-comprehensive income tax base, producing the tax result that Henry Simons described as "digging deep with a sieve."[13] The popular imagination has been caught by recent Treasury studies showing that wealthy taxpayers, ostensibly subject to a marginal income tax rate of 70 percent, often pay only a modest or even trivial percentage of their "total" income—the disparity resulting from a difference between "taxable income" as defined by existing law, and "total" income as defined by the Treasury in calculating the effective rate. In converting the statutory concepts of "adjusted gross income" or "taxable income" into this amended base on which the effective rate is calculated, it is customary to add the untaxed portion of long-term capital gains, exempt interest from state and municipal bonds, excess percentage depletion, and sometimes such other items as personal deductions and unrealized appreciation on property contributed to charities.

---

13. *Supra*, note 9, p. 219.

When the aggregate burden of federal, state, and local taxes is computed as a fraction of this expanded income tax base, our tax structure looks a lot less progressive than if the burden is computed against "taxable income" as defined by existing law. Moreover, if one expands the tax base still more, by adding undistributed trust and corporate income (especially if a broad concept of a corporate income is substituted for corporate income as now defined), or by taking into account unrealized increases in the taxpayer's wealth (e.g., growth in the value of marketable securities, real estate, etc.), the "effective rate" of the federal income tax on wealthy taxpayers falls even more.

It seems reasonable, therefore, to conclude that the aggregate tax burden is pushed in a regressive direction by local property taxes, state and local sales taxes, federal excise and employment taxes, and the corporate income tax to the extent that it falls on consumers and employees. The only counterbalancing elements, then, are the federal personal income tax and the corporate income tax to the extent that it falls on shareholders; and the broader the income tax benchmark used for this calculation, the less impressive is their contribution to progression. * * *

Pending re-examination of this issue on a different set of premises about the appropriate income base—and fully acknowledging that we have no all-purpose, universally-accepted definition of income (a point that I myself have recently argued with vigor)[16]—I wish here only to stress the fact that progression in the federal personal income tax is entirely consonant with the achievement of a national tax burden that is proportional to income. Indeed, given this goal, a significant degree of progression is probably indispensable. To be sure, the broader the income tax base, the less progressive a rate structure will be necessary to achieve proportionality; but if we take account of political realities, * * * the advocates of overall proportionality ought to support progressive income tax rates for some years to come.

A second reason for supporting, or at least acquiescing in, progression is that it is an inevitable consequence of allowing a personal exemption in computing income tax liability. Even if we exempt no more than bare subsistence in computing taxable income, and apply a uniform rate to all income above the survival level, the effective rate on total income will start at zero and rise until it is just short of the nominal rate. Thus, a 10 percent rate on all income above the first $1,000 translates into an effective rate of zero for a taxpayer with $1,000 of total income, 5 percent for the taxpayer with $2,000 of total income, 9 percent for the taxpayer with $10,000 of total income, 9.9 percent for the taxpayer with $100,000 of total income, and so on. This type of progression, resulting solely from the allowance of a personal exemption, has special characteristics, of which the most notable is that it

---

16. Boris I. Bittker, *A Comprehensive Tax Base as a Goal of Income Tax Reform*, 80 HARV. L. REV., 1967, p. 925.

calls for—and permits—only two judgments: the amount to be exempted, and the total amount of revenue to be raised. Once these elements are specified, the tax rate follows automatically; there is no room in the system for comparing the $2,000 taxpayer's ability to pay or his "sacrifice" with the $100,000 taxpayer's ability to pay or his sacrifice. For McCulloch, who did not want to go to sea without a rudder or compass, this form of progression should be quite tolerable, and it would also be comforting to Dan Smith's Montana schoolchild, who could display his skill in arithmetic by deriving the proper tax rate, given the distribution of income, the amount of the exemption, and the total revenue to be raised. * * *

Notes and Questions

1. Is the principle of ability to pay helpful in setting maximum rates? Can it be applied in combination with other considerations?

2. If the range of the highest tax bracket is widened to apply to lower incomes, does this make the tax more progressive or less progressive?

3. Are multiple tax brackets necessary to a progressive income tax system? How many tax brackets are desirable? Over the years the number of brackets has varied from one to 50.

4. Can a three-bracket tax rate schedule be as progressive as a 15-bracket tax rate schedule?

5. Is an income tax more progressive the larger the group of people who have no income tax liability? Is the degree of progressivity of a tax determined by the number of taxpayers subject to its top rate, by the severity of the top rate, by the difference between the top rate and the next lower rate, by the difference between the top rate and the bottom rate, or by some other measure?

6. Can the ability to pay rationale be defended when it focuses exclusively on income without reference to wealth? Consider two individuals with incomes of $1 million. One has received income at this level for 20 years and the other, a college graduate drafted by a National Football League team, has never earned an appreciable amount of income before.

7. Professor McCombs argued that Blum and Kalven focused too exclusively on the importance of money in work decisions. Do you agree with Blum and Kalven that in our society money is the dominant stimulus to work?

8. There is probably a high correlation between jobs that pay well and jobs that offer significant nonmonetary satisfactions. If this is true, what implications does it have for progressive taxation?

9. The McCombs excerpt discussed Professor Simons' idea of government capitalism, such as government purchase of public utilities. Would government capitalism be a practical solution to inadequate private savings and investment?

10. McCombs makes the point that "equality of sacrifice" is not ordinarily used to mean literally the same dollar amount of sacrifice, but, instead, means proportionate sacrifice. If all dollars were of equal satisfaction value (which they are not), this theory would suggest that proportional taxation is appropriate. Only when proportionate sacrifice is determined in the context of the theory of declining marginal utility of dollars—rather than in simple dollar amounts—can it support progressive tax rates.

11. The principle of marginal utility, which is used throughout the study of economics, when applied to the receipt of money, holds that the last dollar received has less utility to the recipient than the next-to-the-last dollar received. Professor Smith points out problems in applying the theory in a useful manner. First, we do not know how much utility declines from the first dollar to the last dollar—i.e., how sharply does the marginal utility curve drop? Without this knowledge, we are reduced to using intuition to determine how steep the progressive tax rate structure should be to achieve proportionate sacrifice among taxpayers with different incomes. Moreover, because we concede that the marginal utility curve varies from one person to another, for whatever reason, we have to adopt a universal (and arbitrary) standard that ignores interpersonal comparisons—treating the miser and the spendthrift alike.

12. What is meant by the theory of "minimum sacrifice" or "minimum aggregate sacrifice"? Why is this theory rejected as the basis for determining the appropriate degree of tax progressivity?

13. The automatic counter-cyclical effect of the income tax, discussed in the Dan Throop Smith excerpt, is also touched on in Chapter One. This counter-cyclical effect, while valid, probably is not large enough to have much impact on the economy.

14. Professor Smith argued that progression in taxation disadvantaged savings vis-a-vis consumption "because of a somewhat higher marginal propensity to save from larger and from increasing incomes"—both of which

are targeted by progressivity. Note that Smith was writing in 1968, when income tax rates (if not the overall impact of the income tax on different income levels) were more steeply progressive than they are now.

15. What is the significance of Dan Throop Smith's observation that "[i]dle capital does not get bored or develop a sense of frustration because of its wasted talents"?

16. Why is the marginal tax rate—not the average tax rate—the determinant in the work/leisure choice?

17. Are special tax breaks "more significant with high and progressive tax rates," as Professor Smith asserts?

18. Lower tax rates on higher incomes since the Smith excerpt was written have reduced the overall revenue loss from tax-exempt bonds. The revenue loss arises from the failure to tax the interest received by the bondholders. Consequently, if tax rates drop, the revenue loss from tax exempts declines.

More important, the yield from tax-exempt bonds is compared, in the marketplace, to the after-tax yield of comparable taxable securities. When tax rates are reduced, the after-tax yield on taxable securities increases, so tax-exempt bonds become relatively less attractive and their price must fall to restore their yield as a percent of cost to a level where it will remain competitive.

19. Dan Throop Smith said that an over-50-percent tax makes tax-saving more important than income-earning. Is this a good reason to place a 50 percent ceiling on tax rates?

20. Professor Smith reverses the usual way percentage increases and decreases in tax rates are viewed. Is it better to compare percentage changes in tax or percentage changes in after-tax income?

21. Most supporters of "flat" rates would provide some degree of progressivity, by providing exemptions (taxed at a zero rate, compared to the single positive rate for income above the exempt level). Why does Smith say that progression arising from exemptions, sometimes referred to as "degression," is simplifying, while progression arising from a progressive rate structure is complicating?

22. What is Smith's antidote to the "each and every" fallacy—the contention that each and every tax should be progressive?

23. Professor Bittker concedes that the case for progression is "uneasy," but he nevertheless supports it. Why?

24. Do you agree with Professor Bittker that the "burden of proof" should not be placed on the proponents of progression any more than on the proponents of proportionality?

25. Professor Bittker uses the head tax as a "straw man," a proposal that virtually no one would support today. Yet, when exactions are in the form of services rather than money, most governments tend toward levying an equal tax upon all. In medieval times, many taxes were in the form of services owed to the king or to nobles.

In the Twentieth Century, the primary example of a "tax" in the form of services is military conscription during wartime. This very large service to the government tends to be meted out fairly equally to all within the relevant group (normally, able-bodied young men).

C. THE TAX RATE STRUCTURE: PRAGMATISM AND EQUITY

For a generation before enactment of the Tax Reform Act of 1986, writers argued that a broader tax base would permit tax rates to be cut drastically without a loss of revenue. Politically, tax rate cuts were offered in exchange for giving up tax shelters and other favored tax treatment. The maximum rate had already been cut from 91 percent to 50 percent over the preceding 22 years. It is doubtful that it would have been possible to impose marginal rates in the 90 percent range to a broad base with no opportunity to escape the top rates. For years political equilibrium had been maintained by imposing high rates to satisfy populist sentiment while simultaneously providing generous opportunities to avoid imposition of high taxes on large segments of personal income.

Charles McLure, an economist, is credited with being the principal author of the 1984 Treasury Study (frequently termed "Treasury I") that was modified and recommended by President Reagan in 1985 ("Treasury II") and eventually led to the comprehensive changes made by the Tax Reform Act of 1986. In the first selection below, Dr. McLure urges that attention be paid to incentives for profit maximization as well as to incentives to stimulate initial investment.

The Shoup Report (so called because it was prepared by a commission headed by Carl Shoup, a public finance professor) was prepared during American occupation of Japan to assist Japan's post-war recovery. This report includes an explicit analysis of reasons to avoid raising marginal tax rates too high.

Focusing on rates and ignoring exclusions, deductions, and tax credits gives only part of the picture of the effect of the income tax—both the impact on taxpayers and the consequences for the economy. The Steuerle and Hartzmark selection, published in 1981, made the point that half or more of personal income in the United States was not subject to the income tax. Even after the base-broadening achieved in the 1986 Act, a huge zero bracket amount continues to be a dominating factor in determining appropriate tax rates.

Finally, the brief selection from the Treasury I recommendations is a reminder that virtually none of the reasons for progression apply to the corporate income tax. This topic is discussed further in Chapter Fourteen.

COMMENTS ON FUNDAMENTAL TAX REFORM
Charles E. McLure, Jr.[*]

National Tax Association-Tax Institute of America

78th Annual Conference 97, 97 (1985)

It is important to reduce marginal tax rates. The advantages of lower marginal rates are easily understood. At lower rates the disincentive effects of taxation are reduced, and whatever inequities and distortions remain are less important.

It seems that the general pattern of rates proposed in Treasury-I would be a reasonable target. Though the number of marginal rate brackets is not important, except as a cosmetic matter, I do not see any reason to have more than four or five rates. From an aesthetic point of view it might be useful to think of rates divisible by five. A top rate as high as 40 percent might not be out of the question from an economic point of view, if restricted only to those with very high taxable incomes, say $200,000 or more. But one must realize that if state and local taxes are not deductible,[e] with a top marginal rate that high the aggregate state and federal marginal rate would not be much lower than under current law.

Thinking about the incentive effects of taxation has undergone a transformation in recent years that may not be entirely beneficial. At one time public finance economists focused on the tendency of high tax rates on business income to distort economic decision making, if only by reducing the pay-off from optimization. * * *

The focus of policy analysis has recently shifted almost entirely to the effects of taxation on investment decisions. Most commonly, such analysis is conducted by calculating the ex ante effective rate of taxation on income from various investments. Such calculations usually take account of the effects of such provisions as accelerated depreciation, the investment tax credit, and marginal tax rates. (The inclusion of interest indexing and the

---

[*]. At time of original publication, Senior Fellow, Hoover Institution, Stanford University.

e. As discussed in Chapter Thirteen, Treasury I proposed ending the federal deduction for all state and local taxes. In the 1986 Act, Congress ended the deduction for sales taxes, but continued the deduction for state and local income and property taxes. (Eds.)

deduction for dividends paid in Treasury-I[f] forced analysts also to consider their effects on effective tax rates.) A common conclusion is that investment tax credits and accelerated depreciation are to be espoused because they reduce the cost of capital. At the very least, these policies are more effective than rate reduction in stimulating investment. * * *

This focus on investment decisions, while generally appropriate, has almost totally diverted attention from issues of incentives for profit maximization and efficient operation, once investments have been made. I believe that more attention should be paid to these traditional questions, along with issues of incentives for investment. Otherwise we will be too sanguine about high marginal rates.
    * * *

REPORT ON JAPANESE TAXATION
Shoup Mission
Vol. 1, at 77-81 (1949)

Taxation of High Incomes

The present Japanese income tax system is superficially a very progressive one. The actual result, however, is somewhat different. There are many ways in which the wealthy taxpayer may legally avoid much of the income tax, through the so-called "loopholes." Also, we have the impression that the administration of the law in the top ranges of income has been relatively ineffective, or at least uneven. Hence many, perhaps most, of the individuals with large incomes are taxed at only a fraction of what the progressive rate schedule seems to indicate. On the other hand, occasional instances arise where seriously excessive burdens have been imposed through overassessment of taxpayers, or even at times merely through the strict application of the law to cases not contemplated when it was enacted.

Among the more serious loopholes in the present law are the exclusion of 50 per cent of capital gains from taxable income, the lack of adequate restraints on the accumulation of earnings in corporations, the flat rates applicable to distributions in liquidation, and the flat rates applicable to certain types of interest, as well as to other forms of income. These loopholes have been adequately closed in the various recommendations made elsewhere in this report. But securing adequate progression is more than a matter of having an adequate law; it requires also that law be administered effectively. Otherwise, beyond a certain point further increases in rates or the closing of loopholes add little or nothing to the progressivity of the tax. The result is merely more evasion and a progressive deterioration of taxpayer morale. Moreover, some of the methods used to evade taxes may be wasteful and hence seriously interfere with the attainment of maximum levels of production. Consequently, in an overzealous attempt to shift the tax burden

---

f. Neither of these proposals was adopted by Congress. (Eds.)

away from the lower classes, the resources available to them are actually diminished.

We conclude that the present top income tax rates in Japan are now much too high in relation to current standards of compliance and enforcement. It is possible that a reduction in these rates, through securing better compliance, would of itself secure a larger revenue from these income classes.

The result would then be an increase rather than a decrease in the real degree of progression, even without any change in methods of administration. In any case, such a reduction of rates is an essential step in securing the greater vigor of administration that is required if substantial improvement in the degree of progression is to be attained. The baneful effects of the various devices resorted to for tax evasion purposes outweigh the slight amount of increased progression that is at present attained by the top rates in practice.

                        * * *

A decision as to whether a given rate is too high or not will always require the exercise of judgment. However, there are two specific considerations that help in forming such a judgment.

The first is the average amount of error in the assessment of income. For example, if we can be reasonably sure that in practically all cases the error in estimating the income for tax purposes is less than 5 per cent, then top rates of 80 per cent or perhaps even 90 per cent may be tolerable. However, it is our impression that at present errors of 10 per cent or 20 per cent in assessing the largest income are almost the rule, and errors of 50 per cent or more are not uncommon. Given these degrees of underassessment, a rate of 80 per cent rather than, say 60 per cent produces only a minor improvement in progressivity compared with the evasion and the increased difficulty of administration. For example, if a certain taxpayer's actual income of 20 million yen is assessed at only 10 million yen, an increase in the tax rate from 60 per cent to 80 per cent decreases the income left to this taxpayer by only one seventh. But it cuts in half the income after tax of the honest taxpayer.

On the other hand, suppose that, in the attempt to achieve a higher average progression, arbitrary overassessments are sometimes made, so that an occasional taxpayer with seven million yen income is overassessed at ten million yen. For such a taxpayer, raising the rates on the assessed income from 60 per cent to 80 per cent means moving from a situation where this taxpayer has at least one million yen left after the tax to one where his tax exceeds his income by one million yen. Under these conditions the administration of the tax tends to deteriorate, so that in the long run higher rates may mean less real progression.

The second consideration is the incentive afforded for avoidance or evasion of the tax. A 50 per cent tax rate on income is equal to a 100 per cent rate on the amount retained by the taxpayer, while a 67 per cent rate on income is 200 per cent on the amount retained, and 75 per cent on income is 300 per cent on the amount retained. This means, for example, that if a corporation is to give an official a net increase in salary of 10,000 yen it will cost only 20,000 yen if the rate is 50 per cent, but 30,000 yen or 40,000 yen if the rate is 67 per cent, or 75 per cent. Under a 75 per cent on individual incomes, the corporate official may much prefer that the corporation spend 40,000 yen on entertainments and other perquisites for him, rather than pay him the same amount in salary. Aside from the tax element, the salary would of course be preferred, since it has the advantage that it can be spent in whatever way the recipient pleases. The company official may consider these perquisites to be worth only a third of what they cost the corporation. Still, receiving the 40,000 yen perquisite is better than getting the 40,000-yen salary, paying the income tax, and retaining only 10,000 yen. If the tax rate is reduced to 67 per cent, the corporate official may consider it to be about an even choice between receiving a certain amount of additional compensation in the form of outright salary or in the form of entertainment and other perquisites, and if the tax rate is only 50 per cent, the corporate official may well prefer the salary increment, even though, after tax, he will have only half the money that it would cost the corporation to give him the alternative, tax-free perquisites.

In cases like this, pushing up the rate of income tax not only loses revenue, but induces wasteful expenditure that does not give as much satisfaction to anyone as would a smaller amount of resources put at the free disposal of the taxpayer. It will always be difficult to check this type of evasion or avoidance, since the line between proper business expenses and personal expenses is impossible to fix with precision.

Other means of avoidance develop under the pressure of high rates. For example, a taxpayer may arrange to take a part of his salary in the form of a loan, with the tacit understanding that it need never be repaid. But if the tax rate is as low as 50 per cent, he may prefer to pay the tax rather than risk liability to repay the loan if the corporation gets into difficulties, or risk investigation by tax officials.

In short, we are of the opinion that under present conditions in Japan it is unwise to push the income tax rate much, if any, above 50 per cent. At least, if the rates do rise substantially higher, they should do so only over ranges of income where the number of taxpayers is small enough to permit of a very thorough investigation and assessment of each taxpayer subject to these higher rates.

Nevertheless, we cannot be satisfied with the degree of high-level progression in the tax system that is reflected by nothing much more than an income tax that is limited to a 50 or 60 per cent top rate. Every progressive tax system worthy of the name must provide a substantial obstacle to the accumulation of huge fortunes that threaten to concentrate the control of the economic system in the hands of a few wealthy individuals. This is a danger of particular significance to Japan. Unless such accumulations are prevented by the tax system, they are almost certain to arise, sooner or later.

An improved form of succession tax will be helpful, but is scarcely enough by itself. Its effect is felt only over a long period of time.

The most satisfactory solution to the problem posed here involves the imposition of an annual, low-rate tax on the net worth of well-to-do individuals.[g]

INDIVIDUAL INCOME TAXATION, 1947-79
Eugene Steuerle[*] & Michael Hartzmark[**]
34 National Tax Journal 145, 147, 151-154, 157-58 (1981)

The Tax Base
* * *

Exclusions from Adjusted Gross Income
Over the past three decades there has been a large growth in the amount of individual income that is not required to be counted as adjusted gross income (AGI). * * *

Deductions, Exemptions, Credits and
Other Nontaxable Adjusted Gross Income
To determine the percentage of personal income which actually comprises the tax base, it is necessary not only to take into account the amount of exclusions from adjusted gross income, but also other deductions, exemptions, and similar exceptions by which the taxpayer reduces taxable income and tax liabilities.

Unlike exclusions from adjusted gross income, the total value of these other exemptions and deductions have declined relative to personal income over time. One reason for this decline is that, relative to personal income, the adjusted gross income of nontaxable individuals decreased substantially from 1947 to the end of the 1960's and then remained relatively constant during the 1970's. Unfortunately, this amount cannot be measured separately from nonreported income of taxable returns and other differences between BEA [Bureau of Economic Analysis] and IRS measures of AGI. The combined measure declined from 19.7 percent of personal income in 1947 to about 9.4 percent in 1979. Because incomes of households have grown faster than tax-exempt levels of income, the decrease in the relative amount of AGI of nontaxable individuals is explained in part by the simultaneous decrease in the percentage of households with AGI below tax thresholds.

The amount of exemptions and deductions relative to personal income has also decreased since 1947. This shrinkage is due almost entirely to the

---

g. Wealth taxes are discussed in Chapter Nine. (Eds.)

*. At time of original publication, Department of the Treasury.

**. At time of original publication, University of Chicago.

drastic reduction in the relative value of personal exemptions.[h] On taxable returns, these exemptions have decreased since the early 1950's from over 24 percent to 9.3 percent of personal income.

Standard deductions * * * also fell in relative value during the 1950's and 1960's, but then rose in the 1970's from less than 2 ½ percent to a high of 7.3 percent in 1977. By 1979, this percentage had dropped to 6.5 because prices and incomes rose faster than the zero bracket amount,[i] which was increased slightly in 1979.

Since 1947 there has also been an increase in the amount of deductions that have been itemized on tax returns. Itemizations grew from 3.7 percent of personal income in 1947 to 10.1 percent in 1969, then declined slightly to 9.0 percent by 1979. Accompanying this decline throughout the early and middle 1970's, however, were the legislated increases in the value of the standard deduction, and a corresponding increase in the number of non-itemizers. Indeed, the decline in itemizations from 1969 to 1979 equaled only 1.1 percent of personal income, while the increase in standard deductions was 4.1 percent.

A final way to reduce individual income tax liability is through the use of credits. By "grossing up" the tax offset by the credit, it is possible to estimate an equivalent amount of income which is made nontaxable. Credits essentially offset taxable income in the lowest brackets first. For example, if a taxpayer has $160 of credits, and if the bracket width is $1,000 for the first two positive rates of 14 percent and 15 percent, then the taxpayer's credits offset $1,000 of income at 14 percent and $133.33 (= $20/.15) at the 15 percent rate.

While credits offset only 1.4 percent of personal income in 1979, that percentage was still substantially higher than any percentage that applied before the 1970's. From 1975 to 1978 a general tax credit was provided to taxpayers in a manner somewhat similar to the personal exemption, that is, it was available to all taxpayers rather than limited to groups of taxpayers with specific characteristics or particular expenditures (e.g., credit for the elderly, child and dependent care credit). Income offset by all credits was at its highest level during that period.

Aggregate Reduction in the Tax Base

When the exclusion amounts are combined with the amount of deductions, exemptions, etc., they result in 49 percent to 66 percent of personal income being excepted from taxation for each year of the period, 1947 to 1979. Thus, no more than 51 percent of personal income was ever in the tax base in the sense of being taxed at a positive rate. This income taxed at a positive rate (or, excluding income offset by credits, taxable

---

h. Personal exemptions are now adjusted annually for changes in the cost of living. Section 151(d)(4). (Eds.)

i. For a few years, including the time when this article was published, the standard deduction was called the "zero bracket amount." (Eds.)

income) actually grew as a percentage of personal income through the 1950's and 1960's, reaching a high in 1969. From 1970 to 1977, there was a decline in the tax base as a percentage of personal income to about the level applicable in the early 1960's, although the trend has been upward again since 1977.

More dramatic than the overall trend has been the combination of factors which produced this movement. For instance, from 1947 to 1979 the tax base increased (or income excepted from taxation decreased) by 6.3 percent of personal income because a decrease of 24.3 percent of personal income principally in the value of personal exemptions and the AGI of nontaxable individuals more than offset an increase of 18.0 percent of personal income in the amount of exclusions, standard deductions, itemizations and credits (see Table 3).

Table 3

AGGREGATE CHANGE IN THE TAX BASE, 1947-79
(As a Percentage of Personal Income)

Increases in Tax Base Due to Decreases In:

Personal Exemptions	14.0%
AGI of Nontaxable Individuals, Nonreported	
AGI & Reconciliation	10.3
Total Increase	24.3

Decreases in Tax Base Due to Increases In:

Net Exclusions from AGI	9.5%
Itemizations	5.3
Standard Deductions	2.1
Income Offset by Credits	1.2
Total Decrease	18.0

Net Increase in Tax Base (or Decrease in	
Income Excepted from Taxation)	6.3%

* * *

Conclusion

Changes in the economy have combined with the actions of Congress, administrators and taxpayers to modify the structure of the individual income tax. Despite the many changes, the average rate of tax has ranged between 9.2 and 12.1 percent of personal income since 1951. For 1981 however, the rate may reach a new high just above 12.1 percent. More significant perhaps than any change in the average rate of taxation has been the shift in the means through which much of income is exempted from taxation or "taxed" at a zero rate and in the rates of tax which apply to the base which remains.

The amount of income excluded from adjusted gross income has been increasing steadily since 1947. The average tax rate on adjusted gross income correspondingly has risen even when the rate on personal income has remained relatively constant. Itemized and standard deductions, along with credits against tax, have also grown at a faster rate than personal income, further reducing the tax base. However, since 1947, these reductions in the base have been more than offset by the decrease, relative to personal income, in the amount of adjusted gross income received by nontaxable individuals and, most importantly, in the amount of personal exemptions.

Exemptions, standard deductions and the general tax credit determine minimum tax-exempt levels of income. Such levels of income for couples with two children have consistently been quite close to official poverty levels; this relationship has been a deliberate policy at least since 1964. Because incomes have grown faster than official poverty levels (or prices), tax-exempt levels have exempted smaller portions of the population from taxation. Additionally, the decreased importance of the personal exemption *vis-a-vis* the standard deduction, along with increases in the standard deduction, has caused the tax burdens of families with dependents to increase relative to those without dependents.

The rates of tax applying to the tax base have also altered substantially. In the early 1960's, only 10 percent of tax returns faced a positive marginal rate of tax other than 20-22 percent. Since then, the marginal rate of tax has risen for tax returns above the median marginal rate and fallen for taxable returns below the median. In general, over the past two decades the combination of tax increases resulting from higher money incomes and legislated tax reductions has resulted in a more progressive distribution of both personal income and individual tax returns in terms of marginal rate of tax.

TAX REFORM FOR FAIRNESS, SIMPLICITY, AND ECONOMIC GROWTH ("TREASURY I")
United States Department of the Treasury
Vol. 2, at 127-28 (1984)

[T]he current progressive rate structure for corporate income serves no affirmative purpose and encourages the use of corporations to gain the advantage of low marginal tax rates. The progressive rate structure for individuals is premised on the ability-to-pay concept, which in turn reflects an assumption that additional amounts of income are increasingly available for discretionary, nonessential consumption. These concepts have no relevance to corporate income, all of which is either distributed or used to produce additional income. Moreover, under current law a small corporation can escape high marginal tax rates on corporate income by electing pass-through treatment as an S corporation. Finally, the Treasury Department proposals include partial dividend relief, which would mitigate the impact of corporate tax rates on all corporations.[j]

The current low rates of tax for certain amounts of corporate income permit the use of corporations as tax shelters for individuals. Thus, an individual may attempt to accumulate investment income within a corporation in order to defer tax on the income at the individual's rate. Where the corporate rate is significantly below the individual's marginal rate, the deferral advantage can more than offset the extra burden of the corporate tax. Current law attempts to limit this use of the corporate form through a surtax on the undistributed income of "personal holding companies." The personal holding company rules are complex and not uniformly effective.

The progressive tax structure for corporate income also encourages multiple corporations in order to maximize income taxed at the lowest rates. The current rules limiting this use of the corporate form are again complex and not consistently effective.

Proposal

The present corporate rate structure would be replaced by a flat tax rate for corporations of 33 percent.

* * *

Notes and Questions

26. In addition to the formal rate structure, there are a variety of back-door techniques for introducing additional progressivity. For example, the floor on miscellaneous itemized deductions (including most employee business expenses) is two percent of adjusted gross income, so expenses that are largely deductible by low-income taxpayers cannot be deducted to any extent by taxpayers with high adjusted gross incomes. Section 68. The treatment of Social Security benefits is another example. Either none of the benefits, 50 percent of the benefits, or 85 percent of the benefits are taxable, depending on the taxpayer's income. Section 86. Similarly, section 151(d)(3) phases out personal and dependency exemptions for high-income taxpayers.

27. Why does Dr. McLure believe more attention should be paid to the effects of taxes on profit maximization and efficient operation once investments have been made, rather than to stimulating new investment?

28. How does the level of income tax rates affect economic distortions caused by the income tax?

---

j. The dividend relief proposals were not adopted. This issue is discussed in Chapter Fourteen. (Eds.)

29. The Shoup Report holds out the possibility that lower tax rates in the upper income brackets, by securing better compliance, might result in more revenue from those with upper incomes. Is this relevant for the contemporary United States?

30. Why did the authors of the Shoup Report think an increase in the tax rate would be especially unfair to the honest taxpayer?

31. The Shoup Report makes the point that the higher an employee's tax rate, the more advantageous it is to the employee (and to the employer) to substitute nontaxable fringe benefits. The employee receives larger after-tax benefits, and the cost to the employer is less than it would be to provide the employee with the same after-tax amount in the form of taxed salary.

32. The Shoup Report addressed a perceived dilemma of reducing income tax rates and still hindering the accumulation of large fortunes. To accomplish this the Shoup Report proposed to supplement the income tax with an annual, low-rate tax on the net wealth of well-to-do individuals. The Report said: "Every progressive tax system worthy of its name must provide a substantial obstacle to the accumulation of huge fortunes that threaten to concentrate the control of the economic system in the hands of a few wealthy individuals." Do you agree? Is this observation relevant to the contemporary United States?

33. Why do Steuerle and Hartzmark say that tax credits essentially offset taxable income in the lowest brackets first?

34. According to Steuerle and Hartzmark, what percentage of personal income was subjected to positive tax rates during the years they studied (1947 to 1979)?

35. Why did the tax burden on families with dependents increase in relation to the tax burden on families without dependents in the period Steuerle and Hartzmark analyzed?

36. Individual income tax rates and corporate income tax rates should be related. In the past they seldom have been. The rationale for a cap on marginal rates is the same for both taxes. It is difficult to get a handle on the relationship so long as corporate earnings are taxed again when paid out as dividends to individuals and any increase in value of corporate stock due to retained earnings is taxed to a selling stockholder. The double tax issue is discussed in Chapter Fourteen.

37. Is ability to pay relevant in setting corporate tax rates? What view is expressed in Treasury I?

38. In determining the appropriate degree of progressivity of the federal income tax, should other federal taxes be taken into account? Should state and local taxes be included? Should adjustments be made for directly related benefits, such as Social Security pensions?

39. Is redistribution of wealth an appropriate objective for the individual income tax? Does it matter whether the gap between high incomes and low incomes occurs in a society where income is largely based on ownership of landed estates or in a society where income is keyed largely to entrepreneurial success?

40. When the overall tax burden is changed because of extrinsic circumstances—i.e., higher taxes in wartime or lower taxes in periods of economic recession—should the relationship between tax brackets remain the same? Be widened? Be narrowed?

41. An income tax that taxes different types of income at different rates is called a *schedular tax*. Should income tax rates vary depending on the source of income, such as earned income versus investment income?

42. What is the role of tax simplification in deciding on tax rates?

43. Suppose society were convinced that progressive taxes are fairer than proportional taxes, but also that at some point of progression they would be less fair—and that we had no way of knowing the crossover point. What should we do?

Selected Bibliography

ANDO, ALBERT ET AL., THE STRUCTURE AND REFORM OF THE U.S. TAX SYSTEM 119-23 (1985).

Atkinson, A.T., *Horizontal Equity and the Distribution of the Tax Burden, in* THE ECONOMICS OF TAXATION 3 (Henry J. Aaron & Michael J. Boskin eds., 1980).

Bankman, Joseph & Thomas Griffith, *Social Welfare and the Rate Structure: A New Look At Progressive Taxation*, 75 CAL. L. REV. 1905 (1987).

BLUM, WALTER J. & HARRY KALVEN, JR., THE UNEASY CASE FOR PROGRESSIVE TAXATION (1953).

Buchanan, James & Geoffrey Brennan, *Tax Reform without Tears, in* THE ECONOMICS OF TAXATION 33 (Henry J. Aaron & Michael J. Boskin eds., 1980).

Feld, Alan L., *Fairness in Rate Cuts in the Individual Income Tax*, 68 CORNELL L. REV. 429 (1983).

GALVIN, CHARLES O. & BORIS I. BITTKER, THE INCOME TAX: HOW PROGRESSIVE SHOULD IT BE? (1969).

GOODE, RICHARD, THE INDIVIDUAL INCOME TAX 11-36, 58-74 (Rev. ed. 1976).

GROVES, HAROLD M., FINANCING GOVERNMENT (3d ed. 1950).

Kornhauser, Marjorie E., *The Rhetoric of the Anti-Progressive Income Tax Movement: A Typical Male Reaction*, 86 MICH. L. REV. 465 (1987).

McCombs, J.B., *An Historical Review and Analysis of Early United States Tax Policy Scholarship: Definition of Income and Progressive Rates*, 64 ST. JOHN'S L. REV. 471 (1990).

McLure, Charles E., Jr., *Comments on Fundamental Tax Reform, in* 82ND ANN. CONF., NAT'L TAX ASS'N 97 (1985).

Minarik, Joseph J., *Who Doesn't Bear the Tax Burden?, in* THE ECONOMICS OF TAXATION 55 (Henry J. Aaron & Michael J. Boskin eds., 1980).

O'Kelley, Charles R., Jr., *Tax Policy for Post-Liberal Society: A Flat-Tax-Inspired Redefinition of the Purpose and Ideal Structure of a Progressive Income Tax*, 58 S. CAL. L. REV. 727 (1985).

Okner, Benjamin A., *Total U.S. Taxes and Their Effect on the Distribution of Family Income in 1966 and 1970, in* THE ECONOMICS OF TAXATION 55 (Henry J. Aaron & Michael J. Boskin eds., 1980).

Scully, Gerard W., *Tax Rates, Tax Revenues, and Economic Growth*, 91 TAX NOTES TODAY 51 (1991).

SHOUP MISSION, REPORT ON JAPANESE TAXATION, vol. 1 (1949).

SIMONS, HENRY, PERSONAL INCOME TAXATION 1-40, 218-20 (1938).

Smith, Dan Throop, *High Progressive Tax Rates: Inequity and Immorality?*, 20 U. FLA. L. REV. 451 (1966).

Steuerle, Eugene & Michael Hartzmark, *Individual Income Taxation, 1947-79*, 34 NAT'L TAX J. 145.

U.S. DEP'T OF TREASURY, 2 REPORT ON TAX REFORM FOR FAIRNESS, SIMPLICITY, AND ECONOMIC GROWTH ("Treasury I"), 127-28 (1984).

U.S. DEP'T OF TREASURY, OFFICE OF TAX ANALYSIS, HOUSEHOLD INCOME MOBILITY DURING THE 1980S: A STATISTICAL ASSESSMENT BASED ON TAX RETURN DATA (1992).

VICKREY, WILLIAM, AGENDA FOR PROGRESSIVE TAXATION (1947).

——, *The Problem of Progression*, 20 U. FLA. L. REV. 437 (1968).

CHAPTER FIVE

TAXING FAMILIES

We expect all persons to make all important decisions in life in light of their tax effect. For the tax-minded young man or woman, with a substantial income, the Code adds to the attractiveness of a prospective spouse without taxable income, and detracts from one with it. Thus the provisions may have an income-leveling effect. But we have no data showing that as yet they operate in that manner. Love and marriage defy economic analysis.[a]

A. HISTORY OF THE TAXING UNIT

This subchapter tells the story of how we got to the present system, which imposes a tax penalty on some marriages and gives a tax reward to others.

The tax policy choice is between a family taxpaying unit (however defined) and the individual as the taxpaying unit. At the outset, the federal income tax was based on the individual as the taxpaying unit, with some recognition of the family unit through allowance of dependency exemptions. In the 1930 *Lucas v. Earl* decision, the Supreme Court, speaking through Justice Holmes, refused to give income tax effect to a contract between husband and wife, valid under state law, providing for income splitting between them:

> [T]his case is not to be decided by attenuated subtleties. It turns on the import and reasonable construction of the taxing act. There is no doubt that the statute could tax salaries to those who earned them and provide that the tax could not be escaped by anticipatory arrangements and contracts however skillfully devised to prevent the salary when paid from vesting even for a second in the man who earned it.[b]

It was not immediately clear, however, how the tax applied in states that had some variation of community property for married couples, and thus provided for income splitting between spouses by operation of law, rather than by private contract. The answer came later in the same year, with the Supreme Court's decision in *Poe v. Seaborn*. As is evident from the first excerpt below, the *Poe* Court seemed to base its decision on one of the "attenuated subtleties" rejected in *Lucas v. Earl*. Anticipatory arrangements

---

a. Judge Philip Nichols, Jr. in Mapes v. United States, 576 F.2d 896, 898 (Ct. Cl. 1978).
b. Lucas v. Earl, 281 U.S. 111, 114-15 (1930).

devised by state legislators would be honored when they prevented a salary from vesting in the spouse who earned it.

The combination of *Lucas v. Earl* and *Poe v. Seaborn* thus disallowed income splitting in the large majority of states following common law property rules while automatically allowing it in community property states, and thereby created politically unacceptable distinctions. The issue is important because of the progressive rate structure: As a general rule, $100,000 of income is taxed more heavily than are two incomes of $50,000 each. The excerpt from the Joint Tax Committee Staff Report summarizes the evolution of the taxation of individuals and couples since *Poe v. Seaborn*. The Report then discusses the near impossibility of reconciling three basic policy preferences.

By cutting tax rates and reducing the number of tax brackets, the Tax Reform Act of 1986 ameliorated the discriminations against single persons and against married couples with similar-sized incomes. According to the article by Messrs. Feenberg and Rosen, the basic contrasts still remained, however, and they were sharpened by subsequent tax increases.

POE v. SEABORN
282 U.S. 101, 108-11, 113, 116-17 (1930)

MR. JUSTICE ROBERTS delivered the opinion of the Court.

Seaborn and his wife, citizens and residents of the State of Washington, made for the year 1927 separate income tax returns as permitted by the Revenue Act of 1926.

During and prior to 1927 they accumulated property comprising real estate, stocks, bonds and other personal property. While the real estate stood in his name alone, it is undisputed that all of the property real and personal constituted community property and that neither owned any separate property or had any separate income.

The income comprised Seaborn's salary, interest on bank deposits and on bonds, dividends, and profits on sales of real and personal property. He and his wife each returned one-half the total community income as gross income and each deducted one-half of the community expenses to arrive at the net income returned.

The Commissioner of Internal Revenue determined that all of the income should have been reported in the husband's return, and made an additional assessment against him. Seaborn paid under protest, claimed a refund, and on its rejection, brought this suit.

    * * *

The case requires us to construe sections 210(a) and 211(a) of the Revenue Act of 1926, and apply them, as construed, to the interests of husband and wife in community property under the law of Washington.

These sections lay a tax upon the net income of every individual.[1] The Act goes no farther, and furnishes no other standard or definition of what constitutes an individual's income. The use of the word "of" denotes ownership. It would be a strained construction, which, in the absence of further definition by Congress, should impute a broader significance to the phrase.

The Commissioner concedes that the answer to the question involved in the cause must be found in the provisions of the law of the State, as to a wife's ownership of or interest in community property. What, then, is the law of Washington as to the ownership of community property and of community income, including the earnings of the husband's and wife's labor?

The answer is found in the statutes of the State, and the decisions interpreting them.

* * *

Without further extending this opinion it must suffice to say that it is clear the wife has, in Washington, a vested property right in the community property, equal with that of her husband; and in the income of the community, including salaries or wages of either husband or wife, or both. A description of the community system of Washington and of the rights of the spouses, and of the powers of the husband as manager, will be found in *Warburton v. White*, 176 U.S. 484.

The taxpayer contends that if the test of taxability under Sections 210 and 211 is ownership, it is clear that income of community property is owned by the community and that husband and wife have each a present vested one-half interest therein.

The Commissioner contends, however, that we are here concerned not with mere names, nor even with mere technical legal titles; that calling the wife's interest vested is nothing to the purpose, because the husband has such broad powers of control and alienation, that while the community lasts, he is essentially the owner of the whole community property, and ought so to be considered for the purposes of Sections 210 and 211. * * *

We are of opinion that under the law of Washington the entire property and income of the community can no more be said to be that of the husband, than it could rightly be termed that of the wife.

We should be content to rest our decision on these considerations. Both parties have, however, relied on executive construction and the history of the income tax legislation as supporting their respective views. We shall, therefore, deal with these matters.

* * *

On the whole, we feel that, were the matter less clear than we think it is, on the words of the income tax law as applied to the situation in

---

1. The language has been the same in each act since that of February 24, 1919, 40 Stat. 1057.

Washington, we should be constrained to follow the long and unbroken line of executive construction, applicable to words which Congress repeatedly reemployed in acts passed subsequent to such construction, (*New York v. Illinois*, 278 U. S. 367; *National Lead Co. v. United States*, 252 U. S. 140; *United States v. Farrar*, 281 U. S. 624), reenforced, as it is, by Congress' refusal to change the wording of the Acts to make community income in states whose law is like that of Washington returnable as the husband's income.

The Commissioner urges that we have, in [principle], decided the instant question in favor of the Government. He relies on *United States v. Robbins*, 269 U. S. 315; *Corliss v. Bowers*, 281 U. S. 376, and *Lucas v. Earl*, 281 U. S. 111.

In the *Robbins* case, we found that the law of California, as construed by her own courts, gave the wife a mere expectancy and that the property rights of the husband during the life of the community were so complete that he was in fact the owner. Moreover, we there pointed out that this accorded with the executive construction of the Act as to California.

The *Corliss* case raised no issue as to the intent of Congress, but as to its power. We held that where a donor retains the power at any time to revest himself with the principal of the gift, Congress may declare that he still owns the income. While he has technically parted with title, yet he in fact retains ownership, and all its incidents. But here the husband never has ownership. That is in the community at the moment of acquisition.

In the *Earl* case a husband and wife contracted that any property they had or might thereafter acquire in any way, either by earnings (including salaries, fees, etc.), or any rights by contract or otherwise, "shall be treated and considered and hereby is declared to be received, held, taken, and owned by us as joint tenants . . ." We held that, assuming the validity of the contract under local law, it still remained true that the husband's professional fees, earned in years subsequent to the date of the contract, were his individual income, "derived from salaries, wages, or compensation for personal service," under §§ 210, 211, 212(a) and 213 of the Revenue Act of 1918. The very assignment in that case was bottomed on the fact that the earnings would be the husband's property, else there would have been nothing on which it could operate. That case presents quite a different question from this, because here, by law, the earnings are never the property of the husband, but that of the community.

* * *

INCOME TAX TREATMENT
OF MARRIED COUPLES AND SINGLE PERSONS
Staff of the Joint Committee on Taxation
Pages J6-J8 (1980)

After *Lucas v. Earl* and *Poe v. Seaborn* were decided, Congress and the Department of the Treasury made several attempts to change the taxation of married couples. The provisions considered and rejected during the 1930s and early 1940s included (1) mandatory joint returns for all married couples; (2) the taxation of community income to the spouse exercising management and control of such income; and (3) mandatory joint returns with a special allowance for the earned income of the husband or wife.

Through 1947, community property spouses continued to benefit from the splitting of income on separate returns. In the early years, however, this advantage over common law spouses was minimized by the relatively low tax rates. For those subject to tax during the years 1913 to 1915, the lowest tax rate was one percent, and it applied to the first $20,000 of taxable income. From 1919 until 1939, the lowest rate ranged from 1.5 to 4 percent and was applicable to the first $4,000 of income. In addition, only a small portion of the population was required to file tax returns because of the relatively high levels of exempt income.[20]

As the tax rates increased, particularly during World War II, the income tax advantage enjoyed by community property spouses increased. Not surprisingly, common law States began to adopt community property laws so that the benefits of income-splitting could be realized by their married residents.[21]

1948-1969

The debate on the taxation of married persons culminated with the enactment of the Revenue Act of 1948. Under the 1948 Act, married couples who filed jointly were in effect taxed as two single persons each reporting one-half the couple's aggregate income. This was achieved by taking half of the taxable income shown on the joint return, determining the tax thereon,

---

20. The pre-World War II portion of the civilian labor force filing Federal income tax returns was as follows:

Total Federal income tax returns as percentage of civilian labor force
Year:
1915 . . . . 0.9
1920 . . . . 17.6
1925 . . . . 9.2
1930 . . . . 7.9
1935 . . . . 8.9
1940 . . . . 26.4

Source: *1941 Statistics of Income*, Table 14, p. 208; *Historical Statistics of the U.S.*, Series D 1-10, p. 126.

21. By 1948, Oregon, Nebraska, Michigan, and Oklahoma had adopted community property laws. Pennsylvania's attempt to adopt community property laws was held unconstitutional by that State's highest court.

and multiplying the result by two. The splitting of all taxable income between a husband and wife was available for all married persons filing jointly. In effect, all married couples were given the benefit which previously had been restricted to community property States.

The Finance Committee Report summarized the intended effects of the income-splitting provisions as follows:

> Adoption of these income-splitting provisions will produce substantial geographical equalization in the impact of the tax on individual incomes. The impetuous enactment of community property legislation by States that have long used the common-law will be forestalled. The incentive for married couples in common law States to attempt the reduction of their taxes by the division of their income through such devices as trusts, joint tenancies, and family partnerships will be reduced materially. Administrative difficulties stemming from the use of such devices will be diminished, and there will be less need for meticulous legislation on the income-tax treatment of trusts and family partnerships.[22] * * *

The 1948 Act was successful in stopping the adoption of community property laws by the common law States. In fact, Nebraska, Michigan, Oklahoma, and Oregon repealed their recently adopted community property laws. To this day, however, community property laws are in effect in Arizona, California, Idaho, Louisiana, Nevada, New Mexico, Texas, and Washington.

The 1948 Act in effect created two rates of income taxation, one applicable to married couples filing jointly and one applicable to all other individual taxpayers. As a result of income-splitting, one-earner married couples paid a much smaller tax than a single taxpayer with the same amount of taxable income.

In 1951, a third set of tax rates was enacted for "heads of households," single taxpayers who maintain households for certain relatives. The new rates applicable to heads of households were calculated to give heads of households approximately one-half of the benefits of income-splitting accorded married couples.

The head of household provisions were extended in the Internal Revenue Code of 1954 to include taxpayers who met certain support requirements with respect to their mother or father, even though the parents did not live in the taxpayer's house. The 1954 Code also extended the full income-splitting benefits enjoyed by married couples to a surviving spouse for 2 years after the death of the other spouse.

1969-present

The last major revision in the comparative income tax treatment of married and single individuals occurred in 1969. Since the enactment of

---

22. S. Rep. No. 1013, 80th Cong., 2d Sess. 25 (1948).

income splitting for married couples in 1948, single persons generally had paid significantly higher taxes than married couples at the same income levels. For example, in 1969, at some income levels a single person's income tax liability was as much as 42.1 percent higher than the income tax liability of a married couple filing a joint return with the same amount of taxable income. In 1969, Congress concluded that, while some difference between the rate of tax paid by single persons and married couples filing jointly was appropriate to reflect the additional living expenses of married taxpayers, the then current differential of as much as 42 percent could not be justified on that basis.

Accordingly, the Tax Reform Act of 1969 included a new rate schedule for single persons effective in 1971. The new rate schedule was designed to impose on middle-income single persons tax liabilities no more than 20 percent above those for married couples.

Another new rate schedule, halfway between the new rate schedule for single persons and the rate schedule for married couples, was enacted in 1969 for heads-of-households. The former rate schedule for single persons was retained for married persons filing separate returns because, if each spouse were permitted to use the new tax rate schedule for single persons, many couples, especially those in community property States, could arrange their affairs and income in such a way that their combined tax would be less than that on a joint return.

With the new rate schedule for single persons, many married couples filing a joint return paid more tax than two single persons with the same total income. This was a necessary result of changing the income-splitting relationship between single and joint returns. At the time, the marriage penalty was justified on the grounds that, although a married couple has greater living expenses than a single person and hence should pay less tax, the couple's living expenses are likely to be less than those of two single persons and, therefore, the couple's tax should be higher than that of two single persons.

* * *

Marriage neutrality versus equal taxation of couples with equal incomes

Any system of taxing married couples requires making a choice among three different ideas of tax equity. One principle is that the tax system should be "marriage neutral"; that is, the tax burden of a married couple should be exactly equal to the combined tax burden of two single persons one of whom has the same income as the husband and the other of whom has the same income as the wife. A second principle of equity is that, because married couples frequently consume as a unit, couples with the same income should pay the same amount of tax regardless of how the income is divided between them. (This second concept of equity should apply equally well to other tax units which may consume jointly, such as the extended family or the household, defined as all people living together under one roof.) A third concept of equity is that the tax should be progressive; that is, as income rises, the tax burden should rise as a percentage of income.

Unhappily, these three concepts of equity are mutually inconsistent. A tax system can generally have any two of them, but not all three. The current tax system specifies the married couple as the tax unit so that couples with the same income pay the same tax, but it thereby foregoes marriage neutrality. A system of mandatory separate filing for married couples would sacrifice the concept of "equal taxation of couples with equal incomes" for the principle of "marriage neutrality" unless it were to forego progressivity. It should be noted, however, that there is an exception to this rule if refundable credits are permissible. A system with a flat tax rate and a per taxpayer refundable credit would have marriage neutrality, equal taxation of couples with equal incomes and some limited progressively.

There is no right or wrong answer to the question of whether "equal taxation of couples with equal incomes" is a better principle than "marriage neutrality." (This discussion assumes that the dilemma cannot be resolved by moving to a proportional or flat-rate tax system.)

Those who hold "marriage neutrality" to be more important argue that tax policy discourages marriage and encourages "living in sin," lowering society's standard of morality. Also, they argue that it is simply unfair to impose a "marriage tax" even if the tax does not actually deter anyone from marrying.

Those who favor the principle of equal taxation of couples with equal incomes argue that, as long as most couples pool their income and consume as a unit, two couples with $20,000 of income are equally well off regardless of whether their income is divided $10,000-$10,000 or $15,000-$5,000. Thus, it is argued, they should pay the same tax, as they do under present law. A marriage-neutral system with progressive rates would involve a larger combined tax on the couple with the unequal income division.

An advocate of marriage neutrality could respond that the relevant comparison is not between a two-earner couple where the spouses have equal incomes and a two-earner couple with an unequal income division, but rather between a two-earner couple and a one-earner couple with the same total income. Here, the case for equal taxation of the two couples may be weaker, because the non-earner in the one-earner couple benefits from more time which may be used for leisure, unpaid work inside the home, child care, and other activities. It could, of course, be argued in response that the "leisure" of the non-earner may in fact consist of necessary jobhunting or child care, in which case the one-earner couple may not have more ability to pay income tax than the two-earner couple with the same income.

The attractiveness of the principle of equal taxation of couples with equal incomes depends on the extent to which married couples actually pool their incomes and single persons do not. In a society where many marriages

last no longer than the typical single person's romance, or where married
couples frequently live apart and single persons frequently live together,
marriage neutrality would clearly be the better principle. However, as long
as differences in lifestyle between married couples and single persons are
pronounced, the issue is less clear.

Census data show that 1.3 million households in 1979 were shared by
two unrelated adults of the opposite sex. Three-fourths of these "unmarried
couples" had no children. Half had never been married before, nearly a third
had been divorced, and the remainder were either widowed or married to
someone else. The number of "unmarried couples" has grown 157 percent
since 1970. The Census report, however, concludes:

> Despite the spectacular nature of the recent increase in this
> unmarried-couple living arrangement, the 2.7 million "partners" in
> these 1.3 million households represent a very small portion of all
> persons in "couple" situations. In 1979, there were an estimated
> 96.5 million men and women who were married and living with a
> spouse. Thus, the partners in unmarried couples represented only
> about 3 percent of all persons among couples living together in
> 1979.

The continuing predominance of marriage among couples suggests that
"equal taxation of married couples with equal incomes" is still an important
concept for many people.

The actual size of the marriage bonus or penalty depends on the
combined effect of all the provisions of the tax law which treat the married
couple as something other than two distinct individuals. However, the most
important factors are the tax rate schedules and the zero bracket amount.[c]
* * *

RECENT DEVELOPMENTS IN THE MARRIAGE TAX
Daniel R. Feenberg[*] & Harvey S. Rosen[**]

48 National Tax Journal 91, 91-95, 99-101 (1995)

Introduction

President Clinton's changes in the personal income tax, embodied in the
Omnibus Budget Reconciliation Act of 1993 (OBRA 93), will affect the tax
liabilities of many Americans. The changes at the two extremes of the
income distribution are particularly important. At the high end, marginal
tax rates have been increased substantially. At the low end, there has been

---

c. The "zero bracket amount," or ZEBRA, was abandoned in the Tax Reform Act of 1986,
when Congress returned to the terminology "standard deduction." The present form of the
standard deduction has the same effect as the ZEBRA, in that it exempts from taxation the same
amount of income for every taxpayer of a given status (principally marital or family status) who
does not itemize deductions. See section 63. (Eds.)

*. At the time of original publication, National Bureau of Economic Research.

**. At time of original publication, Department of Economics, Princeton University.

a major expansion of the earned income tax credit. The impacts of these changes on economic behavior and tax revenues have already been the subject of considerable attention. * * * One issue that has received relatively little analysis is the impact of the new law on the tax consequences of marriage. * * *

We predict that 52 percent of American couples will pay an annual average marriage tax of about $1,244, and 38 percent will receive an average subsidy of about $1,399. Relative to the old law, there is not much of a change in the aggregate marriage tax. But the aggregate figures mask important differences for certain income groups. Specifically, some low-income families will face much higher marriage taxes than before. In this way, they are similar to their counter-parts at the opposite end of the income scale, for some of whom the tax on being married will increase by thousands of dollars. * * *

Background

* * * The basic source of the marriage tax is the fact that key elements of the tax law depend on an individual's family situation, including the rate schedule, the standard deduction, and the earned income tax credit (EITC). Hence, the act of getting married *per se* affects individuals' tax liabilities, even if their work and saving decisions stay the same. As we show below, tax liabilities do not always increase; under some circumstances, the tax system subsidizes marriage.

We now discuss the provisions of OBRA 93 that are most relevant to the calculation of marriage taxes and subsidies. * * *

Rate Schedules

The top of Table 1 shows for 1994 the correspondence between marginal tax rates and taxable income for married couples filing joint returns, * * * married couples filing separate returns, single individuals, and heads of households (unmarried individuals who maintain a household that includes as a member a son, daughter, or any other person eligible to be claimed as a dependent.) * * * For all the filing statuses, the high end brackets are much higher than they were before 1993. Specifically, the higher bracket rate used to be 31 percent; now the maximum statutory marginal tax rate is 39.6 percent.[3]

The schedules in Table I suggest that, just as under previous law, it is possible for marriage to lower a couple's joint tax liability. If X has a taxable income of $30,000 and Y has no income, then if they marry, all of X's taxable income is subject to a 15 percent rate, while before marriage, some would also be taxed at a 28 percent rate. But the possibility of tax liabilities increasing with marriage is also present. If A and B each have taxable incomes of $20,000 and file as singles, then their taxable income is taxed at

---

3. Actual marginal tax rates may be higher due to the personal exemption and itemized deduction phase-outs, and due to the 1.45 percent payroll tax for health insurance.

a rate of 15 percent. But if they marry, then part of their income is taxed at a 28 percent rate. Hence, their joint tax liability increases with marriage *ceteris paribus*.

TABLE 1
TAX PARAMETERS FOR 1994

Rate Schedules
Taxable Income

Marginal Tax Rate	Joint	Separate	Single	Head of Household
15%	$0 - 38,000	$0 - 19,000	$0 - 22,750	$0 - 30,500
28%	38,000 - 91,850	19,000 - 45,925	22,750 - 55,100	30,500 - 78,700
31%	91,850 - 140,000	45,925 - 70,000	55,100 - 115,000	78,700 - 127,500
36%	140,000 - 250,000	70,000 - 125,000	115,000 - 250,000	127,500 - 250,000
39.6%	250,000 -	125,000 -	250,000 -	250,000 -

Earned Income Tax Credit

	Rate	Phase-In Range	Maximum	Phase-Out Range
No Children	7.65	$0 - 4,000	$306	$5,000 - 9,000
One Child	26.3	$0 - 7,750	$2,038	$11,000 - 23,755
Two or More Children	30.0	$0 - 8,525	$2,528	$11,000 - 25,299

Standard Deduction

Joint	Separate	Single	Head of Household
$6,350	$3,175	$3,800	$5,600

Source: Young (1993, pp. 111, 113). The personal exemption is $2,450 regardless of filing status.

Earned Income Tax Credit

The provisions of the earned income tax credit (EITC) are noted in the middle of Table 1. The credit is a percentage of household earnings that depends on the number of children in the family. It ranges from 7.65 percent if there are no children to 30.0 percent if there are two or more. The credit is applied to each dollar of earnings in a phase-in range, reaching a maximum at the end of this range. Then it is implicitly taxed away over a phase-out range. Importantly, if the individual's tax liability is less than the EITC, the difference is refunded.

The key point in the marriage tax context is that on a joint return, eligibility for the EITC is based on the couple's joint earnings. Hence, an unmarried individual with a child may lose part or all of the credit upon marriage.

Standard Deduction

The standard deduction allowed on each type of return is recorded in the bottom of Table 1. Note that the standard deduction associated with two single returns or two head-of-household returns exceeds the standard deduction on a joint return. These differences tend to create a penalty for marrying, *ceteris paribus*.

Some Illustrations

This section illustrates how the provisions in Table 1 determine the tax consequences of marriage. These illustrations assume that all income is from earnings and every return uses the standard deduction. The only other subtraction from AGI to obtain taxable income is the personal exemption of $2450 times the number of people on the return. (The exemption is constant regardless of filing status, although it is phased out for high income individuals.) The calculations also assume that if two-children couples split, each child is claimed as an exemption on one tax return. For the sake of comparison, we also compute what the marriage tax would have been under the old law.[5]

* * * Results for childless couples and couples with two children are reported separately. Negative numbers indicate that tax liabilities go down with marriage.

Taken together, the figures suggest the following observations:

(1) *Except at the high-end of the income distribution, most childless couples face little change in the marriage tax.* Although the new law does introduce for the first time an EITC for childless individuals, it is phased out at such a low income level that most of our hypothetical couples are not affected.

(2) *For many low-income couples with children, the marriage tax is higher under the new law.* The large marriage taxes occur partly because the standard deduction on a joint return is $4,850 less than the sum of the deductions on two head-of-household returns. In addition, the inclusion of both spouses' incomes on the joint return reduces the total EITC.[7] * * *

(3) *The tax law provides a substantial "dowry" for individuals whose incomes are sufficiently far apart.* Suppose, for example, that W, who has an AGI of $50,000, is living with V, who has no income. They have no children. * * * [I]f they marry, W's tax liability decreases by about $3,382.

(4) *Conversely, the tax law penalizes marriage for couples whose incomes are relatively close.* Suppose G and H both have $25,000 incomes. * * * [I]f

---

5. By the "old law" we mean the 1992 law as it would have looked in 1994 after the bracket widths, standard deductions, and personal exemptions were indexed for inflation in the intervening years.

7. Further, the child-care credit is scaled down as AGI increases, another factor increasing the marriage penalty for low-income taxpayers.

they are childless and marry, their joint tax burden increases by $286. This effect becomes quite extraordinary for high income couples.[8] OBRA93 introduced a huge increase in the marriage tax for these couples. It is a consequence of the fact that high-end marginal tax rates have been increased so much by the new law.

Under OBRA 93, then, some couples will experience substantial tax increases upon marriage, others substantial tax reductions. * * *

Conclusion

The changes in the rate schedules and EITC embodied in the new tax law have implications for the tax consequences of marriage. On average, the income tax now imposes a mild tax on marriage of $124, while under the previous law there was a small subsidy of $143. However, the small average figure conceals the fact that some families will be paying substantial taxes or receiving substantial subsidies for being married. In 1994, about 52 percent of U.S. families will pay an average marriage tax of $1,244. This corresponds to a total of about $33 billion. At the same time, about 38 percent of the families will receive a marriage subsidy averaging $1,399 per family; the aggregate amount will be about $27 billion.

Our results lead naturally to the question of whether the new marriage tax will affect people's behavior. As we showed earlier, at least for some low-income couples, the size of the marriage tax is now quite extraordinary, amounting to over 18 percent of total income. An interesting topic for future research will be to see if the incidence of joint filing diminishes in this group. In this context, it is important to note that a reduction in joint filing is not the same thing as a reduction in marriage. It is costly and difficult for the Internal Revenue Service to learn about taxpayers' family situations. One possible response to huge marriage taxes may be that taxpayers will simply not reveal to the IRS that they are married.

Notes and Questions

1. In the Tax Reform Act of 1986 the zero bracket amount was dropped and the standard deduction was restored. Effective beginning in 1988, standard deductions became flat amounts, which are adjusted each year to account for inflation. The 1996 standard deduction amounts were the following:

Single persons - $4,000

Heads of Households - $5,900

Married couples filing jointly and qualified surviving spouses - $6,700

Married persons filing separately - $3,350.

The optional standard deduction was originally enacted as a simplification measure to make it unnecessary for taxpayers to keep track of modest

---

8. For these very-high-income couples, the marriage tax is independent of the number of children because all the personal exemptions are phased out.

itemized deductions and to free the Revenue Service (then called the Bureau of Internal Revenue) from the burden of auditing these itemized deductions. It has gradually come to have a second function (in combination with personal and dependency exemptions) as a poverty line below which the income tax does not apply.

2. Note the radical difference between the tax-favored lifestyles under present law: traditional one-earner married couples on the one hand, and unmarried two-career couples (heterosexual and homosexual) on the other.

3. Do higher tax rates make the marriage tax penalty greater?

4. What income levels are not affected by the differences in income tax rates between married couples and single persons?

5. What tax consequences are there for marriage by persons with incomes so low that they do not exceed the bottom tax bracket whether they marry or remain single?

6. *Poe v. Seaborn* did not impose a constitutional barrier to taxing earned income of a taxpayer in a community property state to the earner rather than to the community. The Supreme Court was construing a statute, not the Constitution. Under present law, employment taxes are imposed on the individual earner even in community property states, not on the community or half to each spouse. Section 1402(a)(5).

7. What would be the result if *Poe v. Seaborn* were to be repealed by Congress, joint returns were made optional, and the special rate schedules for marrieds were to be repealed?

8. Would a flat tax resolve all the issues of marriage penalties and marriage bonuses?

9. Pursuant to section 215 and section 61(a)(8), alimony is deductible to the payor and included in gross income by the recipient. Does this treatment fit the concept of the family as the taxpaying unit or the individual as the taxpaying unit? Alimony is usually thought of as a division of the income of the payor ex-spouse, but it is included in the gross income of the recipient even if the payor has no income. In that respect alimony treats the individual as the taxpaying unit. Insofar as alimony is a division of income (the usual case), it is consistent with the family as the taxpaying unit, albeit a family that has split. Similarly, transfers of property between spouses incident to divorce are treated, under section 1041, as gifts with carryover basis, overriding *United States v. Davis*, 370 U.S. 65 (1962), which had

treated transfers of property incident to divorce in at least some common law states as taxable transactions of property in exchange for relinquishment of marital rights. Although the spouse receiving property under the rule of the *Davis* case got a fair market value basis—as befits a taxable transaction—the Revenue Service never had the courage to be consistent and treat the recipient as having taxable gain equal to the excess of the fair market value of the property received over the zero basis of the marital rights relinquished.

10. Under section 2(b)(1) a person can qualify for head of household filing status if his or her home also is the place of abode of a son, daughter, or other descendant, even though (so long as the son, daughter, or other descendant is not married) the head of household does not furnish over half of the support of the descendant. Should maintenance of the household be sufficient, without regard to a dependency test?

B. CONFLICTING THEORIES OF THE PROPER TAXPAYING UNIT

With the exception of married couples, the federal income tax system generally treats each individual as a separate economic unit. This concept has generated a great deal of debate among commentators. The following excerpts from articles by Professors Boris Bittker, Lawrence Zelenak, Marjorie Kornhauser, and Fred Peel present conflicting theories on the proper unit for imposition of the individual income tax.

Professors Bittker and Zelenak note that the shift from what had been primarily an individual taxpaying unit system to a marital taxpaying unit system was made to reconcile differences in treatment of married couples between common law and community property states. Such a change was essential to overcome the effect of *Lucas v. Earl* with respect to earned income. Even under *Lucas v. Earl* it had always been possible for married couples in common law states to transfer their income-producing property to joint ownership and thereby achieve substantially the same tax treatment on separate returns as married couples in community property states with respect to investment income. Moreover, under present law, such interspousal gifts are exempt from gift tax. Both of these articles consider how the joint return rule, fashioned to meet a pragmatic political problem in an earlier generation, will and should fare in the future, given the economic and social changes in American marital and family arrangements.

Professor Kornhauser stresses changing societal definitions of family and questions the appropriateness of treating married couples differently from many other living arrangements. Peel's article argues that rather than overcoming *Lucas v. Earl* by allowing joint return, Congress should legislatively reverse *Poe v. Seaborn* and tax married residents of community property states on their separately earned income.

The proposed Contract with America Tax Relief Act of 1995, excerpted below in the form in which it passed the House of Representatives, provided a tax credit for married couples based on calculations of the difference between the income tax they would pay on their earned incomes as single filers and the tax they would pay on a joint return, using standardized hypothetical facts.

FEDERAL INCOME TAXATION AND THE FAMILY
Boris I. Bittker[*]
27 Stanford Law Review 1389, 1391-99, 1416-20, 1425-26 (1975)

A persistent problem in the theory of income taxation is whether natural persons should be taxed as isolated individuals, or as social beings whose family ties to other taxpayers affect their taxpaying capacity. From its inception, the federal income tax law has permitted every taxpayer to file a personal return, embracing his or her own income but excluding the income of the taxpayer's spouse, children, and other relatives. On the other hand, married couples may elect to consolidate their income on a joint return, many exemptions and deductions take account of family links and responsibilities, and the income or property of one member of a family is sometimes attributed to another member for a variety of tax purposes. The Internal Revenue Code, in brief, is a patchwork, its history being a myriad of compromises fashioned to meet particular problems.

While this tension between rugged individualism and family solidarity permeates the entire Code, four broad questions capture the major themes:
— Should family members—husbands, wives, children, or others—be required, allowed, or forbidden to amalgamate their separate incomes in order to compute a joint tax liability?
— If amalgamation is either permitted or required, what should be the relationship between the tax liability of a family on its amalgamated income and that of a person living outside any family unit on his or her individual income?
— Should the taxpayer—whether an individual or a family entity—receive a tax allowance for supporting children, parents, or other relatives?
— How should the tax law treat transfers, sales, and other financial and property arrangements between family members, and for what tax purposes (if any) should the law attribute the income or property of one family member to another?

The responses of today's law to these questions are, of course, influenced by the need for revenue, by the Internal Revenue Service's capacity to audit returns and enforce the rules, by legislative and administrative efforts to minimize inconsistencies within the statute and regulations, and by other

---

[*]. At time of original publication, Sterling Professor of Law, Yale University.

objectives, constraints, and values that are "internal" to the tax system. But the impact of these factors on Congress, the Treasury, and the public has always depended on a much more influential context—society's assumptions about the role of marriage and the family.

＊ ＊ ＊

The goal of this Essay is to examine the theories and pressures that shaped today's Internal Revenue Code and to suggest how its provisions may fare in the maelstrom of changing social attitudes toward marriage, women's rights, the two-job couple, communal living patterns, birth control, population growth, and intrafamily rights and liabilities. ＊ ＊ ＊

Consolidation of Family Income

Theoretical Considerations

The case for consolidation

By and large, tax theorists have espoused the doctrine "that taxpaying ability is determined by total family income regardless of the distribution of such income among the members of the family," rather than the contrary theory "that family as a unit has no combined taxpaying ability per se; that its taxpaying ability is composed of the separate taxpaying abilities of its individual members; and that the taxpaying ability of each of these is determined by the amount of income of which he or she is the owner without reference to the income of the other members of the family."[2] The philosophy of consolidation was recently championed in an influential report by the Canadian Royal Commission on Taxation. Its legislative proposals in this area were not enacted, but the Commission's statement in favor of consolidating family income is an excellent exposition of the social premises that underlie this position:

> We conclude that the present [Canadian tax] system is lacking in essential fairness between families in similar circumstances and that attempts to prevent abuses of the system have produced serious anomalies and rigidities. Most of these results are inherent in the concept that each individual is a separate taxable entity. Taxation of the individual in almost total disregard for his inevitably close financial and economic ties with the other members of the basic social unit of which he is ordinarily a member, the family, is in our view [a] striking instance of the lack of a comprehensive and rational pattern in the present tax system. In keeping with our general theme that the scope of our tax concepts should be broadened and made more consistent in order to achieve equity, we recommend that the family be treated as a tax unit and taxed on a rate schedule applicable to family units. Individuals who are not members of a family unit would continue to be treated

---

2. Treasury Department, *The Tax Treatment of Family Income, reprinted in Hearings on Revenue Revision Before the House Comm. on Ways & Means*, 80th Cong., 1st Sess., pt. 2, at 851 (1947).

as separate tax units and would be taxed on a schedule applicable to individuals. . . .

We believe firmly that the family is today, as it has been for many centuries, the basic economic unit in society. Although few marriages are entered into for purely financial reasons, as soon as a marriage is contracted it is the continued income and financial position of the family which is ordinarily of primary concern, not the income and financial position of the individual members. * * *

Where the family grows by the addition of children, further important financial and economic decisions are made in the family as a unit. Questions of the extent of education, time of entrance into the labor force and, frequently, choices of a career are decided on a family basis, although of course there are many exceptions to this statement. In some circumstances the income of the child is added to the family income, and, even where this is not done directly, the fact that a child has income of his own will have some bearing on the main family expenditure decisions. Certainly when the child becomes self-supporting he is normally expected to relieve the family of further expenditure on his behalf. * * * [4]

This rationale implies that the tax on a family with a given amount of consolidated income should be the same regardless of the proportion of each spouse's contribution to their total income, and it also suggests, though less clearly, that the ratio of parent-child contributions should be irrelevant. A corollary of this emphasis on the family's consolidated income is that legal ownership of property and income within the family should be disregarded in judging its taxpaying capacity. For at least 50 years, a major theme in the taxation of income from property transferred within the family has been that bedchamber transactions are suspect because the allocation of legal rights within the family is a trivial matter.

But the persons concerned may have a less cavalier attitude toward their legal rights. Taxpayers pass up many opportunities to reduce their taxes by intrafamily gifts, possibly from ignorance or inertia, but perhaps because they attach more significance to their legal rights than academicians assert. The contemporary women's rights movement is a reminder of the long struggle for married women's property laws, whose underlying premise was that the division of legal rights between husband and wife is a significant matter, not a trivial one. * * * Moreover, at least among upper-income taxpayers, it is not uncommon for separate accounts to be maintained for property owned by each spouse at the time of the marriage, inherited thereafter, or accumulated from earnings or household allowances, especially if the household includes children of a prior marriage. It may be, therefore,

---

4. 3 Report of the Royal Commission on Taxation (Carter Commission) 122-24 (1966).

that tax theorists have excessively downgraded the importance of legal rights within the family, and that a swing of the pendulum is in the offing.

Since 1948, however, the Internal Revenue Code has imposed the same liability on all equal-income married couples, whether the combined income is generated by the earnings or investments of one spouse or both and without regard to the division of ownership between them. So long as family harmony prevails, equal-income married couples can purchase equal quantities of goods and services and probably make their economic decisions in a substantially identical fashion. These common characteristics have been regarded by most theorists as more important in fixing the tax liability of equal-income married couples than differences in their ownership of property, even though technical ownership may become crucial if the marriage is dissolved. For this reason, the 1948 statutory principal of equal taxes for equal-income married couples has been "almost universally accepted" by tax theorists, except for suggestions that a two-job married couple should not pay as much as a one-job married couple with the same joint income.

Tax-equality or marriage neutrality?

There is, however, a cloud on the horizon. It is increasingly argued that the income tax on two persons who get married should be neither more nor less than they paid on the same income before marriage. This call for a marriage-neutral tax system stems sometimes from the conviction that the state should neither encourage nor discourage marriage by a tax incentive or penalty, and sometimes from a belief that ceremonial marriages in today's society are not sufficiently different from informal alliances to warrant a difference in tax liability. * * * Proponents of this reform, however, often overlook the fact that, given a progressive rate schedule, a marriage-neutral tax system cannot be reconciled with a regime of equal taxes for equal-income married couples.

This collision of objectives is easily illustrated. If we assume a rate schedule taxing single persons at the rate of 10 percent on the first $10,000 of income and 25 percent on amounts above $10,000, the taxes paid by four unmarried persons on the amount of taxable income set out in Table I would be as shown therein.

If Alpha marries Beta and Theta marries Zeta, and all four continue to earn the same amount of income as before marriage, the consolidated income of each married couple will be $20,000. If their marriage is to have no effect on their tax liabilities, Alpha-Beta should continue to pay a total of $2,000 and Theta-Zeta a total of $2,900 in taxes. But if this difference in their tax burdens is deemed to be unwarranted, and a new rate schedule is prescribed for married couples that will cause Alpha-Beta and Theta-Zeta to pay the same tax since they have the same joint income ($20,000), marriage will either (1) decrease the tax burden for both couples, (2) decrease it for one and

TABLE 1

HYPOTHETICAL INCOME AND TAXES BEFORE MARRIAGE

	Taxable Income	Tax
Alpha	$10,000	$1,000
Beta	10,000	1,000
Theta	4,000	400
Zeta	16,000	2,500

leave the other's unchanged, (3) decrease it for one and increase it for the other, (4) increase it for one and leave the other unchanged, or (5) increase it for both—depending on the rate schedule applicable to married couples.
* * *

In short, we cannot simultaneously have (a) progression, (b) equal taxes on equal-income married couples, and (c) a marriage-neutral tax burden. A corollary of this conclusion is that a tax system with a progressive rate schedule can be marriage-neutral if individual legal rights over income and property are controlling even after marriage and each spouse reports his or her own income, but not if the tax is based on the couples' consolidated income.

For these reasons, advocacy of a marriage-neutral tax system collides directly and irretrievably with a dominant theme of tax theory for at least 50 years—the irrelevance of ownership within intimate family groups. * * *

The income of children

Returning to the Canadian Royal Commission's rational for taxing families on their consolidated income, it will be recalled that the Commission advocated consolidation of the income of children as well as the income of spouses. In a society whose children are expected to work and to contribute their earnings to the family pool without voicing any opinions on the way funds are used, the case for consolidation is strongest. But even in a society that accords more financial independence to children, their earnings affect the economic behavior of the parents; as the children's income grows, the parents are relieved of pressure to support the children currently and to pass on an inheritance to them. The larger the *aggregate* pool of resources, it is argued, the greater the group's capacity to pay taxes.

The theory is not without appeal. But the justification for consolidating family income is not "tax logic," or any other factors peculiar to the tax system, but rather a social phenomenon—more precisely, the observer's perception of social realities. The Canadian Royal Commission itself implicitly acknowledged this by proposing a series of limits to the inclusion of children's income in the family's consolidated tax base. First, consolidation was to be compulsory only if the children were minors or disabled. Other children, whether living with their parents or not, were excluded, except that students between 21 and 25 years of age could elect to have their income included in the family tax base. Moreover, minors over the school-leaving age could elect to be excluded if employed and living apart from their parents. Finally, regardless of a child's age, gifts and bequests received by him (which were to be included in taxable income under another Commission proposal) could be deposited in an "Income Adjustment Account," a quasi-trust device for holding the property intact until the child's departure from the family unit (usually at 21) and taxing the accumulated income to him at that time. This exception to consolidation was evidently confined by the Commission to property acquired by gift or bequest in the belief that such property is more likely to be treated as sacrosanct by the parents than would be the child's personal earnings. If so, we have one more illustration of the pervasive influence of social customs—actual or perceived—on the tax system.

These exceptions to the principle of consolidation acknowledge that children should eventually be regarded as autonomous persons whose tax paying capacity is independent of their parents. * * *

Defining the group whose income is to be consolidated

If income is to be consolidated, the entity subject to this treatment must be defined, *e.g.*, "married couple," "family," "household," etc. Sociologists may find it useful to study groups that engage in joint decisionmaking or that manifest a common interest in the economic well-being of their members, but it would be difficult if not impossible to administer a law that employed such squishy phrases. Any more precise definition, however, will inevitably exclude groups that are only marginally different, so far as relevant economic or social relationships are concerned, from those within the magic circle. If married couples are taxed on their consolidated income, for example, should the same principle extend to a child who supports an aged parent, two sisters who share an apartment, or a divorced parent who lives with an adolescent child? Should a relationship established by blood or marriage be demanded, to the exclusion, for example, of unmarried persons who live together, homosexual companions, and communes?

The most objective boundary lines are those based on legal characteristics such as marital status, obligation to support, or right to inherit. Under existing law, the principal determinant of the tax burden is marriage, a status that is usually unambiguous. In a society that increasingly questions the legitimacy of traditional legal distinctions, however, one is tempted to substitute social "realities" in defining the boundaries of the group whose income is to be consolidated. But every departure from readily established definitional lines increases the problem of enforcement. If the tax on two unmarried persons depends on whether they live together, for example, how is their status to be verified by the

Internal Revenue Service without an intolerable intrusion into their private lives?[16] * * *

Relative Tax Burdens of Married Couples and Other Taxpayers

The Problem Emerges

The congressional committee reports recommending enactment of the 1948 joint return argued at length that all equal-income married couples should pay the same amount of income taxes, but said nothing about the relationship of that burden to the tax burden on other taxpayers. It is easy to account for this silence. An unspoken premise of the 1948 legislative debate was that married couples in the community property states were not to be subjected to a tax increase; the bruising political fight of 1941, ending in the defeat of two proposals that would have produced such an increase, was still fresh in mind. Given this constraint, Congress was led almost irresistibly to extend the tax advantages of the community property system to married taxpayers in other states. If these taxpayers were to be equalized with community property couples, and the latter were not to be stripped of their historic privilege of paying the same tax as two unmarried taxpayers each with one-half their combined income, the relationship between the tax liability of married couples and that of unmarried taxpayers was predetermined; no discussion seemed necessary.

Once enacted, however, income splitting for married couples came to be seen as a tax allowance for family responsibilities. So viewed, it was assailed as unfair by taxpayers with similar family responsibilities, such as unmarried persons with dependent children or parents, who argued that their taxpaying capacity was no greater than that of a married couple with the same amount of income. To be sure, anyone supporting a dependent was entitled to an exemption, but this allowance ($600 per dependent, under 1948 law) was far less generous than the special rate schedule applicable to married couples filing joint returns.

Acknowledging merit in this complaint, in 1951 Congress prescribed a special head of household ("HOH") rate schedule for an unmarried person maintaining his home as the principal place of abode for a dependent or for a child (or other descendent) even if not a dependent. The new schedule for HOH returns produced a tax liability for a given amount that was midway between the liability of a single person and that of a married couple filing a joint return.

---

16. In Sweden, we are told, the social and legal lines between marriage and informal cohabitation have become quite hazy, but unmarried persons who live together are treated as a tax unit only if they were previously married (in which event the dissolution of their marriage is a suspect "tax divorce") or have borne children. *See* Sundberg, *Marriage or No Marriage: The Directives for the Revision of Swedish Family Law*, 20 INT'L & COMP. L.J. 223 (1971). To aid the enforcement of these provisions, Swedish taxpayers must state annually in their tax returns whether they are living with another person. *See id.* at 223.

Thus, the rate concession to heads of households was only half a loaf, when compared with the tax advantage of the joint return. But the Code does not require HOH taxpayers to amalgamate their income with the income of their fellow householders, and this sometimes enables a two-person household to pay less than a married couple with the same aggregate income. But if the head of household is the only breadwinner, the HOH tax liability is heavier than the tax on a married couple, even if their income and family expenses are identical.

The 1951 reform was reexamined by Congress only 3 years after its enactment. In 1954, the House proposed to extend the full benefit of income splitting to any "head of family," a new concept that was broader in some respect and narrower in others than the term "head of household" as defined by the 1951 legislation. * * *

The Senate Finance Committee recommended a rejection of the House proposal, because it "did not treat all income groups equally and benefits primarily the middle- and upper-income groups."[88] When the bill went to conference, the dispute between the House and the Senate was compromised by expanding the existing HOH provisions to embrace a dependent parent, even if that parent were living separately from the taxpayer, and by according full benefits of income splitting to a "surviving spouse" (defined as a widow or widower whose home is the principal place of abode for a dependent child) for two taxable years after the spouse's death.

The HOH and surviving spouse provisions of 1951 and 1954 responded to the complaint of unmarried taxpayers with dependents that their family responsibilities were comparable to those of married couples. But the provisions did not question—indeed, they implicitly ratified—the tax differential established in 1948 between a married couple and a single person with the same income. * * *

The Insoluble Dilemmas

Some tax theorists have been unable to locate a justification for these differentials. They see income splitting of the 1948 variety as a "subsidy" for getting married and, since the benefits rise with the couple's income, as an "erosion" of the progressive rate structure—even as a "loophole." These pejorative labels imply that the separate rate schedule for married couples is an unjustified departure from a generally accepted standard. What, then, is the "proper" relationship between the tax rates on joint and individual income?

In offering answers to this question, tax theorists have customarily pointed to the following differences between the economic status of single persons without family responsibilities and married couples with the same amount of income, but without agreeing on the weight or even on the relevance of all of these characteristics:

---

88. S. REP. No. 1622, 83d Cong., 2d Sess. 5 (1954).

1. The income of a married couple must support two persons, not one.

2. As compared with two single persons, a married couple benefits from economies of scale—a single kitchen will suffice, for example, and their food can be purchased in larger quantities.

3. If only one spouse is employed, the married couple enjoys the untaxed housework performed by the other spouse.[d]

This summary of differences compares single persons who live alone and have no dependents with one-job married couples. As will be seen there is ample room for disagreement about the relative tax burdens that should be borne by these two polar cases. But, alas, these are neither the only, nor necessarily the most significant, actual living patterns of American taxpayers. Attention must also be given to single persons who support children or other dependents, whether in their own homes or elsewhere, unmarried persons who share the expenses of a single household, two-job married couples, and taxpayers with still other arrangements. Unfortunately, when the debate is enriched by these complexities, the already divergent pathways to reform dissolve into a skein of competing trails.

* * *

MARRIAGE AND THE INCOME TAX
Lawrence Zelenak[*]

67 Southern California Law Review 339, 339, 342-48, 353-66,

368-69, 380-84, 390-93, 404-05 (1994)

Introduction

The federal income tax treats a married couple as a single economic unit. Spouses report their combined income on a joint return, and calculate their tax liability based on that combined income.[2] Married couples will often have a tax liability different from the combined tax liabilities the spouses would have if single. These differences are called marriage penalties and marriage bonuses.

* * *

---

d. The tax treatment of imputed income of housewives is discussed in Chapter Three. (Eds.)

*. At time of original publication, Reef C. Ivey Research Professor of Law, University of North Carolina.

2. Spouses do have the option of filing separate returns, under I.R.C. § 1(d), but the tax rates are designed so that the combined separate-return tax liabilities will be at least as great as their joint-return liability. Separate returns may result in lower total tax liability, however, in the unusual situation where the use of separate returns reduces total taxable income reportable by the couple. This occurs when an expense is incurred by one spouse, and the expense is deductible only to the extent that it exceeds some specified percentage of adjusted gross income. Examples include miscellaneous itemized deductions, I.R.C. § 67(a); casualty losses, I.R.C. § 165(h)(2); and medical expenses, I.R.C. § 213(a). Separate returns can reduce the percentage floor, thus increasing the amount of the deduction and decreasing taxable income. Even then, however, the separate-return advantage of reducing taxable income may be more than offset by the disadvantage of higher rates.

The only way to avoid both marriage bonuses and penalties is to abandon marital status as a tax determinant and to require that spouses file separate returns. However, this would mean that different couples with the same combined incomes, but different income distributions between husband and wife, would be taxed differently. * * *

The Uneasy Case for Joint Returns

* * *

A Historical Review

From its inception in 1913 until 1948, the income tax treated spouses as two separate taxpayers. * * *

In the years following [*Lucas v. Earl* and *Poe v. Seaborn*], a number of separate property states rejected centuries of tradition and adopted community property systems, thus entitling their inhabitants to the benefit of *Poe v. Seaborn*. * * * Husbands in separate property states attempted self-help income splitting, through both gifts of property and by making their wives business partners. This led to controversy and confusion regarding when a husband had given up sufficient control over property to make his wife the tax owner and when family partnerships would be respected for tax purposes. Eventually, in 1948 Congress provided for automatic income splitting between spouses as a matter of federal income tax law. Under the new system, a married couple would have the same tax liability as two single persons, each with half of the couple's income. This automatic perfect income splitting made state marital property law irrelevant, and all the states which had adopted community property after 1930 quickly recanted.

* * *

Rather than being based on bedrock beliefs about the nature of marital sharing, the 1948 legislation was essentially a historical accident—a response to the geographic discrimination and legal confusion resulting from the combination of *Lucas v. Earl* and *Poe v. Seaborn*. If *Seaborn* had not permitted income splitting in community property states, there is no indication that Congress would ever have decided to treat a married couple as a taxable unit.

* * *

After 1948, tax scholars sought a more compelling justification for joint returns than the accident of *Poe v. Seaborn*, and developed theories based on pooling. At best, however, these are after-the-fact justifications for what Congress had done, not explanations for why Congress had done it.

* * *

It is possible, of course, that the joint spousal return is a lovely child, despite its accidental conception. * * * It is still necessary to consider the evidence concerning marital pooling and its relevance to tax policy.

Do Spouses Pool Their Income?

There has been remarkably little empirical research into the income-sharing patterns of married couples. Indeed, a leading scholarly defense of joint returns took it as self-evident that "married couples should be assumed to share their income equally,"[35] and cited no supporting research. * * *

It might be nice if there were more studies of marital pooling beliefs and practices, but whether the focus is on attitudes, reported behavior, or income and expenditure patterns, the evidence of pooled marital income consumption is quite strong. * * *

Shared Consumption or Shared Control?

Given the need for a workable bright-line test, joint returns for married couples (and only for married couples) is the right answer—if the existence of shared consumption is the right question. But *is* that the right question? Proponents of joint returns say it is. * * *

Except for joint returns, the federal income tax *does* determine tax liability according to who controls income, by earning it or by owning the income-producing property. This is the lesson of *Lucas v. Earl* itself, which remains fundamental law outside of the joint-return context.[75] An important application of this rule is the income tax treatment of gifts and bequests as neither taxable to the donee nor deductible by the donor. This treatment separates the income tax liability on the income used to acquire the gifted property (which was imposed on the donor, and which is not shifted by the gift) from the ability to consume (which was transferred to the donee).

Even within the nuclear family, consumption is not treated as the test for taxability *except for married couples*. If shared consumption and a shared standard of living were the key, the taxable unit would be the entire family, including minor children. Except for substantial amounts of unearned income of children under age fourteen, however, the income of children is not aggregated with parental income by the income tax.[77] In keeping with this focus on control rather than consumption, amounts spent to support a child are not deductible by the parent and not taxable to the child.

There is considerable evidence that control over marital income—the power to decide how the income shall be used—is much less shared than the consumption of the income. The spouse who earns the income tends to retain control over how the money is used, even if that spouse's decision results in shared consumption. The higher-earning spouse typically decides whether

---

35. Michael J. McIntyre & Oliver Oldman, *Taxation of the Family in a Comprehensive and Simplified Income Tax*, 90 HARV. L. REV. 1573 (1977), note 13, at 1578.

75. 281 U.S. 111 (1930). The analogous case with respect to income from property is Helvering v. Horst, 311 U.S. 112 (1940).

77. I.R.C. § 1(g) (West Supp.1993), the "kiddie tax," taxes the unearned income of a child under 14, in excess of $1,000 (adjusted for inflation), at the parents' marginal tax rate. For a proposal to treat the family as the taxable unit, see Martin J. McMahon, Jr., *Expanding the Taxable Unit: The Aggregation of the Income of Children and Parents*, 56 N.Y.U L. REV. 60 (1981). Family unit taxation has long been used in France. The French system is described in Louise Dulude, *Taxation of the Spouses: A Comparison of Canadian, American, British, French and Swedish Law*, 23 OSGOODE HALL L.J. 67, 71-73 (1985).

the couple will live frugally or extravagantly, and what its extravagances will be.

* * *

Despite the evidence that consumption decisions are much less shared than the consumption itself, the point may be too controversial with the general public to serve as a basis for tax policy. * * * It is not necessary, however, to reach any decision about * * * the distribution of marital decision-making power * * * in order to apply basic income tax principles to the taxation of spouses. The basic principles are very simple. Earned income is taxed to the earner, and property income is taxed to the owner. The law normally looks no further into questions of power than that, and reasonably so. * * *

If, then, the focus is on consumption of income, a joint-return system is appropriate. If the focus is on control, separate returns are called for. The choice of focus depends on whether consumption or control is a better measure of ability to pay. Ability to pay is crucial because the choice of a taxable unit matters only under a progressive tax system, and progressivity is based on the premise that ability to pay increases more than proportionately with income.

* * *

Refereeing the Battle of the Neutralities

* * *

It might be objected that since we do not have a separate-return system, we cannot know how strong the popular objections would be to such a system. That is not entirely true, however, for three reasons. First, there is the pre-1948 experience with an income tax based on separate returns. The only equity-based complaints with that system concerned the geographic discrimination created by *Poe v. Seaborn* in the taxation of the earnings of *husbands*. There is no indication of any objection to the unequal taxation of one-earner and two-earner couples with equal combined incomes. Second, there is the more recent experience with the two-earner deduction. From 1981 to 1986 the law allowed a deduction of 10% of the earned income of the lower earning spouse (with the deduction not to exceed $3,000). The deduction alleviated, but did not eliminate, the marriage penalty. In so doing, the deduction violated the principle of equal tax on equal income couples. A two-earner couple with two $30,000 earned incomes would have $3,000 less taxable income than a $60,000 one-earner couple.[99] There was no resulting outcry from angry single-earner couples. When the deduction was repealed in 1986, the official explanation was that the reduced progressivity of the rate schedules reduced marriage penalties to the point where

---

99. Because taxes were still determined on a joint-return basis, from 1981 to 1986 the tax system violated both couples neutrality *and* marriage neutrality.

additional relief was not needed. Discrimination against one-earner couples was *not* cited as a reason for change.

Finally, and most significantly, there has been no public outcry against the separate taxation of spouses under the social security wage tax. Under this tax each person, regardless of marital status, pays tax at a flat rate of 7.65% on the first $57,000 of earnings. This means that a two-earner couple may pay much more social security tax than an equal-income one-earner couple. * * * This separate-taxpayer system is not an administrative necessity. Nor is it explicable on the grounds that the social security tax has some features of a retirement savings plan, rather than a pure tax, because marital status *is* relevant in determining eligibility for retirement benefits. Thus, the relationship to benefits suggests the couple *should* be the taxable unit.

* * *

I can only speculate why the non-neutrality inherent in joint returns (marriage penalties and bonuses) bothers people so much more than the non-neutrality inherent in separate returns (different taxes on equal-income couples), but I do have some ideas. First, I suspect that people find marriage neutrality the more compelling of the two principles. They simply believe that it is more important for the tax system not to encourage or discourage marriage (especially the latter) than it is for equal-income couples to pay equal taxes. Second, I think people are more aware of marriage penalties and bonuses than they are of whether equal-income couples are paying equal taxes. Marriage penalties and bonuses can be determined without reference to any other taxpayers. When you get married (or contemplate marriage), you see the penalty (or bonus) without the need to compare yourself to anyone else; so too when you get divorced or contemplate divorce. * * *

There may be another reason why victims of the marriage penalty do not accept the explanation of the need to impose equal tax on equal-income couples (couples neutrality). They may realize that the couples neutrality justification fails even on its own terms, because one- and two-earner couples with equal taxable income are generally not equal in taxpaying ability. The one-earner couple is significantly better off because of its greater imputed income from self-performed services and its lesser nondeductible work-related expenses (such as for clothing and commuting). * * *

The Behavioral Effects of Joint Returns

The discussion thus far has concentrated on equity concerns— whether separate returns would be fairer than joint returns. It turns now to behavioral concerns—whether the joint-return system inappropriately encourages or discourages certain behaviors. If, for example, the system taxes a two-earner married couple more heavily than two single persons with the same incomes, the issue is fairness. If the greater tax burden causes a two-earner couple not to marry (or to obtain a divorce), the issue is behavioral effects. McCaffery criticizes most of the literature on the taxation of spouses for its "focus on static, distributive concerns of what groups pay how much tax," rather than on the behavioral incentives created by the tax rules.[112] The two major behavioral effects are on decisions whether to marry and on wives' decisions whether to work.

The Decision to Marry

Since a man and woman who both work full time will usually pay more tax as a married couple than as singles, the tax laws could discourage such people from marrying (or encourage them to divorce).[113] * * * In the absence of good evidence, it seems likely that the behavioral effect is significant in only two situations.

First, since marital filing status for an entire year depends on whether the marriage exists as of December 31, some couples may delay a marriage from December to January for tax purposes. Even if this effect exists, it is not particularly troubling.

Second, McCaffery suggests that the behavioral effect may be significant on lower income couples, because the marriage penalty at lower income levels is especially severe, and because "legally-sanctioned marriages might be most sensitive to economic conditions" at lower income levels.[117] The special severity is due to the phaseout of the earned income credit, which has the effect of increasing the marginal tax rate over the phaseout range. The marriage penalty created by the credit phaseout is worse than the penalty created by the basic rate structure, because the phaseout range and rate are identical for married and single persons. It is thus the equivalent of a joint filing system with the same rate schedules for marrieds and singles, which creates severe marriage penalties and no marriage bonuses. * * *

Despite these two special situations, widespread effects of the tax laws on decisions to marry are unproven. * * * Equity is, of course, an important tax policy consideration. A two-earner couple that says, "We're not going to get divorced because of the marriage penalty, but we're mad as hell," has a serious complaint, but the complaint is not behaviorally based.

Wives' Decisions to Work

Work Disincentives Caused by Joint Returns

The more serious behavioral concern is the effect of the joint-return system on wives' decisions whether to enter the labor force. If a couple views the wife as the marginal wage earner (in the sense that the husband's job is a given, and the decision to be made is whether the wife should also take a job), then the effect of joint returns is to stack the wife's income on top of the husband's. This means that the first dollar of the wife's earnings will be

---

112. Edward J. McCaffery, *Taxation and the Family: A Fresh Look at Behavioral Gender Biases*, 40 UCLA L. REV. 983, 992 (1993).

113. It is also possible that in situations where marriage would reduce tax liability, because one person has high income and the other little or no income, the tax system may induce some marriages which would not otherwise occur.

117. McCaffery, *supra* note 112, at 1016.

taxed at a high marginal rate—possibly as high as 39.6% under current law, and frequently 28% or higher.[123] This contrasts sharply with the initial tax rates the wife would face under a separate-return system: 0% on the income sheltered by her personal exemption and the standard deduction, and 15% after that.

Many commentators have argued that this stacking effect of joint returns inappropriately discourages women from working. McCaffery's statement of this position is the most recent, and is especially powerful. He notes the strong evidence for the high labor-supply elasticity of married women.[125] That is, wives' decisions whether to work are highly sensitive to their after-tax wages—much more so than the work decisions of husbands and unmarried men and women. Thus the decrease in after-tax wages caused by joint return income-stacking is a significant work deterrent for married women. McCaffery criticizes this result from two perspectives.

The first perspective is that of optimal tax theory. Any tax will discourage the activity subject to tax. If the taxed activity is economically beneficial, the disincentive effect of the tax is inefficient. Optimal tax theory considers how best to limit this inefficiency—how to raise a given amount of revenue with the least possible disincentive effect. The answer is that activities should be taxed in inverse relation to their elasticities. The heaviest taxes should be imposed on activities least sensitive to tax. To an optimal tax theorist, the joint-return system gets things exactly backwards—the first dollars earned by hard-to-discourage husbands are taxed at low rates, and the first dollars earned by easy-to-discourage wives are taxed at high rates.

* * *

Separate returns, although not the optimal optimal tax solution, would be a great improvement over current law in optimal tax terms, and a great improvement over favoritism for wives on fairness grounds. Separate returns would present a married woman with low marginal rates in making the initial decision to participate in the labor force; higher rates would apply when the question is whether to work more or less (rather than whether to work at all) and elasticity decreases. If this is not perfect in optimal tax terms, it is at least good. On the equity side, separate returns are not merely acceptable in terms of fairness; if my earlier analysis is right separate returns will be perceived as much fairer than current law (let alone a tax designed by an optimal tax proponent).

* * *

Designing a Separate-Return System

If spouses are required to file separate returns there must be rules for determining how income (especially property income), deductions, and credits

---

123. Even if the I.R.C. § 1(a) rate schedule indicates the marginal rate is 15%, the true rate will be much higher if the phaseout of the earned income credit is in effect.

125. McCaffery, *supra* note 112, at 1039 n.211 (citing studies).

are allocated between the spouses. For the most part, advocates of separate returns have given scant consideration to these design issues. These issues deserve more consideration than they have received, for two reasons. First, however strong the theoretical case for a separate-return system, the system will be accepted only if fair and workable solutions to the allocation problems can be developed. Second, thinking through the allocation problems affords a good test of the theoretical arguments for separate returns. The allocation problems are not merely practical; they are difficult precisely because there *is* a great deal of marital pooling. Problems of abuse of and disrespect for the tax system arise when behavior of little or no non-tax significance is accorded tax significance. If couples that pool resources consider who owns property or who incurs expenses of no non-tax significance, but the tax system treats those factors as determinative, there will be problems: There will be opportunities for some to manipulate the system and pitfalls for others.

These allocation problems are, in fact, the strongest argument in favor of retaining the joint-return system. * * * [T]his one advantage of joint returns is not enough to overcome the superiority of separate returns in other respects. In addition, a separate-return system avoids one practical problem inherent in joint returns: the need to determine marital status for federal income tax purposes. This determination can be surprisingly difficult in some situations. * * *

Allocation of Earned Income

Taxing earned income to the earner is at the core of the justification for separate returns—both in terms of imposing the tax on the person in control of the income source and in terms of removing the second-earner disincentive of current law. Thus a separate-return system should retain *Earl* and reject *Seaborn*.

In the vast majority of cases there is no question as to which spouse earned a particular item of income, so taxation to the earner will involve neither complexity nor opportunity for abuse. In family businesses, however, there will be some incentive for artificial allocations of earned income to spouses (typically wives). This was also an issue under pre-1948 law, which was addressed by family partnership litigation. It remains an issue today because of the potential for splitting income with family members other than spouses.[208] It does not appear to be a major problem, however. Stanley Surrey opined in 1948 that the courts were "doing a respectable job in separating the wheat from the chaff in this field,"[209] and the area has not been heavily litigated in recent years.
* * *

---

208. In 1951 Congress entered this area by enacting the predecessor of current I.R.C. § 704(e), concerning family partnerships. The focus of the provision, however, is on the taxation of income generated by capital, rather than by services.

209. Stanley S. Surrey, *Federal Taxation of the Family—The Revenue Act of 1948*, 61 HARV. L. REV. 1097, 1111 (1948).

Allocation of Income from Property

The allocation of property income is less important than the allocation of earned income, because there is much less of it and because the most important behavioral effect is on earned income. It is a more difficult problem, however, because there is more opportunity to manipulate a rule that taxes property income to the owner than there is to abuse a rule that taxes earned income to the owner.

There are five important options for the treatment of property income. (1) Tax the income to the owner of the property. This is the general income tax rule. (2) Tax the income according to ownership, except do not give tax effect to interspousal transfers of property. Under this approach, if a husband gave property to his wife, he would continue to be taxed on the income from the property (or any replacement property). (3) Allocate all property income to the higher-earning spouse. (4) Allocate property income between the spouses in proportion to their earned incomes. (5) Allocate property income equally between the spouses.

        * * *

On balance, I find the first option most attractive. It is the only option that achieves true marriage neutrality and thus is fully consistent with the underlying premise of separate returns. The control that goes with ownership has sufficient economic reality to justify respecting ownership for tax purposes, even as between spouses. Although I would not adopt a rule for the purpose of encouraging gifts to non-earning wives, I am happy to accept that encouragement as a side effect. On the other hand, the first option does have a few drawbacks. It places a heavy premium on careful tax planning, it is more complicated to administer than an automatic allocation rule, and it reintroduces a significant work disincentive when the husband has made major gifts to the wife.

I think these drawbacks are tolerable, but someone more troubled by these drawbacks would select the third option (all property income taxed to the higher-earning spouse). It eliminates tax planning concerning property ownership, it is simple to administer, and it creates no work disincentive for the wife. * * *

Allocations of Deductions and Credits

The obvious rule for deductions and credits associated with the production of income (either earned or from property) is to allocate those items to the spouse reporting the related income. It is not obvious, however, how personal deductions and credits (not associated with taxable income) should be allocated between spouses. The possible rules for allocating deductions and credits between spouses are similar to the choices for allocating property income. The important options are: (1) Allocate items to the spouse who incurred the deductible or creditable expense. Thus, for example, medical expenses would be deductible by the treated spouse, state and local taxes would be deductible by the spouse (or spouses) liable for the taxes, and home mortgage interest would be deductible by the debtor spouse (or spouses). Charitable contributions, which do not ordinarily involve the incurring of a liability, would be deductible by the spouse making the payment. (2) Allocate all items to the spouse making the payment, regardless of who incurred the liability. (3) Allocate items according to some formula, without regard to either liability or payment. Possible formulas include allocating items 100% to the higher income spouse, allocating items evenly between spouses, or allocating items in proportion to income.

Only the first option is truly marriage neutral. * * *

There is a serious practical problem, however, with the first option: the possibility that deductions will be lost because the spouse incurring the expense does not have enough income to use the deduction. * * *

Congress may decide that the occasional lost deduction is a price worth paying for marriage neutrality and adopt the first option in its pure form. But consider the likely behavioral effect of that rule, as applied to the home mortgage interest deduction and the property tax deduction. In order to ensure that the deductions were not wasted, one-earner couples would hold their homes (and other assets subject to property tax) solely in the name of the earner spouse. Just as marriage neutral treatment of income-producing property works to the benefit of traditional wives, marriage neutral treatment of deduction-producing property works to the detriment of traditional wives. For the many couples whose most important asset is their home, the detrimental effect on the deduction side is more significant than the beneficial effect on the income side. Although I do not think it is the duty of the federal income tax to encourage transfers of property to non-earning spouses, a rule that actively discourages home (and other asset) ownership by married women is unacceptable.

What, then, of the other options? The second option (allocation of deductions based on payment) would put a tremendous premium on tax planning, and would be almost impossible to enforce. A formula allocation rule is clearly preferable. Among the possible formulas, I would reject a fifty-fifty rule, because it has one of the same problems as the first option: It creates the possibility that one spouse will not have enough income to use the allocated deductions. This problem could be avoided by allocating deductions between spouses in proportion to their incomes. It could also be avoided by the most taxpayer-favorable of all possible rules: Allocate deductions entirely to the higher income spouse until the deductions have equalized taxable incomes, and after that allocate deductions evenly between the spouses.

Either allocation in proportion to income or taxpayer-favorable allocation is a reasonable choice for deductions not associated with the production of income. I would combine one of these rules with allocation of income-related expenses to the spouse taxable on the income.

* * *

Conclusion

There is no absolutely right or wrong way to tax married couples. A system that is right for one time and place may be wrong for another. Whatever the merits of joint returns may have been for mid-twentieth century America, the joint-return system fits poorly with American attitudes and living patterns at the close of the century. The difficult question is when the dissatisfaction will become so great as to overcome the inertia of present law. The answer will depend partly on developments external to the tax system—the evolution of social attitudes and behaviors. It may also depend, however, on the degree of progressivity of the income tax: The more progressive the tax, the larger the marriage penalties and the greater the discouragement of working wives. Increases in the progressivity of the tax will hasten the demise of joint returns. But assuming an income tax with any significant amount of progressivity, the joint return will eventually disappear—the only question is when.

LOVE, MONEY, AND THE IRS: FAMILY, INCOME-SHARING, AND THE JOINT INCOME TAX RETURN
Marjorie E. Kornhauser[*]
45 Hastings Law Journal 63, 63-77, 92-105 (1993)

While tax theorists have debated the appropriateness of the joint return, they have not examined the premise behind the joint return: that married people—and only married people—share not only their hopes and dreams, but also their money.

This Article explores the premise that married couples share or pool their income. It surveys the changing concept and reality of "family." * * * This focus on "pooling" sheds new light on the more commonly asked questions about the joint return: Does it comport with theoretical concepts of income? Does it promote family values? Should it (and the tax system generally) promote family values? Is it justified by other concerns such as economic ones?

Many people believe that the joint return in necessary because it promotes family values. To the extent that the return does so, it does so poorly. The joint return discriminates against many groups that provide their members with the same values of responsibility, caring, sharing, and support that traditional families provide. Moreover, contrary to popular myth, the joint return harms many traditional families, as was highlighted by the debates on the 1993 tax law. Under the new marginal rates, two single individuals living together who each earn $115,000 would pay $4,500 less tax than two married individuals earning the same amounts. By "penalizing" the second worker, the joint return discourages married couples

---

*. At time of original publication, Professor of Law, Tulane School of Law.

from having a second earner (usually the wife), putting both psychological and economic stress on these families, on the wife in particular.

* * *

What is a Family?

As Martha Minow has rightly observed, "The tension between official legal forms and functional families has created issues for centuries."[8] Today those tensions are greater than ever due to rapid changes in society. Minow was primarily concerned with new scientific technology enabling procreation to occur in a variety of unconventional ways. Other changes, however, have affected living arrangements dramatically and increased tension between legal forms of families and functional families. For example, longer life-spans have resulted in a greater population of elderly, many of whom live together as economic units. In the past few decades women's employment opportunities have expanded, in turn affecting their choice of living arrangements and their roles within the family. The current state of the economy requires that more families have two earners for the family to achieve an acceptable living standard. Finally, standards of morality have shifted, removing much of the stigma attached to the cohabitation of unmarried heterosexual couples and to homosexual couples.

The major demographic changes of the past thirty years—declining fertility, rising divorce rates, increasing rates of out-of-wedlock births, aging population—have caused the decline of the traditional nuclear family and an increase in the number of divorces, single-parent families, nonmarried cohabitation, and two-earner families. Nonmarital households in the United States increased nearly 400 percent from 1970 to March 1991.[12] The rapid rise in nontraditional living arrangements calls into question assumptions about patterns of sharing resources, as well as the concept of family itself.

* * *

The household concept encompasses people who physically live together, but who may not be an economic unit because they do not pool resources. Thus, roommates may count as one household for census purposes, but may only share the rent on the apartment. In contrast, two or more people may live together and share all expenses. People may live together either in a platonic or intimate sexual relationship, or they may live in a religious community or a hippie commune. In each situation people can and do share resources. These people functioning as one economic unit must be examined in discussing the taxable unit. However, people may function as an economic unit even if they do not live in the same house. Children may support their

---

8. Martha Minow, *Redefining Families: Who's In and Who's Out?*, 62 U. COLO. L. REV. 269, 270 (1991).

12. U.S. BUREAU OF THE CENSUS, STATISTICAL ABSTRACT OF THE UNITED STATES tbl. 56 (112th ed. 1992). There were 1,094,000 nonfamily households in 1970 and 4,440,000 in March 1991. In 1988, nonfamily households comprised 4.4% of total households, but only 1.7% in 1970.

parents and vice versa. Nonrelated men and women also can support each other.

Flawed as they are, the statistics indicate the decline of the traditional, one-earner nuclear family on which both the joint return and the married couple as taxable unit are based. * * *

If commitment is key, then sexual cohabitation and gender of partners is irrelevant. For instance, two same-sex adults, one adult and her children, or three adult siblings can comprise a family unit.

* * * The commitment definition of family is well suited for the purpose of determining a taxable unit on economic grounds because it is based on functions such as sharing resources, rather than on arguably irrelevant factors such as legal status or bloodlines. Some courts have applied this functional approach to expand the concept of family.

The main problem with such a functional approach is uncertainty. * * * Moreover, as Martha Minow suggests, a functional approach may lead to abuse of the system by those who wish to be treated as a married couple for some but not all purposes. Finally, basing tax liability on a functional approach invites administrative complexity. * * *

Although documentation of pooling involves some administrative complexity, the expanding existence of alternative relationships underscores the growing under-inclusiveness of allowing only marital units to file joint returns.

* * *

Different theories underlie the two basic types of taxable units. If the tax unit is the individual, then tax-paying ability is based solely on each individual's earnings and on income produced by property titled in her name. This position holds that only individuals, not groups, have tax-paying capacity. The contrasting theory holds that the family is the taxable unit since the family, not the individual, is the basic economic unit within which financial resources are shared, regardless of the source of the wage or investment income.

* * *

The justifications for treating the marital unit as the appropriate tax unit are economic unity, marital obligations, and economies of scale.

Economic Unity

The first and most important justification is economic unity. Traditionally, society views a marriage as an economic unit in which the members share the economic resources. * * * There are several criticisms of this justification. First, people other than married couples pool income. This criticism accepts the economic unit theory, but holds that the marital unit is only one type of economic unit. To single it out for special tax treatment is unjust. A fairer approach would be to treat all households or families as economic units, although such an approach has its own problems, such as defining "household" and "family."

Second, some critics attack the underlying assumption of pooling that couples always share income. For example, taxpayers ignore many opportunities to lower their taxes by means of intra-family gifts, not simply because of ignorance or inertia, but possibly because they attach significance to legal title.

Third, the women's rights movement undermines the pooling justification by emphasizing women's increasing access to economic independence as yet another indication that title is significant. More importantly, feminist theory undercuts the very premise that the family is an economic unit. * * *

Finally, the pooling rationale is criticized because it focuses on income consumption, which is more appropriate for a consumption-based tax than an income tax that measures accessions to wealth. * * *

Marital Obligations

Another justification for treating a married couple as a taxable unit is that marriage alters an individual's rights and obligations, thereby justifying treating a married couple as one taxable unit. Critics note, however, that individuals other than spouses have a legal obligation of support, and question why these people are treated differently than spouses. Moreover, spousal support obligations can be viewed as voluntary decisions that should be treated no differently than other voluntary decisions to consume. The rejoinder is that the decision to marry differs greatly from other decisions, such as whether to take a trip or eat a peach.

Economies of Scale

A final justification for treating the married couple as a taxable unit is that economies of scale that result from living together need to be taken into account. * * * Again, the critics reply that people other than two married people live together and share resources. It is inequitable to treat them differently. Moreover, economies of scale are too varied and difficult to measure.

The Dilemma of the Current Situation

* * *

Not only is our present treatment of the taxable unit inconsistent and inaccurate, but it is based on outdated, unexamined premises. In 1948, when the joint return was established, certain assumptions prompted creation of the joint return as a response to perceived inadequacies in the system. First was the assumption that spouses pooled all their resources regardless of who earned or owned them. The second assumption was that sharing of income automatically meant that control of the income was also shared. Finally, the joint return, in order to be helpful to married couples, assumed a "traditional" marriage in which there was only one earner in each family. In today's world, these assumptions are no longer tenable.

Even in 1948 these assumptions were not entirely accurate. If all income were jointly shared, then why had all states not switched to a community property system? Carolyn Jones presents evidence that many states rejected community property laws precisely because they gave rights to spouses who had not earned the income. Nevertheless, pooling of income, at least at the lower levels of income, was generally assumed despite a general absence of empirical evidence to support it. The second assumption concerning equal control, a prerequisite to taxability under general tax principles, lacked universality. The final assumption of one-earner couples also was not uniformly true: In April 1948, 23.1% of all married women participated in the labor force.

These discrepancies are even greater today than they were in 1948. First, many more nonlegal families exist. To the extent that these families are treated differently from married couples, such treatment is inequitable. Furthermore, while the partnership model of marriage may be more true today from a legal standpoint than it was in 1948, pooling, which is a concomitant of the partnership model, is far from universal. Legally, even the community property system still does not require complete joint management and control.

                    * * *

AN APPROACH TO INCOME TAX SIMPLIFICATION
Fred W. Peel, Jr.[*]

1 University of Arkansas at Little Rock Law Journal 1, 17 (1978)

Further simplification could be achieved if Congress would be willing to impose the tax without regard to the assignment of income imposed by statute in the community property states.[104] This would have the additional advantage of solving the nagging problems of tax rate discrimination against unmarried individuals and against married couples when both husband and wife have substantial income. In other words, earned income could be taxed to the spouse who earns it in community property states as well as in common law states (as is already done in the case of the tax on self-employment income)[105] and the spouse who owns an investment could be taxed on the investment income. Married couples in community property states would have some advantage over those in common law states under such a system because of the splitting of investment income from community property, but couples in common law states could be permitted to redress the balance by equalizing their ownership of investment assets by interspousal gifts. Joint returns still could be permitted as a convenience to married

---

[*]. At time of original publication, Professor of Law, University of Arkansas at Little Rock.

104. Poe v. Seaborn, 282 U.S. 101 (1930), holding that the Revenue Act of 1926 did not tax all income to the spouse who earned it in a community property state, involved a question of statutory construction. The Court did not hold that it would be unconstitutional to tax income to the earner before it became property of the marital community. *Cf.* Lucas v. Earl, 281 U.S. 111 (1930).

105. I.R.C. § 1402(a)(5).

taxpayers, but they would be practical only in cases where combining the incomes would not result in a higher marginal tax rate.

* * *

H.R. 1215, THE CONTRACT WITH AMERICA TAX RELIEF ACT OF 1995

House Report No. 84, 104th Cong., 1st Sess., at 13-14 (1995)

Reasons for Change

The Committee is concerned about the inequity of the marriage penalty and the potential work disincentive it causes. As the first step in response to these problems, the Committee believes it is appropriate to allow a credit to married couples who suffer a marriage penalty.

Any attempt to eliminate the marriage penalty involves the balancing of several competing principles, including equal tax treatment of married couples with equal incomes and the determination of equitable relative tax burdens of single individuals and married couples with equal incomes. The Committee believes that relief from the marriage penalty is needed because marriage penalties in the tax laws undermine respect for the family and may discourage family formation.

Allowing married couples to file individual returns according to the rates applicable to single individuals ("optional separate filing") would be very complex because of the necessity for rules to allocate income, deductions, and dependent exemptions between the spouses. With optional separate filing, many married couples would be burdened by having to compute tax liability under both options (jointly and separately) in order to determine which options minimize tax liability. Furthermore, optional separate filing would provide tax reductions with respect to all types of income received by married couples, while the Committee believes that relief should be targeted to wages and salaries received by two-earner married couples.

To avoid these difficulties, the Committee believes it is appropriate to provide relief that can be determined by reference to a table in the tax information materials. The relief is designed to be directed only to those married couples who suffer a marriage penalty through the earnings of both spouses. Consequently, married couples whose distribution of earned income between the spouses currently creates a marriage bonus would not qualify for the credit.

Explanation of Provision

Under the bill, married couples who file a joint return may be eligible for a credit against their income tax liability. The amount of the credit is determined based on the earned income of each of the spouses. The Secretary of the Treasury is directed to issue tables calculating the marriage penalty credit applicable for married taxpayers based on the qualified earned income of each of the spouses.

* * *

The amount of the credit is based on the hypothetical tax liabilities that would result if the individual income tax rates applicable to single filers were applied to each spouse's qualified earned income, allowing for one personal exemption and the standard deduction allowed for single filers. The sum of those hypothetical tax liabilities is compared to the hypothetical tax liability that would result if the individual income tax rates applicable to married couples filing joint returns were applied to the aggregate qualified earned income of the spouses, allowing for two personal exemptions and the standard deduction allowed for joint filers.

If the hypothetical tax liability of the married couple exceeds the sum of the hypothetical tax liabilities of the individual spouses, the married couple is allowed an income tax credit equal to the lesser of that excess or $145, with amounts less than the maximum credit rounded to the nearest multiple of $25. * * *

In general, qualified earned income is earned income within the meaning of the Code sections 911(d)(2) (relating to wages, salaries, professional fees, and other amounts received as compensation for personal services) or 401(c)(2)(C) (relating to dispositions of certain property created by the personal efforts of the taxpayer) less specified deductions allowable under section 62 that are properly allocable to such earned income. Under the bill, qualified earned income does not include any amount that is not includible in gross income, because untaxed income does not give rise to a marriage penalty. * * * [T]he qualified earned income of each spouse is computed without regard to any community property laws; that is, earned income is attributed to the spouse who renders the services for which the earned income is received.

* * *

Notes and Questions

11. Do you agree with the principle that the income tax should be marriage neutral, or should the tax system be designed to encourage marriage?

12. How do present tax provisions affect the choice by spouses between working and staying at home?

13. The tax law is likely to affect not only decisions about earned income, but also the form in which married persons own property. Why did Professor Zelenak express concern that, in moving to a system of separate returns, allowing deductions only to the spouse who made payment might lead couples to transfer ownership of the family home to the higher-earning spouse (usually the husband)? What might be the likely effect of a separate taxing system on the ownership of income-producing property (as distinct

from the home, which produces only tax deductions)? Should the tax system be concerned about these effects?

14. Many states employ a system that allows married persons to file a single return in which the spouses are taxed separately—thus allowing the first dollar of each spouse's income to be taxed at the lowest rate, but without sacrificing the simplicity of the joint return. Typically, spouses filing in this manner jointly report itemized deductions not attributable to the income of either spouse, then allocate these deductions in a manner prescribed by the state, which usually tracks one of the allocation formulas suggested by Professor Zelenak.

15. The Canadian Carter Commission determined that married couples view the family, and not the individual, as the basic economic unit. Do you agree?

16. If the Carter Commission's read on the attitude of married couples is correct, should this resolve the issue of whether the family or the individual should be the taxpaying unit?

17. Is ability to pay affected by family circumstances?

18. Was Professor Kornhauser correct in stating that the joint return was established in 1948 on the assumption that spouses pooled all their resources and that sharing of income automatically meant that control of the income was also shared?

19. How does the old saw, "Two can live as cheaply as one," affect the choice between the family and the individual as the proper taxing unit? Does the widespread acceptance of unmarried couples living together diminish the relevance of this point for tax purposes?

20. If the present differences between separate returns for single persons and joint returns are retained, should joint returns be made available to other joint living arrangements as well as to married couples, as Professor Kornhauser may be implying? What other joint arrangements should be included? How would they be defined?

21. Compare the credit in the 1995 Contract with America proposal that was designed to offset the "marriage penalty" with the pre-1986 provision allowing married couples to deduct ten percent of the earned income of the lower-earning spouse (to a maximum deduction of $3,000).

22. Apart from questions of filing status and rate structure, Congress must repeatedly decide whether to treat married couples as one taxpayer or two, and it acts inconsistently. Many provisions, such as the $17,500 cap on depreciable business assets that can be expensed in the year acquired under section 179, allow the same deduction to single taxpayers and married couples. Many others, such as section 1244 limiting the annual amount of losses on small business stock that can offset ordinary income, give a double benefit to married couples filing joint returns.

C. CHILDREN AND THE INCOME TAX

Children are basically taxed as separate individuals, but they can affect their parents' income tax liabilities in several ways. Tax benefits from children are described in the excerpt from Professor Zelenak's article.

A family's cost of living does not go up proportionately as the number of children in the family increases. The Internal Revenue Code, however, allows the same dependency exemption for the second, or subsequent, child as for the first. The interplay of personal and dependency exemptions, standard deductions, and the poverty line for singles and families of various sizes was discussed by Joseph Pechman.

Another provision designed to assist families with children, the earned income tax credit (EITC), was adopted in 1975. It is a refundable credit designed to assist the working poor. At the outset, it was limited to workers whose household included a dependent child. The EITC was expanded in 1993 to cover some workers without children, though at a greatly reduced level. In a 1994 speech printed below, Alicia H. Munnell, Assistant Secretary of the Treasury for Economic Policy, placed the EITC in the context of a broader income maintenance program.

The final excerpt describes a provision from a bill that passed the House of Representatives in 1995. The bill would have provided a tax credit of $500 per child for most parents, which would have been in addition to the dependency exemption.

CHILDREN AND THE INCOME TAX
Lawrence Zelenak[*]
49 Tax Law Review 349, 350-53 (1994)

All children are not equal under the federal income tax. Under different circumstances, the addition of a dependent child to a taxpayer's household may save the taxpayer in excess of $2,000 to absolutely nothing. At one extreme, the first child of a low income single parent produces a tax benefit of more than $2,700. The first child of an unmarried middle income taxpayer is almost as valuable, resulting in tax savings of almost $2,000. At the other

---

[*]. At time of original publication, Reef C. Ivey Research Professor of Law, University of North Carolina.

extreme, there is no tax benefit from any child of very high income parents or from third and later children of low income parents. Between these extremes, the typical child of middle income parents produces tax savings ranging from about $400 to $700. A dependent child can trigger four tax benefits: the dependency exemption, head of household status, the earned income tax credit ("EITC") and the child care credit. There are different rules concerning the effect of the number of children and of the taxpayers's income level on each benefit.

The enormous variation in the tax consequences attributable to children suggests a need to evaluate how the income tax adjusts for family responsibilities. The issue is timely because there have been numerous legislative proposals in recent years—one of which nearly became law[7]—for major changes in the income tax treatment of children. Although the focus has been more on increasing tax benefits to families with children than on rationalizing the distribution of benefits among families, the legislative interest in the subject presents an opportunity to reconsider both the level and the distribution of these benefits.

This Article * * * begins with a description of current tax benefits for families. * * *

The Four Child Tax Benefits for Children

The most widely available of the four benefits is the dependency exemption. The exemption functions as a deduction of a flat $2,500 for each dependent child,[8] regardless of how many children the taxpayer may have. The tax savings from the exemption depend on the taxpayer's marginal rate. For example, one exemption saves $375 for a taxpayer in the 15% bracket and $700 for a taxpayer in the 28% bracket. Although the size of the exemption for a child does not depend on the number of other dependents, it is sensitive to the taxpayer's income. Phaseout of the exemption begins at parental adjusted gross income ("AGI") of $172,050.[9] Eventually, the exemption is phased out entirely, so that dependents entitle very high income parents to no exemptions.

Unlike the dependency exemption, the benefits of which increase proportionately with the number of children, head of household status produces a large benefit for the first child of an unmarried taxpayer, and no additional benefit for more children. A single person with no dependents is entitled to a standard deduction of $3,900 and is subject to an unfavorable

---

7. Tax Fairness and Economic Growth Act of 1992, H.R. 4210, 102d Cong., 2d Sess. (vetoed by President Bush, Mar. 20, 1992).

8. IRC § 151(d)(1), (4). The amount of the exemption is indexed for inflation, and is $2,500 for 1995. [With the exception of the child care credit, all amounts specified in Professor Zelenak's excerpt are indexed for inflation, and the figures stated are for 1995. (Eds.)]

9. IRC § 151(d)(3). The $172,050 figure is for a married couple filing a joint return. Phaseout begins at $143,350 for a head of household. A taxpayer loses 2% of all exemptions for each $2,500 (or fraction thereof) by which AGI exceeds $172,050 (or $143,350). The phaseout is complete at $294,550 for a joint return and $265,850 for a head of household.

tax rate schedule.[10] A single person living with at least one dependent is entitled to a standard deduction of $5,750 and is subject to a more favorable tax rate schedule.[11] In contrast to the dependency exemption, the benefit of head of household status continues regardless of the taxpayer's income level.[12]

The refundable EITC functions as a wage supplement of low income workers.   Until the 1993 amendments, the credit was available only to a worker living with a "qualifying child." A childless worker is now eligible for a maximum credit of $314.[15] A dependent child makes a dramatic difference, increasing the maximum credit to $2,094.[16] A second child makes a smaller, but still significant difference: The maximum credit rises to $3,100.[17] There is no benefit for additional children. Thus, sensitivity of the credit to the number of children differs from both the dependency exemption, which is equally sensitive to all children, and from head of household status, which is sensitive only to the first child. Like the exemption and unlike head of household status, the credit is tied expressly to the taxpayer's income level. The one child credit is fully phased out at $24,396 AGI, and the two child credit at $26,673.

The child care credit is the only one of the four child-related tax provisions that depends on amounts actually spent on children. The credit is a percentage—20% for most taxpayers[19]—of the amount spent by a taxpayer on child care "to enable the taxpayer to be gainfully employed."[20] The ceiling on expenses eligible for the credit is $2,400 if there is one eligible child, and $4,800 if there are two or more.[21]

* * *

---

10. IRC § 63(c)(2)(C) (standard deduction); § 1(c) (rate schedule).

11. IRC § 63(c)(2)(B) (standard deduction); § 1(b) (rate schedule). The existence of one or more dependents does not affect the standard deduction or tax rate schedule of a married couple.

12. The benefit of the more favorable rate schedule remains at all income levels. The benefit of the larger standard deduction also continues, but it becomes less important at high income levels because most high income taxpayers itemize.

15. The credit is 7.65% of the first $4,100 of earned income, with the credit phased out at 7.65% as AGI exceeds $5,130. See IRC § 32(b)(1) (credit percentages and phaseout percentages), § 32(b)(2) (earned income amounts and the phaseout amounts).

16. The credit is 34% of the first $6,160 of earned income. A 15.98% phaseout begins at $11,290 AGI. IRC § 32(b).

17. The credit is 36% (40% for years beginning after 1995) of the first $8,640 of earned income. A 20.22% (21.06% for years beginning after 1995) phaseout begins at $11,290 AGI. IRC § 32(b).

19. The credit rate is 30% for taxpayers with AGI of $10,000 or less, declining gradually until it becomes 20% for taxpayers with AGI of more than $28,000. IRC § 21(a)(2).

20. IRC § 21(b)(2)(A).

21. IRC § 21(c). A different tax benefit for child care is provided by § 129, which excludes from income (the equivalent of inclusion and deduction) child care provided by an employer pursuant to a dependent care assistance program. This provision is even less sensitive to family size than the child care credit. The maximum amount excludable is $5,000, without regard to the number of children. IRC § 129(a)(2)(A).

FEDERAL TAX POLICY
Joseph Pechman[*]
Pages 83-86 (5th ed. 1987)

Relative Exemptions for Different Family Size

If a family of two must spend x dollars to achieve a certain scale of living, what proportion of x would a single person spend, and how much more than x would families of three, four, five, or more people spend to maintain an equivalent standard? Clearly, the answer depends on the criteria used for measuring equivalence. The standard criteria used by the federal government, which are included in the official poverty-line estimates published annually by the Census Bureau, are based on the amount of income needed to maintain an adequate diet.

Table 4-3. *Indexes of the Minimum Taxable Level under the Federal Individual Income Tax and Estimated Poverty-Level Budgets for Families of Various Sizes, 1989*
Two-person family = 100

Size of Family	Index	
	Minimum Taxable Level	Poverty-level budget
1	56	78
2	100	100
3	122	123
4	143	157
5	165	186
6	187	210

As shown in table 4-3, the financial needs of a household do not increase in direct proportion to the number of people in the household. The relative incomes that would provide roughly equivalent standards of living appear to be in the ratio of 80:100:25 for single persons, married couples, and dependents, respectively. Income tax exemptions plus the standard deduction give a ratio of approximately 55:100:20 for 1989. Although the per capita exemption is too liberal for dependents and too small for single persons, the addition of the standard deduction adjusts the ratio more nearly in line with the relative needs of families of different sizes except for single persons who maintain a separate household.

---

[*]. At time of original publication, Senior Fellow, The Brookings Institution.

Level of Exemptions

The adequacy of the *level* of exemptions may be judged by comparing the official poverty-level incomes with the minimum taxable thresholds for families of different sizes (see table 4-4). The minimum taxable levels equal the statutory per capita exemptions plus the standard deduction. As a result of the passage of the 1986 tax reform, these two elements will be sufficient to raise the minimum taxable levels above the poverty lines for all family sizes except for single persons in 1989, when the increase in exemptions becomes fully effective.

Table 4-4. *Minimum Taxable Level under the Federal Individual Income Tax and Estimated Poverty-Level Budgets for Families of Various Sizes, 1989 Dollars*

Size of family	Exemptions	Standard deduction[a]	Minimum taxable level[b]	Poverty-level budget[c]	Difference
1	2,000	3,120	5,120	6,235	-1,115
2	4,000	5,200	9,200	7,978	1,222
3	6,000	5,200	11,200	9,773	1,427
4	8,000	5,200	13,200	12,527	673
5	10,000	5,200	15,200	14,828	372
6	12,000	5,200	17,200	16,753	447

Sources: Minimum taxable levels are based on the personal exemptions and standard deductions for single and married persons under the Tax Reform Act of 1986. Poverty levels are 1985 data from U.S. Department of Commerce, Bureau of the Census, *Current Population Reports*, series P-60, no. 154, "Money Income and Poverty Status of Families and Persons in the United States: 1985," p. 33, projected to 1989.

a. Adjusted for the estimated increase in the consumer price index from 1988 to 1989.

b. Sum of the first two columns.

c. Poverty-level budgets for 1985 were adjusted for an estimated increase in the consumer price index of 14 percent from 1985 to 1989. [Footnotes a-c are in the original source. (Eds.)]

It is clear from table 4-4 that the standard deduction plays an important role in correcting the inadequacy of the per capita exemption. The purpose of the standard deduction is to augment the regular exemptions at the bottom of the income scale without incurring the heavy cost of raising the exemptions for all taxpayers.

Tax Credits in Lieu of Exemptions

Before 1975 income tax allowances for taxpayers and dependents were generally given in the form of exemptions deducted from income in computing taxable incomes. An alternative method, now used in several states, is to convert the allowance to a credit computed by multiplying the value of the exemption by the first-bracket tax rate or some higher rate. With a 15 percent first-bracket rate, the $2,000 exemption would be converted to a credit of $300; at a 20 percent rate, the credit would amount to $400; and so on. The credit limits the tax value of the exemption to the same dollar amount for all taxpayers. It would increase the tax liabilities for those with taxable incomes above the bracket chosen to calculate the value of the credit and reduce them for those with taxable incomes below that level. * * *

Complete replacement of the exemption by a credit would be generous for large families in the lowest income classes and would reduce the tax differences by size of family in the higher classes. To avoid this effect, it has been proposed that a tax credit be allowed as an alternative to the exemption rather than as a substitute for it. Low-income taxpayers would use the credit, and those in the higher classes would continue to use the exemptions. But an optional credit would complicate the tax return and be confusing to many taxpayers. Moreover, roughly the same effect among income classes could be obtained without narrowing tax differences based on family size by retaining the exemption and adjusting the tax rates in the higher income classes. But proponents of the credit are not persuaded that the rate adjustments would actually be made.

Between 1975 and 1978, Congress departed from previous practice and provided a relatively small per capita credit ($30 in 1975 and $35 in 1976-78) instead of increasing the personal exemptions. The adoption of a small credit was a compromise between those who wanted to replace the entire exemption with a credit and those who preferred to increase the exemption. The credit was eliminated when it became clear that it added to the complexity of the tax return without accomplishing very much.

A Vanishing Exemption

Carried to the extreme, the logic of a tax credit would lead to an exemption that vanished at some point on the income scale. A vanishing exemption is supported on the ground that exemptions are not justified for persons with very large incomes, since at these levels they are not needed to meet essential consumption requirements for the taxpayers and their children.

For the first time in U.S. tax history, the 1986 tax reform bill adopted a variant of the vanishing exemption. The particular device chosen was to phase out the personal exemption at the rate of 5 percent of taxable income beginning when the benefit of the first-bracket tax rate phases out (in 1988, taxable income of $89,560 for single persons, $123,790 for heads of households, and $149,250 for married couples). There is no rationale for phasing out the exemption in this particular way, except to save revenue. A more gradual phaseout that did not raise the marginal tax rate by as much as 5 percentage points would be more appropriate. But, as in the case of the credit, it would be better to retain the personal exemption throughout the income scale and adjust the top tax rate to make up the revenue loss.

* * *

THE COMING OF AGE OF THE EARNED INCOME TAX CREDIT
Alicia H. Munnell[*]

National Tax Association Forum, Winter 1994, at 1-6

The Development of the Earned Income Tax Credit

The Earned Income Tax Credit was introduced as part of the Tax Reduction Act of 1975, a stimulus package designed to combat the deepest recession since the Great Depression. It was originally a very modest program that provided a refundable credit of ten percent of earned income, up to a maximum of $400.

In 1975, three claims were made for the credit:

1. it would stimulate consumption, since it would be paid to persons with high marginal propensities to consume,
2. it would improve the work incentives of people on welfare, by reducing the effective tax rate on earned income, and
3. it would indirectly refund all or a portion of the Social Security contributions paid by low-income workers.

These are sensible goals, but, given that the credit amounted to less than five percent of the stimulus package, it had limited ability to satisfy the first two. It is interesting to note the tie to Social Security, however, because it demonstrates that even at the outset, the EITC was viewed as a component of a broader system of social insurance and income support.

After its introduction, the EITC grew, but very haltingly. After small expansions in 1979 and 1986, the Omnibus Budget Reconciliation Act of 1990 greatly expanded the EITC. The maximum credit was raised to $1,998 when the changes were fully implemented in 1994. Despite provisions in OBRA '90 which simplified eligibility determination for the EITC, other changes in the Act may have led to an increase in complexity for taxpayers. The amount of the credit became dependent on the number of children, whether or not the family paid for health insurance, whether a new family member was born during the year, and whether or not the family may have claimed other tax benefits (for example, claiming the young child supplement could reduce the amount a family claimed under the child and dependent care tax credit).

All of these changes set the stage for the expansion of the EITC enacted in [the 1993] Omnibus Budget Reconciliation Act, which represents the most significant increase in scope yet, but also a simplification in process. In 1996, when the changes are fully implemented, the credit for a two-child family will be increased from 25 percent of the first $7,990 to 40 percent of the first $8,425 of earned income (with the base indexed thereafter). (All dollar amounts are given in 1994 levels.) Families with income between $8,425 and $11,000 will receive the maximum credit of $3,370. The credit will be reduced by 21.06 percent of income (the greater of earned income or AGI) over $11,000 (again indexed), so that taxpayers with incomes of up to $27,000

---

[*]. At time of original publication, Assistant Secretary of the Treasury for Economic Policy.

will receive benefits. Assuming the new law were fully implemented in 1994, 15 million families would receive an average credit of $1,700. When the EITC is combined with food stamps, a family of four, with one full-time earner, will be lifted out of poverty, even if that earner receives barely the minimum wage.

The 1993 legislation not only greatly expanded the earned income tax credit for working families, but also took the revolutionary step of extending the credit to workers without children. The credit for this group, however, is significantly smaller. It is equal to 7.65 percent, the employee's share of the social security tax, up to a maximum of $4,000. This produces a maximum credit of $306. (The credit will be phased out at a rate of 7.65 percent of AGI or if greater, earnings over $5,000. Workers will not be entitled to any credit if they have earnings over $9,000.) Roughly, 5 million individuals will be eligible for this new benefit.

The Role of the EITC in the Income Maintenance System

The expanded EITC fundamentally changes our income maintenance system. First, it represents a major increase in spending on income support for low-income families. This is extremely important, since total spending for cash and near-cash income support as a share of output had dropped off during the 1980s, even when output is adjusted for cyclical variations. (For purposes of this analysis, income support is defined to include food stamps, supplemental security income (SSI), aid to families with dependent children (AFDC), the EITC and general assistance payments. This ignores two other, very large transfer programs—Medicaid and housing assistance—that generally provide in-kind assistance.) * * *

Second, the expansion of the EITC continues a trend toward "federalization" of the income maintenance system. In 1960, the Federal share of these programs was roughly 54 percent. By 1992, the Federal share had risen to 79 percent; by 1996, that share should be 83 percent. The shift is due to three factors: the federalization and consolidation in 1972 of programs for the aged, blind, and disabled into the Supplemental Security Income program, the rapid expansion of the food stamp program, and the introduction and expansion in the EITC.

The shift is profound; we as a nation have decided that we want the federal government—rather than state governments—to provide a basic level of income support. This means federal financing and uniform federally-established benefit levels rather than benefits that vary dramatically from one location to another.

We have also clarified what types of benefits we are most comfortable providing and to whom we want to provide them. We do not want people to starve. Therefore, everyone is eligible for food stamps. Recipients of AFDC and SSI are automatically eligible. Others are eligible as long as they fulfill work registration and training programs.

This work registration provision brings us to the second major decision we seem to have made as a nation. That is,—above food for subsistence—we are quite willing to provide benefits to those who work or to those we deem should not have to work. * * *

Comparison of the Current System with a Negative Income Tax

When I first started thinking about the implications of the major expansion of the EITC, I focused on the federalization of the welfare system and wondered if perhaps we had ended up—thirty years later—with Milton Friedman's negative income tax. As you probably remember, Friedman suggested an extremely simple system: taxpayers would receive a subsidy equal to half the amount by which the total value of the taxpayers' personal exemptions and deductions exceeded their taxable incomes. This yielded a negative income tax for low-income taxpayers, and a marginal tax rate on income of 50 percent until the negative tax is phased out.

Certainly, in terms of procedure, the increasing federalization of income support is a necessary first step toward a system like a negative income tax. With federalization, programs can be consolidated, integrated, and managed in a coherent fashion. More importantly, this federalization has been accompanied by a restructuring of the form of support that incorporates several aspects of income support—most notably the earned income tax credit—into the existing personal income tax system.

Instead of a comprehensive adoption of the negative income tax, however, we have selectively adapted its features for particular segments of the population.

1. Food stamps are available to all, based solely on a means test, and provide a minimum level of support.
2. People who cannot work are eligible for SSI and food stamps, which, in essence, form a negative income tax for this group.
3. The rest of the federalized income support system is premised on work.

We as a society have adopted the premise that individuals who can work should, and that society will ensure that those who work—at least those with children—will be adequately compensated. And we have decided to provide these non-judgmental benefits through the tax system.

Table 1 compares what a two-parent, two-child family have received under Friedman's negative income tax with what they will receive from the combination of food stamps and the EITC. The "disposable income" column depicts a not dissimilar pattern under the two approaches. The noticeable difference, however, is the amount of money we are willing to spend on people with no earnings—that is, the basic guarantee. Our family of four receives $4,900 in food stamps, compared to the $7,800 under the negative income tax.

The greatest difference, however, is the pattern of tax rates, and the level at which benefits phase out. When the negative income tax was introduced, the two basic criticisms against it were that it would cost too

Table 1. Comparison of the Current Income Support System and a Negative Income Tax

| | Current Income Support System | | | | | Negative Income Tax | | |
Earnings	EITC	Food Stamps	Federal Taxes	Disp'ble Income	Marg'l Rate	Federal Taxes	Disp'ble Income	Marg'l Rate
0	-	4,440	-	4,440		(7,800)	7,800	50.0%
2,000	800	4,417	-	7,217	-38.9%	(6,800)	8,800	50.0%
4,000	1,600	3,937	-	9,537	-16.0%	(5,800)	9,800	50.0%
5,000	2,000	3,697	-	10,697	-16.0%	(5,300)	10,300	50.0%
6,000	2,400	3,457	-	11,857	-16.0%	(4,800)	10,800	50.0%
7,000	2,800	3,217	-	13,017	-16.0%	(4,300)	11,300	50.0%
8,000	3,200	2,977	-	14,177	-16.0%	(3,800)	11,800	50.0%
9,000	3,370	2,737	-	15,107	7.0%	(3,300)	12,300	50.0%
10,000	3,370	2,497	-	15,867	24.0%	(2,800)	12,800	50.0%
15,000	2,654	1,297	-	18,952	38.3%	(300)	15,300	50.0%
20,000	1,601	97	660	21,039	58.3%	660	19,340	19,2%
30,000	0	0	2,160	27,840	32.0%	2,160	27,840	15.0%
50,000	0	0	6,863	43,137	23.5%	6,863	43,137	23.5%

much and that it would discourage work by paying people for doing nothing. Both the income effect and the substitution effect under a negative income tax work in the wrong direction. That is, the negative income tax provides a base of support regardless of work effort, which reduces the incentive to work, and it introduces high marginal tax rates over the phase-out range, which also discourage work.

The EITC addresses the work-incentive criticism head on; the credit goes only to those who work. In addition, the marginal tax rate is negative over a substantial range, heightening the incentive to increase income. By greatly reducing tax rates—indeed, turning them into negative tax rates—at the low end, however, the EITC requires much higher tax rates at moderate levels—specifically between $20,000 and $30,000.

Moreover, since the EITC has a low average tax rate, benefits are not phased out completely until much higher income levels. Specifically, under

our example negative income tax benefits would end at $15,600; under the
EITC, benefits go all the way up to $27,000.

In practice, the current system can be viewed as analogous to a
combination of a negative income tax—in the form of food stamps—and an
earned income subsidy for those who are working. Alternatively, it can be
characterized as a negative income tax with a complex set of phase-out rates
that are initially negative.

The Evolving System

No matter how one describes the current federal system in terms of
rates and break-even levels, we are still very far from a negative income tax
in terms of universality—universality in terms of beneficiaries and in terms
of benefits.

Despite the recent extension of the EITC, the current law provides only
minimal support for working individuals and working childless couples.
Consistent with the underlying principle that those who can work should, it
is easy to argue that basic support—unrelated to work effort—for individuals
and couples should be minimal. As a matter of fairness, however, it is
reasonable to provide both income support and additional work incentives to
those workers who are not sufficiently productive to earn a decent wage. In
this context, expansion of the EITC is an attractive alternative to an increase
in the minimum wage, since it provides a decent wage without distorting how
the market sets wages.

The other major group left out of the general system are nonworking
women with dependent children, who receive benefit under the AFDC
program. Indeed, this program is one of the major focuses of the Clinton
welfare reform effort. The consensus within the Administration and within
the country at large is that women with children—beyond some young
age—should work to support themselves like everyone else. Thus the goal
of reform will be to get these mothers off welfare and into employment. To
do this requires making work pay. Work does not pay under the current
system; those who show initiative and seek employment often find
themselves worse off than they were on welfare.

The EITC is an important component of the welfare reform effort. For
a worker with two children, the credit will turn a $4.25 minimum wage job
into one paying $6.00. It will help ensure that people leaving welfare receive
more income working than by staying home. The second key to making work
pay is health care reform. Currently, beneficiaries leaving AFDC have to
worry about losing their medicaid benefits. A universal health care system
will eliminate "medicaid lock" and facilitate the transition from beneficiary
to employee.

Turning finally from beneficiaries to benefits, it is important to note that
one of Friedman's reasons for suggesting a negative income tax was its
simplicity and transparency. In his words, it is directed specifically at the
problem of poverty. It gives help in the form most useful to the individual,

namely, cash. It is general and could be substituted for the host of special measures now in effect. It makes explicit the cost borne by society.

While the EITC has all of these virtues, the rest of the income maintenance programs in our current system, designed to provide general, categorical and in-kind assistance, might very well benefit from consolidation. We are already looking at consolidating the application for food stamps and the EITC. This would reduce transaction costs and eliminate any stigma that may accompany participation. * * *

H.R. 1215, THE CONTRACT WITH AMERICA TAX RELIEF ACT OF 1995

House Report No. 84, 104th Cong., 1st Sess. at 10-11 (1995)

The Committee believes that the individual income tax structure does not reduce tax liability by enough to reflect a family's reduced ability to pay taxes as family size increases. In part, this is because over the last 50 years the value of the dependent personal exemption has declined in real terms by over one-third. The Committee believes that a tax credit for families with dependent children will reduce the individual income tax burden of those families, will better recognize the financial responsibilities of raising dependent children, and will promote family values.

Explanation of Provision

The bill provides taxpayers with a maximum credit against income tax liability of $500 for each qualifying child.

The credit is phased out ratably for taxpayers with AGI over $200,000, and is fully phased out at AGI of $250,000. * * * In calendar years beginning after 1996, the maximum credit amount ($500) and the beginning point of the phaseout range ($200,000) are indexed annually for inflation. * * *

To be a qualifying child, an individual has to satisfy a relationship test, a dependency test, and an age test. An individual satisfies the relationship test if the individual is a son or daughter of the taxpayer, a descendant of a son or daughter of the taxpayer, a stepson or stepdaughter of the taxpayer, or an adopted child of the taxpayer. * * *

An individual satisfies the dependency test if the individual is a dependent of the taxpayer with respect to whom the taxpayer is entitled to claim a dependency deduction. * * *

An individual satisfies the age test if the individual has not attained the age of 18. * * *

Notes and Questions

23. Arguably, it would be a logical extension of the family as the taxing unit to include children as well as spouses. Although Congress has never formally taken this step, the "kiddie tax" of section 1(g), which was adopted in 1986, achieves this tax rate result with respect to the child's unearned

income. The kiddie tax was adopted as a response to the practice of parents
giving income-producing assets to their children to achieve an income-
splitting benefit. The kiddie tax cannot be characterized as reflecting any
deeper consideration of the whole family as a taxing unit—otherwise the
child's earned income would have been included as well.

24. Was Pechman correct in stating that the purpose of the standard
deduction is to augment the regular exemptions at the bottom of the income
scale?

25. Is it proper to characterize a payment made to a non-taxpayer as a
negative income tax, as Assistant Secretary Munnell does?

26. Does the EITC, as presently structured, encourage child bearing by
people unable to financially provide for their children? Does it encourage
divorce?

27. All of the child-related tax benefits are reduced as income rises, and
most—including the $500-per-child credit proposed in 1995 by the Ways and
Means Committee—are eliminated entirely at some maximum level of
income. Is such an approach defensible? Congress recognizes, for example,
that a childless couple with $30,000 income has more ability to pay taxes
than an otherwise similarly situated couple with children. Is it not similarly
true that a childless couple with $500,000 income has more ability to pay
than an otherwise similarly situated couple with children? Would equity be
improved if the tax burden among high-income persons were reallocated by
allowing high-income taxpayers the child-related tax benefits available to
taxpayers of more modest income, and paying for these benefits through
higher tax rates on all high-income taxpayers?

28. Child-related tax benefits can be structured as either credits or
exemptions/deductions. Compare the $500 credit proposed by the Ways and
Means Committee in 1995 to doubling the $2,500 (1995 figure) dependency
exemption. A couple with $20,000 of taxable income would derive more
benefit from the credit ($500 exceeds $2,500 x 15 percent = $375), while the
increased exemption would be more valuable to a couple with $50,000 of
taxable income ($500 is less than $2,500 x 28 percent = $700). What does
the choice of a credit or a deduction imply about the policy basis for a child-
related tax benefit?

29. For taxpayers who are members of a family, what should the proper
taxing unit be—the individual, the husband and wife, or the parents and
minor children? Why?

Selected Bibliography

See also bibliography for Chapter Three.

Alm, James & Leslie A. Whittington, *Does the Income Tax Affect Marital Decisions?*, 48 NAT'L TAX J. 565 (1995).

Alstott, Anne L., *The Earned Income Tax Credit and the Limitations of Tax-Based Welfare Reform*, 108 HARV. L. REV. 533 (1995).

Bittker, Boris, *Federal Income Taxation and the Family*, 27 STAN. L. REV. 1389 (1975).

Blumberg, Grace, *Sexism in the Code: A Comparative Study of Income Taxation of Working Wives and Mothers*, 21 BUFF. L. REV. 49 (1972).

BRADFORD, DAVID F., U.S. DEP'T OF TREASURY, BLUEPRINTS FOR BASIC TAX REFORM 92-100 (1984).

Brazer, Harvey E., *Income Tax Treatment of the Family, in* THE ECONOMICS OF TAXATION 223 (Henry J. Aaron & Michael J. Boskin eds., 1980).

Feenberg, Daniel, and Harvey S. Rosen, *Recent Developments in the Marriage Tax*, 48 NAT'L TAX J. 91 (1995).

Gann, Pamela B., *Abandoning Marital Status as a Factor in Allocating Income Tax Burdens*, 59 TEX. L. REV. 1 (1980).

Harmeling, Philip J., *Marital Status Tax Discrimination After Tax Reform: Proposals to Resolve the Penalty/Bonus Issues*, 26 WILLAMETTE L. REV. 593 (1990).

Jensen, Herbert L., *The Historical Discrimination of the Federal Income Tax Rates*, TAXES, July 1976, at 445.

JOINT COMMITTEE ON TAXATION, STAFF REPORT, INCOME TAX TREATMENT OF MARRIED COUPLES AND SINGLE PERSONS (1980).

Kelley, Marci, *Calling a Spade a Club: The Failure of Matrimonial Tax Reform*, 44 TAX L. 787 (1991).

Kornhauser, Marjorie E., *Love, Money, and the IRS: Family, Income-Sharing, and the Joint Income Tax Return*, 45 HASTINGS L. J. 63 (1993).

McIntyre, Michael J., *Fairness to Family Members Under Current Tax Reform Proposals*, 4 AMER. J. TAX POL'Y 155 (1985).

——, *Rosen's Marriage Tax Computations: What Do They Mean?*, 41 NAT'L. TAX J. 257 (1988).

Munnell, Alicia H., *The Coming of Age of the Earned Income Tax Credit*, NTA FORUM, Winter 1994, at 1.

——, *The Couple versus the Individual under the Federal Personal Income Tax, in* THE ECONOMICS OF TAXATION 247 (Henry J. Aaron & Michael J. Boskin eds., 1980).

Note, *The Case for Mandatory Separate Filing by Married Persons*, 91 YALE L.J. 363 (1981).

O'Kelley, Charles R., Jr., *The Parenting Tax Penalty: A Framework for Income Tax Reform*, 64 OR. L. REV. 375 (1986).

Office of Tax Analysis, *Applications of Optimal Tax Theory to Problems in Taxing Families and Individuals*, OTA Paper 21 (November, 1976).

Pechman, Joseph A., and Gary V. Engelhardt, *The Income Tax Treatment of the Family: An International Perspective*, 43 NAT'L TAX J. 1 (1990).

PECHMAN, JOSEPH A., FEDERAL TAX POLICY 83-86 (5th ed. 1987).

Peel, Fred W., Jr., *An Approach to Income Tax Simplification*, 1 U. ARK. LITTLE ROCK L.J. 1, 17 (1978).

Robinson, Toni, and Mary Moers Wenig, *Marry in Haste, Repent at Tax Time: Marital Status as a Tax Determinant*, 8 VA. TAX REV. 773 (1989).

Rosen, Harvey S., *The Marriage Tax is Down But Not Out*, 40 NAT'L TAX J. 567 (1987).

——, *Is it Time to Abandon Joint Filing?*, 30 NAT'L TAX J. 423 (1977).

Schenk, Deborah H., *Simplifying Dependency Exemptions: A Proposal for Reform*, 35 TAX L. 855 (1985).

SIMONS, HENRY, PERSONAL INCOME TAXATION 136-47 (1938).

Sjoquist, David L. & Mary Beth Walker, *The Marriage Tax and the Rate and Timing of Marriage*, 48 NAT'L TAX J. 547 (1995).

VICKREY, WILLIAM, AGENDA FOR PROGRESSIVE TAXATION 274-305 (1947).

Zelenak, Lawrence, *Children and the Income Tax*, 49 TAX L. REV. 349 (1994).

——, *Marriage and the Income Tax*, 67 S. CAL. L. REV. 339 (1994).

PART II

CONSUMPTION TAXES

Reliance on income as the base for taxation is so well established in this country as to seem almost in harmony with natural law. Indeed, taxes not based on income are frequently evaluated with reference to income. For example, state sales taxes are often criticized as "regressive," a characterization accurate only if the tax is evaluated with reference to income and not to its own tax base.[a] In a sense, the federal government's reliance on consumption taxes long predates the first income tax statute. From the earliest days of the republic, the federal government has levied *excise taxes*, which are consumption taxes imposed only on selected goods and services. At present, for example, the federal government taxes such items as alcoholic beverages, gasoline, interstate long-distance telephone calls, and the portion of the purchase price of a new automobile that exceeds $32,000. In the first 150 years or so of this country's existence, excise taxes yielded an impressive share of the government's total revenue. Given the massive revenue requirements since the Second World War, however, such narrow-based taxes cannot be viewed as realistic alternatives to the income tax as the foundation of federal revenues.[b]

Although the income tax has long been sharply criticized, its dominance makes it the appropriate focus of federal tax policy analysis, and of this book. Nevertheless, rational taxing systems can be based on criteria other than income, and calls for movement away from the income tax are heard with increasing frequency from members of Congress and others who influence federal tax policy. The principal purpose of Chapters Six and Seven is to examine some form of broad-based federal consumption tax as a possible replacement of, or significant addition to, existing federal taxes. Chapter Six focuses on the value added tax, a generally "flat" rate tax, which would be collected and remitted by businesses. Chapter Seven examines a wholly different type of consumption tax, which could be at flat rates or progressive, and which would be paid by individuals on an annual basis in much the same way the income tax now is. The division of the material into two

---

a. The term "regressive" is usually used to mean "regressive with respect to income." Sales taxes normally use uniform rates, so it is technically correct to describe these taxes as "proportional," with respect to their base. Because lower-income persons spend a higher proportion of their income on goods and services subject to sales taxes than do higher-income persons, however, the sales tax is regressive with respect to income.

b. In 1994, federal excise taxes amounted to $55 billion, or less than 4.4 percent of federal receipts. U.S. BUREAU OF THE CENSUS, STATISTICAL ABSTRACT OF THE UNITED STATES, tbl. 518, at 334 (115th ed. 1995).

chapters is artificial to some degree, because many policy issues are common to any consumption tax system. The difficulty of this division carried over to the compilation of the bibliographies (which are, moreover, massive), so any student using the bibliography of either chapter as a starting point for research will be well advised at least to read through the bibliography of the other chapter.

CHAPTER SIX

VALUE ADDED TAXES

As recently as 25 years ago, the VAT existed only in France, and even there in only a very rudimentary form. Since then, adoption of the VAT has been made a prerequisite for membership in the European Community (EC), several European countries that are not members of the EC have adopted the VAT and the tax has spread throughout the Third World.[a]

A. INTRODUCTION

Foreign experience alone suggests that the value added tax, or VAT, merits serious consideration. In 1993, Professor Alan Schenk reported that over seventy nations employed VAT "as a significant source of national revenue" and that "[t]he United States is the only major industrial nation that does not impose some form of broad-based tax on consumption at the national level."[b] Is it possible that the rest of the world is on to something?[c] Or does foreign dependence on VATs simply reflect an inability to achieve a level of income tax compliance comparable to ours?

As will be developed in the excerpts and notes, several systems of taxation can be properly described as VATs. While these variations are not unimportant, the economic impact of each major form of the tax is similar. (The primary variations from country to country derive not from employing different VAT systems, but rather the particular country's deviations from that system, such as allowing certain entities and transactions to be exempted from the tax, or taxed at preferential rates.)

The VAT is not well understood in this country. Many Americans continue to describe it as a national sales tax, which is somewhat misleading. While it is true that the economic effect of a comprehensive VAT should closely approximate that of a comprehensive retail sales tax, the structures of the taxes are quite different. Moreover, in the United States, reference to a "national sales tax" leads one to think of state sales taxes, which are much

---

a. George R. Zodrow & Charles E. McLure, Jr., *Implementing Direct Consumption Taxes in Developing Countries*, 46 TAX L. REV. 405, 407 (1991).

b. Alan Schenk, *Choosing the Form of a Federal Value-Added Tax: Implications for State and Local Retail Sales Taxes*, 22 CAP. U. L. REV. 291, 292 (1993).

c. VAT has scored at least one significant international gain since Professor Schenk's article appeared in 1993. The following year, the Peoples Republic of China completely overhauled its VAT, considerably increasing its reach. See Sabine Stricker, *Tax Reform in China Includes One System for Domestic and Foreign Enterprises*, 5 J. INT'L TAX'N 117 (1994).

less comprehensive than most VATs, especially with respect to the taxation of services.

Thus, it may be well to begin with a very simple illustration of the world's most common form of VAT, the European-style credit-invoice destination-principle VAT. Suppose that the United States imposed such a VAT, at a rate of ten percent; and that a farmer milked a cow and sold a gallon of milk to a dairy for fifty cents, the dairy processed the milk and sold it to a grocery store for eighty cents, and the grocery store sold the milk to a consumer for one dollar. The farmer would collect from the dairy, and remit to the government, five cents VAT (ten percent of fifty cents).[d] The farmer's invoice would reflect a selling price of fifty cents plus five cents VAT. The dairy would collect eight cents VAT from the grocery store (ten percent of eighty cents), but would remit only three cents to the government, because it would receive a credit for the five cents it had paid to the farmer.[e] (Its claim to a credit would be supported by the VAT shown on the invoice for its purchase of milk from the farmer; hence, the terminology "invoice-credit" form of VAT.) The remitted tax, three cents, would be ten percent of the value added by the dairy, which, by its processing and transportation, increased the value of the milk from fifty cents to eighty cents. Finally, the grocery store would collect ten cents from the consumer (ten percent of one dollar), and would remit two cents to the government, because it would receive a credit for the eight cents it paid when it bought the milk. Again, the tax remitted equals ten percent of the value added by the grocery store (twenty cents, the increase from eighty cents to one dollar). Thus, the total tax, ten cents (5¢ + 3¢ + 2¢), equals ten percent of the final sales price. It is reasonable to assume that this tax is passed on by each seller, and is the economic equivalent of a single ten-percent tax paid by the final consumer.[f]

Most American states employ *retail sales taxes (RSTs)*, which are flat-rate taxes on most goods.[g] (Although there is considerable variation from

---

d. In the real world, it is impossible to start at the beginning of a chain of production. In this example, the farmer would have various costs that would reduce the value added at this stage of production. For example, the farmer's purchases of feed, or of milking machines, would generate a VAT credit comparable to the VAT credits described in the text for the dairy and grocery store. This credit would not affect the amount of VAT the farmer would collect from the dairy, but it would reduce the amount of VAT that the farmer would remit to the government.

e. The credit for VAT paid at purchase and the remission of VAT collected at sale might be reported on the same or on different VAT returns; either way, the net effect would be as described in the text.

f. If the milk were sold by the grocery store to a restaurant, which re-sold it, glass by glass, for a total of five dollars, the restaurant would continue the process. It would charge its customers fifty cents VAT, claim a credit for ten cents VAT paid, and remit forty cents. Thus, the government would receive a total of fifty cents—ten cents from the three earlier businesses and forty cents from the restaurant—which amounts to ten percent of the final sales price to the consumer.

g. Many states exempt some items, such as food and prescription drugs, that are deemed most necessary. The resulting tax is less regressive with respect to income than would be a uniform sales tax applicable to all goods.

state to state, services are not subjected to RSTs to the same extent as goods, and in some states are wholly exempt from sales taxes.) Intermediate steps in the production chain are normally not subject to RST. To use the example in the preceding paragraph, a typical RST would not reach the farmer's sale to the dairy or the dairy's sale to the grocery store, but the consumer would pay, and the grocery store collect and remit, RST on the full final price of one dollar.[h]   The ultimate economic effect under either tax should be substantially identical—a total tax of ten cents would be collected, all of which would be borne by the consumer.

Almost all VATs and state RSTs rely on the destination principle. Particularly in the case of a substantial national VAT, this is generally (although not universally) thought to have important consequences with respect to the treatment of exports and imports. The theory of the destination principle is that a VAT is a consumption tax, and that the place of consumption—not the place in which the value was added—should determine whether the tax applies. Thus, to continue with the simple example above, if the retailer (the grocery) exported the milk to Canada, the foreign sale would be "zero-rated." This means that the sale abroad would generate no American VAT to be collected and remitted to the American government by the exporter (the retailer), but that the retailer would still be allowed its credit for eight cents of VAT it had paid. Thus, the entire series of sales, reflecting considerable addition of value in the United States, would generate no net American VAT, because the consumption occurred abroad. By the same reasoning, an imported product would bear the full American VAT, even though most of the value was added abroad, because the consumption took place here. Whether this treatment of exports and imports is a reason to adopt a VAT is a matter of some debate.

Compared to an income tax, VATs and RSTs are relatively simple to administer (as are excise taxes), if for no other reason because fewer entities are responsible for filing returns and remitting tax. Although under both of these taxes the consumer bears the tax (VATs paid earlier in the production/distribution chain are recouped upon resale), no return need be filed by the consumer, because all the tax has been collected by the seller at the point of sale. Thus, the government needs deal only with sellers, which means that a far smaller number of returns are necessary than with an income tax, which reaches virtually every household.

---

h. RSTs do not in operation always allow tax-free purchases before the sale to the final consumer. To the degree RSTs are imposed earlier in the production or distribution chain, they are built into the final price, and included in the RST tax base at final sale. This results in a "cascading," or tax-on-a-tax, effect. Professor Schenk cites sources suggesting that "at least fifteen to twenty-five percent of state sales tax revenue is derived from RST's paid on business inputs," and that the comparable figure for Canadian provincial RSTs is even higher. Schenk, *supra* note b, at 316.

In Subchapter B, Dean Lindholm's article explains the surprising country of origin of this "foreign" tax, and traces its development from theory to practice. Subchapter C, the heart of the chapter, examines the central policy issues related to the consideration of an American VAT. Finally, Subchapter D provides two alternatives to "routine" VAT proposals, one calling for a VAT coupled with measures to achieve progressivity, the other for targeted excise taxes rather than the broad-based VAT.

B. HISTORY OF THE VALUE ADDED TAX

THE ORIGIN OF THE VALUE-ADDED TAX
Richard W. Lindholm[*]

6 Journal of Corporation Law 11, 11-14 (1980)

The value-added tax is not a new idea. Many European countries have utilized the tax for many years. The European experience with the VAT and the hesitancy of the United States to adopt such a tax often obscures the fact that the value-added approach to taxation was first examined, explained and advocated by American fiscal experts. * * *

The early American interest in the value-added tax is at least partially explained by the early embrace by American economists of statistical economic and business analysis. Prior to the development of statistical methods of analysis the study of economics was confined primarily to armchair philosophy and unconfirmed or unverifiable theory. Mathematical formulae enabled economists to put old theories to the test and to measure with relative precision economic trends.

Data based economics was particularly important to the origin of the VAT. At the turn of the century proponents of economic realism, armed with the new mathematical tools of economics, developed the formula for calculating gross national product (GNP). The gross national product is determined by adding the market values of effort expended at each level of the production process. Because GNP represents an increment in value to raw materials as finished products it was all but inevitable that economists and fiscal experts would devise a method of utilizing GNP as a tax base. The method devised was a tax on total production that becomes a part of the cost of consumption of goods and services purchased in the marketplace. In addition to providing the tools to calculate a tax base, data oriented economics made it possible for economists to more accurately predict the various effects that implementation of the value-added tax would have on the economy. This, in turn, provided both proponents and opponents ammunition with which to support or oppose adoption of the tax.

---

[*]. At time of original publication, Emeritus Dean & Professor of Finance, College of Business Administration, University of Oregon.

While the value-added tax has yet to be enacted in the United States, its proponents have been vocal and at times influential. One of the most important early advocates of the VAT was T.S. Adams. Adams supported the value-added approach to taxation as early as 1911. It was in 1921, however, that Adams published a paper in which he set forth his reasons for supporting the VAT. Adams claimed that the value-added tax was the most efficient and desirable method of taxing the business sector of the economy.[5] Later, Dr. Gerhard Colm, a German-trained fiscal expert who became a leading tax specialist for the federal government, published an article in which he discusses the operative aspects of the VAT and then urges that it be adopted on the federal level.[6] In 1940, Paul Studensky, one of the most distinguished tax scholars in the United States, published an article discussing his ethical and philosophical basis for supporting the VAT.[7]
* * *

Adams, Colm and Studensky were important vocal advocates of the value-added tax. Despite their urgings, however, Congress failed to enact the VAT. The response of the VAT proponents was two-fold. First, many proponents began to urge the states to adopt value-added taxes. During the 1930's, for example, the Brookings Institut[ion] urged adoption of the VAT in Alabama and Iowa. With the exception of Michigan, which adopted the VAT in 1953 and again in 1975, the state campaigns met the same fate as the campaign to have a federal VAT adopted. The second approach taken by VAT enthusiasts was to "export" the VAT concept to other countries. For example, shortly after World War II the United States sent a team of tax experts to Japan to assist in the reconstruction of the Japanese economy. The American Taxation Mission[12] strongly urged Japan to adopt a value-added tax. The Japanese Diet did adopt a value-added tax for raising revenue for local governments. A variety of circumstances, however, prevented implementation of the tax and it was later repealed.

Partially in response to the "exportation" efforts of American economists and partially as a result of independent experimentation and initiative, the value-added tax found much greater acceptance in Europe than in the United States. * * *

The French VAT, entitled *taxe sur la valeur adjoutee* (TVA), was implemented to remedy a serious post-World War II fiscal crisis. The roots of the TVA, however, begin much earlier. In 1917 France enacted a general consumption or gross turnover tax which evolved quickly from a luxury tax

---

5. Adams, *Fundamental Problems of Federal Income Taxation*, 35 J. Economics 527 (1921).

6. Brookings Institution, Report on a Survey of the Organization and Administration of State and County Governments of Alabama 319-42 (1932).

7. Studensky, *Toward a Theory of Business Taxation*, 48 J. Political Econ. 621 (1940).

12. The American Taxation Mission has also been known as The Shoup Mission after its leader, Carl A. Shoup of Columbia University.

into a form of sale stamp tax. This, in turn, became part of a larger well-organized stamp duty system. * * * As with the rest of Europe, the end of World War II found France both devastated and at the threshold of economic opportunity. As reconstruction advanced the French economic system took on a new vitality. At the same time, the government had a growing need for revenues to meet the increasing demands being placed upon it by the reconstruction process. In this atmosphere proponents of the TVA urged the French government to adopt the TVA as a part of a broad economic development philosophy. They argued that the TVA was an ideal way to raise the revenue needed by the government without stifling continued economic growth. Moreover, proponents argued that the TVA would provide a more stable source of revenue than the earlier tax system provided. The French government was convinced and adopted the TVA in 1954.
>   * * *

The skepticism of the value-added tax demonstrated in the United States is difficult to explain. It has been demonstrated that the value-added approach to taxation grew out of the American economic and business environment. Calculation of the value-added base is made relatively simple since essentially the same formula for calculating GNP is used to calculate the VAT base. Moreover, the value-added approach to taxation would appear to be consistent with the principles underlying the American free market economy. For example, the VAT avoids, to a large extent, dictating to taxpayers where they should save or invest their resources. Moreover, the VAT does not treat the profits of successful business ventures more harshly than wages or interest income. Lastly, the value-added tax does not favor one method of organizing a business over another. * * *

Notes and Questions

1. When and where was the modern VAT conceptualized? How is VAT related to the computation of gross national product (GNP)? What were the first jurisdictions to enact a VAT?

2. *The Japanese experience.* War—particularly war ending in unconditional surrender and occupation—makes possible political breakthroughs. In 1949, the Shoup Mission, acting under the authority of General Douglas MacArthur, proposed sweeping changes in Japanese tax structure, including a VAT. "The value-added tax became the most controversial single proposal of the *Shoup Report.* It represented a first attempt to put into practice a proposal which had become well known because of a long history in public finance literature."[i] The Japanese Diet

---

i. M. Bronfenbrenner & Kiichiro Kogiku, *The Aftermath of the Shoup Tax Reforms*, 10 NAT'L TAX J. 236, 241 (1959).

    A contemporary reader of the *Shoup Report* might not have suspected that the VAT proposals were particularly important. The report's table of contents makes no reference to VAT,

initially enacted the VAT in 1950, but, perhaps because Japan shortly thereafter regained full control of its domestic tax system, "[t]he enactment date of the value-added tax was postponed twice, and finally the tax was repealed without ever having gone into effect."[j]

The failure of Japan's post-war VAT effort may be attributable to its novelty (in actual practice, although not in academic literature) and to the taint of its being imposed by foreign conquerors, in addition to the usual substantive arguments that can be made against the tax. Nearly forty years passed before, in 1989, Japan enacted a VAT at the modest rate of three percent.[k]

C. THE ULLMAN PROPOSAL AND ITS AFTERMATH

As Dean Lindholm's article explains, serious American interest in the VAT at the academic level dates to the turn of the century. The landmark event that moved VAT to prominence on the national political stage, however, was the strong support given VAT by the most important tax-writing member of Congress—Al Ullman, then Chairman of the Ways and Means Committee. The 1979 Ways and Means Hearing Announcement explains his VAT proposal. Five years later, the drafters of Treasury I examined VAT in some detail—devoting one of its three volumes to VAT—before rejecting the concept. The ABA Committee drafted a model statute and explanation, from which the Ullman bill was the point of departure, without taking any position on whether the United States should enact a VAT. Dr. McLure, on the other hand, unabashedly argued in favor of VAT as a revenue measure. Professor Due examined whether VAT would be a means of taxation friendlier than existing federal taxes to capital formation. Professor Schenk, who was reporter for the ABA Committee's Model Act and the most prolific American writer on VAT, examines both economic and equity issues.

**COMMITTEE ON WAYS & MEANS, HEARING
ANNOUNCEMENT ON THE
TAX RESTRUCTURING ACT OF 1979**
Statement By Representative Al Ullman (D., Oregon)
H.R. 5665, 96th Cong., 1st Sess., WMCP 96-38, at 6-12 (1979)

What is a value added tax?

A value added tax is a tax on consumer goods and services. It is a flat tax—a 10 per cent tax—that falls every time the item passes from one firm

---

which is modestly included in Chapter 13, "Other Local Taxes." The proposed VAT was not to be a national tax, but an improved method of computing the prefectural (provincial) "enterprise tax." The VAT discussion covered only three pages of a four-volume report.

j. *Id.* at 245.

k. Alan Schenk, *Japanese Consumption Tax: The Japanese Brand VAT*, 42 TAX NOTES 1625 (1989); Barry M. Freiman, *The Japanese Consumption Tax: Value-Added Model or Administrative Nightmare?*, 40 AMER. U. L. REV. 1265, 1265 (1991).

to another on the way to the final market place. At every step, the tax is collected and sent to the government. Using a system of rebates on taxes paid along the line, the cumulative tax at the retail level cannot exceed 10 per cent.

The VAT is not a new tax concept. It is used by most of our competitors in the free world—countries that are surpassing us in economic growth.

Many attack VAT as a "national sales tax." A sales tax is imposed only once—at the retail level. If the final seller does not collect the tax, the revenue is lost. A VAT, by contrast, is collected all along the way. It is more efficient than a sales tax, and, consequently, minimizes economic distortion. But, like all taxes on business, the value added tax is ultimately paid by the consumer.

A tax on consumption would give us an even flow of tax revenue. Today's boom and bust cycles have turned tax receipts into a guessing game. Every time we sink into recession, tax revenues fall off because more workers are out of jobs—and, at the same time, federal spending increases to pay for higher insurance protection. A value added tax would be paid all the time—by all the people. And the effect on economic certainty and stability would be dramatic.

The VAT in my bill is virtually a tax without loopholes. Everyone would pay—including those engaged in the "underground" economy. Those who spend more would pay more. Although those with limited budgets typically would pay proportionally more than those with large incomes, a VAT can be shaped into a fair tax—certainly less regressive than the payroll tax which nearly everyone now pays.

* * *

A VAT would also help improve our trade posture by putting American workers and manufacturers on a more equal footing with our trading partners. Unlike payroll and income taxes the VAT could be rebated to manufacturers when products are exported and could be imposed on imported goods. Such border taxes are now levied in most other free world countries, [which] helps to explain our current unfavorable trade balance.

* * *

The choices are few. An American value added tax is not the easiest answer—but it is the most realistic.

* * *

Brief summary of the Tax Restructuring Act of 1979

The bill would restructure our tax system to promote investment and productivity growth. Total tax reductions would equal $130 billion on a calendar year 1981 basis. Net proceeds from the value added tax imposed by the bill would also equal $130 billion.

Tax Reductions

Social Security—$52 billion
- A 2.15-percentage point reduction on the employee and employer rates, with comparable reductions for the self-employed.

Individual Income—$50 billion
- Rate reductions.
- Earned income credit increased.
- Increased AFDC payments.
- Special savings accounts.

Business Income—$28 billion
- Corporate rate cuts.
- Liberalize depreciation.
- Liberalize the investment tax credit.

Value Added Tax

The bill would impose the VAT at each stage of the production and distribution process, including the retail stage. The tax would generally be 10 percent of the value of property or services and would be included in the price which a business charges its customers. Each business in the production and distribution chain would receive a credit for the VAT previously paid on its purchases of property and services from other businesses (including purchases of plant and equipment). Thus, each business would pay a net tax equal to 10 percent of the value it adds to the product, and the total tax paid with respect to sales to consumers would be 10 percent of the retail value of the product.

To avoid narrowing the VAT base, special rules or special tax rates have been limited except where considered absolutely essential. Food, medical care, and residential housing would be taxed at only a five-percent rate at the retail level. Transactions of charities, public and private nonprofit educational institutions, mass transit, and nonretail sales by farmers and fishermen have been given a zero tax rate, which means there would be no tax but the taxpayer would receive applicable VAT credits. Governments and nonprofit organizations other than charities have been exempted from the VAT; they would pay no tax and get no credit. The bill provides special rules for real property, interest transactions, and insurance companies. Also, businesses which have sales of property and services below $10,000 per year could elect to be exempt from the VAT.

The VAT would be imposed on imports. Exports have been zero rated to permit a rebate of VAT previously paid for goods and services associated with the export. This "border tax adjustment" will permit American exporters to compete more effectively with foreign businesses.

* * *

**TAX REFORM FOR FAIRNESS, SIMPLICITY,
AND ECONOMIC GROWTH ['TREASURY I']**
United States Department of the Treasury
Vol. 3, at 5-13, 16-23, 26, 39-42 (1984)

The Nature of the Value-Added Tax

Alternative Forms of Tax

There are three separate types of value-added tax: gross product, income, and consumption. They differ in their treatment of capital equipment that has been purchased from other firms. This difference may be illustrated by assuming that a firm calculates its value added by subtracting its purchases from other firms from its sales and then applying the tax rate to the resulting value added to determine its tax liability, even though this is not the method normally used to calculate tax liability under a value-added tax. For the sake of simplicity and clarity of explanation, this illustration will also not consider the question of whether exports or government purchases would be subject to the tax.

Gross Product Type

In determining its tax liability under a gross product value-added tax, a firm would be allowed to deduct its purchases of raw materials from its sales, but it would not be allowed to deduct the cost of its purchases of capital equipment, or even the depreciation on that capital equipment. Since gross investment purchases (including depreciation) are subject to taxation, the economic base of a gross product value-added tax is similar to gross national product. Capital investment is, in effect, taxed twice under the gross product tax. Capital goods are taxed at the time they are purchased and also when the products they produce are sold to consumers. * * *

A gross [product] type of value-added tax would create significant administrative difficulties in those borderline cases where it is difficult to distinguish expenditures for capital goods from those for items that are exhausted currently in production or for repair and maintenance purposes. * * *

Of the three different types of value-added tax, the gross product version places the heaviest tax burden on capital goods. It would discourage saving, discriminate against capital intensive methods of production, and cause firms to delay modernization and upgrading of plant and equipment by minimizing expenditures on capital assets. The gross product tax is best relegated to the realm of conceptual curiosities and should not receive serious consideration in public policy discussions.

Income Type

Under the income variant of the value-added tax, both purchases of raw materials and depreciation on capital goods would be deducted from sales in computing a firm's value added. Since net investment purchases (gross investment less depreciation) are subject to taxation, the economic base of this tax is similar to net national income. By taxing net investment, this tax would impose a tax burden on net purchases of capital goods. Because this type of value-added tax requires the calculation of depreciation allowances, it would have some of the same administrative problems that arise under an income tax. * * * As long as the United States has an income tax there is no reason to adopt an income-type value-added tax.

Consumption Type

Under the consumption-type value-added tax, all business purchases, including those for capital assets, would be deductible in calculating a firm's value added. Since a full deduction is allowed for gross investment, this alternative would result in a tax base equivalent to total private consumption. A consumption value-added tax avoids the need to distinguish between capital and current expenditures or to specify asset lives and depreciation allowances for capital assets. As noted above, both the gross product and income versions of the value-added tax would penalize capital investment by placing an additional tax burden on capital equipment purchases; the tax would be imposed on the capital good itself and on the output produced by the capital good. In contrast, a consumption-type value-added tax would be neutral between methods of production since substituting capital for labor (or vice versa) would not affect a firm's total taxes; it also would be neutral between the decision to save or consume. Because of these characteristics, the consumption version is the type of value-added tax used in Europe and the only type that should receive consideration in the United States.

Alternative Methods of Calculation: Subtraction, Addition, Credit

Though value added is often thought of as the difference between a firm's sales and its purchases, value-added tax liability may be calculated by three different methods: by subtraction, credit, or addition. These three alternatives are illustrated by the example in Table 2-1. That example assumes an economy with only three firms (one each in manufacturing, wholesaling, and retailing) and in which the manufacturing sector sells all of its output to the wholesale sector; the wholesale sector buys only from the manufacturing sector and sells all of its output to the retail sector. The rate of tax is 10 percent.

Subtraction Method

Under this method, illustrated in the top part of Table 2-1, a firm calculates its value-added tax liability by subtracting its purchases from other firms from its sales and applying the tax rate to th difference. With a consumption value-added tax, the deduction for purchases would include any capital equipment bought during the period. * * *

Table 2-1
Comparison of Three Methods of Calculating
Value-Added Tax Liability
(10 percent value-added tax)
STAGE OF PRODUCTION

	Firm A Manufacturer:	Firm B Wholesaler:	Firm C Retailer:	Total Economy:
1. SUBTRACTION METHOD:				
Sales	$350	$850	$1,100	$2,300
Purchases	100	350	850	1,300
Value added (sales minus purchases)	250	500	250	1,000
Value-added tax	25	50	25	100
2. CREDIT METHOD:				
Sales	350	850	1,100	2,300
Tax on sales	35	85	110	230
Purchases	100	350	850	1,300
Tax on purchases	10	35	85	130
Value-added tax (tax on sales less tax on purchases)	25	50	25	100
3. ADDITION METHOD:				
Factor payments plus net profit				
Wages	150	300	200	650
Rent	50	100	20	170
Interest	25	75	20	120
Profit	25	25	10	60
Total	250	500	250	1,000
Value-added tax	25	50	25	100

Credit Method

The credit, or invoice, method is used by all of the member countries in the European Economic Community (EEC) [now the European Community (EC)] and by most other countries that have a value-added tax. Under the credit method, a firm's tax liability is determined by allowing the firm to subtract value-added tax paid on purchases from tax due on its sales. This method is illustrated in the middle panel of Table 2-1. The amount of deductible tax paid on purchases would include the full amount of tax paid on any capital equipment purchases in the case of a consumption-type value-added tax. * * *

An important characteristic of the credit method is that except in the case of outright exemption of intermediate stages of production the tax on a product depends on the tax rate that prevails at the final taxable stage; this would be the rate levied at the retail stage in the case of a value-added tax that extends through the retail level. Thus, any value-added tax evaded by firms prior to the retail level would result in higher taxes at the retail level; lower tax rates at pre-retail stages would be offset by full collection of the tax at the retail level. * * *

Addition Method

Though value added is equal to the difference between a firm's sales and its purchases, it also is equal to the payments for the labor and capital that generate the value added. Under the addition method, a firm's value-added tax liability is calculated by adding together the components of value added, wages, rent, interest, and net profit, and then applying the tax rate to that sum. It is illustrated in the lower panel of Table 2-1. Since net profit normally reflects a capital depreciation allowance, the addition method is usually associated with an income type of value-added tax. A consumption method value-added tax could be implemented by the addition method only if net profit was based on the expensing or full immediate deductibility of capital equipment purchases. If the objective is a consumption value-added tax, this can be achieved more easily under the credit method than by calculating net profit (with capital expensing) and adding it to the other factor payments. The calculation of net profit involves all of the problems that plague the current income tax.

Analysis and Summary

The subtraction, credit, and addition methods should be viewed as equivalent only in the case of a single rate of tax applying to nearly all goods and services. In such a situation, the three methods would work equally well and would generate the same amount of total tax revenue. A more realistic situation is one in which policy makers may prefer a single-rate value-added tax for administrative and efficiency reasons, but in which it will be necessary to tax some goods and services at special rates. In a world in which all goods and services are not taxed at the same rate, the credit method is superior to either the subtraction or addition alternatives.

Under the subtraction approach, virtually every sector of the economy would exert political pressure for special treatment. This is because ultimate tax liability on a given product would depend on two factors: value added in each sector or industry and the tax rate applied to that value added. Assuming that firms do not incorrectly overstate purchases or understate sales, they would have relatively little control over their value added subject to tax. But they would try to minimize their value-added tax liability by seeking preferential, or perhaps even zero, rates of value-added tax on their own sector or industry.

With the credit method, in contrast, since tax liability on final consumption depends on the tax rate imposed at the final or retail stage, the mining, agricultural, manufacturing, and other non-retail sectors would have less incentive to seek special treatment and be less likely to do so. Because any tax charged on their sales may be credited by their (non-retail) customers, it should (record keeping considerations aside) be a matter of indifference to firms making non-retail sales as to whether or not they are subject to the tax. Indeed, as shown below, exemption from tax would actually be adverse to the exempt firm's non-retail customers.

Special rates, which would be more likely under the subtraction or addition method than under the credit alternative, would have a number of adverse economic consequences. They would unfairly favor those consumers with strong preferences for lightly-taxed goods and penalize those preferring to buy more heavily-taxed items. To the extent that the nonuniform rates induced changes in buying habits, consumer satisfaction would decline and the government would collect less revenue. As explained below, a so-called indirect tax, such as a value-added tax, may be rebated on exports under international trading rules. With differential rates for various sectors or products, it would be virtually impossible under the subtraction method to calculate the correct amount of tax that would be permitted as a rebate on exports and collected on imports. Differential rates would make the tax more complex, both for taxpayers and tax administrators, thus increasing compliance and administration costs.

Though multiple rates are far less satisfactory than a single rate value-added tax, the experience of other countries demonstrates that it may not be possible to avoid them. The credit method is attractive not only because it makes the tax base less vulnerable to erosion from pleas of special interest groups for tax relief, but because it is superior to the subtraction method in accommodating the demands that will be made for tax relief for some goods or services. Under the credit method, goods and services can be freed of tax by simply applying a rate of "zero" at the retail stage and allowing a full credit for pre-retail taxes. In similar fashion, the accurate rebate of tax on exports occurs automatically. The same result could only be achieved under the subtraction method by applying a rate of zero at each and every stage of production or distribution through which the tax favored good or service passes.

* * *

Border Tax Adjustments

In 1983, U.S. exports of goods and services were equal to about 10 percent of the economy's output. In the United States, as in other countries, the design of a value-added tax must take into account the fact that the movement of goods and services across national borders is commonplace.

* * *

[A] value-added tax may be implemented on a destination basis. In this case, value-added tax is imposed only where the good is consumed, not where it is produced. This necessitates a rebate of any tax imposed in the exporting country and a compensatory tax in the importing country to equalize the tax burden with a good that is domestically produced and consumed. The export rebate and import tax, designed to place traded [imported] and domestically-produced goods on an equal tax footing in the country where they are consumed, are known as border tax adjustments. State retail sales taxes are levied under the destination principle. A state retail sales tax is not imposed on goods destined for export out of the taxing state, but is levied on any imports sold to consumers in the taxing state.

The credit method of determining value-added tax liability is superior to either the addition or subtraction approaches for implementing the destination principle. The rebate of tax on exports is accomplished by simply applying a tax rate of zero at the export stage and giving the exporter full credit for any tax paid on inputs purchased to produce the export good.

* * *

Unless the import good is purchased directly by the final consumer, rather than from a taxable firm, it is not even necessary for the importing country to explicitly levy the value-added tax at the import stage to implement the destination principle. Under the credit method, the tax on a product depends on the rate applied on the final sale to the consumer. * * * [P]rovided there is at least one taxable firm between the import stage and final consumer, the credit method will insure that consumption of imports and domestically-produced goods takes place on an equal tax footing, as required by the destination principle.

In contrast to a credit method value-added tax, there are substantial complexities to implementing the destination principle under either the subtraction or addition methods. * * *

If the policy debate in the United States ever focuses on choosing a form of value-added tax, it should concentrate on a value-added tax with the following characteristics:

1. consumption type;
2. credit method of determining tax liability; and
3. destination principle of border tax adjustments.

[T]he tax should also have a broad base, with only minimal and well justified exclusions, and it should be imposed at a single, uniform rate.

Evaluation of a Value-Added Tax

This chapter evaluates a consumption-type value-added tax with tax liability calculated under the credit method from an economic and political perspective. This is the form of tax that has been adopted by the member countries in the European Economic Community (EEC) and would be the most likely candidate for the United States, if a policy decision were made to adopt a value-added tax.

Some of this discussion necessarily involves comparing a value-added tax with other taxes, such as the personal and corporate income taxes and the social security or payroll tax. This is because revenue generated by a value-added tax could also be raised by one of these other levies, or could permit these other taxes to be reduced. * * *

Economic Effects

Neutrality

A neutral tax is one that does not interfere with the economic behavior of individuals or firms. Compared to the situation that would exist if no tax is imposed, a neutral tax would not interfere with the decisions of individuals to work or not work, to save or consume, or to consume one good or another; or with the decisions of firms on what to produce and what production methods to use. A cigarette tax, for example, is not neutral because it may discourage consumers from buying cigarettes. While some taxes are intended to change consumer behavior, neutrality is generally viewed as a desirable objective of tax policy because it is assumed that both the value of economic production and consumer satisfaction will decline if a tax forces either firms or individuals to change their behavior.

Production neutrality

In a market-oriented economy, business firms are motivated by competitive forces to use the most efficient production techniques. In this way, the goods and services demanded by consumers are produced, and at the lowest possible cost. If a tax interferes with these production decisions, resources are used less efficiently and less output is available to satisfy consumer demand.

A consumption-type value-added tax would score high in production neutrality. By allowing a full deduction for the tax paid on purchases of capital equipment it would not distort production or investment decisions. Compared to a no-tax situation, the tax would not encourage firms to favor the use of either labor or capital in the production process. The total tax liability incurred by a firm, consisting of both the tax on its purchases and the tax on its sales (after allowing for the tax on purchases) would be the same regardless of the precise capital-labor mix. The corporate income tax has many distortions, it favors debt over equity finance, noncorporate over corporate products, labor over capital, and consumption over saving. As explained in the next section, a value-added tax would be neutral between consumption and saving. Since purchased consumption goods are subject to taxation, a value-added tax may discourage work effort by those who have the alternative of using leisure time to produce goods and services that would be taxed if purchased. An example of this result would be an individual using leisure time to paint a house or tend a garden. In contrast to a value-added tax, the individual income tax, because it is progressive and applies to both income that is saved as well as the return on saving, may discourage saving and risk taking, as well as work effort. Even though the payroll tax applies to most forms of labor, it probably is not neutral. It may discourage work effort, and the pay-as-you-go financing of social security may reduce saving.

Consumption neutrality

In a market-oriented economy, individuals "vote" for the goods and services they want to buy by signaling the prices they are willing to pay. These price signals are received by business firms, who produce those goods and services valued most highly by consumers. If a tax changes the structure of net relative prices determined in the market place, consumers respond by buying more of some goods and less of others. The end result is reduced consumer satisfaction and a less efficient use of the economy's resources. A broad-based value-added tax, imposed at a single rate, would constitute a relatively uniform percentage of all consumer expenditures. Thus, it would be a reasonably neutral tax. * * *

[I]t is unlikely that a Federal value-added tax would apply to all forms of consumption. Either for social, distributional, or administrative reasons, the tax would probably not apply in full to housing, medical care, insurance and finance, education, and religious and welfare activities. At most, the tax would apply to about 77 percent of total personal consumption expenditures. Exclusions from the tax base would make the tax less neutral and distort consumption and production decisions in favor of the preferentially-taxed items. The experience of other countries indicates that nonuniform coverage and rate differentiation are the prime sources of nonneutrality in the value-added tax. It is for this reason, as well as to avoid administrative complexity, that departures from a broad base should be minimized and that rate differentiation reduction should be avoided, particularly if alternatives exist for alleviating the burden of the tax on lower income groups.

Saving

Unlike an income tax, a value-added tax would be neutral toward the saving-consumption choice. Suppose that in an economy without taxes the interest rate is 10 percent. An individual with $100 of income could either purchase $100 of consumption goods this year or could save the $100 and purchase $110 of consumption goods next year. This individual could consume 10 percent more next year by not consuming (by saving) the $100 now. A value-added tax would not alter the basis for this choice between consumption and saving. Consider a value-added tax rate of 20 percent, levied on the tax-inclusive value of goods and services. Now the choice is between consuming $80 this year and paying $20 in tax or saving the $100 this year, allowing it to grow to $110, and consuming $88 next year and paying the remaining $22 in tax. Note that the net rate of return on saving is not affected by the value-added tax; it is still 10 percent. By postponing $80 of consumption this year, the individual can consume $88 or 10 percent more next year.

In contrast, a tax on income from capital, such as the corporate income tax or the individual income tax on interest or dividends, is not neutral between consumption and saving. * * * Continuing the same example, an individual subject to a 20 percent income tax could, after paying the tax, purchase $80 of consumption goods this year or save the $80 in order to consume $86.40 next year, after paying a 20 percent tax on the $8 in interest earned on the $80 in savings. In the income tax case, the net return to saving is now only 8, rather than 10, percent. * * *

This example demonstrates that a value-added tax is neutral with regard to the choice of whether to consume now or save for future consumption; the value-added tax does not discourage saving the way an income tax does. Assuming any increased saving is absorbed by higher real investment spending, a value-added tax may be superior to an income tax in fostering capital formation and economic growth. The amount of the increase in saving would depend on the responsiveness of saving to higher after-tax rates of return.

Equity

Consumption expenditures, as a percentage of income, fall as income rises. Individuals and families at the middle and upper income levels consume a smaller proportion of their income than those at the lower income levels. Thus, a broad-based value-added tax imposed at a uniform rate would absorb a larger percentage of the income of those at the lower income levels than those at the middle and upper income levels. In other words, a value-added tax would be regressive, assuming no exemptions or differential rates for "necessities" or "luxuries." The individual income tax, in contrast, is progressive, since it allows for personal exemptions and a zero bracket amount and because tax rates rise with income. * * *

[R]egressivity has two facets: the absolute burden of the tax on those below the poverty level and the regressive effect on those above the poverty level. For those with income above the poverty level and subject to the income tax, the regressivity of the value-added tax can be offset by adjusting the income tax rates. But for those who are below the poverty level and not subject to the income tax, this approach is not helpful; the value-added tax could, however, be offset by a refundable tax credit administered through the income tax system or by increased transfer payments.

Generally speaking, reduced rates for purchases of certain commodities and exemptions from the tax base are not a desirable means of alleviating regressivity. * * *

Prices

A value-added tax accompanied by an accommodating monetary policy and no offsetting reduction in other taxes would probably lead to a one-time increase in consumer prices in direct relation to the coverage and rate of tax. * * *

The experience of those countries which have adopted a value-added tax confirms the view that it may generate a one-shot increase in the price level, but not an annual inflationary spiral. * * *

Balance of Trade

It is frequently argued that a value-added tax would improve the U.S. trade balance by making U.S. goods more competitive in world markets. This argument is based primarily on the realization that the value-added tax can be rebated on exports and levied on imports. Though there may be some validity to the argument, it is important to specify clearly the circumstances under which it would prevail.

The General Agreement on Tariffs and Trade (GATT) permits destination principle border tax adjustments for indirect taxes such as sales or value-added taxes, but not for direct taxes such as the corporate or individual income tax or social security taxes. That is, indirect taxes, like the value-added tax, can be rebated on exports and imposed on imports, but no corresponding adjustments can be made for direct taxes.

Imposing a value-added tax without any reduction in the income tax, or some other direct tax, would not directly improve the U.S. balance of trade. Export subsidies and import taxes could, in a system of fixed exchange rates, increase a country's exports and reduce its imports. But, the export rebate and import tax allowed for the value-added tax are merely border tax adjustments required to put the value-added tax on a destination basis. The export rebate merely allows exports to enter world markets free of value-added tax, not at a subsidized price below the pre-tax price. Similarly, imposing a value-added tax on imports merely places imports on an equal footing with domestically produced goods; it does not penalize imports. * * *

The analysis is somewhat different if a value-added tax is part of a revenue-neutral substitution for an existing direct tax, such as the corporate income tax or payroll tax. As noted above, under GATT neither the corporate income nor payroll tax may be rebated on exports and imposed on imports. Under traditional assumptions that these taxes are borne by share-holders or by labor, respectively, reducing them would have no effect on prices, and partially replacing them with a value-added tax would have no effect on the competitiveness of U.S. industry. The substitution of a value-added tax for either of these direct taxes could improve the U.S. trade balance only if the domestic price level remains unchanged, or at least increases by less than the full amount of the value-added tax. This would occur if one of these taxes is shifted to consumers and would be " unshifted" if reduced. Under these circumstances, the export rebate would reduce the price of U.S. exports, and the import tax would increase the price of imports relative to those of domestically-produced goods. In this instance, there would be a tendency for the U.S. trade balance to improve. Even this conclusion, however, requires some important qualifications.

First, it assumes that exchange rates are fixed, or at least are not allowed to adjust fully over time. Exchange rates, of course, have been allowed to adjust since 1971. Thus, any expansion in net exports resulting from the substitution of the value-added tax for the corporate income tax would be dampened by an appreciation of the dollar relative to other currencies. Second, other countries also have payroll and social security taxes. Thus, they could act to offset any expected improvement in the United States trade balance by substituting increases in their (already existing) value-added taxes for these other taxes. Third, even if the partial replacement of the corporate income or payroll tax would improve the U.S. trade balance, the choice of whether to adopt a value-added tax is much too important to be driven by this consideration.

A value-added tax may be associated with an improved U.S. trade balance in a different way. To the extent that it allowed the corporate income tax to be reduced, U.S. industry may become more vigorous and better able to compete in world markets.

* * *

Political Concerns
State-Local Tax Base

A Federal value-added tax or retail sales tax might be viewed as an unwarranted intrusion by the Federal government into the fiscal domain of state and local governments. Forty-five states and the District of Columbia, as well as many local jurisdictions, impose general sales and use taxes, a revenue source which they may view as exclusively their own. Sales and gross receipts taxes account for about 35 percent of overall state and local tax revenue. * * *

While the Federal government should be sensitive to the impact a national sales or value-added tax would have on state and local governments, it is not clear that this should preclude Federal adoption of such a tax. Experience with the income tax, of course, demonstrates that there can be Federal, state, and local government taxation of the same tax base. * * *

Major Design Issues

Zero Rating versus Exemption

Under a value-added tax, commodities, transactions, or firms can receive preferential treatment in two ways, by zero rating or exemption. Under zero rating, all value-added tax is removed from the zero rated good, activity, or firm. In contrast, exemption only removes the value-added tax at the exempt stage, and it will actually increase, rather than reduce, the total taxes paid by the exempt firm's business or non-retail customers. It is for this reason that a sharp distinction must be made between zero rating and exemption in designing a value-added tax.

If a commodity or service is zero rated, no tax applies to its sale and the seller of the zero-rated item receives a credit for the tax paid on the purchase of materials and other inputs used to produce it. By this procedure, the zero-rated commodity is freed of all value-added tax; the user bears no tax with respect to a zero-rated good or service. By contrast, if a commodity is exempted, the sale is not subject to tax, but the seller receives no credit for tax paid on the purchase of materials and other inputs used to produce the exempt item. Users of the exempt item will thus bear some tax.

If a commodity, for example, is exempt only at the retail level, then only the retail level is freed of value-added tax. Although the retailer would not charge value-added tax on its sale, the retailer would not be entitled to a credit for tax paid on the purchase of an exempt item. Thus, exemption of a commodity through all of its production and distribution channels would be necessary to free it of its entire value-added tax burden. But, with zero rating, unlike exemption, only the final sale of the commodity needs to be zero rated, since any tax previously paid would be credited on the last sale.

* * *

The choice between zero rating and exemption should be made on the basis of two principal considerations: (1) Is it desirable to free the users of the good or service completely from value-added tax, or only partially? (2) Is it desirable to exclude certain firms from the requirement to register and file returns? Even from the standpoint of the firms themselves, there are conflicting considerations. Zero rating frees a firm and its customers completely from value-added tax, but the zero-rated firm must register and file a tax return. If a firm is exempt, it is not required to register and file a return, but the customers of an exempt firm bear the tax incurred by the exempt firm on its purchases. This may be particularly objectionable to the exempt firm's business customers who cannot receive credit for this tax. In this instance, exemption would place the exempt-firm at a competitive disadvantage.

One further advantage of zero rating is that it avoids the complications that would arise if a firm handles both taxable and exempt commodities. With zero rating, such a firm receives credit for tax paid on all its purchases, whether for production or distribution of zero rated or of taxable goods. But if some goods are exempted, then the firm selling the exempt items is entitled to a credit only for the tax on those purchases of materials and other inputs that are used to produce taxable (or zero-rated) goods. It does not receive a credit for tax paid on purchases related to the exempt transactions.

* * *

Thus, in general, zero rating is superior to exemption of commodities and services and of transactions, such as exports. Exemption is desirable only for those firms which the government does not wish to register, for administrative or other reasons, and/or does not seek to remove all the value-added tax from their customers. Farmers, small service establishments, sidewalk vendors, and charitable and religious organizations are possible examples of firms for whom exemption may be appropriate.

* * *

VALUE ADDED TAX: A MODEL STATUTE AND COMMENTARY
American Bar Association, Committee on
Value Added Tax of the Section of Taxation
Pages 4-9, 11-15, 38-39, 41, 59-62, 64-65, 68-71 (1989)

Introduction

* * *

Comparison of invoice VAT and BTT

Compared to an invoice method VAT [also referred to as credit-invoice method or credit method VAT], a BTT-type sales-subtractive VAT [also referred to as business transfer tax or subtractive method VAT] has some disadvantages. The BTT, because it is a period tax, does not provide the audit trail available with the transactional invoice method VAT. Under the invoice method, with sales from business-to-business, the sales invoice can be used to verify the seller's output tax liability on sales and the buyer's input tax credits on purchases. It is difficult to rebate the VAT component in export sales under a BTT with the precision that is possible under an invoice method tax. The BTT, as a period tax, is buried in export prices. Unless the BTT is broad-based and levied at a single rate, the BTT component can only be estimated. The invoice method VAT is a transactions tax, with tax on sales listed on tax invoices and tax on purchases eligible for input credit. The precise invoice VAT component in exports therefore can be removed with the zero rating procedure.

If, for administrative reasons, some midstream sales[10] are removed from an invoice VAT base, revenue lost on these sales will be recouped when sales are made at a subsequent stage of production or distribution. On the other hand, if midstream sales are removed from the BTT or other sales-subtractive VAT base, the tax base is reduced permanently, unless the

---

10. The term "midstream sales" is used to refer to sales between taxable businesses at various stages of production and distribution, but it does not include retail sales to consumers.

statute contains an administratively complicated rule that would disallow deductions for purchases that were not subject to VAT earlier in the production-distribution chain. The BTT poses a significant transition problem because it does not provide a mechanism (and cannot do so without unduly complicating the law) upon the introduction of VAT or change in tax rate to tax the full value of goods sold after the effective date at the introductory or new rate. Under an invoice method VAT, sales to consumers after the effective date of a rate change are taxed at the new rate. Because the BTT is buried in the price of goods and services, sales to consumers shortly after the effective date of a rate change will be taxed in part at the old rate and in part at the new rate. The BTT base can be calculated by adjusting accounts maintained for income tax purposes. For some sellers, the cost to comply with a BTT therefore may be less than with an invoice VAT. The principal reason the Model Act adopts the tax invoice method rather than the cost-subtractive method VAT is that the invoice method is a transactions tax rather than a period tax. As such, the invoice VAT avoids many of the negative features of the BTT noted above.

* * *

Comparison of invoice VAT and retail sales tax

The invoice method VAT also has advantages over a single-stage retail sales tax (RST), especially if the combined federal, state and local sales tax rate is high enough to tempt evasion. The Canadian Royal Commission on Taxation estimated this point at 14 percent.[15] A retail sales tax can be designed with the same tax base and the same revenue potential as an invoice VAT.[16] For political reasons, however, the tax bases may differ. Also, the invoice VAT may operate and may have to be administered differently. This report does not thoroughly analyze the differences between a retail sales tax and an invoice VAT. The following material summarizes some of the major differences between these two forms of sales tax.

Under an invoice VAT, most sellers are not required to distinguish between sales to businesses and sales to final consumers. The requirement that the seller charge VAT on sales regardless of the buyer's use of the item purchased simplifies compliance for the seller and administration for the Service. Under a RST, a mechanism such as a resale exclusion certificate is

---

15. *See* 5 Report of the Royal Commission on Taxation, Sales Taxes and General Tax Administration 50 (1966) (the report is commonly known as the Report of the Carter Commission).

16. For an in-depth comparison of VAT and RST, see, Cnossen, *VAT and RST: A Comparison*, 35 CAN. TAX. J. 559 (1987). For other detailed discussions of the differences between VAT and RST, *see* Due, *The Case for the Use of the Retail Form of Sales Tax in Preference to the Value-Added Tax*, in BROAD-BASED TAXES: NEW OPTIONS AND SOURCES 205 (R. Musgrave ed., 1973); Shoup, *Factors Bearing on an Assumed Choice Between A Federal Retail Sales Tax and a Federal Value-Added Tax*, in BROAD-BASED TAXES: NEW OPTIONS AND SOURCES 215 (R. Musgrave ed., 1973).

required in order effectively to identify buyers who purchase for resale and therefore are not subject to the tax.

An invoice VAT provides an incentive for the seller to report sales. To obtain an input credit for tax on purchases, the buyer must obtain a tax invoice from the seller. Pressure from buyers will tend to encourage the seller to report all of his sales, at least to other businesses. There is no comparable incentive under a RST.

If a federal RST or invoice VAT is a consumption-style tax, the tax should be removed from capital goods purchased by taxable businesses. A RST can achieve this result by requiring the seller to monitor the exempt status of sales of capital goods to businesses. Capital goods are more easily eliminated from an invoice VAT base by granting business purchasers input credits for the VAT charged on such purchases. Under a VAT, the buyer, not the seller, bears any cost of recovering the VAT on capital purchases.

* * *

An invoice VAT base probably will include sales of more services than a retail sales tax base, especially if the RST follows the state model. An invoice VAT generally does not distinguish between sales of goods and of services, and therefore taxes all but the services statutorily removed from the base. Theoretically, the same base could be constructed for a RST; but this is less likely to occur.

* * *

Jurisdictional Reach of the Tax

The jurisdictional rules governing international transactions dictate whether a VAT is an origin or destination principle tax. An origin principle VAT imposes tax on value added within the taxing nation, regardless of where the goods or services are consumed. Imports are not taxed, and exports bear tax. A destination principle VAT imposes tax in the nation where the goods and services are consumed, regardless of where the goods are produced or the services are rendered. Under the destination principle, imports are taxed and exports are free of tax. Foreign VATS typically employ the destination principle. The Model Act also is a destination principle tax.

* * *

Inclusion of Capital Goods in the Tax Base

* * * An advantage of a VAT over other forms of consumption tax is that a VAT provides a convenient mechanism (the input credit) to eliminate tax on capital goods. By eliminating tax on capital goods purchased by businesses making taxable sales, a C-VAT imposes tax only once on the goods and services produced with the capital goods. If it is desirable to enact a federal tax on personal consumption, it would be inappropriate for Congress to tax capital goods under a GNP- or NI-variant VAT. Foreign VATs invariably are consumption-style taxes, and the Model Act is a C-VAT.

Guidelines for VAT Project

The VAT committee deliberately refrained from taking a position favoring or opposing the adoption of a VAT. It believes that this is a political issue to be resolved by Congress. Nevertheless, if Congress decides to adopt a VAT, the committee recommends a European-style invoice method VAT with a base of personal consumption.

Former Ways and Means Committee Chairman Al Ullman's proposed VAT served as the springboard for the Model VAT Act, but the Model Act departs from the Ullman bill on many policy issues. * * *

Four general principles have influenced the development of the Model Act. First, the tax should be imposed on a broad tax base to permit the adoption of the lowest possible rate. Congress should accommodate social or economic concerns, such as the regressive effects of a VAT, outside the VAT regime.

Second, the VAT should provide horizontal equity among consumers and should be neutral with respect to consumer choices. Consumers are expected to bear the tax, and the Model Act attempts to tax alike sales of identical goods and services, even if the consumers acquire the goods or services from different sources.

Third, the VAT should not be levied on the same value added to products or services more than once. The Model Act attempts to minimize the grant of VAT exemptions, especially before the retail stage, in order to avoid multiple tax.

Fourth, the Model Act should include only basic VAT rules. Countries outside the European Economic Community generally pattern their VATs on the Common Market-style VAT, a detailed statute that combines features of both our Internal Revenue Code and Treasury Regulations. The Model Act adopts the American tradition of providing basic rules in the statute and leaving many of the details to regulations.

Summary of Model Act

The Model Act is a consumption-style, destination principle, invoice method VAT imposed on the seller's sale of taxable property and services. The Model Act adheres closely to the economic concept of a destination principle tax, taxing imports and zero rating exports of property and services. This report discusses most of the broad policy issues pertaining to a VAT, but it does not attempt to cover all issues that may arise under an American VAT.

The tax is imposed at a single rate on imports by anyone and on taxable sales of property and services in the United States by a taxable person in connection with a business. For example, the lease of property is a taxable service. On the other hand services provided by an employee to his employer are not taxable. Exports are treated as taxable transactions in order to remove all VAT from the price of exports. A casual sale for modest consideration, such as a sale of a used refrigerator to a neighbor, is not taxed; a casual sale of a high-priced item is taxed. * * *

The Model Act zero rates exports and exempts from tax the supply of property and services by income tax-exempt organizations and government entities for which the supplier does not receive consideration other than contributions or general taxes. [T]he Model Act does not provide special treatment for most other sales that were zero rated under the Ullman Bill. The Model Act departs from most foreign VATs by not providing a small business exemption for taxable persons with low quarterly or annual turnover; however, a rule is proposed if Congress decides to grant a small business exemption.

   * * *

Treasury regulations can authorize related businesses to elect to be treated as a single taxable person and can authorize a single business to elect to treat divisions or branches as separate   taxable persons. * * *

Imposition of Tax on Taxable Transactions

   * * *

Transfers to employees

An employer may transfer property or services to an employee as compensation for services. A neutral and comprehensive VAT should tax these fringe benefits the same as the employer's payment of compensation in cash and the employee's purchase of these benefits with his cash salary. Indeed, economic distortions may result if some fringe benefits are removed from the VAT base. * * * *

Under our individual income tax, compensation paid in kind generally is taxable, but, for administrative and other reasons, certain no-additional-cost services, qualified employee discounts, working condition fringes, and de minimis fringe benefits are not taxed. Fringes that are taxable under the income tax should be taxable under the VAT, and the tax should be imposed on their fair market value.

The problem in distinguishing between taxable benefits and working condition fringes under the income tax carries over to a VAT. For administrative convenience or other reasons, Congress may apply the income tax rules to identify transfers treated as nontaxable working condition fringes under the VAT. For administrative or political reasons, Congress also may treat as nontaxable other fringes excludable under section 132. To retain part of the value of these consumption items within the VAT base, Congress could deny employers any input credit for VAT on purchases attributable to these fringe benefits, or it could require employers to charge output tax on these transfers, based on the employer's cost instead of fair market value.

The Model Act taxes compensatory transfers of property or services to employees, except when such transfers are excludable from the employee's gross income for income tax purposes. * * *

Employee services for employer

The cost of labor is part of an employer's value added tax base. An employee's services rendered for his employer therefore does not constitute the sale of services subject to VAT. This rule is included as section 4007(c)(2)(A).

Tax Base Issues—Zero Rated Exports and Zero Rating
Or Exemption for Certain Sales and Sellers

The Model Act * * * removes a small group of transactions from the tax base by designating them as nontaxable transactions. As a destination principle VAT, the Model Act also zero rates exports and taxes imports.

In addition to defining taxable and nontaxable transactions and adopting the jurisdictional rule governing international transactions, the legislature must decide if the tax will be used strictly as a revenue raising measure or will be used also to achieve social, economic, or other nonrevenue goals. If the VAT will serve only the revenue raising function, and regressivity or other economic and social concerns will be addressed through adjustments to the individual income tax or through direct grant programs, VAT should be imposed on all taxable transactions. Foreign VATs typically provide special treatment for some sales to achieve nonrevenue goals. The nature and extent of these exceptions vary from country to country. Some zero rate or exempt a broad range of goods and services. * * * These exceptions add considerably to the complexity of a VAT.

Kinds of exceptions

The exceptions from the rules taxing sales at the standard rate may take three basic forms—sales taxable at a higher or reduced rate, sales taxable at a zero rate, and sales exempt from tax. * * *

Sales of necessities to consumers may be taxable at a lower than standard rate in order to reduce the impact of the VAT on low-income households. Sales of luxuries to consumers may be taxable at a higher rate in order to increase the VAT burden on high income households. The Model Act, except for zero rating exports as required by a destination principle tax, does not impose VAT at a higher or lower than standard rate on any taxable sales. * * *

Zero-rated sales

Sales subject to a zero tax rate are taxable sales. If sales are zero rated at the retail stage only, the final purchaser will buy the article free of VAT. For example, if a retailer makes $1,200,000 of zero-rated sales and has $1,000,000 of purchases on which it pays $100,000 VAT, the retailer does not charge VAT on sales and is entitled to input credits (refunds) for $100,000 VAT on purchases.

* * *

Exempt sales

If a sale is exempt from tax, the seller does not charge tax on the sale and is not entitled to an input credit for tax on purchases attributable to the exempt sale. * * *

De minimis exemption; sales by government and income tax-exempt organizations

Congress, for administrative or other reasons, could provide special VAT treatment for some sellers. For example, to remove small traders from the tax rolls, Congress could add a de minimis exemption for businesses making sales less than a quarterly or annual threshold. The Model Act does not include a de minimis rule. * * *

Taxation of international transactions—in general

A VAT must include jurisdictional rules governing international transactions. The jurisdictional rules may be based on the origin or the destination principle. Under the origin principle, tax is imposed on value added from business activity within the taxing jurisdiction, regardless of where the goods are consumed. VAT is not imposed on imports (value added outside the United States) nor is it rebated on exports (value was added in the United States). Under the destination principle, VAT is imposed on goods and services consumed in the taxing jurisdiction, regardless of where they are produced. VAT is imposed on imports for consumption in the United States, and VAT is rebated on exports to be consumed elsewhere. The Model Act is a destination principle VAT.

Treasury authority to zero rate other sales deliberately omitted

The Ullman Bill authorized the Secretary to issue regulations that zero rated de minimis sales or sales that would not raise sufficient revenue to justify the tax administration and compliance costs. * * *

There may be some taxable transactions that present appealing facts for the administrative grant of zero rate relief; but, if the Ullman proposal were enacted, the Treasury would be deluged with requests to zero rate a wide range of transactions. Without statutory guidance on the kinds of transactions eligible for zero rating on revenue and administrative grounds, it would be difficult for the Secretary to decide which preferences to grant. It is more appropriate for Congress to make these mixed political-administrative judgments. The Model Act therefore does not include any provision delegating to the Secretary authority to zero rate transactions of a de minimis amount or transactions that would not raise enough revenue to justify the administrative or compliance costs associated with the taxation of such transactions. * * *

The Ullman Bill would have zero rated certain food, housing, and medical care, mass transit, interest, and sales by farmers or fishermen.

Food

In 1985, food accounted for approximately 16 percent of all personal consumption expenditures. * * *

The Model Act adopts a broad tax base and does not provide special treatment for necessities to reduce the regressive effects of the VAT. The Act therefore does not exempt or zero rate food. If it is desirable to remove the VAT burden on food purchased by low income households, Congress should use direct grant programs targeted to these consumers, such as increases in food stamp allotments, refundable income tax credits, or reductions in income taxes.

* * *

THE VALUE-ADDED TAX: KEY TO DEFICIT REDUCTION?
Charles E. McLure, Jr.[*]
Pages 10-12 (1987)

Many Americans concerned about fiscal affairs seem to be increasingly convinced that a new source of federal revenue must be found. Although this perception appears to be shared across the political spectrum, a variety of very different reasons probably underlie the common perception.

Many observers, of all political persuasions, believe that the federal budget deficit must be substantially reduced, if not eliminated. Again, concern about the budget deficit has a variety of roots. At one level is the simple intuitive belief that the federal government must pay its own way over the long haul, just as households must, and that continued deficit finance will eventually become inflationary and lead to a need for difficult adjustments to eliminate inflation.

A more sophisticated version of this view is based on the realization that the federal government is not merely borrowing from its own citizens. Rather, because the private saving rate has not risen since the federal government began to run massive budget deficits in 1982, the nation (on combined public and private account) has been borrowing substantial amounts abroad. During 1985 the United States resumed the status of a net debtor—a position more appropriate to a developing country. Thus it can no longer be said sanguinely of the national debt that "we owe it to ourselves." The reduction in net international balances of the United States seems anomalous to many observers. Why, they ask, should the richest nation in the world not be able to pay its own way? Some observers find it unconscionable that the United States should be absorbing so much of the world's scarce supply of net saving, when countries of the third world need capital so badly.

A somewhat different concern has focused on the implications of budget deficits for international trade. The higher real interest rates resulting from the budget deficit have stimulated capital inflows. Borrowing abroad has led to an overvalued dollar, which has made it extremely difficult for American

---

[*]. At time of original publication, Senior Fellow at the Hoover Institution, Stanford University.

business, whether in farming, mining, or manufacturing, to compete in world markets. A substantial reduction of the deficit has been seen as essential to permanent success in the effort to bring the value of the dollar to a more realistic level.

Of course, there is no reason that the present federal taxes could not be used to raise additional revenue. But following that course would necessitate one of two things: income tax rates substantially above those in the recently enacted tax reform; or further base broadening, such as taxation of fringe benefits and repeal or substantial limitation of the itemized deductions for state and local income and property taxes and for mortgage interest.

Many analysts believe that the reduction of the top marginal tax rate to below 30 percent is important for incentive reasons and that a top marginal rate below 30 percent is essential if capital gains are to be taxed as ordinary income. Not only do lower marginal tax rates entail fewer disincentives; they also provide less reward for the uneconomical behavior that has caused so much concern about the tax system and spurred interest in tax reform. Perhaps more important, it is hard to imagine the Congress and the president doing an about-face on rates so soon after cutting them with so much fanfare.

Concern that excessive reliance on the income tax creates too great a bias against saving and in favor of present consumption provides further impetus for interest in a value-added tax. Many observers, including many prominent economists, would like to see a shift from income taxation toward greater reliance on taxes on consumption. Consumption-based taxation could be levied on the personal expenditures of households—for example, through a cash-flow-based tax on consumption—or it could be implemented through indirect taxes on transactions, such as a VAT or other form of general sales tax.

The more liberal members of Congress would use revenues from an alternative source for yet another reason. They would avoid budget cuts such as those mandated by Gramm-Rudman-Hollings. In their more optimistic dreams they would use additional revenues to expand government provision of goods and services.

[I argue in this book] that if a substantial amount of additional revenue is to be raised, it should be through the VAT or some other form of broad-based federal sales tax, rather than through one of the more narrowly based taxes on consumption recently being discussed. The possibility of a broad-based federal sales tax poses a dilemma for both liberals and conservatives. Although many liberals would like to see an important new source of federal revenue introduced to reduce the deficit without sacrificing federal programs, they are concerned about the potential distributional effects of the VAT: because the base of the tax is consumption, the VAT is regressive unless explicit steps are taken to avoid regressivity. Many conservatives would welcome a reduction of the deficit and a shift in the relative emphasis of taxation from income to saving, but they are worried about handing the Congress a new and, they fear, relatively painless source of federal revenue that could be used to expand the scope of government.

The last view is perhaps best epitomized by President Reagan's continued refusal to tolerate proposals for new taxes. He appears to see the threat of continued deficits as the only way to force the Congress to be fiscally responsible. According to this line of reasoning, Congress will exercise fiscal responsibility by reducing expenditures rather than by raising taxes only if no new source of revenue is available. Moreover, if further growth of government is to be avoided, a "money machine" such as a VAT must be kept out of the hands of Congress.

I believe that the federal budget deficit is a major problem and that the American people do not want to see the deficit reduced entirely by cutting federal spending. While I share the concern that revenues from a federal sales tax might lead to greater federal spending than is optimal, I have come to view the continuation of large deficits as a greater threat than the money machine. The regressivity of the VAT or other form of sales tax can probably be dealt with satisfactorily. Problems of intergovernmental relations strike me as being somewhat more serious. Thus I believe that it is time to start seriously discussing the VAT, one type of federal sales tax that might be employed to reduce the deficit to an acceptable level.

* * *

ECONOMICS OF THE VALUE ADDED TAX
John F. Due[*]
6 Journal of Corporation Law 61, 65-70 (1980)

The argument for a federal value added tax centers around economic considerations. Thus, an analysis of economic effects is necessary to properly assess the desirability of the tax. Such an analysis, however, requires assumptions about revenue utilization. There are three principal use alternatives, which can be accepted individually or in combination: (a) substitution of the tax for the corporation income tax; (b) replacement of a major portion of the personal income tax; and (c) replacement of the payroll tax for social security financing. The Ullman bill provides for substitution of a value added tax for portions of the revenues from all three of these taxes. Another alternative is increased federal revenue, absent any further tax reductions. This option is not under serious consideration at present but could become so if defense spending increases significantly. If the tax is to be used to increase federal spending, however, the tax would be an alternative to raising some combination of the other three levies. The analysis of economic effects is thus essentially the same as if the revenue were used to allow reduction in the existing levies.

---

[*]. At time of original publication, Professor of Economics, University of Illinois, Urbana.

* * *

The Relative Effects of a Value Added Tax on Savings and Real Capital Formation

Currently, the argument for a value added tax centers on the capital formation issue. The effects of the VAT, however, must be compared to the consequences of the tax or taxes for which the value added tax is substituted.

Personal Income Tax

The personal income tax is based on income received (assuming no shifting); the value added tax is related to consumption. The relative effects, therefore, are those of income versus consumption related taxes generally. The change would reduce the relative tax on persons whose consumption-income ratio (C/Y) was relatively low and increase the relative burden on those with high C/Y ratios. Liability for the income tax is increased by earning additional income and reduced by earning less; the value added tax liability is not affected by changes in income alone, but instead varies with consumption expenditures. These differences should result in a higher overall savings-income ratio (S/Y), that is, a higher percentage of national income would be saved, for two reasons.

The first reason is that the redistribution of burden from persons with low C/Y ratios to those with high C/Y ratios would force many of the latter to curtail consumption as they have little or no margin between income and consumption. * * *

The second reason is that the change could have some effect upon incentives to save and consume. The income tax not only provides no incentive to save rather than consume, but in a sense it makes savings less attractive by taxing the return earned from such savings. By contrast, the value added tax would give some incentive to save instead of consume. Tax liability could be reduced by so doing, and the interest from the savings would not be directly subject to tax. The interest returns would be taxed only indirectly when they were ultimately spent on consumption. * * *

The only offsetting influence is the possible "income" effect of the income tax. By reducing the return from savings, the income tax may encourage some persons to attempt to save more (rather than less) to have a certain after tax annual return from savings for retirement or other purposes. * * *

The significance of the argument that a switch to a value added tax will increase incentive to save is based upon the assumption that the S/Y ratio—persons [sic] preferences for savings—is highly responsive to the rate of return on savings. This conclusion is still open to question. Traditionally, it was argued that the return to be obtained from savings had only a minor influence on savings. Instead, the motives (such as old age, etc.) are not directly related to the return. A widely quoted study by Boskin at Stanford found the rate of return[10] did have substantial influence on a person's decision to save. Other studies have questioned his econometric analysis, however. The question, therefore, remains unanswered. But quite apart from the incentives, the shifting of relative burden in the direction of persons with high C/Y ratios undoubtedly would result in a somewhat higher percentage of national income saved with the value added tax even if incentives are not affected.

* * *

Substitution of the Value Added Tax
for the Corporation Income Tax

A 10% value added tax would allow complete elimination of the corporate income tax, or, with partial use of the revenue to replace other taxes, a reduction in the corporate rate. A major problem encountered in comparing the effects of the corporate and value added taxes is that the incidence of the corporate tax is unknown. Many studies, econometric and otherwise, have investigated the question, with widely differing results, ranging from complete forward shifting (into the prices of goods and thus distribution on the basis of consumption), to no forward shifting at all, the burden resting on the owners of the corporation.

To the extent that the corporate income tax is not shifted, replacement by a value added tax should result in an increase in the percentage of national income saved. A lower corporate tax (assuming that the tax is not shifted forward) permits either an increase in dividends or an increase in undistributed profits held in the firm. Dividend receivers are concentrated heavily in the higher income group, and have a high propensity to save, relative to the average of the taxpayers whose real incomes are reduced by the value added tax. Corporate undistributed profits are, of course, automatically saved, and thus the ratio of national income saved is increased by replacement of the corporate tax by value added taxation, to the extent that profits are not distributed.

The major problem, however, with complete elimination of the tax on corporate profits is that a major segment of current income would go completely untaxed. The result would be serious distortions in the economy, including a great incentive to incorporate when other circumstances did not dictate this form of organization, and to increase the percentage of profits held in the company. These effects would increase even further the percentage of national income saved, but at the expense of economic distortions and, by usual standards, serious loss of equity. But, as extensively discussed, integration of the tax on undistributed profits into the income tax structure encounters serious complications. Yet, allowing undistributed profits to go completely untaxed, with the relatively light

---

10. M. Boskin, *Taxation, Saving and the Rate of Interest*, 86 J. POL. ECON. S3, S16 (1978).

taxation of capital gains, (apart from the inflation factor) would be politically intolerable.

To the extent that the corporate income tax is shifted forward into prices paid by consumers, it resembles a value added tax in burden distribution, except that the burden will vary widely among different commodities according to the ratio of profits to sales and the ability of the firms to shift. As a consequence, the effects of the two levies on savings are very similar, except that the S/Y ratios of the various groups of consumers are affected differently by the two taxes.

Effects Upon Real Investment

In summary, a shift from either form of income tax (or to some extent, both, as proposed in the Ullman bill), to a value added tax will almost certainly increase the percentage of national income saved. This, in turn, would allow a higher rate of real capital formation, which would then permit a higher rate of growth of labor productivity. But an increase in the S/Y ratio does not automatically increase real investment and the rate of capital formation; it merely makes such increase possible. * * *

[A]n increase in savings should lower the interest costs of borrowing and make more funds available for real investment.

Numerous other factors affect the return from real investment. It is charged that both corporate and personal income taxes, by reducing the rate of return (assuming no or incomplete forward shifting of tax to consumers), diminish the incentive to undertake real investment. Thus, a shift to the value added tax, by lessening the tax on the return from new investment, would lead to increased real investment in the same manner it encourages additional savings. It is argued that reduction in corporate income tax would be particularly effective since this removal would immediately and directly increase the returns from additional capital investment.
        * * *

The critics, however, are not as certain that the change will in fact have much effect on the overall savings ratio. Moreover, they fear that if there is a substantial change, the result will be more unemployment and an even lower rate of capital formation. The evidence is not adequate at this time to determine which view is correct. It must be recognized, in any event, that if there is some current capital shortage, a substantial shift to consumption related taxation could easily tip the balance in the other direction and give rise to significant unemployment.

It should be noted that there obviously are other factors leading to the declining rate of savings in the United States besides income taxes. One is the social security program, which makes savings for old age less essential. The other factor is the fear of continuing inflation, which leads persons to buy now instead of saving for the future. The transition to a value added tax will not alter either of these influences, unless the productivity increase from additional capital formation would be so significant as to slow inflation by increasing supply of goods. Some proponents of the value added tax argue this will occur, but whether this effect will be sufficient to offset the immediate inflationary effect is questionable.

Furthermore, if there is a serious capital shortage, there are other forms of tax adjustments that can increase the percentage of national income saved. A relatively simple step is to exclude from taxable income certain types of interest on savings—for example, a greater portion of dividends than is now allowed, and/or portions of bond interest. At the same time, real investment can be further stimulated by additional investment tax credits and changes in depreciation allowances. There are objections to all such exclusions in terms of overall equity of the income tax system, but they may be preferable to the drastic change involved in the establishment of a value added tax.

     * * *

A Value Added Tax to Replace the Social Security Payroll Taxes

Use of value added tax revenue to replace the payroll taxes, or a portion of the payroll tax revenue, would have less clear cut effects upon the savings/income ratio. A basic problem with this analysis, however, is that the incidence of the payroll taxes is subject to great dispute. A number of studies on this issue have been done, producing results all the way from complete shifting of the entire burden to workers to no shifting of the employer part at all.

If the payroll tax is directed entirely, or primarily at the workers, the change to a value added tax would transfer a portion of the tax burden to nonworkers. The burden would thus be borne, in part, by higher income capital owners, with higher savings ratios on the whole than workers, and partially by lower income persons with low nonfactor incomes. The net result of these transitions is difficult to determine. If the burden rests in part on the employers, it will either reduce profits and thus have a relatively greater effect by reducing savings, or it will be shifted to consumers in the form of higher prices. In the former case, shift to a value added tax will increase the overall S/Y ratio; in the latter, it will have minimal general effect as this portion of the payroll tax is distributed in the same overall pattern (but differently on different consumer expenditures) as the value added tax.

* * *

VALUE ADDED TAX: DOES THIS CONSUMPTION TAX HAVE A PLACE IN THE FEDERAL TAX SYSTEM?
Alan Schenk[*]

7 Virginia Tax Review 207, 260, 263-64, 267-77 (1987)

VAT advocates frequently claim that there are economic advantages of adding this national sales tax to our federal tax system. The analysis in this

---

[*]. At time of original publication, Professor of Law, Wayne State University Law School.

subsection covers the impact of taxes on inflation, capital formation and savings, equity or fairness, and economic efficiency. For purposes of this discussion, it is assumed that federal revenue must be increased. Thus, for each economic issue, the impact of a new VAT will be compared with increases in existing federal taxes. * * *

Inflation and Price Stability

Enactment of a broad-based VAT can be expected to cause a one-time increase in product prices for the taxed items by the rate of the new tax. * * *

[I]f Congress decides to increase revenue and wants the tax increase to serve to stabilize prices and control inflation (or at least not create an inflationary effect), then it should not increase revenue with a new VAT. Quite the contrary, a new VAT likely will increase product prices more than increases in income or payroll taxes, especially a progressive income tax.

Capital Formation and Savings (Economic Growth)

* * *

A VAT ultimately is borne by consumers of taxed items. For individuals choosing between current consumption and saving, the enactment (or increase in rate) of a tax on consumption should provide an incentive to defer consumption—in other words, it should encourage savings.

* * *

A VAT is preferable to existing federal taxes as a fiscal device to encourage savings. Income taxes withdraw funds individuals would otherwise use for consumption or savings. An income tax increase therefore does not encourage savings. Since payroll taxes do not directly burden income from savings or the use of savings for consumption, they do not encourage either. On the other hand, if Congress increased the cost to consume with a VAT (or to a lesser extent selective excise taxes), in effect, it may encourage taxpayers to save rather than consume.

Equity or Fairness

One significant criterion used to measure the quality of a tax system or a particular tax within the system is tax equity or fairness. Explaining the mission's recommended changes in the Japanese tax system following World War II, Carl Shoup, head of the American Tax Mission, noted that a nation's "tax system must satisfy the deep, widespread feelings of the people as to what is fair."[191] He added that "no one remains in the tax field for long without realizing that nothing he recommends will stand up unless it meets the test of fairness in the distribution of the tax burden."[192]

Two economic concepts traditionally have influenced our view of distributive justice—the "benefit" and the "ability to pay" principles. Based on the benefit principle, each taxpayer should contribute to the revenue "in

---

191. See Gen. Headquarters, Supreme Commander for Allied Powers, Tokyo, 1 Report on Japanese Taxation 17 (1949).

192. *Id.* at 16.

line with the benefits which he receives from public services." A tax based on the benefit principle may link revenue to government expenditure policy; for example, highway user taxes and tolls to fund the maintenance of roads, and to some extent social security taxes to fund retirement and disability programs are taxes levied on the benefit principle. Taxes that fund general government services such as defense cannot be explained under the benefit principle. Congress could levy a VAT to finance specific programs. For example, Congress considered the possible adoption of a form of VAT to finance the Superfund to clean up hazardous waste. However this article assumes that a broad-based VAT will be enacted only if substantial revenue is needed either to reduce the budget deficit or to finance general government services. It therefore is more appropriate to judge VAT by the ability to pay principle.

Three broad gauges may be used to measure individual ability to pay taxes—income, consumption, or wealth of a taxpayer or a taxable unit. Since economic income equals the sum of consumption, savings, and taxes, the basic difference between a tax based on income and a tax based in consumption is that under the latter, income not used for consumption is not taxed. Wealth taxes have been viewed as a possible supplementary index of ability to pay, since income does not adequately take account of the fact that wealth represents command over resources. This article does not compare VAT with a possible annual wealth tax.

In the United States, where the economic system distributes income unequally and family responsibilities may affect ability to pay taxes, the income tax tailored to individual differences may effectively distribute the tax burden in accordance with ability to pay concepts. A graduated consumption tax like an annual expenditure tax also may distribute tax burdens in accordance with taxpayers' ability to pay tax.[1]

The "ability to pay" principle is subdivided into two elements of distributive justice—horizontal and vertical equity. To achieve horizontal equity, taxpayers situated equally should be taxed equally. If income (what a taxpayer adds to community resources) is viewed as an appropriate measure of ability to pay tax, then taxpayers with equal incomes should be taxed equally. If consumption (what the taxpayer withdraws from community resources for personal use) is deemed an appropriate measure of ability to pay, then taxpayers with equal levels of consumption should be taxed equally. For this purpose, equity may be measured by individuals' lifetime or annual consumption. In this section, however it is assumed that annual income is a better yardstick of ability to pay taxes.[204]

---

1. See Chapter Seven. (Eds.)

204. Typically, a tax period of one year is used to judge equity in the distribution of the tax burden of a particular tax. See Bradford & Toder, Consumption vs. Income Base Taxes: The Argument on Grounds of Equity and Simplicity, 1976 Proc. of 69th Ann. Conf. on Tax'n of Nat'l Tax Ass'n 25, 30-31. But see J. Pechman & B. Okner, Who Bears the Tax Burden 52 (1974)

Vertical equity assumes that the tax burden should be progressive as to income. For many years, the federal tax system relied on steeply progressive individual income tax rates to implement our concept of vertical equity. However, since the early 1960s, Congress has cut the top individual tax rate from ninety-one percent to twenty-eight percent. Judged by traditional support for a progressive federal tax system, the VAT is not as equitable as progressive income taxes. However, consider (1) the recent dramatic reduction both in the number of brackets and the top rate for the individual income tax, resulting in mildly progressive rates for taxpayers remaining in the tax system; (2) the reduced rate corporate income taxes; and (3) the flat-rate payroll taxes. In light of this new federal tax structure, it is no longer clear that Congress and the taxpaying population would view a single rate, broad-based VAT as providing an "inequitable" distribution of the tax burden.

Broad-based sales taxes are considered regressive because they impose a higher tax burden, as a percentage of income, on lower income groups (especially those below the poverty level) than on higher income groups. But there are two points worth noting. First, there is some evidence that a VAT burden is proportional to income, rather than regressive.[206] Second, the regressivity of one tax may be accommodated by making adjustments in the progressive taxes if, as a result, the overall federal system possesses an acceptable degree of progressivity.

The Treasury Department, in its 1984 report on tax reform, discussed the concept of progressive and regressive taxes. It suggested that there are two equity issues that affect taxes like sales tax or VAT—the regressivity of the tax and the absolute burden of the tax on the poor. Congress can reduce the regressivity of a VAT by granting tax preferences on necessities that account for most or all of the consumption by lower income taxpayers. However, it would be more difficult for Congress to offset the absolute burden of a VAT on the poor, unless Congress grants a refundable tax credit or reduces other taxes that they now pay. With the movement to reduce the number of return-filing taxpayers (individual income tax returns), it is less likely that Congress would offset the burden of a VAT on the poor through refundable credits obtained by filing returns.

Based on principles of horizontal and vertical equity and using income as the standard by which equity principles are measured, VAT does not fare as well as income and payroll taxes. Testing for horizontal equity, the individual income tax scores well. By tailoring the tax to individual

---

(arguing that family economic decisions, such as housing and other consumption choices, tend to [be] made on the basis of expected income over a period of years, and thus "effective rates of tax based on income for a single year may not be representative of the tax burdens of families with unusually low (or high) incomes").

206. Pohmer, Germany, in The Value Added Tax: Lessons from Europe 96-97 (H. Aaron ed. 1981).

circumstances, Congress can tax those with equal taxable incomes equally. Assuming that the corporate tax is borne by shareholders, the corporate tax does not meet the standards of horizontal equity. At various levels of individual income, stock ownership, as well as dividend policy among corporations, vary widely. Assuming that the employer's and employee's share of social security taxes are borne by labor, the payroll taxes deviate somewhat from the standard of horizontal equity. Since they are imposed only on taxable wages, a retired person earning $25,000 income exclusively from social security benefits and from savings is not subject to the social security taxes, while a worker with $25,000 income earned exclusively from wages would be subject to this tax. Testing for horizontal equity, VAT ranks quite low. At the low and middle income ranges, because taxpayers spend most or all of their disposable income on consumption, there is a significant correlation between income and consumption. This is not true at higher income levels, and even within other ranges, taxpayers have different kinds and amounts of consumption expenditures. Selective excise taxes are worse than a broad-based VAT. There are wide variations in the excise tax burden for individuals at any given level of income because it is totally dependent upon their level of consumption of the taxed items.

A progressive individual income tax can be designed to achieve vertical equity. * * *

Selective federal excise taxes and VAT do not fare well when tested by a traditional view of vertical equity, at least when measured annually rather than over a lifetime. Excises on items like alcohol and tobacco tend to be regressive as to income because consumption of these items represents a decreasing proportion of income as annual income increases. If a consumption tax like a VAT has a broad base, it may, at best, be proportional as to consumption. However, the proportion of income used for consumption tends to decline as individual or household income increases. Thus, even if basic necessities are exempt from tax, a VAT or other general consumption tax likely will not become progressive as to income.

Some commentators have suggested that an analysis of equity in the distribution of the tax burden must consider not only the incidence of the tax imposed, but also the distribution of benefits financed by the tax. However, this approach conflicts with the focus of an ability to pay analysis. If (1) it is desirable that lower income families receive benefits that outweigh their tax burden and (2) ability to pay taxes is the appropriate standard, then a VAT is less desirable as a funding source for social welfare programs than income taxes.

Based on traditional views about horizontal and vertical equity, a progressive rate individual income tax permits the most equitable distribution of tax burden, with corporate income and payroll taxes less desirable but better than selective excise taxes. A VAT would rank higher than selective excises, would be difficult to compare with social security taxes, and would be decidedly worse than corporate and individual income taxes. However, while it is too early to make a definitive judgment, in light of the 1986 reforms that dramatically reduced the top corporate and individual income tax rates, and reduced to two the number of individual tax rate brackets, it is possible that taxpayers collectively have changed our concept of vertical equity and no longer consider highly progressive taxes essential to achieve an equitable distribution of the federal tax burden. If so, then a VAT may not rank so poorly, based on ability to pay principles.

Neutrality or Economic Efficiency

A common tax policy goal is to develop a tax system that fosters economic efficiency or neutrality. A tax is economically efficient if it does not distort economic behavior; that is, the tax is neutral as to: (1) a business' choice among various forms of operation; (2) a consumer's choice among possible consumption expenditures; (3) an individual's choice between consuming now or saving for future consumption; and (4) an individual's choice between working or preferring leisure.

If Congress considered increasing the existing income-based individual income tax or enacting a broad-based C-style VAT and neither choice would change relative prices of goods or services, then these alternatives would be neutral as to consumers' choices among consumer items. However, if the VAT were riddled with exemptions or other preferences, it would not foster economic efficiency. Such a VAT would distort choices consumers must make between taxable and tax-preferred consumption items. Similar inefficiency would occur if Congress increased the income tax that incorporated preferences for the consumption of certain goods or services.[219]

Whether or not increases in individual income tax or VAT change relative prices, these tax increases may create other distortions. Compared with a new broad-based VAT, an increase in a progressive individual income tax may distort choices individuals make between current and future consumption or between work and leisure. With the 1986 base broadening and rate reducing reforms, these distortions under the individual income tax have been reduced substantially. However, if the new VAT included a substantial number of "item" preferences, the resulting VAT may distort an individual's decision to consume now or save to consume in the future (the incentive to consume exempt items currently may distort this choice), but to the extent of the preferences, it may be neutral as to an individual's decision to work or prefer leisure, since neither labor income used to consume exempt goods nor the value of leisure would be subject to a VAT.

The corporate income tax is not a neutral tax because it distorts a business' choice of form of operation. * * *

---

219. For example, the existing individual income tax exempts health and accident insurance provided by employers from taxation, thus encouraging workers to take part of their wages in this tax-free form.

It has been asserted that the corporate tax may serve as an umbrella to protect inefficient corporations that otherwise could not compete with profitable taxpaying corporations. To the extent that industry leaders are able to shift part of the corporate tax forward into product prices, this price increase permits the more inefficient corporations to compete with the price setting leaders and thereby remain in business despite their inefficiency. For example, assume the price setting (PS) Corporation shifts its corporate tax (amounting to about $.50 per widget) into the $10.50 price for widgets. An inefficient, competing (IC) Corporation has higher production costs, but still can obtain customers for its widgets if it sells them for not more than $10.50 per unit. At this price, the IC Corporation earns no profit and therefore pays no corporate tax. If the corporate tax were replaced with a VAT, PS Corporation could sell at a pre-VAT ten dollar price and add a VAT on the sale. At this ten dollar pre-tax price, the IC Corporation would sustain losses of $.50 per unit and ultimately may close. Over time, if the corporate tax is shifted, the replacement of the corporate tax with a VAT can be expected to drive the inefficient corporations out of business. However, it is not clear that Congress supports a national goal of promoting economic efficiency in business, if it occurs at the cost of insolvency for marginal businesses. Indeed, new businesses typically are not very efficient during their formative years and national policy promotes capital formation for new enterprises to hire additional workers. The replacement of most or all of the corporate tax with a VAT could produce a federal tax structure that distorts economic decisions on the form of business operation if corporations could become tax shelters for owners to accumulate earnings and avoid the shareholder level tax. However, if Congress coupled the adoption of a VAT with the integration of the individual and corporate income taxes, the tax shelter phenomenon could be avoided.

Payroll taxes are imposed on wages up to a statutory ceiling for covered employees and self-employed individuals and, as taxes withheld from wages, are neutral as to individuals' choices among consumer items and as to individuals' choices between current consumption and savings for future consumption. Since they are imposed on wages up to a statutory ceiling, payroll taxes may create individual preferences for leisure over work until the ceiling is reached; they then do not distort this choice, since they then do not tax either work or leisure. A broad-based VAT does not have any significant efficiency or neutrality advantages over existing payroll taxes, except as to the latter's preference for leisure over work at payroll levels below the statutory cap.

VAT as a Fiscal Tool to Promote Economic Goals

The focus of the 1986 tax reforms was to broaden the base and reduce the top rates for the individual and corporate income taxes. In the process, Congress reduced the role of income taxes in affecting economic or industrial policy. For example, Congress reversed prior tax policy that encouraged the modernization of plants and equipment with the investment tax credit and rapid depreciation, and that had encouraged the investment in research and development and in certain kinds of real estate. It would be ironic if Congress now found VAT attractive as a fiscal tool to promote economic or industrial policy goals. Yet, a VAT can be used as a fiscal tool to affect the economy in very discreet ways.

If Congress enacted a VAT and granted the President the power to alter the VAT rates within a prescribed range (to alter a ten percent VAT rate by twenty percent—up to twelve percent or down to eight percent), then the government may be able to increase the VAT rate to reduce consumption and thereby slow down an overheated economy or may reduce the VAT rate to stimulate a stagnant economy. If Congress retained the power to make these modest short term rate changes, they may be less effective as a fiscal tool. While Congress debated a bill to increase the rate to stifle consumption, consumers could accelerate their purchases to avoid the proposed increase. Likewise, if Congress wanted to cut the VAT rate temporarily to stimulate consumer spending, the normal tax legislative process might delay enactment of the tax cut until it was no longer needed.

Congress could alter VAT rates on selected consumer items to stimulate or dampen demand in particular industries or particular segments of the economy. For example, to reverse a recession in the auto industry, Congress or the President (if the latter is granted power to adjust rates) could stimulate car buying by cutting the VAT rate on automobiles for a limited period of time.

Notwithstanding the attractiveness of a VAT as a fiscal tool to achieve economic, social, or other national policy goals, it would be undesirable to enact a new VAT to serve these functions rather than to serve basically as a revenue raising measure. If the federal government wants to stimulate or dampen the economy, it may find that it would be more effective to rely on monetary than fiscal policy. Congress cannot justify adoption of a broad-based federal tax on consumption just to obtain this potential fiscal tool.

On balance, the economic considerations discussed do not favor the use of a VAT as a fiscal tool. Instead, reliance on existing federal income and payroll taxes is a better course, and a VAT should be considered only as a revenue raising measure.

Notes and Questions

The Ullman proposal

3. Although Congressman Ullman's proposed Tax Restructuring Act of 1979 was never enacted,[m] its introduction marked a political milestone in this

---

m. Congressman Ullman re-introduced his proposal in 1980, again unsuccessfully. H.R. 7015, 96th Cong., 2d Sess., 126 Cong. Rec. 7481.

country's consideration of the VAT. What form of VAT would it have imposed? For what transactions and entities did it propose preferential treatment, what form did the preferential treatment take, and what justification could be offered for such preferential treatment? What use would have been made of the revenue generated by the VAT?[n]

4. Congressman Ullman held the most important tax-writing position in the country—Chairman of the Ways and Means Committee—at the time he proposed the Tax Restructuring Act of 1979. In two important political senses, VAT was dealt a serious setback by Mr. Ullman's defeat in the 1980 general election. First, the new committee chairman did not choose to pick up the VAT flag after Mr. Ullman was felled. Second, other potential supporters of VAT may have been deterred by noting that Mr. Ullman's support of VAT was used against him in the campaign.[o]

5. *Types of VAT: national tax base.* VATs can be categorized in various ways. Treasury I identifies two ways in which VATs might be differentiated from each other. First, we might consider the theoretical national tax base—gross national product, national income, or total private consumption. The difference among the three depends on the treatment of capital equipment. What is the basic difference in the treatment of capital equipment necessary to meet each of these three tax bases? Which does Treasury I find most supportable? Why?

6. *Types of VAT: method of calculation.* Whatever the ideal tax base (let us assume that a consumption-base VAT is chosen), VATs can also be categorized by the method of calculation—addition, credit, or subtraction. As the Treasury I excerpt explains, the addition method assumes that the value added by a given taxpayer, at a given stage of production, can be thought of as the contribution by each of various factors of production. The tax base for each taxpayer thus consists of the sum of the return to the four classic factors of production—land (rent), labor (wages and salaries), capital (interest) and entrepreneurship (profit). The addition method finishes third best on most lists. It seems that the addition method is presented more out

---

n. It should be noted that the 1979 estimates may not be closely reflective of the revenue that a VAT would generate today. In the final excerpt of this chapter, Professor Graetz cites a Congressional Budget Office estimate that in 1996 a five percent VAT (half the level proposed by Congressman Ullman) could have raised between $70 billion and $140 billion, depending on exemptions.

o. Mr. Ullman's support of VAT was criticized particularly by his opponent in the Democratic primary, which Ullman won. However, those attacks may have softened his support in the general election, which he lost. Professors Oldman and Schenk opine that it is inaccurate to attribute Ullman's loss to his VAT proposal. Oliver Oldman & Alan Schenk, *The Business Activities Tax: Have Senators Danforth & Boren Created a Better Value Added Tax?*, 65 TAX NOTES 1547, 1548 (1994).

of a sense of academic tidiness than because it is given serious consideration for adoption. Twenty years ago, the method was rejected by an ABA Committee in a report focusing on the addition method,[p] and there appears to be no more enthusiasm in recent times, either in this country or abroad.

The two remaining methods of computation—the European credit-invoice method and the subtraction method—are serious contenders.[q] The credit-invoice method VAT is a *transactional* tax. The seller in any taxable transaction collects the stated purchase price plus a separately stated VAT, which is computed with reference to the stated purchase price. The invoice for each individual sale should reflect the VAT paid.[r] If the payor is not the ultimate consumer, the payor is entitled to claim a credit for the VAT paid, and can do so in its next return (even before resale). Thus, the *full* VAT is paid on *each* sale, at whatever stage of production. Because any payor other than the final consumer receives a credit for the VAT paid, however, the net tax remitted is based upon the difference between purchase price and sales price—that is, upon value added. The invoice makes the proper amount of the credit definite. In addition, the credit-invoice method should produce a paper trail (now, perhaps, a computer-blip trail) to simplify audit. To use the simple example from the introduction, the dairy, which purchased the milk for fifty cents and sold it for eighty cents would (with a ten percent tax) pay five cents to the farmer, but promptly claim a credit for that amount, then collect and remit eight cents. (When the credit and the tax payment are netted, the dairy should have paid a net tax of three cents—ten percent of its value added—and the entire tax has been passed on to its customer). Observe that the tax to be collected by the dairy from the grocery store does not directly depend on the amount of value added by the dairy—a computation that might be difficult to determine for any single item, especially in a business other than purchasing and reselling—but upon the more-readily-determined selling price.

Under the sales-subtractive VAT, which the ABA committee referred to as the business transfer tax, or BTT, the tax base is not the price paid in each transaction. Instead, each taxpayer in the chain of production pays a tax based upon its value added, as computed by its sales minus its purchases. The taxpayer is not entitled to a credit, because, unlike the invoice method, the tax at each level is not based on total value (i.e., sales price) but on the

---

p. American Bar Association, Special Committee on the Value-Added Tax of the Section of Taxation, *Evaluation of an Additive-Method Value-Added Tax for Use in the United States*, 30 TAX LAW. 565 (1977).

q. The credit-invoice method has been more popular throughout the world and is the preferred form of VAT according to Congressman Ullman, Treasury I and the ABA Committee (all excerpted above). There are, however, serious American BTT proposals—Senator Roth, and Senators Danforth and Boren, have proposed BTTs, and the USA Tax discussed in Chapter Seven includes a VAT component that utilizes the sales subtractive method.

r. Japan has adopted a credit form of VAT that does not depend on an invoice for credit to be allowed. *See* Oldman & Schenk, *supra* note o, at 1550-51 (1994).

value added. Again using the dairy from the introduction, the dairy would compute its value added—the tax base—as eighty cents minus fifty cents—and would remit the tax on the resulting thirty-cent base (three cents, undiminished by any credit). Unlike the credit method, this tax cannot readily be stated separately upon sale, because the tax cannot easily be known by, or demonstrated to, the buyer. The tax depends upon the seller's costs and profit, rather than the selling price. Instead of a separately stated VAT, the seller would simply absorb VAT and pass it along not as a separately stated tax, but rather in the form of a higher price.

Comparison of credit method and
subtraction method / business transfer tax.

7. Both Treasury I and the ABA Committee prefer the credit method to the subtraction method/business transfer tax, for a number of reasons. Why is a BTT more likely to lead to political pressure for exemptions? Why are exemptions under the credit method, even if granted, less likely to cost the government revenue?

8. Why is rebating VAT—such as rebating VAT paid on goods that are exported after some value has been added—easier under the credit method than under the BTT?

9. Under an invoice-credit system, the VAT is clearly stated in every sale, all the way through to the final sale to the consumer. Under the sales-subtractive BTT, the VAT is buried in prices, which are raised by each member of the chain of production and distribution to reflect this additional cost. Assuming the economic effects of the two forms of tax to be substantially identical—i.e., that either tax is ultimately borne by the consumer—what political effect would you expect from the form of the tax, given that the tax is more obvious under the invoice-credit method than under the BTT? Would you regard this effect as an advantage of the invoice-credit method or of the BTT?

10. The fact that the BTT is buried in the price of goods rather than being separately stated might make it easier to coordinate that form of federal VAT with existing state RSTs; see Note 40 below.

Compliance and fraud

11. The invoice-method is said to facilitate compliance. Auditors can follow a paper trail of invoices. Perhaps more important, "downstream" taxpayers other than the ultimate consumer have an incentive to make certain that invoices generated by their purchases properly reflect VAT paid, so that they can claim the VAT credit. Consider the dairy in the example from the introduction. If it failed to obtain an invoice showing VAT paid to

the farmer, it could not claim its credit when it re-sold to the grocery; that accurate invoice, in turn, makes the farmer more likely to remit the VAT due upon his sale to the dairy.

By contrast, a taxpayer's BTT depends not upon VAT paid to each supplier, but upon its total costs of inventory and supplies of goods and services from all suppliers. The tax paid is not reflected on invoices, which may make it easier for upstream suppliers to understate their liability. In his article comparing three forms of consumption taxes—the invoice-credit VAT, the BTT and the retail sales tax (RST)—Professor Sijbren Cnossen gives the nod to invoice-credit VAT with regard to fraud-related problems:

> [F]ictitious claims for refunds through counterfeit invoices, particularly at the export stage,[s] do provide an opportunity for fraud under [the invoice-credit form of] VAT that is not available under RST.   On balance, however, VAT's self-enforcement mechanism and broader control of evasion, lead me to conclude that dishonesty commands a higher price under VAT than it does under RST (or, for that matter, BTT). * * *
>
> Retailers are perhaps the most troublesome sector under VAT. Since consumers are not eligible for tax credits or refunds, neither they nor the retailer have any compelling inducement to ensure that the latter's sales are reported accurately. In other words, VAT's self-enforcement mechanism does not operate at this stage. Still, VAT seems to have an advantage over RST here, since the tax auditor has a presumptively accurate record of the retailer's purchases and therefore can estimate sales on the basis of an average industry mark-up. Moreover, the fact that retailers do have to pay the tax on their purchases makes evasion less likely to succeed for the full amount of the tax. To be sure, they can take credit for the tax on purchases and may file false refund claims, but unless taxable goods are zero rated refund claims should result in a detailed scrutiny of the return.[t]

Observe that even in defending VAT, Professor Cnossen does not fall into the trap of some naive VAT supporters, who seem to believe that a VAT would be almost self-enforcing. Moreover, not all commentators share his view that invoice-credit VAT, while imperfect, is better than its rivals. Professor Mario Leccisotti and Dr. Mauro Mare argue that "VAT, far from emerging as the best way of taxing consumption, appears as a form of taxation with very considerable administrative and compliance costs."[u] They refute Cnossen's

---

s. Because exports are zero-rated, a firm that exports a product not only pays no additional tax but is entitled to a refund of VAT it paid when acquiring the product. This gives an incentive to creation of a fraudulent invoice, which supports an undeserved credit for VAT that was not in fact paid.

t. Sijbren Cnossen, *Broad-based Consumption Taxes: VAT, RST, or BTT?*, 6 AUSTL. TAX F. 391, 418 (1989).

u. Mario Leccisotti & Mauro Mare, *On the Presumed Technical Superiority of VAT*, 9

arguments concerning "the self-policing mechanism and the ease of cross-checks":

> The argument is correct, but it overlooks an essential fact. Although the buyer gains from a high purchase price in the invoice, he or she has a much greater interest in paying a lower tax, but the buyer must pay a higher tax in order to benefit from a higher tax credit. Since the alternatives are a higher tax and a higher credit versus a lower tax and a lower credit, under normal conditions no reasonable person would prefer to pay a higher tax now, in order to be entitled to a higher credit in a more or less remote future.
>
> Moreover, the buyer has very important reasons for desiring to keep the invoice price low, since by reducing costs and turnover for the treasury, the income tax may be evaded more easily.
>
> Given this situation, contrary to the opinion of VAT's supporters, both sellers and buyers have an interest in showing in the invoice a price as low [as] possible. Thus, in all stages the price will tend to be below the true one. * * * [T]he possibility of tax evasion is greatly reinforced by the fact that the final consumer has no interest in paying a higher tax for which he is not entitled to any refund, and asks for a low invoice price.[v]

The student should keep in mind that the realistic goal can never be to create a tax that cannot be evaded. No tax can meet such standards. We seek taxes that are relatively difficult to evade, and that offer relatively low incentives to evasion. How does the credit-invoice VAT compare to more familiar American taxes, such as state RSTs and the federal income tax?

12. VAT offers one attractive opportunity to cheat not matched by the RST. The zero-rated export gives a seller not only an opportunity to evade a tax, but to create phony invoices and thereby obtain a refund for a tax never paid. (The seller is normally entitled to a credit for VAT paid by it to upstream sellers. In the usual case, the credit merely reduces VAT liability. In the case of a zero-rated export, however, the credit results in an actual refund.)

13. The ABA committee suggests that the VAT may be both simpler and less prone to fraud than the RST with respect to sales not to final consumers ("midstream" sales). Under the invoice-credit VAT, such sales are taxable, although the purchaser will later be entitled to a credit. The purchaser has a strong incentive to make the invoice reflect the full selling price and correct VAT, because the invoice will support the purchaser's claim

---

AUSTL. TAX F. 259, 259-60 (1992).
   v. *Id.* at 265.

for VAT credit. Under the RST, the business purchaser will simply be allowed, generally by recording the purchaser's resale exclusion certificate number on the invoice, to purchase without payment of sales tax. Fraud at this stage—by disguising a sale to a consumer as a sale to a business, for example—avoids the entire RST, permanently. In the case of a purchaser claiming RST exemption for a purchase actually intended for the purchaser's personal consumption, it is likely that the purchaser's fraud alone, without participation by the seller, could defeat the RST. False invoices designed to defeat VAT will usually require complicity of both buyer and seller, making this form of fraud less likely.

14. If a retail seller goes bankrupt or simply disappears before remitting taxes, the loss of RST is complete. By contrast, a considerable portion of VAT will have already been collected through sales prior to the retail stage.

15. Perhaps the key to controlling fraud is to keep tax rates low. Higher rates naturally increase the incentive to any form of tax evasion. A significant federal VAT could couple with state RSTs to push the combined rate to a level that would tempt considerably more fraud than would either tax alone. The ABA committee cites Canada's Carter Commission to the effect that a rate of fourteen percent tempts significant evasion,[w] although this obviously will vary widely from taxpayer to taxpayer. Does this argue that there should be many types of taxes, each relatively low? For example, would we expect lower evasion with an income tax of ten percent and a VAT of ten percent than with either tax at twenty percent? But would the imposition of multiple taxes not increase compliance costs for taxpayers and administrative costs for government?

International trade

16. What is the theoretically different tax base under the "destination principle" and its alternative, the "origin principle"? How does the theory chosen affect the taxation of imports and exports?

17. In practice, the destination principle is invariably chosen "[f]or competitive reasons or because international trade is a significant element in the nation's economy."[x] Why might it be expected that a nation's producers—a group with obvious political clout in any country—would prefer that the national VAT embody the destination principle?

---

w. American Bar Association, Committee on Value Added Tax of the Section of Taxation, VALUE ADDED TAX: A MODEL STATUTE AND COMMENTARY 6 (1989), *citing* 5 REPORT OF THE ROYAL COMMISSION ON TAXATION, SALES TAXES AND GENERAL TAX ADMINISTRATION 50 (1966).

x. Alan Schenk, *Value Added Tax: Does This Consumption Tax Have a Place in the Federal Tax System?*, 7 VA. TAX REV. 207, 231 (1987).

18. It seems obvious that exporting firms would be attracted to a destination-principle VAT, because exports are "zero rated." Not only can the exporter sell without having to collect a VAT from its purchaser, but it obtains a rebate for VAT it has paid to its suppliers.

It is perhaps less obvious that the destination-principle VAT is also attractive to firms that do not export, but compete in the domestic market with foreign producers. Why is this the case?

19. The European Community (EC) is moving to implement an origin-principle VAT for trade within the EC, while maintaining the destination principle for trade with the rest of the world.[y] What considerations might prompt this dual approach?

20. The key trade advantage of VAT vis-a-vis other taxes derives from the rules of the General Agreement on Tariffs and Trade (GATT) (which first came into effect in 1947 and since 1994 has been administered by the World Trade Organization). What effect do GATT rules have on the ability of adhering nations (most nations of the world, including the United States and its major trading partners) to support exports? How are these rules applicable to VAT as compared to alternative taxes, such as payroll taxes and corporate income taxes?

21. The favorable effects of an American VAT on this country's international trade are extremely important in the eyes of some VAT supporters, and virtually nil in the view of detractors. Mr. Ullman, for example, claimed that the United States would derive substantial trade advantages from utilizing the VAT. On the other hand, the drafters of Treasury I were considerably more cautious concerning the contributions to the balance of trade to be expected from implementation of a VAT. They not only conclude their discussion of the issue by noting that the decision to implement VAT is too important to be driven by the possible trade benefits, but list two factors that cast doubt on whether the trade benefits would in fact materialize. What are these factors that might rain on VAT's trade-advantage parade?

22. Even VAT supporters question its supposed trade advantages. Gerald Brannon maintains that "[t]here are good arguments for VAT[z] but

---

y. *See* Craig A. Hart, *The European Community's Value-Added Tax System: Analysis of the New Transitional Regime and Prospects for Further Harmonization*, 12 INT'L TAX & BUS. LAW. 1 (1994).

z. *See* Gerard M. Brannon, *The Value Added Tax is a Good Utility Infielder*, 37 NAT'L TAX J. 303 (1984).

balance of trade is not one of them."[aa] In addition to noting the problems
identified in Treasury I, Professor Brannon argues that the trade advantages
accrue only if VAT, which increases prices but is "border-adjusted" (i.e.,
rebated on exports) takes the place of another tax that increases prices but
is not border-adjusted. FICA may or may not increase prices; it depends on
the uncertain question of who—laborer, employer or consumer—bears the
tax. With respect to the corporate income tax, Professor Brannon argues that
the tax is not shifted to the price of the good:

> Why don't firms * * * simply raise the price * * * even without a
> tax? The answer must be that the firm figured the higher price
> would lose enough sales to reduce profit. Now introduce CIT
> [corporate income tax]. It is no more sensible to raise the price
> after CIT than it was before.[bb]

Finally, Mr. Brannon reminds us that even if we are successful in improving
the lot of domestic producers, their benefit may come at the expense of
domestic consumers:

> [T]he higher exports and lower imports will help exporters and
> firms that compete with imports. It doesn't raise the living
> standard of Americans. * * *
>
> The basic policy here, assuming it works, is not much
> different from the protective tariff. * * *
>
> On the export industry side, this switch of VAT for CIT or
> FICA is a pot of pure honey because the VAT is refunded on
> exports.[cc]

Does the "trade advantage" claimed for VAT amount to favoring American
producers over American consumers? Assuming the answer to be "yes," can
a principled defense of VAT nonetheless be maintained?

23. Because GATT rules allow rebate of indirect taxes such as VAT but
not direct taxes such as the corporate income tax, the choice between credit
method VAT and BTT may be important in obtaining whatever advantages
derive from the right to rebate VAT to exporters. Commentators have
observed that the BTT "looks more like a tax on a business than on a
product. * * * Thus, other countries may object to applying the destination
principle to permit rebate of the business transfer tax on exports from the
United States and its imposition on imports."[dd]

---

aa. Gerald M. Brannon, *Does VAT Provide a Balance of Trade Advantage?*, 30 TAX NOTES
1387, 1387 (1986).

bb. *Id.* at 1388.

cc. *Id.* at 1389.

dd. George N. Carlson & Richard A. Gordon, *VAT or Business Transfer Tax: A Tax on
Consumers or on Business?*, 41 TAX NOTES 329, 332 (1988).

24. GATT rules, of course, are not holy writ. Stanley Surrey, who was sharply critical of VAT, suggested that the quest for desirable trade effects should lead us not to adopt a VAT, but to seek an amended GATT:

> One aspect of the reexamination [of GATT] could well be to permit countries not having a high indirect tax system permanently to adopt within limits border adjustments independent of their domestic tax structures if they so desire. It could result also in imposing some upper limits on the total border adjustments countries with indirect tax systems could make. This approach would provide an appropriate international accommodation to the basic question we are considering, that of freedom for domestic tax action without prejudicing a country's trade position.[ee]

To date, however, GATT rules remain unchanged, and American economic influence is probably less than in 1969, when Professor Surrey wrote.

25. *Zero rating vs. exemption.* If a transaction is zero rated, it is a sale within the VAT system. The sale is taxed at a rate of zero percent, but the seller is entitled to claim credit for VAT paid. Exports are zero rated, with the result that the foreign purchaser bears no VAT imposed by the country of production. The same approach could be used to allow any product, such as food, to be sold free from VAT.

If a seller is VAT-exempt, however, the sale is outside the VAT system. For example, small businesses or nonprofit organizations might be exempt. As in the case of zero rating, no VAT liability results from an exempt sale, but the seller is not entitled to a credit for VAT paid. Thus, it may be expected that the selling price reflects VAT paid by the seller.

What are the economic effects on the purchaser and seller of zero rated items? On the purchaser and seller where the seller is VAT-exempt? Why does exemption of midstream sales actually increase VAT liability? What advantages accrue to exemption?

Additional tax or replacement for existing taxes?

26. Why do you think that Professor Due, writing in 1980, viewed VAT as a tax that would replace or reduce existing federal taxes, while Dr. McLure, seven years later, argued in favor of VAT as an additional source of revenue?

27. What political risk do conservatives see in VAT, according to Dr. McLure? Why is McLure undeterred by this risk?

---

ee. Stanley S. Surrey, *A Value-Added Tax for the United States—A Negative View*, 21 TAX EXEC. 151, 171 (1969).

28. The danger of VAT encouraging unwise government expansion may be unfounded. One commentator presented data which led him to conclude that "there is essentially no difference between the behavior of the size of the government sector in VAT and non-VAT countries. This suggests that other political and economic factors are determining the relative size of government."[ff]

Effect on national savings rate

29. Professor Due contended that the argument for VAT "centers on the capital formation issue." Would you expect enactment of VAT, accompanied by equivalent reductions in other taxes, to increase national rates of saving, investment and capital formation?

30. Professor Due's evaluation of VAT generally assumes that federal revenues will be x dollars. Thus, the question is whether the best way to raise x dollars is by use of existing taxes at whatever level is necessary to produce x dollars, or by using a lower level of existing taxes coupled with a VAT. In terms of increasing national savings, how does Professor Due compare VAT to the personal income tax? To the corporate income tax? To payroll taxes? Does it matter whether one assumes that payroll taxes are passed through to a company's customers?

31. VAT proponents contend that saving would increase, not so much because VAT encourages saving but merely because VAT would provide tax neutrality to the saving-consumption choice, as contrasted to the income tax, which encourages consumption.

32. One empirical study of twenty-three nations casts doubt on whether adoption of a VAT would in fact lead to increased national saving: "Although it seems theoretically sound to contend that placing greater reliance on a VAT or consumption taxes to raise government revenue would result in increased saving, we have been unable to find any empirical evidence that happens in practice."[gg]

33. Similarly, some observers suggest that VAT's supposed neutrality should be accepted only with a grain of salt:
> While the VAT is less inherently nonneutral than some taxes, its flexibility makes it possible to mold it into a highly nonneutral tax. The VAT could attain its high potential degree of neutrality only if the Congress made a conscious effort * * * to avoid a major VAT

---

ff. J.A. Stockfish, *Value-Added Taxes and the Size of Government: Some Evidence*, 38 NAT'L TAX J. 547, 549 (1985).

gg. Ken Militzer, *VAT: Evidence from the OECD*, 47 TAX NOTES 207, 207 (1990).

impact on business decisions. Such a conscious effort has not generally characterized the behavior of legislative bodies.[hh]

Equity

34. Unquestionably, the most potent argument of VAT opponents is that the tax flunks the test of vertical equity. At first blush, at least, this argument has considerable force. Why?

35. How did the Ullman bill address such concerns?

36. Is granting of favorable tax rates to food and other necessities a good method of addressing equity concerns? Why do you think this approach was rejected in the ABA committee's Model Act?

37. European countries traditionally have attempted to increase progressivity in their VATs both through low rates on necessities and high rates on luxuries. Common as these provisions are, almost all commentators agree with the ABA committee that they are unwise. Gerald Brannon, in typically irreverent language, observes:

> The most common anti-regressivity "fix" within a VAT or a sales tax is to exempt things like food. This has two very severe drawbacks and one advantage.
>
> The first drawback is that it doesn't do a decent job of reducing regressivity. * * *
>
> A more important problem is that a food exemption greatly complicates the system. * * *
>
> The big advantage of the food exemption in a VAT is that it gives the legislator something that he can tell his middle-class constituents he did for them. This is valuable but it is also hokum since a 4 percent tax without a food exemption is practically indistinguishable for most people from a 5 percent tax with the food exemption.[ii]

Preferences are on the way out in Europe. The EC is now moving toward a single uniform rate with most preferences being phased out.

38. We might couple VAT with changes in the income tax that favored low-income taxpayers, such as an increased standard deduction and personal exemption, or a credit for low-income persons. Why would the credit have to be "refundable" (available to taxpayers with no income to offset)? Are such techniques a good method of addressing equity concerns raised by VAT?

---

hh. L.L. Bravenec & Kerry Cooper, *The Flexibility of the Value-Added Tax*, 55 TEX. L. REV. 453, 469 (1977).

ii. Brannon, *supra* note z, at 306-07.

39. Is the key in proper analysis of the equity of a VAT to evaluate
what the VAT proceeds will be used for? In the words of Professor Arthur
Laffer:

> [I]t is imperative to know the second entry or balancing
> transaction. If a value-added tax were introduced to eliminate a
> poll tax or to increase the pay of conscripted soldiers, it would be
> hard to argue that the VAT package was anything other than a
> progressive package. * * * Similarly, it would be difficult to argue
> that a VAT package was progressive if, in fact, the second entry
> was a reduction in capital gains taxes or a nationwide reduction in
> the upper-income bracket tax rates.[jj]

Federal-State relations

40. In considering a federal VAT, serious consideration must be given
to the fact that 45 states have RSTs. This could lead to political opposition
to a VAT, especially a credit-invoice type of VAT, as opposed to the BTT
form, in which the tax is buried in the price of the product. Professor Schenk
suggests that both political and efficiency concerns could point toward the
BTT form of VAT, rather than the credit-invoice form, if a federal VAT were
to be adopted.

> A state with a high-rate RST may feel that its tax base will be
> threatened more by a European Community-style invoice VAT than
> a BTT because consumers may resist an increase in the combined
> rate of the separately stated RST and European Community-style
> invoice VAT more than the adoption of a federal BTT that is
> buried in the prices of goods and services.
>
>   * * *
>
> If the states were inclined to harmonize their RST's with a
> federal VAT, it may be more likely to occur with a European
> Community-style invoice VAT than a BTT because the invoice VAT
> looks more like a sales tax. It may not be very realistic, however,
> to assume that states will harmonize their RST's with any form of
> federal VAT. * * *
>
> State and local governments' support or opposition to a federal
> VAT ultimately will depend not only on the proposed form of VAT,
> but on such factors as the state's RST rate and the kind of federal
> programs that will be financed with the VAT revenue. * * * [I]f
> the VAT is a hidden BTT that is not added to the consumer's cost
> at the check-out counter, the BTT may not affect the state and
> local governments' ability to raise revenue from [their RST's].

---

jj. Arthur B. Laffer, *The International Impact of a Value-Added Tax*, 6 J. CORP. LAW 119,
119 (1980).

Finally, assuming state and local RST's continue to operate basically in their existing form, a BTT would be more compatible and less costly to administer and compliance costs would be lower than a European Community-style invoice BTT. The reason is that a BTT is hidden therefore does not clash with the separately stated RST's. Is it, however, good public policy to choose a particular form of VAT because it does the best job of masking its identity as a tax on consumption?[kk]

Professor Schenk points out that a federal BTT buried in prices, because it would increase the prices on which state RSTs are based, would actually increase state revenues. Does coordination with state RSTs constitute a significant argument for the BTT form of VAT?

41. Might VAT provide opportunities for federal-state cooperation, rather than rivalry? It has been suggested that upon federal enactment of VAT, states should also move from RST to VAT, with the incentive that the federal government would "collect state taxes piggybacked on the federal VAT, as many states currently collect local supplements to their retail sales tax."[ll] Professor John Miller, on the other hand, suggests that the simpler approach would be for the federal government to adopt RST, and turn collection over to state sales tax authorities.[mm] Federal-state cooperation could lower not only administrative costs for both levels of government, but compliance costs for businesses.[nn]

42. *The underground economy.* VAT proponents, such as Mr. Ullman, claim that VAT will reach the "underground economy," and thus bring in revenue from taxpayers who evade the income tax. Surely drug dealers and prostitutes would not be more likely to collect and remit VAT on their illegal sales of goods and services than to pay income tax on such illegally derived income. In what sense would VAT be successful in reaching the underground economy?

43. Professor Schenk raised but rejected the idea of using VAT as a fiscal tool—that is, increasing rates of VAT taxation to cool an overstimulated economy, and reducing rates to stimulate the economy. Particularly interesting was the observation that Congress acted so slowly in enacting tax law that it might grant to the President the power to vary VAT tax rates, within a specified range. Is this a desirable approach? Is it realistic?

---

kk. Alan Schenk, *supra* note b, at 319-20 (1993).

ll. Charles E. McLure, Jr., *State and Federal Relations in the Taxation of Value Added*, 6 J. CORP. LAW 127, 136 (1980).

mm. John A. Miller, *State Administration of a National Sales Tax: A New Opportunity for Cooperative Federalism*, 9 VA. TAX REV. 243 (1989).

nn. See generally Schenk, *supra* note b.

D.   RELATED PROPOSALS

This subchapter contains excerpts of two recent articles that embrace only certain aspects of the argument favoring a generalized VAT. Professor Isenbergh argues that shifting the primary basis of taxation to consumption is desirable and important due to inadequate saving and capital formation. For that reason, he advocates a VAT, but with significant additional measures that would achieve progressivity at both the high and low ends of the income spectrum. Professor Graetz also sees virtue in increased reliance on consumption taxes. Rather than a broad-based VAT, however, he argues for significantly higher federal excise taxes levied only on specified products.

THE END OF INCOME TAXATION
Joseph Isenbergh[*]

45 Tax Law Review 283, 283-84, 349-56, 360-61 (1990)

[T]he last decade has brought the lowest rates of saving by Americans in our peacetime history. * * *

[C]oncern over our fiscal habits is warranted. The justification for this concern is neither the absolute level of deficits nor the apparent dearth of saving—although these are hardly reassuring—but the specific influence of our indigenous system of income taxation on capital formation. Income taxation, particularly as practiced in the United States, systematically favors current consumption over saving. There is a resulting distortion of individual choices that is not, and cannot readily be, offset by other fiscal actions of government. In short, capital formation in the United States is weaker than it would be with a different tax system.

* * *

A VAT and Progressivity

If a uniform across-the-board VAT were the sole federal tax, it would be open to the immediate objection that it was not progressive with respect to wealth and economic income. Whatever the ultimate merit of this objection, the premise on which it rests is correct. A pure consumption tax does not tend, by its nature, to be progressive. A flat VAT will weigh more heavily on those whose incomes are low, because the lower the income, the greater the percentage that is likely to be consumed currently, if only as a matter of survival. Other forms of tax on consumption can be given a degree of progressivity, but it is not easy to do so across the full range of economic incomes. A tax on consumed income (i.e., an income tax with an unlimited deduction for saving) could, for example, be made progressive on its own base simply by adopting graduated rates, and this would approximate progressivity with respect to income in the ranges of income where the propensity to consume is high. A tax on consumed income, no matter how steeply graduated, does not reach the unconsumed portion, however. The

---

*. At time of original publication, Professor of Law, University of Chicago.

larger the income, the larger the portion that may remain beyond the current reach of the tax.

Progressive taxation has been viewed as everything from the cornerstone of a civilized society to theft. Progressivity can be understood broadly as a measure of the economic redistribution resulting from a tax. It is only a partial measure, however, of the redistributive effect of a fiscal system overall, which depends also on how transfers made *by* government are directed. Because there is no decisive economic argument for or against progressivity (or redistribution generally, for that matter), it remains at bottom an aesthetic question. That does not make progressivity any less important or legitimate a concern. It does mean, however, that the degree of progressivity of a tax system is more likely to reflect the respective success of different constituencies than any irresistible calculus of efficiency. The real constituency for progressive taxation is quite large; the rhetorical constituency larger still.

It is, therefore a reasonable working hypothesis that a reformed system of taxation based primarily on consumption could not itself find a constituency unless it preserved a measure of progressivity. To be sure, there are some who question or oppose the value of progressive taxation, for whom the regressivity of taxes on consumption would be a virtue. But their support for a change would be far weaker than the opposition of those who favor progressivity, because those most opposed to progressive taxation are very nearly the same as those opposed to taxation period, which makes them a reluctant constituency for *any* new tax.

That poses a problem for a proposed tax system built around a uniform VAT. An unalloyed VAT-as-single-tax regime will not sweep the country if it is not modified in some way to the end of greater progressivity. There are different approaches to this end, some that modify the VAT from within, and others that add other taxes and transfers with offsetting effect. The latter, in my view, is the better way. On the low end of the income spectrum, I propose a refund system to offset the amount of VAT paid; on the high end, I propose a flat tax on increases in individual net worth. The next section discusses these proposals.

A Universal Refund

The most obvious way to offset the weight of the VAT on lower incomes, without complicating the tax itself, is to refund the amounts paid by people with low incomes (on the plausible assumption that they spend virtually their entire incomes on consumption). Among the possibilities is a negative income tax: a payment, inversely proportional to income, in an amount designed to reimburse the entire VAT paid in the lowest income bracket, then declining and disappearing as income increases. The idea would be a full refund of the VAT paid by those who are below or at the poverty level, a partial refund for those who are somewhat better off, and none for the middle-middle class and beyond. The amount of the payment would be a function of the rate of the VAT.

Such a system, while by no means impossible, would have its problems. First, people at all levels of income would have to file some sort of return containing a reckoning of their income, although it could be a relatively simple one. Almost inevitably, some people would conceal some of their income to claim a larger refund. Second, this type of negative income tax would reduce the incentive of those in the lower range of income to pursue more.

Therefore, I propose instead what could be called an "exemption system," that is, a universal refund of the amount of VAT paid on consumption up to a basic level, and perhaps a partial refund of additional amounts. The effect would be to leave a minimum amount of consumption wholly or partly exempt from VAT. If, for example, the exempt amount were to be consumption up to the recognized poverty level of income (now roughly $12,000 for a family of four) and the VAT were 25%, a family of four would receive a payment of $3,000. A schedule of refund payments that would fit these numbers would be $1,000 for each adult and $500 for each child. Both to simplify the administration of the refund and to blunt adverse incentives, every man, woman, and child in the United States (if a U.S. citizen or a legal permanent resident) would receive a payment. The payment to adults would be roughly twice the payment to children under 16 which would be paid over to their parents. (And since you ask, yes, Sam Walton, Oprah Winfrey, Carl Icahn, and Gordon Getty would all get a refund payment.) There are roughly 250 million Americans, of whom about 190 million are 16 or over. The cost of the refunds at the levels just indicated would therefore be $220 billion. The cost of these payments would have to be reflected in the rate of the VAT itself (higher, obviously, than if the exemption were smaller or less widespread) and in some measure in the additional tax on increases in net worth discussed below. This system would preserve some incentive to save at all levels of income, because the marginal rate of tax on consumption would be the same for all, while the effective rate would be graduated.

A Net Worth Tax

A universal exemption would make a VAT progressive at the lower end of the income spectrum, but not at the higher end. To reintroduce an element of progressivity at the upper end of the scale of income and wealth one possibility would be to couple the VAT with a tax on annual increases in net worth above a threshold level. The floor of the tax would establish an exempt level of wealth that can be accumulated tax-free in a lifetime. Beyond that, all increases would attract the tax. Every individual who had crossed the threshold of the tax would have a cumulative amount of previously taxed net worth. The total at the end of each year (unless there had been a decline in the year) would be used as the starting point to determine the following year's increase.[291] In order to reach *real* increases in wealth, the annual base of the net worth tax should be adjusted for inflation. That is, the nominal increase would be reduced by a percentage of the taxpayer's total assets tied to some broad-gauged measure of inflation such as the GNP deflator.

Both the level of wealth at which the tax applies and its rate should reflect its main function, which is not to raise large revenues, but to add a measure of progressivity to a system of taxation that nonetheless burdens saving less than the present system. Given this objective, the rate of tax on increases of wealth should be no more than half that imposed on current consumption (12%, for example, if the VAT were 25%). The reason for the rate difference is that even at high levels of income, the immediate tax cost of saving should be less than the tax cost of consuming. Similarly, to remove any tax penalty, even relative, on saving in the middle range of incomes and wealth where the propensity to consume remains fairly high, the threshold of net worth that triggers the net worth tax should be set above a basic middle-class accumulation of wealth. The threshold should not be much lower than $250,000.

* * * The rate of the net worth tax should be half that of the VAT, while the total revenue raised by it should be at the most one-tenth of that brought in by the VAT. Those boundaries would permit, by extrapolation from known data about the amount and distribution of individual wealth in the United States seasoned with a little trial and error, the determination of an exempt level of lifetime wealth.

To set the revenues derived from the net worth tax as no more than one-tenth of those derived from the VAT will doubtless strike some as too little and others as too much. The latter will observe, correctly, that a net worth tax does nothing to advance the cause of capital formation. The former might rejoin that, within appropriate bounds, it would not be fatal to that end either. The merits aside, however, it would be difficult to create a consensus around taxation based solely on consumption.

The tax on net worth just sketched is an *income* tax, despite the vocabulary in which I have clothed it. As such, it imposes a toll charge on deferred consumption through a double tax on saving. This is why the rate of the net worth tax should not exceed half that of the VAT. A rate difference of this degree would at least keep the immediate tax cost of saving below that of consumption, although the ultimate tax cost of saving will be greater. In the range of economic incomes in which it applies, the net worth tax at half the VAT rate would be similar in its effect to the allowance of a tax preference for saving under an income tax. If a flat rate tax on income

---

291. To keep the mechanics of the tax simple, it is probably best not to grant refunds on account of net *declines* of wealth in a given year. Gains that merely retrace previous declines in net worth should be shielded from the tax, however, which would in effect create a system of loss carryovers.

were moved in the direction of a tax on consumed income by allowing a deduction for *half* of amounts committed to saving, the result would be similar to the combination of a VAT and net worth tax I have proposed here. To allow every individual taxpayer a fixed lifetime allowance of fully deductible saving before the half-level deduction for saving would parallel fairly closely the exemption feature of my net worth tax. If the difficulty of framing the tax base of such a system were not considerably greater than in the system I propose here (largely because of problems of realization), it would be an eminently plausible way to shift the base of our present tax system toward consumption.

There is a possible argument of an entirely different order for retaining a component of income taxation in a regime predominantly based on consumption. It is that accumulation (the part of an income tax base that escapes immediate taxation under a VAT) may bring with it some value *as consumption* before it is explicitly converted to consumption. There is, I think, a common suspicion (especially widespread among those not dynastically rich) that simply *having* wealth brings with it consumption value long before that value is realized through exchange. This possibility is obvious, inevitable in fact, when the wealth takes the form of ancestral manors and old master paintings that produce a stream of imputed income, but cannot be dismissed even where the wealth is intangible, to the extent that known wealth may be the catalyst of others' attention, kind regard, even love, as well as an enhanced sense of self. In this light, the net worth tax I have sketched could be conceived as a surtax on the deferred material consumption of those whose wealth brings intangible value in consumption currently. * * *

An obvious difficulty in designing a tax to reach annual changes in net worth is the valuation of property. Except for widely-traded financial assets, the value of property is not self-revealing. * * *

One possibility is to impute some sort of rate of appreciation to assets not readily amenable to specific annual valuation, while using realization events and occasional valuations as a check against large deviations from reality. Another, better to my mind, is to allow, at the election of taxpayers, the deferral of the valuation and taxation of accrued gains in certain classes of assets until a triggering event of realization, such as sale, transfer by gift, or death. The net worth tax attributable to their value would then be paid with an interest factor reflecting the length of the period of deferral of taxation. The amount and vintage of the tax giving rise to interest payments would be determined under the assumption that increases in the value of assets accrued ratably during the period they were owned by the taxpayer.[300]

* * *

---

300. There is a thorough description and analysis of such a system of taxation in Fellows, A Comprehensive Attack on Tax Deferral, 88 MICH. L. REV. 722 (1990).

If stated public positions are any guide, my proposal will go nowhere. Conservatives oppose taxes on consumption, basically because they are taxes, and liberals oppose them because they are efficient.

* * *

One point that gets lost in the current debate over whether and how to change the tax system is that the real level of taxation is not a function of the transfers called "taxes." Real taxation occurs when public claims are asserted against resources. The claims of those who have financed our submarines and bombers, while supplying us with VCRs and BMWs, will not disappear. The debate over what we call "taxation" is ultimately about who will bear those claims and when. Assuming that the claims are to be paid —and neither default nor its cousin, runaway inflation, is a serious option— someone out there will have to be taxed explicitly.[315] How much tax will be paid overall is by now largely determined. What is at stake in the unfolding political contest over taxation is how consumers and suppliers of capital will fare vis-a-vis each other as the United States lurches toward the millennium. It is not yet 1789 (when one of the world's great economic powers came apart after losing its hold on its fiscal destiny), but it is later than you think.

REVISITING THE INCOME TAX VS. CONSUMPTION TAX DEBATE
Michael J. Graetz[*]
57 Tax Notes 1437, 1439-42 (1992)

* * * As has been true throughout the more than two decades that the prospect of value-added taxation has been rising and falling on the national political agenda, its most impressive attribute is its prodigious revenue-raising capacity. The Congressional Budget Office, for example, estimates that a five-percent value-added tax could raise anywhere from $70 billion to $140 billion annually by 1996, depending on whether such things as food, housing, and medical expenses were included or excluded from the value-added tax base.[13]

* * * On the other hand, substantial deficit reduction seems unlikely to occur without a significant revenue-raising component, and such taxes should be levied in the manner most conducive to long-term economic growth: by taxing consumption rather than increasing the tax burden on savings and investment. The question then becomes: Assuming that we are going to tax consumption, how should we do it?

---

315. Even if defaults and inflation are used to depreciate the value of the claims against the public, the losses to the holders of the claims can be regarded as a tax, in the form of a reduction of private wealth representing the cost of public outlays.

*. At time of original publication Justus S. Hotchkiss Professor of Law, Yale University.

13. Congressional Budget Office, Reducing the Deficit: Spending and Revenue Options 335-337 (1992).

There are, I think, three major broad-based consumption tax contenders. First, we might adopt a federal retail sales tax. * * *

Alternatively, the United States could adopt a federal value-added tax of the credit-invoice method commonly used in Europe. * * *

It might well be easier politically to enact a subtraction-method value-added tax—also called a business transfer tax (BTT). * * *

In my view, any of these flat rate, broad-based consumption taxes—with the retention of some relatively low-rate (integrated one would hope) corporate income tax and individual income tax at upper-income levels—would be preferable to a progressive, individualized tax on consumption,[oo] which would probably require sharply progressive and high top rates to satisfy distribution concerns.

Let me, however, echo here the sentiments expressed by Treasury Secretary Andrew Mellon in the 1921 hearings. Secretary Mellon then urged Congress not to replace a long list of federal excise taxes with a broad-based sales tax. Even at that time, this position was contrary to the prevailing economic wisdom. Certainly, at least since the Excise Tax Reduction Act of 1965 (until very recently), it has been quite unfashionable to urge selected federal excise taxes, in either the Academy or to Congress.

Current circumstances, however, make this conventional wisdom wrong. In the 1990 budget negotiations, a broad-based tax on energy consumption was examined in detail but ultimately was not adopted. I will not rehearse here the reasons for increasing the price of energy relative to other commodities and for reducing energy consumption, but instead will simply note that an energy tax is supported by concern both for the environment and reducing our dependence on foreign sources of oil.

The base of a broad energy tax is just over one-quarter the size of a likely value-added tax base (one that has exclusions for housing, food, medical expenses, and the like, or provides a similar measure of low-income relief). This means that a 10-percent energy tax, for example, could raise approximately half the revenue of a five-percent value-added tax, although low-income offsets would be required here as well. The narrower base and higher rates create something of a natural ceiling on the potential revenue raising capacity of an energy tax in contrast to a VAT. A broad-based energy tax, either based on heat (BTU) content or on an ad valorem basis, would distribute more neutrally across the regions of the country than either of its two major competitors: increased gasoline taxes or a carbon tax. * * * If more revenue were required, the combination of, say, a 10-percent broad-based energy tax and additional gasoline taxes would be possible. Unlike gasoline tax increases, however, where there is great pressure to finance additional spending for highway construction, broad-based energy

---

oo. Professor Graetz is referring to the consumption-type personal income tax discussed in Chapter Seven. (Eds.)

taxes could be used for deficit reduction or earmarked to finance extension of health insurance to the uninsured.

There also remains considerable potential for increasing federal taxes on alcohol and tobacco, and well-known good reasons for reducing the consumption of each. For example, the Yale Health Plan recently informed us that cigarette smoking is responsible for 21 percent of all mortality from heart disease and that smoking doubles the incidence of coronary artery disease and increases mortality by about 70 percent.

These taxes are low, both by our own historical standards and in comparison to alcohol and tobacco taxes in Europe or Japan, either as a percentage of revenues or a percentage of price. An additional $5 billion or so a year could be raised by increasing all alcoholic beverage taxes from their current levels to $16 per proof gallon and equalizing the taxes on beer and wine. * * *

Likewise, the tobacco tax could readily be doubled, from the 24-cents-per-pack level (which it is scheduled to reach in 1993) to 48 cents per pack, and another $4 billion of revenue a year would be collected. Indexing both of these taxes for inflation (or converting them to an ad valorem basis) would produce another $1 billion to $2 billion annually, for a total of about $10 billion.

There are a variety of other candidates for specific excise taxes if these three prove inadequate in terms of revenue, although the implementation problems of many of the other environmentally motivated excise taxes signal caution. * * * The federal government could probably raise $1 billion to $2 billion a year by taxing newsprint and the lead in automobile batteries, for example, but to take a contrary example, it seems a practical impossibility to tax virgin materials generally to encourage recycling, as some have proposed.

A 10-percent broad-based energy tax, in combination with the suggested increases in the alcohol and tobacco taxes, would produce about $50 billion of additional tax revenues annually. The major distributional complaint about broad-based consumption taxes, however, applies here as well; these taxes fall more heavily on lower- and middle-income taxpayers than on high-income taxpayers.

This context, however, where taxes are being increased on specific items of consumption that the nation wants to reduce, may create an opportunity for Congress to begin looking at tax distributional issues on a new basis. In contrast to a broad-based consumption tax, people could reduce substantially their tax burdens by shifting to less harmful consumption patterns. If we were to regulate, rather than tax, these items to reduce consumption, Congress would demonstrate little concern for distributional burdens. * * *

Notes and Questions

44. Professor Isenbergh's VAT proposal attempts to help low-income taxpayers by providing *all* families or individuals a payment roughly equal to the VAT that would be paid by a family or individual at the poverty line. Why would he give the payments to millionaires?

45. What role does Professor Isenbergh's proposed net worth tax, which he concedes is really an income tax, play? Why would he include as a feature of this tax a fifty-percent deduction for savings?

46. Professor Graetz argues for sharply increased consumption taxes on specified goods rather than a broad-based consumption tax such as VAT. What goods are singled out for heavy taxation, and why? Do you agree that excise taxes on specific products are better than a VAT? Do you agree that it is proper and desirable for the government to influence consumption patterns through excise taxes? Are you concerned about the regressive impact of the taxes he proposes?

47. Do you think smoking would be significantly reduced if cigarettes cost an additional 24¢ per package?

48. Some medical evidence now suggests that drinking in moderation may be more beneficial to the drinker's health than total abstinence. Would such evidence lead us to reject Professor Graetz's call for increased taxes on alcoholic beverages?

49. Would the logic of Professor Graetz's proposal suggest that other products harmful to health (bacon cheeseburgers, for example) should be subjected to special excise taxes?

Selected Bibliography

See also bibliography for Chapter Seven.

AMERICAN BAR ASSOCIATION, COMMITTEE ON VALUE ADDED TAX OF THE SECTION OF TAXATION, VALUE ADDED TAX: A MODEL STATUTE AND COMMENTARY (1989).

AMERICAN BAR ASSOCIATION, REPORT OF THE SPECIAL COMMITTEE ON THE VALUE-ADDED TAX OF THE TAX SECTION OF THE AMERICAN BAR ASSOCIATION [consisting of reprints of five reports previously published as *Report of the Special Subcommittee of the Committee on General Income Tax on the Value-Added Tax*, 24 TAX LAW. 419 (1971); *Should the United States Adopt the Value-Added Tax?—A Survey of the Policy Considerations and the Data Base*, 26 TAX LAW. 45 (1972); *Technical Problems in Designing a Broad-Based Value-Added Tax for the United States*, 28 TAX LAW. 193 (1975); *The Choice Between Value-Added and Sales Taxation at Federal and State Levels in the*

United States, 29 TAX LAW. 457 (1976); and *Evaluation of an Additive-Method Value-Added Tax for Use in the United States*, 30 TAX LAW. 565 (1977)].

ANDO, ALBERT ET AL., THE STRUCTURE AND REFORM OF THE U.S. TAX SYSTEM 173-82 (1985).

Bickley, James M., *How Much Revenue Could a U.S. VAT Yield?*, 60 TAX NOTES 1273 (1993).

Bloomfield, Mark A., *A U.S. Consumption Tax: The Challenge for President-Elect Clinton*, 57 TAX NOTES 1311 (1992).

BRADFORD, DAVID F., UNTANGLING THE INCOME TAX 59-74, 312-34 (1986).

——, U.S. DEP'T. OF TREASURY, BLUEPRINTS FOR BASIC TAX REFORM (2d ed. 1984).

Brannon, Gerald M., *Does VAT Provide a Balance of Trade Advantage?*, 30 TAX NOTES 1387 (1986).

——, *The Value Added Tax is a Good Utility Infielder*, 37 NAT'L TAX J. 303 (1984).

Brashares, Edith, et al., *Distributional Aspects of a Federal Value-Added Tax*, 41 NAT'L TAX J. 155 (1988).

Bravenec, L.L. & Kerry Cooper, *The Flexibility of the Value-Added Tax*, 55 TEX. L. REV. 453 (1977).

Bronfenbrenner, M., *The Japanese Value-Added Sales Tax*, 3 NAT'L TAX J. 298 (1950).

—— & Kiichiro Kogiku, *The Aftermath of the Shoup Tax Reforms*, 10 NAT'L TAX J. 236 (1959).

Burton, David R. & Don R. Mastromarco, *The National Sales Tax: Moving Beyond the Idea*, 71 TAX NOTES 1237 (1996).

Calkins, Hugh, *The Role of the Value-Added Tax in the Developing United States Tax System*, 6 J. CORP. L. 83 (1980).

Carlson, George N. & Melanie K. Patrick, *Addressing the Regressivity of a Value-Added Tax*, 42 NAT'L TAX J. 339 (1989).

Carlson, George N. & Richard A. Gordon, *VAT or Business Transfer Tax: A Tax on Consumers or on Business?*, 41 TAX NOTES 329 (1988).

Carlson, George N., *Value-Added Tax: Appraisal and Outlook*, 6 J. CORP. L. 37 (1980).

Cnossen, Sijbren, *VAT Treatment of Immovable Property*, 66 TAX NOTES 2017 (1995).

——, *Administrative and Compliance Costs of the VAT: A Review of the Evidence*, 63 TAX NOTES 1609 (1994).

——, *Consumption Taxes and International Competitiveness: The OECD Experience*, 53 TAX NOTES 1211 (1991).

——, *Broad-based Consumption Taxes: VAT, RST, or BTT?*, 6 AUSTL. TAX F. 391 (1989).

——, *The Value-Added Tax: Questions and Answers*, 42 TAX NOTES 209 (1989).

——, *What Rate Structure for a Value-Added Tax?*, 35 NAT'L TAX J. 205 (1982).

Committee on Ways & Means Hearing Announcement on the "Tax Restructuring Act of 1979," 96th Cong., 1st Sess., 6-12 (1979) [Statement by Chairman Al Ullman (D., Oregon) and Brief Summary of bill].

CONGRESSIONAL RESEARCH SERVICE, VALUE-ADDED TAX AS A NEW REVENUE SOURCE, (1994).

——, VALUE-ADDED TAX IN CANADA: BACKGROUND, EVALUATION, AND IMPLICATIONS FOR THE UNITED STATES, (1993).

——, VALUE-ADDED TAX: REVENUE ESTIMATES FOR 1995, (1993).

——, VALUE-ADDED TAX: SHOULD IT BE CALCULATED BY THE CREDIT-INVOICE OR SUBTRACTION METHOD?, (1992).

THE CONSUMPTION TAX: A BETTER ALTERNATIVE (Charls E. Walker & Mark A. Bloomfield eds., 1987).

Due, John F., *Some Unresolved Issues in Design and Implementation of Value Added Taxes*, 43 NAT'L TAX J. (1990).

——, *Economics of the Value Added Tax*, 6 J. CORP. L. 61 (1980).

——, *The Case for the Use of the Retail Form of Sales Tax in Preference to the Value-Added Tax*, in BROAD-BASED TAXES (Richard A. Musgrave ed., 1973).

Fleming, J. Clifton, *Scoping Out the Uncertain Simplification (Complication?) Effects of VATs, BATs and Consumed Income Taxes*, 2 FLA. TAX REV. 390 (1995).

Freiman, Barry M., *The Japanese Consumption Tax: Value-Added Model or Administrative Nightmare*, 40 AMER. U. L. REV. 1265 (1991).

Fuller, Hoffman F., *The Proposed Value-Added Tax and the Question of Tax Reform*, 34 RUTGERS L. REV. 50 (1982).

Galvin, Charles O., *Tax Legislation in the Reagan Era—Movement To or From a Consumption Base?*, 48 LAW & CONTEMP. PROBS. 31 (1985).

——, *The Value-Added Tax—A Proposal for the 80's*, 7 PEPPERDINE L. REV. 505 (1980).

Garber, Harry D., *The Role of Consumption Taxes in Tax Reform Around the World*, 41 NAT'L TAX J. 357 (1988).

Graetz, Michael J., *Tax Policy at the Beginning of the Clinton Administration*, 10 YALE J. ON REG. 561 (1993).

——, *Revisiting the Income Tax vs. Consumption Tax Debate*, 57 TAX NOTES 1437 (1992).

Gravelle, Jane G., *Assessing a Value-Added Tax: Efficiency and Equity*, 38 TAX NOTES 1117 (1988).

Hart, Craig A., *The European Community's Value-Added Tax System: Analysis of the New Transitional Regime and Prospects for Further Harmonization*, 12 INT'L TAX & BUS. LAW. 1 (1994).

Isenbergh, Joseph, *The End of Income Taxation*, 45 TAX L. REV. 283 (1990).

KALDOR, NICHOLAS, AN EXPENDITURE TAX (1955).

Kelly, John F. et al., *Replacing the Social Security Tax with a Value-Added Tax: Policy Perspectives*, 15 U. RICHMOND L. REV. 39 (1980-81).

Kotlikoff, Laurence J., *The Case for the Value-Added Tax*, 39 TAX NOTES 239 (1988).

Laffer, Arthur B., *The International Impact of a Value-Added Tax*, 6 J. CORP. L. 119 (1980).

Leccisotti, Mario & Mauro Mare, *On the Presumed Technical Superiority of VAT*, 9 AUSTL. TAX F. 259 (1959).

LINDHOLM, RICHARD W., THE ECONOMICS OF VAT (1980).

——, *The Origin of the Value-Added Tax*, 6 J. CORP. L. 11 (1980).

Lock, Clarence W. et al., *The Michigan Value-Added Tax*, 8 NAT'L TAX J. 357 (1955).

Massa, Cliff, III, *The "Business Activities Tax"—A Primer*, 64 TAX NOTES 1219 (1994).

——, & David G. Raboy, *The Canadian Value-Added Tax: Does Anybody Care?*, 45 TAX NOTES 480 (1989).

McDaniel, Paul R., *A Value Added Tax for the United States? Some Preliminary Reflections*, 6 J. CORP. L.` 15 (1980).

McLURE, CHARLES E., THE VALUE-ADDED TAX: KEY TO DEFICIT REDUCTION? (1987).

——, *Economic, Administrative and Political Factors in Choosing a General Consumption Tax*, 46 NAT'L TAX J. 345 (1993).

——, *State and Local Implications of a Federal Value-Added Tax*, 38 TAX NOTES 1517 (1988).

——, *State and Federal Relations in the Taxation of Value Added*, 6 J. CORP. L. 127 (1980).

——, *Economic Effects of Taxing Value Added*, in BROAD-BASED TAXES (Richard A. Musgrave ed., 1973).

Militzer, Ken, *VAT: Evidence from the OECD*, 47 TAX NOTES 207 (1990).

Miller, John A., *State Adoption of a Value Added Tax: A Desperate Act in Search of the Proper Occasion*, 71 NEB. L. REV. 192 (1992).

——, *State Administration of a National Sales Tax: A New Opportunity for Cooperative Federalism*, 9 VA. TAX REV. 243 (1989).

Mintz, Jack M., *The Business Transfer Tax as a Consumption Tax*, 9 TAX NOTES INT'L 75 (1995).

Missorten, Walter, *Some Problems in Implementing a Tax on Value Added*, 21 NAT'L TAX J. 396 (1968).

Morris, William H., *A "National Debate" on VAT: The Gibbons Proposal*, 60 TAX NOTES 1259 (1993).

Norr, Martin & Nils G. Hornhammar, *The Value-Added Tax in Sweden*, 70 COLUM. L. REV. 379 (1970).

Oldman, Oliver & Alan Schenk, *The Business Activities Tax: Have Senators Danforth & Boren Created a Better Value Added Tax?*, 65 TAX NOTES 1547 (1994).

Osgood, Russell K., *The Convergence of the Taxation Systems of the Developed Nations*, 25 CORNELL INT'L L.J. 339 (1992).

Raboy, David G., *The Trade Implications of the VAT with Floating Exchange Rates*, 47 TAX NOTES 857 (1990).

SCHENK, ALAN, VALUE ADDED TAX IN THE UNITED KINGDOM (1976).

——, *Taxation of Financial Services Under a Value Added Tax: A Critique of the Treatment Abroad and the Proposals in the United States*, 9 TAX NOTES INT'L 823 (1994).

——, *Choosing the Form of a Federal Value-Added Tax: Implications for State and Local Retail Sales Taxes*, 22 CAP. U. L. REV. 291 (1993).

——, *Administrative Costs of a U.S. Value-Added Tax: A Description and Analysis of the Report of The United States General Accounting Office*, VAT MONITOR, July 1993, at 2.

——, *Japanese Consumption Tax: The Japanese Brand VAT*, 42 TAX NOTES 1625 (1989).

——, *The Canadian White Paper on Sales Tax Reform and the Model Value Added Tax Statute for the United States: A Comparative Analysis*, 26 OSGOODE HALL L.J. 629 (1988).

——, *Value Added Tax: Does This Consumption Tax Have a Place in the Federal Tax System?*, 7 VA. TAX REV. 207 (1987).

——, *The Business Transfer Tax: The Value Added by Subtraction*, 30 TAX NOTES 351 (1986).

Schuyler, Michael A., *Consumption Taxes: Promises & Problems*, 25 TAX NOTES 571 (1984) [a summary of Mr. Schuyler's 1984 book of the same title].

Sheppard, Lee A., *The Consumption Tax: How the Industrial World Does It*, 70 TAX NOTES 142 (1996).

Shoup, Carl S., *Factors Bearing on an Assumed Choice Between a Federal Retail-Sales Tax and a Federal Value-Added Tax*, in BROAD-BASED TAXES (Richard A. Musgrave ed., 1973).

SMITH, DAN THROOP ET AL., WHAT YOU SHOULD KNOW ABOUT THE VALUE ADDED TAX (1973).

Smith, Dan Throop, *Value-Added Tax: The Case For*, 47 HARV. BUS. REV. 77 (1970).

Stockfish, J.A., *Value-Added Taxes and the Size of Government: Some Evidence*, 38 NAT'L TAX J. 547 (1985).

Surrey, Stanley S., *Value-Added Tax: The Case Against*, 48 HARV. BUS. REV. 86 (1970).

——, *A Value-Added Tax for the United States—A Negative View*, 21 TAX EXEC. 151 (1969).

TAIT, ALAN A., VALUE ADDED TAX (1972).

Toder, Eric, *Comments on Proposals for Fundamental Tax Reform*, 66 TAX NOTES 2003 (1995) [statement to Senate Budget Committee].

TURE, NORMAN B., THE VALUE ADDED TAX: FACTS AND FANTASIES (1979).

——, *The Basic Economics of a United States VAT*, 6 J. CORP. L. 49 (1980).

Turnier, William J., *Accommodating to the Small Business Problem Under a VAT*, 47 TAX LAW. 963 (1994).

——, *VAT: Minimizing Administration and Compliance Costs*, 38 TAX NOTES 1257 (1988).

——, *Designing an Efficient Value Added Tax*, 39 TAX L. REV. 435 (1984).

U.S. DEP'T OF TREASURY, TAX REFORM FOR FAIRNESS, SIMPLICITY, AND ECONOMIC GROWTH ["Treasury I"], vol. 3, (1984).

Waldauer, Charles, *Economic Effects of the Tax Restructuring Act of 1979*, 6 J. CORP. L. 103 (1980).

Wetzler, James W., *The Role of a Value Added Tax in Financing Social Security*, 32 NAT'L TAX J. 334 (1979).

Wright, L. Hart, *Personal, Living or Family Matters and the Value Added Tax*, 82 MICH. L. REV. 419 (1983).

Zodrow, George R., *A Direct Consumption Tax as an "Add-On" Tax*, 38 TAX NOTES 1389 (1988).

CHAPTER SEVEN

A CONSUMPTION-TYPE INCOME TAX

*[T]he equality of imposition consists rather in the equality of
that which is consumed than of the riches of the persons that
consume the same. For what reason is there that he which labors
much and, sparing the fruits of his labor, consumes little should be
more charged than he that, living idly, gets little and spends all he
gets, seeing the one has no more protection from the commonwealth
than the other? But when the impositions are laid upon those
things which men consume, every man pays equally for what he
uses; nor is the commonwealth defrauded by the luxurious waste of
private men.*[a]

A. INTRODUCTION

The materials in this chapter examine two related issues. First, should
the principal basis for taxation, and particularly for national taxation in this
country, be consumption or income? This issue was raised in Chapter Six,
but the discussion will be broadened here.

Second, what form should a broad-based consumption tax take? In
comparison to the income tax, and to the forms of consumption tax discussed
in this chapter, value added taxes (VATs) and retail sales taxes (RSTs) are
relatively simple to administer. What, then, is the objection to VAT and
similar forms of consumption taxes? *Fairness.* A hallmark of the federal
income tax is progressivity. It is impossible to operate VATs and RSTs that
are progressive with respect to final consumers without giving up the
administrative simplicity of point-of-sale collection. If the taxpayer buys a
lawn mower from a retailer, for example, the seller has no way of knowing
whether the taxpayer will spend $10,000 or $250,000 during the year;[b] for
that reason, the seller could not be expected to charge the correct tax unless
the tax rate were the same for all purchasers of a given product.

Is it possible to levy *progressive* consumption taxes? In theory, each
taxpayer could be required to keep careful records of all expenditures at the
grocery store, day-care provider, barber shop, restaurant, cigarette vending
machine, etc. At the end of the year, the taxpayer would pay a tax based on
the total of the year's consumption, at progressive rates. It is obvious that

---

a. THOMAS HOBBES, LEVIATHAN 271 (Liberal Arts Press, 1958) (1651).

b. It thus would be impossible to structure the tax so that it would be progressive with
respect to its base, consumption; for similar reasons, it would also be impossible to structure a
VAT or sales tax so that it would be progressive with respect to income.

such a tax would be unworkable, and by comparison would make the present income tax seem a model of administrative simplicity. While most individuals receive income from only a few sources—frequently only one—many of those same individuals make thousands of purchases during the year. A progressive consumption tax on this model would be extremely burdensome on law-abiding taxpayers who would have to keep records of each small expenditure, and it would be impossible for the Internal Revenue Service to police.

Thus, if one is persuaded of the desirability of moving to a system of consumption taxation but without sacrificing progressivity, the challenge is to envision a consumption tax that is both progressive and administratively feasible, and that includes a system for withholding taxes. This has been done.

Most proponents of a progressive consumption tax envision a calculation that would start with income, as at present—indeed, the systems are frequently described as consumption-type income taxes. Withholding by employers and other payors of income would continue. However, certain items would be treated differently—items relating to savings and investment and/or return on savings and investment—to convert the tax base to one more closely approximating consumption than income. The resulting tax base could be taxed at progressive rates, or, even if a flat rate were employed, a considerable element of progressivity could be achieved through personal and dependency exemptions and standard deductions. (Some consumption-type proposals envision a "family allowance" sufficiently generous that many lower-middle-class individuals who are taxpayers under present law would have no liability.) Itemized deductions could be provided as desired under such a system.

In this form, the consumption tax has generated considerable academic interest. More surprising and more important, a number of proposals by political "heavy hitters" mean that there is a real chance that some form of consumption tax could actually replace the present income tax.

B. ACADEMIC EXPOSITION

As this chapter's opening quotation illustrates, utilizing the taxpayer's overall level of consumption as the principal tax base has been discussed for centuries. John Stuart Mill proposed a tax base of income minus saving—essentially the tax base of current proposals—in the Nineteenth Century. In response to the persuasive writing on Nicholas Kaldor in the middle of this century, India and Sri Lanka briefly adopted expenditure taxes.[c]

---

c. Richard Goode, *The Superiority of the Income Tax, in* WHAT SHOULD BE TAXED: INCOME OR EXPENDITURE? 49, 50 (Joseph A. Pechman ed., 1980) (citing Indian and Sri Lankan government reports attributed to Kaldor's writing). *See also* NICHOLAS KALDOR, AN EXPENDITURE TAX (1955).

Nonetheless, Professor Andrews' 1974 article, excerpted below, is frequently and accurately described as "seminal." It has been the catalyst of extensive academic examination of the proper tax base—the Haig-Simons definition of income ("accretion"); consumption; or, as at present, some hybrid of the two.

A CONSUMPTION-TYPE OR CASH FLOW
PERSONAL INCOME TAX
William D. Andrews[*]

87 Harvard Law Review 1113, 1113-25, 1140, 1148-54, 1156-59, 1167-69 (1974)

Serious thought about personal income tax policy has come to be dominated by an ideal in which taxable income is set equal to total personal gain or accretion, without distinctions as to source or use.[1] It will be convenient to call this ideal an accretion-type personal income tax.

Accretion is the sum of personal consumption plus accumulation.[2] This relation is the real counterpart of the accounting identity by which income equals spending plus saving, income being the source of funds whose uses are spending and saving. Computation of money income, however, does not require analysis of its spending and savings components, because income can be independently determined by reference to sources of funds, without regard to uses. Insofar as economic activity is adequately represented by monetary measures and transactions, therefore, it may seem that accretion need not be analyzed or measured in terms of its consumption and accumulation components.

But economic activity is not wholly reflected in monetary transactions. Taxable income in a true accretion-type tax would include money income (as a proxy for purchased consumption and accumulation in the form of investment purchases and money savings) plus unpurchased consumption and unpurchased accumulation. Consumption and accumulation thus serve to identify two categories of adjustments that are needed to get from money income to total real accretion. The tax falls short of the ideal in relation to consumption insofar as it fails to reflect consumption income in kind,

---

[*]. At time of original publication, Professor of Law, Harvard Law School

[1]. H. SIMONS, PERSONAL INCOME TAXATION (1938), is the classic statement. For different views about the usefulness of any general prescriptive model, see B. BITTKER, C. GALVIN, R. MUSGRAVE & J. PECHMAN, A COMPREHENSIVE INCOME TAX BASE? A DEBATE (1968) (mostly reprinted from 80 HARV. L. REV. 925 (1967) and 81 HARV. L. REV. 44, 63, 1016, 1032 (1967-68)). For an argument that even the accretion ideal, properly understood, will admit some distinctions among current uses of funds but none among sources as such, see Andrews, *Personal Deductions in an Ideal Income Tax*, 86 HARV. L. REV. 309, 375 (1972). This Article is in some respects an extension of the argument there.

[2]. H. SIMONS, *supra* note 1, at 50. Arguably accretion should be defined to equal consumption plus accumulation plus the tax itself, since taxable income is computed without any deduction for the income tax itself. * * * But the failure to deduct the tax itself may be viewed as just a computational shortcut, since any particular rate of tax on taxable income is the equivalent of a tax at a higher rate on disposable income—that is, taxable income minus the tax.

whether enjoyed as an incident of employment or as imputed income from services or property, or even the direct enjoyment of leisure time and activities.   Similarly, the tax falls short of the ideal in relation to accumulation insofar as it fails to reflect accumulation in kind in such forms as unrealized capital appreciation and the accrual of pension rights. As we think about the tax in real terms, consumption and accumulation emerge as two distinct components of the underlying subject matter in terms of which the tax should ultimately be understood and evaluated.

Consumption and accumulation adjustments are analytically different in several ways. For one thing, failure to tax an item of unpurchased consumption is a matter of permanent exemption; if it is not taxed now it will not be picked up later on. Accumulation, on the other hand, is essentially a matter of timing; if pension rights are not taxed as they accrue, for example, pension income will be fully taxed if and when it is paid. Moreover, accumulation may be either positive or negative. Consumption, on the other hand, is always positive. Consumption is not always less than accretion; it will be more during any period of net disaccumulation. Indeed even accretion may be negative if disaccumulation exceeds consumption.

If we think about the personal income tax in real terms, as a tax on accretion, and of accretion as consumption plus accumulation (or minus disaccumulation), reflection will show that its worst inequity, distortion, and complexity arise out of inconsistency in the treatment of accumulation. Under existing law, as we shall see, the effect is often to impair the integrity of the tax in relation to consumption as well as accumulation, so that some taxpayers with high standards of living pay limited taxes. But the underlying source of difficulty is with the accumulation component of accretion. Savings out of ordinary income are fully taxed, while accumulation of wealth in kind through appreciation in value of property already owned is not reflected in current taxable income. Further complications arise from this disparity. Some gains, though realized, are unrecognized by reason of special statutory provisions like those governing corporate reorganizations. These are among the most complex provisions in the statute, and have a substantial effect upon the structuring of financial transactions. Recognized long-term capital gains are taxed at not more than half the regular rate.[d] This discrepancy in rates means that realized capital gain income is partially permanently exempted from tax, even if and when devoted to consumption instead of accumulation. Wealth whose accumulation has already been taxed or permanently exempted is not to be taxed again, and so the statute has complex and imperfect provisions for computing and subtracting basis on sales, and for amortizing basis against ordinary income in the case of depreciable property. Distortions in the computation of

---

d. The historical differential between tax rates on ordinary income and capital gains was eliminated in the Tax Reform Act of 1986, and has only partially returned. Under present law, the maximum rate on ordinary income is 39.6%, compared to 28% for capital gains. (Eds.)

depreciation and other items are sometimes grossly magnified by the way borrowing is treated in the case of leveraged investments, so that a limited passive investment may produce an artificial loss which shelters other income from tax even though that other income remains freely available for current consumption or other investments.[e]

The way out of these difficulties, according to the accretion idea, is to make taxable income provide a more comprehensive reflection of real accumulation, and therefore accretion, by including unrealized changes in the value of property in taxable income. Literal achievement of that goal would require that all assets be taken into account at current fair market value at the end of each accounting period. Although practical exigencies may prevent comprehensive inclusion of unrealized appreciation, improvement is thought to lie in that direction.

Another remedy for present difficulties lies in just the other direction. It involves putting the income tax treatment of business and investment transactions more completely on a simple cash flow basis. Investment expenditures would be deductible when made; on the other hand, all receipts from business and investment activities, including loan proceeds, would be immediately and fully includable in taxable income. This would have the effect of treating accumulation consistently by excluding it from taxable income even when it is represented by investment of realized gains or of ordinary income.

On its face this possibility may seem to be a step in the wrong direction, a step further away from fairness and equity as represented by the prevailing accretion ideal. But a cash flow income tax would correspond very closely to another ideal, that of a tax whose burdens are apportioned to current personal consumption expenditures rather than to total accretion. Net cash flow from business and investment activities is a simple and practical measure of cash flow devoted to consumption expenditure. It will be convenient to call this kind of tax a consumption-type personal income tax. Such a tax has been discussed and advocated in the economic literature,[7] and even tried, briefly, in Sri Lanka (formerly Ceylon) and India. But it has been discussed as an alternative or supplement to an income tax, not as an ideal implicit in or appropriate for the personal income tax itself.

Insofar as one thinks of economic activity as adequately represented by money transactions and historical costs, the existing personal income tax is

e. This article was written before enactment of sections 465 (generally limiting deductible losses to amounts at risk) and 469 (limiting passive activity losses and credits). (Eds.)

7. The best and most comprehensive discussion is N. KALDOR, AN EXPENDITURE TAX (1955). Earlier advocates Include I. FISHER & H. FISHER, CONSTRUCTIVE INCOME TAXATION (1942); T. HOBBES, LEVIATHAN ch. 30 (1651); J. S. MILL, PRINCIPLES OF POLITICAL ECONOMY bk V, ch. 1, § 4 (Laughlin ed. 1884); A. PIGOU, A STUDY IN PUBLIC FINANCE, 102-133 (3d rev. ed. 1949); W. [VICKREY], AGENDA FOR PROGRESSIVE TAXATION 329-66 (1947); Marshall, *The Equitable Distribution of Taxation* (1917), *in* MEMORIALS OF ALFRED MARSHALL 340, 350-51 (A. Pigou ed. 1925).

largely an accretion-type tax. Money income is generally taxed whether spent or saved. But in real rather than monetary terms, the existing tax is a hybrid, closer in many respects to a consumption-type than an accretion-type tax. Unrealized capital appreciation and accruals under qualified pension and profit-sharing plans are a large portion of total real accumulation, yet are not taxed. For many persons they represent most real accumulation, and for such persons the existing tax may be well represented by the model of a consumption-type tax.

A person with a moderate amount of income-producing property, for example, may live on the yield without either drawing down or adding to principal. He may take care of the future by investing in securities that will show some appreciation in value as well as current yield. Money income for him provides a close measure of consumption expenditure. Real accretion, however, would also include unrealized changes in the value of his property.

Or an employee may spend his whole salary, without saving or dissaving, if his employer is making adequate provision for his retirement and other emergencies through pension plan contributions and the like. Again, current money income will provide a measure of current consumption expenditure, not of total real accretion which would also have to include the increase in value of accrued pension rights each year.

The question whether our existing personal income tax is better represented by the accretion model or by a consumption model can be restated by asking who to take as typical, an individual whose accumulation is represented by savings bank deposits and interest or one whose accumulation takes the form of unrealized capital appreciation or pension accruals. And the question of whether to prefer the consumption model or the accretion model as an ideal can be restated by asking whose tax treatment to take as a prototype. There is clearly a discrepancy in our present treatment, which ought to be removed, but there is no a priori reason to think the way to remove the discrepancy is by taxing unrealized appreciation and pension accruals. It may well be simpler, fairer, and more efficient to provide generally for tax deferral on savings accounts and other forms of saving out of realized income, while taxing eventual disinvestment from savings accounts and capital assets alike at full, ordinary income rates.

This conclusion may be resisted by one who looks to the income tax as a device for curtailing the accumulation of wealth as well as consumption. But the existing income tax has not been fair or effective in relation to accumulation of wealth, and it would not be easy to make it so. Even if it were practical, it is not clear that we should want to tax the accumulation of fresh wealth without some corresponding imposition on existing stocks of wealth. If we are serious about reaching wealth, therefore, it would be better to strengthen and rely on estate and gift taxes for that purpose, focusing the income tax on the consumption component of accretion where it can be made to be most fair and effective.

Prevailing patterns of thought are reflected in common vocabulary. An accretion-type personal income tax is usually simply called an ideal or comprehensive income tax, personal income being defined to mean accretion.[9] No distinction is thus maintained between practical and ideal bases (money income and real accretion); or at least no name is saved for the former. A consumption-type personal income tax, on the other hand, has been called an expenditure tax, suggesting that it is something quite different from an income tax, indeed somehow its opposite, income and expenditure being contrary notions. This terminology obscures the fact that in practice such a tax would be based on a simple cash flow computation of net yield from business and investment activities, with no more effort to keep direct track of particular consumption expenditures than under the existing income tax.[10]

In this Article, *personal income tax* means any tax whose practical computation is based on personal income transactions. *Income* thus refers primarily to the money transactions that make such a tax a practical possibility. *Consumption, accumulation,* and *accretion* refer to real values, accretion being the sum of consumption plus accumulation. The monetary counterparts of consumption and accumulation, which add up to money income, are called *spending* and *saving*. The prevailing prescriptive model of a personal income tax is called an *accretion-type personal income tax*, and a model in which accumulation is comprehensively excluded is called a *consumption-type personal income tax*. The latter is also called a *cash flow personal income tax* because that describes its practical computation. For shorthand it will be convenient often to refer simply to the accretion model or ideal on the one hand, and the consumption or cash flow model on the other. The existing tax is a *hybrid personal income tax* since it conforms to the accretion ideal in some respects and the consumption ideal in others, but neither with any consistency.

The difference between an accretion-type and a consumption-type personal income tax involves only accumulation, and it is in an important

---

9. The most familiar instance is in H. SIMONS, *supra* note 1, at 50:

Personal income may be defined as the algebraic sum of (1) the market value of rights exercised in consumption and (2) the change in the value of the store of property rights between the beginning and the end of the period in question.

10. There is some tendency to think an expenditure tax base would have to be defined net of tax, since whatever is paid in tax is unavailable for expenditure. Then, to get the equivalent of income tax rates over 50% one would have to have expenditure tax rates in excess of 100%. But there is no more to that point in relation to a consumption-type tax than an accretion-type tax; if tax payments are not part of consumption, they are not part of accretion either. * * * [A]s a matter of computational convenience, it may well be better to define the practical base on a gross basis, as consumption expenditures plus the tax itself. * * * Statutory rates can then be kept on a scale of less than 100%, a scale with which we are familiar, though the effective rate in relation to what is left after tax will sometimes exceed 100% just as it does under present law. *See* note 2 *supra*.

* * *

Throughout this Article it is assumed that in both the accretion and consumption models, as under existing law, taxable income is determined without any deduction for the tax itself.

sense only a difference of timing. If an item of accumulation is not reflected in taxable income, the tax is not waived but only deferred. Under either kind of ideal, what is ultimately subject to tax is the same—funds or wealth available for private consumption.

This difference in timing corresponds to a difference in methods of accounting for business and investment activities. For a consumption-type tax, accounting should be on a pure and simple cash flow basis.[12] For an accretion-type tax, accounting must be put on something approximating fair-market-value accounting for business and investment assets. Our existing hybrid tax can then be defined in relation to these ideals by reference to its method of accounting, in which the cost of business and investment assets is required to be capitalized but subsequent increases in value are not generally taken into account until realization.

Good ex.

The difference in timing between a consumption-type and an accretion-type tax is, however, immensely important in defining the real burden of the tax. Under the accretion ideal capital accumulation and its subsequent yield are both to be taxed as they occur, and such a tax would cast a heavier burden on some taxpayers than if the tax on capital accumulation is deferred until subsequent disinvestment. Consider a farmer who plants and grows 100 fruit trees. A 30% tax on his fruit, if and when it appears for harvest, with no tax on the growth of the trees unless and until they are disposed of, would leave him with the fruit of 70 trees. But if the Government took 30% of the trees themselves as they mature, and 30% of the fruit of the remaining 70 trees, the farmer would be left with the fruit of only 49. Or, similarly, consider an individual setting aside funds for retirement. A 30% tax deferred until retirement will leave him with 70% as much to spend as he would have had in the absence of tax. A 30% accretion-type tax imposed on the funds as earned and also on the yield from investing what is left, will leave substantially less.

Nevertheless, the consumption and accretion ideals reinforce one another in important ways. Consumption is the major component of accretion for most taxpayers most of the time, and therefore under either ideal, the tax is in the long run mostly a tax on household consumption. The principal purpose of the tax, in terms of real goods and services, is to curtail private consumption so that resources will be released for public uses. What makes a personal income tax the fairest tax we have is that its burdens are generally cast in sensible relation to standards of living.

More particularly, the consumption ideal reinforces the main lesson of the accretion ideal: that distinctions should not be drawn, for personal income tax purposes, because items of income accrue from different sources.

* * *

---

12. Cash receipts and disbursements accounting as authorized under the existing income tax corresponds to cash flow accounting with respect to accounts receivable and payable.

I believe, for reasons to be developed, that the consumption model offers better solutions to the question of how to treat accumulation than does the prevailing accretion model. But even if one is not prepared to abandon the accretion model as a goal, the consumption model can help achieve a better understanding of the existing tax by providing another frame of reference for critical evaluation. Indeed, the two models together may provide a kind of binocular or stereoscopic view that will give a better sense of depth and perspective than does either model alone. Studying the model of a consumption-type personal income tax will help us to be more analytic about accretion, separating the problems and implications of taxing its consumption component from those of also including accumulation. That may enable us to see better what can and must be done to preserve the integrity of the tax in relation to the consumption component of accretion, whatever one may further decide to do about accumulation.

The main purpose of this Article is to set forth the model of a *main idea* consumption-type personal income tax as an alternative for understanding the practical potential of the existing tax. * * *

This Article is only about personal taxes. It is almost entirely about the personal income tax, with some limited reference to estate and gift taxes. * * *

The Value of Deferral

It has sometimes been thought that mere deferral of income taxes was not of great importance so long as every element of accretion was eventually accounted for. Sophisticated taxpayers and their counsel, however, have realized that deferral is often of immense importance, and recent writing on matters of tax policy has come to reflect that realization. Some appreciation of the value of deferral is essential for an understanding of the argument in this Article because the difference between accretion and consumption ideals is essentially one of deferral, and because the defects in present law that make it an unacceptable hybrid arise from inconsistencies in matters of timing.

Deferral may be valuable under existing law partly because it leads to ultimate outright exemption or taxation at lower rates. Unrealized appreciation is completely exempted in the case of property held until death, because no income tax will have been imposed on such appreciation and the succeeding owner is given a stepped-up basis equal to value at or shortly after date of death. Income whose recognition is deferred until after retirement is often taxed at lower rates then than if it had been taxed during higher-income, active employment years, and not infrequently the corollary of deferral is taxation at capital gain instead of ordinary income rates.

But the important, underlying fact is that even if rates do not change and nothing is ever permanently exempted, mere deferral can be immensely important. Deferral reduces the burden of a tax because of the time value of money; it requires less than a dollar put aside today to meet a dollar of tax liability in the future. The magnitude of the effect, which is a function of interest rates, tax rates, and length of deferral, can be illustrated by several examples.

Productive Investment

The fruit farmer in the introduction is one example. A 30% tax on the growth of his 100 trees when they reach maturity would leave 70 trees, and an annual 30% tax on the fruit thereafter would leave the taxpayer each year with the fruit from 49. On the other hand, if all tax on the trees could be deferred until the trees were disposed of, with a current tax being imposed only on the fruit harvested, the taxpayer would keep 70% of the fruit of 100 trees, which is 42.9% more than the fruit from 49.

* * *

Retirement Income

Consider a dollar of earnings put aside for retirement. Assume this sum is invested at 9% compound interest, and that it is to be utilized 24 years later. In the absence of tax the one dollar set aside would support eight dollars of retirement consumption 24 years later.

Now consider the effect of a 33% accretion-type tax. This would take away one-third of the original dollar when earned, leaving only 67 cents to invest; and it would cut the rate of growth from 9% per annum to 6%. At 6% per annum for 24 years, 67 cents will produce a retirement fund of only $2.67, as compared with $8.00 in the absence of tax. On the other hand, if the tax were deferred until retirement, the taxpayer would pay only $2.67 tax out of $8.00, leaving $5.33 to spend. Deferral of the tax, without any change in rate, would double what the taxpayer has left to spend.

The effect is greater for higher interest rates, higher tax rates, and longer periods. A dollar held at 12% for 36 years, for example, would produce a fund of $64. A 70% true accretion-type tax would reduce the original dollar to 30 cents, and the rate of growth from 12% to 3.6%. At 3.6%, 30 cents will grow to about $1.07 in 36 years, which represents a reduction from $64.00 of about 98.3%. A 70% tax deferred until retirement would take only $44.80 out of $64.00, leaving $19.80 to spend. This is more than eighteen times the amount left by a 70% tax imposed on a true accretion basis.

* * *

The Existing Hybrid Treatment of Accumulation

* * *

[M]any of the most intractable problems in the personal income tax arise directly out of the hybrid character of our treatment of accumulation. The complexities of corporate distributions and reorganizations, for example, at the individual taxpayer level, all have to do with matters discussed here: realization and nonrecognition, basis determination and recovery, capital gain or ordinary income treatment, and treatment of debt. Other seemingly, simpler provisions like that governing installment sales, have essentially to do with deferral or nonrecognition. The trust and partnership provisions involve complex problems of defining when gain will be recognized by individuals and whether it will be capital gain or ordinary income. The partnership provisions, in particular, have very complex provisions concerning the determination and recovery of basis, and the treatment of partnership borrowing. The whole matter of qualified pension and profit-sharing plans is primarily one of deferral, and other compensation schemes, like stock option plans, are designed to defer recognition of gain and to secure capital gain treatment when recognition occurs. Most of the problems that occupy most of the time of tax practitioners and administrators (not to speak of teachers, students, legislators, and taxpayers themselves) arise immediately out of our failure to take a consistent and comprehensive position with respect to inclusion or exclusion of real accumulation in taxable income.

* * *

True Accretion Treatment of Accumulation

* * *

A true accretion-type personal income tax would be free of many of the complexities and inequities of the existing tax. But a true accretion-type tax is hardly attainable in practice. Even a rough approximation of an accretion-type tax would require an utter transformation of the practical administration and computation of the tax from one depending mostly on cash transactions to one in which current, comprehensive property valuation would play a central role. In practical operation the tax would become largely an incremental net wealth tax as well as a tax on income transactions.

Any partial step in the direction of fuller reflection of total accretion remains a compromise in which inconsistencies are inevitable. Some compromises are undoubtedly better than others, and some of our existing problems could probably be ameliorated by fuller reflection of real accretion, but no practical solution in this direction offers anything approaching the simple practicality of a consumption-type or cash flow personal income tax.

A Consumption-Type Personal Income Tax

A consumption-type personal income tax is often assumed to involve all the practical difficulties of the existing personal income tax plus whatever new ones are involved in getting from income to consumption expenditure. The tax would, of course, be computed on personal income plus or minus net dissavings or savings, and discussion has focused on how much additional difficulty the adjustments for saving or dissaving would produce.

This discussion overlooks the fact that a consumption-type tax would avoid all the difficulties that arise from the failure of money income to provide a satisfactory reflection of real accumulation. Income, to be sure, includes savings, and savings are a partial, imperfect, monetary measure of accumulation. A consumption-type tax requires deductions and additions to eliminate savings and dissavings. But these, being based solely on money transactions, are incomparably simpler than either making adjustments to include unrealized appreciation under a true accretion-type tax or living with the complexity and distortion that result from the existing hybrid treatment of accumulation.

Under a consumption-type personal income tax, capital transactions are treated on a simple cash flow basis. Investments are simply deducted when made and proceeds of sales and other capital transactions are added to income when received. All that is required is to separate business and investment activities on the one hand from personal consumption activities on the other, as under present law, and then to keep track of the former on a cash flow basis. Cash flow accounting for business and investment activities automatically provides a measure of cash spent on consumption activities, which is what we are after.

Precise measurement of current consumption spending would require exact accounting for cash and loan balances which might be something of a nuisance. But in practice there is no need for precision because only short term tax deferral or acceleration and relatively small amounts are involved. Ordinary cash balances, including checking accounts and consumer loans, can therefore be left wholly out of account. In effect, both ordinary cash balances and consumer loans can be treated as falling in the consumption sector of an individual's activity rather than the business or investment sector, without any significant distortion of tax burdens.

A precise measure of current consumption would also seem to require separation of consumption from the investment element in the purchase of consumer durables. Strictly speaking it is the current use value rather than the purchase price of an automobile, for example, that constitutes consumption. But again strict precision is unnecessary. The purchase price for a durable item represents the discounted value of its future usefulness, and the tax burden will tend to be the same in the end whether one is taxed or the other. Therefore, it would be acceptable to deal with the consumer durable problem on a simple cash flow basis, although it may be desirable in some cases to give taxpayers the option of deferring taxation on part of the purchase price with interest. Because purchase price can be taken as a proxy for use value, the consumer durable problem is much more manageable under a consumption-type tax than under a true accretion-type tax. Under the latter, the money invested should be taxed when earned, and the imputed return received in the form of use value should also be taxed.

One of the general advantages of a consumption-type tax is that short-term deferral in the interest of simpler administration can be more readily tolerated than in the case of an accretion-type tax. Under a consumption-type tax the benefit of deferral is offset by a corresponding increase in the amount subject to tax at a rate equal to whatever interest rate the market charges the taxpayer for extensions of credit. No such offset occurs under an accretion-type tax where postponement has the effect of reducing the effective rate of taxation on income. Reverting to the example of the fruit farmer, it makes no difference whether we tax the growth of trees or the fruit under a consumption-type tax, because the ultimate burden is the same either way. Under an accretion-type tax it makes a substantial difference whether we tax the trees because we are supposed to tax the fruit, too, in any event, and a tax on both is substantially more burdensome.

These general observations are elaborated in the following discussion of how particular items would enter into the practical computation of a consumption-type personal income tax.

Ordinary Income

Ordinary income—wages, salaries, fees, dividends, interest, rent, and so on—would be treated exactly the same way under a consumption-type personal income tax as under any other personal income tax. They would be fully includable in taxable income for the period in which received and would continue to form the backbone of the tax. Withholding from salaries and wages could be continued as under the existing tax, and it could just as readily be extended to dividends and interest. Most people spend most of their ordinary income for current consumption, and to that extent a consumption-type personal income tax would be no different from the existing tax. Deductions and additions to reflect savings and dissavings would for most taxpayers be in the nature of relatively minor adjustments that would not impair the general relationship between the tax and ordinary income as its chief determinant and as the source of funds with which to pay it.

Similarly, ordinary, current deductions, business and personal, would be essentially unaffected by the shift to a pure consumption-type tax because they are addressed to the consumption rather than the accumulation component of accretion. Ordinary personal deductions for medical expenses, charitable contributions, and alimony, for example, would have the same justifications and problems as under existing law. Furthermore, personal exemptions and a standard deduction could readily be continued under a consumption-type tax.

Ordinary Investments

The most obvious difference about a consumption-type income tax would be that ordinary investments would be accounted for on a pure cash flow basis. The cost of investment assets would be deductible in the year paid, while the proceeds of sale would be fully included in taxable income in the year received. This does not necessarily mean there would be a large tax in a year when substantial sales are made, since it is likely that taxable proceeds would be largely offset by deductions for reinvestment in that year, or for extraordinary, yearend cash balances.

There is a tendency to think of this treatment of investment assets as involving at least some complication over and above the existing income tax treatment, because in a year when part of a taxpayer's income is invested a deduction must be claimed. But this is viewing the matter in too narrow a time frame. Under the existing income tax the cost of an investment cannot be ignored; it must be recorded for future use as a basis either for amortization or in computing gain or loss on sale or other disposition. Surely it is simpler in the long run, for taxpayer and Government alike, to have deductions based on investment costs paid during the current year rather than on costs incurred in several past periods, some quite long ago. * * * [J]ust as a matter of accurate accounting and reporting, cash flow treatment of ordinary investments would represent a vast simplification.[89]

Moreover, this treatment of ordinary investments would eliminate a whole host of complications in the existing income tax beyond the mere ascertainment of historical costs. Individual taxpayers would no longer compute depreciation or use other forms of cost amortization, since business and investment costs would be simply deducted forthwith. Furthermore, there would be no problems concerning realization and nonrecognition of gain or loss when an individual changes investments. If a taxpayer receives new investment property in exchange for old, or as an increment to old property in the case of a stock dividend or other dividend in kind, it would make no difference whether the transaction is one on which gain is realized and recognized under present law, since any gain recognized would in effect be offset by a deduction for the fresh investment. Thus, in the case of an exchange of securities there would be no need to determine whether it is pursuant to a plan of reorganization, since the deduction for reinvestment would offset any gain recognized. The whole law of corporate reorganizations as it bears on individual investors would be rendered obsolete.

Cash flow treatment of ordinary investments would also resolve present problems about when to account for compensation for services in the form of investment property such as stock bonuses or restricted property.[91] Again, cash compensation that the recipient invests would incur no tax; therefore no tax need be imposed on compensation paid in kind in investment property. Tax would properly await sale of the investment property and devotion of the proceeds to consumption expenditure in either case.

Finally, and above all, this treatment of ordinary investments would eliminate any need for special rates of tax on capital gains. The best justification for capital gain rates is to mitigate the disparity in treatment between unrealized gains and realized but reinvested gains. A cash flow treatment of ordinary investments would eliminate that disparity entirely. Proceeds from the sale of investment property would be taxed only if devoted to personal consumption, in which event there would be no reason to distinguish them from ordinary earned income also directed to consumption.

---

89. Immediate deductibility of capital expenditures, partly for the sake of accounting simplification, is familiar under present law.

91. *See* CODE §83 (dealing with compensation in the form of property to which restrictions are attached).

Less persuasive justifications for capital gain rates would also be inapplicable. The argument based on inflation would be met by the fact that no tax on the accumulation represented by the initial investment would have been paid in uninflated dollars, as it would have been under an accretion-type tax. * * * Even the notion that capital gain rates are justified to offset the hardship, given progressive tax rates, of realizing in one year a gain accrued over many would be met, since only proceeds devoted to current consumption would be subject to tax.

Business and Investment Loans

Business and investment loans would be treated, just like ordinary investments, on a simple cash flow basis. Loan proceeds would be reported as income in the year received, and repayments of interest and principal would be deductible when paid. This treatment is unfamiliar, but would represent a clear net simplification for reasons similar to those favoring a cash flow accounting for ordinary investments.

Cash flow accounting for loans, as for investments, is only a matter of reporting currently events that would have to be recorded for future reference under the present tax or an accretion-type tax. While we do not tax loan proceeds as such under present law, we do tax forgiveness of indebtedness, or satisfaction of indebtedness by the conveyance of appreciated property, even when the result is a substantial tax liability in a year in which there are no cash receipts with which to pay the tax.[95] A record of money received and repaid on account of loans must be accurately kept in order to compute such gains. Cash flow accounting is only a matter of taking each receipt and payment into account in the year when it occurs.

Inclusion of loan proceeds in income would not ordinarily require large tax payments in the year of a loan, because normally such loans are to pay for capital investment that would be immediately deductible under a consumption-type tax. * * *

Consumer Credit

A strict computation of current consumption would seem to require that consumer loans and credit, like business and investment loans, be treated as income when incurred and deductible when repaid. But it is much simpler and quite acceptable just to leave ordinary consumer loans and credit arrangements out of account. The effect of that is to treat payments on account of consumer loans, rather than the use of the loan proceeds, as taxable consumption expenditures. * * *

Consumer Durables

* * *

Theoretically, under a consumption-type tax, the purchase price should be deductible like any other investment, and rental value should be imputed

---

95. *See* Crane v. Commissioner, 331 U.S. 1 (1947); United States v. Kirby Lumber Co., 284 U.S. 1 (1931); Parker v. Delaney, 186 F.2d 455 (1st Cir. 1950), *cert. denied*, 341 U.S. 926 (1951).

to the owner over the useful life. But in practice imputed rental value is adequately reflected, on a discounted basis, by the purchase price. * * * The practical thing to do, therefore, is to treat the purchase of [a consumer durable such as] a personal automobile like any other consumption expenditure, ignoring its investment aspect. This is accomplished by simply leaving such a purchase out of account in computing taxable income, thus making the expenditure subject to tax. * * *

When an automobile is purchased on credit, the loan should be treated as a consumer loan. In practice, therefore, neither the purchase of the automobile nor the loan would enter into the computation of taxable income, and the result would be that consumption use of the automobile would be reflected in taxable income each year in the amount of payments of principal and interest on the loan.

If consumer durable purchases in a particular year were substantial in amount, it might be appropriate to permit a taxpayer to defer them over a limited period, even if they were not financed by borrowing. The procedure would be to claim a deduction in the year of purchase but then to return the deducted amount to income with interest. * * *

Owner-Occupied Housing

Similar general conclusions apply to owner-occupied housing, which undoubtedly represents the most substantial item of consumer durable investment made by most taxpayers. Purchase price, however, is a less acceptable proxy for use value in the case of very longlife items like housing, because tax rates may change and property may go up or down in value for reasons not anticipated at the time of purchase. Nevertheless, it is still the case that the existing treatment of owner-occupied housing is more nearly consonant with a consumption-type model than with a true accretion-type model. Furthermore, whatever accommodations may be made to ease practical computation represent less of a distortion or departure from a consumption ideal than from a true accretion ideal.

A strictly correct treatment of housing would be to allow a deduction for purchase price and capital expenditures, but then to impute full rental value, with periodic changes in imputed rental to reflect market changes. This would involve the difficulties of real estate assessment and valuation on a national scale. It would also involve a duplication of the hardship that is now perceived by some to result from increasing real estate taxes in the case of elderly homeowners who do not have any corresponding increase in money income with which to pay those taxes. The fact is that home ownership during a period of rising real estate prices operates to allow older people to live in houses that are more expensive than they could afford to move into now, and that effect may be judged to be generally desirable. Furthermore, we may feel we do not want our income tax to impair that aspect of homeownership by creating a tax liability that increases over time and that can only be met by having an increasing cash income. The economics of homeownership allow a person to buy a home for a lifetime out of the earnings of his relatively early productive years at price levels prevailing when he makes his initial purchase. It may well be enough for the income tax law to take this economic situation as it is and be satisfied with taxing a person on the cash expenditure it takes to provide lifetime housing, as the expenditure is made.

The treatment of owner-occupied housing then would be virtually the same as under present law, except that there would be no deduction for mortgage interest, and there might be an option to deduct an initial downpayment, returning it to income over a short period of years with interest added annually to the deferred balance at a specified rate.

Proceeds on the sale of a house would present some new problems. The present rule permitting a homeowner to sell at a profit without tax if proceeds are reinvested in another principal residence should be continued.[103] This rule, for example, enables a person to move and purchase comparable housing in another location, without making the additional investment that would be required if he had to pay a tax on the heretofore unrealized appreciation on his first home. Profit on the sale of a house not reinvested in another residence would be included in taxable income, though no tax would be paid if proceeds were invested in any ordinary investment assets.[104] The new question would be whether that part of sale proceeds that represents a return of basis or costs and is not reinvested in housing should be able to be spent for other consumption on a taxfree basis on the ground that it represents a refund of money on which consumption tax has already been paid. The answer to that question should probably be yes, and again that answer is in accord with present law under which the sale proceeds from a house, to the extent they represent return of basis rather than profit, are freely available for consumption spending.[105]

Finally, it should be reemphasized that any practical solution to the problem of owner-occupied housing is more consonant with the consumption model than with the accretion model. The accretion ideal requires that the purchase price of a home come out of after-tax income because it is an item of accumulation, and then it requires that there be further additions to

---

103. CODE § 1034.

104. This would avoid the problem that exists under present law of a recognized capital gain when people sell their home to move into rented quarters. It would largely obviate the need, therefore, for CODE § 121 (gain on sale of residence by a taxpayer aged 65 [now 55] or older partly excluded from taxable income).

105. The law might provide that proceeds from the sale of a house, to the extent that they represent a return of cost or basis, would not be included in taxable income. In addition, if the funds representing a return of cost were invested, the taxpayer would get a deduction for the investment itself, but would be taxed on subsequent disinvestment and consumption. Alternatively, one could grant no deduction for the investment of such funds, but instead give the taxpayer a cost basis in the assets purchased. When the investments were then later liquidated and spent for consumption, the proceeds would be excluded from income to the extent to that basis.

taxable income to reflect both imputed rental income and unrealized appreciation. The existing treatment of housing falls short of the accretion ideal immediately upon purchase and occupation of a home, without any change in value, by reason of failure to include imputed rental income. As a house increases in value, existing treatment falls doubly short by failing to include both an increase in imputed rental income and the appreciation in value as such. By contrast, existing treatment (except for deductibility of mortgage interest) is initially consistent with the consumption ideal since taxation of the purchase price serves as a proxy for taxing imputed rental value. * * *

Fairness and Efficiency

* * *

It may nevertheless be objected that a saver is not to be viewed as a philanthropist contributing more to society than he withdraws. Accumulation is not consumption foregone; it is consumption deferred. Since a saver has not given up the claim against future output represented by his accumulated income, what reason can there be to exempt him from tax upon it?

But the issue as between an accretion-type and a consumption-type tax is not one of exemption; it, too, is only one of deferral. Under a consumption-type tax, deferred consumption is subject to deferred tax. Of course, deferral makes a difference, and in general the burden of a deferred tax is less than that of an immediate tax at the same rate. * * * But to say the burden of a deferred tax is less does not indicate which kind of tax is fairer. The most sophisticated argument in favor of a consumption-type tax is that the lesser burden of a deferred tax is more appropriate because it ultimately imposes a more uniform burden on consumption, whenever it may occur, than does an accretion-type tax. Put the other way around, a consumption-type tax is preferable because an accretion-type tax imposes an excessive burden on deferred consumption.[119] Neutrality with respect to consumption is important not only because it promotes efficiency in the allocation of income, but

---

119. An accretion-type tax is sometimes defended by reference to neutrality, treating saving as just one more thing a person may do with his income. A consumption-type tax, it is said, would impose a penalty on spending as compared with saving. *See* Musgrave, *In Defense of an Income Concept*, 81 HARV. L. REV. 44, 46 (1967). Or, more elaborately, it is said that saving must involve some combination of satisfactions equal to what could have been derived from a little more spending at the margin; otherwise the person would have spent more and saved less. *See, e.g.*, Aaron, *What Is a Comprehensive Tax Base Anyway?*, 22 NAT'L TAX J. 543, 544 (1969).

But this line of reasoning is essentially like an argument against the deductibility of business expenses—one must get as much pleasure from a business expenditure as from a personal consumption expenditure, at the margin, or else he would make more of the latter and less of the former. What we recognize immediately, of course, with respect to a business expense is that satisfactions to be derived from it may be at least one step removed. * * * Saving, similarly, can be viewed as an instrumental expenditure, made as a means of supporting future consumption. The way to achieve neutrality between ultimate ends—future and present consumption—is, as we have seen, to exempt savings, not to tax them.

because it keeps the tax from bearing more heavily on one person than another on account of differences in need or taste for particular goods or services, now or in the future.

Consider again the case of a working person who puts $100 aside for retirement. At 9% compound interest, in 24 years it will grow to $800. A tax of 33% imposed on a consumption basis would take 33% of $800 leaving $533 to spend. A 33% accretion-type tax would cut the $100 to $67 at the outset, and cut its rate of growth from 9% per annum to 6%. At 6%, the $67 would double only twice making $267, or just half what is left under a consumption-type tax. The effective rate of tax in relation to consumption ultimately supported by the earnings in question is thus not 33% but 67%. All this is without even taking account of graduated rates, which are likely to make the relative burden of an accretion-type tax even heavier by subjecting earnings to high-income rates even when put aside to support consumption in low-income retirement years.

The logic of a consumption-type tax is that a 33% taxpayer who would have had $800 to spend in the absence of tax should have $533 after tax whatever combination of earnings and savings may have gone to produce the $800. An accretion-type tax is discriminatory because it will leave much less for the retiree whose potential $800 is the product of work and saving than for another taxpayer with $800 of current income.

Mill called the discrimination of an accretion-type tax against deferred consumption a double tax on savings, once as they accumulate and again as they produce their own return.[121] Unfortunately, ensuing discussion has sometimes focused more on definitional than on substantive issues; the accumulation of savings and earnings of a return on the accumulation represent separate items of income or accretion, it is said, and therefore taxing both does not represent double taxation of a single item. For all the argument, no careful writer seems to have denied that an accretion-type tax imposes a heavier ultimate burden in relation to deferred consumption than to current consumption.

This discussion of neutrality has only to do with neutrality as to expenditures. A personal income tax is not neutral by any means, unfortunately, with respect to questions of productivity—how hard to work and how much, what risks to take with capital, and so on. Either a consumption-type or an accretion-type personal income tax will have substitution effects in favor of leisure over work, and, less clearly, in favor of conservative over risky investment. While both types of taxes are biased with respect to these things, a consumption-type tax is apparently less so.[123] This is an important advantage, though collateral, as it seems to me, to preserving expenditure neutrality between present and deferred consumption.

---

121. J.S. MILL, *supra* note 7, at 545-46.
123. *See* N. KALDOR, *supra* note 7, at 102-14.

Insofar as accumulation is viewed as deferred consumption, a consumption-type tax seems fairer and economically more efficient than an accretion-type tax. If an accretion type tax is to be preferred over a consumption-type tax it must be because accumulation somehow represents something more than deferred consumption, something that would not be adequately captured or reflected or burdened by the deferred imposition of a consumption-type tax if and when consumption ultimately occurs.

* * *

Notes and Questions

1. Why does Professor Andrews term the measurement of income by the Haig-Simons definition an "accretion" measurement?

2. The assertion that the accretion measurement overtaxes savings is central to the proponents of consumption-type taxes. (Professor Gunn's excerpt in subchapter C challenges this assertion.) What examples of asserted overtaxation of savings does Professor Andrews offer?

3. Accretion and consumption are not the only possible models of the ideal tax base. The realization model—which present law tracks to a considerable degree—could be viewed as an ideal. See Chapter Two; see also Professor Gunn's defense of present law (and not of the accretion ideal) in subchapter C. Most scholars, however, now regard present law as a hybrid of the accretion and consumption ideals.

Mechanics of Professor Andrews' proposal

4. The ultimate tax base of the consumption-type income tax is consumption, not income (or accretion). Yet the first step in computing the tax base is quite similar to that of present law—initially including all income in the tax base, without regard to whether the income was consumed or saved. If the tax base is consumption, why start with income?

5. Most taxpayers consume the great bulk of their after-tax incomes. For such taxpayers, the tax base under either an income tax or under the proposed consumption-type tax would be almost the same. "[U]nder either ideal," Andrews observes, "the tax in the long run is mostly a tax on household consumption."

6. Does "consumption" include money paid in taxes? Consider a taxpayer who earned $50,000, but whose employer withheld $10,000 for taxes and paid only the remaining $40,000 to the employee. If the employee spent the $40,000 on consumption, should the taxpayer's consumption-tax base be $40,000 or, as under Professor Andrews' proposal, $50,000?

7. A tax-exclusive base could lead to extremely high nominal tax rates. Suppose the consumption tax base did not include taxes. What rate of consumption taxation would be necessary to equal the effect of an income tax rate of 50 percent for a taxpayer who spent all after-tax income on consumption? What rate would be necessary to equal an income tax rate of 75 percent?

8. Professor Andrews argues that failure to tax consumption results in permanent tax avoidance, while failure to tax appreciation (or "accumulation") generally results only in moving the tax burden to a different year. Why is this generally true? Does this description hold true in all instances of accretion, such as appreciated property held until death?

9. It might be argued that an income base is to be preferred to a consumption base, because tax liability should take account of wealth as well as current living standards. Professor Jeff Strnad argues that two of the principal "norms that have motivated scholars and policymakers to favor accretion taxation" are wealth-based: "The first norm is that intangible benefits from holding wealth should be taxed. The second norm is that the tax system should address disparities in wealth as well as disparities in consumption."[f]

On what grounds does Professor Andrews reject the argument that an income tax effectively and appropriately addresses differences in wealth?

10. Do transfer taxes (estate and gift taxes) have any role to play in Andrews' proposed system?

11. Many advocates of consumption taxation, including Andrews, support transfer taxes. One reason is that the consumption-type tax will not reach income at any time during life, or at death, if the income is not consumed but is passed on to heirs. (Even then, the consumption tax is merely delayed—until consumption occurs by the heir. This delay, however, could extend indefinitely—for generations.)

The Simplification Claim

12. Why does Professor Andrews contend that his consumption tax would be less complex than either current law or the accretion ideal? (Reserve judgment on the simplification issue until you have studied subchapter E, which presents actual proposals for implementation of consumption-type taxation.)

---

f. Jeff Strnad, *Periodicity and Accretion Taxation: Norms and Implementation*, 99 YALE L.J. 1817, 1820 (1990).

13.   Why might such disparate provisions of current law as payments of compensation in the form of stock of the employer, corporate reorganizations, and exchanges of like-kind business or investment property be simplified under a consumption-type income tax?

14.   Why would Professor Andrews count items such as cash balances and checking account balances—amounts clearly not consumed in fact—as consumption? How would you expect taxpayers to react to such a legal rule?

15.   A taxpayer's expenditures for plant and equipment are usually deducted over a period of years (i.e., depreciated) under present law. How would such costs be recovered under a consumption-type tax? Why the different treatment?

16.   Under present law, one source of controversy is whether a given expenditure should be viewed as an ordinary business expense such as a repair (which is "expensed," or immediately deducted), or treated as a capital expenditure (which is capitalized and deducted over time). Under the consumption-type taxing method, the expenditure would be immediately deducted either way, ending this source of controversy.

17.   Under present law, neither loans nor repayments of loan principal have tax effect. Under Professor Andrews' proposal, the proceeds of many loans would be taken into the tax base, while the repayment of those loans would give rise to a deduction. What is the justification for this treatment? What would happen in the case of cancellation of indebtedness, which is generally taxable under current law?

18.   Professor Andrews suggests treating consumer loans differently, giving no tax effect either to the loan or to its repayment. Why?

19.   How should a consumption-type tax deal with consumer durables, such as automobiles, in theory? How would Professor Andrews deal with them? Why?

20.   What is the theoretically correct treatment of housing under Professor Andrews' proposal? What, instead, does he advocate? Why?

21.   What should happen under Andrews' proposal when a taxpayer sells a house?

Capital gains
22   How would capital gains taxation work under the consumption-type tax? What problems of current law would be reduced or eliminated?

23. One of the major justifications of favorable capital gains treatment is that the gain may be illusory, the result of inflation rather than real gain. Traditionally, capital gains have been taxed much more gently than ordinary income, in part due to the inflation factor. Another suggestion is to index the basis of capital assets to adjust for inflation, but complexity, among other problems, would result. (See Chapters Fifteen and Sixteen.)

If the consumption-type tax were in place, the taxation of capital assets would seem devoid of the inflation problem. There would be no basis; at the time of purchase, a full deduction of the amount of the purchase price would be granted, so no inflation adjustment would be justified. Upon disposition, the total amount realized would be taken into account and taxed in that year, and again no inflation adjustment would be necessary.

Suppose this system had been in place for many years, and that a taxpayer who purchased stock in 1960 for $7,000 sold the stock in 1996 for $10,000, thus realizing a nominal gain of $3,000. Obviously, the "gain" would be illusory, because 7,000 1960 dollars would be much more valuable than 10,000 1996 dollars. Assuming a tax rate of ten percent, the taxpayer's "losing" investment would generate $300 tax in 1996. This is troubling under the present income tax; the nominal gain is taxed despite the fact that the transaction resulted in a "real" loss.

Under the consumption-type tax, the problem is automatically cured. Still assuming a 10 percent tax rate, the deduction of $7,000 in 1960 is worth $700 *in 1960 dollars*; when the $10,000 amount realized is taxed in 1996, it results in $1,000 tax *in 1996 dollars*. If, in fact, inflation means that the "real" value of the sales proceeds are worth less than the "real" value of the initial investment, so will the "real" tax on the proceeds be worth less than the "real" value of the deduction granted when the investment was made.

Asserted consistency of consumption-type income tax

24. Why do proponents of consumption taxation contend that unrealized appreciation is more troubling to the income tax system than to a consumption-type system?

25. Is our present federal income tax a consumption tax, or an accretion tax? In what ways does it resemble each?

26. To say that a tax system is entirely coherent and follows its "ideal" pattern at all times is not to say that it is a good system. For example, if our basic system were a head tax, requiring exactly $1,000 in annual tax from each person, there would be no inconsistency about how to handle capital gains or unrealized appreciation or any other of the thousands of perplexing questions under our tax law—the head tax would call for the same amount of tax regardless of any of these events. It does not follow that we should adopt a head tax in place of the income tax.

27. Would a tax in the form proposed by Professor Andrews more closely resemble a point-of-sale consumption tax, such as a comprehensive sales tax or European-style value added tax, or our present income tax? Consider factors such as tax base, vertical and horizontal comparisons of tax liability, and administration.

C. THE INCOME TAX DEFENDED

While the consumption-type income tax has created considerable academic and political interest, many experts defend income as the more appropriate tax base. The excerpts in this subchapter provide a sampling of three very different types of defenses.

Professor Warren analyzes the issue from an extremely academic, and arguably socialistic, perspective. He argues that each member of society who generates income does so as part of a social system; accordingly, society should have first claim on the income produced, and society should decide what portion of that income the individual producer is to retain.

Professor Gunn counters what is perhaps the central justification for consumption taxation—the assertion that an income tax overtaxes saving vis-a-vis consumption. Addressing examples of Professor Andrews and other advocates of consumption taxation, Professor Gunn argues that saving is taxed fairly by the income tax.

Finally, we consider Treasury I, whose drafters found considerable merit in a consumption-type income tax. Ultimately, however, they rejected it for a number of theoretical and practical reasons.

WOULD A CONSUMPTION TAX
BE FAIRER THAN AN INCOME TAX?
Alvin Warren[*]

89 Yale Law Journal 1081, 1090-93 (1980)

Using the Haig-Simons concept of income in order to compute each taxpayer's share of the annual social product, an income tax serves to deflect to the government a progressive portion of each citizen's share of the product otherwise allocated to him by transfers and the marketplace. Whether the tax proceeds are used for public goods and services or for redistribution to some persons, either in cash or in kind, those uses are funded by the output of labor and private capital during the current period. Levying the tax on income is on this view simply a logical concomitant of the proposition that society in general has a claim on its annual product that is prior to the claims of its individual citizens.

The existence of a collective claim on privately produced resources is so well-established as part of our polity that justification may seem superfluous. Nevertheless, economic theorists have formally shown that certain goods and

---

[*]. At time of original publication, Professor of Law, University of Pennsylvania Law School.

services are best produced in the public sector,[31] while political theorists have argued for centuries over the nature and extent of the collective claim for redistributive purposes, a subject that has commanded renewed attention in recent years.[32] But neither the theories of public goods nor those of distributive justice have depended on the source of revenues used for the two analytically distinct governmental purposes. Discussions of redistribution generally either have considered the appropriate distribution of economic resources without identifying the best measure of such resources or have assumed that it is income (as product) that is or is not subject to a collective claim. As a result, existing theories of distributive justice and public goods have little to add to the case for the income tax beyond establishing a social claim on private resources.

Specifying that claim as on social product can be justified on the theory that a producer does not have a controlling moral claim over the product of his capital and labor, given the role of fortuity in income distribution and the dependence of producers on consumers and other producers to create value in our society—factors that create a general moral claim on all private product on behalf of the entire society.[33] This rationale would apply *a fortiori* to other increments in Haig-Simons income, such as gifts and windfalls, which come to the recipient without even the claim due to production. Such a proposition is, of course, no more demonstrable than the proposition that society has a prior moral claim on wealth or consumption rather than on product. As Professor William Andrews has stated, the ultimate choice among these alternatives is not a matter of logical proof but of exposing the assumptions and identifying the consequences of each.[34]

Given that limitation, the case for taxing income can be stated by identifying as a plausible assumption the view that, for the reasons suggested above, the distribution of social product is a matter for collective decision. The collective decisionmaking apparatus of the society is conceived of as deciding both the amount and type of public goods to be produced and the distribution of that portion of private social product that remains after diversion of resources into the public sector to produce those public goods that are not financed by service charges. Whatever after-tax distribution is

---

31. *See, e.g.*, Samuelson, *The Pure Theory of Public Expenditure*, 36 REV. ECON. & STATISTICS 387, 387-89 (1954); Samuelson, *Diagrammatic Exposition of a Theory of Public Expenditure*, 37 REV. ECON. & STATISTICS 350 (1955).

32. The seminal work in rekindling interest in distributive justice is J. RAWLS, A THEORY OF JUSTICE (1971).

33. *See id.* at 72-74, 100-08, 310-15. For a recent argument that treatment of an individual's genetic endowment as an accident devoid of moral significance is inconsistent with basic concepts of individuality, see Posner, *Utilitarianism, Economics, and Legal Theory*, 8 J. LEGAL STUD. 103, 128 (1979).

34. Andrews, *Fairness and the Choice Between a Consumption-Type and an Accretion-Type Personal Income Tax: A Reply to Professor Warren*, 88 HARV. L. REV. 947, 950 (1975).

decided upon, that decision is implemented by the income tax, which is levied on the amount of social product otherwise distributed to each taxable unit.[35]

As anticipated, this argument for the income tax does not appeal to some independently demonstrable principle but is tautological in the sense that it follows simply from the premise of the tax: given a legitimate social concern with the distribution of society's product, the income tax is justified as a means of effecting the desired after-tax distribution. The nature of the desired distribution goes to the content of the tax, rather than to its justification. Extreme egalitarianism would presumably argue for a tax characterized by progressivity, culminating in a confiscatory rate on positive income with corresponding provisions specifying a minimum after-tax income. A social decision to reduce inequality in the distribution of product, but not to the extent of eliminating incentives to work and invest, might lead to less progressivity with rates always under one hundred percent. It is a judgment of this latter type that seems to underlie much current discussion of distributive justice.[36]

Unlike the foregoing argument, the traditional case for the income tax in terms of fairness has appealed to some external standard to establish that income is an appropriate basis for taxation. Generally it has been argued that income is a superior index of an "ability to pay," and that the tax should be structured to result in "equal sacrifice" by taxpayers, the latter being especially relevant to the rate structure. Unfortunately, centuries of elucidation have failed to provide sufficient content to these concepts. For example, ability to pay has been defined as "the capacity of paying without undue hardship on the part of the person paying or an unacceptable degree of interference with objectives that are considered socially important by other members of the community."[37] Such definitions reduce to statements that society should appropriately tax what it should appropriately tax. This approach is no less tautological than the one taken here; it just appears so in that apparently, but not really, independently verifiable grounds, such as ability to pay, are said to justify the tax.

To summarize, the personal income tax follows from, and is justified by, a societal judgment as to the appropriate distribution of social product or personal income. Society's interest in the distribution of income, in turn, depends on the view that the importance of fortuity and the interrelationships of contemporary society deprive producers of a controlling

---

35. This view includes the possibility of negative taxes and assumes that the desired after-tax distribution of income is a function of no personal characteristic other than pretax income. For example, if after-tax income were to be allocated on the basis of weight, intelligence, merit, or whatever, the Haig-Simons definition could be used for collection of revenue, but not for the simultaneous achievement of a given after-tax distribution.

36. *See, e.g.*, A. OKUN, EQUALITY AND EFFICIENCY—THE BIG TRADEOFF (1975); J. RAWLS, *supra* note 32, at 150-61.

37. R. GOODE, THE INDIVIDUAL INCOME TAX 18 (1964).

moral claim to what would be distributed to them in the absence of a tax system.

* * *

THE CASE FOR AN INCOME TAX
Alan Gunn[*]

46 University of Chicago Law Review 370, 370-78 (1979)

Recent studies by the United States Treasury Department[1] and the Meade Committee[2] in England recommend a progressive tax on personal consumption as an alternative to an income tax. Neither adds anything fundamental to the expenditure-tax controversy, but each contains one intriguing feature: a discussion of the practical problems of substituting consumption for income as the tax base.[3] This development may mean that the replacement of the income tax by an expenditure tax should be taken as a serious practical possibility. And even if the possibility of so radical a change in our tax structure is remote, the arguments of the expenditure-tax theorists may encourage changes in the income tax in the form of additional relief for savers or a supplemental tax on expenditure. The time when the expenditure tax could be dismissed as lacking practical significance has long passed.

Arguments based on considerations of equity, administrative convenience, and economic efficiency play an important role in the case for an expenditure tax. I will not address the question of "efficiency" directly, although some of my "equity" arguments may bear on efficiency as well as equity. I will focus on the most important noneconomic issues in the debate between expenditure and income taxation: whether an income tax imposes "double taxation" on savings, [and] how income compares with other bases for taxation in terms of fairness.[5] * * *

The Expenditure Tax, the Income Tax, and the Double Taxation of Savings

The Basis of Expenditure-Tax Theory

The earliest proposal for an expenditure tax that is still cited today was made by Thomas Hobbes. Hobbes thought consumption to be the best tax base because it measures the benefits taxpayers receive from society; an

---

[*]. At time of original publication, Professor of Law, Cornell University

1. DEPARTMENT OF THE TREASURY, BLUEPRINTS FOR BASIC TAX REFORM (1977) [hereinafter cited as BLUEPRINTS]. This report presents two alternative "model tax systems"—an expenditure tax and a comprehensive income tax with rates much less progressive than the existing rates—without choosing between them.

2. INSTITUTE FOR FISCAL STUDIES, THE STRUCTURE AND REFORM OF DIRECT TAXATION (1978) [hereinafter cited as MEADE COMMITTEE REPORT].

3. BLUEPRINTS, *supra* note 1, at 204-12; MEADE COMMITTEE REPORT, *supra* note 2, at 187-92.

5. The tax base defended here resembles that of the existing federal income tax, tidied up somewhat, perhaps, but not fundamentally altered. I have no desire to defend an "ideal" tax based on the Haig-Simons definition.

expenditure tax would charge individuals equally in proportion to the goods they withdraw from the common stock. Hobbes's ideas are recognizable in the position of some modern expenditure-tax theorists that the income tax is unfair to investors and wage earners because it taxes them while not taxing rich people who chose to be economically idle and live off their principal. Few people today accept Hobbes's principle that taxes should be levied in proportion to benefits received, and the idea that only those who spend receive benefits from society seems bizarre.

Modern expenditure-tax theory is closer to the position of John Stuart Mill. Mill viewed an income tax without an exemption for income saved as discriminating against savers because taxpayers would be "taxed twice on what they save, and only once on what they spend."[9] He argued that an income tax taxes savers both upon principal (the money originally earned) and the earnings from investing that principal. This, Mill argued, is unfair to the saver, because "if he has the interest, it is because he abstains from using the principal; if he spends the principal, he does not receive the interest. Yet because he can do either of the two, he is taxed as if he could do both. . . ."[10] Mill's fundamental idea, that the income tax is unfair to savers, is common today, as is the picturesque language with which he expressed this conclusion: the saver is "taxed twice" under an income tax.[11]

Some influential proponents of the expenditure tax have gone beyond Mill in important respects. Mill thought a consumption tax impractical because measuring annual personal consumption directly was impossible. Modern writers have shown, however, that consumption can be measured, perhaps even more easily than income. Irving Fisher pointed the way by demonstrating that modern accounting techniques make it no harder to compute personal savings or dissavings than business savings. He argued for an "income" tax (really an expenditure tax) under which all re-ceipts—including gifts, inheritances, and withdrawals from savings—would enter into the definition of taxable income, but savings would be deductible, thus adding only two steps to present computations.[14] William Andrews has argued, more recently, that a spending tax would actually be easier to administer than an income tax, because the underlying computations would be simpler.[15] His claim is that an expenditure tax would not require the resolution of such troublesome problems of present law as distinguishing

---

9. 2 J.S. MILL, PRINCIPLES OF POLITICAL ECONOMY 407 (1874)

10. Id.

11. E.g., M. CHIRELSTEIN, FEDERAL INCOME TAXATION 260-61 (1977) (presenting the notion that savings are doubly taxed under an income tax as fact, with no suggestion that the conclusion is open to doubt).

14. I. FISHER, THE INCOME CONCEPT IN THE LIGHT OF EXPERIENCE (n.d.) (pamphlet) 14-17, which appears to be Fisher's own translation of a paper originally published in German [in 1927] [hereinafter cited as THE INCOME CONCEPT].

15. Andrews, A Consumption-Type or Cash Flow Personal Income Tax, 87 HARV. L. REV. 1113, 1148-65 (1974).

capital gains from ordinary income, computing depreciation, and drawing a line between business expenses and capital expenditures.

Mill's "double taxation" argument, in the form in which he made it, is circular. To say, as he does, that one who invests money "abstains from using" it is to say, at least implicitly, that consumption is the only "use" of money that should be considered in devising a tax. But modern writers have rescued the "double taxation of savings" argument from circularity. They argue that an income tax discriminates against savers because it makes saving less attractive relative to spending than would be the case in a world without taxes. I will use Andrews's figures to illustrate the argument.[16]

In a world without taxes or with an expenditure tax, a person who decides to save $1.00 of income and invest it at nine percent will have eight times as much to spend after 24 years as he could have spent initially; but with an equivalent income tax he will have only four times as much to spend under the same conditions.

Tax	(1) Available after Taxes if Spent Immediately	(2) Available after Taxes if Spent In 24 Years	Ratio 2:1
No Tax	$1.00	$8.00	8:1
33 1/3% Income Tax	0.67	2.67	4:1
Equivalent Expenditure Tax	0.67	5.33	8:1

Even in this illustration, the expenditure tax does not reproduce the no-tax world in all respects, because any tax, by reducing the total amount a taxpayer has available for saving and spending, will normally affect the proportion he decides to allocate to each use. But to the extent that an individual is influenced by what a dollar saved at the margin can earn, the incentive to save appears the same under an expenditure tax as in a no-tax world and different under an income tax that contains no exemptions for saving.

This argument is convincing only if one accepts a no-tax world as a standard for judging the desirability of a tax. Economists use the model of a no-tax world as a heuristic device to measure the likely effect of different taxes on the economy and as a standard of comparison in measuring

---

16. *Id.* at 1125.

"efficiency." As a starting point in making rough guesses about the effects of changes in existing arrangements, the "tax-free society" device may serve a useful purpose.   But the model rests on so many assumptions about behavior under hypothetical conditions that any conclusions based on it must be problematic and tentative. As Coase has asked in another context:

> In a state of laissez faire, is there a monetary, a legal, or a political system, and if so, what are they? . . . Whatever we may have in mind as our ideal world, it is clear that we have not yet discovered how we get to it from where we are. A better approach would seem to be to start our analysis with a situation which naturally exists, to examine a proposed policy change, and to attempt to decide whether the new situation would be, in total, better or worse than the original one.[19]

Reduction to Present Value and Fairness

Even if we assume, for purposes of argument, that "no-tax society" comparisons are useful in determining economically efficient solutions to complex practical problems, it does not follow that "discrimination" against savings under an income tax (when both income and expenditure taxes are compared to a no-tax society) is unfair. The unfairness argument seems to rest on the notion that people generally prefer to consume as they earn and so must be induced by interest to defer consumption. Interest income is thus merely compensation for delaying consumption. It does not represent a true increase in value to the saver, and a tax on that interest—like a tax on a nominal profit that reflects only monetary inflation—is in reality a levy on capital, a second tax on the earnings whose consumption was delayed. The following example illustrates the thrust of this argument.[21] Two people earn $10,000 in one year. One spends all his after-tax income, while the other saves half his after-tax income the first year and spends it the second. With a flat 30 percent income tax and a 10 percent interest rate, net return after taxes is 7 percent. Ignoring their second-year salaries, we get the following results:

---

19. Coase, *The Problem of Social Cost*, 3 J.L. & ECON. 1, 43 (1960).

21. The example in the text is inspired by Fisher's famous three brothers example. THE INCOME CONCEPT, *supra* note 14, at 12-13. Three brothers inherit $100,000 each. The first chooses to spend only the interest; the second allows his interest to accumulate until his money has doubled, and then spends the interest on this sum; the third buys a $20,000 a year annuity for six years, after which he has nothing left. Fisher assumes a 5 percent rate of return and a 10 percent tax. Under a conventional income tax, the first brother could take care of his future tax burden by setting aside $10,000 in the year of the inheritance, the second would have to set aside $17,140, while the third, "improvident," brother would need only $1,577,30. Under a consumption tax, each brother would have to set aside $10,000.

	Spender	Saver
(1) Spends year 1	7,000	3,500
(2) Tax	3,000	3,000 $(10,000 \times .30 = 3,000)$
(3) Saves	--	3,500 $(7,000 \times .50 = 3,500)$
(4) Interest pre-tax	--	350 $(3500 \times .10 = 350)$
(5) Tax on int.	--	95 $(350 \times .$
(6) Spends Year 2	--	3,745
Present Value:		
of (5) at 10%	--	95
of (6) at 7%	--	3,500
of (1) + (6)	7,000	7,000

Although the "present value" of what the saver and the spender eventually spend is the same, the saver must set aside more for taxes—not only does the saver pay more taxes in total dollars ($3,105 vs. $3,000), the present value of his taxes is greater ($3,095 vs. $3,000). Under an expenditure tax, the present value of their taxes would be the same, no matter how much or how long one saves. The argument that the net interest rate should be used to reduce future consumption and future taxes to their present value, and that, as a consequence, the saver and the spender in the illustration above "really" consumed the same amount but were taxed unequally, is the essence of the modern justification for the view that the income tax is a "double tax" on savings.

Reduction to present value is often an essential step in comparing people's well-being. If two people receive $10,000 each in a taxable transaction, the one who is allowed to pay the tax later needs to set aside less for that purpose than the one who must pay the tax immediately, because money set aside to pay a fixed sum in the future earns interest until the sum is paid. But this type of analysis, so useful for comparing the burden of taxes, cannot be used in a straightforward way as a technique for determining the present value of future consumption to a saver. If a taxpayer can obtain a secure after-tax return of ten percent, he is indifferent whether he pays $1.00 in tax now or $1.10 a year later, and this is true whether the total tax deferred is $1.00 or $1 million. But this does not mean that if a person lends $10,000 at minimum risk for one year at ten percent, he values $11,000 of consumption a year from now no more than $10,000 now.[24]

---

24. The differences between straightforward time-value calculations as applied to the receipt of cash and the same calculations as applied to consumption can be easily shown by a simple if somewhat extreme comparison. Suppose a taxpayer who could expect to receive a secure income of $10,000 a year for the next ten years were offered, as an alternative, a present lump-sum payment of $100,000. Ignoring any possible effects of a progressive income tax, any rational person would accept the offer, since the opportunity for an investment return makes $100,000 now worth more than $10,000 a year for ten years to anyone. But it is surely not the case that any

The interest rate reflects the "time value of consumption," if at all, only at the margin. The interest rate at which a person lends his money measures the value to him of the last dollar he saves. If the interest rate were lower, he would probably still save, although he would probably save a different amount—less or more.[26] The money he would save with a lower rate of interest produces benefits, if invested at the higher going rate, greater than those of current consumption. Use of the after-tax rate of interest to reduce future spending to present value, when applied to measure the present value of savings, ignores that part of a person's interest income that inures to him when he is able to invest part of his savings at a higher rate than he was in fact ready to accept.

Reduction to present value is essential to the argument that the income tax involves "double taxation of savings" and is therefore unfair to savers. Fisher said that it is "unjust" to impose taxes that are different, when reduced to present value, on people whose consumption, also reduced to present value, is the same.[27] This judgment rests on at least two assumptions: first, that a tax is just only if it taxes equal benefits or enjoyments equally;[28] second, that the interest rate measures the benefits forgone by delaying consumption. If the interest rate measures these

---

rational person who expected to consume $10,000 a year for the next ten years and who could give up that opportunity in exchange for $100,000 consumption this year, on condition he consume nothing for nine years, would accept the offer.

26. If consumption had a declining marginal utility for everyone, people would save more as the interest rate went up, and would save less as it went down. This analysis, however, leaves many factors out of account. For example, someone who is saving for a particular goal, such as a college education for his children or a particular level of retirement income, may reduce the proportion of his earnings that he saves as the interest rate goes up. Just as the income tax tends to encourage some people to substitute nontaxable leisure for taxable work (the "substitution effect") and encourage others to work harder to replace money taken in taxes (the "income effect"), a tax with an exemption for income saved would encourage some people to save more while encouraging others, such as those trying to accumulate a fixed sum, to save a smaller proportion of their earnings than they would under an income tax.

27. THE INCOME CONCEPT, *supra* note 14, at 12-13.

28. * * * It should be pointed out here that Fisher's view that it is fair to tax equally—and fair only to tax equally—people whose future consumption reduced to present value is the same assumes, among other things, that the only benefit people get from saving is increased future consumption. But as Guillebaud has pointed out,

> the saver has immediately a new asset in the shape of his savings as a capital sum, in terms of its present exchange value, which is valuable to him not merely, and often not principally, as a source of future income, but as a protection and reserve against emergencies which may at any time befall him. There also comes into the question the prestige value of accumulated wealth, the desire to bequeath large sums at death, the knowledge of the power that derives from the possession of wealth .
> . . .

Guillebaud, *Income Tax and the "Double Taxation" of Saving*, 45 ECON. J. 484, 490-91 (1935). * * *

A person who values accumulation for its own sake will save and, under an expenditure tax, never pay tax on his accumulation, because his enjoyment comes from the possession itself. It is hard to see, on Fisher's own "benefits" approach to taxation, why it is "fair" to tax him less than a person whose benefit comes from consumption, present or future.

benefits only at the margin, this second assumption is undermined and the argument loses much of its force. And a case can be made against reducing postponed consumption to present value, even at the margin, for the purpose of assessing the justice of a tax. As is indicated by the title of the revised (1930) edition of Irving Fisher's famous work on the rate of interest, *The Theory of Interest as Determined by Impatience to Spend Income and Opportunity to Invest It*, interest can be viewed as payment for the cost of postponing consumption—resisting impatience to spend—rather than for the supposedly lesser value of future consumption. To an economist, a forgone benefit is a cost, but not all costs are equivalent for judging the fairness of a tax.

If we view the interest rate as paying the saver for the cost to him of resisting the impulse to spend immediately, the "double taxation" argument becomes an argument for allowing taxpayers who incur the "resisting impatience" cost a tax benefit to put them on a par with current spenders, who do not incur such a cost. But to allow this cost to be taken into account in devising a tax is inconsistent with accepted principles not only of income taxation but of expenditure taxation as well. The psychological cost of deferring consumption is like any other cost of giving up lost opportunities; such costs are not, and could not be, taken into account generally under either an income or an expenditure tax. We do not say that a worker's cost in boredom, or in giving up leisure, or in physical effort should be deducted in computing either his taxable income or, under an expenditure tax, his expenditures from current earnings, even though these things are regarded as costs by economists concerned with predicting behavior. In effect, the "double taxation of savings" argument for expenditure taxation is an argument for allowing a very common kind of cost to be deducted when incurred by savers, but not by those who earn and spend, even though we know that they also incur such costs.

The foregoing discussion does not mean that an expenditure tax is necessarily less desirable than an income tax, but the case for an expenditure tax cannot rest upon the argument that the income tax subjects savings to "double taxation." The justification for abandoning income as a tax base—if indeed there be one—must derive from other considerations of tax policy.

* * *

TAX REFORM FOR FAIRNESS, SIMPLICITY,
AND ECONOMIC GROWTH ["TREASURY I"]
United States Department of the Treasury
Vol. 1, at 30-33 (1984)

Consumption provides an alternative to income as the basis for personal taxation. A personal tax on consumption, or consumed income, would be levied by exempting all saving from tax, allowing a deduction for repayment of debt, *and* taxing all borrowing and withdrawals from savings. Consumed income would be reported on a form much like the present form 1040. Deductions would be allowed for deposits in "qualified accounts" similar to existing individual retirement accounts (IRAs); withdrawals from such accounts would be subject to tax.

Though a flat rate could be applied to the consumption base calculated in this way, most proposals for a consumed income tax postulate personal exemptions and graduated rate schedules. Thus, a consumed income tax could be progressive, if that were desired. Itemized deductions could also be allowed, as under the existing tax.

Administrative Advantages

The current income tax is based on the principle that income should be taxed annually as it is realized. It represents a practical compromise between administrative feasibility and the objective of taxing income as it accrues. Conceptually, accrued income can be defined as the amount a taxpayer could consume without reducing his or her net wealth, that is, as the total of what the taxpayer actually consumes plus the change in his or her net wealth. Many practical difficulties plague application of this conceptual ideal as the basis of an income tax. Compromise between achieving the ideal, on the one hand, and avoiding complexity, on the other, produces a system that departs significantly from the conceptual ideal. Examples of compromise include taxation of capital gains only when they are realized, commonly by sale of an asset, rather than as they accrue. Compromises such as this can allow tax on large amounts of income to be postponed indefinitely, or even avoided altogether, as when appreciated property is transferred at death. On the other hand, efforts to administer the tax on an accrual basis, by levying tax before realization occurs, can introduce significant complexity and hardship. For example, if tax were levied on unrealized gains on closely-held business, valuation would be difficult; payment of tax, moreover, could frequently be required even though there is no cash flow with which to pay the tax.

Because it avoids the problems inherent in accrual taxation, a tax on personal consumption is simpler in many respects than an income tax. The consumed income tax is simpler because all costs of investment are deducted immediately ("expensed"), rather than depreciated over the life of assets; because all costs of creating inventories are expensed, rather than being recognized only as goods are sold; and because capital gains are not taxed, as such. A corporate income tax is not an essential part of an ideal tax system based on consumption; if retained, it would serve only as a withholding device.

The consumed income tax has another major administrative advantage over the income tax. Under the present income tax, the measurement of income is commonly distorted by inflation. Because consumption inherently occurs in dollars of the current year, the measurement of the base of the consumed income tax cannot be distorted by inflation. Since depreciable assets and inventory investments are expensed, inflation cannot erode the value of future deductions because there are none. Interest is not taxed, unless spent on consumption, and thus the inflation premium is not taxed. Purely inflationary capital gains are not taxed, because there is no tax on capital gains, per se.

Economic Advantages

Advocates of a consumed income tax argue that it is preferable to the ordinary income tax on conceptual and economic grounds, as well as on administrative grounds. First, an income tax penalizes saving by inducing taxpayers to consume rather than save for future consumption. By comparison, under certain circumstances, a tax on consumption does not distort the choice between consuming now and saving for future consumption. This is a major attraction of any tax on consumption.

Second, seen from a lifetime perspective, a tax on consumed income is said to be more equitable than an income tax. A taxpayer's total tax burden on consumed income does not depend on when income is earned or spent, at least under fairly restrictive simplifying assumptions. By comparison, an income tax imposes a heavier burden on those who earn income relatively early in life or spend it relatively late.

Despite the manifest attractions of the tax on consumed income, the Treasury Department does not propose it as either a replacement for, or a supplement to, the income tax. Several defects and difficulties of a consumed income tax lead to this conclusion.

Transition Problems

First, the current existence of substantial wealth, much of which has been accumulated from after-tax income, poses difficult transition problems. Taxing all consumption financed from such wealth would constitute a cruel trick on those who did not expect it—especially those who have saved after-tax dollars for retirement. Nor would complete exemption of consumption financed from existing wealth be satisfactory. Such an exemption would either be enormously expensive in terms of lost revenue or entail extremely high tax rates during the transition period. Worse, it would allow wealthy taxpayers to escape taxation for many generations if they consumed only old wealth and saved all current income.

On equity grounds, a compromise between complete exemption and full taxation of consumption from existing wealth would be necessary. Such a compromise might allow each taxpayer above a given age to enjoy a given amount of tax-free consumption during his or her lifetime. But phasing in a consumed income tax in this way would involve transition rules that could complicate the tax system for ordinary taxpayers for a generation.

A different type of transition problem would result from the possibility of avoiding taxes by hoarding money before the effective date of the new tax. After the effective date the taxpayer could either deposit the hoarded funds in a qualified account in order to get a tax deduction for saving or use them to meet living expenses without paying tax. Alternatively, pre-effective date investments in foreign banks could be liquidated after the effective date and reinvested as tax-deductible saving. Even though this would be a temporary problem of transition, it would undermine both the revenue yield and fairness of the tax during that period.

Perception Problems

Even though a taxpayer's standard of living, as reflected by his level of consumption, may be considered by many to be an appropriate base for taxation, the consumed income tax suffers from an important perception problem. Taxpayers presumably would welcome the opportunity to postpone taxes on amounts saved, paying tax only when dissaving and consumption occurs; such is the tax treatment currently accorded saving in qualified pension accounts. But to be consistent, it would also be necessary to tax amounts borrowed and allow a deduction for repayment of loans.   This treatment of saving and dissaving would create a pattern of tax liabilities over the lifetime of the taxpayer that might be perceived to be unfair. Relative to experience under current law, tax liability would be greater during early adulthood and during retirement—periods when financial resources are commonly strained. Tax would be relatively lower during middle age, the time when many taxpayers receive most of their income. The fairness of including amounts borrowed in taxable consumption might be questioned, and this tax treatment might even require a constitutional amendment.

Complexity for Individuals

A consumed income tax would be more complicated than the existing income tax for many individual taxpayers. Under the present income tax, amounts withheld on wages and salaries roughly offset tax liabilities for many taxpayers who have only modest amounts of income from capital. Relatively few taxpayers must worry about estimating liabilities and paying significant amounts of tax in addition to amounts withheld. Under the consumed income tax the situation could be quite different. Withholding might be required on borrowing and withdrawals from savings; if so, "reverse withholding" would be appropriate when a loan is paid off. Even then, far more taxpayers might need to file estimated returns than now, because it would be difficult to adjust withholding rates on financial transactions to the personal circumstances of taxpayers. Moreover, many young adults and retired individuals are not required to file or pay tax under an income tax, but would be required to file and pay tax under a consumed income tax.

Owner-occupied housing would not be treated as an item of consumption, to be taxed in full in the year of purchase. Rather, inclusion of the purchase price in taxable consumption would be spread over the lifetime of the home, in effect, by requiring taxpayers to pay tax as their mortgages were paid off. This could be accomplished through special treatment of mortgages outside of qualified accounts. But purchases of homes from amounts saved in qualified accounts could require special averaging features that would complicate compliance for taxpayers. Ironically, individual taxpayers would, in a sense, be asked to keep accounts resembling depreciation accounts at the same time that such accounts were eliminated for businesses.

The Dilemma of Gifts and Bequests

The proper treatment of gifts and bequests under a tax on consumed income is a fundamental issue. Under one view such transfers would not be taxed to the person making the gift or bequest; they would only be taxed when consumed by the recipient. Under a very different view, transfers would be taxed to the donor, as well as when consumed by the recipient. Advocates of this second approach argue that taxing gifts and bequests is necessary in order to realize fully the beneficial equity and efficiency effects of a consumption-based tax. They refer to this type of tax as a tax on lifetime income, to distinguish it from the conventional tax on annual income. The distributional differences in the two ways of treating gifts and bequests are, of course, substantial. The first approach would allow great fortunes to be passed from generation to generation without tax, whereas the second would subject transfers to tax.

International Aspects

No country has a tax on consumed income, although Sweden and the United Kingdom have considered it, and India and Sri Lanka (then Ceylon) attempted to impose the tax for a brief period following World War II. Any country imposing a consumed income tax would be very much out of step with its trading partners, all of which employ income taxes, and would face the task of renegotiating its foreign tax treaties.

* * *

Notes and Questions

Fairness

28. Professor Warren's analysis relies on conceptions of societal structure that are not universally shared. Do you agree with "the proposition that society in general has a claim on its annual product that is prior to the claims of its individual citizens"? Should annual production in the United States be viewed as societal production ("*its* annual product"), or as the individual production of its millions of citizens (and aliens)?

29. Do you accept "the theory that a producer does not have a controlling moral claim over the product of his capital and labor, given the role of fortuity in income distribution and the dependence of producers on consumers and other producers"?

Fortuity and interdependence are important determinants of income. Professional athletes provide a good example of the dependence of producers on both consumers and other producers. How much would it be worth to throw a ball into a hoop if no one wanted to watch? Or if television had not been invented?

30. Professor Warren asserts that society has a legitimate interest in achieving a desired after-tax distribution of society's product. Social and legal structures are, in effect, means of allocation. An income tax "is levied on the amount of social product otherwise distributed to each taxable unit."

Note that an income tax of general application, regardless of its degree of progressivity (so long as it is less than 100 percent), will leave all taxpayers in the same rank order of after-tax income that they had with respect to pre-tax income.

31. Whether we agree with Professor Warren's position concerning the extent of society's claim against individuals, the legitimacy of any taxing system depends upon the validity of some degree of societal claim. Does Professor Warren demonstrate that this claim should be asserted against income, rather than against consumption or wealth?

32. Professor Charles O'Kelley argued that there can be debate about the relative merits of a consumption tax and an accretion tax only if we assume that the pre-tax division of income is just. If the initial distribution of income is unjust, Professor O'Kelley argued that the accretion tax is the clear choice:

> Consider * * * individual *A* who in year one earns and spends $20,000 and individual *B* who in year one earns $1,000,000, but spends only $20,000. Under a consumption-type income tax *A* and *B* would each have taxable incomes of $20,000, which taxable incomes would not reflect the relative unjustness of *B*'s pre-tax income. Therefore, a consumption-type income tax would be unable to correct an initially unjust distribution of income.[g]

33. Is ability to pay best measured by income, or by consumption? What arguments can be made for each proposition?

"Double tax" on saving

34. John Stuart Mill argued that an income tax taxes savings twice, because "if he has the interest, it is because he abstains from using the principal; if he spends the principal, he does not receive the interest. Yet because he can do either of the two, he is taxed as if he could do both." Professor Gunn labels Mill's argument as circular. What is Gunn's reasoning?

---

g. Charles R. O'Kelley, Jr., *Rawls, Justice, and the Income Tax*, 16 GA. L. REV. 1, 4 (1981).

35. Professor Gunn states that modern advocates of consumption taxation rescue the "double taxation of saving" argument from circularity by comparing the effects of an income tax and a consumption tax to a "no-tax world." While any tax leaves a taxpayer worse off, a consumption tax does not change the relative attraction of immediate consumption versus saving. Gunn illustrates this point through Professor Andrews' example of an investor whose 24-year investment (at nine percent) in a no-tax world would allow eight times as much deferred consumption as would have been available in immediate consumption. A consumption tax would reduce the absolute amount of consumption that would be possible immediately or in 24 years, but would leave the relative attractiveness of saving unchanged—eight times as much consumption would be made possible by saving and waiting. A 33 percent income tax, however, would reduce not only the absolute return on saving but the benefit of saving vis-a-vis immediate consumption—the saver would have only four times as much consumption after 24 years.

36. Does Professor Gunn agree that the best way to evaluate the impact of a tax is by comparison to a tax-free world?

37.   Professor Gunn also acknowledges the argument of consumption-type tax advocates that the excessive tax burden on saving is demonstrated by reducing the tax to present value. Under a consumption tax, the present value of the tax is the same, whether the taxpayer consumes immediately or saves and later consumes both the original principal and the earnings generated by the saving. (See footnote 21 of Gunn excerpt and accompanying text.)   Under an income tax, the present value of the tax is less if the taxpayer consumes immediately than if the taxpayer saves in order to consume more later.

38. In addressing the reduction of tax burdens to present value, Professor Gunn argues that such a reduction would be appropriate only if the saver actually values future consumption less than present consumption at a rate measured by prevailing interest rates—that is, only if the interest at prevailing rates does not really make the saver better off, but merely makes the future consumption equal in value to present consumption.
But, Gunn argues, the saver is actually made better off, and reduction to present value is of little relevance in this context. Indeed, sometimes future consumption is more valued than the same amount of additional present consumption. What argument is Gunn advancing in footnote 24 of his article?

39. Even if reducing future consumption to present value were appropriate, Professor Gunn argues that discounting at prevailing market interest rates would be inappropriate. Why, according to Gunn, do market

interest rates overstate the amount that the saver loses by deferring consumption?

40. Professor Gunn argues, in sum, that additional tax on investment income is appropriate because the saver ultimately has *more* than the nonsaver. It is not the same amount reduced to present value, it is more.

41. Assuming real interest rates are positive (i.e., that interest rates exceed inflation), an individual can choose between consuming x now, or x plus interest at a future time. Professor Gunn argues that this return to investment might be viewed as a payment to the saver for resisting the impatience to consume immediately. Gunn compares the interest payment to a wage paid a worker for resisting the temptation toward leisure. Viewed in this manner, would taxing the interest be overtaxing the saver?

Treasury I

42. Although they ultimately recommended against moving to a consumption-type tax, the drafters of Treasury I acknowledged that it would create a lower, and arguably fairer, tax on saving, and, in theory, that it could be simpler than the income tax. (Simplicity is harder to achieve in concrete proposals than in theoretical proposals. See subchapter E.)

43. A major consideration in adopting a consumption-type tax would be the transition from the present system. Perhaps the most important aspect of the problem concerns accumulated wealth that has already been subjected to the income tax: Would such wealth also be subjected to the new consumption-type tax? Note that either system consistently applied would lead to only one tax—the time of wealth creation under the income tax, or the time of expenditure under the consumption-type tax. Without complicated transition rules, changing forms of tax could result in tax at both occasions. (A corresponding problem is that funds borrowed under the income tax system would have given rise to no income tax, but repayment under the new consumption regime would, absent special provision, give rise to a deduction.) Transition problems are further explored in subchapter E.

44. Treasury I also raises what might be termed the life cycle objection to the consumption-type tax. A typical life pattern is to consume more than is earned during young adulthood (for example, students have been known to take out loans); save during middle age; then consume savings during retirement. Does such a pattern suggest problems in the consumption tax system? Can these problems be met by making the consumption tax system sufficiently progressive?

Gifts under a consumption-type tax

45. As Treasury I points out, gifts present a conceptual challenge under a consumption tax. First, the theoretical problem is whether the donor has "consumed" the money (or money's worth) given. Presenting the "utility" view, which would treat making a gift as an act of consumption, Professor Carolyn Jones observes that "[t]he utility [a donor] derives from making the gift equals or exceeds the satisfaction to be derived from any other use" of the money given.[h] (Else why would the donor have made the gift?)

The competing "preclusive use" approach favored by Professor Andrews holds that the donor has not made use of society's resources in a way that would prevent another from using them, and thus should not be regarded as having "consumed" by making a gift. Satisfaction, Andrews argues, is irrelevant for tax purposes: "Taxing income in the end does not and cannot provide an accurate reflection of either power or pleasure. It is, rather, simply the accumulation or utilization of economic resources, measured at market value, for private consumption."[i]

Which theory is to be preferred? Would the utility approach lead to double taxation?

46. If the preclusive-use theory were adopted, a high-bracket taxpayer could "give" money to a low-bracket family member or friend as part of a fraudulent arrangement (fraudulent if the money were to be spent for the benefit of the high-bracket "donor"). A similar problem exists under present law. Gifts of appreciated property give rise to no tax to the donor, and the donee takes a carryover basis. Upon sale, all gain is taxed to the donee, who may be in a lower bracket than the donor.

Is the fraudulent gift problem any greater under a consumption-type tax than under present law?

D. ANALYZING DIFFERENT TYPES OF SAVING

As Professor Andrews first observed, our income tax is a hybrid, with elements of both consumption and accretion taxation, and the difference between the two lies in the treatment of savings. As we have seen, the proper tax treatment of savings is debated on grounds of fairness and efficiency by advocates of consumption taxation and defenders of income taxation.

In the excerpt below, Professor McCaffery argues that in analyzing income and consumption tax bases we should recognize significant advantages and drawbacks to both ideals. Because the choice between the two ideals turns on the taxation of savings, it is important to realize that we

---

h. Carolyn Jones, *Treatment of Gratuitous Transfers: Unraveling the Case for a Consumption Tax*, 29 St. Louis L.J. 1155, 1171-72 (1985).

i. William D. Andrews, *Personal Deductions in an Ideal Income Tax*, 86 Harv. L. Rev. 309, 356 (1972).

need not automatically assume that all savings must be given equal tax treatment. Instead, each category of savings should be analyzed, to see whether economic and equity goals point toward giving relatively favorable or relatively unfavorable tax treatment to the particular type of savings. It follows that we should be open to the possibility that the ideal tax base may be some hybrid structure that offers more favorable tax treatment to some types of savings than to others.

Professor McCaffery's article should be read not as a proposal for any particular tax structure so much as for a method of analysis. To the degree that his article points toward a particular policy, it may be less important in the income-versus-consumption debate than in the suggestion that estate taxes may undercut important societal goals.

TAX POLICY UNDER A HYBRID INCOME-CONSUMPTION TAX
Edward J. McCaffery[*]

70 Texas Law Review 1145, 1147-48, 1165-67, 1169-73, 1175-79,
1181-92, 1194, 1196, 1198-1213, 1216 (1992)

This Article * * * has several central themes. First, we have a hybrid income-consumption tax, the precise nature of which turns on the treatment of savings. Primarily as an illustration and following the economics literature, this Article divides savings into three categories based on the positive uses of the savings: life cycle, precautionary, and bequest savings. Second, because of the different values we place on the different types of savings, some form of a hybrid may in fact be ideal and not merely a practical necessity. These values come into relatively clear focus when we break analysis down into three broad normative categories: individual welfare, aggregate or macroeconomic welfare, and general equity concerns. Finally, this Article uses these categories to show that we may indeed support a hybrid as an ideal tax scheme. * * *

[T]his Article indicates the types of questions we ought to be asking about tax policy. * * * At the end of this undertaking, much of the work on the road to concrete policy formulation will lie ahead. * * *

The Case Against the Extremes

* * *

The Income Tax

The traditional case for an income tax rests perhaps most strongly on equitable notions of ability to pay. * * *

[A] tax based solely on income may not be ideal.

The individual efficiency concern is that the income tax distorts the choice between consumption and savings by doubly taxing the latter, thus

---

[*]. At time of original publication, Associate Professor of Law, University of Southern California.

causing taxpayers to consume more and to save less than they otherwise would. * * *

A second and logically distinct argument against the income tax is that its double tax discourages saving and leads to too little capital formation. * * * Indeed, a very broad consensus among political economists is that, in the long run, the world would be a better place under a consumption tax. * * *

Finally, there are also fairness arguments against an income tax and for a consumption tax. * * *

Consider the example of retirement savings. * * * Americans would be hard-pressed to understand that, while they certainly ought to save for their own retirement, those who do will be left with half as much, in present value terms, as those who do not![115] But this is exactly what an income tax does to savers. * * * It may be fairer—not just more efficient—to levy a tax based on the resources that taxpayers devote to their own needs, when and as they do so.

The Consumption Tax
* * *

In a partial equilibrium setting that considers only the consumption--savings decision, a consumption tax reduces the consumption-savings distortion and thus leads to a welfare gain and individual efficiency. Yet the partial equilibrium assumption is unrealistic; we must look beyond the consumption-savings choice alone. Given a need for constant revenue, tax rates will almost certainly go up under a consumption tax, at least in the short term. This rate increase will cause a decrease in the after-tax benefit that taxpayers receive from working, thus distorting the tradeoff between labor and leisure and producing an offsetting welfare loss. There is no a priori way of calibrating which set of distortions will be worse. * * *

Like the individual efficiency argument, the macroeconomic argument for a pure consumption tax is not completely persuasive. The inevitable rub with the argument—assuming the validity of all features leading to its basic soundness—lies in the short run, where mere mortals dwell. The argument for greater welfare in the long run is, on its own terms, predicated on reduced consumption in the present. Economists concede that there would be an instantaneous welfare loss under an immediate transition to a consumption tax. To understand what is normally presented as a graph, imagine that we are travelling along at eighty percent of our optimal capacity relative to a pure consumption tax. A change to a consumption tax promises the ultimate attainment of full capacity, but, before getting there, we will

---

115. The example is based on that used by Professors Andrews, Bradford, and Warren. *See* William D. Andrews, *A Consumption-Type or Cash Flow Personal Income Tax*, 87 HARV. L. REV. 1113, 1125 (1974). * * * It compares two workers in the 33% tax bracket with the saver saving for 24 years at 9% interest rates. As fate would have it, these numbers actually appear to be rather realistic by 1992 standards.

have to drop down to some lesser welfare state, perhaps sixty percent of the optimum, for a while. The problem for economists is to answer what "for a while" means—that is, to ascertain the precise period during which we would all be worse off under a transitional regime. Here, the happy consensus of economists breaks down, and the estimates vary from a low of four or five years to a high of one hundred years.

          * * *

Finally, although its advocates make some strong equity arguments for the consumption tax, the income tax proponents are far from defenseless in this debate. * * * A persistent thought in our society and among income tax advocates is that wealth per se matters and ought to be taxed. * * *

Framing Discussion: The Uses of Savings

The hybrid tax system turns on the treatment of savings. * * * There are also different *types* of savings, and no a priori reason why we should treat them all the same way. * * *

Life Cycle Savings

Life cycle savings are those designed solely for the saver's future, selfish needs. The standard economic models discuss this category of use mostly in terms of the young earner's savings to fund future consumption *(e.g.,* retirement savings). Life cycle savings can be generalized, however, to include any future consumption. Saving to buy a car or a house is different only in degree from saving to fund one's retirement: in all cases, one is foregoing consumption now in order to consume later. * * *

Precautionary Savings

Whereas life cycle savings are aimed at smoothing out a consumption path throughout the taxpayer's life for normal consumption purposes, precautionary savings are built up to provide for extraordinary circumstances (*i.e.,* to hedge against risk). The most commonly thought-of risk may be sickness: a taxpayer saves to have money for medical care in the event of future illness. But any risk can lead to precautionary savings, such as risks of interrupted or lessened future earnings, of general economic troubles, or of the early death of someone on whom the taxpayer depends for support. * * * [A] financial vehicle—here, insurance—can perfectly match the precautionary savings need under ideal conditions. Indeed, Medicare and Medicaid are forms of paternalistically provided precautionary savings, analogous to social security's paternalistic life cycle savings. As would be expected with precautionary savings, the economics literature indicates that government-sponsored insurance programs have tended to decrease private savings.

Bequest Savings

Bequest savings represent capital built up to be given away. * * *

Residual Uses

Life cycle, precautionary, and bequest savings may not exhaust all savings motives. Some taxpayers may attempt to accumulate capital for private or public power, for peace of mind, or for lack of other things to do with their money. But ultimately money will be spent in the ordinary course of events, or it will be spent under extraordinary circumstances, or it will be given away. Our mortality assures this. Sooner or later, one of the basic labels will come to fit all savings.

It may appear that a greater problem is the overlap among the uses of savings. For example, taxpayers may save for life cycle reasons while intending that any leftovers be used for bequests. Even so, it may be quite possible, depending on the outcome of our normative exploration, to tailor a system that remains agnostic regarding the classification of savings until the moment of conversion to final use. At that moment, the distinction will necessarily become apparent, and we can tax or not tax accordingly. * * *

The Case Against Identical Treatment of Savings

     * * *

Neutrality Among Different Forms of Savings

Another argument for treating all savings alike is that tax laws should be neutral across different types of savings. For reasons of equity or efficiency or both, we should not relatively encourage or discourage any one type of savings. Whatever playing field the tax law creates, it should at least be level.

This argument confuses and exalts the role of neutrality as an efficiency condition. *Ceteris paribus,* tax laws ought to be as neutral as possible to avoid distortions between choices such as savings versus consumption. But all things are rarely equal, and almost never so in the byzantine world of tax. In a no-tax setting, for example, people might appear to be indifferent between apples and oranges, consuming equal amounts of each. But it does not follow that, in a taxed world, it is efficient or even "neutral" to levy the same tax rate on apples and oranges. Consumer demand for apples at the pre-tax level might be rather inelastic—perhaps because consumers place a premium on consuming enough apples to keep doctors away. At a tax rate of fifty percent on both apples and oranges, consumers might react by continuing to purchase apples and altogether eliminating oranges, for which they have a less strong preference. * * * [A] better, more efficient—and probably even more neutral—approach would have been to tax apples alone, leaving consumers to allocate their reduced after-tax dollars among all goods, including oranges, as they deemed fit.

* * * [E]fficiency does not necessarily dictate taxing all things equally. Rather, a long-standing tenet of optimal taxation has been that when lump sum (nondistortionary) taxation is unavailable, efficiency dictates taxing commodities based on their relative elasticities: the higher the elasticity, the lower the tax. We may call this technique "Ramsey pricing," after its originator. This technique would lead to a high tax on apples, which have a low elasticity, and a low (or no) tax on oranges, which have a high elasticity. It is Ramsey pricing and not a blind adherence to the principle of

neutrality that will maximize efficiency. Neutrality becomes a mere rule of thumb to be followed when no information about the relative elasticities of different goods is available.

Of course, the efficiency norm of Ramsey pricing may yield to equity concerns. Taken to its limit, for example, Ramsey pricing would mean exorbitant excise taxes on necessities. * * *

Life Cycle Savings

This and the next two Parts examine the arguments for and against favoring each type of savings. For the most part, "favoring" will mean taxing the savings under the single, consumption tax model, and "disfavoring" will refer to the double tax, income model. * * *

The Case for Favoring

* * *

Beginning with efficiency arguments, perhaps the easiest and strongest argument for favoring life cycle savings is that the income tax distorts the choice of present versus deferred consumption by double taxing the latter. If we assume that much savings is life cycle—and the economics literature for years has supported this assumption—then the distortion of life cycle savings is particularly important. As mentioned above, a change to a consumption tax on savings leads to an unambiguous welfare gain when the savings-consumption choice alone is considered.

The second efficiency argument for life cycle savings looks to market failure. * * * [A] classic externality may be involved—a failure to provide for one's own future needs may impose costs on society as a whole in the form of increased social-welfare spending. * * *

Finally, there are at least two major equity arguments for favorable tax treatment of life cycle savings. The first is that it is fair, for one reason or another, to tax individuals on their standard of living, or what they appropriate from the common pool for their personal use. * * * The central idea is that only a consumption-type tax preserves the equality of the saver and the spender in an after-tax setting relative to their equality in a no-tax setting. * * *

The second equity argument for favoring life cycle savings is based on the belief that we should tolerate lifetime disparities in wealth because they are earned. This belief leads to a hybrid that favors life cycle and precautionary savings but not bequest savings. We can refer to this hybrid as a "consumption-*cum*-transfer tax" model. * * *

The positions of Mill, Kaldor, Rawls, Andrews, and others are rather interesting in that each favors some form of bequest or inheritance tax in addition to a personal consumption tax. Philosophically, this result is not surprising if we focus on life cycle savings. The equity notion underlying the consumption model becomes a lifetime, individualistic one. The core concept is that it is presumptively fair to allow taxpayers to decide when they should spend their own money. Yet any transfer tax is a tax on accumulation because what is transferred away as a gift or bequest is not consumed by the donor. Mill saw this clearly enough, but he defended a tax on inheritance because he viewed some tax on capital as acceptable and because he considered a tax on bequests as raising no adverse incentive effects: an heir who receives a 1000-pound bequest subject to a ten percent inheritance tax "considers the legacy as only 900 pounds."[200] This latter point, however, reflects an important misconception regarding the incentives for savings. Modern economic scholarship has shown that savers are motivated by a desire to leave bequests.[201] Thus, the adverse incentive effect is at the donor's level, not the beneficiary's. * * * If taxpayers are saving for intergenerational transfers, * * * hindering their ability to make such transfers may indeed reduce savings. We will return to this point when we consider bequest savings more directly.

Bequest saving accumulates income for the purpose of making gratuitous transfers. Gift and estate taxes impose a tax on the accumulated income upon transfer. To the extent that other types of saving are taxed only once under a consumption model, while bequest savings are taxed twice—both initially and on transfer—a hybrid system results. In describing a system of lifetime consumption taxes plus some form of tax on gratuitous transfers, Mill, Kaldor, Rawls, Andrews, and others advocate what is essentially a hybrid system that favors life cycle (and precautionary) savings but not bequest savings—that is, a consumption-*cum*-transfer tax system. * * *

The Case for Disfavoring

Recall that the first efficiency argument supporting consumption tax treatment of life cycle savings rests on the distorting effects of the income tax on the savings-consumption decision. This argument is very persuasive. But it is undermined somewhat by the fact that before-tax interest rates are likely to rise under an income tax, minimizing the welfare loss to individuals. There are two more significant problems with the argument. First, given a constant need for revenue, a move to a consumption tax will result in increased wage taxes in the short term, compounding the labor-leisure distortion. Second, unless we are prepared to go all the way to a pure consumption tax, the questions raised by the hybrid are relative ones—that is, do life cycle savings stand out as an efficient form of savings to tax compared to other forms of savings? Again, this depends on the compensated elasticity, or substitution effect, of the tax. There are some very good intuitive reasons to conclude that life cycle savings have a relatively low elasticity and are therefore a relatively efficient type of savings to tax. Life cycle savers may be motivated to amass a given nest egg regardless of cost.

---

200. JOHN S. MILL, PRINCIPLES OF POLITICAL ECONOMY, bk. V, ch. II, §7, at 822 (W.J. Ashley ed., Logmans, Green & Co. 1909) (1848).

201. *See* Laurence J. Kotlikoff, *Intergenerational Transfers and Savings*, J. ECON. PERSP., Spring 1988, at 41 [and other sources].

Put another way, life cycle savings may be more in the nature of necessities than luxuries.

* * * [A]n expanded social security system might be a more efficient form of favoring life cycle savings than a consumption-style tax. We might even be better able to advance equity concerns through such a public system by better apportioning life cycle savings according to need.
* * *

[F]avoring life cycle savings, especially if we do not also favor bequests, may generate perverse incentives. * * * By definition, a consumption-*cum*-transfer tax hybrid would place an added burden on accumulated capital gratuitously transferred. The flip side of this effect is that such a hybrid will favor consumption during a taxpayer's lifetime over gifts and bequests. The model would create an economic incentive to "spend down" one's resources late in life—exactly the opposite effect desired. * * * Not only would such consumption undermine the macroeconomic argument, it might even be the type of excessive, conspicuous consumption that leads to inequities, both real and perceived.

This analysis brings us to the first of the two equitable arguments against favorable tax treatment of life cycle savings: that the existence of private wealth is somehow inimical to social norms. This raises the central question of what bothers us about wealth. * * *

Instead of possession, however, it may be the private use of wealth that troubles us. This concern leads us to the second set of equitable arguments against consumption tax treatment of life cycle savings. We might share with Thorstein Veblen and others a concern with conspicuous consumption and its attendant problems for the allocation of resources and public morale.[234] Or we might agree with Kaldor that spending power is what matters, or with Andrews that standard of living is somehow the appropriate thing to be taxing. All of this discussion relates to Hobbes's argument and the general cultural case for saving, which favors (or at least does not disfavor) the hard-working saver over the idle consumer. If these were our concerns with wealth, we might logically be heading in quite a different direction than the consumption-*cum*-transfer tax ideal. If we were concerned mainly with the conspicuous consumption aspect of the private use of savings, we would want a persistently progressive lifetime consumption tax and a lower tax or even no tax on transfers by gift or bequest. This combination would directly and indirectly discourage excessive consumption: directly by the progressive tax and indirectly by not discouraging bequests. I will call such a system a consumption-*sans*-transfer tax hybrid.
* * *

---

234. *See* THORSTEIN VEBLEN, THE THEORY OF THE LEISURE CLASS 68-101 (B.W. Huebsch ed., 1918) (1899) (discussing extensively the role an individual's consumption plays in identifying and maintaining his social class, thereby perpetuating the existence of a social hierarchy).

This extended discussion of the possible effects of the consumption-*cum*-transfer tax hybrid has illustrated * * * equity arguments against favoring life cycle savings. * * * [P]articularly if we also had a steep bequest tax, a life cycle consumption model might lead to conspicuous consumption and other real and perceived inequities without creating the optimal incentives for long-term, private savings that might truly alleviate the long-run condition of the worst off. * * *

Precautionary Savings

Precautionary savings are a form of self-insurance. Unlike life cycle savings, which are designed to meet needs in the ordinary course of life and hence to smooth out consumption paths, precautionary savings are designed to meet extraordinary needs. * * *

The Case for Favoring

A good deal of what I have said about life cycle savings applies to precautionary savings. Indeed, the traditional tax policy literature does not separate out the two uses: both fit under what Andrews would call "consumption deferred." * * * [M]any of the equity and efficiency arguments explored above apply with equal force to precautionary savings. * * *

[F]avoring precautionary savings with consumption tax treatment might correct for market failure. Taxpayers may be likely to mis-save for their own future insurance needs either because they wrongly estimate future contingencies or because they fail to consider the social benefits that such savings generate, such as lessened welfare and emergency-care spending. * * *

Finally, the equity case for favorable tax treatment is apparent. In fact, precautionary savings is the category of uses that the law is most likely to put on the favorable no-tax model. * * * [T]axpayers suffering under a hardship may lack the relative ability to pay or the capacity of unaffected taxpayers. Professor Andrews, for example, has made clear that he does not feel that medical expenditures form part of a taxpayer's material well-being.[265]

The Case for Disfavoring

It may at first seem hard to imagine why we would not want to favor precautionary savings, given the strong equity and efficiency appeals of this use. Upon further consideration, however, we can see that there are reasons to stop short of a full-scale consumption model for precautionary accumulation.

Precautionary savings may very well be seen by taxpayers as a type of necessity and thus be a relatively efficient type of savings to tax. This application derives from the Ramsey pricing idea. * * *

---

265. *See* William D. Andrews, *Personal Deductions in an Ideal Income Tax*, 86 HARV. L. REV. 335-37 (1972).

[I]t may very well be that precautionary savers are driven by a desire to obtain a certain quantum of insurance. Tax laws that help savers attain their precautionary goals sooner rather than later might ironically free up resources for consumption. * * *

Perhaps the problems with favoring precautionary savings come into focus most clearly when we look at the choice between government-sponsored and private care. If we prefer private care, then we should encourage private precautionary savings, either through institutional or self-insurance, with consumption tax treatment. But there is no a priori reason to believe that privately funded care is better than government-sponsored care. Indeed, public care may actually be more efficient and more equitable than private care. * * *

The Once and Future Hybrid

We do generally favor precautionary savings with consumption tax treatment. Life, medical, and disability insurance are all taxed essentially under the prepayment model. In the case of life insurance, the tax laws do not allow a deduction for premium payments, but the inside build-up of cash value or whole life policies is not subject to current taxation, and the proceeds or death benefits are not usually taxed. Similarly, for medical insurance, the premium payments are not generally deductible, but the proceeds are tax free. Public care programs like Medicare are also funded with after-tax dollars and the benefits, when received, are not taxed. In certain cases, the Internal Revenue Code even allows deductions for insurance premiums (or exclusions for certain employer-paid premiums), in which case the insurance receives the most favorable, no-tax treatment. * * *

Bequest Savings

* * * [T]his Part looks first at the case for disfavoring [bequest] savings because that side of the debate has dominated the literature. * * *

To clarify one technical matter in advance, favoring bequest savings means not imposing a tax on the transfer itself, either at the beneficiary or the donor level. The beneficiary would take the bequest with a zero basis and would be subject to the consumption tax upon consuming the wealth. We can think of this model as consumption tax treatment of bequests—we are in effect allowing the beneficiary a deduction for saving (i.e., for not spending) the inheritance. I go into this matter here because the literature itself is not consistent on how it uses the term "consumption" in the context of wealth transfers, and it is necessary to make clear a meaning from the start.

The Case for Disfavoring

As seen in Mill, among others, there is a very old case made against gifts and bequests. * * *

The principal equity theme is highly egalitarian: large inheritances create an unlevel playing field. * * *

Consumption tax advocates similarly support gift and estate taxes to assure that wealth is taxed at least once each generation. * * *

The equitable case for favoring some type of bequest taxation is not typically thought to be undercut by economic considerations. If savings are actually motivated largely by precautionary and life cycle uses, taxing bequest savings ought to be relatively efficient. Again, this is an empirical matter of looking at the relative elasticity of bequest savings. Advocates of bequest taxation often seem to believe that such savings are mere leftovers, such that taxing them will not interfere with any important nontax incentives. * * *

In sum, wealth transfer taxes are a favorite in the literature. The most frequently articulated hybrid proposal is the consumption-*cum*-transfer tax model. * * *

The Case for Favoring

The case for disfavoring bequests is appealing and has dominated scholarly debate for centuries. It may nonetheless be wrong. The whole tenor of discussion begins to change when we consider some facts from the economics literature. A good deal, if not most, of savings may be motivated by a bequest motive,[307] and relatedly, bequest savings may be rather elastic to tax law changes.[308] Taxing bequests may indeed interfere with saving incentives at the donor's level. Bequest savings may be the best form of savings to favor * * * as the type of savings having the most elasticity to tax rules and by its nature having the longest, most beneficial time profile. One study has shown that prohibiting all bequests could reduce aggregate United States wealth by as much as fifty percent.[309] * * * Even though taxing bequests is not as onerous as prohibiting them, such a significant effect should give the transfer tax advocates pause. * * *

[Bequest] savings may be a stable source of capital. The marginal propensity to consume out of income appears to be greater than out of wealth, which means that people are more likely to spend their wages than reach into savings or a bequest. * * *

In any event, the various studies and statistics begin to cast considerable doubt on the tendency of the literature to advocate a lifetime consumption-*cum*-transfer tax. This tendency may rest on the naive assumption, evident in Mill, that because bequests represent leftover savings, taxing them would not create adverse incentives and would have little effect on capital accumulation. If people save for the purpose of transferring wealth, however, and if such savings are responsive to the effective tax rate

---

307. *See supra* note 201 and accompanying text.

308. The actual elasticity of bequest savings is an empirical matter that requires further study. However, compared to life cycle and precautionary savings, there are strong intuitive reasons to believe that bequest savings are relatively elastic because of their "leftover" status.

309. *See* Laurence J. Kotlikoff, *Introduction to Part I: Saving Motives, in* WHAT DETERMINES SAVINGS? 39, 41 (1989).

on bequests, then quite a different story emerges. At least to the extent that we are concerned with the macroeconomic and efficiency gains promised by the consumption model, we should be reluctant to impose too high a toll on bequests.

* * *

If we are going to settle for a hybrid, a certain logic argues for choosing the consumption features most likely to achieve long-run benefits. Of all forms of savings, bequest savings may have the greatest payoff in this sense. Indeed, this logic continues to advocate a persistently progressive lifetime consumption tax combined with a reduced or eliminated transfer tax (*i.e.,* a consumption-*sans*-transfer tax hybrid)—precisely the opposite of the balance struck by Mill, Rawls, and others. This may not be simply a matter of preferring efficiency to equity. Instead, it may well be a principled view that, across generations, the best way to advance the cause of the least advantaged may be to allow and even encourage bequest savings.

* * *

The progressive lifetime consumption-*sans*-transfer tax hybrid would allow wealth to stay in private hands, but the public would effectively have a lien on the wealth: if and when savers attempted to consume their savings—that is, to appropriate their wealth for private use—the government would step in to claim its share. In the case of large amounts of savings, under the steep and persistent progressivity that would be an integral feature of this hybrid, the government's share would be generous. This solution would thus allow wealth to be private for the purposes of investment decision, but in an important sense, the law would convert much of the capital into public form.

* * * If the concern is with the private use of wealth rather than with its possession—a position arguably inherent in the logic of the consumption tax theory—then exempting bequests may lessen the offensive excess consumption at the donors' level. Once again, the point comes into sharper focus when we consider the common consumption-*cum*-transfer tax model: by disfavoring bequests relative to consumption, this model encourages private consumption. If we are concerned about accumulating and maintaining a common pool of funds, however, we should do precisely the opposite—steeply taxing conspicuous private consumption and exempting bequests. * * *

Indeed, if it is the possession of wealth and not its use that concerns us, we should confront the possibility that this concern is motivated by envy. Once we have shown that private capital is a form of public good and taken steps to hinder its private appropriation, what further reason do we have to disparage its presence? * * *

If we continue to oppose all bequests, we might have to live with a lower standard of living for all. * * *

Notes and Questions

47. Professor McCaffery states that both efficiency and fairness arguments can be levied against the income tax. What are these?

48. The income tax is said to distort the choice between saving and consumption, but a consumption tax would, at least initially, be expected to have higher rates than an income tax. Why? These higher rates would carry their own distortion—taxpayers would inefficiently substitute leisure for labor.

49. Professor McCaffery notes that economists are in agreement that our economy would be benefitted in the long run by the change to a consumption tax. But we would be worse off "for a while." For how long would we be worse off, according to the economists?

50. Professor McCaffery's article focuses on savings, because the essential difference between the consumption tax and the accretion tax turns on how we treat savings; consumption is part of either tax base. For purposes of analysis, he then divides savings into three components. What are these? How is each described?

51. As Professor McCaffery acknowledges, people frequently save for mixed motives. "For example, taxpayers may save for life cycle reasons while intending that any leftovers be used for bequests." In such cases, which may well account for a large fraction of total savings, does McCaffery successfully explain how we can treat savings differently based upon the motivation for the saving?

52. Professor McCaffery argues that we should not necessarily tax all savings the same. We should, generally, tax more heavily forms of saving that are relatively inelastic (i.e., saving that will tend to occur even in the face of relatively heavy taxation). (Similarly, he states, we should tax apples and not oranges if the demand for apples is relatively inelastic and the demand for oranges is relatively elastic.) Why should we do this? What is meant by Ramsey pricing?

53. Professor McCaffery suggests that "life cycle savers may be motivated to amass a given nest egg regardless of cost." What is the relevance of this observation for tax policy?

54. In discussing life cycle and precautionary savings, Professor McCaffery refers to an "externality" that may lead to undersaving in preparation for old age or disability. What is this externality? In what

direction does it point with respect to treating these forms of savings favorably in the tax system?

55. What are other arguments that suggest the tax system should favor life cycle savings?

56. Professor McCaffery points to several indications in present law that precautionary saving is favorably taxed. What are these present-law provisions?

57. Professor McCaffery suggests that the issue of whether the taxing system should treat precautionary saving favorably may come down to "the choice between government-sponsored and private care." Why might this be the case? Which should the tax system encourage?

58. The consumption tax model as applied to bequest saving would levy no tax at all on the testator who accumulated the wealth, because the testator did not consume; the heir would take a zero basis and therefore pay consumption tax when consumption occurred—which could be a long time.

Professor McCaffery notes that most supporters of consumption taxation also favor transfer taxes. Their "consumption-*cum*-transfer" model is less favorable to bequest savings than the consumption tax alone (the "consumption-*sans*-transfer" model). On the other hand, the combination of consumption and transfer taxes is more favorable to bequest savings than an accretion tax plus transfer taxes—arguably, a three-level tax.

If we imposed a consumption tax plus transfer taxes, which forms of savings—life cycle, precautionary, and bequest—would be favored and disfavored relative to the others?

59. Professor McCaffery views the imposition of estate taxes in addition to the general tax base (income or consumption) as disfavoring bequest savings. What are the traditional arguments supporting such a policy?

60. As noted above, most advocates of consumption-type taxation also favor transfer taxes. Why might the arguments favoring transfer taxes be viewed as stronger under a consumption tax regime rather than an income tax system? Do you think the case for transfer taxation would be stronger under a consumption tax than under the income tax?

61. Professor McCaffery argues that policy should take account of the likelihood that much saving is motivated by the desire to leave a bequest, and that "bequest savings may be relatively elastic to tax law changes." Do you think these propositions are correct? If they are correct, what would be the impact of heavy taxation of bequest savings on national savings?

62. The last sentence excerpted from Professor McCaffery's article argues that opposition to bequest savings could result in "a lower standard of living for all." Why might "all" suffer if only the estates of the wealthiest one or two percent of decedents are subject to estate taxes?

63. Why might discouraging bequest savings—through high transfer taxes, for example—encourage conspicuous consumption? Would that be bad?

64. In general, adoption of a consumption-type tax rather than an income tax tends to favor saving in general.

But what practical use, if any, can we make of analysis of different types of savings? Obviously, the tax system cannot attempt to determine individual motivation in saving, so we cannot tailor a tax provision based on why an individual taxpayer engaged in a particular form of saving. If we concluded that tax law should favor life cycle savings, or precautionary savings, or bequest savings, how might those conclusions be reflected in actual tax provisions?

65. After praising the hybrid, in the end Professor McCaffery exhibits considerable sympathy for a progressive consumption tax coupled with abolition of transfer taxes. He argues that savings are good for society as a whole, and that we should encourage elderly taxpayers to pass along their savings to the next generation rather than engage in conspicuous consumption. If the heirs continue the investment, society is benefitted; if, instead, they liquidate and consume the savings, they will be subjected to a consumption tax "of steep and persistent progressivity."

Readers of the article excerpted above will not be surprised that two years after its publication, Professor McCaffery set forth a detailed proposal for a "progressive consumption-without-estate tax."[j]

66. Keep the issues raised in this subchapter in mind when studying Chapter Ten.

E. PROPOSALS IN THE POLITICAL ARENA

Thus far, this chapter has focused on the academic debate about a consumption-type tax. We turn now to a sampling of the same debate cast in a form directed at Congress and the broader public.

Professor Hall and Dr. Rabushka advocate what they describe as a single consumption tax comprised of two components—an individual tax on wages, salaries, and (when received) pensions; and a business tax. The business tax base allows for deduction of inputs from other businesses and for labor costs, but, notably, no deduction for interest. Both taxes would be

---

j. Edward J. McCaffery, *The Uneasy Case for Wealth Transfer Taxation*, 104 YALE L.J. (1994).

imposed at the same flat rate (the authors suggest 19 percent). Considerable progressivity (more technically, degressivity) would be introduced into the individual tax by allowance of a large, untaxed "personal allowance."

The second excerpt is from an extensive and detailed "prototype" prepared by Alliance USA, a nonprofit corporation urging adoption of the Universal Savings Allowance, or USA, tax proposal. Businesses would be subjected to a flat-rate tax of about 10 percent (a subtraction-type VAT). The USA business tax would have a broader base than the Hall & Rabushka business tax, because USA would allow no deduction for employee compensation. Individuals would pay a progressive tax on income, including not only wages and salaries but income from property, but would be allowed an unlimited deduction for net savings.

Representative Richard Armey (R-TX), the House Majority Leader, has introduced a bill based on the Hall & Rabushka proposal. Senators Nunn (D-GA) and Domenici (R-NM) have offered a bill quite similar to the Alliance USA prototype. References to "the Armey bill" or to "Nunn-Domenici" can generally be understood as also referring, respectively, to the Hall & Rabushka and Alliance USA proposals.

The third excerpt is from an article written by Dr. Rudolph Penner, an economist who consulted in the crafting of the Alliance USA and Nunn-Domenici proposals. In addition to explaining the proposals, Dr. Penner's article discusses the enormous complexity—both technical and political—involved in moving beyond the model of a new tax system to deal with the multitude of issues that must be addressed in constructing an actual new system. Among the most difficult of the practical problems is the transition from present law to the proposed new system; this topic will be further explored in the Notes and Questions.

Finally, a distinguished member of the tax bar, John Nolan, compares proposed consumption-type taxes to present law. While Mr. Nolan finds favorable features in the proposals, he is generally skeptical.

THE FLAT TAX
Robert E. Hall[*] & Alvin Rabushka[**]
Pages 52-64, 71-73, 78-80, 99-100 (2d ed. 1995)

Tax forms really can fit on postcards. A cleanly designed tax system takes only a few elementary calculations, in contrast to the hopeless complexity of today's income taxes. In this chapter, we present a complete plan for a whole new tax system that puts a low tax rate on a comprehensive definition of income. Because its base is broad, the astonishingly low 19 percent tax rate raises the same revenue as does the current tax system.

---

[*]. At time of original publication, Professor of Economics and Senior Fellow at the Hoover Institution, Stanford University.

[**]. At time of original publication, Senior Fellow at the Hoover Institution, Stanford University.

The tax on families is fair and progressive: the poor pay no tax at all, and the fraction of income that a family pays rises with income. The system is simple and easy to understand. And the tax operates on the consumption tax principle—families are taxed on what they take out of the economy, not what they put into it.

Our system rests on a basic administrative principle: income should be taxed exactly once as close as possible to its source. * * *

Under our plan, all income is taxed at the same rate. Equality of tax rates is a basic concept of the flat tax. Its logic is much more profound than just the simplicity of calculation with a single tax rate. Whenever different forms of income are taxed at different rates or different taxpayers face different rates, the public figures out how to take advantage of the differential.

Progressivity, Efficiency, and Simplicity

Limiting the burden of taxes on the poor is a central principle of tax reform. * * * We reject sales and value-added taxes for this reason. The current federal tax system avoids taxing the poor, and we think it should stay that way.

Exempting the poor from taxes does not require graduated tax rates rising to high levels for upper-income families. A flat rate, applied to all income above a generous personal allowance, provides progressivity without creating important differences in tax rates. * * *

Our proposal is based squarely on the principle of consumption taxation. Saving is untaxed, thus solving the problem that has perplexed the designers of the current tax system, which contains an incredible hodgepodge of savings and investment incentives. As a general matter, the current system puts substantial taxes on the earnings from savings. On that account, the economy is biased toward too little saving and too much consumption. * * * In our system, there is a single, coherent provision for taxing the return to saving. All income is taxed, but the earnings from saved income are not taxed further. * * *

An Integrated Flat Tax

Our flat tax applies to both businesses and individuals. Although our system has two separate tax forms—one for business income and the other for wages and salaries—it is an integrated system. When we speak of its virtues, such as its equal taxation of all types of income, we mean the system, not one of its two parts. As we will explain, the business tax is not just a replacement for the existing corporate income tax. It covers all businesses, not just corporations. And it covers interest income, which is currently taxed under the personal income tax.

In our system, all income is classified as either business income or wages (including salaries and retirement benefits). The system is airtight. Taxes on both types of income are equal. The wage tax has features to make the overall system progressive. Both taxes have postcard forms. The low tax rate of 19 percent is enough to match the revenue of the federal tax system as it existed in 1993, the last full year of data available as we write.

Here is the logic of our system, stripped to basics: We want to tax consumption. The public does one of two things with its income—spends it or invests it. We can measure consumption as income minus investment. A really simple tax would just have each firm pay tax on the total amount of income generated by the firm less that firm's investment in plant and equipment. The value-added tax works just that way. But a value-added tax is unfair because it is not progressive. That's why we break the tax in two. The firm pays tax on all the income generated at the firm except the income paid to its workers. The workers pay tax on what they earn, and the tax they pay is progressive.

To measure the total amount of income generated at a business, the best approach is to take the total receipts of the firm over the year and subtract the payments the firm has made to its workers and suppliers. This approach guarantees a comprehensive tax base. The successful value-added taxes in Europe work this way. The base for the business tax is the following:

Total revenue from sales of goods and services

less

purchases of inputs from other firms

less

wages, salaries, and pensions paid to workers

less

purchases of plant and equipment

The other piece is the wage tax. Each family pays 19 percent of its wage, salary, and pension income over a family allowance (the allowance makes the system progressive). The base for the compensation tax is total wages, salaries, and retirement benefits less the total amount of family allowances.

Table 3.1 is a calculation of flat-tax revenue based on the U.S. National Income and Product Accounts for 1993. The first line shows gross domestic product, the most comprehensive measure of income throughout the economy. The next line is indirect business taxes that are included in GDP but that would not be taxed under the flat tax, such as sales and excise taxes. Line 3, income included in GDP but not in the tax base, is mostly the value of houses owned and lived in by families; this income does not go through the market. Wages, salaries, and pensions, line 4, would be reported on the first line of the wage-tax form and would be deducted by businesses. Investment, line 5, is the amount spent by businesses purchasing new plant and equipment (each business could also deduct its purchases of used plant and equipment, but these would be included in the taxable income of the selling business and would net out in the aggregate). Line 6 shows the taxable income of all businesses after they have deducted their wages and investment. The revenue from the business tax, line 7, is 19 percent of the tax base on line 6. Line 8 shows the amount of family allowances that would be deducted. The wage-tax base on line 9 shows the amount of wages, salaries, and pensions left after deducting all family allowances from the amount on line 4. The wage-tax revenue on line 10 is 19 percent of the base. Total flat-tax revenue on line 11 is $627 billion. Lines 12 and 13 show the actual revenue from the personal and corporate income taxes. The total actual revenue on line 14 is also $627 billion. The flat-tax revenue and the actual revenue are the same, by design. We propose to reproduce the revenue of the actual income tax system, not to raise or lower it.

TABLE 3.1
FLAT-TAX REVENUES COMPARED WITH CURRENT REVENUES

Line	Income or Revenue	Billions of Dollars
1	Gross domestic product	$6,374
2	Indirect business tax	431
3	Income included in GDP but not in tax base	217
4	Wages, salaries, and pensions	3,100
5	Investment	723
6	Business-tax base (line 1 minus lines 2 through 5)	1,903
7	Business-tax revenue (19 percent of line 6)	362
8	Family allowances	1,705
9	Wage-tax base (line 4 less line 8)	1,395
10	Wage-tax revenue (19 percent of line 9)	265
11	Total flat-tax revenue (line 7 plus line 10)	627
12	Actual personal income tax	510
13	Actual corporate income tax	118
14	Total actual revenue (line 12 plus line 13)	627

These computations show that in 1993 the revenue from the corporate income tax, with a tax rate of 35 percent, was $118 billion. The revenue from our business tax at a rate of 19 percent would have been $362 billion, just over three times as much, even though the tax rate is not much more than half the current corporate rate.[k] There are three main reasons that the flat business tax yields more revenue than does the existing corporate tax. First, slightly more than half of business income is from noncorporate businesses—professional partnerships, proprietorships, and the like. Second, our business tax does not permit the deduction of interest paid by businesses, whereas the corporate income tax does. Third, the business tax puts a tax on fringe benefits, which escape any taxation in the current system.
  * * *

---

k. Under present law, corporations are subjected to a progressive rate structure, which begins at 15%, for corporations earning less than $50,000, and rises to 35%. Section 11. (Eds.)

Another limitation on our calculations is that we do not consider the way the economy would respond to tax reform. In [a portion of the book not excerpted], we discuss why the flat tax would increase national income and tax revenue. But part of that process might involve a burst of investment, which would temporarily depress flat-tax revenue because of the expensing of investment. Only a detailed analysis using data not available to us would determine whether we have over- or underestimated the revenue from the flat tax. We do not think we are far off, however.

The Individual Wage Tax

The individual wage tax has a single purpose—to tax the large fraction of income that employers pay as cash to their workers. It is not a tax system by itself but is one of the two major parts of the complete system. The base of the tax is defined narrowly and precisely as actual payments of wages, salaries, and pensions. Pension contributions and other fringe benefits paid by employers are not counted as part of wages. In other words, the tax on pension income is paid when the retired worker actually receives the pension, not when the employer sets aside the money to pay the future pension. This principle applies even if the employer pays into a completely separate pension fund, if the worker makes a voluntary contribution to a 401(k) program, or if the worker contributes to a Keogh, IRA, or SEP fund.

* * * To make the tax system progressive, only earnings over a personal or family allowance are taxed. The allowance is $25,500 for a family of four in 1995 but would rise with the cost of living in later years. All the taxpayer has to do is report total wages, salaries, and pensions at the top, compute the family allowance based on marital status and number of dependents, subtract the allowance, multiply by 19 percent to compute the tax, take account of withholding, and pay the difference or apply for a refund. For about 80 percent of the population, filling out this postcard once a year would be the only effort needed to satisfy the Internal Revenue Service. What a change from the many pages of schedules the frustrated taxpayer fills out today!

For the 80 percent of taxpayers who don't run businesses, the individual wage tax would be the only tax to worry about. Many features of current taxes would disappear, including charitable deductions, mortgage interest deductions, capital gains taxes, dividend taxes, and interest taxes. * * *

Anyone who is self-employed or pays expenses directly in connection with making a living will need to file the business tax to get the proper deduction for expenses. Fortunately, the business-tax form is even simpler than the wage-tax form.

Again, we stress that the wage tax is not a complete income tax on individuals; it taxes only wages, salaries, and pensions. The companion business tax picks up all other components of income. Together they form an airtight tax system.

The Business Tax

It is not the purpose of the business tax to tax businesses. Fundamentally, people pay taxes, not businesses. The idea of the business tax is to collect the tax that the owners of a business owe on the income produced by the business. Collecting business income tax at the source of the income avoids one of the biggest causes of leakage in the tax system today: Interest can pass through many layers where it is invariably deducted when it is paid out but frequently not reported as income.

Airtight taxation of individual business income at the source is possible because we already know the tax rate of all of the owners of the business—it is the common flat rate paid by all taxpayers. If the tax system has graduated rates, taxation at the source becomes a problem. If each owner is to be taxed at that owner's rate, the business would have to find out the tax rate applicable to each owner and apply that rate to the income produced in the business for that owner. * * * Source taxation is only practical when a single rate is applied to all owners. Because source taxation is reliable and inexpensive, it is a powerful practical argument for using a single rate for all business income.

The business tax is a giant, comprehensive withholding tax on all types of income other than wages, salaries, and pensions. It is carefully designed to tax every bit of income outside of wages but to tax it only once. The business tax does not have deductions for interest payments, dividends, or any other type of payment to the owners of the business. As a result, all income that people receive from business activity has already been taxed. Because the tax has already been paid, the tax system does not need to worry about what happens to interest, dividends, or capital gains after these types of income leave the firm, resulting in an enormously simplified and improved tax system. Today, the IRS receives more than a billion Form 1099s, which keep track of interest and dividends, and must make an overwhelming effort to match these forms to the 1040s filed by the recipients. The only reason for a Form 1099 is to track income as it makes its way from the business where it originates to the ultimate recipient. Not a single Form 1099 would be needed under a flat tax with business income taxed at the source.

The way that we have set up the business tax is not arbitrary—on the contrary, it is dictated by the principles we set forth at the beginning of this chapter. The tax would be assessed on all the income originating in a business but not on any income that originates in other businesses or on the wages, salaries, and pensions paid to employees. The types of income taxed by the business tax would include:
* Profits from the use of plant and equipment
* Profits from ideas embodied in copyrights, patents, trade secrets, and the like
* Profits from past organization-building, marketing, and advertising efforts

* Earnings of key executives and others who are owners as well as employees and who are paid less than they contribute to the business
* Earnings of doctors, lawyers, and other professionals who have businesses organized as proprietorships or partnerships
* Rent earned from apartments and other real estate
* Fringe benefits provided to workers

All a business's income derives from the sale of its products and services. On the top line of the business-tax form goes the gross sales of the business—its proceeds from the sale of all its products. But some of the proceeds come from the resale of inputs and parts the firm purchased; the tax has already been paid on those items because the seller also has to pay the business tax. Thus, the firm can deduct the cost of all the goods, materials, and services it purchases to make the product it sells. In addition, it can deduct its wages, salaries, and pensions, for, under our wage tax, the taxes on those will be paid by the workers receiving them. Finally, the business can deduct all its outlays for plant, equipment, and land. * * *

Everything left from this calculation is the income originating in the firm and is taxed at the flat rate of 19 percent. In most businesses, there is enough left that the prospective revenue from the business tax is the $362 billion we computed earlier. Many deductions allowed to businesses under current laws are eliminated in our plan, including interest payments and fringe benefits. But our excluding these deductions is not an arbitrary move to increase the tax base. In all cases, eliminating deductions, when combined with the other features of our system, moves toward the goal of taxing all income once at a common, low rate and achieving a broad consumption tax.

Eliminating the deduction for interest paid by businesses is a central part of our general plan to tax business income at the source. It makes sense because we propose not to tax interest received by individuals. The tax that the government now hopes (sometimes in vain) that individuals will pay will assuredly be paid by the business itself.

We sweep away the whole complicated apparatus of depreciation deductions, but we replace it with something more favorable for capital formation, an immediate 100 percent first-year tax write-off of all investment spending. Sometimes this approach is called expensing of investment; it is standard in the value-added approach to consumption taxation. In other words, we don't deny depreciation deductions; we enhance them. More on this shortly.

Fringe benefits are outside the current tax system entirely, which makes no sense. The cost of fringes is deductible by businesses, but workers are not taxed on the value of the fringes. Consequently, fringes have a big advantage over cash wages. As taxation has become heavier and heavier, fringes have become more and more important in the total package offered by employers to workers—fringes were only 1.2 percent of total compensation in 1929, when income taxes were unimportant, but reached almost 18 percent in 1993. The explosion of fringes is strictly an artifact of taxation and thus an economically inefficient way to pay workers. Were the tax system neutral, with equal taxes on fringes and cash, workers would rather take their income in cash and make their own decisions about health and life insurance, parking, exercise facilities, and all the other things they now get from their employers without much choice. Further, failing to tax fringes means that taxes on other types of income are all the higher. Bringing all types of income under the tax system is essential for low rates.

Under our system, each business would file a simple form. Even the largest business (General Motors Corporation in 1993, with $138 billion in sales) would fill out our simple postcard form. Every line on the form is a well defined number obtained directly from the business's accounting records.
* * *

The taxable income computed bears little resemblance to anyone's notion of profit. The business tax is not a profit tax. When a company is having an outstanding year in sales and profits but is building new factories to handle rapid growth, it may well have a low or even negative taxable income. That's fine—later, when expansion slows but sales are at a high level, the income generated will be taxed at 19 percent.

Because the business tax treats investment in plant, equipment, and land as an expense, companies in the start-up period will have negative taxable income. But the government will not write a check for the negative tax on the negative income. Whenever the government has a policy of writing checks, clever people abuse the opportunity. Instead, the negative tax would be carried forward to future years, when the business should have a positive taxable income. There is no limit to the number of years of carry forward. Moreover, balances carried forward will earn the market rate of interest (6 percent in 1995). * * *

Investment Incentives

Expensing investment eliminates the double taxation of saving, another way to express the most economically significant feature of expensing. Under an income tax, people pay tax once when they earn and save and again when the savings earn a return. With expensing, the first tax is abolished. Saving is, in effect, deducted in computing the tax. Later, the return to the saving is taxed through the business tax.

The easiest way to show that expensing investment is a consumption tax arises when someone invests directly in a personally owned business. Suppose a taxpayer receives $1,000 in earnings and turns around and buys a piece of business equipment for $1,000. Under the flat tax, there is a tax of $190 on the earnings but also a deduction worth $190 in reduced taxes for the equipment purchase. On net, there is no tax. The taxpayer has not consumed any of the original $1,000. Later the taxpayer will receive business income representing the earnings of the machine, which will be taxed at 19 percent. If the taxpayer chooses to consume rather than invest again, there will be a 19 percent tax on the consumption. So the overall effect is a 19 percent consumption tax.

Most people, however, don't invest by directly purchasing machines. The U.S. economy has wonderfully developed financial markets for channeling savings from individual savers to businesses who have good investment opportunities. Individuals invest by purchasing shares or bonds, and the firms then purchase plant and equipment. The tax system we propose taxes the consumption of individuals in this environment as well. Suppose the same taxpayer pays the $190 tax on the same $1,000 and puts the remaining $810 into the stock market. For simplicity, suppose that the share pays out to its owner all the after-tax earnings on equipment costing $1,000. (That assumption makes sense because the firm could buy $1,000 worth of equipment with the $810 from our taxpayer plus the tax write-off worth $190 that would come with the equipment purchase.) Our taxpayer gets the advantage of the investment write-off even though there is no deduction for purchasing the share. The market passes the incentive from the firm on to the individual investor.

Another possibility for the taxpayer is to buy a bond for $810. Again, the firm issuing the bond can buy a $1,000 machine with the $810, after taking advantage of the tax deduction.   To compete with the returns available in the stock market, however, the bond must pay the same returns as a stock selling for the same price, which in turn is equal to the after-tax earnings of the machine, so it won't matter how the taxpayer invests the $810. In all cases, there is effectively no tax for saved income; the tax is payable only when the income is consumed.

In our system, any investment, in effect, would have the same economic advantage that a 401(k), IRA, or Keogh account has in the current tax system. And we achieve this desirable goal by reducing the amount of record keeping and reporting. Today, taxpayers have to deduct their Keogh-IRA contributions on their Form 1040s and then report the distributions from the funds as income when they retire. Moreover, proponents of the cash-flow consumption tax would extend these requirements to all forms of saving. Our system would accomplish the same goal without any forms or record keeping.

Capital Gains

* * *

Capital gains would be taxed exclusively at the business level, not at the personal level. In other words, our system would eliminate the double taxation of capital gains inherent in the current tax system. To see how this works, consider the common stock of a corporation. The market value of the stock is the capitalization of its future earnings. Because the owners of the stock will receive their earnings after the corporation has paid the business tax, the market capitalizes after-tax earnings. A capital gain occurs when the market perceives that prospective after-tax earnings have risen. When the higher earnings materialize in the future, they will be correspondingly taxed. In a tax system like the current one, with both an income tax and a capital gains tax, there is double taxation. * * *

Capital gains on owner-occupied houses are not taxed under our proposal. Few capital gains on houses are taxed under the current system—gains can be rolled over, there is an exclusion for older home sellers, and gains are never taxed at death. Excluding capital gains on houses makes sense because state and local governments put substantial property taxes on houses in relation to their values. Adding a capital gains tax on top of property taxes is double taxation in the same way that adding a capital gains tax on top of an income tax is double taxation of business income.

The Transition

* * *

Depreciation Deductions

Existing law lets businesses deduct the cost of an investment on a declining schedule over many years. From the point of view of the business, multiyear depreciation deductions are not as attractive as the first-year write-off prescribed in the flat tax. No business will complain about the flat tax as far as future investment is concerned. But businesses may well protest the unexpected elimination of the unused depreciation they thought they would be able to take on the plant and equipment they installed before the tax reform. Without special transition provisions, these deductions would simply be lost.

How much is at stake? In 1992, total depreciation deductions under the personal and corporate income taxes came to $597 billion. * * *

If Congress chose to honor all unused depreciation from investment predating tax reform, it would take about $597 billion out of the tax base for 1995. To raise the same amount of revenue as our 19 percent rate, the tax rate would have to rise to about 20.1 percent.

* * *

If Congress did opt to honor past depreciation, it should recognize that the higher tax rate needed to make up for the lost revenue is temporary. Within five years, the bulk of the existing capital would be depreciated and the tax rate should be brought back to 19 percent. From the outset, the tax rate should be committed to drop to 19 percent as soon as the transition depreciation is paid off.

Interest Deductions

* * *

Our tax reform calls for the parallel removal of interest deduction and interest taxation. If a transitional measure allows deductions for interest on outstanding debt, it should also require taxation of that interest as income of the lender. If all deductions are completely matched with taxation on the other side, then a transition provision to protect existing interest deductions would have no effect on revenue. In that respect, interest deductions are easier to handle in the transition than depreciation deductions.

If Congress decides that a transitional measure to protect interest deductions is needed, we suggest the following. Any borrower may choose to treat interest payments as a tax deduction. If the borrower so chooses, the lender must treat the interest as taxable income. But the borrower's deduction should be only 90 percent of the actual interest payment, while the lender's taxable income should include 100 percent of the interest receipts.

Under this transitional plan, borrowers would be protected for almost all their existing deductions. Someone whose personal finances would become untenable if the mortgage-interest deduction were suddenly eliminated can surely get through with 90 percent of the earlier deduction. But the plan builds in an incentive for renegotiating the interest payments. Suppose a family is paying $10,000 in annual mortgage interest. It could stick with this payment and deduct $9,000 per year. Its net cost, after subtracting the value of its deduction with the 19 percent tax rate, would be $8,290. The net income to the bank, after subtracting the 19 percent tax it pays on the whole $10,000, would be $8,100. Alternatively, the family could accept a deal proposed by the bank: The interest payment would be lowered to $8,200 by rewriting the mortgage. * * * The deal will be beneficial to both.

* * *

As far as revenue is concerned, this plan would actually add a bit to federal revenue in comparison to the pure flat tax. Whenever a borrower exercised the right to deduct interest, the government would collect more revenue from the lender than it would lose from the borrower. As more and more deals were rewritten to eliminate deductions and lower interest, the excess revenue would disappear and we would be left with the pure flat tax.

Charitable Contributions

Deducting contributions to worthy causes would be a thing of the past under our tax reform. Will the nation stop supporting its churches, hospitals, museums, and opera companies when the tax deduction disappears? We think not. But we should also be clear that incentives matter—the current tax system with high marginal rates and tax deductions provides inappropriately high incentives for some contributions. The immediate effect of tax reform may be a small decline in giving. Later, as the economy surges forward under the impetus of improved incentives for productive activity, giving will recover and likely exceed its current levels.

In 1991, total cash contributions to charitable causes were about $117 billion. Of this, only $61 billion was deducted on personal tax returns. Almost half of all contributions were not affected by the law permitting deduction. We confidently expect that the $56 billion in contributions being made today without any special tax benefits will continue. Further, the bulk of contributions are from people in modest tax brackets—only $28 billion in contributions were deducted in 1991 by families with taxable incomes of more than $75,000. In this connection, it is important to understand that well more than half of all cash contributions go to churches and that these gifts are generally from the middle of the income distribution.

Churches have nothing to fear from tax reform and, like most people and institutions, would have much to gain from better economic conditions brought about by reform. Despite their dominant position in gifts, churches are not the leaders in fighting a tax reform that denies deductions. Instead, institutions serving the absolute economic and social elite—universities, symphonies, opera companies, ballets, and museums—are protesting the loudest. No compelling case has ever been made that these worthy undertakings should be financed by anyone but their customers. * * *

Major tax cuts in 1981 and 1986 cut the top marginal tax rate from 70 percent to 50 percent and then to 28 percent. As a result, major donors shifted from spending thirty-three-cent dollars to spending fifty-cent and then seventy-two-cent dollars for tax-deductible gifts. Despite these major reductions in incentives for the rich to give, donations to charity grew robustly. * * *

UNLIMITED SAVINGS ALLOWANCE (USA) TAX SYSTEM
Alliance USA*
66 Tax Notes 1482, 1487-94, 1514-15 (1995)

The USA Tax System is designed to replace on a revenue-neutral basis the present corporate and individual income taxes in Subtitle A of the IRC of 1986. The proposed new tax system consists of two parts.

A [10%][1] flat-rate Business Tax that applies to all organizational forms of businesses, corporate and noncorporate, and that allows a deduction for business capital investment.

A graduated-rate Individual Tax that applies to individuals and that allows a deduction for personal savings.

The centerpiece of the USA Tax System is the Unlimited Savings Allowance from which the new tax system for America's future derives its name. The concept is a simple but powerful one that views Americans not as payers of taxes but as the producers of the income and the providers of the savings on which a growing economy and higher living standards depend. Everyone has a stake, a large one, in fact, in the national stock of savings whether or not they personally own any of that savings at the present time.

---

*. The paper was prepared for Alliance USA by two legal consultants, Ernest S. Christian and George J. Schutzer, with advice from two economic consultants, Rudolph G. Penner and Barry K. Rogstad, at the request of the Alliance's co-chairmen, Paul H. O'Neill and Robert K. Lutz, and under the administrative supervision of its Executive Director, Barbara W. North.

1. Throughout this document, the drafters placed tax rates in brackets, apparently contemplating that their concept might be used with different tax rates. (Eds.)

Under the USA Tax System, when people earn income, save part of it and add to the national stock of savings, they get a tax deduction. When they take their income out of savings and reduce the national stock, they pay tax on that income. For so long as people have their income invested for everyone's benefit, including their own, they do not have to pay tax on that income.

Putting aside a part of earnings in a savings account, a stock or bond or in their own small business is not the only way that Americans can invest in the future and create even more income for themselves and everyone else. They can and should also invest in human capital. Investment in their own education and training and in the education of their children will produce a large, long lasting return on investment in which everyone will share.

The USA Tax System provides a limited deduction for education expenses. This deduction works in tandem with the Unlimited Savings Allowance. Parents will be able to set aside tax-deferred income for their children's education. When they withdraw the income in the future to pay qualified tuition, the income will not be taxed to the extent offset by the deduction for education expenses.

For lower and middle-income Americans who work for salaries and wages, the existing FICA payroll tax withheld from their paychecks is a heavy burden. The USA Tax System provides a payroll tax credit that phases out as income rises and the payroll tax becomes less of a burden in proportion to income.

The USA Tax System contains important new rules related to imports and exports, and for American companies directly competing in the global marketplace. These innovations are intended to level the international playing field and let American goods, skill and know-how, including emerging new technologies and services, be more competitive.

* * *

The core principles of the USA Tax System are of overriding importance.

In order for there to be income, there must be savings but in order for there to be savings, there must be income.

Human labor and skill is the ultimate source of all income but the amount of income that people produce and enjoy will be less without sufficient savings and investment.

The existing tax system is biased against saving and, therefore, against earning income and the human dignity and well-being that go with it. By allowing people a fair opportunity to save, the USA Tax System removes the bias against earning greater incomes from human effort and skill.

* * *

**Understanding the Business Tax in the Context of
the Individual Tax and Vice Versa**

The Business Tax and the Individual Tax are merely two interrelated parts of a tax applied to a single tax base that happens to appear at two different points in the process by which income is created and received.

The tax base first emerges when businesses create income by producing and selling goods and services. That is when the Business Tax applies. Next, the tax base reappears when individuals actually receive that income, net of the Business Tax, in the form of wages, salaries, interest, dividends and similar distributions to the owners of a business. It is at that point where the Individual Tax applies.

Because the basic operating rules of both parts of the new two-tier tax system are largely interactive, it can best be understood by looking at both the Business Tax and the Individual Tax, separately and in relation to one another, and then by looking at detailed examples where both taxes are applied to illustrative sets of facts.

Basic Operating Rules and Principles of the Business Tax

Rules

Although supplemental rules are needed to make the Business Tax work properly and consistently in all situations, the basic operating rules are few and simple.

1. Every business, incorporated or unincorporated, that is producing and selling goods and services, and, therefore, creating income for its employees, owners and lenders, must file an annual business tax return and pay a [10%] tax on its annual "gross profit" which is a defined term under the Business Tax.

2. In calculating its gross profit tax base to which the [10%] tax is applied, the business adds only the amount it actually received from sales of goods and services and subtracts only the amount it actually paid out to other businesses for the goods and services it had to buy from them (plant, equipment, inventory, supplies, rent, utilities, telephones, fuel, legal and accounting fees, etc.). Excluded from the gross profit calculation are financial receipts and payments. For example, the business neither includes interest and dividends received nor deducts interest and dividends paid. Also excluded are compensation payments to employees. * * *

3. Amounts received from export sales of goods to a purchaser outside the United States and for services rendered outside the United States are excluded from the calculation of gross profit. Correspondingly, a [10%] import tax is imposed on the sale of goods into the United States from abroad. E.g., a foreign business that manufactures outside the United States but sells its products in the U.S. market will pay the import tax.

4. A tax credit is allowed for the 7.65% employer payroll tax (commonly called FICA or Social Security Tax) that businesses must pay on wages paid to employees.

5. The Business Tax is territorial. U.S. businesses will not include in gross profit the proceeds from sales made or services provided outside the United States and they will not subtract amounts paid for the purchase of goods or the provision of services outside the United States. U.S. businesses will not be taxed on dividends paid by foreign subsidiaries. Foreign businesses will include in gross profit amounts received for goods sold or services provided in the United States and will subtract amounts paid for goods acquired and services provided in the United States.

Discussion of General Principles

Because of the special definition of gross profit under the Business Tax, it makes no distinction between that portion of a business's income that is produced and received by its owners and that portion produced and received by its employees. The business calculates its gross profit tax base before paying employees their share, before paying owners their share, before paying creditors their share, and before paying taxes owed by the business.

* * *

The often-drawn line between capital income and work income is, however, indistinct at best. In the case of smaller corporations and partnerships, all or most of the owners also themselves work in the business and receive their shares of the gross profit in part as salary (or "guaranteed payments" or draws) and in part as "dividends" in proportion to their investments of time and effort, as well as capital. Even in the case of large privately held corporations, many of the founders who own all or most of the stock may also work in the business. The key executives of large publicly held corporations nearly always own stock. They too will receive both salaries and dividends out of gross profit.

In the case of the many unincorporated businesses operating as "proprietorships," the owner of the business is almost by definition also the operator of the business. Proprietorships are usually small businesses, such as a farm, retail shop, pharmacy, small-town plumber or electrician, or a doctor or dentist operating as a sole practitioner. The owner-employee is usually the only one who has capital invested in the business (mostly reinvested earnings) and is sometimes the only "employee," although family members may also work full or part time in the business. Here, even for bookkeeping purposes, the distinction between a dollar of gross profit produced and received from working in the business like other employees, and a dollar produced and received for having provided the capital necessary for anyone to earn any income from the business, is as blurred and irrelevant as it is in reality.

The present income tax system makes huge distinctions in the foregoing cases depending on the form of business organization, on the size of the business, on whether income is said to be produced by labor or by capital, and on whether income is said to be received as an employee or as an owner of capital. In the process of making all these fine-spun distinctions, present law imposes vastly different tax liabilities on different parts of what is in fact a single tax base.

In contrast, the Business Tax is even-handed in the amount of tax it imposes on the labor and capital incomes produced by a business. After all, no one, including the Commissioner of Internal Revenue or the President or Congress of the United States, actually knows exactly how much of any business' gross profit is produced by labor instead of by capital, or vice versa, or even has a particularly realistic way of defining either one. We do know that gross profit exists, do know how to measure it in the case of any business and in total for all businesses, and do know that it is ultimately the source of everyone's income. We also know that gross profit is the result of some combination of labor and capital. * * *

The Business Tax responds to the reality of these knowns and unknowns simply by collecting [10%] of gross profit when it is produced at the business level, without distinctions as to who or what contributed more or less to its creation, and leaving to the business' owners and employees, operating within the inexorably accurate forces of the marketplace, to determine who gets and, therefore, who produced, how much of the total.

Applied in this way, the Business Tax serves as a step-one pre-collection of tax even before the respective shares of gross profit are determined, and before people actually receive their respective shares, net of the pre-collection, as wages, salaries, dividends, interest, and mixtures thereof. When people receive their income, the Individual Tax will be collected directly from them. The Business Tax plus the Individual Tax will be the total tax on their shares of what is in reality a single tax base flowing from production (business) to producers (people).

Not only does the Business Tax make no arbitrary distinctions among different dollars of income—based on presumed origins or otherwise—it proceeds from a correct definition of "income" in the first place. All businesses have some capital invested in machinery, inventories, etc. Under the gross profit calculation used in the Business Tax, that cost is subtracted so that the business is first allowed to recover capital. It is only income (not the capital itself) that is included in the business' gross profit tax base and that is ultimately, net of Business Tax, reflected in any person's share of gross profit.

Under the Individual Tax, the counterpart of the business' ability to recover capital before having taxable gross profit, is the ability of a person who receives wages, salaries, dividends, interest, etc. to defer tax on that portion which he or she saves and converts into capital. * * *

Basic Operating Rules and Principles
of the Individual Tax

Rules

Although, here again, some supplementary rules are necessary, the basic operating rules of the Individual Tax are few and simple.

1. All individuals must file an annual return and pay tax at graduated rates ranging from [X to Z%] on their taxable income for the year.

2. In calculating taxable income, the individual generally includes in gross income all amounts received from all sources other than gifts, bequests, the proceeds of loans, and certain income transfers or substitutes received from governments. Thus, gross income would generally include wages, salaries, interest, pensions, annuities, the proceeds of a life insurance contract, dividends, equivalent distributions from a partnership or other unincorporated business, and most amounts received from the sale of assets.

3. If an individual defers receipt of gross income by saving it, i.e., by investing it in a savings asset such as a stock or a bank deposit, the individual is allowed a deduction for that savings. This is called the Unlimited Savings Allowance. This deduction serves to defer tax on income the actual receipt of which the individual has deferred by recontributing it to the national stock of savings. When, later, the individual withdraws savings from the national savings pool, the amount withdrawn is at that time included in the individual's gross income.

4. The individual also deducts from gross income (i) personal and family exemptions, (ii) a Family Living Allowance deduction, and (iii) a few personal deductions generally related to home ownership, charitable contributions and education.

5. Individuals do not deduct on their personal tax returns any "trade or business" expenses such as are now reported on Schedule C of Form 1040. If an individual is self-employed and does incur such expenses, they are reported on a self-employed business tax return along with the gross sales revenues associated with that business entity. Only the net results of that self-employed business, minus the Business Tax, are reported on the individual's personal tax return and, then, only to the extent actually withdrawn from the business.

6. In general, individuals are allowed a credit for the 7.65% employee payroll tax (commonly called FICA or Social Security Tax) that their employers are required to withhold from their wages. Because this credit is phased-out as income rises, some individuals will get only a partial credit and high-income individuals will get no credit. A similar phased-out credit is allowed for self-employed individuals. In addition, employees are allowed a credit for any Individual Tax that is explicitly withheld from their wages or salaries, the same as in the case of present Form W-2 withholding of income tax. In general, W-2 type withholding will operate the same way as under present law.

Discussion of General Principles

The deduction allowed an individual for the purchase of "savings assets" illustrates the interactive combination of the Individual Tax and the Business Tax. That deduction also illustrates the goal of correctly defining income and thereby eliminating the bias under present law against an individual's choice and need to save income and against a business' choice and need to invest in order to create income for its owners and employees. These choices are two parts of the same thing because unless people save, businesses cannot invest and unless businesses invest, people cannot earn income.

Under the Individual Tax, "savings assets" are generally defined as financial assets such as stocks of corporations (and equivalent investments in an unincorporated business by an owner-partner or an owner-proprietor), bonds and notes, both commercial and governmental, annuity contracts, life insurance contracts, and deposits in banks and similar depository institutions.

As defined under the Individual Tax, savings assets do not include properties such as art objects, antiques, classic cars, owner-occupied housing, and land even though such properties may have long-term value in that they may frequently be sold at a later date for as much as or more than the price paid for them. Even though their purchase may be savings in a broader economic definition, there are several reasons why the Individual Tax distinguishes these admittedly valuable properties from such obvious savings assets as stock in a corporation and a bank deposit.

An art object, for example, inherently involves personal enjoyment and pleasure, and derives its value solely therefrom. The more aesthetic enjoyment a painting produces, the "better" it is, and the more valuable it is. Otherwise, it is merely $10 of canvas and paint. Except by price, and the degree and longevity of personal consumption enjoyment and service provided (which is reflected in price), it is difficult to draw the line between a 50 [cent] soft drink, a $50 bottle of wine, and a $5,000 art object. By defining a "savings asset" to include only financial assets such as stocks, bonds and deposits, the Individual Tax eliminates the need to make such distinctions.

This definition of savings assets also serves to allow people who produce and earn otherwise taxable income to defer that tax when they purchase an asset such as a stock that derives its value solely from the fact that it will in the future result in the production of additional income that will also be taxable to the owner-saver. If a person earns a $100X salary and uses current taxable income to purchase a stock that presently has a value of $100X only because it will in the future produce dividends (or the combination of dividends and liquidation or resale proceeds) that have a present value of $100X, and if that person will have to pay tax on the dividends when received (which will be the case), that person must be allowed to deduct the cost of the stock. Otherwise, the $100X of current salary will be taxed twice. In contrast, if the person uses the $100X of currently taxable salary income to purchase an asset (such as an art object, a personal automobile, or a personal residence) that will produce nontaxable income in the form of the personal service or enjoyment it provides, the person should not be allowed to deduct the cost of the asset. Otherwise, the $100X of salary income would not be taxed at all; not even once.

By allowing a savings deduction for the purchase of assets that will produce taxable income in the future, the Individual Tax assures that income is taxed once. If a person buys a savings bond for $25 that will mature in 10 years and pay back $50 ($25 being $50 discounted for 10 years at 7.18%), the Individual Tax allows a deduction for $25 in the year the bond is bought but includes $50 in taxable income in the year the bond matures. * * * Thus, tax is deferred, not forgiven, and all the income is taxed.

> * * *

Deferring tax on deferred income is exactly the concept of the IRA (Individual Retirement Account). Prior to 1987, all individuals could defer tax on up to $2,000 of income per year by depositing it in a special IRA Account at a bank. In general, the funds in the IRA Account can only be invested in financial assets such as stocks, bonds and so forth.

The Unlimited Savings Allowance is the same in concept, although structurally different, more flexible and more efficient. In the case of the IRA, withdrawal had to occur at or during retirement. When withdrawn, the original deposit plus accumulated earnings, such as interest and dividends, were taxed. If withdrawn before retirement age, an additional penalty tax was imposed. Under the Individual Tax, there is no $2,000 limit, no special account is necessary, and the use of saved and deferred income is not restricted to retirement. Income and the earnings thereon can be withdrawn from savings at any time.

> * * *

Basic Example Illustrating the Business Tax and the Individual Tax Operating in Combination—Domestic Business

> * * *

[W]hat might be called "consequential rules" * * * are actually results that inevitably arise from the previously stated basic rules, although these results may not be immediately obvious. Among these, for starters, are the following.

> Compensatory stock awards (or options) to employees will not immediately result in taxable income to the employee even though they are the equivalent of cash and under present law are taxable. Reason: Stock is a deductible savings asset and receiving stock in lieu of cash salary is the same as receiving cash and then buying deductible stock.

> All corporations and their shareholders can have a fully flexible "dividend reinvestment" system where, when the corporation declares a common stock dividend, one common shareholder can receive taxable cash and another can elect to receive either nontaxable stock or nontaxable debt. Reason: Same as above. Even though under state corporate law the electing

shareholder had the "right" to receive cash (which right is taxable under present law), the election to receive stock or debt provides an equal and offsetting deduction for savings.

* * *

Basic Rules That Are Illustrated

In the case of the Business Tax:

The tax rate applies only to the gross profit tax base, which is the net positive result of sales minus purchases from other businesses of goods and services.

Only cash (or the equivalent) actually received or actually paid is taken into account, i.e., the cash method of accounting is uniformly applied.

Positive or negative net cash flow from financial transactions is, however, not taken into account.

Although gross profit is computed without regard to employee payroll cost (or the employer payroll tax paid thereon), a tax credit against the Business Tax is allowed for the 7.65% employer payroll tax.

In the case of the Individual Tax:

An individual's gross income includes wages, salaries, interest and dividends.

Deductions are allowed for the costs of savings assets purchased. * * *

Why [allow deduction for] goods and services purchased from other businesses? The Business Tax is intended to be the first in a two-step process of collecting a tax on income. Therefore, the Business Tax begins with the source—Gross Domestic Product (GDP), which can for this purpose be viewed as the sum of all goods and services produced and sold by all businesses together minus, in order to avoid duplication, those that they bought from one another. * * *

Why Not Also Deduct Employee Payroll? Obviously, Widget Corporation's gross sales of $1,900,000 and gross profit of $1,000,000 were not produced solely by Mr. Founder's entrepreneurial skill and the supplies, inventory and capital equipment bought from Supplier Company in the current and prior years. * * * Widget Corporation's employees contributed a very substantial portion of Widget Corporation's gross profit—just as, by using machinery, equipment and other "tools," employees produce the major portion of total GDP every year measured by what they get paid.

Why, then, not deduct payroll cost? Answer: Employees, as such, are not a business required to file a business tax return and to pay the [10%] Business Tax. If Widget Corporation deducted its payments to them against its business tax base, there would be no corresponding inclusion of that amount in any other business' tax base, and no [10%] Business Tax would be pre-collected on that portion of income.

* * * It is appropriate to deduct [a payment for] accounting "services" where [the payee's] CPA firm is an outside independent contractor that is itself a business subject to the [10%] Business Tax, but it is not appropriate to deduct the salary paid for similar accounting services to an inside employee-accountant who is not a business subject to the [10%] Business Tax. * * *

It is true that the employee's salary will be *included*, when received, in the employee's personal tax return under the Individual Tax but the tax rates under the Individual Tax are lower than they otherwise would be, precisely because of the pre-collection of the [10%] tax. * * *

It is, however, also the case that in addition to the [10%] Business Tax, Widget Corporation must, as under present law, pay a 7.65% payroll tax on wages up to $60,000 per year per employee; whereas in the case of the share of gross profit that goes to interest and dividends, there is only the [10%] tax. It is for this reason that the Business Tax also gives Widget Corporation a full tax credit for the 7.65% employer payroll tax.

It is by a combination of all these means—including splitting the overall tax rate between businesses and individuals—that the Business Tax and the Individual Tax achieve the intended result of correctly measuring income and being even-handed among all forms of income and the recipients thereof.

Why are financial receipts and payments excluded from the gross profit calculation? Part of the answer, at least in terms of the accounting procedure of matching deductions with income and vice versa, has already been stated in explaining that allowing no "deduction" for dividend and interest payments is the same as allowing no "deduction" for wages and salaries to employees.

There are other reasons for excluding all financial receipts and, correspondingly, all financial payments. The heart of the matter goes back to the concept of GDP which fundamentally arises from the production and sale of goods and services. GDP is not increased to a still higher number because of financial flows such as interest and dividends back and forth between businesses or between businesses and individuals. * * *

Therefore, the GDP-based Business Tax for regular, nonfinancial businesses excludes all interest, dividends and similar financial flows among businesses, except to the extent that they may be treated as implicit payments for services. * * *

Under the Business Tax, neither the lender nor the borrower takes into account the transfer or receipt of funds in loan transactions. Loans made are not deducted, repayments received are not included, loan proceeds received are not included, and loan repayments made are not deducted.
* * *

Basic Rules of the Individual Tax
* * *

Deduction for Net Amount Saved

Individuals may deduct, without any dollar limit, their additions to the national stock of savings. * * *

[A] netting calculation will be made. If the netting results in more withdrawals and sales than deposits and purchases of savings assets, the net amount will be included in the gross income line. If the netting results in a net savings deduction, it will be subtracted in the deduction line.

Determining the Net Amount Saved in the Simple Case

Most taxpayers will be able by very simple calculations to determine the net amount saved. * * *

a. When income is earned and deferred by saving, the tax on the income for that year is deferred, generally, by including the amount earned and deducting the amount saved.

b. When in a later year, the income is withdrawn from savings, the amount is included in gross income for that later year.

c. If, however, the withdrawal from savings was merely to shift the same amount of savings from one savings asset to another, the person should not be taxed on the income which, after the shift, is still in the national savings pool.

* * *

Rules to Keep the Calculations Simple
Borrowing

* * * The USA Tax System should not encourage borrowing to save, because that is not really savings. On the other hand, the Individual Tax should be as simple as possible. To balance these competing concerns, the Individual Tax contains special rules for the certain kinds of debt ordinarily incurred by individuals:

i. Mortgage debt on a person's personal residence is not taken into account in determining the net savings deduction.

ii. Debt of up to $25,000 directly related to the purchase of personal property such as furniture, appliances or a family automobile is disregarded.

iii. An additional $10,000 of debt incurred for any purpose is also disregarded in determining the net savings deduction.

* * *

Tax Basis

The simple case calculations will not work properly in cases in which an individual sells a savings asset with a tax basis. If the individual were to then save all of the proceeds, the individual would have no new savings, but if he included in gross income the excess of the proceeds of the sale of the savings asset over the basis of the asset, and deducted the full amount of the proceeds saved, he would have a net savings deduction.

* * *

To minimize the problems caused by tax basis, the Individual Tax rules permit taxpayers who have total tax bases in savings assets of less than $50,000 to elect to assign a zero tax basis to each savings asset and to amortize and deduct their total basis in savings assets ratably over three years. * * *

The tax-basis complication cannot be fairly solved by simply disregarding tax basis in savings assets. Tax basis generally reflects the cost of the assets. Since these assets were purchased with after-tax dollars, the basis reflects amounts of gross income that were previously taxed. To avoid double taxation of income, the basis would have to be taken into account on the sale of assets. By eliminating the basis of most assets and allowing amortization deductions to offset the previously recognized income, the amortization election makes the new tax system simpler.

The amortization election is limited because taxpayer now have substantial bases in savings assets. If all taxpayers were permitted to amortize their tax bases over a short period, there would be a substantial revenue shortfall during the early years of the USA Tax System. * * *

IS RADICAL TAX REFORM IN OUR FUTURE?
Rudolph G. Penner[*]
21 National Tax Association Forum, Spring 1995, at 1, 2-5

At about the same time [1993], Senators Nunn and Domenici were developing a much more radical reform proposal. * * * In it, a subtraction-type VAT replaces the corporate tax and taxes on non-corporate business reflected on Schedule C, and provides a 100 percent credit for payment of employer payroll taxes. The payroll tax structure is maintained to avoid disturbing current social security arrangements.

Businesses total their sales and subtract purchases from other businesses, including investment goods, to arrive at the tax base. In the aggregate, it approximately equals consumption as defined in the national income accounts. Payroll tax payments are then credited against the tax liability. To be revenue neutral in the long run would require a tax rate of slightly less than 10 percent.

The tax is border adjustable. That is to say, it does not apply to exports, but it does apply to imports. Border adjustability has a strong appeal to many businessmen who believe that they are at a disadvantage relative to competitors producing in countries with border adjustable VATS. * * *

The business tax is territorial. That is to say, it only applies to value added generated in the United States. Foreign investments cannot be deducted and the return to them is not taxed. * * *

---

*. At time of original publication, Managing Director of the Barents Group, a subsidiary of KPMG Peat Marwick. Dr. Penner was a consultant to the authors of the substantially identical Nunn-Domenici and Alliance USA proposals.

The proposed business tax is extremely simple compared to the current system. * * *

The individual tax reform is less simple. In the ideal, it would operate on a cash flow basis. Income from wages, rent, interest and dividends would be computed much as it is today. The proceeds from asset sales and borrowing would be added to purchases and asset acquisitions and the repayment of debt and interest would be subtracted. Note that the calculation is equivalent to computing income and deducting saving. It is similar to having a completely unlimited IRA.

The system can be made progressive by increasing the earned income credit and by providing generous exemptions and a large zero-tax bracket. A progressive rate structure can be applied to the remaining tax base. The Nunn-Domenici proposal allows a full credit for the payment of employee payroll taxes.
        * * *

Practical and political considerations prevented Nunn and Domenici from adopting the pure cash flow system. In a pure system, the taxpayer would need to keep track of numerous credit card and accounts payable transactions and of changes in currency balances. This would involve a major effort. Some tax-free borrowing had to be allowed to reduce record keeping and for the purchase of lumpy consumer durables such as cars. The repayment of such loans is not deductible.

Owner-occupied housing represents an immense political and practical challenge to any tax reformer. It escaped the net of [the Tax Reform Act of 1986] and it largely escapes the Nunn-Domenici reform, which retains the current law treatment of the in-kind return and the mortgage and real estate tax deduction. Capital gains on housing sales, however, would be fully taxed to the extent that they are converted into consumption. * * *

Subsequent to the Nunn-Domenici proposal, House Majority Leader Armey proposed a "flat tax" that has gained a great deal of attention. The proposal is based on a design by Robert Hall and Alvin Rabushka, and David Bradford has designed what he calls an "X tax" that has a similar base, but with a tax rate structure that makes it considerably more progressive.

The Armey business tax base is similar to that used by Nunn and Domenici with the important difference that wages are deductible. That means that the tax would not be border adjustable under current GATT rules. Wages are taxed at the individual level. In the Armey proposal, generous exemptions and deductions are combined with a flat rate on what remains. The Bradford proposal would add a progressive rate structure.

These proposals have not been worked out in the same excruciating detail as has Nunn-Domenici. That gives them the appearance of being much simpler. Conceptually, the base of the Armey/Bradford tax is very similar to that used by Nunn and Domenici. It approximately equals value added in the production of consumption goods. It is only a slight oversimplification to say that Armey and Bradford tax income when it is earned; Nunn-Domenici taxes it when it is spent. If all income is spent over a lifetime and tax rates remain constant, the present value of the lifetime tax burden is the same.

Inherently, it may be simpler to tax earnings rather than cash flow, but it is not quite as simple as it seems in the Armey proposal. Because capital income is explicitly exempt at the individual level under the Armey proposal, there is a huge temptation to convey compensation using capital assets. For example, some technique must be designed to handle stock options which can be ignored until converted into cash under Nunn-Domenici.

Nunn and Domenici have elected to try to keep their tax reform distributionally neutral whereas the Armey proposal would result in a large redistribution of the tax burden away from the most affluent.

The rates required for distributional neutrality, however, are extremely difficult to estimate. * * *

An equally disturbing problem is that distributional neutrality cannot be defined without specifying an elaborate theory of tax incidence. Is the current corporate tax largely paid by capital owners or by wage earners because it drives investment abroad? Will the Nunn-Domenici business tax be shifted forward into prices or backward to factors? Who really knows? It is clear that the distributional tables that play such a huge role in political debates over tax policy rest on a foundation of quicksand.

Effect on Saving

Economists are generally skeptical about the use of tax policy to increase private saving and investment. After all, the decline in the saving rate continued in the 1980s in the face of increased saving and investment incentives early in the period and lower marginal rates later. * * *

The effects of a revenue neutral tax reform should, however, be very different from that of a cut in marginal rates. The average taxpayer will be no better off. The same tax will be squeezed out [of] the average person and the only impact will be a greater reward for saving. Moreover, the redistribution of the tax burden within each income class should also increase saving substantially. Those with a high inherent propensity to save will get a tax cut. They should save a relatively high share of it. Those with a high propensity to spend will face a tax increase. They will have to finance it largely by cutting spending. * * *

International Implications

[B]order adjustability is an important issue in the business community. Economists tend to argue that, all else equal, its effects will be washed out by countervailing exchange rate movements. I have never met a businessman who believes this argument.

* * *

Transition and Other Problems

* * * Transition issues have taken more time for the designers of Nunn-Domenici to resolve than any other issues. To my knowledge, transition issues have not been confronted by the proponents of the Armey proposal and proponents of value added taxation generally manage to ignore them.

In the Nunn-Domenici proposal, the most important transition issue involving individuals concerns the treatment of savings accumulated out of after-tax income under the current tax regime. The cost basis of those old savings has already been taxed once. Should it be taxed yet again when it is consumed under the new regime? That would be particularly unfair to retirees.

Ideally, it would be nice to allow the use of old cost basis tax free, both for consuming and for investing in new deductible assets. However, there are trillions of dollars of old cost basis out there and its tax free use might deprive the government of all revenues for several years. Therefore the use of old basis must be limited. But how? * * *

People with less than $50,000 compute their old cost basis on the effective date of the new tax and simply deduct it from their tax base over a limited period, say, three years. The advantage of this approach is that it cannot be gamed. The records underlying it are the same as those now used to compute capital gains taxes.

For those who are wealthy and have complicated investments, * * * the revenue implications of allowing them to write it all off over a limited time period would be very significant since the very wealthy hold most of the nation's wealth.

The designers of Nunn-Domenici have created a fairly simple tax form that allows people to use old basis only to finance consumption in excess of income. Assets acquired by selling old basis are not deductible and the tax form tracks this old basis much as today's tax form tracks accumulated loss carryovers.

The problem with this approach is that many will never consume in excess of their income (e.g. Ross Perot), and will never be able to use old basis tax free. Others with less saving will have an incentive to concentrate the purchase of consumer durables into one year in order to facilitate the use of old basis. This is one of the few distortions in the proposed system, but any system for limiting the use of old basis is likely to inspire intense tax planning.

* * *

THE MERIT OF AN INCOME TAX VERSUS A CONSUMPTION TAX
John S. Nolan[*]

12 American Journal of Tax Policy 207, 207-19 (1995)

The current political debate focuses heavily on the idea of a simple "flat tax"—accompanied by the foolish notion that it could be so simple and at such a low rate that we might even disband the IRS! The real issue lying behind the two major proposals on the table—the Armey flat tax and the Nunn-Domenici USA Tax—is, however, whether we should substitute a consumption form of taxation for our present income tax system. * * *

The most obvious forms of consumption tax are the retail sales tax and the credit-invoice type of value added tax used in Europe. The VAT has exactly the same effect as a retail sales tax; it simply is collected differently. Both forms of tax end up taxing the value of goods and services added by labor, plus "profits" or "rents" in the sense that economists use those terms, which exclude all the normal return on capital investment. Thus capital investment is clearly favored as compared to the impact of an income tax.

The business level USA Tax, and the combined business level/individual level elements of the Armey flat tax, are, in substance, simply subtraction method VAT taxes. As such, they have the same effect as a retail sales tax or a traditional credit-invoice VAT. To illustrate this equivalence, the USA business level tax allows an immediate deduction for all purchases, including the cost of plant and equipment. It allows, however, no deduction for salaries, wages, or fringe benefits. The result is that the tax base, as in a retail sales tax or traditional VAT, is the value added by labor plus profit.

The USA individual level tax then includes wages, salaries, and fringe benefits, as well as dividends, interest, capital gains, and all other forms of income in gross income for tax purposes. The resulting taxable income can, however, be completely offset by contributions to an unlimited IRA account. As a result, the combined USA business and individual taxes are levied on consumption only—that is, they tax income consumed but not income saved.

The Armey flat tax achieves exactly the same effect in a somewhat different way. Unlike the USA business level tax, the Armey business level tax allows a deduction for wages, salaries, and qualified retirement plan contributions, though not for fringe benefits. Like the USA business level tax, it also allows an immediate deduction for all purchases, including the cost of plant and equipment. The Armey individual level tax is then imposed on salaries, wages, and qualified retirement plan distributions, but not on interest, dividends, capital gains, or other investment income. The net result is to tax all forms of income only once, at either the business level or the individual level, just like the USA Tax, except that, in Armey's case, the tax is a single flat rate.

---

[*]. At time of original publication, partner, Miller & Chevalier, Washington, D.C. This paper was presented as the Erwin N. Griswold Lecture to the annual meeting of the American College of Tax Counsel, in New Orleans, on January 19, 1996.

The result in both cases is, as previously stated, to achieve the same effect as a retail sales tax or traditional VAT. The USA Tax taxes salaries and wages at the business level, while the Armey flat tax taxes salaries and wages at the individual level. While the USA Tax includes salaries and wages in the tax base for the individual tax, that tax can be avoided by saving that income, or any other form of income, by use of the unlimited IRA deduction. While the Armey flat tax taxes salaries and wages at the individual level, it does not tax investment income either at the business tax level or the individual tax level.

The key to understanding the basic equivalence of these two systems as being solely taxes on consumption is that the economic effect of not taxing an amount received, but taxing the investment returns on that amount, as in the USA Tax, is exactly the same as taxing the amount received but not taxing the investment returns, as in the Armey flat tax. As a result, both the USA Tax and the Armey flat tax end up being imposed only on income consumed. Each effectively exempts from tax income that is saved.

The political rhetoric focuses upon the flatness of the rate of tax, but that is a red herring. We could obviously achieve that result with our present income tax system, taxing all income, whether saved or consumed, at a single rate. * * *

We are finally moving toward the fiscal discipline of a balanced budget. * * * The tax base would, however, be very considerably narrower under the USA Tax because of the unlimited IRA deduction feature, or, under the Armey flat tax, because of the exclusion of all forms of investment income from the tax base. We will be taking one huge fiscal gamble that the sought-after greater inducements to savings will produce an increase in investment capital sufficient to yield larger or even equal revenues from a narrower tax base.

It is against this background that we should assess the relative merits of our income tax and these proposed forms of consumption tax.

The United States Income Tax

The U.S. income tax is not, of course, a "pure" income tax. Income set aside in qualified retirement plans, or under the limited IRA provisions of existing law, is not taxed to the employee until withdrawn. The investment returns on such savings also are not taxed until withdrawn. These provisions of existing law require a disciplined program for these savings—probably more complex and intrusive than necessary—but nonetheless valuable in a broad sense. For the most part, such savings cannot be withdrawn without penalty until the worker reaches retirement age. These provisions could be substantially simplified and improved. Even so, these provisions have resulted in a substantial volume of savings in the U.S.

Similarly, life insurance, also by its nature a disciplined pattern of saving, is favored; the investment earnings reflected in cash surrender value are not taxed, and the policy proceeds on death are not income. Individuals make regular premium payments every year, and there is effectively a built-in penalty for failing to continue to do so.

Owner-occupied housing, the single most important investment asset held by most Americans, is clearly favored. * * *

Our existing U.S. income tax has also been carefully crafted to serve other valuable economic goals. Employer-provided health insurance, group-term life insurance, disability insurance, and other benefits also represent, in effect, disciplined forms of savings to meet vital needs—burdens which might otherwise fall upon government.

Similarly, our existing income tax serves important social goals. The charitable contributions deduction supports an enormous range of activity that reduces the costs and burdens of government. The refundable earned income tax credit provides welfare-type benefits to low income persons who work to provide for their own needs, but for whom the economy does not provide sufficient support.

All of these other economic and social policy elements of our existing U.S. tax system could, of course, be included in a consumption tax system, but their efficacy might be drastically affected. Thus, for example, the USA Tax allows a charitable contribution deduction. But even under the USA Tax, will the same incentive to give exist in light of the unlimited IRA deduction opportunity? The wealthy can avoid tax completely by saving; the charitable contribution deduction to them loses much of its force.
    * * *

The Armey flat tax allows no mortgage interest deduction and no charitable contribution deduction. The absence of a mortgage interest deduction has an important practical result. The wealthy, who can finance their own home ownership, can still acquire a home but middle class homeowners and prospective middle class homeowners would clearly be disadvantaged.

Both the USA Tax and the Armey flat tax would substantially increase the tax burdens on the middle class. Would this increased tax burden in and of itself adversely affect home ownership?

This is all untested ground.

The Armey flat tax also would repeal the earned income tax credit. Further, nonpension fringe benefits would not be deductible in determining the business level tax and would be includible in income under the individual level tax.

What would be the effect of these Armey flat tax changes? I do not find it sufficiently reassuring to hear that the economy will grow rapidly so that interest rates will fall enough to more than compensate for denying the home mortgage interest deduction. * * * Or to hear that people will give as much to charity without a deduction; major givers, induced by such tax saving opportunities as charitable remainder trusts, are very important to the support of many major charities. Even smaller givers take the tax deduction into account in making charitable contributions. Will employers still provide health, life, and disability insurance with no deduction for such costs? Can we really be sure that wage levels will rise sufficiently that the low income working poor will not need the help that the earned income tax credit presently provides?

* * *

The Advantage Of A Consumption Tax

The consumption tax advantage, to the extent one exists, rests on the proposition that our existing income tax system discourages savings, at least without regard to the retirement income provisions. There has been a substantial decline in U.S. household savings over the past forty years, and this has been correlated to some degree to declining U.S. business investment in real terms in plant and equipment. * * * [I]t is arguable that the decline in savings in the U.S. is caused in some substantial part by the burden of our income tax system on savings.

* * *

A consumption tax, on the other hand, while still reducing the amount available for consumption either today or in the future, eliminates this bias against current saving. Under a consumption tax, either the income saved is not taxed when saved, until it is later consumed, as in the USA Tax, or the returns on the savings are not taxed, as in the Armey flat tax. The result under either type of consumption tax is exactly the same—the present value of the future fund accumulated by saving for later consumption will be exactly the same as the income available for consumption immediately. That being so, there is no bias against saving, as there is in an income tax. As a result, the amount saved, which is available for future consumption, is substantially higher than it would be under an income tax system.

This analysis, however, overlooks an important consideration. Since the income tax is imposed on a broader base, in a perfect world the income tax would be imposed at lower rates to produce the same level of revenue for the government. But tax rates under our income tax system have not been low in modern memory, except for the brief period when the 1986 Act rates remained in effect. * * * [T]he rates under either the USA Tax or the Armey flat tax would very likely be increased after an initial period of euphoria.

* * *

Comparative Advantage

Against this background, we may evaluate the relative merit of an income tax structure versus a consumption tax structure. For this purpose, we apply the four customary criteria—economic efficiency, equity or fairness, simplicity, and administrability.

Economic Efficiency. In a theoretical world, the greatest advantage of a consumption tax is that it will increase savings as compared to an income tax. In the real world in which we live, however, this advantage is greatly moderated by the provisions of the U.S. tax system as to qualified retirement plans, limited IRAs, life insurance, home ownership, and income exclusions and deferrals (fringe benefits, gain on sale of a residence, and others).

A true flat rate tax would have the advantage of eliminating some bracket arbitrage—both between or among years by timing the recognition of income and deductions, and between or among taxpayers. * * * But the USA Tax has progressive rates, and in any event, tax lawyers like us will still find ways under a consumption tax to defer income and accelerate deductions.

Both of the proposed forms of consumption tax would largely eliminate the double taxation of corporate earnings, though by different means. The Armey flat tax simply exempts dividends from the individual tax base. The USA Tax would allow a shareholder to defer the tax on dividends until such income is consumed pursuant to the unlimited IRA deduction.

My greatest concern in this area is that both the USA Tax and the Armey flat tax tend to remove any incentive for employer-sponsored qualified retirement plans and the comparative advantage of permanent plan life insurance versus other forms of savings. While I believe generally in a free market, my enthusiasm for free markets is tempered by some degree of paternalism, at least to the extent of providing a tax incentive for these disciplined forms of saving. * * *

Without employer retirement plans, it is far from clear whether individual workers will maintain the same disciplined pattern of savings throughout their working years. There would be no constraints on using savings for consumption at any time prior to retirement except good judgment, which is not always uniformly exercised in making consumption versus savings decisions. Similarly, by eliminating the comparative advantage of life insurance, largely a form of retirement saving, we would eliminate or reduce the attraction of that form of disciplined saving. In all, we would be embarking upon a wholly untried experiment in free market economics. By abandoning the comparative advantages of these incentives, savings could actually decrease.

Equity. Equity or fairness, like beauty, is largely in the eyes of the beholder. Even so, most Americans instinctively consider it fairer to tax all income, including interest, dividends, and capital gains. * * * Most Americans also feel, despite the political rhetoric being now spewed out, that it is fairer to tax persons with higher incomes at somewhat higher rates pursuant to the ability to pay rationale of our existing system.

In any event, consumption taxes tend to be regressive, as compared to income taxes. Higher income individuals spend a smaller percentage of their income on consumption. Higher income individuals have a higher percentage of their income from savings. To achieve the same distribution of burden by income class, the rate structure of a consumption tax must be more progressive than that of an income tax.

The Armey flat tax attempts to address this concern by a generous personal allowance—$21,400 for a married couple filing jointly, for example —and by a generous personal allowance—$5,000 per dependent. Even so, burden tables recently released by Treasury show disturbing effects by income class of the combined Armey business level and individual level flat taxes. Whether the 17 percent proposed flat tax rate for the business tax and for the individual tax is used, or the 20.8 percent flat tax rate Treasury says is necessary to achieve revenue neutrality, which is a must, the Treasury numbers show an extraordinary pattern of increases in tax burden compared to present law except for high income taxpayers. Persons with incomes over $200,000 would enjoy a significant decrease in tax burden. The heaviest increases in tax burden fall squarely on the middle class.

The USA Tax also addresses the regressivity concern by a substantial standard deduction-type family living allowance and personal exemptions. For a family of four, these would provide a threshold for taxation of $17,600. Unfortunately, however, the lowest nominal rate is 19 percent, rising fairly quickly to 27 percent, and then again fairly quickly to 40 percent. These rates are effectively reduced by the credit for the employee share of payroll taxes—7.65 percent—but even so the net tax rates are very substantial in the middle income range. A family of four will pay an effective rate of 32.35 percent on wage and salary income over $41,600. This 32.35 percent USA Tax tax rate is considerably higher than the 28 percent marginal rate on such income under present law. Just as in the case of the Armey flat tax, middle income families who need their income for basic consumption will pay substantially higher taxes under the USA Tax.

The Armey flat tax has been severely criticized on the ground that middle class working families save mostly by buying a home and then use much of their excess savings to assist their children in obtaining a college education. These investments in "human capital" are ignored under the Armey flat tax. The USA Tax addresses them by its home mortgage interest deduction and a token deduction for higher education expenses up to $2,000 per child per year, with a maximum of $8,000 for all children. God help the Irish and those large families like mine in the younger generation!

Finally, there is also a fundamental fairness issue in changing from an income tax-based system to a consumption tax-based system. Existing U.S. taxpayers have a massive investment in tax-paid savings even apart from qualified retirement plan savings, life insurance savings, and owner-occupied housing. There is a severe degree of unfairness in moving to a system that taxes these savings again in later life when they are consumed.

The USA Tax attempts to address this issue with exceedingly complex transition rules. Unfortunately, in their present form, they would not work and could result in manipulation by the wealthy to their advantage. Al Warren and Marty Ginsburg have demonstrated this all too well in recent papers they have written.[m] The Armey flat tax so far makes no effort to address this problem. It is far from clear that any workable solution can be devised to resolve this transitional unfairness.

Simplicity. The existing U.S. income tax system is inordinately complex for business taxpayers and for individual taxpayers with special circumstances. * * * For the average middle income U.S. taxpayer whose principal source of income is wages or salaries, however, the existing U.S. system is not complicated and in most respects has not fundamentally changed in the last fifty years. * * *

Although the theoretical model of a consumption tax might be simpler in some respects than an income tax, this does not mean, however, that any consumption tax actually enacted will necessarily be simpler than our current income tax system. While any income tax system presents some problems of income measurement, perhaps a greater source of the complexity of the current system is the large body of rules providing preferential treatment for certain types of income or transactions. The same political considerations that prompted Congress to adopt these rules under the income tax may lead to the adoption of similar rules under a consumption tax regime. Therefore, any consumption tax that emerges from the political process may be no simpler than the current income tax system.

In addition, knowing the abilities of this group, I am sure we will have the same arguments as to the definition of consumption, and the timing of consumption that we presently have as to the definition and timing of income.

In my view, the goal of simplification could be achieved through reform of the income tax system without replacing the current system with a consumption tax. In short, the choice between an income and consumption tax should probably be made on the basis of fairness or efficiency rather than simplicity.

Administrability. Administrability depends upon the relative underlying complexity of the system as enacted by, and frequently changed by, Congress. There is no basis for claiming that either the USA Tax or the Flat Tax—as they are likely to be enacted by Congress to serve various interstitial economic and social objectives—will be any simpler to administer than the existing U.S. income tax system.

In several respects, a consumption tax would be more difficult to administer. Withholding the appropriate amount from wages would be more challenging, because the taxpayer's ultimate tax liability would depend on whether the taxpayer uses the wages for consumption or investment. Increased information reporting might be required for transactions involving

---

m. Mr. Nolan is probably referring to Alvin C. Warren, Jr., *The Proposal for an "Unlimited Savings Allowance*, 68 TAX NOTES 1103 (1995), and Martin D. Ginsburg, *Life Under a Personal Consumption Tax: Some Thoughts on Working, Saving, and Consuming in Nunn-Domenici's Tax World*, 48 NAT'L TAX J. 585 (1995). (Eds.)

loans and investment assets, because the taxability of these amounts would depend on the use of the proceeds. It might even become necessary to withhold on the proceeds of these transactions, if not reinvested.

    * * *

We know what we have. It works reasonably well. We should not embark on such a massive experiment without much more assurance that it will be economically more efficient, and at least as fair, simple, and administrable as the present system.

Notes and Questions

Simplification

67. An issue of importance is whether, and to what extent, adoption of a consumption-type proposal would simplify tax law and administration. As we have seen, beginning with Professor Andrews' vision in subchapter B of taxing on "a simple cash flow basis," proponents of consumption-type tax proposals speak of simplification as a major advantage. Even many opponents of consumption-type taxation, such as the drafters of Treasury I (excerpted in subchapter C), concede that, once fully implemented, "a tax on personal consumption is simpler in many respects than an income tax."

Hall & Rabushka make perhaps the most expansive claims of simplification, asserting that every taxpayer, including General Motors, could file a postcard-sized return. Do you think this is possible?

68. Is the primary problem in achieving considerable improvements in simplicity that even an ideal system would have to be fairly complicated? For example, are you confident in the assertions of Hall & Rabushka that their system is "airtight," and that their business tax returns could be postcard-sized because "[e]very line on the form is a well-defined number obtained directly from the business's accounting records"? Or is Mr. Nolan correct that "we will have the same arguments as to the definition of consumption, and the timing of consumption that we presently have as to the definition and timing of income"?

69. Examination of the full presentation of Hall & Rabushka reveals some complications that are not apparent in the excerpted portions of their book. For example, they advise that "[b]usiness meals in restaurants would be fully deductible."[n] We have learned from decades of experience with the income tax law that "business meal" is not a self-defining term. The same complex statutory and regulatory provisions drawing the line between business and personal meals would be necessary under the consumption-type tax.

---

n. ROBERT E. HALL & ALVIN RABUSHKA, THE FLAT TAX 106 (2d ed. 1995).

Similarly, simplicity is missing in the advice Hall & Rabushka give to a travelling saleswoman:

> All self-employed individuals will file Form 2, the business tax form, where they can deduct travel and other business expenses.
>
> To take advantage of the personal allowance, you will want to pay yourself a salary of at least $16,500 if you are married. Report this amount along with your husband's earnings on Form 1, the individual wage tax. In this way you will be able to deduct your legitimate business expenses and receive the personal allowance.
>
> You will need to keep records to document your income and expenses.[o]

The proposed tax treatment entails the artificiality—generally limited to closely held C corporations under present law—of this saleswoman paying herself a salary. She is advised that she can deduct her "legitimate" expenses—but much complexity is entailed in establishing which expenses of a traveling saleswoman are deemed "legitimate," even if there were no concern about fraud. And, of course, Hall & Rabushka recognize the danger of fraud—and thus advise the taxpayer that she is to keep complete records, even though they would not have her reveal the details of those records in her postcard tax return.

Indeed, many of the most difficult questions of current law involve distinguishing business expenses from consumption. In addition to meals and travelling expenses, this issue is raised by expenditures for entertainment, gifts, uniforms, "hobby farms," personal computers, automobile expense, education, "home offices," and club memberships, among others. The complexity of classifying these expenditures would remain. As Professor Andrews observed, "ordinary, current deductions, business and personal, would be essentially unaffected by the shift to a pure consumption-type tax."

70. It is always simpler to describe an idea in generalities than to work out all the concrete details. Dr. Penner argues that the proposals of Armey/Hall & Rabushka and others "have not been worked out in the same excruciating detail as has Nunn-Domenici. That gives them the appearance of being much simpler." The same observation could be made of academic discussion of consumption taxation.

71. Another aspect of the simplification problem is that no proposal—even one worked out in "excruciating detail"—will be enacted intact. It is almost inconceivable that sweeping tax changes of the type discussed in this chapter could be adopted without complications reflecting the input of many affected taxpayers, the political and policy judgments of

---

o. *Id.* at 116-17.

many members of Congress and the Administration, and the conflicting views of many experts. Mr. Nolan and others caution against comparing the present income tax law to an idealized consumption-type proposal.

The income tax could also be made much simpler if a professor were allowed to put together a single, coherent revision. As one example, both the Hall & Rabushka and USA proposals would end the double-tax discrimination against doing business in the corporate form. This discrimination is not inherent to an income tax, however; many proposals have been advanced that would address the problem by revision of the income tax. See Chapter Fourteen.

72. The important issue of simplicity versus complexity can be viewed from different angles. Professor Boyd Kimball Dyer reminds us of the importance of administrative costs, which are not limited to the budget of the Internal Revenue Service: "By far the greater part of administrative costs is what the private sector spends to keep records, file reports, and get answers to questions about taxes. Part of these costs is the cost of keeping transactions from incurring taxes."[p] Professor Dyer concludes that "on the criterion of transaction costs, the consumption base is best because it alone treats each taxable year as sufficient to itself. There is no need for depreciation, keeping track of basis, adjustments for inflation or other concepts that tie one year to another."[q]

Mr. Nolan argues that present law "is inordinately complex for business taxpayers and for individual taxpayers with special circumstances," but is "not complicated" for most middle-income taxpayers. Is that a sufficient goal for simplicity, even if the Internal Revenue Code remains difficult to comprehend?

73. Professor Clifton Fleming devoted a 1995 article to evaluating leading consumption-type proposals in terms of simplicity, coming to the conclusion that "the devil is in the details."[r] He concluded his article with the following paragraphs, which draw an ominous parallel to the adoption of the income tax in 1913:

> A persistent theme of this article has been that the political process is quite likely to deliver a much more complicated consumption tax package than initially seems possible when one reads textbook descriptions of the VAT and the consumed income tax. Consumption tax advocates will probably view this as unduly pessimistic, and they may be correct. However, it is useful to

---

p. Boyd Kimball Dyer, *The Relative Fairness of the Consumption and Accretion Tax Bases*, 1978 UTAH L. REV. 457, 483.

q. *Id.*

r. J. Clifton Fleming, Jr., *Scoping Out the Uncertain Simplification (Complexification?) Effects of VATs, BATs and Consumed Income Taxes*, 2 FLA. TAX REV. 390, 441 (1995).

recall that in 1913, when America stood optimistically poised to adopt a new tax system, the House Ways and Means Committee said:

> In view of the many valuable Governmental purposes to be subserved, those citizens required to do so can well afford to devote a brief time during some one day in each year to the making out of a personal return of income for purposes of taxation. This is done without complaint under the operation of all the general property tax laws of the States. All good citizens, it is therefore believed, will willingly and cheerfully support and sustain this, the fairest and cheapest of all taxes, in order to secure to the largest extent equality of tax burdens, an adjustable system of revenue, and in all respects a modernized fiscal system.[271]

These confident predictions of compliance burdens that would involve no more than a brief period of time on a single day and of warm public support for the income tax now seem laughable. The 1913 income tax proponents, being merely human, could not begin to foresee the complexities that would emerge over time from a system that appeared so promising at the outset. Likewise, unimagined and extensive complications may be lurking in the VAT and the consumed income tax, particularly in the latter, that will make this article's complexity speculations seem naively understated. As our experience with the income tax shows, U.S. tax systems have a way of coming to reflect thoroughly the intricacy of our society and its economy.[s]

Transition problems

74. As we have seen, there are many arguments for and against the adoption of a consumption-type tax. If we concluded that the consumption-type system were superior, we then would face the difficult question of how to get there from here.

The preceding notes have considered the issue of simplification assuming a consumption-type tax had been fully implemented. But there are many transition issues to be considered in a change so massive as moving from present law to a consumption-type system. Even if a consumption-type system might be simpler than present law once in operation, the transition problems are of daunting complexity.[t] Dr. Penner noted that the drafters of

---

271. H.R. Rep. No. 5, 63d Cong., 1st Sess. (1913), reprinted in 1939-1 C.B. (Part 2) 1, 3.

s. Fleming, *supra* note r, at 442-43.

t. In this connection, recall Professor McCaffery's observation in subchapter D that while economists agree we would ultimately be better off under a consumption tax, we would suffer a detriment "for a while"—which various economists estimated could last from four or five years

Nunn-Domenici/USA had spent more time on transition issues than on any others.

75. Perhaps the most important transition issue affecting individuals is the treatment of previously-taxed assets. Consider the simple case of a taxpayer, Alex Bell, purchasing 100 shares of AT&T for $5,000, then selling in a future year for $6,000 (and using the sales proceeds for consumption).

The rules of present law or of any of the consumption-type proposals applied separately are straightforward, and give internally consistent results. Present law would give Alex no deduction and a $5,000 basis at purchase; at sale, he would have $1,000 income. The USA proposal would give Alex a $5,000 deduction and no basis at the time of purchase; when Alex sold, the USA system would tax the entire $6,000.

But suppose Alex purchased under present law—and thus got no deduction for the purchase price—and sold after adoption of the USA system—which, absent some sort of transition rule, would require tax on the entire $6,000 received. This would result in an unfair double tax—a extra tax from changing the tax system that neither system alone would have imposed.

76. The most obvious transition rule would allow taxpayers to keep their basis in assets purchased pre-transition. On post-transition sale of such assets, taxpayers would not be taxed on the entire sales proceeds, but only to the extent the sales proceeds exceeded basis. What is the problem with this approach, according to Dr. Penner?

77. Dr. Penner explains that Nunn-Domenici allows people of modest wealth ($50,000 or less) to deduct their basis in pre-transition assets over a short period, perhaps three years. Having been allowed to deduct their basis, they then would have a zero basis, and have effectively (and fairly) been converted to the new system.

78. For those with more assets, however, the revenue costs to the government of allowing an automatic write-off were deemed too great. So these taxpayers will keep their basis in pre-transition assets.

Without more, this would give the wealthy a great incentive to "churn" their assets. A wealthy taxpayer could sell old assets (with income recognized only to the extent that amount realized exceeded basis), and purchase new assets (with a full deduction under the new USA system). This would cost the government enormous revenue in the early post-transition years.

to 100 years.

Thus, Dr. Penner explained, the USA solution was to allow use of old basis, but not to taxpayers making new investments in the same year; the basis could be used "only to finance consumption in excess of income."

79. Unfortunately, the Nunn-Domenici/USA solution to the pre-transition basis problem may provide the wrong incentive. The proponents of consumption-type taxes want to give incentives to invest, but the most favorable tax treatment for wealthy owners of pre-transition property would go to taxpayers who liquidated investments in order to engage in large-scale consumption.

Another problem is that the system could be manipulated, according to Professor Martin Ginsburg: "[E]veryone decently wealthy will be a net saver in some (perhaps odd-numbered) years and a net dissaver in other years."[u] The reason for this, Professor Ginsburg explained, is that if the wealthy taxpayers show net savings in every year, they can never recoup their pre-transition basis. But by arranging their affairs to show net dissavings in some years, they will be allowed to deduct their pre-transition basis.

80. The drafters (primarily Deputy Assistant Secretary David Bradford) of *Blueprints for Basic Tax Reform*, an influential 1977 Treasury study, discussed various solutions to the transition problem should a consumption-type tax be adopted. Their recommended approach would have required, among other things, that some taxpayers compute their taxes both ways—under the income tax and the new consumption-type tax—for a 10-year period, paying the higher liability each year.[v] For these taxpayers, the promised simplicity of consumption-type taxation would be absent for at least 10 years.

81. The complexity involved in providing comprehensive transition relief to owners of pre-transition property led Professor Michael Graetz to propose very limited transitional relief for elderly taxpayers who would be promptly using pre-transition assets during retirement.[w] As is frequently the case, there seems to be a trade-off between simplicity and fairness.

82. Although less obviously, the same transition issues are presented by substituting any form of consumption tax, including a VAT, for the present income tax. Dr. Penner observed that "proponents of value added taxation generally manage to ignore" transition problems.

---

u. Ginsburg, *supra* note m, at 588.

v. U.S. DEP'T OF THE TREASURY, BLUEPRINTS FOR BASIC TAX REFORM 209-11 (1977).

w. Michael J. Graetz, *Implementing a Progressive Consumption Tax*, 92 HARV. L. REV. 1575, 1653-58 (1979).

Limiting the tax base to consumption

83. The proposals of both Hall & Rabushka and Alliance USA are designed to tax consumption, and thus to avoid the "double tax on savings." Alliance USA follows the route suggested by Professor Andrews in subchapter B—individuals are allowed a deduction for savings in "savings assets," and are taxed on sales proceeds of savings assets (unless the proceeds are reinvested). Interest, dividends and other returns on investment are included in the tax base. The USA approach is comparable to a fully-deductible IRA with no penalty for early withdrawal—making the IRA-like investment gives rise to a deduction, and withdrawals are taxed.

Hall & Rabushka, on the other hand, allow no deduction for investments by individuals not engaged in business, but do not tax their investment returns. The individual tax base is limited to compensation—cash wages, salaries, and pensions (when received).

Both Nolan and Penner describe these forms of taxation as economically equivalent. The form, however, is radically different. Dr. Penner states that, generally, the Armey/Hall & Rabushka proposal taxes income when earned, while the Nunn-Domenici/USA proposal taxes it when it is spent.

84. The economic equivalence of the two proposals is in terms of present value. This can be demonstrated by the two systems' methods of taxing capital gain. Assume that a taxpayer purchases a stock for $100 in Year One, and sells the stock in Year Two for $110 (and uses the sales proceeds for consumption). Assume also that this 10 percent annual appreciation exactly equals the prevailing rate of return in financial markets.

Hall & Rabushka use a very simple approach. They allow no deduction for the purchase; they levy no tax upon sale. Individuals are not taxed on income from property under the Hall & Rabushka system.

Under the USA approach, the taxpayer would be allowed a deduction of $100 in Year One, and would be taxed on the entire $110 sales proceeds in Year Two. Observe that when we apply a 10 percent discount rate, 110 Year Two dollars have a present value equal to 100 Year One dollars. Assuming a constant tax rate—say 20 percent—the $22 tax in Year Two dollars would have a discounted value equal to the $20 tax saving in Year One dollars.

Thus, in this example, the two tax systems would levy a tax that is equal in terms of present value. The USA system taxes an extra $10, but this is offset by the fact that it delays for one year taxing $100.

85. The equivalence would also be present if, in the preceding example, we substituted income produced by the property for income resulting from appreciation in value. Suppose the taxpayer purchased a $100 one-year bond in Year One, which paid the prevailing market rate of 10 percent. One year later, the taxpayer received $10 interest plus $100 principal, all of which was spent on consumption.

Hall & Rabushka would grant no deduction, and levy no tax.

USA would grant a $100 deduction in Year One, resulting in a $20 tax saving (assuming a 20 percent tax rate). In Year Two, USA would tax $110—the interest plus the "dissaving" of using the bond redemption proceeds for consumption. Discounted at 10 percent, the resulting tax, $22, would be equal in present value to the $20 of tax savings one year earlier.

86. In the preceding two notes, it may initially appear that the taxpayer avoids any tax at all, in present value terms, despite ultimately consuming $110. When and how is the tax paid under the USA tax? Under the Hall & Rabushka proposal? (Hint: Assume the taxpayer earned $50,000 in Year One, but consumed only $49,900, and invested the remaining $100.)

87. Hall & Rabushka claim major simplicity advantages for their approach. What is the basis for their claim?

88. Do you agree that the two approaches are in fact economically equivalent? Equivalence may depend upon whether we evaluate from a macroeconomic point of view, or from the vantage point of individual taxpayers. Compare two taxpayers, Gladstone Gander and Donald Duck, each of whom earns the same amount, and each of whom, on the same day, invests $10,000 to purchase common stock. At the time of purchase, the equivalence of market value of the two stocks means that the future expected (by the market) returns of both investments, discounted to present value, equals $10,000. The two investments do not in fact provide the same returns, of course. Gladstone is more skilled, or luckier, in his stock selection. Gladstone's stock, the next Wal-Mart, earns ongoing returns greatly in excess of the expected return, and Gladstone uses these handsome dividends, and ultimately a large capital gain, to increase his standard of living. The company in which Donald invests goes bankrupt; Donald loses the principal amount of his investment, and gets no return whatever.

How would first, Hall & Rabushka, and second, USA, treat these two taxpayers? Which approach is more appropriate? (Assume that from all investors taken as a group the government gets the same overall revenue, discounted to present value, from either approach.)

Capital gains and owner-occupied housing

89. Hall & Rabushka would not tax capital gain, on the theory that doing so constitutes double taxation. They give the example of a taxpayer who purchases stock, the value of which equals "the capitalization of its future earnings." An increase in value merely reflects an increase in anticipated future earnings—hence, taxing both the earnings (dividends, in this case) and the capital gain would result in double taxation. Is this explanation satisfactory in the case of the stock purchase? Is it equally

satisfactory in the case of non-income-producing assets (for example, works of art, precious metals, and jewels). (The important category of owner-occupied housing is discussed below.)

90. The USA proposal indirectly taxes capital gain on "savings assets"—such as stock—by allowing a deduction in the year of purchase, then taxing the entire selling price in the year of sale (unless the sales proceeds are reinvested).

But if a taxpayer invests in a painting by Picasso, expecting it to appreciate in value, the USA proposal would not allow a deduction. Why not? Upon sale of such a "nonfinancial asset," gain would be computed as under present law—amount realized less basis. Is this approach preferable to that of Hall & Rabushka?

91. Consistent with its approach on taxing the gain on sale of the Picasso painting, the USA tax would continue present law by taxing capital gain on owner-occupied housing (assuming the proceeds were not reinvested, either in a replacement residence or in "savings assets").

Hall & Rabushka would not tax an owner-occupier's gain. What is the justification offered by Hall & Rabushka for not taxing the gain on owner-occupied housing?

Which approach do you find more justifiable?

Progressivity and vertical equity

92. A major concern about any form of consumption tax is that it will be perceived as (or in fact will be) unfair to lower-income taxpayers, by comparison to our present income tax. This perceived (or real) unfairness tends to occur because lower-income people spend a larger portion of their income on consumption. How does Nunn-Domenici/USA address these concerns? Is Dr. Penner convinced that the plan achieves vertical equity?

93. The USA proposal envisions a progressive rate structure, and the system is made more progressive by its treatment of Social Security taxes. Employers are granted a full credit for Social Security taxes, and employees a credit that is phased out as income rises. In effect, Social Security taxes are folded into the proposed USA tax, except for high-income employees. Merely ending Social Security taxes would increase progressivity, because Social Security taxes, disregarding benefits, are somewhat regressive. (Looking at Social Security taxes in isolation takes a narrow view; the Social Security *system* of income and benefits combined is markedly progressive.) USA goes even further, by maintaining the tax only for high-income employees.

A simpler approach might have been simply to eliminate the separate Social Security taxes altogether, and address the desired degree of progressivity in the primary tax. Why, according to Dr. Penner, was this approach not taken?

94. Hall & Rabushka acknowledge that a VAT would tax consumption more simply than their proposal, but they term a VAT "unfair because it is not progressive." Assuming progressivity to be necessary to a fair tax (an issue considered at length in Chapter Four), how do Hall & Rabushka address equity concerns while employing a flat rate tax?

Effect on businesses
95. The general approach of both Armey/Hall & Rabushka and Nunn-Domenici/USA is that a business can claim a deduction for purchases from other businesses, on the assumption that the other business will be paying the business-level tax. (Under both systems, the business tax is not limited to corporations, as it is under present law.)

The two proposals take differing approaches with respect to payments of wages and salaries, with Hall & Rabushka, but not USA, allowing a deduction. (USA would allow a deduction for the services of an outside accounting firm, for example, but not for the services of an employee accountant.) What is the theory of each approach?

96. Perhaps the most striking change in business taxation is that neither proposal would allow a deduction for interest, even if paid to another business. Interest and dividends would be treated identically.

97. Consider first the Hall & Rabushka proposal with respect to interest. What is the justification for reversing present law, which generally allows a deduction for interest paid and taxes the recipient, and moving to a no-deduction/no-inclusion model? Business interest, after all, is a business expense. Hall & Rabushka recognize that they may be taxing businesses that are not profitable, but argue that their "business tax is not a profit tax." Would businesses that borrow be hurt? How would Hall & Rabushka deal with existing debt?

98. The USA proposal does not allow the business any deduction for interest (or dividends) paid. Businesses that receive interest need not take it into income, but individual recipients of interest are taxed. What is the justification for denying an interest deduction to a business debtor if the individual creditor is taxed?

99. Dr. Penner points out that the USA business tax is designed to be border adjusted, but that under current GATT rules, the Armey/Hall & Rabushka business tax could not be border adjusted because it allows deduction of wages. As Dr. Penner notes, the economic importance of border

adjustment is debatable, but it is desired by American business. The issues involved in border adjustment are the same under a consumption-type tax as under a European-style VAT, and are discussed extensively in Chapter Six. See Chapter Six, Notes #16-24.

Effect on saving and borrowing

100. A major objective of all consumption-type tax proposals is to stimulate saving and investment, by removing the "double tax on savings." Yet Mr. Nolan expresses concern that abandoning present law might actually undercut saving incentives. Why? Do you share his concern?

101. Alternatively, the problem might be a revenue shortfall attributable to too much saving, at least initially. Hall & Rabushka base their conclusion of revenue neutrality on figures from a past year (1993). Yet a major purpose of moving to a consumption tax is to encourage a change in taxpayer behavior, leading to increased saving and investment. Hall & Rabushka state that they anticipate "a burst of investment, which might temporarily depress flat-rate revenue because of the expensing of investment." They argue that the adverse effect on revenues would be temporary, because increased investment would result in economic growth and thus increased revenues.

Mr. Nolan, on the other hand, fears that under any consumption-type tax, "[w]e will be taking one huge fiscal gamble that the sought-after greater inducements to saving will produce an increase in investment capital sufficient to yield larger or even equal revenues from a narrower tax base."

Would you expect higher or lower revenues?

102. The theory of the USA tax should require borrowed funds to be taxed in the year of borrowing. Why? Why does Nunn-Domenici/USA not fully follow the theoretically correct approach? What approach is taken instead? What problems arise from the approach taken?

103. *Charitable contributions.* Hall & Rabushka would end the charitable contribution deduction, but suggest that any drop in contributions are unlikely to be significant in amount or permanent. They note that of $117 billion contributed in 1991, only $61 billion was deducted "on personal tax returns." (The size of corporate deductions, which also would be ended, is not mentioned.) Nunn-Domenici/USA allows a deduction, but Mr. Nolan questions the importance of the deduction under a tax system that would allow a potential donor the same deduction for simply calling a broker and buying stock.

Do you think adoption of a consumption-type tax would undermine charitable giving? Would that be a reason to oppose adoption of a consumption-type tax?

104. In conclusion: Should the United States adopt some form of consumption-type tax to replace the income tax? If so, what form? Why?

Selected Bibliography

See also bibliography for Chapter Six.

AARON, HENRY J. & HARVEY GALPER, ASSESSING TAX REFORM (1985).

Andrews, William D., *The ALI Reporter's Proposals on Corporate Distributions and Corporate Taxation with a Personal Consumption Tax*, 22 SAN DIEGO L. REV. 333, 342-45 (1985).

——, *Fairness and the Personal Income Tax: A Reply to Professor Warren*, 88 HARV. L. REV. 931 (1975).

——, *A Consumption-Type or Cash Flow Personal Income Tax*, 87 HARV. L. REV. 1113 (1974).

——, *Personal Deductions in an Ideal Income Tax*, 86 HARV. L. REV. 309 (1972).

ATKINSON, A.B., PUBLIC ECONOMICS IN ACTION: THE BASIC INCOME/FLAT TAX PROPOSAL (1995).

Bankman, Joseph & Thomas Griffith, *Is the Debate Between an Income Tax and a Consumption Tax a Debate About Risk? Does it Matter?*, 47 TAX L. REV. 377 (1992).

Bittker, Boris I., *Reflections on Tax Reform*, 47 U. CIN. L. REV. 185 (1978).

Boyer, Daniel J. & Susan M. Russell, *Is It Time for a Consumption Tax?*, 48 NAT'L TAX J. 363 (1995).

BRADFORD, DAVID F., UNTANGLING THE INCOME TAX (1986).

Davies, John H., *Income-Plus-Wealth: In Search of a Better Tax Base*, 15 RUTGERS L.J. 849 (1984).

Doernberg, Richard L., *A Workable Flat Rate Consumption Tax*, 70 IOWA L. REV. 425 (1985).

Domenici, Pete V., *The UnAmerican Spirit of the Federal Income Tax*, 31 HARV. J. ON LEGIS. 273 (1994).

Dyer, Boyd Kimball, *The Relative Fairness of the Consumption and Accretion Tax Bases*, 1978 UTAH L. REV. 457.

Feld, Alan L., *Living with the Flat Tax*, 48 NAT'L TAX J. 603 (1995).

——, *Nunn-Domenici and Nonprofits*, 68 TAX NOTES 1119 (1995).

FISHER, IRVING, NATURE OF CAPITAL AND INCOME (1906).

Fleming, J. Clifton, Jr., *Scoping Out the Uncertain Simplification (Complexification?) Effects of VATs, BATs and Consumed Income Taxes*, 2 FLA. TAX REV. 390 (1995).

Fried, Barbara H., *Fairness and the Consumption Tax*, 44 STAN. L. REV. 961 (1992).

Gale, William G., *Building a Better Tax System: Can a Consumption Tax Deliver the Goods?*, 69 TAX NOTES 781 (1995).

Ginsburg, Martin D., *Life Under a Personal Consumption Tax: Some Thoughts on Working, Saving, and Consuming in Nunn-Domenici's Tax World*, 48 NAT'L TAX J. 585 (1995).

Graetz, Michael J., *Implementing a Progressive Consumption Tax*, 92 HARV. L. REV. 1575 (1979).

Grubert, Harry & T. Scott Newton, *The International Implications of Consumption Tax Proposals*, 48 NAT'L TAX J. 619 (1995).

Gunn, Alan, *The Income Tax, the Consumption Tax and the Deductibility of Interest on Personal Debt, in* THE QUEST FOR TAX REFORM (W. Neil Brooks ed., 1988).

——, *The Case for an Income Tax*, 46 U. CHI. L. REV. 370 (1979).

Hall, Arthur P., *Compliance Costs of Alternative Tax Systems*, 71 TAX NOTES 1081 (1996).

HALL, ROBERT E. & ALVIN RABUSHKA, THE FLAT TAX (2d ed. 1995).

Halperin, Daniel, *Valuing Personal Consumption: Cost Versus Value and the Impact of Insurance*, 1 FLA. TAX REV. 1 (1992).

Jones, Carolyn, *Treatment of Gratuitous Transfers: Unraveling the Case for a Consumption Tax*, 29 ST. LOUIS L.J. 1155 (1985).

Joseph, Richard J., *The "Consumption" and "Flat" Taxes Revisited*, 69 TAX NOTES 211 (1995).

KALDOR, NICHOLAS, AN EXPENDITURE TAX (1955).

Kaplow, Louis, *Recovery of Pre-Enactment Basis Under a Consumption Tax: The USA Tax System*, 68 TAX NOTES 1109 (1995).

——, *Human Capital Under an Ideal Income Tax*, 80 VA. L. REV. 1477 (1994).

—— & Alvin C. Warren, Jr., *Professor Strnad's Rejoinder: Simply Semantics*, 39 STAN. L. REV. 419 (1987).

—— & ——, *An Income Tax by any Other Name—A Reply to Professor Strnad,* 38 STAN. L. REV. 399 (1986).

Kelman, *Time Preference and Tax Equity*, 35 STAN. L. REV. 649 (1983).

——, *Personal Deductions Revisited: Why They Fit Poorly in an "Ideal" Income Tax and Why They Fit Worse in a Far from Ideal World*, 31 STAN. L. REV. 831 (1979).

Knoll, Michael S., *Designing a Hybrid Income-Consumption Tax*, 41 UCLA L. REV. 1791 (1994).

McCaffery, Edward J., *The Uneasy Case for Wealth Transfer Taxation*, 104 YALE L.J. 283 (1994).

——, *The Political Liberal Case Against the Estate Tax*, 23 PHIL. & PUB. AFF. 281 (1994).

——, *Tax Policy Under a Hybrid Income-Consumption Tax*, 70 TEX. L. REV. 1145 (1992).

McGee, M. Kevin, *Alternative Transitions to a Consumption Tax*, 42 NAT'L TAX J. 155 (1989).

McLure, Charles E., Jr., *Substituting Consumption-Based Direct Taxation for Income Taxes as the International Norm*, 45 NAT'L TAX J. 145 (1992).

Merrill, Peter, et al., *Corporate Tax Liability Under the USA and Flat Taxes*, 68 TAX NOTES 741 (1995).

Mieszkowski, Peter, *The Advisability and Feasibility of an Expenditure Tax System, in* THE ECONOMICS OF TAXATION (Henry J. Aaron & Michael J. Boskin eds., 1980).

Moroney, John R. & Lorence L. Bravenec, *Consumption Taxes & Savings Rates: Evidence From Six OECD Countries*, 71 TAX NOTES 235 (1996).

Nolan, John S., *The Merit of an Income Tax Versus a Consumption Tax*, 12 AM. J. TAX POL'Y 207 (1995).

O'Kelley, Charles R., *Rawls, Justice, and the Income Tax*, 16 GA. L. REV. 1 (1981).

PECHMAN, JOSEPH A. (ED.), WHAT SHOULD BE TAXED: INCOME OR EXPENDITURE? (1980).

Penner, Rudolph G., *Is a Radical Tax Reform in our Future?*, NAT'L TAX ASS'N F., No. 21, at 1 (Spring, 1995).

Popkin, William D., *Tax Ideals in the Real World: A Comment on Professor Strnad's Approach to Tax Fairness*, 62 IND. L.J. 63 (1986).

Sabelhaus, John, *What is the Distributional Burden of Taxing Consumption?*, 46 NAT'L TAX J. 331(1993).

Sarkar, Shounak & George R. Zodrow, *Transitional Issues in Moving to a Direct Consumption Tax*, 46 NAT'L TAX J. 359 (1993).

Shachar, Avishai, *From Income to Consumption Tax: Criteria for Rules of Transition*, 97 HARV. L. REV. 1581 (1984).

Sheppard, Lee A., *The Consumption Tax: Borrowing as a Tax Shelter*, 68 TAX NOTES 138 (1995).

——, *The Consumption Tax: Generational Equity*, 68 TAX NOTES 383 (1995).

Steuerle, Gene, *Tax Reform and Private Pensions*, 70 TAX NOTES 1831 (1996).

Strnad, Jeff, *Periodicity and Accretion Taxation: Norms and Implementation*, 99 YALE L.J. 1817 (1990).

——, *Taxation of Income from Capital: A Theoretical Reappraisal*, 37 STAN. L. REV. 1023 (1985).

——, *The Bankruptcy of Conventional Tax Timing Wisdom is Deeper than Semantics: A Rejoinder to Professors Kaplow and Warren*, 39 STAN. L. REV. 389 (1987).

——, *Tax Timing and the Haig-Simons Ideal: A Rejoinder to Professor Popkin*, 62 IND. L.J. 73 (1986).

SULLIVAN, MARTIN A., AMERICAN INSTITUTE OF CERTIFIED PUBLIC ACCOUNTANTS, FLAT TAXES AND CONSUMPTION TAXES: A GUIDE TO THE DEBATE (1995).

UNEASY COMPROMISE: PROBLEMS OF A HYBRID INCOME-CONSUMPTION TAX (Henry J. Aaron et al. eds., 1988).

U.S. DEP'T OF THE TREASURY, 1 TAX REFORM FOR FAIRNESS, SIMPLICITY, AND ECONOMIC GROWTH ["Treasury I"] 30-33, 191-212 (1984).

——, BLUEPRINTS FOR BASIC TAX REFORM (1977).

VICKREY, WILLIAM, AGENDA FOR PROGRESSIVE TAXATION 329-66 (1947).

Warren, Alvin C., Jr., *The Proposal for an "Unlimited Savings Allowance*, 68 TAX NOTES 1103 (1995).

——, *Would a Consumption Tax Be Fairer Than an Income Tax?*, 89 YALE L.J. 1081 (1980).

——, *Fairness and a Consumption-Type or Cash Flow Personal Income Tax*, 88 HARV. L. REV. 931 (1975).

Wolfman, Bernard, *Consumption Tax Issues Under the Nunn-Domenici Consumption Tax*, 68 TAX NOTES 1121 (1995).

Yin, George K., *Accommodating the "Low-Income" in a Cash-Flow or Consumed Income Tax World*, 2 FLA. TAX REV. 445 (1995).

Zodrow, George R. & Charles E. McLure, Jr., *Implementing Direct Consumption Taxes in Developing Countries*, 46 TAX L. REV. 405 (1991).

PART III

DEATH AND TAXES

It is said that "nothing is certain but death and taxes," but tax professionals know that this proverb is only half true. Whatever the certainty of taxation during life, Congress seems to tax wealth passing at death rather gently—excluding from taxable income the proceeds of life insurance policies, providing permanent forgiveness of income tax on unrealized appreciation through stepped-up basis, and imposing estate taxes on the estates of only about one percent of decedents.

Chapter Eight evaluates the tax treatment of the owners and beneficiaries of life insurance policies. The propriety of the rules that deny a deduction for premiums and that exclude proceeds payable at death are considered. The primary focus of the chapter is the proper treatment of "inside buildup"—earnings credited on the cash value of permanent life insurance.

Chapter Nine addresses the income tax treatment of property passing at death. Almost no one attempts to defend present law—stepped-up basis, which permanently forgives tax on unrealized appreciation—but there is no consensus on what should replace it. Several alternatives are discussed in the chapter. Carryover basis, a solution adopted in the Tax Reform Act of 1976 and retroactively repealed, would utilize the technique currently used for taxing gain on property transferred by *inter vivos* gift. Constructive realization would treat death (and perhaps the making of a gift) as a realization event, thus taxing all unrealized appreciation at the time of death (or gift). A more radical approach would tax the recipient of gifts and bequests on the full value of receipts, not merely the appreciation component.

Finally, Chapter Ten considers transfer taxes—primarily, the estate tax. The estate tax is a source of unending controversy, among academics and in Congress. Its proper role—breaking up large concentrations of wealth, serving as a "backstop" to a porous income tax, increasing the progressivity of the overall federal tax burden, or simple generation of revenue—has never been decided. Proposals considered in Chapter Ten range from outright repeal of the tax to strengthening it to provide for confiscation of most estates in excess of $250,000. Other proposals in the chapter would convert present transfer taxes, which are levied on the transferor, to taxes levied on the transferee. The final subchapter considers the imposition of a broad-based tax on wealth, a form of tax never used by the United States Government but common in Europe.

CHAPTER EIGHT

LIFE INSURANCE

Life insurance policies usually combine pure insurance and saving features. * * *

Inasmuch as most forms of investment income are taxable, the present law discriminates in favor of saving through life insurance compared with other forms of saving and financial investment. This discrimination prompts questions of equity and economic policy.[a]

A. INTRODUCTION

This chapter examines the tax treatment of the owners and beneficiaries[b] of individual[c] life insurance policies. Life insurance is designed to reduce the financial risk of death by spreading that loss among a wide number of individuals facing the same risk. The probability of death within the coming year for a healthy 34-year-old man is approximately two in one thousand (2/1000).[d] For any individual, however, death is not a partial event; it either will or will not occur within the year. Thus, if a company agreed with *one* such person to pay his family $500,000 in the event of his death during the coming year, in exchange for a payment of $1,000, the "insurer" would be engaging in a transaction best described as gambling. It would either gain $1,000 or lose $499,000, depending upon an unpredictable result. Insurance companies are not in the business of gambling. Like casinos, insurance companies rely on the "law of large numbers." This mathematical principle holds that a large number of events of given probability, each unpredictable taken alone, becomes eminently predictable as a statistical matter—if a sufficiently large number of insurance policies are issued, or roulette wheels turned. The essence of insurance is the spreading of risk

---

a. Richard Goode, *Policyholders' Interest Income From Life Insurance Under the Income Tax*, 16 VAND. L. REV. 33, 33 (1962).

b. In the main, this chapter ignores the interesting, but far more complex, treatment of life insurance companies. Life insurance companies may be divided into two groups stock and mutual. Stock companies are corporations owned by their shareholders, and policyholders are their customers. Policyholders are both the customers and the owners of mutual companies, which are regarded as corporations without shareholders. Both types of companies are generally taxed as C corporations, with a bewildering set of special rules found in Subchapter L (sections 801 et. seq.).

c. Most of what is said in this chapter is equally applicable to group life insurance. While the premiums on individual policies are not deductible, an employer can deduct premiums on group life insurance provided as a tax-free fringe benefit. Section 79.

d. Commissioners' 1980 Standard Ordinary Table of Mortality, cited in KENNETH BLACK, JR. & HAROLD D. SKIPPER, JR., LIFE INSURANCE 518 (12th ed. 1994).

among many exposed to a risk—of death at age 34, for example—so that the many who avoid the slight risk of loss pay a small amount in order to create a substantial sum for the benefit of the few who sustain the loss. The insurance company does not so much bear risk as facilitate the creation of a pool of risk bearers.

Life insurance policies are issued in thousands of variations by hundreds of companies. An understanding of the principal tax policy issues requires some understanding of two basic models—term insurance and cash-value insurance.[e]

Term life insurance is "pure" insurance comparable to fire insurance or automobile liability insurance. For example, using the figures discussed above, an insurance company might insure a healthy 34-year-old man for $500,000 for one year for a premium of $1,000 (the *mortality charge*), plus an amount to cover the company's expenses and profits (the *loading charge*). If the insured lived through the year, his $1,000 would be lost, just as his fire insurance premium would be lost if his home suffered no fire damage. He would then have the option of insuring his life, or his house, by payment of another year's premium.[f]

The tax treatment of term life insurance is simple and relatively noncontroversial. No deduction is allowed to those who live and "lose" their premiums, and the beneficiaries of those who die do not take the policy proceeds into income.[g]

Term life insurance is significantly different from other forms of pure insurance in that the premium must rise each year, because the risk of death increases with age in a statistically predicable manner. At advanced ages, the premium can become burdensome, prompting many policyholders to forego continued coverage. The policyholders most likely to drop their coverage are those in good health, which tends to increase mortality costs even more for those who continue coverage. (The phenomenon of poorer risks being more inclined than good risks to enter an insurance risk pool, or to remain in the pool, is termed "adverse selection.") In response to this problem, and independent of tax considerations, the life insurance industry

---

e. The explanation provided here is kept as simple as possible, in some cases artificially so, in order to move as quickly as possible from the intricacies of life insurance to a consideration of related tax policy matters. For a fuller explanation of the mathematics of life insurance, and of types life insurance policies not discussed here, see Tommy Thompson, *The Tax Advantaged Treatment of Life Insurance*, 4 TAX L.J. 27, 29-53 (1989).

f. For simplicity, throughout this discussion it is assumed that the insured is the owner of the policy and pays the premiums. In many cases, the policy is purchased by someone other than the insured, frequently the beneficiary. This makes little difference concerning income tax treatment, which is the central subject matter of this chapter.

Ownership is important for estate tax purposes, however. If the owner of the policy is the insured, policy proceeds paid at death are included in the estate.

g. Section 101(a)(1). Section 101(a)(2), which provides an exception to this general rule, is discussed in Notes and Questions #5.

developed *cash-value life insurance*. The traditional model is the level-premium, whole-life policy. The initial premium is considerably higher than for term insurance, but it is never increased. An insurance company issuing a whole-life policy to a healthy 34-year-old man might charge a premium of perhaps $4,000, as compared to the term policy's $1,000 first-year premium (plus loading charges for either policy). From the point of view of the insured, the extra expense would be justified by the knowledge that the premium would never increase; the term policy's premium would increase each year, ultimately to an annual cost greatly in excess of $4,000. From the point of view of the insurance company, the higher initial premium would be necessary to compensate it for providing insurance at the same premium later in the insured's life, when mortality charges would be much higher. Or, stated differently, the insurance company would need to charge a larger premium early in life in order to establish a fund which, together with interest earned by investment of the fund, will cover the face amount of the policy at the inevitable death of the insured.

This extra amount—the difference between the cost of term insurance and whole-life insurance—is placed into the insurance company's "reserves," to provide the fund to meet its future, and ever more likely, obligation to pay the face amount of the policy at the death of the insured. Thus, the cash-value life insurance policy has two components—the cost of pure insurance for the current year, and a saving element to fund the higher costs of protection in future years.[h] The insurance company, of course, invests this savings element during the life of the insured. Although the investment income is received directly by the insurance company, it inures to the benefit of the insured, at least in part, because the insurance company sets its whole-life premiums taking into account the fact that it will be able to invest the extra premiums, probably for many years. Here, as elsewhere, the magic of compound interest is of supreme importance. The earnings attributable to each cash-value policy are referred to as *inside buildup*. The policyholder can borrow the *cash value* of the policy—the portion of premiums not needed for current protection or loading charges plus the inside buildup—with no

---

h. Although the cost per $1,000 of insurance increases throughout life (after approximately age 10), the amount of pure insurance provided decreases as cash value builds in the policy. Thus, if an insurance company agrees to pay $500,000 in the case of the insured's death, but the policy has $50,000 in cash value, the insurance company will actually lose only $450,000 by the insured's immediate death because the insured would have been entitled to $50,000 anyway. The mortality charge will be figured on only $450,000, rather than $500,000. Under a normal whole-life policy, the cash value increases throughout life, and, under the usual industry practice, reaches the face amount of the policy at age 100. (If the insured survives to that age, the company pays him the face value of the policy as if he had died at that time. For tax purposes, however, the transaction is treated as if he had surrendered the policy; see below.) Late in life, the cash value grows so close to the face amount of the policy that the insurance company's amount at risk is relatively small, and, even though the mortality charge per $1,000 at risk is very high, the total mortality charge may be lower than earlier in life.

security other than the policy. Or, the policyholder can simply surrender the policy, stop paying premiums, and pocket the cash value.

The tax treatment of cash-value life insurance is substantially the same as for term insurance—the premiums are not deductible, and section 101(a)(1) allows the beneficiary to exclude the death benefit from income. If policy proceeds are received other than by reason of the death of the insured—if, for example, the policyholder surrenders the policy in exchange for its accumulated cash value—the protection of section 101(a)(1) is not available. In that case, the policyholder has income, but only to the extent, if any, that the amount received exceeds the total premiums paid.[i] Because a substantial portion of the premiums will have been absorbed by mortality charges and loading charges, the taxable element will be much less than the amount of the inside buildup, and in most cases will be zero.

Some insurance policies generate considerably more inside buildup than a whole-life policy. An extreme example is the "single-premium" policy, under which the insured makes a single lump-sum payment for the policy, which the insurance company can then invest—tax-free to the insured—for the remainder of his life.[j]

B. IS LIFE INSURANCE A "SPECIAL" INVESTMENT?

THE INCOME TAX TREATMENT OF INTEREST EARNED ON SAVINGS IN LIFE INSURANCE
Charles E. McLure, Jr.[*]
in THE ECONOMICS OF FEDERAL SUBSIDY PROGRAMS:
A COMPENDIUM OF PAPERS SUBMITTED TO THE
JOINT ECONOMIC COMMITTEE OF THE
CONGRESS OF THE UNITED STATES
Part 3, at 370, 393-94 (1972)

[T]he conceptually most satisfactory way of treating life insurance for tax purposes would be to allow full deduction of all premiums (and interest on loans to pay premiums) and full inclusion of all benefits—whether received by reason of the death of the insured or during his lifetime—in computing income for tax purposes.[71]

---

i. Section 72(e)(5).

j. To prevent life insurance companies from selling tax-advantaged investments with only a nominal insurance element, Congress has defined life insurance for tax purposes in section 7702. As part of the complex definition, section 7702 provides that if the policy's investment component exceeds that of a single-premium policy, the contract is not regarded as life insurance for tax purposes. See Notes and Questions #7.

*. At time of original publication, Professor of Economics at Rice University.

71. Theoretically the deduction for premiums could be allowed in the year in which paid and the proceeds could be included in income when received. This would accord saving in life insurance tax treatment similar to that for qualified pension plans, by allowing postponement of taxation. A more conventional approach would be to allow deduction of total costs in calculating taxable gain at death, surrender, or maturity. This would mitigate both the possibility that

Under this approach the Federal Government would automatically participate in both the pure insurance gains and the interest income components of death benefits, as well as the interest income received on surrender or maturity of policies during the life of the insured. There would be no necessity to allocate premiums between savings, pure insurance protection, and loading, since the entire premium would be deductible. Conversely, there would be no question of distinguishing between pure insurance proceeds, return of principal, and interest income so far as death proceeds are concerned, and no reason to try to identify the interest income component of benefits received during life. All net proceeds would be taxed, regardless of when realized.

It might be argued that this approach would not alter the present tax advantage of being able to offset costs of insurance (including loading) against interest income. This is true, but only half of the story. The present offset is, and would be, of advantage only to taxpayers who had been "unsuccessful" in their bet against the mortality tables and therefore remained alive to surrender their policies before death. There would, of course, be a corresponding group who had died and been taxed upon their insurance gain. Actuarially the two should balance out, with the Federal Government sharing in both mortality gains and losses, as well as interest income.

The problem with this approach is obvious: it would involve levying an income tax on death benefits. That the tax would be levied at progressive rates on interest income earned over a period of years and bunched with the pure insurance proceeds in the year of death of the insured need not be a controlling factor; averaging provisions could be modified to relieve that inequity. Nor is it that a large tax liability would be incurred even on averaged income, since allowance could be made for payments spread over a number of years.[73]

Rather, the problem is simply that there seems to be a decided reluctance to apply income taxation to insurance proceeds realized by reason of death, per se. This reluctance would probably apply almost equally strongly whether the insured were a man of 25 just starting out on a program of cash value life insurance (or covered by term insurance), whose beneficiaries would receive almost entirely pure insurance gain and virtually no interest income and return of [principal], or a man of 95 with a whole life policy, whose beneficiaries would receive virtually no pure insurance gain, the total death benefit representing return of savings and compound interest on it.

---

premium deductions might exceed income in a given year and the problems caused by bunching of income in the year of the insured's death.

73. And one of the usual roadblocks to efforts to tax unrealized capital gains at death—the lack of liquidity—would presumably be less crucial in the case of life insurance, except where a lump sum settlement option had not been elected.

* * *

Notes and Questions

1.   Most criticism of present law has been leveled at the tax treatment of inside buildup. But what of the basic provision in section 101(a)(1), applicable to both term and cash-value insurance, that allows exclusion of death benefits? Suppose 500 people each paid $1,000 for a lottery ticket, and the winner received $500,000. The losers would receive no deduction for their loss, but the winner would be taxed on $499,000.[k] Should the life insurance "winner" be treated more favorably than the lottery winner, given that the "losers" are treated the same?

2.   Professor McLure argued that the gain element—policy proceeds less amounts paid for the insurance—should be included in income. This could be accomplished by either of two methods. First, the United States could follow the practice of some other countries by allowing a deduction for premiums paid, then tax the full amount of the death benefit. Or, instead of allowing a current deduction for premiums paid, the deduction might be deferred until the insured died or the policy was surrendered; at that time, the deduction and inclusion would partially offset.[l] Would either of these approaches be preferred to present law, which allows no deduction for premiums and requires no inclusion of death benefits? Which of the two would be preferable?

3.   X wishes to provide $500,000 for his family in case he dies during the next year. He can purchase a one-year term policy for $1,000. Under present law, he would receive no deduction if he lived, and his beneficiaries would exclude the $500,000 if he died. Assume a constant tax rate of 33-1/3 percent. If the law were changed as Professor McLure proposed, X would be forced to purchase $750,000 in order to provide an after-tax benefit of $500,000. The premium for the larger policy would be $1,500, but his after-tax cost would be the same $1,000. Does this demonstrate that present law is superior to Professor McLure's proposal with regard to term insurance? With regard to cash-value insurance?

4.   The preceding question assumed a constant tax rate. If insurance proceeds were included in income in the year of death, however, there would be a problem of "bunching." For example, a middle-income person might receive a lump-sum payment of $500,000, and face very high marginal rates. Is this a major objection to taxing death benefits?

---

k. Section 165(d) allows losers a deduction for gambling losses during the year, to the extent of gambling gains. This is an itemized deduction. Sections 62, 67.

l. Note footnote 71 of Professor McLure's article.

5. The original purchaser of a life insurance policy can re-sell the policy to a third party. Congress denies the exemption of section 101(a)(1) if the policy was purchased after issuance, with the result that the purchaser (and new beneficiary) has income to the extent the policy proceeds exceed the amount paid for the policy, including premiums subsequently paid by the purchaser.[m] A recent phenomenon is the emergence of companies that make a business of purchasing life insurance policies from AIDS victims and others with short life expectancies; those companies do not enjoy the exclusion of section 101(a)(1). Nor is the policyholder who sells to such a company entitled to the exclusion, because the purchase price does not appear to have been paid "by reason of the death of the insured," as section 101(a)(1) requires. Is this sound tax policy with respect to the company that is purchasing the insurance policy? With respect to the terminally ill person who is selling it? Note that the terminally ill taxpayer is likely to have substantial taxable gain, because, *due to his impending death*, the purchaser will be willing to pay far more than the policy's cash value. A proposed regulation would allow the terminally ill person the benefit of the exclusion by providing that in such circumstances the receipt "is treated as an amount paid by reason of the death of the insured."[n]

C. THE PROBLEM OF "INSIDE BUILDUP"

While the present tax treatment of pure term insurance is rarely questioned (notwithstanding the McLure excerpt in Subchapter B), the treatment of cash value insurance has been the subject of considerable criticism. This criticism has intensified in the past twenty years, as insurance companies have developed "universal life" policies. Purchasers of these policies can vary their premium payments from year to year, or pay a substantial amount and then stop paying for years. This flexibility makes the policy appear more like a term policy coupled with an optional investment component, and provides ammunition to critics who argue that the investment component of cash-value insurance should be currently taxed to the policyowner.

---

m. Section 101(a)(2). The reason for this limitation is sometimes said to be a desire to discourage speculation in the deaths of unrelated parties. A simpler explanation is that Congress is not penalizing a disfavored transaction, but simply refusing to confer a tax benefit where the benefit appears to be unjustified. There is usually little justification for an exclusion if the new beneficiary is sufficiently at arms' length from the original owner (frequently the insured) that consideration is paid for the transfer.

n. Prop. Treas. Reg. § 1.101-8.

REFLECTIONS ON THE MEANING OF LIFE:
AN ANALYSIS OF SECTION 7702 AND THE
TAXATION OF CASH VALUE LIFE INSURANCE
Andrew D. Pike[*]

42 Tax Law Review 491, 524-30, 533-34 (1988)

It is impossible to reconcile the tax treatment of investments made in the form of cash value life insurance with the treatment of other financial investments. The interest or other investment income[171] credited to life insurance contracts is not taxed until (and unless) cash or other property is distributed to the policyholder prior to the death of the insured. For this purpose, a loan from the life insurance company secured by a contract's cash value generally is not treated as a distribution. Moreover, no limitations are imposed on the amount that a policyholder can invest in a life insurance contract.

Interest income generally is included in income currently. The most significant exceptions to this general rule involve interest on state and local bonds and interest income credited to qualified pension plans, individual retirement accounts (IRAs), and deferred annuities. Although qualified pension plans and IRAs receive extremely favorable treatment under the Code, restrictions limit the amount that an individual can invest in these tax favored savings vehicles. In addition, loans from pension plans, individual retirement accounts, or annuities (or loans secured by these assets) are generally treated as taxable distributions and result in the immediate taxation of tax deferred amounts.

Many commentators question the justification for treating interest credited under a life insurance contract differently from other forms of income from savings. Several arguments have been advanced, however, in defense of this favorable treatment. These arguments are discussed and evaluated below.

Would Current Taxation of Interest Credited Under
a Life Insurance Contract Constitute a Tax
on Unrealized Appreciation?

The first argument raised in support of the existing tax treatment of life insurance is that an increase in the cash value of a life insurance contract represents unrealized appreciation: "taxing a policyholder currently on the increase in the cash value of a life insurance policy would be like taxing a homeowner each year on the appreciation in value of the home even though

---

[*]. At time of original publication, Professor of Law at American University.

171. The same tax treatment applies to owners of both variable life insurance contracts and nonvariable life insurance contracts. See H.R. Rep. No. 432, 98th Cong., 1st Sess., Vol. 1, at 145 (1983); S. Rep. No. 169, 98th Cong., 2d Sess., vol. 1, at 572 (1984). In effect, the owner of a variable life insurance contract invests the contract's cash value in assets such as money market funds, bond funds, common stock funds, or real estate funds. K. Black & H. Skipper, Life Insurance 68 (11th ed. 1987).

the home has not been sold."[182] Consequently, it is argued, the interest credited should not be subject to tax until the gain is realized.

* * *

[A]ssuming retention of the general realization requirement, it is questionable whether an increase in a life insurance contract's cash value represents the type of appreciation taxed only upon realization. Treating an increase in cash value as unrealized appreciation ignores the distinction between changes in the value of an asset caused by market forces, which are not taxed until realized through disposition, and those reflecting current compensation for the use of the asset which are currently realized and taxed in accordance with the taxpayer's method of accounting. In many situations, property owners are taxed on investment income that is not received. Partners in a partnership and shareholders of S corporations are taxed currently on their shares of income earned and retained by the business entity. Interest accruing on debt instruments having original issue discount, including a certificate of deposit issued by a bank, is included in income despite the absence of a sale of the instrument.

In each of these examples, the property values reflect income earned but not received by property owners. Current taxation of the property owners in these instances, however, is not premised on the doctrine of constructive receipt. The income is includable irrespective of the taxpayer's ability to command the receipt of cash. For example, limited partners and owners of minority interests in corporations and partnerships often lack either the legal power or the effective ability to convert the income into cash without selling the property.

The cash value of a life insurance contract, like the properties discussed above, is an asset that generates income. A life insurance company's crediting of interest constitutes compensation for its use of the policy's cash value. The cash value reflects the interest credited, just as the values of the partnership interest, the S corporation stock, and the debt instrument with original issue discount also reflect income that has not been severed from the underlying asset. Because income derived from these other forms of property is taxed despite the lack of receipt, actual or constructive, the realization doctrine, standing alone, does not justify treating the owners of cash value life insurance contracts in a different manner.

* * *

Is the Current Tax Treatment of Life Insurance Necessary to Encourage Financial Security?

A second argument in support of the current tax treatment of cash value life insurance is that an incentive is needed to encourage taxpayers to provide for their families' financial security. Though laudable, the objective

---

182. Tax Reform Proposals-XXII, Hearings Before the Senate Committee on Finance, 99th Cong., 1st Sess. 394 (1985) (statement of the American Council of Life Insurance).

of protecting one's family against financial adversity does not, of itself, justify preferential tax treatment. Beyond laudability, two further criteria must be satisfied: (1) Favorable tax treatment must induce changes in taxpayer behavior that significantly advance the perceived social goal; and (2) the behavior likely to be changed must be sufficiently important to justify the revenue loss. The goal of promoting financial security satisfies neither of these requirements.

The preferential tax treatment of investment income earned under a cash value life insurance contract is likely to induce taxpayers to invest more resources in this financial product. How does the purchase of cash value life insurance protect an individual against financial adversity? Cash value life insurance can enhance an individual's financial security by protecting against the loss of two distinct income streams. First, the contractual death benefit provides funds to replace the insured's salary in case of death before retirement. Second, the cash value provides funds that can replace a taxpayer's salary following retirement. The analysis of the current taxation of cash value life insurance requires separate consideration of each function.

Life Insurance as a Source of Post-death Income Replacement

The unique risk shifting function of life insurance relates primarily to the post-death replacement of the insured's income. A parent, for example, may be concerned that the loss of her income would leave her dependents without adequate means of support.

An individual often earns both investment income and income from personal efforts. Because the insured's investment assets remain in existence following her death, cash value life insurance is not needed to replace the insured's investment income. Admittedly, the buildup of the contract's cash value increases the individual's wealth which may generate post-death investment income for an insured's dependents. Saving in the form of a life insurance contract's cash value, however, does not differ from other forms of savings in this regard. Consequently preferential values is not justified.

The portion of the death benefit that consists of term insurance protection provides a fund that can generate investment income to replace the insured's income from personal efforts. The existence of this type of fund undeniably enhances the financial security of the insured's family. Unfortunately, existing tax incentives, perversely, are likely to induce undesirable changes in taxpayer behavior. To the extent that the tax law induces a switch from term insurance to cash value life insurance, the taxpayer is likely to obtain less insurance protection. The premium charged for a level-premium cash value life insurance contract is much larger than the initial premium for a term contract with an identical death benefit. Unless the taxpayer greatly increases the portion of her budget allocated to life insurance, the amount of insurance protection will decline.

Paradoxically, the current tax treatment also provides the greatest tax benefit to taxpayers whose insurance needs are modest: those who can most easily afford to obtain their current insurance protection in conjunction with a savings program. Taxpayers with substantial wealth, who can afford to purchase large amounts of single premium insurance, enjoy the largest tax benefits. Yet, the accumulated wealth of these taxpayers makes it more likely that their families could maintain their standard of living without life insurance protection.

Less, if any, incentive is provided, however, for taxpayers with little wealth. For those taxpayers for whom single-premium policies are too expensive, but who can afford to purchase a level-premium cash value contract, the tax benefits are less generous, but are still substantial. For taxpayers who cannot afford to pay the higher premiums charged under a cash value contract, financial protection is available only in the form of term life insurance, the cost of which, however, is not generally deductible. Because of the irrational inverse relationship between the need for insurance protection and the distribution of tax benefits, existing tax incentives to provide financial security should receive a low national budgetary priority.

Life Insurance as a Source of Retirement Income

Cash value life insurance purportedly enhances an individual's financial security by providing a source of post-retirement income. The same is true, however, of a savings account, taxable bonds, or any other savings vehicle. The income from these alternative savings vehicles generally is fully taxable on a current basis, and the savings feature of cash value life insurance provides no distinguishing characteristic that justifies more favorable tax treatment.

    * * *

Would Current Taxation Create Excessive Administrative Burdens?

A third argument raised in defense of the existing tax treatment accorded life insurance is that taxing the interest as earned would create unmanageable administrative burdens. * * * Although these concerns may have been valid in the past, they have significantly less legitimacy today. * * * The industry's existing computerized record keeping and reporting systems indicate that compliance with a current taxation regime is feasible.

    * * *

Does the Existing Tax Treatment of Cash Value Life Insurance Improve Vertical Equity?

The defenders of preferential tax treatment of cash value life insurance argue, fourthly, that the benefits accrue to the middle class, thereby providing a degree of vertical equity for these taxpayers compared to the wealthy. Even if the current life insurance tax regime primarily benefits the middle class, it is not clear, following the enactment of the Tax Reform Act of 1986, that vertical equity is enhanced by retaining this tax treatment. Enactment of provisions that limit the benefits of most tax sheltered investments, as well as the expanded scope of the alternative minimum tax, limit the extent to which (or at least the ease with which) the wealthy can substantially reduce their tax liabilities. Indeed, investments in cash value life insurance are currently promoted as one of the last remaining tax favored investments.

　　* * *

TAX REFORM FOR FAIRNESS, SIMPLICITY, AND ECONOMIC GROWTH ("Treasury I") United States Department of the Treasury

Vol. 2, at 246-47 (1984)

[T]he favorable tax treatment of inside interest build-up on life insurance policies can be obtained through a contract that provides a relatively small amount of pure insurance coverage.

Interest income on comparable investment vehicles generally is not tax free or tax deferred. Instead, interest income credited on such investments generally is subject to tax whether or not the interest is currently received by the taxpayer. For example, taxpayers generally are subject to current tax on interest credited on certificates of deposit although the interest is not received until the certificate of deposit matures.

Moreover, life insurance is not subject to the significant limitations on the timing and amount of contributions, withdrawals, and loans that apply to other tax-favored investments, such as qualified pension plans and individual retirement accounts (IRAs).

The benefit of deferring or avoiding tax on the inside interest build-up on life insurance policies goes only to individuals with excess disposable income that enables them to save, and particularly to individuals in high tax brackets. This benefit is not available to lower income taxpayers and other individuals buying term insurance since it derives solely from the investment component of a policy (which is not present in a term insurance policy).

The tax-favored treatment of inside interest build-up encourages individuals to save through life insurance companies rather than other financial institutions and perhaps to purchase life insurance that they would not buy except to gain access to the favorable tax treatment of the investment income. This distorts the flow of savings and investment in the economy.

Proposal

Owners of life insurance policies would be treated as being in constructive receipt of the cash surrender value (taking into account any surrender charge or penalty) of their policies. Thus, a policyholder would include in interest income for a taxable year any increase during the taxable year in the amount by which the policy's cash surrender value exceeds the policyholder's investment in the contract. A policyholder's investment in the contract would be equal to the aggregate of his gross premiums, reduced by the aggregate policyholder dividends and other distributions under the policy and by the aggregate cost of renewable term insurance under the policy.

The investment component of a long-term life insurance contract would be eligible for any general savings incentive available to comparable investments. For example, the otherwise-taxable interest income produced by an increase in the cash surrender value of a life insurance contract during a taxable year could be designated as a contribution to an IRA.

Effective Date

The proposal would be effective for all interest build-up credited to policies sold on or after January 1, 1986: In the case of policies outstanding on December 31, 1985, inside interest build-up would continue to be free from tax until December 31, 1990. Beginning in 1991, this proposal would be phased in over a five-year period, so that future inside interest build-up on policies sold before January 1, 1986 would be fully subject to tax starting in 1995. Deferral of untaxed inside interest build-up would continue until withdrawal of funds from the policy. The policyholder's investment in the contract would not be reduced by the cost of term insurance for any period prior to January 1, 1986.

Analysis

Taxing the inside interest build-up on life insurance policies would eliminate the largest tax distortion in the financial services area and would place competing financial products and institutions on more equal footing. This would promote the efficient flow of long-term savings.

Current taxation of inside interest build-up also would eliminate the need for complex rules and restrictions in several areas, including the determination of tax liability when a policy matures or is surrendered and the definition of contracts that qualify as life insurance. * * *

Notes and Questions

6. Advocates of current taxation of inside buildup argue that this form of saving should not enjoy a tax advantage over other forms of saving, such as certificates of deposit. Some commentators, notably William Andrews, question the assertion that the earnings generated by saving are, in fact, generally subjected to current taxation. Professor Andrews points to broad exceptions to this supposed general rule. Note that this issue would disappear under his proposed "consumption-type or cash flow personal income tax" discussed in Chapter Seven. Under the Andrews proposal, current taxation of inside buildup clearly would be incorrect.[o]

---

o. One commentator argues that "life insurance policies are correctly taxed, or even overtaxed, from a consumption tax point of view." C. David Anderson, *Conventional Tax Theory and "Tax Expenditures:" A Critical Analysis of the Life Insurance Example*, 57 TAX NOTES 1417, 1418 (1992). Mr. Anderson goes on to argue that even under an accretion model, life insurance is not undertaxed "when the effects of inflation and policy cancellations are considered." *Id.*

7.   A significant set of tax policy issues revolves around the definition of life insurance. It is possible to envision an arrangement of pure investment, with a tiny amount of insurance thrown in as a "fig leaf" to provide favorable tax treatment. For example, suppose a taxpayer placed thousands of dollars in a "life insurance policy," which provided for a death benefit of an amount $100 more than the cash value. Realistically, this transaction would be designed to provide not insurance, but a place for tax-free compounding of the taxpayer's investment. As Professor Thompson observes, "some definition is required to insure that the tax benefits of life insurance are properly targeted to products with sufficient insurance elements and properly limited savings or investment elements."[p]

Achieving a successful definition of life insurance for tax purposes has proven difficult. Congress has defined life insurance in section 7702, using language so complex that one commentator observes that the statute "sometimes appears to have been co-authored by James Joyce and Casey Stengel."[q] The drafters of Treasury I (in a statement not excerpted above) commented on the limited success of then-existing statutory definition:

> Although the definition of life insurance places some broad limits
> on the use of life insurance as a tax-favored investment vehicle, it
> is still possible to design an insurance policy meeting this definition
> under which the cumulative investment earnings at currently
> prevailing interest rates are projected to be eight times as large as
> the cumulative insurance costs.[r]

Even after changes in the 1980s designed to limit favorable tax treatment to "true" life insurance, continued concern led Congress in 1988 to mandate reports, by both the Treasury and the General Accounting Office, of the policy issues involved in the tax treatment of life insurance products, including "the effectiveness of the revised tax treatment of life insurance products in preventing the sale of life insurance primarily for investment purposes."[s]

8.   Assume that life insurance is defined in a reasonable manner that limits favorable tax treatment to traditional life insurance products. After a thorough analysis, Professor Thompson concludes that "the investment potential of the inside buildup simply is not attractive. The investment

p. Thompson, *supra* note e, at 53.

q. Theodore Paul Manno, *The Federal Income Taxation of Life Insurance, Annuities and Individual Retirement Accounts After the Tax Reform Act of 1986*, 60 St. John's L. Rev. 674, 674 (1986).

r. United States Dep't of Treasury, 2 Tax Reform for Fairness, Simplicity, and Economic Growth 246 (1984).

s. United States General Accounting Office, Tax Treatment of Life Insurance and Annuity Interest 1 (1990). Substantially identical language is found in United States Dep't of Treasury, Report to the Congress on the Taxation of Life Insurance Products 1 (1990).

potential of even a single premium policy is not great enough that a policyholder would purchase the policy for investment purposes."[t] In other words, the mortality charges and loading charges more than offset the tax advantage given inside buildup. Does it follow that present law is correct in not taxing inside buildup?

9. Does neutral application of the realization rule require that inside buildup not be taxed until the owner or beneficiary receives money? In other words, does inside buildup look more like unrealized appreciation of a capital asset, or like interest credited on a long-term certificate of deposit (which is taxed currently)?

10. Tax academics sometimes seem to think that everyone considers the tax considerations of investments with the same care they would. In fact, most purchasers of life insurance are blissfully unaware of the tax treatment of inside buildup, and salesmen do not mention it to any but their most sophisticated clients. Nevertheless, the favorable treatment causes more money to be invested in cash-value life insurance, simply because the favorable tax treatment means that the insurance company can provide the same coverage at a lower premium. Are the principal beneficiaries of the tax benefit the purchasers of policies, or the insurance companies that enjoy a competitive advantage over other entities attempting to attract investors?

11. Professor Thompson argues that Congress has never decided on the policy bases for its taxation of insurance, and that rational taxation cannot be attained without them. He argues, for example, that different tax treatment is more appropriate if Congress seeks to encourage maintenance of permanent insurance protection for beneficiaries than if it seeks to foster saving for retirement.[u]

12. Favorable treatment of inside buildup favors permanent cash-value insurance, but offers virtually nothing in support of term insurance. Is favorable tax treatment of inside buildup justified because it encourages individuals to maintain *permanent* insurance, even later in life when premiums on term insurance might seem prohibitively expensive?

13. Does Professor Pike agree with the proposition that Congress should encourage permanent rather than term insurance? He argues that the tax treatment of inside buildup induces taxpayers to purchase smaller cash-value policies rather than larger term policies. Why might this be so? Assuming this to be correct, is it bad?

---

t. Thompson, *supra* note e, at 157.
u. *Id.*

14.   Is favorable tax treatment of cash-value insurance justified because it encourages saving? Is it sufficient to answer that saving in many other forms is not so encouraged?

15.   Is it important that the tax saving associated with inside buildup will be significant only if the policy is maintained for many years? Congress encourages long-term saving in other areas, such as qualified pensions and individual retirement accounts ("IRAs"). Yet the amounts that can be contributed to those investment vehicles is limited, while taxpayers can purchase life insurance in unlimited amounts.

16.   "Treasury I" would have taxed inside buildup, but allowed it to be regarded as a contribution to an IRA. At the time of the proposal, everyone with $2,000 of earned income could contribute that amount to a deductible IRA. This would mean that very few taxpayers would actually be required to pay tax on inside buildup, if they were willing to reduce their contributions to other IRA investments.[v] Would the Treasury I approach be an improvement even with the present restrictions on deductible IRAs?[w]

17.   If Congress changes its approach to the taxation of insurance, what should it do about insurance policies that are outstanding at the time of the change? Note that life insurance policies tend to be extremely long-term contracts, so a grandfather provision would mean different treatment for holders of insurance policies through most of the Twenty-First century. Treasury I would not have taxed inside buildup for five years, and would have phased in the tax for five years after that.

18.   Some commentators suggest that the complexities of taxing individual policyholders on inside buildup can be attacked indirectly, by taxing the insurance companies more heavily, a cost that would be passed along in higher premiums. This should not be regarded as a panacea; many complexities would be entailed.[x]

---

v. In a portion of Treasury I not excerpted, the drafters estimated that in 1983 families holding cash-value policies had average annual inside build-up of $355. Even among families with economic income in excess of $200,000, average annual inside buildup amounted to only $3,050, an amount less than the $4,000 that then could be contributed to deductible IRAs if both husband and wife had earned income. UNITED STATES DEP'T OF TREASURY, 2 TAX REFORM FOR FAIRNESS, SIMPLICITY, AND ECONOMIC GROWTH ["Treasury I"] 249, Table 1 (1984).

w. Under present law, section 219(g) allows a full deduction of contributions to an IRA only if neither the taxpayer nor his spouse is covered by a tax-favored pension plan, or if adjusted gross income is less than $25,000 single or $40,000 joint. Even if the contribution is not deductible, earnings on the IRA investment are not taxed until received.

x. If the tax were made applicable to reserves covering existing policies, the companies would have to pay the tax and would not have the investment income assumed when the policies were sold; the solvency of some insurers would be imperiled. *See* Goode, *supra* note a, at 54.

A tax on insurance companies as a proxy for taxing policyholders does not take into

This chapter does not cover in detail the distinctions between nonparticipating and participating policies and between stock and mutual companies, but limited discussion of these distinctions may be helpful at this point. Stock companies are owned by shareholders, and policyholders are their customers. Traditionally, they have sold primarily nonparticipating policies, which means that the policyholder is entitled to a fixed return, and any profits benefit the shareholders. Mutual companies are corporations without shareholders; in theory, they are owned by their policyholders. Because the policyholders double as owners, mutual companies have traditionally sold only participating policies, which means that the policyholders share in the profits of the company, usually through a premium reduction. Stock companies can also sell participating policies, and many now do so.

With regard to the issue of increasing taxes on companies as a proxy for taxing policyholders on inside buildup, the problems are wholly different depending on whether we are dealing with participating or nonparticipating policies. If Congress levied a tax on inside buildup against the insurance company, owners of nonparticipating policies would not be affected—they still would be entitled to their contractual rate of return. Such a tax might threaten the solvency of an insurance company that sold only nonparticipating policies, because its expected investment income would be reduced, but its obligations would not be.

The proxy tax would work much better in the case of participating policies. The owners of participating policies would immediately and directly bear the economic cost of the additional tax, because their policy dividends would be reduced.

19. In Canada, the Carter Commission in 1966 recommended taxing policyholders annually on investment income, and taking into account mortality gains and losses at death (or when the policy matured or was surrendered).[y] These proposals were not adopted.

20. The problems discussed in this chapter are in part unique to life insurance, and are in part common to other investments. For example, critics of the present treatment of inside buildup in life insurance policies

---

account different tax rates. All policyholders would bear the tax at the rate imposed on the insurance company. *See* Charles McLure, *The Income Tax Treatment of Interest Earned on Savings in Life Insurance*, in THE ECONOMICS OF FEDERAL SUBSIDY PROGRAMS, A COMPENDIUM OF PAPERS SUBMITTED TO JOINT ECONOMIC COMMITTEE 370, 398 (1972).

Whatever its drawbacks, the proposal has been used. In 1969, Canada adopted "a 15 percent tax on the investment income of life insurance companies in lieu of taxation of policyholders on this income." RICHARD GOODE, THE INDIVIDUAL INCOME TAX 133 (Rev. ed. 1976).

y. 3 REPORT OF THE ROYAL COMMISSION ON TAXATION, 441-55 (1966).

also propose change in section 72, which generally provides the same favorable tax treatment of inside buildup in annuities.

Selected Bibliography

Anderson, C. David, *Conventional Tax Theory and "Tax Expenditures:" A Critical Analysis of the Life Insurance Example*, 57 TAX NOTES 1417 (1992).

BLACK, KENNETH, JR. & HAROLD D. SKIPPER, JR., LIFE INSURANCE (12th ed. 1994).

Carlyle, William M., *Taxation of Life Insurance Proceeds*, 17 CANADIAN TAX J. 321 (1969).

GOODE, RICHARD E., THE INDIVIDUAL INCOME TAX 125-33 (Rev. ed. 1976).

——, *Policyholders' Interest Income From Life Insurance Under the Income Tax*, 16 VAND. L. REV. 33 (1962).

Graetz, Michael J., *Expenditure Tax Design in* WHAT SHOULD BE TAXED: INCOME OR EXPENDITURE? 216-18 (Joseph A. Pechman ed., 1980).

Irenas, Joseph E., *Life Insurance Interest Income Under the Federal Income Tax*, 21 TAX L. REV. 297 (1966).

Krieg, Todd, Note, *Tax Arbitrage and Life Insurance: A Tax Policy Critique of Section 264,* 42 TAX LAW. 747 (1989).

Lent, George E., *The Tax Treatment of Life Insurance, in* HOUSE COMM. ON WAYS AND MEANS, 86TH CONG., 1ST SESS., 3 TAX REVISION COMPENDIUM 1995 (1959).

Manno, Theodore Paul, *The Federal Income Taxation of Life Insurance, Annuities and Individual Retirement Accounts After the Tax Reform Act of 1986*, 60 ST. JOHN'S L. REV. 674 (1986).

McLure, Charles E., Jr., *The Income Tax Treatment of Interest Earned on Savings in Life Insurance, in* THE ECONOMICS OF FEDERAL SUBSIDY PROGRAMS: A COMPENDIUM OF PAPERS SUBMITTED TO THE JOINT ECONOMIC COMMITTEE, CONGRESS OF THE UNITED STATES, pt. 3, at 370 (1972).

Morlitz, Gerald, *Universal Life Insurance: Where Does It Go From Here?*, 46 N.Y.U. INST. FED. TAX'N 54-1 (1988).

Pike, Andrew D., *Reflections on the Meaning of Life: An Analysis of Section 7702 and the Taxation of Cash Value Life Insurance*, 43 TAX L. REV. 491 (1988).

THE PRESIDENT'S TAX PROPOSALS TO THE CONGRESS FOR FAIRNESS, GROWTH, AND SIMPLICITY ["Treasury II"] 253-64 (1985).

3 REPORT OF THE ROYAL COMMISSION ON TAXATION ["Carter Commission"] 441-59, 585-90 (1966).

Skillman, Richard W., *The Impact of TEFRA and the 1984 Act on the "Inside Build-up" Under Life Insurance Products*, 43 N.Y.U. INST. FED. TAX'N 40-1 (1985).

Thompson, Tommy F., *The Tax Advantaged Treatment of Life Insurance*, 4 TAX L.J. 27 (1989).

UNITED SATES DEP'T OF TREASURY, REPORT TO THE CONGRESS ON THE TAXATION OF LIFE INSURANCE COMPANY PRODUCTS (1990).

2 UNITED STATES DEP'T OF TREASURY, TAX REFORM FOR FAIRNESS, SIMPLICITY, AND ECONOMIC GROWTH ["Treasury I"] 244-57 (1984).

UNITED STATES GENERAL ACCOUNTING OFFICE, TAX TREATMENT OF LIFE INSURANCE AND ANNUITY INTEREST (1990).

VICKREY, WILLIAM, AGENDA FOR PROGRESSIVE TAXATION 64-75 (1947).

——, *Insurance Under the Federal Income Tax*, 52 YALE L.J. 554 (1943).

CHAPTER NINE

INCOME TAX TREATMENT OF PROPERTY TRANSFERRED AT DEATH OR BY GIFT

*The most serious defect in our federal tax structure * * * is the failure of the income tax to reach the appreciation in value of assets transferred at death.*[a]

A. INTRODUCTION

While not all tax scholars would agree that the income tax treatment of property passing at death is the worst failing of tax law, it is fair to say that a convention of those who are prepared to defend present law on policy grounds could probably be held in a telephone booth. The law governing the income tax treatment of property transferred by gift and at death is familiar ground to all students who have completed the basic course in taxation. Neither the transferor nor the transferee of either a gift or an inheritance has any gross income or deduction by reason of the transfer.[b] In the case of property that is transferred by gift, the donee usually takes the donor's basis ("*carryover basis*"). Section 1015. (In the case of property worth less than the donor's basis, section 1015 requires the donee to use fair market value for purposes of computing loss.) Even though the gift could constitute a realization event, the theory is that it is appropriate to wait until the donee sells or exchanges the property, then require the donee to take into income the full gain attributable to the donor's period of ownership as well as his own.

In the case of property transferred by death, the general rule is one of "*stepped-up basis*"—the heir normally takes as his basis the fair market value of the property at the date of death.[c] Section 1014. No one ever pays

---

a. Jerome Kurtz & Stanley S. Surrey, *Reform of Death and Gift Taxes: The 1969 Treasury Proposals, The Criticisms, and a Rebuttal*, 70 COLUM. L. REV. 1365, 1381 (1970).

b. Section 102 provides for non-inclusion by the recipient, and, consistently, there is no statutory provision for a deduction by the transferor. Non-taxation of the transferor (on unrealized appreciation accrued to the time of transfer) is not specified by statute, but presumably derives from a traditional and "common-sense" view that transferring property and receiving nothing in return, or at least nothing tangible, does not constitute income.

c. The estate tax is based on the value of the decedent's estate at the date of death, or, if the executor elects, at an alternative valuation date generally six months after death (or the date of sale for property sold within the six-month period). Section 2032. In the event of an election under section 2032, the basis for income tax purposes is the alternative valuation. Section 1010(a)(2). The policy behind the alternative valuation approach is probably not controversial. It is to protect the estate from a high temporary value of assets—resulting, perhaps, from a "spike" in the stock market—which the assets do not retain by the time the estate is settled and tax on any appreciation unrealized at the date of death. Similarly, no deduction is available in the case of depreciated property, whose basis is "stepped-down" at death. While it is difficult to articulate a principled defense for the rule of section 1014—simplicity (by avoiding any difficulty in ascertaining the decedent's basis) is probably the strongest argument available—it is less certain what form a replacement provision should take. There are three leading candidates for reform. First, the rule of carryover basis already applicable to gifts could be extended to inherited property. Second, the transfer of property at death, and perhaps by gift as well, could be treated as a realization event, with the result that the excess of fair market value over basis would be subjected to income tax on the decedent's final return, or on the donor's return. Third, section 102 could be repealed, thus subjecting the heir, and in some cases the recipient of an inter vivos gift, to income tax on the full amount received. The materials in Subchapters B, C, and D discuss each of these options. First, however, the notes and questions immediately below consider present law.

Notes and Questions

1. Why is stepped-up basis—the present rule applied to transfers of property at death, under section 1014—thought to be inequitable?[d]

2. Is it clear that section 1014 is in fact inequitable? From the decedent's point of view, where is the realized gain? The decedent manifestly did *not* realize during life, and claiming that he did so by dying is (arguably) entirely artificial. From the heir's point of view, why should the heir be held accountable for gain that occurred during the period of ownership of another taxpayer (the decedent)? True, it may be argued that the heir realized the principal amount of the inheritance, but that would be equally true regardless of whether the property were appreciated, depreciated, or neither. This suggests that section 102 may be wrong, but says nothing about section 1014.

3. Most modern tax students will instinctively realize that section 1014 is badly out of step with the rest of tax law, but should recognize that such a view was not necessarily present in the early years of the income tax. Initially, the concept of income was tied, much more than today, to trust and accounting concepts, rather than to the more modern principle that economic gain should be taxed even if the gain occurred in a way not ordinarily thought of as income. Only over a period of years was it established that

---

the estate taxes paid. Throughout this chapter, for simplicity, we shall use the term "date of death" to include the alternative valuation date where the election is made.

d. The danger of abuse is controlled by the requirement that the owner die to take advantage of the favorable treatment. Few taxpayers will go to that extent to avoid paying taxes. The gift situation is completely different; see Note #9 below.

economic improvements such as cancellation of indebtedness,[e] payment of the taxpayer's income tax obligations by his employer,[f] and illegally obtained income[g] constituted income. The symbol of this evolutionary process is the Supreme Court's 1955 decision in *Glenshaw Glass*.[h] Keep in mind that this decision, which now seems manifestly correct and which was rendered 42 years after the Sixteenth Amendment was ratified, required reversing the settled position of the Tax Court that punitive damages, even in the business context, were not income.

This history may help us understand how, in the early years of the income tax when many economic gains were not understood to be within the tax concept of "income," the rule that taxed neither the decedent nor the heir might have taken root.

4. Jerome Kurtz and Stanley Surrey, well known tax scholars and Treasury officials during the Johnson administration, emphasized the importance of stepped-up basis in undercutting the progressive tax system. (Keep in mind that the dollar figures are those of a quarter century ago, when income of $100,000 represented a much higher relative income than today.)

> For the group of individuals whose annual economic income (including annual appreciation in asset values) exceeds $100,000, the annual appreciation that is untaxed—and in the end escapes income tax at death—is about equal to all other income, both taxable and exempt, combined. * * * The consequence in the end of not subjecting these large accumulations of income to the income tax is clearly to provide a broad avenue of escape from that tax for the wealthiest families. * * *[i]

5. Is stepped-up basis justified because the estate may be subjected to the estate tax?

6. The stepped-up basis rules of present law are said to result in a "lock-in" effect. A taxpayer who owns appreciated property can sell the property, but must pay a capital gains tax. If he holds the property until death, however, he avoids the tax, as do his heirs. Thus, the taxpayer—especially if he is elderly or for other reasons contemplates death within a few years—will have a considerable incentive to hold the property.

---

e. United States v. Kirby Lumber Co., 284 U.S. 1 (1931).

f. Old Colony Trust Co. v. Commissioner, 279 U.S. 716 (1929).

g. James v. United States, 366 U.S. 213 (1961). *James* overruled Commissioner v. Wilcox, 327 U.S. 404 (1946), which had taken the contrary view.

h. Commissioner v. Glenshaw Glass Co., 348 U.S. 426 (1955).

i. Kurtz & Surrey, *supra* note a, at 1383.

This lock-in creates an impediment on the optimal use of resources. A perfectly functioning market tends to direct property ownership to the person who can most efficiently use the property, because the property is worth more to that person. Thus, the current owner of appreciated property, who by hypothesis is using it less efficiently than the potential purchaser, would have an incentive to sell because the purchaser would be willing to pay more for the property than it is worth to the current owner. The capital gain tax creates an impediment to this efficient transaction, but, absent the rule of section 1014, the owner would know that the tax would have to be paid sooner or later. Under the rule of stepped-up basis, however, the property owner would have a greater incentive to hold rather than sell, because the capital gains tax could be permanently defeated rather than merely postponed.

7. Section 1014 mandates a basis equal to fair market value at death, which can be either more or less than the decedent's basis in the property, and thus can result in stepped-*down* basis. Why is so much more concern expressed about stepped-up basis than about stepped-down basis? Why does the fact that section 1014 mandates both stepped-up basis and stepped-down basis not mean that untaxed appreciation forgiven by section 1014 is roughly balanced by disallowed deductions with respect to assets that have fallen in value? If we thought such a rough balance occurred with respect to taxpayers as a whole (which it does not), would this be sufficient to satisfy the demands of policy, or would it be necessary that each taxpayer's untaxed gains and disallowed losses roughly balance?

8. Real estate and intangible assets, of which corporate stock is the most important, tend to appreciate over time, due to inflation if nothing else.

On the other hand, most tangible personal property owned by taxpayers falls in value as it wears out, so that stepped-down basis occurs more frequently than we usually acknowledge. For example, clothing, automobiles, furniture, etc. normally decline in value after purchase. However, if the assets are personal, no loss would have been deductible anyway (see section 165(c)), so in most cases the stepped-down basis would not adversely affect the heir, and did not represent a loss that could have been deducted by the decedent.

If tangible personal property is used in business or for the production of income, so that losses would be deductible, it is likely that depreciation deductions would have reduced basis below value, so that stepped-up basis, rather than stepped-down, would be the general rule.

9. Why would the rule of stepped-up basis be much more troublesome if applied to gifts than it is when applied to inheritances?

B. CARRYOVER BASIS OF PROPERTY TRANSFERRED AT DEATH

Although this chapter focuses on the income tax treatment of property transferred by death or gift, it is difficult to view the income tax provisions without reference to the transfer taxes (principally estate and gift taxes) dealt with in the next chapter. The interrelated nature of the transfer taxes and the income tax provisions can be seen from the actions of Congress in the Tax Reform Act of 1976. In that statute, Congress increased ten-fold[j] the amount of property that could pass free from transfer taxes. The tradeoff for this benefit was an income tax provision—section 1023, which mandated carryover basis for inherited property. The compromise proved short lived, with the low-tax forces emerging victorious when Congress subsequently repealed section 1023 (retroactively), while leaving intact the liberalized transfer tax exclusion enacted in 1976.

In the excerpt below, the Joint Committee on Taxation explains the 1976 provisions that temporarily implemented carryover basis. Carryover basis sounds simple, but upon closer examination it raises a number of difficult issues; it need not, however, be as complex as it was in the form in which it was enacted in 1976. The complexity of the Joint Committee's explanation reflects the complexity of the law; it was this complexity that provided the ammunition that opponents of carryover basis used to postpone it, and, in 1980, retroactively repeal it.

GENERAL EXPLANATION OF THE TAX REFORM ACT OF 1976
Joint Committee on Taxation
1976-3 C.B. 564-71

Reasons for Change

Prior law resulted in an unwarranted discrimination against those persons who sell their property prior to death as compared with those whose property was not sold until after death. Where a person sells appreciated property before death, the resulting gain is subject to the income tax. However, if the sale of the property could be postponed until after the owner's death, all of the appreciation occurring before death would not be subject to the income tax.

This discrimination against sales occurring before death created a substantial "lock-in" effect. Persons in their later years who might otherwise sell property were effectively prevented from doing so because they realized that the appreciation in that asset would be taxed as income if they sold before death, but would not be subject to income tax if they held the asset until their death. The effect of this "lock-in" was often to distort the allocation of capital between competing sources.

---

j. Prior to the 1976 Act, decedents could pass $60,000 without estate tax. The 1976 Act substituted a unified credit sufficient to offset transfer taxes on taxable gifts and estates of $600,000.

In order to eliminate these problems, Congress believed that the basis of property acquired from or passing from a decedent should have the same basis in the hands of the recipient as it had in the hands of the decedent, i.e., a "carryover basis." This will have the effect of eliminating the unwarranted difference in treatment between lifetime and deathtime transfers.

However, in order to prevent a portion of the appreciation from being taxed by both the estate tax and the income tax, the Congress believed that the carryover basis should be increased by Federal and State death taxes attributable to the appreciation in value. In addition, in order to prevent beneficiaries of smaller estates from paying tax on appreciation accruing before the decedent's death, the Congress concluded that each estate should have a minimum basis in all of its carryover basis assets of at least $60,000. Finally, in order to not subject appreciation arising prior to the Act to income taxation, the Act provides that the basis of assets acquired from a decedent which were held by that decedent on December 31, 1976, shall be stepped-up to their value on that date for purposes of determining gain.

Explanation of Provision

* * *

In the case of property passing by death, it is not possible to selectively transfer only loss assets since all of the assets of the decedent must pass at the death of their owner. Consequently, the Act does not generally limit the adjusted carryover basis to the fair market value of property acquired from or passing from a decedent. Thus, in the case of investment assets held by the decedent, losses as well as gains are to be measured by reference to the basis of the property in the hands of the decedent.

However, the Congress believed that it is inappropriate to permit the losses that typically occur in connection with personal and household assets to offset gains attributable to the investment assets of the decedent. Generally, these losses would have been treated as nondeductible personal losses if they had been realized by the decedent during his life. Thus, the Act provides that, for purposes of computing loss on the sale or other disposition of personal or household effects, the basis of these items cannot exceed their fair market value on the applicable valuation date. Where the amount realized on the sale of a personal item is greater than its fair market value at the date of death of the decedent but less than the basis of the asset in the hands of the decedent, then no gain or loss will be recognized on the transaction. For this purpose, personal and household effects generally include clothing, furniture, sporting goods, jewelry, stamp and coin collections, silverware, china, crystal, cooking utensils, books, cars, televisions, radios, stereo equipment, et cetera.

Definition of Carryover Basis Property

* * *

There are often numerous items such as clothing, etc., which the decedent owned at his death, for which it would be extremely difficult for the executor to determine their carryover bases. Moreover, in most cases, the fair market value of these items is less than their adjusted bases. To deal with this situation, the Act permits the executor of the estate, in effect, to exempt up to $10,000 worth of household and personal effects of the decedent from the carryover basis rules by making an election designating which items are not to receive carryover basis treatment. Where the executor makes such an election, the personal and household effects to which the election applies will receive a stepped-up basis, as under prior law.

Adjustments to Carryover Basis

In addition to a transitional "fresh start" adjustment described below, the Act provides three adjustments that are to be made to the adjusted basis which is carried over from the decedent. Under the first adjustment, the basis is increased by Federal and State estate taxes paid by the estate attributable to the appreciation in the carryover basis property. Secondly, after the adjustment for Federal and State estate taxes, if $60,000 exceeds the adjusted bases of all carryover assets, the bases of appreciated carryover basis property is increased by the excess. Finally, the basis of carryover basis property is increased by any State death taxes which are paid by the distributee of carryover basis property and which are attributable to any remaining appreciation in carryover basis property received by that distributee. However, in no event may the basis of any asset be increased by the three adjustments in excess of its fair market value on the date of the decedent's death.

* * *

Adjustment for "Fresh Start"

Under the Act, the adjusted basis of property which the decedent is treated as holding on December 31, 1976, is increased, for purposes of determining gain (but not loss), by the amount by which the fair market value of property on December 31, 1976, exceeds its adjusted basis on that date. In essence, this modification continues existing law with respect to appreciation in property accruing before January 1, 1977, and provides everyone with a "fresh start."

* * *

In order to avoid the necessity of obtaining an appraisal on all property held on December 31, 1976, the Act contains a provision which requires that all property, other than securities for which market quotations are readily available, is to be valued under a special valuation method. * * *

The appreciation treated as occurring before December 31, 1976, is determined by multiplying the total amount of appreciation over the entire period during which the decedent is treated as holding the property by a ratio. The ratio is determined by dividing the number of days that the property is considered to be held by the decedent before January 1, 1977, by the total number of days that the property is considered to be held by the decedent.

* * *

Under the Act, the December 31, 1976, value of marketable bonds or securities must be determined by their market value on December 31, 1976. Marketable bonds or securities are securities which are listed on the New York Stock Exchange, the American Stock Exchange, or any city or regional exchange in which quotations appear on a daily basis, including foreign securities listed on a recognized foreign national or regional exchange; securities regularly traded in the national or regional over-the-counter market, for which published quotations are available; securities locally traded for which quotations can readily be obtained from established brokerage firms; and units in a common trust fund. The value of such securities is to be determined using the normal methods of valuation for estate and gift tax purposes.

* * *

Any increase in basis permitted by the "fresh start" rule is made before any other adjustments are made to the property's basis for Federal and State death taxes and minimum basis.

Adjustment for Federal and State Estate Taxes

As indicated, the Act increases the basis of carryover basis property by a portion of the Federal and State estate taxes attributable to the carryover basis property. The purpose of the adjustment for Federal and State estate taxes is to prevent a portion of the appreciation from being subject to both the estate tax and the income tax. For this reason, the adjustment is limited to the portion of the Federal and State estate taxes that is attributable to the appreciation in the carryover basis assets. That portion for each individual carryover basis asset is determined by multiplying the net Federal and State estate tax after all credits by a fraction. The numerator of the fraction is the amount of appreciation in the individual carryover basis asset and the denominator is the total value of all property of the decedent subject to the estate tax.

In order to assure that the portion of the appreciation on each particular asset is not also subject to income tax, the appreciation on each asset is not to be reduced by any depreciation or loss in value of any other carryover basis property. In other words, the appreciation is determined on an asset by asset basis; there is no "netting" to determine unrealized appreciation for the estate as a whole. If it were not for this rule, heirs receiving appreciated property might be unfairly disadvantaged *vis a vis* other heirs.

* * *

The adjustment to carryover basis provided under the Act is made only with respect to property which is "subject to tax" for Federal estate tax purposes. For this purpose, the Act contains a special rule with respect to Federal and State estate taxes which provides that property for which a charitable or marital deduction is allowed (sections 2055, 2106 or section 2056) is not considered to be "subject to tax." * * *

In addition, a surviving spouse's share of community property is not considered to be "subject to tax" since it is not included in the deceased spouse's gross estate. Thus, no adjustment is to be made to the basis of the surviving spouse's share of community property.

* * *

Minimum Basis

As indicated above, the Act provides that the aggregate bases of all carryover basis property may be increased (but not above fair market value) to a minimum of $60,000. For this purpose, the determination of whether the aggregate bases of all carryover basis property exceeds $60,000 is to be determined after the increase in basis for "fresh start" and for Federal and State estate taxes (discussed above), but before the increase in basis for State succession taxes. Thus, if the aggregate bases of all carryover basis property in the hands of the decedent was $55,000, and the increase in basis for "fresh start" or Federal and State estate taxes is $5,000 or more, no additional adjustments are permitted under the minimum basis rule.

Once it is determined that the aggregate bases of all carryover basis property is less than $60,000, the difference between that aggregate amount and the $60,000 is then allocated among all appreciated carryover basis property on the basis of the ratio of net appreciation of each appreciated carryover basis asset to total appreciation of all appreciated carryover basis property.

* * *

Notes and Questions

10. Carryover basis is the most familiar reform proposal, because it is already used for gift property and because it was enacted, temporarily, with respect to inherited property as well. It seems to be the first choice of few, however. Even at the time of enactment in 1976, "[c]arryover was the classic compromise that pleased no one."[k] (Note that Representative Ullman, who was Chairman of the Ways and Means Committee in 1976, is quoted to similar effect in footnote 43 of the Zelenak excerpt in Subchapter C.)

11. The seemingly simple idea of carryover basis, as enacted in 1976, turned out to be extraordinarily complex. Critics argued that "the concept was ill-conceived and the statute was prepared with undue haste and lack of consideration of its mechanics," resulting in "a thoroughly unworkable piece of legislation."[l] The 1976 legislation included several qualifications to carryover basis, including: (a) a "fresh start" provision (which included

---

k. Howard J. Hoffman, *The Role of the Bar in the Tax Legislative Process,* 37 TAX L. REV. 411, 442 (1982).

l. Ira H. Lustgarten, Book Review, 78 COLUM. L. REV. 679, 679 (1978) (reviewing THOMAS J. MCGRATH & JONATHAN G. BLATTMACHR, CARRYOVER BASIS UNDER THE 1976 TAX REFORM ACT (1977)).

different rules for publicly traded securities and for other assets); (b) basis adjustments for federal and state death taxes; and (c) a $60,000 "minimum basis." What was the purpose of these provisions? Were they necessary? Were they wise, in terms of equity and workability?

12. Executors objected to carryover basis on the ground that it made the equitable distribution of assets among heirs more difficult. Why would it have this effect?

13. The role of the organized bar, and of the Tax Section of the American Bar Association in particular, in the repeal of carryover basis was portrayed in generally unflattering terms by Howard J. Hoffman, an attorney.[m] Mr. Hoffman begins by stating his views of the proper role of the bar:

> When an attorney participates in the legislative process on behalf of a client, many believe that he is ethically bound—as he would be in a courtroom—to advance the interests of his client unrestrained by considerations of tax policy. An attorney may also participate in the legislative process, however, as an impartial advisor, and offer his expertise of behalf of the tax system rather than on behalf of a client.[n]

Although acknowledging that carryover basis was fraught with problems that may have merited repeal, Mr. Hoffman generally gives the organized bar a failing grade for its role in the debate leading to repeal of carryover basis:

> Overall, however, the Tax Section and other tax groups did not fulfill their role as evenhanded tax experts. During the early part of the debate on carryover, they seemed to stress technical and practical considerations, and to understate other policy concerns. Throughout the debate, they appeared to present a one-sided view of carryover's technical problems and not to treat fairly the merits of cleanup.[o] Their discussion of policy concerns and of alternatives to carryover also seemed one-dimensional. Some of the Tax Section's actions gave the appearance of manipulating the legislative process to facilitate repeal. Although there were many different reasons for the tax group's views, they had given the appearance of taxpayer or client orientation.[p]

Mr. Hoffman quoted the tongue-in-cheek observation of Representative Corman, who was suggesting that the tax bar's complaints about complexity

---

m. Howard J. Hoffman, *The Role of the Bar in the Tax Legislative Process*, 37 TAX L. REV. 411 (1982).

n. *Id.* at 413.

o. "Cleanup" is the term used for the unsuccessful efforts to amend carryover basis in ways to make it more workable and less objectionable than the form in which it was enacted in 1976.

p. Hoffman, *supra* note m, at 492.

were merely an excuse for attempting to protect for their clients (and themselves?) the tax advantages of stepped-up basis:

> We have the wrong people drafting the wrong pieces of the tax code. Whoever drafts tax incentives is very, very good. I have never seen them draft one so complicated you could not live with it, but every time we try to impose taxes, they run in the other team and write it so complex you can't live with it.[q]

What should be the role of the bar in tax legislation?

C. CONSTRUCTIVE REALIZATION: TAXING DONORS AND DECEDENTS ON UNREALIZED APPRECIATION

Carryover basis would not result in income taxes being payable at the time of transfer. The tax would await sale (or other realization event) by the recipient. The tax on the appreciation, including the appreciation during the transferor's period of ownership, would ultimately be taxed to the transferee, at the transferee's marginal rate. Another approach would be to treat the transfer of property as a constructive realization event to the transferor—the equivalent for tax purposes of a sale at fair market value.

TAXING GAINS AT DEATH
Lawrence Zelenak[*]
46 Vanderbilt Law Review 361, 363-75, 409, 414-16 (1993)

The President's Budget estimates the annual revenue loss from the failure to tax gains at death at more than $25 billion.[5] Current law is objectionable also for its lock-in effect: elderly taxpayers are discouraged from disposing of appreciated assets, because if they hold the assets until death, the appreciation will escape income taxation permanently.[6]

This tax forgiveness did not originate as a conscious policy decision.[7]

---

q. *Id.* at 490-91, quoting *Estate and Gift Tax Carryover Basis and Generation-Skipping Trust Provisions and Deductibility of Foreign Convention Expenses: Hearings Before the House Comm. on Ways and Means*, 95th Cong., 1st Sess. 107 (1977).

*. At time of original publication, Professor of Law, University of North Carolina.

5. The Budget of the United States Government for Fiscal Year 1993 estimates the revenue loss at $24.365 billion in 1991, $26.8 billion in 1992, and $28.4 billion in 1993. Office of the President, *Budget of the United States Government for Fiscal Year 1993*, Special Analysis G 2-26 (U.S. Gov. Printing Off., 1992).

6. The lock-in effect discourages gifts as well as sales. A lifetime gift does not trigger tax on the appreciation, but it prevents a step-up in basis upon the donor's death. I.R.C. § 1015.

7. Until 1921, no tax statute specified the basis of property received by gift or bequest. The administrative practice was to give such property a basis equal to its value at the date of transfer. Anita Wells, *Legislative History of Treatment of Capital Gains Under the Federal Income Tax, 1913-1948*, 2 Nat'l Tax J. 12, 16 (1949). In 1921, Congress enacted the predecessors of present I.R.C. §§ 1014 and 1015 (setting a fair market value basis for bequests and a carryover basis for gifts). One commentator has noted that the rationale for the Section 1014-type statute is unclear, and that it appears "to have been merely the legislative adoption of a consistent administrative practice." Louis M. Castruccio, *Becoming More Inevitable? Death and Taxes . . . and Taxes*, 17 UCLA L. Rev. 459, 460-61 (1970).

Rather it occurred almost accidentally from the combination of two ideas that were accepted instinctively during the early years of the income tax: that the mere transfer of property at death did not constitute a realization of gain or loss on the property,[8] and that fair market value basis for heirs was appropriate to prevent taxation of capital, because "'capital' was thought to refer to some tangible thing, whatever its value, rather than to a monetary account keeping track of what has been taxed."[9]

Defenders of the current system have justified it on the grounds that the step up in basis is "paid for" by the estate tax on the appreciation. It is true that appreciation that escapes income tax may not escape estate tax, and the estate tax rate may even be higher than the income tax rate.[11] Nevertheless, there are two problems with this argument. First, the step up in basis applies even to property that is not subject to estate tax (because of the unified credit or the marital bequest deduction). Second, and more important, the income and estate taxes are distinct, both conceptually and practically. Conceptually, there is no reason why appreciation transferred at death should not be subject to both taxes—to the income tax because it is gain, and to the estate tax because it is a gratuitous transfer. Practically, gratuitously transferred income is generally subject to both taxes. If a taxpayer sells appreciated property during life, the gain is subject to income tax, and if at death he transfers the proceeds of the sale (reduced by the income tax paid) to his beneficiaries, the estate tax will apply as well. The treatment of appreciation at death thus produces inequity between taxpayers who realize income during life, and those who transfer unrealized appreciation at death. The inequity is both horizontal (discriminating between different taxpayers of similar income and wealth) and vertical (favoring wealthy taxpayers because a greater portion of their income tends to be in the form of unrealized appreciation transferred at death).

If Congress desires to eliminate the permanent forgiveness of capital gains tax at death, it could do so either by providing that the basis of property transferred at death carries over to heirs and beneficiaries, or by taxing gains at death. During the process that led to the enactment of the Tax Reform Act of 1986, virtually every base-broadening reform with significant support among tax policy experts was discussed by Congress and the administration. The one glaring exception was the forgiveness of gains tax at death.[16] This omission would be astounding,[17] but for some history.

---

8. The leading early case on realization, *Eisner v. Macomber*, 252 U.S. 189 (1920), indicated that gain was realized only when it somehow was severed from capital. Death, of course, does not produce any such severance.

9. Calvin Johnson, *The Undertaxation of Holding Gains*, 55 Tax Notes 807, 813 (1992).

11. Under current law, the highest rate on capital gain is 28%, I.R.C. § 1(h), and the lowest estate tax rate (after application of the unified credit) is 37%, id. § 2001(c)(1).

16. The only mention was a sort of nonmention. The Treasury Department included "capital gains on appreciated assets transferred at death or by gift" in a list of "items not included in the tax reform proposal." 1 *Tax Reform for Fairness, Simplicity and Economic Growth* (Dept. of the

As part of the Tax Reform Act of 1976, Congress enacted Section 1023 of the Internal Revenue Code, which generally provided a carryover basis (rather than a Section 1014 fair market value at death basis) for inherited property. Congress added the carryover basis provision to the Act very late in the legislative process, with little opportunity for either input from interest groups or careful technical drafting. Affected taxpayers and their representatives harshly criticized it, on both technical and policy grounds, and in 1980 it was repealed retroactively. Regardless of one's views on the merits of carryover basis, its short unhappy life was one of the greatest legislative fiascoes in the history of the income tax. This was recent history in 1986, and it is understandable that Congress lacked the fortitude to revisit the issue so soon.

In the past few years, interest in this area slowly has reawakened. As memory of Section 1023 recedes, as pressure to raise revenue without raising rates increases, and as the remaining opportunities for significant base-broadening reform diminish, it becomes more likely that Congress eventually will revisit the area. And when Congress does, it seems much more likely (for reasons discussed below) that it will tax gains at death, rather than revive carryover basis. * * *

Choosing Between Carryover Basis and Taxing Gains at Death

Either carryover basis at death or a death gains tax would prevent the permanent avoidance of gains tax that occurs under current law. At the theoretical level, the argument for carryover basis is that postponing tax until an actual sale of the property avoids the need to appraise the property[26] and imposes tax at a time when the taxpayer is likely to have cash available to pay the tax. The arguments for gains tax at death are that it appropriately limits the maximum deferral possibility to a single lifetime; it enforces the principle that income should be taxed to the person who earned it; it imposes tax at an ideal time in terms of ability to pay (because the decedent has no use for the amount due as taxes, and whatever the heirs or beneficiaries receive is a windfall); and, unlike carryover basis, it solves the problem of lock-in.[28] Congress will not choose, however, between the two

---

Treasury, 1984), at 147.

17. It is especially surprising because the 1986 Act repealed the so-called *General Utilities* doctrine, which allowed liquidating corporations permanently to avoid corporate level tax on the distribution (or, in some cases, even the sale) of their appreciated assets. Tax Reform Act of 1986, § 631, Pub.L. No. 99-514, 100 Stat. 2058 (1986). The *General Utilities* doctrine is the corporate analog of the forgiveness of gains at death, so it is strange that tax reform would repeal one and not even consider the other.

26. If Congress imposes a death gains tax only on estates subject to the estate tax, the gains tax will not involve any additional appraisal requirements. It does increase, however, the tax consequences of an inaccurate appraisal.

28. Carryover basis does lessen the problem of pre-death lock-in because elderly taxpayers know their assets will not receive a stepped-up basis at death. However, carryover basis creates a new problem of post-death lock-in: because the heirs inherit with low carryover basis, they are discouraged from selling the assets. Under either current law or a gains tax at death, the heirs

approaches based on such theoretical considerations. Rather, the key issues will be the complexity of administering the two approaches and the relative amounts of revenue they would raise.

The most serious administrative difficulty—proof of basis—would loom equally large under either system. In other respects, however, a death gains tax would be somewhat simpler to apply than carryover basis. Carryover basis would create a new problem for executors, because their fiduciary duties would require them to make not only an equitable distribution of *value* among beneficiaries, but also an equitable distribution of *basis*. A death gains tax does not present this problem, because all assets (other than assets going to a surviving spouse, if the system permits deferral of gains on such assets) receive a fair market value basis following the imposition of the tax at death. In addition, carryover basis requires the maintenance of basis records across unlimited numbers of generations; a death gains tax does not.

A major complication of carryover basis is the death tax basis adjustment. In order to make the consequences of carryover basis consistent with the tax consequences of selling appreciated property before death, it is necessary to increase the basis of appreciated carryover basis property by the death taxes (federal and state estate taxes, and state succession tax) attributable to the appreciation.[29] Although the principle is easy enough to state, applying it can be very complex. Section 1023(c) calculated the adjustment for each asset by multiplying the appreciation in the asset by the average tax rate for the entire estate. Since the average tax rate for an estate is a function of the value of every asset in the estate, the basis of every appreciated asset in the estate was uncertain as long as the value of even one asset was uncertain.

* * *

Another problem of carryover basis is the need for some method—whether by mechanical rules or executor election—of allocating whatever minimum basis adjustment is allowed. Allocation of the adjustment is necessary under carryover basis because gain on different assets may be recognized at different times and by different taxpayers. By

---

take assets with a fair market value basis, so post-death lock-in does not occur.

29. Suppose, for example, a 50% flat rate estate tax and a 28% flat rate capital gains tax, and a taxpayer with just two assets: $1,000,000 cash, and stock with a basis of zero and a value of $1,000,000. If the taxpayer sold the stock before his death for $1,000,000, the gains tax would be $280,000, and payment of the tax would reduce his estate to $1,720,000. The 50% estate tax would be $860,000, and the beneficiaries would receive $860,000. In order to replicate this result if the taxpayer dies and the stock is then sold by the estate or by the beneficiaries, a death tax basis adjustment is needed. The estate tax liability is $1,000,000 (50% of $2,000,000), of which $500,000 is attributable to the appreciation in the stock. The $1,000,000 cash is used to pay the estate tax, and the beneficiaries receive the stock. The beneficiaries thus take the stock with a basis of $500,000, after the death tax basis adjustment. The gain on a subsequent sale of the stock for $1,000,000 is $500,000, resulting in a tax of $140,000. Reducing the $1,000,000 proceeds by $140,000 leaves the beneficiaries with $860,000—the same amount they would have received if the decedent had sold the stock before death.

contrast, this is not an issue under a death gains tax because all gain is taxed at the same time to the same taxpayer.

Some commentators have argued that a death gains tax with carryover basis for marital bequests would be just as complicated as general carryover basis. They are right that not having a marital exemption is simpler than having one, but they are wrong in arguing that a marital exemption involves all the difficulties of general carryover basis. A marital exemption would require keeping basis records, not over several generations, but only until the death of the surviving spouse. More important, the carryover basis for marital exemption property would be pure carryover basis, without any of the complicating adjustments. There would be no death tax adjustment because the marital bequest would not have been subject to estate tax. No minimum basis adjustment would be allowed for property passing to a surviving spouse, and no transition rule basis adjustment would be made to such property at that time; there would be no need to make either adjustment until the property is actually subject to tax at the death of the surviving spouse.

More important than the modest simplicity advantage of tax at death over carryover basis is the much greater revenue effect of tax at death. The Congressional Budget Office (CBO), for example, estimated that taxing capital gains at death would raise $17.0 billion over four years (1994 to 1997), while carryover basis would raise only $5.2 billion.[39] Part of the reason that Congress was unable to withstand the pressure to repeal carryover basis was that carryover basis did not raise very much revenue. It is difficult to resist impassioned (and plausible) claims that the statute is too complex when the major argument in favor of the statute is that it closes a loophole offensive to some academics. It should be considerably easier to resist the claims that the statute is too complex when a major argument in favor of the law is that it raises very substantial and badly needed revenue.

Although the revenue impact is by far the biggest advantage of the gains tax, it has two additional political advantages over carryover basis. First, it does not carry the historical baggage of carryover basis. The enactment and repeal of carryover basis was such a long and complete fiasco that carryover basis may never be given serious consideration again as long as anyone in Congress remembers that history. Legislators must feel strongly that it has been fully considered and conclusively rejected. Although that history also must color any consideration of a death gains tax, it should not have so conclusive an effect. Second, there are those (primarily academicians, but also some politicians and practitioners) who strongly believe in taxing gains

---

39. Congressional Budget Office, *Reducing the Deficit: Spending and Revenue Options, Part 2* at 315 (U.S. G.P.O. 1990) (*"Reducing the Deficit"*). How much revenue is raised by either a death gains tax or carryover basis will depend, of course, on the extent of relief given to smaller estates. At any given level of relief, however, a death gains tax will raise substantially more revenue than carryover basis.

at death. By contrast, almost no one considers carryover basis the best way of dealing with gains at death.[43]

Taxing Gains at Death: Revenue Implications and Policy Choices

How much revenue would be raised by taxing capital gains at death is unclear, but it is clear that it would be significant. The Budget of the United States for Fiscal Year 1993 lists the failure to tax gain at death as the fourth largest item in the tax expenditure budget, with estimated revenue loss of more than $24 billion in 1991, more than $26 billion in 1992, and more than $28 billion in 1993.[44] By contrast, the CBO has estimated the annual revenue gain from taxing capital gains at death at $5.3 billion by 1997. Much or all of the difference in the estimates derives from the fact that the CBO estimate, unlike the budget estimate, is for a tax with substantial exemptions. The CBO estimate is for a tax with marital and charitable exemptions, with the option of using one-half an asset's date-of-death value as basis, with the availability of the $125,000 exclusion for gain on a primary residence (if not used during life), and with a $75,000 exclusion for any remaining gains. * * *

There are general points worth noting about the revenue effect of taxing gains at death. First, much of the revenue effect would be indirect. That is, without the lock-in effect of forgiveness of gains tax at death, elderly taxpayers would realize much more gain while still alive. Thus, much (perhaps most) of the revenue gain from the death tax would not result from assessing the tax at death, but from tax on dispositions during life which would not have occurred in the absence of a death gains tax. Second, since

---

43. Howard Hoffman, *The Role of the Bar in the Tax Legislative Process*, 37 Tax L. Rev. 411, 442 (1982) (describing carryover as "the classic compromise that pleased no one"). He remarks that during consideration of repeal of carryover, many who favored taxing gains at death gave carryover little support. Id. at 442-43 n.121. During hearings held early in 1976 before the enactment of carryover basis, a panel of experts resoundingly rejected carryover basis. Federal Estate and Gift Taxes, Public Hearings and Panel Discussions Before the Comm. on Ways and Means, 94th Cong., 2d Sess. 1211, 1435 (1976) (*"Federal Estate and Gift Taxes"*) (A. James Casner, stating that "the worst thing to do is . . . a carryover basis"); id. at 1444 (Edward C. Halbach, Jr., calling carryover "the worst of the possible alternatives"; Rep. Ullman, summarizing the testimony: "The carryover basis is obviously very difficult. No one seems to favor it very much.").

44. Office of the President, *Budget of the United States Government for Fiscal Year 1993* (cited in note 5). The exact figures are $24.365 billion, $26.8 billion, and $28.14 billion. Id. at 2-26. The larger items in the tax expenditure budget are the expenditures for retirement savings, medical insurance, and home mortgage interest. The exemption of capital gains at death is unlike the three larger items in that it is unclear what Congress intended the exemption to accomplish. Whatever one may think of the other three expenditures, it is easy to understand why Congress might choose to subsidize retirement savings, medical insurance, and homeownership. It is much more difficult to understand the purpose of subsidizing the holding of appreciated property until death.

Jt. Comm. on Taxation, *Estimates of Federal Tax 1993-1997 Expenditures for Fiscal Years 1993-1997*, 102nd Cong., 2nd Sess. 14.0 (U.S. G.P.O. 1992), estimates the revenue loss from not taxing capital gains at death to be much lower (although still very large): $11.6 billion in 1993, $12.7 billion in 1994, $14.0 billion in 1995, $15.4 billion in 1996, and $17.1 billion in 1997. Neither the Committee's report nor the Budget explains the discrepancy between the estimates.

the income tax liability created by the tax on gains at death logically should be deductible under the estate tax as a claim against the estate, a complete analysis of the revenue impact of the gains tax must consider the partially offsetting reduction in estate tax receipts. Consider, for example, $100 of appreciation held at death, with an applicable capital gains tax rate of twenty-eight percent and an applicable estate tax rate of fifty percent. Compared with no capital gains tax, the gains tax increases income tax revenue by $28, but decreases estate tax revenue by $14 (because the fifty percent estate tax is imposed on $72 instead of $100), for a net revenue gain of $14.

Whatever the amount of revenue raised by the tax, there are three major options for what to do with that revenue: use it to reduce the deficit, use it to offset revenue lost from a decrease in the capital gains tax rate, or use it to reduce or even eliminate the estate tax. Congress also could devote the revenue to various combinations of the three uses.

The deficit reduction option is attractive. As a principled and perhaps politically feasible way of raising substantial additional revenue from the income tax without raising rates, it is a rarity. A death gains tax would result in a top combined income and estate tax burden of sixty-four percent on appreciation held at death, assuming a top capital gains rate of twenty-eight percent and a top estate tax rate of fifty percent. From an historical perspective, that is not a particularly high federal death tax rate—as recently as 1981, the top estate tax rate was seventy percent. Nevertheless, it is questionable whether the current Congress would accept the sixty-four percent combined tax burden that would result if the gains tax were used entirely for deficit reduction.

One economist has estimated that a reduction in the capital gains tax rate to 12.5% and the taxation of gains at death would yield approximately the same revenue as the current twenty-eight percent capital gains rate and forgiveness of tax at death.[52] This proposal is attractive in several ways. Both parts of the proposal would reduce lock-in: the lower rate would decrease resistance to recognizing gains during life, and the death tax would eliminate the incentive to hold assets until death. The proposal also would eliminate the horizontal inequity between taxpayers who sell appreciated assets during life and those who hold assets until death, by moving both groups of taxpayers to the same middle ground. It might fare well as a political compromise between those who feel strongly that there should be a significant reduction in capital gains rates and those offended by the forgiveness of capital gains tax at death. A closely related possibility would use the revenue raised by a death gains tax to pay for indexing of basis for inflation.

---

52. Donald W. Kiefer, *Lock-In Effect Within a Simple Model of Corporate Stock Trading*, 43 Nat'l Tax J. 75, 90 (1990).

The estate and gift taxes raised approximately $12.1 billion in 1992.[53] At least one commentator has suggested replacing the transfer taxes with a capital gains tax imposed on gifts and bequests of appreciated property.[54] As the above discussion indicates, it is unclear whether the revenue lost by repealing the transfer taxes could be replaced entirely by taxing capital gains at death. Assuming, however, that the change could be made revenue neutral, would it be a good idea? The change might appeal to an "academic desire for tidiness,"[55] because it rationalizes the income tax by eliminating perhaps its most glaring loophole. In addition, it repeals a transfer tax system always objectionable for the many omissions from its base.

Notice, however, that the potential tax base for a capital gains tax on gratuitous transfers is substantially smaller than the potential tax base for a transfer tax system—smaller by the amount of the cost bases of the assets gratuitously transferred. Moreover, at current rates the capital gains tax (twenty-eight percent top rate) will raise less revenue from a given dollar amount of tax base than will the transfer taxes (rates ranging from thirty-seven to fifty percent). Thus, for the capital gains tax to raise as much revenue as the transfer taxes, with a smaller potential base and lower rates, it must include in its actual base a much higher percentage of its potential base than do the transfer taxes. Although some of this might be done through loophole closing, the vast majority would have to be done by using much lower exemption amounts than the $600,000 transfer tax exemption created by the unified credit. Thus, assuming revenue neutrality, replacement of the transfer taxes with a capital gains tax on transfers would result in a major shift of tax burden away from the wealthy and the upper middle class, and onto the middle class. I would oppose the regressivity inherent in a such a change, and it seems likely Congress would agree.

* * *

Special Avoidance Concerns

Taxation of Gain on Gifts During Life

Most plans to tax capital gains at death have included taxation of gains on gifts made during life. The reason is apparent: the premise of the tax at death is that gains should be taxed at least once a generation, but gains tax can be deferred indefinitely if appreciated property is transferred from one generation to another by gift and gain is not taxed at that time. A rule taxing gain on assets gifted in contemplation of death, or within a specified time before death, is not adequate to prevent avoidance because many wealthy

---

53. Office of the President, *Budget of the United States Government for Fiscal Year 1993* at 2-3 (cited in note 5). Actual estate and gift tax receipts for 1991 were $11.1 billion. Id.

54. Professor Galvin suggests repealing the transfer taxes and replacing them with either a capital gains tax imposed at the time of gifts and bequests, an accessions tax, or some combination of the two. Charles O. Galvin, *To Bury the Estate Tax, Not to Praise It*, 52 Tax Notes 1413, 1413 (1991).

55. *Commissioner v. Duberstein*, 363 U.S. 278, 290 (1960).

taxpayers will be willing and able to transfer much of their appreciation well before their deaths. Such avoidance will be most practical for the very wealthy, thus reducing the vertical equity of the death gains tax.

It is clear, then, that gifts generally should trigger the recognition of gain. * * *

A Small Estate Exemption

It seems clear that there should be an exemption from a capital gains death tax for small estates. At some point, estates are small enough that the revenue gained from taxing their appreciation does not justify imposing the complexities of a capital gains tax (or, for that matter, of carryover basis). The difficult question is finding that point. One obvious and attractive possibility is designing the exemption to track (so far as possible) the estate tax exemption provided by the unified credit, so that estates not subject to the estate tax also would not be subject to the gains tax, and estates subject to the estate tax also would be subject to the gains tax. For estates not subject to the gains tax, current law—no realization of gain or loss at death, and fair market value basis for inherited property—would continue to apply. This would limit the application of the death gains tax to a small portion of the decedent population.[224]

Would it be appropriate to equate the estate tax and death gains tax exemptions? In considering this question, the current $600,000 exemption amount need not be viewed as unalterable. One may favor a higher or lower estate tax exemption amount, quite apart from considerations related to a new death gains tax. Or the revenue gained from the death gains tax could be used to raise the exemption amount for both taxes. Whatever the precise exemption amount, there are strong arguments for using the same amount for both taxes. Perhaps most important, equating the exemptions would mean that the death tax would not impose any additional valuation requirements: death gains tax would be imposed only on property that already had to be valued for the estate tax. Estates large enough to exceed the exemption amount should have the necessary resources to handle the administrative burdens of the gains tax. And despite affecting only a small percentage of all estates, the tax still would reach much of the appreciation passing at death, since that appreciation is concentrated in larger estates.[225]

---

224. An estimated 45,800 U.S. citizens who died in 1986 had gross estates over $500,000 (the exemption amount for that year). They represented about 2.2% of all U.S. decedents. Slightly fewer than half (about 22,000) of those estates were taxable, after deductions. Barry Johnson, *Estate Tax Returns, 1986-1988*, 9 SOI Bull. 27, 27 (Spring 1990).

225. The leading carryover basis clean-up proposal would have equated the carryover basis exemption with the existing estate tax exemption, by providing an exemption from carryover basis for estates having $175,000 or less of carryover basis property. H.R. 4694 § 2(a) (proposed § 1023(a)(3)). Raising the minimum basis from $60,000 to $175,000 was estimated to reduce the number of estates subject to carryover basis (from 9.4% of all decedents to 2.7%) much more than it reduced the revenue effect of carryover basis (from $833 million to $560 million). Background and Issues Relating to Carryover Basis Hearings Before Joint Comm. On Taxation, 96th Cong., 1st Sess. 35 (U.S. G.P.O. 1979).

Finally, equating the exemptions may be the only way to make the death gains tax politically feasible. The 1976 carryover basis statute was strongly criticized for applying to many estates not subject to the estate tax, and the proponents of carryover basis agreed that the law should be revised to equate the exemption levels.

There are also arguments against equating the exemptions, all of which are based on the fact that a gains tax exemption tied to the estate tax exemption will mean huge amounts of appreciation escaping the tax. * * *

I find the arguments for equating the estate and death tax exemptions persuasive, and I suspect Congress would as well. * * *

BECOMING MORE INEVITABLE?
DEATH AND TAXES ... AND TAXES
Louis M. Castruccio[*]

17 UCLA Law Review 459, 483-91 (1970)

The basic concept of constructive realization provides that gains accrued on capital assets transferred by gift or at death would be subject to the normal capital gains tax.

Economic Aspects

There are some salutary economic results that might arise from the imposition of a capital gains tax at gift and death. * * * It would appear that all lock-in effects, to whatever extent they do in fact exist, would be eliminated because the ultimate attraction of a transfer at gift or death free of capital gains taxation would be removed. The only possible residual tax benefit remaining for those holding capital assets until death would be deferral of payment of the capital gains tax. * * *

Imposition of a capital gains tax at gift and death would increase government revenues. * * * [T]he exact amount of such increase is uncertain. However, it seems reasonable to include as part of such increase not only the taxes collected upon actual transfers at gift and death, but also those taxes resulting from inter vivos sales and exchanges of capital assets which would not have occurred but for constructive realization.

Equitable Aspects

The constructive realization system would appear to remedy the violation of horizontal equity experienced under the present method of treating capital gains at gift and death. Under constructive realization two taxpayers with similar investment goals will in the long run be treated alike in that ultimately the taxpayer who holds his capital assets until death will be subject to exactly the same capital gains tax as the individual who sells or exchanges his capital assets during his lifetime.

---

[*]. At time of original publication, member, California Bar.

To the contrary, it can be argued that the taxpayer who holds capital assets until death is still obtaining more favorable treatment because he can defer his capital gains tax payment until death. This argument can be answered on the ground that the underlying policy of the capital gains tax has always been to leave the timing of the tax creating sale or exchange to the taxpayer's decision and that the purpose of constructive realization is to implement this policy in a meaningful manner. Constructive realization accomplishes this result by defining gifts and transfers at death as very real, and particularly in the case of the latter, final tax creating events. Such an approach will prevent the use of the theory of taxpayer timing of taxable events as a means of completely escaping capital gains tax.

Another criticism of the constructive realization approach is that it would have harsh effects upon closely held corporations and small businesses. It is contended that these concerns, which have often been initiated and built by one or a few individuals, aren't amenable to sale during one's life because of the close relationship between owner and business. On this ground it is argued that a taxpayer who owns a small business is in a completely different position in comparison to those who trade in more readily marketable assets such as securities and real estate. It is further argued that to tax a small business upon the death of its initiator would often force a sacrifice sale.

The contentions that small corporations and businesses are not as amenable to sale as other types of assets and that a sale of such a business to meet tax payments might be disastrous are valid to some extent. * * *

Constructive realization will also bring about some improvement in vertical equity. As previously indicated, the present treatment of capital gains at gift and death results in a lack of vertical equity in that the accrued gains of the wealthy and less wealthy alike completely escape capital gains tax. Imposition of the normal capital gains tax rates upon transfers at gift and death will result in progression between the less wealthy taxed at lower marginal rates and the wealthy presumably taxed at the maximum effective capital gains tax rate. * * *

Major Administrative Problems of Constructive Realization at Gift and Death

There are several major administrative aspects of constructive realization which bear close scrutiny. These items are of such importance that unless Code machinery can be tailored to accommodate them, their negative implications may outweigh all the economic and equity benefits which might otherwise accompany the adoption of constructive realization.

As indicated earlier, there is a danger that imposition of a capital gains tax at death may force the dissolution of closely held businesses. In theory this is not a question of horizontal equity, but unless administrative measures are available to alleviate the problem, it may for all practical purposes become a question of horizontal equity. The same problem was faced in connection with the federal estate tax, and it would seem that the same administrative method used in that instance could be integrated into the constructive realization system. That is, if a closely held business accounts for more than a certain percentage of all the capital gains to be recognized at death, then that portion of the capital gains tax attributable to the gains on such business could be paid in installments over an extended period of time.

* * *

Another formidable administrative problem presented by constructive realization is the treatment of capital losses at death. There are at least three alternative methods available to solve this problem. First, any net losses in the year of the decedent's death, including those recognized under constructive realization, could be offset in full against the decedent's net income in his final tax year. This approach would be unacceptable for at least two reasons. If the decedent was particularly old, had little income in his declining years, yet realized a large capital loss at death, more than likely a great portion of such loss would go unused. Also, if the decedent has a short final year, i.e., a calendar year taxpayer dying on January 10, there would obviously be little income against which to offset any loss recognized under constructive realization.

A second method would allow the net losses recognized under constructive realization, to the extent they exceeded the decedent's final year income, to be carried forward for use by the decedent's heirs or the beneficiaries under his will. It might be argued that this alternative would most nearly parallel the capital loss carryforward available to living taxpayers. At first blush this attempt at similarity of treatment seems quite valid. On closer analysis, however, can it be said that a treatment under which different individuals make use of a decedent's capital losses is at all parallel to a situation where a living taxpayer himself takes advantage of previous losses on his own subsequent tax returns? Beyond this theoretical problem, loss carryforward might cause certain practical problems.

One method whereby losses could be carried forward to survivors would be to allow each separate recipient of a loss asset to also acquire the use of the loss realized upon the transfer of such asset at death. The value of the use of such loss would of course depend in great part upon the tax status of the recipient—whether he had large amounts of capital gains or small amounts, whether he was in a high ordinary income tax bracket or a low one, etc. Potentially more serious problems might arise if a loss asset had to be sold by an estate in order to meet federal estate tax obligations. Would the purchaser of the asset acquire the use of the loss allocable to such asset? If not, would the loss be considered part of the residue of the estate? If it were considered part of the residue, would it have a value for federal estate tax purposes? If it were to be assigned a value for federal estate tax purposes the valuation thereof might depend in some part upon the tax status of the individual residuary beneficiaries.

As can be seen, this loss carryforward approach might become extremely complex. If there is some effective, less involved method of handling net capital losses under constructive realization, it would probably be preferable.

A loss carryback may be superior to a loss carryforward approach. Under a loss carryback system, net capital losses realized under constructive realization would be first applied against all capital gains and then against all ordinary income in the decedent's final tax year. If unused capital losses remained, these could be applied first against capital gains in a set number of previous years and then against all ordinary income in the same number of previous years. To be sure, this would involve reopening back returns. But, the reopening of back returns occurs in many other areas of the income tax law, and if it will improve the overall neutrality of the tax structure, there should be no hesitancy in the use of such a device.

　　　* * *

The more difficult valuation problem created by constructive realization is that which requires the determination of the adjusted basis of assets held by a decedent. The amount of difficulty in this area will depend upon the extent to which the decedent kept records of his capital assets. It is in this area that the Internal Revenue Service will probably have to be particularly watchful in order to determine that reported adjusted bases are accurate. However, this will not be an entirely new problem for the Internal Revenue Service, as it is faced with much the same problem in cases where donees sell property after death of the donor. Neither of the above aspects of the increased incidence of valuation at death should constitute a bar to the adoption of constructive realization. Both problems, though with less frequency, have been a part of the federal estate and gift tax for many years.

It has been suggested that any tax due under constructive realization be deducted from the taxable gross estate. This appears justified on theoretical grounds. * * *

Some Unique Problems of Constructive Realization and Transfers by Gift

If constructive realization were adopted for taxpayers at death but the present carryover method were maintained as to gifts, this latter treatment would take on new importance. Its position as a transaction receiving favored tax treatment would be heightened, as it would represent the last remaining method whereby one could postpone the incidence of the capital gains tax beyond one's death.

A combination of a constructive realization approach at death and a carryover approach as to gifts might create a unique economic lock-in. Faced with this structure, taxpayers might decide to hold their capital assets for an added period of years at the end of which they would transfer such assets by gift. The possibility that this lock-in might develop must be discounted somewhat on at least two grounds. First the tax benefit presented by carryover is merely a tax deferral, an advantage which is much less significant than the complete escape from capital gains tax available under the present treatment of capital gains at death. Secondly, individuals who are actually faced with the prospect of relinquishing ownership of assets often become reluctant to part with them. This latter fact might result in many assets originally planned for transfer by gift actually passing upon an owner's death and therefore subject to constructive realization. Nonetheless, it cannot be denied that capital gains tax deferral * * * would present attractive tax benefits.

Application of constructive realization to gifts would remove such transfers from a favored tax position and would prevent the development of any economic lock-in due to the differentiation in tax treatment between the sale or exchange of capital assets and their transfer by gift. Constructive realization at gift would necessarily eliminate the possibility that the thought of an impending future gift might overcome maintenance of a present optimum portfolio. If constructive realization were applied to gifts the neutrality of the capital gains tax would be assured since it would be imposed upon the sale or exchange of capital assets and upon the transfer of capital assets by gift or at death. There would also be an administrative benefit arising from the application of constructive realization to gifts, since such treatment would avoid the possibility that determination of adjusted basis would take place at a time even further removed from when the donor's basis was actually determined.

Finally, it should be recognized that the application of constructive realization to gifts is very much like the application of the general capital gains tax to sales and exchanges. In both cases there is the imposition of a tax upon a transaction, the timing of which is left to the taxpayer's discretion. Therefore, the treatment of losses and reporting procedures upon transfers by gift could be the same as they are for sales and exchanges. Any dissatisfaction with such procedures should be directed not to constructive realization but to the general capital gains tax itself.

     * * *

ON CONSTRUCTIVELY REALIZING
CONSTRUCTIVE REALIZATION:
BUILDING THE CASE FOR DEATH AND TAXES
Dan Subotnik[*]

38 Kansas Law Review 1, 36-38 (1989)

We come now to our final question: What should be done if, notwithstanding the strong equity case for incorporating CR [constructive

---

[*]. At time of original publication, Professor of Law at Touro College, Jacob D. Fuchsberg Law Center.

realization] into the tax system, our options are limited to choosing between CR and an estate tax? Given our past inability to add a second tax applicable at death, this formulation of the question may be the practical consequence of articles such as this. In an important sense the question is not a real one because our review of CR history has shown that it has attracted only limited interest. Perhaps, however, this is because the estate tax is already in place and none of the proposals that have been advanced has raised the possibility of eliminating the estate tax.

From a revenue standpoint, the choice between CR and an estate tax is a toss-up. The transfer taxes bring in roughly $6.5 billion, while estimates are that CR would bring in about $5 billion.

From a number of other vantage points, however, the Canadian [constructive realization] solution makes more sense. Among the nonrevenue arguments advanced in support of the estate tax, three stand out for our purposes. First, the estate tax is a back-up to the income tax in which (on account of prior practice) there are numerous loopholes. Second, the estate tax helps to break up large estates which, left unchecked, would result in the accumulation of economic and thus political power in the hands of a small number of American families. Finally, the estate tax diminishes the likelihood of formation of an effete "leisure class."

Whatever the persuasiveness of these arguments in the past, it is much diminished now. For one thing, thanks to the Tax Reform Act of 1986 and other recent legislation, the loopholes are fewer and farther between. The passive loss rules, alternative minimum tax, restrictions on the deductibility of "personal" interest, lengthening of depreciation periods, and prescription of the straight-line method for real estate—to name just a few provisions—have combined to ensure that far fewer high gross income taxpayers escape taxation.

At the same time, wealth has spread out so significantly and inflation has had such a profound effect that individuals with asset holdings of over $600,000 can no longer be considered a menace to the republic. Moreover, unlike the apparent situation in Great Britain, far from turning into the idle rich, the sons and daughters of our empire-builders are going to the University of Chicago or Harvard Business Schools so that by working eighty-hour weeks, they can successfully make the family empire "world class."

The matter is clearer yet from the administrative perspective on the estate tax versus CR issue. The estate and gift tax rules are spelled out in about forty code sections. Relating to these sections are innumerable and technical regulations, as well as judicial opinions that frequently are classifiable only as soaring flights of fancy. Estate planning has become so other-worldly and esoteric that it makes up an entire area of professional specialization. If this entire structure could be collapsed and replaced with

a few new code sections (we now know that it *can* be done), Congress would finally be able to boast justifiably that it has simplified the tax system.
　　* * *

Notes and Questions

14. Constructive realization would treat death as a realization event, and assume that the decedent sold all his assets for fair market value. Thus, the decedent's final income tax return would take account of all unrealized appreciation. The heirs would then receive the property with a stepped-up basis, because the gain would have already been taxed. Proposals to treat death as a realization event usually treat making a gift as a realization event as well, as in both the Zelenak and Castruccio excerpts. In part, this is due to the difficulty of administering a rule that death constitutes a realization event but gift does not. However, it also seems that the claimed policy advantages of taxing the transferor of property at death generally apply in the gift situation. Except as noted, the term "constructive realization" in these notes assumes that constructive realization occurs upon either transfer. With respect to gifts in trust, see Note #31 below.

15. Do you agree with Professor Zelenak that constructive realization at death results in levying the tax "at an ideal time in terms of ability to pay"? Is your answer affected by whether an estate tax is also applicable?

16. It seems likely that any constructive receipt proposal would entail an unlimited marital deduction, coupled with carryover basis for the spouse who received the property. This approach seems fully consistent with the recent drift of tax law, notably the adoption of an unlimited marital exclusion under the estate and gift taxes (added to the law in 1981), and the rule of section 1041 that gain and loss is not recognized on transfers between spouses (added in 1984). In a portion of his article not excerpted above, Professor Zelenak discusses problems of this exclusion that may not be immediately apparent, such as whether the law should be concerned about such problems as executors funding marital bequests with low-basis property in order to postpone the death tax until the death of the spouse.[r] The balance, as so frequently, is between simplicity on the one hand, and revenue (and equity?) on the other.

17. Professor Zelenak asserts that constructive realization "appropriately limits the maximum deferral possibility to a single lifetime." Is the propriety of this limitation affected by one's view of the realization rule? By one's view of the family as an economic and social unit?

---

r. Lawrence Zelenak, *Taxing Gains at Death*, 46 VAND. L. REV. 361, 395-401 (1993).

18. One of the problems of current law is the "lock-in" effect created by stepped-up basis (see Note #6 above). What is the basis for the criticism that carryover basis solves one lock-in problem, only to create a new, and arguably worse, lock-in problem? Would constructive realization be better in solving the lock-in problem? Would constructive realization remove all tax incentive to hold appreciated property as long as possible (even to death)?

19. What about losses? Present law sharply limits the deductibility of capital losses, generally allowing deductibility of losses to offset capital gains plus $3,000 of ordinary income, with unused losses being carried forward for life. Sections 1211 and 1212. If we decide to tax gains at death, does it follow that we should allow losses where basis exceeds value? The Castruccio excerpt lists several ways of allowing for losses at death. Which seems best? Should the rule of allowing losses apply to property passing by gift as well as at death?

20. If we are to adopt constructive realization at death, should we extend this rule to charitable bequests? Present law allows taxpayers who make charitable contributions of appreciated property to deduct the full value of the property, and to permanently avoid taxation on the unrealized appreciation. Professor Zelenak contends that "[i]f the gain is not taxed when the property is donated by a living taxpayer, it also should not be taxed when the donation is made at death."[s] Do you agree? And, if so, is the best solution to forgive tax on appreciation in both instances, or to tax it in both?

21. Assuming revenue to be equal from constructive realization and transfer taxes, do you agree with Professor Subotnik that constructive realization is to be preferred?

22. Professor Subotnik's article, only a small sample of which is excerpted, deals at some length with the Canadian experience with constructive realization. Canada adopted a system of constructive realization in 1972, and at the same time repealed its estate tax. The assertion at the end of the excerpt that "we now know that it *can* be done" is a reference to the generally successful Canadian experience with constructive realization.

23. Constructive realization has also attracted serious political interest in the United States. Professor Subotnik traces a number of serious proposals, starting with one made by the Kennedy Administration.[t] Professor

---

s. *Id.* at 401.

t. Dan Subotnik, *On Constructively Realizing Constructive Realization: Building the Case for Death and Taxes*, 2 KAN. L. REV. 1, 2-4 (1989).

Zelenak quotes then President-elect Clinton as saying that constructive realization "probably should be looked at."[u]

D.   TREATING GIFTS AND BEQUESTS AS INCOME TO THE RECIPIENT

Thus far, this chapter has dealt with the failings of section 1014, which allows permanent avoidance of income tax on the appreciation component of property passing at death. Carryover basis would ultimately tax the appreciation to the recipient, while constructive realization would immediately tax the transferor of either a bequest or gift on the unrealized appreciation.

But what of the rule of section 102, which excludes gifts and bequests from the tax base? Should recipients of gifts and bequests—regardless of whether the property appreciated during the transferor's period of ownership—be allowed to avoid including the accession to wealth in their tax base? Professors Dodge and Hudson would tax donees and heirs on the full amount received.

BEYOND ESTATE AND GIFT TAX REFORM: INCLUDING GIFTS AND BEQUESTS IN INCOME
Joseph M. Dodge[*]
91 Harvard Law Review 1177, 1179, 1182-92,
1194-95, 1197, 1199-1200, 1209 (1978)

Legislative Enactment of the Proposal

The enactment of the income tax proposal for gifts and bequests would be accomplished by amending the Internal Revenue Code to repeal the gift, estate, and generation-skipping taxes, and section 102 of the Code, which excludes gifts and bequests from the gross income of the recipient. This would result in gifts' and bequests' being included at some time in the income tax base of the donee or legatee, and thus subject to progressive income tax rates. As under present law, gifts and bequests would not be deductible by the donor or by the decedent's estate.

* * *

**The Justification for Income Tax Treatment
of Gifts and Bequests**

    The Theoretical Basis for the Proposal

        Definitional Models of Tax Base

One or more definitional models of a tax base are necessary to determine whether gifts and bequests should be included by [the] transferee in his tax base, and whether they should be deductible by the transferor. A basic

---

u. Zelenak, *supra* note r, at 367.

*. At time of original publication, Associate Professor of Law, University of Detroit.

proposition is that the justness of a tax system is related to the *apportionment* of the tax burden among the population, and a widely accepted criterion for proper apportionment is that the tax burden should be allocated according to the taxable unit's "ability to pay."

A second proposition is that ability to pay should be determined neutrally, without regard for whether wealth is consumed (spent) or saved. But taxing wealth per se would not neutrally measure ability to pay, since wealth saved would be taxed frequently while wealth consumed would be taxed only once. Two methods have been advanced to construct a more neutral tax base; elements of each are reflected in the current tax structure.

One widely accepted method seeks to tax wealth once in the aggregate by taxing only additions to wealth as they occur. Ability to pay during a taxable period is measured by adding consumption during that period to the increase (decrease) of the unit's stock of wealth during the period. This measurement is the heart of the comprehensive tax base (CTB) model of net income followed by many commentators.[30]

A second method is the "consumption tax" model, which taxes only consumption and not savings. This model postulates that the accumulation and maintenance of wealth are not ends in themselves, but are merely means of providing for future consumption. Consequently, consumption financed through savings should not be taxed more heavily [than] consumption of current receipts, as it is under the CTB model. The consumption tax model, by exempting savings during the taxable period from the tax base, restores equal treatment, and thus neutrality, for present and future consumption.

Under neither of these tax base models should "entities" such as estates, trusts, and corporations be taxed as such. Under the CTB model, though estates and trusts might as repositories of wealth initially be perceived as possessing "ability to pay," this "ability" cannot usually be currently attributed to individuals, since their shares and interests may be unascertainable. If, in contrast, consumption is viewed as the sole measure of ability to pay, then estates and trusts possess no tax base because they do not engage in consumption. Clearly, entities merely serve the ends of individuals; here they serve to facilitate gratuitous transfers. Taxation of entities can therefore be justified only as a means of counteracting the deferral of tax that results naturally from the economic function of these entities.

Source and Nature of Receipt

Under both the CTB and "consumption tax" models, it is axiomatic that receipts should be included in income regardless of source or nature.[34] Thus, both models require full inclusion by the recipient of gifts and bequests.

---

30. The CTB model is sometimes referred to as the "Haig-Simons" definition of income.

34. *But see* Andrews, *Personal Deductions in an Ideal Income Tax Base*, 86 HARV. L. REV. 309, 348-356 (1972).

It has nevertheless been argued that gifts and bequests are not income since they do not represent additions to the existing stock of capital in the economy but rather are mere transfers of capital. This argument, while perhaps partially explaining the historical basis for the exclusion of gifts and bequests, confuses income in the economic sense with income in the tax sense.[37] As previously noted, "income" in the tax sense is the term that has been used to describe the measurement of the taxable unit's capacity to contribute to the public sector relative to other taxable units. It is true that the income tax proposal involves "double taxation" in the economic sense in that the grantor is giving after-tax dollars on which the recipient is again taxed, but whatever hindrance to capital formation may arise from this double taxation can easily be offset in other ways. The area of gifts and bequests is not one where economic considerations should predominate over principles of tax equity.

Deduction to the Donor?

Neither the CTB nor the "consumption tax" model results in a deduction for the donor for gifts and bequests. Those supporting a deduction for the donor indirectly through exclusion by the donee argue that the gift was not part of the income that the donor had available for consumption. This conclusion ignores the basis of the CTB model, since the making of a gift represents the voluntary exercise of the donor's economic power. In other words, the donor's voluntary transfer of the gift itself indicates the donor's ability to pay.

Similarly, under the "consumption tax" model, the fact that a gift may not be "consumption" in the literal sense is no more persuasive with respect to its proper classification for tax purposes than the statement that a gift is not income to the donee under an "income" tax. To begin with, the giving of a gift is more analogous to consumption than to investment. Moreover, the

---

37. The gifts-as-capital argument has been invoked in an attempt to demonstrate that including gifts in income would raise constitutional problems, since gratuitous transfers are not income. *See* Mullock, *The Constitutional Problem of Taxing Gifts as Income*, 53 MINN. L. REV. 247 (1968). Actually, the use of the term "income tax" to describe the present system is misleading; it is derived from historical circumstances relating to the 16th amendment, which authorizes a tax on "income from whatever source derived." However, for a tax to be constitutional it need not be a tax on incomes only but must simply avoid characterization as being an unapportioned direct tax (which is not an income tax). *See* Surrey, *The Supreme Court and the Federal Income Tax: Some Implications of the Recent Decisions*, 35 ILL. L. REV. 779 (1941). Taxes on transfers have long been upheld as indirect (*i.e.*, excise) taxes. *See, e.g.*, Commissioner v. Glenshaw Glass Co., 348 U.S. 426 (1955); Knowlton v. Moore, 178 U.S. 41 (1900). *See generally* Wright, *The Effect of the Source of Realized Benefits upon the Supreme Court's Concept of Taxable Receipts*, 8 STAN. L. REV. 164, 193-201 (1956). Therefore, Congress undoubtedly has the power to include gifts and bequests in income under I.R.C. § 61. *See* J. SNEED, THE CONFIGURATIONS OF GROSS INCOME 115-31 (1967); Del Cotto, *The Constitutional Problem of Taxing Gifts and Bequests as Income: A Reply to Professor Mullock*, 53 MINN. L. REV. 259 (1968); Del Cotto, *The Trust Annuity as Income: The Constitutional Problem of Taxing Gifts and Bequests as Income*, 23 TAX L. REV. 231 (1968); Klein, *An Enigma in the Federal Income Tax: The Meaning of the Word "Gift,"* 48 MINN. L. REV. 215, 219-24 (1963).

equity rationale of the "consumption tax" model is that the future consumption of the person who saves or invests should not be taxed more heavily than current consumption. Since a gift of cash or of a personal asset does not finance or otherwise involve future consumption by the donor, it should not yield a deduction. Nor should a gift in kind of business or investment property or savings account balance yield a deduction, since a deduction will already have been obtained when the investment was made. In fact, because these savings are no longer a means of providing for future consumption by the donor, the earlier deduction should be "recaptured" by the donor and included in the donor's income for the year of the gift.

Even if one should accept the theoretical propriety of deducting gifts, practical difficulties arise. If gifts were included by donees but deducted by donors, wealthy donors could shift income to lower bracket relatives at will, thereby diluting progressive tax rates. Hence, it is argued, the existing exclusion for donees is an imperfect but justifiable approximation of a deduction for donors. Nonetheless, the income shifting problem, while militating against a deduction to the donor, does not necessarily justify ignoring the donee's increased ability to pay.

Finally, permitting the donor to deduct gifts makes no sense if one postulates that gifts and bequests should be treated equally. Because a deduction for bequests would more than shelter all of the decedent's income for his last taxable period, a bequest deduction would have to apply retroactively to the decedent's past income years in order to be fully equivalent to a deduction for gifts. Not only would the administrative difficulties of such a retroactive deduction be considerable, but the deduction would amount to a retroactive exclusion for accumulated savings. If savings are indeed to be encouraged by means of a deduction, a current deduction for savings would be preferable. Of course, under the "consumption tax" model any deduction for the transfer of accumulated savings would be redundant, since that model postulates current deductions for savings.

A Comparison of the Income Tax Proposal
and Specialized Transfer Taxes:
Double Taxation, But in What Form?

Those concerned with double taxation (in the economic sense) under the income tax proposal must acknowledge that double taxation of amounts transferred by gift or bequest has existed since 1916 in the form of the estate tax and its subsequent complements, the gift tax and the generation-skipping tax. Thus the question raised by the adoption of the income tax proposal concerns only the form of "double taxation." Moreover, double taxation is not undesirable if it is consistent with the underlying purposes of the particular tax system.

Under the existing transfer tax system, double taxation is proper because the aim of such taxes is to place a levy on the transfer of wealth. The income tax proposal, on the other hand, has the objective of measuring relative ability to pay, and it therefore considers only the economic position of the individual tax unit when imposing taxes. The method of accession to wealth is irrelevant. Double taxation, that is, taxing the recipient on wealth previously taxed to someone else, is consistent with an attempt to measure each person's ability to pay. While the present system subjects unrealized appreciation both to the transfer taxes and, through the carryover basis mechanism of sections 1015 and 1023,[v] to the income tax of the transferee upon realization, the income proposal taxes it only once because carryover basis would be dropped. The income tax proposal, however, would not preclude additionally taxing the transferor on previously unrealized appreciation, resulting in full double taxation on transfers of appreciated property.

The Objectives of Transfer Taxes

Two primary nonequity objectives of transfer taxes are raising revenue and preventing undue accumulations of wealth. The present transfer taxes focus on the transferor, and constitute a delayed penalty on the accumulation of wealth by the transferor. But it is not clear that undue accumulations are best prevented by a delayed penalty on the accumulating taxpayer. The equally plausible goal of curbing the possibility of reaccumulation of existing wealth by passive means is served by accessions taxes, inheritance taxes, and the income tax proposal. * * *

It might seem that these recipient-oriented taxes would be less effective in raising revenue since the number of transferees is usually greater than the number of transferors. But the effectiveness of any transfer tax scheme in raising revenue—as well as in breaking up accumulations of wealth—depends upon its rates and exemptions. Although the present transfer taxes have considerable potential for accomplishing these goals, recent experience indicates that the political system is unwilling to tap this potential. The income tax proposal, while still subject to some manipulation through exemptions, at least precludes independent tampering with the rate structure. Finally, if any important objective of a transfer tax cannot be accomplished by the income tax proposal, transfer taxes, reduced in scope to bear only on the extremely wealthy, could be retained to supplement the income tax plan.

Tax Base and Rate Structure

Of the recipient-oriented taxes, only the income tax proposal does not contemplate a separate rate schedule for gifts and bequests. Such a separate schedule would contradict a basic premise of the proposal: that the source of receipts should not affect tax liability. * * *

---

v. This article was written after carryover basis—section 1023—had been adopted in 1976, but before its repeal in 1980. (Eds.)

Simplicity of the Proposal: Exclusions, Deductions, and Credits

Adoption of the income tax proposal for gifts and bequests would contribute greatly to the simplification of the tax code. This simplicity of the proposal is both a consequence of its theoretical foundations and an additional justification for its enactment. The existing estate, gift, and generation-skipping taxes would be removed. The portions of subchapter J dealing with the taxation of trusts and beneficiaries would likewise be excised, although those provisions concerned with "grantor trusts" should probably be retained.[69] In addition, the calculation of the basis of in kind property received as a gift or bequest would be vastly simplified for individuals and eliminated for trusts and estates.[70]

The question of what constitutes a gift, now a question of fact which results in much litigation, would be eliminated. Under the income tax proposal, gratuitous transfer exclusions should be allowed only under a de minimis rule to protect the integrity of the tax system in the public eye.[73] Only gifts that are administratively difficult to discover or which are generally not considered transfers of wealth by the public, such as occasional holiday and anniversary gifts, should be excluded from income. Transfers in trust and payments of life insurance premiums, which often qualify—perhaps unjustifiably—for the gift tax present interest exclusion, would not be taxed currently at all under the income inclusion approach. Small distributions from trusts, however, do not fall within the administrative exclusion rationale for small gifts and would therefore be taxed in full.

* * *

In sum, the theoretical basis of the income tax proposal is more easily followed than the theory underlying other transfer tax schemes, which require complicated distinctions and exclusions. In addition, the income tax proposal encourages spreading gratuitous transfers among lower income recipients, who are subject to lower tax rates. Finally, the income tax proposal facilitates compliance and enforcement of taxation on gratuitous transfers by simply including them in income, whereas other transfer tax

---

69. I.R.C. §§ 671-677 (the so-called "Clifford trust" provisions, after Helvering v. Clifford, 309 U.S. 331 (1940), which tax the grantor of a trust because of his retained control, interests, or powers). These provisions would operate independently of the income tax proposal, resulting in taxation of both the grantor of the trust and the recipient.

70. Under the income tax proposal, assets acquired by gift and bequest would normally acquire a stepped-up fair market value basis. Basis would simply be irrelevant with respect to property held by a trust or estate.

73. *See* 3 ROYAL COMMISSION ON TAXATION, REPORT 497-98 (1966) (Canada) ($250 per donee per year exclusion). Under the accessions tax proposal, gifts up to $1500 per donor per year are excluded only if used by the donee for current consumption. *See* Andrews, *The Accessions Tax Proposal*, 22 TAX L. REV. 592 (1967). Consumption items of a modest value are probably not publicly viewed as wealth that should be taxed upon transfer even though they do represent ability of donees to pay under both the CTB and consumption tax models.

schemes require separate returns and, under an accessions tax, separate recordkeeping for prior accessions.

Moreover, if the theoretical basis of the income tax proposal is applied to other tax provisions, further simplification will result. Most important, section 101, which excludes life insurance proceeds and up to $5000 of certain employee death benefits, would be repealed, rendering these amounts taxable to the recipient. Section 117, which exempts scholarship and fellowship grants, should also be eliminated, since it originally was a codification of case law under section 102, the gift exclusion provision. * * *

Problems of the Income Proposal

Deferral With Respect to Trusts

As noted above, trusts and estates would not be taxed and beneficiaries would be taxed only upon distribution under the income tax proposal. The loss to the tax base resulting from the deferral of taxation of trust income, however, will be fully offset by the eventual taxation of trust and estate income and appreciation upon distribution. * * *

In the case of very large trusts, however, this natural disincentive to defer distribution may be ineffective because security and control of wealth are indirect forms of predistribution enjoyment. It may therefore be desirable in some cases to tax trusts prior to distribution. Moreover, such predistribution taxation would counteract the hiatus in revenue collection. For these reasons, a withholding tax on large trusts has been proposed. This proposal requires that any trust distribution be increased by the amount of the tax withheld that is attributable to the distribution, and that the distributee be given a corresponding credit against his income tax in the amount of the withheld tax.

* * *

Gifts and Bequests in Kind

Under a "consumption tax" approach, gifts and bequests of cash are included in income, but the recipient would receive a deduction when the cash is invested in nonpersonal assets. A gift or bequest of business or investment property would not be includible, as these transfers are the equivalent of receipt of cash and full reinvestment. Of course, the asset would have a zero basis, so that the full amount realized upon disposition would be included unless it is reinvested.

Under a CTB approach, gifts and bequests in kind would be included in the income of the recipient as an accession to wealth. Inclusion might, however, create a problem for the recipient of raising the cash to pay the additional tax. This problem of liquidity already poses severe difficulties under the estate tax, and various statutory and estate planning devices exist to deal with it. However, liquidity would be less of a problem under the income tax proposal since legatees could be given more time to pay the tax than an estate, which has a limited duration.

There are, however, additional reasons under the CTB model and income tax proposal for deferral of taxation on gifts in kind by excluding them and assigning them a zero basis. Deferral would avoid the problem of valuing the property upon receipt. Moreover, since income-producing property received by a trust or estate would not be subject to tax until distributed, the same deferral might seem to be equitable where income-producing property is acquired outright by an individual.

Those cases in which deferral is desirable, however, are very limited. Deferral treatment cannot be conferred upon personal assets which represent ongoing consumption. Deferral in the case of depreciable business and investment assets is not particularly compelling since the periodic depreciation deductions would ameliorate the effect of immediate taxation. Marketable securities are not difficult to value or liquidate, so deferral for them would not be necessitated by administrative considerations. What remains is largely real property and small business interests which, as under existing law, plausibly deserve special treatment.

* * *

TAX POLICY AND THE FEDERAL INCOME TAXATION OF THE TRANSFER OF WEALTH
David M. Hudson[*]

19 Willamette Law Review 1, 52-58 (1983)

Proponents of including the receipt of gratuitous transfers in the donee's income tax base are attracted by a number of features which they assert make the approach superior to the present wealth transfer tax system. One of the most appealing advantages is the simplification of the Internal Revenue Code. It would be appropriate to repeal section 102, which excludes the receipt of gifts from gross income, the three chapters of the Code which contain the estate, gift and generation-skipping taxes, and the portions of subchapter J which deal with the income tax treatment of estates, trusts, and beneficiaries. On the other hand, a few words should be added to section 61, specifically enumerating gifts and bequests as items of income. It may be desirable to modify the income averaging provisions or to provide an extended period of time for payment of the tax in order to ameliorate the perceived hardship of having large amounts of taxable income, especially when received by bequest, bunched into a single taxable period.

Second, the improved vertical equity of our tax system is another positive attribute of this income tax proposal. A longstanding fundamental tax policy in this country has been that the ability of the taxpayer to pay should be considered when determining how the tax burden will be allocated; the ability-to-pay concept has been an important criteria in measuring a tax system's overall fairness. Wealth received by gratuitous transfer represents

---

*. At time of original publication, Assistant Professor of Law, University of Florida.

an ability to pay taxes imposed thereon to no different degree than wealth received as compensation for performing services, or as gains from dealings in property, or as prizes or other windfalls. Indeed, the income tax approach is an improvement over the accessions tax in that the income tax is measured by the recipient's *present* ability to pay, rather than on his historical record of receiving gratuitous transfers and the supposition that the greater the cumulative amount, the greater the taxpaying capacity.

The fairness of a tax system refers not only to its vertical equity, but also to the manner in which it operates in practice; whether it is administered and enforced in an evenhanded manner; and whether it is easily avoided or evaded. The present wealth transfer taxes have to a large extent become imposed on the unwary or those who do not wish to arrange their affairs to avoid them. The present system, which the public perceives as unfair, should be replaced by one that is at least less unfair, thereby encouraging public confidence in the system.

The social policy goal of wealth redistribution of the transfer taxes would be enhanced under this income tax proposal for the same reason the accessions tax has been touted as an improvement: donors and decedents would be induced to have less of their wealth paid in tax by transferring it to friends and relatives who are in lower income tax brackets. * * *

Finally, the goal of generating revenue by the taxation of gratuitous transfers could be better accomplished by this income tax proposal. Obviously the amount of tax revenue produced will be a function of the rate structure and any exemptions or deductions allowed, but it has been estimated that by simply including the value of inheritances in income, more than two and one-half times the revenue currently being generated by the transfer taxes would be produced. More importantly, the administration and enforcement scheme for the transfer taxes, which now stands separate from that of the income tax, would be eliminated along with the need for separate returns, forms, basis record-keeping, and other compliance costs.

Two major areas of concern with this income tax proposal are the proper treatment for property left in trust, and the vexing issue of appropriate exclusions and deductions. To be consistent with the approach that people are ultimately the recipients of gratuitous transfers, and that people are the proper taxpayers when they receive such transfers, trusts and estates are merely devices for facilitating transfers and should not themselves be taxpayers. Transfers to an estate or a trust would be tax free; in contrast, distributions to individual beneficiaries would be taxed. Continuing with the conduit theory, income earned with respect to assets held by a trust or an estate would not be subject to income tax when earned, but only when ultimately distributed to beneficiaries. Obviously, wealth that could accumulate in a trust, and the economic power that could be controlled by the trustees, might become enormous. Because of the relatively short duration of estates, the problem seems most acute with respect to trusts. Therefore, a modification has been proposed to impose a tax on the income of large trusts at a rate of fifty percent. A distribution to a beneficiary would be grossed-up by the amount of tax attributable to the distribution, and the beneficiary would be allowed a credit against his income tax by that same amount. In this fashion, the ability to defer tax on income earned by the trust would disappear.

    * * *

The modern transfer taxes have always had some provision for the exemption or exclusion of a certain portion of what would otherwise be a taxable transfer. Currently, transfers of present interests in property to a single donee, up to $10,000 each year, are excluded from the gift tax. The exclusion was originally justified as "obviat[ing] the necessity of keeping an account of and reporting numerous small gifts . . . to cover in most cases wedding and Christmas gifts and occasional gifts of relatively small amounts."[310] Prior to 1977, both the gift tax and the estate tax permitted taxable transfers to be offset by deductions, most recently to a maximum of $30,000 for lifetime gifts and $60,000 in the gross estate. These deductions have been replaced by the unified credit in computing both the gift and estate tax liabilities, but the effect is the same: to permit a certain amount of wealth to be transferred tax free. Finally, neither the gift tax nor the estate tax will be imposed on most transfers to one's spouse or to a qualified charity.

If the income tax proposal is adopted, careful consideration should be given to the adoption of any sort of de minimis exception. Exempting a flat dollar amount that a person could receive each year, whether applied with respect to each donor, or cumulatively, from all donors during the year, would be neither equitable nor necessary. An individual fortunate enough to receive gifts up to the exclusion amount each year would be in a better position economically to pay income tax than an individual who otherwise had the same amount of taxable income, but who received no gratuitous transfers. Instead, the exclusion should be drafted with an eye toward the difference with which the public perceives a gift upon the occasion of some special event, such as a birthday or anniversary, up to a set dollar amount, and a gift which is perhaps motivated by "detached and disinterested generosity," but which is at its essence a transfer of wealth. The horizontal equity of such a tax system would be an improvement over the current one. Similarly, a lifetime exclusion or unified credit would be antithetical to the vertical equity, ability-to-pay element of this income tax proposal.

On the other hand, the marital deduction should be retained in this income tax proposal, as long as the husband and wife are being treated as a unit for income tax purposes by filing a joint return. Transfers to a charity

---

310. S. REP. NO. 665, 72d Cong., 1st Sess. 41 (1932).

which are exempt from income tax would also be tax free, thus effectively continuing present law.

Replacing the wealth transfer taxes with an income tax imposed on the receipt of gratuitous transfers would have the advantages of simplifying the tax laws and bringing to the overall system a greater degree of fairness and equity.   Problems which would be encountered in enforcement, administration and compliance would not be insurmountable, and, indeed, may well be less burdensome than those encountered under the present wealth transfer tax scheme. The revenue which would be derived from the income tax could be at least as great as that presently derived from the wealth transfer taxes. The goal of encouraging wealth redistribution would be more effectively served by this income tax proposal.

　　　* * *

Notes and Questions

24. Professors Dodge and Hudson advocate the repeal of section 102, which excludes gifts and bequests from the recipient's gross income. There would be no deduction for the transferor. Carryover basis would be abandoned, for gifts as well as bequests, and recipients, having taking the full amount of their receipt into income, would have a basis equal to that amount. (The basis of both donees and heirs would thus be the same as the stepped-up basis presently available to heirs under section 1014.)

25. The other reform proposals, carryover basis and constructive realization, deal only with income taxes and are generally silent regarding estate and gift taxes. (It is true that transfer taxes are discussed, and Professor Subotnik explicitly advocates constructive realization in lieu of transfer taxes. Nonetheless, even Subotnik does not advocate abolition of the transfer taxes, but merely notes that this may be the political tradeoff of adopting constructive realization, and argues that such a trade would be a good one.) By contrast, those who propose repeal of section 102 generally envision repeal of the transfer taxes, as do Professors Dodge and Hudson.

26. A generation ago, Professor Thomas Waterbury maintained, in effect, that the case for constructive realization bears a much lighter burden of proof than does full repeal of section 102:

> [T]he case * * * for gains tax realization at death is a case against the exemption of gain from the *first* income tax upon it. A case for including gratuitous receipts in the income of the recipient must be a case for imposing a *second* income tax upon such receipts in any case in which such receipts were previously exposed to an initial income tax in the hands of the transferor.[w]

---

w. Thomas L. Waterbury, *A Case for Realizing Gains at Death in Terms of Family Interests*,

Is this argument persuasive? Stated differently, if A accumulates $1 million of after-tax wealth, then gives it to his son, B, would taxing B be improper double taxation? What is Professor Dodge's response to this objection to his proposal? Which position do you find persuasive?

27. Professor Dodge argues that taxing recipients of gifts and bequests is consistent with either the "ideal" income tax—the comprehensive tax base, or Haig-Simons definition of income—and with the consumption tax base. Note that Professor Andrews, the leading proponent of the progressive consumption tax, disagrees. (See footnote 34 of the Dodge excerpt, and Chapter Seven.) Do you agree that these receipts demonstrate ability to pay? What is Dodge's answer to the argument that gifts and bequests are not properly regarded as income because they are transfers of wealth rather than creations or additions to wealth?

28. In evaluating the proposed repeal of section 102, it may be important whether we look at the family or at the individual. For example, while it is true that a lottery winner has not created new wealth, but has only received a transfer from the losers, surely the winner is to be taxed. If, on the other hand, we look at the transferor and the transferee as two members of the same group—which frequently may be the way at least the transferor looks at it—it may seem that for the group as a whole there is no increase in ability to pay.

On the other hand, the tax law usually treats adult individuals (other than spouses) as entirely separate tax units. Considering the recipient separately from the transferor, it is certainly true that a dollar received as a gift spends as well as a dollar earned by labor or investment.

29. Suppose one were persuaded that the recipient of a gift or a bequest should be regarded as having income, but that the transferor, who has surrendered dominion over the property and received "nothing" in return (true?), should be entitled to a deduction. The Dodge excerpt refers to "[t]hose supporting a deduction for the donor indirectly through exclusion by the donee." If one supported a deduction for the donor, why not provide the deduction directly, rather than by using the recipient's exclusion as a proxy for the transferor's deduction? Is the reason the same whether we are talking of donors or decedents?

30. Professor Hudson argues that the approach of repealing section 102 would encourage donors and decedents to transfer wealth to a greater number of, and to less wealthy, recipients. Why might this happen? Would this be desirable?

---

52 MINN. L. REV. 1, 42-43 (1967) (emphasis in original).

31. Consideration of detailed issues of the taxation of trusts, either under current law or the proposal, is beyond the scope of this book. The issue of transfers in trust requires brief mention here, however, because large transfers of wealth are frequently effected in trust form. As a general rule, the Dodge and Hudson excerpts would exempt the trust from tax, and would tax fully the beneficiary on every dollar received from the trust. That, however, is troubling where a huge trust accumulates income for many years. They propose, in some cases, a withholding tax levied at the trust level.

32. Professor Dodge would carve out a special rule for gifts of property in kind that would largely apply to real estate and closely held business interests. The recipient would have no income and a zero basis (instead of inclusion in income at fair market value, and a basis equal to fair market value). What is his justification for this special treatment? Why is it not extended to consumer goods, such as a new car given to an adult daughter for personal use? To marketable securities? Do you agree with this aspect of the proposal?

33. If you accepted Professor Dodge's treatment of gifts (by including them in income), would you also agree with him that scholarships, whose exclusion grew out of the exclusion of gifts, should be taxed?

34. Professor Dodge explicitly leaves open the possibility of not only taxing the recipient on the entire transfer, but also taxing the transferor on any unrealized appreciation, as through the constructive realization proposal. Assuming section 102 were repealed, would it be appropriate to tax the transferor on the unrealized appreciation as well?

Comparison of the proposals

35. Professor Zelenak observes that theoretical considerations of tax policy will not be of nearly so great concern to Congress as complexity and revenue. These crucial issues always deserve careful consideration.

36. Consider the four proposals—present law, carryover basis, constructive realization, and repeal of section 102—with respect to revenue. It is also relevant to consider the revenue of transfer taxes—the Subotnik excerpt put them at $6.5 billion in 1989—because some of the proposals entail or at least consider repeal of the transfer taxes. Is it fair to say that revenue may be the driving force for change in this area? Is this an opportunity for a hidden tax increase? How would you rank order the proposals in terms of revenue potential?

37. Why might the reform proposals generate additional revenue indirectly, through influencing taxpayer behavior?

38. How do you rank the proposals in terms of complexity, or simplicity? Keep in mind that there are at least two ways to look at simplicity—what simplifies the tax code; and what makes life easier for the Internal Revenue Service, taxpayers, and advisors?

39. Revenue and simplicity are both greatly affected by the levels of exemptions that are provided. What levels of exemptions should be employed, if any? Does your answer vary from proposal to proposal? Note that some of the proposals envision exemptions as large as the present exemption provided by the unified credit under the estate and gift taxes, which allows for tax-free transfers of $600,000.

Selected Bibliography

See also bibliography for Chapter Ten.

Anthoine, Robert, *Tax Reduction and Reform: A Lawyer's View*, 63 COLUM. L. REV. 808, 815-16 (1963).

Carter, George E., *Federal Abandonment of the Estate Tax: The Intergovernmental Fiscal Dimension*, 21 CANADIAN L.J. 232 (1973).

Castruccio, Louis M., *Becoming More Inevitable? Death and Taxes . . . and Taxes*, 17 UCLA L. REV. 459 (1970).

Covey, Richard B., *Possible Changes in the Basis Rule for Property Transferred by Gift or at Death*, 50 TAXES 831 (1972).

—— & Dan T. Hastings, *Cleaning Up Carryover Basis*, 31 TAX LAW. 615 (1978).

Dodge, Joseph M., *Beyond Estate and Gift Tax Reform: Including Gifts and Bequests in Income*, 91 HARV. L. REV. 1177 (1978).

Galvin, Charles O., *Taxing Gains at Death: A Further Comment*, 46 VAND. L. REV. 1525 (1993).

——, *Burying the Estate Tax: Keeping Ghouls Out of the Cemetery: A Reply to Professor Smith*, 56 TAX NOTES 951 (1992).

——, *To Bury the Estate Tax, Not to Praise It*, 52 TAX NOTES 1413 (1991).

Graetz, Michael J., *Taxation of Unrealized Gains at Death—An Evaluation of the Current Proposals*, 59 VA. L. REV. 830 (1973).

Hoffman, Howard J., *The Role of the Bar in the Tax Legislative Process*, 37 TAX L. REV. 411 (1982).

Hudson, David M., *Tax Policy and the Federal Taxation of the Transfer of Wealth*, 19 WILLAMETTE L. REV. 1 (1983).

JOINT COMMITTEE ON TAXATION, GENERAL EXPLANATION OF THE TAX REFORM ACT OF 1976 551-75 (1976).

Kurtz, Jerome & Stanley S. Surrey, *Reform of Death and Gift Taxes: The 1969 Treasury Proposals, The Criticisms, and a Rebuttal*, 70 COLUM. L. REV. 1365 (1970).

Lustgarten Ira H., Book Review, 78 COLUM. L. REV. 679 (1978) (reviewing THOMAS J. MCGRATH & JONATHAN G. BLATTMACHR, CARRYOVER BASIS UNDER THE 1976 TAX REFORM ACT (1977)).

Osgood, Russell K., *Carryover Basis Repeal and Reform of the Transfer Tax System*, 66 CORNELL L. REV. 297 (1981).

Smith, Robert B., *Burying the Estate Tax Without Resurrecting Its Problems*, 55 TAX NOTES 1799 (1992).

Subotnik, Dan, *On Constructively Realizing Constructive Realization: Building the Case for Death and Taxes*, 38 KAN. L. REV. 1 (1989).

Waterbury, Thomas L., *A Case for Realizing Gains at Death in Terms of Family Interests*, 52 MINN. L. REV. 1 (1967).

Zelenak, Lawrence, *Taxing Gains at Death*, 46 VAND. L. REV. 361 (1993).

CHAPTER TEN

TRANSFER TAXES AND WEALTH TAXES

[A]part from its limited base, it is hard to devise a better tax than a death tax. Estates represent ability to pay. And as they are mere windfalls to the beneficiaries, they should be taxed more heavily than any other kind of acquisition.[a]

A. INTRODUCTION AND HISTORICAL ORIGINS

Transfer taxes are imposed on the *transfer* of wealth, at death or by *inter vivos* gift. Wealth taxes, which are less familiar in this country, are imposed on the *possession* of wealth. The income tax, which is principally concerned with the *creation* of wealth, is not a principal focus of this chapter (although, as discussed in Chapter Nine, some scholars would include inheritances and gifts in the income tax base).

Transfer taxes. *Death taxes*, which were used by the ancient Egyptians, Romans, and Greeks, are the most common form of transfer taxes, and have been used by the federal government intermittently since the Eighteenth Century.[b] Since 1916, the federal government has imposed one of the classic death taxes, the *estate tax*. An estate tax is a tax, typically progressive, imposed on an estate and based upon the amount of property passed from the decedent by reason of, or in contemplation of, death. The estate tax is the basic federal transfer tax, but it is bolstered by two other transfer taxes, both of which are best understood as attempts by Congress to protect its policy decision to impose an estate tax. Because it is possible to avoid death taxes by giving property *inter vivos* rather than holding it to death, Congress in 1932[c] added the *gift tax*. The estate and gift taxes, taken in concert, were designed to tax substantial transfers of property from one generation to the next, whether accomplished by death or gift. Significant avoidance of the death/gift tax system could be achieved, however, if, for example, a wealthy individual transferred property in a trust to his children for life, then to his grandchildren for life, with remainder to his great-grandchildren.[d] Such a transfer would result in imposition of estate or gift taxes, but only once. By contrast, if the property were transferred by the more normal route, outright to children, then by the children to their

---

a. Louis Eisenstein, *The Rise and Decline of the Estate Tax*, 11 TAX L. REV. 223, 256 (1955-56).

b. *Id.* at 223, 225-26.

c. A gift tax was temporarily in effect from 1924 to 1926.

d. This assumes that the transfer would not violate the rule against perpetuities.

children, etc., transfer taxes would be due on each transfer, from generation to generation. In response to this avoidance technique, Congress in 1976 enacted the *generation-skipping tax*.[e]

Although the details of the substantive law governing the estate and gift taxes, not to mention the extraordinarily complex generation-skipping tax,[f] are beyond the scope of this book, a few comments are in order. The transfer taxes have never been broad-based taxes; these taxes are borne only by taxpayers who are considerably wealthier than the average. Since 1976, the estate and gift taxes have been unified, and, in effect, progressive rates are applied based upon the current taxable transfer on top of all previous taxable transfers made by the donor or decedent. To ensure that the tax is borne only by the well-to-do, Congress provides that no tax at all is due until a "unified credit"—a single, lifelong credit, which is used to offset both gift taxes imposed on *inter vivos* transfers and estate taxes imposed after death—is exhausted. The present credit protects otherwise taxable transfers of $600,000.[g] Once the credit is exhausted, however, the tax rate is high—it begins at 37 percent and reaches 55 percent when the tax base exceeds $3 million.[h] On a tax base between $10 million and $21,040,000, a "notch" rate of 60 percent is imposed, with the result that for transferors of more than $21,040,000, the benefit of lower brackets and the unified credit is lost, and transfers are taxed at a flat rate of 55 percent.

These high rates, however, are imposed only on taxable transfers. Many devices other than the unified credit are available to taxpayers and their advisors to transfer property without tax. Three major escape routes are worthy of note for our purposes. First, donors can give $10,000 per donee per year (husband and wife donors can combine their exclusion to give $20,000), to each of an unlimited number of donees, without payment of gift tax or utilization of the unified credit.[i] This exclusion—which was increased to $10,000 from $3,000 in 1981—goes considerably beyond the *de minimis* exclusion universally recognized as necessary in a gift tax system. Second, unlimited amounts can be transferred to spouses tax-free, either by gift or at death.[j] The unlimited "marital deduction" also dates from 1981, although

---

e. Section 2601 et seq.

f. One commentator terms the generation-skipping provisions "one of the most complicated sections of an already barely penetrable tax code." G.P. Verbit, *Do Estate and Gift Taxes Affect Wealth Distribution?*, 117 ESTS. & TRS. 674, 674 (1978).

g. The amount of the credit is $192,800. Section 2010. Under the rate schedule of section 2001, this amount of credit protects otherwise taxable transfers of $600,000.

h. Ostensibly, the tax begins at 18%, and includes brackets of 20, 22, 24, 26, 28, 30, 32, and 34% before reaching the 37% bracket. However, the brackets under 37% cover only the first $500,000 of transfers, and cumulatively result in a maximum tentative tax of $155,800. Because this amount is less than the unified credit of $192,800, actual tax is not due unless the cumulative transfers amount to more than $600,000, and at this level the marginal rate is 37%. *See* sections 2001, 2010.

i. Sections 2503(b), 2513.

j. Sections 2056, 2523.

some form of limited marital deduction had been part of the law since 1948. The theory of the current provision appears to be that a transfer from a married couple should be taxed only once, and that the single tax should not be levied until the death of the surviving spouse, when the property finally passes from the married couple.[k] Third, transfers to charity are exempt from transfer taxes, without limit.[l]

Although the federal government has chosen the estate tax, the student of tax policy should be aware of other forms of death taxes. The principal alternatives are the *inheritance tax* and the *accessions tax*. Under both of these, the tax is imposed on the transferee rather than the transferor. (As a matter of administration, state inheritance tax laws may require the executor rather than the individual heirs to make payment, but the tax is computed by reference to each individual heir, not to the estate as a whole.) The difference in technique does more than change the identity of the taxpayer. Under a progressive estate tax, the same tax is imposed whether the decedent leaves his wealth to one heir or fifty, because the tax base is the amount of the taxable estate. Under an inheritance tax, by contrast, the progressive nature of the tax is diminished if the inheritance is divided. Moreover, many state inheritance taxes impose differential rates based on the closeness in kinship of the heir and decedent; the federal estate tax makes no distinction, except for the total exclusion for amounts left to the spouse.

Like the inheritance tax, the accessions tax—which has not gone past the stage of proposal in this country—would tax recipients. The progressivity of the tax, however, would be based on taxable gifts and inheritances received throughout life. Thus, if the taxpayer inherits $1 million this year but had inherited $1 million ten years before, the new inheritance would bear the higher marginal rate applicable to the second million of accessions.

Wealth taxes. Broad-based wealth taxes are virtually unknown in this country, although taxes on certain forms of wealth—especially real estate—are familiar. Broad-based wealth taxes are used by a number of industrialized countries. Instead of a substantial tax infrequently imposed—the model of transfer taxes is to tax wealth once each generation—wealth taxes are imposed much more frequently, typically annually, but at a correspondingly lower rate.

Transfer taxes receive emphasis that seems completely inappropriate for taxes that generate only slightly over one percent of federal revenues.[m]

---

k. The concept of treating the couple as a single entity was subsequently adopted in section 1041. This income tax provision provides that no gain or loss shall be recognized on transfers between spouses (or incident to divorce). The transferee takes a carryover basis.

l. Sections 2055, 2522.

m. In 1994, estate and gift tax receipts totalled approximately $15.2 billion, about 1.2% of total federal receipts. U.S. BUREAU OF THE CENSUS, STATISTICAL ABSTRACT OF THE UNITED STATES, tbl. 518, at 334 (115th ed. 1995).

Virtually every law school offers a separate course on estate and gift taxation. These taxes are central to the practice of many attorneys, and are the object of considerable interest both in academic writing and on Capitol Hill. It is plausible to argue that taxpayers spend more money avoiding the taxes than the government receives from them.

As we shall see throughout this chapter, the merits of transfer taxation tend to be debated—by both advocates and detractors—in terms that have relatively little to do with the revenue they provide. In light of that fact, it is easy to believe that the taxes were never really motivated by a desire to obtain revenue but instead to achieve nonrevenue goals. In the following excerpt, Mr. Eisenstein discusses not only the nonrevenue goals of early estate tax proponents, but also the revenue considerations that actually led to Congressional action.

THE RISE AND DECLINE OF THE ESTATE TAX
Louis Eisenstein[*]

11 Tax Law Review 223, 224-31 (1956)

If we guide ourselves by prevailing notions, the estate tax is animated by a singe purpose—the confiscation of excessive accumulations of wealth. Congressman Kean recently echoed these notions when he approved the tax "entirely on the basis of the social benefit in preventing the piling up of too big estates."[6]

Evidently the estate tax is not regarded as a levy designed to produce revenue. This view of the tax easily implies certain conclusions. As long as the tax prevents estates from "piling up" too high, it presumably does all that can be expected of it. While the tax produces a modest revenue, the revenue is inevitably incidental to its assault upon aggregates of wealth. The tax can hardly appropriate property without gathering some revenue in the process. But its performance is not to be judged by the size of its fiscal haul. Though its yield may be small, it may still be effective.

This understanding of the tax usually satisfies those who applaud it and those who deplore it. The first group can always argue that it is immaterial whether the tax produces much revenue because revenue is not the purpose of the tax; the crux of the matter is that the tax breaks down hereditary estates, and this vital task is sufficient unto itself. On the other hand, the second group is able to argue that the relatively small yield reinforces its conviction that the tax is a pernicious levy; not only does the tax level

---

*. At time of original publication, partner in Paul, Weiss, Rifkind, Wharton & Garrison, New York.

6. *Hearings before the Committee on Ways and Means on Revenue Revision of 1950*, 81st Cong., 2d Sess. 125 (1950). A year later Congressman Kean was of the same opinion. The estate tax, he said, "was not chiefly for the production of revenue, but rather for a social benefit, in order not to allow these great piles of capital to grow and grow." *Hearings before the Committee on Ways and Means on Revenue Revision of 1951*, 82d Cong., 1st Sess. 68 (1951).

wealth, but this evil is not even excusable on the ground of revenue. Both schools are equally loyal to the same error of which neither is aware. It may come as a surprise, but death taxes in the United States were devised to produce revenue. * * *

Though skeptics say that history teaches us nothing, at the very least it may be informative here. Death taxes, no less than other taxes, derived from a desire to obtain revenue. What was true abroad was equally true here. The first federal death tax appeared shortly after the Constitution was adopted. In 1797, amid deteriorating relations with France, Congress levied a stamp duty on legacies and intestate shares of personality. * * *

Federal death duties reappeared during the Civil War. * * * Again Congress was wholly inspired by the revenue required for military exigencies. * * * After the war the death duties were discarded. * * *

Within two decades the scene changed. By the close of the century a death tax movement had emerged [, which] irrevocably identified death duties with the social control of hereditary wealth. "The seething spirit of the times," writes Myers, "was equally concerned with striking hard and deep at plutocracy's wealth as well as its political power." A federal death tax assumed messianic proportions in the minds of those who wished to strike hard and deep. "Steep taxes would tend to shatter great fortunes. They would decrease the number of social drones. Heirs would have less funds to indulge in lavish expenditures." And a death tax "could not be shifted so as to become a tax on the laboring or consuming public."[18]

The propaganda for a death tax soon acquired the invaluable virtue of respectability. In 1889 Andrew Carnegie became a traitor to his class by joining the movement. At the time of his treason Carnegie was worth about $30 million, though he "was not one of the richest Americans." "Why," he asked, "should men leave great fortunes to their children? If this is done from affection, is it not misguided affection? Observation teaches that, generally speaking, it is not well for the children that they should be so burdened." The wealthy who are wise, he declared, should hesitate to provide more than "moderate sources of income" for wife and daughters, and "very moderate allowances indeed, if any, for the sons." The "thoughtful man" would just as soon leave to his son "a curse as the almighty dollar," for "the parent who leaves his son enormous wealth generally deadens the talents and energies of the son, and tempts him to lead a less useful and less worthy life than he otherwise would." In the light of his startling analysis Carnegie welcomed the "growing disposition to tax more and more heavily large estates left at death." It was "a cheering indication of the growth of a salutary change in public opinion." "Of all forms of taxation," he wrote, a progressive death duty "seems the wisest." He found it "difficult to set bounds to the share of a rich man's estate" which the government should

---

18. MYERS, THE ENDING OF HEREDITARY AMERICAN FORTUNES 222-223 (1939).

appropriate. But he was sure that the tax should be graduated; that it should exempt "moderate sums" to dependents; that it should rise "rapidly as the amounts swell"; and that "of the millionaire's hoard" at least 50 per cent should be taken."[21]

* * *

The death tax movement penetrated into the White House. In the spring of 1906 Theodore Roosevelt made a proposal which others found appalling. He recommended "the adoption of some such scheme as that of a progressive tax on all fortunes, beyond a certain amount, either given in life or devised or bequeathed upon death to any individual—a tax so framed as to put it out of the power of the owner of one of these enormous fortunes to hand on more than a certain amount to any one individual."[29] * * *

The tax, he stated, "should increase very heavily with the increase of the amount left to any one individual after a certain point has been reached." The President emphasized that it "is most desirable to encourage thrift and ambition, and a potent source of thrift and ambition is the desire on the part of the bread-winner to leave his children well off." But, he added, this "object can be attained by making the tax very small on moderate amounts of property left; because the prime object should be to put a constantly increasing burden on the inheritance of those swollen fortunes which it is certainly of no benefit to this country to perpetuate." He discreetly refused to say "how far" the tax should, in effect, limit the transmission of "the enormous futures in question."[32]

In 1907 the President saw things more clearly and hence he was more analytical. He focused upon the essential conflict between inheritance of wealth and equality of opportunity. "A heavy progressive tax upon a very large fortune," he declared, "is in no way such a tax upon thrift or industry as a like tax would be on a small fortune. No advantage comes either to the country as a whole or to the individuals inheriting the money by permitting the transmission in their entirety of the enormous fortunes which would be affected by such a tax; and as an incident to its function of revenue raising, such a tax would help to preserve a measurable equality of opportunity for the people of the generations growing to manhood."[33] * * *

Congress, however, refused to be seduced. In 1909 and again in 1913 it disapproved of death taxes.

In three years, as war approached, the picture changed. * * *

The 1916 Act allowed an exemption of $50,000 and fixed rates which ranged from one per cent on the first $50,000 of taxable assets to ten per cent on any amount over $5 million. Within six months the rates were increased

---

21. CARNEGIE, THE GOSPEL OF WEALTH [xxii, 8, 9, 10, 49, 50] (1933).
29. 18 WORKS OF THEODORE ROOSEVELT 578 (Memorial Ed. 1925).
32. 17 WORKS OF THEODORE ROOSEVELT 432-434 (Memorial Ed. 1925).
33. *Id.* at 504-505.

by 50 per cent because of "extraordinary appropriations for the Army and Navy and fortifications."[40] * * *

In another seven months the rates rose once more when Congress imposed an additional war estate tax. The rates now climbed from two per cent on the first $50,000 of taxable assets to 25 per cent on sums over $10 million. * * *

At this point I should pause to generalize. Although the estate tax rates pushed upward for a fleeting period, they made no discernible attempt to level inherited wealth. The tax was initially imposed in response to the need for revenue, and the rates increased as the need increased. The purpose of Congress did not embrace the destruction of large fortunes. Under the 1921 Act the effective rate on an estate of $10 million, before allowance of the exemption, was only 16.7 per cent. Of course, many who urged higher rates were very anxious to regulate wealth and the power which it confers. But what they sought and what they got were not the same. * * *

Notes and Questions

1. The federal estate tax has been in effect since 1916. What were the reasons for its enactment? Which reason predominated at the time?

2. At present, the merits of transfer taxes are usually debated, by supporters and detractors alike, in terms of nonrevenue effects. The primary reason for this is that transfer taxes no longer contribute a significant portion of the budget, and even their defenders think they are unlikely to do so under any politically possible scenario.

From 1935-40, transfer taxes produced more than six percent of federal revenue, compared to about one percent today. This is largely due to the fact that the federal budget has grown so rapidly. That is, although the numerator of the fraction (transfer tax revenues) has risen considerably in absolute terms, the denominator (the federal budget) has exploded. At the same time, it is fair to observe that Congress has rather deliberately moved to reduce transfer tax yield, especially in 1981.

3. Do you think that Congress would repeal transfer taxes except for the associated revenue loss?

4. One of the traditional justifications of inheritance taxes has been the perceived ill effect of inheritances on the recipients. Andrew Carnegie, quoted in the Eisenstein excerpt, opined that undeserved inheritances could constitute a "curse," a view that continues to find support in academic literature. For example, George Gilder, while ultimately concluding that the institution of inheritance should be protected, observed:

---

40. H.R. REP. No. 1366, 64th Cong., 2d Sess. 3-5 (1917).

[Inherited wealth] all too often leaves [heirs] broken and debauched. * * * Supine on expensive piles of pillows, they receive injections of more legal drugs from elegant doctor feelgoods or have their Q-spots probed by maritally ambitious nurses and suave trustees of museums, universities, and environmental societies. * * *

Conservatives who decry the corrupting impact of welfare payments of a few hundred dollars a month will have trouble denying the potential damage to be caused by a trust fund yielding tens of thousands. * * *

Whether money is doled out in foodstamps and spent on booze, or assigned in a bequest and poorly invested, the act of giving may well reduce the total level of wealth, employment and wellbeing in the country.[n]

Obviously, the "victims" themselves do not call for relief. The dominant feeling among potential heirs is perhaps best summed up by the character Tevye in *Fiddler on the Roof*: "May the Lord smite me with the curse! And may I never recover!"

Do you think Mr. Gilder's portrait of the heirs of great fortunes is accurate in many cases? Do you agree that the receipt of unearned, undeserved wealth is a curse for the recipient?

B. THE GOAL OF EQUALIZATION OF OPPORTUNITY

As discussed in subchapter A, one of the primary justifications for the estate tax is the nonrevenue goal of breaking up the largest concentrations of wealth. This is said to serve the egalitarian goal of equality of opportunity. In the following excerpt, Professor Ascher carries the social equality argument to its logical extreme: Our goal should be abolition of inheritance, accomplished through a death tax of one hundred percent (subject to important limitations).

CURTAILING INHERITED WEALTH
Mark L. Ascher[*]

89 Michigan Law Review 69, 70-78, 80-93, 96-104,
106-07, 110, 116-17, 121 (1990)

One of the most dominant themes in American ideology is equality of opportunity. In our society, ability and willingness to work hard are supposed to make all things possible. But we know there are flaws in our ideology. Differences in native ability unquestionably exist. Similarly, some people seem to have distinctly more than their fair share of good luck. Both types of differences are, however, beyond our control. So we try to convince

---

n. George Gilder, *Wealth, Poverty and Inheritance: The Voice from the Coffin*, 11 PROB. LAW. 1, 2-3, 6 (1985).

  *. At time of original publication, Professor of Law, University of Arizona College of Law.

ourselves that education evens out most differences. Still, we know there are immense differences in the values various parents imbue in their children. And we also know there are vast differences in the educations parents can afford for their children. Here too, however, we feel there is little to be done. We respect, if regret, cultural differences that lead some parents to value the education of their children less than others do. And we believe to the bottoms of our souls in the worthiness of the capitalistic game we ask ourselves and our children to play. So we take pride in the fact that some parents can provide their children with the finest educational opportunities imaginable. We have no interest in discouraging excellence in education, even if it is disproportionately available to the children of the fortunate. Instead, we satisfy ourselves with providing an educational safety net for all our children: our taxes support public education and land grant universities, and our charity funds scholarships.

When forced to acknowledge these differences in ability, luck, and educational opportunity, we admit that we do not play on a completely level field. But because each of these differences seems beyond our control, we tend to believe the field is as level as we can make it. It is not. For no particularly good reason, we allow some players, typically those most culturally and educationally advantaged, to inherit huge amounts of wealth, unearned in any sense at all. So long as we continue to tolerate inheritance by healthy, adult children, what we as a nation actually proclaim is, "All men are created equal, except the children of the wealthy."

Meanwhile, [t]he continuing failure of the federal government seriously to address the deficit indicates to many * * * that higher taxes are inevitable. * * * The only real issue is what type of tax could help reduce the deficit least painfully while achieving significant social objectives.

About $150 billion pass at death each year. Yet in 1988 the federal wealth transfer taxes raised less than $8 billion.

Obviously, these taxes could raise much more. If, to take the extreme example, we allowed the government to confiscate all property at death, we could almost eliminate the deficit with one stroke of a Presidential pen.[15] This nation, however, rarely has used taxes on the transfer of wealth to raise significant revenue. Our historical hesitancy in this regard strongly suggests that we as a nation are unwilling to abolish inheritance in order to raise revenue. Nonetheless, thinking about using the federal wealth transfer taxes to abolish inheritance may not be entirely futile. It may permit an entirely new type of analysis. Conventional attempts to reform the federal wealth transfer taxes inevitably bog down in the Anglo-American tradition of freedom of testation. As begrudged intruders upon a general rule, these taxes necessarily end up playing an inconsequential role. One willing, for

---

15. I obviously do not share Michael Graetz's opinion that federal taxes on the transfer of wealth have no significant role to play in dealing with the deficit.

purposes of analysis, to discard freedom of testation could start from the proposition that property rights *should* end at death. Inheritance then would be tolerated only as an exception to that general rule. This article does just that. * * *

My proposal views inheritance as something we should tolerate only when necessary—not something we should always protect. My major premise is that all property owned at death, after payment of debts and administration expenses, should be sold and the proceeds paid to the United States government. There would be six exceptions. A marital exemption, potentially unlimited, would accrue over the life of a marriage. Thus, spouses could continue to provide for each other after death. Decedents would also be allowed to provide for dependent lineal descendants. The amount available to any given descendant would, however, depend on the descendant's age and would drop to zero at an age of presumed independence. A separate exemption would allow generous provision for disabled lineal descendants of any age. Inheritance by lineal ascendants (parents, grandparents, etc.) would be unlimited. A universal exemption would allow a moderate amount of property either to pass outside the exemptions or to augment amounts passing under them. Thus, every decedent would be able to leave something to persons of his or her choice, regardless whether another exemption was available. Up to a fixed fraction of an estate could pass to charity. In addition, to prevent circumvention by lifetime giving, the gift tax would increase substantially.

My proposal strikes directly at inheritance by healthy, adult children. * * * Children lucky enough to have been raised, acculturated, and educated by wealthy parents need not be allowed the additional good fortune of inheriting their parents' property. In this respect, we can do much better than we ever have before at equalizing opportunity. This proposal would leave "widows and orphans" essentially untouched. The disabled, grandparents, and charity would probably fare better than ever before. But inheritance by healthy, adult children would cease immediately, except to the extent of the universal exemption.
　　　　* * *

Inheritance in Principle

John Locke, in his *Two Treatises of Government*, first published in 1690, argued that inheritance was the natural right of children. He derived that right from the fact that children were "born weak, and unable to provide for themselves." Their right to inheritance rested, in Locke's words, on their "Right to be nourish'd and maintained by their Parents."[36]

Despite Locke's powerful influence on those who founded this nation, his conception of inheritance as a natural right never took firm root here. * * *

---

36. J. Locke, Two Treatises of Government bk. 1, § 88, at 206-07 (P. Lassett ed. 1988).

According to Blackstone, inheritance was merely a custom turned into positive law. * * *

Blackstone's positivistic theory, rather than Locke's natural rights theory, has always dominated this country's thinking on inheritance. * * * In 1898 the Supreme Court of the United States bluntly stated, "The right to take property by devise or descent is the creature of the law, and not a natural right . . . ."[49] According to one author, the courts of every state except Wisconsin have reached the same conclusion.[50] Thus, when President Theodore Roosevelt addressed Congress in 1907, he was on solid political and theoretical ground in stating that "[t]he Government has the absolute right to decide as to the terms upon which a man shall receive a bequest or devise from another."[51] * * *

In a letter to James Madison dated September 6, 1789, Jefferson asserted that it was "self evident"

> *"that the earth belongs in usufruct to the living"*: that the dead have neither powers nor rights over it. The portion occupied by an individual ceases to be his when himself ceases to be, and reverts to the society. . . . If [the society has] formed rules of appropriation, those rules may give it to the wife and children, or to some one of them, or to the legatee of the deceased. So they may give it to his creditor. But the child, the legatee, or creditor takes it, not by any natural right, but by a law of the society[63] * * *

Still, the natural rights conception may help to explain Americans' continuing fascination with inheritance. * * *

Inheritance—Property or Garbage?

Locke found an owner's entitlement to property in the labor expended to acquire it:

> The *Labour* of his Body, and the *Work* of his Hands . . . are properly his. Whatsoever then he removes out of the State that Nature hath provided, and left it in, he hath mixed his *Labour* with, and joyned to it something that is his own, and thereby makes it his *Property*. It being by him removed from the common state Nature placed it in, it hath by this *labour* something annexed to it, that excludes the common right of other Men.[65]

---

49. Magoun v. Illinois Trust & Sav. Bank, 170 U.S. 283, 288 (1898).

50. Kornstein, *Inheritance: A Constitutional Right?*, 36 RUTGERS L. REV. 741, 766-67, 789-91 (1984).

51. T. Roosevelt, *Seventh Annual Message* (Dec. 3, 1907), in 16 MESSAGES AND PAPERS OF THE PRESIDENTS 7070, 7084 n.1.

63. 15 T. JEFFERSON, THE PAPERS OF THOMAS JEFFERSON 392-93 (J. Boyd ed. 1958) (emphasis in original).

65. J. LOCKE, TWO TREATISES OF GOVERNMENT bk. 2, § 27, at 287-88 (P. Lassett ed. 1988) (emphasis in original).

Curtailing inheritance in the way I suggest is consistent with Locke's vision of property, because healthy, adult children generally do not participate in the acquisition of the property they inherit. * * *

According to John Stuart Mill, * * * no presumptions in favor of the propriety of inheritance were to be drawn from its antiquity, because Mill believed the feudal family to be fundamentally different from our own. In feudal times, the King dispensed land not to any particular individual, but to a family. The extended family, as a unit, worked on and defended that land. Each family member was in some sense responsible for the productivity of the land. Thus, each had a certain entitlement to the land, regardless of who "owned" it. * * *

In short, in a feudal society, it made sense to think of inheritance as a necessary component of property. But it does not make sense in an industrial society composed of individuals. Instead, according to Mill, inheritance amounts only to the passage of "unearned advantage" to those who "have in no way deserved" it. * * *

Another of the important characteristics of our notion of property is that an owner can give it, during lifetime, to another. Curtailing inheritance would not itself disturb this aspect of property, either. However, if restrictions on inheritance are to be effective, there must also be an ambitious gift tax. Thus, parents could continue to make gifts during their lifetimes to their healthy adult children or anyone else; it would simply become more expensive to do so.

Under current law, property owners also have the right to determine who will own their property after their deaths. Curtailing inheritance obviously would limit this aspect of our notion of property. But allowing those who once owned property to do after death what they were unwilling to do during lifetime has never made sense. When a parent makes a gift to a child, the parent necessarily feels a sentiment something like, "Johnny needs x." Or, "I want Suzy to have y." Curtailing inheritance would not alter parents' ability to satisfy either sentiment at any time during life, for any reason or for no reason at all. What it would disallow is waiting until death to do it. Why? Transferring property at death requires of a decedent neither sentiment. Transferring property by intestate succession requires no sentiment whatever. And transferring property by will requires only a very different sentiment. What a testator says is, "Johnny needs x but can have it only if it is left after my death." Or, "I want Suzy to have y, but she cannot have it until I am completely finished using it." Both sentiments are distinctly less emphatic and less worthy of enforcement by society than those underlying lifetime gifts. They are undeniably secondary sentiments. The primary (and often exclusive) sentiment with respect to death-time transfers is always, "I want x." Or, "I need y." * * * What this proposal eliminates is, therefore, garbage-can parental "giving" to healthy, adult children. A parent would not be allowed to use his or her property until it no longer had any usefulness (to the parent) and then expect the government to collect whatever was left over and deliver it, neatly recycled, to his or her healthy, adult children. Instead, when death placed a property owner's garbage at the curb, the government would simply pick it up.

Constitutional Concerns

* * * In 1942, the Supreme Court of the United States * * * wrote, "Nothing in the Federal Constitution forbids the legislature of a state to limit, condition, or even abolish the power of testamentary disposition over property within its jurisdiction."[79] Since no state has ever attempted to abolish inheritance, all such statements are, of course, merely dicta. These statements are, nonetheless, overwhelmingly in favor of such legislative power.

Concluding that a state legislature could abolish inheritance does not, however, also justify concluding that Congress could do so. * * * But Congress' authority to raise revenue from property passing at death appears to extend to anything less than complete abolition of inheritance. As long as Congress continues to allow every decedent the right to transmit a reasonable amount of property, almost any reform of the federal transfer taxes would appear to pass constitutional muster.

Inheritance as a Matter of Policy

Society's Stake in Accumulated Wealth

Individuals never acquire property on their own. Society plays a crucial role in every individual's acquisitive activities. Society determines the rules by which individuals acquire property. Society also educates (to one extent or another) every individual. And society enacts and enforces laws that protect individuals' enjoyment of what they acquire.

* * * Put another way, the wealth they accumulate is "largely the result of the recipient being favorably positioned vis-a-vis the structure of civilization."[91] Such wealth is, therefore, "in large part produced by society itself."[92] President Theodore Roosevelt put it this way: "The man of great wealth owes a peculiar obligation to the State, because he derives special advantages from the mere existence of government."[93] * * *

Arguments in Favor of Curtailing Inheritance

Leveling the Playing Field

The inequality of accumulation that occurs as the by-product of capitalism is hardly to be despised, as Andrew Carnegie and Theodore Roosevelt well realized. Thus, absolute equality is a goal for which society ought not to strive and that, in any event, society could never even

---

79. Irving Trust Co. v. Day, 314 U.S. 556, 562 (1942).

91. Brannon, *Death Taxes in a Structure of Progressive Taxes*, 26 NAT'L TAX J. 451, 451 (1973).

92. *Id.*

93. T. Roosevelt, *Sixth Annual Message* (Dec. 3, 1906), in 16 MESSAGES AND PAPERS OF THE PRESIDENTS, *supra* note 51, at 7023, 7042.

approximate without eugenics and state socialism. Equality of opportunity, however, is at the very core of American values. Philosophers tend to agree that equality of opportunity is a fundamental good. It is hardly open to debate that inherited wealth contradicts equality of opportunity. According to one authority, "inherited wealth account[s] for half or more of the net worth of every wealthy man and for most of the net worth of equally wealthy women."[102]   How society reallocates accumulated wealth at death is, therefore, a critical determinant of the degree of equality of opportunity succeeding generations will enjoy. Thus, Thomas Jefferson advocated a steeply progressive death tax as a "means of silently lessening the inequality of property."[104]   So did Thomas Paine. President Theodore Roosevelt advocated the predecessor of the current federal estate tax largely on the basis that it would guarantee "at least an approximate equality in the conditions under which each man obtains the chance to show the stuff that is in him when compared to his fellows."[106]

Inheritance nonetheless continues to enjoy widespread support, even from eminent philosophers. F.A. Hayek, for example, writes:

> Egalitarians generally regard differently those differences in individual capacities which are inborn and those which are due to the influences of environment, or those which are the result of "nature" and those which are the result of "nurture...." [N]o more credit belongs to him for having been born with desirable qualities than for having grown up under favorable circumstances. The distinction between the two is important only because the former advantages are due to circumstances clearly beyond human control, while the latter are due to factors which we might be able to alter.
> * * *
> Once we agree that it is desirable to harness the natural instincts of parents to equip the new generation as well as they can, there seems no sensible ground for limiting this to non-material benefits. The family's function of passing on standards and traditions is closely tied up with the possibility of transmitting material goods.[112]

In my opinion, the benefits of the family Hayek dwells on, acculturation and education, are separable from the purely financial advantage inheritance represents. * * *

In short, my proposal attempts to distinguish those types of inequalities that are inevitable in the family context from those that are distinctly less so. * * *

---

102. R. Musgrave & P. Musgrave, Public Finance in Theory and Practice 483-84 (4th ed. 1984).

104. T. Jefferson, *supra* note 63, at 82.

106. T. Roosevelt, *supra* note 51, at 7085.

112. F. Hayek, the Constitution of Liberty 87, 88-89, 91 (1960).

Deficit Reduction in a Painless and Appropriate Fashion

Another reason to curtail inheritance is the prospect of raising revenue. If $150 billion pass at death each year, curtailing inheritance has the potential to raise a substantial amount of revenue. Unfortunately, my proposal would raise nowhere near $150 billion. It contains so many generous exceptions that its very structure limits its promise. Taking those exceptions into account, my best guess is that it might raise $25-30 billion.[120] Even so, it would raise almost four times as much as the federal wealth transfer taxes currently raise. But the exceptions are not the only limitations on the proposal's promise. Its economic effects are unknown. If it decreased incentives to work or save, its revenue yield might be lower still. All these uncertainties suggest that raising revenue is not the most important reason to implement this proposal. On the other hand, a country with a government that insists on consistently spending substantially more than it takes in ought to consider seriously any proposal with reasonable prospects for raising any significant amount of revenue.

Denying healthy, adult children the property that once belonged to their parents is about as painless a tax as one could imagine. * * *

A tax on inheritance by healthy, adult children falls squarely on those whose only claim is by accident of birth. To them, inheritance is little more than a windfall. They, more than anyone else, truly have the ability to pay. And the extent to which a tax is based on ability to pay is widely accepted as a primary measure of a tax's fairness.

Protecting Elective Representative Government

In America, our covenant that "all men are created equal" secures much more than the legitimacy of the capitalistic game we ask ourselves and our

---

120. Forty-five-thousand-eight-hundred estates of decedents dying in 1986 filed returns reporting at least $500,000. Combined, they reported assets of $66 billion. Johnson, *Estate Tax Returns, 1986-1988*, STATISTICS OF INCOME BULL., Spring 1990, at 27. If half of all decedents qualified for (and fully utilized) the unlimited material exemption, the tax base would drop to $33 billion. Assuming all other decedents fully utilized the universal exemption, the tax base would drop an additional $6 billion (one half of 45,800 estates times $250,000). Thus $27 billion would remain. The rough nature of this estimate should be obvious. It ignores four of the exceptions my proposal would allow. Three, however, would be relatively inexpensive: the exemption for dependent lineal descendants, because few parents die with children under age 25; the exemption for disabled lineal descendants, because few beneficiaries are totally and permanently disabled; and the exemption for lineal ascendants, because few parents survive their children. The charitable exemption would be more costly, but I see no way to predict its cost. Each omission suggests the $27 billion figure is too high. Other factors, however, suggest the $27 billion figure is too low. First, the 1986 figures used above reflect only estates exceeding $500,000. This proposal would apply to estates above $250,000. Second, fewer than half of all decedents could and would utilize an unlimited marital exemption. (Only 45% of 1986 decedents whose estates filed estate tax returns passed *anything* to a surviving spouse, despite the fact that all who were married at death automatically qualified for an unlimited marital deduction. Johnson, *supra*, at 48-50 (Table 2).) Third, an invigorated gift tax would yield additional revenue. Fourth, if the amount of wealth passing at death increases as much as some expect, the prospects for future growth in revenue are substantial.

[handwritten in margin: Job wealth threaten representative govt]

children to play.   It also secures the form of elective representative government we cherish. * * *

The existence of billionaires in our country today poses the same dangers the framers sought to avoid by eliminating primogeniture and entail two centuries ago.   If we were willing to curtail inheritance, we could simultaneously eliminate one of the most blatant sources of inequality and improve the prospects for another two centuries of elective representative government in America.

Increasing Privatization in the Care of the Disabled and the Elderly

As the extended family vanishes, it leaves behind many victims.   Elderly parents and grandparents, as well as the disabled, are often, in effect, homeless.   Increasingly, the cost of supporting these individuals has fallen to the government.   The government, however, often provides care for such individuals in a poor and insensitive fashion.   Moreover, the cost of providing such care is an expense we as a nation seem unable to afford.   A system that encourages family members to provide for the care of the elderly and disabled is, therefore, desirable.   Increased privatization would ensure not only better and more sensitive care, but also reduction of the costs borne by the government.

My proposal would encourage private expenditure for the care of the elderly and disabled.   It would allow a generous exemption for disabled lineal descendants.   In addition, it would allow an unlimited exemption for lineal ascendants, most of whom would be elderly. * * *

No doubt the truly wealthy already take care of their elderly and disabled.   Thus, curtailing inheritance might produce little privatization at that level.   Those at lower wealth levels, however, do not always take care of their own. "Divestment planning," a new type of estate planning, caters to clients desiring to shift the costs of caring for elderly and disabled relatives to the government.   By making it much more expensive during lifetime to give large amounts to one's children, and by limiting the amount healthy children could inherit, this proposal would achieve much greater privatization at the "near-rich" level.

* * *

Increasing Lifetime Charitable Giving

* * * Given the incentives for lifetime giving that reallocation at death would create, the allowance of a gift tax charitable deduction would surely result in a marked increase in lifetime charitable giving.

* * *

Arguments Against Curtailing Inheritance

The Effect on the Economy

Several lines of argument suggest that curtailing inheritance might adversely affect the economy.   The adverse economic effects most frequently mentioned fall into three categories: decreased incentives to work, increased consumption leading to decreased savings, and decreased privately held capital.

Incentive to work

One of the first retorts to any proposal to curtail inheritance is the assertion that such a proposal would eliminate incentives to work. According to this line of reasoning, one works in large part for the opportunity to pass something to one's children at death. People, however, work for many other reasons. First are the power and prestige that work and accumulation provide. Money makes the world go round. We work primarily to earn it. Money allows us to feed, clothe, and house ourselves. It also provides us with luxuries and amusement for our leisure. Money provides us with security. * * *

Another of the most important reasons we work and accumulate is to "provide" for others, particularly our children. * * * Curtailing inheritance would have *no effect* on parents' ability to satisfy these desires.

Undoubtedly it is important to ask how curtailing inheritance would affect incentives for work. But with so many other, more important incentives, it is hard to believe curtailing inheritance by healthy, adult children would have any measurable impact. * * *

The failure of the federal government to address the deficit suggests that new or higher taxes are inevitable. The only issue is what type of tax could reduce the deficit with the least adverse economic consequences. Whatever the disincentive effects of an increase in taxes at death, the authorities are all but unanimous that such effects are smaller than those of an increase in the income tax,[180] Congress' traditional tax of choice.

---

180. *See, e.g.*, J. PECHMAN, FEDERAL TAX POLICY 234 (5th ed. 1987) ("[E]ven [critics] would concede that death taxes have less adverse effects on incentives than do income taxes of equal yield."); C. SHOUP, FEDERAL ESTATE AND GIFT TAXES 104 (1966) ("[Transfer taxes] tend less than other taxes to check entrepreneurial drive. They have little tendency to push investors either toward or away from risk taking."); M. WEST, THE INHERITANCE TAX 212 (2d ed. 1908) ("The inheritance tax is less a discouragement to industry than an income tax . . . ."); Harris, *Economic Effects of Estate and Gift Taxation (1955)*, in READINGS IN DEATH AND GIFT TAX REFORM 41,43 (G. Goldstein ed. 1971); Gutman, *A Practitioner's Perspective in Perspective: A Reply to Mr. Aucutt*, 42 TAX LAW. 351, 352 (1989); Graetz, *To Praise the Estate Tax, Not to Bury It*, 93 YALE L.J. 259, 284 (1983) ("[T]axes on bequests are preferable to high tax rates on income."); Brannon, *supra* note 91, at 451-52; Westfall, *Revitalizing the Federal Estate and Gift Taxes*, 83 HARV. L. REV. 986, 989 ("[E]state and gift taxes, unlike the income tax, have a minimal impact on risk-taking, entrepreneurial drive, and resource allocation."); Groves, *Retention of Estate and Gift Taxes by the Federal Government*, 38 CALIF. L. REV. 28, 30 (1950) ("Death taxes reduce savings more than income taxes and impede production and investment incentive less.") *But see* Boskin, *An Economist's Perspective on Estate Taxation*, in DEATH, TAXES AND FAMILY PROPERTY 56, 62 (E. Halbach ed. 1977) ("[O]verall, a substantial decrease in 'expenditures' (saving) for bequests can be expected from increasing transfer taxes relative to income Taxes."); B. BITTKER & E. CLARK, FEDERAL ESTATE AND GIFT TAXATION 1, 3 (6th ed. 1990) ("The personal income tax . . . can accomplish infinitely more in the way of checking inflation than even a confiscatory estate tax."). Of course, none of these authors advocated a death tax with a flat rate of 100%.

Increased consumption and decreased savings

The second economic argument against curtailing inheritance focuses on its supposed tendency to encourage consumption. For years, estate planners have teasingly told their clients that the best estate planning was spending. If inheritance were curtailed, that advice would be truer than ever before. Anyone worried about what would happen to his or her wealth after death could consume it prior to death. If property owners generally followed such advice, curtailing inheritance would raise little revenue. More important, consumption would increase, and savings would decrease.

* * * [U]nder the current system, which itself provides strong incentives to transfer wealth during life, parents almost always keep their money. In short, the incentives to retain property dwarf the incentives to give it away.

Would this parental tendency to retain property change if inheritance were curtailed? * * * [T]he demand for the power, prestige, flexibility, and security money provides seems relatively inelastic—even in persons old enough to be worrying about what happens to their property after death. In short, the instinct for self-preservation would continue to limit spending, even if inheritance were curtailed. Curtailing inheritance might, therefore, increase consumption only slightly. * * *

Curtailing inheritance as suggested in this article would affect less than 10% of the population. Its impact would thus be limited to that group of individuals least likely to engage in additional consumption.

Even if curtailing inheritance did have some adverse impact on savings, the forgoing analysis considers only the behavior of the decedent. It ignores those who, under current law, stand to inherit property. If imposition of a more burdensome tax at death is thought an incentive to consumption on the part of those for whom death is near, ought it not also be seen as an incentive to save on the part of those whose inheritances would be adversely affected? * * *

Looking at the issue from a completely different angle, one is tempted to ask whether an increase in spending would necessarily be bad. The answer would surely depend on what form the additional spending took. * * *

Were I worried about the government appropriating my wealth at death, I would consider insuring myself and my family against all sorts of risks. First, I would want unlimited, lifelong medical coverage, and only the Mayo Clinic or a close equivalent would do. Second, I would want a super "life care contract" that would guarantee nursing-home care in a degree of privacy and quality rarely, if at all, currently available. And only a reputable, thoroughly financially backed institution would do. Third, I would want lifelong access for my descendants to the finest private education available. Each would be expensive, and together they would amount to a significant portion of my wealth, especially if I also tried to provide such protection to collateral relatives or friends. This spending, however, is hardly bad. To the extent I provide, by private means, for medical, nursing-home, and educational needs, I relieve society of the burden of doing so. * * *

Decrease in capital privately held

By reallocating to the government a larger portion of what is owned at death, and by subjecting lifetime transfers to higher gift taxes, this proposal would remove from the private economy a large amount of capital. This concern is, however, irrelevant to a tax providing deficit financing. * * *

Emigration—of Capital and Citizens

Curtailing inheritance may also encourage emigration of both capital and citizens. Much wealth consists, however, of interests in business enterprises or real property. Such wealth generally is not moveable. * * *

As to the movement of citizens, there should be fewer limitations. Nonetheless, to escape the current federal estate tax one must not only cease residing in the United States but also renounce American citizenship. These are drastic measures few would undertake, even under a system that curtailed inheritance. * * *

"Wiping Out the Dream"

* * *

I suggest *curtailing* inheritance, not abolishing it. A universal exemption would allow *every* decedent to bequeath a substantial amount of property. If set at $250,000, this exemption would exempt approximately 98% of the population. Thus, for the vast bulk of society, all my proposal would do is "wipe out the dream" of inheriting a purely imaginary fortune or passing a purely imaginary fortune to healthy, adult children. For the few truly wealthy, my proposal would, of course, represent a major change in the wealth transmission process. But even the truly wealthy could still pass, in addition to lifetime gifts, and in addition to other exempted amounts, $250,000 to whomever they wished. The psychological needs of 2% of the population to control more than that amount of wealth after death ought not prevail over the benefits my proposal promises.

* * *

Notes and Questions

5. Professor Ascher advocates an extreme form of estate tax, claiming that it would achieve both increased revenue and increased social justice. Which of these is more important to Professor Ascher?

6. Professor Ascher contends that his proposal would generate considerable revenue. (See footnote 120.) But suppose we decided that no additional revenue would be obtained from its implementation. For example, hypothesize that the government's cost of administering and collecting the tax would exactly equal the tax revenues derived. Can an argument still be advanced that such a tax would be beneficial to society? Such a tax would have the effect of making some taxpayers (the rich, the near-rich, and their

heirs) poorer without making the government richer. Would such a tax be simply legislating envy into law? Conceding, *arguendo*, that large inheritances by healthy adults are undeserved accessions to wealth, does it follow that society is improved if the wealth is removed?

7. Leaving aside the questions usually raised when any tax proposal is considered—revenue, efficiency, equity, etc.—would outright confiscation of a decedent's property be morally wrong?

8.   Certainly taxes that appear to have as their principal purpose punishment of the taxpayer or his activities rather than revenue have been levied. For example, a state might levy a high tax on illegal narcotics. Regardless of whether we think fines a wise way to combat illegal drugs, we can realize that such a tax would be a thinly disguised form of fine,° and might not be surprised if administering and collecting the fine cost the government as much or more than the money collected. Can transfer taxes, at least in some cases, be justified on a similar theory?   Do you find dispositive the fact that accumulating wealth, unlike trafficking in narcotics, is legal?

9. Professor Ascher acknowledges the inevitability, and in some senses desirability, of inequality arising from differences in important matters such as ability, luck, education, and nurturing. Why would he single out inherited wealth as the area in which to move toward socially mandated equality?

10. Which is the more economically valuable thing to inherit from a parent—$1 million in cash; or the genes, nurturing, and encouragement that will enable one to play professional sports at a salary of several millions of dollars per year? Do you find persuasive the argument of F.A. Hayek (quoted in the Ascher excerpt) that "there seems to be no sensible ground for limiting [parental efforts to benefit their children] to non-material benefits"?

11.   Probably the most important benefits fortunate children receive from their parents—such things as a sense of values; religious faith; self discipline; appreciation of the world, of nature, of people, of art—have little direct economic effect. Why should these major benefits go untaxed, while something as relatively trivial as an inheritance of $1 million is taxed? Does the fact that some children receive these intangible benefits from their parents and others do not, doom taxation as a means of achieving equality of opportunity?

---

o. *See Dept. of Rev. of Montana v. Kurth Ranch*, 114 S. Ct. 1937 (1994). In this case, the Supreme Court held, five-to-four, that imposition of the Montana Dangerous Drug Tax constituted an unconstitutional imposition of double jeopardy, because the taxpayers had already been subjected to criminal punishment of their drug activities.

12. The income tax treatment of parents who choose either additional nurturing time or additional working time—both, let us hypothesize, with the goal of benefitting their children—differs considerably. The nurturing parent generates untaxed imputed income, while the working parent creates taxable income. What might be made of these facts in the debate concerning transfer taxes?

13. An obvious concern with confiscatory taxation is its effect on incentives. Do you agree with Professor Ascher that adoption of his proposal would not materially undercut the incentive to work of parents who would be unable to bequeath their wealth to their offspring? What effect would it have on the working patterns of the sons and daughters who would lose inheritances they otherwise would have received?

14. A related concern is that high death taxes create an incentive toward too much consumption. Some proponents of high death taxes have suggested coupling transfer tax increases with greater reliance on consumption taxation.[p]

15. Professor Edward McCaffery, by contrast, argues for a steeply progressive consumption tax (steeper still if the consumption is out of inherited wealth), but with no transfer tax at all. He maintains that this approach would create optimal incentives and disincentives. It would not discourage (desirable) creation of wealth, but would discourage (undesirable) conspicuous consumption. Using the example of billionaire H. Ross Perot, he argues:

> We may actively want Mr. Perot * * * to work and save, because we value whatever he does to produce that wealth and we appreciate his accumulation of capital, but we may be afraid of his spending his billions personally and quickly. If we are concerned about curtailing his extravagant consumption, however, then we have to let him pass on his wealth. We cannot concede Mr. Perot his earnings while at the same time checking both his consumption and his savings: Something has to give. Under the progressive consumption-without-estate tax with a higher rate schedule on spending out of inheritance, we do not burden Mr. Perot's earnings or savings or wealth transfers *per se*. Instead we monitor the use of the wealth, both at Mr. Perot's and later generation's levels, to make sure that such use is not decadent or offensive, without pushing Mr. Perot to consume it himself.[q]

---

p. *See, e.g.,* Gerald M. Brannon, *Death Taxes in a Structure of Progressive Taxes*, 36 NAT'L TAX J. 451, 452-53 (1973).

q. Edward J. McCaffery, *The Uneasy Case for Wealth Transfer Taxation*, 104 YALE L.J. 283, 353 (1994). See also McCaffery excerpt in Chapter Seven.

16. Professor Ascher would protect the right of even the rich to give property, while sharply curtailing their right to transfer property at death. (Gifts would be subject to transfer taxes much higher than under present law, but still considerably more favorable than the one hundred percent marginal rate he would impose on certain transfers at death.[r]) He justifies the difference, in part, because transfers at death reflect sentiments "less worthy of enforcement by society," and amount to "garbage-can parental 'giving.'" Do you agree with his characterization of transfers at death?

17. Professor Ascher noted but dismissed the argument that taxpayers would emigrate and renounce American citizenship to avoid even a confiscatory estate tax.

State death taxes have raised a somewhat comparable problem. Although the taxes have never approached the 100 percent envisioned by Professor Ascher, considerably less drastic measures were necessary in order to defeat the tax; simply moving to another state sufficed. As a result: "Competition among the states for the aged wealthy was very keen and took the form of outdoing other states in leniency of death taxes."[s] To deal with this perceived problem, Congress enacted a credit against the federal estate tax for state death taxes up to a stated maximum. Section 2011. No state thereafter had any incentive to reduce its death taxes below the amount of the allowable federal credit, because the reduction would benefit not the estate but the federal government.

18. In some respects, Professor Ascher would reduce the burden of death taxes. For example, he would allow a substantial tax-free bequest to a disabled child of any age (he suggests $5 million). Should this general idea be incorporated into whatever form of death taxation is utilized?

C. THE ROLE OF TRANSFER TAXES IN A PROGRESSIVE TAX SYSTEM

Transfer taxes do not exist in a vacuum, but are one relatively minor element of the tax system. In the pair of excerpts in this subchapter, the authors express sharply different views concerning the appropriate role for these taxes. Professor Graetz argues that Congress should retain and strengthen transfer taxes, not because they either bring in much revenue or break up concentrations of wealth, but because they contribute to

---

r. In a portion of his article not excerpted (*see* 89 MICH. L. REV. at 137-48), Professor Ascher proposed gift tax rates that would increase with age (i.e., would increase as the taxpayer approached death and the proposed confiscatory estate tax). The range would be from 100 percent to 300 percent of the amount of the gift. This is still less than a 100 percent estate tax, however. While a 100 percent estate tax is simply confiscatory, a 100 percent gift tax means that a gift can still be made, but that it results in a tax of equal amount.

s. Harold M. Groves, *Retention of Estate and Gift Taxes by the Federal Government*, 38 CAL. L. REV. 28, 32 (1950).

progressivity in the overall tax system. Professor Dobris, by contrast, proposes repeal, pure and simple, arguing that transfer taxes have not and will not fulfill *any* of the roles that supposedly justify their existence, and that they cause myriad problems. (It is interesting to note that each writer expresses pessimism that the change he recommends will be adopted.)

TO PRAISE THE ESTATE TAX, NOT TO BURY IT
Michael J. Graetz[*]

93 Yale Law Journal 259, 259-64, 268-73, 284-86 (1983)

For several decades, total revenues raised by estate and gift taxes have roughly equalled those raised by excise taxes on alcohol and tobacco.[1] Yet no law journal has ever asked me to write on alcohol or tobacco excise taxes. The law firms of America do not routinely have divisions devoted to excise tax planning. We do not hear of the suffering of widows and orphans (or even of farmers and small businesses) because of alcohol and tobacco taxes. Philosophers and economists do not routinely debate the merits of such taxes. Perhaps most significantly, increases in such excise taxes do not arouse fears that we are about to eliminate the concept of private property in this country and embrace socialism, or even communism. The estate tax, however, evokes just such responses.[2]

Recent Trends in Estate Taxation

A review of the most recent history of the estate tax suggests special ironies. Just seven years ago, in 1976, after nearly thirty years of neglect, Congress adopted a series of revisions intended to make the estate and gift taxes apply on a more regular and uniform basis * * *. In 1976, Congress enacted a series of provisions unifying estate and gift taxes into a wealth transfer tax with one cumulative rate schedule and one exemption level, expanding the marital deduction, and establishing a new tax on

---

[*]. At time of original publication, Professor of Law, Yale University.

1. U.S. BUREAU OF CENSUS, STATISTICAL ABSTRACT OF THE UNITED STATES: 1981, at 256 (102d ed. 1981). Actually, the alcohol and tobacco excise taxes together have consistently raised several billion more dollars per year than have the estate and gift taxes. A closer comparison is between revenues from the alcohol excise tax alone and from the estate and gift taxes; the latter exceeded the former only in 1977 ($7.4 billion vs. $5.4 billion) and 1980 ($6.5 billion vs. $5.7 billion). *Id.*

2. *See, eg., Federal Estate and Gift Tax: Public Hearings and Panel Discussions Before the House Comm. on Ways and Means,* 94th Cong., 2d Sess. 390 (1976) (statement of Edward Pendergast) (suggesting that forced sale of small businesses to meet estate tax burdens "encourage[s] people to take the 'safe' route and work for some impersonal monolithic giant"); *id.* at 436-37 (statement of Sen. Gaylord Nelson) (quoting 121 CONG. REC. 22,683 (1975)) (asserting that existing scheme of estate taxation "undermine[s] our values and institutions" and threatens "to change the historic character of our free enterprise system from reliance on independent, imaginative small businesses and family farms to absolute dependence on massive corporations"); *id.* at 548 (statement of Rep. Bill Archer) (equating estate taxation to "the question of the private ownership of property, whether the Government should have the power to confiscate the earnings of a citizen").

generation-skipping trusts. Through that legislation, Congress endeavored to produce a structurally more coherent tax—to move toward a genuinely progressive estate and gift tax, typically to be imposed once each generation without huge tax disparities due to decedents' patterns of lifetime giving. Not all of the structural problems were solved in the 1976 legislation—for example, the gift tax continues to be imposed on a net base exclusive of tax, while the estate tax applies identical rates to a gross base including the tax—but on the whole, the 1976 changes significantly improved the structure of the estate and gift taxes.

In light of subsequent events, however, it requires emphasis that although the 1976 changes—principally the phased-in increase in the size of tax-exempt estates from $60,000 (or $90,000 if the lifetime gift tax exclusion was fully used) to $175,625 and the expansion of the marital deduction for smaller estates—were predicted to lose revenue in the short run, they were to have no effect on revenue over the longer run. The drop in estate tax revenues in the short term from the increased exemption level and marital deduction was, in the long term, to be offset by additional revenues from the new tax on generation-skipping trusts and by application of the carryover-basis rules applicable to appreciated property transferred at death. In fact, the enactment of the carryover basis was an explicit trade-off for the support of the estate tax revisions by crucial Democrats on the House Ways and Means Committee.

The 1976 revisions, of course, were not free of problems. * * * The complexities and technical difficulties that haunted the carryover-basis provision from the outset prompted a delay in its effective date in 1978 and ultimately were a major cause of its demise in the Crude Oil Windfall Profit Tax Act of 1980. The generation-skipping provisions have met with similar technical objections. * * * Nevertheless, in 1976 Congress enacted major structural revisions to the taxation of gifts and bequests in an effort to have these taxes apply in a more even-handed way, *without reducing* the total level of deathtime taxation.

Having moved toward a basically sound and well-structured wealth transfer tax system, Congress then reversed direction a few years later and moved to emasculate it. In 1980, Congress repealed the carryover-basis rules and returned to the unfair and economically distorting step-up of basis to fair market value at death. * * * Then, in 1981, Congress enacted an additional increase in the wealth transfer tax credit to produce immediately a tax-exempt level of $275,625, and phased in further credit increases to produce an exemption for all estates with net worth of $600,000 or less. At the same time, Congress extended an unlimited marital deduction to all estates regardless of size, reduced the top rate of estate tax—applicable only to estates with net worth of ten million dollars or more—from seventy to fifty percent, and increased from $3000 to $10,000 the amount which can annually be transferred to any donee free of gift tax. These changes reduce the deathtime tax base by about seventy percent and reduce the long-term revenue from taxing bequests to at most one-third of that which would have been collected if the 1976 structure had remained unchanged.

When the 1981 changes are fully phased in, the amount of appreciated property transferable at death without being subject to either income or estate taxes will have been increased ten-fold since 1976, from $60,000 to $600,000. With such an exemption level, no more than $3 billion of the more than $20 billion of unrealized appreciation annually passing through estates (at 1979 levels), or only fifteen percent, will be subject to estate tax. The other eighty-five percent will escape both income and estate taxation.

In 1975, the $60,000 estate tax exemption (which had been in effect since 1942) meant that only the wealthiest 6.5 percent of decedents paid estate tax. If the $60,000 exemption had remained unchanged, the estate tax would have applied to about the wealthiest ten percent of decedents in 1982. The 1976 Act's increase to a $175,000 exemption level meant that in 1981 the estate tax applied only to the wealthiest three percent of persons dying that year. The immediate additional $100,000 increase, to a $275,000 exemption level, provided by the 1981 Act resulted in only the top one percent of 1982 decedents being subject to estate tax, and the further phased-in increase to a $600,000 level will exempt all but a small fraction of the wealthiest one percent of decedents from the tax.

In summary, the 1976 legislation, which produced a more rational, more neutral, and fairer tax on gifts and bequests with no long-term reduction in revenues, was followed only five years later by legislation which made the tax all but disappear—not only in terms of the number and percentage of decedents affected, but also in terms of its contribution to federal revenues.

Recent General Trends in Federal Taxation

The schizophrenic attitude of Congress toward the estate tax, manifested by the contrast between the 1976 and 1981 legislation, reflects a fundamental tension in the tax system that has dominated tax policy debates during recent years. Broadly speaking, the tension is one between a desire for structural tax reform, which would move the tax system towards greater horizontal and vertical equity, and a desire for tax provisions designed to stimulate increased savings or capital formation. This tension produces a direct conflict between the need to tax capital or the income from capital in order to achieve a progressive tax burden and the perceived need to exempt capital and capital income from tax in order to induce economic growth.

* * *

Public-opinion polls invariably reflect a public taste for a fairer tax system, but if that taste reflects concern other than a lowering of each individual's own taxes, it seems politically impotent.

* * * [T]he dominant economic factor influencing tax policy today is the projection of very large current and future deficits. If spending is—as seems to be the case—not likely to be reduced further in substantial amounts, the deficit can be narrowed only by additional revenues. Economic recovery may partially close the revenue gap, but, as state and local governments are learning, increased and new taxes will undoubtedly prove necessary. This need for revenues, however, is constrained by great reluctance, by both this Administration and important members of Congress, to increase the tax burden on capital or capital income for fear of stifling economic growth. In contrast, fairness in the distribution of the tax burden seems of little political significance since it currently enjoys no meaningful constituency.

The Role of the Estate Tax

These conditions combine to make the estate tax a very minor player indeed. Since it is a tax on savings, proposals to increase the estate tax run headlong into concerns over "capital formation." Moreover, the estate tax has very limited potential as a source of federal revenues. * * *

The limitation on potential estate tax revenues is an inherent one, not merely a product of political obstacles. Decedents annually transfer a total of about $120 billion in net assets. An average effective tax rate of twenty percent would produce total revenues of about $24 billion, approximately three times the current level.   With any substantial exemption, plus exclusions for certain amounts of property passing to surviving spouses or charities, a higher average effective rate seems unrealistic. The inherent limitation on bequests as a source of revenue cannot be overcome by even a dramatic structural revision of estate and gift taxes, such as converting to an inheritance or accessions tax, or taxing gifts and bequests as income to the recipient (or, in a consumption tax world, as consumption of the donor). A tax on deathtime transfers of wealth will thus not serve as a major source of federal revenues.

So we must look elsewhere than the production of revenues if we are to justify strengthening, rather than eliminating, the estate tax. That place should be its role in the distribution of the tax burden, in particular, its role in providing an important element of progressivity in the federal tax system.

Other than the dramatic increases in total revenues, the most striking characteristic of changes in the federal revenue sources described above is the diminishing relative significance of progressive tax sources. Viewed as a system of purchasing retirement and disability insurance from the government, the huge rise in employment taxes reflects a dramatic increase in taxes grounded in notions of "benefit" rather than "ability to pay." By contrast, if current employment taxes are considered to be taxes on the current generation of workers to fund the current retirement benefits of predecessor generations, rather than insurance purchased by current workers—a view that may well reflect the views of current workers—a far greater share of federal tax is imposed on labor income than in the past. In addition, employment tax ceilings on taxable labor income exempt a portion of the wages of highly salaried individuals. The employment tax increases, in combination with recent cutbacks in the top rates of individual income taxes and reductions in estate and corporate income and capital gains taxes, pose significant threats to the progressivity of federal taxation.

Moreover, the proposals for significant long-term changes in federal taxation that currently enjoy the greatest favor in both academic and political circles—a flat-rate tax and a consumption tax—pose further threats to progressivity. * * *

To view the estate tax, however, as contributing an important element of progressivity to the federal tax system requires shedding a myth which has come to dominate its political discussion. This myth—repeated most recently in the legislative history of the 1981 Act—is that the proper function of the estate tax (as well as its historical role) is only to "break up large concentrations of wealth." The clear implication—indeed, the principal justification for raising the tax-exempt level of estates to $600,000—is that no estate tax should be imposed on "smaller or moderate-sized estates." In 1981, "smaller and moderate-sized estates" meant those of the wealthiest one to six percent. If the 1976 tax-exempt level of $60,000 had been maintained, the estate tax would now apply to the wealthiest ten percent of decedents. The narrowing of the estate tax base that accompanies political acceptance of this myth necessarily defeats the contribution of this tax to the progressivity of the federal tax system. The tax becomes as narrow in its intended function as it is in its contribution to the government's revenue. A strong case can then be advanced for its elimination altogether.

In fact, however, the estate tax has done very little to dilute the greatest concentrations of wealth. The portion of total wealth held by the richest one percent of wealth-holders has remained remarkably stable. They possessed roughly one-fourth of the national wealth in every year from 1958 to 1972. A recent study advances a tentative estimate that their holdings declined from one-fourth to about one-fifth of total wealth between 1972 and 1976. Even assuming that such a decline has actually occurred, however, nothing suggests any significant causal role for the estate tax.

Looking instead at the contribution of the estate tax to the progressivity of the tax system reveals a quite different picture: It has had a significant progressive effect. In 1970, the average ratio of tax to adjusted gross income on individual income tax returns was 13.7 percent. Those taxpayers who were taxed at an average rate of at least 14 paid a total tax of $43 billion. If they had paid their tax at the average rate, the government would have received only $30.5 billion. The total revenue raised through individual income taxes in excess of the average rate was therefore $12.5 billion. By comparison, the fiscal year 1970 estate and gift tax collections from upper-income decedents were just under $3.7 billion. Thus, the estate and gift taxes—despite their low revenue yield—contributed nearly one-third as much to the progressivity of our tax structure as did rates in excess of the average individual income tax even though the estate tax imposed a smaller levy on inheritances than would have been imposed if bequests had been taxed as ordinary income.

* * * Data for the most recent year available, however, reveal a different picture. The average income tax rate had not changed greatly but the revenue raised by the estate tax amounted to only about twelve percent of that raised by income tax rates greater than the average—a far smaller contribution to progressivity than before. With the further increases in the estate tax marital deduction and tax-exemption enacted in 1981, the relative importance of the estate tax will decline even further. Professor Harry Gutman has estimated that if the estate tax changes of the 1981 legislation were fully effective in 1981, "the contribution to progressivity [of the estate tax] would be reduced to approximately 4 percent."[95] Whatever progressivity remains in the federal tax system will be supplied entirely by the income tax.

Reliance on progressive income tax rates as the sole mechanism for ensuring that this nation's tax burden is distributed in accordance with ability to pay poses a number of problems. Realized rates of return apparently tend to fall as wealth increases. Thus, any tax system which relies solely on an income tax to attain progressivity will not sufficiently tax the underlying wealth that generated the income. High income tax rates both create marginal disincentives to productivity and stimulate legal and illegal noncompliance. Moreover, many preference provisions that have long been a part of the income tax exempt certain sources of income from capital.
* * *

The principal reason, therefore, to revise the estate tax is to rescue this mechanism for achieving progressivity, and perhaps to rescue progressivity itself, from both short- and long-term threats. Deciding that restoration rather than repeal is the appropriate course requires three steps: (1) a judgment that progressivity in taxation is just and therefore good; (2) a view that the estate tax can and should play an important role in achieving progressivity; and (3) a conclusion that progressivity should not be abandoned because of the adverse impact of progressive taxation in general (and the estate tax in particular) on capital formation. I shall now turn to an examination of these three propositions.
* * *

What Does This Mean for the Estate Tax?

* * * It is my view, therefore, that the nation's tax laws should move in the direction of the 1976 legislation, not that of the 1981 law, and that the

---

95. Gutman, *Federal Wealth Transfer Taxes After the Economic Recovery Tax Act of 1981*, 35 NAT'L TAX J. 253, 262 (1982). Professor Gutman contends that the Graetz and Treasury methodologies do not provide "a precise measure of the annual contribution of the transfer taxes to progressivity," *id.* at 262, because annual transfer-tax receipts are only "a proxy for aggregate annual individual accruals to discharge future transfer tax liabilities," *id* at 267 n. 42. He suggests that progressivity would be more accurately measured by comparing income and employment taxes paid by an individual today with the present value of the estate tax to be paid by the same individual tomorrow.

estate tax should be rejuvenated and returned to its prior status as an important contributor to the progressivity of the tax system. But having urged this as the direction it *should* go, I cannot close without also examining where it will likely go.

There are two practical barriers to my preferred course of strengthening the role of the estate tax in the federal system. The first I have already described—namely the inherent limitation on the revenue potential of an estate tax. As I have detailed above, there simply is not enough wealth transferred annually to permit a wealth transfer tax (an estate and gift tax) to become a significant source of federal revenue. Given the current and projected levels of federal deficits, only substantial revenue sources seem likely to dominate the political agenda in the near-term. Thus, tax increases grounded predominately on distributional fairness would seem to have little chance of success.

* * *

The most puzzling political obstacle to estate tax revision, however, is that the American people do not seem to like heavy taxes on bequests. George McGovern's proposal in 1972 to confiscate inheritances above a certain amount was not well received, and a recent California initiative to repeal the state's inheritance tax garnered a sixty-four percent positive vote. * * * The only convincing explanation that has occurred to me for this phenomenon lies in the optimism of the American people. In California, at least, sixty-four percent of the people must believe that they will be in the wealthiest five to ten percent when they die.

The combination of these political obstacles to the estate tax's rejuvenation and the tax's inherent limitations as a significant revenue source leads me to conclude that the estate tax seems far more likely to wither than to grow stronger. As I have suggested, this prediction makes me fear the demise of progressive taxation in the United States. * * *

If my prediction (as opposed to my desire) is fulfilled, and the years ahead complete the demise of the estate tax, the federal tax system will have lost more than an important and useful mechanism for achieving progressivity; it will have lost a source of great humor. * * * [J]ust the other day, I heard today's version of thoughtful estate planning advice in the office of a well-known New York practitioner. A client had asked with great anxiety what he might do to minimize the estate taxes of his ninety-year-old widowed mother who had a large fortune, composed of extremely valuable art and cash. The lawyer thought for a great long while, no doubt running through his bag of estate planning tricks, when all of a sudden, with a gleam in his eye, he looked up and said calmly, "Marry her." It would be a real shame if a tax which produces such creative advice were to disappear.

A BRIEF FOR THE ABOLITION OF ALL TRANSFER TAXES
Joel C. Dobris[*]
35 Syracuse Law Review 1215, 1217-26 (1984)

There are meaningful arguments in favor of abolishing all transfer taxes in our federal tax system. They include: (1) the gift and estate tax does not raise a meaningful amount of revenue, (2) the current gift and estate tax does not adequately vindicate any of the social policies it is supposed to, and (3) the tax is costly and inefficient in many ways.

First, the gift and estate tax does not raise a meaningful amount of revenue and never will. Not enough property is transferred to use a transfer tax as a source of revenue, especially if the rates are not confiscatory. After the passage of the Economic Recovery Tax Act of 1981 (ERTA), this low production of revenue has been magnified. Thus, Professor Gutman states that if ERTA had been fully phased-in in 1981 that transfer tax revenue would have been only $2.54 billion.[17] This revenue could be raised in numerous other ways, including a slight increase in the income tax rates.

Second, the current gift and estate tax arguably does not adequately vindicate any of the social policies it is supposed to. Many people believe a gift and estate tax is supposed to break up concentrations of wealth, achieve a more equitable distribution of resources, or assert the hegemony of the common people or the egalitarian nature of our society. Assuming that it is desirable to do any of this, through the tax system or otherwise, then the current gift and estate tax is not a worthwhile tool. The transfer tax does not break up concentrations of wealth. It does not function in a meaningful way to redistribute wealth in order to enhance the quality of life for persons with less wealth. Indeed, it might be said that no politically acceptable transfer tax system can obtain such a result.[26] The tax would have to be confiscatory in order to accomplish this—a politically unacceptable result at the present time.

* * *

If the current system is not working to eliminate concentrations of wealth, that is certainly an argument for reform of the system now in place. Is it, however, an argument for abolition? I believe that it is legitimate to call for the abolition of something that is not working, and has not worked, to achieve one of its important purposes. Moreover, it is not at all clear that

---

*. At time of original publication, Professor of Law, University of California, Davis.

17. Gutman, *Reforming Federal Wealth Transfer Taxes After ERTA*, 69 VA. L. REV. 1183, 1195 (1983).

26. Indeed, the current transfer tax might be categorized as a cruel hoax. *See generally* Boskin, *An Economist's Perspective on Estate Taxation*, in DEATH, TAXES AND FAMILY PROPERTY: ESSAYS AND AMERICAN ASSEMBLY REPORT (E. Halbach ed. 1977) (economic effects of the estate tax). Another understanding of the current situation is that it allows the middle-income taxpayer the illusion that we are taxing the rich and that we have brought the rich to heel. This appears to be the current state of affairs in Great Britain. *See* Wolman, *The Tax That Didn't . . .*, Financial Times (London) March 24, 1984, at 20, col. 3.

people want these concentrations broken up, or that a just America requires it.[34]

The transfer tax does not accomplish another of its social purposes—the importation of progressive taxation into our tax system. * * *

It is clear that the transfer tax does not strongly contribute to progressivity. Moreover, it is unclear if we as a society are committed to progressivity in our tax system or if progressivity is an obvious social goal.[41] * * * Given the failure to obtain progressivity with the current tax and the meaningful uncertainty about progressivity as a tax goal, it is quite legitimate to consider abolition insofar as progressivity is an important policy underlying the tax.

* * *

A third argument favoring abolition is that the tax is costly in many ways, both direct and indirect. The direct costs include both the costs of the constant reform of the tax and the cost of complying with the tax.

Constant reform of the tax is costly. As long as the tax is in existence it seems that it will be changed. Formulating proposals for change, seeing them through the Congress, interpreting the new law, and educating the private and the public sectors to enable them to deal with the new law, all involve substantial costs that repeal would save.

Over recent years, the following pattern has developed. Inflation has increased the face value of property in the hands of "middle-class" taxpayers. As a result, it has appeared that these people would be subject to estate taxes. This situation has forced lawyers to master the estate tax structure in order to service their clients. Congress then changed the law to essentially exempt such taxpayers from estate tax. This wastes the work of many lawyers who plan estates for "middle-class" people, not only because the law is changed, but also because their middle-class clients no longer need estate planning and the lawyers do not have access to richer clients. This waste of time is very meaningful.

Second, taxpayer compliance and the enforcement of compliance also generate substantial direct costs. Taxpayers choose, wisely I might add, to devote substantial time and money to obtaining estate planning and tax-oriented estate administration. Thus, the very existence of the tax places an improper premium on obtaining expert advise. The government also spends substantial amounts on compliance. Abolishing the tax would free

---

34. As Professor Graetz notes, the McGovern proposal "to confiscate inheritances above a certain amount was not well received" and the people of California, in 1982, cheerfully repealed the state's death tax by popular initiative. *See* Graetz, *To Praise the Estate Tax, Not to Bury It*, 93 YALE L.J. 259, 285 (1983).

41. Let us assume there is good in progressivity. One is tempted to ask whether progressivity is inherently good or only valuable if the populace perceives its existence. *See generally* Keene, *What Do We Know About the Public's Attitude on Progressivity?*, 36 NAT'L TAX J. 371 (1983) (outlining the public's varying responses to differently worded questions in public opinion polls on progressivity, and the lack of specific knowledge of the public's attitude toward progressivity).

meaningful numbers of sophisticated Internal Revenue Service personnel for work more likely both to produce revenue and to obtain the goals of the tax system. It is a mistake to allocate substantial resources to an area that does not produce revenue. Abolition would also free large numbers of private sector planners.

* * *

The transfer tax affects, to an unknown degree, the investment decisions of rich people. It can be argued that the planning required to avoid or minimize the tax creates too many intrusions on financial matters and encourages manipulative actions.

It is argued in favor of abolition that an indirect cost of transfer taxation is that death tax discourages savings and encourages consumption, thereby interfering with capital formation via savings. * * * I am not sure I agree that a death tax interferes with capital formation. * * * I believe it requires confiscatory death tax rates, which we obviously do not have, to inspire the kind of unwholesome consumption in lieu of savings that is of social concern.

Repeal might well reduce the amount of money held in trusts. This might well result in more money being invested in riskier investments, which, in turn, might result in economic growth. I am suggesting that many trusts are created only to avoid estate tax, and that trustees invest conservatively. * * *

Another reason favoring abolition is that, arguably, the existence of the current transfer tax is interfering with the efficient functioning of the federal tax system. I believe that legal, proper tax planning will spawn improper tax avoidance schemes if the public fails to see the difference between planning and impropriety. Thus a wise government limits legitimate tax avoidance to limit illegitimate tax avoidance. One way to do this is to limit opportunities for planning. Arguably, repealing transfer taxes wipes out estate planning, thereby reducing the public perception that there is a candy store of tax planning reserved for rich people. The risk is that the repeal of the transfer tax system will be seen as giving a whole other store away.

People, the political system, and the tax system can only accommodate a finite amount of general complexity and, more specifically, complexity in the imposition of tax and complexity occasioned by the imposition of tax. In the face of the growing complexity of our society and of our tax system, perhaps it is a mistake to waste the capacity for accommodation of complexity on a disliked tax that does not raise a great deal of revenue, that does not seem to be accomplishing its social purposes, and that absorbs large amounts of public and private sector effort. Repeal of the costly and complex transfer tax system offers an opportunity to obtain simplification of our tax structure.

* * *

A final argument favoring abolition is that the estate tax creates serious liquidity problems for a small, but economically important, group of decedents—owners of closely held businesses, real estate and farms. * * *

Notes and Questions

Nontraditional justifications of transfer taxes: interplay with the income tax

19. Professor Graetz supports strengthening transfer taxes, despite the "inherent" limitations on the revenue possibilities of those taxes, and notwithstanding the fact that the transfer taxes have done little to break up concentrations of wealth. If the transfer taxes do not fulfill their traditional goals, what policy consideration justifies the transfer taxes to Professor Graetz?

20. Assuming the desirability of greater progressivity in the tax system, why would Professor Graetz prefer to utilize transfer taxes rather than the more obvious route of increasing the progressivity of the income tax?

21. Professor Harry Gutman concludes that the Economic Recovery Tax Act of 1981 "has emasculated the wealth transfer tax as an effective component of our tax system,"[t] a state of affairs he finds particularly distressing given the less-than-comprehensive income tax base:

> That the current tax system excludes large amounts of income from the income tax base provides the most compelling reason for retaining a transfer tax. With a seriously eroded income tax base, a transfer tax is needed to ensure that each taxpayer eventually bears a fair share of the tax burden. The transfer tax serves as a "backstop" to the income tax by taxing the wealth that taxpayers accumulate through tax-preferred income sources."[u]

Do you agree that the transfer tax can and should serve as a "backstop" for the income tax system? Is Professor Gutman adequately answered by the argument that "[t]he flaws of the income tax should be addressed and amended through the income tax laws, not through a dual system of taxation."[v] Professor Gutman wrote prior to the base-broadening changes in the income tax wrought by the Tax Reform Act of 1986. Do the 1986 changes mean that a "backstop" is no longer necessary?

22. Professor Gutman characterizes the transfer tax as a backstop to the income tax as "a second-best solution,"[w] the preferred approach being to

---

t. Harry L. Gutman, *Reforming Federal Wealth Transfer Taxes After ERTA*, 69 VA. L. REV. 1183, 1271 (1983).

u. *Id.* at 1191.

v. Edward J. Gac & Sharen K. Brougham, *A Proposal for Restructuring the Taxation of Wealth Transfers: Tax Reform Redux?*, 5 AKRON TAX J. 75, 87 (1988).

w. Gutman, *supra* note t, at 1212.

broaden the income tax base. And he concedes that structuring the transfer tax system with a role as backstop to the income tax system would be difficult and imperfect:

> Critics of this proposal may also argue that such a rate schedule sacrifices aggregate horizontal equity to achieve tax progressivity. The decedent whose estate is comprised solely of assets purchased with after-tax wage income is subject to the same transfer tax as the decedent whose equivalent estate has been accumulated through inheritance or through the reinvestment of an income-tax-free yield. If the purpose of the transfer tax is principally to recoup unpaid income tax, the former decedent is overtaxed, and the latter remains undertaxed. Aggregate horizontal equity in this regime could be achieved by confining the transfer tax base to assets whose value is traceable to income tax preferences. Alternatively, one could establish a transfer tax credit to compensate for previously paid income tax. Either alternative would require adjustment of the rates. * * * Both alternatives would also create difficult administrative problems. Thus, aggregate horizontal inequity may have to be tolerated.[x]

23. Professor Gutman also suggests that transfer or wealth taxes have a place even if we attain a well designed income tax:

> If one were to design a tax system de novo, one would undoubtedly ask whether an excise on wealth transfers is a necessary component. Commentators have noted that a tax on wealth transfers is indistinguishable from a tax on income because in economic terms wealth is simply the capitalized present value of future income. The argument implies that if economic income were fully taxed, wealth would be fully taxed as well, making a wealth transfer tax unnecessary.
>
> Even if this argument is correct, however, a wealth transfer tax can be justified on a number of other grounds. Suppose, for example, one believed that greater progressivity and higher marginal rates were necessary to accomplish an appropriate redistribution of income and wealth. One alternative for implementing such a goal is simply to tax income at the rates necessary to achieve the desired distribution of the tax burden. An income tax with a high maximum marginal rate, however, might have unacceptable efficiency effects of locking in invested capital and encouraging current consumption rather than saving. Such efficiency concerns have in fact been the basis for recent income tax rate reductions. Many economists also believe that a transfer tax

---

x. *Id.* at 1215-16.

has less allocative impact on investment decisions than an income tax. * * *

Other supporters of the wealth transfer tax have argued that wealth reflects an ability to pay beyond that represented by its future income stream. * * * Still others have contended that a wealth transfer tax should exist to disperse the attributes of economic power and opportunity that are thought to accompany large accumulations of wealth.[y]

Are these arguments in favor of transfer taxes persuasive? Assuming an improved transfer tax (Professor Gutman certainly concedes the need for considerable improvement), could his arguments be countered?

Arguments against transfer taxes

24. Professor Graetz argues that the explanation for popular opposition to death taxes "lies in the optimism of the American people. In California, at least, sixty-four percent of the people must believe that they will be in the wealthiest five to ten percent when they die." Others, including Professor Ascher, similarly appear to attribute popular opposition to death taxes to a combination of unrealistic optimism and ignorance. Do you agree? Is there another explanation for the popular opposition to death taxes? Professor McCaffery argues that "our experience with estate taxation seems to reflect * * * some form of anti-envy. The majority of citizens and our well-evolved practices are opposed to levying a tax exclusively on the wealthiest elite."[z]

25. While Professor Graetz, who has served in tax policy positions in Republican administrations, wishes to strengthen transfer taxes, Professor Dobris, who describes himself as "a person of modest means [and] a registered Democrat,"[aa] argues for their abolition. Professor Dobris agrees with Professor Graetz that transfer taxes generate little revenue and fail to break up concentrations of wealth. While Professor Graetz argues for the taxes because of their contribution to progressivity, however, Professor Dobris questions both the desirability of progressivity and the contribution of transfer taxes to progressivity.

The heart of Professor Dobris' opposition to transfer taxes appears to arise from his conclusion "that the tax is costly in many ways, both direct and indirect." What are some of these costs, according to Professor Dobris? Do you agree that these costs exist? That they justify repeal of transfer taxes?

26. Professor Dobris and other critics of transfer taxes argue that the taxes tend to push assets into trust management, which is said to be

---

y. *Id.* at 1187-88.

z. McCaffery, *supra* note q, at 287.

aa. 35 SYRACUSE L. REV. at 1215.

detrimental because of conservative management. Professor Thomas Robinson, however, observes that trustees are not the worst of all possible money managers:

> This leads to a discussion of trust management, which the wealth transfer taxes have always encouraged. * * * [W]hile it is clear that the qualifications of some professional trustees are professionally adequate, their motivations to maximize benefits from property under their care may be inhibited both by law and by inclination. And a further price of trustee management is often inefficient dead-hand control by the settlor. But since *someone* must manage property, in many cases trustee management is preferable to management by those who would mismanage or squander it, including an incapacitated settlor, his inexperienced wife, or his worthless children.

> Waiting in the wings, of course, is the government, which can be both the best and the worst alternative. * * * [I]f it uses the money so received to displace other revenue sources, particularly those used for income transfer payments, then arguably this is the best of policies, harmonizing both the goal of encouraging good management of the nation's resources and the goal of equally distributing those benefits. * * * Of course, insofar as the government attempts to manage the assets itself, it provides the worst of alternative managers.[bb]

Scope of exemptions from transfer taxation

27. Assuming that transfer taxes in some form should be continued, do you agree with the present tax policy of allowing an unlimited marital deduction? As noted in the introduction, this provision dates only from 1981. What justifications exist for treating a surviving spouse differently from other relatives?

28. As the last sentence of Professor Graetz' article whimsically suggests, the marital deduction opens up the possibility of marriage undertaken in form for the purpose of tax avoidance. An extremely tax-motivated taxpayer could marry a younger family member as the taxpayer approached death; this avoidance technique could be repeated as the young spouse aged, without theoretical limit. (Inexplicable as it may appear to tax professors, many people marry without tax concerns uppermost in their minds. The tax strategy described in this note would raise, among other problems, concerns about bigamy, societal disapproval, and the possibility

---

bb. Thomas A. Robinson, *The Federal Wealth Transfer Taxes—A Requiem?*, 1 AM. J. TAX POL'Y 25, 37-38 (1982).

that a young spouse might die unexpectedly or use the property in a manner not contemplated by the elderly taxpayer.)

While Professor Graetz apparently meant only to end his article on a light note, others have taken the problem seriously. In Canada, the Carter Commission recommended that marriage not protect transfers from tax until the marriage had either lasted five years or resulted in the birth of a child.[cc] Professor Ascher's proposal would not allow a full marital exclusion until the couple had been married twenty years.[dd]

Professor Russell Osgood argues that "[p]olicing the genuineness of marriages seems distasteful at best."[ee] Assuming we agree, is this nevertheless a distasteful problem that should be addressed? (Note that Professor Osgood himself *does* address the problem, by treating a spouse who is more than twelve and one half years younger as a member of a younger generation for purposes of the generation-skipping tax.)

29. Professor Gutman does not challenge the Congressional decision to treat marital partners as a single unit through the unlimited marital deduction. He suggests, however, that the logical extension of this policy should be that when the estates of the spouses are taxed, they should not be treated as separate taxpayers for purposes of the unified credit and the progressive rate structure.[ff]

30. The annual exclusion shields up to $10,000 per year per donee from tax, or even from counting against the unified credit. Married couples can give $20,000 per donee. Such gifts can be made to an unlimited number of donees. Consider a married couple with three married children and nine married grandchildren. The couple could give each of the twelve descendents and each of the descendents' spouses $20,000 each—or a total of $480,000 per year—without touching their unified credits.

All agree that some amount of gift must be allowed tax-free, because Congress has no intention of requiring a gift tax return from a grandmother who sends a $20 birthday check. (Similarly, some *de minimis* exclusion for the recipient would be necessary under an accessions tax.) But is the present exclusion too generous?

Professor Robert Smith argues that Congress allowed the annual exclusion for the purpose of avoiding the necessity of keeping track of numerous small gifts, but that taxpayers routinely use the annual exclusion only with respect to significant transfers of wealth, and simply ignore relatively small birthday and Christmas presents. Such an approach

---

cc. 3 REP. ROYAL COM'N ON TAX'N 146 (1966).

dd. *See* 89 MICH. L. REV. at 123-26.

ee. Russell K. Osgood, *Carryover Basis Repeal and Reform of the Transfer Tax System*, 66 CORNELL L. REV. 297, 322 (1981).

ff. *See* Gutman, *supra* note t, at 1218-39.

subverts the justification for the annual exclusion, Professor Smith asserts. He would lower the exclusion to $5,000 per donee and $20,000 per donor.[gg]

Professor John Steinkamp, on the other hand, defends present law, particularly with respect to limiting gifts on a per-donee, rather than a per-donor, basis. Discussing a 1990 proposal of the Joint Committee on Taxation to impose a $30,000 per donor limitation, he argued: "If Taxpayer A can give each of his three children $10,000 per year free of tax, Taxpayer B should be allowed to give each of his six children $10,000 per year free of tax."[hh]

How, if at all, should the annual exclusion be changed? Should the per-donee annual exclusion be reduced? Should a per-donor limitation be introduced?

31. As discussed in the preceding note, the annual exclusion for gifts can be used to transfer considerable wealth free of transfer taxation. The annual exclusion, unlike the unified credit, is a use-it-or-lose-it proposition. This creates an incentive to transfer wealth early and often. (Other aspects of the transfer tax system encourage early giving; for example, utilization of the unified credit by *inter vivos* gift rather than waiting for transfer at death protects post-gift appreciation from tax.) Professor McCaffery argues that because the transfer tax system encourages giving, and encourages giving early:

> [T]he wealthy young receive their wealth, or become certain of its ultimate receipt, early in life. This wealth may undercut their incentives to work and save. * * * [I]t may be better for them to receive their wealth later in life, say when they are fifty-five years old, than for them to receive it earlier, when their work incentives will be more affected and when their propensity to consume is greater.[ii]

32. The charitable exclusion has generated relatively little academic comment. Note that the exclusion from transfer taxation is not the only tax benefit; the same charitable contribution that protects property from transfer taxes, if made *inter vivos*, also gives rise to an income tax deduction.

A key issue is whether one thinks that the goals of transfer taxation are sufficiently met if wealth is transferred to charities, rather than a large portion (but not all) of that wealth going to the government. A charitable contribution or bequest absorbs the entire amount, while the transfer taxes claim only a fraction; does this mean that the charitable contribution is more effective than the tax itself? On the other hand, is a sufficient public purpose

---

gg. Robert B. Smith, *Should We Give Away the Annual Exclusion?*, 1 FLA. TAX REV. 361 (1993).

hh. John G. Steinkamp, *Common Sense and the Gift Tax Annual Exclusion*, 72 NEB. L. REV. 106, 170-71 (1993).

ii. McCaffery, *supra* note q, at 320-21.

effected if the donor can avoid tax by diverting his wealth to a charitable foundation bearing his name, controlled by his friends, and benefitting causes particularly dear to his heart? On policy grounds, how does the charitable deduction under the transfer taxes compare to the charitable contribution deduction allowed under the income tax?

D. THE ACCESSIONS TAX

The two excerpts below, like the Dobris excerpt in the preceding subchapter, advocate abolition of the estate tax. Unlike Professor Dobris, however, Professors Rudick and Donaldson would replace the estate tax with an alternative form of death tax. Professor Rudick's article, published half a century ago in the maiden issue of *Tax Law Review*, was the first to advocate the accessions tax, which has found considerable favor among academics. The brief excerpt from his article sets out the basics of his proposal.

The excerpt from Professor Donaldson's article explains what he views as the manifest failings of present law, and suggests either of two alternatives, both of which would shift the focus of tax to the recipient. One of his proposed alternatives, excerpted briefly here, is the accessions tax. (The other, treating the receipt of gifts and bequests as income taxable under the income tax, is examined in Chapter Nine.)

A PROPOSAL FOR AN ACCESSIONS TAX
Harry J. Rudick[*]
1 Tax Law Review 25, 25, 30-32 (1945)

This is a proposal for the abolition of the present federal estate and gift taxes and the substitution therefor of a progressive tax on each recipient of money or other property by way of inheritance or *inter vivos* gift. The brackets of tax would progress not according to the size of the donor's taxable dispositions but according to the aggregate taxable acquisitions of the donee, no matter from whom. Tax liability for a particular year would be computed in the same way as under the existing gift tax law,[jj] that is, by first computing a tax on the aggregate taxable acquisitions of the taxpayer during the taxable year and prior years, and then deducting from this figure the tax on the taxpayer's aggregate taxable acquisitions in prior years. For want of a better name, we call the suggested new tax an "accessions tax."

* * *

---

[*]. At time of original publication, Professor of Law at New York University and a partner of Lord, Day & Lord, New York City.

jj. Professor Rudick wrote prior to the "integration" of the estate and gift taxes in 1976. Under current law, the language in the text would describe the estate tax as well as the gift tax, because there is a unified credit and a unified rate structure for all transfers from an individual, whether during life or at death. (Eds.)

Alternative Bases for Death Duties and Superiority of Accessions Tax in Attaining Objective

There are, of course, a number of methods by which, through progressive death duties, the tendency of wealth to concentrate can be counteracted. In considering them we should remember that dead men pay no taxes: the tax depletes what is left for the survivors—they are the real taxpayers. The method we now operate under imposes a graduated tax measured solely by the size of the decedent's estate. Hence, if a man died leaving a net estate of one million dollars, the federal estate tax at current rates would be $325,000, regardless of whether he left the entire million (or rather the residue after death taxes) to one person or twenty persons.

Another procedure—adopted by many jurisdictions including a number of our states—ignores the size of the decedent's estate and graduates the rates according to the amount received by the legatee from the particular decedent. Thus, if a decedent divided his million equally among ten persons, the aggregate tax on these ten people would be very much less than the tax on one legatee who received the entire million. Under this system, no regard is given to any amounts a legatee may have inherited from other decedents. Thus, if a husband died leaving a million dollars to his son and later the widow died leaving another million dollars to the son, the tax would be much less than if the son had inherited the entire two million from one of his parents.

* * *

Examined from the viewpoint of whether they attain their object of deconcentrating excessive accumulations of wealth, each of the * * * devices described above has shortcomings. The first does not in any way encourage the wider distribution of wealth: the tax is the same whether the estate is divided among two or fifty beneficiaries. The second does tend to impel an allotment of smaller shares to more people, but by failing to take into account other inheritances, it does not produce optimum distribution. * * *

It is submitted that the proposal herein will attain, more effectively than the other methods which have been tried, the real objective of death duties, *i.e.*, preventing undue concentration of wealth. Under this proposal no tax will be imposed on the donor or his estate. Instead, each beneficiary of an inheritance or gift will be subject to a progressive tax on his cumulative acquisitions by inheritance or gift. Thus, if A receives a gift of $100,000 from his father in 1946 and a bequest from his mother of $100,000 1947, the tax on the bequest will be at higher rates than the tax on the gift because of the cumulative feature. Donors and decedents will thus have an inducement to transfer their property to those who have previously received or inherited least.

* * *

THE FUTURE OF TRANSFER TAXATION:
REPEAL, RESTRUCTURING AND REFINEMENT,
OR REPLACEMENT
John E. Donaldson[*]

50 Washington & Lee Law Review 539, 540-46, 548-52, 559-60 (1993)

Whether accumulated wealth is a proper subject of taxation is a matter over which economists disagree and is essentially a political question. Assuming that wealth transfer or receipt is a proper base for the imposition of tax, the question of how much revenue should be derived from such base is also a political question. However, the question of whether a particular system for taxing accumulated wealth is useful and worthwhile, though not devoid of political significance, is essentially a practical and utilitarian matter. This essay suggests that as a practical and utilitarian matter, the present estate, gift, and generation-skipping tax system should be abandoned. It acknowledges that the present system can be improved. It suggests, however, that the improvements possible are not sufficient to warrant retention of the old system. It suggests that if wealth is to be taxed upon transfer, two models which focus on the transferee rather than the transferor, are likely to offer more acceptable methods of accomplishing that task. One of these models is an accessions tax. The other treats the receipt of gifts and bequests as taxable income to the recipient. * * *

Goals of the Transfer Tax System

Several goals have, from time to time, been ascribed to the transfer tax system. * * *

Reducing Concentrations of Wealth

However worthwhile the objective of breaking up or reducing concentrations of wealth may be, commentators generally agree that the transfer tax system has been ineffective in this regard. * * *

It is clear that for political reasons or otherwise, Congress has little interest in using transfer taxes as an instrument to reduce concentrations of wealth. Joseph Peckman of the Brookings Institute was probably correct in his observation that "the public does not appear to accept the desirability of a vigorous estate and gift tax system."[24] Professor Graetz, in likewise concluding that the people "do not seem to like heavy taxes on bequests" pointed to the poor reception given to George McGovern's proposal to heavily tax inheritances above a certain amount and to a California initiative to repeal that state's inheritance tax. * * *

The transfer tax system simply has not made a significant contribution to a goal of breaking up wealth concentration. Although in 1992 transfer taxes produced revenues of approximately $12 billion from the wealthiest one percent of the population, that amount is relatively minuscule in relation to

---

[*]. At time of original publication, Ball Professor of Law, College of William and Mary.
24. J. PECHMAN, FEDERAL TAX POLICY 255 (5th ed. 1987).

the objective. Absent a significant change in the political climate, which appears unlikely in the foreseeable future, it is improbable that the system will be called upon to more effectively address perceived problems of wealth concentration.

Production of Revenue

The second, and perhaps the historically more important goal of the transfer tax system, is that of producing revenue. In the mid to late 1930s, the transfer tax system was a major component of the federal tax system, producing more than six percent of total revenues and in one year, 1936, ten percent. * * *   Since World War II, however, transfer tax revenues have rarely exceeded two percent of total federal tax collections and as a result of recent changes, have diminished to approximately 1.1 percent. * * *

Even if there were greater desire to use the transfer tax system as a source of revenue, it is doubtful whether such taxes could be adapted to become a major revenue source. In fact, no country, including those which have more socialistic political values, derives significant revenues from wealth transfer taxation. * * *

Contributing to Progressivity

A third goal, or role, of transfer taxes advanced by some is that of contributing to the progressivity of the federal tax system.[38] However, that role has a more historic than continuing significance. * * * *   In the mid to late 1930s, when estate tax revenues on occasion were as high as twenty-seven percent to fifty-six percent of individual income tax revenues, the transfer tax contributions to the goal of progressivity were substantial. * * *   However, when the affected population drops to approximately one percent, today's level, the role of transfer taxes in contributing to progressivity of the tax system is minuscule.

* * * [E]ven proponents of the progressivity role of transfer taxation are pessimistic that restoration of such a role is politically possible.[46]

Manifestly, current wealth transfer taxation can not be justified by perceived roles either of breaking up or reducing concentrations of wealth or of contributing to the progressivity of the federal revenue system. If these roles are dismissed, a case can be made for repeal of the estate, [gift,] and generation skipping taxes, notwithstanding that they do produce $12 billion in revenue. This revenue, comparatively insignificant, comes at the expense of a "bad" tax system, one that lacks fairness, efficiency, and neutrality.

* * *

---

38. Michael J. Graetz, *To Praise the Estate Tax, Not to Bury It*, 93 YALE L.J. 259, 271 (1983). *See also* Harry L. Gutman, *Reforming Federal Wealth Transfer Taxes after ERTA*, 69 VA. L. REV. 1183, 1185 (1983) (arguing transfer taxes have "traditionally played, and should continue to play, an important role in contributing to the progressivity of the tax system as a whole").

46. Graetz, *supra* note 38, at 271.

Fairness, Efficiency, and Neutrality

Adherence to generally accepted principles of sound tax policy requires that tax systems be fair, efficient, and neutral. The existing transfer tax system severely violates each of these principles.

Fairness

First, the system is not fair, from considerations of both horizontal equity and vertical equity. Horizontal equity suggests that persons transferring equal wealth within the system be taxed in the same manner. Vertical equity (progressivity) suggests that persons of greater wealth be taxed more heavily on their transfers than persons of lesser wealth. Substantial horizontal inequity has been legislated into the system. For example, * * * life insurance proceeds, where the decedent has an incident of ownership, are included in the estate tax base. However, proceeds of life insurance, even when attributable to investment made by decedents, are excluded from the base where incidents of ownership are lacking, or if once possessed, have been yielded more than three years prior to death.

More important to considerations of both horizontal and vertical equity is the simple fact that where transfer taxes that would otherwise have been imposed are avoided or postponed without penalty, equity is violated. A major industry, that pursued by estate planning professionals, has evolved to exploit opportunities for avoidance and penalty-free postponement of transfer taxes that would otherwise have been payable. * * *

A discussion of all of the tax avoidance and postponement devices available to avoid or delay imposition of transfer taxes is beyond the scope of this essay. The literature on estate planning directed to tax avoidance and minimization is extensive. To make the point, however, a mention of several techniques is sufficient. For example, persons having the greatest wealth, and thus benefitting most in circumventing vertical equity, are more readily able than those having less wealth to utilize the gift tax system, with its "tax exclusive"[56] base to reduce the cost of donative transfers. For example, a person who has $10,000,000 of wealth can, while living, more readily transfer $600,000 in assets considered likely to appreciate in value, using the unified credit to avoid immediate imposition of tax, than can [a person] who has only $1,500,000 in wealth. Also, and for convenience, disregarding the unified credit, persons who would otherwise be in the fifty-percent bracket for both immediate gift tax purposes and for eventual estate tax purposes can choose to make a gift of $1,000,000, at a gift tax cost of $500,000 for total transfer related cost (gift plus gift tax) of $1,500,000. If the "fund" of $1,500,000 tapped in giving $1,000,000 to the donee had been retained until death and taxed at the fifty-percent bracket, only $750,000 would remain after tax to pass to objects of bounty. In this example, the transfer tax saving obtained

---

56. Unlike the estate tax, which is "tax inclusive" in its base and allows no deduction for tax in measuring the tax, the gift tax is "tax exclusive" and gift taxes payable on a transfer are not included in the measure of the tax. *Compare* I.R.C. § 2001 *with* §2501 (Supp. 1993).

by using a gift mechanism rather than a testamentary mechanism to pass wealth is $250,000. Another important device for avoiding imposition of transfer taxes is the utilization of the annual exclusion of $10,000 ($20,000 if husband and wife cooperate by using the split-gift election). For example, an individual with three married children and five grandchildren can annually transfer $10,000 to each child, each child's spouse and each grandchild, totalling $110,000 per year, eroding the transfer tax base by that amount and avoiding the imposition of as much of $55,000 (assuming a potential bracket of fifty percent) for each year of such activity. The amounts can be doubled in the case of a married couple. * * *

A corollary to the foregoing observations regarding ease of tax avoidance and its effect on horizontal and vertical equity is the resulting consequence that to a significant extent transfer taxes are "voluntary taxes," paid largely by wealthy persons who are uninformed or ill-advised, or who simply die before putting their affairs in order—all too frequent occurrences. To the extent that the tax burdens those who bear it only because of the want of effective avoidance planning, it is especially unfair. * * *

Efficiency

Second, the transfer tax is inefficient. This is perhaps the system's most serious shortcoming. It requires an inordinate amount of attention at the highest levels of government, especially in relation to the relative insignificance of the revenues generated. * * * The creativity of estate planning professionals imposes a continuing drain on the attention of policy makers and legislators. The tax is comparatively expensive to administer. The system's complexity, coupled with the creative devices employed in estate planning, requires the Internal Revenue Service (IRS) to employ lawyers as estate tax examiners, who are compensated at a higher level than other IRS compliance personnel. While only a small fraction of individual income tax returns are examined, 12,000 of the 56,000 estate tax returns filed in 1989 were examined.

Efficiency is not properly measured by compliance costs to the government alone. The transfer tax system imposes enormous resource and opportunity costs in taxpayer compliance and avoidance endeavors and in the time and energy of lawyers, accountants, trust officers, and financial planners required to understand and apply the system. The magnitude of human resources involved is partially suggested by the American Bar Association's estimate that over 16,000 lawyers consider trust, probate, and estate law as their area of concentration. * * * Lawyers may not cavalierly assume that clients of modest wealth when wills are executed will not have substantial wealth at death. Many clients who will, in fact, not have transfer tax exposure, receive legal services predicated on the possibility that they may face such exposure. * * * Although the transfer tax system is intended to affect only a very small portion of the population, such protective drafting causes the system to affect a substantially larger segment, who prudently,

but often unnecessarily, receive and pay for complex estate planning services.
* * *

There are important consequential costs as well. Prudent fiduciaries are reluctant to distribute and settle decedents' estates before potential estate tax controversies have been settled. The transfer tax system prolongs the administration of estates. Prudent fiduciaries invest conservatively, and prolonged administration delays access to capital by beneficiaries, who may employ it more effectively within the economy. The system also promotes the "trustification" of assets that might otherwise have been transferred outright.

All of the foregoing energy, resources, and opportunity costs are sacrificed on the alter of a tax system that fails to achieve its supposed goals and yields only $12 billion in revenue. A recent study concluded that resources spent in avoiding transfer taxes are of the same magnitude as the revenue produced.[83] The transfer tax system is manifestly inefficient. The resource and opportunity costs generated in relation to revenues obtained are alone sufficient to make the system unacceptable.

Neutrality

* * * A good tax system should be neutral in that it ought to be nonintrusive—it should not alter choices and behavior that would have occurred in the absence of the system. The current tax system is decidedly nonneutral and intrusive. The system encourages lifetime gifts and penalizes the failure to make them. Further, the system virtually compels use of the marital deduction in most cases involving wealthy married couples. In those instances, it thus discourages substantial outright bequests to others. * * * Because life insurance is a form of wealth that is fully realized at the death of the insured, and because life insurance arrangements can be structured to avoid imposition of transfer taxes, even when funded by the insured, the system encourages investment in life insurance products. The transfer tax system discourages the acquisition and retention of life insurance where the insured retains ownership incidents over the policy. Further, the system strongly encourages the obtaining of professional estate planning advice. The system discourages and renders difficult the prompt settlement of decedents' estates. On balance, the system contributes heavily to the "trustification" of wealth and thus channels the flow of substantial capital into arrangements where, given the prudence of fiduciaries, capital is conservatively invested. Thus to a substantial degree, the system operates to prevent people from making desired dispositions of their property and encourages undesired dispositions. The transfer tax system forces use of complex dispositive mechanisms when simple arrangements are desired. The system is severely intrusive in affecting human choices, investment decisions, and dispositive

---

83. Henry J. Aaron & Alicia H. Munnell, *Reassessing the Role for Wealth Transfer Taxes*, 45 NAT'L TAX J. 121, 139 (1992).

arrangements. In penalizing and rewarding different choices and decisions, it restricts investment decisions and donative and testamentary freedom and compromises personal liberty. Consequently, the transfer tax system is decidedly nonneutral.

Summary of Deficiencies

* * *

Congress should repeal the existing estate and gift tax system.

* * *

Transferee Centered Models for Wealth Taxation

The Accessions Tax Model

* * *

The accessions tax, centered and imposed on transferees, is inherently fairer than the existing tax system in that persons whose total gift and bequest receipts are comparable are comparably taxed. Because under any transfer tax system the tax costs are ultimately borne by successors to the transferred wealth, horizontal and vertical equity is best measured in terms of impact on the recipient successors. Under the accessions tax, they are treated equally. Also, being focussed on the transferees, there are no fairness issues arising from aggressive use of, or failure to use, exemptions of the transferor, in that there are no such exemptions. No one is penalized, for example, for failure to use a by-pass trust or other device oriented toward the existing unified credit. * * * The "premium" under the present system associated with equalizing the estates of husband and wife, and the attendant penalty for failure to do so disappears under the accessions tax model. When a child receives accessions of $2,000,000 upon the combined deaths of both parents, it largely matters not whether the bulk of the accession comes from the first or second parent to die. * * *

In addition to its inherent capacity for greater fairness and neutrality than under the present system, the accessions tax model offers the potential for simpler compliance procedures and mechanisms. The administration of the accessions tax can be coordinated with the current income tax system. Additional reporting would be required, but this can be accomplished through the device of appropriate schedules or supplements to the annual Form 1040.

* * *

Notes and Questions

33. As Professor Rudick observed, "dead men pay no taxes." Living people must bear any tax, regardless of the form in which it is levied. Nevertheless, the different forms of the various types of death taxes have substantive importance.

While the federal government has opted for the estate tax, Professor Rudick (not in the article excerpted above) argues that "if the states had not entered the inheritance tax field before the Federal government did, it is not unlikely that we would today have a Federal inheritance tax rather than a

Federal estate tax." Congress in 1916 opted for the estate tax, at least in part, because forty-two states already had an inheritance tax while only one had an estate tax; the Federal estate tax would thus result in "a well-balanced system of taxation as between the Federal Government and the various states." Two years later, in 1918, the Senate Finance Committee suggested, "on grounds of fairness and equity," changing to an inheritance tax, but the Ways and Means Committee refused.[kk]

34. Present federal transfer taxes are levied against the donor or the estate. Inheritance and accessions taxes, by contrast, are, in substance at least, levied against the recipient. (In form, it may prove more convenient to levy inheritance taxes against the executor. At present, state inheritance taxes may be payable by the executor, which is obviously simpler for the state than attempting to collect after the fact from heirs who may not reside in the state.)

35. Assuming a progressive tax structure, why would either an inheritance tax or an accessions tax give a testator an incentive to divide his estate that does not exist under present law?

36. How does an accessions tax differ from an inheritance tax?

37. According to Professor Rudick, an accessions tax would encourage broader distribution of wealth compared not only to an estate tax but also to an inheritance tax. Assuming a progressive rate structure, why might this be so?

38. Assuming that an accessions tax would encourage wealthy people to disperse their wealth among more donees and legatees, is that necessarily desirable? Professor McCaffery expresses concern about the perpetuation of "a very wealthy elite," and observes that "[i]t may not be better for society to have one thousand millionaires, many of them very young, than a single billionaire.[ll]

39. Professor Donaldson argues that the form of a transfer tax, as opposed to the decision to impose such a tax, "is essentially a practical and utilitarian matter." The excerpt from his article encapsulates much of the argument against the present transfer taxes. He argues that the present taxes fail their traditional goals of breaking up wealth and generating significant revenue, and also fail their more modern justification of contributing to progressivity. Moreover, he concludes that these taxes are

---

kk. Harry J. Rudick, *What Alternative to the Estate and Gift Taxes?*, 38 CAL. L. REV. 150, 160 (1950).

ll. McCaffery, *supra* note q, at 324.

unlikely to improve in performance. Is Professor Donaldson on common ground with Professor Graetz, a defender of transfer taxes?

Professor Donaldson argues that in addition to failing to make positive contributions, the present transfer taxes fail in terms of fairness, efficiency and neutrality. He thus calls on Congress to repeal the present structure. Do you concur with Professor Donaldson's dismal assessment of present law?

40. If we are to retain a transfer tax, Professor Donaldson argues that we should move to the accessions tax model. Which of the problems he identified would an accessions tax address?

41. A generation ago, the American Law Institute undertook a project on federal transfer taxes, including as one alternative the accessions tax. The reporter, Professor William Andrews, discussed the proposal in an article published in *Tax Law Review*.[mm] Under the proposal, events that constitute transfers for purposes of the existing transfer taxes generally would constitute accessions for purposes of the accessions tax. The one major exception—and the subject of much of Professor Andrew's article—was the transfer in trust. Under existing transfer taxation, a transfer to a trust normally makes the decedent or donor immediately liable for a transfer tax. But could it be said that the beneficiary had acceded to wealth by the creation of the trust, before any distribution was made to him? The proposal discussed by Professor Andrews took the position that the accession normally occurred when money or property was distributed by the trustee to the beneficiary, a result the ALI "considered to be unacceptable in the case of large estates."[nn] Much of the balance of Professor Andrews' article was devoted to possible solutions to this perceived problem, each of which, of course, would have created its own set of problems.

42. The student should keep in mind an option discussed in Chapter Nine—that of replacing transfer taxes with an income tax option, such as including gifts and inheritances in the taxable income of the recipient.

E. WEALTH TAXES

As we have seen, transfer taxes can be viewed as a form of wealth taxation; indeed, breaking up great concentrations of wealth is one of the traditional goals of transfer tax supporters. These taxes, however, do not tax wealth except on the occasion of its transfer—typically, once each generation, as wealth is passed on either by gift or death.

By contrast, the wealth taxes considered in this subchapter envision taxes on the mere ownership of property, typically annually. The tax could

---

mm. William D. Andrews, *The Accessions Tax Proposal*, 22 TAX L. REV. 589 (1967).
nn. *Id.* at 595.

be compared to familiar real estate taxes, but here we are dealing with broad-based taxes levied on the taxpayer's entire wealth.

Professor Cooper's lengthy article, briefly excerpted below, argues that the present system of transfer taxation is deficient, and that some form of wealth tax would be preferable to any likely reform of current law. In the final excerpt, Professor Posin argues for a wealth tax coordinated with the income tax.

A VOLUNTARY TAX? NEW PERSPECTIVES ON SOPHISTICATED ESTATE TAX AVOIDANCE
George Cooper[*]
77 Columbia Law Review 161, 162-63, 221, 223, 244-46 (1977)

When William du Pont, Jr., great-grandson of the founder of E.I. du Pont de Nemours & Company, died in 1965, each of his five children received an inheritance of more than fifty million dollars. Each will receive an additional sum, worth more than forty million dollars at 1966 values, on the death of his or her aunt, Marion du Pont Scott, who is now 82 years old. Thus these five individuals are the sole inheritors of an aggregate family fortune worth almost a half billion dollars in 1966. Barely a handful of fortunes this large exist in the United States. Yet the total of all estate and gift taxes paid on this aggregation of wealth, from its origins in nineteenth century Du Pont Company profits until its receipt by the present generation, including taxes payable on the aunt's death, will be less than $25 million. This wealth has passed through two generations that died while estate taxes were in effect, meaning that the combined effective tax rate for two generations will be only 5%.

The first purpose of this study is to explain how a phenomenon of this nature has occurred. * * * The second purpose is to explore whether the current generation can continue this pattern of tax avoidance in light of the major estate and gift tax reforms enacted by Congress in 1976. The perhaps surprising conclusion compelled by our findings is that today's multimillionaires, as well as persons of lesser wealth, no more need pay a stiff estate and gift tax than did their predecessors. It may be that the real certainties of this world are death and tax *avoidance*.
    * * *

Reform Possibilities

What are we to make of this? Clearly, the estate and gift tax is not striking terror into the hearts of the very wealthy, nor is it even seriously burdening most persons who devote effort to avoidance. Everyone does not fully exploit the tax avoidance opportunities, it is true. But we can gain little reassurance from this failure of action. Those who remain burdened by the

---

[*]. At time of original publication, Professor of Law, Columbia University.

tax include those who reject tax avoidance for reasons of principle, those who give low priority to engaging in complicated maneuvers solely for tax purposes, those who have no natural alternative to the government for disposition of their fortunes (presumably because they do not have children, do not trust those that they do have, or do not want to burden them with great wealth), and those who die inopportunely.

* * *

In sum, because estate tax avoidance is such a successful and yet wasteful process, one suspects that the present estate and gift tax serves no purpose other than to give reassurance to the millions of unwealthy that entrenched wealth is being attacked. The attack is, however, more cosmetic than real and the economy is paying the price of fettered capital and distorted property ownership for this tax cosmetology. Unless the system can be significantly reformed, consideration should be given to scrapping it, or at least replacing it with a more effective means of accomplishing perceived goals.

* * *

The historical record indicates that the estate and gift tax was originally intended to serve as a revenue producer. This most likely is at least a part of its purpose today, although some would disagree. In addition, a variety of social goals are stated for the tax: supplementing the income tax, breaking up large fortunes, and preventing the creation of a coupon-clipper class.

All of these purposes or goals might better be served by a periodic wealth tax than by the estate and gift taxes. This wealth tax is a tax on net worth imposed recurrently at fixed times, probably annually.[255]

(1) From a revenue viewpoint, a wealth tax is clearly superior to an estate and gift tax. The wealth tax base is not eroded by post-gift appreciation, since wealth in the hands of transferees would continue to be subject to taxation when the next tax period rolled around, rather than shifted out of the clutches of the tax for a generation. This simple fact means that the significance of estate freezing as an avoidance technique would be sharply diminished. (This is not to say that tax revenues might not continue to be affected by intergenerational transfers. Assuming that the wealth tax had progressive rates and was imposed on individuals, rather than family groupings, a transfer of some wealth to a poorer taxpayer would reduce tax collections by reducing the tax bracket, but it could not completely remove property from the tax base. Moreover, the value of intergenerational transfers as a tax avoidance technique would be inherently self-limiting because the more that was given to a person the closer his tax bracket would move to that of the donor. Assuming that a flat top rate would come into

---

255. Such a tax, which would be a "property tax" on personal property as well as real property with an offset for indebtedness, is a standard part of European tax systems. *See* C. SANDFORD, J. WILLIS & D. IRONSIDE, AN ANNUAL WEALTH TAX, app. C. (1975) (tabular summary of existing European wealth taxes).

effect at some level, the super-rich would soon hit that level and thereby have exhausted the tax avoidance opportunities in bracket-lowering transfers.)

(2) As a supplement to the income tax, the wealth tax seems preferable. The primary goal in this respect is to take account of the fact that the existing income tax underrates accumulated wealth as a source of ability to pay because it reaches only the net realized returns on capital; all the indirect benefits of wealth—power, security, appreciation—must be reached by some other tax, if at all. Another asserted income tax supplementary goal is adding to the progressivity of the overall tax system. While the estate and gift tax serves both these goals, it does so only erratically; the wealth tax would do it more consistently and more evenhandedly.

(3) The wealth tax is also far superior in attacking large fortunes because it does so regularly and promptly and cannot be evaded through generational shifting of ownership.

* * *

One other major advantage of the periodic wealth tax should also be mentioned. It has always been difficult for people to accept the idea of having a large chunk of property seized by the government in one fell swoop, particularly when the property is in an illiquid form, and payment of the tax may require disposition of some or all of it. This in large part explains why Congress has consistently been sympathetic to mitigating the estate tax payment duty of farmers and small businessmen and why the courts have been so sympathetic to valuation discounts for closely-held stock. The result of this understandable sympathy has been a substantial complication of the estate tax and an erosion of its base.

This problem could be eliminated under a periodic wealth tax. Because such a tax would be imposed much more frequently than an estate tax, it could carry correspondingly lower rates than the existing scale for estate and gift taxes. For example, an annual net wealth tax with a flat rate of 1% imposed only on net wealth in excess of $200,000 (thus limiting the tax to only the richest 1% to 2% of the population and even as to them exempting the first $200,000) would have produced approximately the same revenue in 1972 as did the estate and gift tax in that year. Given the greatly increased exemption levels and consequent lowered revenue estimates for the post-1976 estate and gift tax, it is probable that this hypothetical 1% net wealth tax on top wealth holders would be a better revenue producer than the new estate and gift tax, as well as being superior for the other reasons discussed above. Such a 1% tax would of course be far easier on holders of nonliquid assets than the existing high rate estate and gift tax.

* * *

TOWARD A THEORY OF FEDERAL TAXATION: A COMMENT
Daniel Q. Posin[*]

50 Journal of Air Law and Commerce 907, 923-28 (1985)

An element that could usefully be hammered onto the federal tax system is a wealth tax. As demonstrated in the preceding discussion [not excerpted], the American income tax is really a combination of income and consumption tax elements. It has thus long since surrendered any claim to theoretical purity and any accompanying advantages of simplicity. Moreover, we are not, as stated previously, likely to develop a theoretically pure tax any time soon. Thus, initiating improvements to the present tax system must involve making *ad hoc* changes to what is already an *ad hoc* system. A wealth tax added to the present system would tap an additional legitimate tax base and add balance to the system. Its contribution to the tax revenues would be substantial. * * *

How a Wealth Tax Works

The wealth tax is levied as a percentage of the taxpayer's net worth. For reasons that I will discuss below, the wealth tax should provide a credit for income taxes paid. The literature on this subject describes two forms of the wealth tax. I believe, however, for reasons set forth below, that the two forms are really one and the same. Before setting forth my own critique, I will describe the two forms of the wealth tax, as seen in the traditional literature.

The two forms of the wealth tax have various names. I will call them for convenience the weak form and the strong form. The weak form of the tax is limited to a relatively small percentage of the taxpayer's net worth. It is designed to exact a tax of less than a normal rate of return from the taxpayer's capital. Rates for this weak form of wealth tax generally hover around 1% or less of the taxpayer's capital subject to the tax.

The strong form of the tax is designed, according to the traditional view, to take more in tax from the taxpayer's capital than is produced by a normal rate of return less income taxes paid. The rate for the strong form is therefore significantly higher than the rate for the weak form. The strong form is said to be a tax directly on capital, according to the traditional view.

My position is that there is in fact no strong form of the wealth tax—no wealth tax is imposed on capital. This is because when a high rate of wealth tax is imposed, the value of capital subject to the tax drops. This in turn decreases the amount of tax that can be collected by the wealth tax to an amount that can be paid out of income.

Some numerical examples may serve to illustrate:

Example (1) Let us say T has capital subject to the tax of $100,000. If this $100,000 is invested in high-grade corporate bonds paying 10% interest,

---

[*]. At time of original publication, Associate Professor of Law, Southern Methodist University School of Law.

T's annual income from this capital will be $10,000. Let us assume further that T is in the 50% marginal income tax bracket. Therefore on T's $10,000 interest income, he must pay income tax of $5,000. Let us say also that T is subject to a "weak" form of the wealth tax, which is imposed at the rate of 1% on his investment. By virtue of this tax, T must pay an additional $1,000 in tax. Thus T's income after the income and the wealth tax is $4000. The tax has been paid out of the income from the bonds. On this set of [facts], a wealth tax has operated like an additional income tax on investment income.

Example (2) The facts are the same as in Example 1, except that T is now subject to a "strong" form of the wealth tax. In this case let us assume that the wealth tax is at a rate of 7% of capital. Once again, T has interest income from his corporate bonds of $10,000. Being in the 50% bracket, he pays income taxes of $5000. However, on account of the strong form of the wealth tax, he now also owes $7000 of wealth tax (7% of $100,000). His total tax is $12,000, which he cannot pay solely out of income. Thus he must dip into capital to come up with the extra $2000. He now has only $98,000 invested. This is the confiscatory aspect of the strong form of the wealth tax, according to the literature.

This analysis, however, is flawed. The day a 7% wealth tax is imposed the value of T's corporate bonds will drop. By how much will they drop? Assume for simplicity that all potential buyers of these bonds are also in the 50% marginal income tax bracket. The bonds continue to pay their fixed amount of $10,000 per year. The income tax on that amount continues to be $5000. However, no one would pay $100,000 for those bonds if the net after tax return was a negative $2000. Therefore the bonds must drop in value by enough to lower the wealth tax to $5000. The bonds will then drop from $100,000 to a value of $71,428. (7% of $71,428 equals $5000). This is a one-time drop. Thereafter, the bonds will continue to trade at around that price and move up and down according to market factors, such as changes in interest rates. In reality, the price will not drop all the way down to $71,428, because some of the potential purchasers of these bonds are not in the 50% marginal bracket. Thus, a taxpayer in the 30% marginal bracket might find these bonds attractively priced at or near $100,000. This would be so because his income tax would be $3000 and his wealth tax would be $7000, if the bonds had a value of $100,000. The bond would not have to drop very much in value for them to have a net positive return to this taxpayer.

What this discussion demonstrates is that there is no such thing as the "the strong form" of the wealth tax. There is no such thing as the wealth tax actually being a tax on wealth. The wealth tax, no matter what its rate, will always be payable out of income from the taxpayer's capital subject to the tax, because the property will drop in value to reflect the imposition of the tax.

Of course, in the case of a wealth tax with a relatively steep rate, such as the 7% in the example above, taxpayers in the 50% marginal bracket have undergone a relatively stiff "tax' on their capital in the sense that their capital has undergone a one-time drop in value on the occasion of the first imposition of the tax. That is a different matter entirely, however, from saying that a wealth tax of relatively high rate is paid out of capital. It is erroneous and leads to incorrect policy decisions to maintain that a wealth tax of relatively high rate is paid out of capital.

Consider, for example, X, an individual, whose wealth is entirely tied up in $10 million worth of undeveloped forest lands. These lands generally appreciate 10% every year. X has no salary and owns no income producing assets. X occasionally sells off some land to meet his modest living expenses. On these facts X has little income (only what may be realized on his occasional land sales). Therefore X pays an inconsequential amount of income tax (assume for simplicity that he pays no income tax). Assume X is subject to a 7% wealth tax. On these facts X has unrealized appreciation on the value of his land of $1 million (10% of $10 million) and pays a wealth tax of $700,000 (7% of $10 million). Thus where X pays little or no income tax, the wealth tax even at a relatively high rate does not cause the value of his assets to fall (at least not to him or others not paying much in income taxes). Indeed, the wealth tax has led to a relatively reasonable result, that a taxpayer of great wealth who would not have otherwise paid any taxes at all, in fact paid some taxes. Note that X in the example given above is a miser with established wealth. Therefore X in the example above would not be significantly reached either by an income tax or a consumption tax.

This discussion leads to the conclusion that a reasonable way to impose a wealth tax of some significant rate is to allow a credit or a partial credit against the wealth tax for income taxes paid with respect to the capital involved. If that were done, then in our Example 2 above, T, having paid $5000 in income taxes on his investment income, would only pay $2000 more in wealth taxes to reach his 7%. That would still leave him with a $3000 after tax return. However, the taxpayer X, above, who owned the forest land, would derive no benefit from the credit for income taxes paid, since he pays no income taxes. As we have discussed, it is appropriate that the wealth tax reach him more heavily.

This discussion has assumed a wealth tax of 7%, which is very much higher than what I would propose or than is in use in Europe or the Indian sub-continent today. Yet even with this relatively high rate, the tax, when combined with a credit for income taxes, works effectively and in a non-confiscatory manner, not overtaxing those who are already paying substantial taxes on income from their capital and yet reaching those who are not otherwise taxed.

While it is not presently on the horizon, the wealth tax may become a useful complement to other methods of federal taxation, in the era of very high budget deficits.

Notes and Questions

43. Professor Cooper's article was published in 1977, between the legislation of 1976 and 1981. The 1976 legislation, it will be recalled, was described by Professor Graetz (in subchapter C) as a shift "toward a basically sound and well-structured wealth transfer system," prior to the 1981 move "to emasculate it." Yet, even in what defenders of the transfer taxes might term a Congressional "lucid interval," Cooper still found that the transfer taxes could be easily avoided by taxpayers.

Professor Cooper contended that the goals of transfer taxes would be better served by an annual wealth tax. What advantages does he identify for a wealth tax vis-a-vis our present system of transfer taxes?

44. Professor Posin describes what he terms a "weak" and a "strong" form of wealth taxation. What is the difference between the two? Why does he contend that the "strong" form does not actually exist?

45. What form would Professor Posin's proposed wealth tax take? Why?

46. Although the United States has not embraced a broad-based wealth tax, Professor Cooper has observed (not in the article excerpted) that "to be without a wealth tax could be said to be the exception rather than the rule in Western Europe."[oo]

47. The wealth tax has attracted some slight support in the American political arena. Ramsey Clark, who was Attorney General under President Johnson, sought the Democratic nomination to become United States Senator from New York in 1976. In the course of his unsuccessful campaign, Mr. Clark advocated a wealth tax of approximately three percent on family wealth in excess of one million dollars, a levy that he declared would combat "economic royalism."[pp]

48. Mr. Barry Isaacs directed the following critique of Mr. Clark's wealth tax proposal, but Mr. Isaacs' cautions—focusing more on practical concerns than purity of policy—may be relevant to many tax proposals, particularly those considered in this chapter:

> Individuals who advocate a redistribution of wealth in America
> often are so irresistibly drawn to any proposal which has as its
> purpose the economic leveling of the wealthiest group of

---

oo. George Cooper, *Taking Wealth Taxation Seriously*, 34 REC. ASS'N BAR CITY N.Y. 24, 24 (1979).

pp. This description is taken from an article criticizing Mr. Clark's proposal, Barry L. Isaacs, *Do We Want a Wealth Tax in America?*, 32 U. MIAMI L. REV. 23, 24-25 (1977-78). Mr. Isaacs referred to "Ramsey Clark/Senate '76, Position Papers 1-2 (1976) (on file with the *University of Miami Law Review*)."

individuals, that they are either unmindful or unconcerned about the inherent problems which will ensue. The wealth tax proposal of Ramsey Clark is no different. It assumes a perfectly designed tax as well as an effectively administered one. It foresees nothing but perfect acquiescence by those affected by the wealth tax. It supposes that the tax can be instituted with modest costs. It dismisses any notion that such a tax could have economically adverse consequences. None of these notions is beyond serious challenge.[qq]

49. The compliance and administrative problems of a wealth tax should not be underestimated. Unless some sort of formula were utilized, annual taxation would require annual valuation. A comprehensive wealth tax could also result in considerable fraud—unlike the familiar real estate tax, which taxes property that is hard to hide and impossible to move, taxpayers might be able to conceal many assets from a wealth tax.

50. It seems quite possible that a federal wealth tax could run afoul of the constitutional bar on direct taxes that are not apportioned among the states according to population.[rr] The meaning of "direct" taxes has been unclear from the outset: "James Madison's Journal of the Constitutional Convention contains the following entry for August 20, 1787: 'Mr. King asked what was the precise meaning of *direct* taxation? No one answered.'"[ss] It is hard to see what might be a more direct tax than a property tax or a wealth tax.

51. *Class warfare?* Professor Ronald Chester argues that "the underlying issue in the inheritance controversy is one of class conflict."[tt] Do you agree? If so, do you think this is any more the case than with respect to many income tax provisions, such as the progressive rate structure and the treatment of capital gains? Professor Chester maintains that "an annual, or even a triennial wealth tax is more productive of equality than a once-in-a-lifetime estate or inheritance tax."[uu]

Australian and Canadian transfer tax repeals

52. Recent Australian history lends credence to the notion that death taxes are not uniformly popular outside the United States. An ordinary citizen—"Sydney Negus, formerly a skilled carpenter and later a smallish

---

qq. Isaacs, *supra* note pp, at 49.

rr. U.S. CONST. art. I, § 9, cl. 4.

ss. ALAN GUNN & LARRY D. WARD, CASES, TEXT AND PROBLEMS ON FEDERAL INCOME TAXATION 2 (3d ed. 1992).

tt. C. Ronald Chester, *Inheritance and Wealth Taxation in a Just Society*, 30 RUTGERS L. REV. 62, 100 (1976).

uu. *Id.* at 69.

building contractor"—started a movement that culminated in Australia's repeal of death taxes, in the process gaining election to the Senate "as an Independent whose single issue campaign was the abolition of death duties."[vv]

53. Canada also abolished death taxes, in 1972, and simultaneously began imposing income taxation on unrealized appreciation of property passed from the taxpayer at death. (For further discussion of Canada's experience with constructive realization, see Chapter Nine.)

In a recent article with the stated goal of reopening the debate, Professor Maureen Maloney observed that the tradeoff between the constructive realization of capital gain and the abolition of death taxes resulted from the perception of avoiding double taxation, a perception that Professor Maloney roundly criticized: "This was a misconception but a politically powerful one. It illustrates a fundamental misunderstanding of the purpose of the two taxes."[ww]

Among the more interesting arguments advanced by Professor Maloney is that high levels of wealth taxation—whether collected annually or by death taxes—are required by justice, apart from the matter of healthy adults inheriting wealth that they did not create: "Even if a perfect market did reward individuals according to ability, effort and talent, the notion that such a distribution is morally just is still unsupportable. * * * People are of equal moral worth. Moral claims to rewards, therefore, cannot rest on the natural abilities with which one is born."[xx]

Do you agree with Professor Maloney that justice requires death taxes? That they are required because market outcomes do not provide morally just outcomes?

Selected Bibliography

See also bibliography for Chapter Nine.

Abbin, Byrle, *The Politics of Transfer Taxation or Watching Sausage Being Made—Is Anyone in Charge?*, 1991 INSTITUTE ON ESTATE PLANNING ¶ 400.

Alexander, John H., *Federal Estate and Gift Taxation: The Major Issues Presented in the American Law Institute Project*, 22 TAX L. REV. 635 (1967).

Andrews, William D., *What's Fair About Death Taxes*, 26 NAT'L TAX J. 465 (1973).

——, *The Accessions Tax Proposal*, 22 TAX L. REV. 589 (1967).

---

vv. Willard H. Pedrick, *Oh, To Die Down Under! Abolition of Death and Gift Duties in Australia*, 14 U. W. AUSTL. L. REV. 438, 438, 440 (1982).

ww. Maureen A. Maloney, *Distributive Justice: That is the Wealth Tax Issue*, 20 OTTOWA L. REV. 601, 606 (1988).

xx. *Id.* at 617.

Ascher, Mark L., *Curtailing Inherited Wealth*, 89 MICH. L. REV. 69 (1990).

Bernheim, B. Douglas, *Does the Estate Tax Raise Revenue?*, *in* TAX POLICY AND THE ECONOMY (Lawrence H. Summers ed., 1987).

Blinder, Alan S., *A Model of Inherited Wealth*, 87 Q.J. ECON. 608 (1973).

Blum, Cynthia, *U.S. Transfer Tax of Nonresident Aliens: Too Much or Too Little?*, 14 U. PA. J. INT'L BUS. L. 469 (1994).

Brannon, Gerald M., *Death Taxes in a Structure of Progressive Taxation*, 36 NAT'L TAX J. 451 (1973).

Brockway, David H., *Comprehensive Estate and Gift Tax Reform*, 67 TAX NOTES 1089 (1995).

Casner, A. James, *American Law Institute Federal Estate and Gift Tax Project*, 22 TAX L. REV. 515 (1967).

Chester, C. Ronald, *Inheritance and Wealth Taxation in a Just Society*, 30 RUTGERS L. REV. 62 (1976).

COOPER, GEORGE, A VOLUNTARY TAX?   NEW PERSPECTIVES ON SOPHISTICATED ESTATE TAX AVOIDANCE (1979).

———, *Taking Wealth Taxation Seriously*, 34 REC. ASS'N BAR CITY N.Y. 24 (1979).

Covey, Richard B., *Possible Changes in the Basis Rule for Property Transferred by Gift or at Death*, 50 TAXES 831 (1972).

Davies, John H., *Income-Plus-Wealth: In Search of a Better Tax Base*, 15 RUTGERS L.J. 849 (1984).

DEATH, TAXES AND FAMILY PROPERTY: ESSAYS AND AMERICAN ASSEMBLY REPORT (Edward C. Halbach, Jr. ed., 1977).

Dobris, Joel C., *A Brief for the Abolition of All Transfer Taxes*, 35 SYRACUSE L. REV. 1215 (1984).

Dodge, Joseph M., *Redoing the Estate and Gift Taxes Along Easy-To-Value Lines*, 43 TAX L. REV. 241 (1988).

Donaldson, John E., *The Future of Transfer Taxation: Repeal, Restructuring and Refinement, or Replacement*, 50 WASH. & LEE L. REV. 539 (1993).

Duff, David G., *Taxing Inherited Wealth: A Philosophical Argument*, 6 CAN. J.L. & JURISPRUDENCE 3 (1993).

Eisenstein, Louis, *The Rise and Decline of the Estate Tax*, 11 TAX L. REV. 223 (1955-56).

Gac, Edward J. & Sharen K. Brougham, *A Proposal for Restructuring the Taxation of Wealth Transfers: Tax Reform Redux?*, 5 AKRON TAX J. 75 (1988).

Galvin, Charles O., *To Bury the Estate Tax, Not To Praise It*, 52 TAX NOTES 1413 (1991).

Gilder, George, *Wealth, Poverty and Inheritance: The Voice from the Coffin*, 11 PROB. LAW. 1 (1985).

Graetz, Michael J., *To Praise the Estate Tax, Not to Bury It*, 93 YALE L.J. 259 (1983).

Groves, Harold M., *Retention of Estate and Gift Taxes by the Federal Government*, 38 CAL. L. REV. 28 (1950).

Gutman, Harry L., *Reforming Federal Wealth Transfer Taxes After ERTA*, 69 VA. L. REV. 1183 (1983).

Hagarman, James, Jr., *The Federal Estate Tax*, 8 A.B.A. J. 92 (1922).

Halbach, Edward C., Jr., *An Accessions Tax*, 23 REAL PROP. PROB. & TR. J. 211 (1988).

Hudson, David M., *Tax Policy and the Federal Taxation of the Transfer of Wealth*, 19 WILLAMETTE L. REV. 1 (1983).

Isaacs, Barry L., *Do We Want a Wealth Tax in America?*, 32 U. MIAMI L. REV. 23 (1977-78).

Kirshberg, Richard D., *The Accessions Tax: Administrative Bramblebush or Instrument of Social Policy?*, 14 UCLA L. REV. 135 (1966).

Maloney, Maureen A., *Distributive Justice: That is the Wealth Tax Issue*, 20 OTTAWA L. REV. 601 (1988).

McCaffery, Edward J., *The Uneasy Case for Wealth Transfer Taxation*, 104 YALE L.J. 283 (1994).

——, *Tax Policy Under a Hybrid Income-Consumption Tax*, 70 TEX. L. REV. 1145 (1992).

Pedrick, Willard H., *Oh, To Die Down Under! Abolition of Death and Gift Duties in Australia*, 14 U. W. AUSTL. L. REV. 438 (1982).

Posin, Daniel Q., *Toward a Theory of Federal Taxation: A Comment*, 50 J. AIR LAW & COMMERCE 907 (1985).

Robinson, Thomas A., *The Federal Wealth Transfer Taxes—A Requiem?*, 1 AM. J. TAX POL'Y 25 (1982).

Ruane, Thomas P., *Federal Estate and Gift Tax Changes Under the Economic Recovery Tax Act: An Ideological Retreat*, 28 LOY. L. REV. 13 (1982).

Rudick, Harry J., *A Proposal for an Accessions Tax*, 1 TAX L. REV. 25 (1945).

——, *What Alternative to the Estate and Gift Taxes?*, 38 CAL. L. REV. 150 (1950).

SIMONS, HENRY, PERSONAL INCOME TAXATION 125-47 (1938).

Smith, Robert B., *Should We Give Away the Annual Exclusion?*, 1 FLA. TAX REV. 361 (1993).

Steinkamp, John G., *Common Sense and the Gift Tax Annual Exclusion*, 72 NEB. L. REV. 106 (1993).

Surrey, Stanley S., *An Introduction to Revision of the Federal Estate and Gift Taxes*, 38 CAL. L. REV. 1 (1950).

Van Doren, John W., *Redistributing Wealth by Curtailing Inheritance: The Community Interest in the Rule Against Perpetuities and the Estate Tax*, 3 FLA. ST. U. L. REV. 33 (1975).

Verbit, G.P., *Taxing Wealth: Recent Proposals from the United States, France, and the United Kingdom*, 60 B.U. L. REV. 1 (1980).

——, *Do Estate and Gift Taxes Affect Wealth Distribution?*, 117 TR. & EST. 598 (part 1); 117 TR. & EST. 674 (part 2) (1978).

Westfall, David, *Revitalizing the Federal Estate and Gift Taxes*, 83 HARV. L. REV. 986 (1970).

Zelinsky, Edward A., *The Estate and Gift Tax Changes of 1981: A Brief Essay on Historical Perspective*, 60 N.C. L. REV. 821 (1982).

PART IV

TAX EXPENDITURES, EXCLUSIONS, AND DEDUCTIONS

Part IV covers issues involving deductions and exclusions in defining taxable income. A large number of individual deductions and exclusions could have been made the subject of a chapter. Three topics have been chosen, for specific reasons.

Chapter Eleven deals with the tax expenditures concept. Conceptually, tax expenditures are special tax benefits—deductions, exemptions, credits, and preferential tax rates—that have much the same effect as direct government outlays. The devil is in the details, however. The chapter illuminates the problems in deciding whether a given tax deduction, exclusion, or credit is "special," or is part of the basic framework of the income tax. Chapter Eleven concludes with challenges to the tax expenditures concept.

Chapter Twelve addresses a particularly difficult issue: the extent to which personal injury awards should be excluded from taxable income. Section 104(a)(2) is perhaps more intriguing than any other exclusion, because its justification is unclear. If the exclusion arises simply from compassion for the injured, it should be analyzed as a tax expenditure. On the other hand, if the exclusion can be justified on the grounds that personal injury awards do not constitute "income," the exclusion merely clarifies section 61. Evolution of the present treatment is described, and various rationales for present law and proposed alternatives are discussed. Finally, particular problems arising from structured settlements are presented.

Chapter Thirteen deals with the interaction of state and local taxes with the federal income tax. In one sense, the issues are common to those of the other major "personal" deductions—medical expense, interest, and charitable contributions. In addition, however, the deduction of state and local taxes raises unique issues in the context of our federalist system of government. The chapter concludes with brief consideration of substituting a federal credit for the current deduction for state and local income taxes.

CHAPTER ELEVEN

TAX EXPENDITURES

Tax subsidies, like their counterparts on the spending side, reduce economic efficiency by substituting political micromanagement for routine market decisions about how capital should be allocated across the economy.[a]

A. INTRODUCTION

Tax expenditures are tax benefits used as incentives or rewards in lieu of outright payments by the government. Tax expenditures include incentive tax credits, exemptions, deductions that are not justified in computing net profit, and lower tax rates on specified types of income.

Not being outlays from the Treasury, tax expenditures are not reflected in government expenditures and are not subject to the annual Congressional appropriation process. They are not items listed in the budget and affect the budget only through tax receipts being lower than they otherwise would be.

Votes for tax expenditures have obvious political appeal for members of Congress. Some discipline in the Congressional procedure for enactment of new tax expenditures or for liberalizing existing tax expenditures has been introduced by a requirement Congress has imposed on itself that bills reducing revenues must contain offsetting revenue increases over a five-year span. Existing, ongoing tax expenditures are not affected. So-called "sunset" rules have been proposed that would terminate existing tax expenditures unless they were explicitly continued. Sunset rules have not been adopted, however.

The Budget Act of 1974 requires the Congressional Budget Committee and the President to present estimates each year of the revenue costs of existing tax expenditures. These annual cost estimates help one appreciate the magnitude of the various tax expenditures.

Although the overall concept of tax expenditures is clear, the precise definition of the term is by no means clear. Furthermore, even the basic concept has been challenged. As respects exemptions and deductions, the debate over tax expenditures merges into the debate over broadening the tax base.

The clearest examples of tax expenditures are the incentive tax credits. These reward taxpayer behavior by credits against tax liability, and are usually calculated as a specified percentage of the taxpayer's expenditure on

---

a. Robert J. Shapiro, *Cut-and-Invest: A Budget Strategy for the New Economy*, PROGRESSIVE POL'Y INST. REP. NO. 23 (1995).

the rewarded behavior. The investment tax credit has been the major tax credit over the years of its off-and-on existence since its original enactment in 1962. Before the credit was sharply restricted in 1986, taxpayers making investments in tangible personal property (and some real property) for business use were permitted to offset their income tax liability by a percentage of the cost of their qualifying investments. Investment tax credits were presented as explicit incentives to invest. As initially proposed by President Kennedy, the credit would have been available only for incremental investments over the taxpayer's normal replacements of business assets, but the incremental investment approach had been abandoned by the time the credit was enacted.

other tax credits

The investment credit was the precursor of a flood of other tax credits. These included a credit for increasing outlays for research and development, a credit for providing low-income housing, a credit for wages paid to workers considered to be disadvantaged in some specified respects, a child care credit, a tax credit for elderly and disabled taxpayers, and an earned income tax credit for low-income taxpayers. Unlike tax credits designed to be incentives, the latter three tax credits are designed merely to provide relief from tax. The earned income credit provides actual cash supplements.

An obvious difficulty with all the tax credits (except the earned income credit) is that they benefit only persons who otherwise would owe income tax. The credits do not provide an incentive to persons whose incomes are so low that they have no tax liability or to businesses that are operating at a loss. One response to this difficulty has been to suggest making the credits "refundable"—i.e., an amount equivalent to the tax credit would be given to persons who qualify for the credit whether or not they have tax liability to apply it against. Thus, a "refund" would be made of a tax that had not been paid. So far, only the earned income tax credit is "refundable." In contrast, the wage withholding tax credit is not referred to as "refundable," because the refund is out of tax withheld from the taxpayer's compensation.

Tax exemptions and deductions from adjusted gross income also can be tax expenditures. As with nonrefundable credits, exemptions and deductions are useful only if the eligible person otherwise would owe tax. Tax deductions and exemptions of specified types of income can be of benefit by increasing net operating losses that are carried over to offset taxable income in other years.

variability of tax expenditures

Unlike tax credits, exemptions and deductions are tax expenditures that vary in value among taxpayers—the higher the potential tax bracket, the greater the tax expenditure. For example, a $1,000 percentage depletion deduction is worth $350 to a corporation with a 35 percent marginal tax rate and only $150 to a corporation with a 15 percent marginal tax rate. If the taxpayer has exhausted the tax basis of the mineral property giving rise to the percentage depletion deduction, the tax expenditure, whether $350 or

$150, is an outright benefit—not merely a postponement of tax—because there is no compensating downward basis adjustment.

It is more difficult to calculate the benefit from tax expenditures that arise from accelerating deductions that a taxpayer eventually would be entitled to under "normal" rules. The value of speeding up such a deduction depends on two factors: how long it would be before the taxpayer would have received the deduction in the absence of the tax expenditure provision, and the time value of the tax deferred by speeding up the deduction. The time value to the taxpayer may be quite different from the cost to the government of postponing its receipt of tax, raising the question of what interest rate should be used to calculate the amount of the tax expenditure.

B. THE TAX EXPENDITURES CONCEPT DESCRIBED

As noted above, in 1974 Congress for the first time began formally evaluating and quantifying tax expenditures. One of the leading advocates of this change was Professor Stanley Surrey, who had been Assistant Secretary of the Treasury for Tax Policy under President Kennedy. His argument for formally evaluating tax expenditures in a manner almost identical to direct expenditures, published the year before the 1974 Act, remains perhaps the best exposition of the concept. The second excerpt provides a recent example of the Office of Management and Budget's annual explanation of the tax expenditures concept in operation.

The proper classification of a given tax provision as a part of the "normal" tax structure or as a "tax expenditure" is not always clear. Does this lack of clarity matter, in the real world? In one sense, the classification is only an academic exercise—dollars saved from a lower tax burden spend just as well whether the lower tax burden results from a tax expenditure or not. On the other hand, the classification as a tax expenditure raises the political exposure of a tax provision. If the provision is viewed as part of the "normal" system, it is less subject to attack than if it is viewed as an "expenditure," which should have to compete for limited federal dollars in a political environment in which it is never possible to spend as many dollars as Congress might wish.

PATHWAYS TO TAX REFORM
Stanley S. Surrey[*]
Pages 6-14, 129-41 (1973)

The Tax Expenditure Budget

The federal income tax system consists really of two parts: one part comprises the structural provisions necessary to implement the income tax on individual and corporate net income; the second part comprises a system of tax expenditures under which Governmental financial assistance programs

---

[*]. At time of original publication, Jeremiah Smith Professor of Law at Harvard University.

are carried out through special tax provisions rather than through direct Government expenditures. This second system is grafted on to the structure of the income tax proper; it has no basic relation to that structure and is not necessary to its operation. Instead, the system of tax expenditures provides a vast subsidy apparatus that uses the mechanics of the income tax as the method of paying the subsidies. The special provisions under which this subsidy apparatus functions take a variety of forms, covering exclusions from income, exemptions, deductions, credits against tax, preferential rates of tax, and deferrals of tax.

These special tax provisions serve ends which are similar in nature to those served in the same or other areas by direct government expenditures in the form of grants, loans, interest subsidies, and federal insurance or guarantees of private loans. The interplay is such that for any given program involving federal monetary assistance, the program may be structured to use the tax system to provide that assistance—where it will usually be called a "tax incentive"—or structured to use a direct Government expenditure. As a consequence of history, design, lack of analysis, and similar factors our present tax system is replete with these special provisions, or tax expenditures, under which many existing Government assistance programs operate through the tax system rather than the direct expenditure route.

The tax expenditure concept in essence considers these special provisions as composed of two elements: the imputed tax payment that would have been made in the absence of the special provision (all else remaining the same) and the simultaneous expenditure of that payment as a direct grant to the person benefited by the special provision. * * *

The Tax Expenditure Budget * * * identifies and quantifies the existing tax expenditures. * * * The list of these tax expenditures here used is based on that published by the House Ways and Means Committee in June 1973, and prepared by the staffs of the Treasury Department and the Joint Committee on Internal Revenue Taxation.

The items in this Tax Expenditure Budget total between $60 and $65 billion—equal to around one-fourth of the regular budget. Yet most of these items seem almost to live a life of their own, undisturbed and unexamined. No agency really studies or controls them. The Office of Management and Budget largely neglects them, for the items are not in *its* budget. The executive departments likewise are usually unconcerned, for the items are not in *their* programs. The Treasury is apparently not evaluating them, but rather is adding new and indefensible items. This is no way to run a tax system and no way to run a budget policy.

These tax subsidies constitute by far the largest element in Government subsidy programs, clearly overshadowing the $12 billion in direct cash payment subsidies, $9 billion in benefit-in-kind subsidies, and $4 billion in credit subsidies. * * *

Tax expenditure analysis and the construction of a Tax Expenditure Budget involve some important structural aspects. Primary among these is the basic matter of definition: Which income tax rules are special provisions representing Government expenditures made through the income tax system to achieve various objectives apart from the tax, and which income tax rules constitute the basic structure of the income tax itself and hence are integral to having such a tax at all? What is required to answer this central question of definition is a normative model for an income tax structure. That normative model in turn will depend on a definition of "income" for income tax purposes. The original Treasury analysis[b] discussed this matter at some length. It indicated the tax expenditures there listed cover "the major respects in which the current income tax bases deviate from widely accepted definitions of income and standards of business accounting and from the generally accepted structure of an income tax."

The Tax Expenditure Budget and underlying analysis drew importantly on the general acceptance of the Haig-Simons approach to the definition of "income," which essentially is based on "gain" or "accretion" and which Simons phrased as follows: "Personal income may be defined as the algebraic sum of (1) the market value of rights exercised in consumption and (2) the change in the value of the store of property rights between the beginning and end of the period in question." This "accretion" approach and the Simons definition cast a very wide net, one reaching in a number of respects further than the coverage of modern income tax systems. The Treasury analysis, while referring to this approach when it spoke of "widely accepted definitions of income," therefore qualified reliance on it by also referring to the "generally accepted structure of an income tax." Thus, contrary to the Simons definition, the noncoverage under the United States income tax, and indeed all other income taxes, of imputed rental income on owner-occupied homes was not listed as a tax expenditure. In addition, the analysis indicated that aspects of our income tax, such as the personal exemptions, rate schedules, and income-splitting for married couples are not considered as "variations from the generally accepted measure of net income or as tax preferences, but as part of the structure of an income tax system based on ability to pay." Hence, they were not treated as tax expenditures but instead were considered as outside the scope of the Treasury study of tax expenditures.

* * *

Comparison of Tax Incentives with Direct Expenditures

The Tax Expenditure Budget thus serves to identify the tax incentives in our existing tax system and so to identify the areas in which Congress has given financial assistance through the tax system to induce desired action.

---

b. The Tax Expenditure Budget for the Fiscal Year 1968, published in the Annual Report of the Secretary of the Treasury for Fiscal Year 1968, at 327, 329-30. (Eds.)

But why through the tax system? Why not through a direct expenditure program? *Given* the Congressional decision to provide the assistance, when should it be furnished through a direct expenditure program and when through a special tax program?

This section of the discussion is concerned with criteria for evaluating the use of tax incentives as compared to the use of direct Government expenditures. This evaluation does not involve the issue whether we should seek to achieve the particular goals for which tax incentives are now used or suggested. * * *

There are * * * a variety of ways to provide Government financial assistance—direct grants, loans, interest subsidies, guarantees of loan repayment or interest payments, insurance on investments, and so on. These methods are here called budgetary or direct expenditures. Skilled tax technicians and budgetary experts can take any tax expenditure and devise a budgetary expenditure approach to serve the same goals as a direct expenditure. For example, the British for some years used an approach under their tax law somewhat similar to our 7 percent investment credit to encourage the acquisition of machinery and equipment. The Labour Government subsequently dropped the tax technique and substituted direct cash payments. The Conservative Government then dropped the direct grants and returned to tax provisions. The existing tax incentive for charitable giving could also be structured as a direct expenditure program, under which the Government would match an individual's contribution to charity with a proportional contribution of its own to the same charity. Tax credits to an employer for manpower training could be structured as grants or contract payments to the employer. Tax benefits to the aged can be structured as cash to the aged. And so on.

It follows that a meaningful comparison between the tax incentive technique and the direct expenditure technique must involve *similar substantive programs*. There is no point to saying that in a particular situation a tax incentive is a more useful approach because it involves no Government supervision over the details of the action to be induced, whereas a direct expenditure involves detailed supervision. To say so is not to compare a tax incentive with a direct expenditure but simply to compare a loosely controlled method of paying out Government funds with a tightly controlled method. Direct expenditures can involve loose as well as tight supervision. Once we decide which substantive program we want, then we can go on to decide which technique—tax incentive or direct expenditure—is preferable for that program.

The matter of what type of substantive program is best calculated to achieve the desired goal lies in the fields of cost-benefit and cost-effectiveness analyses. These methods are being used more and more to devise and test direct expenditures, and they should *a priori* be equally applicable to programs using a tax incentive technique. * * * [T]his has [not] been true

lack of cost bnfts analyses

with regard to tax incentives in the past. Far from it—and therein lie many of the problems with tax incentives. * * *

A meaningful comparison between the two techniques must also be *realistic*. Thus, it must recognize that a tax incentive does involve the expenditure of Government funds. It is often said that a tax incentive is more useful than a direct expenditure because people do not like or will not respond to "subsidies." Such statements always assume that the direct expenditure is the "subsidy," whereas the tax benefit obtained in the tax incentive—the lower tax—is not so regarded. Perhaps we may find that this fiscal illusion has its usefulness, but we should at least be aware of what is the reality and what is the illusion.

portrayal of direct pymts as subsidy but tx expn diture not so portrayed

Some Asserted Virtues of Tax Incentives—Falsely Claimed

Against this general background we can now consider some of the virtues and defects generally claimed for tax incentives and, on the other side of the coin, for direct expenditures. The first level of consideration relates to virtues claimed for tax incentives, but, in the light of the above background, falsely claimed.

Tax incentives encourage the private sector
to participate in social programs

Frequently a tax incentive is urged on the ground that the particular problem to be met is great and that the Government must assist in its solution by enlisting the participation of the private sector—generally business. * * * Thus, a tax incentive for manpower training and employment proposed in the Senate was defended in these terms:[15]

> Tax incentives [are proposed] to encourage the fullest participation of the private sector in employment, upgrading, and training of less skilled people.
>
> * * * [I]n order to encourage business to participate in programs of this nature, Government must be willing to meet business half way. The most convenient form for subsidizing a businessman is through his income tax.
>
> . . . [This bill] enlists the job-creating potential of private enterprise by realistically recognizing the high initial costs involved in hiring, training, and providing supportive services for low-skilled individuals.

But all this is a non sequitur; it points not to the virtue of tax incentives but to the need for Government assistance. The existence of that need has no relevance to the question whether the need should be met by an incentive or by a direct expenditure.

---

15. 115 Cong. Rec. 12,875, 12,876 (1969) (statement of Senator Charles Percy).

> *Tax incentives are simple and involve far less*
> *governmental supervision and detail*

A whole swirl of virtues claimed for tax incentives is summed up in the general observation that they keep Government—that is, the Government bureaucracy—out of the picture: they involve less negotiation of the arrangements, less supervision, less red tape, no new bureaucracy, and so on. The manpower proposal referred to above was supported by this argument:[16]

> The advantages to a tax credit approach are numerous. The most important, however, is that the program can go into effect immediately upon enactment. Employment programs in the past have taken months and years to become operative. . . . Employers who participate in the program will receive a tax credit of 75 percent of the wages paid to the employee for the first 4 months of employment, 50 percent for the next 4 months, and 25 percent for the balance of the individual's first year of employment. This is an uncomplicated program with the minimum of redtape. Any employer who hires a certified employee is eligible for the tax credit—it is as simple as that.

But this merely comes down to saying: "Let's have a manpower program under which the Government pays an employer, who hires a certified employee, an amount calculated as a percentage of the employee's wage." There is nothing so far that indicates whether the payment should be by way of a tax credit or a direct expenditure. Direct expenditure programs can also be structured to pay out Government money with few administrative controls. * * *

A Government that decides it is wise to pay out tax credit money via a simple tax schedule would be highly irrational if it also decided that it would be unwise to pay the same amount directly on the same basis. A dollar is a dollar—both for the person who receives it and the Government that pays it, whether the dollar comes with a tax credit label or a direct expenditure label. Nor is a new bureaucracy needed to pay out these amounts as a direct expenditure—a check-writing process is all that would be needed in keeping with the parallel to the tax credit. Nor, similarly, must there be long negotiations, complex contracts, and the like. It is not the tax route that makes the program simple—it is substantive decisions to have a simple program. In many cases, it is true, direct expenditure programs are probably overstructured and the urging of tax incentives is a reaction to, and a valid criticism of, badly designed expenditure programs. The cure lies of course in better designed expenditure programs.

It should be added, parenthetically, that the alleged simplicity of tax incentives is likely to be illusory. Thus, the argument quoted above states that "[a]ny employer who hires a certified employee is eligible for the tax

---

16. 115 Cong. Rec. 12,875, 12,876 (1969) (statement of Senator Charles Percy).

credit—it is simple as that." But this is not really so, because the legislation actually proposed would have required the employer to be certified by the Secretary of Labor, and to be eligible for certification an employer would have had to prove that the employment program would not impair or depress the wages, working standards, or opportunities of present employees; that the business was not affected by strike, lockout, or similar conditions; that the employees in the program would be afforded an equal opportunity for full-time employment after the expiration of the credit period; that a formal on-the-job training program would be available; and that there would be no discrimination on account of race, color, religion, or national origin. Further complexities were involved in the proposed system for determining the creditable wage base. * * *

The tape is thus present in tax incentive programs and its color is red. * * *

> *Tax incentives promote private decision-making*
> *rather than Government-centered decision-making*

It is said that better progress will be made toward the solution of many social programs if individual decision-making is promoted, and that since tax incentives promote this they should be preferred to approaches that underscore Government-centered decision-making. * * *

[M]any business groups who in urging tax incentives stress the virtues of private enterprise overlook the fact that they are really stressing private enterprise *plus* Government assistance. But wise or unwise, the contentions that private enterprise should be allowed free play, without Government interference, tells us nothing as to the choice between tax incentives and direct expenditures, given the same substantive program. This contention is really a variant of the previous "red tape" argument. Just as we could design a direct expenditure program that provides for reduction of red tape, so we could design one that provides more flexibility for private decision-making and less scope for Government control. For example, the deduction for charitable contributions is sometimes cited as a method of Government assistance that promotes private decision-making—the taxpayer, and not the Government, selects the charity and determines how much to give. But a direct expenditure program under which the Government matched with its grants, on a no-questions-asked and no-second-thoughts basis, the gifts of private individuals to the charities they selected, would equally preserve private decision-making. * * *

It is true that many of the existing tax incentives are less structured than direct expenditure programs. But in part this reflects lack of scrutiny and foresight when the tax incentives were being planned or considered. * * *

Some Asserted Defects of Tax Incentives

Tax incentives permit windfalls by paying taxpayers for doing what they would do anyway

It is generally argued that tax incentives are wasteful because some of the tax benefits go to taxpayers for activities which they would have performed without the benefits. When this happens, the tax credit or other benefit is a pleasant windfall, and stimulates no additional activity. With respect to most, if not all, of the existing and proposed incentives this criticism is well taken, and indeed it is often difficult to structure a tax credit system which avoids this problem without increasing complexity and introducing arbitrariness. But this also is a problem not unique to the tax incentive technique. A direct expenditure program similarly structured would be equally open to the charge. For example, grants or contract payments made to employers who hire unskilled employees as part of a manpower program may go to employers who for one reason or another would have hired those employees anyway.

It may be desirable in particular programs to tolerate this inefficiency or windfall. Or it may be desirable to attempt to eliminate it. * * * The significant question is what sort of substantive program is desired.

Tax incentives are inequitable: they are worth more to the high-income taxpayer than the low-income taxpayer; they do not benefit those who are outside the tax system because their incomes are low, they have losses, or they are exempt from tax

This criticism of tax incentives in terms of their inequitable effects is properly levied against most of the existing tax incentives, and probably most of the proposed incentives. The existing incentives were never really carefully structured and in many instances just grew up, without serious thought ever having been given to the question whether they were fair in these terms. * * *

The fact that tax benefits for the aged and the sick provide no benefits for those aged or ill who are too poor to pay income taxes was not even thought of as a difficulty, since the focus was, as in any positive tax system, on writing the rules for *taxpayers*.[24] The problem was sometimes thought about in the context of an individual who fell outside the tax system because of current losses, and at times a carry-forward of incentive benefits was provided. Thought was occasionally given to the fact that the deduction of

---

24. If we had a *negative* income tax as well as a *positive* income tax, then the direct expenditures involved in the negative income tax payments to those whose incomes were below the level of positive tax would, to that extent, provide some assistance to balance the assistance given to taxpayers through the tax expenditures contained in the positive tax system. And also, of course, direct programs in many fields presently provide assistance to nontaxpayers as well as taxpayers. But the existence of such direct programs and a negative income tax would not make the tax incentives or special tax relief equitable. The jumble of financial assistance these varied methods would provide would only by extreme happenstance provide an equitable continuum of assistance structured to provide funds to those most in need of the assistance.

mortgage interest or charitable contributions is worth more to the top-bracket taxpayer than the low-bracket taxpayer, but the disparity was generally dismissed on the grounds that all deductions had that effect. Sometimes this matter was regarded as worrisome, and a tax credit was used instead of a deduction. * * *

It is clear, then, that most tax incentives have decidedly adverse effects on equity as between taxpayers at the same income level, and also, with respect to the individual income tax, between taxpayers at different income levels. As a consequence of these inequitable effects, many tax incentives look, and are, highly irrational when phrased as direct expenditure programs structured the same way. Indeed, it is doubtful that most of our existing tax incentives would ever have been introduced, let alone accepted, if so structured, and many would be laughed out of Congress. * * *

This difference between the rewards of the marketplace and the rewards of tax incentive also obtains for direct Government grants. Most direct Government economic assistance for business activities is given on a before-tax basis and in one way or another enters as a plus in the income accounts of the person benefited. See for example: agricultural subsidies for domestic activities and exports; manpower subsidies; air carrier and maritime subsidies; land and forest conservation payments; credit subsidies (which reduce interest costs) for agriculture, exports, housing, small business, and other activities. But the tax incentives, as we have seen, do not work that way. * * * The tax incentive thus produces both financial assistance and freedom from taxation. That freedom itself means much more to the well-to-do individual than to one in the lower brackets. * * *

The irony of all this is illustrated by the Treasury Department's first proposing a housing rehabilitation tax incentive and then having to suggest that the incentive is a "tax preference" which must be guarded against by including it in the new minimum tax structure designed to prevent the wealthy from escaping all tax burdens. This inclusion as a tax preference under the new minimum tax[c] thus implicitly characterizes this tax incentive as a special tax benefit for high-bracket taxpayers. The use of the direct expenditure route would have prevented this particular undermining of the tax system.
        * * *

As an aside, we can here see the importance of distinguishing tax expenditures and tax incentives—so-called special tax provision—from those provisions considered a proper and necessary part of the structure of an income tax. If an item is *properly* deductible in the latter sense, it does come off at the taxpayer's top tax rate, and its benefits are confined to those who are taxpayers. Given the decision to have an income tax at all, the result is equitable, within the concept an income tax. An income tax is a tax on *net*

---

c. Sections 55-59. (Eds.)

income and not a tax on gross receipts; therefore the deductions from gross income required to produce net income base must be allowed. Those deductions, generally speaking, are the expenses and costs incurred in the process of producing or earning the gross income received by the taxpayer.

Consider, for example, the deduction for moving expenses: it is a deduction and so benefits a taxpayer (reduces his tax) in accordance with his marginal tax rate. It also benefits only taxpayers; an employee who incurs moving expense, but whose income is so low as not to leave him taxable, does not obtain any benefit or assistance. This is the correct result under a positive income tax system if the moving expense should properly be taken into account in the measurement of net income, as it should be if it is an expense in earning income rather than a personal expense. If it is the latter, the deduction is a subsidy or tax expenditure, inequitably cast, to induce labor mobility. Actually, the moving expense deduction is at the frontier of the positive income tax structure; a gradual shift is occurring, and such expenses are coming to be regarded as a factor proper and necessary to the measurement of net income.[38]

Tax incentives distort the choices of the marketplace and produce unneutralities in the allocation of resources

This criticism is in one sense always valid, because that is what the tax incentive is designed to do. Generally, the critic is also saying or implying that the distortion introduced by the particular incentive is undesirable for various reasons. In large part this criticism is true of many existing incentives for reasons earlier described. The criticism has relevance because the distorting effects of tax incentives often pass unnoticed. But the criticism is of course equally applicable to direct expenditures, some of which certainly are unwise. Again, we are not here concerned with the overall role of Government or the extent to which and under what circumstances financial assistance is desirable to induce private action different from what the marketplace would provide. This criticism thus does not per se tell us when one or the other technique should be used.

It is interesting to note that, even within the area sought to be benefited by the tax incentive, the design of the incentive may push or pull in unneutral directions, which may or may not be desirable. Thus, a tax credit for pollution control facilities focuses on expenditures for machinery as the method of control to the exclusion of other methods, such as different choice

---

38. There is often a hazy line between business expenses properly deducted from gross income for the purpose of an income tax, and personal expenses, which should not be deducted. Thus, commuting expenses are personal, but the expenses of providing comfortable working conditions in an office are business; wearing nice clothes at work is a personal expense, but wearing uniforms is a business expense. The borderlines that evolve are a part of the "generally accepted structure of an income tax" that is used as a standard to identify tax expenditures. We sometimes speak of tax changes designed to provide incentives for taxpayers when what is really involved is the removal of imperfections in the design of a proper tax structure that inhibit their activities.

of materials involved in the manufacturing processes. A tax credit for businesses located in urban slums may focus concentration on monetary assistance to the neglect of the provision of technical assistance.

Further, it is difficult if not impossible to keep tax incentives within proper bounds. Tax incentives for the oil industry or the cattle industry or low-income housing or whatever soon become syndicated tax shelters for doctors, executives, actors, and others far removed from the industry itself. Their only attachment to the industry involved is that the "tax losses" which the ingenious minds can secure for them through bending the tax mechanics of the incentive to the tax shelter device. Tax incentive aid to an industry thus soon becomes a tax windfall to every doctor or other investor who is steered to that industry by tax shelter syndicators and advisers.

    * * *

Tax incentives keep tax rates high by constricting the tax base and thereby reducing revenues

This criticism of tax incentives states a fact that many overlook in their advocacy of tax incentives. The lack of an explicit accounting in the Federal Budget for the tax expenditures involved in tax incentives and the lack in most cases of an accounting in tax statistical data combine to cause many to forget that dollars are being spent. As a consequence, the criticism that is made against direct expenditures—that they keep our tax rates high—is often lost sight of when tax incentives are involved. * * * Tax incentives are usually open-ended: they place no limit on how much tax benefit a taxpayer can earn. Hence it is difficult to foretell how much will be spent by the Government through a particular incentive. * * *

In the end, the issue is whether, as to any particular area, we want direct Government provision of services or goods, Government financial assistance to encourage and assist private action to provide the services or goods, or reliance on private action unaided by the Government. If we choose Government provision or assistance, then public dollars must be spent, and whether they are dollars foregone through lost tax revenues or dollars spent directly through direct expenditures, the effect on tax rates will be the same. So also will the effect on the economy if the Government program succeeds, and the resultant effect on the revenue base and tax rates of the increased economic activity that such success may mean.

Summary of Asserted Virtues and Vices of Tax Incentives

This description of the virtues and vices of tax incentives yields these conclusions: the *asserted disadvantages*—waste, inefficiency, and inequity—are true of most tax incentives existing or proposed because of the way they are structured or grew up. The whole approach to tax incentives—one of rather careless or loose analysis, failure to recognize that dollars are being spent, or to recognize the defects inherent in working within the constraints of the positive tax system—has produced very poor programs. But *if* the problems were recognized and *if* care were taken to design tax incentive programs that one would be willing to defend in substantive terms if the programs were cast as direct expenditure programs, then these disadvantages would not be involved, except to the extent that they are inherent in Government assistance itself. These are large conditions, and in most cases would be hard to bring about. For example, it would not be easy to give tax benefit assistance to groups outside the tax system but performing desired activities, such as local governments or tax-exempt organizations hiring the disadvantaged—direct payments outside the tax system would be needed. And it would not be easy to design tax incentive programs which were not inequitable as between taxpayers in high and low brackets and between taxpayers and non-taxpayers. Indeed, there is no tax incentive in existence or proposed that meets the above standards. But for purposes of comparison we are here assuming that the standards could be met under some tax incentive programs.

Similarly, the *asserted advantages* of tax incentives—greater reliance on private decision-making and less detailed requirements—to the extent that they are true in fact (and they are often only illusory) are really criticisms of the complications and supervision built into direct expenditure programs, or else a reflection of the structural weaknesses of the tax incentive program, depending on the amount of detail and supervision appropriate to the particular program. In a rational world, one should assume that if after careful study it is considered that certain complexities and details are not needed and can be left out of a tax incentive program, then they should and can simply be dropped from the direct expenditure program. This may be a more difficult condition than the description suggests, but it is probably less difficult to bring about than the conditions for repairing tax incentives, or at least no more difficult. Again, for purposes of comparison, we are also here assuming this can be done in direct expenditure programs.

      * * *

ANALYTICAL PERSPECTIVES
BUDGET OF THE UNITED STATES GOVERNMENT
FISCAL YEAR 1995
Office of Management and Budget
Pages 53, 57-61, 64-66 (1994)

Tax expenditures are revenue losses due to preferential provisions of the Federal tax laws, such as special exclusions, exemptions, deductions, credits, deferrals, or tax rates. Tax expenditures are an alternative to other Government policy instruments, such as direct expenditures and regulations. The Congressional Budget Act of 1974 requires that a list of tax expenditures be included in the budget.

      * * *

The Omnibus Budget Reconciliation Act of 1993 (OBRA 93) had a number of effects on income tax expenditures. The Act broadened the tax base by reducing some tax preferences, such as the exclusion for a portion of social security income and the credit available for business income earned in U.S. possessions. Conversely, the Act narrowed the tax base, and increased tax expenditures, by creating, renewing, or expanding several other tax preferences. New provisions include empowerment zones. Certain expired provisions, such as mortgage revenue bonds and the low-income housing tax credit, were extended permanently. Others, such as the research and experimentation tax credit and the targeted jobs tax credit, were extended but not made permanent. Expanded tax expenditures include more generous expensing provisions for small business investments and increases in the earned income tax credit.

OBRA 93 also increased the revenue losses from tax expenditures by raising the top individual and corporate tax rates. As tax rates rise, the revenue losses from deductions and exclusions also increase. For example, raising the top marginal tax rate from 31 percent to 39.6 percent would increase the revenue loss from a $1,000 exclusion in this tax bracket from $310 to $396.

* * *

Tax Expenditures in the Income Tax
Tax Expenditure Estimates

The Treasury Department prepared all tax expenditure estimates presented here based upon income tax law enacted as of December 31, 1993. Expired or repealed provisions are not listed if their revenue effects result only from taxpayer activity in years before 1993.

* * *

As in prior years, two baseline concepts—the normal tax baseline and the reference tax law baseline—are considered for the estimates. For the most part, the two concepts coincide. However, items treated as tax expenditures under the normal tax baseline, but not the reference tax law baseline, are indicated by the designation "normal tax method" in the tables. The revenue losses for these items are zero using the reference tax rules. The alternative baseline concepts are discussed in detail following the estimates.

Table 6-2 reports the respective portions of the total revenue losses that arise under the individual and corporate income taxes. Listing revenue loss estimates under the individual and corporate headings does not imply that these categories of filers benefit from the special tax provisions in proportion to the respective tax expenditure amounts shown. Rather, these breakdowns show the specific tax accounts through which the various provisions are cleared. The ultimate beneficiaries of corporate tax expenditures, for example, could be stockholders, employees, customers, or others, depending on the circumstances.

* * *

Interpreting Tax Expenditure Estimates

Tax expenditure revenue loss estimates do not necessarily equal the increase in Federal revenues (or the reduction in budget deficits) that would accompany the repeal of the special provisions, for the following reasons:

Eliminating a tax expenditure may have incentive effects that alter economic behavior

These incentives can affect the resulting magnitudes of the formerly subsidized activity or of other tax preferences or Government programs. For example, if deductibility of mortgage interest were limited, some taxpayers would hold smaller mortgages, with a concomitantly smaller effect on the budget than if no such limits were in force.

Tax expenditures are interdependent even without incentive effects

Repeal of a tax expenditure provision can increase or decrease the revenue losses associated with other provisions. For example, even if behavior does not change, repeal of an itemized deduction could increase the revenue losses from other deductions because some taxpayers would be moved into higher tax brackets. Alternatively, repeal of an itemized deduction could lower the revenue loss from other deductions if taxpayers are led to claim the standard deduction instead of itemizing. Similarly, if two provisions were repealed simultaneously, the increase in tax liability could be greater or less than the sum of the two separate tax expenditures, since each is estimated assuming that the other remains in force.

The annual value of tax expenditures for tax deferrals is reported on a cash basis in all tables except table 6-3

Cash-based estimates reflect the difference between taxes deferred in the current year and incoming revenues that are received due to deferrals of taxes from prior years. While such estimates are useful as a measure of cash flows into the Government, they do not always accurately reflect the true economic cost of these provisions. For example, for a provision where activity levels have changed, so that incoming tax receipts from past deferrals are greater than deferred receipts from new activity, the cash-basis tax expenditure estimate can be negative, despite the fact that in present-value terms current deferrals do have a real cost to the Government. Alternatively, in the case of a newly enacted deferral provision, a cash-based estimate can overstate the real cost to the Government because the newly deferred taxes will ultimately be received. Present-value estimates, which are a useful supplement to the cash-basis estimates for provisions involving deferrals, are discussed below.

Repeal of some provisions could affect overall levels of income and rates of economic growth

In principle, repeal of major tax provisions may have some impact on the budget economic assumptions. In general, however, most changes in

TABLE 6-2. CORPORATE AND INDIVIDUAL INCOME TAX REVENUE LOSS ESTIMATES FOR TAX EXPENDITURES (In millions of dollars)

	Revenue Loss					
	Corporations			Individuals		
	1995	1996	1997	1995	1996	1997
National Defense:						
Exclusion of benefits and allowances to armed forces personnel	—	—	—	2,030	2,020	2,015
International affairs:						
Exclusion of income earned abroad by United States citizens	—	—	—	895	945	1,000
Exclusion of income of foreign sales corporations	1,400	1,500	1,600	—	—	—
Inventory property sales source rules exception .	1,300	1,400	1,500	—	—	—
Interest allocation rules exception for certain financial operations	95	95	95	—	—	—
Deferral of income from controlled foreign corporations (normal tax method)	1,700	1,800	2,000	—	—	—
General science, space and technology:						
Expensing of research and experimentation expenditures (normal tax method)	2,345	2,515	2,685	45	45	55
Credit for increasing research activities	1,240	730	315	30	10	—
Suspension of the allocation of research and experimentation expenditures	270	—	—	—	—	—
Energy:						
Expensing of exploration and development costs:						
Oil and gas	105	75	45	35	25	15
Other fuels	15	15	15	5	5	5
Excess of percentage over cost depletion:						
Oil and gas	775	790	800	260	265	265
Other fuels	85	85	90	15	15	15
Alternative fuel production credit	820	850	840	150	150	150
Exception from passive loss limitation for working interests in oil and gas properties	—	—	—	50	50	50
Capital gains treatment of royalties on coal	—	—	—	15	15	15
Exclusion of interest on State and local IDBs for energy facilities	70	70	70	105	105	105
New technology credit	65	70	75	*	*	*
Alcohol fuel credit[1]	5	5	5	30	40	45
Tax credit and deduction for clean-fuel burning vehicles and properties	55	55	55	10	10	10
Exclusion from income of conservation subsidies provided by public utilities	85	110	120	60	65	70
Natural resources and environment:						
Expensing of exploration and development costs, nonfuel minerals	45	45	45	5	5	5
Excess of percentage over cost depletion, nonfuel minerals	165	165	170	30	30	30
Capital gains treatment of iron ore	—	—	—	*	*	*
Special rules for mining reclamation reserves ...	45	45	45	5	5	5
Exclusion of interest on State and local IDBs for pollution control and sewage and waste disposal facilities	250	245	240	375	370	360
Capital gains treatment of certain timber income	—	—	—	15	15	15
Expensing of multiperiod timber growing costs ..	415	435	460	160	165	175

	Revenue Loss					
	Corporations			Individuals		
	1995	1996	1997	1995	1996	1997
Investment credit and seven-year amortization for reforestation expenditures	20	20	20	15	20	20
Tax incentives for preservation of historic structures	40	40	35	85	85	85
Agriculture:						
Expensing of certain capital outlays	10	10	10	60	55	55
Expensing of certain multiperiod production costs	10	10	10	75	70	70
Treatment of loans forgiven solvent farmers as if insolvent	—	—	—	10	10	10
Capital gains treatment of certain income	—	—	—	140	145	145
Commerce and housing:						
Financial institutions and insurance:						
Exemption of credit union income	380	420	465	—	—	—
Excess bad debt reserves of financial institutions	40	40	45	—	—	—
Exclusion of interest on life insurance savings	245	265	280	8,485	9,120	9,810
Special alternative tax on small property and casualty insurance companies	5	5	5	—	—	—
Tax exemption of certain insurance companies	110	115	120	—	—	—
Small life insurance company deduction	135	140	145	—	—	—
Exemption of RIC expenses from the 2% floor for miscellaneous itemized deductions	—	—	—	690	810	925
Housing:						
Exclusion of interest on owner-occupied mortgage subsidy bonds	715	705	680	1,070	1,070	1,035
Exclusion of interest on State and local debt for rental housing	365	345	320	555	525	490
Deductibility of mortgage interest on owner-occupied homes	—	—	—	54,800	57,985	61,420
Deductibility of State and local property tax on owner-occupied homes	—	—	—	14,655	15,545	16,425
Deferral of income from post 1987 installment sales	235	240	245	700	710	720
Deferral of capital gains on home sales	—	—	—	14,620	15,195	15,620
Exclusion of capital gains on home sales for persons age 55 and over	—	—	—	4,960	5,155	5,300
Exception from passive loss rules for $25,000 of rental loss	—	—	—	5,775	5,680	5,625
Accelerated depreciation on rental housing (normal tax method)	730	765	815	370	385	405
Commerce:						
Cancellation of indebtedness	—	—	—	110	70	35
Permanent exceptions from imputed interest rules	—	—	—	150	150	155
Capital gains (other than agriculture, timber, iron ore, and coal) (normal tax method)	—	—	—	6,920	7,045	7,120
Step-up basis of capital gains at death	—	—	—	28,305	29,480	30,265
Carryover basis of capital gains on gifts	—	—	—	130	135	140
Ordinary income treatment of loss from small business corporation stock sale	—	—	—	30	35	35
Accelerated depreciation of buildings other than rental housing (normal tax method)	2,415	2,605	2,845	765	820	895
Accelerated depreciation of machinery and equipment (normal tax method)	18,720	18,140	17,965	4,490	4,410	4,365

	Revenue Loss					
	Corporations			Individuals		
	1995	1996	1997	1995	1996	1997
Expensing of certain small investments (normal tax method)	595	470	345	965	765	560
Amortization of start-up costs (normal tax method)	100	105	105	100	105	110
Graduated corporation income tax rate (normal tax method)	3,890	4,140	4,340	—	—	—
Exclusion of interest on small issue IDBs	210	160	125	335	260	200
Deferral of gains from sale of broadcasting facilities to minority owned business	290	305	320	*	*	*
Treatment of Alaska Native Corporations	30	20	15	—	—	—
Transportation:						
Deferral of tax on shipping companies	15	15	15	—	—	—
Exclusion of reimbursed employee parking expenses	—	—	—	1,930	2,015	2,100
Exclusion for employer-provided transit passes .	—	—	—	40	50	65
Community and regional development:						
Credit for low-income housing investments	680	780	885	1,585	1,820	2,060
Investment credit for rehabilitation of structures (other than historic)	25	25	25	55	55	55
Exclusion of interest on IDBs for airports, docks and sports and convention facilities	335	350	370	495	520	545
Exemption of certain mutuals' and cooperatives' income	30	30	30	—	—	—
Empowerment zones	95	130	155	235	310	355
Education, training, employment, and social services:						
Education:						
Exclusion of scholarship and fellowship income (normal tax method)	—	—	—	875	920	965
Exclusion of interest on State and local student loan bonds	120	115	110	185	180	165
Exclusion of interest on State and local debt for private nonprofit educational facilities	300	310	315	450	460	470
Exclusion of interest on savings bonds transferred to educational institutions	—	—	—	5	5	10
Parental personal exemption for students age 19 or over	—	—	—	535	545	565
Deductibility of charitable contributions (education)	670	700	740	1,560	1,640	1,720
Exclusion of employer provided educational assistance	—	—	—	85	—	—
Training, employment, and social services:						
Targeted jobs credit	320	270	50	75	55	10
Exclusion of employer provided child care	—	—	—	725	775	830
Exclusion of employee meals and lodging (other than military)	—	—	—	550	580	610
Credit for child and dependent care expenses .	—	—	—	2,820	2,975	3,145
Credit for disabled access expenditures	130	130	135	30	30	30
Expensing of costs of removing certain architectural barriers to the handicapped	15	15	15	5	5	5
Deductibility of charitable contributions, other than education and health	840	880	930	14,240	14,950	15,700
Exclusion of certain foster care payments	—	—	—	30	35	35
Exclusion of parsonage allowances	—	—	—	290	320	355

| | Revenue Loss | | | | | |
| | Corporations | | | Individuals | | |
	1995	1996	1997	1995	1996	1997
Health:						
Exclusion of employer contributions for medical insurance premiums and medical care	—	—	—	56,265	61,675	67,345
Credit for child medical insurance premiums[2] ..	—	—	—	—	—	—
Deductibility of medical expenses	—	—	—	3,560	3,870	4,195
Exclusion of interest on State and local debt for private nonprofit health facilities	600	615	635	895	920	950
Deductibility of charitable contributions (health)	420	450	470	1,600	1,680	1,760
Tax credit for orphan drug research	15	—	—	—	—	—
Special Blue Cross/Blue Shield deduction	125	140	100	—	—	—
Income security:						
Exclusion of railroad retirement system benefits	—	—	—	400	405	410
Exclusion of workmen's compensation benefits ..	—	—	—	4,455	4,740	5,065
Exclusion of public assistance benefits (normal tax method)	—	—	—	585	605	640
Exclusion of special benefits for disabled coal miners	—	—	—	100	95	95
Exclusion of military disability pensions	—	—	—	130	130	130
Net exclusion of pension contributions and earnings:						
Employer plans	—	—	—	55,540	59,010	59,490
Individual Retirement Accounts	—	—	—	5,290	5,275	5,175
Keogh plans	—	—	—	3,875	4,130	4,400
Exclusion of employer provided death benefits ..	—	—	—	35	35	40
Exclusion of other employee benefits:						
Premiums on group term life insurance	—	—	—	2,880	3,020	3,170
Premiums on accident and disability insurance	—	—	—	140	145	150
Income of trusts to finance supplementary unemployment benefits	—	—	—	35	35	35
Special ESOP rules (other than investment credit)	1,760	1,635	1,545	—	—	—
Additional deduction for the blind	—	—	—	45	45	50
Additional deduction for the elderly	—	—	—	1,555	1,570	1,585
Tax credit for the elderly and disabled	—	—	—	65	70	70
Deductibility of casualty losses	—	—	—	230	230	230
Earned income credit[3]	—	—	—	5,100	5,795	6,435
Social Security:						
Exclusion of social security benefits:						
OASI benefits for retired workers	—	—	—	16,525	17,370	18,140
Disability insurance benefits	—	—	—	1,905	2,105	2,320
Benefits for dependents and survivors	—	—	—	3,730	3,940	4,150
Veterans benefits and services:						
Exclusion of veterans disability compensation ..	—	—	—	1,920	1,855	1,885
Exclusion of veterans pensions	—	—	—	75	70	70
Exclusion of GI bill benefits	—	—	—	65	70	75
Exclusion of interest on State and local debt for veterans housing	35	30	30	50	50	45
General purpose fiscal assistance:						
Exclusion of interest on public purpose State and local debt	4,955	5,095	5,255	7,395	7,595	7,830

| | Revenue Loss | | | | | |
| | Corporations | | | Individuals | | |
	1995	1996	1997	1995	1996	1997
Deductibility of nonbusiness State and local taxes other than on owner-occupied homes	—	—	—	25,640	27,130	28,740
Tax credit for corporations receiving income from doing business in U.S. possessions	2,630	2,680	2,735	—	—	—
Interest:						
Deferral of interest on savings bonds	—	—	—	1,250	1,310	1,380
Addendum—Aid to State and local governments:						
Deductibility of:						
Property taxes on owner-occupied homes	—	—	—	14,655	15,545	16,425
Nonbusiness State and local taxes other than on owner-occupied homes	—	—	—	25,640	27,130	28,740
Exclusion of interest on:						
Public purpose State and local debt	4,955	5,095	5,255	7,395	7,595	7,830
IDBs for certain energy facilities	70	70	70	105	105	105
IDBs for pollution control and sewage and waste disposal facilities	250	245	240	375	370	360
Small issue IDBs	210	160	125	335	260	200
Owner-occupied mortgage revenue bonds	715	705	680	1,070	1,070	1,035
State and local debt for rental housing	365	345	320	555	525	490
IDBs for airports, docks, and sports and convention facilities	335	350	370	495	520	545
State and local student loan bonds	120	115	110	185	180	165
State and local debt for private nonprofit educational facilities	300	310	315	450	460	470
State and local debt for private nonprofit health facilities	600	615	635	895	920	950
State and local debt for veterans housing	35	30	30	50	50	45

Note: Provisions with estimates denoted "normal tax method" have no revenue loss under the reference tax law method. All estimates have been rounded to the nearest $5 million.

* 2.5 million or less.

1 In addition, the partial exemption from the excise tax for alcohol fuels results in a reduction in excise tax receipts of $675 million in 1995.

2. The figures in the table indicate the effect of the child medical insurance premium credit on receipts. The effect on outlays in 1994 is $395 million.

3 The figures in the table indicate the effect of the earned income tax credit on receipts. The effect on outlays in 1995 is $15,795 million.

particular provisions are unlikely to have significant effects on macroeconomic conditions.

Present-Value Estimates

Discounted present-value estimates of revenue losses are presented in table 6-3 for certain provisions that involve tax deferrals or similar long-term revenue effects. These estimates complement the cash-based tax expenditure estimates presented in the other tables in this chapter.

The present-value estimates represent the revenue losses, net of future tax payments, that follow from activities undertaken during calendar year 1994 which cause the deferrals or related revenue effects. For instance, a pension contribution in 1994 would cause a deferral of tax payments on wages in 1994 and on pension earnings on this contribution (e.g., interest) in later years. In some future year, however, the 1994 pension contribution and accrued earnings will be paid out and taxes will be due; these receipts are included in the present-value estimate. In general, this conceptual approach is similar to the one used for reporting the budgetary effects of credit programs, where direct loans and guarantees in a given year affect future cash flows.

The discount rate used for the present-value estimates is the interest rate on comparable maturity Treasury debt. * * *
          * * *

Tax Expenditure Baselines

A tax expenditure is a preferential exception to the baseline provisions of the tax structure. The 1974 Congressional Budget Act does not, however, specify the baseline provisions of the tax law. Deciding whether provisions are preferential exceptions, therefore, is a matter of judgement. As in prior years, this year's tax expenditure estimates are presented using two baselines: the *normal tax baseline*, which is used by the Joint Committee on Taxation, and the *reference tax law baseline*, which has been used by the Administration since 1983.

The normal tax baseline is patterned on a comprehensive income tax, which defines income as the sum of consumption and the change in net wealth in a given period of time. The normal tax baseline allows personal exemptions, a standard deduction, and deductions of the expenses incurred in earning income. It is not limited to a particular structure of tax rates, or by a specific definition of the taxpaying unit.

The reference tax law baseline is closer to existing law. Reference law tax expenditures are limited to special exceptions in the tax code that serve programmatic functions. These functions correspond to specific budget categories such as national defense, agriculture, or health care. While tax expenditures under the reference law baseline are generally tax expenditures under the normal tax baseline, the reverse is not always true.

Both the normal and reference tax baselines allow several major departures from a pure comprehensive income tax. For example:

Income is taxable when realized in exchange

Thus, neither the deferral of tax on unrealized capital gains nor the tax exclusion of imputed income (such as the rental value of owner-occupied housing or farmers' consumption of their own produce) is regarded as a tax expenditure. * * *

There is a separate corporation income tax

Under a comprehensive income tax corporate income would be taxed only once—at the shareholder level, whether or not distributed in the form of dividends.

Values of assets and debt are not adjusted for inflation

A comprehensive income tax would adjust the cost basis of capital assets and debt for changes in the price level during the time the assets or debt are

TABLE 6-3. PRESENT VALUE OF SELECTED TAX EXPENDITURES FOR ACTIVITY IN CALENDAR YEAR 1994 (In millions of dollars)

Provision	Present Value of Revenue Loss
Deferral of income from controlled foreign corporations (normal tax method)	1,640
Expensing of research and experimentation expenditures (normal tax method)	2,035
Expensing of exploration and development costs - oil and gas	275
Expensing of exploration and development costs - other fuels	35
Expensing of exploration and development costs - nonfuels	90
Expensing of multiperiod timber growing costs	235
Expensing of certain multiperiod production costs - agriculture	65
Expensing of certain capital outlays - agriculture	80
Deferral of capital gains on home sales	15,605
Accelerated depreciation of rental housing (normal tax method)	1,140
Accelerated depreciation of buildings other than rental housing (normal tax method)	670
Accelerated depreciation of machinery and equipment (normal tax method)	22,105
Expensing of certain small investments (normal tax method)	3,995
Amortization of start-up costs (normal tax method)	165
Deferral of capital gains from sale of broadcasting facilities to minority-owned businesses	230
Deferral of tax on shipping companies	10
Credit for low-income housing investments	2,055
Exclusion of pension contributions and earnings - employer plans	40,500
Exclusion of IRA contributions and earnings	1,735
Exclusion of contribution and earnings for Keogh plans	2,710
Exclusion of interest on State and local public-purpose bonds	16,140
Exclusion of interest on State and local non-public purpose bonds	8,780
Deferral of interest on U.S. savings bonds	655

Note: Provisions with estimates denoted "normal tax method" have no revenue loss under the reference tax law method.

held. Thus, under a comprehensive income tax baseline the failure to take account of inflation in measuring depreciation, capital gains, and interest income would be regarded as a negative tax expenditure (i.e., a tax penalty), and failure to take account of inflation in measuring interest costs would be regarded as a positive tax expenditure (i.e., a tax subsidy).

While the reference law and normal tax baselines are generally similar, areas of difference include:

Tax rates

The separate schedules applying to the various taxpaying units are included in the reference law baseline. Thus, corporate tax rates below the maximum statutory rate do not give rise to a tax expenditure. The normal tax baseline is similar, except that it specifies the current maximum rate as the baseline for the corporate income tax. The lower tax rates applied to the first $10 million of corporate income are thus regarded as a tax expenditure. Similarly, under the reference law baseline, preferential tax rates for capital gains generally do not yield a tax expenditure; only capital gains treatment of otherwise "ordinary income," such as that from coal and iron ore royalties and the sale of timber and certain agricultural products, is considered a tax expenditure. The alternative minimum tax is treated as part of the baseline rate structure under both the reference and normal tax methods.

Income subject to the tax

Income subject to tax is defined as gross income less the costs of earning that income. The Federal income tax defines gross income to include: (1) consideration received in the exchange of goods and services, including labor services or property; and (2) the taxpayer's share of gross or net income earned and/or reported by another entity (such as a partnership). Under the reference tax rules, therefore, gross income does not include gifts—defined as receipts of money or property that are not consideration in an exchange—or most transfer payments, which can be thought of as gifts from the Government.[2] The normal tax baseline also excludes gifts between individuals from gross income. Under the normal tax baseline, however, all cash transfer payments from the Government to private individuals are counted in gross income, and exemptions of such transfers from tax are identified as tax expenditures. The costs of earning income are generally deductible in determining taxable income under both the reference and normal tax baselines.

Capital recovery

Under the reference tax law baseline no tax expenditures arise from accelerated depreciation. Under the normal tax baseline, the depreciation allowance for machinery and equipment is determined using straight-line depreciation over tax lives equal to mid-values of the asset depreciation range (a depreciation system in effect from 1971 through 1980). The normal tax baseline for real property is computed using 40-year straight-line depreciation.

Treatment of foreign income

Both the normal and reference tax baselines allow a tax credit for foreign income taxes paid (up to the amount of U.S. income taxes that would

---

2. Gross income does, however, include transfer payments associated with past employment, such as social security benefits.

otherwise be due), which prevents double taxation of income earned abroad.
* * *

Other Considerations

Additional tax expenditure analysis may be helpful to policy makers. For example, information on the programmatic and economic effects of tax expenditures could be useful. The outputs and efficiency of tax expenditures could then be compared more systematically with direct outlay programs.

In addition, the tax expenditure analysis could be extended beyond the income and transfer taxes to include payroll and excise taxes. The exclusion of certain forms of compensation from the wage base, for instance, reduces payroll taxes, as well as income taxes. Payroll tax exclusions are complex to analyze, however, because they also affect social insurance benefits. Certain targeted excise tax provisions might also be considered tax expenditures. In this case challenges include determining an appropriate baseline.
* * *

Notes and Questions

1. How does a reduction in income tax rates affect tax expenditures?

2. Is the tax expenditures concept merely a way of framing the issue as to what should be included in the income tax base?

3. If a credit against tax is allowed for purchase of a depreciable asset, should the tax basis of the asset thereafter be the full price paid for it or its cost reduced by the tax credit?

4. Did Professor Surrey make a valid point when he wrote that it was difficult to keep tax incentives within "proper bounds" and prevent them from being used as tax shelters by "doctors, executives, actors, and others far removed from the industry itself"?

5. Professor Surrey argued that almost any tax expenditure could be duplicated, in substantive effect, by a direct expenditure program. Is this correct? What difference would it make? Would direct expenditures be more closely scrutinized?   Would direct expenditures exclude as potential beneficiaries those with so little income that they paid no income tax, as tax expenditures routinely do?

6. Would charities be indifferent if Congress ended the tax deduction for charitable contributions and substituted, as Professor Surrey suggested, "a direct expenditure program under which the Government matched with its grants, on a no-questions-asked and no-second-thoughts basis, the gifts of private individuals to the charities they selected"? Would such a direct expenditure be constitutional if the charity were a church?

7. From the government's point of view, there are important differences between direct expenditures and tax expenditures. Direct expenditures are more closely administered, which means higher administrative costs. However, tax expenditures may cost more because they are likely to benefit an unnecessarily broad class of taxpayers.

Lobbying Congress to adopt a tax expenditure is easier than lobbying for an appropriation for a direct expenditure. Once a direct expenditure program is in place, however, the government agency administering it is likely to lobby for its continuation. In contrast, the Internal Revenue Service will not lobby to sustain a tax expenditure that it has to administer.

8. Why does Professor Surrey not regard the moving expense deduction as a tax expenditure?

9. The structure of a tax expenditure is important. Prior to the Tax Reform Act of 1986, taxpayers over the age of 65 and blind taxpayers were allowed an additional personal exemption, which had the effect of a deduction for all such taxpayers. The 1986 Act, in addition to reducing the amount of the benefit, changed its structure—rather than a personal exemption available to all aged and blind taxpayers, it was restructured as an increased standard deduction, of value only to those who utilized the standard deduction.[d] What policy choices, or what views of the effects of age or blindness, justify one structure as compared to the other? What different decision would be reflected by converting the tax advantage to a "refundable" credit?

10. Why does Congress give a tax advantage to taxpayers who are elderly or blind, and not to taxpayers with other afflictions, such as paraplegia?

11. Professor Douglas Kahn has suggested informally that some personal deductions (such as the medical expense deduction and the additional standard deduction for the aged and the blind) should be regarded not as tax expenditures, but as attempts to refine the very rough utility curve in the progressive tax rate structure to bring it closer to an ideal of equality of sacrifice.

12. In order to identify a tax expenditure, one must have a norm, or reference point. The Office of Management and Budget distinguished between two versions of the normal tax structure—the "normal tax baseline" and the "reference tax baseline." In general terms, what is the difference between the two? What is an item that would be regarded as a tax

---

d. Section 63(f).

expenditure when compared to the normal tax baseline, but not to the reference tax baseline?

13. Tax expenditures arising from deferral of tax liability have been significant over the years, but have attracted relatively little political opposition. The advantages of tax deferral are better understood by the beneficiaries than by the general public. Moreover, such tax expenditures are politically defended on the grounds that the tax is "merely" being postponed.

Tax expenditures arising from deferral are difficult to quantify because the cost to the government depends not only on the amount and length of deferment, but also on the interest rate assumed in computing the time value of money. In measuring these tax expenditures, the Office of Management and Budget uses as a discount rate "the interest rate on comparable maturity Treasury debt." Is this appropriate, or should we look to what the typical taxpayer would have to pay to borrow money?

C. THE TAX EXPENDITURES CONCEPT CHALLENGED

Unless carefully confined, the premise of the tax expenditures concept might be ridiculed by *reductio ad absurdum*: any portion of a taxpayer's income that the government allows the taxpayer to keep would be a tax expenditure. In a slightly less extreme form, under a progressive income tax rate structure, any revenue lost by failure to tax everyone at the top bracket rate might be considered a tax expenditure. The excerpts in Subchapter B are careful to define tax expenditures in such a fashion as to exclude such interpretations. The more limited view of tax expenditures requires the application of normative standards, but these standards are open to challenge, as is demonstrated by the two excerpts, one recent and one written in opposition to the concept of the tax expenditures idea during its pre-1974 gestation.

EXPENDITURE BUDGETS: A CRITICAL VIEW
Douglas A. Kahn[*] & Jeffrey S. Lehman[**]
54 Tax Notes 1661, 1661-63 (1992)

The various tax expenditure budgets prepared in the legislative and executive branches purport to carry out a straightforward task. They claim to identify those situations in which Congress has departed from the "normative," "normal," or "correct" tax rule in a way that is equivalent to the appropriation of public funds. Or, as it is sometimes put, they expose circumstances in which Congress has chosen to subsidize certain activities indirectly, through the Internal Revenue Code.

---

[*]. At time of original publication, Paul G. Kauper Professor of Law, University of Michigan.
[**]. At time of original publication, Assistant Professor of Law, University of Michigan.

Yet, the very statement of the task exposes its Achilles heel. It assumes the existence of one true, "correct," "normative" rule of federal income taxation that should be applied to any given transaction. The collection of all such rules stands as a kind of Platonic Internal Revenue Code, an implicit reprimand to the flawed efforts of our mortal Congress.

We believe that questions of tax policy are more complicated than that. An ideal Internal Revenue Code makes no more sense than an ideal Environmental Protection Act or an ideal Penal Code. An income tax stands inside, not outside, the society that enacts it.

The particular contours of our federal income tax serve to reaffirm public values that are "normative" in every sense of the word except the one used by advocates of tax expenditure budgets. The disallowance of a deduction for illegal bribes confirms that we think they are naughty. Similarly, the limitation on losses from wagering transactions shows that we do not consider them to be an appropriate foundation for a career. Conversely, the exclusion from income of tort recoveries is an expression of public compassion. And our refusal to tax people when their neighbors help them move furniture, or (as some have suggested) when they enjoy a few moments of leisure, suggests a shared sense of a private domain in which even the tax collector will respect people's right to be left alone.

Experts can help to clarify the implications of one tax policy choice over another. They can show how one choice favors one particular set of moral, political, or economic commitments over another. They can argue for greater consistency in the way tensions among such commitments are resolved. They can estimate the differences in the amount and distribution of revenues that would be collected under different regimes. But, the ultimate choice must rest with the citizen and not the oracle.

The Choice Among Utopias

Let us describe a series of perspectives that are frequently presented concerning the ideal nature of an income tax:

(1) For some observers of the tax scene, any tax that alters citizen behavior is terribly unfortunate. Such observers decry any tax that alters individuals' economic incentives from what they would have been in a world with no taxes and a perfect marketplace. They would prefer that the government raise its revenues exclusively by taxing (a) activities that generate negative externalities, and (b) goods for which the demand is entirely inelastic. Since no income tax can pretend to be nondistortional, such observers view all income taxes as tainted by a kind of "original sin."

(2) Other, more practically minded observers, worry that the taxes that would satisfy perspective (1) would not generate enough revenues for the government to finance its current level of operations. They believe that Nicholas Kaldor had it right almost 40 years ago, when he argued that the proper income tax system is what we now call a consumption tax. Such observers are willing to accept the fact that a consumption tax biases

taxpayers' choice between labor and leisure. They console themselves with the observation that at least a consumption tax avoids biasing the choice between savings and current consumption.

(3) Another set of commentators objects that a consumption tax that would satisfy perspective (2) ignores the new economic power reflected in congealed, unconsumed, newly acquired wealth. They contend that all such economic power should be reckoned in the tax base, perhaps as a proxy for an (ideal) wealth tax. For such observers, the touchstone of income taxation must be the sum of consumption and wealth accumulation—what is commonly known as Haig-Simons income.

(4) Still other commentators find fault with the pure Haig-Simons approach endorsed under perspective (3). It would offend such commentators' notions of privacy to tax citizens on unrealized asset appreciation and on imputed income from services or durable goods. Or, at least, it would require a preposterous expenditure of administrative resources in an ultimately futile quest. These observers would prefer that we tax Haig-Simons income to the extent it is realized through market interactions.

(5) Yet another set of commentators finds fault with even the market-delimited, realization-qualified version of the Haig-Simons approach suggested by perspective (4). They believe that such an approach unacceptably distorts investor incentives, leading them to overconsume and undersave, to indulge in too much leisure and not enough work. While they are in sympathy with the political vision that would allocate the tax burden according to accumulating economic power, they favor qualifications to that vision whenever the cost to productive incentives appears to jeopardize economic growth.

(6) Finally, one finds the United States Congress. It apparently believes that even the approach dictated by perspective (5) would leave the American economy in the wrong place. Not enough research and development, not enough low-income housing, not enough money in the hands of working families with children, not enough money in the hands of churches and museums, too many renters and not enough homeowners, etc., etc., etc.

If one is prone to depression, one can view the foregoing list of perspectives from (1) to (6) as identifying a kind of linear decline. Each is one step further from the Garden of Eden of distortion-free taxation. We view them differently. We prefer to see each perspective as emphasizing different elements in a basket of normative values—efficiency (in the neoclassical economic sense), consumption/savings neutrality, privacy, equity, administrability, charity, pragmatism, etc.

What is disturbing about the language of tax expenditures is its tone of moral absolutism. The tax expenditure budget is said to distinguish "normal" tax practice from that which is deviant. Sometimes it is said to distinguish provisions that are "normative" (?) from those that are (presumably) nonnormative (?!). This language is doubly confusing. First, it suggests that provisions that fit *within* the implicit baseline of the tax expenditure budget are somehow pure, safe, and good. They should not be changed because "neutral" principles have blessed them. Conversely, the language suggests that provisions that fall *outside* the implicit baseline of the tax expenditure budget (tax expenditures) are somehow corrupt, dangerous, and evil. They should be changed as soon as possible to conform with the "neutral" position. To flirt with them is to call one's probity into question.

This is, of course, a bit of an overstatement. But, it captures the rhetorical direction of the tax expenditure budget. And that rhetorical direction is grossly misleading. The tax expenditure budget's conception of an appropriate tax base has no legitimate claim to establishing the terms of political debate. * * *

The Illusion of Value-Free Precision—An Example

The reference point for construction of the tax expenditure budget is a measure of taxable income that is close to position (4) above, with some variations. That may be some people's Platonic Internal Revenue Code, but it is obviously not everyone's. The choice among perspectives is a contestable, contingent, political decision. Thus, while the several existing tax expenditure budgets give an appearance of being the products of a highly sophisticated, expert, neutral examination of the tax system, they could just as accurately be characterized as exercises in mystification. They create only an illusion of value-free scientific precision in a heavily politicized domain.

Consider two features of our tax system. First, it grants a form of accelerated depreciation. Second, it does not tax unrealized gains. The first feature appears in tax expenditure budgets. Moreover, as the *Tax Notes* discussion over the past few months has made clear, many proponents of tax expenditure budgets view that as a good thing because they believe that accelerated depreciation is not "normative." Yet the second feature—the refusal to tax unrealized gains—does not appear in any tax expenditure budget.

The tax expenditure budget baseline, which distinguishes between these two features, is "normative" in the sense that it advances a particular moral or political claim. It reflects a particular balance among the ideals of efficiency, equity, neutrality, administrability, privacy, charity, and pragmatism. But, each of the six perspectives enumerated in the prior section is "normative" in precisely the same way. And at most two of the six perspectives (perspective (4) and perhaps some versions of perspective (5)) would distinguish between these two features. The others would treat both as good or both as objectionable.

One can advance plausible arguments in favor of taxing unrealized gains. One can advance plausible arguments against granting accelerated depreciation deductions. One could also argue for the status quo with regard to each of these features. But, there is no *a priori* reason to classify one feature differently from the other, or to allocate a heavier burden of persuasion to those who attack realization or defend accelerated depreciation than one allocates to those who defend realization or attack accelerated depreciation.

* * *

ACCOUNTING FOR FEDERAL "TAX SUBSIDIES" IN THE NATIONAL BUDGET
Boris I. Bittker[*]

22 National Tax Journal 244, 246-57 (1969)

Although Mr. Surrey did not address himself to the mode of presentation, his proposal implied that "tax benefit provisions" would be reported in the Budget as hypothetical expenditures, to be "classified along customary budgetary lines: assistance to business, natural resources, agriculture, aid to the elderly, medical assistance, aid to charitable institutions, and so on."[5]

* * *

Fleshing out Mr. Surrey's proposal, the Treasury has estimated the revenue lost by virtue of "the major respects in which the current income tax bases deviate from widely accepted definitions of income and standards of business accounting and from the generally accepted structure of an income tax." These estimates were published, along with a discussion of the conceptual framework governing the items selected for inclusion, in an exhibit to Secretary Fowler's final report as Secretary of the Treasury, under the title "The Tax Expenditure Budget: A Conceptual Analysis." This study should be regarded as only a first step in achieving the "full accounting" envisioned by Mr. Surrey * * *

It has been a familiar exercise for many years to compute the "cost" of a proposed tax provision by estimating the amount of revenue that would be lost by its enactment; and at first blush, a "full accounting" seems to require nothing more than an aggregation of such estimates, based on existing tax concessions, rather than on proposed ones. If that were its only prerequisite, an expansion of the Treasury's estimating facilities and staff would bring us close to achieving the promise of a "full accounting." To be fully informative, of course, the estimates would have to take account of the fact that tax concessions influence behavior; since the revenue "lost" by virtue of any tax provision depends in part on its absence, its "cost" cannot be accurately measured by merely recomputing the tax liability on the return as filed. It might turn out that the revenue effects of tax incentive provisions, if they succeed in their objective of altering behavior, are especially difficult to

---

*. At time of original publication, Southmayd Professor of Law, Yale University.

5. Surrey, Taxes and the Federal Budget (speech to Financial Executives Institute, Dallas Chapter, Feb. 13, 1968), p. 13. [This was in line with Mr. Surrey's views as expressed in the text in Subchapter A. (Eds.)]

estimate—although these are precisely the provisions that are most in need of cost effectiveness studies. * * *

Even if the Treasury's estimates could be refined to take into account tax-induced changes in behavior, however, a major obstacle in achieving a "full accounting" would remain, viz., the fact that a systematic compilation of revenue losses requires an agreed starting point, departures from which can be identified. What is needed is not an ad hoc list of tax provisions, but a generally acceptable model, or set of principles, enabling us to decide with reasonable assurance which income tax provisions are departures from the model, whose costs are to be reported as "tax expenditures." In this connection, it is important to note that the proposed "full accounting" is evidently intended to embrace every provision that serves as the substitute for an appropriation, including those that are solely or primarily distributive in function (e.g., the extra $600 exemption for the blind and the aged).[e]

In listing the exclusion of social security benefits as a "tax expenditure" that ought to be reflected in the Federal Budget as aid to the elderly, the Treasury analysts very likely had in mind the fact that these receipts constitute income under the Haig-Simons definition. Conversely, their study accepts the deduction of business expenses under §162 as necessary to the accurate determination of net income, with the result that the revenue "lost" by virtue of this provision is not reported as a "tax expenditure" to aid private enterprise. In making this distinction, no value judgment is intended: the deduction of business expenses and the exclusion of social security benefits are not treated differently because one provision is "good" and the other "bad," but because one is helpful or necessary in defining net income, while the other distorts the computation of income. Thus, in asking that the revenue losses resulting from "deliberate departures from accepted concepts of net income and through special exemptions, deductions and credits" be reported as "expenditures," Mr. Surrey noted that these "tax benefit provisions" will have to be separated from provisions that serve to define income accurately: "We should not, of course, overlook the difficulties of interpretation or measurement involved here."[9] * * * In the same vein, the Treasury study seeks to identify the provisions of existing law that deviate "from widely accepted definitions of income and standards of business accounting and from the generally accepted structure of an income tax."

To effect a "full accounting," then, we must first construct an ideal or correct income tax structure, departures from which will be reflected as "tax expenditures" in the National Budget. Although Mr. Surrey is not explicit on the point, his proposal has much in common with the call for a comprehensive income tax base, which similarly presupposes an ideal tax

---

e. Present law no longer provides an additional personal exemption for aged and blind taxpayers; they are entitled, however, to an increased standard deduction. Section 63(f). (Eds.)

9. Surrey, The United Income Tax System—the Need for a Full Accounting (speech to Money Marketeers, Nov. 15, 1967), p. 5.

structure—based on the Haig-Simons definition of income—any departure from which is to be regarded as a maverick that must shoulder a heavy burden of justification.

The call for a "full accounting" does not by itself imply that repeal of all of these provisions is feasible or desirable, but only that the revenue lost by sticking with existing law should be disclosed in the Budget. At the same time, it is not insignificant that Mr. Surrey doubts the "efficiency" of these provisions and their ability to withstand public scrutiny if viewed as expenditures; after all, the purpose of the "full accounting" is to stimulate a re-examination of "tax expenditures," rather than merely to record them for economic historians or antiquarian statisticians. Unless the "full accounting" is to be limited to those provisions that the incumbent Secretary of the Treasury wants Congress to repeal, however, it will require a formidable list of tax provisions to be reflected as "expenditures" if the Haig-Simons definition is to be the criterion for judging the extent of the current Internal Revenue Code's departure from "a proper measurement of net income."

Such a comprehensive list of "tax expenditures" would include a number of items that Congress has so far shown no interest in repealing, despite the magnitude of the revenue "lost" by their preservation. Thus, the cash receipts and disbursements method of accounting for income—which conflicts with the Haig-Simons definition because it does not currently reflect changes in the taxpayer's net worth—can be described as a "tax subsidy," granted for the double purpose of simplifying the income-reporting process for taxpayers with rudimentary records and of easing the payment problem for taxpayers who have rendered services or sold property, but have not yet collected from their customers and clients. Another example of a "tax expenditure" that has hitherto been considered sacrosanct is the exclusion of unrealized appreciation from income, a "preference" that is customarily accepted by even the most confirmed advocates of a comprehensive income tax base on the ground that difficulties in valuing the taxpayer's assets make it administratively impossible to apply the Haig-Simons definition in this area. * * *

A whole-hearted enemy of "backstairs" spending might, I suppose, argue that a disclosure of the cost of the cash receipts and disbursements method of accounting or of the realization concept would be a first step to their elimination. * * *

Favorable legislative action on such proposals is so remote a possibility, however, that one may be inclined to argue for reporting in the National Budget only those "tax expenditures" that Congress is likely to repeal—once they have been brought into the open. But if the "full accounting" is to be limited in this fashion, some of the prime candidates for inclusion on the "expenditure" side might fall by the wayside. I am not at all sure, for example, that percentage depletion and the immunity of state and municipal bond interest are more vulnerable to Congressional hostility than the cash method of accounting. * * *

Assuming a consistent application of the Haig-Simons definition, however, there are many other areas that would generate "tax expenditures" for inclusion in the Budget, including the exclusion from taxable income of gifts, bequests, life insurance proceeds, and recoveries for personal injuries and wrongful death; * * * personal and dependency exemptions; imputed income from assets and housewives' services; the non-recognition provisions (e.g., exchanges of like-kind property, corporate reorganizations, etc.); depreciation deductions that exceed declines in market value * * *; current deductions for expenditures that have value beyond the current year (e.g., research and experimental expenses, institutional advertising, and outlays for industrial know-how); special accounting privileges (e.g., installment sale reporting); the foreign tax credit[15] and other items. The Treasury study—perhaps because it is offered as a "minimum" rather than comprehensive list—makes a number of compromises in applying the Haig-Simons definition in these areas. Thus, it estimates the cost of excluding employers' contributions to pension plans and the interest component of life insurance savings, but not the revenue cost of excluding increases in the taxpayer's net worth resulting from other transactions. Similarly debatable lines are drawn at other points, in that the study estimates the revenue cost of excluding or deducting: public assistance, but not gifts from charitable agencies, friends, and relatives; sick pay and workmen's compensation, but not recoveries and settlements in personal injury suits; child care expenses of employees, but not their moving expenses; accelerated depreciation on buildings, but not straight-line depreciation (even though it too may exceed the property's decline in market value); the expensing of research and experimental expenditures, but not the rapid amortization of such outlays (even if their long-term value is substantial), nor the expensing of comparable outlays for good will, industrial know-how, etc.; nonbusiness state and local taxes, but not foreign taxes. * * *

The revenue cost of the omitted items may have been too difficult to estimate with the data at hand when the Tax Expenditure Budget was prepared; I mention them not to criticize an admittedly "minimum" list for

---

15. The foreign tax credit protects taxpayers with foreign operations against double income taxation; but of all possible ways of accomplishing this end, it is the most costly for the United States. If its cost were reflected as a "tax expenditure," Congress might decide that relief from double taxation could be procured more "efficiently" by hiring more persuasive ambassadors, speaking softly but carrying a big stick, or threatening to reduce our appropriations for foreign aid. In the alternative, Congress might decide that if a deduction is a sufficient recognition of the added burden of a state or local income tax, it is equally sufficient in the case of a foreign tax. The proper treatment of the foreign tax credit is discussed in the Treasury's Tax Expenditure Budget, Annual Report of the Secretary of the Treasury on the State of the Finances (fiscal year ended June 30, 1968) (1969), p. 331; but no estimate of its cost is made because of the complexity of the issues involved.

conforming to its self-description, but to illustrate the scope of the Haig-Simons definition. Because I have recently discussed the ramifications of a consistent adherence to this definition, I will not undertake to list here the many other provisions of existing law that, in my opinion, depart from that definition. Suffice it to say that a "full accounting" for these departures would be a formidable undertaking, comparable to Prof. Charles O. Galvin's challenging proposal for a tax model based on the comprehensive income tax base concept. There is, however, a major difference between the two projects, stemming from the fact that the Haig-Simons definition provides no guidance to many structural issues that must be decided in any income tax law. As to these decisions, the unofficial research model proposed by Prof. Galvin can experiment with alternatives, while the Treasury's "full accounting" will have to select one "correct" model against which to measure existing law. Because I see no way to select such an "official" model for these structural provisions, I am not sanguine about the prospects for a "full accounting."

One such area is the rate structure. In 1964, income tax rates were substantially reduced, for the stated purpose of encouraging economic growth. Since an alternative method of accomplishing this objective was a federal subsidy, should the reduction have been reflected in the Treasury's "Tax Expenditure Budget?" The logic of the "full accounting" approach suggests an affirmative response, so that the cost of this effort to increase economic growth by a rate reduction would be constantly brought to public attention, thus encouraging an annual review of both the merits of its objective and its efficiency as compared with other devices and programs to accomplish the same end. * * *

Once it is decided that a rate reduction may be a form of "back door spending," however, we encounter a troublesome—perhaps an insoluble—problem of measurement. The cost of the 1964 experiment in encouraging economic growth by a rate reduction might, I suppose, be ascertained by computing the difference between (a) the revenue actually collected, and (b) the amount that would have been produced if the old rates had been perpetuated. (Ideally, of course, account should be taken of the effect of the reduced rate on the volume of taxable income; but if this is not done for other "tax expenditures," presumably it would not be done in this instance either.) The aggregate cost of the tax reduction would then be allocated among income classes, to reflect the cost of the tax cut for each such group. This process could be repeated for each tax cut in our history, so that the "tax expenditure" section of the National Budget would report, separately, the "cost" of every such change, classified as an aid to investment, a device to encourage consumer spending, and so on, depending on its purpose. The aggregate to be reported for the current year would thus be the difference between the revenue produced by the rates actually in effect, and the amount that would have been produced if the highest rates in history had been preserved. The benchmark year would vary from one taxable income class to another, of course, since the peak rate applicable to each class would be the standard for determining the "cost" of encouraging that group of taxpayers to engage in investment, consumption, or other tax-favored activity.

                    * * *

Another problem—equally unsolved by the Haig-Simons definition, but equally troublesome to the "full accounting" approach—is the taxable unit to be used in computing the "tax expenditures" that are to be reflected in the National Budget. The problem can be illustrated by a question: should the difference between the tax liability of a married man (or a head of a household) and that of a single individual with the same taxable income be reflected on the expenditure side of the National Budget, as a subsidy to family life, in the interest of a "full accounting"? * * *

It would simplify the search for a "full accounting" to accept the Code's existing classification of taxpayers, disregarding the possibility that structural decisions in this area constitute "tax expenditures." If this were to be done, however, it would seem equally appropriate to me to treat taxpayers who are blind, over 65, or otherwise "different" as appropriate taxpaying units whose exemptions or other allowances are simply devices for imposing rates appropriate to their divergent taxpaying abilities; and the same could be said of taxpayers who have minor children, support aged parents, suffer from illness, or are victimized by fire or theft. * * *

A taxonomic problem that creates similar difficulties for a "full accounting" arises from the separate rate schedules that are applicable under current law to individuals and corporations. Does the fact that the individual rate is lower than the corporate rate at the $5,000 income level mean that the difference is a "tax expenditure" to aid low-bracket individuals? Conversely, since the corporate rate is lower than the individual rate at the $200,000 level, does *this* difference constitute a "tax expenditure" to aid corporate business? Or are the two rate schedules simply not to be compared, on the theory that we have two entirely separate income taxes, each levied on its own self-contained group of taxpayers? * * *

Of course, if the Haig-Simons definition were to be applied to individual taxpayers with rigor, there would be no need to compute the income of legal entities like corporations, since the natural person's net worth computation would have fully taken the corporate activities into account. On this theory, the "tax expenditure" to be reported in the interest of achieving a "full accounting" would take account of the taxes that would be collected from individual shareholders if unrealized appreciation and depreciation on their stock entered into the computation of income. The Treasury's "Tax Expenditure Budget," however, does not attempt such a rigorous application of the Haig-Simons definition, but instead contains estimates of the revenue cost of existing provisions relating to Western Hemisphere Trade

Corporations, the excess bad debt reserves of financial institutions, and the deferral of tax on shipping companies.

The study's working hypothesis, stated without independent discussion, is "[t]he assumption inherent in current law, that corporations are separate entities and subject to income taxation independently from their shareholders." * * * Yet the exemption from corporate tax that is granted to Subchapter S corporations and regulated investment companies is not treated as a "tax expenditure"; evidently it is appropriate to view these corporations as conduits rather than entities. * * * [D]ifficulties in deciding whether corporations are conduits or entities suggest that there simply are no "generally accepted" principles specifying the proper relationship between a corporation's income and its shareholders' tax liability—with the result that it is difficult, if not impossible, to apply the "tax expenditure" concept in this area.

The proper classification of tax-exempt organizations presents another problem for the "full accounting" approach. Should the tax exemptions accorded to educational institutions, churches, charitable organizations, social clubs, and other non-profit institutions be reflected as "tax expenditures" to benefit education, religion, charity, and social intercourse? Or is it more appropriate to view the federal income tax as a device by which the government shares in the profits of activities that are carried on for the personal benefit of individual taxpayers, so that the activities of nonprofit institutions are not a proper subject for income taxation? So regarded, the tax exemption accorded to these institutions is an acknowledgment of, rather than a departure from, the "true nature" of the federal income tax; and hence it is not a "tax expenditure" required for a "full accounting" in the National Budget. * * *

The same question—is tax-exemption an "expenditure" or not?—must be answered with respect to state and municipal governmental agencies, which are not taxed by the federal government on their income, whether derived from taxation, the sale of property or services, investments, or other sources. One might, of course, assert that the immunity from federal taxation that is enjoyed by state and local governments constitutes an "expenditure" because it accomplishes the same result as federal grants to these agencies; and that a failure to acknowledge this infusion of federal assistance understates the federal contribution to their well-being. On the other hand, one is tempted to argue that governmental agencies (even if engaged in activities that compete with private business) do not realize "income" in the Haig-Simons sense, or that, if they do, the federal income tax properly exempts them because it is concerned only with activities carried on for private profit. If this view is accepted, their exemption would not be recorded as a "tax expenditure."

If we conclude that the tax exemption accorded to non-profit organizations and governmental agencies is not a tax expenditure, however, a doubt arises about the proper way to reflect the deductions allowed to individuals for charitable contributions and state and local taxes, as well as the exclusion from taxable income of state and municipal bond interest. To the extent that these tax provisions inure to the benefit of the individual taxpayer, they might be properly classified as tax expenditures. To the extent of the benefit inuring to the non-profit or governmental agency, however, should these exemptions be bracketed with the agency's *own* exemption, and excluded from the list of "tax expenditures"? If the purpose of a "full accounting" is to disclose the cost of all "government expenditures made through the tax system," it would seem desirable to fish or cut bait: either record the tax-exempt organization's tax benefits as "expenditures" whether they derive from its own exemption or from concessions allowed to others that are passed on to it; or disregard these benefits entirely. To pick and choose among these tax provisions, recording some but not others as "tax expenditures," is a way of compromising on a middle ground, but it falls short of a "full accounting."

* * *

Notes and Questions

14. In criticizing the tax expenditures concept, Professors Kahn and Lehman did not mean that every provision in the Internal Revenue Code is normal because it exists, thus depriving us of any standard for judgment. They are saying, in effect, that "normal" is not a useful standard. Virtually every tax provision has political or social implications. In their view, all provisions should be reviewed on their merits, without trying for an automatic rule that will distinguish tax expenditures from normal provisions.

15. Is it fair to treat failure to adopt the Haig-Simons definition of income (discussed in Chapter Two) as a tax expenditure?

16. Are we left with a hopeless standoff between the proponents of the tax expenditures approach and its opponents?

17. Many items generally regarded as tax expenditures are also identified as items of tax preference under the alternative minimum tax provisions (sections 55-59). The AMT provisions demonstrate Congressional ambivalence about these items. Does the existence of the AMT provisions support either the proponents or the detractors of the tax expenditures concept?

18. Virtually every compilation of tax expenditures would include the deduction for home mortgage interest, as a subsidy for housing. Few would count as a tax expenditure the exclusion of imputed income from home ownership. (Even though Professor Bittker argues that consistency should

lead to imputed income being regarded as a tax expenditure, this is just an example in his broader argument that the entire tax expenditures concept is flawed and unworkable.) On the other hand, suppose we view the home mortgage deduction as essential, or at least helpful, in establishing equity *in the measurement of taxable income* (not, as for a classic tax expenditure, solely in the pursuit of a nontax goal), as Oliver argues:

The taxpayer with ready cash can purchase a house outright. Instead of investing his cash to earn a taxable stream of income and then paying nondeductible rent from after-tax dollars, in effect, he can receive a tax-free flow of imputed income from the personal residence. The interest deduction places the taxpayer purchasing his house with borrowed funds in a similar position. For example, suppose each of three taxpayers, *A, B,* and *C,* desires to purchase a personal residence costing $50,000. *A* and *B* each has $50,000 of ready cash; thus, they can purchase their residences for cash, or invest the cash and purchase the residences with borrowed funds. *C* has no available assets and therefore must borrow in order to purchase his residence. Assume further, and somewhat artificially, that the taxpayers can lend or borrow money at 10% interest. Ignoring the transactions described below, the three taxpayers have equal taxable income and will itemize deductions.

A uses his $50,000 cash to purchase his house. He receives neither taxable income nor a deduction as a result of the transaction. The imputed income of the rental value of the house, of course, is not included in income.

Unlike *A, B* chooses to invest his $50,000 cash at 10% interest. He borrows $50,000, also at 10%, to purchase his house. *B* receives taxable income of $5,000 from his investment, but the deduction for the $5,000 interest paid by *B* will offset the interest income. *B*'s taxable income therefore is equal to *A*'s.[184] Because these taxpayers have engaged in transactions that are substantially equivalent in economic terms, their taxable income should be affected in the same way.

C, having no choice, also borrows to purchase his residence. Like *B*, he receives a $5,000 interest deduction. Since *C* has no offsetting income item, *C* has $5,000 less taxable income then either

---

184. *A* and *B* may not have identical taxable incomes since *B*'s offsetting income and deduction may affect other computations. * * *

Of more importance is the assumption that all three taxpayers would itemize deductions even without the interest deduction. If this were not the case, *A* would be in a favored position since a portion of the interest deduction of *B* and *C* would be absorbed by the zero bracket amount, and only the excess would be deductible. *See* I.R.C. § 63.

These refinements, however, do not alter the basic point. The interest deduction, even in the case of interest arising from a purely personal expenditure, assures substantial equity among these three typical taxpayers.

A or B. This result, however, is precisely what we should expect. *A* and *B* each has $50,000 of assets that, given a 10% interest rate of return, will produce $5,000 annually.

$$* * *$$

The denial of an interest deduction thus would favor those with liquid excess cash and the ability to divert it to investments producing only untaxed imputed income. It would disfavor those who borrow to purchase assets that produce imputed income. The interest deduction thus effectively allows those not having sufficient wealth and liquidity to purchase personal assets without borrowing to enjoy the benefits of untaxed imputed personal income.[f]

Do you agree that this analysis justifies the deduction for home mortgage interest? If so, does this mean that that deduction should not be regarded as a tax expenditure?

Selected Bibliography

Bittker, Boris I., *Accounting for Federal 'Tax Subsidies' in the National Budget*, 22 NAT'L TAX J. 244 (1969).

——, *Comprehensive Income Taxation: A Response*, 81 HARV. L. REV. 1032 (1968).

Bradley, William H. & Philip D. Oliver, *The Investment Tax Credit: The Illusory Incentive*, 2 VA. TAX REV. 267 (1982).

Brannon, Gerard M., *Tax Expenditures and Income Distribution: A Theoretical Analysis of the Upside-Down Subsidy Argument*, in THE ECONOMICS OF TAXATION (Henry J. Aaron & Michael J. Boskin eds., 1980).

CITIZENS FOR TAX JUSTICE, THE HIDDEN ENTITLEMENTS (1996).

Feldstein, Martin, *A Contribution to the Theory of Tax Expenditures: The Case of Charitable Giving*, in THE ECONOMICS OF TAXATION (Henry J. Aaron & Michael J. Boskin eds., 1980).

Galvin, Charles O., *More on Boris Bittker and the Comprehensive Tax Base: The Practicalities of Tax Reform and the ABA's CSTR*, 81 HARV. L. REV. 1016 (1968).

Kahn, Douglas A. & Jeffrey S. Lehman, *Tax Expenditure Budgets: A Critical View*, 54 TAX NOTES 1661 (1992).

KING, RONALD F., MONEY, TIME, AND POLITICS: INVESTMENT TAX SUBSIDIES AND AMERICAN DEMOCRACY 261-91 (1993).

NEUBIG, THOMAS & DAVID JOULJAIAN, U.S. DEP'T. OF THE TREASURY, THE TAX EXPENDITURES BUDGET BEFORE AND AFTER THE TAX REFORM ACT OF 1986 (1988).

OFFICE OF MANAGEMENT AND BUDGET, BUDGET OF THE UNITED STATES GOVERNMENT: ANALYTICAL PERSPECTIVES: FISCAL YEAR 1995, 53 *et seq.* (1995).

---

f. Phillip D. Oliver, *Section 265(2): A Counterproductive Solution to a Nonexistent Problem*, 40 TAX L. REV. 351, 394-96 (1985).

Oliver, Philip D., *Section 265(2): A Counterproductive Solution to a Nonexistent Problem*, 40 TAX L. REV. 351, 389-96 (1985).

Pechman, Joseph, *Comprehensive Income Taxation: A Comment*, 81 HARV. L. REV. 63 (1967).

Steuerle, Eugene, *Measuring Expenditure Taxes*, 60 TAX NOTES 1159 (1993).

——, *Building New Wealth by Preserving Old Wealth: Savings and Investment Tax Incentives in the Postwar Era*, 36 NAT'L TAX J. 307 (1983).

SURREY, STANLEY S., PATHWAYS TO TAX REFORM (1973).

—— & PAUL MCDANIEL, TAX EXPENDITURES (1985).

Wolfman, Bernard, Book Review, 99 HARV. L. REV. 491 (1985) (reviewing STANLEY S. SURREY & PAUL MCDANIEL, TAX EXPENDITURES (1985)).

Zelinsky, Edward A., *Efficiency and Income Taxes: The Rehabilitation of Tax Incentives*, 64 TEX. L. REV. 973 (1986).

CHAPTER TWELVE

PERSONAL INJURY AWARDS

The difficulty in interpreting section 104(a)(2) and the inconsistent court holdings and Revenue Rulings of the past seven decades probably comes from the lack of any cohesive tax theory or social policy justifying the exemption. The Service, the courts, and the commentators have failed to find any entirely satisfactory explanation of section 104(a)(2)'s raison d'etre.

> ** * **

Some commentators have called for a repeal of section 104(a)(2), reasoning that all personal injury recoveries should be taxed as a realization of gain. Others favor amending section 104(a)(2) to allow taxation of punitive damages, nonphysical nonpersonal injuries, lost earnings, and/or all economic losses. One commentator suggests that section 104(a)(2) should be rewritten to "use the idea of human capital as the touchstone for exclusion of damages recoveries." Another commentator simply asked Congress to draft a uniform standard for excluding personal injury recoveries from taxation. Congress evidently ignored them all.[a]

A. INTRODUCTION AND HISTORICAL DEVELOPMENT

Section 104(a)(2) excludes from gross income tort awards—"any damages received (whether by suit or agreement and whether as lump sums or periodic payments) on account of personal injuries or sickness." Other provisions in sections 104 and 105 exclude similar financial payments related to personal injury, such as workers' compensation payments,[b] but section 104(a)(2) has always been the focus of interest.

The scope of the section 104(a)(2) exclusion is in flux. Recent Supreme Court decisions in *United States v. Burke*[c] and *Commissioner v. Schleier*[d] offer more restrictive interpretations of what damages are deemed to have been received "on account of personal injuries" than had lower courts in recent years. Meanwhile, in 1995 Congress sent to President Clinton a bill that would have limited the exclusion to compensatory (and not punitive) damages,[e] and then only for cases of physical injury (and not other assertedly

---

a. Margaret Henning, *Recent Developments in the Tax Treatment of Personal Injury and Punitive Damage Recoveries,* 45 TAX LAW. 783, 795-96, 798-99 (1992).

b. Section 104(a)(1).

c. 504 U.S. 229 (1992).

d. 115 S. Ct. 2159 (1995).

e. In 1989, Congress provided that the exclusion would not apply to punitive damages

"personal" injuries, such as defamation, discrimination based on race or sex, or alienation of affections).[f] For reasons unrelated to these provisions, the President vetoed the bill.

The heightened interest in the tax treatment of personal injury awards makes this an interesting time to review the theoretical underpinning of allowing an exclusion, and to consider the proper scope of the exclusion. For example, should damages that compensate accident victims for lost earnings be excluded, as under present law, given that the earnings would have been taxed? Is the present exclusion of awards for pain and suffering appropriate, given the absence of a deduction for those who suffer pain without compensation?

Theoretical considerations must be tempered with practicality. If, for example, it were decided that some elements of personal injury recoveries should be taxed and others not, how should the law allocate amounts received in settlement? The latter question is significant, because the overwhelming majority of receipts come as a result of settlement before trial, or even before suit is filed.

In addition to illuminating an area of tax policy of considerable importance in its own right, the materials in this chapter offer valuable guidance into the nature of income—a fundamental issue for the student of tax policy.

In the immediately following article, Professors Burke and Friel discuss the historical origins of the exclusion, and the growth of the scope of the exclusion, with particular attention to nonphysical injuries deemed "personal." Their article also discusses various theories upon which the exclusion has been justified. Evaluation of these theories, which is the central theme of this chapter, is expanded in subchapter B. In subchapter C, Professor Griffith challenges traditional methods of tax analysis, using the tax treatment of personal injury awards as a case study. Finally, subchapter D considers tax complications arising from timing issues. These issues arise when a lump sum award replaces many years of future expected earnings and expected freedom from pain; particular attention, however, should be given to the tax consequences of "structured settlements," under which, instead of a lump sum, the injured taxpayer receives compensation in a series of payments.

---

awarded in cases not involving physical injury or physical sickness. Section 104(a), final sentence. The vetoed bill referenced in note f *infra* would have ended the exclusion for punitive damages in all cases.

f. H.R. 2491, 104th Cong., 1st Sess. (1995).

TAX TREATMENT OF EMPLOYMENT-RELATED PERSONAL INJURY AWARDS: THE NEED FOR LIMITS

J. Martin Burke[*] & Michael K. Friel[**]

50 Montana Law Review 13, 14-21, 42-47 (1989)

Section 104(a)(2) dates back to Section 213(b)(6) of the Revenue Act of 1918. The history of that original section suggests that Congress intended it to codify then-recent administrative decisions. Treasury regulations promulgated early in 1918 under the Revenue Acts of 1916 and 1917 provided specifically that damages were taxable, stating that an "[a]mount received as the result of a suit or compromise for personal injury, being similar to the proceeds of accident insurance, is to be accounted for as income." However, in June 1918, in response to a Treasury inquiry, an Attorney General's opinion held that accident insurance proceeds were not taxable, based on the theory that the "human body is a kind of capital" and the insurance proceeds represented a "conversion of the capital lost through the injury." Shortly thereafter, based on that Attorney General's opinion, the Treasury determined "upon similar principles that an amount received . . . as a result of a suit or compromise for personal injuries sustained . . . through accident" was not taxable and revoked its prior regulation to the contrary. Against this background Congress enacted Section 213(b)(6) of the Revenue Act of 1918, which provided that the term "gross income" did not include: "(6) [a]mounts received, through accident or health insurance or under workmen's compensation acts, as compensation for personal injuries or sickness, plus the amount of any damages received whether by suit or agreement on account of such injuries or sickness."

Despite the obvious potential breadth of the damages provision, the earliest administrative interpretations were restrictive. In 1919, Solicitor's Memorandum 957, addressing the taxability of damages received by a lawyer for libel of his professional reputation, stated in its entirety that "[m]oney received as damages in libel proceedings is subject to income tax." In 1920, Solicitor's Memorandum 1384 held that damages received on account of alienation of a wife's affections were not within the exemption. This latter opinion conceded that alienation of a wife's affections constituted a personal injury, and that the statutory language "taken by itself, would seem to include any personal injury." Nonetheless, based on the 1918 background to Section 213(b)(6), as well as the statute's reference to accident and health insurance and workmen's compensation, the opinion concluded that it was "more probable . . . that the term 'personal injuries', as used therein means physical injuries only." The opinion further stated:

---

[*]. At time of original publication, Dean and Professor of Law, University of Montana.

[**]. At time of original publication, Professor of Law and Director, Graduate Tax Program, University of Florida.

Probably the provision of the Revenue Act of 1918 in question, so far as personal injuries are concerned, is merely declarative of the conclusions [contained in the 1918 Attorney General's opinion and in the Treasury decision in response to it] thus stated and intended to go no further. These conclusions rest . . . upon the theory of conversion of capital assets. It would follow that personal injury not resulting in the destruction or diminution in the value of a capital asset would not be within the exemption. From no ordinary conception of the term can a wife's affections be regarded as constituting capital.

Thus the earliest administrative opinions rested the statute on a loss-of-capital (or return-of-capital) notion, and suggested that only physical injuries gave rise to such lost capital. Whether judicial interpretations of the damages exclusion would have similarly limited it to physical injuries is unknown. Later in 1920, the Supreme Court, in *Eisner v. Macomber*,[13] held that the stock dividend at issue there was not taxable as income under the Sixteenth Amendment, clearly reaffirming the proposition that income should be defined as the gain derived from capital, from labor, or from both combined. Of course, the Supreme Court subsequently developed a far more expansive view of what constitutes income, a view exemplified by the Court's decision in *Glenshaw Glass*.[14] Nonetheless, with respect to personal injury damages, *Eisner v. Macomber* had a substantial impact.

In 1922, Solicitor's Opinion 132, on the basis of *Eisner v. Macomber*, modified Solicitor's Memorandum 957 (1919), revoked Solicitor's Memorandum 1384 (1920), and held that amounts received as damages for alienation of affections or "defamation of personal character" or in consideration of surrendering custody of a minor child did not constitute income. Opinion 132 noted that "both of these [earlier] rulings . . . were made prior to the decision of the Supreme Court in *Eisner v. Macomber*."
    * * *

Judicial confirmation of the excludability of damages for nonphysical injuries came in the seminal case of *Hawkins v. Commissioner*.[18] The taxpayer in Hawkins was president of a corporation until removed from office by the directors. He subsequently sued the corporation and individual officers of the corporation for having published defamatory statements about him which were injurious to his personal reputation and to his health. That suit plus two other suits brought against the taxpayer by two corporate officers were thereafter settled and dismissed following payment of money damages to Hawkins. The Board of Tax Appeals held that the damages received for libel and slander to personal reputation were indeed nontaxable. It is striking that the court reached this result without any reference to the

---

13. 252 U.S. 189 (1920).
14. *Commissioner v. Glenshaw Glass Co.*, 348 U.S. 426 (1955).
18. 6 B.T.A. 1023 (1927), *acq.*, VII-1 C.B. 14 (1928).

existing statutory exclusion. The taxpayer had argued for exclusion based on the Supreme Court's definition of income as gain from capital, labor, or both, and, in effect, the Board of Tax Appeals agreed:

> This . . . is . . . a case, . . . which in no event involves income. So far as the evidence shows, the amount which petitioner received was wholly by way of general damages for the personal injury suffered . . . . It was compensation for injury to his personal reputation . . . . No suggestion is made that there was special damage paid . . . or . . . punitive or exemplary damages . . . . Even to the economist, character or reputation or other personal attributes are not capital . . . . They are not property or goods. Such compensation as general damages adds nothing to the individual . . . . It is an attempt to make the plaintiff whole as before the injury.

The Internal Revenue Service acquiesced in the *Hawkins* decision, and subsequent rulings and opinions echoed the *Hawkins* analysis of "income." * * * Following *Hawkins*, it was clear that damages for nonphysical personal injuries were excludable from income, and that the exclusion rested on the judicial definition of "income" rather than any statutory analysis.

    * * *

Although *Glenshaw Glass* effectively rejected the *Eisner v. Macomber* formulation of income, it did not mandate a reexamination of the tax treatment of damages for nonphysical personal injuries and, indeed, no reexamination occurred.

The disinclination of the Internal Revenue Service to reconsider the tax treatment of nonphysical personal injury awards became clear in a series of rulings, issued from 1955 to 1958, on war-related damages. In Revenue Ruling 55-132, the Service held that U.S. payments made to World War II prisoners of war under the War Claims Act of 1948 on account of enemy violations of the Geneva Convention relating to provision of food, forced labor and inhumane treatment, were "in the nature of reimbursement for the loss of personal rights" and therefore did not constitute gross income. No authority was cited for the holding, but the loss-of-personal-rights rationale clearly reflects the *Hawkins* emphasis on the nontaxability of compensation for damages to "strictly personal attributes." Revenue Ruling 56-462 held, solely on the authority of Revenue Ruling 55-132, that similar payments made under the War Claims Act to Korean War prisoners were "compensation for the loss of their personal rights" and, as such, not includable in gross income. Revenue Ruling 56-518 dealt with the tax treatment of payments made by the Federal Republic of Germany to former German citizens, now U.S. citizens or residents, who were persecuted by the Nazi regime "because of anti-Nazi persuasion or for reasons of race, faith, or philosophy of life." Citing Revenue Ruling 55-132 as its authority, Revenue Ruling 56-518 held that:

> [T]he compensation paid . . . on account of such persecution which
> resulted in damage to life, body, health, liberty, or to professional
> or economic advancement, are [sic] in the nature of reimbursement
> for the deprivation of civil or personal rights and do not constitute
> taxable income . . . .

On similar facts and reasoning, the Service reached the same conclusions in
Revenue Ruling 58-370 with respect to payments by Austria to former
Austrian citizens persecuted by the Nazi regime. The payments were held to
be reimbursement for the loss of civil and personal rights and, accordingly,
not taxable.

Further evidence of the Service's disinclination to reexamine its historic
view of nonphysical personal injury damages came almost twenty years after
Glenshaw Glass in the promulgation of Revenue Ruling 74-77. The ruling
revisited the tax status of damages received on account of alienation of
affections or in consideration of the surrender of the custody of a minor child,
two of the three issues considered by Solicitor's Opinion 132 over fifty years
earlier. After noting that alienation of affections and custody "relate to
personal or family rights, not property rights, and may be treated together,"
Revenue Ruling 74-77 simply stated that the amounts received as damages
"are not income," and then concluded that "Solicitor's Opinion 132 . . . is
hereby superseded since the position stated therein is set forth under the
current statute and regulations in this Revenue Ruling." The ruling thus
effectively reaffirmed Solicitor's Opinion 132 and, by analogy, *Hawkins v.
Commissioner* as well.

There is a decided irony in this. The teaching of Solicitor's Opinion 132,
Hawkins and the war-claims rulings—that awards for nonphysical personal
injuries such as damage to reputation or deprivation of personal or civil
rights are not includable in income—ultimately becomes part of the fabric of
Section 104(a)(2). But these authorities were based on the *Eisner v.
Macomber* definition of gross income and not on interpretations of Section
104(a)(2) or its predecessors. Indeed, but for the *Eisner v. Macomber*
decision, Solicitor's Opinion 132 and *Hawkins v. Commissioner* might never
have been issued, and the early administrative determinations in the 1919
Solicitor's Memorandum 957 and the 1920 Solicitor's Memorandum 1384—
that the predecessor of Section 104(a)(2) did not encompass nonphysical
personal injuries—might have become the law. * * *

It is curious that a line of authority based on a discredited theory of
gross income which does not rely on or purport to interpret (and in most
cases does not even acknowledge) an existing statutory exclusion should later
be viewed as defining the scope of the statutory exclusion. Nonetheless,
these authorities provide the basis for the unanimous view of the courts and
the Service that the term "personal injury" as used in Section 104(a)(2)
embraces nonphysical as well as physical injuries.
          * * *

Given the history of Section 104(a)(2), only the return-of-capital concept should have any validity today, and even that concept suffers from severe limitations. Under traditional tax principles, application of the return-of-capital theory requires that the taxpayer establish an investment of capital in the asset in question, recognized by the tax code as basis. In the case of a person's corporal and noncorporal attributes—one's body, reputation, mental health, and the like—one presumes that the tax code, ordinarily at least, recognizes no investment of capital, and so no basis. Perhaps money spent over time on food, clothing, shelter, and education, as well as other expenditures necessary for survival or development, might arguably provide a tax basis in one's body and personal rights or attributes. The code, however, has never acknowledged such an investment as constituting basis, and the practical and administrative difficulties inherent in doing so in the general case seem insurmountable. It seems clear that a taxpayer realizes gain on receipt of a personal injury award.[126]

If the receipt of a personal injury award constitutes realization of gain —which, by traditional tax standards, it must—the exclusion of the gain from income can be justified only by substantial policy considerations. One might presume that the involuntariness of the injury sustained is a factor underlying the exclusion, for the taxpayer who consents in advance to the "injury" apparently removes the compensation received from the protection of Section 104(a)(2). Commentators and courts have suggested that personal injury awards are excluded for humanitarian reasons. One writer states that taxing the compensation received "by persons who have been blinded or crippled by accident would no doubt be regarded as heartless, unless their recoveries from tortfeasors were correspondingly increased," but notes that the exclusion extends to "less emotionally charged receipts" as well.[128] Indeed, the Ninth Circuit has suggested that the Commissioner's willingness to exclude personal injury lump-sum awards in their entirety was based on "a feeling that the injured party, who has suffered enough, should not be further burdened with the practical difficulty of sorting out the taxable and nontaxable components."[129]

---

126. Of course, one may conjure up circumstances in which considerations of equity might argue that a specific nondeductible expense has given the taxpayer a basis in some bodily part or personal attribute. But this is surely the aberration, not the norm, and even in the aberrational case, the basis is neither infinite nor elastic; it would have to be established by the taxpayer, not presumed to encompass whatever award is rendered. Assume, for example, that a taxpayer incurs nondeductible expenses for elective cosmetic surgery. If the taxpayer thereafter sustains disfiguring injuries, which essentially undo the cosmetic surgery, and for which damages are awarded, it may not seriously offend one's tax principles to exclude the damages from income to the extent of the nondeductible expenses, or at least to the extent of some prorated ("unused") portion thereof. Of course, if one spies a slippery slope in the vicinity of this example, all bets are off.

128. B. BITTKER, 1 FEDERAL TAXATION OF INCOME, ESTATES AND GIFTS 13-2 (1982).

129. *Roemer v. Commissioner*, 716 F.2d 693, 696 (9th Cir. 1983).

But if humanitarian concerns underlie the exclusion of damages from income, the obvious objection is that not all damages on account of involuntary personal injuries—and perhaps relatively few—warrant such tender treatment. It may, for example, be "heartless" to tax damage awards received on account of severe physical injuries, such as brain damage, paralysis, loss of sight or numerous other terrible injuries. But few conceivable humanitarian reasons exist to exclude damages received for a sprained ankle or a bruised arm; for defamation of personal or business reputation; for violation of free speech rights; for violation of open meeting laws; or for all manner of claims that can plausibly be shoehorned into a personal injury mold. Moreover, why is it only the compensated victim to whom humanitarian tax relief is extended? The uncompensated victim is presumably even more deserving of compassion, and surely administrative burdens could be satisfactorily taken into account in fashioning some tax relief program—an allowance of certain personal injury losses, perhaps—for the uncompensated. The conclusion one is finally driven to is that humanitarian reasons supply a woefully inadequate justification for the breadth of injuries encompassed by Section 104(a)(2).

Of course, in some instances there may be other strong social policy reasons advanced to justify use of the tax code to encourage the victim of injury to pursue and, through the legal system, penalize the tortfeasor. Racial discrimination, for example, might be deemed so abhorrent that some might argue that private action against it ought to receive tax-favored treatment. Nonetheless, Section 104(a)(2) is scarcely limited to personal injuries that strike at a society's fundamental values, nor have the pro-taxpayer results in discrimination cases been justified in those terms. In sum, it seems clear that no policy justifies the breadth of the existing exclusion. Accordingly, it is not surprising that courts, faced with the broad language of Section 104(a)(2) and the absence of any policy moorings, have been willing to permit exclusion to an ever-expanding array of personal injury awards. But the exclusions grow increasingly problematic as Section 104(a)(2) encompasses more and more employment-related awards where traditional tax analysis would lead to the conclusion that taxable compensation was paid.

May the compensation element in such awards be identified and taxed? First, consider the position and role of the courts. As noted, the language of the Section 104(a)(2) is broad; the exclusion extends literally to "any damages received on account of personal injury." Given the return-of-capital concept that prompted enactment of the original statute, it might be argued that the exclusion should apply only where the taxpayer can identify some property interest that has been damaged and is being restored by the award. Such an approach, for example, would clearly eliminate any exclusion for lost wages and punitive damages, and perhaps for pain and suffering as well. But the return-of-capital concept was flawed to begin with. Why overturn settled law in favor of a fundamentally unworkable concept?

Alternatively, the courts might seek to limit the exclusion to physical injuries, consistent with the probable intention of the drafters of the original statute. Such an approach rewrites a statute that Congress has clearly chosen to leave as is. * * * It is for Congress to establish tax policy, and thus it is Congress that must address the burgeoning of the Section 104(a)(2) exclusion.

The Code is replete with provisions that carve out exceptions to general tax rules. There would likely be little quarrel with a Congressional decision to exclude from income for humanitarian reasons a limited category of personal injury awards.[133] * * * Any special treatment provided must be seen as equitable, must be administratively feasible, and must be drafted so that clear guidance is given to taxpayers and the Service as to the specific circumstances that give rise to the favored treatment. The design of the special provisions should also hew as closely as possible to general tax principles underlying the income tax code. For example, increased personal exemptions could be granted to persons with objectively verifiable disabilities; the exemption could vary depending on the degree of disability, and could be phased out beyond certain income levels. Consistent with existing preferences for the blind and elderly, such an approach would have the further advantage of treating disabled persons equally for tax purposes, regardless of the cause of the disability (tortious injury, birth defect, etc.) and regardless of whether compensation had been received for the disability. Under such an approach, all recoveries for personal injuries would be taxable, except reimbursement of nondeductible medical expenses. As an alternative approach, the lost wages component of a damage award could be specifically subject to tax, along with any amount of punitive damages awarded. Such an approach would be consistent with the general tax principle that substitutes for ordinary income shall be taxed as ordinary income, and also with the *Glenshaw Glass* view of income. Where an award compensated for lost wages over a number of years, an income-averaging rule could be adopted to mitigate the bunching effect. As another alternative, an exclusion could be patterned on Section 105(c) and limited to what are

---

133. Even among its related provisions in Sections 104 and 105, Section 104(a)(2) is noteworthy in its breadth. Section 104(a)(1) is limited to workers' compensation awards. Section 104(a)(3) excludes employee-financed accident or health insurance. Exclusions under Section 105 for employer-financed insurance are limited to medical expenses incurred by the employee and to certain permanent disability or disfigurement payments. Whatever the merits of such exclusions—and they are admittedly debatable—embedding them in the context of workers' compensation, or accident or health insurance, surely restrains their expansion and the ease with which they may be manipulated. Section 104(a)(4), as limited by Section 104(b), and Section 104(a)(5) provide exclusions only for certain military disability pensions and certain victims of terrorist attacks, and are clearly quite narrow in their application.

presumably the most serious injuries—those that cause permanent disability or disfigurement.

The final suggestion might offer the most promise of a policy-based tax treatment of damages for personal injuries or sickness. The fundamental difficulty with Section 104(a)(2) is that it is not grounded in any sound tax policy. One solution would be to simply eliminate Section 104(a)(2), so that all such damages are taxed in full, as ordinary income in the year received. Such a solution may lack political appeal; it definitely lacks consistency with companion provisions in Section 104 and 105. The major problems with Section 104(a)(2) can successfully be addressed by narrowing its scope in a manner generally consistent with Sections 104 and 105. The Section 104(a)(2) exclusion for personal injuries or sickness should be no greater than that provided by other provisions of Section 104 and Section 105. Section 104(a)(3) and Section 105 distinguish between the tax treatment of proceeds of health and accident insurance based on whether the insurance is employer-provided or employee-provided. As between the two, the damages received by a tort victim may be better analogized to employer-provided insurance, since in both instances the recipient has no after-tax "investment" attributable to the amounts received. If the analogy is accepted, then consistent with Section 104(a)(3) and 105, the damages received under Section 104(a)(2) should be includable in income—except to the extent they are attributable to amounts expended for medical care in a manner similar to Section 105(b), and except to the extent they are attributable to permanent disability or disfigurement in a manner similar to Section 105(c). Such an approach would end the exclusion for non-physical injuries and for physical injuries that are not serious ones, yet would maintain a compassionate response for recoveries on account of the most serious physical injuries. It remains true, of course, that Section 104(a)(1) would continue to exclude amounts received under workers' compensation acts without limitations such as those contained in Section 105, and workers' compensation may be viewed as employer-provided insurance. Nonetheless, the tax treatment of workers' compensation may reflect its historic concern for employment conditions in or related to the workplace, and the favorable tax treatment is circumscribed by the requirement that compensation be under a workers' compensation act. Whether the distinction warrants different tax treatment may be debatable, but the distinction itself is apparent. The Section 104(a)(2) exclusion may thus be limited in a fashion consistent with Section 104(a)(3) and Section 105, and as a result may achieve a consistency, rationality, and policy basis that it sorely lacks now.

Notes and Questions

1.   What was the background to the initial adoption of the statutory exclusion of personal injury awards?

2. The predecessor of section 104(a)(2) was enacted in 1918. Solicitor's Memoranda in 1919 and 1920 took relatively restrictive views of the scope of the exclusion, ruling that damages for libel and alienation of affection constituted gross income, and expressing the view that the statutory exclusion was limited to cases of physical injury. What was the impact of the Supreme Court's decision in *Eisner v. Macomber*, decided later in 1920?

3. Does the fact that underlying concepts of gross and taxable income have changed since *Eisner v. Macomber* was decided mean that the administrative interpretation of the scope of the section 104(a)(2) exclusion should be reexamined?

4. *Nonphysical personal injuries.* Professors Burke & Friel argue that when first enacted, the predecessor of section 104(a)(2) was interpreted as limiting the exclusion to damages in case of physical injury or sickness. Whatever Congress intended in 1918, Congress now seems ready to adopt that position. As noted above, in 1995 Congress passed legislation, vetoed by President Clinton because of other provisions in the bill, that would have ended the exclusion of damages that compensate for nonphysical injuries or sickness.

Assuming section 104(a)(2) is to be continued in some form, should the exclusion be limited to physical injuries? How would you analyze this question in terms of return of capital? In terms of humanitarian relief? In terms of administrative simplicity? Combining these considerations?

B. HUMAN CAPITAL AND OTHER TRADITIONAL JUSTIFICATIONS FOR THE EXCLUSION

The purpose of this subchapter is to examine in detail the justifications for section 104(a)(2), and, assuming there is to be an exclusion, to consider its proper scope. As Professors Burke and Friel indicated in subchapter A, from the earliest days of the income tax, even before the 1918 enactment of the predecessor to section 104(a)(2), the principal justification for exclusion has been that there is no gain, because the taxpayer's lost capital—his healthy self—has simply been restored by payment of its monetary equivalent. Professor Stephan examines the notion of human capital, giving particular attention to a problem largely ignored when the restoration-of-capital idea first appeared—the taxpayer has no obvious basis in his body, and recoveries for damage to capital usually are tax-free only to the extent of basis.

Perhaps the most questionable aspect of the section 104(a)(2) exclusion is that it protects from tax damages that replace lost earnings, even though the earnings themselves would have been taxed. The excerpt from Professor Brooks' article defends section 104(a)(2)'s treatment of recoveries for lost earnings.

Professor Dodge examines various rationales for section 104(a)(2), with particular consideration of damages to compensate for severe pain and disfigurement. Even in this most appealing case, he finds the justifications for exclusion inadequate. He argues that the tax system should look to objective material resources, not to a subjective notion of utility, as its measure of income.

FEDERAL INCOME TAXATION AND HUMAN CAPITAL
Paul B. Stephan III[*]

70 Virginia Law Review 1357, 1358-60, 1388-99, 1402-03 (1984)

Human capital, in economic terms, is equivalent to the present value of the flow of future satisfactions that an individual can command in the course of his life. Some portion of this capital constitutes endowment, the biological and social inheritance that accompanies a person into the world. The remainder is acquired through individual action, such as education, on-the-job training, migration, and health care, or stems from exogenous changes such as technological or social transformation.[1] When one talks of human capital as a variety of income for taxation purposes, the discussion centers on net changes in the value of human capital over an accounting period rather than the value of capital possessed at any one time.[2]

For example, assume that a college graduate can expect to earn a constant annual income of $20,000 for fifty years. Using a ten percent discount rate (for simplicity more than for realism), these future earnings have a present value of $198,200 (if the salary is paid at the end of each year). Assume also that if the student goes to law school for three years instead of immediately entering the work force, he can earn $40,000 annually for the remaining forty-seven years of his working life. If the student wishes to maximize his wealth and if no other considerations apply, he would attend law school as long as the present value of its costs (forgone earnings plus direct expenses) were less than the present value of the increase in expected earnings. If the only direct expense were annual tuition of $10,000, the

---

[*]. At time of original publication, Associate Professor, University of Virginia School of Law.

1. For the classical treatment of labor inputs to the production process, *see* A. MARSHALL, PRINCIPLES OF ECONOMICS 680-88 (8th ed. 1920); 2 J.S. MILL, PRINCIPLES OF POLITICAL ECONOMY 346-81 (5th ed. 1901); 1 A. SMITH, THE WEALTH OF NATIONS 5-18, 104-24 (J.E.T. Rogers ed. 1880). For more recent discussions of human capital, see G. BECKER, HUMAN CAPITAL (2d ed. 1975); M. FRIEDMAN & S. KUZNETS, INCOME FROM INDEPENDENT PROFESSIONAL PRACTICE (1945); L. Thurow, Investment in Human Capital (1970); Schultz, *Investment in Human Capital*, 51 AM. ECON. REV. 1 (1961); Schultz, *Capital Formation by Education*, 68 J. POL. ECON. 571 (1960).

2. Economic income is generally held to comprise consumption (measured in dollar terms) plus net changes in the value of savings (also reduced to dollar values), during the relevant accounting period (typically one year). See H. SIMONS, PERSONAL INCOME TAXATION 50 (1938). Using this equation, consumption can be defined as income (receipts less the cost of producing current receipts) minus savings (or plus disinvestment). See Andrews, *A Consumption-Type or Cash Flow Personal Income Tax*, 87 HARV. L. REV. 1113, 1120 (1974).

student would "pay" $30,000 a year (because he cannot collect earnings while in law school) for the right to increase his subsequent earnings by $20,000 annually. Because the present value of the return ($148,600) exceeds that of cost ($74,000), he will go to law school unless he has an even more profitable means of investing his time and effort. The increase in human capital produced by his schooling and measured by future earnings constitutes income during the period of acquisition, just as if the student owns securities that grow by a similar amount over the same period.

Under a comprehensive tax on economic income, increases in future earning power of the sort experienced by the law student should produce liability and decreases should produce deductions, even though the investor will also pay tax on earnings when received. Compare changes in human capital to a bond that increases in value as market interest rates decline: under current law the bond's gain will not be taxed unless the holder realizes it by selling the bond, but in theory realization is an administrative concern rather than an essential element of income. Similarly, changes in the value of human capital also constitute economic gain, albeit unrealized.

* * *

Exclusions for Injury Compensation
Current Law and Early Rationalizations
* * *

In the early years of the federal tax the government had difficulty treating any type of capital recovery as income, especially in cases where segregating the portion of gain accrued before adoption of the sixteenth amendment was impracticable. Characterization of the human body as a "kind of capital," albeit based more on analogies to physical goods than on any abstract notion of future income flows, thus led to exclusion of proceeds from the conversion of any part of this asset. When the Revenue Act of 1918 ratified this result by expressly excluding personal injury compensation from taxation, the Solicitor of Internal Revenue explained that Congress meant to endorse the analogy of the human body to a tangible capital asset.

The Concept of Basis Applied to Human Capital
Today the conceptual framework for taxing capital recoveries seems clearer. Unless some nonrecognition provision applies, conversion of a capital asset produces income to the extent that the amount realized exceeds adjusted basis. Adjusted basis, though sometimes dauntingly complex in its calculation, normally equals those acquisition costs not already deducted. Significant exceptions exist for inherited property, which under Section 1014 normally has a basis equal to the property's value at the time of the previous owner's death. * * *

Society might wish to follow this pattern by treating human capital as investment property and by specifying a basis for it. Two problems immediately arise. Should human capital basis reflect the inherited property * * * rules of Sections 1014? * * * To what extent should partial liquidations constitute basis recovery? Answering these formal tax structure questions will suggest a solution to the problem of taxing personal injury recoveries.

The Basis of Endowment

Human capital can be described as having two components: endowment inherited at birth and changes resulting from lifetime events. The endowment component is analogous to inherited property, and therefore might have imputed to it a basis equal to its value at birth. Of course, the rule embodied in Section 1014, generally although not completely accurately described as one of stepped-up basis, has been the target of tax reformers for many years. Its critics see the rule as a loophole through which large amounts of accumulated gain escape income taxation, permitting the small portion of the population that inherits substantial wealth to escape its fair share of the tax burden. It may seem perverse to extend such a principle, under fire in its own domain, to the context of human capital.

An important difference between the two contexts, however, is that for transactions to which Section 1014 applies there exists an alternative rule, by which the recipient of inherited property assumes the previous owner's basis. For the endowment or "inherited" portion of human capital, the alternative of carryover basis is unavailable because no method exists for imputing an individual's biological and social inheritance to a previous owner. As a result, the endowment portion of human capital must have a basis equal either to its value or to zero.

One argument for using a zero basis points to the problem of calculating depreciation. Human capital has an ascertainable useful life, and the normal pattern of capital cost recovery would permit an annual deduction to amortize the taxpayer's basis. If everyone's human capital had a nonzero basis, then separate calculations of these values for depreciation purposes would be necessary. A few ingenious taxpayers have attempted to do just this, but taxing authorities have shown no sympathy for their arguments.

It is possible, however, to accord a positive basis to the endowment portion of human capital while dispensing with a depreciation deduction. We might decide that some combination of the technical obstacles to valuing human capital and the moral difficulties engendered by imputing different opportunities to individuals from birth justifies assigning a uniform value to everyone's endowment. If we then used straight-line methods and a standard, rather than individualized, life expectancy, everyone would have the same deduction every year, in which case the deduction could be ignored.[76] A cruder, but perhaps more satisfying version of this point is that individual differences among ideal human capital depreciation deductions are

---

76. Giving every taxpayer an identical deduction does not mean identical tax savings. Rather, it is equivalent to increasing the zero-bracket amount, a change in rate structure that reduces progressivity. A decision to ignore uniform human capital depreciation implies a choice either to make the system less progressive than it appears, or to compensate by decreasing the nominal zero-bracket amount.

too small to warrant their calculation, but that large variations caused by abnormal disruptions in life patterns might command our attention.

* * *

The Basis of Accumulated Human Capital

As with the endowment component, the rules governing recovery of lifetime human capital investments could try to identify major departures from the normal career path without adjusting for minor variations in taxpayers' gains and losses. The normal pattern for attributing basis to a capital good is to sum undeducted acquisition costs and other undeducted capital expenditures. * * *

So far we have established the plausibility of treating human capital as a kind of investment with a positive but nonamortizable basis. In conventional business environments, the law usually requires taxpayers to document the basis of intangible assets and treats all recoveries as gain if no basis is proved. For the more universal but more complex phenomenon of human capital, however, the system might appropriately assume the existence of some basis and hold in abeyance the issue of value. The assumption that everyone starts with the same endowment, even though it beggars reality, both simplifies the problem and avoids the need for otherwise useless record keeping by the mass of taxpayers who might anticipate accidents. Businesses, by contrast, keep track of costs for reasons besides taxpaying, and hence can more easily bear a documentation requirement.

Timing of Basis Recovery in Partial Liquidations

Only the problem of basis allocation in partial liquidations remains. Life insurance benefits and wrongful death recoveries aside, most injury compensation involves partial impairments of human capital. In the analogous area of incomplete sales of property, a range of rules exists for allocation proceeds between basis and profit. When the transferor separates income interests from remainders, the system often allocates no basis to the income interests. In the case of part-gifts, part-sales to charities, and partial conversions of an asset, it imposes a pro-rata rule that imputes to the sale proceeds the same fraction of basis recovery as the ratio of total basis to the property value. For many transactions, however, the rules treat all proceeds as nontaxable capital recoveries until the basis is exhausted.

The early case of Burnet v. Logan[81] typifies this basis-first rule. * * *

The variety of allocation rules used by the tax system makes impossible the designation of one rule as a norm and disparagement of all others as departures from ideal income taxation. At one time or another Congress has applied variations on all three rules -- income-first, pro-rata allocation, and basis-first -- to annuities, an important standardized transaction. In view of the enormous valuation problems, the basis-first rule makes as much sense as any for partial liquidation of human capital.

---

81. 283 U.S. 404 (1931).

A marriage of the presumption that all taxpayers have a substantial basis in their human capital to a rule allocating the proceeds from partial liquidations first to capital recovery supports the exclusion of most, if not all, individual injury compensation awards. The award, whether a tort or insurance recovery, simply replaces basis, and so as a matter of income definition should fall outside the tax base.

The Problem of Imputed Profit in Human Capital Recoveries

Saying that some, perhaps even the majority, of awards constitute nontaxable capital recoveries does not explain in comprehensive income taxation terms the failure to identify those awards that do exceed whatever basis we might impute to human capital. Recall the hypothetical law student. Half of his human capital upon graduation can be attributed to his law course, and about four-fifths of this component can be attributed either to subsidies or to forgone earnings, neither of which usually produces additions to basis. If a compensable injury suddenly reduced the student's earning potential by two-thirds, a significant portion of the recovery, in the make-believe world where we measure such things, would constitute gain. Yet the present tax system excludes the recovery from income.

Some of this apparent gain is a cashing in of the value of subsidized education, and its taxation might run contrary to the general pattern of not taxing in-kind government transfers. On the other hand, converting an in-kind benefit (education) into cash may eliminate the obvious administrative obstacle of valuation, and there may be no other reason for not taxing the conversion of the subsidy into cash.[86] Just as the recipient of free cheese who turns around and sells his handout theoretically should include the proceeds in income, the realized value of subsidized education embodied in injury compensation might be characterized as a taxable gain.

The dilemma is that identifying the gain portion of a recovery for injury is prohibitively costly in most circumstances. The problem is similar to that of mixed-motive business expenses such as entertainment, business clothing, and commuting, where segregation of personal consumption (nondeductible) and investment (deductible) may be impossible. The choice is between over taxation and under taxation, and one can only guess which rule errs more frequently or more dramatically. Under the basis-first approach it is consistent to assume that a substantial portion of most injury compensation represents a tax-free capital recovery. This presumption of nonincludibility produces fewer "wrong" results—those inconsistent with the model of human capital recovery—than would the opposite rule.

---

86. Cf. Haverly v. United States, 513 F.2d 224 (7th Cir.), cert. denied, 423 U.S. 912 (1975) (free sample of books not included in income until "converted" through charitable contribution).

Some Special Cases

Although the difficulty of identifying profit in human capital recoveries makes a nonincludibility presumption very powerful, it need not be irrebuttable. The next section deals with categories of injuries where the profit element seems strong enough to suggest an opposite presumption. Here I will discuss some forms of recovery that might trigger tax liability regardless of the injury that they compensate.

Imputed Interest

Sometimes injury compensation may take the form of several payments, either a fixed number or regularly for an indefinite period such as the victim's life. Current law permits taxpayers to exclude installment payments of injury compensation if the compensation otherwise is exempt from taxation. Yet such payments have an interest component as the payor takes on a banking role by postponing full realization of the purchase price. When the number of payments is fixed, an internal interest rate can be used to identify taxable income. Outside the area of injury compensation, the trend in recent legislation has been toward accounting for the interest component of installment payments.

* * *

Earnings Replacements

Distinguishing sudden losses of human capital from normal erosion is a more difficult problem. As argued above, a depreciation deduction for normal human capital loss is too costly to implement given the relatively small variance it would produce in individual tax liabilities. Large, lump-sum losses, however, produce greater variations, and employing the presumptions described above, cost little to measure. But when disability payments are contingent on continuing inability to work and extend for roughly the same period in roughly the same amounts as the salary replaced, then the victim may not have suffered a loss. His situation resembles that of an uninjured person, whose human capital erodes gradually with age.

Prolonged earnings replacement payments, however, do not always fully compensate human capital losses. Injuries may affect both the ability to earn and the ability to enjoy. Although market analogues provide less help for measuring the latter than the former, each has a capital value. The victims of such injuries might treat some portion of earnings replacements as recovery of lost future enjoyment even though the payments purport to substitute for earning abilities.

Without a suitable mechanism to assign money value to single-injury losses of earnings and enjoyment capital, it is impossible to develop a tax rule that accurately identifies the capital recovery, and hence the excludible portion of periodic compensation payments. A few rules of thumb might be practicable, however. We could distinguish injuries that affect only working life expectancy, but not life expectancy, as an admittedly rough way to distinguish between earnings and enjoyment capital. * * *

Deductions for the Costs of Injuries

Not all injuries result in compensation. Gaps in insurance or tort coverage will force some individuals to absorb the cost of sudden losses. If the pattern of taxation for injuries to property carried over to human capital, a taxpayer would be entitled to deduct whatever basis he might have in the lost asset. Without a direct method of measuring human capital and its basis, however, the tax system must account for these losses indirectly, if at all. Two costs that may coincide with human capital losses, and so may act as proxies for properly allowable deductions, are insurance and medical expenses. To the extent that deductions for these two items fulfill this function, they are consistent with, rather than departures from, a broad-based tax on income.

Insurance Costs

One way to look at insurance is as a gambling pool where gross "winnings" (compensation for injuries) are something less than total "wagers" (insurance premiums). Although gambling and insurance are opposites in how they distribute risk, they are similar (and formally distinguishable from all other investments) in that they are designed only to distribute risk, and not to seek other gains from trade. It is critical to the comparison that, aside from the service charge levied by the industry, the pool is a zero-sum game. In other words, insurance, like gambling, invites the tax collector to ignore individual risk preferences and to look only at the expected value of the investor's return, which unlike almost all profit-seeking contexts, is invariably a figure less than the investment.

If winnings and losses are distributed randomly across income and marginal-tax-rate levels, a hypothesis that is as plausible as any, and if premium payments are deductible profit-seeking expenses, an assumption to which I return, then absent transaction costs the government will be indifferent between a rule that deducts premium payments and includes compensation in income, and one that does not deduct payments but excludes payments from income. If the enterprise involves only risk distribution, the rules will produce equivalent revenues and will have equivalent distributional effects among income classes, although not among particular individuals. When transaction costs are considered, the no-deduction, no-income rule seems superior. It dispenses with two difficult tax issues that otherwise would increase record keeping, uncertainty, and dispute-resolution costs for many taxpayers.[g]

* * *

Medical Expenses

Medical expenses can not only be investments in future well-being, but can also replace something lost. The amount of medical care may measure, albeit imprecisely, the extent of this loss. One way to look at these expenses

---

g. Compare the discussion in Chapter Eight, especially Note #3. (Eds.)

is as self-compensation in the absence of insurance or tort remedies. A deduction for outlays puts the self-compensator on the same footing as the person who excludes injury compensation provided by others.

[T]he actual deductibility of medical expenses turns on who pays for them. Insurance reimbursements produce no income for the purchaser, and employer-obtained insurance generates deductible premiums. The patient's out-of-pocket payments, whether for medical services or for insurance to cover them, do not qualify for deduction except to the extent that they exceed a sum that grows in proportion to the taxpayer's income.

The rationale for structuring the deduction this way is similar to that for the tax treatment of insurance costs. Expenses covered by an employer more often involve serious injuries rather than self-indulgence, and serious injuries more likely entail human capital losses, especially losses of job-specific capital. If a person is unable to get his employer to pay his expenses, the tax rules in effect insist that he pay for a large portion out of his own pocket to demonstrate the seriousness of the loss. Furthermore, the amount that he must pay to signal seriousness grows with his income, because we believe either that money means less to wealthier people or that their medical expenses tend to involve a larger element of self-indulgence.

* * * [C]urrent law generally conforms to the pattern of human capital taxation outlined in this article. Taxpayers can deduct medical expenses when especially good reasons exist to believe that outlays correspond to a loss of human capital to which we most easily can assign a positive basis. Viewed from this perspective, the medical expense deduction looks less like a departure from a norm of comprehensive income taxation, and more like a refinement of the concept of taxable income to reflect losses of human capital.
* * *

DEVELOPING A THEORY OF DAMAGE RECOVERY TAXATION
Jennifer J.S. Brooks[*]
14 William Mitchell Law Review 759, 769-70, 775-80 (1988)

Excludability of compensatory recoveries makes sense if the payment is a pecuniary restoration of either (1) something the taxpayer had acquired with after-tax dollars (a recovery of basis), or (2) a nontaxable "something" the taxpayer had and lost (a return of nonincludible value). Consider an analogy to recovery for tortious conversion of plaintiff's newly-purchased graphite tennis racket. Because the plaintiff paid $400 in after-tax dollars for the racket, she has a basis of $400, and her recovery of $400 is a nontaxable return of capital. The payment is not a substitute for ordinary income, and because it exactly replaces a racket valued at $400 there is no "accession to wealth;" plaintiff has not received anything more than she had.

---

[*]. At time of original publication, Associate Professor, William Mitchell College of Law.

Her original acquisition of the racket was by a purchase with tax-paid dollars, so the recovery is not a substitute for ordinary income.

Now consider a plaintiff who is injured in an automobile accident and loses the use of his left leg. For simplicity, assume that the injury did not result in lost wages or loss of earning capacity. He accepts a settlement of $500,000. The return of basis analysis that made the previous example easy to resolve does not help this plaintiff. Yet, just as clearly, he has been "restored," if only by a monetary payment, to the status quo. He has not received anything more than he had. The taxpayer did not have a tax-paid basis in the leg, so the question is whether the recovery substitutes for ordinary income or instead for some nonincludible value. It appears that the recovery is a substitute for the nonincludible value of being physically whole—the value of having the leg, the value of its use, and the value of being free from pain.

* * *

The Problem of "Lost Earnings"

A replacement for nonincludible values may not be income, but what if part of a recovery is said to be for lost earnings? Is that part of the payment includible? A case can be made for inclusion. A payment for past lost wages is an accession to wealth that compensates the plaintiff for earnings he did not receive while away from his job during convalescence. If the earnings had been received, they would have been taxable as ordinary income. Thus, the past earnings portion of the settlement appears to be an includible substitute for ordinary income. The same analysis could apply to a payment for lost future earnings: the settlement does not replace something the plaintiff had, but instead confers something new upon him, so he has an accession to wealth; the future earnings would have been includible, so the substitute should be.

There is another way of thinking about this problem. If the "earnings" part of the settlement is conceived of as a recompense for loss of earning *capacity*, then the monetary payment restores the taxpayer to his previous status as a person with income earning potential. Economists have considered whether imputed income derived from the capitalized value of personal earning power should be included in the definition of income. In a nonslave state, personal earning power cannot be bought or sold and is not valued in market terms. Because the imputed income flowing from the earning capacity (as opposed to actual income from the exercise of that capacity) is not capable of objective measure, it is not generally included in the economic definition of income. Human capital does exist as a value; it produces imputed income; but the imputed income is ignored in the measure of taxable capacity until "actual" income occurs from the performance of labor. Other people are not taxed on either the capital value of having income-earning potential or the imputed income that flows from the capacity to earn; neither should the plaintiff in a personal injury case. The tax system really has not dealt with the problem of nonservices exchanges between human capital and market capital, but the fact that the *measure* of human capital loss may be expected future earnings should not alter the result.

A response to this argument might be that most people are taxed indirectly on their earning capacity because they pay tax every year on the monetary income produced by the exercise of their earning capacity in the performance of services. The plaintiff in a personal injury suit could be said to exercise his "earning capacity" by winning a judgment against the defendant (although payment may be in a lump sum rather than in annual increments over the plaintiff's working life). Loss of earning capacity is measured by expected future earnings because this part of the judgment is intended to substitute for ordinary income. Under this analysis, the "lost earnings" portion of an award or settlement should be includible in the plaintiff's income.

It does not seem a satisfactory answer to say that the plaintiff should be taxed on the recovery for lost earning capacity because the pursuit of his claim is the equivalent of the performance of services for another. Suppose it is possible to identify a part of the recovery as representing only the lost capital value of capacity to earn income. People normally enjoy this value tax-free, incurring tax only when the capacity is exercised by work. If an individual chooses not to work, and therefore not to transform the capacity into includible income, the unexercised capacity is not taxable. Put another way, the choice of leisure is not taxable. The capital value of earning capacity can be thought to produce both includible income from labor, and nonincludible imputed income from the choice of leisure. The plaintiff who is injured so that part of his human capital is lost, and who sues for replacement, may be pursuing the only possible course to recover the nonincludible capital values that were damaged. It does not seem to correct to equate the decision to sue with the choice of earning when a person with intact human capital has imputed income from all the human capital values, including earning capacity, and remains untaxed.

* * *

It is possible to argue that excluded capital and income values ought to be includible when the damage recovery transforms them into monetary terms. The argument is * * * based on the idea that imputed income is excluded only because it is hard to measure. Once the income is reduced to monetary values, it ought to be included. This convenience notion of income measurement has some place in the tax law; the realization requirement operates to cause income inclusion only when accretions to income are rendered fairly certain by the happening [of some] event, like a sale or exchange, that clearly identifies an accession to wealth. In the example of the tennis racket, income from the $400 is taxable if it is received as interest on investment of the funds, but excludible if received as imputed income from the use of a consumer durable. It is difficult to measure imputed income from the tennis racket, so it is excluded; the parallel income, interest from the investment, is easy to measure and so is included. Thus, the argument goes, the tax system should include cash recoveries for personal injuries on the theory that cash is includible no matter what its origin.

It is a flaw in the tax system's implementation of the accretion model that easily measured accretions to wealth are included and more difficult to measure values are excluded. An ideal accretion-type tax may be impractical; as long as accretion is a model, adjustments for practical problems of measurement are only to be expected. But the need to adapt the accretion model to everyday use does not compel inclusion of amounts simply because they are there. Returns of basis, for example, may be paid in cash but are not for that reason subject to inclusion. Substantial cash gifts to family members are not includible even though they are easy to measure. Cash payments of child support are not includible. Reference to income theory suggests reasons why these easy-to-reach transfers are excludible; convenience is not the sole arbiter of the tax base.

Exclusion of the imputed annual income from human capital until it has been translated into monetary terms by the performance of services for another provides a consistent basis for the measure of income. * * *

The plaintiff who recovers a personal injury damage award has not received a windfall that ought to be taxed. Nor is the transformation of human capital into money via the judgment a substitute for the performance of services. The injured plaintiff has lost a value that cannot be replaced like a tennis racket, because it is not a value that the economy measures in market terms. Failure to include imputed income from consumer durables is a flaw in the measurement of income that results from practical considerations, but the imputed income from human capital is outside the measurement of income. The plaintiff who recovers for lost human capital and lost imputed income from human capital is recompensed for values that lie without the market. Use of money to replace what is lost does not justify imposing tax on a person who has merely been restored (if that) to a status other taxpayers enjoy tax-free.

　　　　* * *

TAXES AND TORTS
Joseph M. Dodge[*]
77 Cornell Law Review 143, 180-88 (1992)

This Part discusses the policy issue of whether punitive damages and "noneconomic" damages, encompassing both pain-and-suffering damages in

---

[*]. At time of original publication, William H. Francis, Jr. Professor, University of Texas School of Law.

physical-injury cases and nonphysical, noneconomic torts, *should* be excludible from income.

Punitive Damages

As a matter of policy, there is little doubt that punitive damages should be included in gross income. Such damages represent an economic windfall, and do not compensate for any loss whatsoever. Punitive damages represent a pure accretion to wealth.

One argument advanced in favor of excluding punitive damages is that the exclusion might compensate the plaintiff for legal fees and other expenses, and thereby truly make the plaintiff whole. However, punitive damages have no relation, under tort law, to legal fees. The argument for excludibility would be better directed toward reforming tort law to award legal fees to plaintiffs and to create standards for punitive damages. No justification exists for excluding punitive damages in excess of legal fees.

The only other plausible argument for excluding punitive damages is that their inclusion, while retaining exclusions for compensatory damages, would create an administrative problem of distinguishing includible from excludible damages, especially when the case was settled or went to judgment without specification of the punitive damages amount. However, one could also advance this argument in favor of the proposition that compensatory damages should be included in gross income. An allocation by the parties should not control, because their "tax" interests are not necessarily opposed.[177] Nor should the plaintiff's allocation of damages in the complaint control,[178] because tax law should not unnecessarily dictate the behavior of personal-injury lawyers. With no external reference, such as a judicial decree or findings, the allocation must be made on the basis of an independent "tax" examination of the cause of action.

* * *

Recoveries for Noneconomic Harms

Section 104 currently excludes damages for pain and suffering, as well as for purely personal injuries, such as loss of privacy, loss of consortium, intentional infliction of emotional distress, and deprivation of rights. Conceptually, the damages represent a conversion of some nonmaterial benefit, such as lost "normality," peace of mind, or dignity, into cash. This is not a situation in which an exclusion could be justified as maintaining the tax status quo with respect to income from human capital. Since no "basis" exists in any recovery of this type, such damages seemingly should be fully

---

177. The defendant's payment of damages is deductible whether the damages are compensatory or punitive. Even if punitive damages were categorically nondeductible, one would not expect a settlement to accurately embody a proper allocation when the parties are subject to different tax rates.

178. If better evidence of a proper allocation cannot be found, the IRS looks to the complaint. Rev. Rul. 58-418, 1958-2 C.B. 18.

includible as pure accessions to material wealth. The burden of persuasion in the policy sense lies with the proponents of exclusion.

Some argue that these damages should not be taxed because they are a substitute for goods of a nontaxable nature, such as pleasure, pain, or normalcy. However, the "substitute for" analysis is not a policy tool. Rather, it is a doctrinal device employed to ascertain the substance of a receipt in order to determine which statutory category to apply. Moreover, in the doctrinal context, the "substitute for" analysis has limits, which have been imposed in the very area under scrutiny, section 104.[187]

If one were to apply this doctrinal device to the policy arena, it would lead nowhere, because damages for noneconomic harm are not a "substitute for" any other kind of receipt that has tax significance. They are simply damages for noneconomic harm. Nonpecuniary damages are not computed with reference to foregone consumption which would have been purchased in the market. If they were so computed, computing foregone consumption on an after-tax basis would subject the taxpayer to an implicit tax that would be preserved by an exclusion. In fact, pain-and-suffering damages compensate that which cannot be purchased. Thus, it is fundamentally misleading to call these damages "compensation"; they "replace" the irreplaceable.

A variation of the "substitute for" argument is that recoveries for noneconomic harms are mere restorations of a status quo which, in itself, would have been nontaxable as imputed income. Appeals to imputed income, however, are fruitless, because imputed income, by definition, refers to economic benefits that have not been converted to cash or property. In contrast, noneconomic damages result from a conversion to cash. It is also misleading to consider imputed income as nontaxable in the sense of being "excluded"; rather, it is simply ignored. The difference lies in the fact that excluded items are capable of creating a basis. To argue that conversions of imputed income to cash should be excluded is essentially the same as arguing that wages, which involve a conversion of leisure to labor, should be excluded. This argument actually cuts in favor of includibility; noneconomic damages are like wages for a miserable job.

One could argue that damages for noneconomic harms should not be taxed because the recovery merely replaces a loss of intangible benefits. This argument is equivalent to stating that wages are not income because they do not result in "gain," the laborer having "given up" leisure and other psychic goods to obtain wages. Of course, wages are the result of voluntary transactions, whereas pain-and-suffering damages are not. The question squarely raised, then, is whether the involuntariness of the transaction justifies not taxing the accession to wealth. One could argue for no taxation

---

187. *See Roemer v. Commissioner*, 716 F.2d 693 (9th Cir. 1983), *reviewing* 79 T.C. 398 (1982) (defamation damages measured by lost business profits are really for involuntary conversion of human capital).

by analogy to the argument for taxing recovery of lost earning capacity like wages rather than like investments. Involuntariness may be a legitimate rationale for deferral of income or perhaps deductibility of outlay, but not for total and permanent exclusion of a clearly-realized accession to wealth.

* * *

[Another] argument for excluding noneconomic recoveries is simply that the transaction, as a whole, represents a net decrease in the taxpayer's "utility." That is, the plaintiff would be in a worse, not better, position if the recovery for nonpecuniary loss were taxed. Even working in an awful job presumably entails some increase in taxpayer utility; otherwise the employment would not have been undertaken. People do not risk life and limb in the hope of obtaining noneconomic damage recoveries, presumably because such transactions are acknowledged to be "losers" or, at least too risky.

One reason for taxing transactions which generate a utility gain is that the tax, if designed properly, will not unduly inhibit socially desirable activity. It does not follow, however, that involuntary transactions should be exempt from tax. Taxing plaintiffs on noneconomic damages will, if anything, increase deterrence and net social utility, especially if courts and juries shift plaintiff taxes to defendants.

The no-utility-gain argument raises the fundamental issue of the role of "utility" in taxation. Utility in taxation must be distinguished from utility in social welfare. Progressive rates in taxation, for example, have been justified on the theory that sacrificing dollars is less burdensome, in utility terms, on the rich than it is on the poor. Similarly, the desirability of excluding employee fringe benefits can be questioned on economic efficiency grounds. Excluding nonpecuniary damage recoveries has the effect of enriching personal injury plaintiffs relative to taxpayers generally. This kind of subsidy is subject to classic "tax expenditure" analysis, but apparently no welfare economist has undertaken to justify a discrete subsidy to plaintiffs receiving noneconomic damages. Any "economic incentive" justification for the exclusion is totally implausible. A social welfare claim based, at most, on a "hunch" is not a persuasive justification for this aspect of the section 104 exclusion. Finally, the tax rule for nonpecuniary loss recoveries does not ultimately solve the social welfare equation. Even if such recoveries are taxed to plaintiffs, the legal (tort) system can compensate plaintiffs for the incremental tax burden by shifting it to defendants.

We are left with the question of whether the core concept of "income" is ultimately tied to that of "utility." In practice, and ignoring "tax expenditure" provisions, the concept of income is *not* systematically tied to subjective utility, as opposed to changes in objective net wealth. Imputed income from consumer durables, as well as the value of self-provided services and leisure, is ignored. Income is taxed to the person who earns and controls it, not the person who enjoys it. Amounts includible are measured by market transactions, not subjective worth. Deductions, like medical expenses and casualty loss, can be rationalized on a non-utility basis. Other deductions, such as those for charitable contributions and taxes, are allowed despite substantial utility to the taxpayer.[208]

It is not obvious that the income tax *base*, as opposed to government policy in general, *should* be tied to utility in any normative sense, though influential commentators operating out of the tradition of Utilitarian welfare economics have made the connection. Though government policy may rely on utility analysis, and although virtually all items considered to be gross income potentially yield utility to the taxpayer (or to the taxpayer's family and friends), it does not logically follow that the tax base should be equated with utility. The tax base should be equated with material resources that can be appropriated by government for redistributive purposes, or, perhaps, with material resources that represent a claim against society's store of scarce resources. These concepts of the tax base are objective *in principle*, not merely as an expedient. Government, which is supported mostly by taxes, has no interest in appropriating utility directly from taxpayers. Utility is subjective; that is, the utility "curves" of various individuals differ. Therefore, the government cannot transfer utility; it can only deal in money and property. Finally, as a normative concept, "income" is rendered much weaker by burdening it with goals that are unobtainable for practical or political reasons.

* * *

Wrongful Death Recoveries

Recoveries that accelerate tax-free receipts of money or property are *prima facie* candidates for exclusion. The best examples are wrongful death actions, where the recovery is for the lost tax-free support, gifts, and inheritance, which would have derived from the *decedent's* human capital. However, the amount of such support actually received would have been "after-tax" amounts; that is, such sums would have been reduced by the decedent's own income taxes before given to the recipients. Therefore, wrongful death recoveries should be treated like recoveries for other personal injuries.

If the survivor of a deceased plaintiff succeeds to the plaintiff's cause of action, any recovery by the survivor should not be treated as a tax-free bequest or inheritance. Instead, the recovery should be treated as "income in respect of a decedent," meaning that the survivor would step into the decedent's shoes for tax purposes.

* * *

---

208. Utility plays a marginal role in distinguishing "personal" from "business" expenses. *See* Treas. Reg. § 1.183-2(b)(9) (1972) (personal pleasure is one factor in determining whether activity is "not for profit").

Notes and Questions

Return of capital

5.   Numerous arguments beyond tradition are advanced in support of the exclusion of personal injury awards, although critics claim an answer to each. As noted in the Burke & Friel excerpt in Subchapter A, as early as 1918 the return-of-capital theory was put forward by the Attorney General, and this theory remains one of the most-cited justifications of the exclusion. Personal injury awards, it is argued, constitute a return of capital, not a gain but restoration of something the taxpayer already had.

6.   In the usual case, if a taxpayer's capital asset is damaged or destroyed, the loss being compensated by insurance or a tortfeasor, the taxpayer would recognize gain to the extent that the amount received exceeded the taxpayer's basis in the asset. (Recognition of gain might be avoided through a statutory nonrecognition provision, such as section 1033; see Note #11 below.) Assuming the taxpayer received fair market value, which is the usual measure of insurance or tort recovery, the taxpayer would not have gained by the conversion of the capital asset to its monetary equivalent. Nevertheless, the conversion would constitute occasion for taxing unrealized appreciation (value in excess of basis). Given the importance of basis in the normal scheme, what are the implications for the return-of-capital theory as applied to personal injury awards?

7.   Normally, basis equals cost, and taxpayers are usually not regarded as having a basis in their own bodies. Professor Stephan argues that a novel application of accepted principles can lead to a determination that such a basis exists. What role is afforded inherited endowment under Professor Stephan's approach? Once he argues for a basis in a wasting asset (the human body and endowment), what is Professor Stephan's justification for ignoring depreciation? Do you agree that serious moral questions would attach to giving one taxpayer a higher basis than another in the taxpayer's *self*?

8.   If one accepts the human capital concept, yet agrees to ignore depreciation because, in part, of an assumption of a standard life expectancy, should an adjustment be made for taxpayers who die prematurely? Who live longer than expected? Compare Code section 72(b)(2) and (3), which make adjustments in the tax treatment of annuitants depending upon their *ex post* individualized longevity.

9.   Given the difficulty (impossibility?) of computing the taxpayer's basis in his human capital, and given the usual rule that a taxpayer can exclude damages only to the extent of basis, how can Professor Stephan argue that most personal injury awards should be fully excluded?

10. Do you find Professor Stephan's sophisticated approach to the basis problem appealing, or can his arguments be swept aside by the following no-nonsense language of Professor Mark Cochran?:

> The return of capital argument is appealing, especially in the case of damages awarded for loss of a limb or organ. This type of injury graphically illustrates the concept of "human capital." The problem with this analogy is that a return of capital is excluded from gross income only to the extent of the taxpayer's basis. * * * However, in the personal injury context, the taxpayer's basis is zero, because a taxpayer generally does not pay for his limb or organs. * * * Actually, it is unnecessary to speculate about whether a taxpayer has a basis in the various parts of his body. A personal injury award does not pay a taxpayer for the damage to his or her body per se; rather, the taxpayer is compensated for consequent economic loss (i.e., lost earnings) and, in some instances, pain and suffering. Such compensation clearly falls outside the scope of the return of capital concept, since no capital is being exchanged for the award.[h]

11. *Involuntary conversion.* To what degree should we be willing to bend usual rules of taxable income because of the involuntary nature of the conversion of well being into money. Contrast, for example, the voluntary conversion of leisure into earned income.

As discussed in Note #6 above, even in the case of involuntary conversion the usual rule is that income must be recognized if the amount realized from the conversion exceeds the taxpayer's basis in the asset converted. There are some relief provisions—notably section 1033—but the relief is conditioned on replacement of the converted property plus carryover of basis. These limitations suggest that Congress envisioned a postponement of tax rather than a complete forgiveness, such as that granted by section 104(a)(2). Professor Lawrence Frolik has observed:

> One simply does not purchase a new spouse to replace an injured one, and therefore, section 104(a)(2) might be seen as an extension of the principle exemplified in section 1033. * * * Still,
> * * * [w]hile section 1033 merely postpones recognition of the gain,
> * * * section 104(a)(2) permanently excludes the gain. * * *
>
> The expectation that lost consortium or lost parenting will not be replaced evokes two, almost paradoxical, observations. On one hand, it symbolizes the reason for section 104(a)(2). The involuntary nature of the conversion, the lack of satisfactory in-kind replacement services, and the tax-free nature of the services

---

h. Mark W. Cochran, *Should Personal Injury Damage Awards Be Taxed?*, 38 CASE WEST. L. REV. 43, 45-46 (1987).

for which a damage award substitutes, all argue the wisdom, if not the necessity, of section 104(a)(2). Conversely, the receipt of a tax-free damage award presents the claimant with the complete panoply of available consumption choices.[i]

Lost earnings

12. Many tort recoveries compensate the victim for lost past or future earnings. As contrasted with other elements of damage, such as pain and suffering, the compensation takes the place of something that would have been taxed had the injury not occurred. Taxpayers are not taxed on being free from pain, and therefore arguably should not be taxed on receiving the monetary equivalent of this state of well being; by contrast, taxpayers are taxed on earnings, and arguably should be taxed when they receive as tort damages the monetary equivalent.[j] Section 104(a)(2) excludes such damages, but should it?

13. Professor Douglas Chapman repudiates the suggestion that damages for lost earnings should be protected from tax on humanitarian grounds: "[I]t seems only too logical that a plaintiff, fully compensated for injuries not based on earnings, needs no more humanitarianism than any other taxpayer who is required to pay his annual extraction on his earnings."[k]

14. Professor Brooks, in her article excerpted above, argues that recoveries for lost earnings can be thought of as recoveries for harm done to earning capacity, measured by expected future earnings. An uninjured taxpayer has a choice concerning whether this capacity is to be converted into taxable earnings; the tort victim, by contrast, receives monetary damages or nothing. How might this analysis lead one to conclude that a tort recovery for lost earnings merits exclusion? Do you find Professor Brooks' analysis persuasive?

15. *Humanitarian considerations.* An oft-cited observation of a generation ago—still applicable today—is that "the treatment of lost earnings is rooted in emotional and traditional, rather than logical, factors. * * * [I]t is contended * * * that the taxation of recoveries carved from pain and suffering is offensive, and the victim is more to be pitied rather than taxed."[l]

---

i. Lawrence A. Frolik, *Personal Injury Compensation as a Tax Preference*, 37 ME. L. REV. 1, 20-21 (1985).

j. For a forceful repudiation of the "in lieu of what" test in interpreting section 104(a)(2), *see* Patricia T. Morgan, *Old Torts, New Torts and Taxes: The Still Uncertain Scope of Section 104(a)(2)*, 48 LA. L. REV. 875 (1988).

k. Douglas K. Chapman, *No Pain—No Gain? Should Personal Injury Damages Keep Their Tax Exempt Status?*, 9 U. ARK. LITTLE ROCK L.J. 407, 428 (1986-87).

l. Bertram Harnett, *Torts and Taxes*, 37 N.Y.U. L. REV. 614, 626-27 (1952).

Is favorable tax treatment justified on humanitarian grounds, as is frequently contended? Does it matter what sort of injury is being compensated? For example, should favorable tax treatment be reserved for those who suffer severe and permanent physical injury (as Burke & Friel suggested in subchapter A)? Or should the severity of injury merely affect the amount of damages awarded, not their tax treatment? Note that an exclusion based on humanitarian grounds should be viewed as a tax expenditure, while an exclusion based on the return of capital theory could be viewed as neutral application of tax principles.

16. It can be argued very plausibly that victims of personal injury, even after receiving monetary compensation as determined by the tort system, are worse off than before the injury. Does Professor Dodge think that such a decline in the taxpayer's "utility" justifies excluding the monetary damages received?

The uncompensated victim

17. Assume that one concludes that section 104(a)(2) strikes the proper balance between uninjured taxpayers and tort victims who receive monetary compensation. Nevertheless, one is left with the paradox that favorable tax treatment is made available to the compensated tort victim but not to the uncompensated victim.

If the explanation for section 104(a)(2) is tax-free return of capital, the logic of the argument would lead us to expect a deduction for the uncompensated victim's loss of capital. After all, such a deduction need not be limited to income-producing assets; for example, casualty and theft losses of non-income-producing property are deductible.[m]

18. If the explanation for section 104(a)(2) is humanitarian concern—that is, the provision is a tax expenditure—it is extraordinary that this concern should be limited to the most fortunate subset of injury victims, those who are compensated. If one takes into account the vagaries of the tort system, and recognizes that extraneous factors may lead to vastly differing compensation amounts for similarly injured persons,[n] present law becomes even more difficult to defend: The biggest tax benefit goes to the subset of the subset who receive a *large* tort recovery. At the other extreme, tort victims injured by a "judgment proof" defendant—no matter how seriously—not only receive no damages, but also no tax benefit.

---

m. Section 165(c)(3). This is an itemized deduction. Even for taxpayers who itemize, a full deduction is not allowed due to the limitations of section 165(h); indeed, most taxpayers who suffer a casualty loss can claim no deduction due to these limitations.

n. *See, e.g.*, Philip D. Oliver, *Once Is Enough: A Proposed Bar of the Injured Employee's Cause of Action Against a Third Party*, 58 FORDHAM L. REV. 117, 159-71 (1989).

Indeed, why should tax relief be limited to accident victims? What of those who suffer as a result of birth defects or illness?

19. Is the objection to allowing tax benefits to the uncompensated victim only administrative simplicity? Certainly an unlimited deduction for personal injury would be unthinkable. How much deduction for a headache? For tennis elbow? And, if section 104(a)(2) continues to apply to some nonphysical harms, how large a deduction should be allowed for the uncompensated hurt that arises from being "stood up" by a date?

20. Do you find attractive the Burke & Friel approach, discussed in subchapter A, which attempts to tie the tax benefit to the disability, regardless of how it arose?

Punitive damages
21. Almost all commentators agree with Professor Dodge that punitive damages *should* be taxed, even if compensatory damages are excluded. Such damages, he argues in the excerpt above, "represent an economic windfall, and do not compensate for any loss whatever."

22. Professor Patricia Morgan, on the other hand, emphasizes that tort damages defy ready division into damages to make the plaintiff whole and those that punish the defendant. With regard to punitive damages, Professor Morgan points to a recent American Bar Association commission, which recommended that punitive damages in excess of "a reasonable portion of the punitive damages award to compensate the plaintiff and counsel for bringing the action and prosecuting the punitive damages claim" be "allocated to public purposes."[o] Professor Morgan asserts that if the ABA proposal were universally adopted, "the Service would agree that the portion of the 'punitive damages' that is allocated to the plaintiff is compensatory and therefore excludable."[p]

An alternative view might be that the ABA proposal contemplates compensating the plaintiff not for personal injuries, but for industry in prosecuting a claim that benefits the public. (The public benefit is both direct, through obtaining a portion of the punitive award for the public fisc, and indirect, through punishment and deterrence of bad actors.) By this analysis, the punitive award is similar to earned income, and the exclusion of section 104(a)(2) would not be merited.

Which treatment of punitive damages awarded under the ABA proposal would constitute better tax policy?

---

o. Report to the House of Delegates of the American Bar Association Action Commission to Improve the Tort Liability System, 18-19 (February, 1987), *quoted in* Patricia T. Morgan, *supra* note j, at 929.

p. *Id.*

23. The present state of the law regarding taxation of punitive damages in personal injury cases is not altogether clear. The Commissioner appeared to rule in Rev. Rul. 75-45[q] that punitive as well as compensatory damages were excluded by section 104(a)(2), then reverse position nine years later to hold, in Rev. Rul. 84-108,[r] that punitive damages were not excluded.

In 1989, Congress added an ambiguous final sentence to section 104(a): "Paragraph (2) shall not apply to any punitive damages in connection with a case not involving physical injury or sickness." This does not, however, mean that punitive damages in physical injury cases are necessarily to be excluded from income. The statutory language speaks only to cases not involving physical injury, and nothing in the legislative history indicates that Congress considered punitive damages in physical injury cases.

The trend is against the exclusion of punitive damages. As noted earlier, in 1995 Congress enacted legislation that would have explicitly removed the exclusion for punitive damages in all cases, although President Clinton vetoed the bill containing that provision. Even without legislation, courts are restricting the exclusion to compensatory damages, as seems to be required by the Supreme Court's decision in *Schleier*. The Tax Court has abandoned its position allowing punitive damages to be excluded, concluding that *Schleier* "made it clear * * * that damages which are not compensatory but punitive in nature are not excludable."[s]

24. What account should be taken of differences in state tort law? The cool judicial reception given Rev. Rul. 84-108, at least as evidenced by its prompt rejection by a federal district court in Alabama,[t] may be attributable, in part, to the questionable choice of illustrations in the ruling. Oddly, the Commissioner highlighted the least fair application of his new interpretation of section 104(a)(2). Rather than focusing on the usual case of an award of punitive damages to punish the defendant in addition to an award of compensatory damages to compensate the plaintiff, the Commissioner ruled that survivors of decedents in Alabama, whose unusual law provides that all damages in wrongful death actions are punitive, would be taxed on all wrongful death damages. Wrongful death recoveries in other states are typically compensatory, and thus would be excludable. As one commentator argued, "[t]he ruling works an unjustified and inequitable discrimination upon persons recovering for wrongful death under Alabama law, because

---

q. 1975-1 C.B. 47.

r. 1984-2 C.B. 32.

s. Bagley v. Commissioner, 105 T.C. No. 27 (1995). For a Tenth Circuit opinion rejecting the taxpayer's attempt to exclude punitive damages, which discusses decisions from other circuits and the Supreme Court's 1995 decision in *Schleier*, see O'Gilvie v. United States, 66 F.3d 1550 (10th Cir. 1995).

t. Burford v. United States, 642 F. Supp. 635 (N.D. Ala., 1986).

under Alabama law *all* wrongful death damages are considered punitive and beneficiaries receive nothing measured by any 'compensatory' standard."[u]

25. In her evaluation of the interplay of the Service's rulings with substantive tort law governing punitive damages, Professor Mary Jane Morrison contended that, properly interpreted, Rev. Rul. 75-45 provided the correct rule. That ruling properly held that punitive damages *in Alabama* were to be excluded from income, but, in the general case, "did not authorize excluding punitive damages from income."[v] She chided tax experts for reading the 1975 ruling literally, and thus too broadly: "[W]hen there is a choice between a plausible, safe, and reasonable interpretation of a ruling or opinion on the one hand, and an implausible, wild, and unusual interpretation on the other, the more conservative interpretation is preferable."[w]

In Professor Morrison's view, the Service fell from grace when it issued Rev. Rul. 84-108. While the Service properly tried to put to an end the view that punitive damages awarded in personal injury suits were excluded from gross income, the Service went too far in its reaction by asserting that even punitive damages awarded under Alabama law were to be included in income. Proper tax policy, she insisted, requires analysis that goes beyond "the label the state courts put on the awards."[x]

Assuming that compensatory damages are to be excluded, do you agree with Professor Morrison that punitive damages awarded under Alabama's punitive-damages-only wrongful death statute should be excluded? Note that the bill vetoed by President Clinton would have ended the exclusion for punitive damages, *except* in the case of preexisting state law, such as Alabama's wrongful death law, providing "that only punitive damages may be awarded."[y]

26. As Professor Dodge points out, serious administrative problems arise from an attempt to tax punitive damages while exempting compensatory damages. Most personal injury cases are resolved through

---

u. Craig S. Bonnell, *Back and Forth with the I.R.S.: Taxation of Wrongful Death Damages in Alabama*, 17 CUMB. L. REV. 53, 66 (1986). The author argued that the ruling "violates both the technical requirement of uniform application of federal tax statutes, as well as common sense uniformity." *Id.* We find the technical argument dubious, but the common sense argument quite persuasive. The author was an associate in the firm that successfully argued the *Burford* case, in which Rev. Rul. 84-108 was held invalid, and his article is essentially a brief for the taxpayer's position.

v. Mary Jane Morrison, *Getting a Rule Right and Writing a Wrong Rule: The IRS Demands a Return on All Punitive Damages*, 17 CONN. L. REV. 39, 40 (1984).

w. *Id.* at 45.

x. *Id.* at 78.

y. H.R. 2491, 104th Cong., 1st Sess. (1995). The Tax Court interprets the Supreme Court's decision in *Schleier* as requiring inclusion of punitive damages only if they "are not of a compensatory nature." Bagley v. Commissioner, 105 T.C. No. 27 (1995).

settlement. Should the parties' allocations between compensatory and punitive damages be controlling? In that case, we can suppose that all payments would be classified as compensatory, because the compensatory label would save the plaintiff money while costing the defendant nothing; the resulting tax savings would figure into the bargaining, and presumably be divided between the parties.[z]

Should we pay close attention to the pleadings?[aa] By this approach, if the plaintiff in a personal injury case requested $1 million compensatory damages and $1 million punitive damages, then half of whatever was received would be subject to tax. But what do such pleadings prove if the plaintiff subsequently settles for $20,000? What if the case is settled before suit is filed, or if the pleadings simply ask for relief to be determined by the court?

27.   Generally, a tortfeasor can deduct damages under section 162(a), because most tort payments are made for injuries caused in the course of business. Would denial of a deduction for punitive damages be appropriate? Neither fines nor the punitive two thirds of antitrust awards are deductible.[bb]

C. TRADITIONAL ANALYSIS CHALLENGED: EVALUATING THE EXCLUSION OF PERSONAL INJURY AWARDS BY NORMATIVE CRITERIA

Subchapter B is typical of most policy discussion of section 104(a)(2) in its analysis of the exclusion by reference to well established tax rules in analogous areas. For example, analysis of "human capital" is derived from rules governing capital assets, with the concept of basis given corresponding prominence. Similarly, it is argued that immediate inclusion of personal injury awards is inappropriate due to the involuntary nature of the conversion of well being to money, drawing comparison to the nonrecognition rule of section 1033. The exclusion for damages replacing lost earnings is questionable precisely because the most comparable situation—receipt of the earnings themselves—clearly would be subject to tax.

In this subchapter, Professor Griffith takes issue with this mode of analysis for tax policy generally, using as his example the taxation of personal injury awards. He argues that we should structure tax law to achieve an optimal outcome, which should be determined by reference to explicitly acknowledged ethical or normative criteria, without concern for

---

z. Randall Barkan, Comment, *Tax Treatment of Post-Termination Personal Injury Agreements*, 61 CAL. L. REV. 1237, 1252 (1973) criticizes the Tax Court's decision in *Seay v. Com'r.*, 58 T.C. 32 (1972), because it allows favorable tax treatment without a determination that the payment was in fact made for personal injury.

aa. *See* Mark W. Cochran, *1989 Tax Act Compounds Confusion Over Tax Status of Personal Injury Damages*, 49 TAX LAW. 1565 (1990).

bb. Section 162 (f) and (g).

whether the result appears inconsistent with tax principles applicable in other areas.

SHOULD "TAX NORMS" BE ABANDONED? RETHINKING TAX POLICY ANALYSIS AND THE TAXATION OF PERSONAL INJURY RECOVERIES
Thomas D. Griffith[*]

1993 Wisconsin Law Review 1115,

1116-23, 1125-27, 1129-34, 1142, 1145, 1148, 1150-52, 1155-58

Traditional tax policy analysis has focused on whether the particular tax provision under examination is consistent with basic "tax norms" such as horizontal equity, vertical equity, ability to pay and the ideal tax base, typically Haig-Simons income. These norms are not grounded, however, in more general ethical principles. This Article will argue that this is a fundamental flaw and, thus, special tax principles should be discarded as a method of evaluating tax policy. Instead, this Article recommends that the likely consequences of the policies under consideration should be determined and then judged under explicitly stated general normative principles. This approach can lead to tax policy recommendations quite different from those generated by traditional methods.

In order to explore the differences between the traditional and suggested approaches to tax policy, the analysis of the taxation of personal injury recoveries will be examined under both approaches. Under current law, damage awards for personal injuries generally are excluded from an individual's gross income. The exclusion applies to damages received for monetary losses from increased medical expenses and lost earnings, and to damages received for non-monetary losses such as pain and suffering and permanent bodily injury.

The exclusion for personal injury recoveries is a departure from the tax rule applied to business injury claims. For business injuries, courts apply an "in lieu of" test, which looks to the nature of the claim to determine the tax treatment of damages received.

If an "in lieu of" test were applied to personal recoveries, damage awards received for lost earnings presumably would be taxed as ordinary income because they replace taxable wages or salary. The proper treatment of recoveries of medical expenses under such a test, however, is less obvious. Perhaps the recipient should be taxed on the amount received and then granted a medical expense deduction. On the other hand, medical expenses arguably should be given tax-free treatment on the grounds that they replace exempt employer-provided medical services, or because they do not constitute gain because they simply restore the recipients to their pre-injury status.

---

[*]. At time of original publication, Professor of Law, University of Southern California.

Damage awards received for pain and suffering also raise thorny problems under an "in lieu of" test. Full taxation might be proper on the theory that individuals have no tax basis in their body parts, so that all amounts received constitute gain. On the other hand, an exemption might be appropriate under a return of human capital theory or simply because the recipients are no better off than they were before the injury. Excluding pain and suffering recoveries from the tax base also might be supported under an "in lieu of" test on the view that amounts received replace imputed income from good health that ordinarily is received tax free.

Tax scholars have generated a large literature exploring these issues. In general, these commentators have analyzed how personal injury recoveries would be treated under "tax principles" such as the "in lieu of" test mentioned previously, and then have considered whether any "non-tax" reasons exist for departing from these principles. There is a consensus in this literature that personal injury recoveries received as compensation for lost earnings should be fully taxed and that recoveries received for medical expenses should be tax exempt. Scholars are divided, however, regarding the proper tax treatment of recoveries for pain and suffering.

The central theme of this Article is that the basic approach to tax policy taken in the existing literature should be discarded because it is not based on any attractive general normative principles. Instead, a two-step method should be adopted. First, the consequences of alternative tax policies should be considered. Second, those consequences should be evaluated under explicitly stated ethical principles.

* * *

The conclusions reached in this Article regarding the proper treatment of personal injury recoveries are less significant than the methodology. Personal injury recoveries have been chosen not primarily because of their independent importance, but because the existing tax literature on such recoveries provides a good analysis of tax policy under the widely respected tax norms of horizontal equity and the ideal tax base. * * *

Developing a Model of Personal Injury Recoveries

Tax Exemptions as Insurance

The tax exemption for personal injury recoveries can be viewed as a form of insurance which provides additional income to an individual who is injured, at the expense of higher overall rates for individuals not injured. Such insurance provided by the tax exemption is mandatory, since an individual may not choose to forego this tax benefit in exchange for lower rates.

* * *

Viewing tax provisions as a form of insurance is appropriate for many provisions of the Internal Revenue Code. The deductions for casualty losses and for extraordinary medical expenses provide partial insurance against such losses. * * *

The basic function of insurance is to provide additional consumption to an individual in circumstances in which it is more valuable. Additional consumption will be more valuable to an individual in two cases. First, in general, income is worth more to an individual who has a lower level of current consumption. Maintaining a family's normal consumption level, for example, is the primary function of disability and term life insurance. Second, additional consumption is more valuable to an individual who has greater needs. Providing additional consumption in times of greater need is the central purpose of medical insurance.

The model applies these principles to the tax exemption for personal injury recoveries and determines whether the tax exemption allocates additional income to those circumstances in which it is more valuable. Application of the model leads to the conclusion that exempting recoveries for accident-related medical expenses reallocates income to more valuable states, but that exempting recoveries for lost wages and pain and suffering does not.

Normative Criteria

The model incorporates several simplifying assumptions regarding the nature of personal injury recoveries and the way that consumption and other factors influence personal welfare. The model then is used to calculate the impact of alternative tax policies on personal welfare in light of those assumptions.

The main normative criterion adopted is *ex ante* Pareto superiority. A tax policy is *ex ante* Pareto superior if, prior to the time any taxpayer knows his particular circumstances, each taxpayer would prefer that policy. In the context of personal injury recoveries, the *ex ante* perspective means that each individual must choose the tax treatment of such recoveries without knowing whether or not he will be injured.

* * *

Assumptions of the Model

Individual welfare is assumed to be a function of two variables: (1) consumption of goods and services and (2) all other factors that affect individual well-being, such as good health, leisure and job satisfaction. * * * Consumption is assumed to have declining marginal utility, so that the value of additional consumption to an individual falls as the individual's total consumption increases.

It also is assumed that some individuals will suffer personal injuries for which they will recover damages, but the identities of the injured individuals are unknown. Finally, it is assumed that the government has constant revenue needs.

Application of the Model

The model will be applied to three types of personal injury recoveries: (1) lost wages, (2) medical expenses, and (3) pain and suffering. Each will be considered separately.

Lost Wages

The analysis in this section concludes that, for any rate structure and distribution of income, each individual can be made better off *ex ante* by switching from a tax system which provides tax-free recovery of lost earnings to one which taxes lost earnings but which has lower overall rates.

* * *

Imagine a society with two identical individuals each of whom has a pre-tax wage income of $50,000 per year. * * * If $40,000 in tax revenue must be raised, each individual will pay a tax of 40% [or] $20,000, leaving consumption of $30,000. * * *

Now suppose that one of the individuals suffers a personal injury resulting in $50,000 of lost wages for which the individual suffers compensatory damages. If the recovery is taxed, the combined tax base from both individuals will remain at $100,000. Each individual again will pay a tax of $20,000 and will have an after-tax consumption of $30,000. * * *

A different result occurs if recoveries for lost wages are exempt from income. The tax base will be reduced from $100,000 to $50,000, since the $50,000 received by the injured individual for lost wages will not be taxed. To raise the same $40,000 of revenue from this smaller base, the tax rate must be increased from 40% to 80%. The uninjured individual then will be taxed at an 80% rate on an income of $50,000, leading to a tax of $40,000, consumption of $10,000. * * * The uninjured individual will pay no tax and will enjoy after-tax consumption of $50,000. * * *

In sum, providing a tax exemption for wage recoveries has the effect of increasing the injured individual's consumption from $30,000 to $50,000 and reducing the consumption of the uninjured individual from $30,000 to $10,000. A net welfare loss results because $20,000 of consumption is comparatively less valuable in the range of $30,000 to $50,000 than in the range of $10,000 to $30,000. * * *

Medical Expenses

Medical expense recoveries differ from lost wages in that increased medical needs change the marginal value of consumption. Accident victims frequently require expensive medical treatment and receive damage awards to cover these costs. If, as seems reasonable, medical treatment is important enough to an accident victim's welfare that the individual could not be made better off by purchasing something other than medical care, then the marginal value of consumption will vary with an individual's level of consumption *after payment of accident-related medical expenses.* * * * Under these assumptions, it can be shown that it is *ex ante* Pareto superior to exempt medical expense recoveries from taxation.

* * *

Assume there are two individuals, each of whom earns $50,000 in wages. One of the individuals incurs $50,000 of medical expenses as a result of a personal injury and receives compensatory damages. If damages for injury-related medical expenses are fully taxed, the injured taxpayer will have a taxable income [of] $100,000 and the total tax base will increase to $150,000.

If the government must raise $40,000 of tax revenues, a tax rate of 26.67% will be required. The uninjured taxpayer will pay a tax of $13,333 on $50,000 of taxable income and enjoy an after-tax consumption of $36,667. * * * The injured taxpayer will pay a tax of $26,667 on $100,000 of taxable income, leaving consumption of $73,333, allocated between $50,000 for medical expenses and $23,333 for non-medical consumption. * * *

If damage recoveries for medical expenses are tax exempt, the injured and uninjured taxpayer each will [pay $20,000 in tax and] enjoy $30,000 of non-medical consumption [thereby increasing total welfare, again due to the declining marginal utility of money.]

Pain and Suffering

Pain and suffering damages include compensation both for actual pain and for any reduction in welfare due to permanent bodily impairment. Unlike recoveries for lost wages and for injury-related medical expenses, pain and suffering damages compensate individuals for non-monetary losses. Application of the model shows that expected utility is maximized if pain and suffering recoveries are fully taxed.

Pain and suffering recoveries are assumed to compensate an injured party precisely for any harm incurred; that is, the amount received, if not taxed, is assumed to make an injured individual as well-off as before the injury. This assumption is not essential, however, to the results; it is optimal to tax damages for pain and suffering, even if doing so means that injured individuals will not be fully compensated for their losses.
     * * *

Assume a society with two individuals, each of whom earns $50,000 in wages. One individual receives a $50,000 recovery for pain and suffering. If total tax revenues of $40,000 are required by the government and pain and suffering recoveries are not taxed, each individual will pay a 40% tax of $20,000 on a taxable income of $50,000. The uninjured individual will have an after-tax consumption of $30,000 * * * while the injured taxpayer will have consumption of $80,000. * * *

If recoveries for pain and suffering are taxed, the injured individual's income will increase from $50,000 to $100,000 and the tax base will increase from $100,000 to $150,000. The necessary revenue could then be raised by a tax rate of 26.67%. At this rate, the uninjured taxpayer will pay a tax of $13,333 and will enjoy an after-tax consumption of $36,667 * * * while the injured taxpayer will pay a tax of $26,667 and consume $73,333. * * * Thus, elimination of the tax exemption for pain and suffering damages increases expected utility. * * *

The preceding analysis does not take into account any reduction in the welfare of the injured party from the pain and suffering. This omission is appropriate because the welfare loss from pain and suffering is identical whether or not recoveries are taxed. Including the welfare loss from pain and suffering in the calculation would lower expected utility under each tax regime by an identical amount, but would not affect the *marginal* utility of additional consumption and, thus, would not alter any individual's *ex ante* utility maximizing choice.

* * *

Tax Policy and Personal Injury Recoveries

This Part will examine the various ways in which the taxation of personal injury recoveries has been analyzed by courts, the Treasury, and, especially, by tax scholars. In particular, this Part will look at the application of two important traditional tax norms: the ideal tax base and horizontal equity.

The literature on the taxation of personal injury recoveries applies the norm of an ideal tax base by analyzing whether compensatory tort damages constitute "gain." To determine this, commentators often consider whether a basis exists in human ability. Attempts to determine the proper taxation of personal injury recoveries by looking at the treatment of "similar" transactions such as involuntary conversions of property, voluntary sales of personal rights, and the exclusion of imputed income from good health reflect the horizontal equity norm.

Ideal tax base and horizontal equity arguments are viewed as attempts to support the tax exemption for personal injury recoveries on "tax principles." If a tax provision cannot be justified under tax norms, traditional analysis then considers "non-tax" policy justifications. For personal injury recoveries, the most common non-tax justification is sympathy for the victim.

This Article argues that evaluating tax policy in terms of special tax norms that can, perhaps, be overridden by other ethical principles in unusual cases is inappropriate. Instead, * * * the policy maker should determine the likely consequences of the tax policies under consideration and then choose the policy whose consequences are most consistent with explicitly-stated general normative principles.

* * *

Gain, Horizontal Equity and the Ideal Tax Base

Tax commentators generally agree that lost wage recoveries and punitive damages arising from personal injuries cannot be excluded from taxation on a "no-gain" rationale. Punitive damages, they observe, place injured individuals in a better position than if they had never been hurt, while recoveries for lost wages replace gains from labor which ordinarily are taxed.

It is not clear, however, why "gain" should be the touchstone of taxation. A better rationale for taxing punitive damages and lost wages recoveries is that given in this Article—taxing such gains and lowering tax rates to maintain revenue neutrality will increase each taxpayer's *ex ante* expected welfare.

Tax commentators generally support the exclusion for unreimbursed medical expense recoveries. The remainder of this Part, then, will focus on the more controversial issue of the proper taxation of damages received for pain and suffering.

　* * *

The Ideal Tax Base

Evaluating tax policies in terms of their conformity with an ideal tax base is common in tax policy discussions. The two most prominent ideal tax bases are the "normal tax base" and Haig-Simons income.

　* * *

The Normal Tax Structure

The tax exemption for personal injury recoveries generally is viewed as a deviation from the "normal tax structure" and thus is characterized as a tax expenditure. * * *

The inability of tax commentators to develop a satisfactory method of assigning basis to human capital does not arise from measurement problems alone; there is also no consensus on how such basis should be assessed in theory. * * *

Analogies to the taxation of business assets do not seem helpful in answering these questions. * * * Conforming the taxation of human capital to standard basis recovery rules is valuable only if it serves the normative principles underlying traditional basis rules. * * *

Haig-Simons Income

Haig-Simons income is defined as consumption plus change in wealth during a specified period. It is not clear, however, how personal injury recoveries should be taxed under this standard. The argument in favor of taxation is straightforward—if an individual receives a damage award it will increase either her consumption, if spent, or her wealth, if saved. It is less certain whether a personal injury generates an offsetting reduction in consumption or wealth.

A loss of earning capacity from a personal injury might be viewed as a reduction in wealth. Nevertheless, it seems likely that no deduction for lost earning capacity would be permitted under a Haig-Simons standard; no depreciation deduction, for example, presumably is permitted for the decline in an individual's earning capacity over time due to aging. Instead, reduced earning capacity would be reflected by a reduction in Haig-Simons income in future years.

A loss in Haig-Simons income arguably also might be created by pain and suffering associated with an injury. A permanent physical disability might be viewed as a decline in wealth, and temporary discomfort during treatment might be characterized as a reduction in the consumption of imputed income from good health. Similarly, amounts spent on medical expenses might not be viewed as consumption under a Haig-Simons standard because they only restore the injured individual to a baseline level of good health.

* * * Henry Simons, however, saw his definition of income as measuring an individual's control over societal goods and services. He rejected the idea that the tax base should consider mental states. It is unlikely that he would favor a deduction for pain and suffering or physical disabilities.

More broadly, it is not clear why it is relevant, as a matter of tax policy, whether an item is included within the Haig-Simons definition of income. Conforming the tax system to Haig-Simons income or any other tax base is desirable only to the extent such conformity advances more general normative principles. * * *

Horizontal Equity Claims

Horizontal equity is, perhaps, the most widespread norm underlying traditional tax policy analysis. It is also the least helpful. This section argues that horizontal equity cannot provide the answer to the proper tax treatment of personal injury recoveries or, in fact, to any other important tax policy question.

Horizontal equity generally is defined as the principle that "individuals who are in equal positions should bear an equal tax burden." The problem is that all individuals are alike in some respects and different in others. The principle of horizontal equity cannot determine which differences justify different tax treatment.

* * * Consider the application of the horizontal equity principle to the following three taxpayers:

(1) Alice, who earns $50,000 in wages and suffers no injury.

(2) Bob, who earns $50,000 in wages, is injured, and receives damages of $10,000 which precisely compensate him for pain and suffering.

(3) Carol, who earns $60,000 in wages and suffers no injury.

Should Bob be considered equal to Alice, or to Carol? Horizontal equity does not tell us the answer. Rather, the correct comparison depends on which of the following normative principles one finds attractive.

Principle one: Individuals should be taxed in accordance with their utility levels.

Principle two: Individuals should be taxed in accordance with their monetary income.

It is necessary to choose one of these principles *before* one can determine which of the two taxpayers are "equal." If principle one is adopted and utility levels provide the basis for comparison, then Bob is in the same position as Alice, since the welfare he gets from the extra $10,000 of income exactly matches the welfare loss from his pain and suffering. Such "utility level" horizontal equity is implicit in arguments that pain and suffering damages should be tax exempt because they replace imputed income from good health which otherwise would be received tax-free. More broadly, utility level horizontal equity underlies arguments for the exclusion of damages on the ground that such damages do not constitute gain.

On the other hand, if principle two is adopted and cash income levels are the basis for comparison, then Bob is in the same position as Carol because each has an income of $60,000. "Cash income level" horizontal equity underlies the view that an individual who receives damages for the tortious invasion of personal rights should be taxed like an individual who voluntarily sells personal rights (such as privacy rights) because both have reduced those rights to cash.

Horizontal equity is of no help in deciding which comparison is the correct one. Moreover, horizontal equity analysis obscures the underlying principle of decision. Utility level horizontal equity implies that "individuals should be taxed on the basis of their utility levels," while income level horizontal equity implies the principle that "individuals should be taxed according to their level of cash income." It is interesting to note that although horizontal equity arguments implying taxation according to utility levels or cash income levels are common in the tax literature, few, if any, commentators explain why a tax structure based on either principle would be desirable. This is not surprising because neither tax base is appealing. Taxation according to cash income levels would ignore differences in needs. Taxation according to utility levels would require taxing non-monetary factors which affect utility, such as good health and a cheerful disposition. Neither tax base is consistent with any widely-held ethical theory.

* * *

Notes and Questions

28. Professor Griffith argues that "the basic approach to tax policy taken in the existing literature"—which would probably include most of the materials in this chapter—is simply the wrong way to go about analyzing tax policy questions in general and the tax treatment of personal injury awards in particular. Instead of attempting to analogize the particular tax problem to other situations for which the proper treatment seems relatively settled and clear—for example, analogizing personal injury recoveries to property damage recoveries—the policy maker should consider consequences of alternatives, and evaluate the alternatives "under explicitly stated ethical principles."

29. In what sense can a provision such as section 104(a)(2) be viewed as compulsory taxpayer "insurance"? What is the taxpayer's "premium" payment?

30. What is meant by "*ex ante* Pareto superiority" in the tax policy context?

31. The theory of declining marginal utility of money is basic to Professor Griffith's analysis. This theory, which is generally accepted, assumes that each additional dollar of income is worth less to a given individual than the preceding dollar. (As Professor Griffith points out in a portion of the article not excerpted,[cc] the theory is much weaker when used for interpersonal comparisons. That is, while we may readily assume that A's tenth dollar has less utility than his first *to A*, it does not necessarily follow that A's tenth dollar has less utility *to A* than B's first dollar has *to B*.)

32. Assuming *ex ante* Pareto superiority as the primary target in structuring tax policy, and assuming declining marginal utility of money, Professor Griffith argues that—viewed *ex ante*, before each taxpayer knows whether he will become an accident victim—every taxpayer should prefer that damages compensating pain and suffering be taxed. A pain and suffering award does not actually replace freedom from pain, of course; the effect of the monetary award is additional marginal dollars for the victim's consumption. These additional dollars have lower marginal utility to the injured taxpayer than the dollars he already had. Suppose, for example, that a taxpayer with income of $25,000 knows that there is one chance in 1,000 that he will be injured and receive $1,000 for pain and suffering. Would he be better off with a system that excluded $1 from the taxable income of everyone, or a system that would exclude his extra $1,000 award if he were injured? It is crucial to the analysis that the 25,000th dollar is assumed to be of greater utility than dollars 25,001-26,000. Thus, he would prefer the certainty of protecting from tax the more valuable 25,000th dollar than the one-in-1,000 chance of protecting 1,000 less valuable dollars.

33. The same assumptions lead Professor Griffith to conclude that awards for medical expenses, unlike awards for pain and suffering, should be excluded from income. Suppose our hypothetical taxpayer with income of $25,000 had one chance in a thousand of receiving a $1,000 award to compensate for accident-induced unanticipated medical expenses. Would he prefer the certain $1 exclusion (as he would in the case of pain and suffering) or the exclusion of the $1,000 if he turned out to be the accident victim? Professor Griffith argues that awards compensating the victim for medical expenses, unlike pain and suffering awards, do not free up additional dollars for general (i.e., non-medical) consumption. The hypothetical taxpayer would therefore be faced with a system that either protected the 25,000th dollar *available for general consumption* from tax, or that offered one chance in one thousand of protecting dollars 24,001-25,000—dollars that have greater utility than the 25,000th dollar. The rational taxpayer should choose the exclusion this time.

---

cc. 1993 WIS. L. REV., at 1135-37.

34. Does Professor Griffith's analysis take account of the risk-adverse person who might prefer exclusion of even the pain and suffering award, perhaps reasoning along these lines:

> Even in those cases in which I receive full compensation as measured by the tort system, I am going to be worse off after the accident than before, although perhaps not in monetary terms. Even at the cost of lowering my average *expected* return, I am willing to make a small certain sacrifice (forgoing the $1 exclusion) in order to get a significant tax benefit (exclusion of the $1,000 for pain and suffering) if I am an accident victim.

Does Professor Griffith's analysis take account of the good Samaritan who is willing to sacrifice his own best interest to protect those less fortunate than himself, even at some cost of efficiency?

Note, however, that section 104(a)(2) provides relief to the compensated accident victim; risk-adverse persons or good Samaritans might be more concerned with accidents or sickness in which the victim received no compensation.

35. Why does Professor Griffith think it unclear whether personal injury awards are income under the Haig-Simons definition? Why does he think it essentially irrelevant whether such awards fall within that definition?

36. Why does Professor Griffith find the principles of horizontal equity useless—indeed, worse than useless—not only in determining the proper tax treatment of personal injury awards but in tax policy generally?

37. Do you think that Professor Griffith's analysis offers useful insight into how personal injury awards should be taxed?

38. In common with other commentators whose views were discussed in subchapter B, Professor Griffith suggests that some elements of tort awards should be taxed, and others exempted. Is this a practical suggestion?

Let us ignore punitive damages and focus only on compensatory damages. Suppose that we wished to tax only the portion of personal injury awards that represented compensation for lost earnings, and allow exclusion of other compensatory damages. If a jury returns a general verdict for $1 million, how are we to know how much of this total was for lost earnings? This problem might be reduced if state courts began using special verdict forms in all personal injury cases, but even then, we would be left with the overwhelming majority of cases in which the case was settled without trial.

The problems are comparable to those involved in separating punitive and compensatory damages (discussed in Note #26). Actually, the problem dealt with here is more serious, because many tort cases obviously present no issue of punitive damages, but most big-dollar tort cases involve both lost earnings and other damages.

D. STRUCTURED SETTLEMENTS AND OTHER TIMING PROBLEMS

Typically, tort law contemplates payment of a lump sum settlement or award in compensation for all past and future losses. To the extent attributable to future losses, such as future earnings lost to disability, the lump sum is reduced to present value to reflect the potential for investing it. The lump sum is exempt under section 104(a)(2), but the investment income it generates is taxable. This lump-sum method of payment and associated investment income raise timing issues for tax law.

In recent years, settlements—and, more rarely, judgments following trials—of large cases have frequently been paid out over a period of years (perhaps the lifetime of the victim) rather than in a lump sum. The total amount paid is higher than the lump sum would have been, reflecting the fact that the payor (the defendant or insurance company), and not the victim, will have use of the money. This increased total payment can be viewed as the economic equivalent of an investment return on a lump sum. Under present section 104(a)(2), all payments, including those made over a period of many years and representing significant investment income, are exempt from tax. Professor Frolik criticizes this tax treatment of "structured settlements:"

THE CONVERGENCE OF I.R.C. § 104(a)(2), *NORFOLK & WESTERN RAILWAY CO. V. LIEPELT* AND STRUCTURED TORT SETTLEMENTS: TAX POLICY "DERAILED"
Lawrence A. Frolik[*]
51 Fordham Law Review 565, 572-83 (1983)

The above-discussed inequities engendered by section 104(a)(2) might be borne as an unfortunate, but unavoidable consequence of an understandable congressional desire to assist personal injury victims. Other inequities, however—horizontal inequities—exist among personal injury claimants because of the current tax treatment of deferred payment arrangements (structured settlements), which are frequently used to settle personal injury claims. Those claimants who accept a deferred payment arrangement receive more favorable tax treatment than those claimants who accept a lump-sum settlement.

The term structured settlement refers to the practice by which the claimant agrees to be paid over a number of years or to be paid an annuity

---

[*]. At time of original publication, Professor of Law, University of Pittsburgh.

for life rather than accepting a fixed, lump-sum amount. Expenses incurred by the claimant prior to the settlement are usually reimbursed by a lump-sum payment, while future anticipated damages are compensated by subsequent periodic payments. The payments may be a fixed amount, a fixed amount adjustable for inflation, or an amount varying according to the future needs of the claimant. In some instances, the parties may ignore any total calculation of damages and merely agree to a monthly or annual figure sufficient to meet the projected financial needs of the victim.

Once the parties have agreed on the amount of the periodic payment, the defendant is free to seek out the least expensive way to fulfill his obligation. Although some use is made of irrevocable, funded trusts (the claimant being the beneficiary), the preferred method is to purchase an annuity payable to the claimant for the prescribed period of time. Defendants generally hide the actual cost of the annuity from the claimant since it is often considerably less than anticipated by the claimant or less than the lump-sum amount that it supplanted.[dd] The cost of a lifetime annuity may be surprisingly low if the claimant's life expectancy was severely diminished by the accident. However, because of this secretiveness, the parties, and the claimant's counsel in particular, are free to publicly ascribe a large value to the settlement and thereby garner the attendant publicity.

Amended Section 104(a)(2) Fosters Horizontal Inequity

On January 14, 1983, section 104(a)(2) was amended to provide that damage awards received as periodic payments on account of personal injuries are excluded from gross income. The amendment merely codified, rather than changed, the current interpretation of the law. Prior to the amendment, the IRS had held that periodic payments, including the portion of the deferred payments that represents interest earned on the deferred principal, are nontaxable. Thus, the total amount of a deferred settlement payment escapes taxation even though every periodic payment is comprised of a mix of principal and investment income arising from the deferred portion of the principal.[43]

An equitable and consistent income tax should treat a claimant's decision to receive an annuity (or the income from an irrevocable trust) in lieu of outright receipt of the principal sum as providing comparable economic benefit and, therefore, necessitating comparable taxation. Yet this is not the case. If, for example, rather than a deferred payment, the claimant accepted a lump-sum settlement and then invested it, the subsequent interest income would be included in gross income. If the claimant used the lump

---

dd. By "the lump-sum amount that [the structured settlement] supplanted," the author presumably refers to a tentative lump-sum settlement of a tort action, followed by further negotiation resulting in the substitution of a structured settlement for the lump sum. (Eds.)

43. That a deferred payment consists of both principal and interest is most clear in the event that the defendant purchases an annuity, payable to the claimant, as an insured method of payment. Annuities, almost by definition, are a return of principal together with interest.

sum to purchase an annuity, he would be taxed on that portion of the proceeds that represented interest income. In short, section 104(a)(2) does not extend its protection to the income earned on invested damage awards, even though the parties are likely to have anticipated such earnings and calculated the amount of the settlement accordingly.

For purposes of consistency and equity, Congress should tax interest income that is paid to the claimant even though the interest is earned on principal that was not received by the claimant, but rather held or invested for his benefit under a deferred payment plan.[46] The principal need not be retained by the defendant-payor, because the interest is exempt even though earned by and paid through the use of an annuity, or by a funded irrevocable trust.[47] Given the inconsistent taxation of the interest income, the current tax system impels wise claimants to accept a deferred payout of the settlement, thereby obtaining the benefits of the section 104(a)(2) tax exemption for the interest income earned upon the principal sum of the settlement.

Imagine two sixty-year old tort victims, X and Y, both of whom suffer $100,000 in lost future earnings, the $100,000 figure being the discounted value of their lost earnings for the next five years. If X settles for a lump sum of $100,000 and invests it in 10% corporate bonds which mature in 5 years, X would have $10,000 a year taxable income and a return of the $100,000 at the end of the fifth year. X would have consumable income of $150,000 less the income taxes on the interest. If we assume a tax rate of 25%, X will pay $12,500 in taxes ($10,000 x 5 x 25%), leaving net income of $137,500. (A comparable result would occur if X had used the $100,000 to purchase a five-year annuity). If Y, on the other hand, chooses to accept deferred payments of $10,000 per year for five years with a payment of $100,000 at the end of the fifth year, Y's gross income would be $150,000, all of which is tax free. (Again, the same result would occur if Y had accepted a five-year annuity purchased at a cost of $100,000).

---

46. Nor is tax exemption of the interest [consistent] with the treatment of interest arising from other deferred payment arrangements. The interest portion of a taxpayer purchased annuity is taxable. I.R.C. § 72(a) (1976). Any interest resulting from deferred payments of life insurance proceeds are taxable. The exemption for life insurance proceeds applies only to the amount of the at-death benefit. I.R.C. § 101(d) (1976).

47. Deferred payments of damage awards may assume various forms. The purchase of an annuity payable to the claimant is the most widely used form. Moore, *The Use of Annuities in the Settlement of Personal Injury Cases*, 49 INS. COUNS. J. 50, 50 (1982); Sedgwick & Judge, *The Use of Annuities in Settlement of Personal Injury Cases*, 41 INS. COUNS. J. 584, 584 (1974). Another method is an irrevocable funded trust usually with a bank trustee. When the obligation to pay the claimant terminates, usually at the death of the claimant, the trust terminates. The balance of the trust fund then reverts to the defendant or his insurer. Fuller, *Paying Tomorrow's Claims with Tomorrow's Dollars*, 3 LITIG. 27, 29 (Fall 1976). A third possibility is to have the defendant's casualty insurer underwrite its own annuity plan. The insurer would set aside and invest a lump sum, the income from which would be used to fulfill the periodic payment obligation. Verbeck & Michaels, *Structured Settlements and the Uniform Periodic Payments Act*, 29 FED'N INS. COUNS. Q. 17, 19 (1978).

Obviously, such disparate tax treatment finds little justification in economic realities. The chief difference in the above example between X and Y is the retention by X of the power to consume the principal or to choose the form of its investment. X also retained the ability to change investments or to terminate the investment and consume the principal. This "freedom of choice," however, might not exist if X purchased an annuity, or had invested in some similarly restrictive investment. Even an apparently flexible investment might be subject to any number of restraints that would discourage the recipient, as a practical matter, from exercising the freedom of investment that was apparently obtained by the acceptance of a lump-sum settlement. If, for example, the recipient purchased long-term bonds as a means of providing a stable income, and if interest rates subsequently rose, the bonds would decline in value. To change investments, the recipient would have to absorb a loss of principal; something he might not be willing to accept. Still, in our example, X does have continuing "dominion and control" over the damage award, while Y surrendered that control upon agreeing to a deferred payment arrangement. Does that modest difference in control warrant such a difference in tax treatment?

The doctrine of constructive receipt might seem to apply because it calls for taxation based upon underlying economic realities rather than the mere surface arrangements. The relevant Revenue Rulings, however, which seem to be correct, hold that the doctrine of constructive receipt is not applicable to periodic payments of tort settlements. The Regulations define constructive receipt of income as income "not actually reduced to a taxpayer's possession," but which "is credited to his account, set apart for him, or otherwise made available so that he may draw upon it at any time, or so that he could have drawn upon it during the taxable year if notice of intention to withdraw had been given."[51] In short, the taxpayer "may not deliberately turn his back on income and select his year of reporting."[52]

Returning to our example, one might argue that Y constructively received the $100,000 settlement at the moment in the negotiations when, rather than agreeing to deferred periodic payments he could have demanded immediate payment of the $100,000. The argument, although appealing, must be rejected in light of the cases that have considered when and how constructive receipt should apply to deferred compensation arrangements.[53] Suffice it to say that the cases, and the subsequent Revenue Rulings, have decisively concluded that the doctrine of constructive receipt does not govern the transaction merely because the taxpayer negotiated a deferred compensation agreement. Although deferred compensation is not completely

---

51. Treas. Reg. §1.451-2(a) (1979).

52. Metzer, *Constructive Receipt, Economic Benefit and Assignment of Income: A Case Study in Deferred Compensation*, 29 TAX L. REV. 525, 532 (1974).

53. For an exhaustive discussion of the application of the doctrine of constructive receipt to the various forms of deferred compensation, see Metzer, *supra* note 52, at 538-50.

analogous to a deferred payment damage award, the two are conceptually close enough to allow the former to be instructive as to the latter. Hence, the constructive receipt doctrine does not seem to justify taxation of periodic payments in the year of settlement.

A Proposed Solution—The "Economic Benefit Doctrine"

A better solution to the inequities of section 104(a)(2) would be the repeal of the 1983 amendment and the application of the doctrine of economic benefit, which arose in the context of employee compensation,[57] to structured settlements.   The doctrine originated in Old Colony Trust Co. v. Commissioner,[58] which established that the predecessor to section 61 included as income any economic or financial benefit conferred upon the employee as compensation, whatever the form or mode by which it is effected. * * *

Beginning with *Burnet v. Logan*,[65] the economic benefit doctrine has been used to determine the year of taxation for deferred payments from the sale of property.   In *Burnet*, the sale price for stock included deferred payments keyed to the tonnage of iron ore extracted from a mine by the purchaser of the stock. The Court held that no income was realized in the year of the sale because the "promise [of future money payments] was in no proper sense equivalent to cash. It had no ascertainable fair market value." Hence, the transaction was "held open" to await the actual receipt of the future payments before a determination was made as to whether the seller had realized any income.

Although the government lost under the particular facts of *Burnet*, in dicta the court did approve the government's contention that under appropriate conditions deferred payments were taxable in the year of sale. Taxation could precede receipt of the income because the taxpayer received economic benefit equal to the discounted value of the deferred payments.

In the wake of *Burnet*, deferred payment sales agreements are classified either as "open" or "closed" transactions. If the deferred payments have an ascertainable fair market value, the transaction is "closed" and the gain or loss is recognized in the year of sale. * * * IRS regulations hold that "only in rare and extraordinary cases will property be considered to have no fair

---

57. The concept was not formally recognized until the 1945 case of *Commissioner v. Smith*, 324 U.S. 177, 181 (1945), but its antecedents extend at least to Old Colony Trust Co. v. Commissioner, 279 U.S. 716 (1929). The leading case is *Sproull v. Commissioner*, 16 T.C. 244 (1951), *aff'd per curiam*, 194 F.2d 541 (6th Cir. 1952) in which the employer in 1945 paid a bank trustee $10,500 in consideration for the services performed by the taxpayer/employee. The trustee was to pay out approximately one-half the principal and accumulated interest in 1946 and the remainder in 1947. *Id.*, at 245. In holding that the $10,500 was taxable in 1945, the court conceded that it was not a case of constructive receipt. Instead the court held it taxable in the year that the taxpayer received the economic benefit in the form of a cash equivalent. *Id.* at 247; see Rev. Rul. 62-74, 1962-1 C.B. 68.

58. 279 U.S. 716 (1929).

65. 283 U.S. 404 (1931).

market value"[74] and therefore, deferred payment sales are in overwhelming numbers deemed "closed" transactions.

Applying the Doctrine to Structured Settlements

The doctrine of economic benefit has been addressed and surprisingly rejected by the IRS in the context of periodic payment of damage awards.[76] Surely, however, the claimant who agrees to periodic payments does in fact receive economic benefit at the time of the agreement. The transaction must be considered "closed" because the periodic payments have an ascertainable fair market value, particularly if the payments are secured by an annuity or funded irrevocable trust. Thus, applying the doctrine of economic benefit to structured settlements, the claimant would realize income in the year of settlement equal to the discounted value—the ascertainable fair market value—of the future payments.

Generally, the claimant will demand the protection of a fully funded trust (or escrow account) or will require the defendant to purchase an annuity from a financially responsible third party such as an insurance company. In the case of an annuity, the claimant would have income equal to the cost of the annuity to the defendant.[78] If, rather than an annuity, the parties rely upon a funded irrevocable trust or an unsecured promise to pay, valuation would be more speculative, but still determinable. A funded, irrevocable trust, which is required to pay all its income to the claimant, would complicate the valuation problem because the rate of return is uncertain. Nevertheless, a solution might be found by analogy to the field of estate and gift tax, which relies upon valuation tables to determine the present value of future trust income. Even an unsecured promise to pay would have a fair market value, albeit deeply discounted to reflect the risk factor.

The failure of the IRS and Congress to apply the doctrine of economic benefit to periodic payments becomes even more confusing upon examination of applications of the doctrine in analogous contexts. For example, one Revenue Ruling held that the discounted value of prize payments were taxable in the year they were won, even though before the winner was chosen the contest sponsor had placed the prize money in an escrow account to be paid over a two-year period.[80] A similar result was reached in a case in which a father bought a winning Irish Sweepstakes ticket in the names of his

---

74. Treas. Reg. § 1.1001-1(a) (1960).

76. *E.g.*, Rev. Rul. 79-220, 1979-2 C.B. 74.

78. Disclosure to the claimant of the cost of the annuity could cause some problems, however. The issuer of the annuity may be unhappy about the release of its price; disclosure of that information may cost the issuer a competitive advantage if other issuers should learn of the price because the price of an annuity varies from company to company. Defendants also may not appreciate disclosing the price of the annuity because it may have cost less than what the claimant demanded as a lump-sum settlement. The cost of the annuity is keyed to the claimant's life expectancy, concerning which the parties may have quite different opinions.

80. Rev. Rul. 62-74, 1962-1 C.B. 68.

minor children.[81] Pursuant to Irish law, the cash prize was held by the Bank of Ireland until the children reached age 21 or until the bank received an application for release of the funds. The Tax Court held that under the doctrine of economic benefit the prize was taxable in the year it was won, rather than in the year(s) that the children turned twenty-one or in the year in which application was made for the money.

The argument for applying the doctrine of economic benefit to structured settlements is even more compelling than in the above examples. In those situations, the deferred nature of the payments was fortuitous—they could not have resulted from conscious tax planning on the part of the recipient. By contrast, the personal injury claimant plays a major role in determining the nature of the payments he will receive. * * *

Proposed Methods of Taxing Structured Settlements

If deferred payment damage awards were deemed income in the year of the settlement, section 104(a)(2) would come into play, with the result that the fair market value of the settlement would be tax exempt. Thereafter, the tax effect of the later receipt of the periodic payments could take either of two routes. The claimant could be treated as if he had purchased an annuity at a cost equal to present value of the future payments, i.e., the amount exempted by section 104(a)(2). The periodic payments would then be taxed according to section 72. Under that section, each periodic payment would be allocated between a tax-free return of capital—the cost of the annuity—and a taxable investment interest component.

In the alternative, the periodic payments would be taxed as are other closed transactions; the payments would be received tax-free until they totaled the fair market value of the settlement amount. Payments in excess of the amount exempted by section 104(a)(2) would represent taxable income. * * *

Depending on the particular circumstances and the bargaining power of the parties, structured settlements will confer the section 104(a)(2) tax savings upon either the claimant, the defendant or both. To the extent the claimant garners a portion of the tax savings, a horizontal inequity is created among personal injury award recipients. Moreover, the potential shift of some or all of the section 104(a)(2) tax savings to defendants was certainly not one of the purposes behind the section's enactment. By divesting structured settlements of their favored tax treatment both of these effects could be remedied. Deferred periodic payments should be treated as either "closed transactions" or as section 72 annuities.
     * * *

---

81. Pulsifer v. Commissioner, 64 T.C. 245, 245 (1975).

Notes and Questions

Structured settlements

39.   What are "structured settlements"?   What is the tax advantage offered by structured settlements?   Who benefits from this advantage?

40.   Professor Frolik proposes application of the "economic benefit doctrine" to structured settlements.   What effect would this have?

41.   Present law clearly encourages structured settlements.   What non-tax goals are furthered by this favorable tax treatment?   Do the non-tax goals justify present law?

Timing issues in lump-sum awards

42.   Time-value-of-money issues arise not only in the case of structured settlements, but with lump-sum awards as well.   Under tort law, awards that compensate for future losses are "discounted to present value."   Thus, an award that compensates for future earnings or future medical expenses is reduced to reflect the fact that a lump-sum award can be invested until the time of the element of loss it is supposed to compensate.   The investment earnings of the lump-sum award are subjected to tax.

If section 104(a)(2) were repealed, would taxing both the lump-sum award and the earnings generated by the award constitute double taxation?

43.   If section 104(a)(2) is to be narrowed or repealed, *when* should the taxes be levied?   Suppose a taxpayer receives $1,000,000 to compensate for thirty future years of lost earnings and pain.   Assuming the decision to tax the lump-sum award, should it be taxed on receipt or over the thirty-year period?   There are at least two aspects of this problem.   First, does taxing on receipt improperly accelerate tax liability?

Second, does levying all taxes in a single year unfairly tax the tort plaintiff by "bunching" his income, because the lump sum is subjected to high progressive rates?   The seriousness of the bunching argument depends on the degree of progressivity.   For example, the problem would have been far more severe in the 1950s, when marginal rates exceeded ninety percent.   According to one commentator of that era, if a plaintiff received a taxable award of $50,000 to take the place of five years of earning $10,000 per year: "The plaintiff will lose 20% of the full amount of his judgment *simply* because it was all taxable in the year judgment was received.   (Actually 74% of the judgment would go for taxes, but only 20% is caused by the bunching effect.)"[ee]

---

ee. Cutler, Charles R., *Taxation of the Proceeds of Litigation*, 57 COLUM. L. REV. 470, 477 (1957). [From a modern vantage point, perhaps the most striking part of the statement is the overall tax of 74%, rather than the bunching problem. (Eds.)]

Should special relief provisions—income averaging, for example —accompany repeal or substantial limitation of section 104(a)(2)? Professor Malcolm Morris, for example, might combat the bunching problem by levying a tax "equal to five times the tax which would be imposed * * * on one-fifth of the amount."[ff]

Effect of tax law on tort law

44.   If section 104(a)(2) is left intact, should juries be informed that the award is tax-free? If section 104(a)(2) were repealed, should they be told that the award is taxable? Who would benefit in each case, as between plaintiff and defendant? The United States Supreme Court, in a personal injury case brought under the Federal Employers' Liability Act, struck a pro-defendant blow in holding that such an instruction should be given.[gg] The majority position among states, however, continues to be that juries should not be informed that the award is tax-free. Under the *Erie* doctrine,[hh] this view is usually held to bind federal courts deciding diversity cases, which constitute the bulk of tort litigation in federal courts.

45.   Might repeal of section 104(a)(2), or limitation of its application to certain elements of damage, have the unintended effect of increasing the fees of plaintiffs' attorneys? If one supposed that juries would be informed of the tax bite and make allowance by increasing the amounts awarded plaintiffs, a lawyer receiving a percentage contingency fee might see his income rise. Would this be likely to occur? Would this be undesirable?

46.   In conclusion: In what way, if any, would you restructure section 104(a)(2)? Why?

Selected Bibliography

Barkan, Randall, Comment, *Tax Treatment of Post-Termination Personal Injury Settlements*, 61 CAL. L. REV. 1237 (1973).

Blackburn, Joseph W., *Taxation of Personal Injury Damages: Recommendations for Reform*, 56 TENN. L. REV. 661 (1989).

Bonnell, Craig S., *Back and Forth with the I.R.S.: Taxation of Wrongful Death Damages in Alabama*, 17 CUMB. L. REV. 53 (1986).

Boss, Lorraine Stacknowitz, Note, *Taxation and Personal Injury Awards: The Search for Workable Guidelines*, 62 ST. JOHN'S L. REV. 628 (1988).

Brooks, Jennifer J.S., *Developing a Theory of Damages Recovery Taxation*, 14 WM. MITCHELL L. REV. 759 (1988).

---

ff. Malcolm M. Morris, *Taxing Economic Loss Recovered in Personal Injury Actions: Towards a Capital Idea?*, 38 U. FLA. L. REV. 735, 758 (1986).

gg. Norfolk & Western Railway v. Liepelt, 444 U.S. 490, *reh'g. denied*, 445 U.S. 972 (1980).

hh. Erie Railroad v. Tompkins, 304 U.S. 64 (1938), requires federal courts to apply substantive state law in diversity cases.

Burke, J. Martin & Michael K. Friel, *Tax Treatment of Employment-Related Personal Injury Awards: The Need for Limits*, 50 MONT. L. REV. 13 (1989).

—— & ——, *Recent Developments in the Income Taxation of Individuals*, 9 REV. TAX'N INDIVIDUALS 292 (1985).

Chapman, Douglas K., *No Pain—No Gain? Should Personal Injury Damages Keep Their Tax Exempt Status?*, 9 U. ARK. LITTLE ROCK L.J. 407 (1986-87).

Cochran, Mark W., *1989 Tax Act Compounds Confusion Over Tax Status of Personal Injury Awards*, 49 TAX LAW. 1565 (1989).

——, *Should Personal Injury Damage Awards Be Taxed?*, 38 CASE WEST. RES. L. REV. 43 (1987).

Cutler, Charles R., *Taxation of the Proceeds of Litigation*, 57 COLUM. L. REV. 470 (1957).

DODGE, JOSEPH M., THE LOGIC OF TAX: FEDERAL INCOME TAX THEORY AND POLICY 107-13 (1989).

——, *Taxes and Torts*, 77 CORNELL L. REV. 143 (1992).

FROLIK, LAWRENCE A., FEDERAL TAX ASPECTS OF INJURY, DAMAGE, AND LOSS (1987).

——, *Personal Injury Compensation as a Tax Preference*, 37 ME. L. REV. 1 (1985).

——, *The Convergence of I.R.C. § 104(a)(2),* Norfolk & Western Railway Co. v. Liepelt *and Structured Tort Settlements: Tax Policy "Derailed,"* 51 FORDHAM L. REV. 565 (1983).

——, *Personal Injury Compensation as a Tax Preference*, 37 ME. L. REV. 1 (1985).

Griffith, Thomas D., *Should "Tax Norms" Be Abandoned? Rethinking Tax Policy Analysis and the Taxation of Personal Injury Recoveries*, 1993 WIS. L. REV. 1115.

Harnett, Bertram, *Torts and Taxes*, 27 N.Y.U. L. REV. 614 (1952).

Heen, Mary L., *An Alternative Approach to the Taxation of Employment Discrimination Recoveries Under Federal Civil Rights Statutes: Income From Human Capital, Realization, and Nonrecognition*, 72 N.C. L. REV. 549 (1994).

Henning, Margaret, *Recent Developments in the Tax Treatment of Personal Injury and Punitive Damage Recoveries*, 45 TAX LAW. 783 (1992).

Henry, Robert J., *Torts and Taxes, Taxes and Torts: The Taxation of Personal Injury Recoveries*, 23 HOUS. L. REV. 701 (1986).

Kahn, Douglas A., *Taxation of Punitive Damages Obtained in a Personal Injury Claim*, 65 TAX NOTES 487 (1994).

Knickerbocker, Daniel C., *The Income Tax Treatment of Damages: A Study in the Difficulties of Income Concept*, 47 CORNELL L.Q. 429 (1962).

Manns, F. Philip, Jr., *Down and Out: RIFed Employees, Taxes and Employment and Discrimination Claims After* Burke *and* Schleier, 44 KAN. L. REV. 103 (1995).

McIntosh, Stephan Ian, Comment, *Defining the Intersection of Tort Law and Tax Law: Recent Developments Regarding the Exclusion of Personal Injury Damages*, 6 VA. TAX REV. 425 (1986).

Morgan, Patricia T., *Old Torts, New Torts and Taxes: The Still Uncertain Scope of Section 104(a)(2)*, 48 LA. L. REV. 875 (1988).

Morris, Malcolm L., *Taxing Economic Loss Recovered in Personal Injury Actions: Towards a Capital Idea?*, 38 U. FLA. L. REV. 735 (1986).

Morrison, Mary Jane, *Getting a Rule Right and Writing a Wrong Rule: The IRS Demands a Return on All Punitive Damages*, 17 CONN. L. REV. 39 (1984).

Palmer, Timothy R., Note, *Internal Revenue Code Section 104(a)(2) and the Exclusion of Personal Injury Damages: A Model of Inconsistency*, 15 J. CORP. LAW 83 (1989).

Stephan, Paul B. III, *Federal Income Taxation and Human Capital*, 70 VA. L. REV. 1357 (1984).

Vaughan, Randall G.,Comment,*Tax Issues of Personal Injury and Wrongful Death Awards*, 19 TULSA. L. REV. 702 (1984).

Willoughby, David D., Comment, *The Taxation of Defamation Recoveries: Toward Establishing Its Reputation*, 37 VAND. L. REV. 621 (1984).

Yoran, Aharon, *Tax Aspects in Tort Compensation*, 22 ISR. L. REV. 37 (1987).

Yorio, Edward, *The Taxation of Damages: Tax and Non-Tax Policy Considerations*, 62 CORNELL L. REV. 701 (1977).

CHAPTER THIRTEEN

FEDERAL TAX TREATMENT OF STATE AND LOCAL TAXES

If, among deductions allowed under the Federal income tax, veneration is a function of age, then State and local taxes constitute the most venerable of all deductions. Together with Federal taxes, they were the only deductions specifically provided for in the Income Tax Act of 1861. Every income tax statute enacted since 1861 has continued their deductibility.[a]

A. INTRODUCTION

The language above should not lead the reader to conclude that the scope of the deduction for state and local taxes (S-L taxes) has remained unchanged. In the pre-1913 income tax statutes, and in the first years of the income tax under the Sixteenth Amendment, virtually all taxes were deductible. Prior to 1917, even the federal income tax itself was deductible.[b] Until 1964, all taxes were deductible unless specifically barred; in the Revenue Act of 1964, Congress reversed this approach so that taxes were not deductible unless specified allowed. The 1964 Act substantively narrowed the deduction, principally by not including S-L "sin" taxes (excise taxes on alcoholic beverages and tobacco products) in the list of deductible taxes. In 1978, motivated in part by petroleum shortages, Congress ended the deduction for gasoline taxes. The most recent change, and the most important, is the provision in the Tax Reform Act of 1986 that ended the deductibility of S-L sales taxes. At present, the only deductible S-L taxes are income taxes, real property taxes, and ad valorem personal property taxes.[c] (Other S-L taxes are deductible if they constitute expenses "in carrying on a trade or business or an activity described in section 212."[d] This chapter, however, deals with the deductibility of S-L taxes outside the business/income-producing context.)

There is no reason to think that section 164 is immune from more change, or even outright repeal. Over the years, widely varying proposals,

---

a. Harvey E. Brazer, *The Deductibility of State and Local Taxes Under the Individual Income Tax, in* HOUSE COMM. ON WAYS & MEANS, 86TH CONG., 1ST SESS., 1 TAX REVISION COMPENDIUM 407 (1959).

b. For example, payment of 1915 taxes would have been made in 1916, and, under the cash method, would have been deductible in computing 1916 taxes.

c. Section 164(a)(1)-(3).

d. Section 164(a).

with differing and conflicting justifications, have been put forward by a large number of commentators, as well as by the Treasury and members of Congress. The excerpts below give a sampling of these divergent viewpoints.

B. DEDUCTION OF STATE AND LOCAL TAXES

TAX REFORM FOR FAIRNESS, SIMPLICITY, AND ECONOMIC GROWTH ["TREASURY I"]
United States Department of the Treasury
Vol. 1, at 78, 80; vol. 2, at 66-67 (1984)

Itemized deduction[s] for State and local taxes are not required for the accurate measurement of income. Many years ago, with top rates in the neighborhood of 90 percent, the deduction was perceived to be necessary to prevent the sum of the marginal tax rates for Federal and State income taxes from exceeding 100 percent. Given the present levels of tax rates, such an argument is no longer relevant. The deduction is sometimes defended as a subsidy that is required to reduce the taxpayer's net cost of paying State and local taxes. Some would argue that the deduction has the advantage of encouraging greater expenditures by State and local governments.

Expenditures by State and local governments provide benefits primarily for residents of the taxing jurisdiction. To the extent that State and local taxes merely reflect the benefits of services provided to taxpayers, there is no more reason for a Federal subsidy for spending by State and local governments than for private spending. Both equity and neutrality dictate that State and local services should be financed by taxes levied on residents or on businesses operating in the jurisdiction, in the absence of evidence that substantial benefits of such expenditures spill over into other jurisdictions. There is no reason to believe that most expenditures of State and local governments have such strong spillover effects that they would be greatly under-provided in the absence of the deduction for State and local taxes. There is no reason to have high Federal tax rates and provide implicit Federal subsidies to spending of State and local governments by allowing deduction for their taxes. It would be better—fairer, simpler, and more neutral—to have lower Federal tax rates and have State and local government services—like private purchases—funded from after-tax dollars.
* * *

The three most important sources of State and local tax revenue in the United States are the general sales tax, the personal income tax, and the property tax. There may be a tendency to believe that itemized deductions should be eliminated for some of these taxes, but retained for others. The Treasury Department rejects this view, because the degree of reliance on these three tax bases varies widely from state to state. Five States have no general sales tax, and six have no personal income tax. Moreover, local governments in various States make widely different use of the property tax;

in 1982 the tax represented from below 40 percent to almost 100 percent of total local tax collections in various states. To allow itemized deductions for some of these revenue sources, but not others, would unfairly benefit residents of the States levying the deductible taxes, relative to those who live elsewhere. Moreover, it would distort tax policy at the State and local level away from the non-deductible revenue source. Current law does this by allowing deductions for certain taxes but not for many fees and other taxes.

Moreover, because the deduction for State and local taxes leads to higher federal tax rates for all, there is a net benefit only for States (and localities) that levy above-average taxes. Residents of States (and localities) with below-average taxes are worse off than if there were no deduction.

* * *

Reasons for Change

The current deduction for State and local taxes in effect provides a Federal subsidy for the public services provided by State and local governments, such as public education, road construction and repair, and sanitary services. When taxpayers acquire similar services by private purchase (for example, when taxpayers pay for water or sewer services), no deduction is allowed for the expenditure. Allowing a deduction for State and local taxes simply permits taxpayers to finance personal consumption expenditures with pre-tax dollars.

Many of the benefits provided by State and local governments, such as police and fire protection, judicial and administrative services, and public welfare or relief, are not directly analogous to privately purchased goods or services. They nevertheless provide substantial personal benefits to State and local taxpayers, whether directly or by enhancing the general quality of life in State and local communities. * * *

It is argued by some that State and local taxes should be deductible because they are not voluntarily paid. The argument is deficient in a number of respects. First, State and local taxes are voluntary in the sense that State and local taxpayers control their rates of taxation through the electoral process. Recent State and local tax reduction initiatives underline the importance of this process. Just as importantly, taxpayers are free to locate in the jurisdiction which provides the most amenable combination of public services and tax rates. Taxpayers have increasingly "voted with their feet" in recent years by moving to new localities to avoid high rates of taxation. Indeed, taxpayers have far greater control over the amount of State and local taxes they pay than over the level of Federal income taxes. Nevertheless, Federal income taxes are nondeductible.

The subsidy provided through the current deduction for State and local taxes is distributed in an uneven and unfair manner. Taxpayers in high-tax States receive disproportionate benefits, while those in low-tax States effectively subsidize the public service benefits received by taxpayers in neighboring States. Even within a single State or locality, the deduction of

State and local taxes provides unequal benefits. Most State and local taxes are deductible only by taxpayers who itemize, and among itemizers, those with high incomes and high marginal tax rates receive a disproportionate benefit.

* * *

Proposal

The itemized deduction for State and local income taxes and other taxes that are not incurred in carrying on a trade or business or income-producing activity would be phased out over a two-year period. * * *

SENATE COMMITTEE ON FINANCE

Senate Report No. 99-313, 99th Cong., 2d Sess., at 56-57 (1986)

Reasons for Change

The committee believes that, as part of the approach of its bill to reduce tax rates through base-broadening, it is appropriate to disallow the itemized deduction for State and local sales taxes. A number of additional considerations support the committee's decision.

First, itemized deductions already are not allowed under present law for various types of State and local sales taxes—such as selective sales taxes on telephone and other utility services, admissions, and sales of alcoholic beverages, tobacco, and gasoline. Also, present law does not allow consumers any deduction to reflect the inclusion in selling price of taxes levied at the wholesale or manufacturers' level. The committee believes that extending nondeductibility to all State and local sales taxes will improve the consistency of Federal tax policy by not providing an income tax benefit for any type of consumption.

Further, to the extent that sales taxes are voluntary costs of purchasing the consumer product or other items to which the taxes apply, the deduction is unfair because it favors taxpayers with particular consumption patterns, and is inconsistent with the general rule that costs of personal consumption by individuals are nondeductible.

Second, although the committee is aware of arguments that eliminating the sales tax deduction will provide unwarranted encouragement for States to shift away from these taxes and will be unfair to States that retain them, the committee did not find persuasive evidence for this view. On the contrary, it is significant how small a portion of general sales taxes paid by individuals actually are claimed as itemized deductions. Data from 1984 show that less than one-quarter of all such taxes levied are claimed as itemized deductions. By contrast, well over one-half of State and local income taxes paid by individuals are claimed as itemized deductions. The fact that the large majority of sales tax payments already are not claimed as itemized deductions under present law alleviates any effect of repealing the deduction on the regional distribution of Federal income tax burdens or on the willingness of State and local governments to use general sales taxes as revenue sources.

Third, for itemizers who do not rely on the IRS-published tables to estimate their deductible sales taxes, the deduction for sales taxes involves substantial recordkeeping and computational burdens, since the taxpayer must determine which sales taxes are deductible, must keep receipts or invoices showing the tax paid on each purchase, and must calculate the total of all deductible sales taxes paid. * * * Thus, repealing the deduction advances the committee's goal of simplifying the tax system for individuals.

For itemizers who do rely on the IRS tables, the amount of deductions that individuals can take without challenge from the IRS may vary significantly in particular instances from the amount of general sales taxes actually paid to State and local governments. The tables do not provide accurate estimates for individuals who have either lower or higher levels of consumption than the average, and do not reflect the fact that an individual may purchase items in several States having different general sales tax rates. Accordingly, use of the tables neither accurately measures the amount of disposable income an individual retains after paying general sales taxes, nor accurately provides an appropriate Federal tax benefit to residents of States that use general sales taxes.

* * *

LIMITING STATE-LOCAL TAX DEDUCTIBILITY: EFFECTS AMONG THE STATES
Nonna A. Noto & Dennis Zimmerman[*]
37 National Tax Journal 539, 542, 546 (1984)

This paper starts from the premise that the Congress has decided to raise a specified amount of additional revenue from the federal individual income tax by limiting the deductibility of state and local (S-L) taxes through one of four proposals which surfaced in the discussions surrounding TEFRA[e] and subsequent to it. One proposal would completely eliminate the deductibility of the general sales tax. A second would treat all eligible S-L tax deductions in combination and impose a floor, set as a percent of AGI: only S-L tax payments in excess of the floor would remain deductible. A third proposal would impose a ceiling on the combined tax deductions, set as a percent of AGI: S-L taxes in excess of that ceiling amount would no longer be deductible. A fourth proposal would disallow from deduction a percentage of otherwise deductible tax payments.

* * *

The precise dollar and percentage limits were calculated so as to make the floor, ceiling, and percent disallowance proposals revenue-equivalent to

---

[*]. At the time of original publication, both authors were affiliated with the Congressional Research Service.

e. Tax Equity and Fiscal Reform Act of 1982. (Eds.).

the sales tax proposal, which would have raised approximately $3.7 billion in additional federal revenue in 1980. Accordingly, the floor in proposal two would be 1.08 percent of adjusted gross income. The ceiling in proposal three would be 6.32 percent of AGI. The disallowance in proposal four would be 14.6 percent of taxes currently eligible for deductions.

> * * *

Policy Conclusions

Drawing upon all of the above theoretical and empirical considerations, our conclusion is that if S-L tax deductibility is to be limited, the preferred alternative is the percent of AGI floor.

The proposal to repeal the deductibility of the sales tax, the alternative most frequently mentioned in popular and political discussions, is unattractive on all of the grounds considered. First, this approach to raising federal revenue is anticipated to create unnecessary variability among the states in its effect on after-tax income, and consequently on S-L revenues, because of the differing dependence on the sales tax as a S-L revenue source. Second, it is expected to have income *and* substitution effects and consequently cause a greater S-L revenue loss per dollar of federal revenue gain than the floor approach, which is expected to have just an income effect. Furthermore, as a result of the substitution effect anticipated if deductibility were repealed, S-L revenue officials could be expected to reduce their reliance on sales taxes relative to other taxes remaining eligible for deduction. This would be an unnecessary federal influence on S-L revenue choice. The foregoing conclusions are not unique to the sales tax. They would apply to any proposal to repeal the deductibility of a particular S-L tax.

It is difficult to have a "fair" ceiling if it must be expressed uniformly nationwide. Because of the tremendous variation among states in the S-L tax burden as a percent of AGI, a ceiling set at a given percent of AGI might not affect taxpayers in some jurisdictions at all but might affect taxpayers in other jurisdictions by a substantial amount. Another consequence of these differences in tax burdens is that the ceiling proposal has by far the greatest variability among the states in terms of expected effect on after-tax income and therefore S-L revenue. * * *

The percent disallowance proposal sounds evenhanded in the sense of disallowing the same fraction of deductions for all itemizers, unlike either the floor, ceiling, or sales tax proposals. In practice, however, it resembles the ceiling proposal in imposing a greater increase in federal tax liability on itemizers in states with high tax effort. * * *

A floor emerges as the preferred alternative. The floor approach is expected to have a less damaging effect on S-L own-source tax revenue than the sales tax, ceiling, or percent disallowance approaches because it is expected to have only an income effect, and not a substitution effect, if the floor is set below the S-L tax burden in even the lowest-tax jurisdiction.

Furthermore the floor proposal ranked as most evenhanded among the states in terms of federal impact on after-tax incomes.

     * * *

EVALUATING PERSONAL DEDUCTIONS IN AN INCOME TAX—THE IDEAL
William J. Turnier[*]

66 Cornell Law Review 262, 262-63, 294-95 (1981)

The role of personal deductions in our income tax system has generated considerable debate among individuals who have criticized personal deductions as unwarranted erosions of the tax base. * * *

This dim view of personal deductions is unwarranted for a number of reasons. First, although critics generally agree on the definition of income, they have failed to define its key components. As a result, they leave unresolved the question of whether personal deductions are necessary to assure that only income is taxed. Moreover, in focusing exclusively on the extensiveness of an income tax, these critics overlook the role that our society intends this tax to play. Consequently, critics ignore the capacity of deductions to insure that the base is compatible with the principal reasons underlying society's adopting the income tax. Finally, critics also ignore the role that personal deductions can play in insuring the primacy of fundamental social, economic, and political values. In so doing, these critics elevate values implicit in a comprehensive income tax above all other values.

This Article proposes a three-tiered test to evaluate the propriety of personal deductions. First, one should measure all deductions against a generally accepted definition of income to determine if they are essential in arriving at the goal of taxing income. Second, an examination of deductions is necessary to determine whether their continued existence is related to the basic reasons why our society adopted and maintains an income tax. Third, one should ascertain whether deductions are required to insure the primacy of fundamental social, economic, and political values. Judging the validity of a given deduction involves balancing all the above factors; none of them alone should be determinative.

     * * *

Personal deductions exempt from taxation expenditures or losses that do not constitute consumption; receipts, so adjusted, equal [Haig-Simons] income. The deduction for state and local income taxes represents such an essential adjustment. On the other hand, the deduction for state and local gasoline taxes is an example of a deduction that was unwarranted: these expenditures constituted consumption. The deductions for state and local sales and property taxes are not easily categorized. Although such taxes

---

*. At time of original publication, Associate Professor of Law, University of North Carolina at Chapel Hill.

represent funds that are not consumed by the taxpayer, but rather by the general public, they are arguably incidents of consumption. As such, they are similar to many other taxes that are indirectly borne by consumers. * * *

Considering the principal reasons for adopting and maintaining an income tax system, one recognizes the need to insure that our tax structure is geared toward an individual's ability to pay. As a result, the involuntary nature of state and local income taxes makes them ideal candidates for deduction. Both property and sales taxes are involuntary only to the extent they are imposed on true essentials; therefore the deductibility of a vast majority of these taxes cannot be justified on the ground that they impair one's ability to pay. * * * Although at least two other reasons support an income tax—its role as an economic stabilizer and its capacity to raise substantial amounts of revenue in an efficient fashion—neither suggests that a further erosion of the tax base is required to accommodate the base to these considerations. A deduction for income, sales, and property taxes does not present substantial administrative and compliance burdens and their continued deductibility cannot be rejected on that ground. Moreover, the continued deductibility of these taxes probably has a mild positive impact on the role of the income tax as an economic stabilizer.

Considering the role of section 164 in a federal system, one must conclude that complete repeal of section 164 would produce a neutral environment in which the states could shape their legislative programs. However, because the existence of section 164 facilitates the states' revenue raising efforts, repeal would probably impair the ability of a number of states to fund programs adequately, thus placing more of the burden of funding programs on the federal government. Partial repeal of the deduction would render some of the states' principal sources of revenue nondeductible and others deductible. Arguably, states should not be subject to this indirect form of pressure in determining the composition of their revenue raising programs. However, because * * * repeal of the sales tax deduction would probably not produce a significant shift away from this tax toward the income tax, this consideration may merit little weight. * * *

After weighing the above competing considerations, this author suggests retaining the deduction for state and local income taxes. Moreover, because it is unclear whether the state sales and property taxes represent nonconsumption expenditures, and because state finances would be adversely affected if the taxes were repealed, one might conclude that the deduction for sales and property taxes should continue. Ultimate resolution of that issue, however, should hinge on whether another adequate accommodation to the revenue interests of the states can be found. If such an accommodation exists, repeal of the deduction for either the sales or property taxes would probably be desirable. * * *

A NEW FEDERAL TAX TREATMENT
OF STATE AND LOCAL TAXES
J B McCombs[*]

19 Pacific Law Journal 747, 748-50, 753-55, 759-62, 764 (1988)

The Haig-Simons definition of income is widely accepted as describing the theoretically ideal income tax base. It defines income as the sum of the taxpayer's consumption of goods and services plus the net increase in his or her savings and investments during the year. There is no serious argument that state and local tax payments represent any form of savings or investment by the individual taxpayer. Therefore, the focus throughout this article is on their possible characterization as a form of consumption by the taxpayer.

One plausible view of a sales tax is that it is an integral part of the cost of consumption. Because consumption is one component of the Haig-Simons definition of income, that view leads to the conclusion that sales tax payments are part of one's income, and should not be deductible for federal income tax purposes. In other words, the sales tax on a new stereo is no different, economically, than the actual purchase price of the stereo. From this viewpoint, the recent change[f] improves the theoretical soundness of the law.

The foregoing argument appears to be correct, if one views the issue through a close-up lens. This author looks at the big picture and comes to a different conclusion.

In a world where the average individual taxpayer spends ninety-eight percent of his earnings, there is very little practical difference between an income tax that takes five percent from the taxpayer as he earns it, and a sales tax that takes five percent from the taxpayer as he spends it. The taxing government receives an essentially identical pound of flesh under either system. In both cases, the taxpayer has the same amount of after tax income remaining to purchase the goods and services he desires to consume. Although the two systems as found in practice have somewhat different impacts due to their differing deductions and exemptions, as a general proposition sales tax and income tax are more alike than different in their real economic effect. They represent government attempts to take water from the same stream, but simply at different points along its course. The theoretical argument to distinguish them breaks down when transferred to the real world where saving approaches zero and income virtually equals consumption.

The similarity between sales and income tax increases when a consideration of the property tax is added to the analysis. One major difference between the economic impact of an income tax and that of a sales

---

*. At time of original publication, Assistant Professor of Law, University of Nebraska.

f. Professor McCombs is referring to the repeal of the deduction for S-L sales taxes made by the Tax Reform Act of 1986. (Eds.)

tax is that the dollars used to buy[6] or rent a home are subjected to the income tax, but are not normally reached by the sales tax. The real property tax, by taxing those dollars at the expenditure end of the stream, fills this gap left by the sales tax structure. A property tax can be viewed as a massive sales tax on the construction and sale of a new home, which is collected (with interest) over the life of the home. Sales and property taxes, viewed together, tax nearly all dollars as they are spent. The income tax reaches nearly all dollars as they are received. An income tax dips from the taxpayers stream of money at one point, while the sales and property taxes together take from the same stream at a different location. Therefore, any federal distinction between these three types of general revenue taxes is not well founded in theory.

The foregoing argument is not meant to imply that all forms of state and local taxes are economically equivalent and should receive consistent federal tax treatment. The basic similarity between the three principal types of tax systems does not carry over to a sales or excise tax imposed on a narrow category of goods or services. The taxes imposed on liquor and cigarettes are not at all comparable to an income tax, because a class of people who all have the same income will spend widely varying amounts on alcohol and tobacco. * * *

Furthermore, the separate treatment of gasoline taxes is similarly defensible. In addition to the preceding analysis of narrow based sales taxes, which does apply to the gas tax, another difference between the gas tax and the three principal types of taxes is the fact that a gas tax is intended as, and has the effect of, a toll for the use of the roads. The more one drives, the more one pays. It is economically equivalent to having a toll booth on every road in the state, but is much simpler and more efficient. * * *

A Closer Scrutiny of State and Local Tax Payments,
In Light of Benefits from State and Local Governments

Professor Turnier states that "economists are in wide agreement that payments of state income taxes do not provide taxpayers with benefits which are in any way commensurate with the tax paid."[17] Nevertheless, each taxpayer does receive some level of direct benefits from state and local government programs, and it seems fair to presume that such direct benefits were funded with a portion of that particular individual's state and local tax payments. The fact that the payment is often much greater than the benefit is not sufficient reason to totally ignore the benefit.
* * *

A more appropriate test is the directness of the benefit. When Mr. and Ms. Taxpayer pay their state and local taxes, and some of those dollars are

---

6. I am referring here to the actual purchase price, to the extent paid in cash, or principal payments on a home loan.

17. Turnier, *Personal Deductions and Tax Reform: The High Road and the Low Road*, 31 VILL. L. REV. 1703, 1717 (1986).

used to provide assistance to the handicapped, Mr. and Ms. Taxpayer have a benefit, which is the satisfaction of living in a compassionate society. That benefit is extremely indirect. The government's primary intention in making that particular expenditure was to benefit the handicapped persons who qualify for the particular program. On the other hand, if some of the dollars paid by Mr. and Ms. Taxpayer are used to educate their children, the benefit to them is extremely direct. * * *

This argument is leading, first, to the point that the value of goods and services provided by a state or local government to a direct beneficiary should be included in the definition of consumption, as that term is used in the Haig-Simons definition of income. From that conclusion, this author makes the argument that, as a theoretical ideal, tax payments to state and local governments should not be deducted for federal income tax purposes to the extent of the taxpayer's receipt of direct benefits from those governments. * * *

If one can assume that taxpayers who itemize their deductions are found primarily in the middle class and above, the scope of inquiry into direct benefits can be narrowed.

The task is to identify the major state and local government programs from which the middle class and above (hereinafter, for simplicity, the middle class) receive at least their pro rata share of the benefits. For example, if a city of 1,000 residents spends $40,000 to provide police protection, it is fair to say that the average middle class resident enjoys approximately $40 of police protection. If this city spends $15,000 for its symphony, one would be certain that the average middle class resident will enjoy more than $15 of symphonic performance, because the poor generally do not partake of such services in proportion to their numbers. * * * Finally, if this city spends $25,000 on its welfare program, it is neither accurate [nor] fair to say that the average middle class resident receives $25 in direct benefits from that program. * * *

Some fairly obvious nominees to the category of programs that directly benefit the middle class are education,[g] roads, health and hospitals, police protection, and fire protection. * * *

This approach can now be applied to some actual figures for government spending. In 1984 the state and local governments of America spent a combined total of $145.3 billion (from their sales, property, and individual income tax revenues) on the following programs: education, roads, health and hospitals, police protection, and fire protection. Based on a population of 236 millon, this translates into an expenditure of $616 per capita. * * * Until some rigorous empirical study and statistical analysis are conducted, let us

---

g. Professor McCombs acknowledged, and discussed at some length, the possible distortions in computation arising from the fact that most S-L taxes are spent on public education, which is utilized at inconsistent rates by itemizing taxpayers. (Eds.)

assume that at least 80% of the itemizing taxpayers receive direct state and local government benefits in the amount of $500 or more each year.

* * *

[T]his article is proposing that a minimum floor of $500 in state and local tax payments be nondeductible, with any excess remaining deductible.

* * *

Progressivity

Another possible modification is to calculate the proposed floor as a percentage of adjusted gross income (AGI), as is currently done with the medical, casualty, and "miscellaneous itemized" deductions. That would eliminate the admittedly regressive effect of the proposal made by this article. * * *

Notes and Questions

1. Is the deduction for S-L taxes, or some of them, necessary for accurate measurement of income, or is section 164 best viewed as a subsidy? Would you give the same answer for all types of S-L taxes?

2. Is the deduction for S-L income taxes justified on the theory that the taxes are essentially indistinguishable from "ordinary and necessary" income-producing expenses deductible under sections 162 and 212?

3. Is it sufficient answer to the preceding question to note that federal income taxes are even harder for the taxpayer to avoid than S-L income taxes, yet federal taxes have not been deductible since 1917? Or is Professor Turnier correct in arguing that "one can characterize the 1917 changes as nothing more than a significant increase in the tax rate,"[h] which therefore tell us nothing about the propriety of a deduction for S-L income taxes?

4. A generation ago, marginal federal income tax rates stood at 91 percent. With some states imposing income tax rates of 10 percent or more, the deduction was thought to be necessary to prevent confiscatory taxation. Assuming this problem arose in the future, is the more appropriate solution for the federal government to allow deduction of S-L taxes, or vice versa? (Either route avoids the possibility of combined taxes rates in excess of 100 percent.) At present, some states allow deduction of federal income taxes in computing state income tax liability.

5. Assuming that the deduction for S-L taxes is viewed as a subsidy, who are the beneficiaries—high-tax states and localities, or high-bracket taxpayers who itemize deductions? Section 103's exclusion from federal

---

h. The quoted language, which is not part of the excerpt reprinted above, is found at 66 CORNELL L. REV., at 267.

income tax of interest paid by S-L governments is generally viewed as a boon for the issuers of the bonds, not their holders. Does section 164 lend itself to the same analysis?

6. Or might the beneficiaries be low-income people in high-tax states, who receive higher welfare benefits from S-L taxes made politically possible by the deduction?

7. How would you expect the elimination of the federal deduction for gasoline taxes to have affected consumption? In 1978, Congress ended the deductibility of S-L gasoline taxes, in part because "in view of the pressing national need to conserve energy and reduce oil imports, the Federal government should not in effect partially subsidize nonbusiness consumption of motor fuels through a deduction for State-local taxes on such fuels."[i] A dozen years before, however, the Senate Finance Committee had defended the deductibility of the gasoline tax, in part arguing that "to deny the deduction of [the gasoline] tax while allowing the deduction of property, income, and general sales taxes tends to encourage States to use other than automotive taxes as their more important revenue sources."[j] If removing the deduction for S-L gasoline taxes had no effect on S-L tax policies, then ending federal deductibility would increase the after-tax cost of gasoline and discourage its consumption. But if states and localities reacted to the removal of federal deductibility by lowering gasoline taxes (or, much more likely in the real world, by refraining from increasing those taxes), then the removal of deductibility might have had the unintended effect of making gasoline consumption cheaper than it otherwise would have been.

8. Quite apart from energy and environmental concerns, deductibility of gasoline taxes is almost uniformly condemned because the taxes are viewed as user fees, and are usually earmarked for highway construction and maintenance. But if one state finances its highways with income taxes while another employs gasoline taxes, should that difference mean that the first state, but not the second, should be able to shift part of its burden to the federal government? Or, if a state should choose to adopt high gasoline taxes to finance, let us say, education, why should the form of the tax bar the deduction?

9. Congress has been solicitous of the homeowner in the tax laws, through provisions such as section 163(h)(2)(D) (excluding most home mortgage interest from the definition of nondeductible personal interest); section 1034 (allowing tax-free rollover of gain from the sale of a principal

---

i. H. Rep. No. 1445, 95th Cong., 2d Sess., at 42 (1978); S. Rep. No. 1263, 95th Cong., 2d Sess., at 58 (1978).

j. S. Rep. No. 830, 88th Cong., 2d Sess., at 54 (1964).

residence); and section 121 (allowing taxpayers over age 55 an exclusion from income for up to $125,000 of gain from the sale of a principal residence under certain circumstances). Moreover, the imputed income arising from home ownership goes untaxed. See Chapter Three. Is the deduction for property taxes on owner-occupied residences an additional subsidy for homeowners vis-a-vis renters?[k] Could one argue instead that the renter automatically gets the benefit of the landlord's deduction for property taxes in the form of lower rent—and without the requirement of itemizing deductions?

10. Is the problem one of economic efficiency rather than equity? Perhaps the housing market has adjusted to the property tax deduction with the result that housing is overvalued, as compared to its value in a non-tax world. It might be argued that home buyers are not really benefitted by the deduction, because they have paid for it in the form of higher purchase prices. Is the principal problem that the deduction artificially increases housing values and thus diverts resources to housing of all types?

11. On the other hand, perhaps it is the S-L real estate taxes themselves, rather than the federal deduction for those taxes, that distorts the allocation of resources, and distorts it *against* real estate investment. Real estate taxes tend to be much heavier than property taxes on other forms of wealth, such as securities and other forms of intangible wealth. Real estate taxes owe much to tradition, and to the fact that real estate is very difficult to conceal either from the assessor or the collector. It may be that such taxes distort resources away from real estate investment, and that the federal income tax deduction of those taxes has the salutary effect of reducing that distortion. Do you find this argument persuasive?

12. In general, should the form of the S-L tax be as important as it is under present federal tax law, which allows full deductibility of some S-L taxes and no deduction for others?

13. Writing before the federal deduction for S-L sales taxes was repealed in 1986, Dr. Noto and Dr. Zimmerman identified several revenue-neutral alternatives to abolition of the sales tax deduction. What were these alternatives? Which alternative did they prefer? Do you agree with their conclusions?

---

k. There may be historical irony to the S-L tax deduction, now thought to favor homeowners. Professor Turnier, in a portion of his article that is not excerpted, suggested that the original deduction for taxes may have been designed to avoid unfairly favoring renters vis-a-vis homeowners. Congress allowed a deduction for rent in tax statutes enacted to finance the War Between the States, and Professor Turnier concluded that "the personal deduction for taxes probably arose out of a desire to equalize the tax treatment of renters and nonrenters." 66 CORNELL L. REV., at 269.

14. There is considerable difference of opinion concerning whether principles of federalism suggest that the federal government should allow deduction either of all major S-L taxes—income, property and general sales taxes—or of none. For example, in the Revenue Act of 1964, both the Ways and Means Committee and the Finance Committee concluded that if income and property taxes were to be deductible, the deductibility of sales taxes should be continued, because "it is important for the Federal Government to remain neutral as to the relative use made of these three forms of State and local taxation."[1] In 1986, Congress changed this policy. Is Congress improperly favoring states that rely on income and property taxes rather than sales taxes?

15. Assuming Congress' denial of a deduction for sales taxes is viewed as interference with S-L decision making, can such interference be justified as a federal attempt to discourage S-L use of regressive taxes?

On the other hand, note the antiprogressive effect of making S-L income taxes deductible. The ostensible degree of progressivity in S-L income taxes is reduced by the federal deduction. For example, a nine percent state income tax amounts to only six percent if the taxpayer itemizes and is in a 33 percent federal bracket.

16. If you agree that the federal government should "remain neutral," by treating major S-L taxes the same, should this be extended to *all* S-L taxes? In the recent past, S-L taxes such as "sin" taxes and gasoline taxes were deductible.

17. How much weight should be given to administrative concerns? It is relatively easy for taxpayers and the Internal Revenue Service to ascertain the amount of S-L income and property taxes paid. At the other extreme, it would be almost impossible to keep track of "sin" taxes and amusement taxes, and one might expect liberal guesses (a kinder, gentler term for fraud) from taxpayers, with the amounts being so small that the Service would rarely challenge them. Even the most conscientious taxpayer would have difficulty keeping track of gasoline taxes, except by reference to tables corresponding to mileage driven during the year, or of sales taxes, except by reference to tables based on income and family size.

18. The tax policy issues concerning deductibility of S-L taxes become enmeshed in broader issues about the proper scope of government and the means of financing it. For example, if only some S-L taxes are to be deductible (and thus encouraged by federal law), one might expect liberals

1. H. Rep. No. 749, 88th Cong., 1st Sess., at 49 (1963); S. Rep. No. 830, 88th Cong., 2d Sess., at 54 (1964).

to encourage deductibility of the income tax, which is typically progressive, and to argue against deductibility of the sales tax, which is typically regressive with respect to income. In the same vein, it may not be surprising that President Reagan, who is strongly identified with a preference for lower taxes at all levels of government, proposed an end to the deductibility of all S-L taxes. Treasury I argued that this would end an inappropriate subsidy to high-tax states, and an improper bias in favor of taxes rather than user fees. Critics of President Reagan's proposal saw it as an indirect method of attacking the social spending of high-tax states. If section 164 makes raising S-L taxes easier politically, does this argue in favor of retaining or repealing the provision?

19. Perhaps a federal subsidy to high-tax states can be justified if the high taxes are a means of dealing with a national problem that impacts some states more severely than others. Consider the following argument from Professor Edward Yorio:

Whenever a state imposes an above-average tax burden on its citizens, the excess may be due to one (or more) of the following factors: (1) the state provides more goods and services to its citizens than do other states; (2) the state is less efficient than other states; * * * (3) the cost of living in that state and hence the cost of government goods and services is higher; (4) citizens of that state endorse a higher level of government responsibility for solving social problems than citizens of other states; or (5) the state has been forced—or has chosen—to expend tax monies to alleviate a national social problem.

Of these explanations for variations in tax burdens among the states, only the last justifies a deduction for state and local taxes. * * *

[A]bove average rates of taxation in a particular state may be due to the state's assumption of a national burden, such as the costs of providing for an unusually large number of illegal aliens. Where state spending produces spillover benefits for the rest of the nation, the case for a deduction for state taxes is strong.[m] * * *

Assuming one accepts Professor Yorio's argument, How does one separate item 4 from item 5 if, for example, a high-tax/high-social-benefit state attracts, and provides for, a disproportionate share of the nation's homeless? In addition, keep in mind that costs and benefits are usually more complex than they initially appear. For example, employers in states with large numbers of illegal aliens (the example chosen by Professor Yorio) benefit from a supply of low-cost labor.

---

m. Edward Yorio, *The President's Tax Proposals: A Major Step in the Right Direction*, 53 FORDHAM L. REV. 1255, 1279-80 (1985).

20. Do you agree with Treasury I's characterization of S-L taxes as a form of consumption? Does it matter?

21. Do you agree with Treasury I's assertion that S-L taxes should not be viewed as truly involuntary assessments because of the taxpayers' control over the political machinery that levies the taxes? Professor Turnier (not in the article excerpted above) ridiculed this suggestion: "On the basis of that sort of reasoning, one can conclude that military conscription in a democracy results in an all volunteer army or that the victims of capital punishment in a democracy have committed suicide."[n] Professor Due, on the other hand, argued that the taxes are "mandatory payments, and particular individuals may strongly object. * * * But for the community as a whole, state and local tax payments constitute voluntary payments for services rendered and are as discretionary as the purchase of new cars or suits of clothes."[o]

22. Do you agree that the ability of S-L taxpayers to relocate to a different taxing jurisdiction means that their S-L taxes should not be regarded as involuntary?

23. Canada allows no deduction for provincial taxes. For a brief comparison of Canadian and U.S. practice, including a brief discussion of "equalization payments * * * paid by the Canadian federal government to the poorer provinces," see pages 157-67 of Professor Bale's article cited in the bibliography.

C. A FEDERAL CREDIT FOR STATE AND LOCAL TAXES?

Virtually all debate on the federal tax treatment of S-L taxes has centered on whether such taxes should give rise to a *deduction*. A deduction, however, merely reduces the sting of S-L taxes. On the other hand, it is certainly possible to envision a federal *credit* for S-L taxes. To the extent a federal credit were available, a taxpayer would be indifferent to the level of S-L taxes, because the burden would be offset by a dollar-for-dollar reduction in federal taxes. For example, under a ten percent credit, a taxpayer with pre-credit federal income tax liability of $5,000 would be allowed a credit of the lesser of $500 or his state income tax liability. An immediate consequence of such a system would be that all states would enact income taxes sufficient to absorb the credit, because this would give the states additional tax revenue without additional cost to their taxpayers. A generation ago, Professor Walter Heller, while arguing that S-L taxes other

---

n. William J. Turnier, *Personal Deductions and Tax Reform: The High Road and the Low Road*, 31 VILL. L. REV. 1703, 1735 (1986).

o. Due, John F., *Personal Deductions, in* COMPREHENSIVE INCOME TAXATION 37, 51 (Joseph A. Pechman ed., 1977).

than income taxes should not even be deductible, offered the Ways and Means Committee a detailed proposal of a limited federal income tax credit for state income taxes:

DEDUCTIONS AND CREDITS FOR STATE INCOME TAXES
Walter W. Heller[*]

House Comm. on Ways and Means, 86th Cong., 1st Sess.

1 Tax Revision Compendium 419, 423-27 (1959)

The Case for a Federal Credit

The case for a Federal credit for State income taxes paid does not rest on the removal of income tax deductibility. Retention or removal will affect the form which the credit should take, but not the underlying case for it. That case rests on (1) the need for drawing on the superior taxing power of the Federal Government to undergird the strenuous State tax efforts required to meet the severe financial strains on State and local budgets today and in the years ahead; (2) the need to reduce interstate differentials in income taxation and thereby to allay the fears of interstate migration of industry and wealth which plague the States in their efforts to make full use of their tax potential; (3) the need for Federal fiscal support in a form that will reduce rather than increase income inequalities among the States.

   * * *

The Fear of Interstate Competition

Another important cause of favorable action on a Federal tax credit is the impact that fears of driving out industry and wealth have in choking off the full use of State tax resources. Although every unbiased study of location factors ranks taxes well below such considerations as skill and productivity of the labor force, closeness to markets, availability of plentiful water and low-cost power, the fear of interstate competition continues to be a major, even a growing, influence in the politics of State taxation. And the State income tax movement bears the full brunt of taxpayer threats to seek haven in friendlier tax territory. This process of playing off one State against another has the net effect of weakening the financial base of responsible self-government and striking hard at the tax which responds most readily to economic growth. * * *

Congress should follow the precedent it established 35 years ago when it enacted a Federal estate tax credit to bring to an end the vicious competitive rate cutting which had threatened to run State death taxes into the ground. A Federal income tax credit averaging 5 or 10 percent would not remove the interstate competition threat entirely, but it would put a substantial noncompetitive floor under State income taxes and reduce the struggle for competitive advantage which has retarded the use of the outstanding growth tax in the State revenue system.

---

*. At time of original publication, Professor, University of Minnesota.

Interstate Equalization

Either substitution of a Federal credit for deductibility, whether as a flat percentage of the Federal tax or on a sliding-scale basis, or supplementation of deductibility by a sliding-scale credit would serve to reduce somewhat the existing interstate inequalities of income. * * * [T]he protective impact of deductibility is greater, the wealthier the state; the higher the brackets a State's taxpayers are in, on the average, the larger the percentage of the State income tax burden that can be "exported" to the Federal Government.

* * *

[S]ubstitution of a flat credit would materially improve the distribution of benefits by income groups in the sense of sharing a larger portion of the benefits with the lower bracket taxpayers than they receive at present under deductibility. * * * A corresponding improvement in the interstate impact of the allowance for State income taxes would also take place with the substitution of the credit for the deduction. Proportionately, the residents of the poorer States would get a substantially larger part of any given benefit in the form of a tax credit than they now get in the form of a deduction from income. The net effect would be a shift in Federal support from the wealthier to the poorer States.

This shift could be magnified by the adoption of a sliding-scale credit of the type illustrated in table 3. Here, the credit would be 20 percent of the first $200 of Federal income tax, 10 percent of the next $300, and 1 percent of the remainder. If Federal deductibility were retained, it would be imperative to put a Federal credit in this negatively graduated form in order to balance somewhat the bias of deductibility in favor of high incomes. Even if the deduction were eliminated, the desire to build a positive interstate equalizing effect into the credit for State income taxes might well lead to some form of the sliding scale.

Table 3 demonstrates the equalizing effect. The central column shows that State taxpayers in Mississippi and Montana would get almost twice as large an average credit against their Federal tax as those in Delaware, and about one-third more than those in New York, Michigan, and Illinois. Since the average credit allowed in each State depends on both the average size and the distribution of income, the suggested sliding-scale credit would not accomplish the perfect inverse correlation between size of credit and per capita income that might be desired. But its general effect would be the desired one: to provide more fiscal support to the poorer, and less fiscal support to the wealthier, States.

Concluding Comments

* * *

As to the Federal revenue loss, this would depend on the size of the credit and the action taken on other State and local tax deductions. Removal

Table 3 - *Allowable Credit Against Federal Income Tax Under a Sliding-scale Credit Plan: 20 percent against the first $200 of Federal tax, 10 percent against the next $300, and 1 percent against tax in excess of $500, Selected States, 1956*

States	1956 Federal individual income tax liability	Total Federal tax credit allowable to residents of each State under sliding scale credit plan	
		Amount	As percent of Federal liability
Arkansas	$133,344	$13,228	9.9
California	3,373,902	269,593	8.0
Delaware	161,748	8,600	5.3
Florida	644,329	51,198	7.9
Georgia	385,097	36,781	9.6
Illinois	2,611,643	203,751	7.8
Kansas	303,256	29,435	9.7
Louisiana	388,475	32,513	8.4
Maryland	646,807	57,981	9.0
Michigan	1,839,256	143,024	7.8
Minnessota	526,262	50,349	9.6
Mississippi	119,728	12,010	10.0
Missouri	746,046	65,349	8.8
Montana	97,412	9,790	10.1
New York	4,232,431	327,914	7.7
Ohio	2,149,144	181,794	8.5
Pennsylvania	2,373,040	207,911	8.8
Rhode Island	166,319	15,313	9.2
Tennessee	377,869	35,355	9.4
Texas	1,404,530	114,278	8.1
Wisconsin	686,386	63,210	9.2

of all such deductions would make possible a Federal credit averaging 5 percent without any appreciable revenue loss. * * *

Finally, what of the coercion issue? The crediting device represents a paradoxical combination of freedom and coercion. Its most fundamental purpose is to protect the power of the purse underlying State sovereignty and local independence. Moreover, Federal credits, while certain to bring about greater uniformity not only in income tax burdens but also in the structure of income taxation at the State level, leave ample room for variations in State definitions of income, exemptions, and tax rates. At the same time, the credit would strongly induce if not force [states without an income tax] to adopt at least minimum, credit-absorbing personal income taxes. On balance, it seems fair to conclude that the Federal tax credit, particularly if substituted for the present deduction for state income taxes, offers the States a large gain in fiscal integrity and independence in exchange for a relatively small loss in freedom of taxation.

Notes and Questions

24. It is important to remember that Professor Heller wrote over 35 years ago. Obviously, the dollar amounts must be updated for inflation. More important may be the political and policy implications of the long and unbroken string of large federal deficits. In developing the idea that the federal government should use its "superior taxing power" in support of the states, Professor Heller pointed to "[p]rojections for the next decade [which] generally forecast rising surpluses for the Federal Government, rising deficits for State-local governments." Such projections seem anachronistic in the current era of 12-digit federal deficits.

25. The Internal Revenue Code provides taxpayers their choice of a deduction (section 164) or a credit (section 901) for income taxes paid to a foreign country. Normally, the credit proves more beneficial. Thus, if a U.S. citizen owns stock in a British company that pays dividends taxable by Great Britain, the taxpayer must include the dividends in U.S. income, but receives a credit for British tax paid or withheld (not to exceed the U.S. tax attributable to the British-source income). Presumably, Congress allows the credit in order to avoid double taxation—the same income being taxed by both Great Britain and the United States. Why do considerations of equity lead us to allow a credit with respect to foreign income taxes, but not for S-L income taxes? (Superficially, it might appear that a New York resident taxed by both New York and the federal government was being subjected to double taxation on the same income, in the same way as the U.S.-citizen recipient of British dividends.)

26. States *inter se* normally provide a credit comparable to the federal foreign tax credit, for income taxes paid to another state. For example, if an Arkansas resident works part of the year in Missouri and is subjected to Missouri income tax, Arkansas requires inclusion of the Missouri-source income but then allows a credit for the Missouri tax paid (not to exceed the Arkansas tax attributable to the Missouri-source income).

27. Why would an unlimited federal credit for state income taxes be completely unworkable?

28. In part, Professor Heller justified his proposal as an effort to discourage both relocation by taxpayers, and actions by states and localities to affect relocation decisions. Why might enactment of his proposal have that effect? Does your answer depend upon whether the state's income tax is imposed at a rate in excess of the allowable federal credit?

29. Do you agree with Professor Heller that S-L efforts to attract industry with preferential tax rates are objectionable? Professor Heller states that tax considerations are less important than factors such as "skill and productivity of the labor force, closeness to markets, availability of plentiful water and low-cost power." Should states with less able labor forces, and less favorable locations and resources, be able to compete for industry by offering lower taxes?

30. Interstate tax competition is not limited to S-L *income* taxes, of course. Indeed, Professor Heller referred to the early competition among states for the wealthy elderly, who might be attracted by a low rate of death taxes. Congress responded by allowing a credit against the federal estate tax for state death taxes up to a certain level. This level became the minimum state death tax, because a state could no longer provide an advantage to its decedents by lowering the state death tax below the level that would be fully offset by the federal credit. See section 2011. For further discussion of this credit, see Chapter Ten, Note #17.

31. What of competition arising from other preferential tax treatment, notably the property tax? And what of a state or locality providing a free building, such as a stadium to attract (or retain) a professional sports franchise?

32. Enactment of Professor Heller's proposal would mean that all states not having an income tax, or not having a tax high enough to absorb the federal credit, would immediately change their laws to take advantage of the federal credit. In this sense, Professor Heller acknowledged that his proposal entailed, "a large measure of federal coercion." On the other hand, he argued that his proposal "represents a paradoxical combination of freedom and coercion." In what sense might a state find greater freedom of action under this proposal?

33. Focusing on individuals rather than states, a federal tax benefit structured as a credit probably would be of more value than an itemized deduction to low-income taxpayers, and of less value to high-income taxpayers. Does this argue in favor of the credit?

34. Professor Heller would prefer a sliding-scale credit, which would allow low-income taxpayers a relatively higher credit. For example (writing a generation ago), he suggested a credit of 20 percent of first $200 of federal income tax, 10 percent of the next $300, and one percent of the remainder. What justifications did he offer? Do you agree?

Professor Heller appeared to focus at least as much on high- and low-income *states* as on high- and low-income *individuals*. Is the effect on rich and poor states a relevant concern?

Selected Bibliography

Bale, Gordon, *The Treasury's Proposals for Tax Reform: A Canadian Perspective*, 48 LAW & CONTEMP. PROBS. 151 (1985).

Brazer, Harvey E., *The Deductibility of State and Local Taxes Under the Individual Income Tax*, in HOUSE COMM. ON WAYS AND MEANS, 86TH CONG., 1ST SESS., 1 TAX REVISION COMPENDIUM 407 (1959).

Break, George F., *Tax Principles in a Federal System*, in THE ECONOMICS OF TAXATION 317 (Henry J. Aaron & Michael J. Boskin eds., 1980).

Courant, Paul N. & Edward M. Gramlich, *The Impact of the Tax Reform Act of 1986 on State and Local Fiscal Behavior*, in DO TAXES MATTER? THE IMPACT OF THE TAX REFORM ACT OF 1986 243 (Joel Slemrod ed., 1990).

Due, John F., *Personal Deductions*, in COMPREHENSIVE INCOME TAXATION 37 (Joseph A. Pechman ed., 1977).

GOODE, RICHARD E., THE INDIVIDUAL INCOME TAX 168-71 (Rev. ed. 1976).

Gramlich, Edward M., *The Deductibility of State and Local Taxes*, 38 NAT'L TAX J. 447 (1985).

Heller, Walter W., *Deductions and Credits for State Income Taxes*, in HOUSE COMM. ON WAYS AND MEANS, 86TH CONG., 1ST SESS., 1 TAX REVISION COMPENDIUM 419 (1959).

Janiga, John M. & Louis S. Harrison, *The Case for the Retention of the State Death Tax Credit in the Federal Transfer Tax Scheme: "Just Say No" to a Deduction*, 21 PEPP. L. REV. 695 (1994).

McCombs, JB, *New Federal Treatment of State and Local Taxes*, 19 PAC. L.J. 747 (1988).

Noto, Nonna A. & Dennis Zimmerman, *Limiting State-Local Tax Deductibility: Effects Among the States*, 37 NAT'L TAX J. 539 (1984).

THE PRESIDENT'S TAX PROPOSALS TO THE CONGRESS FOR FAIRNESS, GROWTH AND SIMPLICITY 62-69 (1985) ["Treasury II"].

Steuerle, Gene, *The State and Local Tax Deduction*, 71 TAX NOTES 389 (1996).

Turnier, William J., *Evaluating Personal Deductions in an Income Tax—The Ideal*, 66 CORNELL L. REV. 262 (1981).

——, *Personal Deductions and Tax Reform: The High Road and the Low Road*, 31 VILL. L. REV. 1703 (1986).

U.S. DEP'T. OF TREASURY, 1 TAX REFORM FOR FAIRNESS, SIMPLICITY, AND ECONOMIC GROWTH, 78-81 (1984) ["Treasury I"].

PART V

TAXATION OF BUSINESS AND INVESTMENT INCOME

Part V discusses the income tax in relation to the major components of our business economy. Chapter Fourteen covers issues involving corporations and dividends. These issues require facing the fundamental question of who bears the corporate income tax: shareholders, employees, customers, the return on capital in the economy generally, or the corporations themselves. Assuming that all, or the major share, of the corporate income tax is borne by the shareholders, the next question is what, if anything, should be done about the double tax borne by shareholders. The numerous solutions that have been offered to the double tax are described. Finally, the implications of interest deductions by corporations and the retained earnings of corporations are discussed.

Chapter Fifteen deals with a perennial high-profile tax policy issue, the tax treatment of capital gains and losses. The unsettled history of their treatment is described. Unique features of capital gains are discussed, as are peripheral areas where capital gain treatment is accorded to income on the borderline between ordinary income and capital gains. Restrictions on use of capital losses are discussed. The politically-charged assertion that the tax treatment of capital gain is an important factor in determining national rates of saving and investment is explored. Finally, capital gain treatment is related to the treatment of gain and loss on sale of taxpayers' homes.

Chapter Sixteen goes to the fundamental question of how to measure taxable income in a climate of changing price levels. Present inflation adjustments to the tax rate structure are described. The more complex issue of whether, and how, to apply inflation adjustments to the measurement of gains, losses, interest deductions, and investments in debt instruments are discussed. Also, questions are raised as to the accuracy of existing measures of price level changes.

CHAPTER FOURTEEN

CORPORATIONS AND DIVIDENDS

*During the 1980s Congress produced five major facelifts of Subchapter C. * * * Each enactment reflected the noble goal of structural tax reform; none represented an obvious attempt to satisfy special interests. Yet despite these efforts, * * * calls for restructuring corporate taxation seem even more urgent.*[a]

A. INTRODUCTION

The taxes considered in this chapter generate significant revenue. The corporate income tax currently yields approximately 11 percent of total federal tax revenues, as compared to 43 percent for individual income taxes and 37 percent for social insurance taxes.[b] Moreover, dividends paid by C corporations and taxed to individual shareholders account for over three percent of taxable income under the individual income tax.[c]

The preeminent policy issues in the taxation of corporations and shareholders relate to the degree to which tax law should follow nontax law to treat corporations and their shareholders as separate taxable entities. C corporations are taxable entities, separate from their shareholders, in contrast to partnerships[d] and S corporations.[e] Because corporations are not allowed a deduction for dividends paid, and the dividends are fully subject to tax in the hands of individual shareholders, the result is a double tax on income earned by a corporation and distributed as dividends to its individual owners.

The second tax cannot necessarily be avoided by a corporate policy of not paying dividends, even if one ignores the slight possibility of imposition of the

---

a. Paul B. Stephan, III, *Disaggregation and Subchapter C: Rethinking Corporate Tax Reform*, 76 VA. L. REV. 655, 655 (1990).

b. In 1994, federal receipts from corporate income taxes were $140 billion, individual income tax receipts were $543 billion and social insurance tax receipts were $462 billion. Total federal receipts amounted to $1.258 trillion. U.S. BUREAU OF THE CENSUS, STATISTICAL ABSTRACT OF THE UNITED STATES, tbl. 518, at 334 (115th ed. 1995).

c. In 1992, dividends included in the adjusted gross income of individuals amounted to $78 billion; total taxable income of individuals was $2.396 trillion. *Id.* tbl. 533, at 345. (Not all adjusted gross income becomes taxable income, of course, because some is offset by deductions and personal and dependency exemptions. Nevertheless, it is the case for most individuals that if dividends were not included in the tax base, taxable income would be reduced by the amount of the dividends.)

d. Some publicly traded partnerships are treated as taxable entities under the same provisions that apply to corporations and their shareholders. Section 7704. *See infra* Note #8.

e. Hereinafter, the term "corporation" should be understood to refer to a C corporation unless otherwise indicated.

accumulated earnings tax.[f] To the extent that common stock of a corporation appreciates in value because of undistributed income that has been earned and taxed to the corporation, sale of the stock by the shareholders at a gain produces a second tax, though generally in the form of a capital gain. This does not occur, however, if a shareholder dies owning stock that has appreciated in value because the stock then takes a basis equal to its value at the date of the decedent's death. See section 1014 and Chapter Nine. The portion of a capital gain tax that is a second tax due to accumulated earnings is difficult to isolate and measure because the market value of common stock is affected by so many other factors.

Corporate shareholders are largely exempt from the second, shareholder-level, tax. The dividends-received deduction in section 243 reflects a decision largely to exempt the passage of earnings from one corporation to another until distribution is finally made to a noncorporate shareholder, who normally would be fully taxed. Such dividends are entirely tax free if the corporations are members of an affiliated group, which requires an 80-percent-ownership relationship while the earnings are accumulated and distributed. Otherwise, 80 percent of deductions can be deducted by a corporate shareholder that owns at least 20 percent of the stock of the dividend-paying corporation, and 70 percent of dividends are deductible if the corporate shareholder owns less than 20 percent of the payor. See section 243 and Note #5 for details and limitations.

Similar to the individual income tax, the corporate rate structure of section 11 is graduated, except for specified categories of personal service corporations. A corporation is taxed at 15 percent on the first $50,000 of income, 25 percent on income between $50,000 and $75,000, and 34 percent on income between $75,000 and $10 million. When a corporation's taxable income exceeds $100,000, however, a tax of five percentage points in addition to the 34 percent standard rate is applied to its income until this five-percentage-point tax amounts to $11,750. At this point, when the corporation's taxable income is $335,000, the five-percentage-point "notch" tax rate has absorbed all the advantage from the 15 percent rate and the 25 percent rate on the corporation's first $75,000 of income. The tax rate on income in excess of $10 million is 35 percent. Another notch rate of three additional percentage points, or a total rate of 38 percent, is applied to income in excess of $15 million until it absorbs the advantage of the 34 percent rate.

Notes and Questions

Tax rates

1. Discussion of corporate tax rates must take place against the

---

f. Sections 531 et seq. impose a tax on accumulations of earnings "beyond the reasonable needs of the business," but only if accumulations exceed $250,000.

background of substantially higher tax rates in a not-so-distant past. Before
the Tax Reform Act of 1986 the top corporate tax rate was 46 percent and the
top tax rate for individuals was 50 percent. The 1986 Act not only lowered
rates for both individuals and corporations, but reversed the previous pattern
of taxing corporations at rates lower than the top individual tax rate. Under
the 1993 Act, however, the top individual tax rate (39.6 percent) again is
higher than the top corporate rate (35 percent). Assuming that corporations
should be taxable entities, what relationship (if any) should be maintained
between corporate income tax rates and individual income tax rates?

2.   In addition to the regular income tax, section 59A imposes a tax of
0.12 percent on income in excess of $2 million. The tax is designed to finance
the fund to clean up the environment and is called the environmental tax.
The income subject to this tax is a modified version of the corporation's
alternative minimum taxable income.

3.   All income of some personal service corporations is taxed at a flat
35 percent rate. These corporations perform health, law, engineering,
architectural, accounting, actuarial, art performance, or consulting services.
Such corporations are viewed as the alter egos of their typically high-income
owner/employees, and the high flat rate prevents these individuals from
benefitting from the graduated corporate tax structure.

4.   There is no connection between a corporation's tax rate and the tax
rates of its individual shareholders. Should there be such a connection?
Should the corporate income tax have progressive rates?

5.   *Dividends-received deduction.* The broad outline of the dividends-
received deduction of section 243 is subject to qualifications. The deduction
is reduced in the proportion that stock ownership is debt-financed. The
apparent reason is to block a corporation's using debt financing to combine
an interest deduction and dividend income taxed at preferential rates.

The 100 percent dividends-received deduction normally allowed if both
the corporation paying the dividend and the corporate shareholder are
members of the same affiliated group—that is, affiliated through 80 percent
ownership—is limited to dividends paid out of earnings accumulated after
1963 while the two corporations were affiliated.

This treatment is flawed in that the definition of earnings out of which
dividends are paid is not consistent with the definition of taxable income.
Consequently, some dividends eligible for a dividends-received deduction
have not been taxed at the corporate level at an earlier stage. If section 243
were perfected to reach only dividends paid out of previously taxed earnings,
one might ask whether all such dividends (and not merely those paid to
members of affiliated groups) should be eligible for the 100 percent

dividends-received deduction.

Affiliated corporations

6. Groups of affiliated corporations are permitted to file consolidated income tax returns instead of reporting income or loss separately. Dividends are eliminated when paid within an affiliated group of corporations filing a consolidated return. Treatment of consolidated returns is governed by extensive "legislative" regulations issued pursuant to section 1501.

7. Even if a consolidated return is not filed, if a corporation owns 80 percent or more of the stock of one or more other corporations, these corporations are combined for purposes of applying the graduated income tax rates. Section 1561. Corporations that are owned by the same small group of individuals also are combined for purposes of applying the graduated tax rates. Section 1563(a)(2). What is the purpose of these provisions?

8. *Entities taxable as corporations.* A corporation may have only one shareholder. Professional associations organized under a state's corporate laws can qualify as C corporations for tax purposes. Associations can be taxable as corporations even though they are not incorporated. Among the associations taxable as corporations are trusts with transferable interests. So long as they are not publicly traded partnerships described in section 7704, partnerships, even limited partnerships, generally do not fall in the category of associations taxable as corporations. Neither do organizations set up as limited liability companies. In Notice 95-14,[g] the Treasury Department proposed to allow associations to choose between partnership and corporation treatment (so long as they are not publicly traded partnerships described in section 7704).

In some instances dummy corporations set up to facilitate title transfers and the like are disregarded for tax purposes. If a corporation engages in any substantial activity, however, it is required to file a corporate income tax return and is treated as a separate taxable entity.

Limitations on deductions by corporations

9. *Interest.* The limits placed on interest deductions by individual taxpayers do not apply to most corporations, because interest paid by corporations ordinarily is considered paid in the course of trade or business. There are, however, some limits on interest deductions by corporations. In some instances interest in excess of $5 million a year on subordinated indebtedness incurred to permit the debtor corporation to acquire stock or a substantial majority of the operating assets of another corporation may not be deducted. Section 279. Interest on debt between related corporations and

---

g. 1995-1 C.B. 297.

between corporations and their over-50 percent owners may not be deducted until reported in income by the related creditor. Section 267. Also, corporations—as is the case with individuals—may not deduct interest on loans used to finance investments in tax-exempt bonds. Section 265(a)(2).

10. *Charitable contributions.* Section 170(b)(2) permits corporations to deduct charitable contributions in amounts up to 10 percent of taxable income.

11. *Losses.* Losses on transactions with over-50 percent shareholders are denied by section 267.

12. This Chapter does not discuss the alternative minimum tax, which applies lower tax rates to a broader base. Section 55 et seq. The Contract with America Tax Relief Act of 1995, in the form in which it passed the House of Representatives, provided for repeal of the alternative minimum tax on corporations after the year 2000.

B. WHO BEARS THE CORPORATE TAX?

FEDERAL TAX POLICY
Joseph A. Pechman[*]
Pages 135-37, 141-45, 151-54 (5th ed. 1987)

The corporation income tax was enacted in 1909, four years before the introduction of the individual income tax. To avoid a constitutional issue, Congress levied the tax as an excise on the privilege of doing business as a corporation. The law was challenged, but the Supreme Court upheld the authority of the federal government to impose such a tax and ruled that the privilege of doing corporate business could be measured by the corporation's profits.

The corporation income tax produced more revenue than the individual income tax in seventeen of the twenty-eight years before 1941, when the latter was greatly expanded as a source of wartime revenue. From 1941 through 1967 corporation income tax receipts were second only to those of the individual income tax, but they were overtaken by payroll taxes in fiscal year 1968 and have since been declining in importance. The corporation income tax accounted for about 8 percent of federal receipts in 1986, compared with 28 percent in 1956. Since the end of World War II, the corporate tax rate has been reduced from a peak of 52 percent in 1952-63 to 34 percent beginning July 1, 1987. Corporate tax receipts should increase as a share of total tax collections as a result of the reforms enacted in 1986, but the share will remain significantly lower than it was in earlier postwar years.

---

[*]. At time of original publication, Senior Fellow, The Brookings Institution.

A business enterprise enjoys special privileges and benefits when it operates in the corporate form. These include perpetual life, limited liability of shareholders, liquidity of ownership through marketability of shares, growth through retention of earnings, and possibilities of intercorporate affiliations.   Moreover, the modern corporation—particularly the large "public" corporation in which management and ownership are separated—generates income that nobody may claim for personal use. The growth of the corporate sector could not have taken place if the corporation had not been endowed with these valuable privileges. The Supreme Court's acceptance of the constitutionality of the corporation income tax was based on the view that the corporation owes its life, rights, and power to the government.

Few experts accept this rationale for a substantial tax on corporate profits. Instead, one justification seems to be that the corporation is a mechanism for accumulating capital that is managed by the corporate officers and directors, and is not really subject to the control of the owners—the stockholders. Proponents of the corporation tax believe that the earnings and economic power derived from this large stock of capital are a proper base for taxation.

Another reason for the corporation income tax is that it is needed to safeguard the individual income tax. If corporate income were not subject to tax, people could avoid the individual income tax by accumulating income in corporations. Short of taxing shareholders on their shares of corporate income whether the income is distributed or not (a method that has been proposed from time to time), the most practical way to protect the individual income tax is to impose a separate tax on corporate income. * * *

Despite its long history in the United States, the corporation income tax is the subject of considerable controversy. In the first place, there is no general agreement about who really pays it. Some believe the tax is borne by the corporations and hence by their stockholders. Others believe it depresses the rate of return to capital throughout the economy and is therefore borne by owners of capital in general. Still others argue that the tax is passed on to consumers through higher prices or may be shifted back to the workers in lower wages. Some believe that it is borne by all three groups—stockholders, consumers, and wage earners—in varying proportions. This uncertainty about the incidence of the tax makes strange bedfellows of individuals holding diametrically opposed views and often puts them in inconsistent positions. Some staunch opponents of a sales tax vigorously support the corporation income tax even though they profess to believe it is shifted to the consumer, while many who say that the corporation tax is "just another cost" (and is consequently shifted) demand that the tax be reduced and some form of consumption tax substituted for all or part of it.

Second, the proper relation between individual and corporation income taxes has never been settled in the United States. At various times, dividends have been allowed as a credit or deduction in computing the tax on individual income. Currently, there is no deduction for dividends, but there is still considerable agitation to moderate or eliminate the so-called double taxation of distributed corporate earnings.

A third set of issues has to do with the effect of the corporation tax on the corporate sector and on the economy in general. It has been argued that the tax places a heavy burden on corporations and thus curtails business investment and reduces the nation's growth rate. Since interest paid is deductible in computing taxable corporation profits but dividends paid are not, the tax is said to favor debt over equity financing and to encourage the retention of earnings rather than paying them out in dividends. Some question the desirability of a tax that discourages the corporate form of business; others believe that alternative tax sources yielding the same revenue would be more harmful to the economy.

Fourth, the introduction of tax incentives for investment has sharply reduced the yield of the corporation income tax. When corporate income was not measured or taxed uniformly, effective rates of tax varied widely among firms and industries. Beginning in 1987, the elimination of the investment tax credit and the adoption of depreciation rates that more nearly resemble economic depreciation will greatly reduce the variation in tax rates. However, the corporate tax continues to distort the allocation of investment and reduce economic efficiency.

* * *

Shifting and Incidence of the Tax

There is no more controversial issue in taxation than the question, "Who bears the corporation income tax?" On this question, both economists and businessmen differ among themselves. The following quotations are representative of these divergent views:

> Corporate taxes are simply costs, and the method of their assessment does not change this fact. Costs must be paid by the public in prices, and corporate taxes are thus, in effect, concealed sales taxes. (Enders M. Voorhees, chairman of the Finance Committee, U.S. Steel Corporation, address before the Controllers' Institute of America, New York, September 21, 1943.)

> The initial or short-run incidence of the corporate income tax seems to be largely on corporations and their stockholders. . . . There seems to be little foundation for the belief that a large part of the corporate tax comes out of wages or is passed on to consumers in the same way that a selective excise [tax] tends to be shifted to buyers. (Richard Goode, *The Corporation Income Tax*, Wiley, 1951, pp. 71-72.)

> . . . The corporation profits tax is almost entirely shifted; the

government simply uses the corporation as a tax collector. (Kenneth E. Boulding, *The Organizational Revolution*, Harper, 1953, p. 277.)

It is hard to avoid the conclusion that plausible alternative sets of assumptions about the relevant elasticities all yield results in which capital bears very close to 100 percent of the [corporate] tax burden. (Arnold C. Harberger, "The Incidence of the Corporation Income Tax," *Journal of Political Economy*, vol. 70, June 1962, p. 234.)

. . . An increase in the [corporate] tax is shifted fully through short-run adjustments to prevent a decline in the net rate of return [on corporate investment], and . . . these adjustments are maintained subsequently. (Marian Krzyzaniak and Richard A. Musgrave, *The Shifting of the Corporation Income Tax*, Johns Hopkins Press, 1963, p. 65.)

. . . There is no inter-sector inefficiency resulting from the imposition of the corporate profits tax with the interest deductibility provision. Nor is there any misallocation between safe and risky industries. From an efficiency point of view, the whole corporate profits tax structure is just like a lump sum tax on corporations. (Joseph E. Stiglitz, "Taxation, Corporate Financial Policy, and the Cost of Capital," *Journal of Public Economics*, vol. 2, February 1973, p. 33.)

. . . If the net rate of return is given in the international market place, the burden of a tax on the income from capital in one country will not (in the middle or long run) end up being borne by capital (which can flee) but by other factors of production (land, labor, and to a degree, perhaps, old fixed capital). (Arnold C. Harberger, "The State of the Corporate Tax: Who Pays It? Should It Be Replaced?" in Charls E. Walker and Mark A. Bloomfield, eds., *New Directions in Federal Tax Policy for the 1980s*, Ballinger, 1983.)

Unfortunately, economics has not yet provided a scientific basis for accepting or rejecting one side or the other. This section presents the logic of each view and summarizes the evidence.

The Shifting Mechanism

One reason for the sharply divergent views is that the opponents frequently do not refer to the same type of shifting. It is important to distinguish between short- and long-run shifting and the mechanisms through which they operate. The "short run" is defined by economists as a period too short for firms to adjust their capital to changing demand and supply conditions. The "long run" is a period in which capital can be adjusted.

The Short Run

The classical view in economics is that the corporation income tax cannot be shifted in the short run. The argument is as follows: all business firms, whether they are competitive or monopolistic, seek to maximize net profits. This maximum occurs when output and prices are set at the point where the cost of producing an additional unit is exactly equal to the additional revenue obtained from the sale of that unit. In the short run, a tax on economic profit should make no difference in this decision. The output and price that maximized the firm's profits before the tax will continue to maximize profits after the tax is imposed. (This follows from simple arithmetic. If a series of figures is reduced by the same percentage, the figure that was highest before will be the highest after.)

The opposite view is that today's markets are characterized neither by perfect competition nor by monopoly; instead, they show considerable imperfection and mutual interdependence or oligopoly. In such markets, business firms may set their prices at the level that covers their full cost *plus* a margin for profits. Alternatively, the firms are described as aiming at an after-tax target rate of return on their invested capital. Under the cost-plus behavior, the firm treats the tax as an element of cost and raises its price to recover the tax. (Public utilities are usually able to shift the tax in this way, because state rate-making agencies treat the corporation tax as a cost.) Similarly, if the firm's objective is the after-tax target rate of return, imposition of a tax or an increase in the tax rate—by reducing the rate of return on invested capital—will have to be accounted for in making output and price decisions. To preserve the target rate of return, the tax must be shifted forward to consumers or backward to the workers or partly forward and partly backward.

It is also argued that the competitive models are irrelevant in most markets where one or a few large firms exercise a substantial degree of leadership. In such markets, efficient producers raise their prices to recover the tax, and the tax merely forms an "umbrella" that permits less efficient or marginal producers to survive.

When business managers are asked about their pricing policies, they often say that they shift the corporation income tax. However, even if business firms intend to shift the tax, there is some doubt about their ability to shift it fully in the short run. In the first place, the tax depends on the outcome of business operations during an entire year. Businessmen can only guess the ratio of the tax to their gross receipts, and it is hard to conceive of their setting a price that would recover the precise amount of tax they will eventually pay. (If shifting were possible, there would be some instances of firms shifting more than 100 percent of the tax, but few economists believe that overshifting actually occurs.)

Second, businessmen know that should they attempt to recover the corporation income tax through higher prices (or lower wages), other firms would not necessarily do the same. Some firms make no profit or have large loss carry-overs and thus pay no tax; among other firms, the ratio of tax to gross receipts differs. In multi product firms, the producer has even less basis for judging the ratio of tax to gross receipts for each product. All these possibilities increase the uncertainty of response by other firms and make the attempt to shift part or all of the corporation income tax hazardous.

The Long Run

In the long run, the corporation income tax influences investment by reducing the rate of return on corporate equity. If the corporation income tax is not shifted in the short run, net after-tax rates of return are depressed, and the incentive to undertake corporate investment is thereby reduced. After-tax rates of return tend to be equalized with those in the noncorporate sector, but in the process corporate capital and output will have been permanently reduced. Thus, if there is no short-run shifting and if the supply of capital is fixed, the burden of the tax falls on the owners of capital in general. If the depressed rate of return on capital reduces investment, productivity of labor decreases and at least part of the tax may be borne by workers.

Where investment is financed by borrowing, the corporation tax cannot affect investment decisions because interest on debt is a deductible expense. If the marginal investment of a firm is fully financed by debt, the corporation tax becomes a lump-sum tax on profits generated by previous investments and is borne entirely by the owners of the corporation, the stockholders. In view of the recent large increase in debt financing (see the section on equity and debt finance below), a substantial proportion of the corporation income tax may now rest on stockholders and not be diffused to owners of capital in general through the shifting process just described.

The Corporation Tax in an Open Economy

The foregoing analysis assumed that the corporation tax was imposed in a closed economy. In an open economy, the rate of return on capital is set in the international marketplace. If the tax in one country is higher than it is elsewhere, capital will move to other countries until the rate of return is raised to the international level. Thus the burden of the tax would not be borne by capital but by other factors of production (land, labor, and old fixed capital) that cannot move. Since labor is the largest input into corporate products, wage earners would bear most of the burden of the corporation tax through lower real wages.

In the years immediately after World War II, most countries imposed tight capital controls and currencies were not convertible. As capital controls were dismantled and many foreign currencies other than the U.S. dollar became acceptable in international transactions, the open economy model became more realistic. During this later period, the effective corporation tax rates have been declining in the United States. It follows that recent U.S. tax policy has probably reduced any adverse effect of the corporation income tax on real wages, not increased it as some allege.

* * *

Equity and Debt Finance

Corporations are allowed to deduct interest payments on borrowed capital from taxable income, but there is no corresponding deduction for dividends paid out to stockholders in return for the use of their funds as equity capital. At the 34 percent tax rate, a corporation must earn $1.52 before tax to be able to pay $1 in dividends, but it needs to earn only $1 to pay $1 interest. This asymmetry makes the cost of equity more expensive for the corporation than an equal amount of borrowed capital. In fact, in combination with the accelerated cost recovery system and the investment tax credit, the allowance of an interest deduction provided a substantial subsidy to investment in the early 1980s.

* * *

Financial experts discourage large amounts of debt financing by corporations. Debt makes good business sense if there is a safe margin for paying fixed interest charges. But business firms may be tightly squeezed when business falls off, and the margin will evaporate rapidly. At such times, defaults on interest and principal payments and bankruptcies begin to occur. Even though borrowed capital may increase returns to stockholders, corporations try to finance a major share of their capital requirements through equity capital (mainly retained earnings) to avoid these risks.

* * *

Resource Allocation

If the corporation income tax is not shifted in the short run, it becomes in effect a special tax on corporate capital. This does not necessarily mean that the tax permanently reduces rates of return on capital in the corporate sector relative to returns in the noncorporate sector. Capital may flow out of the taxed industries into the untaxed industries, and rates of return will tend to equalize. In the process, the allocation of capital between corporate and noncorporate business will be altered from the pattern that would have prevailed in the absence of the tax.

How much capital, if any, has left the corporate sector as a result of the corporation income tax is not known. It is possible that the corporate form of doing business is so advantageous for nontax reasons that, for the most part, capital remains in the corporate sector despite the tax. To the extent that corporate investment is financed by debt, the corporation income tax does not affect investment incentives because interest on debt is deductible as a business expense. The same is true if the capital-consumption allowances are so liberal as to be the equivalent of expensing (as they were before the Tax Reform Act of 1986 was passed). In addition, the preferential treatment of capital gains under the individual income tax provided an offsetting incentive to invest in the securities of corporations that retained earnings for reinvestment in the business. These earnings showed up as increases in the price of common stock rather than as regular income. In any case, the corporate sector has been getting larger, both relatively and absolutely, for decades. The discouragement of investment in the corporate form induced by the tax system, if any, must have been comparatively small. * * *

Distortions may also take place if the tax is shifted in the short run. If prices increase in response to an increase in the tax, they rise in proportion to the use of corporate equity capital in the various industries. Consumers will buy fewer goods and services produced by industries using a great deal of corporate capital because the prices of these products will have risen most, and they will buy more goods and services produced by industries with less corporate capital. Within the corporate sector, profits will fall in the "capital-intensive" industries as a result of the decline in sales and will rise in the "labor-intensive" industries. In the end, not only will less capital be attracted to the corporate sector, but less will be attracted to the capital-intensive industries in that sector, and the economy will suffer a loss in efficiency as a result. The quantitative effect of this process is heavily dependent, of course, on the degree to which the noncorporate form of doing business can be substituted for the corporate form and production can be transferred from capital-intensive to labor-intensive industries. As in the nonshifting case, even a shifted corporate tax would tend to distort the composition of output.

Major distortions were introduced by the pre-1986 allowances for investment and the deduction for interest on borrowed capital. The depreciation allowances under the accelerated cost recovery system (ACRS) plus the investment credit were equivalent on average to expensing of capital equipment, which can be shown to be equivalent to a zero tax on investment under certain conditions. If the investment was financed by debt, the tax was actually converted to a subsidy. Moreover, the investment tax credit was allowed only for equipment, and the depreciation allowances under ACRS were much less generous for buildings than for equipment. The result was that machinery was treated much more favorably than plant and other structures, inventories, and intangibles. Thus the effect of the capital allowances and the interest deduction differed greatly among different assets and industries. * * * These distortions were greatly reduced, though not entirely eliminated, by the tax reforms enacted in 1986.

Notes and Questions

13. In deciding who bears the corporate income tax, consider the possibility that the incidence of the tax might be changed by changing the structure of the tax or the tax treatment of other business entities, such as partnerships.

14.   Is a business corporation an appropriate taxable entity in its own right? Is the decision to tax it based on anything more than administrative feasibility?

15.   What different categories of people might conceivably bear all or a portion of the burden of the corporate income tax?

16.   State regulators allow public utilities to pass on their corporate income taxes to their ratepayers as a cost of operations. Who bears the corporate tax imposed on public utilities?

17.   What is the incidence of the tax on corporations that are in direct competition with individual proprietors, partnerships, limited liability companies, and S corporations that do not owe corporate tax?

18.   In the long run, who bears the burden of income tax imposed on corporations for which capital is not a significant income-producing factor?

19.   Dr. Pechman stated that the corporate tax will not adversely affect investment incentives if capital investments can be "expensed," or fully deducted when made, "as they were before the Tax Reform Act of 1986 was passed." This assertion requires explanation on two points. First, although pre-1986 law did not allow capital expenditures to be expensed (except for relatively small amounts under section 179), Pechman apparently agrees with economists who argued that the combination of the short depreciation periods and the 10 percent investment tax credit then in effect were as favorable as expensing.

The second point is to examine why immediate expensing of capital expenditures is said to completely eliminate, and not merely reduce, the impact on investment incentives of any income tax (including the corporate income tax). The detailed explanation of Professors Alan Gunn and Larry Ward follows:

> [A]llowing an immediate deduction for the cost of a long-lived income-producing asset produces the same effect as capitalizing the cost and exempting the income the asset earns from taxation. * * * Consider a taxpayer who pays $100,000 for a machine with a ten-year life and no salvage value. The machine will generate $20,000 in revenue each year (a 20-percent pre-tax return on the $100,000 cost), all of which (except for income taxes) the taxpayer will spend on consumption. Assume that the taxpayer has a large amount of other income, and that the taxpayer is subject to a flat-rate 40-percent income tax. If the taxpayer capitalizes the cost of the machine and takes straight-line depreciation, the taxpayer's decision to purchase the asset rather than to spend its purchase

price on consumption amounts to a decision to give up $100,000 of consumption in the year the machine was bought in exchange for $16,000 annual consumption[c] over a ten-year period.

Now suppose the taxpayer is offered a tax exemption for the earnings from the machine. Because the machine produces no taxable income, no depreciation is allowed. The taxpayer will be able to spend $20,000 a year for ten years.

If, instead of an exemption for the machine's earnings, an immediate deduction for the purchase price of the machine (and of similar machines) were allowed, the taxpayer would still be able to spend $20,000 a year for ten years. We have assumed that the taxpayer was willing to give up $100,000 of current consumption to buy a non-deductible machine. If the cost of machines is deductible, the taxpayer can buy $166,666.67 worth of machines by giving up $100,000 of consumption (because the out-of-pocket cost of an immediately deductible $166,666.67 investment to a 40-percent taxpayer is $100,000). The gross return on this investment will be $33,333.33 (20-percent of $166,666.67) a year. This amount will be fully taxable (no depreciation being allowed because the cost of the machine was deducted at the time of purchase). Therefore, the taxpayer will be able to spend 60-percent of this sum, or $20,000, each year.

The equivalence between an immediate deduction and an exemption for return on investment holds for any constant rate of return and tax rate.[h]

C. THE DOUBLE TAX ISSUE

The six excerpts of this subchapter discuss varying answers to the same core question: Assuming the present "double tax" system imposed on corporations and their individual shareholders to be improper, what tax treatment should replace it? The mechanics of the various alternatives for ending or reducing double taxation of corporate earnings are illustrated by this example: Suppose a corporation starts with one shareholder who contributes $1,000 for stock. In the first year the corporation has $100 of taxable income, after deducting interest and other expenses. Under present law suppose the corporate tax is 34 percent, or $34, leaving current earnings and profits of $66. If the entire $66 is paid out as a dividend and the

---

c. The machine will generate a $20,000 annual cash return, but only $10,000 in taxable income (because of the $10,000 annual depreciation deduction). Each year's income tax will be $4000, leaving the taxpayer $16,000 to spend. [Footnote c was in the original source. (Eds.)]

h. ALAN GUNN & LARRY D. WARD, CASES, TEXT AND PROBLEMS ON FEDERAL INCOME TAXATION 280-81 (3d ed. 1992). Professors Gunn and Ward state that "[t]he equivalence between current deductibility and exemption of return was first noted in Brown, Business-Income Taxation and Investment Incentives; in L. Metzler et al., Income, Employment and Public Policy; reprinted in R. Musgrave & C. Shoup, Readings in the Economics of Taxation (1959)."

shareholder is taxed at 39.6 percent, the individual income tax on the dividend will be $26.14, leaving a net amount after taxes of $39.86. Total taxes will take $60.14, or 60 percent of the $100 net income.

One method, that of "pure integration," would tax corporations as though they were partnerships—i.e., income and deductions completely integrated with those of the shareholder. If the corporation described above were so taxed, the entire $100 of corporate taxable income, whether or not distributed, would be taxed at the individual shareholder's 39.6 percent tax rate, for a total tax of $39.60. (If the corporation had a loss for the year, presumably the shareholder could deduct it currently—a privilege not now available to shareholders of C corporations.)

Another technique for integration of distributed income is to treat the corporate tax apportioned to dividends as a tax withheld from the shareholder's dividend, similar to the wage withholding tax. In the example, if the entire $100 were declared as a dividend, the entire $34 of corporation tax would be treated as withheld tax. The shareholder would report as income the $66 net amount received plus the $34 withheld, or a total of $100. (This treatment of the amount of tax paid by the corporation on the shareholder's behalf as part of the dividend is referred to as a grossed-up dividend.) The shareholder's tax on $100 at 39.6 percent would be $39.60, and the shareholder would claim a credit of $34 (the amount withheld at the corporate level) against this tax liability. If the shareholder's marginal tax rate were below 34 percent, presumably the additional tax withheld would be allowed as a credit against the shareholder's tax on other income or would be refunded to the shareholder.

A simpler alternative would be to allow corporations to deduct dividends, much as they deduct interest now. In the example, payment of a $100 dividend would reduce corporate taxable income to zero, shareholder income would be $100, and tax on that amount at 39.6 percent would be $39.60. In this example, the result would be the same as partnership treatment, but if a corporation did not pay out all its earnings as dividends the result would be vastly different because, under partnership treatment, the shareholder would be taxed whether earnings are distributed or not.

Another alternative would be to exclude dividends from the individual shareholder's income; thus, the double tax would be eliminated, and the sole tax would be paid by the corporation. To assure that the dividends bear a full tax at one level, the exclusion could be limited to dividends paid from corporate earnings that have borne tax at the top corporate rate. In the example, a dividend of $100 paid from earnings that have been taxed at 34 percent would be excluded from the shareholder's income, so the total tax would be $34.

Yet another alternative would be to exclude dividends from the individual shareholder's income; thus, the double tax would be eliminated, and the sole tax would be paid by the corporation. To assure that the dividends bear a full tax at one level, the exclusion could be limited in the case of dividends that have not borne a corporate tax equal to the top individual rate. In the example, 34/39.6, or 85.86 percent, of the $100 dividend paid from earnings that have been taxed at 34 percent would be excluded from the shareholder's income. The shareholder, therefore, would be allowed to exclude $85.86, and would be taxed on the remaining $14.14. This would result in a corporate tax of $34 and a shareholder tax of $5.60, so the total tax would be $39.60.

TAX REFORM FOR FAIRNESS, SIMPLICITY, AND ECONOMIC GROWTH ("TREASURY I")
United States Department of the Treasury
Vol. 1, at 118-19 (1984)

With a comprehensive corporate income tax base, income derived from equity investment in the corporate sector would be taxed twice—once when earned by a corporation and again when distributed to shareholders. The double taxation of dividends has several undesirable effects. It encourages corporations to rely too heavily on debt, rather than equity finance. By increasing the risk of bankruptcy, this artificial inducement for debt finance increases the incidence of bankruptcies during business downturns.

The double taxation of dividends also creates an inducement for firms to retain earnings, rather than pay them out as dividends. There is however, no reason to believe that firms with retained earnings are necessarily those with the best investment opportunities. Instead, they may have more funds than they can invest productively, while new enterprises lack capital. If retained earnings are used to finance relatively low productivity investments, including uneconomic acquisitions of other firms, the quality of investment suffers. In addition, both corporate investment and aggregate saving are discouraged, because the double taxation of dividends increases the cost of capital to corporations and reduces the return to individual investors.

These problems cannot be solved by simply eliminating the corporate income tax. If there were no corporate tax, dividends would be taxed properly, at the tax rates of the shareholders who receive them, but earnings retained by the corporations would not be taxed until distributed, and thus would be allowed to accumulate tax-free. As a result, there would be a substantial incentive to conduct business in corporate form, in order to take advantage of these benefits of tax exemption and deferral.

Nor can the corporate and individual income taxes be fully integrated by treating the corporation as a partnership for tax purposes. Technical difficulties * * * preclude adoption of this approach. The Treasury Department thus proposes that the United States, following the practice of many other developed countries, continue to levy the corporate income tax on earnings that are retained, but provide partial relief from double taxation of dividends.

There are two alternative ways to provide dividend relief. The approach more commonly employed in other countries is to allow shareholders a credit for a portion of the corporate tax attributable to the dividends they receive. The credit is generally available only to residents, although it is sometimes extended to foreigners by treaty. The credit can be denied tax-exempt organizations, if that is desired.

The simpler method, and the one proposed by the Treasury Department, will allow corporations a deduction for dividends paid similar to the deduction for interest expense. Dividends paid to nonresident shareholders will be subject to a compensatory withholding tax, equivalent to the reduction in tax at the corporate level. The proposal will not impose such a compensatory tax where it would be contrary to a U.S. tax treaty; nor will the compensatory tax apply to dividends paid to U.S. tax-exempt organizations. However, the initial decision to extend the benefits of dividend relief to these two groups of shareholders will be subject to continuing review.

Despite the advantages of full relief from double taxation of dividends, the Treasury Department proposal would provide a deduction of only one-half of dividends paid from income taxed to the corporation. This decision is based primarily on considerations of revenue loss, and can be reconsidered once the proposal is fully phased in.

The deduction would not be allowed for dividends paid from income that had not been subject to corporate tax; firms wishing to pay out tax-preferred income will not receive a deduction, but dividends will be presumed to be paid first from fully taxed income. For this purpose, income that did not bear a corporate tax because of allowable credits, including foreign tax credits, will not be eligible for the deduction.

Reduction of the double taxation of corporate equity income will tend to increase initially the market value of existing corporate shares of companies that distribute an above-average proportion of current earnings as dividends. It will reduce the current tax bias against equity finance in the corporate sector and make equity securities more competitive with debt. Because dividend relief will also reduce the tax bias against distributing earnings, corporations will be likely to pay greater dividends and to seek new funds in financial markets. Corporations will therefore, be more subject to the discipline of the marketplace and less likely to make relatively unproductive investments simply because they have available funds. Similarly, the pool of funds available to new firms with relatively high productivity investment opportunities will be larger. As a result, the productivity of investment should be improved substantially.

Dividend relief will be phased in gradually in order to match the phase-in of the correct rules for measurement of corporate income and to minimize unjustified windfall profits to current shareholders. Moreover, phasing in dividend relief will prevent a large loss of tax revenue and any associated reduction in the tax burden of high-income shareholders.

* * *

AMERICAN LAW INSTITUTE
REPORTER'S STUDY OF CORPORATE TAX INTEGRATION:
SUMMARY AND PROPOSALS
Alvin C. Warren,[*] Reporter

Pages 1-8, 12 (1993)

The United States has long had what is usually called a classical income tax system, under which income is taxed to shareholders and corporations as distinct taxpayers. As a result, taxable income earned by a corporation and then distributed to individual shareholders as a dividend is taxed twice, once to the corporation and once to the shareholder on receipt of the dividend. Corporate taxable income distributed as dividends to exempt shareholders is taxed only at the corporate level. In contrast, earnings on corporate debt capital are nontaxable at the corporate level to the extent they are distributed as deductible interest payments. Whether interest is taxed to the recipient depends on the recipient's status, with foreign and tax-exempt lenders generally nontaxable on such receipts.

Integration of the individual and corporate income taxes refers to various means of eliminating the separate, additional burden of the corporate income tax, in favor of a system in which investor and corporate taxes are interrelated so as to produce a more uniform levy on capital income, whether earned through corporate enterprise or not. *The integration proposals in this study would convert the separate U. S. corporate income tax into a withholding tax with respect to income ultimately distributed to shareholders.*

There are two principal reasons for studying this subject. First, the current system has long been the subject of criticism, for which integration has often been offered as a solution. * * *

The second reason for studying the subject is that most other major developed countries have in recent decades adopted various forms of integration. As the American economy becomes less separable from these other economies, it becomes more important to understand the potential advantages and disadvantages of integration for the United States and for U.S. companies.

* * *

The approach throughout the study is to develop proposals that provide as complete a response as possible to the defects of current law by converting the corporate tax into a withholding device. * * *

Defects in Current Law

In general, the classical system can (a) discourage individual investors

---

[*]. At time of original publication, Professor of Law, Harvard University.

from investing in new corporate equity; (b) encourage corporations to finance new projects with retained earnings and debt, rather than by issuing new stock; and (c) encourage corporations to distribute earnings in tax preferred transactions, such as redemptions, rather than by paying dividends. Whether the classical system encourages retention or distribution of corporate earnings depends on the rate relationships among corporate, shareholder, and capital gains rates, as well as assumptions about the operation of the capital markets. The tax-induced distortions of current law are undesirable to the extent they have deleterious economic effects (such as over reliance on debt finance by corporations) or create unadministrable legal distinctions (such as that between debt and equity). Integration would reduce or eliminate these undesirable effects.

System of Integration

There are a variety of ways in which the individual and corporate income taxes could be integrated to reduce the distortions of current law. The corporate tax could, for example, be repealed and shareholders taxed currently on all corporate earnings, but that approach would require annual attribution of undistributed corporate income to a myriad of complex capital interests. Alternatively, the corporate tax could be repealed and shareholders taxed annually on changes in stock values, which would require abandonment of the realization criterion of income taxation. Another approach would be for shareholders simply to exclude corporate dividends from their taxable income, but that approach would preclude application of graduated shareholder tax rates to dividend income. Finally, on receipt of a dividend, shareholders could receive a tax credit for corporate taxes previously paid with respect to that dividend. Shareholder credit integration along these lines is the approach most widely adopted abroad and is the system developed in this study. If withholding on dividend payments is considered desirable for compliance purposes, a corporate deduction for dividend payments is essentially equivalent to the recommended form of shareholder credit integration.

The proposed approach would convert the separate corporate income tax into a withholding tax with respect to dividends. Because some dividends will not have borne a corporate tax prior to distribution, an auxiliary dividend withholding tax is necessary to assure that shareholders do not receive tax credits for taxes that have never been paid at the corporate level. No double tax would result, because payments of regular corporate tax would be considered prepayments of this auxiliary tax. On the other hand, certain dividends may be free of corporate tax as a result of deliberately enacted corporate tax preferences that should be passed through to shareholders. Finally, in order to minimize differential treatment of debt and equity, a withholding tax on corporate interest payments would be desirable. Four proposals implement this basic system of integration:

1. A withholding tax will be levied on dividend distributions;

payments of corporate tax will be fully creditable against this withholding tax.

2. Shareholders will receive a refundable tax credit for the dividend withholding tax.

3. Certain corporate tax preferences can be passed through to shareholders.

4. A withholding tax will be levied on payments of corporate interest; that tax will be fully creditable by and refundable to the recipients of such interest payments.

Retained Earnings

If the corporate income tax became part of a withholding system, retained earnings would present two problems. First, shareholders whose marginal tax rates were below the corporate rate would be disadvantaged by corporate retentions, creating a tax incentive for distributions of corporate earnings. Second, taxation of shareholder capital gains due to retained corporate earnings could, as under current law, constitute multiple taxation of the same gain. The second problem could be eliminated by preferential taxation of gains on corporate stock, but such a preference would be overbroad because not all gains on corporate stock are due to taxable corporate earnings. Both problems would be addressed by a constructive dividend option, under which shareholder tax credits would be available to shareholders without the requirement of an actual dividend distribution. If the withholding and corporate tax rates were equal to the highest individual rate, such constructive dividends could only benefit shareholders, who would either pay no taxes or receive a refund. The increase in shareholder basis due to the constructive reinvestment would eliminate the potential of double taxation on sale of the stock. These ideas are implemented by Proposals 5 and 6, which can be summarized as follows:

5. Corporations could make shareholder credits available to shareholders at any time through constructive dividends and reinvestments.

6. Sales of stock will be fully taxable to shareholders, with deductions for stock losses limited to dividends, realized stock gains, and the excess of realized stock losses over net unrealized stock gains.

Nondividend Distributions

There are a variety of transactions other than dividends by which corporate income can be distributed to shareholders, including repurchases by a corporation of its stock, purchase by one corporation of stock in a second corporation from noncorporate shareholders, and payments in liquidation. Under current law, the tax treatment of such nondividend distributions to individuals is usually less onerous than that of dividends, because basis recovery and a capital gains preference may be available with respect to the former, but not the latter. Corporate shareholders, on the other hand, would generally prefer to characterize distributions as dividends to take advantage of the dividends received deduction. In a shareholder credit system of integration, the principal issue presented by nondividend distributions is the extent to which shareholder credits will be available In such distributions. The approach taken in Proposal 7 is to maintain the distinction under current law between dividends and exchanges, with the latter generally carrying out a portion of previously paid corporate taxes. Where it is difficult to identify the recipient of a nondividend distribution, the appropriate tax credit will be available to the distributing corporation.

> 7. Nondividend redemptions and liquidations will be treated as exchanges with basis recovery, and will carry out a *pro rata* portion of previously paid corporate taxes. Other nondividend distributions will result in a refund to the corporation of previously paid corporate taxes.

Intercorporate Transactions

In general, shareholders that are corporations can be treated like other shareholders under integration. However, a special problem arises in the case of intercorporate dividends of previously untaxed corporate income because application of the dividend withholding tax would require payment of a corporate tax prior to distribution of corporate earnings to noncorporate shareholders. Proposal 8 provides for an election to defer this tax in the case of significant intercorporate investment until a distribution is made to noncorporate shareholders:

> 8. Major corporate investors will have the option to treat intercorporate dividends as nontaxable and noncreditable.

Exempt Shareholders and Creditors

Nominally exempt suppliers of corporate capital, such as charitable organizations and pension funds, do not always receive their share of corporate income free of tax under current law. The portion of corporate income distributed to such investors is sometimes taxed (due to the corporate tax on income distributed as dividends) and sometimes not (due to the corporate deduction for interest payments and to corporate preferences for some income distributed as dividends). Because one of the goals of integration is elimination of such discontinuities, any comprehensive system of integration will necessarily affect currently exempt shareholders. The approach of these proposals is to maintain a single level of tax on corporate income received by such investors, and to rationalize that tax to eliminate tax-induced distortions in investment decisions. Accordingly, entities that are nominally exempt under current law would be subject to an explicit tax on corporate investment income, against which the shareholder and creditor withholding credits could be used, with any excess refundable. The basic idea of this proposal is that the rate of tax on income from corporate investment received by an exempt entity should be uniform and explicitly determined as a matter of tax policy. That rate could be set to maintain the same level of revenue that is currently collected on corporate income distributed to exempt shareholders, or at a higher or lower rate. The resulting proposal can be summarized as follows:

9. A new tax will be imposed on the corporate investment income of exempt organizations, which will be allowed credits for corporate taxes on the same basis as other investors.

* * *

Transition

As with any major change in tax law, integration could be made immediately effective, phased-in over time, or subject to certain exceptions for per-existing transactions. With respect to the last possibility, it is sometimes argued that integration should be available only for corporate equity acquired after the date of enactment, on the theory that capital markets have already discounted the price of pre-enactment corporate equity to reflect the classical system, so that integration for pre-enactment equity would result in unjustified windfalls to current shareholders. The proposals are not limited to post-enactment corporate capital, in part because recommendations implementing such limitations have already been developed in prior Institute studies. Instead, Proposal 12 develops a method for transition to full integration over time. * * *

The net effect of the * * * proposals summarized above is that the US. corporate income tax would no longer function as a separate, additional tax. Rather, it would be part of an integrated system under which investors in corporate enterprise would be taxed once, but only once, on income from investment in corporate capital. The only rate of tax ultimately applicable to corporate income distributed to a shareholder or creditor would be that investor's rate. * * *

[W]hat follows is a long and complicated study[i], but it is based on a simple and straightforward idea: *conversion of the separate U.S. corporate income tax into a withholding tax would reduce economic distortions and troublesome legal distinctions that arise under current law.*

STATEMENT OF TAX POLICY: INTEGRATION OF THE CORPORATE AND SHAREHOLDER TAX SYSTEMS
American Institute of Certified Public Accountants
Pages 18-19, 63-67 (1993)

The Objectives of Integration

A system of integration would lower the cost of capital and mitigate many of the distortions and inequities created by the present classical system by taxing corporate income only once. There are several methods or approaches available to relieve the double taxation of corporate profits.

In evaluating the alternative methods available, the AICPA has

---

i. Professor Warren is referring to the entire Reporter's Study. Only the Summary and Proposals are excerpted. (Eds.)

identified five basic objectives that an integrated system should seek to achieve:

* A more uniform taxation of income earned in the corporate and noncorporate sectors
* A reduction in the tax bias favoring debt financing
* A reduction of tax incentives for corporations to retain rather than distribute their profits
* An easy interface with foreign integrated tax systems
* No significant additional complexity for the tax system

Brief Overview of Alternative Methods

This study analyzes the three principal alternative methods of implementing an integration system: (1) the flow-through method; (2) the dividends-paid deduction method; and (3) the shareholder-credit method. However, three variants of these principal methods have also been considered: (1) the repeal of the corporate tax; (2) the split-rate corporate-level tax; and (3) the dividend-exclusion method.

A brief overview of the three principal alternatives follows. * * *

Flow-Through Method

The flow-through integration method achieves complete integration of all corporate earnings by allocating all items of income to shareholders in a manner similar to the allocation of partnership and S corporation income under the current system. This method taxes all income at the shareholder level when earned, whether or not distributed. The flow-through method represents the purest form of integration because it subjects all corporate income to only one level of tax, at the shareholder rates.

Dividends-Paid Deduction Method

The dividends-paid deduction method allows a corporation to deduct all or part of dividends paid from taxable income. Under this method, the benefits of integration inure to the corporation, since shareholders still report dividends received as income. To the extent that corporations make fully deductible distributions, one level of tax at the shareholder's tax rate should result. This method does not extend integration benefits to retained earnings.

Shareholder-Credit Method

The shareholder-credit method imposes a corporate-level tax on all earnings, but grants a credit to shareholders for a portion of the corporate tax paid that is allocated or imputed to dividends. This method generally requires shareholders to "gross up" their dividend income by the amount of credit allowed. Integration is achieved by eliminating or reducing the tax on dividends at the shareholder level. Therefore, the benefits of integration inure to the shareholder. As with the dividends-paid deduction method, double-tax relief applies only to distributed income. Therefore, integration benefits are not granted to retained income.

* * *

Conclusions and Recommendations

Each of the three principal methods has been evaluated to determine whether it achieves five basic objectives for an integrated system and whether and how easily it can be designed to handle certain key issues. Each of these principal methods would achieve more neutral taxation by (1) providing more uniform taxation of income between the corporate and noncorporate sectors; (2) reducing the tax bias favoring debt investment; and (3) reducing the incentives to retain rather than distribute earnings. Accordingly, the AICPA believes that an integration method must be chosen primarily on the basis of its ease of administration, its compatibility with foreign integrated systems, and its flexibility in addressing the key issues of tax preferences, tax-exempt investors, and international transactions.

Theoretically, the flow-through method is the purest form of integration; however, it would be considerably more difficult to administer and implement. Broadening the eligibility of the S corporation election by expanding the number of allowable shareholders would offer one alternative to the use of the flow-through method, but the use of the S corporation rules would not be practical for large, widely held corporations. Moreover, if policy makers were to decide not to extend integration benefits to tax-exempt and foreign shareholders, the flow-through method would need to include an appropriate withholding mechanism, further complicating implementation of the method. After careful review, the flow-through method was not chosen as a viable option because of the numerous problems in administering the method, its lack of flexibility in dealing with the key issues, and its incompatibility with foreign integrated systems.

Both of the other two alternatives, the dividends-paid deduction and the shareholder-credit methods, would offer a more practical and realistic means of achieving integration. The public's perception of the equity of each method may be an important factor in determining whether either is adopted. The public may perceive that the dividends-paid deduction method would confer all of the benefits on the corporation. The shareholder-credit method is likely to be more acceptable, since the public may perceive that the shareholder would receive a greater benefit than under the current system or the dividends-paid deduction method. On the other hand, the public may perceive that integration benefits only high-income taxpayers.

The United States could adopt either the deduction or the credit method with substantially the same tax results.[99] However, to achieve this equality, it must be assumed that the corporate-dividend policy would be comparable under both methods. In addition, the deduction method would be assumed to include a withholding mechanism and credits under both methods would be refundable.

Proponents of the dividends-paid deduction method argue that (1) it is simpler and easier to administer than the shareholder-credit system, (2) it handles the debt-equity problem more effectively, and (3) it can more easily restrict integration benefits to new equity. The simplicity and ease of administration of the dividends-paid deduction method is its most significant advantage. However, the modifications (including withholding) required to implement adjustments for foreign and tax-exempt shareholders, credits, and tax preferences would complicate this method greatly. Without these modifications, greater revenue loss, reduced compliance, and a decrease in the value of tax preferences could result. Consequently, such a modified deduction method would provide no significant advantages over a shareholder-credit method.

Another advantage of the dividends-paid deduction method is that it would provide for more neutral tax treatment of debt and equity. The shareholder-credit method would not achieve the same result, since the shareholders, not the corporation, would receive the benefits of integration. Therefore, under the credit method, corporations may continue to prefer debt because interest would be deductible, whereas dividends would not.

Proponents of the shareholder-credit method argue that it is preferable to the dividends-paid deduction method because (1) it would achieve a higher level of compliance with less effort, (2) it would be more flexible in dealing with foreign and tax-exempt shareholders and corporate tax preferences, (3) it would more easily conform to the integrated systems of other countries,

---

99. For example:

	Credit	Deductions
Corporate Level		
Net income	$1,000	$1,000
Cash dividend	660	1,000
Dividend deduction	0	1,000
Taxable income	1,000	0
Corporate tax (34%)	340	0
Withholding tax (31%)	0	310
Shareholder Level		
Cash dividend received	$660	$690
Gross-up inclusion	340	310
Shareholder income	1,000	1,000
Tax before credit	310	310
Credit	340	310
Refundable credit	(30)	0
Net Cash to Shareholder	$690	$690

and (4) it would not affect the corporation's financial statements.

The shareholder-credit method should have a higher level of compliance than the dividends-paid deduction method, unless the deduction method includes a withholding mechanism. The level of compliance would be higher under the credit method because taxpayers would report dividend income before receiving the benefit of the credit, whereas under the deduction method, the corporation would be permitted to take a deduction for dividends even if some shareholders failed to report the dividend income.

The shareholder-credit method can more easily be designed either to extend or to limit benefits for foreign and tax-exempt shareholders, and either to pass through or to limit the pass- through of tax preferences to shareholders. Although the deduction method, too, can be designed to address these issues, the credit system would handle them with far less complexity. A special provision for corporate tax preferences would make both methods more complex, but implementation of rules relating to tax preferences would be more difficult under the dividends-paid deduction method.

If policy makers decide not to extend integration benefits to tax-exempt shareholders, the shareholder-credit method could make the credit nonrefundable to tax-exempt organizations, whereas the dividends-paid deduction method would have to tax dividends as unrelated trade or business income (or include a withholding mechanism) to achieve the same result. Making the credit nonrefundable is easier to implement, and certainly less complex, than requiring withholding or taxing dividends as unrelated trade or business income.

The shareholder-credit method also can be more easily tailored to other specific types of shareholders. This feature is especially important when determining the proper treatment of foreign shareholders, and may be the reason why other countries have preferred the shareholder-credit instead of the deduction method. Conversely, the main drawback to the dividends-paid deduction method is that it would apply to all categories of shareholders equally. Under the credit method, the United States could make the credit nonrefundable to foreign shareholders and extend integration benefits to foreign shareholders only through bilateral treaty negotiations. The only way to prevent the granting of integration benefits to foreign shareholders under the deduction method would be to increase the withholding rate on dividends paid to such shareholders. However, such an increase could be very difficult, if not impossible, to achieve under the provisions of many existing tax treaties.

Another advantage of the shareholder-credit system is that it would not change the amount of net income a corporation reports in its financial statements. Because the corporate income tax liability would not change under this method, there would be no consistency problems with reporting the prior year's operations and cash flows, such as those that would occur under the deduction method.

International conformity, however, may be the most important advantage of the shareholder-credit method. All other major industrialized nations that have adopted integration use this method. This international experience not only would benefit the United States in designing and implementing an integration system, it also would make it easier to interface the U.S. system with foreign systems. Adopting the shareholder-credit method also would facilitate bilateral treaty negotiations on providing reciprocal integration benefits.

In summary, since both the credit and deduction methods can be structured to produce substantially equivalent tax results, the United States should consider other advantages and disadvantages when selecting the appropriate method. The single most important factor in this decision seems to be the international ramifications, particularly the method's ability to work within the framework of bilateral tax treaties. Flexibility in treaty negotiations, particularly in dealing with foreign tax credits and the extension of integration benefits to foreign shareholders, would give the credit system a decisive advantage.

The shareholder credit also would allow for greater flexibility in handling the key policy issues involved in the treatment of tax preferences and tax-exempt investors. This flexibility would facilitate the adoption of an integrated system, because it would more easily allow policy makers to reach the compromises that necessarily are a part of the legislative process. Although some forms of the shareholder-credit method may be relatively complicated to implement, international experience suggests that even the most complex forms of the method can be administered without substantial difficulty.

On balance, the AICPA concludes that the shareholder-credit method best achieves the objectives of an integrated system, and therefore recommends its adoption by the United States.

REPORT ON INTEGRATION OF THE INDIVIDUAL AND CORPORATE TAX SYSTEMS
United States Department of the Treasury
Pages vii-x (1992)

Currently, our tax system taxes corporate profits distributed to shareholders at least twice—once at the shareholder level and once at the corporate level. If the distribution is made through multiple unrelated corporations, profits may be taxed more than twice. If, on the other hand, the corporation succeeds in distributing profits in the form of interest on bonds to a tax-exempt or foreign lender, no U.S. tax at all is paid.

The two-tier tax system (i.e., imposing tax on distributed profits in the hands of shareholders after taxation at the corporate level) is often referred to as a classical tax system. Over the past two decades, most of our trading partners have modified their corporate tax systems to "integrate" the corporate and shareholder taxes to mitigate the impact of imposing two levels of tax on distributed corporate profits. Most typically, this has been accomplished by providing the shareholder with a full or partial credit for taxes paid at the corporate level.

Integration would reduce three distortions inherent in the classical system:

(a) *The incentive to invest in noncorporate rather than corporate businesses.* Current law's double tax on corporations creates a higher effective tax rate on corporate equity than on noncorporate equity. The additional tax burden encourages "self-help" integration through disincorporation.

(b) *The incentive to finance corporate investments with debt rather than new equity.* Particularly in the 1980s, corporations issued substantial amounts of debt. By 1990, net interest expense reached a postwar high of 19 percent of corporate cash flow.

(c) *The incentive to retain earnings or to structure distributions of corporate profits in a manner to avoid the double tax.* Between 1970 and 1990, corporations' repurchases of their own shares grew from $1.2 billion (or 5.4 percent of dividends) to $47.9 billion (or 34 percent of dividends). By 1990, over one-quarter of corporate interest payments were attributable to the substitution of debt for equity through share repurchases.

These distortions raise the cost of capital for corporate investments; integration could be expected to reduce it. To the extent that an integrated system reduces incentives for highly-leveraged corporate capital structures, it would provide important non-tax benefits by encouraging the adoption of capital structures less vulnerable to instability in times of economic downturn. The Report contains estimates of substantial potential economic gains from integration. Depending on its form, the Report estimates that integration could increase the capital stock in the corporate sector by $125 billion to $500 billion, could decrease the debt-asset ratio in the corporate sector by 1 to 7 percentage points and could produce an annual gain to the U.S. economy as a whole from $2.5 billion to $25 billion.

Prototypes

This Report defines four integration prototypes and provides specifications for how each would work. Three prototypes are described in Part II: (1) the dividend exclusion prototype, (2) the shareholder allocation prototype, and (3) the Comprehensive Business Income Tax (CBIT) prototype. * * * For administrative reasons that the Report details, we have not recommended the shareholder allocation prototype (a system in which all corporate income is allocated to shareholders and taxed in a manner similar to partnership income under current law). Simplification concerns led us to prefer the dividend exclusion to any form of the imputation credit prototype.

In the dividend exclusion prototype, shareholders exclude dividends from income because they have already been taxed at the corporate level. Dividend exclusion provides significant integration benefits and requires little structural change in the Internal Revenue Code. When fully phased in, dividend exclusion would cost approximately $13.1 billion per year.

CBIT is, as its name implies, a much more comprehensive and larger scale prototype and will require significant statutory revision. CBIT represents a long-term, comprehensive option for equalizing the tax treatment of debt and equity. It is not expected that implementation of CBIT would begin in the short term, and full implementation would likely be phased in over a period of about 10 years. In CBIT, shareholders and bondholders exclude dividends and interest received from corporations from income, but neither type of payment is deductible by the corporation. Because debt and equity receive identical treatment in CBIT, CBIT better achieves tax neutrality goals than does the dividend exclusion prototype. CBIT is self-financing and would permit lowering the corporate rate to the maximum individual rate of 31 percent[j] on a revenue neutral basis, even if capital gains on corporate stock were fully exempt from tax to shareholders.

Policy Recommendations

In addition to describing prototypes, the Report makes several basic policy recommendations which we believe should apply to any integration proposal ultimately adopted:

(a) *Integration should not result in the extension of corporate tax preferences to shareholders.* This stricture is grounded in both policy and revenue concerns and has been adopted by every country with an integrated system. The mechanism for preventing passthrough of preferences varies; some countries utilize a compensatory tax mechanism and others simply tax preference-sheltered income when distributed (as we recommend in the dividend exclusion prototype). Both of these mechanisms are discussed in the Report.

(b) *Integration should not reduce the total tax collected on corporate income allocable to tax-exempt investors.* Absent this restriction, business profits paid to tax-exempt entities could escape all taxation in an integrated system. This revenue loss would prove difficult to finance and would exacerbate distortions between taxable and tax-exempt investors.

(c) *Integration should be extended to foreign shareholders only through treaty negotiations, not by statute.* This is required to assure that U.S. shareholders receive reciprocal concessions from foreign tax jurisdictions.

---

j. The top corporate rate no longer exceeds the top individual rate. The maximum corporate rate is now 35% (excluding notch rates), compared to a maximum individual rate of 39.6%. (Eds.)

COMPARISON OF THE FOUR PRINCIPAL INTEGRATION PROTOTYPES

	DIVIDEND EXCLUSION	SHAREHOLDER ALLOCATION	CBIT	IMPUTATION CREDIT
Rates a) Distributed Income	Corporate rate	Shareholder rate[1]	CBIT rate (31 percent)	Shareholder rate[1]
b) Retained Income	Corporate rate (additional shareholder level tax depends on the treatment of capital gains)	Shareholder rate[1]	CBIT rate (additional investor level tax depends on the treatment of capital gains)	Corporate rate (additional shareholder level tax depends on the treatment of capital gains)
Treatment of non-corporate businesses	Unaffected	Unaffected	CBIT applies to non-corporate businesses as well as corporations, except for very small businesses.	Unaffected
Corporate tax preferences	Does not extend preferences to shareholders. Preference income is subject to shareholder tax when distributed.	Extends preferences to shareholders.	Does not extend preferences to investors. Preference income is subject to compensatory tax or investor level tax when distributed.	Does not extend preferences to shareholders. Preference income is subject to shareholder tax when distributed.
Tax-exempt investors	Corporate equity income continues to bear one level of tax.	Corporate equity income continues to bear one level of tax.	A CBIT entity's equity income and income used to pay interest bear one level of tax.	Corporate equity income continues to bear one level of tax.
Treatment of debt	Unaffected	Unaffected	Equalizes treatment of debt and equity	Unaffected (unless bondholder credit system adopted)

1. Plus 3 percentage points of corporate level tax not creditable because the prototype retains the 34 percent corporate rate but provides credits at the 31 percent shareholder rate. [The 34% and 31% rates were the maximum corporate and individual rates when this report was published. (Eds.)]

(d) *Foreign taxes paid by U.S. corporations should not be treated, by statute, identically to taxes paid to the U.S. Government.* Absent this limitation, integration could eliminate all U.S. taxes on foreign source profits in many cases.

A table summarizing the characteristics of each of the prototypes [is on the preceding page].

A PROPOSAL FOR ELIMINATING DOUBLE TAXATION OF CORPORATE DIVIDENDS
Fred W. Peel, Jr.[*]

39 Tax Lawyer 1, 1-6 (1985)

Introduction

This article develops in detail a proposal for eliminating double taxation of corporate dividends by excluding dividends from gross income at the individual shareholder level if the dividends are paid from income previously taxed at the corporate level. In brief, the proposal is to adopt a single corporate income tax rate equal to the maximum individual tax rate and permit shareholders to exclude from income dividends paid out of corporate earnings that have been taxed at the single corporate rate. It is submitted that the proposal would advance tax simplification, while taxing corporate profits on a more rational basis.

The past decade has seen wide discussion of methods integrating the corporate and individual income taxes—either completely or partially. Full integration would treat corporate income as though it had been earned initially by the shareholders as individuals. Partial integration plans are designed to achieve that result for all or part of the dividends distributed to individual shareholders, either by crediting the shareholders with the corporate tax or by allowing corporations to deduct all or part of their dividends.

Exclusion of dividends from the income of individual shareholders heretofore has generally been dismissed out-of-hand.[5] There appear to have been three reasons for the lack of interest in the dividend exclusion approach. First, until the maximum individual tax rate on investment income was reduced to 50%, the wide disparity between the corporate tax rate and the higher individual rates would have meant that exclusion of dividends would discriminate unacceptably in favor of corporate income. With a maximum individual tax rate of 50%, however, the gap has been narrowed significantly. Now it is feasible to suggest that the two rates be made the same, at some rate between 46% and 50%, or perhaps at some lower rate if one of the current base-broadening plans is enacted.[k] Regardless of the adjustment, the

---

[*]. At time of original publication, Professor of Law, University of Arkansas at Little Rock.

[5]. *See, e.g.,* C. McLure, Must Corporate Income Be Taxed Twice? 5 (1979).

[k]. Since this article was written, the maximum rate applicable to individuals has fallen from 50% to 39.6%, and the maximum rate applicable to corporations has fallen from 46% to 35%.

proposed dividend exclusion requires a nonprogressive corporate tax rate that equals the maximum individual rate.

Second, because some dividends, defined in terms of earnings and profits, may not have been taxed at the corporate level, exclusion of all dividends would permit some corporate income to escape tax altogether. The proposal here will exclude dividends at the individual shareholder level only when distributed from previously taxed income, and only from income earned by the corporation after the proposal has been put into effect.

Third, there has been widespread confusion between two different policy objectives—integration of corporate and shareholder taxes, on the one hand, and elimination of double taxation of dividends, on the other hand. Although their consequences overlap to some degree, the objectives of integration and of elimination of double taxation differ sharply. For example, full integration, by treating corporate income as though earned directly by the shareholders, would not merely eliminate the double tax but also all tax when the shareholder is an exempt organization (unless the tax is reimposed on exempt organizations as a corollary to the tax on unrelated business income, or as an extension of the tax now imposed on investment income of some exempt organizations, such as social clubs). In essence, integration assumes that the corporation is not an appropriate taxpayer and that its role should be, at most, that of a tax withholding agent for its shareholders. In contrast, eliminating double taxation of dividends treats the corporation as a viable and appropriate taxpayer. After the corporate tax has been imposed, however, no further tax should be imposed on the same income when, diminished by the corporate tax, it is distributed to the shareholders

The Objections to Double Taxation

Put simply, the double tax on corporate dividends is unfair. It violates the principle of horizontal equity. A shareholder who is taxed on a dividend out of earnings that already have been taxed at the corporate level is bearing a heavier tax burden than an individual in the same tax bracket receiving equivalent income through an S corporation, through a partnership, or directly as a sole proprietor.

It is true that in some circumstances the C corporation shareholder may be treated better than his counterparts, at least when the income is initially earned. This occurs when the corporation's earnings are not distributed as dividends and the tax paid at the corporate level is at a lower rate than the shareholder would pay if he or she had received the income directly. For this reason, the present system has been described as biased in favor of retained corporate earnings. This bias has been reduced by the 50% maximum individual rate and would be eliminated altogether under the proposal by taxing corporate income in full at the maximum individual rate.

Accordingly, the proposed equalization now would presumably fall in the range of 35% to 39.6%, the marginal corporate and individual rates. (Eds.)

In addition to its unfairness, the incidence of the double tax is inconsistent because of the escape routes open to some shareholders in lieu of receiving taxable dividends. For example, the second tax can be cut by 60% by selling the stock at a capital gain equivalent to the accumulated corporate earnings.[l] The same result can be achieved by liquidating the corporation or by stock redemptions within the bounds of section 302(b). Some publicly held corporations have combined tender offers for, or market purchases of, their own stock with a policy of declaring little or no cash dividends.[15] In addition, if a shareholder holds stock in a corporation until his death and the value of the stock reflects the accumulated earnings, the basis of the stock will be stepped up by the amount of the accumulated earnings so that the stock can be sold or redeemed by the heirs without any second tax on earnings accumulated during the decedent's ownership.

Individual shareholders of publicly held corporations can sell their stock and attempt to realize a capital gain equivalent to their share of the accumulated earnings. If, however, the stock is sold to other individuals who are no better positioned to extract the accumulated earnings without dividend tax, the stock price will be discounted by the potential of an eventual dividend tax. Individual investors who hold stock in publicly held corporations and have chosen dividend-paying stocks in order to have current income are the principal victims of the double tax. There is no compelling policy reason for penalizing these people as a class.

The dividend tax, therefore, seriously distorts the pricing mechanism for stock in publicly held corporations. In essence, there are at least two markets for the stock, with widely divergent prices. One market is made up of individual investors, who must discount the value of the dividend income stream by the individual income tax they will have to pay. The second market is comprised of corporations that, at most, must discount the value of the dividend income stream by a tax on only 15%.[m] (Exempt organizations, such as pension trusts, might be considered as composing another market.)

If a corporate buyer acquires 80% or more of the stock of a target corporation, it may elect a 100% dividends-received deduction on distributions of future earnings of the target. Alternatively, the acquiring corporation may file a consolidated return with the target, eliminating all dividends from it, or liquidate the target and receive the earnings from its operations directly thereafter. The corporate buyer can recover the cost of

---

l. Under present law, long term capital gain income is taxed at a maximum rate of 28 percent, or 71 percent of the 39.6 percent maximum tax rate on ordinary income. (Eds.)

15. For example, Teledyne, Incorporated, a corporation that does not pay dividends, repurchased 8.66 million shares of its own common stock for $200 a share under a June 1984 tender offer.

m. When this article was written, corporations could deduct 85 percent of dividends received from other corporations (100 percent if the corporations were affiliated.) Under present law the general deduction is 70 percent. Section 243. (Eds.)

stock of a target corporation tax free through dividends paid by the target corporation out of the latter's earnings, whereas an individual buying and holding stock must recover his or her investment out of after-tax dollars from dividends. A takeover bid by another corporation lifts the stock out of the low-priced market of individual investors who must pay tax on their dividends and places it in the market of corporate buyers who can recover the price of the shares out of tax free dividends. For this reason, among others, we have the phenomenon of sudden increases in the price of stocks when corporations become takeover candidates. This possibility, in turn, encourages investors to seek out corporations that are likely to become takeover candidates.

The double tax clearly discourages dividends by publicly held corporations. From the point of view of corporate management, retained earnings are available for reinvestment in the business after bearing only one tax. Distributed earnings, however, are diminished by the second tax at the shareholder level. Consequently, even if distributions are put back in the distributing corporation, the amount available for reinvestment is much smaller. Many shareholders invest willingly in publicly held corporations that pay few or no dividends, preferring to gamble that retained earnings will increase the value of the stock. By deferring tax until sale, they can realize capital gains at lower rates rather than incurring an immediate tax on dividends at ordinary income rates. This confers upon corporate management the power to direct investment of corporate earnings, rather than allowing shareholders to exercise that power through reinvestment of dividends.

The additional corporate tax on unreasonable accumulations is designed to curb corporate retention of earnings and to force dividend payments. It applies only to accumulations that cannot be justified by the needs of a new or existing busin ss, however, and in any event a business corporation may accumulate $250,000 without penalty. In the vast majority of cases, a business use can be found for accumulated earnings. The postponement or eventual avoidance of the double tax, however, is as real and advantageous as for the shareholder of a corporation that accumulates earnings without a business use. Meanwhile, the Service is saddled with the tremendous administrative job of finding and penalizing the corporations that cannot adequately excuse their accumulations. Although in the past the tax on unreasonable accumulations was applied only to closely held corporations, it may now apply to publicly held corporations as well.

The double tax on dividends also distorts the corporate choice between debt and equity financing. Because interest on debt is deductible, corporate earnings applied to payment for the use of borrowed capital are taxed only once—to the lender. Debt and equity capital are by no means interchangeable when the debt is owed to persons other than shareholders, so the choice in that case between the two types of financing is not based merely on tax considerations. Moreover, the tax differential can be minimized by not paying out dividends. Nonetheless, for a corporation that *must* pay dividends for use of its equity capital, the double tax on dividends favors raising capital by borrowing.

It might be thought that the bias would remain under the proposal because dividends still will not be deductible by the corporation. If there is a sufficiently close identity between corporate management and shareholders, however, exclusion by the shareholder is as good as deduction by the corporation. Even in the absence of identity between management and ownership, the cost of equity capital will be reduced as a result of the dividend exclusion, balancing the ability to deduct interest paid on indebtedness.

In addition to distortion of the debt-equity ratio for corporations borrowing from persons other than their shareholders, the present tax treatment of corporate debt and equity has created an apparently insuperable problem of distinguishing between debt and equity owned by the same persons. It is advantageous for shareholders in closely held corporations to hold as much of their investment as possible in the form of debt to avoid double tax on payments for the use of the capital and to permit additional withdrawals to be characterized as repayment of debt. Short of treating all debt owed to controlling shareholders as equity, there does not seem to be any workable (or logical) standard that can be applied to distinguish shareholder-owned debt from equity. Congress' attempt in 1969 to delegate authority to draw the line by regulation so far has failed.[26] The problem appears to be unavoidable so long as interest is taxed once and earnings paid out as dividends are taxed twice.

* * *

SELF-HELP INTEGRATION (LLCs) OR OTHERWISE
Bernard Wolfman[*]
62 Tax Notes 769, 769-70 (1994)

By year-end 1993, 36 states had passed laws authorizing limited liability companies (LLCs). The number doubled in only one year. In the past two months alone, the IRS has published revenue rulings holding that firms formed under the recently adopted LLC statutes of close to 10 states would be treated as partnerships (and not as associations taxable as corporations). Yet until 1988, when the IRS put its imprimatur on a Wyoming LLC, the Service had declined to approve any.

For almost two decades, the Service, with the Tax Court's blessing, has

---

26. The Treasury Department has so far been unsuccessful under section 385, added by section 415(a) of the Tax Reform Act of 1969, Pub. L. No. 91-172, 83 Stat. 613, in issuing regulations to distinguish stock from indebtedness. Regs. § 1.385-1 to -10 were finally adopted in 1980, but were later withdrawn by T.D. 7920, 1983-2 C.B. 69.

*. At time of original publication, Fessenden Professor of Law, Harvard University.

made it possible to organize partnerships that possess up to two of the four characteristics that are the usual marks of a corporation (and not historically those of an unincorporated business) without being treated as a corporation for federal income tax purposes. The four familiar attributes are limited liability, transferability of interest, continuity of life, and centralized management. The test is simply arithmetical, not at all qualitative. With up to two of those attributes but no more, the entity avoids tax treatment as a corporation; with more than two, the entity enters the double tax world of the C corporation.

The most popular and customary form used to achieve partnership status, while assuring the nonmanaging investors that their liability will be limited to their investment, has been the limited partnership formed under the Uniform Limited Partnership Act. Those entities can easily avoid continuity of life if they wish, and they may provide for a restricted form of transferability of the limiteds' interests. Usually they avoid centralized management and limited liability. Although management is vested in the general partner, that vesting is by reason of his status as general partner and not by appointment or election of the generals and limiteds together. The limited partners, to be sure, are not exposed to liability beyond their investment in the firm, but since the general partner is liable for partnership debts without limitation, the partnership is not treated as having the corporate attribute of limited liability.

The code does not restrict the number of partners a partnership may have and still receive partnership treatment, but it provides that the organization will be treated as a corporation if its interests are publicly traded (section 7704). An S corporation will avoid the "double taxation" of the C corporation and its shareholders, and it will assure limited liability to its investors along with centralized management (through a shareholder-elected board), but an S corporation may not have more than 35 shareholders or foreign shareholders or more than a single class of stock. Both the partnership and the S corporation limit the passthrough of losses to the investor's basis, but in the case of the partnership (and not the S corporation) the investors include in basis their share of "inside" (partnership) liabilities.

The LLC is fast becoming the vehicle of choice, especially for real estate and personal services. The recent increase in the top marginal tax rate of individuals, above the top corporate rate, may slow the pace of change for other profitable businesses for which the C corporation may provide a degree of shelter.

In states where the LLC is available, it provides a form of self-help integration, a "single tax" enterprise without a fixed statutory limit on the number of members, where outside basis is augmented by inside liabilities, and the "special allocation" rules of subchapter K provide the flexibility generally available to limited partnerships. Transferability of interest can be avoided by requiring membership approval before a transferee may be recognized as such and acquire the perquisites of membership, although a transferee will be entitled to the distributions and profit interest of the transferor without membership approval. The IRS will treat delegation of management to an appointed or elected manager or management committee as creating centralized management, but centralized management may be avoided by providing for management to be vested in all of the members. Since there is limited liability for all investors (no "general partner" or equivalent need be liable beyond his investment in the firm), two of the other three corporate attributes must be shunned to achieve partnership tax status. Although I am unaware of any statistics on the subject, my impression is that many LLCs opt for transferability of interest and, of course, limited liability, but they avoid continuity of life and centralized management, while others adopt a form of centralized management and limit transferability of interest sufficiently to avoid being tainted with that corporate attribute. As with partnerships generally, of course, public tradeability of members' interests would, by itself, bring on corporate tax status.

Until all of the states, or at least all of the leading commercial and financial states, adopt legislation recognizing or authorizing LLCs, there will be hesitation about adopting the LLC form if the enterprise will be doing business in a non-LLC state or if it has members living or doing business in such a state. The reason is that it is unclear whether, as a matter of law, a non-LLC state must recognize the limited liability status of an LLC investor. * * * Lawyers' opinions on this issue differ, and there is no governing judicial precedent. There is no federal law to resolve the question, but by the end of 1994 it may well be that California, New York, Pennsylvania, and Massachusetts will themselves have adopted LLC legislation—they and others are now considering it, and if Jimmy the Greek were asked he might well quote odds that point to approval.

Because publicly traded partnerships will be treated as C corporations and because S corporations are limited to 35 shareholders, current law does not offer an integrated "single tax" regime to corporations with a substantial number of shareholders or to publicly traded partnerships. Proposals have been made to increase the permissible number of shareholders in S corporations, and some of them may be adopted, but no pending legislation will eliminate the double tax for publicly held enterprises. To do so, it will be necessary for Congress to face head-on the issue of integration, the elimination in one way or another of a federal income tax hitting both the entity and the investor.

Two major studies have emerged in the past few years proposing integration schemes, one by the Bush Treasury and the other by an American Law Institute (ALI) Reporter.[n] The ALI study would convert the corporate

---

n. Both studies are excerpted earlier in this subchapter. (Eds.)

tax into a withholding tax under which shareholders would take credit on their Forms 1040 for their share of the corporate tax after grossing up their dividends to include the corporate tax paid. The Treasury would permit domestic shareholders to exclude dividends from their gross income. This is but a simplistic contrasting summary of the two most important integration studies. They deserve the careful attention of tax professionals. The issue of integration will not go away, but it will not receive full congressional consideration until the professionals and their clients have given it theirs and then urge Congress to take the subject seriously.

Not all students of the subject favor integration for publicly traded enterprises, faulting both the Treasury and the ALI proposals. Indeed, an earlier ALI study (1989) makes a strong, persuasive case for a reformed, "double tax" subchapter C, but one in which corporations would be able to deduct both interest on debt and, with respect to newly contributed equity, dividends as well—in effect, a proposal for a form of partial integration. Just as they have neglected the major integration studies, however, tax professionals have not paid sufficient attention to basic reform of subchapter C. Until they do, neither their clients nor Congress will.

Corporate tax simplification and subchapter C restructuring ought not be viewed as polar antagonists. They can and they should go together. For the non-publicly traded firm, the evolving LLC is a reform being achieved without congressional participation, and it is one that promises integration, simplification, and flexibility. Until there is sustained congressional focus on comprehensive corporate tax reform, however, including the proposals for partial or full integration for publicly traded companies, piecemeal code amendments, hit-or-miss legislation, further complexity, and a lack of coherence are likely to remain the order of the day.

Notes and Questions

20. Tax rate changes in recent years, by bringing the top rates for individuals and for corporations closer together, have made ending the double tax on dividends more acceptable.

21. Is a double tax eventually imposed on corporate earnings that are retained and reinvested? Is the capital gains tax on sale of corporate stock a double tax where reinvested earnings have increased the market price of a corporation's stock?

22. Can the double tax be avoided or minimized by closely held C corporations? How?

23. Treasury I asserts that by encouraging use of debt rather than equity, present law leads to increased numbers of bankruptcies during recessions. Why might this be so?

24. If the double tax were ended, would the attitude of stockholders be changed toward management's choice between retaining earnings and paying them out as dividends?

25. If corporations could deduct dividends, as they can deduct interest now, could corporate management resist pressure to distribute earnings?

26. Adoption of any of the proposals would be likely to encourage more liberal dividend policies, because corporate directors could no longer point to the double taxation of dividends as a reason to retain earnings. Corporate expansions would more often be financed by issuing new debt or equity rather than through retained earnings. Would these developments be desirable, as Treasury I asserts?

27. Professor Warren writes that adoption of his proposals "would convert the separate U.S. corporate income tax into a withholding tax with respect to income ultimately distributed to shareholders." What does this mean?

28 If shareholders were allowed to credit corporate income tax allocable to their dividends, why should the shareholders be required to "gross up," or increase, the dividends they receive by the amount credited? For example, if a corporation earned $100, paid $34 in tax, and distributed the remaining $66 in dividends, the shareholders would be required to report $100 of dividends, rather than $66, and would be granted a $34 credit against tax.

29. Why does Professor Warren propose that corporations that have not distributed dividends be allowed to make "constructive distributions," which then would be deemed to have been reinvested in the stock of the corporation?

30. The AICPA asserts that addressing the double tax problem through the shareholder-credit method would result in a higher level of taxpayer compliance than would the dividend-deduction method. Why?

31. According to the AICPA, what is the most important reason to prefer the shareholder-credit method over the dividend-deduction method?

32. The first paragraph of the excerpt from the 1992 Treasury proposal refers to the distribution of profits in the form of interest on bonds. This is overly broad. Interest paid to bondholders is a cost, not a distribution of profits, unless the bondholders also own the equity interest in the distributing corporation—in which case the distinction between profit and

interest expense can be considered artificial.

33. Should dividends paid from income that has been subject to foreign corporate income tax be eligible for whatever shareholder credit or exclusion is provided? What is the view of the 1992 Treasury proposal?

34. Peel argues that the double tax on dividends makes it possible for another corporation to offer a higher price for stock of a target corporation than individual stockholders would offer. Why?

35. Like other proponents of change, Peel argues that the present double-tax system leads to various economic problems. He also asserts, however, that the classic treatment of dividends—separate taxes at the corporate and shareholder level—is "unfair." Do you agree?

36. How should tax-exempt organizations be treated if the double tax system is ended? Under present law, if Irene Individual and the First Methodist Church each owns 100 shares of AT&T stock, each bears the same portion of the corporate tax, but only Irene pays a shareholder-level tax. Should integration or dividend relief result in the church being relieved of all tax with respect to AT&T earnings?

37. Under the shareholder-credit model, the corporation would pay the corporate income tax, which would generate a credit for shareholders. If this model were adopted, should a tax-exempt shareholder receive a refundable credit (and thus a check from the government, because it presumably would not have any tax liability to absorb the credit)? Note that Professor Warren would impose a tax on dividends (as well as interest) received by tax-exempt organizations, then allow the credit with any excess credit being refundable.

38. Can a fully integrated system—taxing shareholders on all corporate income, distributed or undistributed—be devised that is practical? Would it help to make the corporation a withholding agent for its shareholders?

39. Professor Wolfman explains how the recent emergence of limited liability companies (LLCs) has changed the taxation landscape. Why? Why are publicly held companies not able to achieve the benefits of LLCs?

40. One consequence of the Hall-Rabushka flat tax proposal, which is excerpted in Chapter Seven, would be to eliminate tax on dividends whether or not they are paid out of previously taxed corporate earnings.

41. Can it be argued that present stockholders are not penalized by the double tax because the price they paid for their stock already reflects a

discount for the double tax? Would a change in the law be a windfall for such shareholders?

42. Of the various reform proposals to address the problem of double taxation, which do you find most attractive? Why?

D. INTEREST DEDUCTIONS AND RETAINED EARNINGS

In contrast to the usual focus on the double tax on shareholders, Professor William Andrews, Reporter for the American Law Institute's Subchapter C Project, took the second, or shareholder, tax as given and derived from that assumption the conclusion that the system is biased in favor of equity capital to the extent the shareholder tax is postponed by the corporation retaining and reinvesting earnings that have borne only corporate tax. This point had more force before the 1981 Act, when the top corporate tax rate was substantially lower than the top individual tax rate, so that retained and reinvested corporate earnings bore substantially less tax than income earned and reinvested by partnerships or sole proprietors. The differential before the 1981 Act was 20 percentage points (70 percent versus 50 percent). As a result of the 1981 Act the differential fell to four percentage points (50 percent versus 46 percent), and is now 4.6 percentage points (39.6 percent versus 35 percent).

Section 302 treats as a sale, thus allowing capital gain treatment, stock redemptions by a corporation "if the redemption is not essentially equivalent to a dividend." Examples of qualifying redemptions are those in which the shareholder's entire interest is redeemed, or the shareholder's proportionate ownership is reduced to such a degree that the redemption is "substantially disproportionate."[o] This treatment seems correct if we focus only on the redeeming shareholder. However, Professor Andrews looks at the shareholders as a group, and is concerned that a redemption enables them to remove earnings from the corporation without imposition of a second tax at ordinary income rates. Some of Professor Andrews' proposals are directed at this perceived abuse.

The shift from equity to debt in corporate financial structures was of particular concern to Professor Michael Graetz (Assistant Secretary of the Treasury for Tax Policy in the Bush Administration) because such a large share of corporate bonds is owned by organizations that pay little or no tax on their interest income. Thus, the corporate deduction for interest expense is not compensated for by tax at the creditor level. The net result is no tax, as contrasted to the double tax on corporate earnings paid out as dividends

---

o. Section 302(b). Even if the shareholder's interest is not entirely ended by the redemption, a redemption is normally "substantially disproportionate" if, after the redemption, the shareholder owns less than 50% of the stock, and his percentage ownership is less than 80% as great as his pre-redemption percentage ownership.

to taxed shareholders. (This situation may call for a reexamination of tax exemptions for charities, pension funds, and foreign investors, as well as for study of the policy of allowing corporations to deduct their interest expense.)

**AMERICAN LAW INSTITUTE
REPORTER'S STUDY OF THE TAXATION OF CORPORATE
DISTRIBUTIONS,
APPENDIX TO SUBCHAPTER C PROPOSALS
William D. Andrews,[*] Reporter**

Pages 327-33 (1982)

Throughout this century the United States has pursued the classical system of taxing corporate earnings, in which corporations and shareholders are treated effectively as separate income taxpayers. Corporations are taxed as such on corporate income, whether or not distributed. Shareholders, on the other hand, are taxed on their dividends without any significant credit for corporate taxes paid on the earnings from which they come. Distributed corporate earnings are therefore said to be doubly taxed, first to the corporation that earns them and then to the shareholders to whom they are distributed.

This treatment of dividend income is to be contrasted with the treatment of corporate interest payments and nondividend distributions to shareholders. Interest on corporate debt is fully taxable to the recipient, but it is deductible by the corporate payor; corporate revenue distributed as interest is therefore only taxed once, to the investor-distributee, not to the corporation. * * *

These differences in tax treatment generate both economic distortions and legal problems. The deductibility of interest and nondeductibility of dividends create an inducement to raise money by issuing debt instruments rather than stock, and they generate a legal problem of differentiating between debt and equity interests. Similarly, capital-gain treatment of nondividend distributions creates an inducement to seek nondividend modes of distribution and avoid paying dividends, and generates a problem of differentiating between nondividend and dividend-equivalent distributions. These problems are central problems in the taxation of corporations and shareholders and are the subject of this Study.

One approach to these problems would be to accept as given the treatment described for each of these modes of distribution, but try to provide a better definition of the boundary lines between them. In particular, this would involve constructing a better way to differentiate between debt and equity for tax purposes, and better ways of measuring dividend equivalence in the case of boot and redemption distributions.

This approach has been taken in much valuable prior work. The trouble

---

[*]. At time of original publication, Professor of Law, Harvard University.

with this approach, however, is that it cannot eliminate or even much mitigate the disparities in treatment with which it deals; wherever the lines are drawn, substantial disparities will persist along with the economic and legal pressures they generate.

A bolder approach, widely discussed in the recent past, would seek to temper these disparities by eliminating or reducing double taxation of distributed earnings through integration of corporate and individual shareholder taxes. * * *

Any of these methods of integration would indeed reduce disparities among modes of distribution, by eliminating or reducing the double taxation of dividend income. But that objective would only be accomplished at a substantial cost in revenue and progressivity, since a high proportion of dividends flow to high-income, wealthy individuals. The initial effect of complete dividend relief would be almost to double the after-tax income of shareholders from dividends if aggregate corporate disbursements for taxes and dividends were held constant.

The approach explored in this Study runs along less familiar lines somewhere in between more general integration and mere refinement of existing boundaries. The basic distribution of tax burdens imposed by the existing classical system has been taken as given, and there is no proposal, therefore, to eliminate or even reduce the burden of double taxation on dividend income from existing equity investment. On the other hand, it has not been taken as given that the existing disparity in treatment between debt and equity or between dividend and nondividend distributions should be maintained. Rather than redefining boundaries between debt and equity or between dividend and nondividend distributions, this Study proposes that disparities in treatment be reduced by making substantive changes. Specifically, it is proposed to reduce or eliminate the disparity between debt and equity by giving particular limited relief for dividends on newly issued shares, and to reduce the disparity between dividend and nondividend distributions by imposing a compensatory excise on the latter.

The proposals in this Study * * * are published here solely as a Reporter's Study. One main reason for pursuing this course is the close relationship between these proposals and more general integration, which made it unrealistic to seek formal approval of the former without a full-scale study of the latter. On the other hand, these proposals are somewhat more radical than some would be prepared to approve under the banner of mere refinement of the existing system.
> > >   * * *

Summary of Reporter's Distribution Proposals

This Study deals with the tax treatment of corporate distributions to investors. The subject includes deductibility by the corporation—deductible interest and rent as compared with nondeductible dividends. It also includes taxability to the investor—ordinary income treatment of dividends as compared with capital-gain treatment of nondividend distributions. Finally, it embraces the special problems surrounding intercorporate investments and distributions—the intercorporate dividend deduction and cognate provisions. There is one proposal on each of these three topics.

1) *Newly contributed equity capital.* Existing law discriminates in favor of debt over newly issued equity by allowing a deduction for interest payments but not for dividends. This bias is familiar in theory and in practice, and it lies at the root of the seemingly intractable legal problem of differentiating satisfactorily between debt and equity for tax purposes.

Less obviously, perhaps, existing law also discriminates in favor of internally generated equity capital over contributed capital, by deferring individual income taxes on accumulation of the former. The effect of that deferral is similar to the benefit that would be conferred if individuals were allowed a deduction for purchasing newly issued shares. This bias is less familiar, stated this way, than the bias in favor of debt, but it is equally consistent with common experience. The main source of equity capital for most corporations other than regulated utilities is accumulation of earnings.

Because of this second bias, the existing discrimination in favor of debt can be defined more narrowly than at first appears. In effect, it is only a discrimination against newly contributed equity capital, not all equity, since accumulated earnings enjoy the compensatory advantage of individual tax deferral.

Reporter's Proposal R1 is to relieve this discrimination, thus narrowly defined, by treating newly contributed equity capital like debt, allowing a deduction for dividends paid up to some specified rate on the amount of capital contributed. In effect, the proposal is to treat all newly contributed debt and equity capital alike by making its cost largely deductible.

This proposal bears some resemblance to schemes for partially integrating corporate and individual taxes by allowing some deduction or credit for all dividends. But the focus of this proposal is narrower, and its revenue cost and redistributional impact are very much less, since it would not permit any deduction for dividends attributable to income from capital accumulated by retention of earnings. Moreover, it is not even proposed to allow any deduction for dividends from earnings on contributed capital invested prior to the proposal's effective date. The primary aim of the proposal is simply to remove the bias against future equity contributions; it is too late to pursue that objective with respect to past contributions.

By mitigating or eliminating the bias against new issues of stock, the proposal would go a long way toward resolving the legal problem of differentiating between debt and equity. The proposal would go even further in that direction by introducing limitations on the corporate interest deduction to correspond with limitations in the proposed deduction for dividends on newly contributed equity capital.

2) *Nondividend distributions.* Much of existing law is built around the

notion that a distribution in complete redemption of a shareholder's interest in a corporation is to be taxed in the same manner as proceeds from a sale of his shares to another investor. This entails a subtraction of basis from the redemption proceeds and application of relatively favorable capital-gain rates to any remaining profit. Less-than-complete redemptions may be taxed like complete redemptions or like dividends, primarily according to their effect on proportionate ownership rights. Drawing the line between redemption distributions to be taxed as sales and those to be taxed as dividends has been a continuing source of difficult controversy.

But even a complete redemption, when viewed in a broader perspective than that of the redeeming shareholder alone, has important similarities to a dividend, which distinguish it from a sale to new investors. Like a dividend, any redemption distribution has the effect of liberating the distributed funds from the prospective burden of a corporate income tax on earnings from their investment. Moreover, any redemption distribution has the exact effect of a dividend together with purchases and sales of shares among shareholders. As a result, even complete redemptions serve as a substitute for dividend distributions, in practice as well as theory. For many corporations long-range plans are made and carried out whose effect is to substitute share redemptions for dividends to a very considerable extent.

The substantial disparity in tax treatment between dividend and nondividend distributions, despite these functional similarities, creates, for many corporations, a strong bias against the former and in favor of the latter. This bias imposes uneven tax burdens on shareholders in different corporations, presumably distorts behavior, and generates considerable controversy in differentiating between dividend and nondividend distributions.

It is proposed in this Study to deal directly with this bias by raising the level of tax on nondividend distributions to something more nearly like that on dividends. There are several ways this could be done.

One possibility would be just to make the capital-gain rates inapplicable to stock redemptions. But that would induce low-basis shareholders to sell to other investors from whom the corporation could redeem shares at little gain. Alternatively, it could be provided that a proportionate part of accumulated earnings would be taxed as a dividend on any redemption, whether or not at a gain. But that would create an inducement for corporations to make redemptions from tax-exempt or low-bracket shareholders, and for other shareholders to sell to tax-exempt investors.

Another possibility is to tax any nondividend distribution as a dividend pro rata to all shareholders (or to continuing shareholders), as if there had been a dividend together with purchases and sales of shares among shareholders. Such a tax might not be readily understood or accepted by shareholders who merely hold their shares while others redeem, but the likely effect of such a provision would be to deter corporations from making redemption distributions in any event.

Another possibility is a simple, flat-rate excise on nondividend distributions, to be paid by the distributing corporation. The purpose and effect of such an excise would be to make burdens on dividend and nondividend distributions roughly comparable, without getting into the complications of treating a distribution to one shareholder as a dividend to another. This would have the effect of drastically reducing distortions of behavior and inequities of treatment under existing law while preserving the radical simplicity of the rule that shareholders are only taxed on what they receive. Moreover, this would permit repeal of much of the present law of dividend equivalence, so that a shareholder could treat a sale of shares as a sale without regard to the identity of the purchaser.

Reporter's Proposal R2 is to impose a compensatory excise on nondividend distributions. As a corollary, the proposal would also simplify standards of dividend equivalence in several respects.

3) *Intercorporate investments and distributions.* Dividends paid by one corporation to another that holds its shares are wholly or largely exempt from income tax by reason of the dividend-received deduction. The rationale for this deduction is that the earnings from which such dividends are paid have already been subject to corporate income tax, and that one round of corporate tax is enough.

But exemption of intercorporate dividends creates distortions when a corporation simply invests surplus funds in shares of other corporations, because it means that the corporate investor can secure a tax-free return on investments whose price is likely to be based on market evaluation of a taxable return. Moreover, a corporate purchase of all the shares of another corporation is equivalent in effect to a purchase of assets and liquidation of the transferor. It is in effect another means by which corporate funds can be distributed to noncorporate investors without being taxed as a dividend.

Reporter's Proposal R3 is to curb the intercorporate dividend deduction by disqualifying mere portfolio investments, and to treat payment for the acquisition of any direct investment, which still qualifies for the deduction, as a nondividend distribution subject to the excise in Proposal R2. Reporter's Proposal R3 also deals with the technical problem of coordination between a dividend-received deduction and the deduction in Proposal R1 for dividends paid on newly contributed capital.

THE TAX ASPECTS OF LEVERAGED BUYOUTS AND OTHER CORPORATE FINANCIAL RESTRUCTURING TRANSACTIONS
Michael J. Graetz[*]

42 Tax Notes 721, 721-26 (1989)

There apparently is little evidence that recent mergers and acquisitions have been predominantly motivated by tax reasons. * * * The tax aspects of leveraged buyouts (LBOs) and other corporate financial restructuring, however, play a very significant role in how the transactions are structured, and are a worthy subject for congressional attention for both long- and short-term reasons.

Corporate Tax Base Problems

The immediate fiscal problem is the potential erosion of the corporate tax base. * * *

From both an immediate and a longer term, or structural, perspective of the corporate income tax, the most serious problem seems to be the long-lamented fact that the tax burden on income earned by a corporation and distributed to shareholders as dividends bears a heavier tax burden than corporate income distributed in other forms or to other suppliers of capital —most importantly, amounts distributed to bondholders as interest. Unlike dividends, interest is deductible at the corporate level and, therefore, bears no corporate income tax. This disparity creates tax incentives for raising corporate capital through debt rather than equity and for substituting debt for equity. * * * [D]uring the period 1984 through 1987, corporate equity apparently decreased by more than $300 billion, while corporate debt increased in excess of $600 billion. These numbers alone obviously portend major revenue effects from substitutions of corporate debt for equity and, potentially, from restructuring the corporate income tax law.

The tax issue is further complicated by the relationship of tax burdens on retained versus distributed earnings and by the tax consequences of various corporate financial transactions to the recipient. With regard to the latter, amounts of corporate income distributed to suppliers of capital as interest and dividends generally are taxed in a similar manner to the recipient—as ordinary income, subject to rates ranging from a low of zero on pension funds and other tax-exempt organizations to a high of 33 percent [now 39.6 percent] for some individuals. In contrast, earnings distributed by corporations to their shareholders in exchange for stock typically are treated as stock purchases and sales, and an offset is allowed to the recipient for her basis in the stock, with any gain taxed at the shareholder's normal tax rate [now not in excess of 28 percent]. Amounts distributed to bondholders as principal repayments are untaxed.

Needless to say, this number of potential variables, coupled with great

---

[*]. At time of original publication, Justice S. Hotchkiss Professor of Law, Yale University.

flexibility in structuring corporate finance, make it extremely difficult either to obtain and maintain a firm grasp of the matters at stake or to devise a solution that cannot readily be undone by tax planners for the corporate and investment communities. These difficulties are further compounded by our general reliance on similar tax rules to govern the taxation of huge multinational corporations and small corporate businesses.

Substituting Debt for Equity

Such complexities, however, should not be permitted to obscure the potential impact of corporate financial restructuring on the Federal revenues. A back-of-the-envelope calculation demonstrates the critical points. The corporate income tax today generates nearly $100 billion of revenues, and additional revenues are produced by shareholder and creditor level taxes on dividends, interest, and stock and bond sales. These also are significant potential sources of revenues for state governments, many of which are confronting fiscal crises of their own.

At the extreme, $100 of corporate income distributed as dividends to a shareholder taxed at the top 33-percent marginal rate can produce as much as $55.78 of Federal income taxes ($34 at the corporate level plus $21.78 at the shareholder level (33 percent of the distributed $66 of after-tax income)). If the dividends are distributed to a 28-percent shareholder, the Federal government collects $52.48 of taxes ($34 plus $18.48); if the dividends are distributed to a tax-exempt shareholder, the government collects only the $34 of corporate income taxes. By comparison, $100 of corporate income distributed as interest to bondholders bears no tax at the corporate level and is subject to a maximum of $33 of total Federal tax if distributed to the highest marginal bracket individual, $28 if paid to a 28-percent taxpayer, and no tax at all if distributed to a tax-exempt creditor. Corporate income that is retained at the corporate level normally bears a 34-percent corporate income tax.

Depending on the corporation's method of raising capital, therefore, the Federal government's taxes on corporate-source income can range from zero to nearly 56 percent. If a single level tax were levied either in the form of a corporate income tax or at the top marginal rate applicable to individuals, the Federal government's tax would be roughly equal to one-third of the income, while about two-thirds would stay in private hands.

In 1985, the last year for which IRS data is available, corporate taxable income before interest deductions for domestic nonfinancial corporations totaled nearly $440 billion. A single Federal tax imposed at a 33-percent rate on such income would have produced about $145 billion of revenues, a number that seems to be at least as great as that year's combined corporate and individual level income taxes on all corporate-source income (by which I mean, simply, the net pretax income earned by corporations before it is divided among those who have contributed to the corporation the capital with which the income was earned, *viz.* the creditors and shareholders).

Federal Reserve estimates suggest that about one-half of corporate equity at the end of 1987 was held by individuals, while the other half was held by charitable organizations, pension funds, foreign investors, or life insurance companies, which are likely to receive favorable Federal income tax treatment. By contrast, only about five percent of corporate bonds are thought to be owned by individuals. Thus, a shift from equity to debt as a source of corporate capital will serve to avoid corporate income taxes and, in addition, will tend to reduce or eliminate individual income tax revenues.
* * *

Inadequate Solutions

It is no small irony that this year marks the twentieth anniversary of two well-known "solutions" to the kinds of problems we are discussing here today. The first is section 385, added to the Internal Revenue Code in 1969, which, as every schoolchild knows, delegated to Treasury regulatory authority to resolve the question how to distinguish between debt and equity. The Treasury Department failed to produce as much as a whimper in this regard until it issued proposed regulations in 1980 that ultimately were withdrawn in 1983 when the enterprise attempting to distinguish debt from equity based on their economic substance once again returned to a moribund state.

The 1969 Tax Reform Act also added section 279 to the Code in an effort to restrict deductibility of interest on acquisition indebtedness, apparently on the view that, like construction period interest, such interest is in the nature of a capital expenditure. Corporate financiers, however, apparently have not found section 279 to be even a tiny barrier to corporate financial restructuring or LBOs.

The two decades of experience with these laws suggest great caution in attempting to enact solutions that require the recharacterization of debt as equity or that attempt to limit a disallowance of interest to indebtedness incurred for a particular purpose, such as a hostile (or even any) takeover. The past two decades also teach that there is little gain and no stability to be had from such marginal tinkering as opposed to beginning to address the underlying fundamental income tax problems. One cannot help but wonder where we would be today if Congress in 1969 or even in 1978—when Congressman Ullman, then chair of the House Ways and Means Committee, advanced such a proposal—had begun to phase in an integrated corporate tax that eliminated, or at least narrowed, the corporate income tax treatment of debt and equity.
* * *

A Single Tax on Corporate Income

Congress should reject gerrymandered ad hoc solutions designed to preserve the status quo, and, instead, seize this opportunity to move—slowly perhaps, but with a clear sense of direction—toward true corporate income tax reform by embarking on a path that ultimately would provide equal corporate income tax treatment for debt and equity—in other words, to move in the direction of an integrated corporate income tax.

What needs to be done, I think, is to begin now to move toward a single tax on corporate-source income—by which I again simply mean a single tax on the net pretax income earned by a corporation before it is divided among the creditors and shareholders who have contributed to the corporation the capital with which the income was earned. As indicated earlier, such a single tax should produce revenues at least equal to the combined corporate and individual income taxes now imposed on all corporate-source income, and, in addition, would ensure that the Federal government would share in any future growth in such income.

I do not mean to suggest by this observation that this is an appropriate occasion for raising additional revenues from taxes on corporate income, although it does seem the proper moment to halt the ongoing disappearance of the corporate tax base. There are a variety of revenue-neutral ways to begin to move toward the goal of a single tax on corporate income, and I think that it is important that steps be taken clearly in this direction now, indeed, far more important than the precise contours of such steps. My preferred solution, however, would be to phase in a shareholder-credit type integration of corporate dividends, financed through an identical bondholder-credit approach to interest payments. This would be an important first step toward equal treatment for corporate debt and equity.

Such a proposal is grounded in the lessons learned from thinking in some detail about corporate tax integration. In particular, we have learned that a dividend and interest deduction or, as an alternative, a shareholder and bondholder credit are essentially equivalent methods of eliminating the corporate tax burden on distributed earnings with respect to debt or equity contributed or owned by shareholders or bondholders who are allowed the credit.

In brief outline, a tax credit could be provided to shareholders for some portion or all of the corporate tax paid with respect to corporate earnings distributed to shareholders as dividends. Likewise, in lieu of the interest deduction, a similar tax credit could be provided to bondholders for some portion or all of the corporate tax paid with respect to corporate earnings distributed to bondholders as interest. The shareholder or bondholder would include both the amount of the tax and the cash dividend or interest in income and receive a tax credit for the amount of the tax.

* * *

To be sure, if the credit were not refundable, much of the burden of shifting from an interest deduction to a bondholder credit system would be borne by foreign creditors and tax-exempt bondholders, while the benefits of the shareholder credit would tend to accrue to individual shareholders who now bear the burden of the double corporate tax. However, many of the benefits of elimination of the corporate tax from substitution of debt for equity in leveraged buyouts and other corporate recapitalization transactions are now accruing to those same nontaxable persons and entities. Moreover, to the extent that the tax would be borne by corporate defined benefit pension plans, corporations and their shareholders, rather than the beneficiaries of such plans, would tend to suffer the tax. In any event, the result of such a proposal, as mentioned earlier, would be to take a major step in the direction of a single tax on corporate income without regard to who contributed to the corporation the capital with which the income was earned, and regardless of whether the capital contributed was debt or equity.

Previous proposals for corporate tax integration, whether through dividend deductions or shareholder credits, have received a lukewarm reception from the corporate community. But much of the corporate community's previous opposition to corporate tax integration may have been due to the fact that on every prior occasion where such integration has been before Congress, it would have been financed through tax increases on *retained* earnings, in particular through reduction or repeal of investment tax credits or of accelerated depreciation or through higher corporate tax rates. Needless to say, corporate managers prefer not to reduce the tax on income distributed to shareholders as dividends at the cost of higher taxes on income they retain in corporate solution. Today, however, we are talking about financing a tax reduction for shareholders by increasing taxes on another form of *distributed* earnings, namely, amounts paid to bondholders as interest. The reception in the corporate community might well be more positive, although it may be naive to expect the corporate and investment communities to welcome any effective barrier to their ability to shed the corporate income tax through restructuring their financial systems or by leveraged buyouts. As Treasury Secretary Brady told the Senate Finance Committee, the corporate community seems to have found its own way to integrate the corporate tax.

In any event, this idea merits the serious attention of Congress, because it implies a corporate income tax that would not distinguish between debt and equity and that, by providing such equal treatment, would eliminate the potential provided by current law to erode the corporate tax by substituting debt for equity. It has the additional advantage of abandoning the fruitless quest of the past two decades for a workable distinction between debt and equity. It would represent an important step toward neutrality between corporate and noncorporate investments, neutrality between debt and equity finance at the corporate level, and neutrality between retention and distribution of corporate earnings. At the same time, it avoids any effort to permit or disallow interest deductions based on the purpose of incurring a debt; such an enterprise is inevitably complex and ultimately will prove unsuccessful. If some basic structural change along these lines suggested here is not begun now, I fear that we simply can look forward to future years and perhaps decades of half-solutions or nonsolutions.

* * *

Notes and Questions

43. Corporations postpone the double tax by retaining and reinvesting earnings and, for most years, pay a single income tax at a rate lower than the top individual income tax rate. Does this justify imposing an additional corporate tax when corporations distribute their accumulated earnings in liquidation?

44. How does present law discriminate in favor of debt financing as contrasted with equity financing?

45. Professor Andrews points out that a nondividend redemption distribution has the effect of liberating the distributed funds from the burden of a corporate income tax on future earnings from their investment. Does this justify imposing a tax at the time of the stock redemption?

46. Professor Andrews is concerned with potential avenues of escape from a full tax on corporate earnings at the shareholder level. His concern arises from the ability of corporations to reinvest their accumulated earnings without their having been subjected to a second tax at the shareholder level.

47. Should discrimination against corporate equity compared to corporate debt be ended by denying corporations the right to deduct bond interest as well as dividends, and perhaps allowing credit to both bondholders and stockholders for corporate tax paid? Would such treatment have to be extended to interest on other types of corporate debt as well? Would similar treatment have to be given to partnerships?   To sole proprietorships?

48. If corporations were denied a deduction for interest payments, would it also be necessary to deny a deduction for rent? After all, interest is simply rent for one category of property—money. What would prevent shareholders who wanted to keep personal ownership of property used by the corporation, and remove money from the corporation in a form deductible by the corporation, from achieving these ends by renting property to a corporation rather than lending it money at interest?

49. As discussed in Note #9, present law contains several limitations on interest deductions by corporations.

50. Professor Graetz makes a significant point that much of the corporate community has opposed previous legislative attempts to ameliorate the double tax on dividend income. Given a choice, corporate management

would prefer a cut in corporate income tax rates.

Selected Bibliography

AMERICAN LAW INSTITUTE, REPORTER'S STUDY OF CORPORATE TAX INTEGRATION (1993).

ANDO, ALBERT ET AL. THE STRUCTURE AND REFORM OF THE U.S. TAX SYSTEM 143-65 (1985).

Andrews, William D., *The ALI Reporter's Proposals on Corporate Distributions and Corporate Taxation with a Personal Consumption Tax*, 22 SAN DIEGO L. REV. 333 (1985).

Bradford, David F., *The Incidence and Allocation Effects of a Tax on Corporate Distributions*, 15 J. PUB. ECON. 1 (1981).

Feldstein, Martin & Daniel Frisch, *Corporate Tax Integration: The Estimated Effects of Capital Accumulation and Tax Distribution of Two Integration Proposals*, 31 NAT'L TAX J. 37 (1977).

Goode, Richard, *Rates of Return, Income Shares and Corporate Tax Incidence, in* EFFECTS OF CORPORATION INCOME TAX (Marian Krzyzaniak ed., 1966).

Gourevitch, Harry G., *Corporate Tax Integration: The European Experience*, 31 TAX LAW. 65 (1977).

Graetz, Michael J., *The Tax Aspects of Leveraged Buyouts and Other Corporate Financial Restructuring Transactions*, 42 TAX NOTES 721 (1989).

Gravelle, Jane G., *The Corporate Income Tax: Economic Issues and Policy Options*, 48 NAT'L TAX J. 267 (1995).

Harberger, Arnold C., *The State of Corporate Income Tax: Who Pays It? Should It Be Repealed?, in* NEW DIRECTIONS FOR FEDERAL TAX POLICY FOR THE 1980S (Charls E. Walker & Mark A. Bloomfield eds., 1984).

Integration of the Corporate Shareholder Tax Systems, AMERICAN INSTITUTE OF CERTIFIED PUBLIC ACCOUNTANTS, STATEMENT OF TAX POLICY (1993).

KRZYZANIAK, MARIAN & RICHARD A. MUSGRAVE, THE SHIFTING OF THE CORPORATE INCOME TAX (1963).

Kwall, Jeffrey L., *The Uncertain Case Against the Double Taxation of Corporate Income*, 68 N.C. L. REV. 613 (1990).

MCLURE, CHARLES E., JR., MUST CORPORATE INCOME BE TAXED TWICE? (1979).

——, *Integration of the Personal and Corporate Income Taxes: The Missing Element in Recent Tax Reform Proposals*, 88 HARV. L. REV. 534 (1975).

Nadeau, Serge J. & Robert P. Strauss, *Taxation, Equity, and Growth: Exploring the Trade-Off Between Shareholder Dividend Tax Relief and Higher Corporate Income Taxes*, 46 NAT'L TAX J. 161 (1993).

PECHMAN, JOSEPH A., FEDERAL TAX POLICY 135-89 (5th ed. 1987).

Peel, Fred W., Jr., *A Proposal for Eliminating Double Taxation of*

Corporate Dividends, 39 TAX LAW. 1 (1985).

Poterba, James M. & Lawrence H. Summers, *The Economic Effects of Dividend Taxation, in* RECENT ADVANCES IN CORPORATE FINANCE 227 (Edward Altman & Marti Subrahmanyam eds., 1985).

Reporter's Study of the Taxation of Corporation Distributions, Appendix to ALI SUBCHAPTER C PROPOSALS (1982).

SIMONS, HENRY, PERSONAL INCOME TAXATION 185-204 (1938).

Snoe, Joseph A., *The Entity Tax and Corporate Integration: An Agency Cost Analysis and a Call for a Deferred Distribution Tax*, 48 U. MIAMI L. REV. 1 (1993).

Sorensen, Peter B., *Changing Views of the Corporate Income Tax*, 48 NAT'L TAX J. 279 (1995).

Stephan, Paul B. III, *Disaggregation and Subchapter C: Rethinking Corporate Tax Reform*, 76 VA. L. REV. 655 (1990).

U.S. DEP'T OF TREASURY, REPORT ON INTEGRATION OF THE INDIVIDUAL AND CORPORATE TAX SYSTEMS (1992).

——, 1 REPORT ON TAX SIMPLIFICATION AND REFORM ["TREASURY I"] 118-19 (1984).

——, OFFICE OF TAX POLICY, RESTRUCTURING THE U.S. TAX SYSTEM, AN OPTION FOR FUNDAMENTAL REFORM (1992).

VICKREY, WILLIAM, AGENDA FOR PROGRESSIVE TAXATION 150-63 (1947).

Warren, Alvin, *The Relation and Integration of Individual and Corporate Income Taxes*, 94 HARV. L. REV. 719 (1981).

Wolfman, Bernard, *Self-help Integration (LLCs) or Otherwise*, 62 TAX NOTES 769 (1974).

Yin, George K., *Corporate Tax Integration and the Search for the Pragmatic Ideal*, 47 TAX L. REV. 431 (1992).

Zodrow, George R., *On the "Traditional" and "New" Views of Dividend Taxation*, 45 NAT'L TAX J. 497 (1991).

Zolt, Eric M., *Corporate Taxation After The Tax Reform Act of 1986: A State of Disequilibrium*, 66 N.C. L. REV. 839 (1988).

CHAPTER FIFTEEN

CAPITAL GAINS AND LOSSES

Tax lawyers spend about a third of their time converting ordinary income into capital gain.[a]

A. HISTORY, DEFINITIONS, AND TAX TREATMENT

The proper tax treatment of capital gains and losses is a staple of any course in tax policy. Perhaps more than in the case of any other area of tax law, the policy debate on this issue has gone beyond academic disputes to become a significant political issue for policy makers. Since the Tax Reform Act of 1986, when Congress almost eliminated the favorable treatment of capital gain vis-a-vis ordinary income that had prevailed for the preceding 65 years, the issue has made its way into television newscasts and presidential campaigns.

Treating capital assets differently from other items generates complexity in the income tax. Intricate statutory and regulatory provisions are necessary to describe differential treatment and to limit its exploitation. These rules often are difficult to understand. Significant amounts of time and resources have long been spent searching for the rewards from achieving capital gain or ordinary loss treatment; this seems to be the case at present, even though the benefits are smaller than they were before 1986. Perhaps more seriously, the capital gains and losses rules are difficult for the Revenue Service to police and to administer. In 1973, Professor Boris Bittker called the treatment of capital gains and losses "perhaps the single most complicating aspect of existing law."[b]

Capital gains and capital losses are gains and losses from the sale or exchange of capital assets. Section 1221 defines capital assets, using the technique of considering all assets that are not excluded by the provisions of that section to be capital assets. The two major categories of assets that are excluded from the definition of capital assets are (1) stock in trade or inventory of taxpayers and (2) property used in taxpayers' trades or businesses that is either depreciable property or real property. Most other assets are capital assets. Capital assets include stocks and bonds (except stock in trade of brokerage firms), land held for investment purposes, and property held for personal use such as a taxpayer's home, automobile, jewelry, and clothing.

---

a. Statement attributed to Walter Blum.

b. *General Tax Reform: Panel Discussions before the House Comm. on Ways and Means*, 93rd Cong., 1st Sess. 118 (1973).

In general, Congress has sought to give capital gain and loss treatment to most sales of property, while denying such treatment to sales where the proceeds represent earned income or income from ordinary business operations. As the excerpts in this chapter demonstrate, even when Congress has not intentionally deviated from this general pattern, it has been difficult to draw lines consistently.

For example, section 1235 provides that gain by inventors on the sale of their patents is to be treated as capital gain. On the other hand, section 1231(3) provides that gain by authors on sale of their copyrights is to be treated as ordinary income.

Although corporate stock ordinarily is a capital asset, pursuant to section 341, if a person owns more than five percent of the stock of a "collapsible" corporation, gain on sale or exchange of the stock will be treated as ordinary income. In general terms, a collapsible corporation is one formed or used with a view to liquidating it or selling its stock before it has realized at least two-thirds of the anticipated income from its manufacturing, constructing, or inventory-holding operations.

An interest in a partnership is a capital asset, but the portion of a taxpayer's gain from sale of a partnership interest that is attributable to "unrealized receivables" is treated as ordinary income under section 751. A major component of unrealized receivables, which is a defined term, is the value of the right to compensation for services the partnership has rendered or will render and the right to payment for goods delivered or to be delivered by the partnership.

Although depreciable business assets and real property used in business are not capital assets, section 1231 generally treats gains on these assets that have been held for more than a year as capital gains if these gains (plus involuntary conversion gains in excess of involuntary conversion losses) exceed losses from similar assets. Section 1231 gains include income from timber sales, coal and iron ore royalties, and some livestock sales, as well as gains from sale of unharvested crops sold along with land that has been held for more than a year.

The scope of capital gain treatment under section 1231 is narrowed substantially by other Code provisions, such as sections 1245 and 1250, which provide for ordinary income treatment of realized gain to the extent of deductions taken against ordinary income in earlier years ("recapture").

The magnitude of the major sources of capital gains of individuals is described in the first excerpt by Ms. Gravelle and Professor Lindsey. Professor Calvin H. Johnson's article examines the serious peripheral problems with the capital asset definition and with the interaction of preferential treatment of capital gains and related deductions from ordinary income.

CAPITAL GAINS
Jane G. Gravelle[*] & Lawrence B. Lindsey[**]
38 Tax Notes 397, 398-99 (1988)

Types of Capital Gains Assets

The asset most closely associated with capital gains in the popular debate is corporate common stock. Some analysts have gone so far as to ascribe the primary determination of the level of capital gains realizations to changes in the stock market. In general, too much emphasis has been placed on common stocks as being typical of the assets on which capital gains are realized.

Even at the stock market's peak this August, common stocks comprised only 20 percent of the value of the assets in the household sector. Not all assets are likely to register capital gains. Some household assets are either liquid, such as cash or checking accounts, or held by fiduciaries, such as pension funds. One measure of the capacity to realize gains is tradable household wealth,[2] which includes all household assets on which capital gains are likely to be realized, including stocks, real estate, and the value of unincorporated businesses. Common stocks comprised 27 percent of tradable household wealth at the end of 1986.[3]

Detailed data from the Department of Treasury[4] indicates that corporate stock comprises only about one quarter of realized capital gains, and 35 percent of all gains other than those on personal residences. In 1977 corporate stock comprised 23 percent of gross capital gains and 15 percent of the net capital gains reported that year. In 1981 the corresponding figures were 28 percent of gross gains and 25 percent of net capital gains. In short, although it is an important component of capital gains, corporate stock hardly can be considered typical of capital gains assets.

Corporate stock changes in value over time in line with how the market values the firms represented by the shares. The changes in value of corporate stock can be broken into three components: (1) an inflation component due to the rise in the price of corporate assets along with other prices; (2) a rise (or fall) in the real valuation of corporate assets with market conditions; and (3) an increase in corporate assets due to the reinvestment

---

[*]. At time of original publication, Specialist in Industry Analysis, Congressional Research Service, Library of Congress

[**]. At time of original publication, Assistant Professor of Economics at Harvard University and Research Fellow at the National Bureau of Economic Research.

2. Tradable household wealth includes the value of corporate equities, real estate, and unincorporated businesses.

3. Data computed from the Federal Reserve Board's "Balance Sheets of the U.S. Economy and Flow of Funds."

4. Clark, Bobby and David Paris, "Sales of Capital Assets, 1981 and 1982" in Statistics of Income Bulletin, Winter, 1984, p. 65. The calculation notes that while corporate stock comprised 28 percent of all gains, 21 percent of gains were personal residences that are untaxed. Thus, the 35 percent figure represents the share of corporate gains in all gains except for the sale of personal residences.

of retained earnings. For the sake of future discussion, we will term these the inflation, risk, and reinvestment components of corporate capital gains. It is the reinvestment component of capital gains on corporate stock that renders it unique.

The second largest component of capital gains in 1981 was from the sale of personal residences, comprising 21 percent of the gross gain and 25 percent of the net gain reported that year. (Recent changes in compliance provisions with respect to sale of real estate indicate that these figures are probably understated.) Although the reported net capital gain on real estate is roughly as large as that on common stock, most of this gain is not subject to tax. The tax law excludes the gain on the sale of residences from taxation if the seller purchases a new residence equal to the cost of the old.[c] Taxpayers also may take a one-time exclusion of $125,000 from the sale of a residence if they are over 55 years of age. In practice, very little capital gain from owner-occupied housing is taxed. Like corporate stock, capital gains on residential real estate accrue due to inflation and risk. Additional investment in residential real estate increases the tax basis of the property, and thus is not taxed.

Non-business real estate comprises the next largest category of capital gains. Much of the gain in this component is due to inflation, although there is also likely to be a component of real appreciation in the value of land and other real estate over time. Gains also may occur if the depreciation of the asset used for tax purposes overstated the true economic decline in the value of the asset. Unlike corporate stock, there are no retained earnings that are reinvested in the asset. Any new investment in this type of asset increases the basis, or initial purchase price, of the asset and so is excluded from capital gains tax.

The fourth category of capital gains represents a catch-all of gains on unincorporated business assets. Although no single component of this catch-all category is large, collectively gains on unincorporated business assets are nearly as great as gains on common stock. Like other assets, gains on these assets may accrue either due to inflationary price increases, because of a change in the real value of the assets due to market conditions, or because of a mismatch between tax depreciation and economic depreciation. Unlike corporate stock, earnings are not explicitly retained and reinvested by these business entities. Instead, all profits are taxed to the individual owner in the year they occur. The owner then may reinvest part of the after-tax profits back into the firm. These reinvested earnings increase the basis, or initial purchase price, of the asset and so are excluded from capital gains tax.

---

c. The authors' statement of law is not correct. In order to be allowed nonrecognition treatment, the taxpayer must reinvest in a new residence the amount of the sales proceeds from the old residence, not merely the cost of the old residence. *See* section 1034. (Eds.)

There are two other relatively minor categories of assets on which capital gains occur. One is gains on interest yielding assets such as bonds, whose value changes with the interest rate. Any gain or loss offsets future changes in income from this type of asset. If the interest rate falls, the value of a bond yielding a given return rises. The seller receives a gain, and the purchaser has an increased basis for the return of principal.

The other type of asset that yields gains is an asset that appreciates in value naturally, such as timber. The economic income of such an asset is a result of the natural appreciation in value. As a tree grows, its value increases. There are both real and inflationary components of this income.

In sum, there are a wide range of assets that yield capital gains. Although corporate stock comprises only about a quarter of all capital gains, such stock has a unique attribute. The reinvestment of after-tax profits in a corporate enterprise does not increase the basis, or initial purchase price, of the investor's asset. This reinvestment becomes subject to capital gains taxation when the corporate shares are sold. Although the taxpayer did not pay personal income tax on the profits, the corporate tax rate on the reinvested earnings is at least equivalent to the personal rate that would be paid on a similar reinvestment in an unincorporated enterprise. The capital gains taxation on this reinvestment of corporate retained earnings constitutes, in our view, an important distinction between corporate stock and other types of assets.

* * *

SEVENTEEN CULLS FROM CAPITAL GAINS
Calvin H. Johnson[*]

48 Tax Notes 1285, 1285-99 (1990)

Congress needs to simplify the law of capital gains to clean out some of the deadwood. The common understanding of "capital gain" is that it represents appreciation over time of investment property, such as land or corporate stock. * * * The existing law of capital gains has anomalies and complexities unrelated to any policy for giving special rates to capital gains.

* * * When the cows are crossed over the river to the land of low rate capital gains, there are some things that need to be culled from the herd. Following are seventeen reforms that need to be made to the law of capital gain * * * None of the proposals is intended to endorse preferential rates for capital gains nor to imply the case for any preference has been made.

* * * Some of the proposals have important revenue impact; some just foreclose future abuses or achieve academic neatness. But for almost all, if not all, of the proposals, there is or would be a strong consensus within the

---

[*]. At time of original publication, Arnold, White & Durkee Centennial Professor of Law, University of Texas.

academic community that these items should be culled from the definition of capital gains. The list is not, however, exhaustive.

* * *

Proposal 1: Self-Produced Assets

Current law. Capital gain is understood to arise from the market appreciation of capital invested by the taxpayer rather than from value added by the personal efforts of the taxpayer or taxpayer's agents, but literally any "property" is a capital asset unless the property is "held primarily for sale to customers in ordinary course of a trade or business." IRC section 1221(3) (withdrawing capital asset treatment from assets created by personal efforts of the taxpayer) applies only to literary or artistic works.

Proposal. Exclude all self-produced assets from the definition of "capital asset" by amending now section 1221(3) to read:

"(3) property, whether real or intangible, where the personal efforts of the taxpayer or the taxpayer's agents created or substantially enhanced the value of the property."

Conform IRC section 1231 by replacing IRC section 1231(b)(1)(C) with the above language.

Reasons for the Change. A taxpayer who makes or improves an asset with his or her own personal efforts receives compensation for services when the asset is sold at a profit. Thus, for example, the sale of furniture made by an amateur cabinet maker is salary or compensation and not capital gain as a matter of economics, even if the cabinet maker does not have enough activity to be in a trade or business.

* * *

Section 1221(3) was adopted "to close the loophole," recognizing that gain on self-produced assets was supposed to be ordinary (S. Rep. No. 2375, 81st Cong., 2 Sess. 43 (1950), but the exclusion was narrowly drawn to cover only literary or artistic works. Under the proposal here, "capital asset" would exclude all real and intangible property created or improved by the taxpayer, not just artistic works.

* * *

Proposal 2: Property Without Substantial Investment

Current law. Receipts from sale of income items are held not to constitute "property" within the definition of capital asset under IRC section 1221, even though the items qualify as "property" under state law, where the taxpayer has no basis or capital investment in the income item disposed of. Commissioner v. Gillette Motor Transp. Inc., 364 U.S. 130,134 (1960); *Luna v. Commissioner*, 42 T.C. 1067, 1079 (1964).

Proposal. Add the italicized wording to the first lines of IRC section 1221: "(T)he term 'capital asset' means property held by the taxpayer (whether or not connected with his trade or business), *in which the taxpayer has a substantial capital investment*, but does not include, . . . " Add IRC section 1221(b) to define 'capital investment' to include capital expenditure, carryover basis, or basis by reason of prior taxation of the receipt of the property, even if adjusted basis is zero by the time of sale. Value on death (IRC section 1014) would not be a capital investment, although an heir would have a substantial capital investment if the decedent did. Conform IRC section 1221.

Reasons for the Change. If the taxpayer has no substantial investment in an asset, then none of the doctrinal or policy reasons for a preferential tax rate apply to sale of the asset. Capital gain is the gain attributable to appreciation in value over a period of years of capital invested by the taxpayer; if the taxpayer has no investment, his or her gain cannot be explained by appreciation. Lowered rates cannot create an incentive for the formation of capital nor for mobility of capital if there is no capital investment involved. * * *

Proposal 3: Sale of Name, Likeness, or Waiver of Privacy of Living or Dead Person

Current Law. Sale of the rights to use the name, image, likeness, biography or private facts or images of a living or dead person were held not to qualify as a sale of "property" within the meaning of the section 1221 definition of a "capital asset" by *Miller v. Commissioner*, 299 F.2d 706 (2d Cir. 1962) *cert. denied* 370 U.S. 923 (1962) (waivers by heirs for "Glenn Miller Story"), but the decision depends in part on failure of state law to treat sold rights as property rights.

Proposal. Codify *Miller* excluding the rights from the definition of capital asset, even if rights to name, image, likeness, or biography qualify as "property rights" under state law. Add a new (6) to IRC section 1221 and new (f) to section 1231(b)(1), excluding: "rights to use the name, image, likeness, voice, signature, or private or biographical facts of a living or dead person, acquired by the taxpayer other than by arm's-length purchase."

Reasons for the Change. The *Miller* decision treated the proceeds of sale by heirs of rights to use the name and biographical facts of Glenn Miller as ordinary income. But the decision rested heavily on the fact that the heirs had no property under state law. * * *

Federal tax results cannot be made to rest on state law recharacterizations of a transaction. State lawmakers have no loyalty to federal revenue concerns and will readily alter state characterizations if that will save their state citizens some federal tax. Federal tax characterizations are moved by policy reasons independent of the policies behind the state law characterization. * * *

As a matter of history, capital gains were accorded to those things that were considered to be allocable to the corpus or principal account at common law because there was originally some doubt that the corpus could be taxed under an "income" tax. But rights to name, likeness, biographical facts, et al., were not corpus or property rights under the common law.
  * * *

Proposal 4: Expensed Asset is an Ordinary Asset

Current law. Expensed assets are sometimes treated as not "property," for instance, within the meaning of statutes giving nonrecognition upon sales of property. See, e.g., *United States v. Bliss Dairy Inc.*, 460 U.S. 370 (1983)(disposal of expensed prepaid feed was recovery of tax deduction, notwithstanding statutory rule that capital gain on sale of property was not recognized). But in general, assets may qualify as capital assets even though the cost of the asset was deducted upon acquisition of the asset ("expensed").

Proposal. Assets, the cost of which was expensed upon acquisition, would be excluded from the definition of capital asset, by adding a new section 1221(b), defining substantial "capital investment" required for a capital asset (see Proposal 2), to exclude from "capital investment" costs that had been deducted upon acquisition of the asset.

Reasons for the Change. Capital gain is conceived of and debated as a reduction of tax on economic profit, which, however, collects tax at the lower rate. But when a misaccounting is allowed under which the inputs into a transaction are deducted from ordinary income whereas the gross revenue from the transaction qualifies for capital gain, there is an accounting mismatch that ends up giving the transaction treatment better than tax exemption, that is, a negative tax.

Assume, for instance, that a $100 investment (such as for feed or to enhance goodwill) paid by a 33-percent bracket taxpayer is expensed (deducted immediately) by the investor when acquired. Assume that the investment generates gain of $100 (such as by sale of livestock or the business) considered to qualify as capital gain. Assume the $ 100 capital gain (computed from zero basis) is subject to a new lower 15-percent rate. The $100 transaction bears tax of $15 and saves tax of $33 for a total negative tax (tax savings) of $18.

Given the negative tax, revenue of up to 220 percent of costs would go untaxed ($ 220 x 15% tax on revenue less $ 100 x 33% tax savings from the expense equals zero net tax) and the taxpayer could willingly incur economic losses of 27 percent of receipts and still break even with the negative tax. ($100(1-15%) after-tax revenue less $127(1-33%) after-tax expense equals zero net cost.)

* * *

Proposal 5: Recapture of S Corporate Losses

Current Law. Ordinary losses incurred by an S corporation pass through and are deducted by the shareholder, up to the amount of the shareholder's basis in the S corporation stock. IRC section 1366(a), (b) & (d). S corporation stock is a capital asset, sale of which will generate capital gains, even when the gain represents shareholder recovery of the prior deductions. (IRC section 341(f), moreover, will exempt S corporations from collapsible corporation rules.)

Proposal. Enact a new IRC section 1369 to provide that gains from sale of S stock are recaptured (ordinary) gain to the extent of prior losses passed through under IRC section 1366.

Explanation. The simplest way to convert ordinary income from a general investment that does not qualify for any special rule into capital gain is through an S corporation. * * *

Gain from a sale for an amount greater than the adjusted basis of the stock represents a recovery of the passed-through losses that the shareholder has previously deducted. Over the course of the entire transaction, the shareholder has not suffered economic loss because the reported tax losses are reimbursed on sale or because the taxpayer has never borne the losses. The gain, between adjusted basis and original cost, is not market appreciation on the taxpayer's original investment, but rather an artificial gain that identifies an artificial loss never in fact suffered.
 * * *

Proposal 6: Recapture Prior Expenses

Current Law. Depreciation is recaptured in part or full when depreciable property is sold (IRC sections 1245 & 1250), but expenses contributing to the taxpayer's gain are not. In *Allan v. Commissioner*, 856 F.2d 1169 (8th Cir. 1988) *aff'g* 86 T.C. 655 (1986), the court held that nonrecourse liabilities for accrued and previously deducted expenses that were forgiven in a sale of a capital asset were capital gain to the seller, notwithstanding the tax benefit rule.

Proposal. Amend section 111 to add a new subsection (a):

"(a) General Rule. Except as provided in subsection (b), gross income includes amounts received in recovery of a tax benefit, the reversal into income of a prior deduction because of the happening of events fundamentally inconsistent with the original deduction, including the forgiveness of or assumption of a liability to pay an accrued expense previously deducted."
 * * *

Enact new IRC section 1258 providing for recapture as ordinary income of deductible expenses, forgiven, paid or accrued by reason of the sale of a capital asset. Recapture expenses and interest accrued to maintain or carry the asset for the prior two tax years.

Reasons for the Change. The deduction of expenses that make capital gain possible, combined with reduced tax rates for amounts realized as capital gain, will cause a negative tax. The deduction of the expense from ordinary income combined with capital gain for the gross revenue will mean that profitable transactions reduce tax, rather than incurring tax. * * *

Proposal 7: Conversion into Capital Asset by Gift or Contribution

Current law. Literary and artistic works created by the author or artist remain ordinary assets in the hands of a donee or other person with a carryover basis from the creator (IRC section 1221(3)(C)), but otherwise a new taxpayer may establish that property is a capital asset even if it is inventory or other ordinary asset in the hands of a predecessor from whom basis carries over.

Proposal. Ordinary asset will remain an ordinary asset if the seller carries over basis (for gain) from a person or entity in whose hands the asset was ordinary. Add new section 1221(7) to read "property held by a taxpayer who has a carryover of basis in whole or in part, for purposes of determining gain on a sale or exchange, from a taxpayer in whose hands the property is an ordinary asset." Conform IRC section 1231(b)(1) by adding the same exception.

Reasons for the Change. Literally, a taxpayer with inventory, property held for sale to customers in the ordinary course of a trade or business, or any other ordinary asset can avoid the adverse tax results of the ordinary asset character by transferring the property to a related taxpayer in a tax-free transaction. The donee or corporate transferee would carry over the basis and holding period of the original taxpayer, but there is no provision for general carryover of the ordinary asset character. * * *

Proposal 8: The Installment Method

Current Law. Under the installment method, a seller of property reports gain from sale of property for debt obligations of the purchaser only as the debt obligations are paid. The installment method is not available for sale of marketable securities, inventory, and real property held for sale to customers in the ordinary course of business, nor for sales of depreciable property to controlled corporations, nor if the buyer's obligations are payable on demand or are in a form readily tradable on established market. Recaptured depreciation is taxable immediately on sale. IRC section 453. A seller must pay interest to the government (nondeductible by an individual seller) on tax deferred beyond sale on many kinds of installment obligations if seller's outstanding installment obligations exceed $5,000,000. IRC section 453A (1987).

Proposal. Prevent the combining of tax reductions under both capital gain and installment reporting, by adding subsection (8) to IRC section 1221, to provide that capital asset shall not include any asset reported under the installment method of IRC section 453(a), unless the taxpayer elects out of the method under IRC section 453(d).

Reasons for the Change. Given the size of the deficit * * *, the function of capital gains rate cuts is to maximize government revenue. Congress will attempt to cut nominal capital gains rates to reach the optimal point, i.e., the point where voluntary realizations increase such that the product of the nominal capital gains rate times the rate of voluntary realization will generate the highest possible effective tax on capital appreciation. If nominal capital gains tax rates are inadvertently reduced below the optimal revenue point, then that will exacerbate the deficit crisis, incurring real revenue losses to the benefit of those taxpayers least in need of redistribution.

The installment sale provisions reduce the effective or economic burden of tax by allowing the taxpayer to delay tax beyond sale until the payments are received. Because of the time value of money, mere deferral of tax reduces the economic burden of the tax. Assume, for instance, that Taxpayer A sells property for a note of $1,000,000 payable in 10 years and the tax on the gain computed under optimal, revenue-maximizing rates would be $150,000. The ability to defer the $150,000 tax for 10 years means under current FMV interest rates that a mere $75,000 set aside will grow after tax to be sufficient to pay the $150,000 tax when due. The real burden of the tax has thus been cut in half (from $150,000 to $75,000) and the effective tax rate imposed on the gain has been cut to half of the optimal rate. When Congress debates an optimal rate for sales, it cannot simultaneously reach the optimal rate for sales that are taxed immediately and for sales that have been tax deferred under the installment method.

* * *

Proposal 9: Open Transactions

Current Law. In *Burnet v. Logan*, 283 U. S. 404 (1931), the Supreme Court held that sales of property for assets that had no ascertainable value would not be taxed in the year of the sale based upon mere conjecture, but that the transaction would be kept "open" and taxed only when the seller received the cash (or property that had ascertainable value.) Once the open transaction doctrine applies, the first cash is tax-exempt recovery of basis up to seller's original basis and gain thereafter is generally considered to be capital gain. * * * The regulations claim open transactions are available only in rare and extraordinary circumstances involving contingent payments, but the courts are sometimes more generous. See, e.g., *Gralapp v. United States*, 458 F.2d 1158 (10th Cir. 1972).

Proposal. Make amounts taxed under the open transaction doctrine ordinary income, by adding a new subsection (b) to IRC section 1222: "(b) SALE OR EXCHANGE. The term 'sale or exchange' shall not include amounts received in a year after the year of sale reported under the open transaction doctrine." Conform IRC section 1222.

Reasons for the Change. The open transaction doctrine reduces the effective tax on the sale of property by allowing the tax to be deferred until cash (or property of ascertainable value) is received. * * *

Gain under the open transaction doctrine is also appropriately excluded from gain from a sale or exchange for independent reasons. The taxpayer receiving open transaction payments has not liquidated his or her interest. Instead the taxpayer is receiving amounts, spread out over many years, that are usually contingent upon normal business operations or interest or other normally ordinary income events. For instance, in Burnet v. Logan, a shareholder sold stock by liquidation of her corporation in exchange for a royalty interest in a mine distributed by the corporation. Because the royalty interest had no ascertainable value, the sale of stock was "open." Although

Logan itself involved a year before capital gains were taxed at a lower rate, it is assumed that now the gain would be taxed as capital gain. But the royalty income would normally have been ordinary income, and there was no policy reason why the fact that the taxpayer had originally received the interest in a transaction accounted for in an advantageous way should have also converted the character of the ordinary royalty income into capital gain. The character of the income from the asset should be determined independently of whether it was possible to value the asset when received. * * *

Proposal 10: Limitation to Fair Market Value

Current Law. Current law provides that nonrecourse liability forgiven on sale of a capital asset is capital gain in full even though the nonrecourse liability exceeds the fair market value of the capital asset. Tufts v. Commissioner, 461 U.S. 300 (1983) *reh'g denied* 463 U.S. 1215. IRC section 7701(g).

Proposal. Amend IRC section 7701(g) to provide that for the purpose of determining gain or loss, the amount realized with respect to the sale or exchange of a capital asset shall not exceed the fair market value of the asset at the time of the sale, but that the excess of the outstanding nonrecourse liability over value of the capital asset shall be treated, except as provided in section 108, as cancellation of indebtedness income.

Reason for the Change. The proposal limits the amount of capital gain on a sale of a capital asset to the fair market value of the capital asset. Market appreciation of a capital asset explains the gain economically only to the extent of the fair market value. The remainder of the canceled or forgiven nonrecourse liability is ordinary income, subject to the deferred tax recognition given to forgiveness of indebtedness by section 108 in certain hardship cases. Forgiveness of tax-recognized indebtedness is generally ordinary income because the taxpayer has previously received proceeds of borrowing without paying tax on them or took depreciation or other deductions without bearing any economic cost. The proposal, bifurcating the total economic gain into a capital gain element and an ordinary (or section 108) element, brings the treatment of nonrecourse liability into accord with the treatment of a recourse liability forgiven on sale. Treas. Reg. section 1.1001-2(c), Example (8) (1980). If the capital asset has declined in value below adjusted basis, but the outstanding nonrecourse liability exceeds adjusted basis, the bifurcation approach generates capital loss and added forgiveness of indebtedness.

Current law, treating the gain as entirely capital gain, is based on legal fictions adopted to prevent the excess of outstanding liabilities over value from slipping out from under tax entirely. Prior to the Supreme Court's decision in Tufts, there was some doubt as to whether the excess of an outstanding nonrecourse liability over the fair market value of the sold property was a taxable amount of any character. * * * To prevent the accounting mistake of ignoring the gain over value entirely, section 7701(g) adopted a legal fiction that the nonrecourse liability is in fact adequately secured and Tufts adopted a legal fiction that there was no economic difference between a recourse and nonrecourse liability on sale. * * * The legal fictions adopted pragmatically to explain the amount of gain on sale misdescribe the character of gain.

* * *

Finally, the excess liability can be taxed under the tax benefit theory: Nonpayment of a debt is an event fundamentally inconsistent with the accrual and depreciation deductions given only on the assumption that the liabilities justifying the deduction would be paid.

* * *

Proposal 11: Corporate Distributions Not from E&P

Current Law. Current law provides that a corporate distribution on stock in excess of its earnings and profits and the shareholder's basis will be treated as a sale or exchange by the shareholder, even when the distribution effects neither a liquidation nor a meaningful reduction in the shareholder interest. IRC section 301(c)(3).

Proposal. Repeal IRC section 301(c)(3)(A) so that corporate distributions not out of earnings and profits would have to qualify under the redemption or liquidation rules to qualify as capital gain.

Reasons for the Change. Corporate distributions on stock are normally ordinary income rather than capital gain because "(t)he shareholder retains his underlying investment interest, and neither his voting power or rights to future income have been altered." Cohen, Surrey, Tarleau & Warren, A Technical Revision of the Federal Income Tax Treatment of Corporate Distributions to Shareholders, 52 COLUM. L. REV. 1, 5 (1952). Distributions described by section 301(c)(3) (but no other sale or exchange rule) are not sales or exchanges in fact nor reductions in the shareholder's interest in the corporation.

The fact that a distribution exceeds corporate earnings and profits and shareholder basis provides no independent reason for the capital gain advantage. Distributions falling under section 301(c)(3) are not subject to double tax on corporate income: If the corporation had paid corporate tax on the amounts distributed, the corporate income would have increased earnings and profits and made section 301(c)(3) inapplicable to the distribution.

* * *

The shareholder has recovered all of his capital before section 301(c)(3) can apply so that the shareholder has no capital that needs to be indexed for inflation. Since the shareholder has withdrawn and recovered all his capital for section 301(c)(3) to apply, the distribution cannot fairly be attributed to a return on or appreciation of the shareholder's already-taxed capital. * * *

Proposal 12: Incentive Stock Options

Current Law. Nontransferable "incentive stock options" issued to executives as compensation are not taxable to the executives when issued nor when exercised [if certain conditions are satisfied]. The executive's gains are taxed as capital gains only if and when the stock is sold. The corporate employer gets no compensation deduction. IRC section 422A [now section 422].

Proposal. Repeal IRC section 422A [now section 422.]

Reasons for the Change. Under general law, an executive must pay ordinary income tax on property received in connection with the performance of services. IRC section 83. * * * As a fundamental principle, "capital gain" does not encompass compensation (see Proposal 1) and stock options given in return for the employee services are compensation.

* * *

Proposal 13: Sales of Patents

Current Law. An inventor whose efforts created a patent and an individual (other than employer or related party) who paid for an interest before the invention was reduced to practice has capital gain on sale of the patent, even though the sale price is contingent on future actual use of the patent. IRC section 1235. Research and experimental costs are deducted when incurred, even if they are really investments. IRC section 174. There is a 20-percent credit for increased research and experimentation costs for use in a trade or business over base amounts, but section 174 deductions are reduced by the amount of the credit. IRC section 41, 280C(c).

Proposal. Repeal IRC section 1235.

Reasons for the Change. For the inventor whose personal effort created the patent, the gain from the sale of the patent is salary or compensation. Lower tax rates on some kinds of compensation received by some kinds of taxpayers create a special caste or status system inconsistent with the equality of all people before the law. In a free market system, incentives for compensation come from pretax income—paid by the people who understand and can value the services provided—and not from government subsidies.

* * *

Proposal 14: Timber

Current Law. The fair market value of timber cut in the ordinary course of the timber business is deemed to be capital gain. IRC sections 631(a), 1231(b)(2). But the costs of timber are ordinary deductions if they are for management or maintenance of timber or reforestation. (IRC section 194 (reforestation costs); *Kinley v. Commissioner*, 51 T.C. 1000 (1969)(shaping of Christmas trees, amounting to 50 percent of labor costs of tree nursery, were expenses; insect control deductible); *Barham v. United States*, 301 F. Supp. 43 (M.D. Ga. 1969) *aff'd. per curiam*, 429 F.2d 40 (5th Cir. 1970) (brush clearing deductible); *Union Bag-Camp Paper Corp. v. United States*, 325 F.2d 730 (1963) (marking trees for cutting was part of overall forest management expenses); Rev. Rul. 68-281, 1968-1 C.B. 22 (temporary road gave ordinary deductions)). Timber is exempted from uniform capitalization. IRC section 263A(c)(5).

Proposal. Repeal capital gain for timber by repealing section 1231(b)(2). Absent repeal, capitalize all costs connected with the timber business, including overhead, management, and interest costs stacked first to timber.

Reasons for the Change. The paradigm of the income account at common law was the harvest from the land (or fruit from the tree). The harvest was never a corpus or capital item. Timber is a harvest from the land. It is the product of capital (i.e. yield or income) and not the capital or principal or corpus that generated the product.

* * *

Proposal 15: Coal and Iron Ore

Current Law. Sale of coal and iron ore by an owner (who does not mine the coal or ore) is capital gain, even if it is inventory and even if the lease by which it is sold would not otherwise be a sale or exchange. IRC sections 631(c), 1231(b)(2). Exploration expenses are expensed, even if investments, although they are recaptured from sale or production. IRC section 617. Development expenses, incurred after commercially marketable quantities have been disclosed, are expenses, and not recaptured, even though they would otherwise be inventoried or capitalized costs. IRC section 616.

Proposal. Repeal sections 616, 617, and 1232(b)(2), so as to treat coal and iron ore as inventory.

Reasons for the Change. Capital gain for the coal and iron industry is an off-budget hidden government subsidy because it gives capital gain to inventory, which is ordinary income under normal principles, and because it gives capital gain to leases, which do not qualify as sales or exchanges under normal principles. * * * There has never been any attempt to justify the capital gain for coal and iron in terms of normal tax doctrine or wise expenditure of government costs.

* * *

Proposal 16: Livestock and Crops

Current Law. Sale of livestock (but not poultry) held for draft, breeding, dairy or sporting purposes will be capital gain. Cattle and horses must have been held for 2 years, other livestock for 1 year. Costs of feed, seed and fertilizer are expenses when made by a farmer, even if otherwise inventoried costs (IRC section 180, Treas. Reg. section 1.162-12(1972), section 1.471-6(a)), but nonfarmers face an array of barriers to access to the benefits of expensing that farmers can get. * * *

Proposal. Repeal section 1231(b)(3) and (4).

Reasons for the Change. Capital gain for sale of livestock converts ordinary deductions into capital gain because the costs of feeding livestock are ordinary expenses, while the gain from sale of the livestock [is] capital gain. Capital gain under IRC section 1231(b)(3) is not available for livestock raised for sale or slaughter, but it does apply to livestock even though held "for sale to customers" because of the amount of the activity. Treas. Reg. section 1.1232-2(b)(2) Ex. (3)(1971). The mismatch between ordinary deductions for the inputs and capital gain for the revenue remains within the scope allowed. Assuming the capital gain rate drops to 15 percent, a farmer could plan to lose 27 percent of his or her costs economically on transactions benefitting from the mismatch of ordinary deductions and capital gain and still break even after tax.

The tax advantages mean that farmers face an onslaught of outside capital which drives up the price of feed and farm labor and drives down the sale price of livestock. Farmers who are not in high enough tax brackets to use the negative tax fully are then driven into failure. On the other hand, the current attempts to block outside capital, while retaining the advantages for true farmers with mud on their boots, if successful, blocks whatever benefit the economy might get from the negative tax. It is only by driving down the pretax profit from farming that the public at large gets any benefit from the farm subsidies.

Expensing of farm investments first arose under Treasury regulations issued in 1915. The most plausible historical explanation for the expensing of farm costs that would otherwise be inventoried or capitalized is that the regulation drafters thought that the timing did not make any difference. Johnson, Soft Money Investing Under the Income Tax, 1989 ILL. L. REV. 1019, 1089 (1990). But when combined with capital gain for the product of the expense, expensing has the impact of less than no tax.

The proposal would also repeal IRC section 1231(b)(4), which now provides that sale of an unharvested crop with the underlying farmland is capital gain. Crops are expiring assets that must be sold or left to rot, so there is no possibility of causing significantly earlier realizations of crop gain by reducing the tax rate. Absent IRC section 1231(b)(4), the crop would be an ordinary asset even though sold with the land. *Watson v. Commissioner*, 345 U.S. 544 (1953).

Proposal 17: Section 1231

Current Law. Gains and losses on the sale of section 1231 assets are aggregated for the year. Net gain is capital gain. Net losses are ordinary losses. Assets brought within section 1231 includes real estate and depreciable property used in a trade or business (other than inventory and artistic compositions), timber, coal, iron ore, and livestock. Net gains (from insurance) on property lost to casualty or theft, but not net losses, are included in the section 1231 aggregation. IRC section 1231.

Proposal. Repeal section 1231. Treat gain or loss from market fluctuations of invested capital as capital in either direction. Gain from created or improved assets (including livestock, trees and mined assets) would be ordinary. Depreciation deductions and recapture would be ordinary. Casualty gain (from insurance) would benefit from rollover (section 1033), but would otherwise be ordinary income.

Reasons for the Change. Gains and losses on assets brought within section 1231 are treated asymmetrically. If market fluctuations cause gain, the gain will benefit from the lower rate on capital gains; if they cause loss, the loss saves higher-rate tax on ordinary income. The asymmetry benefits assets expected to fluctuate, vis a vis more stable assets and more stable sources of income. For losses, moreover, section 1231 allows taxpayers to avoid the section 1211 limitations on deduction of discretionary losses, even when the taxpayer has full control as to whether to show or hide the changes in value of the assets.

* * *

Section 1231 is no longer very important as to depreciable property because rapid depreciation now makes it unusual that depreciable property will be sold below basis and depreciation recapture of the depreciation usually makes the gain ordinary. Gain or loss on unimproved land (i.e., nondepreciable real estate) is market fluctuation that should be capital gain or capital loss in theory. Proposal 14 (timber), Proposal 15 (coal and iron ore) and Proposal 16 (livestock) would repeal other important parts of section 1231. Section 1231 is complicated; it has a convoluted form (Form 4797) all its own. The tax effects it accomplishes are not worth the complexity it generates.

With the repeal of section 1231, capital or ordinary character would be determined by general theory. Gain from self-created or improved assets and gain on property the taxpayer had no investment in would be ordinary (Proposals 1 and 2). Gain from the appreciation of invested capital would be a capital gain.

Gain from insurance proceeds covering casualty losses or thefts would usually be ordinary because of recapture of depreciation. Such gain, moreover, is involuntary. * * * Section 1033 of the Code gives the taxpayer the ability to avoid recognition of gains from casualties or thefts if the insurance proceeds are reinvested. Since sales proceeds that fail to meet the reinvestment requirement of section 1033 are consumable income (not timeable by the taxpayer), there is no policy reason for the differentially lower rate.

Notes and Questions

1. Although Professor Johnson does not endorse the idea of preferential tax treatment for any capital gains income, his approach implies that there is such a thing as a true, or ideal, capital asset. The concept of the ideal capital asset is pervasive in the legal profession. It may have its basis in the distinction in property law and trust law between capital and income. While essential there to draw a line between the rights of income beneficiaries and the rights of remaindermen, it is not necessarily relevant to tax treatment.

Excluding assets for personal consumption by the taxpayer and assets considered to have intrinsic value in and of themselves (such as art objects), the market value of capital assets reflects present value of capitalized future income streams. Such future income will be taxed as ordinary income. To justify favorable treatment of capital gains requires finding a conceptual basis for treating advance realization of income differently because it is accomplished by sale of assets that are expected to produce ordinary income, rather than by holding the assets and receiving the ordinary income they generate.

2.   In his first proposal, Professor Johnson would expand the present exclusion of copyrights, etc. created by the taxpayer from the definition of capital assets. He proposes exclusion of amounts received for all types of property created by the taxpayer or the taxpayer's agents. What would be the impact of this proposal?

3.   In Professor Johnson's Proposal 8, he would prohibit capital gain treatment for sales reported on the installment method. He supports this proposal with an example in which property is sold for a $1,000,000 note payable in 10 years. Professor Johnson assumes a $150,000 tax, and asserts that the capital gain tax is being cut in half because, with current interest rates, $75,000 set aside currently will be sufficient to pay the $150,000 tax 10 years later. Is his example valid?

4.   In his Proposal 11, Professor Johnson would deny capital gain treatment to distributions from corporations with no accumulated corporate earnings after the stockholder's basis in the stock has been exhausted. Is his argument for this convincing?

5.   Assuming a general rule that capital gains are to be afforded favorable tax treatment, how would you rank Professor Johnson's proposals in terms of the persuasiveness of his argument that favorable capital gains treatment is not justified in those particular cases?

6.   *Historical development.* Over the years since the present federal income tax was first imposed in 1913, the attitude of Congress toward treatment of capital gains can best be characterized as ambivalent. Prior to the Revenue Act of 1921, capital gains were taxed the same as ordinary income. Under the 1921 Act, short-term capital gains continued to be taxed as ordinary income, but a maximum tax of 12.5 percent was set for long-term capital gains. In the Revenue Act of 1934, a set of five graduated holding periods was enacted, with 100 percent of gain taxed on disposition of assets held for one year or less, 80 percent taxed for assets held from one to two years, 60 percent taxed for assets held from two to five years, 40 percent

taxed for assets held five to 10 years, and only 30 percent taxed for assets held over 10 years. In the 1938 Act, the number of holding periods was cut to three, with a maximum tax rate of 15 percent on assets held more than 24 months.

The Revenue Act of 1942 set a maximum tax of 25 percent for gain on capital assets held longer than six months and enacted the first version of present section 1231. Individuals became entitled to deduct 50 percent of their net long-term capital gains.

The Internal Revenue Code of 1954 initially provided for deduction of 50 percent of net long-term capital gains. In the 1976 Act the holding period for short-term capital gains and losses was increased from six months to one year. In the 1978 Act the deduction from net long-term capital gains was increased to 60 percent.

The Tax Reform Act of 1986 taxed net long-term capital gains at the same rates as other income, ending 65 years of favorable treatment for long-term capital gains. The statutory rules defining capital assets and computing capital gain were left intact in the 1986 Code, however, apparently as a token of the sincerity of the promise by Congress (codified in section 1(h)) that the tax rate on long-term capital gains would not be increased if ordinary income tax rates subsequently were raised above their level under the 1986 Act. Consequently, when the top bracket income tax rate was increased above 28 percent in 1990, and still higher in 1993, the maximum tax on net long-term capital gains was kept at 28 percent. Because the statutory rules had been left intact, return to more favorable treatment of capital gains was very simple technically and did not require reexamination of the various special types of capital gains, such as those described by Professor Johnson.

B. UNIQUE FEATURES OF CAPITAL GAINS AND LOSSES

Capital gains and losses are not taken into account until they are realized. Timing of realization of both gains and losses on capital assets ordinarily is within the taxpayer's control. This probably is the most important distinction between capital gains and other types of income. By and large, ordinary income must be taken when the opportunity arises: sales of inventory that are foregone in this Christmas season are lost permanently and a major league baseball pitcher who sits out a season has lost that season's salary forever.

The role of realization in the income tax has been challenged, as discussed in Chapter Two. More particularly, proposals have been made for taking into account currently for tax purposes appreciation or depreciation in market value of investment assets that have easily ascertainable market values.[d] These proposals are criticized in the following excerpt:

CAPITAL GAINS: FALLING SHORT
ON FAIRNESS AND SIMPLICITY
Fred W. Peel, Jr.[*]
17 University of Baltimore Law Review 418, 424-25 (1988)

An unrealized gain unaccompanied by current benefit is, in common terminology, a "paper profit." Entirely aside from the administrative problems of annual valuation involved in applying the Haig-Simons definition, the principal problem with such definition is the absence of any benefit to the owner that justifies the imposition of an income tax on an unrealized accretion in value. Thus, the theoretical basis for this component of the Haig-Simons definition of income is at least questionable.

Some commentators have proposed taking into account in the tax base appreciation or depreciation in market value of investment assets that have easily ascertainable market values.[37] This concept, called "mark-to-market," was initially advanced in pursuit of the Haig-Simons ideal. Since the enactment of TRA '86, however, the use of mark-to-market for a limited category of assets has been proposed as one way of reducing the potential for cherry-picking[e] sufficiently to permit unlimited allowance of capital losses.[39] The proposal is to mark property to market if it is "marketable," a characteristic of stocks and bonds listed on stock exchanges or publicly traded in the over-the-counter market. Publicly traded stocks and bonds may include those issued by corporations or partnerships already identified by registration under the Securities Exchange Act of 1934, as amended.

The limited mark-to-market proposals are flawed in several respects. First, as discussed earlier,[f] taxation of unrealized appreciation under the Haig-Simons definition of income is of questionable validity.

---

d. See sources cited in footnote 37 of Peel excerpt immediately following. Broader proposals for taxation without realization include David J. Shakow, *Taxation Without Realization: A Proposal for Accrual Taxation*, 134 U. PA. L. REV. 1111 (1986); and Martin D. Ginsburg et al., *Reexamining Subchapter C: An Overview and Some Modest Proposals to Stimulate Debate, in* INVITATIONAL CONFERENCE ON SUBCHAPTER C 1, 6-7 (1987).

*. At time of original publication, Ben J. Altheimer Professor of Law Emeritus, University of Arkansas at Little Rock.

37. *See* Slawson, *Taxing as Ordinary Income the Appreciation of Publicly Held Stock*, 76 YALE L.J. 623 (1967); Note, *Realizing Appreciation Without Sale: Accrual Taxation of Capital Gains on Marketable Securities*, 45 STANFORD L. REV. 857 (1982).

e. The term "cherry-picking" refers to taxpayers selling depreciated assets to realize and deduct losses, while not selling appreciated assets that would result in the realization of taxable gains. (Eds.)

39. Ginsburg, Canellos, Levin, Eustice, *Reexamining Subchapter C: An Overview and Some Modest Proposals to Stimulate Debate*, INVITATIONAL CONFERENCE ON SUBCHAPTER C 3, 6 (1987).

f. A portion of this earlier discussion is found in another excerpt from this article in Chapter Two. (Eds.)

Second, the imposition of a tax on unrealized appreciation and the limitation of such imposition to a designated type of investment asset would create a serious bias in capital markets. The bias against stock of publicly held corporations would be particularly acute. Because of the double taxation of dividend income, such stock is already under a tax handicap compared with debt obligations, stock of S corporations, stock of closely held C corporations that do not declare significant dividends, and interests in partnerships that are not taxed as corporations. Singling out investment in publicly held corporations for mark-to-market treatment would undermine the United States securities market.

Third, taxation of unrealized appreciation in securities would put the taxpayer in a position of having to liquidate a substantial portion of his investment in order to pay the tax. This forced liquidation would create an unfair hardship and would have an artificial, adverse effect on the market price of the securities. This prospect alone would deter closely held expanding companies from making public offerings of their stock. A hypothetical illustration is the case of one individual who owns all the outstanding stock of a corporation—one million shares with a basis of $1 per share. The corporation has bright prospects, and a public offering by the corporation of an additional one million shares could yield $10 per share. If the effect of the public offering is to bring the stock under a mark-to-market regimen, the market value of $10,000,000 for the original shareholder's stock would produce a $9,000,000 taxable gain based on the unrealized appreciation of his stock. At a 28% tax rate, the cost in taxes of the corporation's public offering to such an individual would be over $2,500,000.

Finally, the mark-to-market concept might be unconstitutional. In *Eisner v. Macomber*,[41] the Supreme Court assumed that realization was necessary for a constitutional tax on income.[42] The precedent is old, perhaps even obsolete. In TRA '86, Congress adopted a mark-to-market method of dealing with a special abuse situation: the taxation of futures contracts held by the taxpayer at the close of the taxable year.[43] The courts could uphold mark-to-market in these limited circumstances as constitutional. They could nevertheless decide under *Eisner* that, because unrealized appreciation is not income and thus is not encompassed by the sixteenth amendment, a tax imposed on broad-based mark-to-market is a direct tax that requires apportionment.

* * *

---

41. 252 U.S. 189 (1920).
42. *See* id. at 213-15. *See also* Helvering v. Independent Life Ins. Co., 292 U.S. 371, 378 (1934) (dictum).
43. I.R.C. § 1256.

Notes and Questions

7. Taxpayer control over timing the taxation of capital gains has caused the lock-in problem. Normally, an investor would be expected to shift from investing in one asset to investing in another asset offering a better percentage yield. A rational taxpayer will not do so, however, if tax on gain from the sale of the first asset reduces the net amount remaining for investment in the replacement asset to a point where the total yield on the replacement investment, albeit at a higher percentage rate, is less than the total yield on the initial investment. For example, suppose a taxpayer has an asset with a basis of $100 and a market value of $500 that is yielding a five percent return, or $25. The taxpayer is tempted to sell the asset and invest the proceeds in another asset with an annual yield of six percent. Sale will result in a gain of $400 ($500 minus $100), however, and assuming the gain will be taxed at 28 percent, will result in a tax of $112, leaving only $388 to reinvest. The yield on the new $388 investment at six percent will be only $23.28, which is less than the five percent yield on the first asset. This tax deterrent to a shift in investment, or lock-in, means that the market does not allocate resources in the economy with optimum efficiency.

Stockbrokers have argued that the one-year holding period to qualify for favorable long-term capital gain treatment has an adverse lock-in effect. This is a stretch, however, because a few months' delay in shifting investments is unlikely to have much effect on the long-term allocation of resources in the economy. Long-term graduated holding periods that reward taxpayers with lower and lower taxes—as the law provided in the 1930s and as is still occasionally proposed—certainly would make the lock-in effect worse.

The worst problem with lock-in is the reward of total exemption from tax for capital gains on assets held until death. The basis step-up at death is discussed in Chapter Nine.

As noted in the Peel excerpt above, some commentators, most notably Mr. David Slawson (see article cited in note 37 of Peel excerpt), have argued for currently taxing unrealized appreciation in traded securities; this proposal would solve the lock-in problem for those assets. As Peel argued, however, the solution might be worse than the problem.

8. What is meant by mark-to-market as applied to capital gains taxation? Why is mark-to-market more feasible for listed securities than other capital assets? Apart from increased revenue, what advantages, if any, would derive from adoption of mark-to-market?

9. Why does Peel oppose mark-to-market for listed securities?

10. Lock-in could be avoided by broad allowance of tax-free rollover of appreciated investments. Rollover has been proposed.[g] Tax-free rollover is permitted under present law for a limited list of tax-free exchanges, of which the most obvious examples are corporate reorganizations. Unlimited rollover of investments tax-free would approximate conversion of the income tax into a consumption tax, because persons with gains on appreciated assets would be taxed only on the gains they consumed rather than reinvested. For discussion of this form of consumption tax, see Chapter Seven.

Tax-free rollover of investments already is allowed in several areas. Section 1031 permits tax-free exchange of property held for productive use or investment, but is not applicable to stock in trade, stocks or bonds, partnership interests, certificates of trust, or other choses in action. Section 1033 permits tax-free replacement of property lost through involuntary conversion. Section 1034 permits individuals to roll over gain tax-free on sale and replacement of their homes. Section 1043 permits tax-free rollover of property sold to comply with conflict of interest rules, as where a government official places assets in a blind trust.

C. TREATMENT OF CAPITAL LOSSES

Capital losses may be deducted in full against capital gains. For this purpose, there is no distinction between long-term and short-term capital gains and between long-term and short-term capital losses. In the case of individuals, estates, and trusts, for a year in which capital losses exceed capital gains, up to $3,000 of the excess capital loss may be deducted against ordinary income (only $1,500 if an individual is married and filing a separate return). Corporations may deduct capital losses only to the extent of capital gains. Section 1211.

Unused capital losses of individuals, estates, and trusts may be carried forward to succeeding years until they are exhausted. Unused capital losses of corporations may be carried back three years and carried forward five years. Section 1212.

When special treatment of capital gains was terminated by the Tax Reform Act of 1986, the limits on deduction of capital losses were not changed. In the first excerpt below, Peel argues against limiting capital losses, particularly if capital gains are taxed the same as ordinary income. Next, Professor Martin Ginsburg and former Assistant Secretary of the Treasury for Tax Policy Kenneth Gideon discuss an area of concern in allowing unlimited deduction of capital losses: due to taxpayer control over realization of capital gains and losses, taxpayers may let their potential capital gains ride without realization while realizing their capital losses to avoid tax on ordinary income ("cherry-picking").

---

g. DAN THROOP SMITH, FEDERAL TAX REFORM 151-55 (1961).

CAPITAL GAINS: FALLING SHORT ON FAIRNESS AND SIMPLICITY

Fred W. Peel, Jr.[*]

17 University of Baltimore Law Review 418, 418-19 (1988)

Fair treatment of capital gain and loss requires that each be treated the same as ordinary income and loss, respectively, because the economic benefit from a dollar of capital gain is the same as the economic benefit from a dollar of ordinary income, and a dollar of capital loss has the same effect as a dollar of ordinary loss. There is no intrinsic difference between capital assets and other assets that justifies special treatment for either capital gains or capital losses. Taxpayers invest in capital assets to profit from their use or their eventual disposition. Such assets may yield current income through rents, royalties, dividends, or interest. Even those assets held for personal use—homes, pleasure boats, etc.—yield imputed income to their owners. Capital assets held for eventual profit through sale at a gain really are being held for sale even though they escape the narrower classification of inventory or property held for sale to customers in the ordinary course of a trade or business. The thinness of the distinction between capital assets and business assets is demonstrated by the anomalous treatment in section 1231 of the Internal Revenue Code of depreciable assets and land used in a trade or business.

Unlimited allowance of capital losses may be justified in theory even when net capital gains are given favorable tax treatment.[10] Certainly, theoretical justification exists for unlimited allowance of capital losses when capital gains are fully taxed at the same rate as ordinary income. It is no longer possible to defend restrictions on the allowance of capital losses by arguing that such treatment is justified because it is parallel to the treatment given capital gains.[11]

The parallel treatment argument was specious from its outset except in the case of gains and losses realized by the same taxpayer. Restriction of one taxpayer's use of an economic loss cannot be justified by pointing to another taxpayer's benefit from special treatment of capital gains. An extreme example is the unfortunate individual who has one large capital loss in a lifetime and no present or foreseeable capital gains. Even if this taxpayer should live long enough to recoup the loss through small annual deductions of the unused capital loss carry forward each year, such recoupment will not accurately reflect the current cost of the initial loss to the taxpayer.

* * *

---

[*]. At time of original publication, Ben J. Altheimer Professor of Law Emeritus, University of Arkansas at Little Rock.

[10]. *See* Warren, *The Deductibility by Individuals of Capital Losses under the Federal Income Tax*, 40 U. CHI. L. REV. 291, 295 (1973).

[11]. The parallel treatment argument was used by the Committee on Ways and Means in its Report on the Revenue Act of 1924. *See* H.R. Rep. No. 179, 68th Cong., 1st Sess. 57 (1924).

DISCUSSION BY CCH TAX ADVISORY BOARD ROUNDTABLE
Vol. 79, Number 26, Part 2, May 27, 1992, pp. 5-6

Martin Ginsburg: A common concern or shared objective in what has been said so far is tax simplification. Certainly I am a great believer, as who is not. But it struck me that neither in Ken's opening, ground-laying discussion nor in any of the comments that followed did I hear a reference to the taxation of capital gains. Does this reticence reflect a general belief that a taxing regime that awards special treatment to capital gains and losses cannot earn the simplification merit badge? * * * We have already seen the return of a rate preference, albeit a small one. Is more to come?

Ken Gideon: I think that capital gains at this point has undergone apotheosis into the political firmament. That means that issues that concern tax practitioners like simplification are really not even on the charts in terms of consideration of capital gains. Capital gains is viewed as religion by one side for whom it is a sure-fire cure for the economy, and as the embodiment of the devil by the other side for whom it is the sure-fire assurance that the wealthy will get all the money in America.

I must say, having viewed this debate up close for awhile, I have difficulty with both propositions. I'm not sure that it is an instant cure for the economy and I'm equally sure that going back to a system that we successfully lived with for virtually the entire history of the income tax is unlikely to upset the distribution of wealth in the Republic forever.

Having said that, returning to your question about its simplification effects, I guess my response to that, Marty, would be it's difficult for me to see how it is particularly complicating. As long as we have the fundamental rule in the Code—which we are not about to abandon because we can't afford to—that we are going to classify capital losses and limit them so that we've got to keep track of what's a capital item already, it's hard for me to see that there is a significant complication added by giving a preferential rate for capital gains. And this is wholly apart from whether a capital gains cut would be good, bad, or indifferent. I'm simply saying I don't see that on the simplification scale you really can put much weight on one side or the other.

Martin Ginsburg: Ken has nicely framed one side of the issue. Let me just try to lay out what I believe is a counter-position and then hear from crowds of supporters and detractors. Ken's reference to capital losses urges the question, isn't there something more sensible we can do with the tax treatment of capital losses, more sensible than the present arrangement of limiting deductibility to offsetting capital gains plus $3,000 of ordinary income? I do agree that in allowing greater deductibility of capital losses, the revenue concern is the real one but the problem is not amorphous or abstract, it is a problem of cherry picking which, essentially, centers on property for which there is a quoted price and a ready market.

If I have enough money, a surplus $400 million say, I will probably never have to pay taxes again if there is unlimited deductibility of capital losses. I will invest $1,000,000 in each of 400 different publicly traded stocks. With good luck 360 of them will go up in value, 20 will stay the same, and 20 will go down in value. Then, abusing our realization system, I will sell the 20 depressed stocks to generate a large loss while retaining the 360 good ones with their appreciated value unrecognized and intact. Permitted freely to do so, I will offset [all taxable income by] the large cherry-picked loss. * * *

Notes and Questions

11. Why might the potential for "cherry-picking" have led Congress to limit deduction of capital losses?

12. Treatment of capital losses has varied wildly over the years. Under the 1913 Act, losses were allowed in full if incurred in trade--otherwise, no losses were allowed. In the 1918 Act, all losses were allowed on transactions entered into for profit. Under the 1924 Act, the tax saved by using capital losses to offset ordinary income was limited to 12.5 percent of the losses, matching the maximum tax rate then imposed on long-term capital gains. The 1932 Act limited deduction of short-term losses to short-term gains. Under the 1934 Act, only $2,000 of capital losses in excess of capital gains were allowed to offset ordinary income. Under the 1938 Act, only 30 percent of capital losses could be used to offset tax on ordinary income. Under the 1942 Act, individuals were allowed to deduct only $1,000 of capital losses from ordinary income. The present limitations date from 1986.

D. EFFECT OF TAXING CAPITAL GAINS ON INCENTIVES

Commentators have advanced various economic theories to support favorable tax treatment of capital gains. A charge frequently made against taxing capital gains (or against taxing them in full) is that it deters risk-taking. A 1990 study by the Congressional Budget Office, the first excerpt below, discussed the impact on risk-taking of the tax treatment of capital gains and losses. In order to stimulate investment, President Bush consistently, and without success, sought modifications of the income tax provisions governing capital gains. His administration's case for special treatment of capital gains as an incentive for increased saving and investment was made by Michael J. Boskin, Chairman of the President's Council of Economic Advisers, before the Senate Finance Committee in 1990. A portion of Dr. Boskin's testimony follows the excerpt of the CBO study.

Both increased savings and more efficient capital markets were given as reasons for a deduction of 50 percent of net capital gains in the excerpt from the Ways and Means Committee report on the Contract with America Tax Relief Act of 1995. In contrast to such broad, generalized arguments that lower taxes on capital gains stimulate savings and investment, James M.

Poterba's analysis of sources of venture capital concluded that across-the-board reductions in individual capital gains tax rates would have little effect on the tax burden on venture capital financiers, while providing large benefits to owners of many other assets. Mr. Poterba explains his position in the final article of this subchapter.

INDEXING CAPITAL GAINS
Congressional Budget Office
Pages 39-42 (1990)

Capital Gains Taxes and Risk-Sharing

A tax on capital gains lowers the after-tax return from investing in risky assets. By itself this would discourage risk-taking. So long as capital losses are also deductible, however, a capital gains tax also lowers the variability of returns, which makes risky assets relatively more attractive.

Under current law, capital losses are fully deductible against capital gains, and up to $3,000 of capital losses in excess of capital gains may be deducted against ordinary income. For investors with both gains and losses, or only small net capital losses, current law amounts to taxation of capital gains with full loss offsets. Thus, the net effect on risk-taking of current law is ambiguous, and the presumption that current law deters risk-taking may be unwarranted. Furthermore, current law favors assets that pay returns in the form of capital gains over income-producing assets because of the ability to defer taxes. Since risky assets are more likely to pay their returns in the form of capital gains, current law taxes the gain to risky investments relatively favorably, although less so than before the 1986 tax reform.

A capital gains tax preference such as indexing or an exclusion is sometimes rationalized as a subsidy to encourage risk-taking by raising expected after-tax returns on risky investments. However, the two forms of tax preference would have much different incentive effects. As compared with present law, an exclusion would reduce risk less than an otherwise equivalent indexing scheme because it would reduce the effective marginal tax rate on capital gains, whereas indexing does not affect the marginal rate. For example, for assets held for the same length of time, a 30 percent exclusion at a 28 percent statutory tax rate on capital gains would increase the variance of return by 25 percent as compared with indexing or present law. An exclusion that fully offset inflation (on average) would be larger and it would increase variance even more. Thus, in the absence of loss limitations, indexing would encourage risk-taking more than an equivalent (on average) exclusion.

In addition, a major source of risk in investment is inflation. The effective tax rate under an exclusion increases with inflation whereas under indexing the effective tax rate is invariant with respect to inflation (for a given holding period). Thus, the variance in after-tax returns resulting from unexpected inflation is much smaller under indexing than under an exclusion.

One qualification must be made. Since indexing would treat yield assets much more favorably than would an exclusion, indexing might shift investment away from growth assets into yield assets. If yield assets are inherently less risky than growth assets, indexing might result in less aggregate risk-taking than a similar exclusion. However, it is important to note that this would occur because yield assets would be penalized less, not because risky assets would be penalized more.

Effect of Loss Limitations

As noted above, current law limits deductions for realized capital losses in excess of realized capital gains. Under a capital gains tax based on realization, a limitation on the deductibility of losses is needed. Otherwise, taxpayers with diversified portfolios could achieve negative effective tax rates on capital gains by realizing capital losses and deferring capital gains whenever possible. However, a loss limitation, when it was binding, would affect riskier investments much more than less risky investments since the former would be more likely to produce losses.

* * *

Diversified investors can often avoid current loss limitations by using capital losses to offset other capital gains. The loss limitation would be a serious constraint primarily on undiversified investors—for example, on those who invest heavily in their own businesses. However the special indexing loss limitation would affect any risky investment that faced a possibility of real losses. Such a limitation would discourage risk-taking even more than full taxation of capital gains and losses.

To see this, consider two investments: one is safe and always yields a gain of $100; the other is risky and yields no gain or a gain of $200 with equal likelihood. Both have the same expected (average) return of $100. Under present law, both would also face the same average tax of $28 at a 28 percent rate. An investor who was not concerned about risk (risk-neutral) would be indifferent between the two investments. Now suppose that inflation erodes the initial investment by $50, so the real return is $50 for the certain investment. Because of inflation, the risky asset produces a real loss of $50 and a real gain of $150 with equal probability. The tax on the safe investment under indexing would be $14 (28 percent of the real gain of $50). The loss limitation would disallow the real loss on the risky investment, if it occurred, so the tax would be $0 or $42 with equal probability. The average tax for the risky asset would thus be $21, or 50 percent higher than the tax for the riskless investment. The risky asset would be relatively penalized by the indexing loss limitation, even though its average tax liability would fall relative to full taxation. The penalty would arise because the tax on the riskless investment would fall by more than the tax on the risky investment.

Notice that the disincentive effect of the indexing loss limitation occurs because of the asymmetric treatment of gains and losses. Since partial indexing—for example, allowing only $25 of inflation indexing in the preceding example—treats gains and losses symmetrically, it would not produce this bias against risk-taking.

TAX INCENTIVES FOR INCREASING SAVINGS AND INVESTMENTS
Testimony of Michael J. Boskin[*]

Hearings Before the Senate Committee on Finance, 101st Cong., 2d Sess. 40-43 (1990)

I appreciate the opportunity to present the Administration's views on the capital gains tax provisions of the Savings and Economic Growth Act of 1990.[h] The key component of that Act is the restoration of the capital gains tax differential which existed prior to the Tax Reform Act of 1986. This proposal is an important part of a package of Administration initiatives designed to remove impediments to savings and investment, to encourage innovation and entrepreneurship, and to enhance economic growth.

The American economy is the largest, most productive economy in the world. We are in the eighty-eighth month of the longest peace-time expansion in our history. We cannot, however, take continued economic growth merely for granted. * * * We must redouble our efforts to enhance economic growth.

The Administration's foremost priority is to sustain the highest possible rate of economic growth. That goal, sir, is not just an abstraction, it is how we create rising living standards for the bulk of the population, how we develop the resources to uplift those most in need, how we provide economic and social mobility to our citizens, how we leave a better legacy to our children, and how we maintain America's leadership in the world.

The faster economic growth is going to require movement on several fronts, but it will make more social and private goals attainable. Increasing the rate of growth of living standards will require higher rates of savings and investment. Longstanding Government policies * * * such as the budget deficit, as well as tax policies, impede national savings and investment.

Partly because of these policies Americans save and invest a smaller fraction of gross national product than their counterparts in other industrialized countries. According to the World Bank the United States' investment rate ranks last among the 22 Western industrialized economies.

A major reason for the relatively low rate of investment in the United States is the high cost of capital. Some studies estimate the cost of capital in the United States is almost twice that in Germany or Japan. Taxes, a large component of the cost of capital, produce a bias against equity finance

---

[*]. At time of original testimony, Chairman of the President's Council of Economic Advisors.

[h]. This proposed Act was not enacted. (Eds.)

in the United States. Taxes on capital gains increase capital costs for equity finance while reducing the returns to investors.

Lowering the capital gains tax rate will lower the cost of capital. As a result of the Tax Reform Act of 1986, the overwhelming bulk of which was quite favorable, the United States unfortunately now taxes capital gains at the same rate as other income for the first time since 1921. The United States is burdened with a higher capital gains tax rate than almost every one of our major competitors. Most of them tax capital gains at a lower rate than ordinary income. Many of them do not tax capital gains at all—for example, West Germany, Italy, and most of the newly industrialized economies of the Pacific Rim.

Most of these nations also have numerous other tax provisions—such as partial or complete integration of personal and corporate income taxes—that reduce the overall taxation of capital income. The high cost of capital is a particularly onerous problem for new ventures and small businesses that have only limited access to traditional sources of finance.

Much of the return to entrepreneurs who bring new products to market, particularly through new business formation, comes through increasing the value of the business. Reducing the tax rate on capital gains will reward those who bring successful ideas to market and will help improve the climate to invest in new technologies and products, thereby creating jobs.

During the current record breaking expansion, as throughout U.S. history, most new jobs have been created by small and medium size firms. Lowering the capital gains tax rate will encourage entrepreneurs to start new businesses, to develop new products for new markets here and abroad. Lower capital gains tax rates will encourage risk taking, raise investment, improve competitiveness and spur economic growth.

These important issues, notwithstanding, much discussion has been focused on the more narrow question—how will the President's proposal or any other proposal affect Federal revenues?

Congress and the Administration are naturally concerned about the revenue consequences of any proposal, particularly during this period of necessary budget stringency and our joint responsibility under the Gramm-Rudman-Hollings law. While the economic benefits of capital gains tax reduction are likely to outweigh any reasonable estimate of its cost, let me briefly state some issues with respect to the revenue impact of the capital gains tax reduction before turning to its broader impact on economic performance.

    * * *

A capital gains tax rate reduction affects revenues in five ways. Therefore, one has to estimate each of these five to get an estimate of the total impact of the capital gains tax rate reduction on Federal revenues.

First, the lower capital gains tax rate will induce greater realization of capital gains, as investors sell after they become unlocked from the higher capital gains rate. Many of these gains would escape taxation completely or at least defer it substantially. It is well documented that lowering the capital gains tax rate will reduce this lock-in effect, freeing investors to find more productive investments, increasing realizations of capital gains and raising revenue due to higher voluntary tax payments.

The second effect reduces revenue, as the tax rates on capital gains that would have been realized anyway are lower.

Third, over time there will be some restructuring of return to investments from ordinary income into capital gains. And with the reduced tax rate, that will reduce revenue.

Fourth, the President's proposal raises revenue through provisions to recapture depreciation allowances on investments sold for capital gain and to include capital gains as a preference item for alternative minimum tax purposes.

* * *

Fifth, and most important, the capital gains rate reduction will spur growth, increase incomes and GNP, leading to additional revenues.

While opinions can differ on each of these five factors, our best estimate of the bottom line is that the Administration's proposal to reduce capital gains tax rates is likely to raise Federal revenues in both the short run and over the longer horizon. The Office of Tax Analysis of the Treasury estimates that the President's proposal will gain $12.5 billion over the next 5 years. The Joint Committee on Taxation estimates that the President's proposal will lose $11.4 billion.

Neither of these estimates captures the favorable effects of economic growth on Federal receipts which would offset JCT's estimated losses or enhance OTA's estimated gains.

It is my own view, by the way, that OTA's revenue estimates are more representative of the extensive research on the effect of changes in capital gains tax rates on realizations.

Let me turn now for a few moments to discuss the impact of capital gains tax rate reductions on economic performance. The United States is faced with challenges to increase saving and investment, raise technical innovation and productivity growth, and improve our international competitiveness. The President's proposal on capital gains is one part—a central, important part—of a program to lower the barriers to meeting these goals.

Reducing the tax rate on capital gains will foster more rapid economic growth. To estimate the likely size of this effect, the CEA [Council of Economic Advisors] has done a standard computation of the impact of lower capital gains tax rates on the economy. The computation traces through the effect of lower tax rates on the cost of capital, capital formation and the resulting increase in productivity and GNP.

This computation may well be conservative since it ignores some important effects of capital gains, such as the reallocation of capital to higher productivity uses as the result of the reduced lock-in, increased entrepreneurial activity and so on.

Despite its limitations, it provides a rough, useful estimate of the magnitude of the likely effect and is comparable to other estimates. Over the past 2 years there have been a variety of estimates to the effect of reducing capital gains tax rates on national output and other costs of capital.

Put on a basis consistent with the Administration's proposal, a survey of these suggested that GNP will ultimately rise by between two-tenths of a percent and 1.2 percent per year.

The Council of Economic Advisers' estimate is that the effect lies roughly in the middle of this range, with GNP ultimately rising by about six-tenths of a percent as the result of adopting the Administration's proposal, which would amount to about $60 billion per year in the year 2000. This would be a rise equivalent to current Federal spending on education, training, employment and social services combined and roughly four times private sector spending on basic research.

Over the next 5 years, cumulatively, we estimate the President's proposal would increase GNP by roughly speaking $60 billion, over the next 10, cumulatively, by about $280 billion.

As I stressed in my opening remarks, increases in GNP represent new jobs, better opportunities and better standards of living for Americans. It also means higher Federal revenues. The estimated revenue dividend from the growth induced by the capital gains proposal would be roughly $12 billion over the next 5 years and probably over $50 billion over the next 10 years.

* * *

HOUSE REPORT 104-84

H.R. REP. NO. 84, 104th Cong., 1st Sess., pt. 1, at 35-37 (1995)

The Committee believes it is important that tax policy be conducive to economic growth. Economic growth cannot occur without saving, investment, and the willingness of individuals to take risks and exploit new market opportunities. The greater the pool of savings, the greater the monies available for business investment in equipment and research. It is through such investment in equipment and new products and services that the United States economy can increase output and productivity. It is through increases in productivity that workers earn higher real wages. Hence, greater saving is necessary for all Americans to benefit through a higher standard of living.

The net personal saving rate in the United States averaged 4.8 percent of gross domestic product (GDP) in the 1980s, below the 5.5 percent rate of the 1970s, and far below the rates of Japan, Germany, Canada and other major trading partners. The net personal saving rate reported by the Department of Commerce for 1990 through 1992 averaged only 3.5 percent of GDP. The Committee believes such saving is inadequate to finance the investment that is needed to equip the country's businesses with the equipment and research dollars necessary to create the higher productivity that results in higher real wages for working Americans. A reduction in the taxation of capital gains increases the rate of return on household saving. Testimony by many economists before the Committee generally concluded that increasing the after-tax return to saving should increase the saving rate of American households.

American technological leadership has been enhanced by the willingness of individuals to take the risk of pursuing new businesses exploiting new technologies. Risk taking is stifled if the taxation of any resulting gain is high and the ability to claim losses is limited. The Committee believes it is important to encourage risk taking and believes a reduction in the taxation of capital gains will have that effect.

Reduction in the taxation of capital gains also should improve the efficiency of the capital markets. The taxation of capital gains upon realization encourages investors who have accrued past gains to keep their monies "locked in" to such investments even when better investment opportunities present themselves. All economists that testified before the Committee agreed that reducing the rate of taxation of capital gains would encourage investors to unlock many of these gains. This unlocking will permit more monies to flow to new, highly valued uses in the economy. When monies flow freely, the efficiency of the capital market is improved.

The unlocking effect also has the short-term and long-term effect of increasing revenues to the Federal Government.   * * * [C]urrent Congressional estimates project that revenue losses to the Federal Government will arise from the reduction in the tax rate on capital gains beginning in fiscal year 1997. The Committee observes, however, that the conservative approach embodied in such estimates does not attempt to account for the potential for increased growth in GDP that can result from increased saving and risk taking. Many macro economists have concluded that reductions in the taxation of capital gains will increase GDP and wage growth sufficiently that future tax revenues from the taxation of wages and business profits will offset the losses forecast from the sale of capital assets.
* * *

The Committee rejects the narrow view that reductions in the taxation of capital gains benefit primarily higher-income Americans. Traditional attempts to measure the benefit of a tax reduction for capital gains are deficient. Typically, the classification of individuals in such studies measure the individuals' incomes including any capital gains realized. Many Americans realize only one or two capital gains during their lifetime, for example upon the sale of family business upon retirement. Including the gain on such a one-time sale in the income of the individual makes the individual appear, for that one year, to be a higher-income taxpayer when, in other years, the taxpayer would appear to be solidly middle class. Another deficiency is that such studies classify taxpayers only by their current economic condition. Studies show that there is substantial economic mobility in the United States. An individual who might be counted as lower income now may in a decade be higher income.

        * * *

Explanation of Provision

The bill allows individuals a deduction equal to 50 percent of net capital gain for the taxable year. The bill repeals the present-law maximum 28-percent rate. Thus, under the bill, the effective rate on the net capital gain of an individual in the highest (i.e., 39.6 percent) marginal rate bracket is 19.8 percent.

        * * *

The bill reinstates the rule in effect prior to the 1986 Tax Reform Act that required two dollars of the long-term capital loss of an individual to offset one dollar of ordinary income. The $3,000 limitation on the deduction of capital losses against ordinary income continues to apply.

        * * *

CAPITAL GAINS TAX POLICY TOWARD ENTREPRENEURSHIP
James M. Poterba[*]

42 National Tax Journal 375, 375-85 (1989)

The need to subsidize risky new ventures is frequently cited as a reason for taxing capital gains at rates below other types of income. This paper investigates the efficacy of lowering individual capital gains tax rates as a device for subsidizing such ventures, particularly those which are funded through the organized venture capital process.

The paper makes two central points. First, more than three quarters of the funds that are invested in start-up firms are provided by investors *who are not subject to the individual capital gains tax*. Funds committed by untaxed investors, notably pension funds, have expanded more rapidly than funds from taxable investors in the years since the 1978 capital gains tax cut. A significant fraction of the funds supplied to venture firms is therefore unaffected by the individual capital gains tax.

Second, the overwhelming majority of taxable capital gains results from investments in activities *other* than start-up firms. Less than one third of reported gains are the result of appreciation of corporate equity, and only a small fraction of the gains on equity are related to venture capital investments. An across-the-board capital gains tax cut is therefore a relatively blunt device for encouraging venture investment. If policy makers

---

*. At time of original publication, Massachusetts Institute of Technology and National Bureau for Economic Research.

wish to subsidize venture investments, some form of targeted capital gains reduction would be a more attractive option.

* * *

Capital Gains Taxation and the Supply of Venture Capital Funds

The source of funds for start-up enterprises is a central issue in assessing the importance of capital gains tax changes. Start-up firms receive capital from many sources. The corporate founder and other employees usually contribute capital, much of this in the form of equity that is ultimately subject to individual capital gains taxation. * * * In 1976, organized venture capitalists accounted for less than 15 percent of total funding. By comparison, equity from insiders and unaffiliated individuals amounted to 24.9 percent of the initial capital for technology-based firms. Approximately 54 percent of the funds for these small firms was supplied as equity. For non-technology firms, the equity share was 29.7 percent with insiders and other individuals supplying 20.7 percent of total capitalization.

The importance of organized venture capital has almost surely grown since the 1976 survey. Nevertheless, the common view that start-up enterprises rely exclusively on equity finance seems incorrect. Although small firms appear to use relatively more equity than their larger counterparts, many start-ups rely heavily on debt finance. One recent study commissioned by the Small Business Administration found that 57.8 percent of start-up businesses did not use *any* of the founders' saving. Debt, either from banks or from friends and relatives, accounted for more than 80 percent of capitalization in 24.8 percent of the start-ups.

The "bottleneck theory" of equity finance may apply to some classes of start-up firms, although the importance of this view remains to be demonstrated. This theory implies that without a certain amount of equity finance at a critical early stage, many firms would never be viable. If the suppliers of this equity capital, who may be the corporate founder or friends and relatives of the founder, are discouraged by high capital gains tax rates, then the amount of start-up activity could decline in response to higher capital gains tax rate even if most of the funds flowing to more mature start-up firms are unaffected.[2] There is some evidence, however, that the organized venture capital market can be used to avoid this bottleneck: 45 percent of commitments by organized venture capital firms in 1985 were to firms in the start-up or pre-start-up stages.

The rapid growth in organized venture capital funding during the last decade has been widely cited as demonstrating the sensitivity of the supply of venture funds to capital gains tax policy. The evidence traditionally used to bolster this view, namely the rapid growth in organized venture capital

---

2. None of the available data sets on startup firms are adequate for determining whether, and in what circumstances, the bottleneck theory is correct.

partnerships, is not particularly supportive of this view. Taxable individual investors have supplied relatively little of the capital these funds have invested.

Organized venture capital consists of three classes of institutions: independent venture capital funds, Small Business Investment Companies (SBICs), and corporate subsidiaries. Independent venture funds are the most important financing channel. They usually involve a general partner or partners who screen potential investments and assist the management teams the partnership has invested in, as well as limited partners who provide financial capital. At the end of 1988, the total capitalization of the venture industry was $31 billion, with almost $25 billion of the total supplied through independent venture partnerships. Commitments to such partnerships have increased fifteen-fold during the last decade, while funds channeled through SBICs and corporate subsidiaries have not even doubled.

Small Business Investment Companies are licensed and regulated by the Small Business Administration (SBA). They are essentially closed-end investment trusts which provide both capital and managerial assistance to start-up firms. The 1958 legislation authorizing SBICs allowed these entities to borrow three dollars at Treasury interest rates for each dollar of equity capital they raised. Because the investment income of SBICs is not taxable until it is distributed to shareholders, SBICs provide an attractive investment vehicle for banks or insurance companies wishing to defer taxable income. Individuals may invest through SBICs, but they have not been primary suppliers of capital through this channel.

Corporate subsidiaries enable large corporations to become involved in developments at start-up firms. They are designed to provide diversification or innovation for their corporate parents. Venture capital investments through corporate subsidiaries face corporate tax rates, so they should be much less sensitive to changes in the individual income tax treatment of capital gains than investments though independent venture partnerships.

* * * Individual investors account for less than one quarter of the capital invested in the organized venture capital industry. Moreover, their share of the *new investment* flow has declined through time, from more than one third at the end of the 1970s to only 8 percent in 1988. Although individuals supplied less capital to independent venture funds after the 1986 capital gains tax increases took effect, it is difficult to attribute this decline to changes in their tax burdens. Individuals committed $392 million in new capital in 1986. This amount *increased* to $501 million in 1987 (after the new higher rates were in effect), and then declined by fifty percent—to $236 million—in 1988. This decline cannot be traced solely to capital gains tax burdens on capital suppliers, however, since commitments by pension funds also declined by 20 percent, those by foundations by 25 percent, and those by foreign investors declined by 33 percent between 1987 and 1988.

Corporations emerge as the single most important category of capital supplier. The corporate category * * * includes both nonfinancial corporations investing through subsidiaries or SBICs, as well as financial corporations (principally insurance companies). Of the 37.2 percent of the venture capital pool supplied by firms at the end of 1988, 20.5 percent was due to insurance companies and 16.7 percent was from nonfinancial corporations.

After corporations, the second most important group of capital suppliers are tax-exempt investors such as pension funds and foundations. They accounted for 32.5 percent of the stock of funds in 1988, and were even more significant (59 percent) in the flow of new money in that year. The importance of untaxed investors in this market suggests that pretax returns have not been reduced by the favorable tax treatment of venture capital gains to individuals. If this subsidy were central in this market, then untaxed investors would be paying an implicit tax by investing in venture projects. These investors avoid other assets with substantial implicit taxes (such as tax-exempt debt) and their presence in this market suggests that the current tax subsidies are not overwhelming. Finally, 13 percent of the venture funding pool in 1988 was supplied by foreign investors. These investors are unaffected by the United States' capital gains tax.[3]

The finding that more than 80 percent of the funding for venture capital projects is from investors who are not affected by the personal income tax casts doubt on the view that changes in the capital gains tax rate affect the supply of funds to new ventures. * * *

There may be an important link between capital gains tax rates and the *demand* for venture capital funds operating through the occupational decisions of potential entrepreneurs. These individuals can work as middle or high-level managers for large firms, or they can start their own firms with a senior management position. A given worker's compensation package is likely to involve a larger share of capital gains at a start-up firm than at a larger, more established firm. By altering the relative tax burdens on wage and capital gains income, reductions in the capital gains tax make entrepreneurship more attractive.
* * *

Although it is premature to draw any strong conclusions on the effect of the 1986 Tax Reform Act on the supply of entrepreneurs, Table 4 presents four summary measures of start-up activity during the last two decades. The various data series provide very little support for the view that the supply of entrepreneurial activity has declined in the last two years. The first column reports the Commerce Department's Index of Net Business Formations. It is higher in 1987-1988 than in the previous four years, but not as high as

3. Several nations that account for substantial inflows of equity investment to the U.S., notably Japan, the Netherlands, and West Germany, do not tax long-term capital gains on corporate equities.

during the late 1970s (when capital gains tax rates were high). This index
is very sensitive to cyclical conditions, however, and its strength since 1986
may simply be a reflection of macroeconomic conditions.

The second column in Table 4 reports the number of new incorporations
in each year since 1965. This series shows a substantial decline after 1986.
It is difficult to link new incorporations with entrepreneurial activity,

Table 4: Indicators of Business Start-up Activity 1965-1988

	Index of Net Business Formations	New Incorporations	Self-Employment (Percent of Labor Force)	New Venture Capital Commitments
1965	99.8	204.1	8.2	—
1966	99.3	200.3	7.9	—
1967	100.0	206.8	6.7	—
1968	108.3	233.4	6.5	—
1969	115.8	274.0	6.5	1546.3
1970	108.8	263.8	6.3	787.6
1971	111.1	287.5	6.3	690.2
1972	119.3	317.4	6.1	410.6
1973	119.1	329.1	6.1	327.5
1974	113.2	319.0	6.1	279.9
1975	109.9	326.3	6.1	40.6
1976	120.4	374.1	6.0	179.9
1977	130.8	437.4	6.2	123.3
1978	138.1	480.0	6.3	1648.7
1979	138.3	524.3	6.3	695.5
1980	129.9	531.5	6.4	1365.3
1981	124.8	581.2	6.4	2107.5
1982	116.4	565.8	6.6	2578.3
1983	117.5	601.9	6.8	5971.0
1984	121.3	635.1	6.9	5186.7
1985	120.9	662.8	6.8	3843.4
1986	120.4	701.7	6.7	4968.5
1987	121.2	685.4	6.8	5066.5
1988	124.1	682.9	7.0	2100.0

Source: Column 1 is an index (1967 = 100) calculated by the Commerce
Department and reported in *Business Conditions Digest*. Column 2, measured in thousands of
incorporations and based on IRS data, is also reported in the *Business Conditions Digest*. Column
3 is the percent of total employment in self-employment and is drawn from various issues of
Employment and Earnings. Column 4 is drawn from the *Venture Capital Yearbook* and is
measured in thousands of 1988 dollars, with deflation by author using the GNP deflator.

however, because incorporations merely reflect legal change of existing business with no effects on real activity. This is particularly true with respect to personal service corporations. Since the corporate tax rate is currently higher than the top personal income tax rate, there is a strong incentive for using partnerships or sole proprietorships when possible to avoid corporate tax burdens. The third column in Table 4 presents the aggregate self-employment rate, another indicator which may bear on the extent of entrepreneurial activity. It shows a small increase between 1986 and 1987, with a larger increase in 1988. Once again, however, this may be an unreliable indicator of start-up activity since many self-employed individuals are not starting businesses with much capital at risk. The self-employment rate is also sensitive to changes in the relative demand for the output of different industries, and it is affected by macroeconomic conditions.

Finally, the fourth column in Table 4 shows total venture capital commitments in 1988 dollars. Commitments in 1987 exceeded their level in 1986, and then declined in 1988. Even this variable, which is probably the single best indicator of activity by start-up firms, can be difficult to analyze over time periods of several years. In 1987, for example, there was a shift from early-stage seed finance to later stage "mezzanine" financing. Thus the increase in commitments does not ensure that the level of start-up activity has increased, it could simply reflect funding being channeled to enterprises that were already started but are now in later stages of development.

The data in Table 4 do not yield a consistent picture of changes in start-up activity since 1986. * * *

The Small World of Venture Capital

An across-the-board cut in capital gains tax cut is a relatively blunt instrument for encouraging venture activity. Most of the benefits of such a tax reduction would accrue to investors in assets besides venture capital firms. In 1981, for example, the most recent year for which the IRS published detailed tabulations, only one third of taxable capital gains reflects appreciation on common stock. Venture activity is only a small share of this equity component. Real property accounts for a larger share of net gains than does common stock in each of the survey years. This underscores an important point for capital-gains policy making: a systematic reduction in capital gains tax rates will benefit many investments besides equity-financed venture capital activity.

The pool of venture capital funds under management in 1988 totaled approximately $31 billion, or approximately one percent of the value of U.S. equity markets. * * *

On Targeting a Venture Capital Subsidy

The relatively small amount of realized venture gains suggests that if one were to design a policy to aid high-risk start-up firms, the policy should be targeted so as to avoid substantial revenue loss without substantial benefit to start-up firms.[4] A number of issues of practical tax design arise in crafting such a targeted policy.

Targeting by Enterprise Size

One option is to design tax policies to provide lower capital gains burdens on investments in small firms. It may be difficult, however, to distinguish between genuine new ventures and pre-existing ventures that have been spun-off into new enterprises. A lower tax rate on capital gains in start-up firms would distort organizational structure away from large firms and toward many small enterprises. Many of the same problems that arise in policing transfer pricing between multinational subsidiaries would arise in transfers between existing firms and start-ups in which they owned equity. There would be strong incentives for established firms to transfer patents or other valuable assets to startup firms that would qualify for more favorable tax treatment.

The case for encouraging small firms at the expense of larger enterprises is not clear. Several indicators suggest that workers fare better at large than small firms. * * * [S]maller firms tend to pay lower wages. Workers at larger firms are less likely to be injured in the workplace, and they are more likely to be covered by a pension plan and health insurance. Offsetting these disadvantages for employees are the potentially greater flexibility of smaller firms and the higher research and development intensity of smaller firms. It is likely to be very difficult to compare these various aspects of industrial structure in deciding what constitutes optimal governmental policy.

Targeting by Enterprise Risk

A second possibility is to target high risk ventures. As the difficulty in designing regulations for debt versus equity securities suggests, it is difficult to objectively measure the riskiness of an investment. A risk-based targeting scheme might encourage many individuals providing services, such as doctors, lawyers, and tradesmen, to incorporate and find ways to bear risk in order to take advantage of favorable tax rates. Many of the implementation problems which would arise in this case have strong parallels in existing contexts such as the design of rules for personal holding companies.

Lower tax rates on capital gains may not be the most effective way of subsidizing high risk ventures. If it were possible to distinguish risky activities, some attention should also be devoted to current loss-offset provisions, since these might have substantial value to potential entrepreneurs. Phillips and Kirchoff (1989) report that 23.7 percent of start-up firms fail within two years, 51.7 percent within four years, and 62.7

---

4. Any targeted policy will have adverse incentive effects in distorting the organization of economic activity. The efficiency costs of such distortions would need to be far larger than reasonable calculations would suggest in order to offset the revenue losses from an untargeted capital gain reduction.

percent in six years. The implementation problems associated with more generous subsidies for large losses may be smaller than the corresponding problems with lower tax rates on certain classes of gains, so these options may warrant exploration.

Conclusions

The policy debate concerning the links between capital gains tax rates and venture capital activity has been largely misplaced. It is simply not credible to argue that a substantial fraction of the growth in organized venture capital markets since the late 1970s is the result of lower capital gains tax rates on investors, since most of the funds have come from investors who do not face the personal capital gains tax. Across-the-board reductions in individual capital gains tax rates would have a small effect on the total tax burden on venture capital financiers, while conveying large benefits on many assets other than venture capital investments.

While the links between the supply of venture capital funds and the level of capital gains tax rates has been much discussed, two issues which are central for policy evaluation have received very limited attention. First, there is very limited evidence on the extent to which the supply of entrepreneurial activity responds to the relative tax burdens on capital gains and labor income. Interviews suggest that taxes may affect employment venue, which in turn could link capital gains tax rates with the *demand* for venture capital funds by potential entrepreneurs. Economists understand very little about the entrepreneurial process, and this makes it difficult to analyze the potential effects of tax changes.

A second neglected issue is the feasibility of designing a targeted tax subsidy for the high-risk start-up sector. Neither the practical tax issues nor the more theoretical questions of whether policy *should* subsidize small or risky firms have been resolved. Policy discussion has focused almost exclusively on the rate of capital gains taxation, while other instruments such as loss offset rules or change in estate and gift tax provisions on equity in start-up firms should also be explored.

Notes and Questions

13. The Internal Revenue Code already contains provisions designed to minimize the consequences of risk-taking in making investments. Section 1244 allows an individual shareholder in a small business corporation to deduct $50,000 of losses on the corporation's stock from ordinary income each year ($100,000 if the shareholder files a joint return). Also, election of Subchapter S treatment permits losses of corporations to be passed through to individual shareholders without the losses being transmuted into capital losses.

14. Speculation on the effect of capital gains taxes on the flow of capital for investment tends to ignore the role of retained earnings and of tax

exempt entities, such as pension and profit-sharing funds. Recall Professor Ruggles' conclusion (in Chapter One) that, over the long run, households were not net lenders to enterprises or to government. Consequently, Ruggles argued, capital formation must come from capital consumption allowances, retained earnings, and pension funds, making much of the speculation as to the effect of capital gains taxes on savings and investment irrelevant. In the excerpt from Dr. Boskin's testimony, he concedes that established corporations rely largely on debt or retained earnings for new investment.

15. Are Dr. Boskin's conclusions as to the economic effect of lower capital gains taxes predicated on increased savings or increased investment?

16. One important aspect of the debate concerning capital gains taxation is the effect on revenue. Respectable economists can be found to support widely differing interpretations. (Economists working for Democrats who oppose broad-based preferential treatment for capital gains generally forecast long-term revenue losses, while economists working for Republicans who support such preferential treatment tend to forecast long-term revenue gains.)

Initially, it must be noted that the revenue argument has two components. The first is applicable to tax rates on any form of income. Lower taxes always stimulate increased economic activity. While lower capital gains rates may stimulate more investment and more willingness to realize gains, it is also true that lower tax rates on ordinary income will make taxpayers willing to take second jobs, work longer hours, etc. So the question is whether there is something special about capital gains tax rates that is not present in taxation of ordinary income.

The key is the realization rule. It is difficult to utilize labor without currently realizing income. Thus, taxpayers in the labor force are likely to continue working and generating taxable income, with any impact from variations in tax rates being relatively minor, affecting only marginal conduct. A decision not to utilize labor means the income is lost, not postponed.

Income from unrealized capital gains that is not realized, however, is not lost. The asset, with its value in excess of basis, can be kept, and the tax postponed. Under present law, if the asset is held until death, the tax is not merely postponed but permanently avoided. (See Chapter Nine.) The decision to realize and pay taxes is much more likely to be sensitive to tax rates than is the decision to work more. Lower capital gains tax rates, therefore, may stimulate greater increases in realization of capital gain than would lower rates on ordinary income stimulate additional labor. The extra realizations could generate sufficient additional revenue to pay for the capital gains tax cut. It is generally agreed that revenue would increase initially; as noted above, economists disagree concerning long-term revenue effects.

17. Critics of preferential treatment argue that any significant favorable revenue effect will be temporary, and that thereafter lower capital gains rates will translate into lower tax revenues. Why might this be the case?

18. Mr. Poterba's article is an attempt, using the limited data available, to measure the actual effect of capital gains taxes on the flow of funds from investors to new ventures. This is a refreshing contrast to the usual generalized, and often politicized, arguments over the effect of capital gains taxation.

19. Is an across-the-board capital gains tax cut a cost-effective way to encourage investment in new ventures?

20. The Poterba article points to evidence that workers are better off in large firms. Does this counter the frequently-asserted view that it is desirable for the income tax to be structured to favor small businesses?

21. First, assume that you are persuaded that equity should lead us to tax capital gains income at the same rate as ordinary income. Second, assume that you are persuaded that the government would get as much revenue, over the long term, if it lowered capital gains tax rates and kept rates on ordinary income the same (but not if it lowered rates on both types of income). Under this pair of assumptions, do you think that Congress should enact preferential tax treatment of capital gains, or tax capital gains and ordinary income equally?

E. RELATION OF CAPITAL GAIN TREATMENT TO OTHER ISSUES

A frequent complaint against taxing capital gains is that the tax is imposed on ostensible gains that, in reality, merely reflect a decline in the value of the dollar. The complaint often is valid, though its force is diminished to the extent the investor financed the purchase of the capital assets with borrowed funds. Then it is the lender who suffers from the decline in the value of the dollar. The problem is broader than one of fair measurement of taxable gain on capital assets. This issue is discussed in greater detail in Chapter Sixteen.

Taxpayers who own their own residences clearly own capital assets. The tax system is lenient toward such assets in several respects. Not only does section 1034 permit gain on sale of one's residence to be postponed if the sale proceeds are rolled over into the purchase of a replacement residence, but section 121 provides an outright exemption for a substantial amount of gain (up to $125,000) on sale of a senior citizen's principal residence. Property taxes on a taxpayer's residence may be deducted from ordinary income if the taxpayer itemizes deductions. Unlike interest to finance other personal expenses, interest on a home mortgage also qualifies as an itemized deduction. Above all, homeowners are not required to include in income the imputed rental value of their homes. See Chapter Three.

Professor Gerard M. Brannon's article gives an economist's view of the tax treatment of homeowners. The brief excerpt from House Report 104-84 explains a novel provision in the Contract with America Tax Relief Act of 1995, which would treat a loss on the sale of a taxpayer's personal residence as a deductible capital loss rather than as a nondeductible personal loss.

BRINGING TAXES HOME: CAPITAL GAINS ON RESIDENCES
Gerard M. Brannon[*]
in THE CAPITAL GAINS CONTROVERSY:

A TAX ANALYSTS READER 413 (1974)

A pesky issue in tax policy is capital gains on residences. Some legislative proposals would eliminate such taxation entirely. Very frequently, homeowners complain that it is unfair to permit no deduction for capital losses on homes. The actual truth of the matter is that the tax law as applied to residential housing is a compromise with logic but is, nevertheless, a noteworthy combination of simplicity and generosity to home owners.

In a well-ordered tax system, the provision of housing services would be regarded as a business in which the taxpayer provides housing services to himself. The rental value of the home would be in income and the costs of providing these services would be a deduction. Among the costs would be, of course, depreciation.

For reasons which are compelling to somebody, Congress has never seen fit to treat housing this way nor has any administration told Congress that this is what it should do. This particular falling away from tax logic turns out to be fairly simple. Home ownership is simply ignored except that two of the costs of this nonincluded income are still allowed as deductions: property taxes and mortgage interest.

When a home is sold, it is not so simple to get away from the logic of the accounting. If we had done things properly all along the sales transaction would be routine. The taxpayer would report as gain net sales proceeds reduced by original cost less depreciation.

By analogy to accounting for gain on the sale of commercial real estate, some of the gain due to depreciation might be "recaptured" at ordinary income rates but would be taxed as either capital gain or ordinary income.

The complication in the sale of a home in the system that we have is that the taxpayer has not maintained a depreciation account. Assume a taxpayer buys a house for $50,000 and assume that we know for sure that

---

[*]. At time of original publication, Professor, Georgetown University.

the useful life of the house is exactly 50 years. If our taxpayer sells the house for $40,000 after he has lived in it for 40 years, then certainly he has had a substantial capital gain. He has not lost anything. He used up 4/5th of his investment living on the house. The cost less depreciation should be down to $10,000 and the sale should represent a $30,000 gain.

It is not very compelling to say that the taxpayer should not have to reduce the cost basis for depreciation because the taxpayer didn't take depreciation. In a correct accounting procedure depreciation would have only offset part of the imputed rental income and there was a tax benefit from not having to include the imputed rent.

If we had depreciation accounts for homes, it would be logical to allow capital losses on sale when the house is sold for less than cost adjusted for depreciation.

If there is not [a] logical reason for not reducing basis in the house by depreciation, there is a practical reason; namely, that the taxpayer has not kept depreciation records.

Given the practical problem of no depreciation accounts, the tax law takes a very broad swipe at the problem. The tax law solution is to deliberately understate the gain (by not requiring a depreciation adjustment) and to deny any "loss" that may be indicated by this peculiar calculation. This solution may not be elegant but, by God, it's simple! (Remember that the next time somebody yaks at you about how complicated the tax law is.)

Being generous in the tax law doesn't save the Congress from trouble. Having decided that most gains in houses will be covered over by funny accounting, it seems unfair that a taxpayer who has not lived in his house long enough for the value to fall below cost will pay a capital gains tax if he moves into a bigger house. To take care of this case the Congress had to invent a rollover provision which lets a taxpayer who perhaps for reasons of age, cannot move into another house and takes an apartment. To limit this tax liability for the capital gain, Congress said taxpayers over 65 don't have to recognize part of the gain for tax purposes.[i]

At the root of all this is the question of whether an individual has greater ability to pay when his house increases in value. The answer, I think, must be yes. He is better off than someone who hasn't had such a gain.

HOUSE REPORT 104-84

H.R. REP. NO. 84, 104th Cong., 1st Sess., pt. 1, at 44 (1995)

Generally, under present law if a taxpayer sells the taxpayer's principal residence for less than the taxpayer's adjusted basis in that asset the

---

i. In addition to section 1034, the rollover provision that is available to all taxpayers who sell their homes and that can be used repeatedly, section 121 allows a permanent, one-time exclusion of up to $125,000 of gain ($62,500 if married filing separately). Section 121 was amended in 1978 to lower the qualifying age to 55. (Eds.)

taxpayer is treated as having a nondeductible personal loss. In contrast, when a taxpayer sells an investment asset for less than the taxpayer's adjusted basis in that investment asset, the taxpayer may be eligible for capital loss treatment on the sale. That capital loss is available to offset the taxpayer's capital gains and $3000 of ordinary income annually. The Committee believes that it is inappropriate to allow the capital loss on the sale of the investment asset but not on the sale of the principal residence. Further, the Committee believes that the proper measurement of economic income under the Code requires a recognition of the large out-of-pocket loss that a taxpayer incurs when a taxpayer's principal residence is sold at a loss.

Notes and Questions

22. A flaw in taxing capital gains when realized is that, absent a maximum cap on capital gains tax rates, some individuals will be taxed at a higher rate in the year they realize a sporadic capital gain than their average tax rate on ordinary income. A flat, preferential capital gains tax rate has been defended as a substitute for averaging, though its benefits would not be limited to taxpayers whose average tax rates are lower.

The potential for inequitable treatment of individuals with sporadic capital gains was diminished by the Tax Reform Act of 1986, because it drastically broadened tax brackets and reduced individual income tax rates overall. In fact, coincident with the broader tax brackets and the lower rates, the 1986 Act terminated the rather complex income-averaging provisions.

23. Capital gains on sale of corporate stock reflect, among other factors, after-tax accumulations of earnings and profits at the corporate level. If and when these accumulated earnings are distributed as dividends, they are subjected to a second income tax at the individual shareholder level. (Double taxation of corporate earnings distributed as dividends is discussed in Chapter Fourteen.) If stock is sold before dividends are distributed, gain is subjected to double tax to the extent the gain is attributable to the accumulated earnings. It is difficult, however, to know what portion of the gain should be attributed to the corporation's accumulated earnings. In most instances the primary factor in determining a stock's price is the corporation's anticipated future earnings. These future earnings are valued after corporate tax. The discount for anticipated corporate tax reduces the sales price of the stock, so that the seller indirectly bears it. All of this may be too speculative to justify a preferential tax on gain from sale of the stock.

24. If the Code were to be changed to provide that dividends distributed from previously taxed corporate earnings were to be excluded from the income of stockholders, would there be double taxation of corporate earnings when a shareholder sold stock at a gain before the corporation distributed its earnings?

25. Professor Brannon pretends to be puzzled that Congress has not included the rental value of taxpayers' homes in income. Why has Congress not provided for inclusion?

26. Is Professor Brannon correct in saying that, if we had depreciation accounts for our homes, it would be logical to allow a capital loss when a home is sold for less than its adjusted basis?

27. Is there a logical basis for distinguishing the loss on the sale of a taxpayer's home from the situation in which a taxpayer buys a suit of clothes for $400, uses it until it wears out, and then sells it for two dollars?

Selected Bibliography

Auerbach, Alan J., *Retrospective Capital Gains Taxation*, 81 AM. ECON. REV. 167 (1991).

——, *Capital Gains Taxation and Tax Reform*, 42 NAT'L TAX J. 391 (1989).

Brannon, Gerard M., *Bringing Taxes Home: Capital Gains on Residences*, *in* THE CAPITAL GAINS CONTROVERSY: A TAX ANALYSTS READER, 413 (1974)

CCH Tax Advisory Board Roundtable: 1992 Tax Issues and Trends, 79 Stand. Fed. Tax Rep. (CCH) No. 26, at 1 (May 27, 1992).

CONGRESSIONAL BUDGET OFFICE, EFFECTS OF LOWER CAPITAL GAINS TAXES ON ECONOMIC GROWTH (1990).

CONGRESSIONAL BUDGET OFFICE, INDEXING CAPITAL GAINS (1990).

Cunningham, Noel B., and Deborah H. Schenk, *The Case for a Capital Gains Preference*, 48 TAX L. REV. 319 (1993).

DAVID, MARTIN, ALTERNATIVE APPROACHES TO CAPITAL GAINS TAXATION (1968).

Feldstein, Martin et al., *The Effects of Taxation on the Selling of Corporate Stock and the Realization of Capital Gains*, 1980 Q. J. ECON. 777.

Gillingham, Robert & John S. Greenlees, *The Effects of Capital Gains Tax Rates on Capital Gain Tax Revenues: Another Look at the Evidence*, 45 NAT'L TAX J. 167 (1992).

GOODE, RICHARD, THE INDIVIDUAL INCOME TAX 176-211 (Rev. ed. 1976).

Gravelle, Jane G., and Lawrence B. Lindsey, *Capital Gains*, 38 TAX NOTES 397 (1988).

Halperin, Daniel I., *Capital Gains and Ordinary Deductions: Negative Income Tax for the Wealthy*, 12 B.C. INDUS. & COM'L L. REV. 387 (1971).

Johnson, Calvin H., *The Undertaxation of Holding Gains*, 55 TAX NOTES 807 (1992).

——, *The Private Advantage of Money-Losing Investments Under Cut-Rate Capital Gains*, 55 TAX NOTES 1125 (1992).

——, *The Consumption of Capital Gains*, 55 TAX NOTES 957 (1992).

——, *Seventeen Culls From Capital Gains*, 48 TAX NOTES 1285 (1990).

Kiefer, Donald, *Lock-in Effect Within a Simple Model of Corporate Stock Trading*, 43 NAT'L TAX J. 75 (1990).

Kornhauser, Marjorie E., *The Origins of Capital Gains Taxation: What's Law Got to Do with It?*, 39 SW. L. J. 869 (1985).

Landsman, Wayne R. & Douglas A. Shackelford, *The Lock-in Effect of Capital Gains Taxes: Evidence from the RJR Nabisco Leveraged Buyout*, 48 NAT'L TAX J. 245 (1995).

Mariger, Randall P., *Taxes, Capital Gains Realizations, and Revenues: A Critical Review and Some New Results*, 48 NAT'L TAX J. 447 (1995).

Peel, Fred W., Jr., *Capital Losses: Falling Short on Fairness and Simplicity*, 17 U. BALT. L. REV. 418 (1988).

Poterba, James M., *Capital Gains Tax Policy Toward Entrepreneurship*, 42 NAT'L TAX J. 375 (1989).

Shaviro, Daniel N., *Uneasiness and Capital Gains*, 48 TAX L. REV. 393 (1993).

SIMONS, HENRY, PERSONAL INCOME TAXATION 148-69 (1938).

Skinner, Jonathan & Daniel Feenberg, *The Impact of the 1986 Tax Reform on Personal Savings, in* DO TAXES MATTER? THE IMPACT OF THE TAX REFORM ACT OF 1986 50 (Joel Slemrod ed., 1990)

Tax Incentives For Increasing Savings and Investments: Hearings before the United States Senate Committee on Finance, 101st Cong., 2d Sess. 40-43 (1990) (statement of Boskin, Michael J.).

U.S. CONG. BUDGET OFF., HOW CAPITAL GAINS TAX RATES AFFECT REVENUES: THE HISTORICAL EVIDENCE (1988).

U.S. DEP'T OF TREASURY, REPORT TO CONGRESS ON THE CAPITAL GAINS TAX REDUCTIONS OF 1978 (1985).

VICKREY, WILLIAM, AGENDA FOR PROGRESSIVE TAXATION 136-63 (1947).

Waggoner, Michael J., *Eliminating the Capital Gains Preference, Part 1: The Problems of Inflation, Bunching and Lock-In*, 48 U. COLO. L. REV. 313 (1977).

Weiss, Deborah M., *Can Capital Tax Policy Be Fair? Stimulating Savings Through Differentiated Tax Rates*, 78 CORNELL L. REV. 206 (1993).

Wells, Anita, *Legislative History of Treatment of Capital Gains Under the Federal Income Tax, 1913-1948*, 2 NAT'L TAX J. 12 (1949).

Wetzler, James W., *Capital Gains and Losses, in* COMPREHENSIVE INCOME TAXATION 115 (Joseph A. Pechman ed., 1977).

Zodrow, George R., *Economic Analysis of Capital Gains Taxation: Realization, Revenues, Efficiency and Equity*, 48 TAX L. REV. 419 (1993).

CHAPTER SIXTEEN

RESPONDING TO PRICE LEVEL CHANGES

Taxes rise with inflation, however caused or to whatever extent, whether temporary or permanent.[a]

A. INTRODUCTION

For the past sixty years overall changes in price levels have invariably been upward. Conceivably price levels might drop, but for all practical purposes responding to price level changes means responding to price level increases. In common parlance and in most of the literature, this is called inflation.

Inflation affects an income tax in two ways. First, it changes the meaning in real terms of the amounts expressed in the law as specific dollar figures. Thus, personal exemptions and standard deductions expressed as specific dollar amounts become less valuable to the taxpayer as a result of inflation. Also, the upper and lower limits on tax brackets apply to smaller real income amounts than originally intended.

Congress has addressed the effect of inflation on tax brackets, exemptions, and various other dollar amounts specified in the Code. Annual adjustments to the tax rate tables are provided to correct for changes in the cost of living, measured by the Consumer Price Index, so that inflation will not result in tax increases in real terms. Similarly, the dollar amounts of dependency exemptions, the standard deduction, and limits on contributions and benefits under qualified pension plans are adjusted for estimated changes in the cost of living.

The second major effect of inflation on the income tax is to distort measurement of gains and losses and of income and deduction items. The typical example is the taxpayer who sells her home for more than she paid for it, but finds that the dollar proceeds from the sale are worth no more (and possibly worth less) than the purchasing power of the dollars she paid for the house originally. Another example, less frequently recognized, is a lender-taxpayer who lends money to a borrower-taxpayer. When the loan is repaid in a subsequent year in dollars that have less buying power than the dollars originally lent, the detriment to the lender is equalled by a benefit to the borrower.

Price level changes distort the measurement of interest income, interest deductions, debt repayment, capital gains and losses, and depreciation

---

a. Nathan Clifford, quoted in 69 TAX NOTES 1667 (1995).

deductions. By and large, taxable income from service activities is calculated in current dollars and consequently is not affected by price level changes.

Income from sales of inventory is distorted for taxpayers who use the FIFO convention, but taxpayers have the option to elect LIFO. By calculating income from inventory sales by matching sales receipts against the costs of the most recently acquired inventory a taxpayer who maintains inventory levels is measuring income using current dollar costs. If inventory levels fall, however, so that the taxpayer is drawing down inventory bought in earlier years at lower price levels, part of the inventory profit will be due to inflation that occurred after the inventory was acquired.

So far Congress has not attempted to deal explicitly with the distortion that price level changes cause in the measurement of gains, losses, income items, and deductions. Most of the discussion of the distorting effect of inflation on measurement of taxable income has focused on capital gains.

INFLATION AND THE INCOME TAX
Henry J. Aaron,[*] ed.
Pages 5-6 (1976)

All tax systems distort economic decisions. Indexing makes these distortions the same regardless of the rate of inflation. An inflation-free, or indexed, income tax system is one that imposes the same real tax burden on a particular amount of real before-tax income regardless of the rate of inflation. For given real before-tax income the real tax base and the rate structure must be unaffected by inflation. Whether indexing is desirable depends on whether in its absence inflation improves or worsens the particular set of distortions a tax system contains. Indexing the tax system cannot eradicate, although it may offset, consequences of inflation not related directly to the tax system, such as the reduction in the demand for money and the consequent effects on interest rates, savings, and investment.

Inflation affects income tax liabilities in two distinct ways. First, inflation distorts the tax base—the measures of current-dollar business and personal income from which personal exemptions and deductions are subtracted and to which personal and corporate income tax rates are applied in order to compute tax liabilities. Second, inflation changes the rate structure, loosely defined to include the real value of all nominal quantities in the Internal Revenue Code, most notably personal exemptions and dollar-limited credits, the standard deduction, * * * the refundable credit on earnings, and the size of the income brackets to which the personal income tax applies. * * *

In general the distorting effects of inflation on the tax base are important because they cause a taxpayer to pay a different amount of tax

---

[*]. At time of original publication, Director, Economic Studies Program, The Brookings Institution.

than he would pay on the same real income in a noninflationary world. Moreover, this distortion will vary among taxpayers. In contrast, the distorting effects of inflation on the rate structure are important principally because they change the relative tax liabilities of taxpayers who would be in different brackets in a noninflationary world.

Tax Base

Economists generally define income as the sum of consumption plus additions to real net worth (for individuals) or as the excess of receipts over costs, where costs include the replacement of capital consumed (for businesses). Some individuals receive both business income—in the form of dividends, profits, rents, interest, or capital gains—and earnings, in the form of salaries and wages.

Inflation negligibly distorts the measurement of earned income but creates serious problems in the measurement of business income. Business income is the residual after subtracting from receipts a variety of expenses. Since receipts and associated expenses may occur at widely separated times, the purchasing power of the dollars in which they are measured may differ widely. When inflation is occurring, earnings received at the beginning and end of the year also are denominated in dollars of different purchasing power and are not strictly comparable; but in most cases these effects are relatively small. Earnings paid evenly throughout the year are denominated *on the average* in midyear dollars. Unless some earners are paid mostly at the beginning of the year or mostly at the end, *relative* earnings will not be affected by inflation.

In principle, the definition of income just enunciated requires that all changes in real net worth be taxed as accrued. In fact, the Internal Revenue Code generally requires realization of gains or losses on capital assets before they become subject to tax, but permits (and generally requires) businesses to accrue receipts and expenses in measuring business net income. Whether this distinction should be preserved if adjustments are made for inflation (or if they are not) raises difficult questions, because inflation simultaneously affects current expenses and receipts and the value of capital assets.

Inflation-sensitive elements of income include (1) capital gains and losses and interest payments and (2) business deductions for depreciation and the cost of materials used.

* * *

Notes and Questions

1. There was strong opposition to enactment of a system of automatic adjustments to tax brackets, exemption amounts, etc. to correct for inflation. What caused this opposition?

2. Congress has not provided inflation adjustments for all dollar amounts specified in the Internal Revenue Code. For example, the tax

brackets for the graduated corporate income tax are not adjusted, nor is the $2,000 maximum limitation on contributions to Individual Retirement Accounts. The $5,000 exclusion for employee death benefits allowed by section 101(b) has not been adjusted for inflation since its adoption in 1954, demonstrating that, over a long period, inflation can convert a significant exclusion into a *de minimis* provision. There does not appear to be a coherent policy distinction between the amounts that are adjusted for inflation and those that are not.

3. The cost-of-living adjustment in section 1(f) of the Internal Revenue Code is a one-way street. No downward adjustments are provided in case price levels should drop.

4. It is generally thought by economists that the Consumer Price Index, which is the most common benchmark for indexing for inflation, overstates the effect of inflation. Revision of the means of computing the CPI, or abandoning the CPI for some other inflation measuring stick, might result in smaller adjustments for tax purposes and with respect to important nontax matters such as cost-of-living adjustments (COLAs) paid to retirees and others. The impact of inflation varies according to consumption patterns, however, and thus varies greatly by age, income level, geographic location, and individual tastes in consumption. The process of revision of the CPI would be likely to cause sharp divisions among affected interest groups.

5. How does application of inflation adjustments to tax rates, personal exemptions, etc. affect the contra-cyclical influence of the individual income tax?

6. Why does Aaron say that inflation only negligibly distorts the measurement of earned income?

7. It is difficult to see why indexing should lead to a reappraisal of the present requirement that capital gains and losses be realized before they are taken into account in computing taxable income, as Aaron implies. If gains were required to be taken into account before realization, under the Haig-Simons mode, pressure to correct the definition of gain for inflation would be intensified. The Treasury I proposal, though complex, provides one way to apply indexing in the framework of a tax system keyed to realization.

B. INFLATION AND CAPITAL GAIN

TAXATION OF CAPITAL GAINS—LET'S BE FAIR
Calvin Engler[*] & Mitchell L. Engler[**]
50 Tax Notes 1303, 1303-04 (1991)

Capital gains are now taxed at a maximum rate of 28 percent while other income is taxed at a maximum rate of 31 percent [now 39.6 percent]. This tax relief does not solve the problem of fairness when taxing capital gains, and now that President Bush indicated in his State of the Union message that he plans to pursue further capital gains tax reductions, it is appropriate to examine the need for capital gains tax relief. The relief thus far granted fails to consider the effects of inflation during the period of time property is held. Inflation will have a markedly different effect on property held for a short period of time, say a year or two, compared to property held for a long period of time—20 or more years. In contrast, the three-percent rate reduction applies equally to property held for a short period or long period of time.

A cure for this inequity in taxation would be to index capital gains. Indexing capital gains was in the forefront of the recent round of tax negotiations, and it is almost certain that the issue of indexing capital gains will emerge again in the near future. Indexing of personal exemptions and the standard deduction are already a part of income tax law, and the need for indexing capital gains is illustrated by the following example.

Example 1: Assume a taxpayer purchases shares of capital stock for $100,000 and sells the shares a year later for $110,000. The inflation rate during this holding period—the time between the purchase and sale of the property—was 10 percent. Under present tax law the taxpayer would be taxed on a capital gain of $10,000. The imposition of a tax on these facts is unjust to the taxpayer because the taxpayer merely maintained his/her purchasing power and did not have a real economic gain of $10,000; rather, the differential was all due to inflation. Indexing capital gains would correct this inequity by limiting the tax on capital gains to the true economic gain. This would be accomplished by adjusting the taxpayer's basis (i.e., cost of the asset) for the amount of inflation during the holding period. On the facts of Example 1, the taxpayer's original basis of $100,000 would be multiplied by 110 percent giving the taxpayer an adjusted basis of $110,000. Therefore, the taxpayer would not be subject to any tax since the sales proceeds would be equal to the taxpayer's adjusted basis.

However, this indexing of capital gains would create a windfall to the taxpayer if any part of the $100,000 purchase price was financed through borrowed funds. This can be illustrated by the following example.

---

[*]. At time of original publication, Professor of accounting, Iona College.

[**]. At time of original publication, recent recipient of LL.M. in Taxation at New York University Law School.

Example 2: Assume the same facts as in Example 1 except that the taxpayer borrowed the full $100,000 purchase price at an interest rate of 10 percent. When the taxpayer sells the stock for $110,000, he/she uses the full $110,000 to pay off the lender ($100,000 toward principal and $10,000 toward interest). Indexing only the gain side of the transaction would allow the taxpayer a net deduction of $10,000. Once again the taxpayer would have no taxable gain on the sales proceeds because the adjusted basis would be $110,000, but the taxpayer would be allowed an interest deduction of $10,000 (assuming for the moment that it is qualifying interest). Therefore, the taxpayer would have a net deduction of $10,000 from a transaction that was an economic wash. Bear in mind that the taxpayer did not use any personal funds to achieve the $10,000 tax deduction. * * * Indexing only the gain side of the transaction irrespective of the source of the funds used to purchase property would merely substitute one inequity for another inequity.

Since many taxpayers purchase stock securities on margin and almost all purchases of real estate are financed in part through the use of mortgages, the failure of existing proposals to consider the interaction of borrowed funds with purchases raises substantial concerns of equity in taxation. * * * Henry Aaron, of the Brookings Institution, * * * suggests that all loan transactions should be adjusted for inflation to prevent a taxpayer from earning a tax arbitrage by using borrowed funds to acquire property.

An alternate solution would be to allow a taxpayer the benefits of indexing capital gains only to the extent that the taxpayer's basis is attributable to nonborrowed funds. This proposal would accomplish the goal of providing indexation where needed and would avoid the complexity of adjusting all loan transactions for inflation.

At the simplest level our proposal would work as follows:

Example 3: Assume the same facts as in Example 2 except that only the portion of basis attributable to nonborrowed funds is indexed for inflation. Since the purchase price was financed entirely by borrowed funds, none of the basis is indexed and remains at $100,000. Therefore, when the taxpayer sells the securities for $110,000 he/she will have a taxable gain of $10,000 and a tax deduction of $10,000 for interest. Thus, the taxpayer will not have a tax benefit from a transaction that is an economic wash. Of course, this proposal, if enacted, would require that the three-percent rate differential be eliminated.

Our proposals also would achieve the same equitable result in more realistic scenarios. For example:

Example 4: A taxpayer purchases a building on January 1, 1990 for $500,000 using a down payment of $100,000 and assumes a mortgage of $400,000. Principal payments for 1990 and 1991 amount to $20,000 and are payable at the end of each year. The inflation index at January 1, 1990 is 100; at January 1, 1991 it is 110; and at January 1, 1992 it is 121. The taxpayer sells the property for $700,000 on January 1, 1992. If the basis of the property is indexed, the taxable gain would be:

Selling price	$700,000
Basis ($ 500,000 x 121%)	$605,000
Taxable gain	$95,000

As described earlier, this would create an inequity for fairness in taxation. The way to avoid this inequity is to index only nonborrowed funds. This would be accomplished as follows:

Example 5:

Average Invested Funds			Indexed Amount
$100,000	x	21%	$21,000
20,000	x	10%	2,000
20,000	x	0%	0
			$23,000

Under this approach, the taxpayer's basis would be $523,000 ($500,000 + $23,000) leaving a taxable gain of $177,000 ($700,000 - $523,000). Thus, a taxpayer would be prevented from reaping an arbitrage windfall from leveraging (borrowing) against purchased property.

Some observers undoubtedly will argue that it is difficult to separate borrowed basis from nonborrowed basis. In the case of stock securities purchased on margin or real estate purchased with a mortgage, however, this separation can be accomplished easily. Since most real estate transactions and many purchases of stock fall within these categories, the source of the purchase price will be obvious. For those transactions where tracing the borrowed funds would be necessary, existing regulations of the Internal Revenue Code already provide a method for allocating borrowed funds to various expenditures.

In sum, while the indexation of only nonborrowed basis would not eliminate all inequities in the Internal Revenue Code arising from inflation, our proposal would be a relatively simple procedure to alleviate inequities in connection with the taxation of capital gains.

REPORT ON INFLATION ADJUSTMENTS TO THE BASIS OF CAPITAL ASSETS
New York State Bar Association Section on Taxation
Ad Hoc Committee
48 Tax Notes 759, 759-60, 773-75 (1990)

Introduction

In the ongoing debate regarding the implementation of some form of preferential taxation of capital gain income, many legislative alternatives will be considered. One such alternative is adjusting or "indexing" the basis of certain capital assets to reflect general price level inflation, thereby attempting to tax only "real" as opposed to inflationary gains. This Report discusses the issues, problems, and other considerations raised by the indexing of the basis of capital assets.

      * * *

The Weak Theoretical Basis for Indexing

All the complexity and exposure to significant erosion of the revenue base would be problematic even under a perfect indexation system, because the primary theoretical bases supporting indexation of the tax system are themselves problematic.

Inexact Nature of Adjustments

The main premise underlying any indexing proposal, i.e., that indexing the basis of an asset will result in the taxation of only real appreciation, is highly questionable. The four factors discussed below contribute to this conclusion. Given the reality that any inflation adjustment would be imprecise at best, we believe * * * that any form of indexation would be extremely bad tax policy.

First, the use of any particular inflation index will offer inexact relief to the owner of any particular asset. For example, if the consumer price index is used, exact relief will be given only to an owner who plans to use the income from the asset for consumption, as opposed to business or investment purposes, and then only if the composition of the owner's planned or actual consumption matches that of the basket of goods whose price level is measured in composing the index. Although it may be said that consumption is the ultimate goal or at least use for all income, it nevertheless is true that for certain periods, investment goals may predominate. This has caused some to question whether use of an index other than the consumer price index would be appropriate.

Second, the price of an asset and the returns available from that asset already may be adjusted to account for inflation. For example, if a lessor charges higher rents to compensate for the overtaxation attributable to inflation, basis adjustments would provide the lessor with redundant relief.

For this reason, it is unclear whether it would be preferable to index basis for actual or expected inflation.[57]

Third, deferring basis indexation adjustments until disposition creates arbitrary results where income-producing property generates periodic returns in excess of the "real" rate of return. For example, if the current income generated by property were sufficiently high, there would be relatively little real or nominal appreciation in that property. All the currently received income would be treated as ordinary income to the recipient, notwithstanding the fact that in an inflationary environment, a portion of that income in economic terms would represent a return of principal. Thus, indexing basis would be of limited usefulness to the holder of this type of property for whom property appreciation attributable to inflation would be recognized as ordinary income over the period the property is held, accompanied by a capital loss (if losses are allowed) or diminution of capital gain on disposition.[58] Ironically, the benefit of basis indexation is greater for property that does not generate current income and that as a result already enjoys the benefit of tax deferral.

Finally, even assuming that the proper measure of inflation in an asset can be determined with reasonable precision, it can be demonstrated that in most cases actual basis adjustments will match inflationary increases only by happenstance. This unfortunate result occurs because in the absence of gain realization, annual adjustments are made to the basis of the asset without regard to its fair market value. Nevertheless, inflation in any period by its nature will increase the nominal price of an asset relative to its value at the beginning of the measurement period.

For example, assume that Ms. A purchased an asset for $1,000. After one year the asset is still worth $1,000. After two years, Ms. A sells the asset for $1,300. Inflation in each year is 10 percent. Under an indexation system, Ms. A would have a basis in the asset at the time of sale of $1,210 (i.e., $1,000 plus $100 for the first year and $110 for the second year). Although Ms. A's inflation adjustment of $100 for the first year is appropriate, her inflation adjustment for the second year should be limited to $100. Price level increases in the second year only inflated the actual value of her asset, not the asset's adjusted basis. Ms. A's taxable gain is $10 less

---

57. Halperin & Steuerle, *Indexing the Tax System for Inflation,* in *Uneasy Compromise: Problems of a Hybrid Income-Consumption Tax* 366-368 (H. Aaron, H. Galper & J. Pechman, eds., Brookings 1988).

58. This result is most easily understood in the context of an investment in nonparticipating preferred stock. For example, individual Investor A pays $1,000 for $1,000 face amount of XYZ Corp. preferred stock, which has a 10 percent annual dividend. Inflation of five percent is anticipated in determining the dividend rate and inflation actually occurs at that rate. A's stock is redeemed after 10 years for $1,000. At that time, A's indexed basis in the stock is $1,629, resulting in a capital (and economic loss of $629. This loss occurs because each unindexed dividend payment represents economically a return of capital in part. Cf. section 1059(f). The same phenomenon occurs with respect to depreciable property if basis is indexed only on disposition and depreciation deductions are not indexed.

than her "real" gain. By comparison, Mr. B purchases an asset for $1,000.
The asset is worth $1,200 after one year and is sold for $1,300 after two
years. At the time of sale, Mr. B's basis also would be $1,210, but his
inflation adjustment for the second year should have been $120 rather than
$110, resulting in tax of $10 of gain in excess of real gain.

Accordingly, the basis adjustment for an asset will exactly equal the
measure of its price inflation (assuming that the exact amount of price
inflation can be measured in any event) only where the asset appreciates at
exactly the rate of inflation. Basis adjustments will be inadequate to adjust
for inflation where an asset appreciates faster than the rate of inflation, and
basis adjustments will be excessive where an asset appreciates at a rate
slower than inflation.
* * *

Neutral Taxation of Capital Income

Another often-stated premise underlying indexation proposals is that
indexation is needed to achieve neutral taxation of income from capital as
compared to other sources, i.e., to prevent capital income from being taxed
more heavily than other income by reason of including inflationary as well
as real gains in the tax base. This premise too is false. It is well understood
that the current system taxes income from capital more favorably than
income from other sources because gain from the appreciation of capital is
not taxed unless realized and avoids tax altogether if the asset is held at
death. Other advantages include accelerated depreciation, the availability
of interest deductions on related indebtedness, and LIFO inventories. Thus,
unless these other benefits are eliminated, indexing of basis will allow income
from capital to enjoy an even more favored tax status relative to income from
other sources than it now enjoys.

Conclusion

It is our position that the implementation of any indexation system as
a part of a modification of the present tax system would be highly
inadvisable. * * *

Appendix: Indexing in the United Kingdom

In 1982, following the high inflation of the 1970s and after several years
of discussion, the U.K. indexed the basis of certain assets in an attempt to
avoid the taxation of inflationary gain. Announcing the measure, the
Chancellor of the Exchequer said in his Budget speech:

> I come now to the incidence of capital gains tax on inflationary
> gains. This is a matter which has rightly given rise to a great deal
> of discontent. No one has yet succeeded in finding a solution to this
> problem. Innumerable proposals for full indexation, for tapering
> and other ingenious devices have been put forward.   None,
> unfortunately, overcame all the practical difficulties. I cannot,
> however, allow this injustice to continue. It is intolerable for people

to be permanently condemned to pay tax on gains that are apparent but not real—that exist only on paper.

Thus, acknowledged at the outset that the measure was imperfect, basis indexing was created in the U.K. Since its introduction, the basis indexing provisions have undergone two major revisions, the second of which, in 1988, was part of a larger revision of the capital gains tax ("CGT").

The U.K. indexing rules provide for adjustment to the basis of an asset upon its disposal. On the disposal of an asset, an indexation allowance is given, equal to relevant allowable expenditure multiplied by a fraction, the denominator of which is the retail price index ("RPI") for the month of disposal and the numerator of which is the RPI for the month of disposal less the RPI for the month of acquisition. The indexation allowance is treated as a deduction from the gain or loss computed under general CGT rules. It may reduce a gain, turn a gain into a loss, or increase a loss.

* * *

A continuing problem with the U.K. indexing provisions has been the complexity of identifying the assets that have been sold to determine their eligibility for the allowance, and the correct cost basis to be attributed to them, especially in the case of securities. Because of the relevant effective date provisions, assets had to be divided between those acquired before March 1982 and after. Another allocation had to be made initially for assets held for less than one year, which were not eligible for the allowance. In 1985, the one-year rule was abandoned, but the taxpayer was given the ability to choose whether to calculate the allowance for assets acquired before March 1982 using the base cost on acquisition before March 1982 or the fair market value of the asset in March 1982, requiring further allocations. Expenditure on property after March 1982 itself qualified for a separate calculation to determine the allowance due in respect of it. Part disposals also had their own rules. The effect has been to impose a considerable administrative burden on taxpayers who generally have been unable to compute their basis adjustments without professional help. The shifting of basis of all assets to their value on March 1982 is expected to ease that burden somewhat, but carries with it obvious administrative problems of its own.

In 1985, the rules were revised to allow the allowance even when it created a capital loss. Attempts to take advantage of this have resulted in legislation to prevent abuses.[7] For example, the Finance Act of 1988 contains provisions preventing linked companies from manufacturing an artificial loss through the sale of certain intercompany debts. Other problems include the

---

7. For example, the distortion caused by indexing gains on securities, while fully taxing interest as income, will result in transactions and devices designed to convert the return on securities from income (unindexed) into capital gains (indexed). In the U.K., this has led to a series of anti-avoidance legislation.

failure to index gains or losses on debt, creating arbitrage possibilities, and resulting in frequent legislative action to stop it.

Notes and Questions

8. The Engler and Engler article illustrates the complexity of indexing gains and losses without taking into account the distorting effects of inflation on the use of borrowed money to finance the purchase of assets. Does inflation not distort *any* debtor-creditor relationship? If a taxpayer borrows $1,000 in 1990 for five years and repays the loan in 1995 with $1,000 that have purchasing power equal only to 60 percent of 1990 dollars, has not the borrower enjoyed a gain, and the lender suffered a loss, of $400 in real terms?

9. Engler and Engler point out that indexing capital gains would result in a windfall for the taxpayer who acquired an asset with borrowed funds. Consider whether the effect of inflation on taxes could better be broken down into two problems: what to do about debt repaid with cheap dollars and what to do about assets whose real value is eroded by inflation. For example, suppose A borrows $5,000 to finance a trip to Europe (using a home equity loan secured by his personal residence) and repays the loan in later years with cheap dollars. Also suppose B borrows $5,000 that he invests in common stocks and repays his loan in later years with cheap dollars. Both A and B have benefitted from repaying their debts with cheap dollars. If A does not have income from the transaction, would it be fair, as Engler and Engler propose, to deny B an inflation adjustment to his stock market gain because he got the same benefit as a borrower that A got?

10. Engler and Engler state that, if an inflation adjustment is provided for gain derived from nonborrowed funds, "of course" any capital gain rate differential would be eliminated? Does this conclusion follow as a matter of course?

11. Are Engler and Engler correct in saying in their conclusion that their proposal would be a relatively simple procedure?

12. The critique by the New York State Bar Committee points up the fallibility of all inflation indices. Neither the Consumer Price Index nor any other index reflects precisely the change in purchasing power of a dollar over time to any particular person. In addition to subjective differences, problems lurk in the composition of each price index. One common failure is the difficulty they have in adjusting for quality changes. Another is their inability to take into account the introduction of new products.

Some of the problems with indexing can be avoided by giving up on attempts to adjust depreciation deductions annually. In computing a taxpayer's gain or loss on eventual disposition of an asset the focus shifts from the effect of price changes on the particular asset to the effect of price changes on the dollar proceeds the taxpayer receives from sale of the asset, which the taxpayer may spend on other, different assets the prices of which have been affected by inflation.

13.   Is the New York State Bar Committee Report correct in characterizing accelerated depreciation, interest deductions on related indebtedness, and LIFO inventory treatment as tax advantages for income from capital compared with income from other sources?

14.   The New York State Bar Committee Report asserts that, for purposes of determining gain or loss upon disposition of an asset, an inflation adjustment should be made on an asset-by-asset basis, to take account of that particular asset's inflation experience.   Read again with care the example involving Ms. A and Mr. B.

The Committee's description of indexing appears to be flawed, and thereby to exaggerate the difficulties in indexing the basis of capital assets. The Committee appears to have forgotten the purpose of indexing for inflation, which, at least for capital assets sold at gain or loss, is to measure the gain or loss in a manner that accounts for inflation.   Inflation adjustments during the period of ownership are irrelevant.   Thus, A and B each started into their transactions with 1,000 *dollars* and finished up with 1,300 *dollars*.   The question is, how much are the dollars received at time of sale worth in comparison to the dollars expended at time of purchase.   The answer must be the same for A and B.   What the assets were worth at any time during the holding period sheds no light on the problem.

15.   The Contract with America Tax Relief Act of 1995, in the form in which it passed the House of Representatives, contained a provision for indexing the basis of assets for purposes of computing gain (but not loss). The adjustment was based on quarterly changes in the Gross Domestic Product (GDP) deflator.   The bill applied only to assets acquired after 1994. The indexed assets were common stock of C corporations and tangible property, including both capital assets and property used in trade or business.   Benefits flowed through to the owners of S corporations, partnerships, and common trust funds.   To be eligible,   assets must have been held for at least three years.

No adjustments were provided for the basis of debt obligations, and there were no offsets against indexing benefits when the taxpayer's eligible assets were debt financed.   Indexing benefits were not made available to C corporations, perhaps because gain on sale of their common stock was eligible for indexing.   This is puzzling, however,   because C corporations are taxpayers in their own right.

C. INFLATION AND DEBT

Most discussion of the tax effect of inflation has centered on overstatement of profit upon sale of assets. In addition, there is concern over the failure of depreciation reserves to cover the cost of replacement assets. Surprisingly little attention is paid to the failure of the income tax to reflect gain or loss on repayment of indebtedness. The two excerpts of this subchapter address this almost-forgotten aspect of the problem.

The 1984 Treasury I proposal, in addition to indexing gains on sale of assets, treated the impact of inflation on debt as a separate issue. Treasury I, while not treating borrowers as having income as a result of inflation, did reduce deductible interest payments by a price inflation adjustment and excluded corresponding amounts from the interest income of creditors.

Indexing to correct the measurement of income in debt transactions is complex. To some degree the market for debt instruments adjusts for anticipated inflation and its tax consequences through higher interest rates. Furthermore, it is unlikely that denial of a portion of interest deductions, as in the Treasury I proposal, would be readily accepted, and treating debt satisfaction in cheaper dollars as creating income would be even less popular. Professor Durst's article discusses the effects of inflation on borrowing transactions and relates it to the Treasury I proposal.

REPORT ON TAX REFORM FOR FAIRNESS, SIMPLICITY, AND ECONOMIC GROWTH ["Treasury I"]
Vol. 2, pp. 190-197 (1984)

Reasons for Change

Over time inflation erodes the value of a creditor's claim for repayment of an indebtedness with a fixed principal amount, and the debtor's liability to repay principal is correspondingly reduced. Debtors and creditors routinely take account of the anticipated effects of inflation on a lending transaction by adjusting the rate of interest charged. Thus, nominal interest rates typically include an inflation component which compensates the lender for the anticipated reduction in the real value of an obligation of a fixed dollar amount; as to the borrower, this payment is an offsetting charge for the inflationary reduction in the value of the principal amount of the borrowing.

Because the inflation component of nominal interest payments is, in effect, a repayment of principal, the current treatment of nominal interest payments as fully deductible by the debtor and fully taxable to the creditor mismeasures the income of each. These inaccuracies in the measurement of income distort a variety of investment decisions, greatly increasing the significance of tax considerations in such matters as the allocation of investment funds between debt and equity and between long-term and short-term financing. Moreover, in a progressive tax system, overstatement of interest expense and income accentuates the existing incentive for lower tax-bracket taxpayers (including tax-exempt institutions) to be net creditors and higher tax-bracket taxpayers to be net borrowers. This so-called "clientele effect" occurs because the tax savings from interest deductions is greater for high-bracket borrowers than is the increased tax liability from interest income to low-bracket lenders. This clientele effect is aggravated during times of high inflation and corresponding high nominal interest rates.

The failure of the current tax system to recognize and measure the inflation component of nominal interest payments also accentuates the economic effects of variable inflation on debtors and creditors. If the rate of inflation increases unexpectedly, a creditor with fixed-interest indebtedness suffers an economic loss, and the debtor has a corresponding economic gain. These changes in economic position are compounded by the treatment of interest under current law, since the entire amount of nominal interest payments remains deductible or includible in income regardless of changes in the inflation rate. The resulting mismeasurement of income in an economy with variable inflation spawns economic uncertainty. Such uncertainty likely contributes to reduced levels of savings, investment and risk-taking.

Finally, the overstatement of interest under current law encourages borrowing for investments in which income is tax exempt or tax deferred. For example, the investment of borrowed funds in capital assets produces a current deduction for interest expense but no realization of the increase in value of the capital asset until its sale or disposition. This mismatching of income and expense from related transactions understates current income and thus permits the deferral of tax. Overstatement of interest expense thus increases the extent to which debt-financed tax shelter investments can be used to offset taxable income from other sources.

Proposal

Interest would be indexed for tax purposes by excluding a fractional amount of interest receipts from income and denying a deduction for a corresponding fraction of interest payments. For example, with a fractional exclusion rate of 25 percent, taxpayers would include in income only 75 percent of otherwise taxable interest receipts and deduct only 75 percent of otherwise deductible interest payments. The fractional exclusion rate would be based on the annual inflation rate, as explained below.

In general, the proposal would apply the fractional exclusion rate to a taxpayer's net interest income or net interest expense, subject to the following exceptions. First, an individual would deduct any mortgage interest on indebtedness secured by or allocable to his or her principal residence. Qualifying mortgage indebtedness for this purpose could not exceed the fair market value of the principal residence. Next, an individual would net aggregate gross interest expenses (excluding home mortgage interest) against aggregate gross interest income (excluding tax-exempt interest). An individual with net interest expense would apply the fractional exclusion rate to the amount of interest expense. * * * An individual with net interest income would apply the fractional exclusion rate to such net interest income. Interest income, after reduction by the fractional rate would be includible in income.

All of a corporation's interest income and expense would be subject to the fractional exclusions. Interest incurred by a partnership or other pass-through entity would be treated as incurred by the partner or other person to whom the payments are allocable.

Interest received by a partnership or other pass-through entity would be treated as received by the partner or other person reporting such payments.

Tax-favored retirement plans, such as an individual retirement account or qualified pension plan, which earn interest income would not be able to pass on the benefit of the fractional exclusion to the plan beneficiaries. Thus, the fractional exclusion rate could not be claimed with respect to distributions from tax-favored retirement plans.   * * *

The fractional exclusion rate would be modified annually to reflect changes in the rate of inflation, as measured by the Bureau of Labor Statistics' Consumer Price Index.   The proposed relationship between fractional exclusion rates and inflation rates is set forth in Table 1.   The proposed relationship set forth in Table 1 is based on an assumption of a constant six percent real, before-tax interest rate. Assumption of lower real interest rates would result in higher exclusion rates for any given inflation rate. The fractional exclusion rate for a taxpayer that uses a functional currency other than the U.S. dollar should be based on the inflation rate in the foreign currency.

The proposal would not alter the current law definition of interest. The current law rules which impute interest income in certain transactions would also be retained.
        * * *

Analysis
Indexing Interest Rather than Principal

An ideal measure of real economic income for tax purposes would recognize the inflationary reduction in principal on a loan as creating loss for the creditor and income for the debtor on an annual basis. That ideal system departs from the realization doctrine of current law, however, under which mere changes in the value of an asset, including a debt instrument, do not trigger income or loss.   Abandonment of the realization doctrine in this context would introduce substantial costs in complexity and recordkeeping.

Inflation's impact on indebtedness may be indirectly accounted for, however, without departing from the realization doctrine. Instead of computing inflationary gain or loss on principal, the effects of inflation can be approximated by indexing interest payments and receipts through application of the proposed fractional exclusion rate.

Table 1
Fractional Exclusion Rule Rate

InflationRate (Percent)	Fractional Exclusion Rates (Percent) 1/
0	0
1	14
2	25
3	33
4	40
5	45
6	50
7	54
8	57
9	60
10	62
11	65
12	67

Office of the Secretary of the Treasury   November 30, 1984
    Office of Tax Analysis

1/ Fractional exclusion rate is determined by assuming a constant, six percent real interest rate (rate of return).

For example, A borrows $100 from B on January 1, agreeing to pay back the principal plus ten percent interest on December 31. Over the course of the year, there is four percent inflation and the real, pre-tax rate of return is six percent. On December 31, A satisfies its indebtedness by repaying the $100 principal and $10 in interest. B's receipt of the $100 in principal actually represents a loss of $4 in real purchasing power. B's receipt of $10 in nominal interest, however, actually represents a $6 real return on the loan, plus a $4 inflationary component which offsets the reduction in the value of the $100 principal. Thus, in this example, a fractional exclusion rate of 40 percent would be appropriate.

The example demonstrates that, in theory, the effects of inflation on indebtedness may be reflected for tax purposes either by indexing principal or indexing interest. Indexing interest retains the realization rules of current law, and is a much more administrable system.

Determining the Fractional Exclusion Rate

In a world with but one nominal interest rate, real interest income and expense would be accurately measured by a fractional exclusion rate equal to the ratio of the inflation rate to the nominal interest rate. With such an exclusion rate, the excluded interest payments and receipts would correspond to the inflationary component of nominal interest.

The proposal's single fractional exclusion rate for each inflation rate obviously oversimplifies the relationships between inflation and nominal interest rates in a diverse economy. The real rate of return earned on indebtedness will differ from lender to lender. The proposal's economy-wide fractional exclusion rate, however, allows a more accurate measurement of real economic income than does current law, which implicitly provides a zero fractional exclusion rate for all interest.

Effects on Nominal Interest Rates

The proposal would likely result in lower nominal interest rates than would prevail under current law for any given set of economic conditions. For any expected inflation rate, lenders would not demand as high an inflation premium since the inflation component of nominal interest receipts would not be taxed. Similarly, borrowers would be less willing to pay a high inflation premium, since the inflation component of nominal interest payments would not be tax deductible. Accordingly, nominal interest rates would likely fall, relative to levels that would prevail under current law for any given economic conditions. * * *

The proposal also likely would result in reduced volatility of interest rates with respect to changes in inflation. Under the proposal, a change in inflation should induce a smaller change in nominal rates than would occur under current law.

Effects of the Exceptions to Fractional Exclusion Rate

The proposal would not apply the fractional exclusion rate to all deductible interest payments, resulting in some asymmetric treatment of borrowers and lenders. Homeowners would be permitted full deduction of mortgage interest on a principal residence, while mortgagees would be entitled to apply the fractional exclusion rate to interest received on home mortgages. All individuals would be allowed full deduction (without indexing) of the first $5,000 of other net interest expense. Although these exceptions depart from theoretical symmetry for all interest payments and receipts, their retention facilitates the transition from an unindexed to an indexed tax system. The exception for home mortgages, however, would create an incentive for taxpayers both to mortgage the existing equity in their homes, and to disguise consumer, investment or business indebtedness

as increases in home mortgages. These opportunities for tax arbitrage present serious revenue concerns, and it may be necessary to develop strict rules to prevent such schemes from circumventing the intent of the exception.
   * * *

Interaction with Other Proposals

Indexing interest receipts and payments is consistent with the Treasury Department proposals relating to inflation indexing for capital gains, RCRS property and inventories. * * *

INFLATION AND THE TAX CODE: GUIDELINES FOR POLICYMAKING
Michael C. Durst[*]
73 Minn. L. Rev. 1217, 1251-56 (1989)

The Basic Effects of Inflation on the Tax Burdens of Lenders and Borrowers[117]

Consider first the very simple situation of a person, whether or not an asset holder, who borrows $100 for a period of one year. In the absence of anticipated inflation, the lender will charge the borrower annual interest equivalent to the lender's "time value of money"—the price the lender will demand for forgoing alternative uses of the borrowed funds during the year. For example, in the absence of anticipated inflation, the annual interest rate charged to a reasonably creditworthy borrower might amount to five percent.

Adding inflation to the equation complicates the picture. The lender will demand, in addition to compensation for the time value of money, compensation for the erosion that inflation will cause in the value of the borrower's repayment obligation during the course of the year. If inflation occurs during the year at an annual rate of ten percent, the real value of the borrower's repayment obligation would shrink at the rate of ten percent during the year, a result that would enrich the borrower at the expense of the lender. To compensate for this enrichment and to make the lender "whole," the parties must find some way of effectively increasing the amount of the repayment obligation during the year.

To accomplish this adjustment in practice, lenders commonly require that interest payments include compensation for the time value of money (as well as for any risk of default), and an additional amount designed to compensate for the erosion of the value of the loan principal anticipated from inflation. Thus, in the above example, if the parties expected inflation to occur at a rate of ten percent per year, the borrower would be responsible for interest not of five but of fifteen percent: five percent to compensate the lender for the time value of money, plus ten percent to compensate the lender

---

[*]. At time of original publication, Associate Professor, Notre Dame Law School.

117. The discussion in this subsection follows, in substance, the analysis in 1 U.S. TREASURY DEP'T, TAX REFORM FOR FAIRNESS, SIMPLICITY, AND ECONOMIC GROWTH (1984) [hereinafter U.S. TREASURY DEP'T], at 77, and 2 *id.* at 193-200.

for the erosion in the value of the borrower's repayment obligation. Interest thus commonly includes two components: a "real" component designed to compensate the lender for the time value of money and for bearing any risk of nonpayment, and an "inflation" component designed to offset the effects of inflation on the value of the principal.

To measure net income properly under an accretion-model tax system, Congress should permit a borrower who uses loan proceeds for income-producing purposes to deduct the true economic cost of maintaining the loan. In periods of inflation, the borrower's economic cost of maintaining the loan is the *difference* between the borrower's total interest expense (including both the time value of money and inflation components of interest, as well as any risk premium charged by the lender) and the economic benefit the borrower receives from the erosion of the real value of the repayment obligation. Thus, under a pure accretion system, if Congress permitted the borrower of a loan for income-producing purposes to deduct in full all interest paid on the loan, Congress also should require the borrower to include in gross income the amount by which inflation lowers the real value of the borrower's repayment obligation.

The proper tax treatment of the lender, under an accretion-model system, mirrors that of the borrower. Congress should require the lender to include in gross income all interest payments received from the borrower. In addition, as the borrower receives an economic benefit from inflation's erosion of the real value of the repayment obligation, the lender suffers an economic detriment. Congress should permit the lender to deduct the amount of this detriment.

In actual operation, the tax laws depart radically from the accretion model in their treatment of debt. Although the tax code does not include in gross income the economic benefit the borrower enjoys from the erosion in the value of the repayment obligation, the Code generally does allow the taxpayer to deduct the entire amount of interest payments made, including the inflation premium. As a result, the borrower can deduct inflation-related costs without paying an offsetting tax on inflation-related benefits. Conversely, the lender must include all interest payments in gross income, but does not receive any deduction for inflation's erosion of the value of the repayment obligation.

These imperfections in the tax treatment of debt would have no significant consequences if the borrower and lender shared the same marginal tax rate. The Code's undertaxing of the borrower as a result of inflation then would match precisely the overtaxing of the lender. In a competitive market for loans, lenders would pass their tax costs to borrowers in the form of additional interest, so that the cost of borrowing would be the same as it would be under a tax system that adjusted both interest deductions and receipts for inflation. The borrower and lender would be left in the same economic positions they would occupy if the Code conformed to the accretion model.

Borrowers and lenders, however, often do not face the same marginal tax rates. In many loan transactions, the lender faces an unusually low marginal rate or is entirely tax-exempt. Thus, in many instances, the borrower's tax advantage from deducting the inflation component of interest will not match the corresponding tax detriment to the lender and inflation will result in an overall tax reduction.

In keeping with Treasury I's policy of adhering closely to the accretion model, the proposal would have implemented for the first time a system of explicit indexation for debt. On grounds of feasibility, Treasury I rejected the theoretically exact approach of computing the outstanding balance of each loan on an annual basis, and of including in the borrower's gross income, and excluding from the lender's gross income, the amount by which inflation had caused the real value of the loan principal to decline during the year. Treasury I instead employed the admittedly rough assumption that the "real" component of interest on long-term debt averages approximately six percent per year, and that interest paid in excess of six percent constitutes an inflation premium.[126] Treasury I would have used this assumption to estimate the proportion of interest payments and receipts during the year that was attributable to inflation.

For example, if the average long-term interest rate in the economy during the year was thirteen percent, Treasury I would have assumed that six percent represented real interest, and seven percent represented an inflation component. Based on this assumption, Treasury I would have permitted borrowers to deduct only six-thirteenths of any interest payments made during the year, and would have excluded from gross income an equivalent proportion of lenders' interest receipts.

The Administration dropped Treasury I's debt-indexation proposal from the Treasury II reform plan, thus rendering interest indexation an early casualty of the legislative process that led to the 1986 Act. In large measure, the failure of the interest indexation proposal resulted from its sheer novelty to many participants in the tax reform process, as well as from opposition from the real estate industry, which relies heavily on debt financing. * * *

A concern over prospective revenue losses also contributed to the rejection of interest indexation in the 1986 Act. A significant portion of interest paid consists of interest on federal government debt. The payer of this interest—the government—is tax-exempt, but the recipients comprise a mixture of taxable and tax-exempt entities. The indexation plan's reduction

---

126. 2 U.S. TREASURY DEP'T, *supra* note 117, at 194-98. "The formula's use of 6 percent—a rate that is high relative to historical real interest rates—was chosen to err on the side of a smaller than appropriate disallowance of interest deductions (although this decision also implied a relatively small interest income exclusion)." McLure & Zodrow, *Treasury I and the Tax Reform Act of 1986: The Economics and Politics of Tax Reform*, 1 J. ECON. PERSP. 37, 52 (1987).

of interest deductions therefore would not have raised tax revenue from this interest, but the exclusion from gross income of a portion of receipts would have reduced tax revenue.   As the principal author of Treasury I subsequently has pointed out, the net effect on government revenues probably would have been limited, because the partial exclusion from gross income of receipts probably would have permitted the government to lower the rate of interest paid on its debt.   Despite this argument, however, revenue concerns apparently helped to account for the rejection of Treasury I's interest indexation proposals.

     * * *

Notes and Questions

16. Indexing bases to measure gain for tax purposes is complex, perhaps too complex to use to respond to moderate inflation.   How high should inflation be in order to justify indexing?

17. In a portion of his article not excerpted, Professor Durst proposed a "safety-valve" inflation adjustment to be allowed in computing depreciation allowances.   The basis for Professor Durst's proposal is that Congress had a given level of moderate inflation—Professor Durst argues this was four percent—in mind as one reason for allowing depreciation write-offs that otherwise were too generous to reflect economic depreciation.   Only if inflation significantly exceeded that anticipated amount would any adjustment at all be appropriate:

> The safety value would compensate for the effects of inflation only to the extent that inflation *exceeds* the rate assumed in setting the 1986 Act's depreciation schedules.   Thus, unless inflation accelerates to unforeseen levels, the safety-valve adjustment would have no revenue cost at all.   The safety value would have some revenue cost in periods of high inflation, but the revenue cost very likely would be lower than the costs of other measures that Congress would implement if high inflation were to recur and Congress had not previously set in place protections against its effects.[b]

Professor Durst's safety valve proposal—which he acknowledges to be a "compromise"[c]—is no panacea.   The proposal assumes that the accelerated depreciation schedules adopted by Congress in fact constitute an adequate response to moderate, anticipated levels of inflation.   This is not self-evident.   Moreover, while accelerated depreciation is available to borrowers and non-borrowers alike, Professor Durst's proposal would apply only to borrower-owners of depreciable assets.   Finally, accelerated depreciation does nothing

---

    b. Michael C. Durst, *Inflation and the Tax Code: Guidelines for Policymaking*, 73 MINN. L. REV. 1217, 1266 (1989).
    c. *Id.* at 1267.

to meet the problem of lenders who are repaid in dollars cheapened even by moderate inflation.

18. Note that the Internal Revenue Code contains provisions that limit to some degree the ability of taxpayers to generate current interest deductions that result in mismatching of income and expense. See sections 163(d) and 265(a)(2).

19. In proposing to reduce interest deductions by an inflation quotient, why did Treasury I make an exception for interest on mortgage indebtedness secured by a taxpayer's principal residence?

20. Professor Durst implies that the only difficulty with the failure of the market to produce interest rates that will compensate for the effect of inflation on borrowers and lenders is the overall loss of revenue to the government, a problem that would disappear "if the borrower and lender shared the same marginal tax rate." Do you agree, or would you still be troubled by unfairness in tax treatment of individual borrowers and lenders?

Selected Bibliography

ADVISORY COMMISSION ON INTERGOVERNMENTAL RELATIONS, THE INFLATION TAX: THE CASE FOR INDEXING FEDERAL AND STATE INCOME TAXES (1980).

Brinner, Roger, *Inflation, Deferral and the Neutral Taxation of Capital Gains*, 26 NAT'L TAX J. 565 (1973).

CONGRESSIONAL BUDGET OFFICE, INDEXING CAPITAL GAINS (1990).

Durst, Michael C., *Inflation and the Tax Code: Guidelines for Policymaking*, 73 MINN. L. REV. 1217 (1989).

Engler, Calvin & Mitchell L. Engler, *Taxation of Capital Gains—Let's Be Fair*, 50 TAX NOTES 1303 (1991).

Galvin, Charles O., *Indexing The Internal Revenue Code*, 48 TAX L. REV. 661 (1993).

Halperin, Daniel & C. Eugene Steuerle, *Indexing the Tax System for Inflation*, *in* UNEASY COMPROMISE: PROBLEMS OF A HYBRID INCOME-CONSUMPTION TAX (Henry J. Aaron et al. eds., 1988).

Hoerner, J. Andrew, *Indexing Capital Gains: The British Experience*, 46 TAX NOTES 988 (1990).

INFLATION AND THE INCOME TAX (Henry J. Aaron ed., 1976).

McIntyre, Michael J., *Problems with "Contract" Scheme for Partial Indexing of Nominal Capital Gains*, 70 TAX NOTES 749 (1996).

Mick, Joel, *A Proposal for the Indexation of Debt for Inflation*, 140 U. PA. L. REV. 2051 (1992).

New York State Bar Association, Tax Section Ad Hoc Committee, *Report on Inflation Adjustments to the Basis of Capital Assets*, 48 TAX NOTES 759 (1990).

Note, *Inflation and the Income Tax*, 82 YALE L.J. 716 (1973).

Rosenn, Keith S., *Adjusting Taxation of Business Income for Inflation: Lessons from Brazil and Chile*, 13 TEX. INT'L. L.J. 165 (1978).

Shuldiner, Reed, *Indexing the Tax Code*, 48 TAX L. REV. 537 (1993).

STEUERLE, C. EUGENE, TAXES, LOANS AND INFLATION, chs. 7, 14 (1985) .

U.S. DEP'T OF TREASURY, 2 REPORT ON TAX REFORM FOR FAIRNESS, SIMPLICITY, AND ECONOMIC GROWTH ("Treasury I") 190-97 (1984).

Young, James C., *Every Little Bit Helps: An Analysis of Inflation Adjustments Impacting Individual Taxpayers in 1992*, 52 TAX NOTES 1657 (1991).

PART VI

ENACTING TAX LAW

This book has been concerned with the issue of what particular provisions of tax law *should* be. The book concludes, however, with a single-chapter part that explores how tax law is in fact made and changed. Chapter Seventeen attempts to provide a framework of understanding the legislative process in the tax area. The objective is to describe how present tax provisions came to be and what is involved in changing them. The mechanics of the process are described, as are the constraints imposed by budget consequences. Revenue estimates frequently can make or kill a tax proposal, and the discussion of the revenue estimating process shows that the process itself is imprecise and often lacks objectivity. The Tax Reform Act of 1986 is used to illustrate the factors influencing wholesale tax revision. Finally, the role of lobbying in making tax laws is discussed.

CHAPTER SEVENTEEN

TAXES AND THE LEGISLATIVE PROCESS

The less people know about how sausages and laws are made, the better they'll sleep at night.[a]

A. MECHANICS OF THE TAX LEGISLATIVE PROCESS

To understand the legislative process for enacting (or refusing to enact) tax legislation requires understanding the interplay of the Treasury Department and Congressional staffs. The activities of the two staffs principally concerned are discussed in articles by Kenneth Gideon, former Assistant Secretary of the Treasury for Tax Policy, and Ronald Pearlman, who served as Assistant Secretary of the Treasury for Tax Policy and later as Chief of Staff of the Joint Committee on Taxation.

TAX POLICY AT THE TREASURY DEPARTMENT: A 20-YEAR PERSPECTIVE
Kenneth W. Gideon[*]
57 Tax Notes 889, 889-891 (1992)

The first assistant secretary for tax policy of the Treasury, Stanley Surrey, took office just over 30 years ago. Whether motivated by fear of this innovation or Surrey himself, the Finance Committee demanded Secretary Dillon's pledge always to accompany his new assistant secretary whenever he appeared before that Committee. Since then, incumbents have been allowed to testify alone (although the Surrey arrangement has looked like a fine idea to most of his successors on at least a few occasions during their tenure). Institutional concern for tax policy at Treasury is much older. Joint Committee documents from the 1920s make references to Treasury's tax experts. The tax legislative counsel's position dates back to the 1930s, and a number of assistants to the secretary before 1961 had primary responsibility for tax issues. But the modern form of the Office of Tax Policy dates from Surrey's appointment by President Kennedy.

Initially, the single deputy assistant secretary was an economist and supervised the Office of Tax Analysis (OTA), the cadre of career economists who perform the critical tasks of economic studies and revenue estimating. Later, * * * a second deputy assistant secretary for tax policy was added on

---

a. Otto von Bismarck, *quoted in* George Anastaplo, *Legal Realism, The New Journalism, and* The Brethren, 1983 DUKE L.J. 1045, 1066 n.44.

*. At time of original publication, partner in Fried, Frank, Harris, Shriver, & Jacobson, Washington, D.C.; formerly, Assistant Secretary of Treasury for Tax Policy.

the legal side. These officials and the OTA economists have a fine reporting relationship to the assistant secretary.

In contrast, the lawyers on the tax policy staff report (in long honored tradition and theory) to the general counsel. In fact, they work for the assistant secretary. So long as everyone concerned understands this, the system works well as it has on most occasions over the past 30 years. To avoid such dual allegiance, what is now the International Tax Counsel's Office was initially organized as a group of special assistants to the assistant secretary. With the adoption of the title "international tax counsel" under Ed Cohen's tenure came the dual relationship that had previously prevailed with respect to the tax legislative counsel. The third counsel staff, the Office of the Benefit Tax Counsel, was organized early in my tenure as assistant secretary to meet the needs for a specialized legal staff addressing pension, health, and similar benefit issues.

Relationship to the Secretary

Officially described as the Treasury Department's spokesman on matters of tax policy, the assistant secretary's influence derives from serving as the secretary's principal adviser on tax issues. In contrast to my experience at the IRS, where contacts with the secretary's office outside regular staff meetings were limited and typically concerned issues such as the Service's budget, the assistant secretary is literally "on call" at any time. While technology has eliminated John Connolly's strolls down the hall (now there is a direct, push-button telephone line from the secretary's office that bypasses all other secretaries), the immediate and frequent nature of the contacts have not changed. When not at the office, the secretary's operators (who rival their White House counterparts in the ability to find anyone, anywhere, anytime) can always get the call through.

These ubiquitous contacts—ranging from two-minute phone calls to almost endless briefings or budget sessions—are the transmission system for tax policy concerns into the public policy decisionmaking process. Maintaining such direct access to the secretary and through him to the White House, is critical if the assistant secretary is to be a credible spokesperson within the administration for Treasury and for the administration before the taxwriting committees. Over the years, various proposals have been made to have the assistant secretary report to the secretary through one of the undersecretaries. It's a bad idea. Unless the undersecretary is prepared to function as the assistant secretary (in which case, the proposal amounts to a change in title, not function), regular and direct access must be maintained for the Tax Policy office to do its job.

Legislation

Perhaps no aspect of the work of the Office of Tax Policy has seen more change in the past 20 years than its role in the legislative process. In 1972, the office could look back on a primary role in the initiation and enactment of the Tax Reform Act of 1969. That participation was itself a function of a more compact legislative process in Congress. Chairman Mills headed a Ways and Means Committee of 25 members (compared to 36 today) with no subcommittees. His committee also served as the Committee on Committees and thus controlled committee assignments for the whole House. The Senate Finance Committee had 16 members then as compared to 20 today, and it, too, had no subcommittees. In that era, if the chairman of the Ways and Means Committee and the chairman of the Finance Committee and their staff at the Joint Committee on Taxation concurred with a Treasury proposal, it was virtually an accomplished fact.

Modern practice is very different, in part because there are so many more active participants in the process and, in part, because the politics of the process have become bitter, but more fundamentally because the issue of revenue has moved from an occasional concern of the Congress, usually left to its specialist committees, to a fundamental limitation in all congressional action. Exploring why this occurred would require a paper of its own (although elimination of the automatic revenue dividend that arose from bracket-creep before indexation of the brackets and the changes in congressional staffing after Watergate would be high on any list of causes).

Now there are many more players. Five active technical staffs on the Hill are engaged with any piece of tax legislation (a majority and minority staff for each tax-writing committee in addition to the Joint Committee staff). All are considerably larger now than they were in 1972 (the Treasury staff is larger, too—but Treasury staff growth has not matched congressional staff growth.) In addition, a member of either taxwriting committee is now likely to have a tax technician on their personal staff (who often takes issue with the committee staffs and Treasury). The organization of the tax writing committees into subcommittees has significantly multiplied the number of subjects that can be addressed at any given time (thereby forcing Treasury to devote time to those issues as well). Treasury finds itself, in this environment, one voice among many.

On a broader scale, Treasury and the taxwriting committees have found Congress and other executive departments less willing to cede authority over revenue issues to their expertise. Budgetary constraints drive other congressional committees and executive departments to seek "revenue offsets" for their programs. Deprived of the steadily increasing revenue base provided by bracket creep, the Congressional Budget Committees and the Office of Management and Budget must assert themselves in defining at least the size of revenue requirements to fulfill their budgetary responsibilities.

But Treasury's core legislative roles remain. Treasury remains a critical initiator of tax system revision, even if its ultimate influence on outcomes has diminished because there are more participants and because the politics of the moment from time to time exclude it from the final decisionmaking process. Treasury studies and initiatives have been precursors not only to major tax reform, but to a variety of less sweeping, but significant changes. Treasury views on legislation are always sought and often heeded. Treasury remains the tax system's primary gatekeeper on "member" issues, saying "no" when it needs to be said (often when others are politically unable to do so).[b]

Tax Administration

Organizationally, the relationship between the Office of Tax Policy and the IRS has changed little in the last 20 years. The commissioner and the assistant secretary each report directly to the secretary and not to each other. The precept of leaving individual case matters to the Service while focusing the Tax Policy staff on issues of general guidance remains intact (and indeed was recently strengthened by Treasury's withdrawal from formal participation in the letter ruling process). Both the commissioner and the assistant secretary must approve a regulation and Treasury staff reviews published rulings and revenue procedures.

But, within these bounds, there has been constant experimentation with the goal of making the guidance process work "better." The objective content of "better" has shifted from time to time. Often "better" means faster—issuing guidance as promptly as possible after significant legislation and avoiding long delays between "proposed" and "final" regulations. At other times, "better" has referred to the quality of the guidance. But what constitutes "quality" guidance has itself undergone cyclic variation. When I served as chief counsel from 1981 to 1983, we were urged to provide "meaningful" guidance (which meant answering as many questions as possible rather than providing broad, general rules). Products of the "meaningful guidance" era were criticized for "hyperlexis," bringing on the current era of "simplification." It will be no surprise to find today's products criticized in the future as insufficiently "meaningful."

Issuing guidance faster is unambiguously desirable. The difficulty has been to balance the need for adequate review with the need for speed. From an institutional standpoint, this has led to an evolution from informal "policy" meetings between senior Treasury and IRS officials, which occurred on an "as needed" basis 20 years ago, to the current structure in which senior officials regularly set priorities for guidance projects and make general policy decisions in response to a staff-generated "issues memorandum" at the commencement of a regulation project. This assures that the general form of a regulation is likely to be acceptable to those who must ultimately approve it and prevents the waste of staff time on approaches having little chance of ultimate publication. After a brief interlude of guidance by "notice" (compelled by the need for massive guidance after the 1986 act), Treasury and the IRS have returned to traditional "notice and comment" rulemaking.

---

b. This refers to a long-standing practice in the Ways and Means Committee of occasionally reporting out a bill containing one provision desired by each committee member and accepted by the whole committee with only cursory review. (Eds.)

The long-run desirability of this change may largely depend on whether proposed regulations are in fact made final on a prompt basis.

Charting the boundaries between not interfering in individual cases at the Service and making general policy at Treasury may, however, become a significant issue for future tax policy staffs. Significant individual cases can drive policy results, particularly if they become engraved in stone as Supreme Court decisions. A recent case, *Arkansas Best*, illustrates the difficulty: Although the Supreme Court's decision in *Arkansas Best* was rendered with respect to a quite different set of facts, the language of the decision has proved to be a significant impediment to achieving an appropriate policy solution for liability hedges. A mechanism for better harmonizing the positions taken by government litigators, particularly before the Supreme Court, with policy positions of the Treasury Department would be a welcome development.

Revenue Estimating

Treasury has always made revenue estimates, but the significance of this task changed dramatically with the enactment of the Gramm-Rudman-Hollings budget reforms. Revenue neutrality became a legal requirement, enforceable by across-the-board sequester. As the official administration scorekeeper for revenues, OTA's estimates have become critical determinants of policy in the last decade. Because the revenue estimates have become so much more important, there has been increased focus on the revenue-estimating process.

Over time, the process has changed with both OTA and its Joint Committee counterpart seeking to improve their ability to make "dynamic" estimates (i.e., those that account for changes in taxpayer behavior caused by the proposed change rather than simply measuring the impact of the proposal on the current "static" bases). The most notable example has been in capital gains estimating and that example illustrates the difficulties of attempting to predict changes in behavior.

There has been substantial pressure in recent years to include "feedback" effects in the estimates as well (i.e., to estimate the expansion of the overall economy that would occur if a particular proposal were enacted). Thus far, "feedback" estimates have been resisted because the estimators doubt that economic measurements of the overall economy are sufficiently accurate to permit reasonable quantification of such impacts and because there is doubt that growth from a proposal can be distinguished from sector shifts involving little or no overall change in the economy. On a more practical level, "feedback" estimates could undermine budget discipline by providing pork barrel proponents with the argument that the cost of their projects should be offset by the "growth" they will produce.

Studies

Some of Treasury's best work over the past 20 years has arisen from integrating its economic and legal staffs to produce studies. Some are legendary: for examples *Blueprints* and the 1984 tax reform study.[c] But the range of studies has been very wide and their impact as precursors of legislative change is apparent. The principal change over the last 20 years has been the increasing tendency of Congress to award mandated studies as consolation prizes to disappointed legislative hopefuls. Good and worthwhile studies typically require substantial staff effort and a great deal of time (often two to three years). They cannot be mass produced and ought not to be trivialized.

Tax Treaties

The most noticeable change since 1972 with respect to treaties has been the heightened concern about treaty abuse. This concern has led to both legislative action and treaty renegotiations to limit treaty shopping and, in a few notable cases, to treaty terminations. The pace of substantive law legislative change has also created an environment in which treaty modernization, either through the negotiation of protocols or complete renegotiation (e.g., the German treaty), now consumes as much or more of the staff's time than the negotiation of new conventions. While the treaty process has benefited from the talents of a succession of talented lawyers on the ITC [International Tax Counsel] staff over the past 20 years, the senior Treasury economists who work in the treaty area have been in place during the entire period since 1972 and have furnished an invaluable store of knowledge, experience, and institutional memory.

Staffing

The professional staff of the Office of Tax Policy is approximately 30 percent larger today than it was in 1972. Career tenure for the economic staff is in transition. In 1972, most OTA professionals expected to make a career of government service. Significantly more attractive financial opportunities in the private sector have led to higher turnover in OTA in recent years and may in time cause recruiting for the OTA staff to more closely resemble recruiting for the legal staff. As was true in 1972, the legal staff is recruited by finding the best young lawyers in the country and attempting to lure them to Treasury for a two- to three-year tour. Unlike 1972, the invitation now almost invariably requires financial sacrifice since Treasury pay scales seldom allow the Office to match outside compensation.

* * *

---

c. U.S. DEP'T OF TREASURY, BLUEPRINTS FOR BASIC TAX REFORM (1977); U.S. DEP'T OF TREASURY, REPORT ON TAX REFORM FOR FAIRNESS, SIMPLICITY, AND ECONOMIC GROWTH (1984) ("Treasury I"). Treasury I was the study that formed the basis for the Tax Reform Act of 1986. (Eds.)

THE TAX LEGISLATIVE PROCESS: 1972-1992
Ronald A. Pearlman[*]
57 Tax Notes 939, 939-43 (1992)

Since 1972, five major pieces of tax legislation have been enacted, including the Tax Reform Act of 1986, which has been characterized as the most significant reform in the history of the income tax. In addition, at least 16 other pieces of tax legislation of varying significance have been adopted. Indeed, beginning with 1975, tax legislation has been enacted in every year through 1992. It is not surprising, therefore, that taxpayers, as well as tax professionals both within and outside government, have been overwhelmed by the thousands of changes in the law. It also should not be surprising that an 18-year period of annual tax legislation has resulted in considerable instability in the law.

There are a number of possible explanations for the explosion in the volume and complexity of tax legislation. To an important extent, it may be attributable to changes in the tax legislative process.   The following commentary focuses on several of the more significant changes in the process since 1972. They are: (1) the emergence of the budget deficit as an issue of intense public debate and the changes since the mid-1970s in the federal budget process; (2) changes in the size and organization of the taxwriting committees and the size, sophistication, and responsibilities of the various congressional tax staffs; and (3) at least since 1986, the diminution in the role of the Treasury Department in the tax legislative process.

The Deficit and the Budget Process

The fiscal year 1972 budget deficit was $ 23.4 billion. Although not very large when compared to $ 290.2 billion for fiscal year 1992, the fact of increasing annual budget deficits concerned congressional budget policymakers in the 1970s and particularly impacted the tax legislative process in the 1980s.[6] In fact, the deficit and changes in the budget process beginning in 1974 may well be the two developments that have resulted in a tax legislative process today that is so different than that of the early 1970s.

Three budget-related developments have influenced the tax legislative process: (1) changes in the budget process itself; (2) the refusal of the Reagan and Bush administrations to support tax-rate increases but a willingness to agree to loophole closures, base broadeners, and certain other "indirect" revenue increases; and (3) the indexing of tax brackets and personal exemptions in 1981, thereby eliminating the annual increase in federal revenues resulting from bracket creep.   * * * [M]uch of the tax

---

[*]. At time of original publication, partner in Covington & Burling, Washington, D.C.; formerly, Assistant Secretary of Treasury for Tax Policy; formerly, Chief of Staff of Joint Committee on Taxation.

6. The first budget reconciliation legislation was enacted as the Omnibus Reconciliation Act of 1980, Pub. L. No. 96-499, 94 Stat. 2599 (1980).

legislation of the 1970s was designed, at least in part, to offset bracket creep.[9]

Since 1972, three major pieces of budget legislation have been enacted: the Budget Act of 1974, the Gramm-Rudman-Hollings enforcement mechanisms,[11] and the expenditure caps and pay-as-you-go enforcement feature of the 1990 Budget Act. The impact on the tax legislative process, particularly during the 1980s, of the budget deficit and changes in the budget process is reflected in at least four developments during this period. First, in recent years, the budget process frequently has required the taxwriting committees to adopt revenue-increasing tax legislation in response to mandated budget reconciliation resolutions without regard to whether members of the committees thought that changes in the tax law were appropriate either as a matter of policy or timing.[13]

The second effect on tax legislation has been the relatively recent emergence of the concept of revenue neutrality. The Treasury Department adopted revenue neutrality as one of the benchmarks of its 1984 tax reform recommendations to the president as a means of constraining a process that easily could have turned into a massive deficit increasing exercise. President Reagan also adopted this standard in his 1985 tax reform recommendations to Congress and, since then, revenue neutrality has been honored informally as a legislative constraint by the taxwriting committees. A revenue neutrality restriction was formalized in the "pay-as-you-go" provisions of the 1990 Budget Act.

The revenue-neutrality constraint has been a double-edged sword. It has limited the number and size of revenue-losing changes in the tax law that might have further increased the deficit or represented bad tax policy. However, it also has restricted the ability to enact revenue-losing proposals that were considered to be economically sound or were designed merely to correct substantive defects in existing law. Revenue neutrality also has complicated the design of new substantive tax law changes, even those intended to increase revenues. This has been true particularly when such initiatives were included in a revenue-neutral tax package of revenue losers and revenue raisers as often occurred in the late 1980s. When a new proposal that was part of such a package initially was represented as raising a certain amount of revenue, it became very difficult to change the proposal during the course of the legislative process in response to public comment if the proposed change reduced the revenue raising potential of the proposal. This frequently was the case even if the change was intended merely to make

9. Leonard, "Perspectives on the Tax Legislative Process," 38 *Tax Notes* 969, 971-72 (1988).

11. Balanced Budget and Emergency Deficit Control Act of 1985, Pub. L. No. 99-177, 99 Stat. 1037, section 200, et seq. (1985).

13. The 1974 Budget Act required the Congress to adopt annual budget reconciliation resolutions that directed the taxwriting committees to increase revenues by specified dollar amounts.

the proposal more administrable or to provide appropriate transition relief. As a result, the ultimate substantive design of revenue proposals enacted during this period, even when grounded in sound tax policy, has been distorted by the revenue neutrality constraint.

The third effect of the current budget process on the development of tax legislation is the importance now attached to revenue estimates. In 1972, revenue estimates were more or less an afterthought, considered after policy decisions were made. The relative unimportance of revenue estimates at the time is evidenced by the minor resources devoted to revenue estimates by the Joint Committee on Taxation, Congress' official revenue estimator. In 1972, the Joint Committee employed three revenue estimators and one revenue analyst. The Joint Committee estimators did not have access to a computer model and their data sources were very limited. (Treasury estimators had been using a computerized individual tax model since the mid-1960s.) Today, there are 14 revenue estimators and four computer analysts on the Joint Committee revenue estimating staff. Moreover, the estimating process is dependent on a greatly expanded data base and on sophisticated computer analyses. The revenue estimating staff serving in Treasury's Office of Tax Analysis (OTA) in the early 1970s was larger than that of the Joint Committee (in 1972, seven estimators and three statisticians) in large part because OTA had the responsibility to estimate receipts for budgeting purposes. However, even at Treasury, there has been a rather substantial growth in the size of the estimating staff. Today, there are 14 revenue estimators and 10 computer modeling specialists on the OTA staff.

A fourth outgrowth of changes in the budget process is the increase in the number of people on Capitol Hill who are indirectly involved in the tax legislative process. The 1974 Budget Act created the House and Senate Budget Committees and the Congressional Budget Office (CBO). The two budget committees are responsible for developing and implementing the annual congressional budget resolution and, therefore, have a direct interest in revenue legislation and an ability to influence the tax legislative process through revenue-raising reconciliation instructions. It also has become increasingly common for individual members of the budget committees to put forth specific tax legislative proposals. In addition, as an adjunct to CBO's responsibility to estimate annual budget receipts and the revenue effects of certain nonincome tax legislative proposals, its staff of 19 professional tax policy analysts have assumed an active role in the tax policy process through the publication of CBO's annual compendium of revenue options[17] and other periodic tax policy analyses.[18] Although these budget-related organizations

---

17. *See, e.g., Reducing the Deficit: Spending and Revenue Options* (Congressional Budget Office, 1992).

18. *See, e.g., The Changing Distribution of Federal Taxes: 1975-1990* (Congressional Budget Office, 1987) and *The Changing Distribution of Federal Taxes: A Closer Look at 1980* (Congressional Budget Office, 1988).

have played a relatively modest role in effecting specific substantive changes in the tax law when compared to the role of the taxwriting committees and the traditional congressional tax staffs, their role in the budget process has enabled them to broadly influence the tax debate.

Changes in the Size and Composition of the Taxwriting Committees and Congressional Tax Staffs

The most dramatic changes since 1972 relating to people involved in the tax legislative process are reflected in the increased size of the taxwriting committees, the creation of subcommittees, the growth and increased prominence of the taxwriting committee professional tax staffs, and the employment of tax legislative assistants on the taxwriting committee members' personal staffs.

In 1972, the Ways and Means Committee was comprised of 24 members. Today, the committee is almost 50 percent larger with a membership of 35. The Senate Finance Committee also has increased in size since 1972 (from 16 to 20 members), but not as dramatically as the Ways and Means Committee. In 1972, neither the Ways and Means Committee nor the Finance Committee had subcommittees.[19] In late 1974, the Ways and Means Committee formed the Oversight Subcommittee and, in 1977, the Miscellaneous Revenue Measures Subcommittee, the predecessor to the present Select Revenue Measures Subcommittee. The Finance Committee first organized a Subcommittee on Administration of the Internal Revenue Code in 1975 and the Subcommittee on Taxation and Debt Management in 1977. Currently, among its eight subcommittees, two are primarily tax related, the Subcommittee on Taxation and the Subcommittee on Private Retirement Plans and Oversight of the IRS. * * * [T]he Ways and Means subcommittees, and particularly the Oversight Subcommittee, have played important roles in initiating certain tax legislation. The Finance Committee subcommittees, on the other hand, have no legislative authority and no separate staffs and, therefore, have played a less important role.

In examining the relative roles of the congressional tax staffs, it is clear that in 1972, the Joint Committee on Taxation was dominant both in terms of size and influence and that Dr. Lawrence Woodworth, the Joint Committee Chief of Staff since 1964, was the most influential tax staff member on Capitol Hill. The Joint Committee staff was comprised of 19 professional members, excluding the lawyers responsible for refund cases within the committee's jurisdiction. The Ways and Means Committee tax staff, on the other hand, was comprised of two individuals on the majority side and one on the minority side, and the Finance Committee tax staff was comprised of two individuals who served both the majority and minority members of the committee. Substantive responsibility for the design of tax legislative

---

19. The Ways and Means Committee previously had subcommittees until the early 1960s, when they were disbanded until the mid-1970s.

proposals and implementation of the committees' tax policy decisions rested almost exclusively with the staff of the Joint Committee and the House and Senate Legislative Counsel. As late as 1974, for example, the Ways and Means Committee tax staff did not attend legislative drafting sessions.

Although the Joint Committee staff has expanded during the 21-year period and presently numbers 51 professionals, the growth and increased influence of the taxwriting committee staffs and the employment of tax legislative assistants on the personal staffs of the members of the taxwriting committees are most noteworthy. Today, the Ways and Means Committee majority tax staff is comprised of eight individuals, and there are five professional members of the minority tax staff. In addition, the Ways and Means Oversight Subcommittee majority staff has seven professional members, and the minority staff has one professional member. The Finance Committee tax staff also has increased in size since the early 1970s. Today, the Democratic [majority] staff is comprised of seven individuals and the Republican [minority] staff, of four individuals.

In 1972, the taxwriting committee members did not employ tax legislative assistants on their personal staffs. Since the early 1980s, however, most Ways and Means Committee members have employed individuals who devote most of their time to tax matters,[20] and since the beginning of the 101st Congress, a portion of the salaries of committee members' tax legislative assistants has been paid out of the Ways and Means Committee budget, thereby enabling the committee members to hire more experienced individuals. Members of the Finance Committee began employing specialized personal staff members in 1977, after Senators received budget authority to increase the size of their personal staffs. Today, the House and Senate taxwriting committee members' legislative assistants often are directly involved in the development of legislation of particular interest to the members for whom they work. These legislative assistants look to, and expect support from, the taxwriting committee and Joint Committee staffs in implementing the members' objectives.

The General Accounting Office (GAO) and the Congressional Research Service (CRS) are not directly involved in the development of tax legislation but are indirectly involved in the tax policy process. The Tax Policy and Administration Division of GAO undertakes a large number of tax studies at the request of members of Congress, the taxwriting committees, and the congressional tax staffs and serves as a major investigative and data resource. Presently, the Division employs 75 professionals based both in Washington and in other locations; in 1972, the Division was not even in existence. The CRS employs approximately 20 economists and lawyers in its American Law and Economics Divisions (as compared to approximately five

---

20. Previously, on occasion, several Ways and Means Committee members would pool resources to employ a professional tax legislative assistant.

individuals in the early 1970s). These individuals, who are tax specialists, serve as legal and policy resources to members of Congress and regularly publish analyses of important current tax policy topics.

The increase in the size of the taxwriting committees, particularly on the House side, and the existence of subcommittees has resulted in a somewhat increased democratization of the committee legislative process during the past 21 years, although it would be inaccurate to understate the continued substantial influence of the committee chairmen. Compared to 1972, when the staff of the Joint Committee dominated the scene, the expanded size and increased quality of the taxwriting committee tax staffs, as well as the addition of tax legislative assistants on the committee members' personal staffs, has significantly increased the number of people involved in the development of tax legislation and has served to diffuse the decisionmaking process at the staff level. Some have suggested that the increases in the size of the taxwriting committees and the number of congressional tax staff have themselves contributed to the increased volume of tax legislation on the theory that the job of a legislature is to legislate.

Role of the Administration and the Treasury Department

The administrations of five presidents have had the opportunity to influence federal tax policy during the past 21 years. Surely, President Reagan's 1981 tax reduction initiatives and his 1985 tax reform initiatives put him at the forefront during this period in influencing the course of federal budget and tax policy.

The Treasury Department's Office of Tax Policy (OTP) has served as the administration's tax policy professional staff throughout the period. In 1972, the OTP was comprised of approximately 73 professionals; today, the professional staff, including members of the Office of Tax Analysis, numbers 93. It would be inaccurate to attribute the increase in the size of the OTP staff solely to its legislative responsibilities because a large part of the office's work relates to, among other things, regulatory and other interpretative responsibilities, the administration of the U.S. tax treaty network, and other international tax policy matters. However, there have been times during the past 21 years when pending tax legislation was the staff's highest priority and strained the office's resources.

One aspect of the structure of the Treasury Department generally, and of the OTP specifically, that largely goes unnoticed has been the relative lack of continuity, particularly when compared to the congressional tax leadership and tax staffs. Since 1972, no secretary of the Treasury has served more than four years, whereas the chairmen of the taxwriting committees typically have served for longer periods. For example, Wilbur Mills served as chairman of the Ways and Means Committee for 19 years and Dan Rostenkowski, the current chairman, is completing his twelfth year. On the

Senate side, Russell Long chaired the Finance Committee for 14 years and Lloyd Bentsen, the current chairman, is completing his sixth year.[d]

At the staff level, it is not uncommon to find individuals on the congressional staffs who have been there for 10 or more years, and there is a relatively large number who have served from five to 10 years. In contrast, the tenure of the lawyers in the OTP typically is two to four years. Although traditionally, there has been a greater degree of longevity and, thus, continuity within the Office of Tax Analysis, comprised of the OTP's economists, even here the turnover has increased during this period.

The lack of continuity both at the secretarial level and within the OTP, particularly among the lawyers who are active in the legislative process, puts Treasury at a disadvantage when dealing with the committee leadership and congressional staff. It simply is not possible to understand the inner workings of the legislative process and establish the necessary interpersonal relationships on Capitol Hill during a relatively brief tenure. In addition, many of the legislative initiatives that are active at any point in time have been considered previously. Yet, anyone new to the tax legislative process, whether at Treasury or on Capitol Hill, may not be familiar with recent history, let alone understand what happened five years ago.

     * * *

Notes and Questions

1.   The Joint Committee on Taxation (JCT) was the first joint Congressional Committee established on a permanent basis with a professional staff. The Joint Congressional Budget Committee was modeled after it.

The JCT staff is not duplicative of the staffs of the Ways and Means Committee and the Finance Committee. Historically, the JCT staff has provided the advantage of continuity, because it did not change when control of Congress shifted from one party to the other. The JCT staff provides a different sort of continuity by following revenue bills from the House to the Senate. By custom, JCT staff members have been left to develop a level of professionalism and expertise that could not be duplicated in the staff of a House or Senate committee, who are more closely tied to the political fortunes of the chair.

2.   Both the Tax Legislative Counsel (TLC) and the JCT have functions in addition to tax legislation, but these do not detract from the performance of legislative duties. The TLC staff reviews drafts of Treasury Regulations which ordinarily are written in the Internal Revenue Service. This review gives the TLC staff a broader perspective on tax issues. (Unfortunately,

---

d. Representative Rostenkowski and Senator Bentsen are no longer in Congress. A chairman's tenure is dependent, among other things, upon his party continuing in the majority. (Eds.)

attention to tax legislative issues often results in inordinate delays in reviewing and clearing regulations.)

The JCT reviews large tax refunds before they are paid by the Revenue Service. While this requires final review by the Chief of Staff, most of the refund review work is carried out by a separate division of the staff that does not ordinarily work on legislation.

3. The elimination of "bracket creep" is described in Chapter Sixteen. Mr. Gideon makes an important point concerning the political impact of adjusting tax brackets to reflect changes in price levels. Because indexing deprives the government of automatic "real" tax increases caused by inflation, Congress no longer has the periodic opportunity to enact politically easy tax cuts. This, in turn, has heightened the pressure on Congress to cut expenditures or increase taxes.

4. The Treasury's influence on tax legislation appears to have lessened in the past 25 years or so. Why?

B. THE ROLE OF BUDGET CONSTRAINTS AND REVENUE ESTIMATES

Since enactment of the budget-busting 1981 revenue act, tax legislation has been under severe revenue constraints. There is pervasive public concern with the budget deficit and the mounting public debt. Congress now operates under a self-imposed restriction that requires revenue-losing tax legislation to be accompanied by offsetting estimated revenue increases or expenditure reductions. Revenue estimates have acquired enormous importance. In the excerpts in Subchapter A, both Messrs. Gideon and Pearlman emphasized the role of budget constraints.

Revenue estimating is not an exact science. There are two official sources of revenue estimates: the Office of Tax Analysis (OTA) in the Treasury Department and the Staff of the Joint Committee on Taxation (JCT). Their estimates are based, respectively, on projections for the overall economy by the Office of Management and Budget (OMB) and the Congressional Budget Office (CBO). Even when the OTA and JCT estimates coincide they are not always correct. When they are at variance with one another the estimators find themselves involved in tax policy disputes. The revenue effect of a 1990 proposed cut in capital gains tax rates, discussed in the excerpt from Mr. Bopp's article, is a case in point. Professor Strahan's article points up deficiencies in the attempt by Congress to set ground rules for its own taxing and appropriation behavior.

THE ROLES OF REVENUE ESTIMATION AND SCORING
IN THE FEDERAL BUDGET PROCESS
Michael D. Bopp[*]

56 Tax Notes 1629, 1645-47 (1992)

Problems With the Existing Revenue Estimation Processes

Though the revenue estimating process is challenged by a number of problems, this section focuses upon two—the inaccuracy and politicization that threaten the efficacy and integrity of revenue estimates. These two "problems" might also be thought of as symptoms of other, underlying difficulties, upon which the following discussion will elaborate. Both the OTA and the JCT, as well as private revenue estimators, are, in varying degrees, faced daily with these problems.

As a starting point for discussion, this section will focus upon the accuracy and politicization considerations raised by the recent controversy over capital gains revenue estimates. The controversy embraced elements of both problems and has helped incite efforts to reform the process.

When two government entities derive significantly different revenue estimates for the same legislative proposal, the controversy threatens an erosion of public confidence. Revenue estimation is the practical application of a social science—economics—to the inner workings of the U.S. tax system. Revenue estimation differs from more theoretical applications of economics in that the former practice demands quantification of behavioral assumptions. But, predicting and quantifying people's behavior is inherently speculative, and revenue estimators possess no particular clairvoyance into the minds of individuals. And when the JCT and the OTA derive different estimates of behavior effects, charges of politicization are inevitably raised.

The JCT and the OTA produced well-publicized, disparate estimates of President Bush's capital gains proposal in late 1990.[181] The JCT believed that the proposal would lose $11.4 billion in Treasury receipts over five years, whereas the OTA estimated a $12.5 billion revenue increase.[e] What explains the greatest share of the disparity between these estimates is a divergence in assumptions regarding the effect of the proposal on realizations, or the elasticity of realization response with respect to taxes. * * *

Problems of Inaccuracy

The different assumptions adopted by the JCT and the OTA might be explained by structural problems that plague government revenue estimation. One could reason that revenue estimation is inherently

---

*. At time of original publication, associate in the firm of Kutak Rock, in Washington, D.C.

181. The proposal afforded an exclusion from income for capital assets held for at least one year. The exclusion increased from 10 percent for assets held at least one year, but less than two years, to 30 percent for assets held three years or more.

e. In 1990, OTA was part of President Bush's Treasury Department. JCT, on the other hand, was a joint committee drawn from the two tax-writing committees, both controlled by Democrats who opposed the Republican President's capital gain tax proposal. (Eds.)

inaccurate and is unworthy of the imprimatur of science. Ironically, this position is bolstered by the JCT admission that "the choice of an elasticity is ultimately a judgment call,"[185] and by acknowledgments that both elasticity assumptions are reasonable. The effects of these acknowledgments are ironic, because they attempt to restore confidence in the revenue estimating process, though they ultimately betray the speculative nature of the undertaking.

The accuracy of both the JCT's and the OTA's elasticities has been called into question by a recent study. The study, conducted by Congressional Research Service economist Jane Gravelle, indicates that both government revenue estimating bodies adopted elasticities figures that are too high.[187] Gravelle's results "imply a revenue loss from a gains cut which is at least twice what the JCT projects, and probably more than five times as great."[188]

Gravelle's study, it might be argued, assumes particular importance in light of the difficulties associated with evaluating the accuracy of revenue estimates. These difficulties stem from an inability to hold constant all revenue influences other than the provision being examined; an inability to isolate a single tax law change. Only aggregate revenue figures are determined with certainty. Thus, when GAO analysts attempted to ascertain, on the basis of Statistics of Income data, the accuracy of prior OTA revenue estimates, they confessed an inability to "claim any added measure of accuracy for our projected baseline of what revenues might have been had tax provisions not been introduced or altered."[191] The authors nevertheless did attempt to measure the accuracy of a number of OTA estimates, including an estimate of the relaxation of IRA requirements in 1981. They found substantial inaccuracies in the OTA estimates, concluding that the OTA's revenue estimate of legislation providing for IRAs was off "by a factor of at least four."[192] The GAO analysts concluded that "[w]hen a change in a provision allows taxpayers a number of alternative responses, economic models are less likely to yield an accurate prediction of how the change will play out in the 'real world.'"[193]

In contrast to this rather gloomy appraisal of government revenue estimation [stand] a number of arguments made in its defense. * * *

---

185. Staff of Joint Comm. on Taxation, 101st Cong., 2d Sess., *Explanation of Methodology Used to Estimate Proposals Affecting the Taxation of Income from Capital Gains* 7 (Comm. Print 1990).

187. Gravelle, *Can a Capital Gains Tax Cut Pay for Itself?* 14 (CRS Report for Congress, March 23, 1990).

188. Hoerner, "'Treasury and JCT Both Off Mark in Estimating Revenue Effects of Capital Gains Cut, CRS Finds,'" 50 *Tax Notes* 1329 (March 25, 1991).

191. Vehorn, McCool, and Jantscher, "Revenue Estimating: A More Prominent Part of Tax Policy," *The GAO Journal* 64, 68 (Summer 1988).

192. *Id.*

193. *Id.* at 71.

The GAO analysis is similarly subject to a criticism. The analysis is undermined by the argument that ex post facto analyses of revenue estimating accuracy are conjectural endeavors.[196] More specifically, it has been argued that it is impossible to quantify the decrease in tax revenues attributable to IRA provisions because "[t]here is no way to know whether monies placed into IRAs were fully taxable under prior law, partly taxable, or sheltered."[197] In short, there are too many variables imbedded in the Internal Revenue Code to know with certainty what a taxpayer would have done had one variable been added or taken away.

Some commentators and estimators have suggested that problems of revenue estimation inaccuracy can be ameliorated with fairly straightforward improvements. The chief explanation for the difference between Gravelle's and the government estimators' elasticity figures centers upon time, one former OTA estimator noted. Government revenue estimators do not possess enough of it to delve into all of the assumptions that they must determine. And the trend has been such that revenue estimators have increasingly less time to spend per estimate. A number of revenue estimators perceive that the solution to this predicament is to increase the resources of the JCT and the OTA. It seems not implausible that 550 revenue estimates is too heavy a burden for the Joint Committee's 10 estimators to shoulder in one year. Indeed, most revenue estimates engender complex and time consuming activities including data gathering, economic formulations, and computer modelling.[202]

Another possible, partial solution, is to improve the available data. Revenue estimators could better determine behavioral variables if they had access to different forms of data. This point is no more apparent than in the context of estimating the revenue effects of a change in the tax treatment of capital gains. Efforts to refine and improve revenue estimating data have focused mainly on creating a more complete, though static, picture of U.S. taxpayers. What is lacking is longitudinal data, data that traces the tax status of individuals over a number of years. One analyst, who helps disseminate and package data used by both government and private revenue

---

196. It is also contradicted by another ex post facto assessment of revenue estimating accuracy, one performed by the CBO. The CBO's analysis attempted to assess the OTA's overall revenue estimating accuracy for the period, 1963-1978. It concluded that OTA receipts estimates were accurate "to within one percent of actual collections" after adjusting for inaccuracies in the economic forecast and the fact that proposed tax legislation was not enacted. A Review of the Accuracy of Treasury Revenue Forecasts, 1963-1978 17 (CBO Staff Working Paper, Feb. 1981).

197. Barry L. Dennis, Remarks at the Tax Executives Institute 41st Midyear Conference (March 26, 1991).

202. If adding to the staffs of JCT and OTA would not solve the problems of inaccuracy, perhaps a better solution is one suggested by commentator Rob Bennett. He posits that "[i]t might even be a good thing if lawmakers were told they could not obtain an unlimited number of estimates. The fact that JCT estimates are a 'free good' seems to have created an unquenchable thirst for ever more estimates." Bennett, "About Those 'Technical Differences,'" 50 Tax Notes 891, 892 (Feb. 25, 1991).

estimators, has noted the need for longitudinal data in examining taxpayer behavior with respect to capital gains. He argues that:

> [T]he policy implications are quite different if, on the one hand, most people realize gains at only a few points in their lives (e.g., selling a home or a business, or cashing in assets post-retirement) or if, on the other hand, they typically realize gains every single year (e.g., stock market speculators). . . . [N]o amount of data analysis of single-shot, one-year tax returns can shed any light on this matter. . . . Thus, whether to analyze existing tax systems or to be ready to analyze future tax systems, it is imperative that we acquire more longitudinal information on taxpayers.[204]

But, better data and a heavier staff would not, by themselves, cause the JCT and the OTA to produce the same capital gains revenue estimate. A factor that accounts for $2 billion, or eight percent of the discrepancy between the existing JCT and OTA estimates, is the baseline amount of realizations assumed by each estimating body. The "baseline" figure predicts the amount of realizations that will occur over the next five years under current law. The OTA used OMB figures, which forecast $1,466 billion in realizations between 1990 and 1995. The JCT adopted the CBO baseline figure, which predicted $1,604 billion in realizations, or 9.4 percent more realizations than expected by OMB.

One might wonder why the JCT and the OTA use such divergent baseline figures when this practice is guaranteed to produce similarly divergent revenue estimates. The answer is simple: Congress allows this practice. Congress has not specified which baseline figures either government body must employ. Their different practices are explained by their respective positions within the government, and, hence, the locus of their loyalties. The JCT is a congressional committee, created to assist the Senate Committee on Finance and the House Committee on Ways and Means and ordered by Congress to maintain a symbiotic relationship with the CBO. The OTA, conversely, is situated within the executive branch of government and its internal practices are controlled by Congress only by means of a long and permissive leash.

It is thus arguably a part of the congressional budget scheme to permit the two government revenue estimators to derive differing revenue estimates on a variety of tax legislation. Indeed, the BEA [Budget Enforcement Act of 1990] contemplates differing estimates through its pay-as-you-go enforcement plan. When a piece of tax legislation is enacted, the OMB must first consider the CBO's revenue estimate of the provision before issuing to Congress its own estimate. Moreover, the OMB must explain any differences between its and CBO's estimates.

---

204. Bristol, "Tax Modelling and the Policy Environment of the 1990s," 8 *SOI Bulletin* 115, 116 (Fall 1988).

This congressionally authorized scheme, however, is not without its shortcomings. Disagreement on one issue can breed further disagreement on others. One Joint Committee revenue estimator maintains that the inherent disagreement between the JCT and the OTA on baseline figures and other macroeconomic estimates provides a disincentive for estimators at the two organizations to agree *ex ante* on other factors relating to the methodology behind a given revenue estimate. If the estimates are going to differ anyway, the reasoning proceeds, why bother ironing out methodological concerns? Unfortunately, the JCT estimator sees no practical solution to this problem.

* * *

DISCUSSION: GRAMM-RUDMAN-HOLLINGS AND TAX POLICY
Randall Strahan[*]

National Tax Association-Tax Institute of America

82nd Annual Conference 49, 49-51 (1989)

Two basic issues are addressed in the papers that have been written for this panel: 1) what have been the effects on tax legislation of Gramm-Rudman-Hollings and other budgeting procedures during the 1980s? and 2) have these effects been positive or negative ones for the federal tax system? The authors of all three papers agree that some undesirable patterns in tax policymaking have emerged or at least become more pronounced in the 1980s. These include instability, increased complexity, and a tendency to focus primarily on the short-term revenue effects. The papers also point out that developments in tax policymaking during the 1980s have not all been pathological. Gramm-Rudman-Hollings and revenue pressures created by large deficits have helped produce a more disciplined tax policy process in which tax expenditures have been subjected to greater scrutiny and we have achieved some gains in equality and efficiency in the 1986 Tax Reform Act.

To this list of new developments I would add changes in the role of the Senate in the tax legislative process. In contrast to its traditional role of reacting to tax policy changes initiated by the House, the current budget process has allowed the Senate to take a more active role in initiating legislation. Gramm-Rudman-Hollings has also produced a much more disciplined tax legislative process in the Senate by requiring a three-fifths vote to waive points of order that may be raised against legislation that increases the deficit beyond the level approved in each year's budget resolution.

Regarding the negative developments that have occurred in tax legislation during the 1980s, together these papers call into question the assumption that budget procedures—either Gramm-Rudman-Hollings or earlier changes in the congressional budget process—should be viewed as the principal cause of these developments. The paper by Peter Merrill, Stanley

---

[*]. At time of original publication, Department of Political Science, Emory University.

Collender, and Eric Cook points out that many of the problems that have been noted by the critics of the current tax legislative process appeared prior to the enactment of Gramm-Rudman-Hollings and are traceable to pressures for new revenues that have existed since the 1981 tax cuts. George Zodrow's paper points out that the tendency during the 1980s to revisit the tax base repeatedly rather than adjust the rates reflects not budget procedures but political constraints defined by presidential opposition to rate increases. Finally, Al Davis's paper emphasizes that the undesirable features of the tax legislative process during the 1980s are due primarily to a political stalemate on tax policy rather than the procedures created by Gramm-Rudman-Hollings.   In Davis's view, Gramm-Rudman-Hollings may contribute to problems such as an overemphasis on short-term revenue gains, but is not the principal *cause* of these problems. Instead, these developments reflect the "political impasse to no new taxes." "Tax and fiscal policy," he argues "are not going to improve much until this impasse is broken."

* * * [I]t is the question of the effects of budget procedures on the tax legislative process that I wish to focus on in my comments. I agree with Al Davis that both Gramm-Rudman-Hollings *and* the instability that has been present in tax policy in recent years are in fact symptoms of a deeper problem in American politics today. Davis argues that the problem is an impasse over the question of new taxes. I would argue that this impasse reflects an even more fundamental disagreement among the nation's political leadership over the proper role of government in American society.

Gramm-Rudman-Hollings is merely one symptom of a breakdown of consensus among policy makers on what some political science types would call a "public philosophy." By the late 1970s a liberal public philosophy that stressed federal government activism to reduce social inequality and reduce the risks associated with a market economy had ceased to define the national agenda. In the 1980 presidential election Ronald Reagan proposed a program based on an alternative public philosophy that emphasized private initiative and unfettered markets as the primary sources of social progress.   The Reagan administration skillfully took advantage of political and economic conditions in 1981 to win passage of massive tax cuts and some of the budget cuts it sought to implement the new conservative public philosophy, but with large increases in defense spending and the onset of a major recession, the result, of course, was massive budget deficits.

After 1981 a governing coalition to carry out additional cuts in domestic programs consistent with a new public philosophy could not be assembled in Congress, but nor would the president accept major changes in his tax program to reduce deficits. The result since 1982 has been a recurring pattern of deficit politics in which the White House has refused to initiate any major tax policy changes to increase revenues, while congressional Democrats sympathetic to a liberal public philosophy have sought to protect domestic programs by proposing increased taxes and a slowdown in defense spending. * * *

During the 1980s large deficits have created pressures for government to set priorities, but our political leadership has been locked in an unresolved debate over the proper role of government in society. Long time observers of budgetary politics such as Aaron Wildavsky argue that the extent of conflict and polarization over budgetary goals during the Reagan years was unprecedented. The problems of governing under these conditions where the president has held to one public philosophy and majorities in one or both houses of Congress to another, have produced a whole series of new organizational and procedural forms, including so-called "gangs," bipartisan "summits," and finally, Gramm-Rudman-Hollings. Gramm-Rudman-Hollings has certainly been important at times in defining the scope of deficit reduction proposals, but it is not the *cause* of our current fiscal instability or of the problems that have been present in tax policymaking. These reflect instead the breakdown of consensus on a public philosophy among those who occupy our national governing institutions.

What, if any, are the prospects for a resolution of the political impasse that now exists on tax and fiscal policy? Though it is difficult to judge the long term goals of the Bush administration at this point, I would argue that a transformation of this pattern of deficit politics which might in turn introduce some degree of stability to federal tax policy is likely to occur only in the context of some dramatic event or economic shock that renews a sense of crisis about large deficits. Although events of this type are unpredictable, there appears at present to be nothing of this type on the horizon. "Budget deficits are passe subjects on Wall Street," observed former Senate Budget Committee staffer Stephen Bell in a recent article (October 6, 1989) in the *Wall Street Journal.* "They won't let you into a party in Manhattan if you talk about the budget deficit." Until a sense of crisis reemerges—and Manhattan cocktail party chatter may be a pretty good leading indicator here—each side in this unresolved debate over the proper role of the federal government will likely continue to press for its broader policy goals rather than focusing on the possible negative effects of deficits or further instability in the tax system. Under these conditions Gramm-Rudman-Hollings will continue to encourage gimmickry and policy changes driven by short-term revenue concerns. This pattern may be good for business for those of us who make our livings deciphering the complexities of tax policy and politics, but over the long term it will probably be bad for the economy and for the goals of simplicity and stability in the tax system.

Notes and Questions

5. Would it be better to insulate revenue estimating from both the Treasury and the JCT by creating a separate office of estimators? If so, should it be part of the executive branch, part of the legislative branch, or an

"independent" body akin to, or conceivably part of, the Federal Reserve System?

6. Is Professor Strahan's point valid that present constraints imposed by revenue and budget considerations encourage gimmickry and policy concerns driven by short-term revenue concerns?

7. Excerpts in this chapter attest to the frequent impasses resulting from the political climate in recent years when the President was a Republican while Democrats controlled Congress. As this book goes to press, the parties have reversed positions, but the impasse continues.

8. Professor Strahan offers a gloomy assessment of the prospects for an end to political impasse. Can the problem be resolved over the long haul, short of adoption of a parliamentary system?

C. THE TAX REFORM ACT OF 1986: A CASE STUDY IN TAX REVISION

The Tax Reform Act of 1986 was the most ambitious attempt in a generation to fix the income tax. Unlike other revenue acts that focussed on a few specific segments of the tax system, the 1986 Act attempted to revise the whole system in one convulsive effort. Even if it failed to do all one might have hoped for and even though some of its changes were reversed in subsequent years, enacting a sweeping tax revision was an enormous, and surprising, accomplishment.

Professor Witte's article, written just after a dramatic breakthrough in the Senate Finance Committee that led to the 1986 Act, puts that Act in the context of tax history and tax policy. Mr. Birnbaum, who observed the process from the vantage point of a *Wall Street Journal* reporter, gives what is probably the best explanation of how the 1986 Act came to pass. Dr. Brannon's article is a critical and cynical analysis of what the 1986 tax revision accomplished.

A LONG VIEW OF TAX REFORM
John F. Witte[*]
39 National Tax Journal 255, 255-59 (1986)

Beyond the simple excitement of tax politics, I also have a modest personal stake in the result, primarily because of a passage, written late in an evening during a particularly depressing period in tax politics following the 1981 tax cut. I committed that passage to print, and made the further error of italicizing it. It occurs at the end of a long, and perhaps tedious, but I think scholarly treatment of the politics, development, and consequences of

---

[*]. At time of original publication, professor at University of Wisconsin-Madison.

the federal income tax. The passage follows a description of the then most popular tax reform proposals, Bradley-Gephardt, Kemp-Roth, and Hall-Rabushka. It reads as follows:

> There is nothing, absolutely nothing in the history or politics of the income tax that indicates that any of these schemes have the slightest hope of being enacted in the forms proposed.

Later, just before the book went to press in January 1985, I added an epilogue, which was a reaction to the first Treasury reform proposal. At this point I was facing the embarrassing prospect of having a prediction go to press which would already have been proven wrong. So I did what any intelligent person would do—I carefully waffled.

> The central argument of this book has been that our political system has, to this point, been incapable of producing such lasting reform. This time the chips seem about to fall, but that has happened before—in 1969 and 1976—and they did not. Instead, what followed the 1976 effort was wholesale retreat from tax reform. * * * [P]roposals are not laws and I remain highly skeptical that these proposals will become and remain law over the long run. More likely, I would predict some curtailing of tax expenditures (although elimination of very few), a reduction in the number of brackets (which simplifies nothing and will reduce progressivity), and then, in the years ahead, a return to the more natural political impulses of conferring both broad and specialized benefits through the tax system. Lasting tax reform will not come without lasting political reform.

Until about three weeks ago those passages looked pretty good . . . now I am not so certain. I have never claimed that these prognoses were very imaginative or analytically astute. A relatively quick reading of the major historical trends in tax policy, which I will render in very brief form today, suggests these results. Indeed I would offer them as an example of the deadly phrase used by social psychologists: "My mother could have told you that."

Today, however, I am faced with a dilemma: stick with the prognosis and argument and discuss why *lasting*, comprehensive tax reform will not become a reality given our present political process; or cave in and discuss what went wrong with my bleak analysis and what led to this potentially monumental reform which seems to be on the threshold. I chose the former approach, and leave to my respondents and the audience the opportunity to raise all the interesting and hopeful prospects of recent events.

I chose to remain with my basic argument. * * * First, it is very important, particularly for tax policy which undergoes continuous change (a very serious problem in its own right), to have some grasp of the longer-term factors and basic incentives that drive tax politics. Second, I still think I am basically correct. * * * [O]ne bill does not insure lasting tax reform. The political and financial incentives I conceive as so obvious and apparent in tax politics will not be changed; and the actors, including those legions whose lives and fortunes have come to be tied to our tax system, are not about to pack their bags and go home.

In what follows I will first sketch the long-term patterns in income tax policy, particularly as they relate to the prospects for tax reform. I then will discuss the deeper problem as it relates to the general structure of politics which nurtures the development of tax policy in directions that produce the litany of defects that we all know so well.

Historical Trends and Tax Reform

Two essential facts are critical to understanding the historical development of the income tax in the United States. The first is the importance of periods of war; and the second is the incremental process of change which shapes tax policy. As is well known in this audience, the initial income tax enacted in 1913 was a modest piece of legislation. Given the exemption level of $4,000 for a family of four, and thus the very small number of people required to file, an irate Henry Cabot Lodge correctly labelled the act as "the pillage of a class." * * *

World War I radically changed the very modest provisions of that initial act. Those changes established the potential of the income tax as a major source of revenue and created the first truly progressive tax structure in our history. In the years 1914 and 1915, the percentage of federal revenue derived from income taxes was minuscule. However, by the end of the war the combined individual and corporate income taxes, including excess profits taxes, accounted for approximately 60 percent of all federal revenues. At the same time the nominal rate structure was ballooning from an initial top rate of 7 percent to a war-ending top bracket rate of 77 percent.

Between the wars, these dramatic increases were largely undone, as both the progressivity and the revenue capacity of the taxes were considerably reduced (although never to pre-war levels). However, with the onset of World War II, the income tax again became the mainstay of our tax system, accounting for over 75 percent of revenues. The magnitude of revenues far outstripped any other period in our history. In 1938 revenues from each income tax were less than 1 percent of GNP; by 1942 they each were approximately 8 percent of GNP. Progressivity was drastically altered not only by raising rates to an historical high of 94 percent, but more importantly by shifting the definition of bracket widths so that large numbers of people paid at these higher marginal rates.[1] Finally, and most importantly, the war eliminated the elite nature of the income tax. World War I produced an increase in the percentage of the work force paying

---

1. For example, the 77 percent rate during World War I only affected income over $1 million, and Roosevelt's famous Wealth Tax of 1935 had a top rate of 81 percent for incomes exceeding $5 million. On the other hand, the top World War II rate applied to incomes over $200,000.

income taxes from less than 1 percent to 13 percent. That percentage then declined throughout the 1920s, increasing in the 1930s to approximately 7 percent in 1938. By war's end, 70 percent of the labor force were paying taxes and almost 90 percent were filing returns. That wartime system, which was reenacted for the Korean War, was largely kept intact with the writing of Internal Revenue Act of 1954, to which all subsequent income tax laws are amendments.

Because the modern structure of the income tax, and thus the foundation of our system of public finance was created as a response to war, it is not implausible to suggest that the basic features of that system would not have resulted from the more normal political process that governs tax policy-making in other periods. I have argued that the normal process is an excellent example of the incremental model of decision-making as first set out in detail by Charles Lindblom. In non-war periods, and to some degree also in wartime, the legislative process produces an almost continuous series of marginal changes in the status quo, often presented as remedies for current problems either internal to the tax system ("abuses") or as an answer to the plight of specific groups. Provisions are endlessly tinkered with, with new provisions introduced modestly and over time rather than in one grand sweep orchestrated by an overall plan for tax revision or reform.

What is important for this discussion of the long-term prospects for tax reform are the results of this combination of rapid, almost uncontrolled change induced by outside forces, set against a "normal" process of incremental political bargaining. The first important result is that the high level of taxes and the progressivity of that system were induced under abnormal circumstances. Indeed, the normal result of peacetime tax legislation has been almost perfectly consistent in reversing this trend. Through 1981, only one major income tax bill in history legislated a total tax increase, and that was in 1932 as a response to an effort to balance the budget as a remedy for the depression. Beyond that, whether a reform bill or not, politicians of both parties have always been able to claim that their actions "cut taxes." Walter Mondale can attest to the political power of such claims.

A second trend resulting from the incremental changes in tax policy that follow wartime periods—a trend which continues to this very day—is a constant downward ratcheting of marginal rates. Although there is severe difficulty in making accurate estimates of historical effective rates, the political intent again appears to be quite obvious; leading me to the conclusion that the often discussed national commitment to a progressive tax system was never a real commitment at all, but rather a backdoor result of war.

Finally, although incremental changes are by definition non-radical departures from the status quo, it is a major error to interpret the longterm result of this process as conservative or producing little change. The reason is that modifications are *cumulative*. This simple fact has produced the policy results with which we are all so familiar—a hopelessly large tax code, that is unbearably complex, and riddled with particularized sets of benefits for all ranges and types of taxpayers. The wealthy benefit from these cumulative changes in a greater proportion than those not as fortunately situated, but there is almost no group that is left without an important set of provisions which lower their tax burden.

My personal situation may exemplify this latter point. * * * My family income over the last seven years has rapidly regressed toward the national mean. By whatever definition of income, the Wittes are middle class. However, considering provisions in isolation, other than rate, exemption and standard deduction levels there are six changes in the present Packwood bill which would have considerable consequences on my tax status . . . and, from a very narrowly self-interested perspective, there are many more that affect my family that remain untouched. Tax politics is not simply, or even mainly, a welfare program for the rich. If it was, the task of reforming it would be substantially less difficult.

What these basic trends and patterns in tax history mean for the prospects of major, lasting tax reform, have to this point been relatively obvious. The prospects are not good. Major tax reforms implies radical, comprehensive change, which is anathema to the normal incremental process. However, the historical trends also suggest major problems even if the political process could be controlled to generate and sustain the power needed to overcome incremental impulses. It is very difficult to conceive of tax reform and overall tax increases at the same time. In the past, tax reform has been purchased, and thus sold on the back of tax reduction. In addition, tax reform must also contend with the counter-trends of reduction in marginal rates and continuous expansion of the tax expenditure system.

Additionally, the base political incentives producing each of these trends are very strong. A politician's perfect world is to deliver a speech that proclaims his or her efforts for overall tax reduction, lower tax rates, and an added particular benefit (or protection of a benefit) for the specific audience at hand (elderly, teachers, developers, farmers, military personnel, small businesses . . . the list is endless). Ironically, that same politician is very likely to end the speech with an attack on the tax system, which may vary depending on current conditions, but usually includes problems of complexity, fairness, and the drag of the tax system on the growth of the economy, which in turn explains the economic malaise of the nation, and probably at the same time the success of the Japanese. The speech may well end with a call for tax reform as an immediate priority . . . immediately after the election.

* * * I want to explore this anomalous situation, which I do not believe is based on hypocrisy or a deviant political process. If I was in their position, and you must trust that I am not hypocritical, I would do the same thing . . . and so would all but the most courageous, or perhaps the dimmest of you.

The Deeper Problem

The difficult road to tax reform rests on a larger set of political problems than simple extrapolations of historical trends or assumptions concerning political incentives. These problems have to do with the basic design and workings of our representative system. And while I believe these flaws directly affect tax policy and add to explanations of the obstacles to tax reform, they are also more general and affect other bases of public policy as well.

Our initial representative system, which has undergone remarkably little structural change in over two hundred years, was based on a notion of government as a necessary evil. Following the failure of the Articles of Confederation, a majority emerged in favor of a stronger central government and federal system that would establish uniformity in and enforcement of laws, particularly those involving parties in different states. Provisions were also made for rudimentary services such as the coining of money and postal services, that obviously made more sense on a national level. The intent was to use government only to the point of establishing some certainty in economic and social transactions, and of course protecting the rights of property and contract. A central government was also viewed as essential in protecting the nation and individual states from foreign aggression and possible internal insurrection.

Discussion during the Constitutional Convention, and afterward during the process of ratification, repeatedly returned to the dangers of government and the need to proceed with caution. States' rights extremists, such as Patrick Henry, did not even ascribe to the limited role of a central government as outlined above. Federalists, such as Madison and Hamilton, often couched their arguments in language that admitted the possibility of excessive government and the need to guard against it. The most famous of the federalist papers, number 10 written by James Madison, argues for an encompassing federal system because it would limit factions from coming together to form majorities which would then use government to tyrannize minorities. The design of our system of fragmented and divided powers, between branches of the federal government and between state and federal governments, followed from this fear of government and the need to limit its powers and actions.

Beginning in the latter part of the nineteenth and the early part of the twentieth century, and greatly accelerating during the depression, that conception of government changed in a dramatic way. Government began to be viewed as the answer to national problems as well as the problems of specific groups. * * * The transition from government as a necessary evil, to a much larger government, that is a much more necessary good, is the major political fact of our age.

Now what does all this have to do with the prospects for tax reform? I believe a great deal, because the system first established to protect against government, is not as effective in dealing with government as a benefactor. The issues, for tax policy and other matters, are two-fold. First, why are policies that clearly benefit only a narrow minority ever approved by a majority that must eventually bear at least a marginal cost? And second, why is it often impossible to radically restructure a policy, such as a tax code, when the vast majority agree on the basic designs for reform?

There are several plausible answers to the first question, which for tax politics explains the proliferation of specialized tax expenditures. The most often cited explanation is that because specialized benefits (such as tax expenditures) are of large value to a few, while costs are widely dispersed, opposition will be weak. This is a variant of Madison's original argument—if the countervailing interests are widely enough dispersed, it will be difficult to form a majority. The shift has come in what the majority is anticipated to be doing. In the original formulation, the system was designed to prevent the majority from damaging the minority. However, in the modern state, the absence of majority will allow minority factions to secure benefits for themselves. Madison's logic remains intact, but that he wrongly conceived the problem is taking its toll.

Additionally, the underlying assumption that majorities will form and act on a sole expression of self-interest is also questionable. People may listen with empathy to special pleadings, particularly when they can conceive of themselves affected at some point by similar pleas. The aged are vulnerable; small businesses can be victimized by large corporations; students may need aid as they advance their education; and even those involved in oil production may need help when the Arabs fail to cooperate.

This prospect is even more important for elites who represent constituents; constituents who may or may not be carefully watching the actions of government. The gain for an elected politician from opposing specialized benefits requested by colleagues is likely to be minimal, particularly if the request is relatively marginal, as most are. On the other hand, the cost of isolating oneself through opposition may be high particularly when it is their turn to propose or assume credit for a benefit. Thus empathy may force inaction either through genuine agreement or as a calculated strategy.

Last, the torturous path to governmental action, institutionalized as fragmented and divided power, provides a possible explanation for both of the problems. The obstacles imbedded in the system may work to the benefit of narrow interests because success requires a diligence and perseverance that intense gain will engender (repeal of the withholding of interest comes to mind). Additionally, the lack of majority opposition to narrow, marginal gains increases the likelihood of passage, particularly when considered over the long term.

On the other hand, appeals to widely shared majoritarian concerns, such as tax reform, are much more difficult when the cost is potential disruption of acquired benefits. If a majority is faced with a clear prospect of harm, one can easily imagine a consensual coalition. However, when confronted with a complicated, confusing and uncertain shift of benefits, that coalition is much harder to form and to hold. And all of the fragmentation, potential for delay, and devices to kill an action will be brought into play.

    * * *

SHOWDOWN AT GUCCI GULCH
Jeffrey H. Birnbaum[*]
40 National Tax Journal 357, 357-61 (1987)

With Alan Murray, I have written a book for Random House that carries the same name as this speech: *Showdown at Gucci Gulch*. The title is meant to convey that taxwriting is NOT a bore. * * * The Tax Reform Act of 1986 proves that, and our book details it.

    * * *

There is more than one Gucci Gulch. The term is simply the nickname for the hallways outside of the Ways and Means and Finance Committees where hundreds of people stood for two years waiting for the members of Congress and their aides to decide the fate of the nation's income tax. These denizens of the hallway, mostly lobbyists and journalists, believed that they were outsiders looking in, powerless to do anything about the decisions that were being made secretly inside. Our book chronicles these deliberations.

In fact, forces that were working well beyond even the people inside the room, were what was pushing tax reform forward. What I hope to describe to you today are the conclusions that Alan and I have reached about what propelled this very unlikely piece of legislation forward, and what forced so many of us to wear out our heels on those marble floors, in Gucci Gulch, for so long.

In brief, I believe tax reform passed not because anyone really wanted it. Indeed, it was the bill that nobody wanted. It succeeded because so few people were willing to kill it once it got rolling. Put another way, no one wanted the dog to die on his doorstep.

At the end of 1983, when the Reagan administration was debating whether to put tax reform at the top of the next year's agenda, White House Chief of Staff James Baker asked pollster Richard Wirthlin for his view. Wirthlin was decidedly unenthused. He knew that tax changes always create more anger among potential losers than gratitude among winners. Moreover, he said, "the words 'tax reform' for a lot of Americans mean 'tax increase.'"

The next three years proved Mr. Wirthlin's point. Despite soaring rhetoric and whistlestop tours around the country, neither President Reagan nor Senator Bill Bradley was ever able to excite audiences with their plans to overhaul the nation's income tax. Mr. Reagan boldly labeled the effort a

---

[*]. At time of original publication, reporter for *The Wall Street Journal*.

"second American revolution." Senator Bradley used more restrained, but no less compelling terms. Some Republican analysts even predicted that tax reform would bring about a grand "realignment" of political loyalties. Sen. Bradley, and later Chairman Dan Rostenkowski of Ways and Means, warned about the Republicans' plan and prepared to fight back for the good of their own Democratic Party.

But, for the most part, absolutely none of that happened. The country reacted with a yawn. The parties remained pretty much aligned as they always had been.

Even after the new law was enacted and hailed as a legislative miracle of sorts the public remained ambivalent. When asked to name the most significant event of 1986, only 9 percent of those asked picked the passage of tax reform. Far more people chose the explosion of the space shuttle, the U.S. sale of arms to Iran, and the bombing of Libya.

Tax reform, as Chairman Rostenkowski put it, was "the bill that nobody wanted." It was opposed by armies of Washington lobbyists. Lawmakers were equally unimpressed; many of them feared that they would be forced to vote against groups that kept their campaign coffers filled. Even the men who shepherded the bill forward—Treasury Secretary James Baker, Senate Finance Committee Chairman Bob Packwood and Chairman Rostenkowski—approached the task reluctantly. The only natural constituency for reform was the great mass of voters who paid their taxes each year without the benefits of shelters and tax gimmicks—and even they were skeptical.

A few months after President Reagan unveiled his plan to overhaul the tax system, Rep. Richard Gephardt, a cosponsor of the seminal Bradley-Gephardt plan, encountered a reporter on a plane. The Missouri legislator was surprised to find the journalist still writing about the tax issue.

"It's not that good a story," he said. Like almost everyone else in Washington, Rep. Gephardt had concluded that revamping the federal income tax was an impossible dream.

To be sure, most polls taken in 1985 and 1986 showed that a majority of Americans favored reform. But their support tended to be uninformed and thin. Although the bill promised tax cuts to two-thirds of the nation's taxpayers, most people thought their own taxes would not be reduced. Moreover, when poll-takers explained which tax breaks were being threatened, support quickly evaporated. Most taxpayers were worried about losing deductions, even if lower tax rates more than made up for the loss.

Take the case of poor Ron Pearlman. Back in 1985, when he and others at the Treasury were putting together what would later be called Treasury II, he was paid a visit by an army of armed-services veterans. The group was led by Chad Colley, national commander of the Disabled American Veterans, who had lost both legs and one arm while fighting in Vietnam.

Pearlman started the meeting by asking the triple amputee, "Why should veterans' disability payments be treated differently than any other income?" The meeting went downhill from there. Pearlman's question was heresy to a world accustomed to lenient treatment by the income tax. The red-faced Treasury official tried to dig himself out of the hole he had dug for himself, but to no avail. The veterans left his office and went on the warpath.

They demanded a second meeting at Treasury, this time with Pearlman's boss, Jim Baker. They brought with them a full-page advertisement that they were planning to run in three national newspapers. It had a huge picture of Commander Colley in a wheelchair, his missing appendages painfully evident. At the top of the page, in large, bold letters, the copy read: "What's so special about disabled veterans?" And it continued: "That's what a top Treasury official said to Chad Colley."

Baker called Pearlman into his office a little later. He said, "I think we'll have to drop this one."

With few people actively supporting it, and lots of powerful groups lined up against it, how did tax reform become law? The answer requires a more complex understanding of taxes and the way the public and lawmakers view them. While polls showed no abiding interest in the bill, per se, they also showed profound dissatisfaction with the existing tax code, and the political system that brought it into being. Politicians with their ears to the ground feared a public backlash might engulf anyone who was perceived as opposing the effort. Few legislators wanted tax reform, but even fewer wanted to be responsible for killing it. It was this decidedly negative motivation that was largely responsible for the enactment of the most sweeping overhaul of the federal income tax in history.

As a result, once President Reagan put the bill into motion, and Chairman Rostenkowski joined him making the effort bipartisan, tax reform acquired supernatural momentum of its own. As Senator Alan Dixon of Illinois put it: "This thing breathes its own air."

Or put another way. No one wanted the dog to die on his doorstep.

The income tax was enacted three-quarters of a century ago in an attempt to bring fairness to the U.S. tax system. At the close of the nineteenth century, the government raised all of its revenue from tariffs and excise taxes, which placed a heavy burden on low-income Americans. "If taxation is a badge of freedom," declared William Jennings Bryan, an early income-tax advocate, "let me assure my friend that the poor people of this country are covered all over with the insignia of freedom."

   * * *

The idea that the income tax is, by and large, a fair tax persevered for many decades. When a Fortune magazine survey asked people to name the most unjust tax in 1938, only 8 percent fingered the income tax. Even as late as 1972, when the Advisory Commission on Intergovernmental Relations asked Americans which tax was the most fair, the federal income tax came out on top.

The 1970s, however, saw a steady erosion of taxpayers' faith in the federal income tax. To a large degree, the decline reflected the effects of inflation, which distorted the tax system in many ways, and pushed the poor and the middle class into higher tax brackets. But the dissatisfaction also reflected a growing awareness of tax shelters and ever larger tax loopholes that were used by the wealthiest, and most advantaged among us.

The 1981 tax bill was, in part, a response to this swelling dissatisfaction. But the response was flawed. While tax rates were cut deeply that year, new tax breaks were put into the code that provided powerful fuel for the proliferation of even more tax shelters, and enabled many large and profitable corporations to escape taxes altogether.

Roscoe Egger, the commissioner of the Internal Revenue Service during the first five years of the Reagan administration, recognized this public frustration and saw that it posed a major threat. He said: "People were rapidly becoming disenchanted with the whole system. We began to see the emergence of tax protesters. Groups refused to file, backyard churches began to claim income as charitable contributions, and tax shelters reached entirely different proportions. One couldn't fail to recognize that this was a reflection of deepseated unhappiness with the entire tax system. By 1983, we even began to see people in the lower-income levels, with incomes of only $18,000 or $20,000 a year, buying into phony tax shelters. . . . They listened to this siren song and said: 'Gee, everybody else is doing it. Why not me?'"

Horror stories about millionaires and large corporations that paid no tax became commonplace. Many Americans began to perceive that the income tax was not very progressive. It sometimes seemed that the average man on the street paid a higher portion of his income than the typical millionaire, rather than the other way around.

Gary Hecht, an assistant principal for a school in New York City, reflected the sentiments of millions of Americans in a December 1984 discussion group conducted by the *Wall Street Journal*: "My feeling with the federal tax goes back to the same old story. The rich get richer, the poor stay poor, and the middle class gets poor too. Because of the loopholes, this is going to constantly occur."

By January 1984, when President Reagan called for his tax reform study, no one could doubt that the American people were harboring a huge reservoir of resentment toward the income tax. It promised to be a powerful political force if ever effectively tapped.

The problem, though, was that the American public was also deeply cynical. They were upset by the tax system, but doubted that the President or Congress could fix it. As pollster Wirthlin had predicted, many people feared that tax reform would, for them at least, be a tax increase in disguise.

The ambivalence over taxes was recognized by most of the members of the House Ways and Means Committee, who were forced to confront the issue in 1985. Tax reform was a hot topic in Washington, but in the members' districts it remained a sleeper. * * * [H]ardly anyone mentioned tax reform, and when they did it was to complain. * * *

Republican Representative Bill Frenzel concluded, "It's obvious that for every friend you make with tax reform, you are going to make a few enemies."

Even Speaker Tip O'Neill, a backer of the bill, noticed the trend. "I have found very little sentiment. The people in the street, they never mention it."

Members of the Ways and Means Committee began serious consideration of tax reform in the fall of 1985. Aware of the public's apathy, they proceeded to rip the measure apart. Heeding the requests of special-interest lobbyists, they voted to restore tax breaks, one after the other, that both the President and Ways and Means Chairman Rostenkowski had slated for elimination. With little public support, tax reform was headed for the rocks.

The turning point for the House bill came on Tuesday Oct. 15, 1985. An amendment was offered in the committee by Alabama Democrat Ronnie Flippo to expand the deduction for bad debt reserves—the biggest tax break enjoyed by financial institutions. Flippo's amendment was the antithesis of reform; it represented old-time tax legislation at its worst, giving out goodies to favored interests, rather than taking them away. And to the surprise of Chairman Rostenkowski, the amendment passed, 17-13. Out in the hallway, a jubilant bank lobbyist shouted triumphantly, "We won! We won!"

The next day, the national newspapers attacked the committee for the vote, and vividly reported the glee of the gloating lobbyist. Whether these reports made their way into the nation's heartland is unclear. But their message was obvious enough. If the Ways and Means members allowed tax reform to die, they would take a heavy beating in the press, and probably in public opinion as well. Reminded of that threat, lawmakers slowly began to turn. No one wanted the dog to die on his doorstep.

Rostenkowski discovered a new willingness to compromise among his members. Within a week, in fact, the bank vote was reversed and the bill was on its way to passage. One savvy aide said at the time: "The last thing that any of these guys want is for it to be written that tax reform dies in the Ways and Means Committee because sleazebag politicians want to take care of First National City Bank so the average public gets screwed."

At about this time, members who had opposed the chairman's drive began to worry that they would be left behind, and left out. Indeed, those who had battled against the chairman, like Sam Gibbons of Florida, had reason to fear they might be the subject of the chairman's revenge in the final bill. * * *

For his part, Chairman Rostenkowski spoke of the tax bill as the "Phoenix Project," after the mythological creature that rose from its own ashes. He understood that tax revision gained its greatest strength after it appeared to have failed.

In the Senate, the bill followed a similar course. Aware of scant public support, (and ample private opposition), members of the Senate Finance Committee at first ripped into the bill. Even the committee's chairman, Oregon Republican Bob Packwood, had little interest in the measure. He had hoped it would die in the House. When it didn't, he felt bound to make an attempt to pass it in the Senate. But clearly, his heart wasn't in it. He allowed his committee to vote to retain one tax break after another, until, by April 18, 1986, the bill was "in ruins," as Democratic Senator Daniel Patrick Moynihan so aptly put it.

Like the House Ways and Means Committee, the Senate Finance Committee took a beating in the press for its behavior. Packwood, in particular, felt the sting. A month away from what he knew would be a bruising primary race back in Oregon, Packwood was pounded by a political opponent for "floundering" in his first major test as chairman. Oregon newspapers chided him for taking huge campaign contributions from dozens of groups with an interest in the tax bill. He rapidly gained a reputation as "Mr. Special Interest." The *New Republic* magazine dubbed him "Senator Hackwood."

Worried about the potential damage to his career, Senator Packwood and his top aide, Bill Diefenderfer, retreated to a Capitol Hill saloon and began plotting a truly radical overhaul of the tax system—one that would bring tax rates even lower than the President's plan. This new approach was mostly a political ploy. Neither Packwood nor his aide, who downed two pitchers of beer at lunch, believed that the radical approach would do much more than call the bluffs of the other committee members who claimed they wanted "real reform" while voting for special interests.

Senator Packwood himself described the boozy lunch and its product as being like the end of the movie "The Wild Bunch." In the film, a gang of bandits sells out a young member of their crew to the other side, but later decides to undo the deed. As Packwood describes it, "The next morning they get up and look at each other and strap on their guns and go to get the kid. They know they're going to be killed, but they've got to do this, they've got to try it. Bill and I just felt, OK, this is something we've got to try. If we fail, we fail at a great enterprise. No guts, no glory."

But to the surprise of almost everyone, a small group of Packwood's colleagues, some of whom had suffered similar second thoughts due to the public outcry, decided to join in the radical new approach to tax reform that emerged from that desperate lunch. And again a bill began to take shape, born NOT out of a belief that the public would applaud such an effort, but rather out of fear that the public would punish failure.

They didn't want the dog to die on their doorstep.

SOME ECONOMICS OF TAX REFORM, 1986

Gerard M. Brannon[*]

39 National Tax Journal 277, 277-79 (1986)

My colleagues on the panel have analyzed the current tax reform efforts in political terms, the circumstances of Gramm-Rudman-Hollings, the effect of the Great Communicator,[f] etc. I would like to contribute an economic perspective to what explains the success of the present tax reform.

A key element in the current process is the outcome of some highly sophisticated economic analysis relating to effective marginal tax rates. This economic analysis story starts 30 years ago.

In the 1950s the views about investment among the prevailing Keynesian economists changed from the earlier concern with over-saving and pessimism about investment. The new view emphasized the importance of investment for economic growth. This shift to Neo-Keynesianism was critical to the adoption of the investment credit, an invention of the economic advisers to President Kennedy.

The view at that time was that the investment credit was a neutral way to improve the level of investment. The investment credit was thought to be uniform between various kinds of equipment. It particularly seemed more neutral than the gadgety changes in depreciation that were the alternatives for encouraging more investment.

After the adoption of the credit, something important happened back at the ranch called public finance theory. It was discovered that the investment credit was not very neutral after all. That credit operates like a uniform reduction in the price of equipment but in truth the price of equipment hasn't been reduced. Leading investors to think that equipment is cheaper than it is will distort investment toward more short-lived equipment. When capital seems very cheap one tends to waste it, to spend more on capital that wears out fast.

The critical economic discovery was that the important test of neutrality was not a uniform cost reduction for equipment, but a uniform effective marginal tax rate. An efficient tax incentive for investment should uniformly reduce the tax burden on investment. This led directly to the proposal to repeal the investment tax credit and lower the business tax rate. The efficiency gain involved made it possible to use less revenue on rate reduction than was gained by repeal of the investment credit and still generate enough capital investment to improve productivity over what it would be under present tax laws.

This different kind of fiscal dividend made it possible to package a reform program based on investment credit repeal which would contain individual tax reduction which Professor Witte regards as the sine qua non

---

*. At time of original publication, Professor, Georgetown University.

f. A reference to President Reagan. (Eds.)

of non-emergency tax legislation. Treasury I and II built on this core by adding several other corporate reforms that had this efficiency bonus. These changes alone were enough to pay for substantial individual tax reduction but the Treasury plans went further by adding selected individual loophole closers (fringe benefits, State and local taxes etc.) to make the individual rate cuts quite spectacular.

The response to all this in the Democratic House was quite close to a standard political prediction. A proposal from a Republican Administration to raise business taxes and to provide substantial relief for low incomes was manna from heaven. The real problem was get some share of the credit. The House bill: rejected most of the individual reforms; used the business tax increase to pay for the full relief program at low incomes; and, adopted only modest tax rate reductions. Significantly the House bill had sufficient individual reforms to pay for a sharp cut in the top tax rate, the only rate that gets mentioned in the press summaries. Due to the juggling of the brackets, there was not much overall rate reduction. This was a neat bit of symbolism about which we will have more to say later.

One aggregate description of the Senate bill makes it close to the political tradition. The Republican Senate opted for less business tax increase and less individual tax reduction than the House bill. The Finance Committee took the easy investment credit repeal and some other business tax reforms, but rejected others (revision of mineral and timber taxation). The remarkable thing about the Finance Committee bill is that despite the lower individual tax relief, it accomplished more rate reduction than the House bill. This is the one part that doesn't fit any traditional formula.

When one looks closely at the loophole closers that the Finance Committee used to cover its rate reductions some familiar patterns re-emerge.

Denial of deduction for State and local sales taxes is an almost classic compromise. Sales tax was the safest of the big three taxes to pick on. Property tax runs into the homeownership lobbies. Income tax can be very large for some taxpayers and it can be a big thing for some powerful States.

* * *

Increasing the capital gains rate, another Senate Committee bill feature, is a traditional tax change. We have diddled with this rate innumerable times. Significantly the bill says nothing about the serious loophole in the capital gains area, the tax free step up in basis at death. So long as this loophole remains, capital gains is virtually a voluntary tax. Ample research has demonstrated that increases in the capital gains rate will reduce realizations. The question is only whether there will be any appreciable increase in revenue.

The new limitation on the deduction of consumer interest is in the timid compromise pattern. Most consumers have the opportunity to finance consumer goods purchases by adding to their home mortgage the interest on which will still be deductible. There is reform here but a reform crafted to avoid hurting anybody very much.

The disallowance of passive tax shelter losses also fits into another established pattern, i.e., dealing with problem areas by increased complexification. There is good reason to argue that some business situations are allowed excessive deductions but the bill doesn't remove the excessive deductions, per se, it only disallows some deductions when they are packaged in a certain way, i.e., for outside investors. This provides a sporting challenge to tax lawyers and accountants to repackage the investments. My money is on the lawyers and accountants.

Another big revenue source for the Finance Committee is the minimum tax, a tax which is more reform by complexification. A variety of special tax benefits is provided in the law to encourage activities like mining. If a company concentrates in one or more favored activities its average rate will be low and it will be hit by minimum tax. The same benefits are there if a low tax company merges with a high tax company but then the minimum tax is avoided. Again we have a provision that hangs on how things are packaged and invites tax practitioners to repackage. This is in the historical tradition of tax reform.

In an economic vein, I worry about the solidity of revenue estimates from these reforms that don't go to fundamentals but leave so much room for taxpayer maneuvering.

In a political vein, I am struck by how much symbolism there is in this. The essence of the minimum tax and the tax shelter amendments is to deal with public perceptions of tax abuses. A specific minimum tax proposal in the Finance Committee bill goes to the very statistic, book profit, which is used to compute the headlines about low effective average tax rates of this or that company. There is no underlying analysis as to why this is a sensible tax base; the provision is only designed to deal with what some parts of the public consider to be a symbol of tax abuse.

The other anti-symbol reform, the limitations on tax shelter deductions, is in a logical sense the opposite of the minimum tax. In the minimum tax case, the taxpayer who gets punished is the one who concentrates in a favored activity, thereby reducing the average tax rate. In the tax shelter case the typical taxpayer who gets punished is the one already paying a high rate who finds it attractive to invest on the side in a tax favored activity. Any underlying economic theory escapes me. The indications are that our tax law in the future should be designed after consultation with public relations experts.

Notes and Questions

9. What are the relative merits of an incremental approach to tax reform versus a convulsive, overall revision of the sort carried out in 1986?

10. Why is Professor Witte pessimistic about the long-term prospects for tax reform?

11. According to Mr. Birnbaum, the Tax Reform Act of 1986 passed against all odds. Why?

12. According to Professor Brannon, what was the political effect of the economic conclusion that a cut in corporate income tax rates was a more efficient stimulus to investment than was the investment tax credit?

D. HOW TAX LAW IS MADE

Discussion of taxes and the legislative process requires discussing the role of lobbyists. In narrow terms, lobbying means attempting to influence legislation by dealing directly with members of Congress. In practice, lobbying objectives also are accomplished by communicating with Congressional staff, and Treasury staff, and, occasionally, with Revenue Service personnel. In the broadest use of the term, lobbying includes grassroots lobbying: attempts to persuade constituents of members of Congress and to influence voter initiatives and referendums.

Lobbyists perform useful functions. Existing tax law needs to be challenged constantly, to justify its relevance and its fairness. Legislative tax proposals should be scrutinized and criticized. Taxpayers affected by existing law or by proposals are in a good position to know how they will be affected, whether favorably or unfavorably, and they are entitled to be heard.

Professor Stanley S. Surrey had a wealth of experience with lobbyists when he was Tax Legislative Counsel during the Truman administration and Assistant Secretary of Treasury for Tax Policy during the Kennedy and Johnson administrations. As such, he was in an unique position to write the article excerpted here.

THE CONGRESS AND THE TAX LOBBYIST—
HOW SPECIAL TAX PROVISIONS GET ENACTED
Stanley S. Surrey[*]
70 Harvard Law Review 1145, 1145-55, 1181-82 (1957)

The development of a proper tax structure for an economy as large and as complex as ours is a task of the first magnitude. Given the dimensions of the task and the political arena in which it must be undertaken, the Congress has performed the essential work successfully. It has shown remarkable collective wisdom in shaping our federal tax structure, and its accomplishment in this field may be measured favorably against the tax systems of other countries. Since we live in an era when both professional learning and public opinion regard a progressive income tax as the most

---

[*]. At time of original publication, Professor of Law, Harvard Law School.

appropriate method of raising governmental revenue, and since the progressive income tax is the mainstay of our tax structure, this accomplishment is remarkable. For a progressive income tax is also the most complicated and difficult of taxes to maintain. It places a premium on sensitivity to economic changes and to public attitudes. It demands high technical skills on the part of those who shape the legislative structure, who administer and interpret its provisions, who advise the public how to order its business and family affairs under the tax. It requires a literate citizenry with a respect for law and a willingness to shoulder fiscal burdens. Our over-all successful record in relying on the progressive income tax is thus a noteworthy achievement in public finance.

The continuation of this success with our federal-tax structure demands, however, constant alertness to the correction of faults as they appear. Recently there has been considerable criticism directed against the existence in our tax laws of provisions granting special treatment to certain groups or individuals. This criticism is aimed at both the increasing number of new provisions of this kind and the continuation of old provisions the significance of which has become far more important with passage of time. Some, it is true, have irresponsibly resorted to criticisms of this character as a justification for discarding the income tax. But nearly all who have voiced objections to special-treatment provisions have done so in the hope that a considerations of the problem would result in a strengthening of the income tax.

The criticisms on the whole involve these assumptions: (1) that it is essential under a progressive income tax, and also progressive estate and gift taxes, to adhere as far as possible to the criterion of equity or fairness. Stated simply, this criterion demands that the income-tax burden should as far as possible apply equally to persons with the same dollar income; (2) that the Congress has not always followed this criterion in tax legislation; and (3) that there are a good many instances in the income, estate, and gift taxes in which the failure to follow this criterion is not properly justified by the requirements of other criteria. As illustrations, the critics point to such matters under the income tax as the present exceedingly preferential treatment of capital gains and especially its application to employee stock options, pension-trust terminations, coal and timber royalties, patent royalties, growing crops, livestock, and so on; percentage depletion; the exemption of interest on state and local obligations; the continual expansion of deductions for personal expenses unrelated to profit-seeking activities; the provisions for the blind and the aged; and the exemption of certain fringe benefits. In the estate-tax area, reference is made, for example, to the exemption of employee annuities and of transferred life insurance. In addition to these provisions involving certain groups in our society, the criticisms are of course directed against those special provisions which can affect only a handful of taxpayers, or even only one or two, such as the so-called "Louis B. Mayer amendment."[4]

Often these provisions are spoken of as "loopholes" or "special tax privileges." Of course, the use of the appellation "loophole" is a matter of viewpoint. What is a "tax loophole" to a CIO or an ADA meeting is merely "relief from special hardship or intolerable rates" to an American Bankers Association or NAM meeting—and vice versa. Obviously we do not all feel the same way about each of the examples mentioned above. But despite an absence of consensus on any particular list of provisions there seems to be considerable agreement that Congress in its tax legislation has adopted provisions favoring special groups or special individuals and that these provisions run counter to our notions of tax fairness. Moreover, the tendency of Congress to act this way seems to be increasing.

Against this background, the purpose of this article is to consider the question of why the Congress enacts these special tax provisions, to use a fairly neutral term. * * * [I]t may be useful to speculate about some of these factors and to see if there are ways in which the consideration of tax legislation could be altered for the better. It may help first to sketch some of the major factors that are operative in tax legislation. I propose to do this only briefly, since these factors are generally well recognized.

Some Major Factors

High Rates of Tax

The high rates of the individual income tax, and of the estate and gift taxes, are probably the major factor in producing special tax legislation. This is, in a sense, a truism, for without something to be relieved of, there would be no need to press for relief. The point is that the average congressman does not basically believe in the present rates of income tax in the upper brackets. When he sees them applied to individual cases, he thinks them too high and therefore unfair. Any argument for relief which starts off by stating that these high rates are working a "special hardship" in a particular case or are "penalizing" a particular taxpayer—to use some words from the tax lobbyist's approved list of effective phrases—has the initial advantage of having a sympathetic listener. Put the other way around, an advocate of the "Louis B. Mayer amendment" would simply make no headway with a congressman who firmly believed in a ninety-one-per-cent top tax rate. But most congressmen apparently do not believe in such a rate—certainly not in the concrete and perhaps not even in the abstract. Since they are not,

---

4. Under this provision amounts received from the assignment or release by an employee of over twenty-years employment of his rights to receive, after termination of his employment and for a period of not less than five years, a percentage of future profits or receipts of his employer are taxed at capital-gains rates if the employee's contract providing for those rights had been in effect at least twelve years. Clearly the blueprint for compliance with this section is quite detailed. It is generally assumed that the amendment at the time covered only two persons, Louis B. Mayer, retired vice-president of Loew's, Inc., and one other executive in the company, and that the amendment saved Mayer about $2,000,000 in taxes.

however, willing to reduce those rates directly, the natural outcome is indirect reduction through special provisions.

The United States is not unique in this regard. Students of the British tax system, for example, state that the very high rates of that system are considerably ameliorated in a number of ways through which the wealthy can escape the full impact of those rates.[6] The exclusion of capital gains is one broad method. The estate tax offers a number of avoidance possibilities. Indeed, it may be said that both here and abroad, as various pressures have driven tax rates to top levels, the refuge of the wealthy has been in the brains of their tax lawyers and in the technicalities of the tax law. Governments are generally aware of these escape routes but are reluctant to close them and enforce with vigor the excessively high tax rates. In effect, a sort of political paralysis appears to be forming in countries relying strongly on income taxation, under which no clear way has appeared to move away from the combination of high rates tempered by many avoidance possibilities. The obvious solution would seem to be simultaneous lowering of the rates and closing of the escape routes. But conservative governments fear the political consequences of rate reduction for the wealthy although their effective tax burden would not be lessened. They may also fear that, once the system were tightened and stabilized at a lower tax-rate level, political pressures might drive the rates up again, this time with a much more severe effect. Liberal governments fear that they cannot persuade their supporters to accept tax-rate reductions for the wealthy in such clear terms as reduction of a ninety-per-cent rate to fifty per cent or sixty-five per cent, especially when the starting rates are high and the compensating factor is merely the closing of a number of loopholes which the public cannot understand. This is obviously a dilemma which the income tax must solve in the years ahead.[7]

Tax Polarity

The existence of two rate structures in the income tax * * * permits a congressman to favor a special group by placing its situation under the lower rate structure or the less effective tax. Thus, the presence of the twenty-five-per-cent capital-gains rate enables Congress to shift an executive stock option from the high rates applying to executive compensation to the lower capital-

---

6. Professor Carl Shoup, an informed observer of the Japanese tax system, asserts that the same trend is evident in that country. [The Shoup Mission's REPORT ON JAPANESE TAXATION is excerpted in Chapter Four. (Eds.)]

7. The dilemma should be solved solely in the context of the income tax, but must be considered in the light of the entire tax structure. Thus, those who believe that stabilizing the income tax at levels of 50-65% does not leave a sufficient over-all burden on the wealthy would urge a concomitant strengthening of taxes on capital. In other countries this may mean a resort to net-worth taxes restricted to upper levels and further development of estate taxes. In this country constitutional requirements may restrict the effort to a strengthening of the estate tax. Looking further ahead, there may be experimentation with expenditure taxation for the upper brackets, as contrasted with the current sales taxes that reach all levels but with greater impact at the lower ranges.

gains rate. If there were no special capital-gains rate, or if we did not tax capital gains at all, this shift could not be made, since a congressman would not completely exempt the stock option. * * *

Technical Complexity

The high rates of tax, the complexities of modern business, the desires of the wealthy and middle-income groups for clear tax charts to guide their family planning, the Government's need for protection against tax avoidance, the claims of tax equity, and various other factors have combined to make the income, estate, and gift taxes exceedingly complex in technical detail. These technicalities involve the drawing of countless dividing lines. Consequently, a case on the high-tax side of a line may closely resemble the cases on the other side receiving more favorable tax treatment. The result is a fertile around for assertions of inequity and hardship as particular taxpayers desire legislation to bend the dividing lines and thereby extend the favorable treatment to their situations. Also, faulty tax planning, ill-advised legal steps, or transactions concluded in ignorance of tax law can produce severe tax consequences. These "tax penalties" could have been averted under an informed tax guidance that would have taken the taxpayer safely through the technical tax maze. In these circumstances, the taxpayer facing severe monetary hurt because of a "mere technicality" (to use the phrase that will be pressed on the congressman) is quite likely to evoke considerable sympathy for his plight.

History and Politics

The accidents of tax history also play a major role in the existence of special provisions. Tax-exempt securities in large part achieved their favored status through the vagaries of constitutional interpretation and not through any special desire to relieve the wealthy. Percentage depletion for oil and gas and the deduction of intangible drilling expenses have their roots in legislative compromises and administrative interpretation which for the most part do not appear to have been planned as special-interest relief. It is only later that the extent of the tax generosity inherent in such provisions is comprehended. But by then they are in the law, the problem of the group benefited is one of defense rather than attack, and the strategic advantages are all with that group. This is especially so when the area involved touches on major political matters, as in the case of percentage depletion and tax-exempt securities.

Political considerations naturally overhang this whole area, for taxation is a sensitive and volatile matter. Any major congressional action represents the compromises of the legislator as he weighs and balances the strong forces constantly focused on him by the pressure groups of the country. Many special provisions—capital gains, for one—are caught in these swirling pressures. The response of the legislator to issues raised by these provisions is like his response to the general level of tax rates or to personal exemptions, a political response of considerable significance. It is an important part of the fabric of political responses which determines whether he will remain a congressman and whether his party will control Congress. In this group of provisions highly affected by political considerations are those "tax relief" provisions which have a broad public appeal and are thus likely to be regarded by the congressman as useful "vote-getters"—a "baby-sitter" deduction, the exclusion of "retirement income," or an extra exemption for the "aged." The political appeal of favorable action on these issues is quite likely to outweigh what a congressman would regard as "technical" tax arguments to the contrary.

Separation of Executive and Legislative Branches of Government

But many of the tax provisions we are considering do not lie at this political level. They are simply a part of the technical tax law. They are not of major importance in their revenue impact. But they are of major importance to the group or individual benefited and they are glaring in their departure from tax fairness. The inquiry, therefore, must here be directed toward some of the institutional features in the tax-legislation process which may be responsible for special provisions of this technical variety. Lacking direct knowledge, I must leave to others the task of describing the types of pressure from constituents or other groups which may be operative in a particular case. While these pressures may explain why the congressman who is directly subject to the pressures may act and vote for a special provision, they do not explain why other congressmen, not so subject, go along with the proposal. We must look for reasons beyond these pressures if we are to understand the adoption of these special tax provisions. A number of these reasons lie in the institutional aspects of the tax legislative process.

Basic to a consideration of these institutional aspects are the nature of our governmental system and the relationship between the Congress and the executive. A different Governmental structure might give the legislator little or nothing to say about tax provisions. Under a parliamentary government, the revenue department retains tight control over the statutory development of tax law. It is responsive only to the broad political issues that require decisions of a party nature. Beyond these, the governmental tax technicians mold the structure, so that the tax lobbyist pressing for special legislative consideration or the legislator seeking to ease a constituent's problem by special tax relief is not a significant part of the tax scene. Thus, under the British practice, finance bills are framed by the Treasury and the Board of Inland Revenue. The bills are debated in the Committee of Ways and Means—the entire House of Commons sitting under another name and with different rules of procedure. Here is an opportunity for anyone sufficiently concerned, who can persuade a Member of Parliament to voice his proposals, to have these proposals considered in the debates on the bill. Such discussion may focus attention on weaknesses in the bill or law, and if the proposal is considered meritorious by the minister in charge of the bill a change will be made. But if the government does not accept a member's amendment, party discipline is such that the minister is always supported and the amendment defeated.   In practice, consequently, finance bills generally emerge in about the same form as introduced.

The United States picture is quite different, for here Congress occupies the role of mediator between the tax views of the executive and the demands of the pressure groups. This is so whether the tax issue involved is a major political matter or a minor technical point. The Congress is zealous in maintaining this position in the tax field. A factor of special importance here is article I, section 7, Of the Constitution, which provides that "All Bills for raising Revenue shall originate in the House of Representatives." The House Committee on Ways and Means jealously guards this clause against possible inroads by the Senate.   It also protects its jurisdiction over revenue legislation from encroachment by other House committees. When senators and other congressmen must toe the line, the executive is not likely to be permitted to occupy a superior position. Further, a legislator regards tax matters as politically very sensitive, and hence as having a significant bearing on elections. It is no accident that the tax committees are generally strong committees, whose membership is carefully controlled by the party leaders.

The Congress, consequently, regards the shaping of a revenue bill as very much its prerogative. It will seek the views of the executive, for there is a respect for the sustained labors of those in the executive departments and also a recognition, varying with the times, of the importance of presidential programs. But control over the legislation itself, both as to broad policies and as to details, rests with the Congress.   Hence a congressman, and especially a member of the tax committees, is in a position to make the tax laws bend in favor of a particular individual or group despite strong objection from the executive branch. Under such a governmental system the importance to the tax structure of the institutional factors that influence a congressman's decision is obvious.

* * *

Conclusion

The consideration of any legislation is a complex matter and tax measures are no exception. But the institutional factors in the tax legislative process do differ from those in other legislative areas, and the differences have affected the end product. The growing concern with the integrity of our tax system may well force a substantive re-examination of many of the special provisions now in the law. This concern should also extend to the tax legislative process itself. The situation is a serious one, and the solutions are far from clear.

It is suggested that the executive branch take affirmative action to attack the problem through a strong program led by the President or the Secretary of the Treasury designed to focus public consideration on special provisions and their interaction with the rate structure. The Treasury's tax officials and technicians should engage in intensive research on these matters and the results of their studies should be made public. In the Congress, consideration should be given to changes in the methods of obtaining information on tax problems, to improvements in the conduct of hearings, and to a re-examination of the staff arrangements. Procedures should be adopted under which proposals for amendment of the tax laws limited in application to a single person or a small group, especially when retroactive in nature, would be treated as private-relief claims. These claims should be considered by the tax committees under special procedures similar to those applicable to private-relief bills generally. In respect to the bar, both bar associations and lawyers generally should consider how, consistently with the traditions of the profession regarding the protection of a client's interests, the wisdom and experience of the tax bar can be made available in the public interest to aid the Congress by objective guidance. The sum total of these suggestions is that the Congress, the Treasury Department, and the tax bar equally bear a responsibility to reappraise their roles and activities in the tax legislative process.

Notes and Questions

13. In many ways Professor Surrey's 1957 article reads as though it were written last week, but in some important ways it does not. The top marginal individual income tax rate exceeded 90 percent at that time, and the most important consequence of tax legislation in the late 1970s and the 1980s was to bring the top rates down below 40 percent. This change not only reduces the equitable appeal of a taxpayer asking for relief, but it lowers the stakes: a taxpayer presumably is less concerned about petitioning Congress to avoid a tax of less than 40 percent compared to a tax of over 90 percent.

14. Is the "loophole" label a useful tool for tax policy analysis?

15. Professor Surrey rejected use of the loophole label, but said provisions favoring special groups or special individuals run counter to our notions of tax fairness. Was he acting fairly when he assumed that tax provisions were unfair if they applied to special groups, particularly small groups?

16. Professor Surrey compares the American system for legislating taxes to the British parliamentary system, where the executive branch and the legislative branch are not separate and revenue bills pass through Parliament virtually unscathed. Would we have a better income tax if we had a parliamentary form of government?

17. The issue of whether lobbying expenses should be deductible when they are ordinary and necessary business expenses deserves attention. Originally, Congress did not deal explicitly with the issue. Deduction of expenditures to influence legislation was denied by regulation, which the Supreme Court upheld against a challenge that it was inconsistent with the Code provision allowing deduction of ordinary and necessary expenses.[g] In 1962, Congress responded with section 162(e), which allowed deduction of certain lobbying expenses when they were ordinary and necessary business expenses. No deduction was allowed for expenditures on grassroots lobbying.

In the 1993 Act, section 162(e) was amended to deny deduction of lobbying expenses even though they are ordinary and necessary business expenses. (Section 162(e)(5)(A) made clear that the business expenses of conducting the business of lobbying on behalf of others remains deductible.)

18. Suppose Ms. Macbeth, a real estate developer, lobbies the state legislature to repeal a law that blocks her plans to subdivide Burnham Wood into quarter-acre lots for single family dwellings. Suppose Mr. McDuff, an individual with no business interest in the matter, is dismayed by Ms. Macbeth's proposal because he likes to walk through Burnham Wood to escape the noise of the city. Clearly Mr. McDuff cannot deduct any expenses he has in lobbying the state legislature by using ecological arguments on the issue because, for him, the expenses are personal and not business-related. Should Ms. Macbeth be able to deduct her lobbying expenses?

19. Our final observation is that the process of writing tax legislation, and the factors that influence it, reflect the legislative process in all areas. For example, the differences between the United States system and a parliamentary system are present in all types of legislation.

Selected Bibliography

Aaron, Henry, *Lessons for Tax Reform, in* DO TAXES MATTER?: THE IMPACT OF THE TAX REFORM ACT OF 1986 321 (Joel Slemrod ed., 1990).

—— & HARVEY GALPER, ASSESSING TAX REFORM (1985).

Barker, Rosina B. & Jasper L. Cummings, Jr., *Interview with the Hon. Dan Rostenkowski*, 15 ABA Sec. of Tax'n Newsl. 11 (Winter, 1996).

Birnbaum, Jeffrey H., *Showdown at Gucci Gulch*, 40 NAT'L TAX J. 357 (1987).

—— & ALAN S. MURRAY, SHOWDOWN AT GUCCI GULCH: LAWMAKERS, LOBBYISTS, AND THE UNLIKELY TRIUMPH OF TAX REFORM (1987).

Bopp, Michael D., *The Roles of Revenue Estimation and Scoring in the Federal Budget Process*, 56 TAX NOTES 1629 (1992).

---

g. *Cammarano v. United States*, 358 U.S. 498 (1959).

Brannon, Gerard M., *Some Economics of Tax Reform, 1986*, 39 NAT'L TAX J. 277 (1986).

Doernberg, Richard L. & Fred S. McChesney, *Doing Good or Doing Well? Congress and the Tax Reform Act of 1986*, 62 N.Y.U. L. REV. 891 (1987).

Gideon, Kenneth W., *Tax Policy at the Treasury Department: A 20-Year Perspective*, 57 TAX NOTES 889 (1992).

Gravelle, Jane G., *Behavioral Feedback Effects and the Revenue-Estimating Process*, 48 NAT'L TAX J. 463 (1995).

Leonard, Robert, *Perspectives on the Tax Legislative Process*, 38 TAX NOTES 969 (1988).

McLure, Charles E., Jr., *The Budget Process and Tax Simplification/Complexification*, 45 TAX L. REV. 25 (1989).

——, *The 1986 Act: Tax Reform's Finest Hour or Death Throes of the Income Tax?*, 41 NAT'L TAX J. 303 (1988).

Pearlman, Ronald A., *The Tax Legislative Process: 1972-1992*, 57 TAX NOTES 939 (1992).

STEUERLE, C. EUGENE, THE TAX DECADE (1992).

Strahan, Randall, *Discussion: Gramm-Rudman-Hollings and Tax Policy*, in NAT'L TAX ASS'N-TAX INST. OF AM. 82ND ANN. CONF. 49 (1989).

Sunley, Emil M., *A Tax Preference is Born: A Legislative History of the New Jobs Tax Credit*, in THE ECONOMICS OF TAXATION 391 (Henry J. Aaron & Michael J. Boskin eds., 1980).

Surrey, Stanley S., *The Congress and the Tax Lobbyist—How Special Tax Provisions Get Enacted*, 70 HARV. L. REV. 1145 (1957).

—— & Paul R. McDaniel, *The Tax Expenditure Concept and the Legislative Process*, in THE ECONOMICS OF TAXATION 123 (Henry J. Aaron & Michael J. Boskin eds., 1980).

THE PRESIDENT'S TAX PROPOSALS TO THE CONGRESS FOR FAIRNESS, GROWTH, AND SIMPLICITY 1-30 (1985) ["Treasury II"].

WITTE, JOHN F., THE POLITICS AND DEVELOPMENT OF THE FEDERAL INCOME TAX (1985).

——, *A Long View of Tax Reform*, 39 NAT'L TAX J. 255 (1986).